# shakespearean criticism

"Thou art a Monument without a tomb,
 And art alive still while thy Book doth
    live
 And we have wits to read and praise to
 give."

*Ben Jonson, from the preface
to the First Folio, 1623.*

*Frontispiece to the First Folio (1623). By permission of the Folger Shakespeare Library.*

ISSN 0833-9123

Volume 48

# shakespearean criticism

## Yearbook 1998

A Selection of the Year's Most Noteworthy Studies
of William Shakespeare's Plays and Poetry

### Advisers

Ralph Berry, *University of Ottawa*
Graham Bradshaw, *University of St Andrews*
William C. Carroll, *Boston University*
S.P. Cerasano, *Colgate University*
Sidney Homan, *University of Florida*
MacDonald P. Jackson, *University of Auckland*
Randall Martin, *University of New Brunswick*
T. McAlindon, *University of Hull*
Yasuhiro Ogawa, *University of Hokkadio*

**GALE GROUP**

**Detroit
San Francisco
London
Boston
Woodbridge, CT**

## STAFF

Michelle Lee, *Editor*

Kathy Darrow, *Associate Editor*

Janet Witalec, *Managing Editor*

Maria Franklin, *Permissions Manager*
Kimberly F. Smilay, *Permissions Specialist*
Kelly A. Quin, *Permissions Associates*
Erin Bealmear, Sandy Gore, *Permissions Assistant*

Victoria B. Cariappa, *Research Manager*
Cheryl Warnock, *Research Specialist*
Tamara C. Nott, Tracie A. Richardson, *Research Associates*
Phyllis Blackman, Patricia Love, *Research Assistants*

Gary Leach, *Graphic Artist*
Randy Bassett, *Image Database Supervisor*
Robert Duncan, Michael Logusz, *Imaging Specialists*
Pamela A. Reed, *Imaging Coordinator*

---

Since this page cannot legibly accommodate all copyright notices, the acknowledgments constitute an extension of the copyright notice.

While every effort has been made to ensure the reliability of the information presented in this publication, Gale Research neither guarantees the accuracy of the data contained herein nor assumes any responsibility for errors, omissions or discrepancies. Gale accepts no payment for listing; and inclusion in the publication of any organization, agency, institution, publication, service, or individual does not imply endorsement of the editors or publisher. Errors brought to the attention of the publisher and verified to the satisfaction of the publisher will be corrected in future editions.

This publication is a creative work fully protected by all applicable copyright laws, as well as by misappropriation, trade secret, unfair competition, and other applicable laws. The authors and editors of this work have added value to the underlying factual material herein through one or more of the following: unique and original selection, coordination, expression, arrangement, and classification of the information.

All rights to this publication will be vigorously defended.

Copyright © 2000 Gale Group, Inc.
27500 Drake Rd.
Farmington Hills, MI 48331-3535
Gale Group and Design is a trademark used herein under license.

All rights reserved including the right of reproduction in whole or in part in any form.

---

This book is printed on acid-free paper that meets the minimum requirements of American National Standard for Information Sciences—Permanence Paper for Printed Library Materials, ANSI Z39.48-1984.

Library of Congress Catalog Card Number 86-645085
ISBN 0-7876-3143-4
ISSN 0883-9123

Printed in the United States of America
Published simultaneously in the United Kingdom
by Gale Research International Limited
(An affiliated company of Gale Research)
10 9 8 7 6 5 4 3 2 1

The Gale Group

# Contents

Preface vii

Acknowledgments ix

List of Plays and Poems Covered in *SC* xi

**Comedies**

Huston Diehl, " 'Infinite Space': Representation and Reformation in *Measure for Measure*" ............ 1

Stephen B. Dobranski, "Children of the Mind: Miscarried Narratives in *Much Ado about Nothing*" ............ 14

Sidney Homann, " 'What Do I Do Now?' Directing *A Midsummer Night's Dream*" ............ 23

Lisa Hopkins, "Marriage as Comic Closure" ............ 32

Cynthia Marshall, "The Doubled Jaques and Constructions of Negation in *As You Like It*" ............ 42

Mary Janell Metzger, " 'Now by My Hood, a Gentle and No Jew': Jessica, *The Merchant of Venice*, and the Discourse of Early Modern English Identity" ............ 54

Ruth Nevo, "Motive and Meaning in *All's Well That Ends Well*" ............ 65

Linda Rozmovits, "Shylock: The Infamous Secret Jew," ............ 77

**Histories**

Harry Berger, Jr., "The Prince's Dog: Falstaff and the Perils of Speech-Prefixity" ............ 95

Douglas A. Brooks, "Sir John Oldcastle and the Construction of Shakespeare's Authorship" ............ 117

Edward Gieskes, " 'He Is But a Bastard to the Time': Status and Service in *The Troublesome Raigne of John* and Shakespeare's *King John*" ............ 132

Michael Goldman, "History-Making in the Henriad" ............ 143

Maurice Hunt, "The Hybrid Reformations of Shakespeare's Second Henriad" ............ 151

Paola Pugliatti, "Shakespeare's Historicism: Visions and Revisions" ............ 167

Kathryn Schwarz, "Fearful Simile: Stealing the Breech in Shakespeare's Chronicle Plays" ............ 175

**Tragedies**

Geoffrey Aggeler, "Nobler in the Mind: The Dialect in *Hamlet*" ............ 195

Rick Bowers, " 'The Luck of Caesar': Winning and Losing in *Antony and Cleopatra*" ................ 206

Tom Clayton, "Who 'Has No Children' in *Macbeth?*" ................................................................ 214

Catherine S. Cox, " 'An excellent thing in woman': Virgo and Viragos in *King Lear*" ................ 222

William M. Hawley, "*Coriolanus:* Punishment of the Civil Body" ............................................... 230

Dennis Kezar, "*Julius Caesar* and the Properies of Shakespeare's Globe" .................................. 240

Kaara Peterson, "Framing Ophelia: Representation and the Pictorial Tradition" ......................... 255

Sid Ray, " 'Rape, I fear, was root of thy annoy': The Politics of Consent in
*Titus Andronicus*" ............................................................................................................................ 264

Martin Scofield, "Shakespeare and Clarissa: 'General Nature', Genre and Sexuality" ................ 277

**Romances and Poems**

A. D. Cousins, "Subjectivity, Exemplarity, and the Establishing of Characterization
in Lucrece" ........................................................................................................................................ 291

John G. Demaray, "On the Symbolism of *The Tempest*" ............................................................... 299

Nora Johnson, "Ganymedes and Kings: Staging Male Homosexual Desire in
*The Winter's Tale*" ........................................................................................................................... 309

Michael Keevak, "Shakespeare's Queer *Sonnets* and the Forgeries of William
Henry Ireland" .................................................................................................................................. 325

Jennifer Laws, "The Generic Complexities of *A Lover's Complaint* and Its Relationship
to the Sonnets in Shakespeare's 1609 Volume " ............................................................................. 336

Malabika Sarkar, "The Magic of Shakespeare's Sonnets" ............................................................. 346

David Schalkwyk, "What May Words Do? The Performative of Praise in Shakespeare's
Sonnets" ............................................................................................................................................ 352

David Skeele, "*Pericles* Reconstructed" ......................................................................................... 364


Guide to *Shakespearean Criticism* Series  377

Cumulative Character Index  379

Cumulative Critic Index  389

Cumulative Topic Index  427

Cumulative Topic Index, by Play  445

# Preface

*S*hakespearean Criticism *(SC)* provides students, educators, theatergoers, and other interested readers with valuable insight into Shakespeare's drama and poetry. A multiplicity of viewpoints documenting the critical reaction of scholars and commentators from the seventeenth century to the present day derives from the hundreds of periodicals and books excerpted for the series. Students and teachers at all levels of study will benefit from *SC*, whether they seek information for class discussions and written assignments, new perspectives on traditional issues, or the most noteworthy analyses of Shakespeare's artistry.

## Scope of the Series

Volumes 1 through 10 of the series present a unique historical overview of the critical response to each Shakespearean work, representing a broad range of interpretations. Volumes 11 through 26 recount the performance history of Shakespeare's plays on the stage and screen through eyewitness reviews and retrospective evaluations of individual productions, comparisons of major interpretations, and discussions of staging issues. Beginning with Volume 27 in the series, *SC* focuses on criticism published after 1960, with a view to providing the reader with the most significant modern critical approaches. Each volume is ordered around a theme that is central to the study of Shakespeare, such as politics, religion, or sexuality.

## The *SC* Yearbook

*SC* compiles an annual Yearbook, collecting the most noteworthy contributions to Shakespearean scholarship published during the previous year. The essays are chosen to address a wide audience, including advanced secondary school students, undergraduate and graduate students, and teachers. Each year an advisory board of distinguished scholars recommends approximately one hundred articles and books from among the hundreds of valuable essays that appeared in the previous year. From these recommendations, Gale editors select examples of innovative criticism that represent current or newly developing trends in scholarship. The 32 essays in the present volume, *SC-48,* the *1998 Yearbook,* provide the latest assessments of the Shakespeare canon.

## Organization and Features of the *SC* Yearbook

Essays are grouped on the basis of the genre of the Shakespearean work on which they focus: Comedies, Histories, Tragedies, and Romances and Poems. An article examining the symbolism in *The Tempest,* for example, appears in the Romances and Poems section of the yearbook.

- Each piece of criticism is reprinted in its entirety, including the full text of the author's footnotes, and is followed by a complete **Bibliographical Citation.**

- The *SC Yearbook* contains the following indices:

    **Cumulative Character Index**: Identifies the principal characters of discussion in the criticism of each play and non-dramatic poem in *SC*.

**Cumulative Critic Index**: Identifies each critic that has appeared in *SC*.
**Cumulative Topic Index**: Identifies the principal topics in the criticism and stage history of each work. The topics are arranged alphabetically, by topic.
**Cumulative Topic Index, by Play**: Identifies the principal topics in the criticism and stage history of each work. The topics are arranged alphabetically, by play.

## Citing the *SC Yearbook*

Students who quote directly from the *SC Yearbook* in written assignments may use the following general forms to footnote reprinted criticism. The first example pertains to material drawn from periodicals, the second to material reprinted from books.

[1]Michael Neill, "Unproper Beds: Race, Adultery, and the Hideous in *Othello*," *Shakespeare Quarterly,* 40 (Winter 1989), 383-412; reprinted in *Shakespearean Criticism,* Vol. 13, Yearbook 1989, ed. Sandra L. Williamson (Detroit: Gale Research, 1989), pp. 327-42.

[2]Philip Brockbank, "*Julius Caesar* and the Catastrophes of History," in *On Shakespeare: Jesus, Shakespeare and Karl Marx, and Other Essays* (Basil Blackwell, 1989), pp. 122-39; reprinted in *Shakespearean Criticism,* Vol. 13, *Yearbook 1989,* ed. Sandra L. Williamson (Detroit: Gale Research, 1991), pp. 252-59.

## Suggestions Are Welcome

The editors encourage comments and suggestions from readers on any aspect of the *SC* series. In response to various recommendations, several features have been added to *SC* since the series began, including the topic index and the sample bibliographic citations noted above. Readers are cordially invited to write, call, or fax the editors: *Shakespearean Criticism,* The Gale Group, 27500 Drake Rd., Farmington Hills, MI 48331-3535. Call toll-free at 1-800-347-GALE or fax to 1-248-699-8049.

# Acknowledgments

The editors wish to thank the copyright holders of the excerpted criticism included in this volume and the permissions managers of many book and magazine publishing companies for assisting us in securing reproduction rights. We are also grateful to the staffs of the Detroit Public Library, the Library of Congress, the University of Detroit Mercy Library, Wayne State University Purdy/Kresge Library Complex, and the University of Michigan Libraries for making their resources available to us. Following is a list of the copyright holders who have granted us permission to reproduce material in this volume of *SC*. Every effort has been made to trace copyright, but if omissions have been made, please let us know.

**COPYRIGHTED EXCERPTS IN *SC*, VOLUME 48, WERE REPRODUCED FROM THE FOLLOWING PERIODICALS:**

*AUMLA*, n. 89, May, 1998. Reproduced by permission of the publisher.—*Comparative Drama*, v. 32, Spring, 1998. Copyright © 1998, by the Editors of *Comparative Drama*. Reproduced by permission.—*Criticism*, v. XL, Spring, 1998. Copyright © 1998, Wayne State University Press. Reproduced by permission of the publisher.—*ELH*, v. 65, 1998. Copyright © 1998 by The Johns Hopkins University Press. Reproduced by permission of The Johns Hopkins University Press.—*English Literary Renaissance*, v. 28, Winter, 1998. Copyright © 1998 by *English Literary Renaissance*. Reproduced by permission.—*English Studies: A Journal of English Language and Literature*, v. 79, November, 1998. Reproduced by permission of Swets & Zeitlinger Publishers.—*Modern Philology*, v. 96, November, 1998 for " 'An Excellent Thing in Woman': Virgo and Viragos in *King Lear*" by Catherine S. Cox. Copyright © 1998 by The University of Chicago. Reproduced by permission of the University of Chicago Press and the author.—*Mosaic: A Journal for the Interdisciplinary Study of Literature*, v. 31, September, 1998. Copyright © Mosaic 1998. Acknowledgment of previous publication is herewith made.—*PMLA*, v. 113, January, 1998. Copyright © 1998 by the Modern Language Association of America. Reproduced by permission of the Modern Language Association of America.—*Renaissance Studies*, v. 12, June, 1998 for "The Magic of Shakespeare's Sonnets" by Malabika Sarkar. Copyright © 1998 The Society for Renaissance Studies and Oxford University Press. Reproduced by permission of Oxford University Press and the author.—*Shakespeare Quarterly*, v. 49, Winter, 1998; v. 49, Spring, 1998; v. 49, Summer, 1998; v. 49, Fall, 1998. Copyright © The Folger Shakespeare Library, 1998. All reproduced by permission of *Shakespeare Quarterly*.— *Shakespeare Studies: An Annual Gathering of Research, Criticism, and Reviews*, v. 26, 1998 for "Ganymedes and Kings: Staging Male Homosexual Desire in *The Winter's Tale*" by Nora Johnson. Copyright © 1998 The Council for Research in the Renaissance. Reproduced by permission of the author.—*Shakespeare Survey: An Annual Survey of Shakespearian Study and Production*, v. 51, 1998 for "Shakespeare and Clarissa: 'General Nature', Genre and Sexuality" by Martin Scofield. Copyright © Cambridge University Press, 1998. Reproduced with the permission of Cambridge University Press and the author.—*Studies in English Literature, 1500-1900*, v. 38, Spring, 1998. Copyright © 1998 William Marsh Rice University. Reproduced by permission of The Johns Hopkins University Press.

**COPYRIGHTED EXCERPTS IN *SC*, VOLUME 48, WERE REPRODUCED FROM THE FOLLOWING BOOKS:**

Aggeler, Geoffrey. From *Nobler in the Mind: The Stoic-Skeptic Dialectic in English Renaissance Tragedy*. University of Delaware Press, 1998. Copyright © 1998 by Associated University Presses, Inc. All rights reserved. Reproduced by permission.—Clayton, Tom. From "Who 'Has No Children' in *Macbeth*?" in *Shakespearean Illuminations: Essays in Honor of Marvin Rosenberg*. Edited by Jay L. Halio and Hugh Richmond. University of Delaware Press, 1998. Copyright © 1998 by Associated University Presses, Inc. All rights reserved. Reproduced by permission.—Demaray, John G. From *Shakespeare and the Spectacles of Strangeness: The Tempest and the Transformation of Renaissance Theatrical Forms*. Duquesne University Press, 1998. Copyright © 1998 by Duquesne University Press. All rights reserved. Reproduced by permission.—Goldman, Michael. From "History-Making in the Henriad" in *Shakespearean Illuminations: Essays in Honor of Marvin Rosenberg*. Edited by Jay L. Halio and Hugh Richmond. University of Delaware Press, 1998. Copyright © 1998 by Associated University Presses, Inc. All rights reserved.

Reproduced by permission.—Hawley, William M. From *Shakespearean Tragedy and the Common Law: The Art of Punishment*. Peter Lang Publishing, Inc., 1998. Copyright © 1998 Peter Lang Publishing, Inc. All rights reserved. Reproduced by permission.—Homann, Sidney. From "'What Do I Do Now?' Directing *A Midsummer Night's Dream*" in *Shakespearean Illuminations: Essays in Honor of Marvin Rosenberg*. Edited by Jay L. Halio and Hugh Richmond. University of Delaware Press, 1998. Copyright © 1998 by Associated University Presses, Inc. All rights reserved. Reproduced by permission.—Hopkins, Lisa. From *The Shakespearean Marriage: Merry Wives and Heavy Husbands*. Macmillan Press, 1998. Copyright © Lisa Hopkins 1998. All rights reserved. Reproduced by permission of Macmillan Press Ltd. and the author. In North America by St. Martin's Press, Incorporated.—Nevo, Ruth. From "Motive and Meaning in *All's Well That Ends Well*" in *Strands Afar Remote: Israeli Perspectives on Shakespeare*. Edited by Avraham Oz. University of Delaware Press, 1998. Copyright © 1998 by Associated University Presses, Inc. All rights reserved. Reproduced by permission.—Pugliatti, Paola. From "Shakespeare's Historicism: Visions and Revisions" in *Shakespeare and the Twentieth Century: The Selected Proceedings of the International Shakespeare Association World Congress, Los Angeles, 1996.* Edited by Jonathan Bate, Jill L. Levenson, and Dieter Mehl. University of Delaware Press, 1998. Copyright © 1998 by Associated University Presses, Inc. All rights reserved. Reproduced by permission.—Rozmovits, Linda. From "Shylock: The Infamous Secret Jew" in *Shakespeare and the Politics of Culture in Late Victorian England*. The Johns Hopkins University Press, 1998. Copyright © 1998 The Johns Hopkins University Press. All rights reserved. Reproduced by permission.—Skeele, David. From *Thwarting the Wayward Seas: A Critical and Theatrical History of Shakespeare's Pericles in the Nineteenth and Twentieth Centuries*. University of Delaware Press, 1998. Copyright © 1998 by Associated University Presses, Inc. All rights reserved. Reproduced by permission.

# List of Plays and Poems Covered in *SC*

Volumes 1-10 present a critical overview of each play, including criticism from the seventeenth century to the present. Beginning with Volume 11, the series focuses on the history of Shakespeare's plays on the stage and in important films. The Yearbooks reprint the most important critical pieces of the year as suggested by an advisory board of Shakespearean scholars. Beginning with Volume 27, each volume is organized around a theme and focuses on criticism published after 1960.

**Volume 1**
*The Comedy of Errors*
*Hamlet*
*Henry IV, Parts 1 and 2*
*Timon of Athens*
*Twelfth Night*

**Volume 2**
*Henry VIII*
*King Lear*
*Love's Labour's Lost*
*Measure for Measure*
*Pericles*

**Volume 3**
*Henry VI, Parts 1, 2, and 3*
*Macbeth*
*A Midsummer Night's Dream*
*Troilus and Cressida*

**Volume 4**
*Cymbeline*
*The Merchant of Venice*
*Othello*
*Titus Andronicus*

**Volume 5**
*As You Like It*
*Henry V*
*The Merry Wives of Windsor*
*Romeo and Juliet*

**Volume 6**
*Antony and Cleopatra*
*Richard II*
*The Two Gentlemen of Verona*

**Volume 7**
*All's Well That Ends Well*
*Julius Caesar*
*The Winter's Tale*

**Volume 8**
*Much Ado about Nothing*
*Richard III*
*The Tempest*

**Volume 9**
*Coriolanus*
*King John*
*The Taming of the Shrew*
*The Two Noble Kinsmen*

**Volume 10**
*The Phoenix and Turtle*
*The Rape of Lucrece*
*Sonnets*
*Venus and Adonis*

**Volume 11**
*King Lear*
*Othello*
*Romeo and Juliet*

**Volume 12**
*The Merchant of Venice*
*A Midsummer Night's Dream*
*The Taming of the Shrew*
*The Two Gentlemen of Verona*

**Volume 13**
1989 Yearbook

**Volume 14**
*Henry IV, Parts 1 and 2*
*Henry V*
*Richard III*

**Volume 15**
*Cymbeline*
*Pericles*
*The Tempest*
*The Winter's Tale*

**Volume 16**
1990 Yearbook

**Volume 17**
*Antony and Cleopatra*
*Coriolanus*
*Julius Caesar*
*Titus Andronicus*

**Volume 18**
*The Merry Wives of Windsor*
*Much Ado about Nothing*
*Troilus and Cressida*

**Volume 19**
1991 Yearbook

**Volume 20**
*Macbeth*
*Timon of Athens*

**Volume 21**
*Hamlet*

**Volume 22**
1992 Yearbook

**Volume 23**
*As You Like It*
*Love's Labour's Lost*
*Measure for Measure*

**Volume 24**
*Henry VI, Parts 1, 2, and 3*
*Henry VIII*
*King John*
*Richard II*

**Volume 25**
1993 Yearbook

**Volume 26**
*All's Well That Ends Well*
*The Comedy of Errors*
*Twelfth Night*

**Volume 27**
Shakespeare and Classical Civilization
*Antony and Cleopatra*
*Timon of Athens*
*Titus Andronicus*
*Troilus and Cressida*

**Volume 28**
1994 Yearbook

**Volume 29**
Magic and the Supernatural
*Macbeth*
*A Midsummer Night's Dream*
*The Tempest*

**Volume 30**
Politics
*Coriolanus*
*Henry V*
*Julius Caesar*

**Volume 31**
Shakespeare's Representation of Women
*Much Ado about Nothing*
*King Lear*
*The Taming of the Shrew*

**Volume 32**
1995 Yearbook

**Volume 33**
Sexuality in Shakespeare
*Measure for Measure*
*The Rape of Lucrece*
*Romeo and Juliet*
*Venus and Adonis*

**Volume 34**
Appearance versus Reality
*As You Like It*
*The Comedy of Errors*
*Twelfth Night*

**Volume 35**
Madness
*Hamlet*
*Othello*

**Volume 36**
Fathers and Daughters
*Cymbeline*
*Pericles*
*The Winter's Tale*

**Volume 37**
1996 Yearbook

**Volume 38**
Desire
*All's Well That Ends Well*
*Love's Labour's Lost*
*The Merry Wives of Windsor*
*The Phoenix and Turtle*

**Volume 39**
Kingship
*Henry IV, Parts 1 and 2*
*Henry VI, Parts 1, 2, and 3*
*Richard II*
*Richard III*

**Volume 40**
Gender Identity
*The Merchant of Venice*
*Sonnets*
*The Two Gentlemen of Verona*

**Volume 41**
Authorship Controversy
*Henry VIII*
*King John*
*The Two Noble Kinsmen*

**Volume 42**
1997 Yearbook

**Volume 43**
Violence
*The Rape of Lucrece*
*Titus Andronicus*
*Troilus and Cressida*

**Volume 44**
Psychoanalytic Interpretations
*Hamlet*
*Macbeth*

**Volume 45**
Dreams
*A Midsummer Night's Dream*
*The Tempest*
*The Winter's Tale*

**Volume 46**
Clowns and Fools
*As You Like It*
*King Lear*
*Twelfth Night*

**Volume 47**
Deception in Shakespeare
*Antony and Cleopatra*
*Cymbeline*
*The Merry Wives of Windsor*

**Future Volumes**

**Volume 48**
1998 Yearbook

**Volume 49**
Law and Justice
*Henry IV, Parts 1 and 2*
*Henry V*
*Measure for Measure*

# Comedies

# "Infinite Space": Representation and Reformation in *Measure for Measure*

## Huston Diehl, *University of Iowa*

*Measure for Measure* is a deeply dissatisfying comedy, so problematic that, as Jean Howard argues, it "puts critics under stress."[1] They typically respond by judging, finding fault with the play's structure, the Duke's elaborate manipulations, Isabella's ethical choices, Shakespeare's use of the bed-trick, and, especially, the final trial scene, with its exaggerated theatricality, its failure to effect any real reformation, and its unsettling subversion of the conventional comic ending.[2] Identifying a pattern of failed, inadequate, and problematic substitutions in *Measure for Measure,* Alexander Leggatt, like many other critics, concludes that the play is flawed:

> I am not saying that Shakespeare, in order to make a point about the imperfection of his art, deliberately wrote an imperfect play.... He seems, however, to have found *Measure for Measure* a harder struggle than most, and as he faced the gap between conception and embodiment, his imagination generated image after image of representations that are vivid but not quite adequate, and substitutions that are revealing and fascinating but incomplete.[3]

Taking Leggatt's disclaimer as my starting point, I want to examine Shakespeare's representational strategies in *Measure for Measure,* and the dissatisfaction they arouse, in order to make precisely the opposite claim. I will argue that Shakespeare deliberately calls attention to the imperfection of his art, and I will show how the inadequacy of the multiple substitutions is a crucial factor in Shakespeare's conception of his drama, producing—not undermining—the play's meaning as well as its peculiar power. What Leggatt attributes to a breakdown in the creative process—resulting in the proliferation of incomplete and inadequate substitutions and the contrived nature of the final revelations—are, I think, better understood as products of the playwright's experimentation with a Protestant aesthetic of the stage.

Shakespearean criticism has long been alert to the play's religious themes, biblical allusions, and theological subtexts. The references to the Sermon on the Mount and to St. Paul; the dramatization of the conflict between law and mercy; the association of the Duke with divine providence; the parodies of the Annunciation and the Last Judgment; the language of grace, ransom, and remedy; the appropriation of such religious genres as hagiography, parable, and *contemplatio mortis*: scholars have discussed these and many other theological aspects of *Measure for Measure,* though without arriving at any consensus about how Shakespeare employs this theological material or to what end.[4] But to a surprising degree, scholars who focus on the play's religious dimension ignore the contested nature of religion in early modern England, preferring to speak of a universal Christianity in ways that obscure the controversies fracturing the Christian church during the Reformation.[5] And critics who take issue with these attempts to read *Measure for Measure* in terms of Christian themes are much more likely to insist on the play's having a secular or even antireligious nature than to evaluate the historical assumptions about religion that inform such studies.[6] Even those new historicists who use *Measure for Measure* as a key text in their studies of early modern English culture tend to treat religion as a conservative and stable orthodoxy in the service of the state and monarchy.[7]

But, of course, in post-Reformation England Christianity was in crisis, religious ideology unstable, and theological doctrines vigorously disputed. Even among English Protestants religious beliefs and practices were so much the subject of contentious debate that one of James's first acts as the king of England was to convene in January 1604 a conference of bishops and puritans at Hampton Court to try to resolve some of their long-standing differences and perhaps "to begin a further reformation of the Church."[8] Yet to illustrate my point, that historical event goes unmentioned in virtually all treatments of *Measure for Measure* as a play written for or about James even though Shakespeare's 1604 comedy, in staging a conflict between a rigid reformer and a woman intent on entering a strict Roman Catholic religious order, rehearses the extremist views—radical puritan and Catholic—that James sought to suppress at the Hampton Court conference.[9] According to Kenneth Fincham and Peter Lake, James used the conference, on the one hand, "to construct and support a common Protestant front against Rome" and, on the other, to contain radical puritanism by "driving a wedge between the moderate and radical wings of Puritan opinion."[10]

I mention King James's ecclesiastical policy not to argue that Shakespeare advocates or allegorizes it but rather to suggest how fully *Measure for Measure* engages many of the religious controversies of Jacobean England, exploring theological issues—about monasticism, celibacy, idolatry, auricular confession, merit, righteousness, hypocrisy, reformist zeal, and moral discipline—that trouble and divide James's subjects in the early years of the seventeenth century. Set in the

Roman Catholic city of Vienna and featuring a number of characters who are, desire to be, or pretend to be members of the Roman Catholic clergy, the play questions the possibility of achieving either celibacy or a disciplined withdrawal from the world. By using the clerical habit of the friar as a disguise that the Duke puts on and off and eventually discards, the play also demystifies monasticism, perhaps even reinforcing Protestant associations of friars with a fraudulent theatricality, their "humblest habits" with "a false disguise."[11] At the same time, the play depicts the very pressing urban problems that preoccupied the Protestant authorities of Jacobean London and critiques the draconian measures proposed by radical puritans to reform human behavior, revealing these measures to be both inhumane and ineffective. It also exposes the moral depravity and hypocrisy of a character associated with these extreme reformist policies—the precise and legalistic Angelo. Thus marking Vienna for its early modern London audiences as a setting simultaneously alien and familiar, papist and puritan, *Measure for Measure* identifies Isabella's monastic vocation and Angelo's reformist zeal with a false—or counterfeit—righteousness. Angelo's hypocritical and tyrannical behavior, to be sure, is depicted as far more abhorrent than Isabella's idealistic, if excessive, commitment to the rigid rules observed by "the votarists of Saint Clare" (1.4.5). But efforts to read the play as either pro-Catholic or nostalgic for a Catholic past fail to address the ways in which Shakespeare appropriates the representational strategies of English Calvinism, distancing his theater from a fraudulent theatricality widely associated in Protestant England with the Roman Catholic Church while also challenging the vehement antitheatricality of radical Protestants.[12]

There was, most historians agree, a Calvinist consensus within the national church under King James, who sought at the beginning of his reign to win over moderate puritans "through the incorporation of evangelical Calvinism into the Jacobean establishment."[13] Indeed, Patrick Collinson asserts that "Calvinism can be regarded as the theological cement of the Jacobean church . . . 'a common and ameliorating bond' uniting conformists and moderate puritans."[14] But although Calvinism is the cement that binds together different factions of the Jacobean church, various segments of the population appropriated and adapted it to their own needs and interests—"consumed" it in Michel de Certeau's sense of this word.[15] Calvinism was employed in the service of competing authorities and rival political factions and invoked to achieve a range of multiple and even conflicting goals, not all of them religious in nature.

A case in point is the battle over the legitimacy of the stage. As literary scholars have frequently noted, antitheatricalists often draw upon Calvinist distrust of theatricality in their attacks on the stage, tapping into their Protestant readers' deepest anti-Catholic sentiments by aligning the London theaters with the "false" ceremonies, "idolatrous" spectacles, and "cunning" theatricality of the Roman Church.[16] But apologists for the stage also appropriate basic tenets of Calvinist theology to wield against their opponents, a phenomenon that has for the most part been ignored in the critical literature. In his refutation of Stephen Gosson's *Schoole of Abuse*, Thomas Lodge, for example, counters Gosson's point that Plato banished the poets from his republic by accusing Plato of idolatry, thus attempting to undermine Plato's authority by associating him with the "idolatrous" Roman church; he also insists that poetry is a gift from God, an argument that Calvin and his followers repeatedly use to justify certain kinds of art.[17] Lodge is just one of many writers who appropriate Calvinist arguments and tropes to defend the stage. They charge the antitheatricalists with employing Roman Catholic modes of interpretation, argue that the stage exposes rather than produces the fraudulent kind of theatricality Calvinism distrusts, and apply Calvinist notions of the conscience to their theories of dramatic art.[18]

Shakespeare, I suggest, participates in these efforts to legitimate the theater by aligning it with the moderate Calvinism of the established English church. At the same time, he raises provocative questions about the challenge of knowing, judging, and reforming in a Calvinist universe. In a sustained exploration of the power and limits of representation, including his own theatrical representations, Shakespeare formulates an aesthetic of the stage that marks and preserves the gap between the sign and the thing signified, arouses and frustrates the desire to know directly and fully, and compels his audiences to confront both the inadequacy of all human knowledge and their own imperfect judgment. By eliciting an enabling kind of dissatisfaction in *Measure for Measure,* he claims for the theater the project of reforming human behavior even as he acknowledges the limits of that project and distances his theater from the extremist views of radical puritanism.

## Knowing

Rather than assume that Shakespeare's play is flawed because the substitutions staged in the course of *Measure for Measure* are inadequate or incomplete, I propose to examine its pattern of substitutions in terms of Calvin's insistence that the physical world is itself a *representation*. English Calvinists encourage the faithful to discern in the visible world signs of another truer and more real world, to find in the transient present images of a permanent future, and thus to see how the world they inhabit mirrors (however imperfectly) the divine. Calling the created world "painted tables, by which al mankinde is provoked and allured to the knowledg" of God, Calvin argues that "God doth in the mirror of his workes shew by representation both himself and his immortall kingdome," and he urges his readers to discern "certaine markes" and "ensignes" of God's glory that God has "graven" and "displaid" in the "whole workmanship of the world."[19] Indeed, Calvin imagines the world as a magnificent theater and its inhabitants as spectators capable of knowing God indirectly by beholding the beauty of his creation. "For what else is the world," he asks in a sermon on Ephesians, "but an open stage wheron God will haue his majestie seene?"[20] Man, he asserts in the *Institutes,* "is set as it were in this gorgeous stage to be a beholder" of God's works.[21]

To take an example that might shed light on Shakespeare's duke and deputy, in such a construction of the world a magistrate is in a sense always a representation of the divine judge—God's substitute, if you will—and always to be viewed in terms of both his likeness to the divine (his authority, power, and capacity to judge and punish) and the limitations of that comparison. Calvin defines civil magistrates as "deputies of God" who "altogether beare the person of god, whose stede they do after a certaine maner supply." Ideally, they "are true examplars and paternes of hys bountifulnesse" in whom "the lord himself hath emprinted and engraved an inuiolable maiesty."[22] The practice of hanging paintings of the Last Judgment directly above the magistrate's seat in the law courts of Northern Europe visually reinforced the notion that the magistrate was an earthly proxy for the divine judge.[23] But to see the magistrate as an image of the all-judging God was to understand not only how he derives his authority from God but also how inadequate he is in relation to God. Even as he urges magistrates to "represent in themselues unto men a certaine image of the providence, preservation, goodnesse, good wil, & righteousnesse of God," Calvin addresses the problem of tyrannical, severe, deceitful, vengeful, and violent rulers, noting how far they have strayed from the God they should figure.[24] The comparison between the earthly magistrate and the divine Judge thus inevitably produces dissatisfaction, a longing for that which is represented but absent, the God who cannot be seen in this world face to face.

The peculiar way in which the characters of *Measure for Measure* seem to point beyond themselves to divine things, even as their flaws firmly locate them in the human world of Vienna, may well reflect Shakespeare's attempt to represent the physical world as it was understood in the age of Reformation, to write not an allegory but a play about living in an allegorized world. For if, as Calvin teaches, the world that humans inhabit is understood to be a theater in which God manifests himself indirectly through images and signs, then Shakespeare's theatrical practice—in the Globe, no less—is a representation of a representation, one that engages its spectators in the challenge of knowing indirectly, partially, by means of signs. In *Measure for Measure* characters repeatedly define the human condition in representational terms, describing themselves as figures, mirrors, coins, stamps, prints, and forms that image something else. Even Angelo's name, which calls to mind both the spiritual creature and the English coin stamped with the image of the archangel Gabriel, reminds Shakespeare's audiences that a deputy bears the image of the divine and gains his value from that image. The spectators in the Globe of 1604, I am suggesting, were encouraged to engage in acts of interpretation that replicated the way the established English Church—in sermons and catechisms—had taught them to interpret the world. "Because he [God] hath made hym self knowen unto us by his woorkes," the child in an English catechism is taught to respond, "it is necessarie for vs to seeke hym out in them. For our capacitie is not able to comprehende his Diuine substaunce, therefore he hath made the worlde as a Glasse, wherein wee maie beholde hym in such sorte, as it is expedient for us to knowe hym."[25] Central to this mode of experience is a profound sense of the gap between the fallen world and the celestial one it can only shadow.

For early Protestants the challenge of living in a world where human knowledge is partial, indirect, and limited centered on the need to curb the all-too-human tendency to mistake the sign for the thing it signifies. According to Calvin and his English followers, people are always prone to confusing the substitute with the original because they long for direct knowledge and they overvalue the things of this world. "Even the children of God," a 1581 English catechism warns, "feele themselves so intangled in the delight of earthly things which of themselves are good" that they commit idolatry, attributing "that to the creature which ys due to the creator."[26] The Protestant reformers identify this as one of the chief errors of papistry, evidenced in the doctrine of transubstantiation, the cult of the saints, and the worship of images. In their attack on "idolatrous" theater, the antitheatricalists accuse playwrights of perpetuating this error, claiming that stage plays tempt spectators "to giue that which is proper to God, unto them [the players and their theatrical illusions] that are no gods."[27]

In *Measure for Measure* Shakespeare seems intent on guarding against this danger, both by thematizing it and by marking his own representations as representations. From the opening scene when the Duke deputizes Angelo, to the bed-trick when Mariana is substituted for Isabella, to the complicated substitution of Ragozine's head for the unrepentant Barnardine's so that it in turn can be substituted for Claudio's head, to Elbow's comic malapropisms (substitutions that force the audiences to listen for the gap between the literal word and the intended meaning), to the dizzying proliferation of substitutions in the last act: Shakespeare not only explores the capacity of the substitute to stand in for the original but also nurtures a highly self-reflexive awareness of the nature of representation and the problem of indirect knowledge. To illustrate, let me briefly discuss three key episodes: Angelo's sudden and inexplicable lust for Isabella, which I interpret as a classic example of idolatry; the bed-trick and the subsequent playing with the notion of carnal knowledge, which I read as an inquiry into the nature of embodiment; and the often-overlooked but highly significant substitution of the Duke's seal for the deputy's death-warrant, which I see as a test of faith.

In the fascinating and disturbing scene in which Isabella, goaded by Lucio, pleads with Angelo for her brother's life, the righteous deputy who has never before experienced sexual passion finds himself overwhelmed by desire for a woman who wishes to enter a convent. Many scholars interpret this sudden and unexpected eruption of sexual desire in Angelo in psychoanalytical terms. Focusing on the relation between repression and desire, they argue that for Angelo "prohibition is aphrodisiac"; but the widely held assumption that "Angelo desires a woman because she is forbidden" obscures, I think, the way this scene locates the origin of Angelo's sexual desire for Isabella in his sense of his own righteousness, identifying his lust for the virtuous woman with his love of virtue.[28] "Dost thou desire her foully," Angelo asks himself incredulously after Isabella departs, "for those things / That make her good?" (2.2.178-79).[29] Imagining that the devil uses a saint to ensnare him in his own saintliness, he concludes:

> O cunning enemy, that, to catch a saint,
> With saints dost bait thy hook! Most
>   dangerous
> Is that temptation that doth goad us on
> To sin in loving virtue. Never could the
>   strumpet,
> With all her double vigour—art and nature—
> Once stir my temper; but this virtuous
>   maid
> Subdues me quite.
>
>                    (ll. 184-90)

How can loving virtue be the source of sin?

Shakespeare, I submit, depicts Angelo's lust for Isabella as idolatry, for when the deputy is aroused by the novice's saintliness—that is, for the way she images the divine—he immediately seeks to know that saintliness directly and carnally. In other words, he substitutes the woman who reflects divinity for God himself, a substitution that simultaneously "foul[s]" Isabella and alienates him from God. Once he is aroused by Isabella's virtue, he can think of her only with a lust he himself identifies with misplaced devotion:

> When I would pray and think, I think and
>   pray
> To several subjects: heaven hath my empty
>   words,
> Whilst my invention, hearing not my tongue,
> Anchors on Isabella. . . .
>
>                    (2.4.1-4)

Enacting the error of idolatry as it was understood by early Protestants, Angelo is, in effect, "so snared with . . . affection" for one of the "creatures that God hath made for our use" that "the Lord is . . . altogether . . . thrust out of place."[30] His imagination "[a]nchors on Isabella" and not the God who created her. Angelo's attempt to "know" Isabella's virtue by "knowing" her body, however farfetched it may sound to us today, conforms to a pervasive early Protestant belief that idolatry—perceived as misplaced devotion, a substitution of the creature for the Creator—leads directly to physical lust and "abominable concupiscences" because it privileges the carnal over the spiritual.[31] To interpret Angelo's lust as a misplaced desire to know God directly and carnally—that is, to understand it in theological rather than psychoanalytic terms—is not therefore to deny the utter perversity of it; rather, it is to recognize how dangerous, how fundamentally depraved, the idolater in the Calvinist schema was believed to be. English reformers equate idolatry with "spirituall fornication," and they warn that the idolater—alienated from God, paradoxically, by trying to physically possess the divine—inevitably falls into "carnall fornication, and all uncleannesse," indulging in "Sodomie," "the stewes," "whoredoms and fornications."[32] The idolater, in other words, was understood to be someone who, like Angelo, gives his "sensual race the rein" (2.4.160).

If we understand Angelo's fundamental error as epistemological—a confusion of the sign for what it signifies, a misidentification of the substitute as the original—we can see how provocatively Shakespeare explores the problem of knowing in the bed-trick, where he literalizes Angelo's error in order to expose its absurdity. When the Duke substitutes Mariana for Isabella, tricking Angelo into sleeping with the woman he has wronged and rejected, he exploits Angelo's tendency to apprehend—as the Duke says of Barnardine—"no further than this world" (5.1.475) and forces a recognition of the danger of equating the image with the truth. The bed-trick thus does not simply trap Angelo in his own perverse lust, hypocrisy, and betrayal; it also reveals his central epistemological error, an error that he is in danger of repeating endlessly: mistaking his limited power for absolute power and confusing his asceticism with perfection, as well as desiring Isabella in place of God.

Before she reveals her identity in the trial scene, the veiled Mariana speaks enigmatically, first declaring "I have known my husband, yet my husband / Knows not that ever he knew me" and then claiming to the startled onlookers that Angelo is her husband and the man "Who thinks he knows that he ne'er knew my body, / But knows he thinks that he knows Isabel's" (ll. 184-85, 198-99). Her riddles, like Lucio's comic assertion "I know what I know" (3.1.390) earlier in the play, call to mind an enigmatic passage from First Corinthians in which Paul, preaching against idolatrous practices, questions the validity of all human knowledge and insists that "loue" rather than knowledge "edifieth": "If any man thinke that he knoweth any thing," Paul declares, "he knoweth nothing yet as he oght to knowe."[33] In appropriating this Pauline text, which identifies any belief in one's own capacity to know with vanity, pride, and idolatry, Mariana unsettles Angelo, for she not only denies his version of the truth but also challenges the very ground upon which he has passed judgment on others. She plays, too, of course, with the double meaning of the word *know,* a joke that underscores Angelo's epistemological error, highlighting his presumption that what he knows carnally is valid and emphasizing that the very nature of embodiment impedes direct and full apprehension. Through the bed-trick Angelo thus quite literally experiences the partiality and inadequacy of corporeal knowledge, in the "shadow and silence" (3.1.239) mistaking the substitute for the woman he illicitly desires.

The play, I suggest, produces a similar experience for theater audiences, who are simultaneously invited to believe that what they see embodied on the stage is true and reminded that the theater, after all, is nothing but a "fantastical trick" (l. 340) involving masks and disguises, lies and indirections, shadows and substitutions. But while the artifice of the bed-trick calls attention to the gap between representation and reality, eliciting dissatisfaction in audience members who prefer drama to achieve greater verisimilitude, Shakespeare never entirely demystifies his representations but rather promotes a faith in signs as well as a skepticism about theatrical illusions. Indeed, in one particularly significant scene, he casts as heroic the character who acts solely on the basis of faith in a sign.

I refer to the scene in which the Provost receives Claudio's death warrant from Angelo. Having arranged the bed-trick in order to save Claudio, the disguised Duke is unprepared for this turn of events. Rather than reveal his true identity, he asks the Provost to disobey his superior and delay the execution, thereby risking his own death. Refusing, at first, to violate his oath, the Provost changes his mind when, told that the Duke approves the delay, he is shown "the hand and seal of the Duke" and encouraged to recognize "the character . . . and the signet" (4.2.177-78). Replying simply, "I know them both" (l. 179), the Provost chooses to honor the signet of the absent Duke and to ignore the deputy's death warrant. Except for the Duke's seal and handwriting, the "amazed" Provost has only the assurance of an obscure friar that the Duke's approval of this dangerous course of action is "a certainty" (l. 173). Although the friar promises that the truth will eventually be revealed and the Provost's actions vindicated, he speaks in cryptic and mysterious riddles, offering only more signs to interpret. "Look," he tells the Provost, "th'unfolding star calls up the shepherd" (ll. 185-86). In this scene Shakespeare explores the challenge of exercising faith in the absence of direct proof. This was a central concern of early Protestantism and one that English reformers, articulating the tenets of a Calvinist covenant theology, frequently addressed by using the analogy of the king's seal or signet.[34] Shakespeare champions the character who has the capacity to recognize, interpret, and trust the sign of an absent authority, and he constructs as heroic the ability to act on the basis of faith in such a sign even though one's own knowledge is indirect and incomplete. In the end Claudio's life is spared not (as in Shakespeare's source) because the lustful deputy was provided with a sexual partner but because a seal and signet were honored by the faithful and courageous Provost.

The last act promises to resolve the problem of indirect, partial, and imperfect knowing through the anticipated comic resolution, but, significantly, that promise is not fully realized.[35] Shakespeare stages a fictional moment in which the gap between sign and thing signified is eradicated and substitution gives way to identity: the hooded friar *is* the Duke; the veiled Mariana, the woman who slept with Angelo; the muffled man, Claudio. But the desire for direct knowledge that the play has aroused in the audiences is thwarted, the promise deferred, by Shakespeare's stagecraft. Although the multiple unveilings invoke the Pauline promise of direct knowledge and clear vision, the scene insists on its own dark and fantastical artifice. The Duke's plan resembles a comic script too complex and contrived to be credible; the return of the Duke requires the disappearance of the friar he has been playing, highlighting the theatrical convention of doubling and its attendant problems; the Duke and Friar Peter rehearse the ending with Mariana and Isabella, coaching them on how to relate their story, perform their roles, and "veil full purpose" (4.6.4); and Lucio serves as a skeptical audience member, stripping away the theatrical disguise of the friar, refusing the fiction. Even the stunning revelation that Claudio lives is made ambiguous by the Duke's odd insistence that the muffled man resembles and stands in as a substitute for Claudio rather than actually being Claudio. Presenting the mysterious prisoner "As like almost to Claudio as himself," the Duke withholds any assurance of certainty, telling Isabella that "If he be like your brother, for his sake / Is he pardoned" (5.1.483, 484-86), thereby reintroducing a gap between the substitute and the longed-for original.

By calling attention to the artifice, the staginess, of his comic resolution, Shakespeare denies his audiences the pleasure of believing, even for a moment, that the image and the thing imaged are one. The promised revelations are, after all, only theatrical illusions, reminding the audiences that the players cannot escape their own bodies or the play its own representations. But the resulting dissatisfaction, I suggest, is energizing and productive. The trial scene arouses the audience members' deepest desire for completion and revelation, direct knowledge and certainty. By eliciting a longing for certainty that is promised but perpetually deferred, the play does not merely frustrate; it encourages its audiences to view both the world they inhabit and the fictional world of the play as representations, which are inadequate, to be sure, but also potentially significant, even powerful.

## JUDGING

Scholars interested in Shakespeare's treatment of the law in *Measure for Measure* have examined English ecclesiastical and civil laws pertaining to marriage, adultery, and fornication in some depth, but they generally ignore Reformation theories of the law and, in particular, Calvin's emphasis on the epistemological function of the law. And yet Shakespeare seems far less interested in details of the English legal system—one critic calls the law of Vienna "story-book law"[36]—than in exploring the relation between law, broadly defined, and the problem of knowing and judging. Central to his play's inquiry into the law, I suggest, is a Calvinist insistence that self-knowledge can be achieved only by recognizing one's utter inability to fulfill the law, a recognition that necessarily precludes passing judgment on others.

Emphasizing the immeasurable gulf between any individual and perfection, Calvin teaches that no one is capable of obeying the law. His discussions of the law focus not on ethical behavior, discipline, and punishment but on knowledge. "By the law," he writes, "is the knowlege of sinne."[37] For him, the law does not correct or control sin but rather represents it, showing people the multiple ways they have transgressed. The law, he writes, is a "loking glasse" that "representeth unto us the spottes of our face," a mirror that reveals to people how utterly they have defaced the divine image in which they were made.[38] English Protestant catechisms of this period invariably advance Calvin's interpretation of the law, rehearsing the notion that the law is a "glasse" that teaches "that we be imperfect in all our workes," thereby making us aware of "our naughtiness sinne and defectes."[39] That awareness, moreover, is productive, for it creates the conditions for repentance and redemption. "And so by our own euells we are stirred to consider the good things of God," Calvin writes, "and we can not earnestly aspire toward him, untill we begin to mislike our selues."[40] For Calvin, the law thus serves a vital function: by revealing our inherent sinfulness, it produces dissatisfaction with the self, a dissatisfaction that, because it initiates the process of repentance, is essential for salvation.[41]

When Calvin defines the law as a mirror that works to "admonish, certifie, proue gilty, yea and condemne euery man of his owne unrighteousenesse," he declares any belief in one's own righteousness a fantasy; insisting that none "shall come to the mark of true perfection, unlesse he be loosed from the burden of his body," he warns that to presume that one has "any woorthinesse" or "any meane or abilitie to doo good (of himself:)" is "too step intoo Gods place," that is, to confuse one's own powers with God's, usurping the place of the Creator.[42] The law thus serves as a continual reminder that "there is none righteous, no not one" (Romans 3:10) by enabling people to see their transgressions, imperfections, and failings. Calvin insists that the person who believes himself to be righteous is deluded by self-love,

> so long as he measureth it [his strength] by the proportion of his own will. But so sone as he is compelled to trie his life by the balance of the law, then leaving the presumption of that counterfait righteousnesse, he seeth himself to be an infinite space distant from holinesse: againe, that he floweth full of infinite vices, wherof before he semed cleane. For the evels of lust are hidde in so depe and croked privuie corners, that they easily deceiue the sight of man.[43]

Setting aside the tantalizing linguistic echoes of this passage in *Measure for Measure,* I want to suggest how Calvin's theory of law informs Shakespeare's play and, in particular, its theatrical insistence on the gap, the "infinite space," between "counterfait righteousnesse" and "holinesse."

*Measure for Measure* dramatizes a conflict between two characters who trust in their own capacity to obey the law and to lead virtuous lives: a reformist magistrate smugly confident of his own righteousness and a Roman Catholic novice earnestly preparing to join a strict religious order. Through their confrontation both discover the "infinite space" between their behavior and perfection. Angelo commits a crime far more repugnant than the one for which he has condemned Claudio, and in the trial scene he is forced to acknowledge the distance between the laws he administers and his own rapacious and unruly appetites. Isabella experiences a range of conflicting emotions when she is confronted with Angelo's terrible proposition that requires her to choose between her chastity and her brother's life. Passionately pleading for her brother's life, actively participating in the duplicitous bed-trick, and deliberately giving false testimony against Angelo in order to take her revenge on him, she, too, fails to live up to her ideals of purity and holiness.

The play's insistence that neither the rigorous discipline of the religious novice nor the severe laws of the precise puritan can produce a state of righteousness surely must have resonated in a powerful way with the audiences of post-Reformation England, where questions of human merit, good works, and righteousness were vigorously debated. Protestant reformers vehemently denounce the clerics and saints of the Roman Church because they "most shamelessly call" their lives "Angelike, doing herein verily so great injurie to the Angells of God" when in reality they are nothing more than "whoremongers, adulterers, and somwhat ells muche worse and filthier."[44] And satiric attacks on radical Protestantism skewer puritans for assuming they could attain a state of righteousness, exposing that belief to be a grand delusion and exposing them as contemptible hypocrites.[45] Many recent critical readings of the play, however, ignore these contemporary religious controversies and especially the intense anti-Catholic and anticlerical sentiments they generated in Jacobean London. Feminist criticism in particular tends to valorize Isabella's commitment to a monastic life of celibacy and saintliness, viewing the cloistered life of a nun as an admirable assertion of "female autonomy" that is inherently subversive of patriarchal society. From this perspective, Isabella's public humiliation in the final act is an inexcusable violation of both Isabella's independence and her religious vocation, a shameless "shaming of a nun."[46]

For these critics the play's ending, which turns on Isabella's capacity to forgive the man who tried to coerce her into having sex with him, is profoundly disturbing, for that forgiveness represents to them not an admirable willingness to relinquish a "counterfait righteousnesse" but a regrettable surrender to patriarchal authority; and the Duke's subsequent pardon of Angelo constitutes a nullification of the grievous wrongs committed against Isabella. Declaring the final trial scene "aesthetically and intellectually unsatisfying . . . [and] personally infuriating," Harriett Hawkins, for one, complains that "the Duke's decision to grant mercy to everybody revokes the rule of law, and to revoke the rule of human law is to revoke the idea of consequence, of necessity."[47] Such an intense resistance to the play's resolution provides insights into late-twentieth-century democratic notions of law and justice, criminals and victims, power and submission. But it may also illustrate the way *Measure for Measure* challenges traditional notions of merit that were being contested in Shakespeare's own day. The play arouses but thwarts a deeply felt desire for "justice, justice, justice, justice!" (5.1.25), eliciting a profound dissatisfaction, a dissatisfaction inherent in Calvin's premise that the law exists not to control the dangerous behavior of a few but to reveal everyone's imperfections.

In deliberately violating the conventions of poetic justice, Shakespeare not only challenges traditional belief in human merit but also interrogates his own theatrical practices. Many critics have noted that the final trial scene resembles a play that the Duke carefully scripts, rehearses, and stages. The insistent metadrama of this final scene, I suggest, underscores how theatrical representation can thwart self-righteous judgment and compel self-knowledge.

In compliance with the Duke's script, the chaste (and chastened) Isabella plays the role of the defiled woman in the trial scene and publicly proclaims that she has slept with Angelo. Although Shakespeare depicts her as self-conscious about the role she reluctantly agrees to play, heightening his audience's awareness of the pretense, he insists on the value of her role-playing. Isabella experiences her theatrical performance as profoundly humiliating, but her public humiliation enables her to identify and empathize with Mariana. Required to step into Mariana's place, Isabella, "with grief and shame" (l. 96), declares herself a "fallen" woman and is treated as an object of scorn and approbation. Imaginatively reversing the earlier physical substitution of Mariana for Isabella, a substitution that put Mariana at risk in order to save both Isabella's brother and her chastity, the Duke's casting thus forces Isabella to recognize that she, like the woman she plays, is vulnerable, conflicted, passionate, imperfect, and at risk. It is this recognition, the product of a theatrical fiction, that enables Isabella to join Mariana in pleading for Angelo's life.

The Duke's theatrics force Angelo, too, to acknowledge his imperfection. When Isabella and Mariana accuse Angelo of terrible crimes and demand justice, the Duke, in a shocking move, turns the legal proceedings over to the accused, placing him in the seat of judgment and telling him, "be you judge / Of your own cause" (ll. 165-66). Rather than reasserting his authority, the Duke delegates his power of judgement to his deputy, the very man whom he knows to have flagrantly abused that power and who is the subject of judicial inquiry. The Duke then stages an elaborate theatrical performance, one in which Angelo is positioned as both dramatic protagonist and judging spectator. Shaken and exposed by this performance, Angelo confesses his crimes and repents. If Shakespeare calls attention to the contrived and scripted nature of Angelo's trial, he nevertheless attributes its efficacy—its capacity to make Angelo's transgressions visible to himself and others and to elicit self-examination and confession—largely to the Duke's representational strategies: his use of indirection; his substitution of Isabella for Mariana; his deployment of a paradoxical riddle; his teasing theatrical presentation of a mysterious, veiled woman; his own complicated doubling as friar and Duke; and the way he forces Angelo to pay attention to the discrepancies between what Angelo thinks he knows and what is. By foregrounding the confusing gaps between language and meaning, knowledge and truth, the substitute and the person she stands in for, the disguise and the person in disguise, the Duke's theater disrupts and confounds its spectators, ultimately revealing to them what has been hidden, denied, or misunderstood.

In *Measure for Measure,* as in *Hamlet,* Shakespeare insists on the capacity of theater to activate the conscience, arouse guilt, and elicit confessions of wrongdoing. In both plays he draws on Calvinist theories of the conscience to explain the powerful affect of theater, and in both he nurtures as well as thematizes the interiorized, reflexive, and self-disciplinary gaze that those theories seek to inculcate. According to the many English Protestant tracts on the conscience which proliferated in the wake of the Reformation, the conscience enables a person to see his or her actions from God's perspective and therefore to render " 'a man's judgment of himself, according to the judgment of God of him.' "[48] Angelo confesses his crimes and declares his heart "penitent" as soon as he realizes that the Duke, "like power divine," has been privy to his most secret acts and private transgressions—that is, as soon as he imagines his actions from the viewpoint of a judging authority:

> O my dread lord,
> I should be guiltier than my guiltiness
> To think I can be undiscernible,
> When I perceive your grace, like power divine,
> Hath looked upon my passes.
>
> (5.1.358-62)

It is, significantly, the Duke's theater that provides Angelo with this perspective by positioning him as a spectator and judge at his own trial. In this scene, as in the performance of "The Murder of Gonzago," Shakespeare claims for the stage the power to activate the conscience—that internalized and self-regulating spectator, "God's spy," "man's . . . overseer," and a keeper "ioyned to man, to marke and watch all hys secretes"—that Protestant reformers taught has the power "to prescribe, prohibit, absolue and condemne *de iure.*"[49] In a play that questions the capacity of any individual to achieve righteousness, he imagines a theater that nurtures reflexivity, produces guilt, and thwarts the impulse to judge others.

### Reforming

Inasmuch as the Duke's theater seeks to initiate an internal reformation in its spectators by arousing dissatisfaction with the self, it conforms to the kind of art approved by Protestant theologians. Although they condemn as idolatrous images and plays that seduce, dazzle, and trick the beholder, the English reformers routinely defend art that "provoke[s]" us "to consider ourselves . . . and to condemn and abhor our sin," that serves as "stirrers of men's minds," and that enables its viewers "to remember themselves, and to lament their sins"; and they approve of art that awakens the conscience and nurtures moral self-examination.[50] In his defense of the stage, written a few years after Shakespeare's comedy, Thomas Heywood fully articulates a theory of dramatic representation based on these Protestant defenses, arguing that theater has the capacity to "new mold the harts of the spectators" by enabling them to "see and shame at their faults."[51] Louis Adrian Montrose asserts that the arguments advanced by Heywood and other apologists for the stage "remain constrained within the terms of the dominant antitheatrical discourse" and thus "do not fully comprehend the cultural practice" they seek to defend.[52] He looks instead to the antitheatrical tracts, and especially their pervasive fear of the seductive pleasures of the stage, for a more accurate sense of theater's power over its spectators. But I would like to suggest that, by the beginning of the seventeenth century, Shakespeare and his fellow playwrights were actively appropriating Calvinist theories of representation and creatively exploring the disciplinary potential of their medium in an effort to legitimate the stage in the face of virulent antitheatrical attacks.

Steven Mullaney also takes Heywood's claims seriously, using them to illustrate how the early modern stage was understood to be "a potent forum for the reformation as well as the recreation of its audiences." However, he associates the dramatic practice of inducing apprehension and shame with the suppressed Roman Catholic practice of auricular confession, arguing that early modern playwrights appropriate the "internal drama" of the forbidden sacrament, which was "performed before a judgmental authority, at times harrowingly silent, at times sharply inquisitorial."[53] Certainly auricular confession is, as he suggests, a "specter" that haunts *Measure for Measure,*[54] but Shakespeare's play questions its efficacy and, in the final scene, stages another kind of confession, a public and communal rehearsal of mutual guilt that conforms much more closely to Calvinist than to Roman Catholic rituals of confession.

In eliminating the sacrament of auricular confession and instituting a reformed confession, the English Protestant Church substituted one form of apprehension for another. In fact, what the Calvinist reformers most strenuously objected to in the Roman Catholic sacrament of auricular confession was not so much that it aroused apprehension and shame, as Mullaney argues, as that it relieved it in a particularly offensive way. Calvin complains that

> men hauing made confession to a Priest, think that they may wype their mouth and say, I did it not. And not onely they are made all the yeare longe the bolder to sinne: but al the rest of the yeare bearing themselves bolde upon confession, they neuer sighe vnto God, they neuer return to themselues, but heape sinnes vpon sinnes, til they vomit vp all at once as they thinke. And when they haue once vomited them vp, they thynke themselues

discharged of their burden, and that they haue taken away from God the iudgemente that they haue geven to the Priest, and that they haue brought God in forgetfulnesse, when they haue made the Priest priuie.[55]

For him the Catholic sacrament is "pestilente" because it confers on the priest the power to absolve sin, a power he insists resides only in God.[56] He seeks instead to devise religious practices that provoke men to "sighe unto God" and "return to themselves," to feel their guilt continuously and reflect on divine judgment.

Calvin privileges the individual's private and internal confession of sins before God, but he also imagines that such a confession will naturally be followed by a voluntary and public confession before men "not only to whisper the secret of his heart to one man, and once and in hys eare: but oft and openly, and in the bearing of al the world simplye to rehearse . . . his own shame."[57] Indeed, he imagines an ideal Protestant community as one in which all members share publicly the knowledge of their own failings, rehearsing their shame. "We shoulde lay our weaknesse one in an others bosome," he writes, "to receiue mutuall counsel, mutual compassion & mutual comfort one of an other: then that we be naturally priuie to the weaknesses of our brethren; shoulde praye for them to the Lorde."[58] Far from being eliminated from Protestant confessions, then, shame is understood to be shared, and its rehearsal in public is believed to be salutary, arousing the desire for an absolution that no human can confer, nurturing a continual process of self-reflection and repentance, and fostering a sense of community.

In the final scene of *Measure for Measure*, Shakespeare stages just such a public rehearsal of shame, one in which the comic ending is governed by mutual confessions of weaknesses and transgressions and repeated requests for forgiveness rather than the conventional triumph of love and mirth. Even Escalus and the Provost, who appear relatively blameless, and Isabella, who was clearly wronged, confess their faults and ask—publicly—to be pardoned for their behavior; and Angelo, the most obviously guilty character, not only requests forgiveness but is also asked to forgive the Provost for sending him the head of Ragozine instead of Claudio. Indeed, the Duke himself, having discarded his clerical disguise along with all pretense that he has the power to absolve sins, asks to be pardoned, confessing to Isabella that he is responsible for the supposed death of her brother and even declaring his kinship with the condemned man (5.1.487). All of these confessions are offered spontaneously and openly to the entire community after Lucio inadvertently reveals that the friar is, in truth, the Duke. To the extent that these confessions nurture a sense of community based on shared guilt—that is, a Calvinist community of sinners—they may be understood to liberate Isabella, Angelo, and the other characters from the isolation of their counterfeit righteousness.[59]

But that community, forged out of the painful awareness of a common guilt, is necessarily imperfect. As many critics have pointed out, the Duke does not achieve the complete reformation he desires. Isabella struggles to forgive Angelo, making a reluctant and qualified plea for his life; Angelo marries Mariana under duress, never speaking a word of affection to her; Lucio resists the Duke's order to marry Kate Keepdown, his wit still directed toward the bawdy and subversive; Barnardine stubbornly refuses all efforts to reform him; and Isabella does not answer the Duke's marriage proposal, her silence unsettling the comic ending. Although he asserts the power of theatrical representation to arouse guilt and produce the conditions for repentance, Shakespeare questions the capacity of the stage to reform its spectators.[60] When, in the final act, he makes his own activity as dramatist visible through a Duke who constructs fictional narratives, traffics in substitutions, manipulates desire, cleverly scripts comic endings, and seeks to reform his audiences, he depicts his central character as an imperfect, even a bungling playwright.[61]

Why might Shakespeare create a figure of a playwright who cannot be trusted, who devises tricks that raise troubling ethical questions, who employs an improbable and highly contrived script, and who cannot even produce the conventional comic ending, unable as he is to reform the transgressors or persuade his romantic heroine to assent to the traditional marriage proposal? One answer may be that, by calling attention to the imperfection of his own art, Shakespeare deliberately cedes the reforming powers of the artist to a higher, divine authority and sacrifices the satisfactions of a comic ending in order to create a felt need for grace. It is surely significant that grace in Shakespeare's play is on everyone's tongue (in the repeated utterance of the words *grace* and *gracious*) yet is so noticeably absent.[62] The persistent references to grace, like the pattern of inadequate substitutions, function to arouse desire for what the play cannot, on its own, achieve; for in *Measure for Measure* authority remains stubbornly outside both the world of the play and the realm of the author. Like the law as Calvin conceives it, the play can only reveal, not correct, imperfection, and it thus arouses a longing for what it acknowledges it cannot deliver: divine forgiveness. But even as he exposes the inadequacies of his representational theater, Shakespeare brilliantly exploits them. By portraying an imperfect playwright-Duke, by marring his own comic ending, and by depicting a series of inadequate but evocative substitutions, Shakespeare cultivates a knowledge of lack that is not only dissatisfying but also productive. He creates in his audiences a profound sense of the infinite space that separates them from the divine.

## Notes

[1] Jean E. Howard, "*Measure for Measure* and the Restraints of Convention," *Essays in Literature* 10 (1983): 149-58, esp. 149.

[2] See, for example, Rosalind Miles, who argues that "there remains an unshakeable sense that it [the trial scene] fails to conclude the play in a way that leaves us entirely content; it does not fully resolve the issues and release the dramatic tensions which the course of the play has created" (*The Problem of* Measure for Measure: *A Historical Investigation* [New York; Barnes and Noble, 1976], 250); Anthony Dawson, who argues that "the elaborate restitution at the end of *Measure for Measure* is more hoax than reaffirmation" ("*Measure for Measure,* New Historicism, and Theatrical Power," *Shakespeare Quarterly* 39 [1988]: 328-41, esp. 341); Robert N. Watson, who sees the final revelation as "an illusion manipulated by a fake holy man for his own aggrandizement" and argues that "all the strategies of secular immortality, all the fantasies (religious, artistic, familial) of resurrection . . . lie mortally wounded amid the formulaic resurrections of the final scene" ("False Immortality in *Measure for Measure:* Comic Means, Tragic Ends," *SQ* 41 [1990]: 411-32, esp. 423); and Richard Wheeler, who comments on "Shakespeare's inability to find an ending that responds fully to the whole action" (*Shakespeare's Development and the Problem Comedies: Turn and Counter-Turn* [Berkeley: U of California P, 1981], 12).

[3] Alexander Leggatt, "Substitution in *Measure for Measure,*" *SQ* 39 (1988): 342-59, esp. 359.

[4] See, for example, Katharine Eisaman Maus, *Inwardness and Theater in the English Renaissance* (Chicago: U of Chicago P, 1995), 172-77; Louise Schleiner, "Providential Improvisation in *Measure for Measure,*" *PMLA* 97 (1982): 227-36, esp. 227; Julia Reinhard Lupton, *Afterlives of the Saints: Hagiography, Typology, and Renaissance Literature* (Stanford, CA: Stanford UP, 1996), 110-40; and Michael Flachmann, "Fitted for Death: *Measure for Measure* and the *Contemplatio Mortis,*" *English Literary Renaissance* 22 (1992): 222-41. For earlier treatments of the play's religious content, see also Roy W. Battenhouse, "*Measure for Measure* and Christian Doctrine of the Atonement," *PMLA* 61 (1946): 1029-59; Darryl J. Gless, Measure for Measure, *The Law, and the Covenant* (Princeton, NJ: Princeton UP, 1979); and George Wilson Knight, *The Wheel of Fire: Interpretations of Shakespearian Tragedy, with three new essays* (London: Methuen, 1949).

[5] Elizabeth Pope, for example, explicitly argues that in *Measure for Measure* Shakespeare "touches . . . only on such elements of traditional theology as were shared by Anglican, Puritan, and Roman Catholic alike" ("The Renaissance Background of *Measure for Measure*" in *Aspects of Shakespeare's 'Problem Plays',* Kenneth Muir and Stanley Wells, eds. [Cambridge: Cambridge UP, 1982], 57-73, esp. 71). Making no distinctions between Roman Catholic and Protestant views of chastity, Jonathan Dollimore assumes that "the Church" approves of Isabella's renunciation of her sexuality; see "Transgression and surveillance in *Measure for Measure*" in *Political Shakespeare: Essays in Cultural Materialism,* Jonathan Dollimore and Alan Sinfield, eds. (Ithaca, NY: Cornell UP, 1985), 72-87, esp. 82. Leggatt remarks that were a duke to disguise himself as a friar and go "around hearing confessions," he would create "a major scandal in an actual Catholic community" (344), but he never considers how a dramatic representation of such an action might play to a Protestant audience in early modern England. Carolyn Brown does not address the radically different views of Roman Catholics and Protestants on religious flagellation, asserting instead that the practice of flagellation "did not die in the Middle Ages but, to the contrary, survived and flourished through the sixteenth century in most of Europe" ("Erotic Religious Flagellation and Shakespeare's *Measure for Measure,*" *ELR* 16 [1986]: 139-65, esp. 141).

[6] Watson, for example, ignores Protestant condemnation of vows of chastity when he argues that because the play makes "a mockery of the pious notion that virginity is a plausible or even permissible way to pursue immortality," it is subversive of all religion, and he suggests that the play is "potentially heretical, even blasphemous" (426 and 415). Harriett Hawkins suggests that the play reveals how "organized religion itself . . . provide[s] solutions that are false, ways out that are too easy" (" 'The Devil's Party': Virtues and Vices in 'Measure for Measure' " in Muir and Wells, eds., 87-95, esp. 95).

[7] See, for example, Dollimore, 72-87; Jonathan Goldberg, *James I and the Politics of Literature* (Baltimore: Johns Hopkins UP, 1983); Stephen Greenblatt, *Shakespearean Negotiations: The Circulation of Social Energy in Renaissance England* (Berkeley: U of California P, 1988); and Leonard Tennenhouse, "Representing Power: *Measure for Measure* in Its Time," *Genre* 15 (1982): 139-56.

[8] I quote from Frederick Shriver, "Hampton Court Re-Visited: James I and the Puritans," *Journal of Ecclesiastical History* 33 (1982): 48-71, esp. 48; see also, William Barlow, *The Summe and Substance of the Conference . . . at Hampton Court* (London, 1604).

[9] "James's ecclesiastical policy was often conceived and presented as a via media between these two extremes" of puritanism and papistry, write Kenneth Fincham and Peter Lake, who note that "the king himself never tired of pointing out the equivalence of these

two menaces" ("The Ecclesiastical Policy of King James I," *Journal of British Studies* 24 [1985]: 169-207, esp. 170). They argue that "James I not merely identified and opposed the threats of popery and Puritanism but also endeavored to emasculate the political dangers that both contained" (171).

[10] Fincham and Lake, 175 and 172.

[11] See, for example, in Henry Peacham's *Minerva Britanna* (London, 1612), the emblem of a hypocrite, who wears a friar's habit and carries a rosary and staff (198); Peacham identifies the friar's "humblest habits" with "a false disguise" that cloaks his "hidden villainies."

[12] In her fascinating analysis of what she calls "the relics of hagiography in Shakespearean drama," Julia Reinhard Lupton finds in this play "a residually *Catholic* discourse not fully subject to its Reformation into secular literature" (140). She argues provocatively that *Measure for Measure* stages "the founding of secular literature on the supersedure of Christian forms" (135), but in identifying the Protestant Reformation with the "classicizing . . . humanist, rationalist, and empiricist initiatives of the Renaissance" (xxxii), she is, I think, too quick to equate early English Protestantism with the secularizing impulses of modernity.

[13] Fincham and Lake, 207.

[14] Patrick Collinson, *The Religion of Protestants: The Church in English Society 1559-1625* (Oxford: Clarendon Press, 1982), 82.

[15] Michel de Certeau, *The Practice of Everyday Life,* trans. Steven Rendall (Berkeley: U of California P, 1988).

[16] See, for example, Louis Adrian Montrose, "The Purpose of Playing: Reflections on a Shakespearean Anthropology," *Helios* 7 (1980): 51-74; and Michael O'Connell, "The Idolatrous Eye: Iconoclasm, Anti-Theatricalism, and the Image of the Elizabethan Theater," *ELH* 52 (1985): 279-310. Both argue that the early modern London theater develops in reaction against Protestantism, a religion they assume is hostile to all theater. Montrose has recently distanced his position from O'Connell's; see Louis Adrian Montrose, *The Purpose of Playing: Shakespeare and the Cultural Politics of the Elizabethan Theatre* (Chicago: U of Chicago P, 1996), 32n.

[17] Thomas Lodge, "A Reply to Stephen Gosson's *Schoole of Abuse:* In Defence of Poetry Musick and Stage Plays" (1580?) in *The Complete Works of Thomas Lodge,* 4 vols. (Glasgow: Robert Anderson for the Hunterian Club, 1883), 1:A4$^r$, A7$^r$, and B2$^r$. I would even suggest that it is Lodge, in his reply to Gosson, who first formulates a position on the stage that draws on Calvinist theology. It is only when Gosson answers Lodge's critique of his first tract that he fully develops the relation between antitheatricality and Protestant theology.

[18] For a detailed discussion of these Calvinist defenses, see my book, *Staging Reform, Reforming the Stage: Protestantism and Popular Theater in Early Modern England* (Ithaca, NY: Cornell UP, 1997), 71-72 and 205-7.

[19] John Calvin, *The Institution of Christian Religion, written in Latine,* trans. Thomas Norton (London, 1562), Bi$^v$ and Avi$^r$. Subsequent references to the *Institutes* follow this sixteenth-century edition.

[20] John Calvin, *The Sermons of M. John Calvin, upon the Epistle of S. Paule too the Ephesians,* trans. Arthur Golding (London, 1577), fol. 87.

[21] Calvin, *Institutes,* Biiii$^v$, Gi$^{r-v}$, and Niii$^v$-Niiii$^r$. Calvin elsewhere laments that most men are blind to these signs, preferring to "rest in beholding the workes without hauing regard of the workeman" (Bi$^v$).

[22] Calvin, *Institutes,* QQQvii$^r$, RRRv$^v$, RRRvii$^v$, and SSSi$^r$.

[23] For a discussion of these pictures, see Craig Harbison, *The Last Judgment in Sixteenth-Century Northern Europe* (New York: Garland Press, 1976), 52-61.

[24] Calvin, *Institutes,* RRRi$^r$. In an extended discussion of civil government, Calvin raises many of the central issues that Shakespeare explores in *Measure for Measure,* including the problems caused by too severe and too lenient administration of the law.

[25] John Calvin, *The Catechisme, or maner to teache Children the Christian Religion* (London, 1580), A4$^v$.

[26] William Wood, *A Fourme of Catechising in true religion* (London, 1581), C1$^r$. For Calvin, G. R. Evans writes, "The signs are present in this world, seen by our eyes and touched by our hands. Calvin's fear is that if this spatial separation of sign and thing signified is not emphasized there will be idolatry" ("Calvin on signs: an Augustinian dilemma," *Renaissance Studies* 3 [1989]: 35-45, esp. 40). Early Protestants repeatedly define idolatry in terms of substitution: see, for instance, Calvin, *Institutes,* Biii$^r$; "An Homilie Against perill of Idolatrie, and superfluous decking of Churches" in *Certaine Sermons or Homilies Appointed to be Read in Churches in the Time of Queen Elizabeth I . . . A Facsimile Reproduction of the Edition of 1623,* ed. Mary Ellen Rickey and Thomas B. Stroup (Gainesville, FL: Scholars' Facsimiles and

Reprints, 1968), 11-76, esp. 49; and William Perkins, *A Treatise of Mans Imaginations* (Cambridge, 1607), B12$^v$-C1$^r$.

[27] Stephen Gosson, *Playes Confuted in fiue Actions* (London, 1582), D7$^v$.

[28] Maus, 164 and 163. See also Janet Adelman's discussion of "the battle within [Angelo] between fierce repression of sexual desire and equally fierce outbursts of degrading and degraded desire"; Adelman concludes that for Angelo "desire is necessarily the ravishing of a saint" ("Bed Tricks: On Marriage as the End of Comedy in *All's Well that Ends Well* and *Measure for Measure*" in *Shakespeare's Personality*, Norman N. Holland, Sidney Homan, and Bernard J. Paris, eds. [Berkeley: U of California P, 1989], 151-74, esp. 164).

[29] Quotations of *Measure for Measure* follow *The Norton Shakespeare, Based on the Oxford edition*, ed. Stephen Greenblatt et al. (New York: W. W. Norton, 1997).

[30] Wood, B8$^v$-C1$^r$.

[31] "An Homilie Against perill of Idolatrie," 49.

[32] "An Homilie Against perill of Idolatrie," 49; and William Perkins, *A Warning against the Idolatrie of the last times. And an Instruction touching Religious, or Diuine worship* (Cambridge, 1601), F6$^r$.

[33] 1 Corinthians 8:1-2. Biblical quotations in this essay follow the 1560 *Geneva Bible* and will hereafter be cited parenthetically in the text.

[34] See, for instance, Calvin, *Sermons upon Ephesians*, fol. 85.

[35] Although he does not discuss this play in terms of Calvinist theology or the Reformation, R.L.P. Jackson makes a similar observation in "Necessary Ambiguity: The Last Act of *Measure for Measure*," *The Critical Review* 26 (1984): 114-29, esp. 117.

[36] Margaret Scott, " 'Our City's Institutions': Some Further Reflections on the Marriage Contract in *Measure for Measure*," *ELH* 49 (1982): 790-804, esp. 794. For interesting discussions of civil and ecclesiastical law and *Measure for Measure*, see Victoria Hayne, "Performing Social Practice: The Example of *Measure for Measure*," *SQ* 44 (1993): 1-29; and Maus, 157-81.

[37] Calvin, *Institutes*, Diii$^v$.

[38] Calvin, *Institutes*, Diii$^v$. According to John T. McNeill, "the term 'law' for Calvin may mean (1) the whole religion of Moses . . . ; (2) the special revelation of the moral law to the chosen people . . . ; or (3) various bodies of civil, judicial, and ceremonial statutes." He notes that "Of these, the moral law, the 'true and eternal rule of righteousness' . . . is most important" (John T. McNeill, ed., *Institutes of the Christian Religion*, trans. Ford Lewis Battles, 2 vols. [Philadelphia: The Westminster Press, 1960], 1:348n).

[39] Edmond Allen, *A shorte Cathechisme: A briefe and godly bringinge up of youth in the knowledge and commandementes of God.* ([Zurich] 1550), C5$^v$ and D3$^v$. See also *A Short Catechisme, or Playne Instruction* (London, 1553), B5$^v$, John Dod and Richard Cleaver, *A Plaine and familiar Exposition of Ten Commaundments, with a methodicall short Catechisme* (London, 1605), Ff4$^v$; and Stephen Egerton, *A Briefe Method of Catechizing* (London, 1631), A5$^r$-A7$^r$ and C6$^r$.

[40] Calvin, *Institutes*, Ai$^r$.

[41] Alexander Nowell writes that the law "striketh their heart with a wholesome sorrow, and driveth them to . . . repentance" (*A Cathechisme written in Latin* [1570], trans. Thomas Norton, ed. G. E. Corrie [Cambridge: Parker Society, 1854], 141).

[42] Calvin, *Institutes*, Diii$^r$ and Dii$^v$, Calvin, *Sermons upon Ephesians*, fols. 77$^v$-78$^r$.

[43] Calvin, *Institutes*, Diii$^v$.

[44] Calvin, *Institutes*, GGGiiii$^r$.

[45] See, for instance, Ben Jonson's portrayal of the Anabaptists in *The Alchemist* (1610) and of the puritan Zeal-of-the-Land Busy in *Bartholomew Fair* (1614).

[46] Mario DiGangi, "Pleasure and Danger: Measuring Female Sexuality in *Measure for Measure*," *ELH* 60 (1993): 589-609, esp. 596; Laura Lunger Knoppers, "(En)gendering Shame: *Measure for Measure* and the Spectacles of Power," *ELR* 23 (1993): 450-71, esp. 462. Knoppers believes that Isabella's desire to enter a convent is "threatening" to patriarchal society (464). See also Brown, who laments that the Duke's shaming of Isabella "prevents her from ever returning to the protection of the convent" (216).

[47] Harriett Hawkins, *Likenesses of Truth in Elizabethan and Restoration Drama* (Oxford: Oxford UP, 1972), 70 and 68. See also Richard Ide, who writes: "For Barnardine to be forgiven along with Claudio also seems an abuse of justice on the part of the lenient Duke" ("Shakespeare's Revisionism: Homiletic Tragicomedy and the Ending of *Measure for Measure*," *Shakespeare Studies* 20 [1987]: 105-27, esp. 119).

[48] William Ames, *Conscience with the Power and Cases Thereof* (London, 1639), B1$^r$. For a discussion of early

Protestant notions of the conscience, see John S. Wilks, *The Idea of Conscience in Renaissance Tragedy* (New York: Routledge, 1990).

[49] Jeremiah Dyke, *Good Conscience or A Treatise Shewing the Nature, Meanes, Marks, Benefit, and Necesity thereof* (London, 1624), B7$^r$, Calvin, *Institutes*, DDDi$^v$; Richard Carpenter, *The Conscionable Christian* (London, 1620), Hi$^r$.

[50] Thomas Cranmer, *The Bishop's Book* (1537), quoted here from John Phillips, *The Reformation of Images: Destruction of Art in England, 1535-1660* (Berkeley: U of California P, 1973), 57; "The Contents of a Book of Articles devised by the King," quoted here from *The Actes and Monuments of John Foxe* (1570), ed. Stephen Reed Cattley, 8 vols. (London: R. B. Seeley and W. Burnside, 1937-41), 5:163.

[51] Thomas Heywood, *An Apology For Actors* (London, 1612), B4$^r$ and F4$^r$, see also G1$^v$-G2$^r$. For a detailed discussion of Heywood's defense of the stage and Protestant theories of conscience, see my book, *Staging Reform*.

[52] Montrose, *The Purpose of Playing*, 44-45.

[53] Steven Mullaney, *The Place of the Stage: License, Play, and Power in Renaissance England* (Chicago: U of Chicago P. 1988), 95, 98, 101, and 100.

[54] Mullaney, 99.

[55] Calvin, *Institutes*, CCvii$^v$-CCviii$^r$

[56] Calvin, *Institutes*, CCvii$^v$.

[57] Calvin, *Institutes*, CCiiii$^r$.

[58] Calvin, *Institutes*, CCii$^v$.

[59] In "The Politics of Theatrical Mirth: *A Midsummer Night's Dream, A Mad World, My Masters*, and *Measure for Measure*" (*SQ* 43 [1992]: 51-66) Paul Yachnin argues that *Measure for Measure* represents "theater as the place of private conversional work rather than as the gathering-placc of politically reconciliatory mirth," and he contends that Jacobean comedy, in sharp contrast to Elizabethan comedy, seeks "to exert itself with respect to the individual *as individual* rather than as a member of the community" (62). But he ignores the way the final scene's public rehearsal of mutual guilt creates a community of sinners. Victoria Hayne, in "Performing Social Practice," argues that "the audience is repeatedly invoked as witness, compurgator, congregation, jury" (21); and it might be possible to argue along these lines that the final act positions Shakespeare's audience as a congregation, witnessing these public confessions. But while she examines puritan emphasis on the congregation's judgmental role, I focus on Calvin's emphasis on the importance of the congregation's identification and compassion.

[60] Noting that Viennese "society seems singularly unaffected" by the Duke's efforts to inflict "anxiety for ideological purposes," Stephen Greenblatt argues that "salutary anxiety is emptied out in the service of theatrical pleasure," thereby calling into question the Duke's goals (141 and 138). Greenblatt argues that the pleasure the audience experiences is "bound up with the marking out of theatrical anxiety as represented anxiety—not wholly real, either in the characters onstage or in the audience" (135). But I want to suggest that salutary anxiety, rather than simply being emptied out, has both an aesthetic and a disciplinary function.

[61] Anne Righter Barton makes a similar observation in *Shakespeare and the Idea of the Play* (London: Chatto and Windus, 1962) when she notes that "the Duke's managerial rôle flatters neither himself nor the theater" (178).

[62] The word *grace* or *graces* occurs twenty-five times in *Measure for Measure*, the words *gracious* and *graciously* eight times; see T. H. Howard-Hill, ed., *Oxford Shakespeare Concordance:* Measure for Measure (Oxford: Clarendon Press, 1969).

---

Source: " 'Infinite Space': Representation and Reformation in *Measure for Measure*," in *Shakespeare Quarterly,* Vol. 49, No. 4, Winter, 1998, pp. 393-410.

# Children of the Mind: Miscarried Narratives in *Much Ado about Nothing*

## Stephen B. Dobranski, *Georgia State University*

An idea for a short story about people in Manhattan who are constantly creating these real unnecessary neurotic problems for themselves 'cause it keeps them from dealing with more unsolvable, terrifying problems about the universe.

—Woody Allen, *Manhattan*

When Beatrice first speaks in *Much Ado about Nothing,* she inquires after Benedick: "I pray you, is Signior Mountanto returned from the wars or no?" (I.i.28-9).[1] That her first concern is Benedick's welfare suggests an interest in him beyond their ongoing "skirmish of wit" (I.i.58). Like Benedick's assertion that Beatrice exceeds Hero "as much in beauty as the first of May doth the last of December" (I.i.178-9), her question looks ahead to their open acknowledgment of love and concluding nuptials. That Beatrice refers to Benedick as "Signior Mountanto" (I.i.28)—literally, "Lord Upward Thrust"—also implies, through a bawdy innuendo, the erotic nature of their "merry war" (I.i.56).

We thus meet Beatrice and Benedick *in medias res,* the two having already developed an antagonistic attraction: "I know you of old," Beatrice cryptically apostrophizes (I.i.133-4). As they quarrel, compete, and court, their veiled allusions to the past do more than provide a context for their war of words. Suggesting images of sex, birthing, and loss, Beatrice's language—particularly in II.i—evokes possible causes for their mutual animosity and hints at ominous events from their past that lend depth to the play's comic tone. I want to posit a history for Beatrice and Benedick, a history to which the text alludes but always deflects. I further wish to suggest, in the second part of my reading, that such deflection is itself the subject of comedy: at the core of the play lies a haunting sense of loss that the characters, especially Beatrice, communicate obliquely.

This technique of alluding to an undeveloped, possible history represents a neglected strategy of Shakespeare's dramaturgy: he convinces us of the worlds that he creates by intimating suggestive details of his characters' past experience. I am not concerned whether Benedick and Beatrice actually lived the history that the text implies; rather, I think it important that Shakespeare contextualizes the fiction that he dramatizes by evoking another fiction that he does not.

I

Hinting at events that precede the play, the multiple allusions to Hercules in *Much Ado about Nothing* color Benedick's conversion from soldier to lover as his relationship with Beatrice progresses. To understand how these images may have been intended to influence our perception of his character, we need first to recall that Hercules was born when Zeus tricked the virgin Alcmene into sleeping with him.[2] Enraged by another of her husband's infidelities, Hera tried to prevent Hercules' delivery by having the goddess of childbirth sit outside Alcmene's room with her legs and fingers crossed; when that plan failed, Hera attempted to murder the child by sending two serpents to strangle him in his crib.

The theme of infanticide recurs in the story of Hercules: struck by Hera with a fit of madness, Hercules murdered his own children, two of his nephew's children, and in some versions of the myth, his wife. He performed his twelve labors as punishment from the Pythia, the prophetess of Apollo at Delphi. To absolve himself, she stipulated that he must visit King Eurystheus and do whatever tasks the ruler demanded.

Hercules' reputation as a child killer later prevented his marriage to Iole, the daughter of another king, Eurytus. Eurytus had put up Iole as the reward in an archery contest, but after Hercules defeated the king and his sons, Eurytus reneged on his offer because of Hercules' past crimes. Hercules vowed revenge, and when Iphitus, the eldest son of Eurytus, requested Hercules' aid in searching for the king's missing horses, Hercules killed again. He flung Eurytus' son off the walls of Tiryns. As punishment, the gods inflicted Hercules with a disease, and so a second time he sought the Pythia's advice. She told Hercules that he could cure his malady and receive absolution if he were sold as a slave to Omphale, Queen of Lydia. According to some Roman authors, Hercules had to dress in women's clothes while in Omphale's service and tend to domestic chores, such as providing music and spinning yarn.

In *Much Ado about Nothing,* Benedick allies himself with Hercules by comparing Beatrice to Omphale. She is so unreasonable, he quips, that "She would have made Hercules have turned the spit, yea, and have cleft his club to make the fire too" (II.i.236-8). Initially he suggests a series of Herculean labors to escape Beatrice: when she enters with Claudio after the dance, Benedick frantically beseeches Don Pedro to send him away; he will do even the most absurd task—"the slightest errand" (II.i.248)—to avoid her company. Benedick's exaggerated request for permission, even when playfully performed, not only calls attention to Beatrice's independence in her ensuing rejection of

Don Pedro, but also casts Benedick as a burlesque version of the Greek hero. He rattles off a list of pointless, Herculean labors: "I will fetch you a toothpicker now from the furthest inch of Asia," he offers, or "bring you the length of Prester John's foot" (II.i.250-2). Thus, as Beatrice enters, Benedick suggests that he would prefer this kind of futile activity so as to escape the consequences of his earlier gibes—or, in terms of the play's title, he introduces the idea of a great deal of work for nothing.

By the end of the play, however, Benedick offers to perform such labors on Beatrice's behalf. When Claudio slanders Hero at their wedding, Beatrice laments the decline of manhood by caustically observing, "He is now as valiant as Hercules that only tells a lie and swears it" (IV.i.320-1). Motivated in part by his own belief that Claudio has wronged Hero, Benedick accepts Beatrice's challenge, agreeing to "Kill Claudio" and thus defend Hero's honor (IV.i.288). He has moved from his own parody of a militant Hercules, eager to fetch Don Pedro "a hair off the great Cham's beard" (II.i.252), to a love-struck version of the overachieving hero. For Beatrice, he will do anything; he pledges to "live in thy heart, die in thy lap, and be buried in thy eyes" (V.ii.94-5).[3]

Although we cannot know what previously occurred between Beatrice and Benedick, the play's allusions to Hercules suggest the need for atonement: just as Hercules depends on the Pythia and must serve Omphale, Benedick eventually places himself in a woman's control to find forgiveness for his own past crime.[4] Hinting at the nature of this crime, Beatrice explains that Benedick, like Hercules challenging King Eurytus, had attempted to rival "Cupid at the flight; and my uncle's fool, reading the challenge, subscribed for Cupid, and challenged him at the bird-bolt" (I.i.36-8). Although we do not know for certain the identity of her "uncle's fool," Beatrice calls her own heart "poor fool" (II.i.295); and as Benedick's verbal adversary, she seems the likeliest candidate to have encountered him on Cupid's behalf. In addition to its association with the god of love, the phallic shape of a "bird-bolt," a blunt arrow, implies a sexual challenge.[5]

The "flight" to which Benedick challenged Cupid during his previous visit presumably refers to the flight of an arrow, but "flight" also can denote an act of fleeing or an extraordinary display of something, such as fancy, or in the case of Cupid, love. Thus, in this one speech, Beatrice subtly justifies her hostility toward Benedick: she compresses into a whimsical narrative hints that he seduced and abandoned her, using one word, "flight," to connote both. Beatrice conjures the image of Benedick striding into town, advertising his interest in love ("He set up his bills here," I.i.35)—but taking "flight" at the first sign of her challenge. As Carol Cook notes, when the play opens Beatrice "already seems to be nursing wounds from some abortive romance with Benedick."[6] I will argue that the play is more suggestive than Cook describes, and that Cook's own diction—"nursing" and "abortive"—unconsciously echoes the text's allusions to Beatrice and Benedick's previous romance.

II

We get perhaps our best glimpse of Benedick and Beatrice's pre-history during Beatrice's conversation with Don Pedro. She explains that she puts Benedick down "[s]o I would not he should do me, . . . lest I should prove the mother of fools" (II.i.267-8). Just as she earlier alluded to Benedick's visit as a sexual encounter—a challenge "at the bird-bolt" (I.i.38)—the verbs "do" and "put down" also suggest a sexual conquest; her concern with becoming a "mother of fools" points to a real, potential outcome of letting down her guard. More subtly, the lack of punctuation in her remark signals a complexity that Beatrice's humor masks. Without a comma, the dependent and independent clauses collide: the sentence "So I would not he should do me" suggests, on the one hand, "If *I did not* insult him, he would put me down" and, on the other, "I insult him, so that *he should not* put me down."[7] Although both versions convey the same general meaning, the possibility that "not" can attach itself to the "I" clause or the "he" clause subtly obscures responsibility for putting down the other person. The negation of "not" acts as a hinge between Beatrice and Benedick, knotting them together while, as a negation, keeping them apart.

The full implications of this "not" / "knot" become clearer as Beatrice discusses "the heart of Signior Benedick": she says that Benedick "lent it me awhile, and I gave him use for it" (II.i.259-62). The word "use" can mean interest (as in usury), but it also denotes employment or maintenance for sexual purposes (as when "using someone" means having sex). Beatrice seems to say that Benedick temporarily loved her, and she responded to his advances.

We need to doubt, of course, that Beatrice and Benedick once had a sexual relationship, but her diction momentarily teases us into questioning what previously transpired. As Sandra Cavallo and Simona Cerutti note, a man's promise to marry a woman in early modern Europe—especially if he were a man of honor—was often enough to initiate a sexual relationship: "a woman pledged her sexuality, obtaining from the man, through his promise of marriage, the guarantee of a new condition that assured her a permanent state of honor."[8] The deception to which women were susceptible in this exchange "was so frequent and endemic" that it acquired a specific vocabulary in Italian: "*dare la burla* (to give the trick); *gettare la burla* (to throw the trick); or *burlare* (to trick or deceive in the sense of making a fool of)."⁹ A man had the power, in other words, to rescind a promise of marriage simply by turning it into a "trick" and thus mocking the woman and those with her who had foolishly believed him.

Balthasar alludes to this practice of false wooing when he sings about the "fraud of men" who "were deceivers ever" (II.iii.63, 72) and advises women to "sigh not so, but let them go, / And be you blithe and bonny" (II.iii.66-7). Such tricks also occur frequently in Shakespeare's other comedies. Bertram in *All's Well that Ends Well* breaks his promises to both Helena and Diana: he flees from Helena before consummating their marriage and abandons Diana after (apparently) seducing her. Similarly, in *Measure for Measure,* Claudio impregnates Juliet before their marriage, Lucio breaks his promise to marry Kate Keepdown after she becomes pregnant, and Angelo gives Mariana the trick "in chief / For that her reputation was disvalu'd" (V.i.219-20).

When Beatrice complains to Benedick that "You always end with a jade's trick, I know you of old" (I.i.133-4), she suggests a scenario in which Benedick "gave the trick" to negate a promise of marriage. Although *Much Ado about Nothing* could not support an explicit reference to this kind of deception, the hint of such duplicitous behavior, common as it was, is sufficient to darken briefly the comedy's light-hearted tone. Beatrice's words "always" and "of old" suggest that Benedick characteristically retreated when he felt threatened by her, as he does during the dance when she approaches with Claudio and as he does during their badinage after volleying a last insult.

Again and again, Beatrice conflates her feelings for Benedick with sex and pregnancy. Explaining to Don Pedro that she once gave Benedick "a double heart for his single one" (II.i.261-2), she conjures a metaphor of considerable intimacy. By "double heart" she may be referring to the union of her heart with Benedick's, or to the compounded interest that she earned on his borrowed affection. The metaphor carries the added implication that in return for Benedick's "single" heart, she could have given him two, hers and a child's. The "not" that ties her and Benedick together would then signify a miscarriage or abortion—that is, an absent child who remains unspoken, but nevertheless haunts her conversation about Benedick and marriage. The play's frequent references to Hercules, who murdered his children, his nephew's children, and King Eurytus's son, subliminally evoke, at least, the idea of lost children and the need for forgiveness. Although the predominant tone of the play cannot support more than this furtive suggestion, that suggestion is enough.

Even the title of *Much Ado about Nothing* subtly suggests as part of the play's metaphoric structure the idea of a lost child. In the seventeenth century, "nothing" could signify a nobody as well as something or someone destroyed or non-existent; according to the editors of the OED, Shakespeare established the first usage of several meanings of this word.¹⁰ We also ought to recall that Shakespeare would have likely been thinking about a dead child while composing the play, for he wrote it around the middle or later part of 1598, soon after losing Hamnet, his only son.¹¹ The term "ado" in the title not only meant action or fuss, but also signified labor or work forced upon a person, as in Hercules' labors or the labor of childbirth; the editors of the OED identify its usage as "labour, trouble, difficulty" as early as 1485.¹² Thus the phrase "much ado about nothing" includes among its various implications the tragedy of miscarriage or the death of an infant, for which a woman suffered much without producing a living child.¹³

In Beatrice's conversation with Don Pedro, her thoughts turn naturally from Benedick to childbirth. When Don Pedro presumes she must have been "born in a merry hour" because she is so "pleasant-spirited," she takes him literally, responding with uncommon candor about the pain of birthing: "No, sure, my lord, my mother cried" (II.i.314, 320, 315).¹⁴ That Beatrice, too, has experienced such pain remains—and, to preserve the play's comic atmosphere, *must* remain—virtually impossible. Yet, she obscures the outcome of her and Benedick's previous romance:

> *Don Pedro.* Come, lady, come, you have lost the heart of Signior Benedick.
>
> *Beatrice.* Indeed, my lord, he lent it me awhile, and I gave him use for it, a double heart for his single one. Marry, once before he won it of me with false dice, therefore your Grace may well say I have lost it.
>
> (II.i.259-64)

Although "it" signifies Benedick's heart in the first two phrases—"he lent it me" and "I gave him use for it" (II.i.261-2)—its subsequent meaning is less clear. Logically, "he won it of me" ought to refer to Beatrice's heart, which Benedick claimed under false pretenses (i.e., "false dice"). But grammatically we expect the antecedent to remain consistent and "it" to signify still Benedick's heart. Substituting "Benedick's heart" for "it," however, makes little sense: once before he won his own heart from her? Beatrice may, of course, mean that Benedick had won his heart *back* from her, but the passage's ambiguity at least temporarily reunites Beatrice's and Benedick's hearts: her explanation grammatically re-creates the "double heart" that she describes.

Like the half-disclosed events that precede the play, Beatrice's antecedents are teasingly unclear; that the "it" signifying Benedick's heart becomes unstable insinuates that he was unfaithful to her. In the final phrase "I have lost it," Beatrice may mean that she has lost her heart to Benedick or that she lost Benedick's heart. The ambiguity in the previous usage of "it" now allows a flood of possibilities to rush in. We can no longer say with certainty what Beatrice has lost from her past relationship with Benedick—his heart? her heart? her virginity? a child? Perhaps "it" means that she has lost the game of courting, the metaphor she introduces in the phrase "he won . . . with false dice."

Beatrice's claim that "I am sunburnt" (II.i.300) suggests still another kind of loss. By sunburnt, she observes that, unlike the "fair Hero" (II.i.280-1), she is dark-complexioned and, therefore, not attractive enough to marry, according to Renaissance notions of beauty. "Burnt" in early modern England, however, also meant parched or dried up, as from a sexually transmitted disease.[15] Beatrice specifically complains that she is "sick" when she learns that Benedick loves her. Margaret's punning prescription, "distilled *carduus benedictus*" (III.iv.68), refers to a general cure-all used during the sixteenth and seventeenth centuries that had a special application for women.[16] The herbalist William Langham claimed that *carduus benedictus* "helpeth the matrix" and "provoketh . . . the termes," and in his guidebook for midwives, Jacob Rueff notes the tradition that "If a woman take the juyce of Carduus, and shall cast it up againe being taken, it is supposed to be a certaine signe of conception."[17] Beatrice's complaint that "I am stuffed" (III.iv.59) thus warrants Margaret's remedy; like Benedick's sexually suggestive name, her diction has a sexual innuendo. Triggering a series of other bawdy puns—"prick'st," "thistle" (III.iv.71)—the word "stuffed" and the reference to *carduus benedictus* together evoke sex and pregnancy, which, although not literally true, reveal how Beatrice thinks about a relationship with Benedick.

Throughout the play, Beatrice uses metaphors of disease to refer to Benedick. If she suffers, he is to blame, for she has caught "the Benedick," a sickness that, she jokes, costs a thousand pounds to cure (I.i.81). Scorning his new friendship with Claudio, Beatrice playfully warns that Benedick "will hang upon him like a disease" and that Benedick "is sooner caught than the pestilence, and the taker runs presently mad" (I.i.78-80). Even at the wedding, Beatrice finally relents only because, she tells Benedick, "I was told you were in a consumption" (V.iv.96). Though couched in these humorous remarks, Beatrice's association of Benedick with disease suggests that their previous relationship has caused her considerable injury. The final allusion also recalls Hercules' relationship to Queen Omphale: just as the diseased Hercules obtains absolution by serving as Omphale's effeminized slave, Benedick, too, may be seeking forgiveness when he submits to Beatrice's charge.

Benedick is the one character who seems to recognize Beatrice's unhappiness perhaps because, the play suggests, he knows its cause. Whereas Don Pedro especially misunderstands Beatrice—he ignores her repeated attempts to change the subject to her cousin[18] and overlooks her insulting reference to his bastard brother, "Hath your Grace ne'er a brother like you?" (II.i.304)—Benedick intimates that he and Beatrice know a great deal about each other.[19] Referring to Beatrice's "base (though bitter) disposition" (II.i.193), for example, Benedick may be alluding to her hurt feelings from their previous encounter.[20] Rather than implying a causal relationship between the two words—i.e., that Beatrice is bitter because of her poor quality—Benedick positions them as two contradictory facts, "base (*though* bitter)," as if the latter somehow restricted or qualified the former. The adversative phrase "though bitter" thus suggests that he sympathizes with Beatrice; while belittling her, he parenthetically acknowledges what no one else in the play realizes: she is nevertheless full of affliction.[21]

Similarly, as Benedick attempts to write Beatrice a poem, his poor rhymes create provocative word associations. Benedick keeps stumbling on "very ominous endings": he "can find out no rhyme to 'lady' but 'baby,'" and all he can think of for "scorn," is the "hard rhyme" of the cuckold's "horn" (V.ii.35-9). His frustration not only implies the limits of conventional poetry, but also hints at the circumstances of some half-disclosed, failed affair.[22] Just as Beatrice conflates her feelings for Benedick with sex, pregnancy, and disease, he thinks about their relationship in these "ominous" terms; when he tries to articulate his love, his mind immediately turns to images of a child, rejection, and unfaithfulness.

The couple's final rapprochement within a comic framework requires, however, that such grim events remain ambiguous. Any attempt to argue that Beatrice and Benedick had a child or that they once had a sexual relationship would be to push into literalism the characters' wordplay and metaphors—or, again in terms of the play's title, to make too much ado about nothing. On the contrary, Shakespeare teases us: the characters of Beatrice and Benedick, as predominantly drawn, could not have experienced the darker, more realistic history that their language implies. Beatrice affirms, after all, that she is still a virgin when she imagines the devil addressing her, "Get you to heaven, Beatrice, get you to heaven, here's no place for you maids" (II.i.41-2). But when Beatrice envisions her death, she first goes, not to heaven, but to the gates of hell: "and there will the Devil meet me like an old cuckold with horns on his head" (II.i.39-40). With the placement of "like an old cuckold," she could be describing the devil or comparing herself to a man whose wife has committed adultery. Once again, her language encourages us to question momentarily her sexual experience. When Beatrice says that she will "lead his apes into hell" (II.i.37), she refers, on the one hand, to the peculiar proverb that virgins escort apes in the underworld. On the other hand, at least one version of this proverb, the ballad "The Maid and the Palmer," describes a maid who must "lead an ape in hell" as part of her penance for having buried her illegitimate children.[23]

### III

This strategy of evoking a fragmentary, undeveloped history, which enriches the relationship between Beatrice and Benedick, arises repeatedly in *Much Ado about Nothing.* Dogberry elliptically refers to the losses he has endured (IV.ii.82), Leonato's wife, Innogen, appears in only two scene headings (I.i and II.i), and Beatrice's parents remain absent and undiscussed. Leonato inquires after Antonio's son (I.ii.1) and claims that Claudio "hath an uncle here in Messina" (I.i.17), but neither character is incorporated into the play. We do not know against whom Don Pedro, Claudio, and Benedick have been fighting in their recent battle, nor can we explain with certainty whether Don John is their prisoner or a disgruntled ally. More information about Margaret's former relationship with Borachio might help us comprehend how she would agree to dress in Hero's clothes, stand in Hero's window, be addressed as Hero, and bid Borachio as Claudio "a thousand times good night" (III.iii.142-3).[24] In an attempt to account for such inconsistencies, John Dover Wilson and Arthur Quiller-Couch have argued that the ambiguities in the text represent vestiges of an older play that Shakespeare was hurriedly revising. According to Wilson and Quiller-Couch, Shakespeare reworked the play into its surviving state by emphasizing the plot of Beatrice and Benedick, but retaining as much of the older version as possible.[25]

Regardless of its origin—Shakespeare's artistry or the traces of an unknown source-text—this technique of partial information characterizes Shakespeare's dramaturgy: the details of the characters' pasts hover on the periphery of the plays, spied from the corner of our eyes, but frustrating any attempt to specify what has previously transpired. We cannot pinpoint, for example, whether the ghost lies to Hamlet about Claudius's adultery; we are not even told why the crown passed to Claudius, and can only speculate about the exact nature of Hamlet's relationship to Ophelia before his father's death. In *King Lear,* the absent mother receives scant attention; in *Othello,* Iago inexplicably refers to Cassio's "fair wife";[26] and in *The Winter's Tale,* the events of Polixenes' nine-month visit to Sicily remain ambiguous as do the pressing matters that he cites when he tries to depart. In *Romeo and Juliet,* the Montagues and Capulets are feuding—but why?

Such shadowy narrative contexts draw us into the dramas by tantalizing us with what has already occurred. We believe that the characters have a past because they do not enter with neat, packaged explanations of their previous experiences; the plays seem more realistic because the characters' lives exceed the boundaries of the stage. As Norman Rabkin argues, Shakespeare's artistic achievement lies in his ability "to create illusory worlds which, like the world we feel about us, make sense in ways that consistently elude our power to articulate them rationally."[27] According to Rabkin, we must understand the worlds of the plays intuitively because they "cannot be reduced to sense."[28] Writing on the *Henry IV* plays, John Rumrich also emphasizes this kind of "organic messiness" inherent in the "evocative idiom of the dramas"; he suggests that Shakespeare's play-making depends on its "life-like mingling of significance and irresolvability," which often defies the restrictive categories imposed by a critical analysis.[29]

More specifically, the genteel world of Shakespeare's comedy cannot accommodate the volatile passions to which the characters allude. No one in Messina, for example, is able to confront the emotional events that precede the play: except for the messenger's terse account of Don Pedro's victory, we learn little about the recent battle, and the characters can only refer to painful memories covertly. Describing what she calls Messina's "sophisticated, graceful, almost choreographic social forms," Carol Cook notes that its inhabitants often rely on humor to communicate their aggression; the "tight rein kept on emotions" makes "them difficult or dangerous to express."[30]

Such dangerous emotions receive a fuller and more open treatment in Shakespeare's later comedies. If we doubt that he would have crafted such a cruel history for Beatrice and Benedick, we should recall that Shakespeare often built his comedies around tragic or potentially tragic circumstances. In *Troilus and Cressida,* Pandarus encourages his niece to become Troilus's mistress. In *All's Well that Ends Well,* Bertram callously rejects Helena, cruelly tortures his follower Parolles—and shows scant signs of repentance at the play's end. The third of the "problem comedies," *Measure for Measure,* focuses on prostitution, capital punishment, and premarital intercourse.[31] Claudio tries to escape execution by persuading his sister Isabella to gratify Angelo sexually, and Angelo covers up his sexual exploits by ordering Claudio's death.

Although in *Much Ado about Nothing* Messina, like Beatrice, appears "pleasant-spirited" (II.i.320), it too harbors these darker sentiments. When Claudio, Leonato, and Beatrice successively release their pent-up hostility at the wedding, we momentarily witness the intense emotions that have been percolating beneath Messina's decorum.[32] These feelings remain for the most part offstage, however, or lurk in the play's humor and imagery. Just as we do not know what has previously transpired, we must infer what will happen after the final act. Benedick tells Don Pedro not to think about the captured Don John "till tomorrow; I'll devise thee brave punishments for him" (V.iv.125-6). He then immediately exclaims, "Strike up, pipers!" which is followed by the single stage-direction, *"Dance"* (V.iv.126). Such celebrating suggests a cathartic release, but it also represents an artful dodge: the inhabitants of Messina, in particular Benedick, make "much ado" so as to escape serious consequences. Benedick's promise displaces the torture of Don John, as if Messina could not tolerate such violence; the play cannot linger over his treachery for it to sustain its comic tone. Don John flees after Hero allegedly dies, Hero copes with her public humiliation by hiding, and Don Pedro assuages the pain of Beatrice's rejection by distracting himself with his elaborate match-making. Again and again, the characters turn away from difficult situations; they even brush aside Margaret's complicity, rationalizing that she helped Borachio "against her will" (V.iv.5).[33]

Benedick most consistently embodies the play's strategy of fleeing from serious consequences. He wears a mask to speak with Beatrice, for example, and cowers in the arbor to avoid Don Pedro and Claudio. He takes flight whenever he feels threatened—at the dance, during his conversation with Beatrice, and during his past visit to Messina. That Benedick should speak the final line is thus fitting: the play leaves us with the threat of violence—Don John's "brave punishments"—but just as the comedy persistently averts its attention from a sense of loss, these punishments remain deflected, put off indefinitely until a "tomorrow" that will never come.

In like manner, Beatrice and Benedick's past is there and not there, alluded to but absent. Rather than depict (or even fully explain) the couple's previous, failed relationship, Shakespeare constructs a parallel narrative with less emotionally complex lovers, Hero and Claudio, whose losses are visible and potentially more devastating than what Beatrice and Benedick have endured. Presumably, because this pair of lovers quickly recovers, so can Beatrice and Benedick. The plot of Hero and Claudio thus represents the present displacement of Beatrice and Benedick's earlier romance; like the jokes that the characters use to sublimate their passions, the story of Hero and Claudio furtively suggests the pain of Benedick and Beatrice. Within Hero's plot, a loss of virginity results in a child's death, and Claudio, like Hercules, must perform a series of prescribed tasks to achieve absolution: he must clear Hero's name, "Hang her an epitaph upon her tomb, / And sing it to her bones," and then marry Leonato's fictitious niece (V.i.278-9). This plot does not entirely correspond to Beatrice and Benedick's; it refracts and compresses parts of the narrative I have been suggesting.[34] Hero supposedly loses her virginity, for example, the "child" that dies is Leonato's, and, of course, Leonato only pretends that Hero dies. But these discrepancies render Beatrice's possible loss all the more poignant, for the play implies that she may have truly suffered what Leonato feigns and, unlike the fair Hero, she may have truly lost her virginity.

The irony lies in the play's title, "much ado about nothing." It refers to the characters' strategy for denying serious consequences by occupying themselves with futile activity, and, as we have seen, it specifically describes Beatrice's suffering—she endured much ado and she has come away with nothing. The title applies to the relationship between Claudio and Hero because he creates a great deal of fuss over nothing: in fact, Hero has not lost her virginity and she only pretends to die.[35] "Nothing" also means the absence of a "thing," and "thing" in the Renaissance euphemistically signified a penis; this sense applies to the play in that Claudio makes a fuss about Hero's sexual organ. But Beatrice, too, has experienced a great deal of labor/ado because of her "no thing"—because of her womanhood and perhaps because of a lost child. Her emotional response to Hero's ostracism at the wedding becomes even more touching when we acknowledge that Beatrice may empathize with Hero. Beatrice, too, has suffered.

Throughout the play, we encounter metaphoric shades and echoes of "nothing," such as Hero's virtual silence in the opening scene, the watch's orders to do essentially nothing (III.iii.25-80), and Don John's inability to devise any mischief without Borachio's prompting. In addition to its many instances of deflection, *Much Ado about Nothing* depends on trickery and lying (Don John's machinations, Claudio's false accusation, the ruse to bring together Benedick and Beatrice), words full of sound, veiling their characters' fury, and signifying not the thing that they pretend to represent. The absence of Benedick and Beatrice's child and, more generally, their shared past suggests another manifestation of this theme. By only glimpsing Benedick and Beatrice's previous romance, we can appreciate their "merry war" while remaining distanced enough to find their plight humorous. For us to laugh rather than sympathize, they must make much ado about "nothing"; the source of their pain must remain offstage, just beyond our comprehension.

The technique of implying an undeveloped, fragmentary history for Benedick and Beatrice corresponds to the imagined lost child that haunts their relationship: the details of their previous romance represent a miscarried fiction that complements the fully-conceived narrative, occupying the stage. "I was born to speak all mirth and no matter," Beatrice explains to Don Pedro after rejecting his marriage proposal (II.i.310-1). She is pretending that she is light-hearted, but her explanation also implies that she cannot speak any "matter": she suggests that, because she was born a woman, everything she says is interpreted as mirth. Or she may be hinting that as a woman she must cloak her real feelings with humor. The genre of comedy also demands that she speaks "all mirth" and that what "matters" to Beatrice be communicated in densely allusive language, which continually threatens to undercut the play's light-hearted tone, but can never be explicitly articulated.[36]

*Notes*

[1] William Shakespeare, the Arden Edition of *Much Ado about Nothing,* ed. A. R. Humphreys (London: Routledge, 1981). Future references will appear parenthetically in the text by act, scene, and line number. In all cases I have checked the text against the first quarto, *Much adoe about Nothing* (London, 1600), at the Harry Ransom Humanities Research Center at the University of Texas at Austin (STC 22304; Pforz 819).

[2] This and all subsequent information regarding the myth of Hercules is taken from Edward Tripp, *The Meridian Handbook of Classical Mythology* (New York: New American Library, 1970), pp. 275-95. I have also consulted Douglas Bush, *Mythology and the Renaissance Tradition in English Poetry* (New York: Pagent Book, 1957); and Jean Seznec, *The Survival of the Pagan Gods: The Mythological Tradition and Its Place in Renaissance Humanism and Art,* trans. Barbara F. Sessions (New York: Pantheon Books, 1953).

[3] Ironically, Benedick resembles Hercules not through his feats of strength during the war, but in his acceptance of a woman's sovereignty. He appears most heroic when, at Beatrice's prompting, he severs his friendships with Claudio and Don Pedro, and thus resigns from the battlefield. The two kiddingly taunt Benedick to distract themselves from their "high-proof melancholy," but he remains serious and reserved, gallantly thanking Don Pedro for his "many courtesies" and formally announcing that "I must discontinue your company" (V.i.123, 185-7).

[4] Accepting Beatrice's charge, Benedick, like Hercules under Queen Omphale, is made effeminate though still forceful. Beatrice claims that if she were married to a husband without a beard, she would "Dress him in my apparel and make him my waiting-gentlewoman" (II.i.30-1). After learning of Beatrice's love for him, Benedick complies—he shaves, and thus submits, at least symbolically, to her authority. Borachio explicitly refers to a "shaven Hercules" when he contrasts the clothes of "Pharaoh's soldiers" with "Bel's priests" and "the shaven Hercules in the smirched worm-eaten tapestry, where his codpiece seems as massy as his club" (III.iii.130-4). This image seems to conflate the myth of Hercules with the story of Samson. By simultaneously evoking Hercules' virility and blind Samson's emasculation, the image captures the paradoxical nature of Benedick's changed status. After accepting Beatrice's love, Benedick is both cowed and potent: he shaves according to Beatrice's preference, but in complying with her command he bravely challenges Claudio and defends Hero's honor.

[5] Rather than choose the lance or long-distance arrow, Beatrice mocks Benedick's manhood by arming and countering him with this modest weapon.

[6] Carol Cook, "The Sign and Semblance of Her Honor': Reading Gender Difference in *Much Ado about Nothing,*" *PMLA* 101,2 (March 1986): 186-202, 191.

[7] Neither the quarto nor the First Folio version punctuates this line.

[8] Sandra Cavallo and Simona Cerutti, "Female Honor and the Social Control of Reproduction in Piedmont between 1600 and 1800," in *Sex and Gender in Historical Perspective,* ed. Edward Muir and Guido Ruggiero, trans. Margaret A. Gallucci (Baltimore: Johns Hopkins Univ. Press, 1990), pp. 73-109, 76, 77-8. For the frequency of prenuptial fornication, see Martin Ingram, *Church Courts, Sex, and Marriage in England, 1570-1640* (Cambridge: Cambridge Univ. Press, 1987). Ingram claims that the "[a]ttitudes to antenuptial fornication are best summed up as ambivalent but, especially before the end of Elizabeth's reign, tending towards tolerance" (p. 230). For example, the Duke in *Measure for Measure* (ed. J. W. Lever [London: Routledge, 1992]), claims that Mariana may sleep with Angelo, for "He is your husband on a pre-contract: / To bring you thus together 'tis no sin" (IV.i.72-3).

[9] Cavallo and Cerutti, p. 78. As Ralph A. Houlbrooke observes in *The English Family 1450-1700* (London: Longman, 1984), such "private agreements or promises . . . might be highly informal" and therefore "could not be enforced at law" (pp. 81-2).

[10] For an example of the definition that I am applying here, see Lysander's comment during the rustic's play in *A Midsummer-Night's Dream,* ed. Harold F. Brooks (London: Routledge, 1991): "Less than an ace, man; for he is dead, he is nothing" (V.i.297). See also Cardinal Wolsey in *King Henry VIII,* ed. R. A. Foakes (London: Routledge, 1991):

> So looks the chafed lion
> Upon the daring huntsman that has gall'd
>   him;
> Then makes him nothing.
>
>                               (III.ii.206-8)

As an example of "nothing" meaning "a nobody," see Imogen's outburst in *Cymbeline* (ed. J. M. Nosworthy [London: Routledge, 1991]):

> No court, no father, nor no more ado
> With that harsh, noble, simple nothing,

> That Cloten, whose love-suit hath been to me
> As fearful as a siege.
>
> (III.iv.133-6)

[11] We can only speculate how devastating Hamnet's death may have been for the author: as the biographer S. Schoenbaum notes, with Hamnet "died Shakespeare's hopes of preserving the family name according to the common way of mankind" (*Shakespeare's Lives* [Oxford: Clarendon Press, 1991], p. 12). From the parish records we learn that the twins Hamnet and Judith Shakespeare were christened on 2 February 1585, and that Hamnet was buried on 11 August 1596.

[12] *The Historie of the Pitifull Life, and Unfortunate Death of Edward the Fifth* (London: William Sheares, 1641; Wing M2688A), Thomas More writes, for example, that "the Dutches had much adoe in her travell, that shee could not be delivered of him uncut, and that hee came into the world the feet forward" (B3$^v$). Similarly, in *Thystorye and Lyf of the Noble and Crysten Prynce Charles the Grete Kynge of Frauuce* (1485; STC 5013), William Caxton writes "And made no more a-doo to bere hym, than dooth a wulf to bere a lytel lambe."

[13] Based on the methods of delivery described in sixteenth- and seventeenth-century guidebooks, the woman whose child died in the womb experienced considerably more pain than the woman who had a "normal" delivery. In *The Expert Midwife, Or An Excellent and most necessary Treatise of the generation and birth of Man* (London, 1637; STC 21442), for example, Jacob Rueff recommends (and includes pictures of) scraping and pulling devices that appear more torturous than useful.

[14] Beatrice's reference to her mother's crying may imply, more generally, her cultural disappointment in giving birth to a daughter, especially such a strong-willed daughter as Beatrice proves to be. But we ought not to underestimate her literal meaning, given that no anesthetics were used during the Renaissance to alleviate the pains of birthing. In *Child-birth, or The Happy Deliverie of Women* (London, 1612; STC 12496), Jacques Guillemeau only recommends that the laboring woman, "as soone as she feeles her selfe stirred and prouoked with throwes and paines," ought to "walke vp and down the chamber, and then lay herselfe down warm in her bed," repeating this action until "the water bee gathered, and the Matrice be opened" (L4$^r$).

[15] William Robertson cites the expression "a burnt whore" in *Phraseologia generalis* (Cambridge: Daniel Browne, 1693; Wing R1617A), p. 289.

[16] According to herbalist encyclopedias, *carduus benedictus* was used, among other applications, to assuage fevers, comfort the brain, prevent the plague, induce appetite, cure halitosis, improve the memory, relieve snakebites, and "strengtheneth all the principall partes of the bodie" (see Thomas Cogan, *Haven of Health* [London, 1584; STC 5478], G3$^v$-G4$^r$; and William Langham, *The Garden of Health* [London, 1597; STC 15195], E8$^r$-F3$^r$).

[17] Langham, E8$^v$, F2$^r$; Rueff, N6$^r$).

[18] See II.i.268, 296, 317.

[19] In light of all the implications in Beatrice's speeches—sex, childbirth, disease, and loss—her rejection of Don Pedro, which may initially surprise readers, now seems logical. He proposes while she reflects upon the suffering she endured in her past relationship with Benedick and, more generally, the pain associated with being a woman. In this frame of mind, she would not likely accept any man, even a prince.

[20] I am following the punctuation of the first quarto, C1$^v$. In the Arden Edition of *Much Ado about Nothing*, Humphreys uses commas to set off the phrase "though bitter."

[21] Interestingly, the word "base" not only meant of poor quality, but also denoted illegitimacy, as in Edmund's soliloquy in *King Lear* (ed. Kenneth Muir [London: Routledge, 1991]): "Why bastard? Wherefore base?" (I.ii.6). Benedick's diction playfully suggests one possible explanation for Beatrice's missing parents. For this definition of "base," see also Henry Cornelius Agrippa, *The Commendation of Matrimony*, trans. David Clapham (London, 1534), B8$^r$: "For he is base borne, and is the sonne of the people, yea rather the sonne of no man, which is the chylde of a woman not laufully maryed."

[22] Susan C. Shapiro in "The Originals of Shakespeare's Beatrice and Hero" (*N&Q* 25, 2 [April 1978]: 133-4), argues that Penelope Devereaux, the strong-willed wife of Lord Rich, served as a model of Beatrice. Reportedly Devereaux was so independent that she refused to live with her husband "except at odd intervals." If we accept Shapiro's claim, Benedick's "halting sonnet" (V.iv.87) to his lover becomes that much more humorous, for Lady Rich served as the model for Sidney's "Stella," and more generally, as a patron of literature, she often had poems addressed to her. That she bore five children by her lover Lord Mountjoy—which echoes Beatrice's nickname for Benedick, "Signior Mountanto"—suggests that the potential inspiration for Beatrice did not let the niceties of social expectations deter her, even in pursuing her sexual desires.

[23] Francis James Child, ed., "The Maid and the Palmer," in *The English and Scottish Popular Ballads*, 5 vols. (New York: Folklore Press, 1956), 1:232. See also Humphreys, ed., *Much Ado about Nothing*, p. 111, for other references to this proverb. For the common problem of women abandoning or murdering their illegiti-

mate children so as to avoid the severe consequences of bastardy, see R. V. Schnucker, "The English Puritans and Pregnancy, Delivery and Breast Feeding," *History of Childhood Quarterly* 1, 4 (Spring 1974): 637-58.

[24] We learn the details of the deception piecemeal. I have combined here Borachio's original description of the plot (II.ii.33-50), his boastful conversation with Conrade (III.iii.139-47), and his confession to Don Pedro and Claudio (V.i.225-38).

[25] "The Copy for *Much Ado about Nothing,* 1600," in *Much Ado about Nothing,* ed. Sir Arthur Quiller-Couch and John Dover Wilson (Cambridge: Cambridge Univ. Press, 1962), pp. 89-108.

[26] *Othello,* ed. E. A. J. Honigmann (Walton-on-Thames, Surrey: Thomas Nelson and Sons, 1997), I.i.20.

[27] Norman Rabkin, *Shakespeare and the Common Understanding* (New York: The Free Press, 1967), p. 13.

[28] Ibid.

[29] John P. Rumrich, "Shakespeare's Walking Plays: Image and Form in *1* and *2 Henry IV,*" in *Shakespeare's English Histories: A Quest for Form and Gene,* ed. John W. Velz (Binghamton: Medieval and Renaissance Texts and Studies, 1996), pp. 111-41, 112, 113.

[30] Cook, p. 193.

[31] Richard P. Wheeler, *Shakespeare's Development and the Problem Comedies: Turn and Counter-Turn* ([Berkeley: Univ. California Press, 1981], pp. 2-3), neatly summarizes the various uses of the label "problem comedies." Applying the term only to *All's Well that Ends Well* and *Measure for Measure,* Wheeler argues that these two plays "occupy a transitional place in Shakespeare's development of comic form" (p. 2).

[32] Responding to critics who have complained that Claudio's violent denunciation at the wedding mars the play's comic tone, Cook argues that this eruption of "naked emotions" is intended to startle us (p. 193).

[33] To account for Margaret's participation, Borachio claims that she "knew not what she did" (V.i.295), and Leonato offers the terse, unsatisfactory explanation that

> Margaret was in some fault for this,
> Although against her will, as it appears
> In the true course of all the question.
>
> (V.iv.4-6)

[34] We glimpse the difference between the two stories in the stringency of the two men's punishments: whereas Claudio's labor seems, by his own admission, "overkindness" (V.i.287), Benedick's labor requires that he "Kill Claudio" (IV.i.288). Beatrice's bluntness and alliteration emphasize the severity of what she asks.

[35] The word "nothing" also connotes something that is not very much, like a failed romance, which could apply equally to Claudio and Hero as well as Benedick and Beatrice.

[36] For advice and encouragement in the writing of this essay, I would like to thank Eric Mallin, Shannon Prosser, and John Rumrich.

---

Source: "Children of the Mind: Miscarried Narratives in *Much Ado about Nothing,*" in *Studies in English Literature, 1500-1900,* Vol. 38, No. 2, Spring, 1998, pp. 233-50.

# "What Do I Do Now?" Directing *A Midsummer Night's Dream*

## Sidney Homann, *University of Florida*

"What do I do now?" my Hippolyta asked me, the first day of rehearsals for a production of *A Midsummer Night's Dream* I was directing for the Florida Theatre.[1] "After those first four lines, I've got nothing until act 4—and that's after intermission. So, do I just stand there like an idiot while Theseus talks to Hermia? Waiting around for my exit?" She was right about the lines—as far as the character of Hippolyta was concerned—for, like any actor, the moment she got her part and was handed the script she had highlighted Hippolyta's lines and knew that they were precious few Besides 1.1. and 4.1 (the conversation with Theseus about hunting dogs), there is Hippolyta's observation at the start of the last act (" 'Tis strange, my Theseus, that these lovers speak of") that sends Theseus into a twenty-one-line harangue against poets, lovers, and madmen, after which she contends that, nevertheless, their stories "grow to great constancy," until the lovers' arrival halts the debate. Finally, during the performance of *Pyramus and Thisby* Hippolyta makes a few cynical observations about the actors before retiring to consummate the marriage.

Actually, my Hippolyta had more lines than this, for, like many other modern directors, I had doubled her part with Titania's—and, for good measure, doubled those of Theseus and Oberon, and old Egeus and Puck. This was part of a larger reading of the play, the "director's concept," that underscores the irony of Theseus, who has no sympathy for anything beyond the pale of his Athenian reason, having a doppelgänger in the King of the Fairies. Hippolyta's problems with the Duke echo on a cosmic scale the quarrel Titania has with Oberon. Like the doubling, that concept suggested that the play itself, our own imaginative collaboration with the playwright, whether as actor, director, or audience, unites the seeming opposites of its comic world: court / forest, left brain / right brain, reason / imagination, male / female, reality / illusion, *homo sapiens / homo ludens*. Peter Brook, to be sure, was just over my shoulder here.

So my Hippolyta was not confined to Hippolyta's lines, and her small part in that opening scene notwithstanding, she would appear moments later in 2.1, charging Oberon with unfound jealousies and swearing to forswear "his bed and company" (62). Still, my experience has been that actors, even when playing double roles, focus on the character at hand, on how to make him or her live and breathe, to *be* something each moment. Valuable to set and lighting designers and to the costumer, the director's concept—that larger reading of the play most resembling the sweeping, after-the-fact interpretations of Shakespeareans—may be a subject for conversation in some Brechtian discussion with the cast after rehearsals, but it is generally avoided by actors. As an actor-friend, who is also a fine Shakespearean scholar, once told me, "When I'm onstage, I'm just trying to make it to the next line. To win the moment both as a character, with a distinct view of the situation, and as an actor aware of the audience just offstage."

-I-

"What should you do?" I asked.

"Yeah, you've got me downstage-left with Theseus, the court upstage, and here comes five new characters, with a complaint that Theseus has to solve—and I've got nothing else to say."

"We'll find the motivation to move you in those opening lines."

I had, of course, my own reading of that ten-line interchange between Theseus and Hippolyta, yet I knew enough to wait for my Theseus and Hippolyta, to see what they would come up with. Now, I must admit at the first read-through with the cast to having colored their approach to some degree by a series of questions I had raised. Hippolyta has been a queen, leader of a band of warrior women in Brazil, bonding with her sisters and not needing the company of men. Theseus brings her back to Athens as his Duchess, but the decision was his, not hers: "Hippolyta, I wooed thee with my sword, / And won thy love, doing thee injuries" (1.1.16-17). How does she feel about this? For her, is going to Athens a step up—or down?

Hippolyta empathizes with the lovers, finding their story "strange" (as in "wondrous"). Theseus feels the need to correct her; his "strange" means "absurd" or "irrational." But after his harangue, she still finds the story "admirable," and while he dismisses the lovers' accounts of the night, all of which agree, despite the fantastic events of which they tell, she insists that the combined stories grow "to something of great constancy" (5.1.1-27). If she agrees with his sense of "strange," she quickly adds her own "admirable." The conversation—debate? would we want to hear more of it? could Theseus stand anymore?—is abruptly halted with the entry of the lovers. So, how harmonious is this couple? To what degree is Hippolyta arguing with, resisting Theseus and his view of what is real or rational? And, more important, if she is resisting, then why?

In act 4 she recalls hunting in the woods of Crete with Hercules and Cadmus, "with hounds of Sparta." Theseus has just proposed to go to the mountaintop and there listen to his own dogs barking in the valley below, their sound one of "musical confusion" (4.1.112-30). With the anticipated consummation on his mind—indeed, on his mind for four days now—Theseus sees the outing as a way to pass the time. But might it also be taken as self-congratulatory? He is proud of having picked his brace of dogs with care, their distinct barks forming a perfect chord on the scale, a chord to be amplified by the echoing hills. He may take Hippolyta's reference to Hercules and Cadmus as name-dropping, her pointed reference to Sparta—famous for its hounds—as competitive. Quick to assert that his hounds are also "bred out of the Spartan kind," he goes on to brag of how low to the ground they run, right on the scent, how they are powerfully built like Thessalian bulls, careful or dogged in pursuit ("slow"). He even expands on the quality of their barking: they are "matched in mouth like bells," and no cry "more tunable" has ever been heard "in Crete, in Sparta, or in Thessaly."

To make this passage something more than scene-painting, or references to hunting that will drive the editor into copious footnotes, to make the passage live onstage, actors will need to find the characters' objects here, their motivations. What are they after? Could it be that Theseus and Hippolyta have two very different objects? Perhaps she relishes her past, life before Theseus came to Brazil, that time when the dogs' barking seemed to link "the groves, / The skies, the fountains, every region near" (118-21) so that nature itself became "all one mutual cry," a moment when opposites were united: "So musical a discord, such sweet thunder."

In effect, here Hippolyta seems at one with the play itself, where dichotomy gives way to unity, where opposites dissolve. For a time the lowly Bottom becomes a fairy queen's lover; youthful, irrational lovers have a mystical experience denied more sober, rational adults like Theseus. And a potential *Romeo and Juliet* (Hermia = Juliet = Thisby; Lysander = Romeo = Pyramus; Old Egeus = Old Capulet) is at once saved by a comic ending in which three couples are married even as it dissolves into an unintentionally funny, poorly acted melodrama staged before the Duke. Theseus' object, again, may be that of asserting his status as a hunter, as a man, annoyed as he is when a woman he has conquered brings up her own days as a huntress. His dogs attest his status. How solid, therefore, is the union of Theseus and Hippolyta? To be sure, Hippolyta is on his turf; yet how cowed is she? As with the debate about the stories in the final scene, the conversation here is aborted when Theseus spies the sleeping Athenians.

How does Theseus view women? Hippolyta? Does he think she "owes" him something for the decision to marry, rather than execute her in Brazil? Does she have any reservations about being here, about giving up her former life?

-II-

Not so much armed with these questions as being willing to entertain them, the three of us (two actors and a director), after an hour or so of "table work" (or discussion before taking the stage), decided to *try*—for rehearsals are periods of experimentation, as signaled by the well-worn phrase "the rehearsal process"—the following objectives in the play's opening moment.

Theseus is dying to consummate the marriage; his first word "Now" rides a subtext something like: "I want you *now,* not four days from now. I deserve your body; you owe me that much for I could have left you dead in Brazil." He alternates between exposing his private desires and being socially discrete. So, one second the sexual act he yearns for is euphemized as a "nuptial hour," the next as a slow horse drawing on "apace." The moon—feminine, the goddess of chastity, Hippolyta's former symbol—bears the brunt of his anger born out of frustration: while four "happy days" will bring in the new moon of the marriage night, the fact is that tonight's moon wanes too slowly. The mutual "nuptial act" of the first line shrinks to "my desires," as if only Theseus' own sexual satisfaction were now at issue. Most telling is the clumsy metaphor with which he describes his condition. He is the young man, living with a maiden aunt, waiting for the old lady to die so he can collect his inheritance, yet she goes on living and living, and with each passing day uses up the money he thinks rightfully his for having endured life with a "stepdame, or a dowager."

A director-friend wryly observes, "Any actor can say lines. The real test is what to do onstage when you aren't speaking." As Theseus speaks, Hippolyta—at least in our construction of the moment, with the caveat that our option is just one of many—thinks to herself subtextually: "I gave up Brazil for this? This isn't that handsome would-be conqueror-turned-lover who swept me off my feet. Here's a self-centered MCP, concerned about *his* glands, his sexual satisfaction. As if I didn't exist! As if I, a woman, had no desires, no needs of my own! Well, I can't go back to Brazil. Here's a world where males have all the power. I'm a survivor. I'm stuck here. Let's see what I can do to soften this self-absorbed lover."

As we staged it, Hippolyta moved toward Theseus with "Four days will quickly steep themselves in night," saying, in effect: "It's only four days, not twelve, not twenty, and so the time will pass relatively quickly for *both* of us. Don't forget, it's four days for me as well." She gets no response from Theseus, even though she appeals to his accountant's mentality with "four days." Self-centered, Theseus has turned away from her on "young man's revenue." His visual, gestural subtext is a crude, petulant one: "If I have to wait too much longer, if these four days continue to pass so slowly, to draw on 'apace,' I'll become old with frustration, withered, impotent." The fact is that Hippolyta also looks forward to the consummation or—to be more accurate—*was* looking forward to it, yet her first concern here is Theseus. She ups the stakes, this time putting a consoling, almost maternal hand on his shoulder as she doubles her reassurance to him: "Four nights will quickly dream away the time." But Theseus is not to be consoled, and, somewhat irritated by him, in part giving up, she crosses downstage-right to find some space of her own, as she unleashes her own metaphor of the sexual act, as expansive, as beautiful, as "poetic" as Theseus' was constrictive, mundane, "un-poetic." For Hippolyta, the wished-for wedding night is not something owed, or her right, but, as she returns to her roots as a huntress, one where the male is the silver bow, bent and about to discharge, the consummation (their "solemnities") taking place under the moon's watchful eye.

Does he hear her own erotic hymn to the marriage night? Does she even care at this point? All that we know is that Theseus, rather than responding to her, barks out orders to Philostrate. My Theseus linked the moon and, by implication, Hippolyta's serene, cosmic picture with melancholy. He'll have none of this "pale companion," but wants, instead, a public celebration. Thinking Hippolyta is still at his side, not having noticed that she had left his presence after he rejected her attempts to console him, he turns around, expecting to find her on his right. She, instead, has now strolled to far downstage-right, with the results that his "I wooed thee . . . with reveling," spoken over a void, lacks intimacy. My Theseus added the following subtext to his paradox of war's turning to love, the initial plan to do "injuries" to a wedding "in another key": "I'm not sure just why you left my side. Is something bothering you? I can't imagine what. Surely, *I've* done nothing. If anything, you *owe* me your constant presence. I'll have to handle this later because here come Egeus and the lovers—I know he's going to insist that I support Demetrius for Hermia's hand."

Thus, by working with the two actors, by allowing them to establish this dark cloud in the relationship between Theseus and Hippolyta, one that would not dissolve until four days later when, Theseus' anxieties gone, they could enjoy a play together before going to bed, we had found the motivation for Hippolyta's cross, getting her out of the way in time for Egeus' angry entrance. She would have no more lines—that is true—but now, in her own "space" downstage-right, she could observe Theseus, assess him, sympathizing with her "sister" Hermia, as Theseus, supporting her crabbed father, delivers the ultimatum: either marry the man of your father's choice, or be sent to a nunnery or—worse yet—your death. Careful not to upstage the actors to her left, she could still "speak" with her face, her posture, a slight gesture or two. Her expressions implied: "So this is what Athens is like, this world where males have all the power? From what I see, Helena looks like a perfectly fine woman. (Hippolyta would even exchange glances with both Helena and Hermia.) Why would Demetrius reject her? Lysander and Demetrius look like generic, eligible young men, handsome, intelligent, equal in every way. Why can't Egeus be content with Lysander?"

With his frail body plagued by arthritis, unsteady on his feet, our Egeus brought onstage an enormous large black law book, so large that it dwarfed him and he had great difficult carrying it. On "And, my gracious Duke" (38), he managed to unload the volume on Theseus, who later, on "Either to die the death, or to abjure" (65), turned to the specific section where these harsh edicts were inscribed. I suggested that halfway through the conversation between the Duke and Hermia, Hippolyta cross to stage-left and, while the Duke was talking to Hermia on the left, take the volume from him, crossing back with it to her downstage-right position. She chose Theseus' "For disobedience to your father's will" (87) for that cross. Absorbed in his conversation with Hermia, Theseus could still feel her lift the book from his right arm, would catch her in the periphery of his eye and, distracted by Hippolyta, falter a bit on his next line. His subtext here was something like: "I'm not sure why you interrupted me the middle of my talk with Hermia. Why would you, a woman, want to look at a law book? Well, I can't deal with this now; we'll talk about it later—in private." As our stage manager suggested, Theseus has something of the E. F. Hutton mentality: when he speaks, everyone listens. Now back in her space downstage-right, Hippolyta could thumb through the law book, reading there a confirmation of her suspicions about Theseus' supposedly brave new world. Every once in awhile she would look up from her reading, sympathizing with her sisters, feeling for Lysander, looking contemptuously at Egeus and Demetrius, and—most certainly—showing increasing doubts about the man who, at the top of the scene, had reminded her of the consummation four days away.

One day in rehearsal Hippolyta accidentally slammed the law book shut on Theseus' "Or else the law of Athens yields you up" (119), making a sound that, given the size of the book, boomed across the stage. Startled, the actor playing Theseus looked in her direction, and I promptly suggested that he deliver the next line to Hippolyta (they were twenty-five feet apart): "Which by no means we may extenuate." With the line said to Hippolyta rather than Hermia, Theseus' subtext was: "Why did you slam that book, right in the middle of my speech? Why did you take it in the first place? Don't you understand that I'm just doing my job. I can't ignore or water down ('extenuate') the law. I'm the Duke. It's my job to enforce the laws in that book you're reading. What I personally think about the law is not relevant. We'll speak about this later."

He crossed stage-right to Hippolyta on "Come, my Hippolyta" (122); his line to her, "What cheer, my love?" had the modern sense of: "Why so glum? Why out of spirits?" After his final four lines, where he promises to confer with Egeus and Demetrius on "something nearly that concerns" them, Theseus, facing upstage with his profile to stage-right, offered his left arm to Hippolyta, his eyes saying: "It's time to go, and I need to discuss this strange behavior of yours as soon as we are in private quarters." Turning toward him, her profile to stage-left, Hippolyta, instead of linking her arm with his as he expected, put the law book in Theseus' left hand, the action speaking loudly: "Snuggle up with that tonight, honey." He glared at her, angry that she was embarrassing him in front of the courtiers, who were now whispering among themselves on stage-left. Then she glanced down at whatever women were in the front row's audience left—we added this Brechtian touch the second week of rehearsals—as if addressing them: "Sisters, this male will wait an eternity for me until I give him my right arm [Theseus had since passed the book to his right arm and was conspicuously holding his left arm open in invitation]. What do you think I should do? What would you do, if you were I?" Then, much to Theseus' relief but, by the delay, asserting her integrity and such power as a woman could have in this– patriarchal world, she gave him her arm so they could exit.

-III-

Not coming out of a vacuum, still, my actress's "What do I do now?" had been the first in a chain of events, options, experiments that, taken together, pushed our *A Midsummer Night's Dream* toward a feminist concept, or statement (in critical terms). Here the women, especially Hippolyta and Titania, were at the play's imaginative center, able to entertain the idea of a world beginning with but expanding far beyond Athens, a world where dichotomies of the genders, of reason and imagination, reality and illusion, were dissolved. Earlier scholarship on the play had stressed the conflict between reason and passion. It saw the play as a debate, the rational Theseus as the center of value, Bottom with his ass's head representing the absurd depth to which man sinks when he abandons Athens.[2] In the 1960s Jan Kott would challenge that judgment: Athens and Theseus are the establishment, a constraint on our imagination; the trip into the forest, far from being a step down, as earlier readings would hold, is a step up. For Kott, Theseus' kingdom represents the "censorship of the day," the forest "the erotic madness liberated by night."[3] There, in the darkness, however fleeting on this summer solstice, men and women discover their true selves. Without negating either of these readings, our production offered another option—just another option and nothing more: a single, expansive world, embracing dichotomies, constructed of both reason and the imagination, merging them into a whole greater than the sum of its two parts.

But I stress, again, that word "option," for the theater as I see it, does not argue, let alone prove; it explores, tests out possibilities, stages and includes rather than argues against or excludes. Even as Shakespeare played on such sources as he had for *A Midsummer Night's Dream,* the director and actors play on Shakespeare, and their performance is in turn played out before an audience, who come to it with their own agendas, their own needs and idiosyncrasies.[4]

The option we had chosen shaped the rest of the production. That area downstage-right soon became a "woman's place," a retreat from the male world, an area of imagination or introspection occupied only by the women. With its own special lighting, no male in the cast was allowed to occupy it.

-IV-

Given the doubling, the tension between Theseus and Hippolyta, as we had staged it in the opening scene, returned in 2.1 as the quarrel over the changeling boy between Oberon and Titania (118-43). His three and a half lines demanding that she hand over the boy offer the actor, if not the scholar, a wonderful challenge. Oberon's strategy here changes from demanding the boy for no other reason than that women, in his view, do whatever men tell them to do ("Do you amend it, then; it lies in you"), to a rather childish question expressing his shock that a woman would behave so unwomanly ("Why should Titania cross her Oberon?"), to what must seem to Oberon a compromising of his demand with a justification: he isn't asking for the moon but only for "a little changeling boy." Like his other half, Theseus, Oberon speaks here with the posture of male superiority, but he cannot know how much, and why, Titania values the changeling boy. her "Set your heart at rest" had something of the blue-collar television character Archie Bunker's "Stifle it!" With "The fairy land buys not the child of me" our Titania rose and started to cross to that woman's spot downstage-right. As she did, we took the lights off Oberon center-stage, so that the ensuing speech became something of a soliloquy, an introspective moment Titania shared directly with the audience, especially any women on audience-left. She would not cross back to Oberon—nor would full stage lighting return—until the speech's coda: "And for her sake do I rear up her boy, / And for her sake I will not part with him." The equation she makes between a ship, its hold full of cargo, its sails puffed out by "the wanton wind" looking like a pregnant woman, with a pregnant woman who resembles a ship "rich with merchandise" was at one with that union of seeming dichotomies informing our production, from the doubling of roles to the questions raised in Theseus' character about the limits of reason and the significance of the imagination. Like that of Hippolyta in 4.1, Titania's vision is one of union, "all one mutual cry," as the inanimate ship is linked with the doubly animate pregnant woman. No less, Titania recalls an exquisite moment when two women bonded, one mortal and heavy with child, the other supernatural. The changeling boy is the sign of that bonding, and, Titania's explanation completed, Oberon's reply must be, for her, tawdry and grating: "How long within this wood intend you stay?" A businessman, like Theseus with his "young man's revenue," Oberon focuses only on schedules and time allotment! He has heard nothing she has said; little wonder that he cannot understand the boy's true value and meaning.

-V-

"A court scene at the start and the end, surrounding the main set in the forest"—this was the set designer's pithy assessment of his task. And he was right. In our production, the play began in a rigid, unimaginative male world, where cranky fathers, backed up by authority figures who, being lovers as well, ought to know better, control their daughters—a revisiting of *Romeo and Juliet,* which Shakespeare's company was possibly performing around the same time (1595). The intervening forest world, what Helen Gardner would call "a green world,"[5] is neither male nor female but one of dissolutions and mergings, fluidity, rich confusion, a world that Bottom struggles to recall and in his failure recalls eloquently, however unintentionally: an indistinct place, a dream "past the wit of man to say what dream it was," where eyes can hear and ears see, a place profound "because it hath no bottom" (4.1.298-309). It is, above all, a world where opposites, antitheses, categories, hierarchies—all are abolished: the lowly, half-ass Bottom is loved by the Queen of the Fairies; the rejected Helena is for a time pursued by two men; compounds such as Peaseblossom and Mustardseed take animate form while humans in turn are reduced to a kind of arithmetic where "two of both kind makes up four" (3.2.438). It can be a magical world for men as well as for women, or rather for the man who, recognizing the "woman" in him, celebrates his own feelings and intuition, and even the irrational—a world for the male lover that Theseus himself is, when he isn't playing the patriarchal tyrant. Appropriately, Bottom, who gains entrance to this world, specializes, as he tells us, in playing both lovers and tyrants—though his preference is for the tyrant.

When the court world returns in the final act, it too is changed, transformed by our mutual journey—whether we be actor, character, or audience—through that intervening forest world. Our lighting designer signaled the change with a subdued, more suggestive atmosphere, as did the costume designer who replaced the sterile, Star Trek-like uniforms of the opening scene with multicolored, softer evening attire.

In 4.1 Egeus demands "The law, the law upon [Lysander's] head" for having robbed Demetrius of a bride and himself of the right to dispose of his daughter (4.1.157-62). But it is a gentler, kinder Theseus who now dismisses the old man, whose character has not changed, with a simple, "Egeus, I will overbear your will." Theseus, and Hippolyta no less, can be cynical and condescending about the actor's performance, yet the Duke has also mellowed somewhat, suggesting that "If we imagine no worse of them than they of themselves, they may pass for excellent men" (5.1.216-17). His anxieties of four days ago replaced by thoughts of the imminent consummation, concerns with his own needs or more serious matters now diverted by the amateur production, Theseus is—in a phrase—more human, less the tyrant who earlier could not extenuate the laws of Athens. Now he is just another lover, one among five lovers, watching a poorly staged play about tragic lovers that reminds us, if not its onstage aristocratic audience, of the *Romeo and Juliet* that *A Midsummer Night's Dream* would have become if it had not been for the forest. Theseus' other half, Oberon, has also reconciled with his Titania; the initial source of their contention, the changeling boy, is now his, without any explanation from playwright or character. In that final scene our Hippolyta had no problem with her lines or with her stage position. There would be no quarrelsome old men or frustrated lovers to rush on and upstage her. In her own words, "I like Theseus a little better in the final act."

I did give her one unvoiced "line" in the closing moments. Holding what well may be "Bottom's Dream," the epilogue, as told to Quince, he promised to deliver at Thisby's death "peradventure to make it the more gracious" (4.1.221-22), Bottom steps out of his role as Pyramus to ask the Duke if he would like "to see the epilogue" (again, as in 4.1, confusing eyes and ears). Eager to get to bed, joking with his fellow aristocrats about the wretched performance that is beyond excuse—though the thick-witted Bottom takes the barbs as compliments—Theseus has no time for an epilogue. Then, he suddenly reverses himself by taking Bottom's second choice, a Bergomask dance. Why, we asked, would he do this? After all, he is eager to consummate the marriage, has been eager for four days, and the dance will take at least as much time as an epilogue. The Duke, once again, is being selfish. In our production, Hippolyta, noticing how eager Bottom is to honor theatrical tradition by adding an epilogue or a dance, as a sort of aesthetic "chaser" to the performance, crossed to her husband. More sensitive to the feelings of others than the Duke, however mellow he may be at this point, Hippolyta whispered something in her husband's ear, to the effect: "Look at that poor man. He wants to add something. Be kind. If you don't want the epilogue, at least let him dance." Eager to please his wife, acknowledging this small display of her power or rights, he concedes, first asking for the Bergomask and then, saving face, adding "Let your epilogue alone."

Perhaps a hopeful sign that Hippolyta will continue to assert herself, is in scenes beyond what Shakespeare has given us? Still, it is unfortunate that Theseus declined the epilogue, because *if* it did chart Bottom's "translation" in the forest and *if*—a big "if" here—Theseus were attentive and willing to consider its message, then he would have heard—or, rather, "seen"—an account of that larger imaginative reality, dwarfing his own Athens, which would have radically altered his attitude toward everything from reason to the imagination. But this is to speak of a play we do not have. It is enough that Theseus, perhaps at his wife's urging (the option chosen in our production), is willing for a few minutes to forego his own pleasure, his desires that have been "lingered" since the opening scene, to watch a dance by actors—*fellow* actors, if he only knew the truth of his own imaginative reality.

-VI-

My actress's "What do I do now?" came back to haunt me in the staging of *Pyramus and Thisby*. This time I was the one delivering that line, and yet once again a seeming problem became a challenge that, in turn, both affected and was at one with the concept of the production. The producer had told us in no uncertain terms that he could afford only eight Equity actors for the production. "You'll have to double or eliminate parts, or do whatever you can—just keep it to eight." This was fine with me since I had wanted to show the rational Theseus' other, magical side in Oberon, as well as the irony of having a single actor play both the imaginative Puck and that legalist Egeus, who can think of no other reason for Hermia's choice than Lysander's having bewitched "her fantasy" with everything from "feigning voice" to "knacks, trifles, nosegays, sweetmeats, [and] messengers" (1.1.28-34).

Besides, doubling Hippolyta and Titania would give focus to the feminist motif of the production. In a larger sense, doubling would call attention to the play's insistent metadramatics that underscored multiple role-playing, the limits of realism and the virtues of imagination, and the presence of the stage (even if it be parodied in the Quince-Bottom production). In the final scene we watch Puck and Oberon watch Theseus and his court watch a wretched production of *Pyramus and Thisby*. Secure in his realism, condescending to attend a stage performance that for him serves only "to ease the anguish of a torturing hour" (5.1.37), Theseus cannot know that he himself owes his life to the theater.[6] Like Bottom's confusion of the five senses, the rustics' inability to separate stage and reality—they fear the ladies will confuse Snug with a real lion, and they bring on a character to designate moonshine as an aid to the audience's imagination—is also a virtue, when compared to Theseus' own rigid distinction between the two.

Only Bottom (Pyramus in the inner-play) could not effectively be doubled with any other character. However, besides the doubling of Theseus and Oberon, Hippolyta and Titania, Egeus would be Puck and Snug (Lion in the inner-play); Lysander, Flute (Thisby in the inner-play) and Cobweb; Hermia, Robin Starveling (Moonshine in the inner-play); Helena, Tom Snout (Wall in the inner-play) and Mustardseed; and Demetrius, Quince (Prologue in the inner-play). We deleted Moth and gave Philostrate's lines to Egeus in the final scene.[7] We could not afford the luxury of "Other Fairies attending their King and Queen" or "Attendants on Theseus and Hippolyta." To stress the multiple role playing, and the larger fact, as Bert O. States suggests,[8] that an audience responds both to the story and its enactment, both to theme and the actor's craft, we made little attempt to disguise characters. Indeed, when Theseus came onstage shortly after Oberon's exit in 4.1, Oberon simply froze in position, without leaving the stage, while a stagehand brought in the "Theseus robe," which was then, in full view of the audience, exchanged for the "Oberon robe."

In the final scene there were only Theseus and Hippolyta to constitute the onstage audience, since Hermia, Helena, Lysander, Demetrius, and Egeus would join Bottom in *Pyramus and Thisby*. Curiously, Hermia and Helena have no lines in this scene; I reassigned those of Lysander and Demetrius to that "audience" of two. Egeus (or Philostrate) makes no commentary during the performance. To preserve some sense of illusion, we had planned to have Egeus (assuming Philostrate's lines) exit with Theseus' "Go, bring them in; and take your places, ladies" (84). He would not return; we deleted Philostrate's line on his re-entrance, "So please your Grace, the Prologue is addressed" (106), and changed Theseus' "Let him approach" to "I see the Prologue approaches." This, of course, allowed

Egeus to go backstage and change into Snug's Lion costume. Demetrius stood close to the upstage-right exit and during Theseus' long speech before the Prologue enters ("The kinder we, to give them thanks for nothing" [106]), he would exit and change into Quince's Prologue costume. As he emerged from stage-left for his "If we offend, it is with our good will" (108), stage-right would be darkened, allowing Hermia, Helena, and Lysander to exit unseen, change into the costumes of Moonshine, Wall, and Thisby, and be ready, with time to spare, for their stage-left entrances. (I should add that since Snug, doubled with Puck, has no lines in the rehearsal scene, which Puck interrupts, I simply did not bring him onstage in 3.1.) At the end of *Pyramus and Thisby,* Theseus and Hippolyta could cross to the lit stage-left side for his "No epilogue, I pray you" (including her "whispered" line that he should at least let the actors do a Bergomask dance). His call to the other two couples ("Sweet friends, to bed" [307]) would only imply that Lysander, Hermia, Demetrius, and Helena were still on stage-right. Theseus and Hippolyta would exist stage-left, as did the actors after the Bergomask dance, with Snug's (formerly Egeus) having just enough time to change into his Puck costume and re-emerge stage-right for "Now the hungry lion roars" (373). That speech would in turn allow Theseus and Hippolyta to be recostumed as Oberon and Titania, with Peaseblossom, Mustardseed, and Cobweb returning for the "song and dance" promised by the now united King and Queen of the fairies.

In a production eschewing illusion or, conversely, calling attention to the art of the theater through its obvious doubling, our one moment of illusion here in the final scene depended, therefore, on darkening stage-right to the degree that two actors would be able to represent an audience of seven. The darkened stage was also essential since, with the exception of the "hunting scene" (4.1), here within a single scene actors would need to make unseen exits as one character and visible entrances as another.

We had rehearsed for four weeks in a hall some blocks from the Florida Theatre; because of other productions, we would not be able to rehearse on its stage until three days before opening night. The lighting director had been assured that the facilities were "top-notch," the board itself "*almost* state-of-the-art." The day we moved to the main stage, however, he told us the bad news. Mounted on the high ceiling above the house were five lights, relics of the theater's vaudeville days, that were essential for our basic stage lighting but which could not be adjusted during a production so that half the stage would be dark. Given the lights' primitive state, it was all or nothing with them. The real audience would therefore be able to see that our onstage audience excluded the four young lovers and Egeus; nor would darkness conceal their exits to reappear in *Pyramus and Thisby.* Our one attempt at full-blown illusion—"stage magic," to invoke the cliché—was doomed.

Having launched our voyage now rich with theatrical "discoveries"—a word dear to actors and directors, signaling that moment when some combination of thought, emotion, accident, and necessity suggests a new slant on a character or the delivery of a line—our Hippolyta came to the rescue. "You know, we haven't done much to pull the wool over their [the audience's] eyes; why worry now?" She was right. Not trying to use costumes as a disguise, rejoicing in multiple role-playing, celebrating that blurred line between onstage and off, allowing actors to address the audience directly in that special "woman's spot" downstage-right—hadn't we been doing everything possible to include the audience in the production, to make them collaborators in such illusion as our meager stage and small cast could afford? Why worry now? Why not ask the audience to make the ultimate in imaginative collaborations with the actor and director—to believe in an invisible audience (shades of Ionesco's *The Chairs!*), to "allow" five actors to change characters before their eyes?

Therefore, we would not darken stage-right—a conscious decision that usurped whatever necessity had forced on us. The actors would not go backstage to change into rustic actors; instead, they would cross to stage-left and change costumes in full view of the audience. After all, we had set a precedent in the onstage costume changes of Oberon/Theseus and Titania/Hippolyta in 4.1.

Denying the illusion of an aristocratic audience watching a production by their social inferiors would, paradoxically, only underscore the potency of the theater. What we know is an illusion, a fraud, is still significant, for the change from frustrated to requited love is a wished-for event in our own reality, where patriarchs, a rigid legal system, or conflicts between reason and the heart are all too common. Confessing the patent unreality of the stage, as we would be doing, only made of it an "honest woman" or "man." The titles of Shakespeare's plays themselves beg us to dismiss them as of no or little consequence, a mere *Midsummer Night's Dream,* something *As You Like It* or *What You Will,* little more than a *Winter's Tale* told by the fire. For Genet, such theatrical honesty distinguishes the stage from life; for the latter, which is nothing but role playing, mistakenly assumes that it is real and thereby superior to the theater.[9] The confession of illusion is inseparable from the theater's celebration of its own significance, for the stage characters have been enacted by fellow humans, with their own life stories, needs, and desires. Taking place in space and time, the production is witnessed, ratified by fellow humans in the house, occupying precisely that same space and time. In this sense, the theater is the most real, the most tangible and literal of the arts. However impoverished, *Pyramus and Thisby* only reminds us of what would have been the lovers' fate—what is often our own fate—in a world without dreams, where there is no forest of transformation or potentiality. Theater itself is a two-way process, where the audience as well as the actor have a vital role. Or, as I tell my own actors, to be onstage speaking lines with no audience in the house is to be in rehearsal only, not in a production. Their presence validates ours; the ascription works both ways.

By design, by necessity, we had asked the audience to assist us in the production of *A Midsummer Night's Dream*. Onstage, humans had acknowledged the presence of fellow humans offstage. Now, with an audience in the house watching an audience onstage watch a performance, we were pushing that collaboration to the limits. I believe it worked. Or, as one audience member said to me, "Watching that actor who played Demetrius rush across that stage and become Quince . . . well, you know, you made me feel that we were all in it together. If you were willing to make believe, so were we." Another audience member put it more succinctly: "I felt that I was a part of the performance."

"What do I do now?" The actress's question, for me, describes the mutual role of actor and audience. For the actor portrays a character who, not knowing the story, must live and breathe line by line, can know only the "now" as he or she pushes his or her object through dialogue with fellow characters. Likewise, the audience, even if they know the story, know how the play turns out, nevertheless abandon such omniscience—at least, in a production that captures their interest—and respond beat by beat with that illusory character onstage who, a fraud, mere words, words, words, reminds them of and, in a more profound way, represents themselves. I have asked myself that same question—"What do I do now?"—in all of the plays, Shakespearean and otherwise, I have directed since *A Midsummer Night's Dream*.

## Notes

[1] *A Midsummer Night's Dream* was produced by the Fable Factory in Gainesville, Florida, in February 1985. By a lucky coincidence I also co-directed a production of *Romeo and Juliet* at the Hippodrome State Theatre the next month, and thus had the experience of being involved with two plays which, most likely, Shakespeare's own company had staged—perhaps back to back—in 1595. The text for *A Midsummer Night's Dream* is edited by Wolfgang Clemen in *The Complete Signet Classic Shakespeare,* gen. ed. Sylvan Barnet (New York: Harcourt, 1972).

[2] For studies celebrating Theseus and his reason over the imaginative forest see Paul Olson, "*A Midsummer Night's Dream* and the Meaning of Court Marriage," *English Literary History* 24 (1957): 113; Peter F. Fisher, "The Argument of *A Midsummer Night's Dream*," *Shakespeare Quarterly* 8 (1957): 307-10; and E. C. Pettet, *Shakespeare and the Romance Tradition* (London and New York: Staples Press, 1949), 234.

[3] Jan Kott, *Shakespeare Our Contemporary* (Garden City, N.Y.: Doubleday), 234.

[4] Marvin Rosenberg's books on Shakespeare's four great tragedies, besides proving invaluable to people working in the theater as each traces the play's onstage history, also remind us of a very basic distinction between actual theater practice and literary criticism of Shakespeare. Too much of dramatic criticism seems caught up in "search-and-destroy" syndrome, the assumption being that there is a single "mystery" at the heart of each play which, despite efforts of past critics, the present critic can best solve. Put another way, the assumption is that the world of the play, as reconstructed by a particular critical approach—an approach, I should add, that usually treats the play as literature rather than as something meant for enactment in a theater—is somehow more significant than worlds fashioned by other methods, especially those no longer in fashion. However, as Rosenberg records and comments on the numerous options that directors, over the centuries, have exercised in the staging of the plays, and the choices made by actors challenged with giving that illusory theatrical "life" to characters who are otherwise just words on the page, he shows us, instead, how theater practice is a collaborative art, one involving playwright, director, actor, and—ultimately—the audience. Here, rather than asserting a single meaning, or the superiority of a particular critical method, the focus is on options, choices, process, and discoveries, both in rehearsal and performance.

[5] Helen Gardner, "*As You Like It,*" in *More Talking of Shakespeare,* ed. John W. P. Garrett (London: Longmans, 1959), 17-32.

[6] I think the best discussion of the play's theatrical commentary and of the division between reason and imagination remain David Young's *Something of Great Constancy: The Art of "A Midsummer Night's Dream"* (New Haven: Yale University Press, 1966); and James Calderwood's *Shakespearean Metadrama: The Argument of the Play in "Titus Andronicus," "Love's Labour's Lost," "Romeo and Juliet," "A Midsummer Night's Dream," and "Richard II"* (Minneapolis: University of Minnesota Press, 1971).

[7] See Philip McGuire's discussion of Egeus' presence in the play, particularly in the final act, in "Intentions, Options, and Greatness: An Example from *A Midsummer Night's Dream,*" in *Shakespeare and the Triple Play: From Study to Stage to Classroom,* ed. Sidney Homan (Lewisburg: Bucknell University Press, 1988), 177-89.

[8] Bert O. States, *Great Reckonings in Little Rooms: On the Phenomenology of Theater* (Berkeley: University of California Press, 1985).

[9] Jean Genet, *Reflections on the Theater, and Other Writings,* trans. Richard Sever (London: Faber and Faber, 1972), 79.

---

Source: " 'What Do I Do Now?' Directing *A Midsummer Night's Dream*," in *Shakespearean Illuminations: Essays in Honor of Marvin Rosenberg,* edited by Jay L. Halio and Hugh Richmond, University of Delaware Press, 1998, pp. 279-96.

# Marriage as Comic Closure

## Lisa Hopkins, *Sheffield Hallam University*

The most outstanding feature of Shakespearean comedy is its pervading obsession with marriage. In many instances single or multiple marriages are used to provide comic closure, as in *As You Like It* and *Love's Labour's Lost*, in which four couples marry or are expected to marry, *A Midsummer Night's Dream* and *Twelfth Night*, in each of which three couples marry, and *Much Ado About Nothing* and *Two Gentlemen of Verona*, in each of which two couples marry. In other examples the very fact of marriage is used as the mainspring of the comedy, as in *The Merry Wives of Windsor*, where the very title of the play indicates the importance of marriage, or, to a lesser extent, *The Comedy of Errors*, *The Merchant of Venice* and *The Taming of the Shrew*, in each of which a marital relationship plays a central part. Indeed, marriage is so central a topic in Shakespearean comedy that it is the presence of marriages in their plots which has problematised the genre classifications of both the late romances and the two 'dark' comedies, *Measure for Measure* and *All's Well that Ends Well*, and which provides the main justification for whatever claim they are accorded to be treated as comedies.[1] We know, moreover, that many of Shakespeare's comedies bear clear marks of having been written expressly for performance as part of the celebrations surrounding the solemnisation of actual marriages, so that the connection would have been still more obvious to their original audiences.

But for all that the plays can indeed be grouped together with reasonable accuracy into these broad classifications, to do so obscures both some significant and some interesting differences between them, and also the problematic ways in which marriage is generally treated in these plays. For one thing, despite the traditional view that marriage provides comic closure, this is, in fact, very rarely achieved.[2] The idea is of course drawn on—the audience is repeatedly encouraged to expect that the proceedings will be appropriately closed with a wedding—but these expectations are then either disappointed, or gratified in such a way that the spectator will be forced to question both the meaning of the events he or she has witnessed and also the assumptions underlying his or her response to the events.

Marriage is appropriate as a provider of closure for comedy because it focuses primarily on the experience of the group, as opposed to the individualist, isolationist emphasis of tragedy. The tragic hero lives and dies a fundamentally lonely figure, traumatically separated from his God, his society and his surroundings. Marriage both counters this element of separation by showing humans in a relationship which is, in theory at least, one of indissoluble bonding, and also holds out the promise of renewed life in the birth of offspring (referred to both in the words of the marriage ceremony and in Elizabethan wedding customs, and assumed to be the inevitable product of all heterosexual intercourse).[3] The ultimate polar opposite of the tragic closure provided by death would of course be birth itself, which is indeed sometimes used in this symbolic sense (*All's Well that Ends Well* may be taken as an example of this); but birth, too, places primacy on the experience of the isolated individual, and the social ritual of marriage, with its stress on continuity and group survival, therefore provides a more effective counterbalance to the finality implied in the death of the tragic individual.

Such an emphasis on continuity is undoubtedly present in much of Shakespeare's work. It can be traced explicitly through the first 18 of his sonnets, and it can also be detected in Oberon's blessing of the bridal bed in *A Midsummer Night's Dream,* and in Rosalind's reference to Orlando, almost as soon as she sees him, as 'my child's father'.[4] It is also possible to discern in Shakespeare's comedies clear signs of the conservatism which is so often felt to flourish in comedy: the lovers in *A Midsummer Night's Dream* may flee from Athens at the outset of the play in rebellion against the patriarchal order articulated by Theseus and Egeus, but they do so only to find themselves in a wood ruled by a patriarch just as powerful (a point neatly made by the theatrical tradition of using the actor who plays Theseus to double Oberon), and at the end of the play the two couples willingly return to the society from which they had fled to take their allotted parts as leading members of it and, no doubt, to assist in its perpetuation. In similar fashion, Rosalind, Celia, Oliver and Orlando return from the Forest of Arden, where they had so briefly glimpsed a world in which traditional gender roles could be reversed and the patriarchal system of property division overturned by Oliver's renunciation of his patrimony in favour of Orlando, to take their places in the hierarchy of the court; and in *The Two Gentlemen of Verona* the excursion into the forest of Valentine, Proteus, Silvia and Julia merely enables them to return to the city properly established as clearly defined couples. In *Hamlet* and *King Lear, Othello* and

*Macbeth,* worlds may be broken and assumptions overturned; in the comic universe, however, the world not only remains fundamentally the same, but is indeed reinforced by the reaffirmation of that most basic of all props of social and patriarchal order, marriage.

Although these elements of conservatism may doubtless be traced, other factors, far more radical, are also at work. It is noteworthy that although single or multiple marriages are almost invariably the obvious goal of Shakespearean comedy and are clearly signalled from the outset, either by such transparent devices as the King of Navarre's misogyny,[5] which is clearly riding for a fall, or by the even more obvious sign of a crucially placed, slow-paced meeting between the hero and heroine such as that between Rosalind and Orlando, this expected telos is only very rarely attained within the confines of the play itself. The truism that Shakespeare's comedies all end with marriages is not true. There was of course no theoretical prescription that all comedies should end thus—indeed, comedy in general lacked a theory such as that supplied by Aristotle for tragedy—but there was nevertheless a growing tradition which established marriage as the goal at least of romantic comedy. That tradition Shakespeare habitually disrupts.

## AS YOU LIKE IT

*As You Like It* may appear to contradict this assertion immediately, since it closes with not one but four weddings: those of Rosalind and Orlando, Celia and Oliver, Silvius and Phebe and Touchstone and Audrey.[6] But although the audience certainly perceives these couples as having been finally united and receives the appropriate sense of comic closure, the weddings do not take place on stage, or indeed within the timescale of the play at all. Rosalind and Celia are brought on to the stage by what the New Penguin editor terms 'a masquer representing Hymen'.[7] In the theatre this part is usually taken by the actor who plays Corin, one of the few named characters who does not have to appear on stage at this time; but there is some residual ambiguity about whether we are to perceive this as a metatheatrical doubling or one operating and acknowledged within the fictional world of the play—whether we are to see it as one actor doubling two parts which have no necessary connection between them other than the fact that they never appear on stage at the same time, or whether we are to assume that Rosalind and Celia, having no one else to whom they can turn, have taken Corin into their confidence and asked him to represent Hymen in the masque that they wish to stage.[8] Trivial though this point may seem, it may nevertheless be of some interest; if the masquer is obviously Corin in disguise, and is visibly perceived as such by the other characters on stage, then the whole affair is going to seem very much less mysterious than it might otherwise do. The supernatural elements which Rosalind has earlier tried to invoke with her claim to be the nephew of a magician will be at once debunked, and it will even be apparent to the quick-witted where Rosalind has been hiding all this time, and how the whole scene has been stage-managed. (That this *is* apparent to the characters seems clearly suggested by the fact that nobody ever troubles to explain it, and by Phebe's immediate exclamation 'If sight and shape be true, / Why then, my love adieu!') However, to have Corin taking part in a masque will provide a visual blending of country character with courtly form, offering an image of that utopian mingling of classes which Arden may initially have seemed to promise but which it has never, until now, achieved, so that a sense of magic lost in one area may perhaps be miraculously regained in another.

Whoever plays Hymen, however, one thing is certain: he is not competent to perform a marriage. Indeed he explicitly admits as much in his words to the Duke:

> Good Duke receive thy daughter,
> Hymen from heaven brought her,
>    Yea brought her hither,
> That thou mightst join her hand with his
> Whose heart within his bosom is.
> 
> (V.IV.110-14)

The god of marriage, then, seems to be transferring his responsibilities to the Duke; but the Duke is no more able than he to conduct the ceremony. It would, of course, be normally expected that he would have to give his consent, but even that seems to be pre-empted when, immediately after Hymen's speech, Rosalind intervenes:

> *Rosalind* [*To the Duke.*] To you I give
>   myself, for I am yours.
> [*To* Orl.] To you I give myself, for I am
>   yours.
> 
> (V.IV.115-16)

At the same time as she reinscribes herself within the patriarchal order by investing her rights in herself in her father, she also challenges it by asserting her desire for Orlando; Diane Elizabeth Dreher comments of this moment that 'discovering her animus or inner authority, she performs what has traditionally been the father's function, arranging her marriage and those of the other couples'.[9] Fortunately, the Duke is unlikely to prove a demanding father; he will accede happily to her wish to marry the son of his own old friend, and neither he nor the audience is liable to pick up on any potentially disturbing undercurrents in Rosalind's words. Unlike the story of Cordelia, where the divided selfhood which must attempt to please both father and husband becomes a source of anxiety, the emphasis here is less on the division implied by Rosalind's phrasing than on the reintegration and reconstitution of the family. The potential disharmony of the double promise is left unexplored. But it is there.

More obviously an issue, though, is that no one has come forward who has the authority to sanction and legitimate the weddings. As Celia says when Rosalind entreats her to conduct the mock marriage, 'I cannot say the words' (IV.I.121)—or rather, she can utter them, but in her mouth they have no performative validity. Diane Elizabeth Dreher feels that this exchange 'not only assures Rosalind of Orlando's love, but also approximates a legal marriage';[10] but this seems an odd view to take of it given Celia's own disclaimer of competence in the matter. Only a priest can speak the words of the marriage service, and priests in the forest are few and far between. Indeed clerics in general prove elusive in the play: there is the 'old religious man' who converts Duke Frederick, but his whereabouts are unknown, and there is Sir Oliver Martext, whom Richard Wilson sees as the outlaws' Friar Tuck,[11] but he, as Touchstone and Jaques agree, 'is not like to marry . . . well' (III.III.82-3). Just as in the mock marriage performed by Celia—which can indeed be read as foreshadowing this difficulty—so here at the time of the real marriage there is no-one who can say the words. Hymen's declaration that ''Tis I must make conclusion / Of these most strange events' (V.IV.125-6) has its claim to finality undercut when 170 lines later the Duke pronounces the end of the play proper with a rhyming couplet of his own: 'Proceed, proceed. We will begin these rites, / As we do trust they'll end, in true delights' (V.IV.196-7). Here, closure deconstructs itself with its emphasis on proceeding and beginning; and even this sense of beginning is in turn eroded by Rosalind's immediately following remark that 'It is not the fashion to see the lady the epilogue' (V.IV.198). Into this slippage of time, paradoxically caught between conclusions, beginnings and epilogues, the weddings themselves disappear. They have not been performed by the end of the play; and when Rosalind with her epilogue returns the audience to the real world of time, the play no longer has any future in which they could still take place. So although the marriages may be promised, implicit and assumed, they can never happen.

Moreover, the whole idea of marriage itself becomes an issue in the play. Touchstone has earlier attempted to disrupt the traditional pattern of comedy by having his marriage to Audrey performed in the very middle of the play (III.iii) but in fact his aim in attempting to arrange such a marriage is paradoxically not to achieve closure, but to leave open in his life possibilities which marriage is seen as precluding: Jacques exhorts him not to have his marriage performed by Sir Oliver Martext because 'This fellow will but join you together as they join wainscot; then one of you will prove a shrunk panel, and like green timber, warp, warp' (III.III.77-80). If marriage is traditionally used to achieve closure, then Touchstone's sentiments call into question the very possibility of such closure by his insinuation that marriages are prone to dissolution, and not just by the hand of God removing one of the partners.

Nor is Touchstone's an isolated perspective on his situation: Hymen sings ironically that he and Audrey are 'sure together / As the winter to foul weather' (V.IV.134-5), while Jacques tells him 'thy loving voyage / Is but for two months victuall'd' (V.IV.190-1). Granted that what is envisaged here is not so much divorce as squabbling within marriage (as Rosalind in more playful mood also forecasts for herself and Orlando [IV.I.135-54]), even so Touchstone's earlier resolution to be married by Sir Oliver has explictly addressed the question of termination of marriages, and it is even possible to see it hinted at when Orlando agrees to go through the mock-wedding ceremony with Ganymede 'now, as fast she can marry us' (IV.I.127), where 'fast' can be taken to refer not only to the speed but also to the validity of the ceremony. And of course another form of the dissolution of marriages is figured in the plot not only of this play alone but of virtually all Shakespeare's comedies: while both Rosalind and Celia have living fathers and Orlando has one who was alive recently enough for his memory to be green, no one in the play has a living mother.[12] The male partner, it seems, may survive after marriage, but the female partner has borne her children and then disappeared, her identity so utterly effaced that we do not even know what happened to her.[13] The implication may well be that within their marriages a similar fate may lurk to obliterate the vivacity even of a Rosalind or a Celia. Certainly, it would be possible to cast a sceptical eye over the likely effects on Phebe's health and life expectancy of the perpetual pregnancy and parturition forecast for her in Jacques' valediction to Silvius, 'You to a long and well-deserved bed' (V.IV.189).

But if a constant and life-threatening involvement in the processes of pregnancy and childbirth is the inevitable destiny of the married woman, the married man too has an unpleasant fate which he cannot avoid and which is repeatedly foreshadowed for him in the course of the play: cuckoldry. It forms the standard theme of Rosalind's teasing of Orlando: the snail, she tells him, brings its destiny with it, and when he inquires what that is she replies 'Why horns—which such as you are fain to be beholding to your wives for; but he comes armed in his fortune, and prevents the slander of his wife' (IV.I.56-9)—with perhaps an implication that even where cuckoldry itself is not present in a marriage, the rumour of it is bound to be. It is seen by Touchstone as not only unavoidable, but in some sense even acceptable:

> As horns are odious, they are necessary. It is said, many a man knows no end of his goods. Right. Many a man has good horns and knows no end of

them. Well, that is the dowry of his wife,'tis none of his own getting. Horns? Even so. Poor men alone? No, no. The noblest deer hath them as huge as the rascal. Is the single man therefore blessed? No. As a walled town is more worthier than a village, so is the forehead of a married man more honourable than the bare brow of a bachelor; and by how much defence is better than no skill, by so much is a horn more precious than to want.

(III.III.45-57)

Indeed, as Touchstone has earlier pointed out, the very environment of the forest is full of reminders of cuckoldry: contemplating his imminent marriage, he remarks, 'A man may, if he were of a fearful heart, stagger in this attempt; for here we have no temple but the wood, no assembly but horn-beasts' (III.III.42-4).

This is a point raised again in the short and bizarre scene in which Jaques and the Lords celebrate the deer-killer with a song:

*What shall he have that kill'd the deer?*
*His leather skin and horns to wear.*
*Then sing him home. The rest shall bear*
*This burden.*
*Take thou no scorn to wear the horn,*
*It was a crest ere thou wast born.*
  *Thy father's father wore it,*
  *And thy father bore it.*
*The horn, the horn, the lusty horn,*
*Is not a thing to laugh to scorn.*

(IV.III.10-19)

The scene seems to be introduced solely to allow for the singing of this lyric, which, like Jaques' speech, both affirms and defuses the inevitability of cuckoldry by representing it as natural, figured even in the idyll of the pastoral by the horns of the deer, which become a badge of potency—the sign of the deer-killer—simultaneously with their more normal role as signifiers of shame. This song also, though, addresses one of the most fundamental of all aspects of cuckoldry, the threat it poses to the transmission of land and property from undoubted father to undoubted son. The spectre is raised in the sixth line ('it was a crest ere thou wast born') simultaneously evokes the pride of ancestry symbolised by heraldry, and casts doubt on the line of descent by associating birth and cuckoldry so intimately. However, the threat has no sooner been raised than it is triumphantly defused: the fear of not being able to identify the father is countered with the assurance that in this matter all fathers are alike—all are cuckolds. A kind of collective identity is thus asserted which can take precedence over the ultimately unknowable individual identity of any one father. Male bonding has triumphed over the apparent threat to patriarchal and class power posed by women's sexual infidelity.[14]

*As You Like It* does, indeed, then, take marriage as a central theme; but just as the structural patterning of the play resists closure, so does the apparent ideological fixity of the meaning of marriage itself break down under the pressure of the meanings imposed on it by the play. Even the play's Edenic overtones work ultimately to undermine the stability of the marital ideal that is apparently held up at its end: for all the return to a prelapsarian state in the duchy (a theme obviously signalled by Adam's name), this is an Eden with a snake, and, moreover, a lioness (interestingly changed from a lion in Shakespeare's source);[15] and if the couples at the end in any sense figure Adam and Eve, they must equally image the collapse of the pastoral ideal and of marital harmony which was to occur in that first of all marriages. Rather than a device to close the play securely, to ensure female subordination to patriarchal power and to secure the transmission of property between members of the elite, marriage is revealed as allowing interference with all three elements. But while the male characters of the play seem able to accept and even to embrace these contradictions within marriage, for the female characters the absence of mothers—the fact that the previous generation of married women have apparently vanished without trace—postulates a less hopeful future.

A MIDSUMMER NIGHT'S DREAM

In *A Midsummer Night's Dream* the difference in the nature of the experiences offered by marriage to men and to women is signalled right at the outset, in the opening dialogue between Theseus and Hippolyta. The couple seem to be united in their eagerness for the approach of their ensuing wedding:

*The.* Now, fair Hippolyta, our nuptial hour
Draws on apace; four happy days bring in
Another moon: but O, methinks, how slow
This old moon wanes! She lingers my desires,
Like to a step-dame or a dowager
Long withering out a young man's revenue.
*Hip.* Four days will quickly steep themselves
  in night;
Four nights will quickly dream away the
  time;
And then the moon, like to a silver bow
New bent in heaven, shall behold the night
Of our solemnities.[16]

In fact, Hippolyta's lines are susceptible of a very different interpretation, as was shown by the way that Penny Downie played the role at Stratford-upon-Avon in 1982. Her Hippolyta was a deeply reluctant, indeed sullen, bride: her statements that the time would pass quickly were motivated not by joy but by a disempowered acceptance of the inevitable, and her flat future tenses, without any use of the optative, reflected this sense of despairing entrapment.

Such a reading also serves to highlight the fact that Theseus insistently perceives all the blocking figures to their marriage as female. He alludes, in turn, to the moon (most usually figured in Elizabethan discourse in her classical personae as Cynthia, Diana, Dictynna or Artemis, and as such associated with the Virgin Queen herself), a stepdame and a dowager.[17] Hippolyta, in marked contrast, concurs in imaging the moon as female, but views it as a symbol of empowerment, a representation of the 'bow' (I.I.9) which was once her weapon. Theseus' assumptions are even more remarkable in a play where the blocking figures are in fact uniformly male— Egeus, who objects to his daughter's marriage, and, arguably, Oberon, though, like Theseus, he himself constructs the cause of the quarrel between the fairies as the opposition of Titania—and where the women tend to be unusually powerless for representatives of the comic feminine.[18] But if the plot of the play minimises the power of women, its imagery maximises it, and concomitantly figures men as weakened, clearly suggesting a deep-rooted fear, as in Titania's elegiac comment that 'the green corn / Hath rotted ere his youth attained a beard' (II.I.94-5). Even the play-within-the-play may encode a fearful female. 'Ninny's tomb' may be funny, but it also memorialises Ninus, King of Assyria, whose wife, as Sir David Lindsay of the Mount recorded in his attack on female rulers, was the 'proude and presumptious' Semiramis,[19] who is one of the examples Lindsay cites to prove the innate unfitness of women to occupy posts of power.

The idea briefly indicated in Hippolyta's speech that women may be unwilling to marry recurs throughout the play.[20] In many of Shakespeare's romantic comedies, the women are seen as being very actively in search of a husband: Viola has barely landed in Illyria before she is enquiring about Orsino's marital status, Olivia rapidly proposes marriage to the supposed Cesario, and Feste is able to tease Maria by alluding to the possibility of Sir Toby marrying her; both Julia and Silvia in *The Two Gentlemen of Verona* actively seek their lovers out, and Rosalind in *As You Like It* effectively engineers her own marriage when Orlando, blinded by her male disguise, does not take the initiative. In *A Midsummer Night's Dream,* Helena does indeed actively pursue Demetrius, but whereas the other heroines who do this are presented as spirited and determined, and invariably preserve their dignity and their self-respect, she is seen as merely ridiculous:

> I am your spaniel; and, Demetrius,
> The more you beat me, I will fawn on you.
> Use me but as your spaniel, spurn me, strike me,
> Neglect me, lose me; only give me leave,
> Unworthy as I am, to follow you.

> What worser place can I beg in your love—
> And yet a place of high respect with me—
> Than to be used as you use your dog?
> (II.I.203-10)

Titania, who (although for very different reasons) similarly pays court to the man of her choice, is equally seen as a butt of jokes. Far more popular, both with the men of the play and generally with audiences and critics, is Hermia, who, unlike the majority of Shakespeare's heroines, shows a distinct concern for propriety—'Nay, good Lysander; for my sake, my dear, / Lie further off yet; do not lie so near' (II.II.42-3). In fact, if Hermia and Lysander had decided to perform a contract of *per verba de futuro* in front of a witness such as Helena and had then consummated their marriage in the woods, it would have become immediately legal; but that is never suggested, and Hermia's behaviour is presented instead as the polar opposite to Helena's. When attitudes such as this are highlighted, the decision to set the opening scene of the 1982 Stratford-upon-Avon production in the Victorian period becomes a highly suitable one.

Hermia's concern to protect her virginity has previously gone even further, when, unamazed by the choice she is offered between enforced marriage, execution, and the cloister, she unhesitatingly chooses the lifelong chastity of sisterhood rather than marriage with Demetrius.[21] Here, of course, her decision is perfectly understandable, since the partner offered her is one she has no liking for; but taken along with other instances of women not wishing to marry or to live within marital relationships in the play, it may nevertheless be seen as significant. Titania may be eager enough for Bottom, but she is undergoing what seems to be an effective separation from her 'lord' Oberon; and whatever Hippolyta's feelings for Theseus may be now, we are told clearly enough what they must have been initially when Theseus reminds her 'Hippolyta, I woo'd thee with my sword, / And won thy love doing thee injuries' (I.I.16-17). Moreover, the play even includes more or less direct reference to that ultimate refuser of marriage, 'the imperial votress' (II.I.163) herself, Elizabeth I, whose decision to remain single had given rise to the cult of the Virgin Queen.[22]

As if this were not enough, the play clearly warns of the possible dangers of marriage: a wife risks quarrels and the curbing of her will, such as occurs in the relationship of Titania and Oberon, and death in childbirth, as happens to the mother of the changeling boy; or her children may be deformed—although the fairies promise that this will not happen to any of the couples in the play, their mere mention of deformity nevertheless serves to confirm it as a real possibility.[23] This last is an issue that would affect the husband too, and the death of both Pyramus and Thisbe in the mechanicals' playlet could perhaps serve as a reminder that love offers perils for both sexes. Nevertheless, neither Demetrius nor Lysander is threatened with anything like the dreadful choice that is offered to Hermia, and both Theseus and Oberon end the play with very much the upper hand in their relationships: Titania has been thoroughly humiliated by the discovery of her love for an ass (an ironic and radically reductive rewriting of Theseus' much more heroic adventures with the Minotaur), and Theseus at the banquet firmly overrules Hippolyta's distaste for the mechanicals' play with her first lesson in theatre criticism and public behaviour (V.I.89-105).

Moreover, in this play too the marriages do not provide closure by occurring at the end of the play.[24] Almost all the plot material has been used up by the opening of Act V: Titania and Oberon are reconciled, the lovers have come together in mutually agreeable couples, returned to the city and been reconciled with Theseus and Egeus, Bottom has been transformed back to his normal shape, and all that remains is for the mechanicals to perform their play. We may perhaps wonder to what extent the fairies Titania and Oberon can be considered bound by the human rite of marriage at all—especially since each accuses the other of having effectively conducted an open relationship. As for the marriages of the mortals, they appear to have taken place between IV.I and V.I: in the first of these scenes Theseus announces that 'in the temple by and by with us / These couples shall eternally be knit', and in the second all are looking forward to the advent of the evening which will allow them to consummate the marriages. It would in fact be perfectly possible in narrative terms to end the play after Act IV.I.

What comes after that point is obviously important in terms of providing a suitably celebratory finale, but it offers too a comment on what has occurred. The tragic story of Pyramus and Thisbe may serve to remind us how very easily the events of the play could have developed along the lines of *Romeo and Juliet;* the fairies' final benediction can be seen as indicating how much such a blessing may be needed. Marriage then is not seen as some sort of transcendental signifier which automatically confers meaning on events: its own meaning is open to probing and exploration. Even when closure does finally occur, its meaning is unmade even as it is made:

> If we shadows have offended,
> Think but this, and all is mended,
> That you have but slumber'd here
> While these visions did appear.
> And this weak and idle theme,
> No more yielding but a dream,
> Gentles, do not reprehend:
> If you pardon, we will mend.
> And, as I am an honest Puck,

> If we have unearned luck
> Now to 'scape the serpent's tongue,
> We will make amends ere long;
> Else the Puck a liar call.
> So, goodnight unto you all.
> Give me your hands, if we be friends,
> And Robin shall restore amends.
> (V.I.409-24)

Puck's paradoxes both return the play to the real world and, at the same time as they offer a final comment on the play, they deny the possibility of making any such comment at all, since the making of meaning must finally be in our hands. In offering itself for approval the play finally abdicates control over its own authority; and thus, although it has been careful to present itself as an ostensible celebration of marriage, the diametrical antithesis of the 'some satire, keen and critical, / Not sorting with a nuptial ceremony' (V.I.54-5) which Theseus fears, it ultimately acknowledges that the meaning-making audience is equally free to construct out of it as potentially subversive a critique as it wishes of contemporary marriage, and, above all, of the role of women within it. As Christopher Brooke, in his history of marriage, observes of the idea that *A Midsummer Night's Dream* was an occasional play feting an actual wedding, 'I am glad it was not my wedding it celebrated, for it proceeds by showing us the lowest view of human marriage we have so far encountered'.[25]

If both *As You Like It* and *A Midsummer Night's Dream* seem to offer sympathy for the position of women within marriage, it must not be forgotten that the issue of men's role within marriage has, even if only marginally, also been addressed in them.[26] In *The Two Gentlemen of Verona,* as later in *The Merry Wives of Windsor* where Herne the Hunter functions as a recuperative figure in exactly the same way as the horn song does, this becomes of far greater importance.

### THE TWO GENTLEMEN OF VERONA

In *The Two Gentlemen of Verona,* the character who in many ways appears the most vulnerable is not Valentine, whose good faith leads him into banishment, nor Silvia, distressed and frightened though she undoubtedly is by the attempted rape, nor even Julia, forced to witness the faithlessness and villainy of her lover, but Proteus himself, the man who causes the suffering of all of them. Proteus says of himself, 'I do as truly suffer, / As e'er I did commit'.[27] These lines, and Proteus' part in general in this scene, have often been considered badly underwritten, but Barry Lynch's moving delivery in the 1991 Swan Theatre production by David Thacker at Stratford-upon-Avon showed that they can in fact be seen as more than adequate to the situation, since what they suggest is that Proteus' own suffering is directly proportional to that experienced by all the other three lovers in combination. Indeed, it could even be argued that he has undergone more than they have had to do: for whereas they have throughout the play been firmly locked into stable, unshakeable identities, Proteus has undergone a most violent and radical attack on his very sense of selfhood, bordering almost on what might now be termed a form of schizophrenia.

This is seen clearly in II, VI, where, like Richard III before Bosworth, Proteus effectively falls apart. Given, in modern editions, the whole scene to himself, he soliloquises:

> I cannot leave to love; and yet I do;
> But there I leave to love, where I should
>   love.
> Julia I lose, and Valentine I lose;
> If I keep them, I needs must lose myself;
> If I lose them, thus find I by their loss:
> For Valentine, myself; for Julia, Silvia.
> I to myself am dearer than a friend,
> For love is still most precious in itself,
> And Silvia (witness heaven, that made her
>   fair)
> Shows Julia but a swarthy Ethiope.
>
> (II.VI.17-26)

Underlying the apparent arrival at a decision here is a terrifying sense of the dizzying relativity of all available senses of identity. The first line sets up a logical impossibility which the balanced syntax can do no more than leave as paradox. It may be glossed over by the sophistry of the second, but that also introduces another, equally worrying, idea: 'I' is no longer absolute, standing unbounded as subject of the sentence, but modified and compromised by its physical location—'there', 'where'.

'I' finds itself even further destabilised in the third line when both Julia and Valentine successively usurp the apparent subject position of their respective phrases, and in the fourth line the issue is explicitly addressed when Proteus admits to himself the awful possibility that he may 'lose myself'. This is hastily dismissed when a swift change of object alters the situation to losing not himself but 'them'—a safely demonised, externalised group which leaves his own sense of identity apparently unthreatened and intact. But Proteus, as his Protean name suggests, has exposed a far more radical possibility than that of simple self-loss: lurking behind the exchange of persons which he now proposes is the spectre that he may have no self to lose. If Julia can replace Silvia and Proteus Valentine, and if Julia's former self is indeed modified and devalued by the mere existence of Silvia, as suggested in the two closing lines, then in what sense can any of these people be presented as a 'self'? In this sense Proteus' 'I do as truly suffer / As e'er I did commit' is a statement which is both admirably expressive and a profound psychological restorative, for in it he has finally achieved an assertion of the coherence of the two parts of his previously shattered self: what 'I' has done, 'I' is also paying for, and the payment is small price for the reintegration of self which the language enables him to assert. Looked at in this light, the 'marriage' which seals the end of the play is less one between Proteus and Julia than between Proteus and his estranged selfhood, or perhaps with Julia as a manifestation of that former, regretted state of psychological unity.

The play does end with the promise of other, more conventional marriages. Valentine assures his regained friend:

> Come, Proteus, 'tis your penance but to hear
> The story of your loves discovered.
> That done, our day of marriage shall be
>   yours,
> One feast, one house, one mutual happiness.
>
> (V.IV.168-71)

All is apparently well that ends well, and Valentine's extraordinary offer of his own interest in Silvia to Proteus could also be read as indicating that the friendship of the two gentlemen will, despite all the strains to which it has been subject, survive and even prosper. Nevertheless the darker notes are there. The ring which Julia produces as a token both of her own identity and of Proteus' former affection for her may serve to remind us that bonds sealed by rings have been broken before and could be again. Moreover, while the two women have shown themselves eager for marriage throughout the play, the behaviour of both Proteus and Valentine can be seen as registering a rather more ambivalent attitude. When we first meet them, in I.I, love is already a force which threatens to pull their friendship apart: Proteus will stay at home because of it, losing the chance of adventures and finding himself separated from his friend. And it remains throughout the play the single greatest threat to male bonding, not only disrupting the relationship of Proteus and Valentine but also falsifying and eventually undermining their interactions with the male authority figure, the Duke.

It would be plausible to see Proteus' sudden switch to Silvia as operating effectively as a continuation of that movement away from love which has already been inaugurated by his decision to leave Julia: subconsciously, he has chosen the most inaccessible of all possible females, the beloved of his friend. It is a move guaranteed to precipitate the crisis which has until now been only latent, to force a radical choice between the two parts of his fissured identity. As in *The Two Noble Kinsmen,* so much later in Shakespeare's career, what we see here is the crippling psychological cost in terms of the loss of personal and social selfhood which men may fear will be the price of marriage.[28]

Another fear, too, can be seen as lying behind both this play and others of Shakespeare's apparently 'happy' comedies. Finding himself unable to persuade Silvia to yield to his advances, Proteus decides to rape her. This is not only his own lowest psychological point; it is also devastatingly revealing about his attitude to marriage. Obviously no modern feminist can admit any sort of defence of his act, but it may be possible to look at in a light rather different from that in which it is customarily considered. If Proteus himself regards marriage as a threatening, dangerous state, he might well project such feelings of reluctance onto his female partner—and this could lead him to regard not only Silvia but *all* women as quite simply needing to be raped in order to make marriage possible at all. We can read his action less as an individual, isolated act of violation than as the emblem of his views of all relationships, in which either others or the self must always be lost; in one sense, it is himself that he tries to rape. The idea of female reluctance to marry, which had figured so threateningly in *A Midsummer Night's Dream,* thus recurs here, raising the question of whether it could be that the universal assumption of women's desire to cuckold their husbands by incessant sex actually masks in general the repression of a deeper fear too threatening even to voice—that female participation in sex is reluctant.

Frigid women, who are at the same time impossible to keep chaste; fragmented men in danger of losing their selves, their honour and their friends; incompetent or unavailable priests and defective ceremonies; savage uncivilised settings in which wild beasts roam as the fitting emblem of the human condition—the makings of marriage in Shakespearean comedy are not promising ones. But it is, of course, precisely the innate instability of its personnel and character that make the institution such a vital one. The radical fissuring that splits selves and societies can be kept from cracking only by the constant repetition and reduplication of social and ideological bonds that marriage alone is seen as capable of providing, forming as it does the one framework in which the behaviour of each partner is constantly visible, constantly subject to policing by the other. The Shakespearean 'happy' comedies do not celebrate marriage: they reveal its crucial functioning in the maintenance of society and also the internal stresses and contradictions to which it is constantly subject—an instability instanced by the repeated structural decentring of marriage from its supposed position of comic closure. And contrary to so much of the misogyny and the marital ideology of the time, they powerfully reveal that outside the institution of marriage both men and women are adrift, while inside it both must pay a high price for their security.

*Notes*

[1] See Ejner J. Jensen, *Shakespeare and the Ends of Comedy* (Bloomington: Indiana University Press, 1991), p. 2, on the importance attached by the critical tradition to the ends of comedies.

[2] This is noted by Nigel Wood ('Endpiece', in *Theory in Practice: Hamlet,* ed. Peter J. Smith and Nigel Wood [Buckingham: Open University Press, 1996], pp. 24-54, p. 137), in response to Brian Vickers' assertion to the contrary.

[3] For the Elizabethan expectation that the birth of a child would inevitably result from sex, see Lisa Jardine, *Still Harping on Daughters: Women and Drama in the Age of Shakespeare* (Brighton: Harvester, 1983), p. 130.

[4] William Shakespeare, *As You Like It,* ed. Agnes Latham [1957] (London: Routledge, 1987), I.III.11. All future quotations from the play will be taken from this edition and reference will be given in the text.

[5] Katharine Eisaman Maus, in 'Transfer of Title in *Love's Labour's Lost:* Language, Individualism, Gender', in *Shakespeare Left and Right,* ed. Ivo Kamps (London: Routledge, 1991), pp. 205-23, sees Navarre's academy as an attempt to repress 'the involvement of women in the process of title transfer' (p. 215).

[6] The extent to which *As You Like It* is generally perceived as a play riddled with marriages is interestingly indicated by the Oxford and Cambridge 'O' level board question on the play cited by Alan Sinfield, 'Write an editorial for the *Arden Gazette* on the recent outbreak of marriage in the district' ('Give an account of Shakespeare and Education, showing why you think they are effective and what you have appreciated about them. Support your comments with precise references', in *Political Shakespeare,* ed. Jonathan Dollimore and Alan Sinfield [Manchester: Manchester University Press, 1985], pp. 134-57, p. 150).

[7] William Shakespeare, *As You Like It,* ed. H.J. Oliver (Harmondsworth: Penguin, 1968), V.4.104s.d.

[8] That there is a genuine ambiguity here is something that has become very clear to me when teaching this text, and an assumption either way can produce very different readings, as in Malcolm Evans' discussion of the play in *Signifying Nothing: Truth's True Contents in Shakespeare's Texts,* 2nd edition (Hemel Hempstead: Harvester Wheatsheaf, 1989), where it is taken for granted that it is indisputably the god Hymen who appears. (Evans does not discuss the performance aspect.)

[9] Diane Elizabeth Dreher, *Domination and Defiance: Fathers and Daughters in Shakespeare* (Lexington: University of Kentucky Press, 1986), p. 123.

[10] Dreher, *Domination and Defiance*, p. 122.

[11] See Richard Wilson, *Will Power: Essays on Shakespearean Authority* (Hemel Hempstead: Harvester Wheatsheaf, 1993), p. 75.

[12] See Adelman, *Suffocating Mothers*, pp. 13-14.

[13] Barbara J. Bono points out, however, that the forest of Arden echoes the maiden name of Shakespeare's mother Mary Arden, and that the play encodes a recognition of human origin in a maternal body which precludes knowledge of the father ('Mixed Gender, Mixed Genre in Shakespeare's *As You Like It*', in *Renaissance Genres: Essays on Theory, History, and Interpretation*, ed. Barbara Kiefer Lewalski [Cambridge, MA: Harvard University Press, 1986], pp. 189-212, pp. 194 and 211). On absent mothers in Shakespearean drama generally, see most particularly Mary Beth Rose, 'Where are the Mothers in Shakespeare? Options for Gender Representation in the English Renaissance', *Shakespeare Quarterly* 42:3 (Fall 1991), pp. 291-314.

[14] See Richard Wilson, Will Power: Essays on Shakespearean Authority (Hemel Hempstead: Harvester Wheatsheaf, 1993), p. 76, on the patriarchal values encoded in 'thy father's father'.

[15] See Louis Adrian Montrose, ' "The Place of a Brother" in *As You Like It*: Social Process and Comic Form', *Shakespeare Quarterly* 32 (1981), pp. 28-54, p. 50. Montrose also offers a brilliant analysis of the workings of male bonding mechanisms in the play in general and in the horn song scene in particular, which he terms a 'charivari' (p. 49). He sees the play as a whole as working to diminish the power of women. For additional comment on the snake and lioness, see Valerie Traub, 'Desire and the Differences it Makes', in *The Matter of Difference*, ed. Valerie Wayne (Hemel Hempstead: Harvester Wheatsheaf, 1991), pp. 81-114, p. 105.

[16] William Shakespeare, *A Midsummer Night's Dream*, ed. Harold F. Brooks (London: Methuen, 1979), I.1.1-11. All further quotations from the play will be taken from this edition and reference will be given in the text.

[17] For the argument that Shakespeare might be alluding here to the presence of actual dowagers in the audience, see Steven May, '*A Midsummer Night's Dream* and the Carey-Berkeley Wedding', *Renaissance Papers* (1983), pp. 43-52, pp. 46-7.

[18] For an ingenious reading of *A Midsummer Night's Dream* as structured around the fear and avoidance of older women, see Terence Hawkes, 'Or', in *Meaning by Shakespeare* (London: Routledge, 1992). On the absence of mothers in Shakespeare's plays, see Carol Thomas Neely, *Broken Nuptials in Shakespeare's Plays*, 2nd edition (Urbana, IL: Illini Books, 1993), p. 171.

[19] See Paula Louise Scalingi, 'The Scepter or the Distaff: The Question of Female Sovereignty, 1516-1607', *The Historian*, 41:1 (1975), pp. 59-75, p. 64. Semiramis is referred to twice in *Titus Andronicus* (II.I.22 and II.III.118), and so is Pyramus (II.III.231), which increases the probability of an allusion to her in *Dream*.

[20] On lesbian desire in the play, see Valerie Traub, 'The (In)significance of "Lesbian" Desire in Early Modern England', in *Erotic Politics*, ed. Susan Zimmerman, pp. 150-69, p. 157. For an argument that all Shakespearean comedy is fundamentally informed by homoeroticism, see Jardine, *Still Harping on Daughters*, pp. 20-9.

[21] For discussions of the difficulties of ascertaining whether, in this and similar situations, the sympathies of the audience would be engaged on behalf of the unruly lovers or of the patriarchal order which they challenge, see Michael Hattaway, 'Drama and Society', in *The Cambridge Companion to English Renaissance Drama*, ed. A.R. Braunmuller and Michael Hattaway (Cambridge: Cambridge University Press, 1990), p. 110, and Richard Levin, *New Readings vs Old Plays* (Chicago: University of Chicago Press, 1979), pp. 151-3.

[22] For an account of some pertinent aspects of the cult, see Roy Strong, *The Cult of Elizabeth* (London: Thames and Hudson, 1977); Susan Bassnett, *Elizabeth I: A Feminist Perspective* (Oxford: Berg, 1988); and my own *Elizabeth I and Her Court* (London: Vision Press, 1990). On its potential implications for the play, see particularly Louis Adrian Montrose, '*A Midsummer Night's Dream* and the Shaping Fantasies of Elizabethan Culture: Gender, Power, Form', reproduced most conveniently in *New Historicism and Renaissance Drama*, ed. Richard Wilson and Richard Dutton (Harlow: Longman, 1992), pp. 109-30. For discussion between the relationship between the cult of Elizabeth and comic closure in general, see Peter Erickson, 'The Order of the Garter, the cult of Elizabeth, and class-gender tension in *The Merry Wives of Windsor*', in *Shakespeare Reproduced*, ed. Jean E. Howard and Marion F. O'Connor (London: Methuen, 1987), pp. 116-40, p. 130. Philippa Berry comments on the tension between the strong emphasis on marriage in Protestant ideology and Elizabeth's refusal of it, and offers a reading of *A Midsummer Night's Dream* as attempting to restore Elizabeth to 'the control of the patriarchy' (*Of Chastity and Power: Elizabethan Literature and the Unmarried Queen* [London: Routledge, 1989], p. 143) and as mounting a 'challenge [to] the Platonism of Elizabeth's cult by its emphasis upon female heterosexuality and the subordination of woman in marriage' (pp. 143-4). My own reading would agree that women are shown to be subordinated in marriage

but would suggest that the implications of this fact may be a possible locus for debate, and hence that it is not being uncritically endorsed.

[23] Hawkes (*Meaning by Shakespeare,* p. 20) comments that 'a motif of disfiguring, translating change is all-pervasive'.

[24] Though Stephen Greenblatt suggests that the Fairies' use of fielddew at the end of the play is indeed evocative of the marriage blessing ('Resonance and Wonder', *Bulletin of the American Academy of Arts and Sciences,* 43 [1990], pp. 11-34; reprinted in Stephen J. Greenblatt, *Learning to Curse: Essays in Early Modern Culture* [London: Routledge, 1990], p. 163).

[25] Christopher Brooke, *The Medieval Idea of Marriage* (Oxford: Oxford University Press, 1991), p. 231.

[26] The importance of directing critical attention to the male characters as well as the female ones, even and perhaps especially for a feminist reading, has been stressed by, amongst others, Walter Cohen, who characterises as one of the achievements of American feminist criticism 'a psychoanalytically inspired sensitivity to the costs repeatedly exacted in the course of the plots not only from women but, given the constricting norms of male identity, from men as well' ('Political Criticism of Shakespeare', in *Shakespeare Reproduced,* p. 23). He goes on to question Linda Bamber's division into comic women, tragic men (p. 24).

[27] William Shakespeare, *The Two Gentlemen of Verona,* ed. Clifford Leech (London: Methuen, 1969), V.IV.76-7. All further quotations from the play will be taken from this edition and reference will be given in the text.

[28] For a discussion of this as a central concern in *The Two Noble Kinsmen,* see Kathleen McLuskie, *Renaissance Dramatists* (Atlantic Highlands, NJ: Humanities Press International, 1989), p. 13, and Bruce P. Smith, *Homosexual Desire in Shakespeare's England: A Cultural Poetics* (Chicago: University of Chicago Press, 1991), p. 72.

---

Source: "Marriage as Comic Closure," in *The Shakespearean Marriage: Merry Wives and Heavy Husbands,* Macmillan Press, 1998, pp. 16-33.

# The Doubled Jaques and Constructions of Negation in *As You Like It*

## Cynthia Marshall, *Rhodes College*

So thoroughly does Shakespeare's work encompass our sense of textual possibility that even his apparent missteps take on interest and meaning. The Fool's unexplained disappearance from *King Lear,* for instance, has famously come to serve as an emblem of Shakespeare's writerly economy—a character disappears when no further use exists for him—and has been formally linked with the king's own descent into a Foolish view of things.[1] Yet, as psychoanalysis tells us, the structure of language itself has a capacity to open up crevices in a surface of meaning, to trick a wily practitioner into showing a hand he may not realize he holds, so that "mistakes" may serve as pathways to recesses within the text. Jacques Derrida has alerted us to the paradoxical way that a "trace" or "track in the text" both testifies to authorial presence and erases the writer's authority as point of origin.[2]

The particular "misstep" here begins with an issue most teachers of *As You Like It* have faced: the inclusion of two characters named Jaques in the dramatis personae. It is not entirely accurate to say that the two are "in the play," since only one, the melancholy Jaques who serves Duke Senior, is addressed by name in the course of the action. The other, Orlando and Oliver's brother Jaques de Boys, is identified in the Folio text as "Second Brother" when he appears in the closing moments of Act 5. But because Orlando has referred to "my brother Jaques" (1.1.5) in the opening speech, Jaques de Boys exists as a palpable source of confusion for readers and viewers, haunting the play as a kind of double for the melancholy Jaques.[3] Or, as I will argue, it is more precisely the melancholy Jaques who serves as a double, standing in for the absent second son of Sir Rowland de Boys. In a play so intimately concerned with names and with substitutions, this elliptical blocking of an absent Jaques with a present one provides a signal instance of the symbol's capacity to compensate for loss. But Jaques is not just any symbol, nor does he have just a garden variety of uncanny textual effect. Rather, the requirement of a melancholy Jaques, so crucial to the play's emotional equilibrium, testifies to an undertow of sadness in it that is brilliantly held at bay by a Shakespearean game of *Fort/Da,* and thus Jaques reveals how the carefully managed relation between melancholy affect and textual representation enables this comedy to function.

Psychoanalysis may seem extraneous in relation to so balanced a work as *As You Like It,* but the nature of textual equilibrium here and elsewhere is part of my interest. The Freudian *Fort/Da* has stood at the center of debates about the purpose and meaning of psychoanalysis—roughly speaking, about its status as either a structural or poststructural discourse. My essay situates itself on this divide, reading the constructions of negation in Shakespeare's comedy as evincing a compensatory principle that brings about a satisfying harmony and closure to the play, but also finding in the play's traces of melancholy a pathway that leads toward the eroding consequences of cultural repressions. Using the psychoanalytic concept of negation to probe the structure of *As You Like It* and some of its particular fixations, this essay will show that the unconstrained gender play in Arden (which has received a great deal of critical attention in recent years) as well as other sorts of liberty exhibited within the play are linked to the presence of the melancholy Jaques. But while my argument takes its cue from the doubleness of Jaques, I do not focus on him as a character; indeed because he wears a melancholic mask, I see him as largely unavailable in terms of characterological depth.[4] My concern instead is with Jaques as the most obvious example of the structural and linguistic compensations the play repeatedly makes. I aim to extend the classic understanding of the compensatory nature of comedy by showing how language is imbricated in comic structure, using contemporary psychoanalytic theory to probe the connections in early modern texts between melancholia, gender, and language. In order to advance such a psychoanalytic reading, I propose that Jaques's doubled existence within the play and his ultimate departure from it serve as intratextual markers of theory's possible relation to the text.

I

It has been suggested by Harold Jenkins that the two Jaqueses are the result of an uncorrected error of composition, that Shakespeare originally intended for the melancholy fellow encountered in the forest to be the second son of Sir Rowland de Boys.[5] The suggestion makes a great deal of sense: the one thing we know about brother Jaques is that he has been away at school, a site—as the nearly contemporaneous *Hamlet* witnesses—where melancholy appears to flourish. Though denying that his is "the scholar's melancholy" (4.1.10), Jaques expresses the easy disdain and the hunger for "matter" (5.4.184) of an educated person. Indeed a viewer watching the play or a reader encountering it for the first time has no way to know that the melancholy Jaques is *not* Jaques de Boys prior to Second Brother's late arrival in Arden. For most of the play, the two characters named Jaques are severed by a single fact: Orlando's failure to recognize the melancholy fellow in Arden as his brother.[6] This failure, however, is not in itself indicative. Leaving aside the fact that the raillery between Orlando and Jaques seems not at all uncharacteristic of that between brothers, one is struck by Orlando's utter unreliability as a witness to the events and people around him. Orlando, after all, fails to recognize Rosalind, his proclaimed love, during their extensive interactions in Arden. Might he not also fail to recognize his brother, especially if that brother has been changed, translated, by melancholy?

A reader or viewer need not contemplate the exact logic of Orlando's failure; the point is that many will silently compound the one Jaques with the other, at least until Second Brother's appearance. Agnes Latham suggests that a difference in pronunciation may let Shakespeare off the hook: the name of melancholy Jaques, as several verse lines indicate, is disyllabic (Jake-is or Jack-is); the single mention of Jaques de Boys, however, might call for monosyllabic or "English" pronunciation, "in so far as prose rhythms are discernible."[7] Although other editors similarly distinguish the two characters by pronunciation of the name, Latham herself seems rather dubious about the method's accuracy: "If this is so, it clears Shakespeare of a maladroit duplication of names. If, on the other hand, the names by some oversight were identical, there is little harm done."[8]

In fact, his name is not the only peculiar thing about the melancholy Jaques. As has frequently been observed, his exuberant spirits belie his nominal complaint. Harold Jenkins says his melancholy is "not the fatigue of spirits of the man who has found the world too much for him, but an active principle. . . . His misanthropy is a form of self-indulgence."[9] Latham sees him as more misplaced than melancholic: "his railing against the wicked ways of the world keeps before us the truth that, outside the charmed circle, the ways of the world are wicked. It is only in Arden that his cynicism looks ridiculous. At Elsinore it would be a different matter."[10] This is a character who pursues his desire aggressively: "More, I prithee more. I can suck melancholy out of a song, as a weasel sucks eggs. More, I prithee more" (2.5.11-13); who exults over his meeting with Touchstone by laughing, "sans intermission, / An hour by his dial" (2.7.32-33); who intrudes upon the intended mar-textual wedding of Touchstone and Audrey to counsel "a good priest that can tell you what marriage is" (3.3.76-77). Claiming to love melancholy "better than laughing," he pridefully notes the particularity of his malady: "it is a melancholy of mine own, compounded of many simples, extracted from many objects, and indeed the sundry contemplation of my travels" (4.1.4, 15-18). Yet Jaques shows little sad or brooding affect: melancholy is for him rather a pose, a role, a set of prescribed behaviors. As the present absence of melancholy, Jaques serves as a kind of placeholder, standing in for the missing second brother, Jaques de Boys, but also, more importantly, standing in for the acknowledgment of loss and sadness missing in Arden's merry crew. He functions, that is, to forestall the threat of melancholia, but in (successfully) doing so, he also figures melancholia's threatening estrangement of self from self.

The logic at work here is that of negation, a subject's method of striking a balance with otherwise disruptive or even destructive energies. Negation, Freud writes, provides "a way of taking cognizance of what is repressed," permitting "the content of a repressed image or idea" to become conscious "on condition that it is *negated*." The result is an "intellectual acceptance of the repressed, while at the same time what is essential to the repression persists."[11] Where true repression threatens to crack under the weight it must bear in order to maintain psychic equilibrium, negation affords a healthy-seeming acknowledgment of what has been repressed. The censor allows troubling material to pass, masking it with a negative judgment. Negation is a trick of comedic function—in fact it seems central to the functioning of comedy—and it bears a close resemblance, as we will see, to the mastery of loss Freud found emblematized in the *Fort/Da* game. Yet where the game commemorates an acknowledged loss, negation remains poised on a gulf of repression: it is a process that fails to deliver mastery of what is repressed, so that the subject must appeal to language in order to trick herself. The trick, however, is a productive one, enabling not only a patina of psychic order but an enriched functioning: "With the help of the symbol of negation, thinking frees itself from the restrictions of repression and enriches itself with material that is indispensable for its proper functioning."[12] Freud stakes no less than the proper functioning of thought itself on the "symbol of negation." Without the ability to have things two ways at once, to confirm through denial, thinking would remain brittle, univalent, impoverished, gripped by repression.[13] For many the concept of negation has had a bad rap recently, having been reduced to Freud's masterful refusal to hear his patients when they said "no." Certainly his brag, that "there is no stronger evidence that we have been successful in our effort to uncover the unconscious than when the patient reacts to it with the words 'I didn't think that,' or 'I didn't (ever) think of that,'" is a chilling document of clinical practice.[14] Yet an ideological distrust of Freud should not blind us to his brilliant analysis of linguistic symbol-making, especially as his insights into speech and language have been further elucidated by Jacques Lacan. The central ideas on which my essay relies are available in Lacan's "The agency of the letter in the unconscious or reason since Freud," although the function of the linguistic signifier is basic to all Lacan's work, as evidenced by his familiar reference to *"the unconscious . . . structured like a language."*[15] Before turning to the specific content—

melancholia—that demands repression in *As You Like It*, I need to consider in more detail the linguistic and characterological techniques of disguise and substitution.

## II

The melancholy Jaques makes his living, we might say, by cheerfully lampooning what he could be but is not. The linguistic principle he practices is by no means particular to him. The very nature of language, as Lacan and others have unfolded it, is to cloak a meaning that may or may not exist. Building on the work of Ferdinand de Saussure, Lacan refers to the "incessant sliding of the signified under the signifier" as an effect creating a "chain of discourse." The chainlike structure of language in turn allows the possibility "to use it in order to signify *something quite other* than what it says."[16] Or, in Joan Copjec's words, "*Since signifiers are not transparent, they cannot demonstrate that they are not hiding something behind what they say—they cannot prove that they do not lie.* Language can only present itself to the subject as a veil that cuts off from view a reality that is other than what we are allowed to see."[17] For Lacan, language acquisition introduces a split within the subject; as "the discourse of the Other," the unconscious functions linguistically but inaccessibly.[18] *As You Like It* returns again and again to the ability or propensity of language, and in particular of names, to veil an inaccessible zone, a "reality that is other than what we are allowed to see" and is taken for reality precisely because we are unable to see it.

Consider, for instance, the "new news at the new court" in Act 1, which is nothing "but the old news," specifically that "the old Duke is banished by his younger brother the new Duke" (1.1.96-100). The wordplay unsettles the political structure whose machinations it documents: there is a certain obvious equivalency between old and new news, between old and new dukes, but the placement of Duke Senior away from court, outside of power, underlines his authority as the "real" duke. The keen nostalgia that inspires Charles's comparison of the old duke to "the old Robin Hood of England," fleeting the time "as they did in the golden world" (1.1.116, 118-19), furthers the image of an authoritative, originary, but utterly inaccessible reality. The play's world becomes one of substitutions, where duke replaces duke, brother challenges brother, cousin threatens to unseat cousin, fool topples oaf in the affections of Audrey, Ganymede supplants Silvius in those of Phebe; in the midst of all this, the old duke's namelessness testifies to his unique place outside the linguistic chain of replacements. That he, moreover, embraces pain for its capacity to "feelingly persuade me what I am" (2.1.11) seems to indicate further that he is one character (and the only one, it seems to me, other than Touchstone and the melancholy Jaques) not at least intermittently in the grip of repression.

In contrast to the duke's placement outside the linguistic turnstile, Rosalind fully occupies it. Ganymede's success at standing in for Rosalind is the showpiece of the play's set of substitutions. "Nay, you must call me Rosalind" (3.2.422): what is the love-cure but a glorification of the symbol's substitutive power, an intoxicating revelry in the capacity of language to construct a character, a relationship, a love affair? Ganymede's reiterated claim "And I am your Rosalind" (4.1.62) is accepted on a linguistic basis by Orlando: "I take some joy to say you are, because I would be talking of her" (ll. 85-86). But the claim underscores a sense that Ganymede's Rosalind is *only* a creation of words. In contrast to Rosalind's transformation into Ganymede, which requires a costume and altered behavior, Ganymede adopts the Rosalind role simply and only through conversation with Orlando. Such a demonstration of the character's purely linguistic reality is gravely taxing to theatrical mimesis. In the face of the dissolution threatened by Ganymede as reminder that all the characters are but verbal artifice, the play emphasizes instead the gendered frisson, the apparently stubborn presence of the male Ganymede rather than the female Rosalind enacting amorous play with Orlando. Ganymede indeed protests too much that "he" is really "she," highlighting for viewers the gendered gap between Orlando's actual and virtual love partners. Even Orlando's late signal that he is weary of the game—"I can live no longer by thinking" (5.2.50)—offers no certain escape from the dilemma of equivocal gender: where, and how, might one live without thinking? How can he opt out of the social arrangements born of cognitive ordering? If Orlando's comment does suggest a preference for the physical reality of Rosalind over that of Ganymede, and if the wedding with which the play closes seems to grant his wish, the theatrical condition of the original performance by an all-male cast nevertheless works to undermine this heterosexual ordering.

Ganymede's masquerade as Rosalind opens up the equivocacy of Orlando's desire: it is apparent during the loveplay in Arden that Orlando desires both of them. The compression of male and female personae into one character functions like the symbol of negation, allowing Orlando to acknowledge a repressed idea—"I desire him"—on condition that the idea is negated—"I desire her, not him." Orlando's increased vividness testifies to his enrichment through this symbol of negation. Whereas his first encounter with Rosalind at Duke Frederick's court strikes him dumb, Orlando's interaction with Ganymede/Rosalind shows how, to quote Freud again, his "thinking frees itself from the restrictions of repression and enriches itself with material that is indispensable." But, perhaps because of the arrival of Oliver and his immediate assertion of a heterosexual claim on Celia, Orlando quails from continued "thinking" of this free and enriched sort. His demand of a settled arrangement of heterosexual coupling reinstates the repression of his desire for Ganymede.[19]

Desire, as Freud was well aware, involves identificatory wishes as well as possessive ones; it can take the form of wishing to be the object or wishing to have it. Not only are Orlando and those readers or viewers who primarily identify with him allowed to acknowledge the titillating possibility of a boy lover, but Rosalind and those who identify with her are likewise allowed the fantasy of being male. This wish seems, to most viewers, not at all surprising: in a masculinist society, who wouldn't choose to be male? Yet I think it's not enough to read the politics of gendered privilege in the Ganymede disguise; we also need to see how erotic play is pressured and manipulated. Rosalind's decision to maintain the Ganymede persona in her interactions with Orlando suggests that she does not wish to participate only as a female in a heterosexual couple. She also wishes to be a boy interacting with Orlando; perhaps she wishes to be, or at least to be *like,* Orlando himself. Recognizing this erotic tendency allows us to see desire as something other than lack. The Ganymede disguise, once again, lifts the barrier of repression, allowing temporary acknowledgment of illicit erotic desires that are safely veiled by the symbol of negation: not Rosalind but Ganymede; not Ganymede but the pretended Rosalind; and, most encompassingly, not us but Shakespeare's fiction.

In spite of the contrast between Rosalind and her father, between her subordination to linguistic order and her father's placement outside it, there is a sense that what is banished in both their cases takes on greater reality. The old duke is the real duke, and the disguised Rosalind is, or more precisely becomes, the real Rosalind. Rosalind's low spirits in the opening act of the play, that is, make her seem less "herself"—the exuberant, inventive character whom viewers cherish—when she appears before us as a girl than during her lengthy period in drag. Celia's pleading tones suggest that her cousin's gloom is uncharacteristic: "I pray thee Rosalind, sweet my coz, be merry" (1.2.1); "my sweet Rose, my dear Rose, be merry" (ll. 21-22). Melancholy has displaced Rosalind from herself. By means of her banishment and subsequent disguise, she recovers her spirits. The trip to Arden and the entry into male dress constitute an adventure, of course, but we should also notice that disguise and substitution—veiling her identity—allow Rosalind's return to happiness. Viewers, along with Orlando, know Rosalind better when she is hidden beneath Ganymede than when she appears as herself. Displacement is shown to be the key to characterological recognition, even though all such recognition is bracketed: the tantalizing promise of a reality hidden by the veiling signifier cannot be confirmed; the signifier cannot prove that it does not lie.

This bracketing of linguistically constructed reality means that banishments, displacements, and disguises are never totally realized in *As You Like It.* Inevitably some trace of what they repress remains behind. I here use *trace* as both noun and verb, as a suggestive bit left behind and as the action of following the outline or shape of something. Understanding the emotional logic of *As You Like It* requires attending to such traces, because the play achieves its much-admired balance by covering up with one hand what it reveals with the other. Thus Rosalind's first-act sadness re-emerges momentarily when as Ganymede she sighs that "men have died from time to time and worms have eaten them, but not for love" (4.1.101-3). While she is disguised, her feminine excitability comes to the fore during private exchange with Celia (3.2.215-220; 3.4.1-35; 4.1.195-207). By the same token, Ganymede's ambivalent gender and rhetorical cleverness re-emerge in the Epilogue. *As You Like It* is unlike a lighter comedy such as *A Midsummer Night's Dream,* which simply banishes melancholy ("Turn melancholy forth to funerals: / The pale companion is not for our pomp" [1.1.14-15]), and unlike a heavier one such as *Measure for Measure,* which takes account of the cost of repression on both individual and societal levels. *As You Like It* achieves its vaunted balance by admitting troubling ideas but cloaking them so as to limit their impact. Joseph Westlund says the play "is sane and wonderful, and it makes us feel that we are too."[20] This complexly satisfying effect may suggest a triumphalist plot in which evil is overcome, but *As You Like It* is not a heavily plotted play. As Jenkins observes, it contains a "minimum of action" and most of it occurs in the first act.[21] Instead, what *As You Like It* offers are symbolic conversions of troubling material. The process starts early, with the mutation of Orlando's fratricidal anger into the recreational rhythm of the wrestling match.[22] It includes Duke Senior's conversion of exile into sabbatical and Rosalind's interpretation of banishment as adventure. Repeatedly, painful events are mastered through their symbolic reorganization. As Touchstone says, "when I was at home I was in a better place, but travellers must be content" (2.4.13-14).

Most important to note, the rhythm at work in these repeated instances of painful emotion converted to positive gain is that of the Freudian *Fort/Da.* Observing his grandson cast a toy away (*Fort* ["gone"]) only to drag it back (*Da* ["there"]) by an attached string, Freud found an emblem of the compensatory psyche.[23] He partially answered the problem of why the child would repeat a painful experience of loss by noting the mastery achieved in the game and hence, by implication, over the painful departures of his mother that the game supposedly symbolized. But the triumphant ego is ultimately less significant in Freud's analysis of the game than the vexing fact of repetition; and by the end of "Beyond the Pleasure Principle," Freud is led to propose both a death instinct and primary masochism.[24]

The problem with Freud's *Fort/Da* formulation, as Lacan allows us to see, is that he overlooks the step of converting actual loss (the mother's departure) into symbolic loss (casting away the toy and assigning words to the enactment). Reading the two as equivalent, Freud proposes a mechanical repetition of emotions on the part of the little boy. Lacan, however, places the crucial step in the process of symbolizing loss, for the positions of absence and presence are reversed through "the introduction of the symbol." "[D]on't forget," Lacan writes, "when he says *Fort,* it is because the object is here, and when he says *Da* the object is absent." Language thus effects not a simple repetition but an inversion, so that "absence is evoked in presence, and presence in absence." Far from understanding this as accident or coincidence, Lacan labels it the essence of human discourse; the introduction of the symbol "opens up the world of negativity, which constitutes both the discourse of the human subject and the reality of his world in so far as it is human."[25] Where a mechanistic reading of the *Fort/Da* scenario finds only compulsion to repeat and master, Lacan sees a symbolic conversion that opens up a world of negativity, a linguistic reality in which "the thing" accords imperfectly with "the symbol." If under this order nothing is ever quite what it seems, if reality is displaced by language, a world is nevertheless opened up by the symbolic process. As Lacan puts it, the *"subject does not just in this master his privation . . . but he also raises his desire to a second power."*[26]

Lacan goes on to link the "primal masochism" Freud had mentioned in "Beyond the Pleasure Principle" with "this initial negativation . . . this original murder of the thing."[27] Freud found masochism an intensely troubling concept because it contradicted his fundamental premise of an essentially self-protective (and pre-linguistic) psychic economy; over the course of his career he changed his mind several times about the existence and status of primary masochism.[28] Lacan's recognition of language as a fundamental third term of psychic reality complicates the idea of primary masochism. Rather than simply implying self-destructiveness, Lacan's sense of an "initial negativation" founded in the symbol develops, and takes us back to, Freud's recognition that "the symbol of negation" proves "indispensable" for thinking. Lacan views the *Fort/Da* episode, I am suggesting, not in terms of mastery but as an instance of Freudian negation. The synchronic structure of language complicates the diachronic order of events.

Now, *As You Like It*'s Arden, that impossible realm of pastoral possibility, is itself "a world of negativity." This "golden world," with its "tongues in trees, books in the running brooks, / Sermons in stones, and good in everything" (2.1.16-17), is the universe of discourse opened up by symbolic conversion.[29] Here language in its various forms proliferates: Corin counsels Silvius and debates with Touchstone; Orlando becomes a poet, "character[ing]" his thoughts in the bark of trees; Jaques orates his view of the "seven ages of man"; and Rosalind/Ganymede uses verbal pretense to engage in courtship with Orlando. All this is predicated on an initial Lacanian "murder of the thing," a willingness to sacrifice a sure reality for the linguistic *If* whose powers Touchstone documents late in the play (5.4.102). I have discussed already the erotic expansion and possibility enabled by the replacement of Rosalind with Ganymede's personified "Rosalind." The border-crossing "conversion" of Oliver from villain to lover is another signal instance of symbolic inversion. Viewers complain that Oliver's transformation is unrealistic because unmotivated, but his is only the most abrupt of a sheaf of similar changes. He, moreover, narrates his own alteration:

> CELIA  Was't you that did so oft contrive to kill him?
> OLIVER  'Twas I. But 'tis not I. I do not shame
> To tell you what I was, since my conversion
> So sweetly tastes, being the thing I am.
> (4.3.134-37)

The point is not that Oliver's essence has been miraculously altered, any more than Rosalind's feminine nature has been replaced by Ganymede's boyish one. Instead it is a matter in each case of new symbolic or linguistic possibilities being opened up through the process of negation: " 'Twas I. But 'tis not I."

What of the part of the melancholy Jaques in this world of negativity? I am arguing that Jaques, even more than Ganymede's Rosalind, exemplifies the power of a symbol to hold at bay a repressed and troubling idea. The melancholy affect of Rosalind is overdetermined in Act 1: her father's banishment has left her unable and unwilling "to remember any extraordinary pleasure" (1.2.5-6); her sudden passion for Orlando produces "burs . . . in [her] heart" (1.3.16-17); the duke banishes her, on pain of death, for the simply stated reason "that I trust thee not" (1.3.51). Orlando, too, grieves for multiple causes; not only has he been barred from "the place of a brother" (1.1.19), but his successful wrestling is "misconster[ed]" by the duke (1.2.255) and Oliver treacherously plots to kill him. All this, together with the old duke's banishment in Arden, constitutes a weighty burden of gloom at the play's start, a weight that must somehow be acknowledged despite the changed conditions of Orlando and Rosalind when they reappear in Arden. The absent Jaques de Boys becomes the emblem of the severing of family that troubles both Orlando and Rosalind, merging with the melancholy Jaques, who thereby takes on the melancholic burden set down by the other characters upon their entry into Arden.

Freed from the weight of melancholy, both Rosalind and Orlando become extremely verbose. Although Orlando seemed to have no difficulty expressing dismay to Adam or outrage to Oliver, eros then struck him dumb: on first meeting Rosalind, Orlando feels his passion hangs "weights upon [his] tongue," rendering him mute, "a mere lifeless block" (1.2.247, 241). In Arden, however, passionate verses drip from his pen, and he "carve[s] on every tree" (3.2.9) the notation of his love. The samples provided of his poetry indicate that writer's block is not his problem. Rosalind, too, appears somewhat reticent at the start of the play; at one point Celia chides, "Cupid have mercy, not a word?" and Rosalind replies, "Not one to throw at a dog" (1.3.1-3). Although Rosalind acquits herself well enough linguistically during Act 1, she demonstrates none of the loquaciousness that characterizes the Ganymede persona. Arden, we can say, affords a lightening of spirits that brings increased verbal facility. How then can we account for the fact that in the closing moments of the play—specifically, with the arrival of Hymen—Rosalind silences herself? To determine the significance of her movement into and back out of verbal expressiveness, the cultural assumptions linking melancholia, speech, and gender must be investigated. Exploring these connections reveals the stubborn survival of material that resists the censorship of negation, the troubling remnants of cultural prohibitions on maternal connection and on same-sex desires. This emotional debris proves so destabilizing that contemporary theorists maintain that it causes melancholy, and at momentary junctures it unsettles the happy construction of *As You Like It*. Jaques, once again, enables our investigation.

### III

As I mentioned earlier, Jaques makes a point of carefully defining his melancholy:

> I have neither the scholar's melancholy, which is emulation; nor the musician's, which is fantastical; nor the courtier's, which is proud; nor the soldier's, which is ambitious; nor the lawyer's, which is politic; nor the lady's, which is nice; nor the lover's, which is all these; but it is a melancholy of mine own, compounded of many simples, extracted from many objects, and indeed the sundry contemplation of my travels, in which my often rumination wraps me in a most humorous sadness.
>
> (4.1.10-19)

The method of his self-diagnosis reveals as much about early modern notions of melancholia as it does about the character: the malady, in its various forms specified here, seems ubiquitous. Jaques's confidence that his melancholy is distinctively individualistic yields to our sense that the complaint is endemic within the culture. How particularized can its manifestations be? And, to anticipate the conclusion of *As You Like It*, what happens when the self-assigned keeper of melancholia departs? How could he carry away all traces of a melancholia so various and so widespread?

In his encyclopedic *Anatomy of Melancholy* (1621), Robert Burton echoes Jaques in attempting to define and describe versions of the complaint. Burton generally associates melancholy with mental frenzy, leading to prophecy, speech in strange languages, and proliferating discourse (such as his own book). Burton marks many distinctions in how the affliction affects its sufferers. For one thing, men and women display different symptoms. In contrast to the typical male melancholiac's verbosity, female melancholiacs are described as confused and complaining, "so stupified and distracted" in their suffering that "many of them cannot tell how to express themselves in wordes, or how it holds them, what ailes them; you cannot understand them, or well tell what to make of their sayings."[30] With this distinction Burton participates in the Renaissance "gendering of melancholia" that Juliana Schiesari has recently analyzed.[31] Yet, as Burton himself acknowledges, melancholy can call into question firm differentiation by gender: love-melancholy, he says, "turns a man into a woman."[32] The anatomist's efforts to segregate male and female melancholy are subverted by the malady's own disintegrative powers.

In Jaques's self-diagnosis and in Burton's *Anatomy*, melancholy paradoxically both inscribes difference and testifies to universality. Like the concept of the autonomous subject to which melancholy bears a close (and in some ways mutually-constituting) relation, the affliction isolates its victim; yet the marks of this isolation closely resemble those suffered by other victims. Like subjectivity, melancholy separates into sameness, marking individual boundaries without reliably guaranteeing individuality. Perceiving a connection between melancholia and the development of subjectivity, post-Lacanian theorists—notably Julia Kristeva and Judith Butler—have posited the continuing impact of early experiences of attachment and loss. Both theorists build on Lacan's concept of the split subject, which can be usefully illustrated here by a further Lacanian comment on Freud's *Fort/Da* episode. Lacan observes that the toy that is cast away and retrieved "is not the mother reduced to a little ball. . . . it is a small part of the subject that detaches itself from him while still remaining his, still retained."[33] This reading suggests, briefly, how radically the subject may invest itself in others and how divided its emotional life may be. In their investigations of the split subject in relation to melancholia, Kristeva and Butler have different agendas: Kristeva pursues the link between overpowering emotion, speech, and loss of the mother, while Butler is interested in the formation of gender, which she argues is a melancholic formation. Both connections are relevant to *As You Like It*. Neither theorist denies the shaping influence of cultural valuations in determining perceived differences between, for instance, men's and women's melancholia, but both seek a psychological motivation for the evolved cultural scenario.

Kristeva, like Burton, follows tradition in valorizing melancholia's proximity to aesthetic creativity. But what Burton wants to see as the specifically female type of melancholia becomes the norm in Kristeva's analysis. She observes that the speech of melancholiacs tends to be repetitive and monotonous, and she maintains that, in its extreme forms, melancholy is linked with aphasia or asymbolia. Kristeva sees this breakdown of linguistic function as specific and meaningful. Language proceeds from the process of negation: a symbol replaces a lost or absent object, so that negativity is "coextensive with the speaking being's psychic activity." Melancholiacs, however, "*disavow*" negation. Rather than allowing the absent object to be replaced with a sign, they "nostalgically fall back on the real object . . . of their loss, which is just what they do not manage to lose, to which they remain painfully riveted."[34] Melancholic artists are able to bypass or even capitalize on their symbolic collapse by creating semiotic representations of their experience, but for ordinary sufferers the condition is painfully disintegrative.

Kristeva's analysis suggests that Orlando's and Rosalind's verbal ease in Arden exhibits, once again, the success of negation. With the melancholy Jaques serving as the symbol for melancholia, the other characters are freed to practice the proliferating substitutions of happy linguistic function. Yet Jaques will eventually depart, and as if in preparation for his exit, Rosalind, with her final words in the play, gives herself to the duke ("I'll have no father, if you be not he") and to Orlando ("I'll have no husband, if you be not he") and announces to Phebe that she will "ne'er wed woman, if you be not she" (5.4.121-23). Positioning herself in relation to father and husband, Rosalind enters the culturally mandated silence of femininity. The line with which she bars herself from ever "wed[ding] woman" is ordinarily played with a comic turn, but it signals that the descent of prescribed gender roles entails prohibition as well as partnership. The easy erotic attractions that proliferate earlier in the play cease with the movement into organized, marriageable couples. The presiding figure for this nuptial ceremony is Hymen, god of marriage and hence of conjunction, but also, through irreducible linguistic association, evoking virginity and hence obstacle or limit. Marriage involves loss as well as gain, and "virginity" names only part of what is lost; Rosalind also leaves behind the Ganymede persona, the affiliated habit of linguistic ease, and the possibility of a primary bond with a(nother) woman. Thus the arrival of Hymen confirms not only heterosexual coupling,[35] but also the correspondent movement away from parents and in particular from mothers.

Why mothers? Rosalind's rejection of Phebe closes down the possibility of an intimate relationship with another woman. In terms of the plot, of course, Rosalind's close female friend is Celia not Phebe, but Phebe's erotic attraction has raised the specter of union between two women. Such a union would recapitulate an early bond with a mother. Part of the "confusion" that Hymen "bar[s]" (l. 124), in other words, is the confusion of identities threatened by even this remote suggestion of a maternal bond. Hymen's descent thus points, elliptically, to the profound absence of mothers from *As You Like It*.[36] In her important article "Where Are the Mothers in Shakespeare? Options for Gender Representation in the English Renaissance," Mary Beth Rose argues that Shakespeare's romantic comedies eliminate mothers in their dedication to an "oedipal plot" whereby separation from the mother is the crucial "enabling condition" for satisfactory adulthood.[37] Where the maternal role does find its way into Shakespearean drama, it proves distinctly problematic. For Rose, Rosalind's giving of herself to Orlando signals her "voluntary future subordination" as wife and mother, "clarif[ying] a basic structural principle underlying Shakespeare's comic interpretation of marriage and the family: the harmonious, stable, wished-for society is based upon the sacrifice of the mother's desire."[38] This picture of the basic outline of Shakespeare's romantic comedies is indisputable, although pursuing the threads of melancholy in the text suggests to me that mothers have been banished only imperfectly from *As You Like It*. Even this happy comedy reveals the cultural and individual costs of repressing early attachments.

Although the trope of the absent mother is familiar in Shakespearean drama, it is striking to find, in the words of Mario DiGangi, only one "mention of a mother [3.5.35-37] in a play that continually returns to fathers."[39] I suspect that disavowed mourning for the mothers whose acknowledgment is forcefully effaced from the play drives the need for a melancholic safeguard who can hold at bay any recognition of emotional loss. The idea that a child's relationship to its nurse can be a precipitating cause of melancholy goes back to Burton: "From a child's Nativity, the first ill accident that can likely befall him, in this kinde is a bad Nurse, by whose meanes alone hee may bee tainted with this malady from his cradle."[40] Kristeva gives the idea modern expression, claiming in *Black Sun* that melancholia is fundamentally linked with the subject's loss of the mother; it is *"impossible mourning for the maternal object."*[41] Indeed in her view, language itself proceeds from such a loss:

> "I have lost an essential object that happens to be, in the final analysis, my mother," is what the speaking being seems to be saying. But . . . since I consent to lose her I have not lost her (that is the negation), I can recover her in language.[42]

This is a troubling crux in Kristeva's thought: having equated melancholia with inadequate movement into the symbolic realm and having traced that failure to unsuccessful separation from the mother, she suggests the necessity of "matricide" as the "*sine-qua-non* condition of our individuation."[43] Schiesari argues that Kristeva's "murderous rhetoric of violence against women" reproduces the misogyny of masculine tradition.[44] Certainly Kristeva's miming of a nostalgic voice (" 'I have lost . . .' ") can imply a regressive fixation on the lost mother. But reading Kristeva as more closely aligned with Lacan renders a different emphasis: that mothers are lost because the primal bond with them occurs prior to linguistic acquisition. Thus where Schiesari finds *Black Sun* evincing Kristeva's "own ambivalence, if not hatred, toward women,"[45] Lynn Enterline suggests that the text contains a more technical error, Kristeva's apparent ascription of maternal identity to a connection that both logically and developmentally must precede any such notation of identity. She observes that in other texts Kristeva, following Lacan, presents the link between melancholia and the entry into the symbolic in recursive terms, since the mother becomes intelligible only within the symbolic order.[46] It seems Kristeva may intentionally ambiguate her argument, since to claim full command of the signifier would, according to her theory, enact the abjection of maternal flesh.

Although questions remain about the degree to which Kristeva valorizes, diagnoses, or participates in hatred of the mother, *As You Like It* exhibits clear traces of misogyny, which make it difficult to believe that in the creation of this fiction mothers were simply forgotten. At certain moments the misogyny in *As You Like It* resembles that in *Black Sun,* however one chooses to explain Kristeva's position. Ganymede, for complex reasons, voices numerous negative remarks about Rosalind, inspiring Celia's charge "You have simply misused our sex in your love-prate" (4.1.191-92). Ganymede also attacks Phebe in distinctly gendered terms ("Who might be your mother . . . ?" "'Tis such fools as you / That makes the world full of ill-favour'd children" [3.5.35, 52-53]). Jaques exhibits profoundly homosocial habits, refraining from ever addressing a female character, although he addresses the "pretty youth" Ganymede (4.1.1).[47] So while the presence of Jaques blocks melancholia in Arden and opens up a certain degree of gendered freedom for Rosalind/Ganymede and Orlando, the absence of mothers suggests, in line with Rose's argument, something closer to repression—an attempt to hide the troubling effort to resist maternal entanglement by keeping mothers altogether out of the picture.[48] The presence of melancholy Jaques, figuring the fact of loss without its eroding consequence, forestalls acknowledgment of the ongoing presence of certain desires that cannot be claimed or expressed, but the play does not thereby create an ideal site of gendered or psychological equality.[49] Its design and its accommodations are imperfect as well as temporary.

Anne Barton observes that Jaques's "withdrawal at the end impoverishes the comic society. . . . Like a ship which has suddenly jettisoned its ballast, the play no longer rides quite evenly in the waves."[50] Certainly I agree that Jaques's presence is crucial to the balance of the play, but I see his departure as disruptive because of what he leaves behind rather than what he takes away with him. Before his departure Jaques announces an inheritance to each of the male characters on stage: his "former honour" to the duke, "love" to Orlando and Oliver, "a long and well-deserved bed" to Silvius, "wrangling" to Touchstone (5.4.185-90). Jaques's bequest here returns the play to the issues of inheritance with which it began but does so within a more overtly gendered arrangement, since four of the five inheritors stand as part of a newly married couple. It is an odd speech, not only because "considerations of rank ought to have assigned" it to the duke,[51] but because it is difficult to know what Jaques could have to "bequeath" (l. 185)—other than his melancholy. Melancholy is what I understand him to be redistributing over the four couples, in the strongly prescribed gender formations in which Hymen has left them.

Why should melancholy return at this point, as experiential fact rather than as name? An association seems to exist between marriage and melancholy, although the issue that induces sadness seems less marriage per se and more the shutting-down of gender play. As I have suggested, Rosalind gives up the freedoms and possibilities of Ganymede in order to marry Orlando: she strongly embraces femininity as a limit. Rosalind's final appearance as the Epilogue, whose words unsettle the relationships between boy actor, Ganymede, and Rosalind, testifies to the diminution effected by Rosalind's marriage. Characteristically, the play gives back in the Epilogue part of what has been taken away by the nuptial resolution. The Epilogue's careful separation of viewers into men and women, however, maintains the gender opposition ordained by Hymen.

For many viewers a sense of loss pervades the closing moments of the play, sadness that a joyous romp is over but more specifically, I think, sadness that Arden's fluid erotic arrangements have yielded to a traditional, fixed structure. We might gain insight into this response through the link Judith Butler has suggested between gender and melancholia. Furthering Freud's concept of identification as a way of preserving a loved object, Butler understands gender to result from disavowed grief. Indeed, in Butler's strong interpretation gender itself is a melancholy construction. An object that is prohibited—typically in our culture the same-sex object—is incorporated into the ego and thus consolidated as "masculinity" or "femininity."[52] Butler is most interested in how same-sex desire escapes recognition in a heterosexual culture. Following this line of thought, it is possible to argue that Ganymede/Rosalind permits into consciousness the recognition of same-sex desire, desire both to have and to be, as I have suggested above. As far as male subjects go, Butler's concern with the heterosexual imperative does not accord perfectly with the culture in which *As You Like It* was written. In the patriarchal, masculinist world of early seventeenth-century England, "marriage did not necessarily curtail homoerotic desire," for men at least, because "the constitution of the early modern household and the absence of a distinct ideology of heterosexuality" opened the door to a variety of sexual practices.[53] However, in this world an emotional attachment to the mother would have been disavowed by young men at their breeching and later at school, leading us back to Kristeva's sense of melancholia as *"impossible mourning for the maternal object."* As Gail Kern Paster shows, the image of melancholia resulting from disrupted early attachment is present in Jaques's reference to the infant "Mewling and puking in the nurse's arms" (2.7.144); acutely noting that the nurse, not the mother, holds this infant, Paster suggests that the image implies the "extended gastrointestinal trauma," with its accompanying psychological consequences, experienced by babies who were wet-nursed.[54] For women the cultural picture with regard to maternal connection is somewhat more ambiguous than for men, although within the play we have noted that Rosalind's movement into marriage involves assigning herself to her husband and father, barring herself from "wed[ding] woman," and embracing silence. Both Kristeva's and Butler's theories of melancholy appear relevant in Rosalind's case, and thus both melancholic foreclosure of the mother's loss and melancholic gender formation are inscribed within the play.

Evidently something about the bleeding edges of melancholia as a construction make it difficult to limit. Both Kristeva's and Butler's theories of melancholy present a problem of adducing limits. Kristeva indicates a particularized condition when she diagnoses mourning for the maternal object, but when she links language itself to this cause, the particularity evaporates and one can less easily charge her with a pathological misogyny. Butler, on the other hand, sees melancholia as ubiquitous in a gendered culture, but the problem becomes in application a slightly more particular one of disavowed attachment to the same-sex object within heterosexist culture. This is not simply a problem with postmodern theories of melancholy: similar slippage characterizes early seventeenth-century discussions. Jacques Ferrand's *Treatise on Lovesickness* (1610, 1623) manages to avoid clearly differentiating between the particular excesses of erotic mania and a more general view of love as a disease or disruptive force. When Ferrand cites, for instance, the power of passionate love to transform women into men, the condition would seem particularized; but his recitation of surgical, pharmaceutical, and empirical cures for love suggests that the condition is endemic.[55] As a practicing physician, he may have intended his book to build his clientele, and he was no doubt documenting the suffering caused by sexual repression in early modern society. Burton's monumental *Anatomy* is even more precariously perched on the divide between generality and specificity. Burton begins by distinguishing between melancholy as a "Disposition," part of the mixed and various experience of human life and "in this sense . . . the Character of mortalitie," and the more settled, intrinsic "habit" of melancholy as "a Chronicke or continuate disease."[56] Yet the distinction quickly crumbles, since the passing disposition of individuals is traced to the very condition of mortality and hence can scarcely be escaped. Promising in the title to explain "what it is, with all the kinds, causes, symptomes, prognostickes & severall cures of it," Burton's book proliferates details to such an extent that the condition becomes universalized. As Schiesari notes, his "systematizing reason is contradicted by Burton's key assertion that 'all the world' is mad from melancholy."[57]

In Kristeva, Butler, Ferrand, and Burton the repeated movement between the particular and the universal supports a sense that melancholia is not just difficult to define but that it is intrinsically linked with language, that the concept itself is part of the process of symbolic substitution. The particular is replaced by another particular: thus the deferral of the signifier accounts for absence through language. Lacan, as we recall, found "primal masochism" in the subject's willingness to engage in symbolic substitution. Permitting or even inviting loss in order to taste the complex pleasure of sweet sorrow, a lovesick swain such as Silvius or Orlando falls under the spell of poetry. The sort of masochism Lacan speaks of is distinctly purposeful: it yields pleasure. So, too, the melancholic lover of the Renaissance engaged in suffering as a means of refining his spirit; it was "a quest of the spirit that passe[d] through the dangers of psychic decomposition in an act of ultimate self-affirmation."[58] To see masochism simply as pain that is sought, or melancholy as pain that is welcomed, avoids both the full complexity of these acts of psychic compensation and, evidently, their full reward. The rich wordplay of *As You Like It* illustrates how successfully (though never completely) language can substitute for lost objects and repressed desires.

At the end of *As You Like It,* then, when Orlando has tired of "thinking" (both in his own sense and in the one Freud indicates as a benefit of negation) and invited the reassertion of gendered order and heterosexual coupling, the melancholic truth of gender emerges with Ganymede's disappearance and Hymen's arrival. Both Orlando and Rosalind must disavow an aspect of desire that has emerged in Arden so that a proper marriage can occur. Significantly, the melancholy Jaques here departs, replaced by the Second Brother, who appears as through a revolving door. We miss the point if we suppose that the melancholy Jaques leaves because he finds the concluding happiness inimical to his interests. The doubling of the two Jaqueses should make us suspicious of just such an emphasis on character at the expense of symbolic patterning. Rather, by serving as the placeholder for melancholy, the melancholy Jaques has helped to keep gender questions open; more broadly, he has allowed an opening-up of discourse, an enriched thinking. By enabling the function of negation, he has made the play a comedy.

The arrival of Jaques de Boys with news from abroad that spurs the departure of the melancholy Jaques also reveals the relation of Arden to the "real" world of the court. If Arden, the place of banishment, is *Fort,* the arrival of the Second Brother would seem to announce *Da,* the completion of the pattern, the return to reality, and the end of the play. The doubling of the two Jaqueses partially unsettles, however, any closure the pattern might promise, for it is difficult to know which Jaques we should consider prior—the first we hear of? the first we see?—so that *Fort* and *Da,* absence and presence, tend to reverse themselves, according to the Lacanian linguistic structure I have noted. The logic of negation is double, not linear.

Since, as Derrida claims, "the writing of a *fort/da* is always a *fort/da,*"[59] this demonstration of the pattern's relevance to *As You Like It* might deliver a sense of closure and mastery—at least until we remember that Freud, by the time he finished writing about the *Fort/Da,* came to doubt his own insistence on the pleasure principle and reached the conclusion that, in Derrida's words, "instead of one unknown, now we have two."[60] However it might have seemed to Freud, for later generations the *Fort/Da*'s completed pattern and its promise of mastery hold less significance (and, perhaps, less satisfaction) than the discursive opportunity it presents. So, too, at the end of *As You Like It* any number of unsettling questions remain about the disposition of the characters toward one another and toward themselves, about the connection between Ardenic freedom and a return to court, about the desirability of gendered ordering—in the most encompassing sense, about the degree of closure the play attains. As the figure whose presence opens up, sustains, modifies, and partially replaces the narrative and symbolic logic of the play, Jaques functions like "theory": he appears inexplicably within the text but is finally extruded from it. He doubles or supplements another figure with a more legitimate link to the play's fiction, a figure who claims the authority of the real world when he appears late in the play. Like theory or like a construction of negation, Jaques's melancholic presence does not so much explain the play as enrich our thinking about it.

*Notes*

This essay originated in a seminar at the 1997 meeting of the Shakespeare Association of America; it was revised with support from the Rhodes College Faculty Development Endowment. I appreciate the helpful comments of Bob Byer, Jennifer Brady, Christy Desmet, Richard Finkelstein, Martha Ronk, Chris Stroffolino, and especially Amy Hollywood and *Shakespeare Quarterly*'s editors and anonymous readers.

[1] See, for instance, William Hazlitt, *Characters of Shakespeare's Plays* (London: C. H. Reynell, 1817), 158-59; Jan Kott, *Shakespeare Our Contemporary,* trans. Boleslaw Taborski (New York: W. W. Norton, 1966), 168.

[2] Jacques Derrida, *Of Grammatology,* trans. Gayatri Chakravorty Spivak (Baltimore: Johns Hopkins UP, 1976), 61.

[3] Quotations from *As You Like It* follow the Arden edition by Agnes Latham (New York: Methuen, 1975). Quotations from other Shakespeare plays follow *The Riverside Shakespeare,* ed. G. Blakemore Evans (Boston: Houghton Mifflin, 1974).

[4] Cf. Juliana Schiesari's comment that "melancholia, as a cultural category . . . if not as a medical category, is essentially theatrical" (*The Gendering of Melancholia: Feminism, Psychoanalysis, and the Symbolics of Loss in Renaissance Literature* [Ithaca, NY: Cornell UP, 1992], 236).

[5] See Harold Jenkins, "As You Like It," *Shakespeare Survey* 8 (1955): 40-51, esp. 42.

[6] At the beginning of 5.4, Oliver also confronts the melancholy Jaques with no apparent sign of recognition, but the plots are winding down by this point.

[7] Latham, ed., lxviii.

[8] Latham, ed., lxviii. See also *The Norton Shakespeare,* ed. Stephen Greenblatt et al. (New York: W. W. Norton, 1996), 1612n: and Evans, ed., 376n.

[9] Jenkins, 45

[10] Latham, ed., lxxvi.

[11] Sigmund Freud, "Negation" in *The Standard Edition of the Complete Psychological Works of Sigmund Freud,* trans. James Strachey, 24 vols. (London: Hogarth Press and the Institute of Psychoanalysis, 1961), 19:233-39, esp. 235-36.

[12] Freud, "Negation," 236.

[13] Cf. Martha Ronk Lifson's emphasis on the play's use of lies, "which open up possibilities to minds which might otherwise be enclosed, narcissistic, narrow" ("Learning By Talking: Conversation in *As You Like It,*" *SS* 40 [1987]: 91-105, esp. 92). I agree with Ronk

about the play's affirmation of pretence and complex truths, but I see the characters as subject to language and its effects rather than as masters of their conversational fates.

[14] Freud, "Negation," 239.

[15] Jacques Lacan, *The Four Fundamental Concepts of Psycho-Analysis,* ed. Jacques-Alain Miller, trans. Alan Sheridan (New York: W. W. Norton, 1981), 20. Lacan's "The agency of the letter" appears in *Écrits: A Selection,* trans. Alan Sheridan (New York: W. W. Norton, 1977), 146-78. See also Jacques Lacan, *Speech and Language in Psychoanalysis,* trans. Anthony Wilden (Baltimore and London: Johns Hopkins UP, 1968). For an accessible explanation of Lacanian theory, see Bruce Fink, *The Lacanian Subject: Between Language and Jouissance* (Princeton, NJ: Princeton UP, 1995).

[16] Lacan, *Écrits,* 154 and 155.

[17] Joan Copjec, *Read My Desire: Lacan against the Historicists* (Cambridge, MA: MIT Press, 1994), 54.

[18] Lacan, *Écrits,* 172.

[19] For discussion of how the play's acknowledgment of multiple and shifting erotic desires works against the concluding image of heterosexual marriage, see Valerie Traub, *Desire and Anxiety: Circulations of Sexuality in Shakespearean Drama* (New York: Routledge, 1992), 122-30, esp. 123. For the argument that Rosalind/Ganymede's doubled gender is necessary for the play's happy ending, see Susanne L. Wofford, " 'To You I Give Myself, For I Am Yours': Erotic Performance and Theatrical Performatives in *As You Like It*" in *Shakespeare Reread: The Texts in New Contexts,* Russ McDonald, ed. (Ithaca, NY: Cornell UP, 1994), 147-69.

[20] Joseph Westlund. *Shakespeare's Reparative Comedies: A Psychoanalytic View of the Middle Plays* (Chicago: U of Chicago P, 1984), 69.

[21] Jenkins, 42 and 41. Anne Barton similarly observes that "the play's plot barely exists" (" 'As You Like It' and 'Twelfth Night': Shakespeare's Sense of an Ending" in *Shakespearian Comedy,* David Palmer and Malcom Bradbury, eds. [London: Edward Arnold, 1972], 160-80, esp. 162).

[22] See Cynthia Marshall, "Wrestling as Play and Game in *As You Like It,*" *Studies in English Literature* 33 (1993): 265-87.

[23] Freud, "Beyond the Pleasure Principle," *Standard Edition,* 18:1-64, esp. 15.

[24] Freud, "Beyond the Pleasure Principle," *Standard Edition,* 18:38 and 54-55.

[25] Jacques Lacan, *The Seminar of Jacques Lacan: Book I: Freud's Papers on Technique 1953-1954,* ed. Jacques-Alain Miller, trans. John Forrester (New York: W. W. Norton, 1988), 173-74.

[26] Lacan, *Seminar I,* 173.

[27] Lacan, *Seminar I,* 174.

[28] In "Three Essays on the Theory of Sexuality" (1905) Freud views sadism and masochism as congruent; in "Instincts and Their Vicissitudes" (1915) he questions the existence of primary masochism, but his claim that sadists identify with their victims essentially posits a hidden masochism; in "The Economic Problem of Masochism" (1924) Freud theorizes that a conjunction of the death instinct with the libido produces the various forms of masochism.

[29] William Kerrigan similarly observes that "Arden is a text. . . . a forest of literacy, teeming with heteroglossia" ("Female Friends and Fraternal Enemies in *As You Like It*" in *Desire in the Renaissance: Psychoanalysis and Literature,* Valeria Finucci and Regina Schwartz, eds. [Princeton, NJ: Princeton UP, 1994], 184-203, esp. 194).

[30] Robert Burton, *The Anatomy of Melancholy,* ed. Thomas C. Faulkner, Nicolas K. Keissling, and Rhonda L. Blair, 3 vols. (Oxford: Clarendon Press, 1989-94), 1:415.

[31] See Schiesari, 243-56.

[32] Burton, 3:142. See also Schiesari, 252.

[33] Lacan, *Four Fundamental Concepts,* 62.

[34] Julia Kristeva, *Black Sun: Depression and Melancholia,* trans. Leon S. Roudiez (New York: Columbia UP, 1989), 45 and 43-44.

[35] See Traub, 127.

[36] Interestingly, Derrida reads the bedclothes into which young Ernst Freud threw his spool as "the *hymen* of the *fort:da,*" the marker of loss and distance while also the marker of the mother whose absence first inspired his game. Although many readers assume the child himself is in the bed, Derrida points out that the child must be located outside the bed in order to throw the toy through the curtains into the bed; thus "the bed . . . is *fort*" (*The Postcard: From Socrates to Freud and Beyond,* trans. Alan Bass [Chicago: U of Chicago P, 1987], 316 and 315).

[37] Mary Beth Rose, "Where Are the Mothers in Shakespeare? Options for Gender Representation in the English Renaissance," *Shakespeare Quarterly* 42 (1991): 291-314, esp. 301.

[38] Rose, 302 and 303.

[39] Mario DiGangi, "Queering the Shakespearean Family," *SQ* 47 (1996): 269-90, esp. 284.

[40] Burton, 1:328. Burton goes on to describe bad nurses in some detail, furthering his misogynistic agenda. By contrast, Kristeva's focus is on the relationship between child and mother rather than on the latter's overt deficiencies.

[41] Kristeva, 9.

[42] Kristeva, 43.

[43] Kristeva, 27 and 28.

[44] Schiesari, 80.

[45] Schiesari, 91.

[46] See Lynn Enterline, *The Tears of Narcissus: Melancholia and Masculimity in Early Modern Writing* (Stanford, CA: Stanford UP, 1995), 32-38.

[47] I owe this point to Chris Stroffolino.

[48] This sense of the play draws on Janet Adelman's observation that in Shakespeare's plays written before *Hamlet*, "masculine identity is constructed in and through the absence of the maternal" (*Suffocating Mothers: Fantasies of Maternal Origin in Shakespeare's Plays,* Hamlet *to* The Tempest [New York: Routledge, 1992], 10). Kerrigan has also recently argued that *As You Like It* deals with "maternal menace." In his Kleinian reading, Arden corresponds to "the mother of infancy," specifically to Shakespeare's mother (Mary Arden) and Shakespeare's infant experience of "being displaced at the breast" by his brother Gilbert (194-97, esp. 195 and 196).

[49] Lynn Hunt makes the important point that the tendency to idealize the Renaissance, and in particular to idealize it as a site of "polymorphous eroticisms and loosely constructed gender boundaries," needs to be resisted and countered by a realistic attention to "connections between sexuality and power" ("Afterword" in *Queering the Renaissance,* Jonathan Goldberg, ed. [Durham, NC: Duke UP, 1994], 359-77, esp. 373).

[50] Barton, 171.

[51] Barton, 166.

[52] See Judith Butler, "Melancholy Gender / Refused Identification" in *Constructing Masculinity,* Maurice Berger, Brian Wallis, and Simon Watson, eds. (New York: Routledge, 1995), 21-36; see also the earlier version of the argument in Judith Butler, *Gender Trouble: Feminism and the Subversion of Identity* (New York: Routledge, 1990), 57-65.

[53] DiGangi, 289.

[54] Gail Kern Paster, *The Body Embarrassed: Drama and the Disciplines of Shame in Early Modern England* (Ithaca, NY: Cornell UP, 1993), 218.

[55] See Jacques Ferrand, *A Treatise on Lovesickness,* ed. and trans. Donald A. Beecher and Massimo Ciavolella (Syracuse, NY: Syracuse UP, 1990), 230.

[56] Burton, 1:136 and 139.

[57] Schiesari, 247.

[58] Beecher and Ciavolella, eds., 157.

[59] Derrida, *Postcard,* 321.

[60] Derrida, *Postcard,* 22.

---

Source: "The Doubled Jaques and Constructions of Negation in *As You Like It,*" in *Shakespeare Quarterly,* Vol. 49, No. 4, Winter, 1998, pp. 375-92.

# "Now by My Hood, a Gentle and No Jew": Jessica, *The Merchant of Venice*, and the Discourse of Early Modern English Identity

## Mary Janell Metzger, *Western Washington University*

Jessica, the other Jew in *The Merchant of Venice,* is doubly distinguished.[1] Unlike her father, Shylock, she is said to be "gentle": at once noble and gentile. Yet as the "now" quoted in my title signifies and as Jessica readily admits, she remains "a daughter to [Shylock's] blood" despite her conversion (2.6.51, 2.3.18). Distinguished from Portia and Nerissa, whose marriages work to secure the social standing of the men they love, she is more saved than saving in her marriage to Lorenzo. Indeed, representations of Jessica, unlike those of other characters in the play, turn on alternating characterizations of her as a latent Christian and as a racialized and thus unintegrable Jew.[2]

Until recently, discussions of race or Jewishness in *The Merchant* tended to focus on Shylock alone. These readings suggested that critics could deal with religion, gender, or class but not with all three. There were no attempts to understand how such categories are, as Carol Neely puts it, "inseparable, unstable, disunified, and mutually constitutive" (303).[3] Critics like Neely, however, imply that reading Jessica both as a wealthy white woman who is thus coded as gentile and as "issue to a faithless Jew" (2.4.37) should highlight the interconnectedness of discourses of difference in Shakespeare's time.[4] This critical project has been considerably advanced by James Shapiro's *Shakespeare and the Jews,* which challenges assumptions about the significance of real and imagined Jews for early modern English audiences. By documenting both the actual lives and fictive representations of Jews in Shakespeare's England, Shapiro eliminates the distinction between theology and race implicit in G. K. Hunter's argument that Shakespeare and Marlowe did not depict "real" or "racial" Jews but, rather, portrayed a "moral condition" rooted in a "theological rather than ethnological framework" (215). Similarly, Kim Hall's studies of early modern representations of race and gender show how, in an age of soaring population and foreign immigration, English fears of uncontained female sexuality found expression in a "narrative of alien culture" that fused notions of blacks, Jews, and women (*Things* 39).

Yet like critics before them, Hall and Shapiro do not see Jessica as a central figure in *The Merchant* or in the play's discourse of racial difference. Although Shapiro grants that "the battle over *The Merchant of Venice* is a battle over the nature of Englishness itself and who has the right to stake a claim to it," he dedicates but a few pages of his book to Jessica (4). She does not appear in his index. More sensitive than many new-historicist critics to issues of gender, Shapiro nevertheless explains the focus on Jewish men in the texts he examines (and thus in his text) by noting "that Jewish men were represented as endowed with male and female traits" (38). Unfortunately, representations of men subsume those of women once again. Like Shapiro, Hall acknowledges the significance of Jessica as a figure of conversion. Yet while she skillfully traces the ambivalence present in the travel narratives she reads and in the imagery associated with Shylock, she finds Jessica's conversion an unambiguous portrayal of "a successful type of cross-cultural interaction" ("Guess" 102). Hall registers her uneasiness with this position, admitting that "glorifying" the transgressions of women like Jessica and Portia, as feminist critics often have, "may serve only to obscure the very complex nature of difference for a changing society in which racial categories developed along with changing organizations of gender" (103-04).

Hall's discomfort with readings that fail to acknowledge Jessica's ambivalent status in the play echoes my own. Indeed, I have long thought that Jessica's multiplicitous nature—as Jew and Christian and as "fair" beloved descended from blackened Chus, her father's "countrym[a]n" (2.4.39, 3.2.285)—constitutes an emblematic figure for the play's renowned discontinuities. The ambiguous mix of comedy and tragedy, humanism and racialism, patriarchal imperialism and festive rebellion in *The Merchant* corresponds to the inherent incompatibility of the identities Shakespeare attempts to unite in Jessica. Indeed, the nature and effects of Jessica's difference can illuminate how Shakespeare may have struggled with competing notions of Jewishness circulating in early modern England and how he worked to resolve them by creating not one Jew but two. In what follows I argue that only attention to the shifting emphases on discourses of gender, class, and religion in Shakespeare's representation of Jessica can elucidate *The Merchant*'s relation to early modern England's emerging ideology of race and to the bitter effects of that ideology that persist even today.[5]

Any discussion of conversion in Shakespeare must involve the Jew, just as any discussion of the Jew in Shakespeare inevitably involves the meaning of conversion in early modern England. As Hunter rightly observes, theology is central to the analysis of the early modern theatricalization of Jews because of the "long and torturous tradition" of interpreting Christianity *adversus Judeos*—that is, in opposition to Judaism (213). More simply, early modern Christian notions of what it means to be subject to God inevitably entail an account of the Jewish refusal to receive Christ as the Messiah. The English Reformation complicated Christians' response to Jews by offering an unqualified promise of conversion within a discourse shaped by the oppositional rhetoric of anti-Semitism. Further, as historical documents attest, the problem of the Jew in Christian England intersected with an emerging ideology of race to affirm a notion of English identity in which color, religion, and class converged.

In succeeding editions of *Actes and Monuments,* perhaps the most prevalent religious text in Elizabethan England excepting the Bible, the Protestant John Foxe offers "a complete history of the lives, sufferings and deaths of the Christian Martyrs from the commencement of Christianity to the present period" (1563 ed., title p.)—that is, the stories of men and women who met death rather than assert as true what they believed false. Foxe emphasizes the role of reason in the practice of the "true" Christian faith. Describing his text as an "[e]cclesiastical history" from which "the people may learn the rules and precepts of doctrine," Foxe takes a pedagogical tone: "They that be in error, let them not disdain to learn" (1570 ed., 4r). Or as he puts it in the 1563 edition. "Ignorance is the mother of all errors" (EE3v). Yet for Jews, the original recusants, choosing the truth was a matter not simply of learning but of a prior belonging that was denied them: "For like as the nature of truth so is the proper condition of the true church, that commonly none seeth it, but such only as be members and partakers thereof" (3r). Foxe argues even more ambivalently in the 1570 edition that Jews are to blame for their failure to choose wisely—"who should rather have known and received him than the Pharisees and Scribes of that people who had his law"? (E1r). He also repeatedly characterizes them as inherently unable to make such a choice. Foxe presents Jews both as "more tolerable than Papists" (1563 ed., K1v), who abandon their poor and worship idols and bread, and as "enemies to Christians" (1570 ed., index), as child murderers whose historical and bloody destruction confirms their rejection by God (1563 ed., E1r).[6] This ambivalence finds an analogue in *The Merchant,* where Jews are characterized as unwilling and unable to see the truth of the Messiah in Jesus, driven by their base natures, as Gratiano says with characteristic hyperbole, to pursue their "wolvish, bloody, starv'd, and ravenous" desires (4.1..138).

Foxe's apparent need to account for Jewish belief may be as old as Christianity itself, but the sixteenth century constitutes a specific and particularly significant moment in that history (see, e.g., Gerber; Netanyahu; Friedman; Shapiro). For the first time Jewishness was legally defined through Spain's pure-blood laws "not [as] a statement of faith or even a series of ethnic practices but a biological consideration" (Friedman 16). In England, as Foxe's text illustrates, the question of the Jews took on new importance in the light of Reformation struggles among Christians over the proper path to God's truth. How could one discern, as Foxe puts it, between "antiquitie and novelty" (1570 ed., iiv), between false worship and true faith? The Protestant emphasis on the inability of the individual to effect his or her own salvation, which Foxe's text elaborates, challenges the promise of Christianity made explicit in baptism. Called to "learn" and to "choose" rightly, one nevertheless could not "see" unless elected a "member or partaker thereof" by God's grace.

Readers like Hunter have been inclined to dismiss the import of such questions by asserting the relative scarcity of Jews in England in Shakespeare's time.[7] But the presence of crypto-Jews (converts to Christianity who secretly practiced Judaism) in Elizabethan England has been acknowledged since Lucien Wolf's discovery in the early twentieth century of a mostly Portuguese community of Jews. In fact, *The Merchant* followed fairly closely on the trial and execution of the most connected member of that community, Elizabeth's chief physician, Roderigo Lopez,[8] and Shylock's principal antagonist takes the name of the man whose political aspirations provided the context for Lopez's alleged treason: Don Antonio, pretender to the throne of Portugal following the death of the cardinal-king Henry. Such allusions would have been easily recognized by Shakespeare's audience.

According to Wolf, this Portuguese community "could not have remained altogether unknown to the general public, while to the Government, with its vigilant watch of all strangers hailing from Spain and Portugal, it must have been in every sense an open secret" (21); indeed, Wolf documents the government's knowledge in the correspondence of Lord Burghley, the queen's secretary of state, and his son Robert Cecil. But more important, Wolf argues that the Portuguese community of Jews was tolerated because they served the state without causing a stir—that is, because of economic interest: "they appear to have been, on the whole, quite decent folk, who worked honestly and unobtrusively at professions, trades and handicrafts which added appreciably to the well-being of the country" (22). Living and working "honestly and unobtrusively" meant becoming invisible as "former" Jews and convincingly performing the prerequisites for integration into English society. The cases of Joachim Gaunse on the one hand and of Bernard Leavis and Pedro Frere on the other illustrate this. Gaunse, a German Jewish mining chemist who worked in England for eight years, was expelled in 1598 on the grounds that he had challenged Christian doctrine in debating the status of Jesus with a Protestant minister from Bristol.[9] Portuguese agents pursuing prohibited

Spanish goods on behalf of English traders, Frere and Leavis were accused by Mary May, a Christian investor, who claimed that their Jewishness was a principal cause of her losses. Though much evidence of their "secret practices" was procured from servants and acquaintances, the court did not expel them; rather, it was "moved with the losses and trobles which the poore straungers indured" as a consequence of doing English business (Sisson 51).[10] As long as Jews did not publicly insist on their Jewishness, economic interests prevailed.

As other deportations suggest, notions of religious and racial conformity may have contributed to the emerging concepts of the English subject and of its requisite other, the alien. In 1596, the year *The Merchant* was probably written, Elizabeth I wrote to the Privy Council to request the aid of the mayor of London, his aldermen, and "all the other Maiours, Sheryfes, etc." in deporting eighty-nine blacks, to be given to a Lubeck merchant in exchange for his return of an equal number of English prisoners of war held by Spain and Portugal (*Acts* 16). Elizabeth distinguished "people of our owne nation," "the subjectes of the land and Christian people, that perishe for want of service, whereby through labor they might be mayntained," from "those kinde of people," meaning blacks, brought to live and work in England (16, 20-21). As Elizabeth's equations among color, faith, wealth, and nationality confirm, to be black was to be a common laborer, non-Christian, and consequently not English.

While European Jews may appear to have had the adventage over blacks in their ability to pass, as it were, as white and Christian and hence English, analogies between blackness and Jewishness were long-standing. As Anthony Barthelemy has shown, the association of blackness with sin and evil, which dates from the ancient world, was adopted by Christianity and overlaid with a narrative of salvation and damnation: white became the color of the saved, black the color of the damned. First among the damned would, of course, have been the Jews, as a 1604 biography of Spain's Charles V demonstrates:

> Who can deny that in the descendent of the Jews there persists and endures the evil inclination of their ancient ingratitude and lack of understanding, just as in Negroes [there persists] the inseparability of their blackness? For if the latter should unite themselves a thousand times with white women, the children are born with the dark color of the father. Similarly, it is not enough for a Jew to be three parts aristocrat or Old Christian for one family-line [i.e., one Jewish ancestor] alone defiles and corrupts him.
>
> (Friedman 16-17)

Shakespeare's Jessica anticipates this equation when she describes her father as a countryman "[t]o Tubal and to Chus" (3.2.285), for the first is a Jew and the second the mythical originary black African.[11]

The connection between blacks and Jews as alien others helped construct the racialized notion of Englishness. Because of color privilege, however, the converted Jews of London were not always perceived as threats to emerging notions of English identity, as Roger Prior's discovery of an integrationist Italian Jewish community in Tudor London indicates. Like the Portuguese Jews, the Italian Jews owed their presence in England to royal patronge, engaged in trade, and had connections to Jews in Antwerp. They lived in the same places in and outside London as their Portuguese counterparts did, but they integrated into English society far more thoroughly through marriage to Christians (see Prior 138). According to Prior, Shakespeare draws distinctions between converted Italian Jews, like Emilia Bassano—better known now as the poet Emilia Lanier—the woman alleged to be the dark lady of his sonnets, and Portuguese converts like Lopez whose resistant Jewishness was seen as a threat to English identity.[12] Whether or not Prior's claims about Emilia Bassano are true, the history of the Italian Jewish community suggests that competing notions of Jewishness existed at the time Shakespeare wrote and staged *The Merchant*. The construction of Jews as "deserving" (as they would later be labeled in the state documents calling for their readmission to England) or alien may have functioned to authorize the social and political agendas of British imperialism and the racialism it depended on.[13] Foxe's concerns may be seen, then, as representative of larger political questions: How would the English distinguish resistant and finally unintegrable Jews like Lopez or Gaunse from more cooperative and thus "truly" convertible Jews like Bassano? How could they affirm this distinction without denying the meaning and promise of conversion to Christianity? And how could English Christians define the Jew's difference both as a difference of nature and as a difference of faith involving the act of will faith requires? These issues constitute Shakespeare's challenge in *The Merchant of Venice*—a challenge he meets by presenting Jessica as a "fair" Jewish alternative to Shylock.

Initially Launcelot describes Jessica as a "[m]ost beautiful pagan, [a] most sweet Jew," and her embodiment of such conjunctions is an obvious source of comic tension in the play. Significantly, however, Launcelot's oxymorons depend on anti-Semitic assumptions that are impressed on the audience when Shylock first appears onstage as the incarnation of the inherently evil Jew of medieval and early modern Christian legend: he is scheming ("If I can catch him once upon the hip . . ." [1.3.46]), greedy ("He lends out money gratis, and brings down / The rate of usuance" [1.3.44-45]), satanic ("The devil can cite Scripture for his purpose. . . . O, what a goodly outside falsehood hath!" [1.3.98, 102]), and eager for Christian blood ("[the] fair flesh, to be cut off and taken / In what part of your body pleaseth me" [1.3.150-51][14]).

Jessica must overcome these images if she is to be integrated into the world of the play, which is largely defined in opposition to the malevolent Jewish otherness of Shylock. The difficulties of doing so, however, become quickly apparent. Alone onstage at the end of her first scene, Jessica presents the audience with the first of several arguments for her convertibility.

> Alack, what heinous sin is it in me
> To be ashamed to be my father's child!
> But though I am a daughter to his blood,
> I am not to his manners. O Lorenzo,
> If thou keep promise, I shall end this strife,
> Become a Christian and thy loving wife!
> (2.3.16-21)

That Jessica distances herself from sin by blatantly disregarding her father's authority may be necessary, but it is also problematic. For Shakespeare's audience, patriarchal authority was divinely ordained, and it secured the right of princes as well as that of fathers.[15] Jessica's disregard for that authority thus creates the first obstacle to a Christian audience's acceptance of her as a Christian.

The late-sixteenth-century debate over the role of parental authority in choosing a spouse would have been equally familiar to Shakespeare's audience.[16] Moreover, texts such as Andrewe Kyngesmill's "Godly Advise Touchyng Mariage" (1580) and Charles Gibbon's *How to Bestow Children in Marriage* (1591) reveal that the contest between individual will and patriarchal authority in the choice of spouses was often most intense when marriages were proposed between "believers and nonbelievers" (Kyngesmill Jiv). Gibbon lays out the competing views about such marriages in a fictional debate between Philogus and Tychias. Philogus argues that a Christian should not "be unequally yoked with infidels for what fellowship hath righteousness & what communion hath light with darkness?" Tychias counters that "the unbelieving husband is sanctified by the believing wife" and vice versa (C2r-v).[17]

In this context, acceptance of Jessica's marriage to Lorenzo would require a Christian audience to conclude either that she is a believer before her marriage or that she is, as she insists, "sanctified" through her marriage. In fact, Jessica lays claim to both arguments. Distinguishing between her own and her father's manners to resolve the "sin" and "strife" implicit in her rebellion, she underscores her preconversion difference. She nullifies the claims of filial attachment by insisting that she is a different kind of Jew, one whose manners take precedence over blood and who thus can see the truth of Christianity. Conversely, she equates Shylock's blood and manners, asserting a racial notion of Jewishness that she claims not to share. To extend an argument Frank Whigham makes, material and aesthetic distinctions between the powerful and the powerless take on both moral and bodily force and thus reveal to the audience a "natural" social hierarchy in which men subordinate women and Christians subordinate Jews (95, 103). Indeed, though Jessica clearly prefers a Christian life, she is saved not so much by her own choice as by Lorenzo's choice to marry her. By uniting her willingness with the willingness of others to find her integrable, she combines the blessings of Christian grace with individual will.

The need to guarantee Jessica's willingness is demonstrated in the scene following her soliloquy, in which Lorenzo, Gratiano, Solanio, and Solerio plan how Jessica, along with "what gold and jewels she [shall be] furnished with," will be taken "from her father's house" (2.4.31, 2.4.30). Jessica's wealth and her willingness to spend it constitute the first of several distinctions that guarantee her integration into Christian society. The next is articulated by Lorenzo when he receives her letter setting the time of their elopement:

> I know the hand; in faith, 'tis a fair hand,
> And whiter than the paper it writ on
> Is the fair hand that writ.
> (2.4.12-14)

The stress Lorenzo places on "fair" is echoed by Gratiano and again by Lorenzo before the scene concludes (2.4.28, 2.4.39). Early modern uses of *fair* combine the senses of color and beauty, and Lorenzo's direct reference to whiteness suggests color is related to his assertion of Jessica's worth.[18] Thus, while the scene establishes the means for Jessica's liberation from Shylock's house, it creates a color difference between father and daughter that justifies her removal, and it casts that difference as a source of comedy instead of tragedy: consider, for example, Desdemona's fate after eloping. Why color might be a prerequisite to differentiation from the Jewish stereotype is suggested later, in the seemingly comic debate between Launcelot and Jessica about the effectiveness of Jewish integration through marriage. In an awkward quotation of Exodus 20.5, Launcelot warns Jessica that "the sins of the father are to be laid upon the children" (3.5.1-2). She answers by repeating her earlier argument: "I shall be saved by my husband. He hath made me a Christian" (3.5.19-20). The power of her response is manifest not only in its simplicity, which contrasts with Launcelot's comic misprisions, but also in the representation of marriage as a force for order. But Lorenzo clarifies the bodily requirements for marriage as a means for the "making of Christians," as Launcelot puts it, when Jessica relays Launcelot's claims (3.5.23). "I shall answer that better to the commonwealth," Lorenzo warns Launcelot, "than you can the getting up of the Negro's belly; the Moor is with child by you, Launcelot" (3.5.37-39).

Jessica's defense and Lorenzo's rebuttal show how her whiteness and femaleness make possible her reproduction as a Christian in the eyes of the "commonwealth." As Hall notes, the scene reflects that institution's investment in "sexual practices" ("Guess" 89). Moreover, Jessica's marriage reconstitutes her as a body, for according to Christian ecclesiastical and legal authorities, a woman was incorporated into the body of her husband in marriage, becoming both one with and subject to him. As Portia says after Bassanio has successfully negotiated the prenuptial test devised by her father, "Myself, and what was mine, to you and yours / Is now converted" (3.2.166-67). In a play concerned with the conversion of Jews, Portia's terms make explicit the analogy between the transfer of her person and property to Bassanio and the incorporation of Jessica's person and property into Lorenzo. Like Portia's conversion from "lord," "master," and "[q]ueen" to "an unlessoned girl" ready "to be directed / As from her lord, her governor, her king" (3.2.167, 3.2.168, 3.2.169, 3.2.159, 3.2.164-65), Jessica's conversion from dark infidel to fair Christian is required by the play's ideology of order through marriage. As Jessica argues early in the play, becoming one with the body of Christ requires not only her marriage to a Christian but also the conversion of her body in distinctly racial and gendered terms (2.3.16-21).

It is in this context that Lorenzo's celebration of Jessica as "whiter" than the paper she writes on becomes significant. For unlike the offspring of Launcelot and his absent black lover, those of Jessica and Lorenzo will not differ bodily from the normative white Christian subject. Drawing on the work of Kim Hall and Janet Adelman, Lynda Boose explains the significance of this distinction:

> In terms of the ideological assumptions of a culture such as that of early modern England, the black male-white female union is not the narrative that requires suppression. What challenges the ideology substantially enough to require erasure is that of the black female-white male, for it is in the person of the black woman that the culture's preexisting fears both about the female sex and about gender dominance are realized. Through her, all free-floating anxieties about "the mother's dark place" contaminating the father's designs for perfect self-replication become vividly literal.
> ("Getting" 45-46)

Like Lorenzo, Hall and Boose consider Jessica visually white and therefore integrable within the racial and religious ideologies of early modern English patriarchy. But this view obscures the process of racialization in the play and thus the intersection of religion and gender in the production of racial ideology. In an inversion of the hierarchy of flesh and blood that Portia uses to incriminate Shylock, Jessica's "Jewish blood" is subordinated in the course of the play to her "fair" and hence convertible flesh (see 3.1.37-42). After her marriage, she will "appear," to quote Wolf, to be one of the "decent folk" who constitute Christian society.

In this context, Shylock's attempts in act 3 to defend himself against the attacks of Solanio and Solario take on new significance. Shylock appears to fail when he asserts, as Normand Lawrence writes, "that his daughter partakes of the same physical substance as himself, and so shares the same racial identity" (58): "I say my daughter is my flesh and blood," he declares (3.1.37). Solanio returns:

> There is more difference between thy flesh and hers than between jet and ivory, more between your bloods than there is between red wine and Rhenish.
> (3.1.39-42)

Whereas Shylock merely cites the relation between his body and his daughter's, Solanio emphasizes a transformation in Jessica whereby color and gender combine to overcome less discernible differences of blood.

Shylock, like Launcelot's black child, cannot undergo such a transformation. The reasons for his inability to do so help explain the unsettling effect of the final order for his conversion.[19] For Shylock's body, like the body of any Jewish man, would "convert" a Christian bride. Further, unlike Jessica, Shylock bears the mark of Judaism on his body—circumcision—and the Jewish body lies at the center of early modern anti-Semitic discourse. Though this bodily difference is never explicitly referred to in the play, the representation of Shylock as a devil intent on the apportionment of a Christian body is part of a tradition of anti-Semitic discourse in which Jews were said to be horned, tailed, and bearded like goats, to emit a distinct smell, and to be the source of leprosy and syphilis. According to this discourse, Jewish men, unlike Christian men, shared the mark of women's sexual difference: menstruation,[20] a feminizing trait that would effectively erase the patriarchal authority inscribed literally and figuratively on Jewish men. The male Jew incarnated the power of naming attributed to all men: this power became particularly threatening in a Jewish man because in placing his name on a Christian woman, and thus on future generations, he embodied the danger of the annihilating, consuming other.

For Shapiro, Christian obsession with circumcision and with the sacred covenant it symbolizes "shapes the final confrontation between Shylock and Antonio": thus Antonio's demand that Shylock "presently become a Christian" "metaphorically uncircumcise[s] him" (130).[21] The new covenant, represented by symbolic circumcision of the heart, supersedes the old, thus resolving the troubled relation between physical attributes and social identity through baptism.[22] As critics have noted, Shylock's conversion occurs only after the play ends, and it is cast as an act of submission on his part—"I pray you give me leave to go from hence, / I am not well. Send the deed after me, / And I will sign it" (4.1.395-97)—a portrayal that weakens the representative power of the transformation. In contrast, Jessica is to be incorporated into Venetian society because she has been excluded from the practice of circumcision. According to Shapiro, this exclusion "helps explain why Jewish daughters like Jessica in *The Merchant of Venice* and Abigail in *The Jew of Malta* can so easily cross the religious boundaries that divide their stigmatized fathers from the dominant Christian communities. The religious difference of women is not usually imagined as physically inscribed in their flesh" (120). But as I have argued, female difference was inscribed in the flesh not only by religious discourse but also by ideologies and emerging notions of race and nationality, which converged to define the "proper" English person.

From this perspective, the unsettling effect of Shylock's forced conversion can also be traced to the tension in Foxe's writing between the notion of free will implicit in baptism and the drive to delimit and thus control the oppositional other implicit in Christian imperialism. Like Othello, Shylock inspires feeling about his fate only insofar as he is capable of choosing Christian "goodness." Moreover, Shylock's malevolence depends on the shifting inscription of Jessica as racial Jew and freely choosing Christian. Jessica's incorporation into Christian society is essential to defining her father's alien status. Indeed, her nature in act 5 may be said to offer something of a reverse image of her father's in his final scenes: represented initially as her father's daughter, ruing her rebellion but longing for salvation through subordination in Christian marriage, she becomes the cool wit who seeks to "outnight" Lorenzo, trades the tokens of her mother's love for a monkey, and gains the trust of Portia in her plot against Bassanio (5.1.23). Shylock, by contrast, evolves from the resistant other to the raging and then nearly silent Jew of the fourth act and finally to a converted but unwilling, powerful yet alien figure, the image of the other against which English identity could be inscribed as white and Christian.

Still, such distinctions between Shylock and Jessica are perhaps too easy. As Lorenzo's attempt to claim the perceptual difference of Jessica's fairness makes clear, the logical incompatibility of the play's representations of Jews is impossible to sustain and requires endless permutations. Consequently, the Jessica of act 5 *may* be read not as an alternative and fully integrated Jew but as a homeless figure that suggests the dangers of consummating a relationship across such differences. In this reading she becomes an emblem of postcoital regret, ruing not her rebellion against patriarchal authority but the terms of her new commitment to it and the meager possibilities for unalienated pleasure they provide. In act 5, both Jessica and Lorenzo look to the past to make sense of their relationship. Further, the relationships with which they allegorize and thus make sense of their own all end tragically because of confusion and conflicting aims: Troilus and Cressida, Pyramus and Thisbe, Aeneas and Dido, Jason and Medea. Then, as if to illustrate and thus anticipate the potential for tragedy in their own union, Jessica and Lorenzo offer individual memories of the fateful night of their elopement. "In such a night / Did Jessica steal from a wealthy Jew, / And with an unthrift love did run from Venice, / As far as Belmont" (5.1.14-17), says Lorenzo, using metaphors of wealth, poverty, and thievery to underscore Jessica's betrayal of her father and the loss of security their mutual commitments guaranteed her. Playful or bitter, Jessica's version of the night hints at the difficulty of establishing trust between persons of different religions, colors, classes, and especially genders that is played up in the rest of act 5: "In such a night / Did young Lorenzo swear he lov'd her well, / Stealing her soul with many vows of faith, / And n'er a true one" (5.1.17-20).

These two distinct readings of the final act of *The Merchant* are both predicated on the idea that Jessica's difference—from her father and from the Christian characters—is crucial to the play's meaning. As the excluded other whose resistance to the truth of Jesus serves to delineate the essential, impermeable nature of the Christian story, the converted Jew could function to guarantee simultaneously both the promise of freedom implicit in baptism and the incontrovertible difference of white, Christian, and, by analogy turned equation, English forms of being. Indeed, only by taking Shylock's measure in the light of his daughter's difference—a difference that combines shifting representations of gender, color, class, and religion—is it possible to account for the play's inscription of contradictory notions of Jews. If *The Merchant*'s representation of Jews continues to haunt us—as the numbers of productions and critical responses to the play suggest it will and the survival of its racial discourse in contemporary politics suggests it should—we may get closer to the meaning of such ghosts by examining more closely the nature of their differences.

*Notes*

I am grateful to Janet Adelman, Michael Galchinsky, and Bruce Goebel, who read this essay at significant stages in its development and offered that combination of enthusiasm and critical insight we value in the best of colleagues and teachers.

[1] Tubal is the only character other than Shylock described as "a Jew" in the dramatis personae. He is also Shylock's only friend and the source of the funds that guarantee Shylock's bond. Although Tubal is certainly worthy of study, I focus here on the play's major characters.

[2] I use the term *integration* to refer to the acceptance of (forcibly or willingly) converted Jews by English Christians rather than *assimilation,* which in modern usage implies the freedom to continue practicing Judaism, an option unavailable to Jews in Shakespeare's England.

[3] Compare, for example, the work of McKewin; Boose, "Comic Contract"; Leventen; and Newman, "Portia's Ring" with that of Whigham; S. Cohen; Moisan; W. Cohen; Oz; and Ferber. Though there are differences in the ways each group of critics sidesteps the issues raised by the intersection of gender, race, and class, Newman and Ferber both illustrate the problems such critical choices raise. Each addresses the issue in a footnote. Newman states that she has "chosen deliberately to leave Shylock out of [her] reading . . . to disturb readings of the play that center their interpretive gestures on the Jew." She "recognize[s] the suggestive possibilities, however, of readings . . . which link Shylock and Portia as outsiders by virtue respectively of their race and sex" ("Portia's Ring" 19). Ferber declares, "A fuller treatment of ideology than is possible here would take up 'male ideology' from a feminist standpoint. I omit it here because I think the issue of the status or rights of women is not foregrounded in the play, and the peculiarly male way of doing things is only passingly and obliquely indicated" (460). Both comments appear to acknowledge the importance of the critical claims they choose to ignore, then contradict their initial claims. Newman leaves Shylock out because he has somehow enabled readings that fail to account for the play's women, but her reference to other "possibilities" suggests that elision of Shylock's "race" in favor of his gender, which is implicit in her reasoning, is problematic. Jessica, who is a woman and a Jew, is not mentioned at all. Ferber's claims are manifestly absurd given the importance the play assigns to marriage and gender roles, such as father, daughter, brother, husband, and wife. When considered at all, Jessica is often presented solely as a contrast to Portia's image of filial feminine duty: "where Portia gives, Jessica takes; where Portia accepts constraints, Jessica rebels" (Leventen 62).

[4] See, e.g., Boose ("Getting") and Callaghan, who argue for "the inherent interrelatedness" of categories of difference and its importance for any interpretation of Jews in *The Merchant* (Callaghan 170). Still, neither explains what a reconsideration of the terms *race* and *Jew* might mean for reading Shakespeare.

[5] There is an important distinction between racism as an identifiable mode of twentieth-century thought and the racialist roots of this ideology in early modern culture. Others have made the same distinction (see Neill; Bartels; Boose, "Getting"; Erickson).

[6] Foxe's attitude toward Jews seems to take a turn for the worse after the 1563 edition. While in that edition Jews frequently serve to point up the errors of Catholics (see, e.g., "Jewe's Reasoning with Master Wysehart" [NNiir]), in the 1570 edition Jews appear most often as ridiculous and deserving targets of violence, willing victims like the "Jewe fallen into a privey [who] would not be taken out for kyping hys Sabboth day" (Nir).

[7] See, e.g., Greenblatt, "Marlowe," and Ferber. On the historical presence of Jews in England, see Katz, *History* and *Philosemitism;* Rabb; Gwyer; Wolf; Roth; Samuel; Hyamson; Prior; Shapiro. Others who attempt to account for the representation of human difference in early modern Europe include Bartels; Mullaney; Pratt; Hulme; Brown; Said; Greenblatt, *Marvelous Possessions;* Erickson.

[8] Hotine cites the publication in 1594 and possibly early 1595 of the popular account of Lopez's trial, *A True Report of Sundry Horrible Conspiracies to Have Taken Away the Life of the Queenes Majestie,* which along with Marlowe's *Jew of Malta* documents the popular taste for anti-Semitic representations that preceded Shakespeare's *Merchant.* See Hotine for a useful chronology of the revival of Marlowe's *Malta* that preceded and followed Lopez's trial in 1594; the play was revived yet again in early 1596 the year in which it is generally agreed Shakespeare wrote *The Merchant.* More recently, David Katz, the foremost historian of English Jews, has argued that "Lopez, the model for Shylock, had far greater influence in the long run on moulding public views and prejudices about the Jews than the worthy efforts of all the English Rabbis put together" (*History* ix). Katz argues for Lopez's guilt. For a competing interpretation of the case against Lopez, see Gwyer.

[9] For more on Gaunse, see Feuer; Abrahams; Shapiro.

[10] For the story of Frere and Leavis, see Sisson.

[11] A 1578 adaptation of the biblical narrative of Ham and his sons by George Best, an English traveler, is a possible source for Jessica's reference to Chus. See Hakluyt for Best's complete text. For useful discussions of Best's representations of race, see Newman, "Ethiop" 78-82; Boose, "Getting" 43-48; Hall, *Things* 11-15.

[12] For more on the influence of Lopez, see Katz, *History.*

[13] The term *deserving* is used in a 1656 document in which a committee of the Council of State argues

for the readmission of Jews to England. For a copy of the document, see Samuel.

[14] For studies of the representation of the Jew in medieval and early modern European culture, see Trachtenberg; Poliakov; Edwards; Baron; Yardeni; Felsenstein; Shapiro. Tractenberg suggests that the equation of Jews with devils was the product of Christian legends in which "the inexorable enemies of Jesus . . . were the devil and the Jew." "It was inevitable," he argues, "that the legend should establish a causal relation between them" (20). Shapiro claims that "by the late sixteenth century the widespread medieval identification of Jews and the devil had virtually disappeared in England" (33), yet he locates the medieval myth of abduction and ritual murder in Shylock's desire to feast on his Christian enemies (110).

[15] On patriarchalism in early modern England, see Schochet; Ezell.

[16] On marriage without parental consent during the sixteenth century, see Ingram.

[17] Kyngesmill's text takes up the topic under the heading "Certain places of Scripture touchyng ungodly matchyng in Mariage" and focuses on marriage to "women of a wicked kinred and Religion." Such marriages are inadvisable, he argues, because unbelieving wives don't properly fear and submit to their husbands and thus "overruleth the beleevyng husbande and causeth hym to make a plaine shipwracke of faith . . ." (4iiv).

[18] On early modern constructions of the term *fair*, see Hall, *Things* and "Black-Moor."

[19] Shylock's distaste for Christians is based on the historical practice of ritual separateness. As Johnson explains in his history of the Jews, "Circumcision set [Jews] apart and was regarded by the Greco-Roman world as barbarous and distasteful. But at least circumcision did not prevent social intercourse. The ancient Jewish laws of diet and cleanliness did" (133-34). Thus, Shylock's declaration "I will buy with you, sell with you, talk with you, walk with you, and so following; but I will not eat with you, drink with you nor pray with you" (1.3.33-35) can be read as evidence that Shakespeare's knowledge of Jewish practice and perspective went beyond stereotypes.

[20] Poliakov claims that Christians believed in Jewish male menses; he cites late-fifteenth-century documents concerned with Jewish ritual murder (143). Foa discusses how sixteenth-and seventeenth-century beliefs in a Jewish cause of syphilis were related to the discourse of sexual difference long applied to women. In a study of the nineteenth-century British equation of usury and prostitution, Gilman documents the continuity of the practice of feminizing male Jews (cf. Gallagher).

[21] Shapiro argues for a relation between circumcision—the ritual reenactment of God's covenant with Abraham—and Christian fears of castration and death in early modern England.

[22] As Shapiro explains, Paul's letter to the Romans attempts to promote symbolic circumcision of the heart without condemning the trimming of the foreskin. Shapiro argues convincingly that the shift in *The Merchant*'s representation of the terms of Shylock's bond, from "fair flesh, to be cut off and taken / In what part of your body pleaseth me" (1.3.150-51) to "A pound of flesh, to be by him cut off / Nearest the merchant's heart" (4.1.232-33) involves a "double displacement" of Paul's text: "For circumcision verily profiteth, if thou keep the law: but if thou be a breaker of the law, thy circumcision is made uncircumcision" (Rom. 2.25). Thus, Shapiro continues, "Shylock will cut his Christian adversary in that part of the body where the Christians believe themselves to be truly circumcised: the heart" (127). The heart takes the place of the penis, the spirit the place of the letter. However, as Shapiro notes, such a displacement depends on a distinction between the symbolic and the literal, between the spirit and the flesh, that Paul's text does not sustain. Paul's terms conflate the categories by begging the question of interpreting God's law. Instead of solving the problem of Jewish and Christian identity, Paul's concern with circumcision becomes a touchstone for obsessions about the relation between physical attributes and social identity.

*Works Cited*

Abrahams, Israel. "Joachim Gaunse: A Mining Incident in the Reign of Queen Elizabeth." *Transactions of the Jewish Historical Society of England* 4 (1899-1901): 83-101.

*Acts of the Privy Council.* Vol. 26 (1596-97). Ed. John Roche Dasent. London: HMSO, 1902.

Adelman, Janet. *Suffocating Mothers: Fantasies of Maternal Origin in Shakespeare's Plays,* Hamlet *to* The Tempest. New York: Routledge, 1992.

Baron, Salo Wittmayer, ed. *A Social and Religious History of the Jews.* 2nd ed. Vol. 4. New York: Columbia UP, 1957.

Bartels, Emily C. *Spectacles of Strangeness: Imperialism, Alienation, and Marlowe.* Philadelphia: U of Pennsylvania P, 1993.

Barthelemy, Anthony. *Black Face, Maligned Race: The Representation of Blacks in English Drama from Shakespeare to Southerne.* Baton Rouge: U of Louisiana P, 1987.

Boose, Lynda E. "The Comic Contract and Portia's Golden Ring." *Shakespeare Studies* 20 (1987): 241-54.

———. "'The Getting of a Lawful Race': Racial Discourse in Early Modern England and the Unrepresentable Black Woman." Hendricks and Parker 35-54.

Brown, Paul. "'This Thing of Darkness I Acknowledge Mine': *The Tempest* and the Discourse of Colonialism." *Political Shakespeare: New Essays in Cultural Materialism*. Ed. Jonathan Dollimore and Alan Sinfield. Ithaca: Cornell UP, 1985. 48-71.

Callaghan, Dympna. "Re-reading Elizabeth Cary's *The Tragedy of Miriam, Faire Queene of Jewry*." Hendricks and Parker 163-77.

Cohen, Stephen. "'Is This the Law?': Legal Ambiguity and Its Effects in *The Merchant of Venice* and *Measure for Measure*." *The Language of Power, the Power of Language: The Effects of Ambiguity on Sociopolitical Structures As Illustrated in Shakespeare's Plays*. Cambridge: Harvard UP, 1987. 80-118.

Cohen, Walter. "*The Merchant of Venice* and the Possibilities of Historical Criticism." *ELH* 49 (1982): 765-89.

Edwards, John, ed. *The Jews in Christian Europe, 1400-1700*. New York: Routledge, 1988.

Erickson, Peter. "Representations of Blacks and Blackness in the Renaissance." *Criticism* 35 (1993): 499-527.

Ezell, Margaret. *The Patriarch's Wife*. Chapel Hill: U of North Carolina P, 1987.

Felsenstein, Frank. "Jews and Devils: Anti-Semitic Stereotypes of Late Medieval and Renaissance England." *Journal of Literature and Theology* 4.1 (1990): 15-28.

Ferber, Michael. "The Ideology of *The Merchant of Venice*." *English Literary Renaissance* 20.3 (1990): 431-64.

Feuer, Lewis S. "Francis Bacon and the Jews: Who Was the Jew in the *New Atlantis?*" *Transactions of the Jewish Historical Society of England* 29 (1988): 1-25.

Foa, Anna. "The New and the Old: The Spread of Syphilis (1494-1530)." *Sex and Gender in Historical Perspective*. Ed. Edward Muir and Guido Ruggiero. Trans. Margaret A. Galluci with Mary M. Galluci and Carole C. Galluci. Baltimore: Johns Hopkins UP, 1990. 26-45.

Foxe, John. *Actes and Monuments*. London, 1563. Rev. ed. 1570.

Friedman, Jerome. "Jewish Conversion, the Spanish Pure Blood Laws and Reformation: A Revisionist View of Racial and Religious Antisemitism." *Sixteenth Century Journal* 18 (1987): 3-29.

Gallagher, Catherine. "George Eliot and Daniel Deronda: The Prostitute and the Jewish Question." *Sex, Politics, and Science in the Nineteenth-Century Novel*. Ed. Ruth Bernard Yeazell. Baltimore: Johns Hopkins UP, 1986. 39-62.

Gerber, Jane S. *The Jews of Spain: A History of the Sephardic Experience*. New York: Free, 1992.

Gibbon, Charles. *How to Bestow Children in Marriage*. London, 1591.

Gilman, Sander. *The Jew's Body*. New York: Routledge, 1991.

Greenblatt, Stephen. "Marlowe, Marx, and Anti-Semitism." *Learning to Curse: Essays in Early Modern Culture*. New York: Routledge, 1990. 40-58.

———. *Marvelous Possessions: The Wonder of the New World*. Chicago: U of Chicago P, 1991.

Gwyer, John. "The Case of Dr. Lopez." *Transactions of the Jewish Historical Society of England* 16 (1952): 163-84.

Hakluyt, R. *The Principal Navigations, Voyages Traffiques, and Discoveries of the English Nation*. Ed. Walter Raleigh. London, 1600.

Hall, Kim F. "Guess Who's Coming to Dinner? Colonization and Miscegenation in *The Merchant of Venice*." *Renaissance Drama* 23 (1992): 87-111.

———. "I Rather Would Wish to Be a Black-Moor: Beauty, Race and Rank in Lady Mary Wroth's *Urania*." Hendricks and Parker 178-94.

———. *Things of Darkness: Economies of Race and Gender in Early Modern England*. Ithaca: Cornell UP, 1995.

Hendricks, Margo, and Patricia Parker, eds. *Women, "Race," and Writing in the Early Modern Period*. New York: Routledge, 1994.

Hotine, Margaret. "The Politics of Anti-Semitism: *The Jew of Malta* and *The Merchant of Venice*." *Notes and Queries* 38.1 (1991): 35-38.

Hulme, Peter. *Colonial Encounters: Europe and the Native Caribbean, 1492-1797*. London, Methuen, 1986.

Hunter, G. K. "The Theology of Marlowe's *The Jew of Malta*." *Journal of the Warburg and Courtauld Institutes* 27 (1964): 211-40.

Hyamson, Albert. *The Sephardim of England.* London: Methuen, 1951.

Ingram, Martin. *Church Courts, Sex, and Marriage in England, 1570-1640.* London: Cambridge UP, 1997.

Johnson, Paul. *A History of the Jews.* New York: Harper, 1987.

Katz, David S. *Jews in the History of England.* Oxford: Oxford UP, 1994.

———. *Philosemitism and the Readmission of the Jews to England.* Oxford: Oxford UP, 1982.

Kyngesmill, Andrewe. "Godly Advise Touchyng Mariage." *A View of Man's Estate.* London, 1580. Jiv-L8v.

Lawrence, Normand. "Reading the Body in *The Merchant of Venice*." *Textual Practice* 5 (1991): 55-73.

Leventen, Carol. "Patrimony and Patriarchy in *The Merchant of Venice*." *The Matter of Difference: Materialist Feminist Criticism of Shakespeare.* Ed. Valerie Wayne. Ithaca: Cornell UP, 1991. 59-79.

McKewin, Carole. "Counsels of Gall and Grace: Intimate Conversations between Women in Shakespeare's Plays." *The Woman's Part: Feminist Criticism of Shakespeare.* Ed. Carol Ruth Swift Lenz, Gayle Greene, and Carol Thomas Neely. Chicago: U of Illinois P, 1980. 117-32.

Moisan, Thomas. " 'Which Is the Merchant Here? And Which the Jew?': Subversion and Recuperation in *The Merchant of Venice*." *Shakespeare Reproduced: The Text in History and Ideology.* Ed. Jean E. Howard, Marion F. O'Connor, and Margaret Ferguson. New York: Methuen, 1987. 188-206.

Mullaney, Steven. *The Place of the Stage: License, Play, and Power in Renaissance England.* Chicago: U of Chicago P, 1988.

Neely, Carol Thomas. "Circumscriptions and Unhousedness: *Othello* in the Borderlands." *Shakespeare and Gender: A History.* Ed. Deborah Barker and Ivo Kamp. New York: Verso, 1995. 302-15.

Neill, Michael. "Unproper Beds: Race, Adultery, and the Hideous in *Othello*." *Shakespeare Quarterly* 40 (1989): 383-412.

Netanyahu, B. *The Origins of the Inquisition in Fifteenth Century Spain.* New York: Random, 1995.

Newman, Karen. " 'And Wash the Ethiop White': Femininity and the Monstrous in *Othello*." *Fashioning Femininity and Renaissance Drama.* Chicago: U of Chicago P, 1991. 79-93.

———. "Portia's Ring: Unruly Women and Structures of Exchange in *The Merchant of Venice*." *Shakespeare Quarterly* 38 (1987): 19-33.

Oz, Avraham. " 'Which Is the Merchant Here? And Which the Jew?': Riddles of Identity in *The Merchant of Venice*." *Shakespeare and Cultural Traditions: Selected Proceedings of the International Shakespeare Association World Congress, Tokyo, 1991.* Ed. K. Tetsuo, R. Pringle, and S. Wells. Newark: U of Delaware P, 1994. 155-73.

Poliakov, Leon. *The History of Anti-Semitism.* Vol. 1. Trans. Richard Howard. New York: Vanguard, 1965.

Pratt, Mary Louise. "Scratches on the Face of the Country; or, What Mr. Barrow Saw in the Land of the Bushmen." *Critical Inquiry* 12 (1985): 119-43.

Prior, Roger. "A Second Jewish Community in Tudor London." *Transactions of the Jewish Historical Society of England* 31 (1990): 137-52.

Rabb, Theodore K. "The Stirrings of the 1590s and the Return of the Jews to England." *Transactions of the Jewish Historical Society of England* 26 (1979): 26-33.

Roth, Cecil. *A History of the Jews in England.* Oxford: Oxford UP, 1964.

Said, Edward. *Orientalism.* London: Routledge, 1978.

Samuel, Edgar. "The Readmission of the Jews to England in 1656, in the Context of English Economic Policy." *Transactions of the Jewish Historical Society of England* 31 (1990): 153-70.

Schochet, Gordon. *The Authoritarian Family and Political Attitudes in Seventeenth-Century England: Patriarchalism in Political Thought.* New Brunswick: Transaction, 1988.

Shakespeare, William. *The Merchant of Venice. The Riverside Shakespeare.* Ed. G. Blakemore Evans. New York: Houghton, 1974. 254-85.

Shapiro, James. *Shakespeare and the Jews.* New York: Columbia UP, 1996.

Sisson, C. J. "A Colony of Jews in Shakespeare's London." *Essays and Studies* 23 (1938): 38-51.

Trachtenberg, Joshua. *The Devil and Jews: The Medieval Conception of the Jew and Its Relation to Modern Anti-semitism.* New Haven: Yale UP, 1943.

Whigham, Frank. "Ideology and Class Conduct in *The Merchant of Venice*." *Renaissance Drama* 10 (1979): 93-115.

Wolf, Lucien. "Jews in Elizabethan England." *Transactions of the Jewish Historical Society of England* 11 (1924-27): 1-91.

Yardeni, Myriam. *Anti-Jewish Mentalities in Early Modern Europe.* New York: UP of America, 1990.

---

Source: " 'Now by My Hood, a Gentle and No Jew': Jessica, *The Merchant of Venice,* and the Discourse of Early Modern English Identity," in *PMLA,* Vol. 113, No. 1, January, 1998, pp. 52-63.

# Motive and Meaning in *All's Well That Ends Well*

## Ruth Nevo, *Hebrew University of Jerusalem*

*All's Well That Ends Well* has been classified among the problem comedies, perhaps mainly because Bertram has failed to captivate; he has been found even more devoid of charm than Angelo in *Measure for Measure,* the companion "problem" comedy. Bertram is, as my students invariably inform me, a creep. And in this they have the critics on their side: that he is "a thoroughly disagreeable, peevish and vicious person" (Lawrence 1931, 61) seems to be the consensus. One is hard put to it, indeed, to think of a fictional character less popular than the young Count of Rossillion. Yet Helena has come in for her share of criticism too. She is forward, obstinate, manipulative, opportunistic. She does not heal the King out of patriotic fervor but because she has an eye for the main chance. And so on. To rebellious, feminist Katherine Mansfield,

> Helena is a terrifying female. Her virtue, her persistence, her pegging away after the odious Bertram (and disguised as a pilgrim—so typical!) and then telling the whole story to that good widow-woman! And that tame fish Diana. As to lying in Diana's and enjoying the embraces meant for Diana—well, I know nothing more sickening. It would take a respectable woman to do such a thing. The worst of it is I can so well imagine ... acting in precisely that way, and giving Diana a present afterwards.... But to forgive such a woman! Yet Bertram would. There's an espece of mothersboyisme in him which makes him stupid enough for anything. (Mansfield 1927, 274)

Critics who, on the other hand, fall in love with Helena—Coleridge, it will be recalled, found her "Shakespeare's loveliest character" (Raysor 1970, 2:113)—attempt desperately, for her sake, to exculpate Bertram of at least the worst of his lies and infidelities. Those who scold her for being a shameless hussy forcing himself (twice!) upon an unwilling partner feel that a thoroughly unattractive couple, evidently conceived by Shakespeare "in a time of illness or mental disturbance" (Nicoll 1952, 116) get, in each other, no more than they deserve.

On the face of it, and considered in terms of the modular properties it shares with the festive comedies and their New Comedy paradigms, *All's Well* would not seem to be in line for presenting a problem at all. It possesses, conspicuously, many of the features of its distinguished predecessors. It has a resourceful heroine; an autocratic father-figure to be eluded or outwitted; true love which doesn't run smooth; a comic device involving mistaken identities which through its deception reveals a truth; a wonderful fop who is resoundingly exposed; and a fool whose ribaldries provide a low-life counterpoint to the concerns of his betters. And there is a final matchmaking that puts the recalcitrant young man firmly in his place in the scheme of things by making an honest father of him. To make of it a problem because its male protagonist is a callow youth and its female protagonist determinedly in pursuit of her man (which of the comic heroines, save Beatrice, is not?) is surely nonsense as criticism, reducing our expectation of a Shakespearean play to the level of a tabloid magazine.

Yet generic uneasiness, a sense of generic impropriety, remains. The paradigm ground plan outlines as many problems as it sets out to skirt. For the play seems to break as many rules as it keeps. It starts, not with young men and women in search of a mate but with the death of a father, two fathers indeed, and with mourning. A foster-father is at once provided, but instead of constituting the obstacle to a match desired by the young he positively forces a marriage upon his resistant foster-son. Instead of the canonical *senex* of the Terentian New Comedy formula, whose law or writ or interference with young lovers must be overcome or evaded, we have a blocking son. This too is a clash between a father, or father figure, and a son, but upside down, as it were. Similarly topsy-turvy, the young woman, enterprising and triumphant trickster-heroine of the earlier comedies, is a victim-bride (like her single precursor, Hero) who must be done to death before resolutions can be found, and she plays the role of therapeutic, even thaumaturgic, quasi daughter to the King which becomes canonical for daughters only in the later romances.

Then again, though it looks like a courtship comedy, it is one which is constrained to get along without courtship, since the young man takes flight to the Italian wars, and the young woman follows him to Italy, but not, as previous comedies might have led one to anticipate, in page disguise. One has only to imagine Helena in pursuit of her Bertram in page disguise, with the opportunities thus offered for masked witty courtship, for a playful battle of the sexes in which a balance, for both sexes, between pursuit and defense, winning and losing, is articulated, to see that this device might well have transformed *All's Well* into the supreme successor to *Two Gentlemen of Verona, As You Like It,* and *Twelfth Night.* I make the point not because one would expect or wish a dramatist simply to go on repeating his inventions, but to throw into prominence the peculiar distribution of differences with which we are presented in *All's Well*. For what we have instead of the page disguise is the pilgrim disguise and the bed-trick, a mock death and a trick consummation. And the bed-trick notoriously pleases no one. On the contrary, it crystallizes the general sense of impropriety, and throws into relief the split in critical opinion concerning Helena: saint or strumpet, and the near-unanimous critical repudiation of Bertram, tricker tricked, but not, it is felt, thereby improved.

For all these reasons the festive end is felt to be a flop, or a merely mechanical or superficial closure. And it lacks the grand harmonic completion the festive comedies have accustomed us to. The King, cured of his wasting disease in act 1, and "of as able body as when he number'd thirty" (*All's Well,* 4.5.77-78), remains unmatched, though the widowed Countess, it would seem, is an available and ideally suitable partner for her. "You shall find of the king a husband," says Lafew, incorrigible matchmaker, already in line 6 of act 1, but that carefully planted option is not taken up. Nor is a mate found for the virtuous and good-hearted Diana. There is even another unmarried young woman, possibly jilted, in the wings at the play's end. The play provides all the constituents for a grand celebratory wedding closure in which "individual fulfillment, marital intimacy and communal renewal are celebrated" (Wheeler 1981, 3), but it is felt to be a question whether there are any truly festive marriages at all, or rather quite the contrary: a disillusioned rendering (for good or ill—some will praise the absence of illusion) of a cynical and sterile world. *All's Well,* it is generally agreed, has no commanding center, does not integrate its realism (which is usually admitted to be of a power and veracity equal to Shakespeare's peak period) either with its folklore motifs—the Healing of the King, the Clever Wench, the Fulfillment of the Tasks[1]—or with conventional expectations, and produces an effect of unease and confusion.[2] *All's Well* is unable, it seems to make up its generic mind. It is neither fish, flesh, nor good red herring; neither comedy, tragedy, nor romance.

I would like to submit that *All's Well,* so far from having to be apologized for, can be seen as a particularly interesting successor to the festive or, as it might be better to call them, the maturation comedies; that the critics' problems are often reflections of their own unaware masculine or feminine identifications, embodying defenses and resistances which themselves repeat the conflicts dramatized in the play; and that therefore, the better to understand both critics and play, we must attempt to read, as we say, between the lines, and to hear with a third ear. The space between the lines is the psychic space of evocation and resonance shared by both audience and dramatis personae. It is the space of precipitation by the text into consciousness of the normally unconscious. It is there that we can find what Peter Brooks calls the "complex history of unconscious desire, unavailable to the conscious subject but at work in the text" (Brooks 1980, 516). This, "the self's other story," is what we must set out to discover if we wish to do justice to the drama enacted in *All's Well* and to see as significant the anomalies just mentioned. The complaint, for example, of the Arden editor that the play lacks a "central, acceptable, and unified viewpoint" to define its values, and to integrate its incompatibilities (p. xxxv), acquires a different kind of truth when we perceive that *All's Well* places itself at a node where three dreams cross: the dream of the elders, reliving their lives through their children; the dream of the young man escaping parental domination; and the dream of the young woman desiring a child and a father. And these dreams neither coincide nor harmonize.

In *All's Well,* still in outline and plan a courtship comedy, parents have become, if not central as in the romances, at least not completely instrumental. The point of view is predominantly of the young, but since the parents, with their own problems of aging, of holding on, and letting go, are not mere obstacle figures, their point of view is operative too. They exist within the play both in their own right, and as their wills, desires, fantasies, and memories intermesh with those of the younger generation. This intermesh is a feature neither of the festive comedies nor of the romances, and it is what gives to *All's Well* its peculiar richness and density.

If there is a problem in this text, it is to be found in the unfinished business—unresolved tensions or repressed fears and desires that every play, every text, leaves in its wake to motivate the writing of the works to follow. But so far as its comic project is concerned, it quite triumphantly contains, while it also reveals, its potentially explosive and painful material.

Comedy, Chaplin once said, "is at its best when it flirts with death, plays with it, mocks it, pokes its nose into it." If there is validity in the view that comedy is the mode of drama which defers, denies, evades, or overcomes death, then one can see the play's opening not as an abrogation of comic conditions, but as a foregrounding of them. The deaths of the two fathers are undone by the adoption of Bertram and of Helena by the King and Countess respectively. The initial mourning, already past as the play begins, suggests precisely such a denial, renewal, or overcoming. But if death is thus vigorously defended against at the very start, its shadow remains to haunt the play. If we listen, as perhaps we always should, with half-closed eyes to the verbal texture of the opening scenes, we become aware of major themes that are the older generation's: nostalgia, the vulnerable body, the dereliction of time, impotence. "In delivering my son from me," says the Countess, "I bury a second husband" (*All's Well,* 1.1.1). The King's disease—that mysterious fistula—is immediately introduced, together with the wishful fantasy of his restoration to youthful fitness. A strangely skeletal image—"virtue's steely bones

/ Looks bleak i' th' cold wind' (1.1.101-2)—appears in Helena's defense of Parolles; the consequences she envisages should her gamble for Bertram fail are vividly imagined: "Let the white death sit on thy cheek for ever" (2.3.71). Parolles' adjurations on the subject of virginity not unexpectedly turn the age-old carpe diem theme into a very explicit memento mori: "Your date is better in your pie and your porridge than in your cheek; and your virginity, your old virginity, is like one of our French wither'd pears: it looks ill, it eats drily; marry, 'tis a wither'd pear" (1.1.154-59).

The peculiar anxiety the play's body language expresses lies in a vacillation between images of desire and of decrepitude. The passionate Helena, who has loved (though it was "a plague" to do so) "To see him every hour; to sit and draw / His arched brows, his hawking eye, his curls" (1.1.91-92), who longs to "feed [her] eye . . . / To join like likes, and kiss like native things" (1.1.217, 219) grieves that "wishing well had not a body in't / Which might be felt" (1.1.177-78). This vehemence is curiously echoed by Bertram, newly wed and in flight, as he parts from one of his new companions: "I grow to you, and our parting is a tortur'd body" (2.1.36). We have the unvarnished plain speaking of Lavatch (of Touchstone's ilk) to drive the point home, as he seeks permission to marry his Isbel: "My poor body, madam, requires it; I am driven on by the flesh, and he must needs go that the devil drives"; "Service is no heritage, and I think I shall never have the blessing of God till I have issue a' my body; for they say barnes are blessings" (1.3.26-28, 21-24). "Issue of the body" is the leitmotiv of the King's elegy for his own, and for his old friend's, youth:

> But on us both did haggish age steal on,
> And wore us out of act. . . .
> (1.2.29-30)
>
> Would I were with him! . . .
> "Let me not live", quoth he,
> "After my flame lacks oil, to be the snuff
> Of younger spirits, whose apprehensive senses
> All but new things disdain; whose judgments are
> Mere fathers of their garments. . . . "
>   This he wish'd.
> I, after him, do after him wish too,
> Since I nor wax nor honey can bring home.
> (1.2.52, 58-65)

"Oil" for his flame, "wax" or "honey" for the hive, suggest that the loss of sexual potency underlies the melancholy of this Fisher King. We note his resigned reply to the courtier's "You're loved, sir": "I fill a place, I know't" (1.2.67, 69). The lewd Lafew leaves no room for doubt about the nature of the King's disease, or at least its symptomatic manifestation. He himself refers to his task—the bringing of the physician's daughter to her royal patient—as a pandar's role: "I am Cressid's uncle / That dare leave two together" (2.1.96-97); describes what "Doctor she" will achieve in language which barely cloaks its sexuality; and takes a salacious pleasure in persuading the melancholy King to attempt the cure:

> O, will you eat
> No grapes, my royal fox? Yes, but you will
> My noble grapes, and if my royal fox
> Could reach them. I have seen a medicine
> That's able to breathe life into a stone,
> Quicken a rock, and make you dance canary
> With spritely fire and motion; whose simple touch
> Is powerful to araise King Pippen, nay,
> To give great Charlemain a pen in hand
> And write to her a love-line.
> (2.1.68-77)[3]

It is precisely the King's virility that Helena restores. After his recovery, he is "lustique" enough to lead his "preserver" in a coranto (2.3.41). "Your dolphin is not lustier," Lafew informs us (2.3.26). This restoration by the daughter of his old friend is the magic fulfillment of a wishful fantasy; but it also provides the King with—what? a surrogate daughter as well as a surrogate son? An Avishag for his declining years? A greater warmth, perhaps, than one would feel for one's physician is to be caught in the King's resolve to become her patient: "more to know could not be more to trust" (2.1.205). His violent repudiation of the recalcitrant Bertram, the transformation of "My son's no dearer" (1.2.76) into

> Check thy contempt;
> Obey our will. . . .
> Or I will throw thee from my care for ever
> Into the staggers and the careless lapse
> Of youth and ignorance; both my revenge and hate
> Loosing upon thee in the name of justice.
> Without all terms of pity
> (2.3.157-66)

is the provision of the tyrannical *senex* of New Comedy with a vengeance. But if he is, as we intuit, more than half in love, not any longer with easeful death, but with a young woman who promises rejuvenation, it is not difficult to understand the intensity, and the ambivalence, of his emotional investment in this match.

By the same token we recall the words of the widowed Countess, as the play opens with the dispatching of Bertram to Paris: "In delivering my son from me," says the Countess, "I bury a second husband." On the face of it, this is the patrician gesture of a dignified and courtly lady distancing with art a double sorrow. This second "birth" is a second death, she says. But in the rhetorical condensation may we not descry a telltale parapraxis? The Countess is in mourning for her husband; she is also, we perceive, rather more than half in love with her son.[4]

The Countess's second exchange with her fool, which follows Helena's confession and her departure for Paris, is similarly revealing. She is sending him off in Helena's wake to the King's court and is prepared, with good-natured irony, to indulge his scapegrace effrontery. On the whole she treats his scurrilities with much the same matronly indulgence as Olivia does Feste's, but the open sexuality of his bawdry this time, it seems, is provocative of more than cool irony. His "answer," he says, fits all questions "like a barber's chair that fits all buttocks" (2.2.16); is as fit

> as ten groats is for the hand of an attorney, as your French crown for your taffety punk, as Tib's rush for Tom's forefinger, as a pancake for Shrove Tuesday, a morris for Mayday, as the nail to his hole, the cuckold to his horn, as a scolding quean to a wrangling knave, as the nun's lip to the friar's mouth; nay, as the pudding to his skin. . . . From below your duke to beneath your constable it will fit any question.
>
> (2.2.20-30)

"It must be an answer of most monstrous size that must fit all demands," is the Countess's reply; and then suddenly, in the midst of the thrust of parry and repartee, comes a striking non sequitur: "To be young again, if we could" (2.2.37).

They are mourning their youth, this autumnal pair, it seems. And in consequence they are projecting upon their children (or their adopted children) their longing to relive their lives. It is no wonder that currents of ambivalence will crisscross this inverted family romance.

Read in this light the testing scene between the Countess and Helena becomes as iridescent as Helena's tears. The Countess receives the steward's confirmation of Helena's love for Bertram with an immediate, motherly empathy, shadowed, however, in its reference to "faults," by the hint of a jealous reservation:

> Even so it was with me when I was young; . . .
> this thorn
> Doth to our rose of youth rightly belong. . . .
> Such were our faults, or then we thought
>   them none.
>
> (1.3.123-25, 130)

The scene that follows is masterly in its representation of ambivalence, of simulation and dissimulation, between the two women, both contenders for Bertram's love. "You know, Helen, / I am a mother to you" (1.3.132-33) is the Countess's opening ploy, and it serves her purpose of eliciting response and testing intention excellently when Helena replies, with modestly disavowing emphasis, "Mine honourable *mistress*" (*my italics*):

> Nay, a mother.
> Why not a mother? When I said a "mother",
> Methought you saw a serpent. What's in
>   "mother"
> That you start at it? I say I am your mother,
> And put you in a catalogue of those
> That were enwombed mine. . . .
> You ne'er oppress'd me with a mother's
>   groan,
> Yet I express to you a mother's care.
> God's mercy, maiden! does it curd thy blood
> To say I am thy mother? what's the matter,
> That this distempered messenger of wet,
> The many colour'd Iris, rounds thine eye?
> —Why, that you are my daughter?
>
> (1.3.134-48)

The Countess exploits Helena's embarrassed feint—"The Count Rossillion cannot be my brother . . . must not be my brother" (1.3.150, 155) to point out that Helena as her daughter-in-law would solve the semantic problem, and she drives home her advantage:

> God shield you mean it not! daughter and
>   mother
> So strive upon your pulse. What! pale again?
> My fear hath catch'd your fondness; now I
>   see
> The myst'ry of your loneliness, and find
> Your salt tears' head. . . .
>     Speak, is't so?
> If it be so, you have wound a goodly clew.
>
> (1.3.163-67, 176-77)

She is playing the role of indignant matron that she has set herself. But in doing so, she is playing it out. The ambiguous irony of "you have wound a goodly clew" allows us to register simultaneously the angry resentment she is professing, and the compensatory acceptance she is working her way toward. Since she cannot have a husband in her son, she will identify with the girl who would be his wife, and so transform her love for Bertram into a double maternal solicitude. This is an admirable solution: it is indeed the way of women in Shakespearean comedy to resolve their inner conflicts more successfully, more benignly, than do the men.

At the end of the scene, Helena has the Countess's leave and love and approval for her project. But in order to understand Helena in the testing scene we must retrace our steps.

The predicament that is developed in act 1 of *All's Well* offers a powerful exemplification of Freud's observation upon family quadrangles. "I am accustoming myself," he wrote in a letter to Fleiss in 1899, "to regarding every sexual act as an event between four individuals." "Every sexual thought" perhaps he should have said. Much of interest emerges when we turn our attention to the Countess's foster daughter, also, like Bertram, in mourning for a father: "The remembrance of her father never approaches her heart but the tyranny of her sorrows takes all livelihood from her cheek" (1.1.45-47), we are told. We are immediately alerted by a scene curiously reminiscent of the opening scenes of *Hamlet* but with the sexes reversed. "I do affect a sorrow indeed, but I have it too" (1.2.50) is Helena's reply to the Countess's chiding: "No more of this, Helena; go to, no more; lest it be rather thought you affect a sorrow than to have—" (1.2.47-49). Helena, it seems, like Hamlet, has something to hide, something that presses for utterance and chafes at the need for dissimulation. Helena, like Hamlet, as we speedily learn, is "too much in the *son*":

> I think not on my father,
>
> And these great tears grace his remembrance more
> Than those I shed for him. What was he like?
> I have forgot him; my imagination
> Carries no favour in't but Bertram's.
>
> (1.1.77-81)

The lines are obscure, but possibly uncannily shrewd. To make sense of the antithesis we must read "remembrance" as a metonymy for "remains"—all that remains of her father is her memory of him. So: the great tears grace his memory more than those she shed at his funeral, tears shed "for *him*," (*my italics*) still, so to speak, present in the flesh. This is very condensed, more particularly since "grace" carries with it its subliminal contrary—"disgrace." Surely a considerable tinge of guilt colors Helena's acknowledgment of the displacement, in her passionate affection, of father by beloved. The denials, like most denials, are self-betraying. What the speech tells us is that she is very far from having forgotten her father; but that her love for Bertram has, quite literally, and not without guilt, taken the place of her love for her father, the one image overlaying the other. If so, it is no wonder that her love is perceived by her as unattainable, out of reach, never to be consummated. Yes, he is socially above her, and this provides the ostensible reason for her despair. But since nothing, we are told, is fortuitous in the world of the mind, Helena's choice of the object of her affections could be in accordance with a deeply ambivalent inner need. If it is her father she loves, and therefore a father that she seeks in the mate she chooses, the latter will be, for that very reason, impossible, untouchable, a forbidden *prince lointain*: "twere all one / That I should love a bright particular star / And think to wed it" (1.1.83-85).

We are offered a great deal more data for the fathoming of Helena's complex motivation in the dialogue with Bertram's friend, Parolles, whom she loves "for his sake" though she knows him for the liar, fool, and coward that he is. With Parolles she enjoys a relationship of ironic equality despite her lowly birth and his complacent patronizing. "Save you, fair queen" is his greeting, and her reply, "And you, monarch!" (1.1.104-5), shows, as does the flyting that concludes their conversation (1.1.187-200), that she can give as good as she gets in this power game. Helena is shrewd and self-reliant as the scene makes very clear: it ends with her bold resolve to seek the remedies that "in ourselves do lie" (1.1.212):

> Who ever strove
> To show her merit that did miss her love?
> The king's disease—my project may deceive me,
> But my intents are fix'd, and will not leave me.
>
> (1.1.222-25)

She is also preoccupied, as the scene makes clear, with the very subject Parolles, with preternaturally cunning complicity, has chosen for their conversation.

Parolles is a mine of information on the subject of virginity, which is the topic he first provocatively launches. Helena parries his provocation to good effect, but in the process of inquiring of Parolles, who should know, how one may "barricado it" against man the enemy, Helena also inquiries, "How might one do, sir, to lose it to her own liking?" (1.1.147). Parolles' diatribe against withered pears concludes with the challenge "Will you anything with it?" (1.1.159-60), and is followed by an elliptical speech from Helena, perhaps half to herself, which has proved no less a challenge to interpreters:

> Not my virginity; yet. . . .[5]
> There shall your master have a thousand loves,
> A mother, and a mistress, and a friend,
> A phoenix, captain, and an enemy,
> A guide, a goddess, and a sovereign,
> A counsellor, a traitress, and a dear.
>
> (1.1.161-66)

The ellipsis, a characteristic of Helena's which suggests a reflective inwardness, is open to a number of interpretations. Are we to hear an emphasis upon "my" virginity? Is the implied other virginity, if any is implied, Bertram's? Is "yet" temporal or concessive? Whatever is unspoken crystallizes finally upon what is evidently the dominant preoccupation—"your master": "There shall your master have a thousand loves." But where shall this take place? In Paris? Or in "my virginity," the immediate antecedent for the anaphoric "there"? However we read what follows, whether as an envious and ironic catalog of sonneteering epithets (a denigration of the loves Bertram will find in Paris) or as an ardent outdoing even of the chivalric passions of the sonneteers (and so a valorization of the love that she can offer), immediately after "a thousand loves" there occurs an oddity we can surely only interpret as another astonishing slip of the text. What follows is "a mother, and a mistress, and a friend." For while one has encountered fantastic, hyperbolic, even outrageous, epithets in High Renaissance sonnets, even the most assiduous reader of these confections will be hard put to it to recall a mother among them. No occurrence, the Arden editor assures us, is on record.

Why has this "mother" entered Helena's mind? Has she perceived the bond between the Countess and Bertram? And, seeking herself a father surrogate in her love, does her wise unconscious fear a contrary quest in Bertram? Or, on the contrary, is it her wish too to "mother" Bertram? These are the questions which resonate further in the testing scene between the Countess and Helena, which we will consider now from Helena's point of view.

The Countess's outburst:

> does it curd thy blood
> To say I am thy mother? what's the matter,
> That this distempered messenger of wet,
> The many-colour'd Iris, rounds thine eye?
> —Why, that you are my daughter?
> (1.3.144-48)

receives the opaque reply, "That I am not." Helena, elliptical as ever, may mean by this "I am not *that*," by way of emphatic disavowal, or "Because I am not" by way of concession. How are we to read the elliptical Helena? Does she inadvertently reveal her true feelings, or cannily mask her feelings with a declarative equivocation? The reason she gives for her continued insistence is disingenuous: "Pardon, madam, / The Count Rossillion cannot be my brother":

> My master, my dear lord he is; and I
> His servant live, and will his vassal die.
> He must not be my brother.
> (1.3.153-55)

Embarrassed, Helena falls into confusion as she struggles between the Scylla of impoliteness or ingratitude and the hypothetical Charybdis of brother/sister incest:

> You are my mother, madam; would you were—
> So that my lord your son were not my
>   brother—
> Indeed my mother! or were you both our
>   mothers

> I care no more for than I do for heaven,
> So I were no this sister.
> (1.3.156-60)

It can surely escape no one that Helena's double bind here is factitious. The Countess can be her mother only metaphorically. Certainly the semantic absurdity does not escape the Countess, who, as we have seen, uses it to drive home her advantage.

Helena's agitation serves the Countess's testing purposes, and she is trapped into the confession the Countess wants to hear. But we must seek a deeper reason for her extreme discomposure. Her ostensible reason—the desire not to be Bertram's sister since she wishes to be his wife—since it is absurd, can only be a screen upon which we can read an inner conflict. That she is made so nervous by the idea of being Bertram's forbidden sister could well be symptomatic of the deeper taboo. Daughter and mother so strive upon her pulse in a sense truer than the Countess knows: shall she continue to be her father's docile daughter, submissive and self-effacing, or become her lover's active pursuer, challenger and replacer of his mother? That it is the father's daughter that at this point dominates her mind is to be inferred from the posture of helpless, hapless adoration from afar that she expresses, in excess, one feels, of what is required to pacify the Countess, but in keeping with the masochistic note we have already heard ("The hind that would be mated by the lion / Must die for love" [(1.1.89-90)]):

> I know I love in vain, strive against hope;
> Yet in this captious and inteemable sieve
> I still pour in the waters of my love
> And lack not to lose still. Thus, Indian-like,
> Religious in mine error, I adore
> The sun that looks upon his worshipper
> But knows of him no more. . . .
>     O then, give pity
> To her whose state is such that cannot choose
> But lend and give where she is sure to lose;
> That seeks not to find that her search implies,
> But riddle-like lives sweetly where she dies!
> (1.3.196-202, 208-12)

Richard P. Wheeler says that Helena's main task is to overcome a difficulty "that originates in Bertram's revulsion from her" (Wheeler 1981; 15). But this is surely not so. Helena's main task is to overcome a difficulty that originates in the Oedipal taboo. She is as passionate a woman as she is an affectionate daughter, but not yet able to break the father's spell. The phoenix image fantasizes a sublime self-immolation, but pursuit of Bertram to Paris is seductive, too. The will to pursue Bertram to Paris under the guise of healing the King, since it is also the will to heal the King under the guise of pursuing Bertram, is for her a wonderfully composite and legitimizing wish fulfillment. Using the craft of her own father, she will restore a proxy father figure to health, and receive, at his grateful hand, a husband.

Helena consciously conceives her problem as a conflict between boldness and self-effacement, or presumption and modesty, in terms both of the social hierarchies and the maidenly proprieties, but also in terms of chastity and sensuality. "Loving dearly," for Helena, is no matter for platonic abstractions and Diana, her much invoked goddess, was, it will be recalled, the goddess of childbirth as well as of virginity. But it is Diana, not of the Ephesians but of virgins, whom she invokes in order to formulate her plight at this point:

> My dearest madam, . . . if yourself,
> Whose aged honour cites a virtuous youth,
> Did ever, in so true a flame of liking,
> Wish chastely and love dearly, that your Diana
> Was both herelf and love—
>
> (1.3.202-8)

Only later, and, typically, when she steels herself for possible humiliation in the self-exposure of the choosing scene, does she see herself as deserting Diana for "imperial Love, that god most high" (2.3.75).

Helena's fantasied plot of success, in which she will choose her man and the King-father will sanction her choice, fails. It is at the French court, following the triumph of her cure of the King, that humiliation—the "Tax of impudence, / A strumpet's boldness, a divulged shame" (2.1.169-70) which, she told the King, she was ready to venture, in other words, had deeply feared, as the consequence instinctively associated for her with sexual love—becomes indeed her lot. In a way she has tempted Providence, for her replies to the reluctant courtiers are self-abasing: "Love make your fortunes twenty times above / Her that so wishes"; "I'll never do you wrong, for your own sake. / . . . in your bed / Find fairer fortune if you ever wed!"; "You are too young, too happy, and too good, / To make yourself a son out of my blood" (2.3.82-97). We conceive the drama that she has conceived, empowered by her father's power: the response she hoped for from Bertram would have reversed the situation, dignified her humility by triumphantly vindicating her intrinsic worth. But at her grand moment of choice, she is despised and rejected, punished, if you will, by a chauvinist text. The choice-of-a-suitor scene has understandably troubled critics, both on her behalf and on Bertram's. The latter indeed has troubles of his own, to which I now turn.

They interestingly mirror Helena's. For where Helena seeks, and struggles with, a father in her love, Bertram fears, and flees, a mother in his. Understanding this, we will understand the pathos of the crossed vectors of desire, the knot of conflicting needs which this comedy of maturation must untie.

Critics scold Bertram for being so unchivalrous about Helena, but we should surely register the authenticity of his resistance to a marriage forced upon him by a foster father, to the socially inferior, and domestically familiar, receiver of his mother's patronage. Even to a kind of sister—Helena's anxiety on this score can alert us to his. That he chafes is hardly to be wondered at. Bertram has emerged from beneath the maternal wing only to fall under the sway of a new paternal authority. It is surely incumbent upon us to see the matter from his point of view when he bursts out with

> My wife, my liege! I shall beseech your
>   highness,
> In such a business give me leave to use
> The help of mine own eyes.
>
> (2.3.106-8)

And seeing it thus we may perceive the bind in which he is placed. It would hardly make things better for Helena if his repulsion were so great as to make him defy the King's threatened "revenge and hate." His surrender has been construed as abjectly, cynically opportunistic. But it could also be read as a bitter acceptance of force majeure:

> Pardon, my gracious lord; for I submit
> My fancy to your eyes. When I consider
> What great creation and what dole of honour
> Flies where you bid it, I find that she, which
>   late
> Was in my nobler thoughts most base, is now
> The praised of the king; who, so ennobled.
> Is as 'twere born so.
>
> (2.3.167-73)

It depends where we locate the irony, whether we monopolize that commodity as a critical prerogative, or allow the dramatized persona access to the sarcasm that is the defense of the powerless. And Bertram *is* powerless. That he is "not yet old enough for a man, nor young enough for a boy" (as Malvolio says of Cesario in *Twelfth Night* [1.5.158-59]) is the play's generational starting point.

Already in act 2 Bertram's plight is presented as one of extreme frustration. He is

> commanded here, and kept a coil with
> "Too young", and "The next year" and " 'Tis
>   too early". . . .
> I shall stay here the forehorse to a smock,
> Creaking my shoes on the plain masonry,
> Till honour be bought up, and no sword worn
> But one to dance with.
>
> (2.1.27-33)

Seeking honor in battle, action, and manhood, he is kept childishly at home by a King who is as patronizing as he is paternal. And this situation reaches a crisis when even freedom of marital choice is denied him.

But more is at stake for Bertram than freedom of marital choice. Lafew's comments throughout the scene of Helena's choice brand all the reluctant courtiers as beardless boys, objects of his macho contempt before their lackluster performance. "Do all they deny her? And they were sons of mine I'd have them whipp'd, or I would send them to th' Turk to make eunuchs of" (2.3.86-88). They are "boys of ice . . . bastards to the English; the French ne'er got 'em" (2.3.93-95). In particular he despises Bertram, and in terms which suggest the condescending arrogance of the grown man for the sexually immature youth. "There's one grape yet. I am sure thy father drunk wine; but if thou be'st not an ass, I am a youth of fourteen; I have known thee already" (2.3.99-101).

In the scene which follows, the mutual hostility between Lafew and Parolles also hinges specifically upon the question of manliness: Lafew excoriates Parolles for his effeminate clothes—he is a "good window of lattice" (2.3.212)—and for his foppish airs and affectations—"I must tell thee, sirrah, I write man; to which title age cannot bring thee" (2.3.197-98). And his insinuations go further than aspersions cast merely upon Parolles' sartorial foppishness: "Why dost thou garter up thy arms a' this fashion? Dost make hose of thy sleeves? . . . Thou were best set thy lower part where thy nose stands" (2.3.245-48). To Lafew, aggressively male, Parolles is "a hen." As far as Lafew is concerned, it seems, Parolles is nothing but a male punk and he cannot stand him. Parolles for his part throws Lafew's "antiquity" in his face, and, once Lafew is safely absent, swears "Well, thou hast a son shall take this disgrace off me; scurvy, old, filthy, scurvy lord! . . . I'll beat him, by my life, if I can meet him with any convenience" (2.3.231-35). It is to this braggart "sweetheart" that Bertram turns for sympathy when he enters, "Undone and forefeited to cares for ever!" (2.3.263). Parolles' bravado, characteristic defense of the sexually and personally insecure, presents the refuge of a homoerotic attachment as a valorization of the male camaraderie of warfare:

> To th' wars, my boy, to th' wars!
> He wears his honour in a box unseen
> That hugs his kicky-wicky here at home,
> Spending his manly marrow in her arms,
> Which should sustain the bound and high
>   curvet
> Of Mars's fiery steed.
>
> (2.3.274-79)

And off to the wars go the bachelor companions in perfect agreement that "A young man married is a man that's marr'd" (2.3.294).

For Bertram, frustrated by his forced marriage, Mars is a welcome substitute for Venus. But that a fear of impotence lies just beneath the surface of his martial posture is suggested not only by the Parolles connection but by his own telltale envoi:

> I have writ my letters, casketed my treasure,
> Given order for our horses; and tonight,
> When I should take possession of the bride,
> End ere I do begin.
>
> (2.5.23-26)

Effeminate Parolles, "jackanapes with scarfs" (3.5.85), is Bertram's refuge from "the dark house [a displaced image of female enclosure?] and the detested wife" (2.3.288). The danger, bawdy Lavatch informs us, is in "standing to 't': in battle, "that's the loss of men"; elsewhere, "the getting of children" (3.2.40-41). Bertram, who runs away, the clown's irony seems to suggest, has double indemnity. Lavatch's caustic comment is important because it links the two masculine prerogatives, and puts them both in question vis-à-vis Bertram. But we must ask our own questions of the text that represents Bertram.

First of all, we note, the nearly universal critical prejudice against him leads to a cardinal misjudgment. Bertram does in fact exhibit prowess in battle. And he does not, at this stage at least, lie to Helena. He does not declare to her a love he does not feel. He will not kiss her even when they part, and she pleads for at least a formal embrace.

Moreover, the riddle with which he sets Helena her impossible task: *"When thou canst get the ring upon my finger, which never shall come off, and show me a child begotten of thy body that I am father to, then call me husband"* (3.2.56-58) is double-tongued, like all riddles. It states an apparent impossibility but represents an unacknowledged desire. To see this, one has only to suppose the conditional *form* changed, not the primary substance; to read instead of "When thou canst, . . ." "If only thou couldst. . . ."[6]

And when he dispatches her to his mother, it is with almost a plea on his part for her understanding:

> And rather muse than ask why I entreat you;
> For my respects are better than then seem,
> And my appointments have in them a need
> Greate than shows itself at the first view
> To you that know them not.
>
> (2.5.65-69)

The need "Greater than shows itself," as Richard P. Wheeler persuasively demonstrates, stems from the fact that Helena is ineluctably bound up in his mind with his mother: "A son's affection for a mother is directed by Bertram toward the countess; a son's fears of female domination and of his own Oedipal wishes are aroused in Bertram by Helena" (2.5.42). Hence "I cannot love her nor will strive to do't" (2.3.145). Wheeler concludes, however, that the play's "comic purpose, to free Bertram from anxieties that originate in family ties," is not achieved. "The action of *All's Well*," he says, "dramatizes neither a liberation from nor a transformation of obstacles that obstruct the marriage to Helena" (2.3.80).

It is at this point that my own reading of *All's Well* diverges from Wheeler's. He reads into the play the problems of the Sonnets, with Helena as a screen figure for the humiliated and self-humiliating lover and Bertram as the Sonnets' young man, presented now with a savage mockery the self-excoriating author of the Sonnets could not permit himself. My own reading is dramatically opposed. I see these two as chiastic doubles, mirrors of each other. Where Helena seeks a (forbidden) father in her love, Bertram fears a (forbidden) mother; but the text also inscribes their shared desire for sexual enfranchisement, for fatherhood and motherhood, and provides the means for its attainment.

The reversals, which will make possible the happy ending, occur in the play's middle act. Helena's great speech of renunciation is worth quoting at length for the subtlety with which it articulates a momentous transformation.

> Nothing in France, until he has no wife!
> Thou shalt have none, Rossillion, none in France;
> Then hast thou all again. Poor lord, is't I
> That chase thee from thy country, and expose
> Those tender limbs of thine to the event
> Of the none-sparing war? And is it I
> That drive thee from the sportive court, where thou
> Wast shot at with fair eyes, to be the mark
> Of smoky muskets? O you leaden messengers,
> . . . do not touch my lord.
> Whoever shoots at him, I set him there;
> . . . I am the cause
> . . . No; come thou home, Rossillion,
> . . . I will be gone;
> My being here it is that holds thee hence.
> Shall I stay here to do't? No, no, although
> The air of paradise did fan the house
> And angels offic'd all. I will be gone,
> . . . Come, night; end, day;
> For with the dark, poor thief, I'll steal away.
> (3.2.100-129)

In the parting scene Helena begged for her kiss "like a timorous theif, [who] most fain would steal" (2.5.81) what is legally hers. Now she will herself steal away, so only she be no obstacle to Bertram's return. It is to be noted, too, that in thus renouncing him she refers to him in his own patronymic right, as Rossillion. It is a turnabout for the determined young woman who has outfaced a king and a court to gain her end, and gained it. But what the accents of the speech tell us is that this self-abrogation, which springs no doubt from the masochism of infantile taboo, has undergone a transformation. Her guilt here is reality-tested, objective, since she really is the cause of Bertram's escape into soldiering. The tenderly maternal solicitude that we hear in this speech is a transference wonderfully, and movingly, caught. Helena has broken the spell of the father in this fantasy of herself as a mothering, protective figure to the man she desires.

It is for this reason, I suggest, that there is no page disguise in *All's Well*. Helena's problem has not been the sorting out, balancing, and harmonizing of masculine and feminine components in her own personality as it was for her hermaphrodite sisters of the earlier comedies. They had to reconcile themselves to a woman's role without loss, if possible, of the adventurous, maverick male attributes they also possessed, and cherished. She has had to free her sexuality from the archaic bond of infancy, to undertake a pilgrimage into mature sexuality. It is beautifully in keeping with this trajectory of "the other plot" that we are following that disguise as a girl called Diana, women's camaraderie, and the bed-trick mark her achievement of the passage from virgin chastity to marital sexuality.

The bed-trick represents enabling fantasy for both partners. For Helena it offers camouflage—anonymity, invisibility—under cover of which she can transcend the inhibitions of a threatening sexuality. For men, conversely, bed-trick fantasies represent fears of being tricked in bed. But for Bertram the bed-trick is his sexual conquest of the woman he believes to be Diana and so fulfills an analogous liberation. Helena is dead. We do not know the nature of the change that came over Bertram when he received the news of Helena's death, but "on the reading it he chang'd almost into another man" (4.3.3-4). Already in his wooing of Diana, he was liberated enough to be able to contemplate, and to exorcise by invoking, a primal scene: "now you should be as your mother was," he says, "When your sweet self was got" (4.2.9-10). Now, in bed with a light o'love—Fontybell!—and therefore unhampered by any honorable intentions whatsoever, "he fleshes his will" (4.3.15), confirming his potency. Thus Bertram outgrows Parolles. Or rather, he is in a position to outgrow Parolles. His repudiation of his erstwhile "sweetheart," however, is still to be brought about.

Parolles, often seen as a quasi vice figure in a morality play contest with virtuous Helena, and about whom Wheeler, oddly, has very little to say, is perhaps the most brilliant dramatic invention in *All's Well*. Bertram's virtual sibling, brother-at-arms, alter ego, he is our essential vehicle for an understanding of Bertram's rake's progress as an authentic reflection of masculine adolescence. Perhaps too much so for the comfort of spectators, male and female, who cannot free themselves from masculine idealizations of romantic protagonists.[7] But let us examine the exposure of the inimitable Parolles.

The exposure of Parolles in act 4 marks, together with the bed-trick, the remedial phase of the Shakespearean comic plot. Characteristically, folly, become hyperbolically excessive, extrudes itself, exposes itself, or is exposed, exhausts, and so eliminates itself.[8] The lords have a double remedial project in hand in the gulling scene. Parolles, "most notable coward, an infinite and endless liar, an hourly promise-breaker" (3.6.9-10), is to be openly and palpably disgraced, but Bertram, too, is due for chastisement for the brazen callousness with which he has received the news of Helena's death and for his seduction of "a young gentlewoman . . . of a most chaste renown" (4.3.13-14). The French lords will "gladly have him see his company anatomiz'd, that he might make a measure of his own judgments wherein so curiously he had set this counterfeit," and they economically set their trap so that each will be "the whip of the other" (4.3.30-35). The first stage of the trap exposes Parolles, in sham pursuit of his lost drum, as the fraud and coxcomb, the "counterfeit module" (4.3.96) and craven informer that he is. The second stage turns the tables upon the now indignant, and betrayed, Bertram. The latter appears, in extremely high spirits after his rendezvous with Diana, and that he deserves what he gets is underlined by his airy account of the "sixteen businesses" he has dispatched (4.3.82-89) since the news of Helena's death.

Parolles, having surrendered unconditionally at the first syllable of the Lords' "terrible language," is now beyond shame—"If ye pinch me like a pasty" (4.3.119-20), he says, he can betray no more military intelligence than he possesses, which, when it comes to a run-down on the French commanders, he is determined to embellish with details that will, he is confident, endear him to his interlocutors. Thus it comes about that the trickster Lords, including Bertram—"a foolish idle boy, but for all that very ruttish" (4.3.207)—hear no good of themselves. The blindfold removed, face-to-face with the objects of his "pestiferous" slanders, Parolles' exposure is complete.

The "cure" proves wonderfully effective; more so than Malvolio's even, perhaps because Parolles has had a measure of self-knowledge all along concerning at least his "foolhardy tongue": "Tongue, I must put you into a butter-woman's mouth, and buy myself another of Bajazeth's mule if you prattle me into these perils" (4.1.41-43). But he goes on paroling himself into perils, and that it is by the Lords' gobbledygook—"choughs' language" (4.1.19)—that a meanspirited braggart is undone is no more than poetic justice. Or homeopathy. Self-knowledge, self-acceptance can hardly go further than that of Parolles, shamed beyond words, disgraced, despised, but alive:

> Yet am I thankful. If my heart were great
> 'Twould burst at this. Captain I'll be no
>   more,
> But I will eat and drink and sleep as soft
> As captain shall. Simply the thing I am
> Shall make me live. . . .
> Rust, sword; cool, blushes; and Parolles live
> Safest in shame. . . .
> There's place and means for every man alive.
>                                    (4.3.319-28)

But what of Bertram vis-à-vis his ex-alter ego? He repudiates him of course. He is now, "A pox upon him! . . . a cat" (4.3.254-55)—whom he detests. But does he see anything of himself in this unmasking? "What a past-saving slave is this!" "Damnable both-sides rogue!" (4.3.135, 214), he says, failing to recall that the only afterthought he had about Diana was a fear of ever hearing of her again. We might adapt the courtier's rhetorical question regarding Parolles: "Is it possible he should know what he is, and be that he is?" (4.1.44-45). Is it possible that Bertram knows what Parolles is, and be as *he* is?

Bertram's own exposure, indeed, is still to come. At present he still "thinks himself made" (4.3.16-17) by his battle honors and bed victories. If the gulling of Parolles dramatizes the demise in Bertram of Parolles the effeminate tongue-man, Parolles the feather-man remains to be demolished. Parolles himself, though he smells, is still very much alive—on handouts from the contemptuous Lafew. He must still run the gauntlet of Lavatch's olfactory insults, just as Bertram will run the gauntlet of the women's unmasking. The foppish kinship between them is neatly brought out by Bertram's affectation of a velvet patch (we have not heard that he was wounded) upon which Lavatch lavishes his scurrilous witticisms.

The final scene has the curious effect of a replay, only this time with the young women firmly in charge of the act. The elders are once more engaged in matchmaking, Lafew's daughter and Bertram this time, an opportune circumstance Bertram seizes with alacrity. Once more paternal benevolence turns into ferocity when Diana's possession of Helena's ring, given her, we recall, by the King as a pledge of his gratitude, makes the King suspect foul play, even murder, on Bertram's part.

And Bertram, trapped between rings, the inherited, patrilinear ring that he gave, the virginal, betrothal ring that he took? Yes, he lies, and wriggles and prevaricates. His snobbery is distasteful; chivalry was never his strong point. Like Parolles, in his recognition scene he is disgraced, left with no face to save, his "champion Honour" exposed for the broken reed it is.

But what, after all, do his critics expect? He is trapped, as he was at the beginning; he has a face, a life, to try to save.

He too is restored by Helena, who, like Mariana in *Measure for Measure,* wants no other, nor no better, man. Her "O my good lord, when I was like this maid / I found you wondrous kind" (5.3.303-4)[9] is, for his wounded ego, the one most restorative thing she could say. The bed-trick, it turns out, served his fantasy of virile masculinity, and trumped it. For he finds in the woman he seduced, the woman he fled—a nurturing, saving presence, a sexually compatible bride and the mother of his child. He is still bewildered when he says to the King, "If she, my liege, can make me know this clearly / I'll love her dearly, ever, ever dearly" (4.3.309-10). But I myself do not find his "Both, both. O pardon!" (5.3.302) necessarily perfunctory. Certainly an actor need not make it so.

Are they a mismatch? More, or less, than anyone else in life or in literature?

Is *All's Well* a "problem" play, and as such deserving of relegation to second-class status? It has been my claim that no such special category is required for the elucidation of *All's Well.* It exhibits a firm structural family resemblance to the earlier maturation comedies, and if it anticipates in certain aspects a late romance like *Cymbeline,* it is no more problematic for that reason than any other play in the Shakespearean opus (or any other), each play being manifestly transitional between its precursors and its successors.

Certainly the vicissitudes of motive and meaning of fear and desire, which are caught and displayed in the web of its text engage our closest attention. Its complexities, its psychological depth and finesse, its brilliant mirroring of intra-psychic conflicts as these are acted out, and paralleled, in confrontations between characters might well admit it once more into the canon of Shakespeare's most admired plays. Where, to adapt once more Parolles' famous self-summation: simply the thing it is shall make it live.

## Notes

[1] See Lawrence, *Shakespeare's Problem Comedies.*

[2] See, for example, Richard A. Levin, "*All's Well* and All Seems Well," *Shakespeare Studies* 13 (1980): 131-42.

[3] Wheeler, 75, quotes Eric Partridge, *Shakespeare's Bawdy* (New York, 1955) on the sexual suggestiveness of "stone," "fire," "motion," "touch," "[a]raise," and "pen."

[4] Otto Rank noted the Oedipal motif in the very first lines of the play as early as 1912, and found "the tabooed relationship of mother and son underlying a good deal of the play." See Holland, 154. Literary critics, on the other hand, have made surprisingly little of suggested unconscious motivations. Significantly, however, Bernard Shaw, in whose "deeper affections" the play was "rooted" found the Countess "the most beautiful old woman's part ever written": *Shaw on Shakespeare,* ed. Edwin Wilson (London, 1961), 10.

[5] G. K. Hunter provides an account of the textual problem in his commentary on the lines in the New Arden edition.

[6] Cf. Helena's "riddle" in 1.3.212: "But riddle-like lives sweetly where she dies," in which the wit masks a wish by way of the Elizabethan *double entendre* in "dies." Phyllis Gorfain, "Puzzle and Artifice: The Riddle as Metapoetry in *Pericles,*" *Shakespeare Survey 29* (1976), makes the interesting suggestion that the paradoxes and contradictions out of which riddles are contrived constitute a "schema of marriage"—children being born of male and female, and mediating between past and future. See also Freud's account of the *aliquis* "riddle" in *The Psychopathology of Everyday Life,* (Pelican Freud Library 5, 46-49).

[7] G. K. Hunter admits Parolles' stage success as a humor character but finds no way to "fit him into this play," or "to balance him against the different kind of reality" of Helena (xlviii). But see Rogers, *Psychoanalytic Study of the Double in Literature,* chap. 8 passim, for a very useful account of character "doubling," especially the latent, "secret sharer" kind, as "a fundamental mechanism" for the representation of psychic conflict.

[8] I have attempted to develop a theory of exorcist Shakespearean comic form in *Comic Transformations in Shakespeare* (London, 1980).

[9] "Sexually responsive" was one of the many nuances of the word in Elizabethan English, which included the archaic "natural" and the modern "well-intentioned" or "good-natured."

## Bibliography

Brooks, Peter. "Repetition, Repression and Return: *Great Expectations* and the Study of Plot," *NLH* (1980).

Frye, Northrop. *Anatomy of Criticism* (Princeton, N.J.: Princeton University Press, 1957).

Holland, Norman. *Psychoanalysis and Shakespeare* (New York: Farrar, 1979).

Lawrence, W. W. *Shakespeare's Problem Comedies* (New York: Macmillan, 1931).

Mansfield, Katherine. *Journal,* ed. John Middleton Murray (1927, reprint; London: Constable, 1954).

Nicoll, Allardyce. *Shakespeare* (London, 1952).

Raysor, T. M., ed. *Coleridge's Shakespeare Criticism* (London: Dent, 1960).

Rogers, Robert. *A Psychoanalytic Study of the Double in Literature* (Detroit: Wayne State University Press, 1970).

Ure, Peter. *Shakespeare: The Problem Plays* (London: Longman, 1961).

Wheeler, Richard P. *Shakespeare's Development and the Problem Comedies* (Berkeley and Los Angeles: University of California Press, 1981).

---

Source: "Motive and Meaning in *All's Well That Ends Well,*" in *Strands Afar Remote: Israeli Perspectives on Shakespeare,* edited by Avraham Oz, University of Delaware Press, 1998, pp. 113-37.

# Shylock: The Infamous Secret Jew

## Linda Rozmovits, *University of East London*

I

Despite its deliberate failure to meet the Victorian vogue for spectacular theater,[1] Henry Irving's Lyceum production of *The Merchant of Venice* set "a record without precedent in the annals of the stage" (L. Irving 356). Mounted and rehearsed in the space of three weeks—Irving having opted to avoid "hampering the natural action of the piece with any unnecessary embellishment" (H. Irving, *MV* preface)—the production, which opened on 1 November 1879, ran for seven straight months, or two hundred and fifty consecutive performances. During the course of that season it was estimated that "330,000 people had visited the Lyceum," generating receipts amounting to some fifty-nine thousand pounds (L. Irving 357). Subsequently, Irving revived the production "nearly every season, took it on every tour, played it perhaps a thousand times, and was still playing it the week he died, more than twenty-five years after the first night" (Hughes 227).[2] On 14 February 1880 the fact that *The Merchant* had "for the first time in history [been] played for a hundred nights in succession" (*Theatre* 1/3/80, 188) was celebrated with dinner for three hundred at the Lyceum at a cost of six hundred pounds (L. Irving 357). And nearly ten years after it opened, the production still had enough cachet that Irving was summoned by the Prince of Wales to perform the trial scene from *The Merchant of Venice* along with *The Bells* (also a play about a Jew) on a specially prepared stage at Sandringham. With one minor exception it was the only theatrical entertainment that Queen Victoria had attended in the twenty-eight years since the death of Prince Albert (512).

Undoubtedly, Irving's star status contributed to the success of the production, but there seemed to be more to it than that; the favorable reception of Irving's Shakespearean offerings was by no means assured. He had had only middling results with both *Coriolanus* and *Twelfth Night* (Hughes 226) and was widely considered to have failed outright with *Macbeth* (E. M. Moore 209). Yet, with *The Merchant of Venice,* Irving "made Shakespeare [truly] popular—an achievement of which but few of his predecessors . . . could boast" (*Theatre* 1/12/79, 292). Thus, the phenomenon seems to be one that cannot be accounted for by cult of personality alone. Moreover, the fact that the production "provoked a controversy" over which both Irving's supporters and detractors "took up extreme positions" (Hughes 225) suggests that something else lay at the heart of it all. That something else, without a doubt, was Irving's treatment of the figure of Shylock, for in Henry Irving's Lyceum production of *The Merchant of Venice,* in all but the most literal of senses, Shylock wins the trial.

While aspects of Irving's Shylock were recognizably indebted to theatrical predecessors such as Charles Macklin and Edmund Kean, Irving was considered to have utterly redefined the role. In popular terms he was widely perceived to be "the first star actor to play Shylock for sympathy" (Maude 172). In an earlier age the part of Shylock had been a two-dimensionally villainous one; as a sort of stock evil buffoon, Shylock was traditionally fitted out with a grotesque red wig and made exaggerated gestures meant to convey the immeasurability of his inhumanity and greed. Moreover, in performance a farcical piece entitled *The Jew of Venice* was actually favored over *The Merchant* from the time of the Restoration until 1741, when "Macklin persuaded the management of Drury Lane to restore Shakespeare's text in place of George Granville's adaptation" (J. R. Brown 187). Challenges to this long tradition of farce had been made by sophisticated interpreters who realized that to play the role entirely in this spirit was to diminish its dramatic interest. But Irving had taken this idea further than anyone before him, moving beyond the difference in degree to effect a striking difference in kind. Irving's Shylock

> was venerable, lonely, grieved, austere: he moved with pride and grace; his humour was coldly cynical, rather than sardonic; his thought was meditative, not sullen, and his anger was white and tense; in defeat he called forth pity and awe. (194)

In other words, under Irving's direction *The Merchant of Venice* had ceased to be a comedy and, as one worried critic noted, "foster[ed] the delusion that the play is a tragedy" (*Athenæum* 8/11/79, 605), with Shylock emerging "as something very like a tragic hero" (Hughes 226). To viewers of the Lyceum production, "as in the writing, so in the acting of the play, the first and highest merit . . . [was] the presentation of its tragical element" (E.R.R., "Henry" 16).

It is sometimes suggested that Irving's sympathetic portrayal of the Jew was opportunistic in that he had no choice but to dispense with the traditional histrionic reading of Shylock, since he was not particularly robust and therefore had "not sufficient physical force for such clamorous exhibitions" (Cook 224). An observer at rehearsals for the production once claimed that, although Irving "'shot' for Shakespeare's Shylock," he found that "at least two of the scenes were beyond his powers," forcing him to "develop . . . a 'Shylock' he *could* compass" (Barnes 104). This seems unlikely at best. There were plenty of dramatic moments in Irving's repertoire which required physical force, and discussion of his intentions for the role of Shylock was ongoing for years after the production first opened.[3]

Similarly, claims that Irving's sympathetic Shylock "grew less sympathetic over the years" may be dispatched (J. Gross 141).[4] A review of the 1887 London revival of *The Merchant* confirms that, in the long term, Irving stood his ground. "Mr. Irving's view of the character of Shylock and his subtle appeals for sympathy on the Jew's behalf," the reviewer wrote, "remain of course unchanged. Right or wrong, his is a noble ideal of the part, and he is not likely in any way to lower it" (review [Enthoven]). Indeed, at times Irving's determination to play Shylock as he had developed him at the Lyceum was cause for consternation. On his American tour of 1883 Irving felt that, though the critics consistently applauded his performance, audiences were somewhat taken aback.[5] Joseph Hatton has noted that American spectators expected "in his Shylock a very hard, grim, and cruel Jew":

> Many persons hinted as much to him before they saw his impersonation of this much-discussed character . . . Singularly sensitive about the feelings of his audiences, and accustomed to judge them as keenly as they judge him, he fancied . . . [they] were not stirred as they had been by his other work in response to his efforts as Shylock. (262-63)

Irving himself expressed the fear that the audiences were not with him:

> I always feel, in regard to this play, that they do not quite understand what I am doing. They only responded at all . . . where Shylock's rage and mortification get the better of his dignity. (Qtd. in ibid. 263)

Hatton sought to reassure Irving by pointing out that audiences were so strongly accustomed to a histrionic Shylock that they were "probably a little disappointed" by a "view of the part [which] forbids anything like . . . the strident characteristics of most other Shylocks" (263-64). Irving was unwavering in his reply:

> I never saw Kean's Shylock, nor Phelps's, nor, indeed, anyone's. But I am sure Shylock was not a low person; a miser and usurer, certainly, but a very injured man . . . I felt that my audience to-night had quite a different opinion, and I once wished the house had been composed entirely of Jews. I would like to play Shylock to a Jewish audience. (264)

Yet, while the production was an unprecedented popular success, for Irving's antagonists there was still plenty to fault. It was suggested, for example, that the physical mannerisms and affectations of speech displayed by Shylock were not the product of inspired interpretation but were, in fact, simply Irving's own. Both Irving and Ellen Terry, one critic observed, "have strange mannerisms; they never divest themselves of them, and hence . . . are successful where the parts . . . they play lend themselves to mannerisms . . ." (*Truth* 6/11/79, 568). *Punch*'s theater critic liked the production and so "dismiss[ed] Mr. Irving's peculiarities of gait and utterance with . . . [the] remark that they are [at least] less noticeable in *Shylock* than in any part in which I have hitherto seen him" (*Punch* 15/11/79, 225). While George Bernard Shaw, not a fan, summed up the general objection by saying that "the truth is that he [Irving] has never in his life conceived or interpreted the characters of any author except himself" (Shaw, *Dramatic Opinions* 56). The most strenuous objections to Irving's *Merchant of Venice,* however, were reserved for his editorial treatment of the text.

Irving's acting version of the play reduces Shakespeare's text by approximately 25 percent, cutting nearly six hundred lines. Some critics have argued that this was a conventional and logistically motivated editorial intervention, that Irving's text was simply based on Charles Kean's published version of 1858, and that all Irving did was reduce the number of scene changes and eliminate material that failed to advance the plot significantly (Hughes 227). Some of Irving's detractors, however, have argued to the contrary that the cuts he made to the text of *The Merchant of Venice* were anything but superficial. Irving "does not merely cut plays," it was said, "he disembowels them" (Shaw, *Dramatic Opinions* 55). And in this case what Irving's antagonists claimed he did was excise "passages [and]—indeed, whole scenes—which tended to discredit Shylock" (E. M. Moore 203). While these objections to Irving's textual alterations are often questionable insofar as they take the form of ad hominem attacks on a man arrogant enough to have tampered with Shakespeare's text, they do nevertheless raise an interesting question.[6] In isolation, eliminating gratuitous remarks about Shylock's evil nature or reducing the amount of raving about the loss of his ducats would not be gestures drastic enough to alter the play radically. But, in combination with a staging strategy that made Shylock the center of attention and a use of stage business which mitigated the conventional crudity of many of his remaining lines, these cuts *can* be seen as part of a systematic transformation of the text. Whether one approves or disapproves of Irving's editorial conduct, its overall effect was, clearly, to tender an account of Shylock which valorized the character's sufferings rather than confirmed his status as an object of scorn.

The two most obvious alterations Irving made to his acting version of *The Merchant of Venice* were that, first, he consolidated the scenes involving Portia's suitors, pretty clearly in order to reduce the number of scene changes; and, second, predictably, he edited out virtually all references to sex. The first group of changes has no obvious effect on Shylock's part unless one considers that cutting back on Portia's speeches increases proportionally the amount of time given over to Shylock, while the second eliminates only the small handful of insults against the Jew which are bawdy in addition to being racial. But several outstanding alterations fall into neither of these categories and, for a number of reasons, suggest that something more than directorial pragmatism or prevailing standards of good taste may well have been at stake. For, although they are extremely limited in terms of the number of lines they constitute and could hardly be described as essential to the narrative, these passages, as I shall argue, could have attacked the very foundations of Irving's monumental success. All three of these passages concern Shylock's relationship to his daughter, Jessica.

In order of their appearance the relevant omissions consist of all of act 2, scene 3, which is only twenty-one lines long and includes a brief exchange between Jessica and the clown Launcelot Gobbo; act 2, scene 8, lines 12-24, which is a conversation between two minor characters; and act 3, scene 1, lines 22-37, which is a continuation of this same conversation, which by this time includes Shylock. The impact of the absence of these lines, however, is best appreciated if the passages are considered in terms of their content rather than their chronology, so I will begin by considering the latter two passages first.

The first part of the conversation between Salerio and Solanio (friends of Antonio) recounts Shylock's discovery that he has been robbed and abandoned by his daughter:

*Solanio:*
I never heard a passion so confused,
So strange, outrageous, and so variable
As the dog Jew did utter in the streets:
"My daughter! O my ducats! O my daughter!
Fled with a Christian! O my Christian ducats!
Justice! The law! My ducats and my daughter!
A sealèd bag, two sealèd bags of ducats,
Of double ducats, stol'n from me by my daughter!
And jewels, two stones, two rich and precious stones,
Stol'n by my daughter! Justice! Find the girl!
She hath the stones upon her and the ducats!"

*Salerio:*
Why, all the boys in Venice follow him,
Crying his stones, his daughter, and his ducats.

Of this exchange Irving retains only the first six lines, therefore editing out both the belabored farce of Shylock's apparent inability to distinguish between his ducats and his daughter and Salerio's description of the spectacle of the anguished Shylock taunted and pursued by "all the boys in Venice." The effect of this is, arguably, considerable, since, by ending the exchange as he does, Irving effectively replaces a raving burlesque with the cynical reporting of what now appears to be a comparatively sympathetic, rational, and not unwarranted call by Shylock for "Justice! The Law! My ducats and my daughter!"

The second passage follows from the previous exchange but now includes the presence of Shylock, who confronts the two men about their having known of his daughter's intended flight:

*Shylock:*
You knew, none so well, none so well as you, of my daughter's flight.
*Salerio:*
That's certain. I for my part knew the tailor that made the wings she flew withal.
*Solanio:*
And Shylock for his own part knew the bird was fledged, and then it is the complexion of them all to leave the dam.
*Shylock:*
She is damned for it.
*Salerio:*
That's certain, if the devil may be her judge.
*Shylock:*
My own flesh and blood to rebel!
*Solanio:*
Out upon it, old carrion! Rebels it at these years?
*Shylock:*
I say my daughter is my flesh and blood.
*Salerio:*
There is more difference between thy flesh and hers than between jet and ivory, more between your bloods than there is between red wine and Rhenish

In this instance Irving cuts everything after Shylock's exclamation "My own flesh and blood to rebel!" and moves directly to the discussion of Antonio's losses at sea which follows. While the excised material might seem merely to prolong the already well-established exchange of hostilities between the Venetians and the Jew, it becomes apparent under scrutiny that the omission of the half-dozen lines significantly alters the exchange. For to end on Shylock's lament for his faithless daughter is to construct the issue as one of female disobedience, as a crisis of gender, while to end on Salerio's denial of the legitimacy of Shylock's paternal claim—"There is more difference between thy flesh and hers than between jet and ivory, more between your bloods than there is between red wine and Rhenish"—is to introduce the question of race.

If we look to the final omission from the text, the matter becomes even more explicit, as Jessica considers the twin evils of female disobedience and racial disavowal and in so doing raises the prospect of something more harrowing than either, namely, miscegenation:

> Alack, what heinous sin is it in me
> To be ashamed to be my father's child.
> But though I am a daughter to his blood,
> I am not to his manners. O Lorenzo,
> If thou keep promise, I shall end this strife,
> Become a Christian and thy loving wife.

Whatever the personal intentions of a theatergoer at the time, the experience of watching Irving's *Merchant of Venice* could hardly do less than bring to mind two of the most prominent social crises of the day. The first, as we saw in the previous chapter, is embodied in the figure of Portia and concerns the increasing claims of women over their futures and their social mobility. The second, embodied in the figure of Shylock, evokes the specter of race—the stranger in our midst. The importance of Jessica, as these omissions from the text show, is that she is the figure in which these crises of race and gender are most provocatively manifest for being most perilously entwined. And yet Jessica is an extremely difficult character to pursue, from a historical perspective, because the evidence of attitudes toward her tends to be circumstantial rather than direct. Nevertheless, I would argue, she is pivotal in many ways, and appreciating her importance means that we need to understand not just what people were saying about her but also why they were saying so little when they were saying anything at all.

One obvious difficulty in approaching the character of Jessica is the extent to which she is overshadowed, legendarily, by her larger-than-life father but even more so by the cult of Portia, a difficulty considerably compounded by the popular association of the two characters with figures as charismatic in their own rights as Henry Irving and Ellen Terry. Indeed, in Irving's production the sidelining of Jessica was clearly reinforced by the casting of the role. For at the Lyceum the part was played by an actress named Alma Murray, who was apparently so young and undistinguished that a reviewer for *Blackwood's Magazine* complained of its having been "regarded of as so little importance as to be intrusted to . . . [a young lady] who would be weak in the smallest of comediettas" (12/79, 651). As we shall see, this marginalization of Jessica served a particular function in relation to Irving's production, but the character's diminished status was by no means limited to that context alone.

In a literary culture so heavily dominated by character criticism, for example, Jessica was seldom the focus of substantial interest in her own right. Partly this was due to the prevailing conventions, which tended to focus on leading roles, and partly to the associated bias in favor of characters who lent themselves to the endorsement of an exemplary nature. Thus, when she is acknowledged, it is often just in passing or in an aside as the lesser party in an unfavorable comparison with Portia. Anna Jameson's reference to Jessica simply as one of "the other female characters of 'The Merchant of Venice'" who deserves our notice, primarily because "something of the intellectual brilliance of Portia is reflected on [her]" is fairly typical (39). It's not that Jessica is seen to be utterly unworthy of attention. Indeed, "in any other play," Jameson consoled her readers, and,

> in any other companionship than that of the matchless Portia, Jessica would make a very beautiful heroine of herself . . . Nothing can be more . . . elegant than the scenes between her and Lorenzo . . . Every sentiment she utters interests us for her . . . And the enthusiastic and generous testimony to the superior graces and accomplishments of Portia comes with a peculiar grace from her lips. (39-40)

The most commonly held perception of Jessica, then, was that, if she were herself short on virtue, at least she could detect it in others. "One of the things we like best in Jessica," one commentator wrote, "is her genuine admiration of Portia . . . It augurs the development of her own character . . . into something ampler and more responsible" (Verity xxxiii). Helena Faucit held a similar view. That Jessica can, "despite her training, appreciate goodness and virtue," she wrote, "may be inferred from what she says of Portia" (Martin 36).

Occasionally, Jessica would be acknowledged for other reasons, but this was usually done with considerable resentment—much as one would acknowledge the winner of a door prize—for being the character who gets to have the beautiful poetry of the last act of *The Merchant of Venice* spoken to her, although she has done nothing special to deserve it. As one particularly peeved reviewer put it, Jessica was someone "to whom one always grudges the loveliest love-lines ever spoken" (qtd. in Hughes 232).

Where we do find evidence of a less backhanded interest in Jessica, suggestively, the emphasis is often placed on the utility of her part rather than on its moral content or iconic significance. In a society intent on emphasizing the structural perfection of Shakespeare's plays, in other words, one way of dealing with Jessica was clearly to relegate her to a role that, if morally treacherous, was at least structurally recuperable for linking the casket and bond stories together or for providing the contrast needed to develop other characters. Thus, the Jessica-Lorenzo plot was seen as "assisting" the main plot by "bridging over the three months' interval between the signing of the bond and its becoming due" or by "occupy[ing] some of the superfluous characters of the Merchant's story" (Barnett 10). Similarly, its relation to the "main drift of the drama" was explained in terms of its furnishing "a contrast to the graver love-story of Bassanio and Portia" or illuminating the character of Shylock, giving greater insight into his "avarice," his "motive in pressing for the execution of the bond," and showing him "in his domestic relations, which we would not otherwise see" (Verity 119).

On all counts, then, it was difficult for Jessica to compete. She could hardly command the interest of a Portia or a Shylock, and, however key she might appear with hindsight, from a late Victorian perspective she was notable mainly for her failings, "properly kept subordinate" (Jameson 39) and recuperable only through her structural utility and awareness of the superiority of those around her. But, this being said, there is evidence that points in another direction and which suggests that there were aspects of the character that could not be so easily dismissed. For, despite her obvious and deliberate marginalization in popular attitudes, in pedagogy and literary scholarship, but especially in Irving's high-profile theatrical production, there is a palpable anxiety about Jessica which far outweighs her ostensible lack of importance.

One place we immediately get a sense of this is in discussions of Jessica which take place in the notes accompanying school editions of *The Merchant of Venice,* possibly because this is a forum in which moral issues would be difficult to ignore. And here we begin to get a sense of the true depth of feeling associated with the character and of the terrible dilemmas her situation must have posed for a late Victorian audience. Specifically, one is struck by the resonant and highly contested way in which the theme of public accountability extended beyond the parameters of Shylock's story to encompass that of his daughter, the notion of judgment figuring centrally throughout. "Jessica's conduct stands at the bar of judgment," wrote one editor. "Although she describes her home as a hell, and from Shylock's nature that can well be believed, there could not be baser ingratitude in a Jewess than to steal her father's jewels and money, and take flight with a Christian" (Crook lv-lvi). Or, contrastingly, "Jessica is not to be judged by any present-day standard of morality," wrote another:

> The poet himself evidently intended her failings to be regarded with much leniency, and we must endeavour therefore to view her in the light of a . . . lively young girl, driven to rebellion by the oppression of her father and the joylessness of her life at home. Otherwise we shall be unable to justify such glaring transgressions as the appropriation of her father's ducats and her desertion of him in his old age. (Wood, Manuals 16-17)

Clearly, the difficulty with the story of Jessica was that it presented a litany of what to a late Victorian audience would have been highly charged moral concerns in an uncomfortably complicated set of relations to one another—female disobedience, racial and religious disloyalty, the effects of an unsuitable domestic environment, premeditated deception, conversion, and, of course, miscegenation.[7] And, like the question of Portia's feminism or lack of it, it thus occasioned substantial disagreement about Shakespeare's intentions in representing the character and her actions as he did.

Sometimes, Jessica's disregard for family loyalty is seen to be mitigated by her genuine feeling for her lover, so that, while she is censured for not even making the "pretence of being a dutiful daughter to the Jew, whom she deceives with the lightest conscience," she is redeemed for being genuinely in love with Lorenzo" (Wood, Manuals 16-17). But at other times no such allowance is made, and, despite "all her . . . love of Lorenzo," she is declared to be "but a heartless beauty" (Meiklejohn 4). Likewise, while Jessica's Jewishness is in some cases seen to be enacted through her disobedience, at others it is an attribute made tragic by actions declared to be uncharacteristic of this normally loyal race. Thus, we are told in one instance that "there could not be baser ingratitude in a Jewess than to steal her father's jewels and money and take flight with a Christian" (Crook lv-lvi), while in another we are assured that "to rob her father of his ducats and precious stones . . . was a touch of Judaism too much for Christian forgiveness" (Meiklejohn 4). In another still, Jessica's mercurial racial identification itself becomes the key to her redemption, since, it is claimed, "she is not a Jewess in heart and feelings . . . and will readily become a Christian when she marries her lover" (Wood, Manuals 16-17).

It is perhaps not surprising, then, that Henry Irving opted to sever rather than untangle the Gordian knot of racial and domestic affiliations which Jessica brings to the text of *The Merchant of Venice.* For it is harder to imagine anything that would more immediately provoke a late Victorian audience than the suggestion that a faithless daughter could become a faithful wife; that the endowment of manners could be distinguished from the inheritance of blood; that a Jew of discreditable family could become a Christian; and, perhaps most disturbingly, that, in spite of it all, Jessica was a serious marriage prospect by virtue of her dowry, regardless of how it was obtained. What is crucial to recognize here is that in this marginalized and, as we have seen, easily excised character, whose own shortcomings serve primarily to endorse our adoration of the heroine, is constituted a site of significant struggle. And what I am arguing about Henry Irving's *Merchant of Venice* is that its fantastic attractions must be understood in terms of the conflicts and social anxieties it strategically excised when it selectively redefined the representation of Shylock's relationship to his daughter.

Irving's phenomenally successful bid for Shylock as tragic hero is substantially underwritten by his portrayal of the character as a benevolent patriarch betrayed by his thankless child. Audiences saw a Shylock who was "tenderly attached to his daughter" (Hawkins 194), a father who loved Jessica "with no ignoble love" and "feels bitterly her desertion of him and her renunciation of the old faith" (F. Marshall, "Introduction" 251). In order to gain this effect Irving had to play quite deliberately against the text, even after having excised so many lines. And he apparently did so without reserve:

> after Shylock's outburst in III, i, "I would my daughter were dead at my foot," etc. (lines 88 ff.), Irving paused, hid his face in his hands, and murmured an anguished "No, no, no, no!" ... in the subsequent self-pitying lines on his losses, he opened his robe and smote himself continually, slowly, and heavily on his bare breast ... after Jessica's elopement ... the curtain ... rose on Shylock silently walking in the moonlight across the bridge and deserted streets to his home. Originally, the curtain fell as he reached his door, later only after he had knocked several times. (E. M. Moore 201-2)[8]

While the gender politic is thus exploited in order to gain sympathy for Shylock, the racial element is, for the same reason, deliberately downplayed. Irving all but eradicated any suggestion of the Jew's conventionally anticipated obsession with money. Indeed, "to one alert listener at an early performance ... [Shylock] spoke 'with the reflective air of a man to whom money means very little.'" This was apparently more than Irving had intended, and he was compelled to amend his reading of the character in order to convey at least the fact that money was indeed important to Shylock "as a shield against persecution" (Hughes 230). This greatly modified relation of the character to money was something that many viewers were moved to comment upon. Rather than endorse the customary view that Shylock's greed was an inevitable manifestation of his racial identity and a quid pro quo for the play, commentators sought, instead, the mitigating circumstances that had led Shylock to be so. "His avarice," it was argued, was "a vice forced upon him by circumstances" (Hawkins, "Shylock" 194). And, they said, "that it was not personal avarice is ... proved when Shylock scorns thrice his principal proffered to cancel his bond" (Conway 836). Moreover, the sort of reading which sought and found in the character an impressive display of family feeling further identified Shylock as the jealously maligned self-made man. According to some, Shylock cared about money

> not for the pleasures it can purchase for him, nor with that narrow-minded vanity in the sense of possession which the mere miser feels; but rather because it is the evidence of his own thrift and industry, the ... witness, in one respect at least, to his superiority over the Christians who despise and persecute him. (Marshall, "Introduction" 251)

We can see, then, the extent to which Irving's sympathetic portrayal of Shylock depends on a disavowal of race mobilized by the vilification of Jessica. To have allowed the racial question to stand would have been to engage the single element most liable to undermine Irving's carefully wrought appeal. The stage having thus been set, the tragic hero was now free to play out his final moments of glory in the trial scene. For the Jew, safely divested of all but the most sentimental attributes of race, was now eligible to occupy high moral ground.

Drawing on Charles Kean's conception of a diagonal staging, "the design for the trial scene fulfilled the major function of centring the action on Shylock" (Foulkes, "Staging" 317). It was here that Irving was most liberal with his use of innovative stage business, introducing "a crowd of Jews ... to emphasize the ... persecution theme" (E. M. Moore 202), and that the originality of his performance was at its most striking. "Unlike other Shylocks, Irving made his strongest effects in the Trial Scene. Here his dignity had its full scope" (J. R. Brown 194):

> At the end of Portia's verdict he dropped the scales and stood as though mesmerized ... his lips murmured incoherent words as his whole body resumed a dreamy, motionless attitude. When Shylock grasped the severity of his sentence, his eyelids became heavy as though he was hardly able to lift them and his eyes became listless and vacant. The words "I am not well ..." were the plea of a doomed man to be allowed to leave the court and to die in utter loneliness. But Gratiano's ill-timed jibe governed Shylock's exit. He turned. Slowly and steadily the Jew scanned his tormentor from head to foot, his eyes resting on the Italian's face with concentrated scorn. The proud rejection of insult and injustice lit up his face for a moment, enough for the audience to feel a strange relief in knowing that, in that glance, Shylock had triumphed. (L. Irving, qtd in. E. M. Moore 202-3)

The strength of Irving's performance in the trial scene was so overwhelming that it generated difficulties for the other actors and, in particular, for his co-star, Ellen Terry. Terry's own popularity had been greatly enhanced by her debut performance of Portia in the Bancroft's production of *The Merchant of Venice* four years earlier. Visually stunning but otherwise undistinguished, the production had been praised mainly for Terry's performance, and, undoubtedly, this was something audiences had in mind when they purchased their tickets for the Lyceum *Merchant of Venice.* But Irving's Shylock was heroic to the extent that it necessitated a radical revision of Ellen Terry's carefully thought out and established interpretation of her role. In effect, Irving's Shylock made Ellen Terry's Portia impossible. "I am," she wrote, "of the mind that Portia in the trial scene ought to be very quiet... But as Henry's Shylock was quiet, I had to give it up. His heroic saint was splendid, but it wasn't good for Portia" (qtd. in Taylor 191).

Another objection arising out of Irving's portrayal of Shylock in the trial scene was that the representation of the Jew so altered people's expectations of the play that it became virtually unrecognizable. Although his Shylock was "undoubtedly a great piece of acting," it was seen to be "un-Shakespearian if not anti-Shakespearian" (Jones, qtd. in Sprague, "Irving" III). "There was no question... of a bad Shylock or a good Shylock... when... [Irving's] own creation came into conflict with Shakespeare's he simply played in flat contradiction to the lines and acted Shakespeare off the stage" (Shaw, *Dramatic Opinions* 56). As one anonymous reviewer put it, "Before a persecuted Hebrew prophet for hero, a dull ill-mannered Christian for villain, and an incomparable Portia flinging in her lot with the might-is-right party, Shakespeare retired discomfited" (qtd. in Taylor 191). These sorts of opinions were far from quibbling. Where you stood in relation to Irving's Shylock was a matter upon which people staked their personal reputations. And on at least two notable occasions prominent members of the audience went to extreme lengths to dissociate themselves from Irving's reading of the play.

The first such incident actually took place at the dinner celebrating Irving's one hundredth performance of *The Merchant.* Lord Houghton, known as an after-dinner speaker and seated to Irving's right, had been asked, according to custom, to propose a toast. Rather than inviting the assembled guests to join him in celebrating the achievements of Irving and his company, however, Lord Houghton reprimanded Irving "for following the example of some contemporary historians in white-washing and rehabilitating the established villains of the drama." "He for one could not accept Shylock as 'a gentleman of the Hebrew race with the manners of a Rothschild'" (qtd. in L. Irving 354-55).

Even more striking, perhaps, was a comparable incident involving John Ruskin. After attending a performance of *The Merchant,* Ruskin had been invited to meet Irving backstage. At that meeting Ruskin praised Irving's performance, describing it as "noble, tender, and true." The compliment was somehow relayed to Clement Scott, editor of *Theatre* magazine, and found its way into the pages of that publication a short time later. By the next day, however, Ruskin had decided that he had only praised Irving out of politeness and thus wrote to the actor in order to express his views "with more accuracy and frankness." What those views consisted of, primarily, was the belief that Irving's Shylock was, precisely, un-Shakespearean, or, as Ruskin put it, "not... in harmony with his [Shakespeare's] design" (L. Irving 346). But this retraction was conveyed too late to stop the compliment he had paid Irving from appearing in the pages of *Theatre,* and Ruskin was so vexed by this that he once again felt compelled to reply. Here the story becomes truly baroque, for, while Ruskin was clearly incensed about being represented as approving of Irving's *Merchant of Venice* and was accordingly anxious to retrieve his reputation, he suddenly declared himself to be in poor health, too ill to carry on the debate, and so engaged a Mr. Laister to continue the correspondence with Irving on his behalf. In the event Laister wrote to Irving, communicating Ruskin's views, and it is worth noting here the more specific meanings that the phrase "not in harmony with Shakespeare's design" began to reveal once Ruskin had handed over the disagreeable task of being specific on the subject of Shylock to someone else. "You are probably aware," Laister wrote,

> that the Play in question, as revived, has given rise to a vast deal of public teaching, the moral of which Mr. Ruskin and others greatly deplore; and he naturally desires to correct any wrong impression which the unqualified publication of the paragraph in *The Theatre* might create. (Qtd. in L. Irving 348)

Ruskin had told Laister about the original letter he had sent to Irving and directed him to request that "*the whole* of that letter" be published in the *Theatre* as a retraction. Irving's response, not surprisingly, was to "decline to enter into correspondence with a stranger" and to inquire why "Mr. Ruskin... does not write to me in person... if he has any communication to make to me" (349). Despite these considerable difficulties, a version of Ruskin's letter finally did appear in *Theatre,* allowing him to have his say. And what he actually did say at that point was: "I entirely dissent (and indignantly as well as entirely) from his [Irving's] general reading and treatment of the play." Furthermore, Ruskin went on to suggest that anyone interested in a fuller rendering of his views on Shakespeare's meaning in *The Merchant of Venice* should consult his essay "Munera Pulveris," in which he argued that "[the inhumanity of mercenary commerce] is the ultimate lesson which the leader of English intellect meant for us" (*Theatre* 1/3/80 169).

Such incidents are telling, particularly in light of the fact that, for most of the hundreds of thousands of spectators attending the Lyceum production, Irving's *Merchant of Venice* was a triumph and Shylock's exit from the trial scene "the crowning glory" of the play; for most it was the ultimate tragic exit, "and many of the audience actually wept" (Hughes 238). At one point during the opening run Irving cut the entire fifth act, thus ending the play with Shylock's exit from the trial. While the piece was only acted in this form for two months, in order to allow Ellen Terry to star in a one-act version of *Iolanthe* appearing on the same bill, the gesture gave rise to an apocryphal legend. Whenever Henry Irving played *The Merchant of Venice,* people liked to believe, he played it that way.

But even more powerful than the objection that Irving's Shylock was un-Shakespearean was the fear that it was not. For, if Irving were right, then the bard of Avon might indeed have written the play as a plea for toleration toward the Jews.[9] Moreover, once the conventions governing dominant representations of Jews had been exposed and the possibility raised that Shylock was neither grotesque nor merely a clown, the attention of the Victorian public was forced away from the artificiality of the theater to the world outside its doors. The problem with Irving's sympathetic Shylock was that it tended to dispel Victorian nostalgia for the Elizabethan age, leaving nothing in its wake but the threat of internationalism and the increasing pressures of modernity. It admitted the presence of Jews in modern English society and asked, in a way that could not be ignored: If Shylock were not the loathsome and primitive buffoon he had long been held to be, then who was he? How did he get here? And where did he come from?

The simplest and perhaps, for that reason, one of the most popular answers to these questions was that Shylock had come from "somewhere else." The character was declared to be manifestly un-English, the invention of foreigners, undoubtedly having gained entry into England by unconventional means like a dangerous foundling taken in by an unsuspecting English couple. "The Germans have started a theory," one critic wrote,

> that in Shylock Shakespeare wished to portray a sort of noble and dignified martyr to popular prejudice, and this nonsense has been still further elaborated by some of our own critics, who ask us to believe that the Jew of Venice is the embodiment of the spirit of toleration. (*Truth* 6/11/79, 569)

Another line of argument contested the sympathetic Shylock by construing him as a logical impossibility, in effect, as an anachronism whose admission to the realm of possibility invidiously altered the terms of the debate. "To say that . . . [Irving's] was the Jew that Shakespeare drew," wrote one commentator, "would be to quote Pope's doggerel inopportunely." Rather, he argued, "it was the Jew idealized in the light of the modern Occidental reaction against the *Judenhetze,* a Jew already conscious of the Spinozas, the Sidonias, the Disraelis, who were to issue from his loins" (Walkley 136). The un-Shakespearean Shylock altered the balance of power in ways that, up to this point, had been inconceivable, and he rudely exposed the extent to which the inner sanctums of politics and finance had been penetrated by Jews. In the words of one of Irving's first reviewers:

> Irving has . . . impart[ed] to his impersonation . . . the ruling feelings of a Jew such as Shakespeare has drawn . . . [and] these . . . reveal a lofty consciousness such as once manifested to an English constituency by a candidate "descended from a line of Jewish merchants who had . . . told the electors that his ancestors had been princes and statesmen when theirs were staining their bodies with woad." (E. R. R., "Henry" 16)

Yet another response to the question "Who is Shylock, and where did he come from?" was generated in literary-historical circles in which the matter was taken up as a question of genealogy seeking out the origins of Shylock. But, while, in one sense, this was simply the predictable academic response to Henry Irving's "admirable impersonation" of Shylock and the interest it rekindled in a subject that "had long been a bone of contention among critics" (Lee, "Original" 185), in other ways it was more than just another round of debate about literary representations of Jews. As we shall see, the ostensibly editorial task of locating the "original of Shylock" became a search for origins in a number of far-reaching and unforeseen ways, suggesting—at least to a contemporary cultural historian—that the critical exigency here lies not with discovering the historical origins of Shylock but, rather, with examining the motivations of late-nineteenth-century Shakespeareans.

II

> A Jew, in the dictionary, is one who is descended from the ancient tribes of Judea, or one who is regarded as descended from that tribe. That's what it says in the dictionary; but you and I know what a Jew is—*One Who Killed Our Lord* . . . All right. I'll clear the air once and for all, and confess. Yes, we did it. I did it, my family. I found a note in my basement. It said: "We killed him. signed, Morty." And a lot of people say to me, "Why did you kill Christ?" . . . We killed him because he didn't want to become a doctor, that's why we killed him. (Bruce 40-41)

Ruy Lopez, a Jewish Portuguese doctor and personal physician to Elizabeth I, was accused of conspiring to poison the monarch, found guilty, and publicly hanged in June 1594. The affair was widely considered to have inspired both the figures of Shylock and of Marlowe's Barrabas, since it was believed to be roughly contemporaneous with the first productions of both *The Merchant of Venice* and *The Jew of Malta*. While it now seems possible that Lopez was indeed involved in espionage and had, in fact, intended an attempt on the queen's life,[10] what is at issue here is not Lopez's demonstrable innocence or guilt but, rather, the manner in which his story, as it was understood at the time, seized the attention of a number of critics and historians in the latter decades of the nineteenth century. I shall return to those accounts of the Lopez affair later on. For the moment, however, it will be helpful to define the story's parameters and to provide a basis for understanding why it was that people, three hundred years later, wished to find in Lopez a prototype of the figure of Shylock.

Lopez is believed to have settled in England in 1559. He "rapidly reached the highest places in the medical profession in London [and] was the first to hold the office of house physician at St. Bartholomews' Hospital." By 1575 he was listed as one of "the chief London doctors" and shortly afterward served as physician to the household of the Earl of Leicester. In 1586 he was appointed personal physician to Queen Elizabeth, who, in addition to bestowing the honor of his appointment, granted Lopez "a monopoly for the importation of aniseed and sumach into England" (Lee, *Lopez* 132-33). Lopez's success excited a considerable degree of envy, a fact witnessed by the derisory accounts of his rise to public prominence set out in the pamphlets of the day. Gabriel Harvey described him as a man who "by a kind of Jewish practis hath grown to much wealth and sum reputation as well with ye queen herself as with sum of ye greatest Lordes and Ladyes" (qtd. in Lee, *Lopez* 133). One of these lords was the Earl of Essex, whose increasing animosity toward Lopez seems to have been central in contributing to his demise.

Essex attempted to engage Lopez in gathering political intelligence about Spain. Lopez declined, however, and compounded Essex's irritation by disclosing details of his activities to the queen. The intrigue that ensued is unimaginably complicated and cannot be entered into here, but, in briefest outline, a plot was hatched in which Spanish spies in London were alleged to be conspiring to poison both Queen Elizabeth and Don Antonio of Spain. As alleged conspirators were arrested and made statements under torture or threat of torture, Lopez was brought under suspicion. Essex "insisted on his guilt," and Lopez was imprisoned and tried. "The prosecution was conducted by Sir Edward Coke . . . who described the prisoner as 'a perjured and murdering villain and Jewish doctor, worse than Judas himself.' " After Lopez's conviction the queen "delayed signing the death-warrant for three months" but was ultimately unable to prevent his execution. Even in death, however, to those at court Lopez appeared to maintain his privileged vicinity to the center of power; "the queen is said to have worn at her girdle until death . . . [a] jewel given to Lopez by Philip of Spain" (Lee, *Lopez* 134).

There are two powerful metaphors at work in the story of Dr. Lopez which merit particular attention. One is the metaphor of Marranism, or the secret profession of Judaism, to which I will return. The other is the metaphor of the Jewish doctor in an otherwise Jewless state.

At the time that Lopez was appointed personal physician to Queen Elizabeth, England had been, technically speaking, Jewless since the year 1290, when the Jews were expelled by King Edward I. In fact, Jews had been secretly settling in England at least since their expulsion from Spain in 1492. More to the point, however, as Gil Harris has noted, in acquiring a Jewish doctor for the monarch, England was participating in a long-standing if "seemingly inexplicable tradition" of popes and Christian rulers "receiving care from Jewish physicians" (8). This custom posed more than just the obvious paradox of entrusting the well-being of the head of state or the head of the church to an individual whose entire race had been banished for political and spiritual undesirability. For, renowned as they were for their skills in curative medicine, Jews were also commonly believed to be experts in the art of poisoning; and Jewish physicians, it was assumed, participated in a secret but nonetheless somehow universally acknowledged program of "diabolical revenge against Christianity."[11] "The Vienna Faculty of Medicine believed that a private code adhered to by Jewish physicians obliged them to murder one patient in ten [while,] according to Spanish authorities, the figure was one in five" (7). The very Jewishness of the physician was seen to embody "semi-magical properties" (8) so that, absurdly, the attraction of the Jewish court physician was precisely the danger he or she brought to bear. Harris's analysis of the phenomenon is persuasive. The point in employing a Jewish doctor, he says, was that, "as in a modern-day vaccination," the presence of a Jewish physician at court enacted a regulated exposure of the body politic to a toxic substance (9). If Jews could not be hermetically excluded from the state, then at least their secret and powerful presence within it could be harnessed and controlled. When England purged Dr. Lopez from its body politic, it reasserted the integrity of its political boundaries, expelling what was undesirable while appropriating the doctor's seemingly ominous powers for itself.

The issues surrounding Lopez's Marranism are similarly intriguing. Marranos were enforced Jewish converts to Christianity. Yet, though these people were, strictly speaking, fully Christian, in practice the term was perceived to be "synonymous with the secret profession of Judaism" (Lipman I), and the case of Dr. Lopez typifies the Marranos' habitual fate. For, while he had "been baptized, and was a professing member and communicant of the Church of England," according to his enemies "he was said to be no Christian at heart" (Dimock 440-41). On the scaffold Lopez protested his innocence, affirming, up until the moment of his death, his loyalty to church and queen. Yet, though

> with his last words he emphatically insisted that he had loved his mistress better than Christ Jesus . . . coming from one believed to be in secret a Jew by religion as he was by race, this did but excite the derisive laughter of the multitude. (469)

Of all the ways in which Lopez's story prefigures the institutional anti-Semitism of late-nineteenth- and early-twentieth-century commentators on Shakespeare, it is the issue of his Marranism, I would argue, that comes closest to providing a root metaphor for it all. It is a metaphor that I would now like to explore.

In Spain during the Middle Ages Christians, Muslims, and Jews coexisted successfully, if at times uneasily, for centuries. With the Catholic reconquest of Spain, however, the social position of the Jews became increasingly difficult to resolve. For, while Jewish participation in the consolidation of the Catholic state was, on the one hand, considered to be crucial, on the other, it was an enduring point of convergence for popular resentment. On the most basic level the allegiance of the Jews had to be secured in order to ensure that they did not side with the Muslims, but their position was considerably more complex than that. Barred from certain trades and professions, Jews had tended, historically, to earn their living by the provision of services and, as a result, possessed administrative and diplomatic skills that the state was anxious to deploy on its own behalf. Moreover, as occupants of the cultural space between Muslims and Christians, Jews were particularly well placed to serve as "intermediaries" in the adaptation of Muslim institutions to Catholic forms of administration (Poliakov 110). But this Jewish participation in the unification of the Catholic state, effective as it was, gave rise to a dilemma. For, the more successful the mediation and thus the stronger and more unified the state, the more conspicuous became the position of Jews as infidels outside the Catholic Church. And, the more pronounced the infidelity of the Jews seemed, the more it appeared that there was something nefarious about their influential position within Spanish society. Over time perceptions of the social position of Spanish Jews deteriorated into the classic anti-Semitic trope that conveyed the belief that Jews constituted a privileged urban economic caste who exercised a disproportionate influence within the nation, "earning their living without much labour while sitting on their bottoms" (Bernáldez, qtd. in Kamen, *Spanish* 10). And, not surprisingly, the long-standing oscillation between tolerance toward the Jews and discrimination against them eventually degenerated into one of the most protracted catastrophes in Jewish history, culminating in the Inquisition and the expulsion from Spain.

The mounting hostility toward the Jews in Spain expressed itself in conventional ways. Jews were prohibited from participating in trade and commerce, their social mobility and literal freedom of movement were severely restricted, and they were subject to massacres and innumerable smaller-scale physical attacks. Some official efforts were made to ensure the safety of the Jews, but these were effective only in limited ways and in the short term. Significant numbers of Jews converted to Christianity over the years in order to escape persecution, but, as they tended to maintain their associations with unconverted Jews, it was felt that the menace to the Catholic state endured. Many of the converts "lived close to the Jewish quarter to which they still felt a cultural affinity; they retained traditional characteristics in dress and food . . . [and] some returned actively to the practice of Judaism" (Kamen, *Spanish* 27). In 1492 the situation was declared to be intolerable, and it was decreed that the presence of Jews in Spain would no longer be allowed. In July of that year an ultimatum was issued: submit to conversion or be expelled. Hundreds of thousands of Jews fled, initially mainly to Portugal, where they enjoyed a brief period of security. Unfortunately, this only lasted for five years as one of the conditions of a marriage, negotiated between King Manoel of Portugal and Isabel, daughter of Ferdinand and Isabella of Spain, was that the Jews of Portugal convert to Christianity or face expulsion. The Marranos were those who, rather than suffer the terms of exile, chose to convert to Catholicism and stay in Spain.

Once a Jew had become a convert and was no longer subject to political and religious disabilities, there was nothing to impede his or her progress in Spanish society. Understandably enough then, given that they were now free of long-standing restrictions, converts rapidly made their way into the professions, especially law and medicine, the political and financial administration, the municipal councils, the legislature, the army, the universities, and even the church (Roth 21). Moreover, "commercial agility and a . . . disposition to mutual help . . . put them in the vanguard of the new urban bourgeoisie and, in the next century, of the protocapitalist and entrepreneurial class that was then budding in Spain and Portugal" (Yovel 16-17). But, while this successful absorption of the Marranos into every aspect of life should, at least in theory, have satisfied the terms of the act of homogenization which the Spanish state had so forcefully sought, in fact, it merely recast ancient hostilities. For, where once the objection to their presence lay in the question of religion, it now came to be expressed in terms of blood. The Marranos, it was said, were tainted, inferior, impure.[12] And, like the unconverted Jews before the expulsion, they were considered to be exercising an undue influence over Spanish affairs.

By the mid sixteenth century, for example, "it was reputed that most of the Spanish clergy resident in Rome in search of preferment were of Jewish origin" (Kamen, *Spanish* 22) and that a considerable number of Spanish bishops were, in reality, converted Jews. Wealthy Marranos "intermarried with the highest nobility of the land . . . [so that] within a couple of generations, there was barely a single aristocratic family in Aragon, from the royal house downwards, which was free from the 'taint' of Jewish blood" (Roth 21). The Marranos, or New Christians as they were sometimes called, appeared to have finessed their way "into the heart of Christian society, into the ranks of the aristocracy and the Church" (Kamen, *Spanish* 22). And, willfully blind to the role that the enforced conversions had played in creating this situation, popular prejudice held that an alien infestation was hollowing the nation out from the inside.

What the Marranos found themselves confronting was the paradox of assimilation in its most overt form. For, in choosing to submit to conversion in order to avoid expulsion or death, the Marranos had responded to the tacit assurance conveyed by the state's ultimatum: "Become like us—abandon your difference—and you may be one with us." But assimilation is, precisely, a paradox, and the offer of undifferentiated acceptance is thus, by definition, always falsely tendered. "The more you are like me," says the dominant culture, "the more I know the true value of my power, which you wish to share, and the more I am aware that you are but a shoddy counterfeit, an outsider" (Gilman, *Jewish* 2).

While the church could not officially sanction the shunning of Marranos, since the mass conversions had been undertaken at its behest, and to deny their legitimacy would be to deny its own jurisdiction, in practice there was little if any distinction maintained between Marranos and unconverted Jews. The Franciscan Alfonso de Espina gave voice to a widespread belief when he declared that "there were two types of Jews, public Jews and hidden Jews, and that both had the same nature" (Poliakov 181). Unconverted Jews suddenly seemed preferable, since there was at least little doubt about their identity. The problem with the Marranos was that they claimed to be Christians, which, of course, they were—except that everyone knew that they weren't. Jews outside the church were infidels, but they had been dealt with, expeditiously, by the general expulsion. False Christians, which is to say secret Jews inside the church, however, were heretics, and this was by far the greater menace. It was a situation that only the Inquisition could resolve.

The methods of the Inquisition are well documented, and there would be no point here in reiterating the fate of the Marranos at its hands. What is germane to this discussion, however, is the question of how the Inquisition identified its subjects, for deciphering the secrecy of the Jews and learning to deal with their "inherent duplicity" was, as we shall see, a preoccupation that the Inquisition shared with a great many cultures, late Victorian literary society among them.

Historiographically speaking, the secret life of the Marranos is a subject of considerable debate, but, for the time being, the traditional account of their existence is the one that matters here and runs as follows. Publicly, the Marranos lived as Christians, and while there were some "who had not been over-sincere in their attachment to Judaism, and did not find much difficulty in accommodating themselves . . . to their new religion . . . the vast majority," it was believed, "had accepted Christianity only to escape death, and remained at heart as completely Jewish as they had ever been" (Roth 19):

> Outwardly they lived as Christians. They took their children to church to be baptized, though they hastened to wash off the traces of the ceremony as soon as they returned home. They would go to the priest to be married, though they were not content with the ceremony and, in the privacy of their houses, performed another to implement it . . . Their disbelief in the dogmas of the Church was notorious, and . . . not always concealed. They kept all the traditional [Jewish] ceremonies, in some instances down to the last details. They observed the Sabbath so far as lay in their power; and it was possible to see, from a height overlooking any city, how many chimneys were smokeless on that day . . . they married exclusively amongst themselves . . . In race, in belief, and . . . in practice, they remained as they had been before conversion. They were Jews in all but name, and Christians in nothing but form. They were moreover able to transmit their disbelief to their children, who, though born in the dominant faith and baptized at birth, were as little sincere in their attachment to it as their fathers. (20)

The problem with the Marranos, then, was considered to be twofold, a fact that is evident in the twin discourses that arose antagonistically around them and engaged, in tandem, notions of racial predisposition and of the pernicious exploitation of the private sphere. Jews can never be anything other than Jews, it said. Their race is the most important thing about them; they cannot form alliances or make commitments as anything other than Jews.[13] No matter what they say or do in public, in the privacy of their homes they will revert to their innate identity. Their participation in public ceremonies and their declarations of loyalty to persons or institutions outside their own ranks mean nothing, since at home they will simply wash away any trace of these commitments and cease to be their public selves. Jews only marry other Jews. Jews have Jewish children, to whom they communicate, by both biological and social means, the essence of deceit.

The reputed cunning and boundlessness of the Marrano conspiracy set the Inquisition a special challenge, for it found the greatest perils in the greatest semblance of order and the truth to be indistinguishable from lies. Thus, the more mundane and normal the behavior of a Marrano, the more likely he or she was to be brought under suspicion. "Edicts of Faith" were issued which "summoned . . . the faithful . . . to denounce to the . . . authorities any person . . . guilty of . . . heretical offenses" (Roth 99-100). But, as these offenses were necessarily secret, and therefore might not appear to be heretical at all, the edicts included detailed descriptions of the sorts of behaviors true Christians ought to look out for. Some of these behaviors constituted forms of religious observance which would, indeed, identify a practicing Jew, but others, like the smokeless chimneys on Saturdays, were not overt acts but merely absences or actions so commonplace that it was only in the Inquisitorial imagination that they could have significance at all. People were denounced for not eating hare, cuttlefish, or pork; for "putting on clean or festive clothes"; and for "cleaning their houses on Friday." Adherents to the Edicts of Faith were solemnly informed that Jews had a tendency to wash their hands (100-101), creating a social climate in which the "mere regard for personal cleanliness might be enough to convict a person of secretly practising Judaism . . . and so cost him his life" (105).[14]

I will return to the question of how late Victorian commentators on Shakespeare approached the Marrano Lopez and the matter of his relation to the figure of Shylock. But, before doing so, it will be helpful briefly to clarify several points of historiography.

The story of the Marranos is, as I have indicated, a traditional narrative that presents an epic of steadfast belief in the face of insuperable adversity, but, as Miriam Bodian has argued, the tendency to locate the problem of Marranism so firmly within the sphere of religion is reductive on several counts. The overemphasis on religion tends to discount questions of commercial and economic interest and to ignore the complexities of social and familial relationships and of self-perception and definition in a context in which people were subject to protracted and contradictory pressures. Thus, the Marranos are unified into a coherent group and the ineffable complexities of their Marranism reduced to a matter of religious fidelity or infidelity and, occasionally, even further to one of personal sincerity or insincerity.

Even more worrisome, however, is the extent to which the traditional account of the Marranos and their secret faith replicates the logic of Inquisitorial paranoia. For, although historians such as Cecil Roth embrace the cause of the Marranos, valorizing their crypto-Judaism, in order to do so they must leave intact the notion of the racial predisposition of Jews to duplicity. To put it another way, the concept of the Marranos' unshakable loyalty to Judaism is as tied as the tropes of the Inquisition are to the belief that Jewishness is a function of biology or of social characteristics so profoundly embedded that they are effectively quasi-biological. So, while these narratives champion rather than denounce the Marranos, they nevertheless participate in a discourse about Jews which attributes their social and political behavior to their race. More recent work has moved away from this presentation of crypto-Judaism as a coherent phenomenon.

Increasingly, for example, it has been recognized that "patterns of converso behaviour did not simply emerge from some primordial Jewish stratum of consciousness" and that Marrano identity, therefore, needs to be understood "as a changing cultural construction evolving over many generations and answering a variety of needs" (Bodian 50-51). Rather than secretly returning to Judaism at any cost, and with biologically programmed inevitability, Jewish converts to Catholicism displayed a wide range of responses to their respective situations, responses that varied tremendously, from generation to generation and from individual to individual, even among members of a single family. Moreover, compounding these differences were the relative levels of acceptance or rejection which Marranos experienced within their social and religious communities of resettlement and the variety of their relationships with the Jews and Gentiles they encountered outside the Iberian Peninsula. Most profoundly, however, as Yirmiyahu Yovel has argued:

> people do not discard their past simply because they make new decisions or embark upon a new course; a being endowed with consciousness and memory cannot simply return to the point of departure, even when reverting to a position once held in the past and then abandoned. The Marranos had lived among Christians for generations, partaken of their mores and education, practised their customs—at least outwardly—and internalized the same symbolic universe and mode of thinking. (41)

Thus, whether they believed themselves to be true Christians, Christians in name only, or once and forever Jews, the Marranos clearly bore with them enduring confusions of identity which made them, at best, the subjects of benign curiosity and, at worst, of opprobrium and oppression. Only by recognizing these complexities can we begin to appreciate the enduring fascination and treacherous promise attached to figures such as Ruy Lopez and the Shylock he may or may not have inspired.

## III

The question of the Lopez affair and its relation to the figure of Shylock drew the attention of a number of critics and historians in the latter decades of the nineteenth century.[15] These accounts portray Lopez's treachery, his influence on the design of Shylock, and Shakespeare's intentions in representing the Jew. The study I would like to focus on, however, is the one that addressed itself most directly to the Victorian Shakespeare establishment and which was, most obviously, part of the wave of response to Irving's *Merchant of Venice,* appearing as it did in the *Gentleman's Magazine* in February 1880, about halfway through the production's opening run. Moreover, the essay, entitled "The Original of Shylock," deserves particular notice here not only for "attract[ing] . . . the attention of Shakespearean scholars" (*SSL* 3) but also for its part in launching one of the Victorian era's most distinguished literary careers. The eighteen-year-old undergraduate author of the essay went by the forenames Solomon Lazarus. But, for the sake of his career he changed his name, it is popularly believed, on the advice of Oxford's Benjamin Jowett, ironically, a man who had himself been accused of excessive displays of religious radicalism.[16] As an eminent Shakespearean, editor of the *Dictionary of National Biography,* first biographer of Queen Victoria, fellow of the British Academy, founding member of the English Association, and member of the Athenæum Club, to name only a few of his distinctions, Solomon Lazarus was better known to the world as Sidney or, more fully, as Sir Sidney Lee.

In his search for the original of Shylock, Sidney Lee posits four categories of evidence pertaining to the putative links between Shylock and his historical prototype. In outline he argues that the date of composition of *The Merchant of Venice* more or less coincides with the date of the alleged conspiracy and its aftermath; that the text of *The Merchant* contains topical references; that Shakespeare's protagonist, the merchant Antonio, was likely drawn with the protagonist of the Lopez affair in mind; and that Shylock and Lopez display similarities of character too great to be coincidental. As general categories of evidence, these seem fair enough, and, indeed, at the time of the article's publication they greatly impressed established authorities in Elizabethan studies such as J. O. Halliwell-Phillips and F. J. Furnivall. In the context of this study, however, the evidence that Sidney Lee offers with regard to Lopez and his relation to Shylock is compelling primarily in ways that the author and his contemporaries probably did not intend. Rather, what is remarkable from this vantage point is the extent to which the perception of a significant relation between the two figures is, effectively, inevitable, as are the particular narrative formulations mobilized in telling the story of Lopez and Shylock. It was a story that had been told before.

Sidney Lee's most straightforward argument is that pertaining to *The Merchant*'s date of composition, his claim being that the play "appeared for the first time not much more than three months after Lopez's famous execution" (Lee, "Original" 198). But, while it seems unlikely that Shakespeare—or, for that matter, anyone living in London at the time—would have been unaware of so public an event as the execution of the queen's personal physician, Lee's dating of the play and his connection of the two events is largely speculative. Nonetheless, at the time this would have constituted a scholarly argument. His remaining points, by way of contrast, display increasingly prominent elements of fantasy amid the learned speculation.

Lee's identification of topical references, for example, suggests that the connections he was arguing for were, in some imaginative sense, already in place. A conventional allusion to "the rack," which occurs as part of an exchange between the lovers Portia and Bassanio, is taken, without question, to allude to the fate of those implicated in the plot against Elizabeth,[17] while an anachronistic reference to trial by jury—a procedure not known in Venice during the time in which *The Merchant* is set—leads him directly to conclude that it must have been intended to suggest "the way in which an English court of law would treat a Jew" (Lee, "Original" 199). As far as the link between the protagonist of the play and the protagonist of the Lopez affair is concerned, somewhat fantastically, Lee's evidence here consists of little more than the fact that they were both called Antonio. Pointing out that "the name Antonio . . . was very common among the Portuguese"—the protagonist of the Lopez affair was Don Antonio, pretender to the Portuguese throne—it is not "by any means," Lee argues, "so ordinary an Italian one as Lorenzo or Ludovico" (197). It is difficult to know how to respond to this assertion, especially considering the stir it caused in the Shakespearean academic community at the time. To respond insofar as possible in the spirit of the author, however, one can only point out that, with the exception of certain "Citizens," "Servants," "Soldiers," "Ladies," "Gentlemen," and "Ghosts," Antonio is, as a matter of record, the single most commonly occurring name in all of Shakespeare's oeuvre.

Finally, there is Sidney Lee's claim that the similarities of character between Lopez and Shylock are too great to be coincidental. While Lee concedes that not much can be said definitively of Lopez's character, since his "extant correspondence is very incomplete, and gives us only glances here and there of his characteristics," he is nevertheless willing to comment, with authority, on points of character. Firstly, although he doesn't say why, Lee asserts "with some probability" that "the spirit of revenge in the doctor's case was similar in calibre to that in Shylock's." Even more to the point, however, he commits himself with "certainty" to the following claim:

> In their devotion to their family the two Jews closely resemble each other. Neither Lopez nor Shylock, in good fortune or in bad, fail to exemplify the Jewish virtue of domesticity. Lopez excused his attendance at court on the ground that the illness of his wife detained him at home. His Dutch correspondents never omit to send his family affectionate remembrances from his Jewish friends in Holland, whatever be the subject of the letter, and he never omits to return them. Similarly, Shylock's love for his daughter and for his wife Leah, whose memory he piously cherishes, are touches of character which theories of dramatic art only incompletely explain. (Lee, "Original" 198-99)

There are two chronically recurring narratives at work here, the first of which is the story of "the Jewish virtue of domesticity," a virtue that, as we have already seen, necessarily connotes hidden vice. The fact that Lopez's correspondence includes conventional greetings and inquiries after the welfare of friends abroad or that, as a husband and doctor, he should have attended his wife in illness is to Sidney Lee, as they would undoubtedly have been to the Inquisition, signs of the innately suspect nature of Jews. Here, as everywhere else, Jewish participation in the commonplace is a sign of secret goings-on. Thus, the fact that Shylock loves his daughter and reveres the memory of his dead wife cannot possibly be taken at face value. They are enigmatic signifiers, "touches of character which theories of dramatic art only incompletely explain."

The second narrative at work here is one that Sidney Lee authored but did not, in any ordinary sense, write. For, like a man holding up a mirror while looking in the mirror, Sidney Lee, in rooting out the story of Lopez embedded in the figure of Shylock, manifested yet again the infinitely regressive life of the secret Jew. The story of Lee's own life is the story of a great public figure, a man who made his way, by virtue of his talent and industry, to the top of the Victorian intellectual establishment; it is the story of a man deemed fit to write the life of the queen. Considering the accomplishments he could list by the time he died, one would hardly remember that what had launched his career was nothing more than an essay exposing the relation of an infamous Jewish villain to a secret Jew, a great public figure who, like Lee himself, had made *his* way, by virtue of his talent and industry, to the top of the Elizabethan establishment and who, until he was found out, had been deemed fit to guard the life of the queen. Even less would it be remembered that until he had written that essay, as a young man, Sir Sidney had gone by another name.

## Notes

[1] On spectacular production, see Michael Booth, *Victorian Spectacular Theatre, 1850-1910* (London: RKP, 1981); Richard Foulkes, ed., *Shakespeare and the Victorian Stage* (Cambridge: Cambridge UP, 1986), esp. "Part 1: Shakespeare in the Picture Frame"; William E. Kleb, "Shakespeare in Tottenham-Street: An 'Aesthetic' *Merchant of Venice*," *Theatre Survey* 16.2 (1975): 97-121.

[2] The dominance of Irving's interpretation is further indicated by the fact that no notable production of the *Merchant* which did not feature Irving in the role of Shylock was mounted in London until 1905. For a complete list of notable productions and revivals, see Freda Gaye, ed., *Who's Who in the Theatre* (London: Pitman, 1967), 1434. For a more general overview of Jews on the late Victorian stage, see Shearer West, "The Construction of Racial Type: Caricature, Ethnography, and Jewish Physiognomy in Fin-de-Siècle Melodrama," *Nineteenth Century Theatre* 21.1 (1993): 4-40.

[3] Irving's first public defense of his Shylock appeared in *Theatre* on 1 Dec. 1879 (254-55), as part of a symposium on the character. For a lengthy reassertion of his original intentions several years into the history of the production, see Joseph Hatton, *Henry Irving's Impressions of America*, vol. 1 (London: Sampson Low, Marston, Searle and Rivington, 1884), 262-75.

[4] John Gross's claim that "it is generally agreed that his [Irving's] interpretation grew less sympathetic over the years" (141) is unsupported by any convincing evidence. Virtually the only critic to express this view was William Winter, a notorious American theater critic and by Gross's own admission an extremist, who was known as an arch-conservative and a bigot, consistently antagonistic toward non-Anglo-Saxon foreigners on the American stage (*Oxford Companion to the Theatre* 897). Winter's account of Irving's Shylock, in *Shakespeare on the Stage*, appears to be Gross's source. But what Gross fails to take into account is Winter's own reading of *The Merchant* by which he then measures the legitimacy or illegitimacy of subsequent interpretations of Shylock's role. The lurid language Winter uses to describe his ideal of a convincing Jew, coupled with his belief that "the true Shylock of Shakespeare" must be "hard, merciless, inexorable, terrible" (178), strongly suggests that Irving's softening of the role did not sit well with Winter's own feelings about Jews. The two men were friends for many years, and it is likely that Winter was reading into Irving's performance what he wished were there but, as other evidence would suggest, manifestly was not.

[5] For a selection of reviews of Irving's American tour of 1883, see *Mr. Henry Irving and Miss Ellen Terry in America: Opinions of the Press* (Chicago: John Morris, 1884).

[6] Edward Moore, in his essay "Henry Irving's Shakespearean Productions" (*Theatre Survey* 17.2 [1976]:

201), says, for example, that Irving "cared nothing about realizing a play as written, but only about making his effects; and splendid as these no doubt were, most of us would rather have Shakespeare's."

[7] On the importance of conversion as a cultural motif and of the father-daughter relationship in this context, see Michael Ragussis's compelling *Figures of Conversion: "The Jewish Question" and English National Identity* (Durham: Duke UP, 1995).

[8] Robert Hichens, in his essay "Irving as Shylock" (in *We Saw Him Act,* ed. H. A. Saintsbury and Cecil Palmer [London: Hurst and Blackett, 1939], 168), remarks on how unforgettable this bit of stage business was.

[9] For an example of just such a discussion, see Frederick Hawkins, "The Character of Shylock," *Theatre* (1 Nov. 1879): 191-98; and the roundtable discussion involving numerous commentators, including Irving himself, the following month (*Theatre* [1 Dec. 1879]).

[10] For a recent account of Lopez, see David Katz, "The Jewish Conspirators of Elizabethan England" *The Jews in the History of England, 1485-1850* (Oxford: Clarendon P, 1994): 49-106.

[11] See also, Sander Gilman. *Jewish Self-Hatred* (Baltimore: Johns Hopkins UP, 1986): 37 ff., 61 ff.

[12] On changing perceptions of Marranism, see Miriam Bodian, " 'Men of the Nation': The Shaping of *Converso* Identity in Early Modern Europe," *Past and Present* 143 (1994): 48-76.

[13] See Gilman, *Jewish Self-Hatred,* chap. 3, esp. 83 ff.

[14] On this point, see also Moshe Lazar, " 'Scorched Parchments and Tortured Memories': The 'Jewishness' of the Anussim (Crypto-Jews)," in *Cultural Encounters: The Impact of the Inquisition in Spain and the New World,* ed. Mary Elizabeth Perry and Anne J. Cruz (Berkeley: U of California P, 1991), 182 ff.

[15] See Arthur Dimock, "The Conspiracy of Dr. Lopez," *English Historical Review* (July 1894): 440-72; and John W. Hales, "Shakespeare and the Jews," *English Historical Review* (Oct. 1894): 652-61.

[16] See C. H. Firth, *Sir Sidney Lee, 1859-1926,* in Proceedings of the British Academy (London: Humphrey Milford, 1929), 15:3.

[17]   *Bassanio:*
      Let me choose,
  For as I am, I live upon the rack.
  *Portia:*
    Upon the rack Bassanio? Then confess
    What treason there is mingled with your love.
  *Bassanio:*
    None but that ugly treason of mistrust
    Which makes me fear th'enjoying of my love.
    There may as well be amity and life
    'Tween snow and fire, as treason and my love.
  *Portia:*
    Ay, but I fear you speak upon the rack,
    Where men enforced do speak anything.
  *Bassanio:*
    Promise me life and I'll confess the truth.
  *Portia:*
    Well then, confess and live.
                      (III.ii.25-39)

## Bibliography

PRIMARY SOURCES

*Examination and Study Guides and Other Editions of Shakespeare and* The Merchant of Venice

Barnett, T. Duff, ed. *Shakespeare's Merchant of Venice.* London: Bell, 1893.

Crook, C. W., ed. *The Merchant of Venice.* London: Ralph, Holland, 1907.

Meiklejohn, J. M. D., ed. *Shakespeare's* Merchant of Venice. London: Chambers, 1879.

*The Merchant of Venice.* As presented at the Lyceum Theatre under the Management of Mr. Henry Irving. London: Chiswick, 1881.

Verity, A. W., ed. *The Merchant of Venice.* Cambridge: Cambridge University Press, 1912.

Wood, Stanley. Supplement to *The Merchant of Venice. Questions and Notes.* Dinglewood Shakespeare Manuals. Manchester: Heywood, 1891.

*Other Primary Sources*

Bruce, Lenny. *The Essential Lenny Bruce.* New York: Ballantine, 1967.

Conway, Moncure D. "The Pound of Flesh." *Nineteenth Century* May 1880: 828-39.

Cook, Dutton. *"The Merchant of Venice": Nights at the Play.* London: Chatto and Windus, 1883. 2:223-27.

Dimock, Arthur. "The Conspiracy of Dr. Lopez." *English Historical Review* July 1894: 440-72.

E. R. R. "Ellen Terry as Portia." *Theatre* 1 Jan. 1880: 49.

———. "Henry Irving as Shylock." *Theatre* 1 Jan. 1880: 16.

Hatton, Joseph. *Henry Irving's Impressions of America.* 2 vols. London: Sampson Low, Marston, Searle, and Rivington, 1884.

Hawkins, Frederick. "The Character of Shylock." *Theatre* 1 Dec. 1879: 260-61.

———. "Shylock and Other Stage Jews." *Theatre* 1 Nov. 1879: 191-98.

Irving, Henry. "The Character of Shylock." *Theatre* 1 Dec. 1879: 254-55.

Jameson, Anna. "Portia." *Characteristics of Women, Moral, Poetical, and Historical.* London: Saunders and Otley, 1833.

Lee, Sidney. "The Original of Shylock." *Gentleman's Magazine* Feb. 1880: 185-200.

———. "Roderigo Lopez." *Dictionary of National Biography.* London: Smith, Elder, 1909. 132-34.

Marshall, Frank. "The Character of Shylock." *Theatre* 1 Dec. 1879: 256-57.

———. "Introduction." *The Merchant of Venice. The Henry Irving Shakespeare.* Ed. Henry Irving and Frank Marshall. London: Blackie, 1888.

Martin, Helena Faucit. "Portia." 1 Sept. 1880 (for private circulation). British Library Catalogue 11763 cc18.

Shaw, George Bernard. *Dramatic Opinions and Essays.* Vol. 2. New York: Brentano's, 1906-7.

SECONDARY SOURCES

Barnes, J. H. " 'Irving Days' at the Lyceum." *Nineteenth Century* Jan. 1923: 99-116.

Brown, John Russell. "The Realization of Shylock." *Early Shakespeare.* Ed. John Russell Brown and Bernard Harris. London: Arnold, 1961. 187-209.

Foulkes, Richard. "Helen Faucit and Ellen Terry as Portia." *Theatre Notebook* 31 (1977): 27-37.

———. "The Staging of the Trial Scene in Irving's *The Merchant of Venice.*" *Educational Theatre Journal* 28 (1976): 312-17.

Gilman, Sander L. *Difference and Pathology: Stereotypes of Sexuality, Race, and Madness.* Ithaca: Cornell UP, 1985.

———. *Jewish Self-Hatred: Anti-Semitism and the Hidden Language of the Jews.* Baltimore: Johns Hopkins UP, 1986.

Gross, John. *Shylock.* London: Chatto and Windus, 1992.

Hughes, Alan. *Henry Irving, Shakespearean.* Cambridge: Cambridge UP, 1981.

Irving, Laurence. *Henry Irving.* London: Faber, 1951.

Kamen, Henry. *The Spanish Inquisition.* London: Weidenfeld and Nicolson, 1965.

Lipman, V.D. *A History of the Jews in Britain since 1858.* Leicester: Leicester UP, 1990.

Maude, Cyril. "Irving as Shylock." *We Saw Him Act: A Symposium on the Art of Henry Irving.* Ed. H.A. Saintsbury and Cecil Palmer. London: Hurst and Blackett (1939): 171-73.

Moore, Edward M. "Henry Irving's Shakespearean Productions." *Theatre Survey* 17 (1976): 195-216.

Poliakov, Leon. *The History of Anti-Semitism.* Vol. 2. Trans. Natalie Gerardi. London: RKP, 1974.

Roth, Cecil. *A History of the Marranos.* New York: Meridian, 1959.

Sprague, A. C. "Irving as Shylock." *Shakespearian Players and Performances.* London: Black, 1954.

Taylor, George. "Shakespearean Interpretation." *Players and Performances in the Victorian Theatre.* Manchester: Manchester UP, 1989. 173-91.

Walkley, A. B. "Henry Irving" (1892). Rowell, *Victorian* 134-37.

Yovel, Yirmiyahu. *Spinoza and Other Heretics: The Marrano of Reason.* Princeton: Princeton UP, 1989.

---

Source: "Shylock: The Infamous Secret Jew," in *Shakespeare and the Politics of Culture in Late Victorian England,* The Johns Hopkins University Press, 1998, pp. 61-95.

# Histories

# The Prince's Dog: Falstaff and the Perils of Speech-Prefixity

## Harry Berger, Jr., *University of California, Santa Cruz*

Throughout the two *Henry IV* plays, from his first appearance in the second scene of Part 1, Falstaff knowingly collaborates with Harry on the scenario entitled "The Rejection of Falstaff," subplot of "The Return of the Prodigal Son." Harry's resounding "I know thee not, old man" near the end of Part 2 (5.5.47) fulfills the scenario he entertained in the "I know you all" soliloquy that concluded the second scene of Part 1 (1.2.189-211).[1] But Falstaff had already anticipated the scenario, alluding to it several times during conversations leading up to the soliloquy. Consider, for example, his sanctimonious parody at 1.2.89-96:

> O, thou hast damnable iteration, and art indeed able to corrupt a saint. Thou hast done much harm upon me, Hal, God forgive thee for it. Before I knew thee, Hal, I knew nothing; and now am I, if a man should speak truly, little better than one of the wicked. I must give over this life, and I will give it over. By the Lord, an I do not I am a villain. I'll be damned for never a king's son in Christendom.

Substituting "Falstaff" for "Hal" in this passage makes it clear that the sentiments he utters in the first person are those he attributes to Harry. They indicate his awareness that Harry will sooner or later run bad humors on the knight and that the rejection of Falstaff will be necessitated by a Puritan impulse to self-purgation in the prince. Falstaff impersonates Harry's response to his report that "An old lord of the council rated me the other day in the street about you" (ll. 82-84), and this suggests that he already anticipates Harry's famous "I do, I will" (*2 Henry IV*, 2.4.476) and his more famous "I know thee not, old man." He knows from the beginning both that Harry has chosen him to play the role of misleader and that his misrule must have an end. He also recognizes the particular version of the Prodigal Son story that will best accommodate not only Harry's political needs but his moral needs as well: the naïf victimized by misleaders. That he knowingly, ironically, accepts this role turns out to be motivated by his own need for the Judgment he seems so enthusiastically to flout and thus to ask for. His deliberate assumption of the role in the second scene of Part 1 sharpens its challenge and its risk by giving Harry the moral advantage along with the chance to misuse it.

I find it difficult, therefore, to interpret his excited rush toward the royal presence in Act 5 of Part 2 as motivated only by a simple desire for preferment. Everything about the episode vibrates uneasily with the desire to bring his carnival to an exorcistic conclusion, to make himself "bait for the old pike" (3.2.329) and get his comeuppance. This orgiastic prospect spurs him to transgression and provocation: "Master Shallow, my lord Shallow—be what thou wilt, I am fortune's steward. . . . I know the young King is sick for me. Let us take any man's horses; the laws of England are at my commandment" (5.3.132-39). His plan to greet the king "stained with travel and sweating with desire to see him" is explicitly voiced as a histrionic fantasy: "to ride day and night, and not to deliberate, not to remember, not to have patience to shift me . . . thinking of nothing else, putting all affairs else in oblivion, as if there were nothing else to be done but to see him" (5.5.20-27).[2] That he thinks the newly crowned king will appreciate his "zeal . . . to see him," his "earnestness of affection," his "devotion" (ll. 14, 16, 18), is hardly credible in view of his previous knowing assessments of Harry. If he is in a state of "inflammation" similar to the one he mockingly ascribes to the "operation" of sack in the soliloquy at 4.3.95-115, it is because he has prepared himself for the long-deferred expulsion or sacrifice that will end the "lingering act" (1.1.156) of his carnival.

This is not to suggest that Falstaff's behavior in this scene fails to display any hope of advancement. That hope rides on the rhetorical surface of his excitement. But the message conveyed by the totality of his utterances and actions up to this point is that he also wants to put both his hope and Harry to the test; he wants to see how far Harry will let him go, to probe the limits of transgression, to expose himself to the risk of the rejection and punishment he half looks forward to. And it is further confused by another motive: he knows the king needs a public occasion, a ritual of exorcism, to dramatize his reformation, and he cooperates in provoking it. Yet even as he yields to the temptation to offer himself up to Harry, he continues Being Bad. For if Harry shifts responsibility in calling Falstaff his misleader, Falstaff's provocation gives him the opportunity and makes the king appear solely responsible for the rejection the two had been conspiring to bring about from the start. It is in the context of this discursive tug of war that one can begin to appreciate the ethical constraints on Harry and the meaning of his response to it.

"I know thee not, old man. Fall to thy prayers. / How ill white hairs becomes a fool and jester" (5.5.47-48). These words signal Harry's rejection not only of

Falstaff but also of the knowledge of what really went on between them. The distance of the refusal to know is increased by the generic appellation "old man," which Harry's subsequent words interpret in a religious context so that "old man" becomes synonymous with "my former self." (These connotations reverberate in *Henry V* in Canterbury's scary characterization of the king's violent conversion: "Consideration like an angel came / And whipped th' offending Adam out of him" [1.1.29-30].) "I know thee not" asserts the reality of Falstaff's sinfulness by forcefully and publicly rejecting it and asserts the validity of Harry's conversion. This seeming knowledge keeps Harry from submitting to an unknown or half-known fear of himself, but of course it does so by a strategy that must reactivate the fear, since he is at this very moment falsifying the hopes of his corruptibility that he earlier aroused.

Without such knowledge Harry could win the crown of England but could not ensconce himself on the throne of his self-esteem. Therefore he rejects the ironic Falstaffian voice that refuses to sanction this knowledge and stubbornly reminds him he was a falsifier of hopes. Yet even here the traces of guilt and his need to manage it are registered in the sentence he passes. Those who criticize Harry for the harshness of his treatment of Falstaff, for the narrowing of his sensibility, for the sacrifice of humaneness demanded by the royal office, perhaps overlook the character of the sentence. Given the severity of his rhetoric, it is oddly anticlimactic:

> When thou dost hear I am as I have been,
> Approach me, and thou shalt be as thou wast,
> The tutor and the feeder of my riots.
> Till then, I banish thee, on pain of death,
> As I have done the rest of my misleaders,
> Not to come near our person by ten mile.
> For competence of life I will allow you,
> That lack of means enforce you not to evils.
> And, as we hear you do reform yourselves,
> We will, according to your strengths and
>   qualities,
> Give you advancement.
> (5.5.60-70)

Because "I banish thee, on pain of death" sounds so threatening, the actual terms of banishment specified two lines later seem surprisingly lenient, producing at the rhetorical level the effect of a feint toward strict justice countered by a gesture of clemency.[3] The sentence is proclaimed in words that express the speaker's full assurance of his moral superiority. But what he brandishes is a carrot, not a stick.

I view this maneuver as an act of moral self-protection. The motivation behind it may be suggested by comparing a section of Harry's first soliloquy in Part 1 with the declaration in Part 2 that precedes the passage quoted above:

> So when this loose behavior I throw off
> And pay the debt I never promisèd,
> By how much better than my word I am,
> By so much shall I falsify men's hopes. . . .
> I'll so offend to make offense a skill,
> Redeeming time when men think least I will.
> (*1 Henry IV,* 1.2.202-11)

> Presume not that I am the thing I was,
> For God doth know, so shall the world
>   perceive,
> That I have turned away my former self;
> So will I those that kept me company.
> (*2 Henry IV,* 5.5.56-59)

Since these two passages represent a promise and its fulfillment, they dramatize the singleness, the integrity, of the speaker's purpose over time. Thus they contradict the assertion that he is not the thing he was. He knows he never *was* but only *played* the prodigal, that he *was* and therefore *remains* the misleader of his misleaders and the falsifier of the hopes he falsely planted in others. That this is something he has not been able conveniently to forget is evidenced by the continuing traces of anger and violence his language betrays from the time of his interview with his dying father to the end of *Henry V*.[4] *Henry V* as a whole reflects the consequences of Harry's need to produce and maintain a ten-mile trouble-free zone around his conscience. This may be sensed in the language with which he protests to the French ambassadors that "We are no tyrant, but a Christian king," whose passion "is as subject [to our grace] / As is our wretches fettered in our prisons" (1.2.241-43), an odd analogy that exposes his dim view of his passion. The anger he directs toward Henry, Falstaff, and the French is rooted in what I have elsewhere described as the self-purging fury with which he "scours [the] faults" of others while persisting in his famous disclaimers of responsibility.[5] These signs of anxious concern for moral solvency indicate his abiding suspicion that he may be more sinning than sinned against. It is in this general context that I view Harry's tempered rejection of Falstaff as a defensive maneuver of self-exculpation, part of a pattern in evidence from their first appearance together in the second scene of *1 Henry IV*.

Nothing in this interpretation of Harry's language would surprise the speaker who emerges from my reading of Falstaff's language. His awareness of the prince's project and of his own relation to it is suggested from the beginning, conveyed by such teasingly indirect means as the parody of sanctimoniousness discussed above. It peeps forth with equal diffidence before the Gadshill robbery when he complains about the removal of his horse:

> I am accursed to rob in that thief's company. The rascal hath removed my horse and tied him I know not where.... Well, I doubt not but to die a fair death for all this, if I scape hanging for killing that rogue. I have forsworn his company hourly any time this two-and-twenty years, and yet I am bewitched with the rogue's company. If the rascal have not given me medicines to make me love him, I'll be hanged; it could not be else—I have drunk medicines. Poins! Hal! A plague upon you both!
>
> (2.2.10-20)

This passage is ambiguous for two reasons. First, as David Bevington points out, though Poins is the obvious referent of the complaint, "much of what Falstaff says . . . about the rascal's bewitching company applies no less aptly to Hal."[6] Second, until the outburst at the end, it isn't clear what kind of speech act it is. This can be determined only—like the "open silences" Philip McGuire discusses in *Speechless Dialect*—by the way it is staged.[7] The speaker could utter or mutter it to himself. He could say it loud enough to indicate that he wants to be overheard, and those at whom it is directed could be either offstage or visibly within earshot. If he aims his vexation at potential eavesdroppers, he could do so simply to register a complaint; but he could also do it to keep the game in play by telling his persecutors what they want to hear. It becomes clear as he continues—and even clearer if we note the echoes of the previous scene with Gadshill and the carriers—that he is *performing* the victim's discourse, exploiting its dialectical turnings, the alternation of its rhetoric between the specious probity of injured innocence and the villain's compensatory bluster:

> I'll starve ere I'll rob a foot further. An 'twere not as good a deed as drink to turn true man and to leave these rogues, I am the veriest varlet that ever chewed with a tooth. Eight yards of uneven ground is threescore-and-ten miles afoot with me, and the stony-hearted villains know it well enough. A plague upon it when thieves cannot be true one to another! . . . A plague upon you all! Give me my horse, you rogues, give me my horse, and be hanged!
>
> (ll. 21-29)

When a speaker echoes the words and sentiments uttered in an episode from which he was absent (in this case, 2.1), it usually means that he is inscribed in the same discourse. Here, Falstaff articulates the discourse and inscribes himself in it. Allowing himself to be set up, pretending to be an unwilling victim, and feigning indignation at the disloyalty of thieves, he stages the complicity and self-deception that drive the intertwined discourses of the victim-revenger and the villain. He parades himself as an example of what he mocks.[8]

The structure of eavesdropping in this performance is complex, but it is considerably clarified by the sense Bevington conveys of the staging of the episode. In his account of the textual difficulties that make for indeterminate stage directions, he speculates that since Harry "comes forward to torment Falstaff about his horse, . . . he presumably overhears with Poins the soliloquy of comic grumbling that Falstaff directs at them. Conventions of darkness on the Elizabethan stage allowed the audience to suppose that Falstaff could not see those who are teasing him and overhearing his complaint."[9] Falstaff, then, is listening to them listen to him, and letting them know it. The speech is itself a kind of eavesdropping performed by someone who rustles conspicuously behind the arras. Since, in the analogy this metaphor suggests, Falstaff resembles Polonius less than Harry resembles Hamlet, I am attracted to Bevington's suggestion that his opening remarks easily bounce from their putative target, Poins, to Harry.[10] What he says is not "I love him" but "he has made me love him; it's his fault; he has bewitched me, seduced me, misled me, victimized me; he is indeed able to corrupt a saint." This is another piece of innuendo by mimicry. It continues Falstaff's knowing parody in 1.2 of the purposes subsequently revealed in the "I know you all" soliloquy.

If, then, he submits "with comic grumbling" to the project he mimics, a project that (the mimicry suggests) will victimize him sooner or later and of which the present episode is a proleptic parody, an anamorphic reduction, is it because he believes what he says: "I am bewitched with the rogue's company"? Does he believe it about Harry? About himself? Is he expressing what he thinks Harry feels or what he thinks Harry pretends to feel? What he himself feels or what he pretends to feel? Is he—and this is a possibility the Shakespearean soliloquy always promotes—eavesdropping on himself as well as the others, testing his ability, his desire, to believe the sentiments he utters? His ability and desire to deceive himself and justify yielding to the affection he knows will undo him? And if the innuendo by mimicry is intended for Harry's ears, is he prompting Harry to listen to him listen to Harry so that Harry will understand "I know you all" has been overheard? And, understanding that, will perceive that Falstaff perceives "I know you all" supplies the real force, the real meaning, behind the comic colting/uncolting of Falstaff?

At this point we can do little more than sift aimlessly through these questions because they encode the unresolved condition and ongoing interrogations of the bond between Falstaff and Harry. They represent questions I imagine Falstaff continually to ask himself, to ask Harry, and to ask Harry to ask himself; questions asked through the safely indirect medium of practical jokes and wit wars, questions that aren't yet answerable and whose darker implications are lightly broached in Falstaff's soliloquy, then carefully thrown away by the comic form the episode as a whole gives to the victim's discourse. The spectacle of Falstaff colted and uncolted condenses, displaces, reduces—in a word, *detextualizes*—those implications and thereby controls them. But because they are very much alive in the illocutionary fireworks of the soliloquy, their latent power overshadows the spectacle. Its comic circumstances anamorphically foreshorten the deep encounter embedded in the textual conditions of the scene's language. This limitation has strategic value: it enables Falstaff and Harry to go on colting and testing each other, sounding each other out, circling about each other.

I have been at this game long enough to know that the preceding analysis of interlocutory and illocutionary action is not something readers are inclined to accept at face value, especially those readers whose interests tend to be stage-centered and who are impatient with what they view as needlessly complexifying accounts of language intended to be spoken and heard in real-utterance time. Since I stand by the defense of decelerated close reading worked out in *Imaginary Audition,* I won't repeat it here. But there are some methodological premises informing my view of speakers' relations to their language and language games that may seem counterintuitive enough to violate conventional assumptions about the interpretation of speech acts in theatrical texts, and especially of two aspects of deixis: the direction and recipients of address in speech marked as soliloquy, and the reflexivity of address in speech acts of any kind. What does it mean for a fictional speaker to address a theater audience? Can a speaker who performs for and before others be shown to address himself as one of those others? What theoretical distinctions and moves are necessary to orient reading toward the signs of self-representation and self-auscultation in dialogue as well as in monologue and soliloquy?

METHODOLOGICAL INCIPIT

*The Old Law:* In the beginning Shakespeare created the script and the characters, and the script was inky-still and unsound, while the characters were without body; whereupon he created actors and performances to give soundness to the script and body to the characters.

*The New Law:* In the beginning is the speech prefix, and the speech prefix is with the text, and the text is speech. *And the text transforms its speech prefix into the name both of the object represented by the speech and of the subject that represents itself through the speech.*[11] And neither the object nor the subject named by the speech prefix is with body until the actor's manlike or boylike body fills the words with sound. Nor does either have a character or become a character until speech as script is uttered by the actor and speech as text is interpreted by a reader. And the first reader is the actor, who performs his interpretation before an audience. And from the totality and multiplicity of performances and interpretations unrolling or scrolling across the horizon of time will be revealed the authorial Last Thing, the Omega that validates them all by being rewritten as their Alpha, the speech prefix "Shakespeare."

From the New Law flow many potent precepts, propositions, definitions, and guidelines to perplexity, but in this essay my immediate purpose is to explore the implications of the italicized sentence in order to reexamine the coordinates of the interlocutory territory that environs a single speech prefix, the name Oldcastle/Falstaff, which will from now on be abbreviated to Falstaff.[12] My contention is that our maps of the territory are constructed according to imprecise interpretive cartographies that reflect various designs on Falstaff's ownership of his name and region, efforts to reduce him to a figurehead representing interests other than his own. I contend, in other words, that when critics, by means of their interpretations, transform the speech prefix into a speaker and a subject, the subject is dissociated from the speaker: the real subject is not the character but the playwright, the actor, the audience, or the culture—whatever is presumed to speak through the character Falstaff; and the character, dethroned from the subject position, is reduced to an object, a symbol, an iconograph, the bearer of the meanings of others.

In the playscripts there is no presence on the other side of the representational medium of speech, only a speech prefix. Therefore what actors present is a more aggressive mode of representation: not a *re*-presentation but an interpretation, and one that may depend for its effect on the charismatic force of presentation—an interpretation of the character that may reduce it (her, him) to the medium, vehicle, or reflection of the performance and its context, may reduce it (her, him) to the *re*presentation of a presentation so that the character is more the object than the subject of the speech assigned to the speech prefix. This problem invariably confronts playwrights who work within a star system, and the existence of something like an Elizabethan star system is indicated by the fact that in early Shakespeare texts, in which the same speaker may be denoted by speech prefixes other than the character's name, the actor's name is one of the frequent alternatives.[13] As Randall McLeod notes during his discussion of the implications of this "polynomial" practice, there were plays "in which the actor's own personality and sometimes his name were as much part of the stage business and audience response as was his fictive role."[14] In Elizabethan times as in our own, the star system encouraged audiences "to identify themselves with the 'star' actors, to wish the characters portrayed . . . 'as if the personator were the man personated.' "[15]

Were playgoers drawn by the prospect of seeing Burbage as Hamlet, Tarleton as Dericke, and Kempe as Falstaff, or did presentation so outweigh representation as a performance value that these preferences were inverted and Shakespearean theater aspired to the condition of opera? You don't go to hear Joan Sutherland's Norma or Placido Domingo's Otello or Maria Callas's Tosca; you go to hear Tosca's Callas, Otello's Domingo, and Norma's Sutherland. Of course, any composer/librettist familiar with that audience predilection is perfectly capable of standing it on its head and representing characters who carry on as if they were opera singers trapped in and frustrated by the stereotypes identified with The Tenor, The Soprano, etc., that is, by the cultural representations produced when opera conventions transform vocal registers into ethical discourses. So, too, the playwright confronting the charismatic dominance of the Actor over the Character may respond by displacing the tension between Actor and Character to a tension within Character. Imagine Morris Carnovsky telling Shakespeare that when he plays Lear, "it is *my own* indignation, *my own* frustration, *my own* anger, *my own* dawning sympathy with the world . . . that I communicate."[16] If I were Shakespeare, I would ask Carnovsky whether he would also be willing to communicate at least a little of his own complicity, his own self-contempt, his own self-love, his own fear of death and emasculation, his fear especially of being unworthy of the love he needed and demanded from his children. Or perhaps I wouldn't ask him to do all that; I would simply write it into his language as everything he disowns or evades by emphasizing the indignation, frustration, anger, and dawning sympathy of the victim and fool whose suffering brought him knowledge and love. I would thus displace the tension I discerned between Carnovsky's Lear and mine into a tension within Lear. The effect of this shift would be to embed the conditions of theater within the dramatic illusion so that Character would be less the object of Actor's speech and more the subject of his or her own speech.

Such a displacement is indeed the theme of the story of Elizabethan drama told in various ways by theater historians as they explore the changing relations between presentation and representation, theatrical interaction and dramatic illusion, the staging of community rituals and the staging of dramatic fictions. But there is a problem in the way the story is told, and the problem turns on a difficulty in conceptualizing and maintaining the distinction between Actor's and Character's relations to their respective audiences. In his indispensable *Shakespeare and the Popular Tradition in the Theater,* Robert Weimann gives social and ideological substance to the story through his account of the transformation of what were initially upstage and downstage locations (*locus* and *platea*) in the medieval theater to modes of *"Figurenposition,"* the orientations of stage presence by which the actor "establishes a special relationship between himself and his fellow actors, the play, or the audience, even when direct address has been abandoned."[17] Weimann immediately goes on to illustrate this with a discussion not of actors but of characters, Hamlet and Apemantus, and their relations to their "fellow actors." Is Hamlet as Hamlet aware of his fellow actors or of his fellow characters? When he moves downstage and seems to accost the audience, is it the same audience as the one addressed by the actor playing Hamlet?

The second question crops up during the course of Weimann's stimulating and persuasive analysis of the complex organization of behavior, stage position, dress, and language that allows Hamlet to establish "audience contact without departing from his role."[18] Shakespeare's accomplishment is to make

> Hamlet's special *Figurenposition,* his being apart from the *locus* (and the "illusion") of court society . . . [have] a real (theatrical) as well as an imaginative (characterizing) significance. And so, spatial position assumes a moral function: the actor's rejection of illusion is turned into the character's honesty "which passes show."

> Thus, traditional forms of dramaturgy are turned into modern modes of characterization; the paradox being that Hamlet, who knows no "seems," has to develop his *platea*-like *Figurenposition* within the "seems," that is, the illusionistic frame of the Renaissance play.[19]

But the "traditional actor-audience relationship" is maintained by the deployment of "verbal conventions" that "break the dramatic illusion and create the so-called 'extra-dramatic moment,'" sustaining the impertinent authority of theater as an upstart institution.[20] On the one hand Weimann demonstrates that the spectacle in which actors present themselves representing characters to an audience is gradually internalized or fictionalized until it infiltrates and haunts the language and actions of the characters. On the other hand he demonstrates that the traditional relation persists in the modern one, and that an alienating or defamiliarizing power results from the mixing of modes. These different emphases are held together by Weimann's premise that in moments of direct audience contact, the character and the actor both address the same audience, the one consisting of the actual spectators in the actual theater. Not only does this premise limit Weimann's conception of, and interpretive engagement with, the displacement of the actor's *"platea*-like *Figurenposition"* to the character; it also leads to at least one questionable inference, namely, that the character intermittently behaves as if he or she knows he or she is in a theater performing before an audience, an effect that may give charismatic actors a chance to go Operatic and strut their stuff at Character's expense.[21]

I want to modify this premise but not reject it. That the Elizabethan theater is both participatory (or collaborative) and representational (or illusionistic) can hardly be denied.[22] But both modes are equally conventional, being inscribed in a conventional structure of theatrical practices that defines each mode in terms of and over against the other. And insofar as the use of scripts or "sides" and promptbooks are among those practices, both modes are fictional: to the extent that participatory episodes—prologues, epilogues, asides, soliloquies, stand-up monologues, clown acts—are scripted, the audience they engage is a fiction, a virtual audience constituted by the direction and express motivation of address and thus pre-existing any actual audience. This holds true for minor as well as major characters—for clowns and choruses no less than for such villainous *platea* addicts as Richard III and Iago. But of course the latter have more scope to make the transition from functioning *as* actors to functioning *like* actors—more scope, that is, to internalize the actor-function and, as characters, to be the subjects of the speech through which they present themselves representing themselves to themselves and others. Such variations in the intensity of self-representation as occur between minor and major speakers correlate with modal shifts between collaborative and illusionistic emphases, in which the collaborative often seem to serve up metatheatrical critiques of the illusionistic, and they call for corresponding flexibility in the intensity of linguistic or rhetorical interpretation.

One way to imagine the variable state of this theatrical structure is to plot it diagrammatically along a polar continuum:

```
Collaborative<------------------------------->Illusionistic
     1         2            3              4          5
   actor     actor    character/actor   character  character
           character                      actor
```

Metatheatrical negotiations between theatrical presentation and dramatic representation go on across the range of the three middle positions (2-4) between the pure poles, the idealized points, of the actor and the character, neither of which appears in a staged play. The actor-qua-actor (not representing a character) appears only outside the play—before it, after it, or in the tiring house—and the character-qua-character (unrepresented by an actor) appears only in unstaged texts of plays.[23] My claim is that the theatricality of minor speakers or minor speech acts such as asides tends to be more collaborative and non- or counter-illusionistic, while the theatricality of major speakers or speech acts such as soliloquy tends to be more illusionistic. The former includes the speaker's awareness of the theater audience, while the latter doesn't, which is to say that in position 4 on the diagram, the speaker may perform before other characters or before an invisible audience he imagines and that these fictionalized audiences are not to be confused with the theater audience. On these grounds I would argue that skeptical critiques of the editorial desire for consistency of characterization such as those polynomially claimed by Random Cloud and Randall McLeod should not be applied across the board. Polynomial speech prefixes may reflect the variability and stroboscopic alternation that mark relations between actor and minor character—Tarleton and Dericke, Sinklo and Clown—in the collaborative mode of positions 2 and 3, but to extend the critique to such major figures as Falstaff is trivial and potentially counterproductive. The chief aim of this study is to illustrate effects produced by the formulation and isolation of position 4 on the approach to interactions between speech and speech prefix. The focus on this position and its differentiation from positions 3 and 2 provide the basis for the analysis of what I call the subjective and objective aspects of those interactions.

The fictionalization of the audience may be linked to changing forms and uses of extradramatic address in Tudor drama before Shakespeare. Anne (Righter) Barton observes that after 1550, in conjunction with an increasing emphasis on self-contained illusion, audience address tended to be "set apart from the body of the play" and to assume "the quality of incidental amusement, an expedition across the space which separates two worlds."[24] Within the body of the play, stand-up monologues mutated into soliloquies:

> [T]he solitary reflections of characters other than the Vice begin to move out of the category of extra-dramatic address. As soliloquy, they belong now to the self-contained world of the play. By the time of Shakespeare, it was understood that almost all speeches of this kind were overheard by the spectators *as the result of stage convention, not through conscious intent on the part of the speaker.* Nevertheless, they retained an ambiguous and, in the new context, enormously valuable memory of their original position. The soliloquy continued throughout Elizabethan and Jacobean drama to imply a certain rapport with the audience, a rapport that was indefinite and deliberately vague. . . .[25]

Barton quotes a wonderful example of an earlier moment of hesitation archly performed by the Vice in *Kyng Daryus:* after he "opens the performance by hailing the audience in what seems to be the old manner. . . . he deliberately and rather slyly withdraws this initial recognition of the spectators" in the following lines:

> But softe, is there no body here?
> Truly, I do not lyke thys gere;
> I thought I should haue found sum bodie.[26]

This perfectly expresses the pathos and desire of the character who longs for an audience he can't see even though it is right before the actor's eyes.

Theater history is all on the side of monologue against soliloquy—on the side of the presentational high jinks of the stand-up Vice, Clown, and Villain cavorting on what they know is a stage before what they acknowledge as a theater audience. But the premise that actor and character address the same audience is a theoretical solecism. It may not make much practical difference in the case of the Vice and Clown, but its impact on the response to principal characters is deleterious. It jeopardizes the idea of a character constructed by his speech as its subject in the specific sense of a speaker capable of representing himself to himself as well as to others, a speaker who can speak as if from the *platea* and absorb the actor's charisma fully into his fictive substance without appearing to surrender his *locus*-like *Figurenposition,* a speaker who may behave like an actor in need or search of an audience but who has absolutely no knowledge that he is performing or being performed onstage. Weimann's adoption of the premise tends to subvert his own distinction between *Figurenposition* and the material *locus/platea* structure of earlier stage practice. By insisting that the character functions *as* an actor rather than *like* an actor, he in effect rematerializes and detextualizes the *locus* and *platea.* To guarantee the character both his rights and his innocence, I posit the following distinction: when the actor seems to speak directly to *the* (theater) audience, the character he plays speaks *as if* to *an* audience. The character's audience is always a fiction:[27]

> In theater signifier and signified, pretense and pretender, draw unusually close. Or, as Peter Handke more interestingly puts it, in the theater light is brightness pretending to be other brightness, a chair is a chair pretending to be another chair.
>
> A dog on stage is certainly an object; but the act of theatricalizing it . . . neutralizes its objectivity and claims it as a *likeness* of a dog.[28]

Similarly, an audience offstage is certainly an object, but the act of theatricalizing it neutralizes its objectivity and claims it as a likeness of an audience.

This distinction is obviously modeled on the basic move of reader-response theory. The initial (but hardly the only) distinction which that theory makes between the actual and the virtual reader is transferable to theater, where it correlates nicely with the distinction between the audiences addressed respectively by actor and character. I have discussed this four-way relation—actor : audience :: character : "audience"—in *Imaginary Audition,* where I suggest that the presence of the theater audience to the actor should be construed not merely as an analogy but as a contrastive analogy, a metaphor that figures the absence of the audience to the character, who is thereby depicted as being his or her own audience. The relation has the form of a chiasmus—an actor plays a character who performs as if he were an actor—and the specular reversal inherent in the trope accentuates the force of the negation that deprives the character-as-actor of the very conditions he needs in order to resemble the actor-as-character he desires to be. Formulating the relation in this manner opens up what is at least a structural possibility: not only is the speaker who performs on the *platea* his own audience; he is also his own audience by default. "Truly, I do not lyke thys gere; / I thought I should haue found sum bodie"; if the presence of the theater audience signifies the absence of the virtual audience, the character's downstage address may valorize that absence and establish the missing audience as the object of his desire.

In this revised version of Weimann's analysis, the theatrical relations that are always (already) "outside" the field of illusion they produce and support take on a special interpretive function when considered as relations "inside" the field. Recursively embedded in the speech and behavior of characters, they enhance the impression of reflexivity conveyed by speakers who seem "aware of their own theatricality" even if we deny them awareness that they are dramatis personae onstage in a theater.[29] The impression is further enhanced in Shakespearean drama when the "active and self-advertising presence of language in use" denotes self-advertising or -dramatizing tendencies in characters.[30] Something of the histrionic self-presentation of the actor as charismatic performer rubs off on the character he performs, and something of the playwright's delight in the sound, the verve, and the tropical bravura of his own language transmits itself through the actor to the character. Even amid the declamatory thunder of tragic climaxes, speakers seem to be listening to themselves and to the way others listen to them. In that respect every dialogical speech act contains within it an element of monologue or soliloquy. And every monologue or soliloquy is dialogical because it represents the *I* that speaks as performing before the *I* that listens.

Yet if we premise that the *I* is the object created by its utterance as well as the subject that uses and commands it, we may find ourselves opening up a gap between what speakers do with their language, what they mean by it and hear in it, and what their language does with (or to, or for) them, what it says and does regardless of what they say, do, mean, and hear. This is the gap—or collision—between theatrical performance and linguistic performativity, between the presentational practice in which subjects of speech try to represent themselves and the pressure of those textual and illocutionary forces by which language acts on the speech prefix, interprets it, transforms it into an object that may not be congruent or coterminous with the *I* as subject.

But just what does "textual and illocutionary forces" mean? In the present context I use the phrase to denote the characterizing work done by clusters of images, topics, and tropes that twist and twine like rhizomes through the language of the play's speech community. Consider, for example, the many occurrences of *horse* in *1 Henry IV* and its multifunctional capacities as an epithet (the matter of jokes and put-downs), a referential sign (means of transportation, bearer of burdens, implement of war), and a symbol (of chivalry, nobility, honor, manhood). The horse enters into a set of comparisons between the ease of riding and the labor of walking and between the relative security of the former and the exposed condition of the latter. These comparisons implicate differences of political status, social class, and gender. Images, topics, and tropes exfoliating from the signifying node of the horse intermingle with those exfoliating from the sign of woman. The tokens of a cultural iconography, they branch through the text, appearing and reappearing in the utterances of one or another speaker, often in seemingly incidental or accidental relation to the main purposes of those utterances. Thus what they characterize is not so much the individual speaker as the way diverse inflections of the community ethos speak through speakers who may or may not be aware of the messages their language conveys. Speakers become sites through whose language is enunciated the habitus of the play's community, its understandings about positional or hierarchic differences, its anxieties and the language games (the ethical discourses and scenarios) they motivate. It is in this particular sense that speakers are objectified by their language; they become sites of interpretation by others whose readings of linguistic performativity may cut across the grain of the performances in which the speakers represent themselves as the subjects of their speech.

CRITIQUE

The aim of this methodological exercise has been to set up and render explicit an interpretive framework that, in addition to dissociating the character's audience from the actor's, makes possible a double articulation of the speech prefix into the subject of the speech acts it performs and the object of the language that performatively interprets it. My emphasis is on the articulation of the speaker as the subject of his speech because my survey of several major treatments of Falstaff leads me to believe that their failure to give the subject's performance its due occasions what is simultaneously an oversimplification and an overvaluation of the object educed from their interpretations of the speech. And as I shall try to show in the seven samples of object-oriented analysis contained in this section, this result is usually connected with a failure to insulate the virtual audience constructed by the character's speech from the empirical audience hypothesized by the critic.

1) "[T]he difficulty of establishing the Right in . . . an England under no rightful king, is paralleled and parodied throughout in Falstaff's 'manner of wrenching the true cause the false way.' "[31] "Parodied . . . in Falstaff's manner" could mean "parodied *by* Falstaff's manner"—that is, by Falstaff—but in this sentence it doesn't because A. P. Rossiter is concerned with Falstaff's manner, or behavior, only as a symbolic factor contributing to the network of parallels and contrasts that constitute the plays' multiple-plot structure. Rossiter's interest in the way the playwright uses his craft of plot construction to send messages to the audience leads him to reduce Falstaff to a symptom of defects in the social body the play represents and thus to reduce him to an object constructed by his speech. This focus tends to marginalize other possible relations of speech to speaker. One might, for example, entertain the possibility that speech may function reflexively and construct a speaker who, like an actor, presents himself representing himself as the kind of symbol Rossiter discusses.

2) "Falstaff represents to Hal not an alternative paternal image but rather a projected fantasy of the pre-oedipal *maternal,* whose rejection is the basis upon which patriarchal subjectivity is predicated."[32] The opening construction is loose enough to let it mean that Falstaff represents himself to Hal as a maternal (rather than paternal) figure, but it doesn't mean that here. Traub is concerned in this essay with what Harry sees in Falstaff, and she thus discusses Falstaff as the object of Harry's representations but not as the subject of his own. Her purpose is to reposition a psychoanalytic approach to the Harry/Falstaff relation, first, by factoring in the previously excluded scapegoat function the play assigns to the fantasy of the female reproductive body mapped onto Falstaff, who "is figured in female terms," and, second, by asking what it shows about "both the Shakespearean and psychoanalytic dramas" that "the parent who is rejected, metaphorically killed, is figured in the iconography of the female body."[33] How would this double purpose be affected if we redirected our attention to the victim's— the metaphoric mother's—discourse of self-representation? This question about Falstaff is in fact modeled on Traub's question about Katharine in *Henry V.* After having discussed Katharine as "the object of Henry's discourse" and shown how "*Henry's* subjectivity and sexuality are predicated upon his repression of Katharine's linguistic power," she asks, "what of Katharine as the subject of her own discourse?" and goes on to give a concise account of the princess's limited resistance to the imperatives of the traffic in women.[34] Nowhere in her study does Traub pay comparable attention to Falstaff as the subject of his own dis-

course, or to the implications for her larger theoretical claims of the possibility that he, the victim and metaphoric mother, may be complicit in his victimization.

3) With characteristic brilliance William Empson picked out an analogy between the Falstaff/Harry relation and that of the speaker and addressee of the sonnets. Actually, he expressed the analogy in genetic terms: the relation between the poet and friend or patron of the sonnets is the model for that between Falstaff and Harry. Thus in *Some Versions of Pastoral* he plays with the notion that Shakespeare might have projected into Harry "a grim externalisation of self-contempt as well as a still half-delighted reverberation of Southampton," and into Falstaff "an attack on some rival playwright or on Florio as tutor of Southampton as well as *a savage and joyous externalisation of self-contempt,*" and he concludes that "only the second of these alternatives [Falstaff as Shakespeare] fits in with the language and echoes a serious personal situation."[35] In other words, any particular topical reference as site of displacement presupposes a generic moment of self-interpretation and representation, the recognition that an attack on the referent externalizes an attack on oneself. By "generic," of course, I mean discursive. The radical structure of what Empson describes is the complex interaction of the sinner/villain's and victim/revenger's discourses. This pattern, in which self-contempt oscillates with self-wounding impulses to Be Bad and Get Had, is not merely mediated into discourse but given shape within the pre-existing discourse network. The language games that inform the moment of self-interpretation enable it to be represented, explored, developed, varied, and revised in discursive media that include lyric and drama, literature and theater, biography and history, experience and life. To embrace this standpoint is to readjust the relation between topical and extratopical references from genetic accounts of cause and effect within a diachronic field to analogical accounts of parallelism and variation within a synchronic field no less constitutive of actual (topical) than of fictional objects of interpretation.

In his revised essay on Falstaff, Empson resorts to the parabolic mode of genetic fantasy:

> It seems inherently probable that the humiliation of Shakespeare's dealings with his young patron, which one can guess were recently finished, would get thrown into the crucible in which the Prince's friends had to be created. Falstaff looks to me like a secret come-back against aristocratic patrons, marking a recovery of nerve after a long attempt to be their hanger-on. . . . The point is not that he was like Falstaff but that, once he could imagine he was, he could "identify" himself with a scandalous aristocrat, the sufferings of that character could be endured with positive glee.[36]

This fantasy is reversible in the sense that Empson's reading of Falstaff may be taken as the source of his insight into Shakespeare and his patrons. But my interest is in a different reversal: where Empson collapses Falstaff into Shakespeare, collapsing Empson's "Shakespeare" into Falstaff internalizes the savage and joyous self-contempt so that it is the scandalous aristocrat who endures his own sufferings with positive glee.

4) Something else has to be thrown into the crucible to fuse the savagery with the joy: Falstaff "clamours for love," "regularly expresses love towards the young men who rob *for* him, and . . . this is a powerful means of leading them astray."[37] Deleting the italicized word converts Empson's insight into the thesis Jonathan Goldberg develops in *Sodometries* on the basis of Empson's comparisons of Falstaff with the sonneteer and of Harry with the young patron: Falstaff expresses love toward the young men who rob him because from

> their first scene together, . . . [he] stands to be abused. It's often said that we desire Falstaff's resurgence . . . , but it is his condition throughout the play, and if we desire his repeated comebacks it is because it is on his desire that ours floats. . . . That desire is, importantly, the desire to take abuse. *If we accept his banishment, it is then because we take it up as our position, because we have been accepting it all along, and because it is part of the way in which we need never give up desiring Hal.*[38]

The "we" in this passage signals the ironic mimicry of critique; it activates the shifter formula "*we* minus *I* equals *they.*" "We" are the critics who continue to be charmed by Harry and thus to reproduce the incipient heterosexist discourse of homophobia/misogyny visible in his "engrossing" of Hotspur and Falstaff.[39] I wish not to take any exception to this critique but, on the contrary, to extend it back into the play so that Goldberg's irony may be seen as a reflection of the playwright's. But I would like to displace his insight from the critics to Falstaff, rewriting the italicized passage in a form that brings out the mordancy lurking in the phrase "Falstaff stands to be abused": "If Falstaff accepts his banishment, it is then because he takes it up as his position, because he has been accepting it all along, and because it is part of the way in which he need never give up desiring Hal." "Stands to be abused" means "solicits, desires, offers himself to abuse, is complicit in getting himself abused," but this kind of "standing to be" implicates the exhilaration of risk-taking, the search for opportunities both to seduce and outwit the abuser, a practice of dilation or delation that prolongs the pleasure and defers the anticipated consequences of the desire for self-abuse.

5) How much and what kind of interpretive control can the speech prefix have over the speech that interprets it and over the interpreters who use the speech to convert the speech prefix into a character? For example, how would my revision of Goldberg's phras-

ing be affected by replacing the name "Falstaff" with the name "Oldcastle," or by keeping "Falstaff" but reading the dispersed traces of the Oldcastle/Brooke affair as allusions by means of which the censored text of the play remarks "the censored name and even the agents of that censorship"?[40] Gary Taylor argues that the play brings together "two opposing conceptions of Oldcastle current in the sixteenth century," Oldcastle the soldier and martyr versus Oldcastle the "robber, traitor, heretic and hypocrite," in such a way as to produce "a deliberate and brilliant caricature of the dead Oldcastle," a caricature effected in part by "conflat[ing] the historical Oldcastle with the theatrical Vice." To assign the words that evoke this rich structure of "historicity and ambiguity" to the name "'Falstaff' fictionalizes, depoliticizes, secularizes, and in the process trivializes the play's most memorable character," thus robbing it "of that tension created by the distance between two available interpretations of one of its central figures."[41]

By now it would be redundant to belabor Taylor's shaky presuppositions about authorship and authority, the simplistic opposition he draws between the historical and the fictional, or a method and practice of reading for which I have little sympathy and which I have examined elsewhere.[42] My concern here is restricted to the effect of Taylor's renaming on the possibility that the speaker of the words assigned to Oldcastle may be constructed as both the subject and the object of his speech, a subject capable of representing himself as an object and of presenting that self-representation to himself and others. If those words are construed as a "caricature of the dead Oldcastle," the portrait of "a Protestant martyr as a jolly hypocrite" whom the author "deliberately lampooned,"[43] I submit that their speaker is perforce reduced to the object of the representations of others. The method of interpretation implied by this reduction is one that necessarily rules out a whole range of linguistic, rhetorical, and—I insist—theatrical effects that other approaches to close reading make available. I have no objection to any speech prefix that doesn't shut down these possibilities in the name of old or new historicist and bibliographical fantasies.

Taylor's construal puts Falstaff in the position of the innocent dupe or dope whose relation to author, actors, and audiences is the same as that of the native to the outside observer, the one supposed-to-know in the classic but long-discredited mode of ethnographic narrative. But why, it may be objected, couldn't the caricature of the historical Oldcastle be attributed to the fictional Oldcastle, construing the words and behavior of the character as *his* deliberate lampoon of his namesake, and thus letting the speaker in on the secret? There would then be two different Oldcastles, I and II, the former the historical butt, the latter the fictional lampoonist. Or would there instead be a single figure, Oldcastle I/II, who, self-divided, makes fun of himself? But the point is that both Oldcastle II and Oldcastle I/II would differ from Oldcastle I—unless, of course, the historical Oldcastle is represented in the record as someone given to self-parody, which, as far as we know, he wasn't (and if he was, why would the Lords Cobham have objected to Shakespeare's portrait?).[44] Therefore if the representation of Oldcastle I were performed in the spirit of parody or self-parody, it would make sense to mark and stabilize the difference between the performer and the performed by changing the speech prefix from Oldcastle to—for example—Falstaff.

The hilarity of seeing Falstaff as the historical butt Oldcastle I would be at Falstaff's expense and without his knowledge; he would be neither the subject nor the object of his discourse; he might as well be called Oldcastle—or Shakespeare. The hilarity of seeing him as lampoonist Oldcastle II would be shared by Falstaff but in a way that makes the latter's function as character structurally subordinate to that of the actor who presents his satiric representation of another to a theater audience. Oldcastle, not Falstaff, would be the object of his discourse, and the subject position would be co-occupied by Falstaff and the actor. The hilarity of seeing Falstaff as the self-divided Oldcastle I/II would be preemptively modified by the reflexive and self-dividing force of speech in which the speaker is related to his discourse as both its subject and its object, and also as the monitor, the interpreter, of that relation. Under this construal two things happen to Oldcastle: one, since the satire is reflexively internalized in this manner, the centrifugal force of its topical or referential energy tends to diminish. Topicality is contained and turned around: instead of seeing Falstaff as Oldcastle, Oldcastle through Falstaff, you assimilate what you know about Oldcastle to the interpretation of Falstaff. If the satire on Oldcastle-the-historical-figure lingers on, it does so only as an extra, added attraction. Two, as I argued at the beginning of this essay, Falstaff uses puritan rhetoric and discourse to target both Harry's moral scenario and his own indulgence in it. To the extent that such passages of mimicry work as allusions to the Bible-quoting proto-Protestant martyr and/or hypocrite, the figure of Oldcastle becomes less a historical person and more a personification, a caricature of the misuse of puritan discourse.

6) Taylor's proposal has recently been rejected by Kristen Poole in an argument similar to Goldberg's but based on more specific historical objections:

> To annihilate the effects of Shakespeare's contemporary censors is to rewrite history in a disturbingly Orwellian fashion and to deny the text's sociopolitical setting. In addition, if, as Taylor effectively argues, Elizabethan and Jacobean

audiences were highly aware of Falstaff's "real" identity as Oldcastle, then part of the pleasure of this theatrical experience would have been the knowledge that one could read the clandestine identity hidden behind the name. . . . In short, rather than depoliticizing the play or robbing it of tension, the presence of the name "Falstaff" *combined with* the knowledge of the character's "true" identity heightens awareness of the political circumstances of the play.[45]

Poole goes on to shift the emphasis from the portrayal of a particular historical figure to the broader context of antipuritan discourse—the Martin Marprelate controversy—in which the figure of Oldcastle works to transpose Falstaff "into a register of religious/political language familiar to his Elizabethan audience."[46] This shift is compatible with the transition to the more complex construction of Falstaff as Oldcastle I/II described above. Does this strategy then enable her to avoid the reduction produced by Taylor's thesis?

"In Falstaff, as in Martin Marprelate," Poole asserts, "social and discursive orders are undermined and overturned."[47] Does "*In* Falstaff" = *by* Falstaff? Through the figure or symbol of Falstaff? In the person of Falstaff? Is Falstaff as the subject of his speech the source of subversive discourse, or is he, as the object constructed by his speech, the comic embodiment of subversion in the carnival figure of the grotesque puritan? Poole wants to have it both ways, but her polemic against critics who assume Falstaff self-consciously mocks puritans leads her to emphasize his function as an object of satire: she argues that an audience attuned to "stage lampoons of Martin Marprelate" and to the history of Oldcastle "would have laughed not only *with* Falstaff but simultaneously *at* him." She goes on to concede that he is also a satirist who "articulates overtly subversive sentiments, freely criticizing—even mocking— king and prince," but she is careful to restrict the scope of his satire to generalized social critique by reducing king and prince to symbols of rank and hierarchy, and metonyms of the "social and discursive orders" that Falstaff, like Martin Marprelate, irreverently puts down.[48] This is in fact a double restriction: if it is deemed unlikely that Falstaff would criticize puritans, it is deemed equally unlikely that he would criticize himself. Both exclusions are motivated by respect for the expectations the critic imputes to the theater audience. Thus she rejects the opinion that "Falstaff's tendency to speak in biblical idiom and puritan jargon . . . is intended as active mockery of the puritans" on the grounds that it would "not make much sense" to "an audience that identifies Falstaff with Oldcastle": "The parody would have to be self-reflexive, with Sir John ridiculing his own religious inclinations—those same beliefs for which the historical Oldcastle was martyred."[49]

In a passage illustrating Falstaff's recourse to puritan jargon, Poole notes that he "compares himself to a 'saint,' " that he "speaks of his 'vocation,' " that he mimics biblical rhetoric, "makes references to psalm-singing," and "wishes he 'were a weaver.' "[50] This series implies not simply that he is or symbolizes but that he *performs* the role of the grotesque stage puritan. It provides the basis for a study of the discursive registers through which Falstaff as the agent or subject of his speech constructs and deconstructs, represents and interprets, himself and his relation to Harry. We may then ask for whose laughter and pleasure, for whose mockery and contempt, he presents this representation. To answer with Poole that the audience the character addresses is an audience actually or potentially in an Elizabethan theater—or, typologically, *the* Elizabethan theater—effectively bypasses the dramatic center of the ambivalence and ambiguity it is one of the virtues of her essay to articulate.[51] I want to answer that Falstaff, obviously, performs for Harry's pleasure and for his own. Perhaps less obviously, his puritan parody targets the self-righteous rationale he predicts Harry will resort to in casting off his misleader, but, as we have seen, it may at the same time be part of a performance perversely aimed at soliciting Harry's contempt, giving the prince further incentive to cast him off, and thus keeping open the possibility that he will eventually receive his just if bitter deserts. This is an account of Falstaff-as-object different from the one Poole gives; not, that is, the symbolic object of some form of iconographic analysis, not a representation of *X* constructed by and for others, but an object characterized and interpreted by the speaker's own speech, educed from the analysis of its linguistic performativity and set over against his performance as subject.

7) Even when critics pick out particular passages or scenes for extended comment that elucidates interactions between performance and performativity, their romance with the audience diverts their attention from the subject of those interactions. The implications of Falstaff's verbal behavior in the Coventry scene (*1 Henry IV*, 4.2) have been brilliantly but problematically illuminated by William Empson and Charles Whitney. Problematically because both read the soliloquy that dominates the scene as an address to the audience. Here, first, is Empson:

> Falstaff has just boasted that he took bribes to accept such bad recruits ("I have misused the King's press damnably"—and the audience would not think him a coward here, but that it took a lot of nerve to be so wicked) and he boasts later that he got them killed to keep their pay . . . but this makes his reply all the more crashing, as from one murderer to another. . . .[52]

The reply Empson mentions is Falstaff's "Tut, tut, good enough to toss; food for powder, food for powder. They'll fill a pit as well as better. Tush, man, mortal men, mortal men" (4.2.64-66). This is, he claims, "the most unbeatable of all Falstaff's retorts to Henry."[53] But to whom has he just boasted that he took bribes? Empson's aside on what the audience would think reinforces my suspicion that he reads the retort as part of an ongoing flyting contest staged for the benefit of a collective third party offstage: Falstaff performs his wickedness in order to score another point and win another round of applause. If, in making himself a mirror and example of Harry's irresponsibility, his utterance conveys any bitterness, any note of irritable self-reproach, it is occluded by Empson's focus on performance.

This swerve from character to audience is elevated to a methodological principle and exhibited as an interpretive strategy in Charles Whitney's reading of the soliloquy. In one sequence, for example, an initial series of acute and compelling comments bring out the reflexive implications of Falstaff's speech:

> Falstaff's treatment of his recruits and his use of the word "prodigal" may express his own feelings of apprehension about being abandoned by Hal; what Hal may do to him, he will do to the recruits. Such behavior on Falstaff's part parallels the "displaced abjection" of carnival violence that scapegoats those lower in the social scale rather than those who are responsible for the revellers' abjection.

> With his line "food for powder" Falstaff performs . . . [a] festive inversion, shifting responsibility for the recruits' fate from himself to Hal. . . . "Whose fellows are these that come after?" Hal asks. "I never did see such pitiful rascals." As Falstaff answers, the nobles' faces show consternation which grows the more they stare and the more they hear the words of reassurance meant to have an opposite, horrific effect. . . . The irony of "food for powder" is so massive that here one tends to find Falstaff sympathizing with his recruits, where just before he was cackling at them. The irony suggests that Hal, as a leading member of the elite, has some responsibility for beggars being sent into battle; Sir John here contrives to become the wry spokesman for the very lower orders he is fond of exploiting.[54]

Though this perception about the displacement of responsibility is standard, it has seldom been applied to Falstaff's discursive practice here, and it invites closer attention to Falstaff as the auditor to whom "the wry spokesman" addresses his ironies and evasions. His sympathizing with those he exploits, for example, may comment on his own as well as Harry's displacement of responsibility. He isn't only Being Bad. He is showing himself up. There is anger in his words, but it is not aimed solely at the prince. The soliloquy solicits self-reproach.

This direction, however, is not the one Whitney takes. In fact he sets it up as a possibility only to turn away from it in his next words:

> One may say that here Falstaff is simply demonstrating his ability to avoid responsibility for his actions. But a kind of representation typical of festivity—mimicry—seems to fit him well here. The character has a marvellous self-awareness about his impersonations, one that has sometimes been hailed as a sign that he is truly a rounded and coherent character, but is actually a sign that, as Dryden said, he is really a "miscellany of humors or images, drawn from so many several men"—a miscellany played . . . by an actor exploring comic roles.

The festive multiplicity emphasized by this latter reading helps to explain how Falstaff "manages to be both exploiter and spokesman for the exploited"—and at this point Whitney delivers the coup de grâce to what he depicts as a holdover from fictive (and liberal?) ideals of coherent well-rounded individualism by appealing to Bakhtin: Falstaff's "lines exhibit a double-voicing or doubly-oriented speech that suggests the speech's unhinging from individual persons."[55] That is, he is a mimic, an impersonator of the miscellaneous alterities that speak citationally through him. Not merely like an actor, but as an actor, Whitney's Falstaff materializes the *platea* and regales the theater audience with witty cynicisms that reflect and appeal to their baser instincts:

> Falstaff's joy is evident in his main speech (11-48), . . . [which] directly addresses the playgoers as if all were cronies in a tavern chuckling over Falstaff's particularly clever ruse. That ruse turns out to embody the subversion of fellowship. . . . Falstaff smirkingly confesses that he is ashamed of his soldiers, but his pleasure in what he has done is evident, and contagious—perhaps to our horror, we are clearly supposed to laugh with him.[56]

It is in the context of an emphasis on the carnivalesque features of the Coventry scene that Whitney depicts Falstaff working his theater audience with the presentational awareness of a stand-up comic.[57] In terms that recall the accounts of Weimann and Barton, Whitney grounds his emphasis historically:

> Carnivalesque play includes the playgoers and encourages the diversity of response that already seems to have been a common feature of playgoing. Shakespearean theater is in a process of evolution from a semi-professional drama enacted during holidays, in which playgoers were interactive participants, to a commercial, representational drama staged daily. Carnivalesque forms in this theater often still encourage participation of the playgoers, allowing for interpretive authority to be dispersed among them. . . . In this situation there can still exist a theatrical encouragement and accommodation of topical responses.[58]

Hence Whitney's interest in taking up Taylor's line on Oldcastle as one of a number of possible—and conflicting—interpretations to be expected from a heterogeneous audience.

For Whitney, then, the cash value of Dryden's view of Falstaff ("a miscellany of humors or images, drawn from so many several men") lies in its mirroring of the thesis that carnivalesque play allows "interpretive authority to be dispersed among" Elizabethan playgoers who represent diverse social and political interests. This centrifugal thesis depends on the exclusionary strategy of reading that underlies the structure and argument of Whitney's essay: he produces the effect of carnival by taking the scene out of its narrative/dramatic/textual context and treating it as an isolated moment embedded in the synchronic space of an imaginary theater he populates with "diverse playgoing groups"—pro-war supporters of the Essex faction, plebeians, burghers—each of which gives the scene's topical allusions a different interpretive skew.[59] Falstaff, whom Whitney imagines as directly addressing these groups, becomes their Rorschach test. The problem this poses for me is how to retain Whitney's insights into carnival while replacing his exclusionary and centrifugal reading with one that recentralizes interpretive activity and desire in Falstaff as the self-testing subject of his speech.

As the preceding examples show, out of the language that constructs speakers interpreters may draw characters who are more the objects than the subjects of their speech, characters who are not objects for themselves, who do not present their self-representations as characters to themselves or to others. To imagine Falstaff as subject is to imagine the speaker on the model of the actor, imagine him performing like the actor (but not as an actor) in that he presents his representation of himself as the object he interprets, and in that he continuously audits and monitors this performance. Yet it stands to reason that the speech of only some, perhaps relatively few, speakers lends itself to such "thick" interpretation. In my discussion and critique of Weimann, I suggested that variability not only between minor and major speaking parts but also between collaborative or participatory and illusionistic *Figurenpositionen* calls for corresponding flexibility in the choice of interpretive strategies. Of course I may be overstating the problem: we're not in danger of being swamped these days by an outpouring of thick and close interpretation. Given the tendencies of the critical projects sampled in my critique, the opposite is more likely to be the case. There is a danger of reductive reading in which major speakers' relation to their language is characterized by extension of or projection from the analysis of minor speaking parts.

To illustrate this problem, I turn once again to Weimann, this time to his appendix on *Two Gentlemen of Verona,* in which he tries to define a comic position that gives the character more parity with the actor—the position of characters the audience laughs with as opposed to those it laughs at. His example is Proteus's servant, the clown Launce, whom he distinguishes from Speed in that, while Speed's asides provoke laughter at others, Launce "and his family experience are the objects of his own mirth." Since he can join the audience in laughing at himself, he is the "free and willing subject" of his mirth: "Launce, much like Falstaff, is not merely witty in himself but the reason that others have and enjoy their own wit."[60] Weimann's point is two-fold. In the traditional situation the audience laughs with the actor at the comic figure the latter plays, and the character who laughs with the audience at himself assimilates the perspective and position of the actor: "The real performance of the actor and the imaginative role of . . . [Launce] interact. . . . Within this unity the character's relations to the play world begin to dominate, but the comic ease and flexibility of these relations are still enriched by some traditional connection between the clowning actor and the laughing spectator," a connection that extends the character's awareness, "his implicit insight into and criticism of the action of the play," and that brings together actor, audience, and character in the utopian "laughter of solidarity."[61]

Weimann's coupling of Launce with Falstaff in terms of presentational role—of their common function as critical "countervoices" embodying "a *platea*-like position"[62]—is symptomatic of a failure to distinguish between what I referred to earlier as different intensities of self-representation. If we find in the language of both speakers "implicit insight into and criticism of the action" of their respective plays, do we also find that the insight and criticism are equally attributable to both speakers as the subjects of their speech? Weimann's reading practice follows the track of his social history of theater, hence particular passages of analysis are often narrowly constrained by their function as examples of the theme. The treatment of Launce is no exception. He is used to illustrate Shakespeare's contribution to the changing structure of relations between theatrical and fictional "worlds": Launce as subject is like the actor sharing with his audience the genial laughter occasioned by (his performance of) Launce the object. Meredith Skura takes Weimann to be arguing that Launce's "ridiculousness within the play's world—his shame and isolation—are thus mitigated by the actor Kempe's connection" to the spectators, who "laugh at Launce but identify with Kempe."[63] This is a distortion of Weimann's claim, which is that they identify with Launce, or Kempe-in-Launce. But her distortion accurately registers the fact that his argument for the integration of actor with character combines with his underinterpretation of the language that represents the character to deny the character the richness or complexity he clearly wishes to confer on it.

Skura's critique of Weimann's utopian optimism is based on a closer and darker reading of Launce's soliloquies, a reading contextualized within a study of the Elizabethan actor's subculture which differs from Weimann's both in the greater attention it pays to the effects on the actor of his precarious social position and in the greater subtlety with which it analyzes the play of those effects in Shakespeare's texts. She likens Launce's speech in 2.3, in which he complains about his "cruel-hearted cur," Crab (he "has no more pity in him than a dog"), to the "introductory monologue" of the "typical Elizabethan clown." Launce is

> a kind of comic Aeneas, stepping forth to tell his sad tale to the only Dido he has: to us, the spectators in the audience. . . . In soliciting our response, Launce's soliloquy foregrounds his ambiguous relation to the audience, who both are and are not there: he calls attention to the precariousness of the actor's position and to the audience's multiple roles in validating it.[64]

This precariousness is comically intensified by the uncertainties—behavioral as well as ontological—connected with the presence onstage of a real dog representing Launce's dog, Crab (but not presenting itself as representing Crab).[65] While noting that Weimann "also finds Launce an epitome of theatrical precariousness," Skura goes on to observe that he avoids the "dystopian implications of clowning" and its social cost to the performer by confining his comments to the first and lighter of Launce's two monologues about Crab.[66] Weimann, who never mentions the dog, doesn't deal with the more humiliating moment in 4.4 when Launce "literally takes on the dog's identity—at least takes on his sins"—and makes the audience laugh at his "self-abasement . . . like a player 'playing the fool,' as Thomas Nashe sneered, to earn a few pennies—and our laughter."[67]

As a clownish servant, Launce is a boundary figure in the sense that he dramatizes the paradoxes inherent in the theater's edgy negotiations with illusion and reality. The audience he conjures up through extradramatic address is invited to laugh not only at him but also—through the network of puns that bind his language in 2.3 echoically to that of Julia and Proteus in 2.2—at the serious knots and plots of the main action, the deceptions, desires, self-delusion, and self-abasement inscribed in the language games of romance and friendship, the conventionality of which *Two Gentleman* continually indexes by the conspicuousness of its citational play.[68] This makes Launce more important as a precipitator of irony directed reflexively by the play at itself than he is as the subject of his own speech.

Skura nevertheless succeeds in depicting him as a complex version of the clown figure—a kind of metaclown—by identifying the theatrical pressures his monologue exhibits with the clown/actor's occupational vulnerability. She focuses on the social dependency, the ethical self-abasement, and the psychic cost attendant on "the use the clown makes of himself in order to secure unity with society"; and she notes that such "self-deprecating humor" as Launce displays when he "takes on the role of 'dog' " may elicit from the audience laughter that is "tinged with sadism even in its solidarity."[69] This amounts to an acerb revision of the bland praise Weimann bestows on Launce because, "much like Falstaff, [he] is not merely witty in himself but the reason that others have and enjoy their own wit." Skura is careful not to lump Falstaff together with Launce; she devotes a chapter to the former, six pages to the latter. Nevertheless, as we'll see, she focuses on something they have in common—their canine connection. A transition from Launce to Falstaff is easily made in terms of her analysis by noting that the evocation of "laughter tinged with sadism" may reflect the tinge of masochism in a character divided between suffering—even enjoying—his haplessness and wanting to be put down for it. Thinking of Launce, Falstaff, and Crab, I'm tempted by a fortuitous analogy to confuse small things with great by mentioning the last words of Joseph K. as he watches (not feels) "the final act" in the putative ending of *The Trial:* "'Like a dog!' he said; it was as if he meant the shame of it to outlive him."

Fortuitous and confused as it may be, it is nevertheless the spirit of Joseph K. that I invoke in turning back, finally, to the Falstaff of Part 1, whom, Skura reminds us, "W. H. Auden identified as 'the prince's dog,'" an epithet she unpacks in the following comment:

> Falstaff knows there are benefits in being a loser. He dosen't merely become "the prince's dog": he plays it for all it's worth—just as he plays dead on the battlefield. The posture brings safety, material gain, and, most of all, what Falstaff needs even more than food: an appreciative audience. So long as the exchange holds ("I'll make a fool of myself if only you'll laugh"), his resentment is kept at bay. It's an actor's bargain. In fact, Falstaff's greatest moments are triumphs of recovery from humiliation; he succeeds by lying or charming his way out of traps. The moments we most remember when we think of Falstaff's vitality are escapes, rather than escapades.[70]

To this concise profile I add only two minor qualifications: first, that the traps Falstaff lies or charms his way out of are traps he sets for himself, and, second, that his resentment is diffusely, confusedly directed toward both himself and Harry. That is, I want to push a little harder on the idea that Falstaff as the subject and primary auditor of his speech performs the role of prince's dog for himself as well as for Harry, and that he is a less appreciative audience than the prince.

If Harry plays the prodigal to distance and decontaminate himself from the dubious legitimacy of his father's accession, Falstaff targets that project by playing the buffoon, the figure of carnival misrule, to dramatize the complicity of the prince in the sins he displaces onto his subjects. But at the same time, in making himself the mirror and example of Harry's bad faith, he dramatizes his own complicity. This double play is strikingly evident in the Coventry soliloquy in *1 Henry IV*, 4.2. There he links his abuse of his military assignment to the irresponsible motive behind the prince's appointing him to lead "a charge of foot." The soliloquy is an uneasy performance of the villain's discourse, edged with anger and with what may be more than mock-penitence. "If I be not ashamed of my soldiers, I am a soused gurnet. I have misused the King's press damnably.... I pressed me none but such toasts-and-butter, with hearts in their bellies no bigger than pins' heads, and they have bought out their services" (ll. 11-22), and he replaced them with unsoldierly riffraff. What happens when we redirect the monologue from the theater audience toward the virtual audience that includes the internal auditor for whose benefit the discourse is performed? Is Falstaff telling himself that it takes a lot of nerve to be so wicked? Does he find the spectacle of his wickedness only admirable or also irritating? His contempt for the all-round haplessness of the "scarecrows" he victimized is predictable, but more surprising is his contempt for the cowardice of those who weaseled out—as if he is angered by the complicity he encouraged and by the ease with which they could be (as he expected) corrupted. But "look what they got away with!" only reflects "look what I got away with!" which in turn reflects "look what my betters let me get away with!"

And who are his betters? They emerge in the following sequence:

> We must all to the wars, and thy place shall be honorable. I'll procure this fat rogue a charge of foot, and I know his death will be a march of twelve score. The money shall be paid back again with advantage.
>
> (2.4.539-42)

> A hundred thousand rebels die in this!
> Thou shalt have charge and sovereign trust
>     herein.
>
> (3.2.160-61)

> O my sweet beef, I must still be good angel to thee. The money is paid back again.... I am good friends with my father and may do anything.... I have procured thee, Jack, a charge of foot.
>
> (3.3.177-86)

> Jack, meet me tomorrow in the Temple Hall
> At two o'clock in the afternoon.
> There shalt thou know thy charge, and there
>     receive

> Money and order for their furniture.
> The land is burning. Percy stands on high,
> And either we or they must lower lie.
>
> (3.3.199-204)

> PRINCE ... tell me, Jack, whose fellows are these that come after?
>
> FALSTAFF Mine, Hal, mine.
>
> PRINCE I did never see such pitiful rascals.
>
> FALSTAFF Tut, tut, good enough to toss; food for powder, food for powder. They'll fill a pit as well as better. Tush, man, mortal men, mortal men.
>
> WESTMORELAND Ay, but, Sir John, methinks they are exceeding poor and bare, too beggarly.
>
> FALSTAFF Faith, for their poverty, I know not where they had that, and for their bareness, I am sure they never learned that of me.
>
> PRINCE No, I'll be sworn, unless you call three fingers in the ribs bare. But, sirrah, make haste. Percy is already in the field.
>
> (4.2.60-74)

> I have led my ragamuffins where they are peppered. There's not three of my hundred and fifty left alive, and they are for the town's end, to beg during life.
>
> (5.3.35-38)

This sequence charts the transgressive convergence of the "serious" and "comic" plots at the same time that it shows Harry moving away from Falstaff toward his father and Percy. But his method of moving away is peculiar. The repeated coupling of the "charge of foot" with the return of the stolen money suggests that the central joke of the robbery scene, the colting and uncolting of Falstaff, is being replayed.[71] The picking of Falstaff's pocket, which Harry carefully has someone else do (2.4.525ff), effectively repeats the purse-taking of the Gadshill escapade, which he carefully had someone else do; but in claiming that he has cleaned up the mess Falstaff made (3.3.176), the princely "good angel" implicitly clears himself.[72]

Even as Harry mounts up from prose to the iambic pentameter that gathers speed near the end of 3.3, and rides off toward the dawning glitter of his reformation, his practices confuse the gesture of disengagement by extending the tavern tour and its carnival prodigality into his father's wars. Falstaff's thievery, his self-indulgence, his vulnerability, and his cowardice are all recalled in a context that makes them the basis of the next joke: they are the qualifications that will determine the nature of his war service; the argument of his running away recommends him for a charge of foot. Thus the "charge and sovereign trust" (3.2.161) Harry receives from his father is used to promote another lark aimed at keeping Falstaff close to the sullen ground or making him lard the lean earth: "his death will be a march of twelve score" (2.4.541), but his march will be the death of almost eight score.[73]

Falstaff responds immediately to Harry's announcement of the "charge of foot." He reads it as both a continuation of the uncolting joke and another invitation to highway robbery: "I would it had been of horse. Where shall I find one that can steal well? O, for a fine thief, of the age of two-and-twenty or thereabouts! I am heinously unprovided" (3.3.187-90).[74] In 4.2 his tart "food for powder" comment shows that his misuse of the commission is in part a way of talking back to Harry, even, as Whitney observes, of making his own irresponsibility rub off on the prince—"what Hal may do to him, he will do to the recruits."[75] It is in the context of the carnival extension of the tavern tour to the battlefield that I want to reconsider and revise Whitney's audience-centered reading of the carnivalesque features of the Coventry monologue. Recall his assertion that Falstaff addresses the theater audience as if they were "cronies in a tavern."[76] The rules of theatrical disengagement I discussed above suggest the following revision: first, replace the actual theater audience with a virtual audience addressed and (therefore) constructed by the monologue; then, in line with Whitney's suggestion, let that audience, imagined by Falstaff, consist of his Eastcheap cronies.

The effect of revision is to displace the carnival relation from the contact between author/player/play and theater audience mediated through the character to the contact between the character and the virtual audience that includes such Corinthians as Poins and Harry—and Falstaff himself. In this new scenario, Falstaff revives the interlocutory swash of the earlier tavern games, fulfilling the wish he had perversely chimed out in the teeth of Harry's inspiring call to arms:

> PRINCE  ... The land is burning. Percy stands on high,
> And either we or they must lower lie.
> FALSTAFF  Rare words! Brave world! Hostess, my breakfast, come!
> O, I could wish this tavern were my drum!
> (3.3.203-6)

His first words in 4.2 are a request to Bardolph to "get thee before to Coventry" and "fill me a bottle of sack." Following this, he resumes his role as the cowardly braggart and outrageous teller of tall tales who can count on his cronies to appreciate not only the gusto with which he boasts of misusing "the King's press" (l. 12) but also the opportunity he gives them to put him down for the roguery he confesses.[77] And if I pretend to listen to the monologue as a report Falstaff imagines himself giving Harry, I hear it—with Empson and Whitney—less as a boast than as a reproach. When he compares his pitiful rascals to "tattered prodigals lately come from swine keeping, from eating draff and husks" (ll. 34-36), one thinks of the play's chief Prodigal. But the real prodigal is a greenhorn, a victim, a "younker": "What, will you make a younker of me? Shall I not take mine ease in mine inn but I shall have my pocket picked?" (3.3.77-79). Both he and his soldiers are victims of the false Prodigal, and, as Whitney perceptively observes, Falstaff is taking his victimization out on them even as his self-proclaimed villainy makes a statement about his betters:[78] "Let me show you how bad *you* are by showing how bad *I* am." This is the force of "food for powder. They'll fill a pit as well as better," which Empson calls his "crashing" reply, "as from one murderer to another: 'that is all you Norman lords want, in your squabbles between cousins over your loot, which you make an excuse to murder the English people.'"[79] In addition, "let me show you how bad I am" is inextricable from its presentational sine qua non, "let me show *myself* how bad I am." To listen to his utterance as a piece of bravery he tries out on himself is to hear it as a performance that solicits self-reproach. For then the bitterness in his words is keener, the anger sharper, the words surging violently back and forth between the villain's swagger and the sinner's disgust. As in *Twelfth Night*'s festering festival, its protracted whirligig declining into a sink-a-pace, Falstaff's reprise of the tavern holiday brings out its darker undertones.

His comparison of his recruits to the ragged "Lazarus in the painted cloth, where the glutton's dogs licked his sores" (4.2.24-26), recalls his earlier remark that Bardolph's face makes him "think upon hellfire and Dives that lived in purple" (3.3.31-32). The echo helps him to merge with Dives in the glutton's position, and Whitney aptly notes that the parable "slips from its appropriator's grasp" for it "unmistakably . . . implies that Dives stands for Falstaff, who will get his just desserts [sic] in hell, as Dives did, for what he is doing to his recruits on earth."[80] Thus "while Falstaff's parables mock his recruits, they mock Falstaff as well." But Whitney goes on to speculate that "the festively Satanic Falstaff" may be

> aware of his scriptural citations' ominous implications, and . . . be laughing at the whole idea of salvation and divine retribution. . . . [He] will gaily accept his own death and affirm the pleasures of life meanwhile. . . . Shakespeare has some sympathy for this view. He allows Falstaff to be both Lazarus and Dives. . . . From the perspective of grotesque realism, the biblical references in Falstaff's speech suggest a cycle of earthly pleasures: the individual may die, but the festive community lives on. This "old, white-bearded Sathan" turns apocalypse into carnival.[81]

I second the emphasis on the speaker's awareness but resist the happy Bakhtinian/Rabelaisian account of his tone on the grounds that the perspective of grotesque realism, or any other perspective that produces so optimistic a reading, responds less to the continuity of the text and the dramatic fiction than to this isolated moment of theatrical reception. That is, the consoling Saturnalian fantasies of Whitney's hypothetical plebeian playgoers are privileged over the bitterness of the speaker, whose biblical reference suggests that there may be some sort of compensatory resurrection for the slaves but none for the glutton who profits from their loss.

In her brilliant account of Falstaff's growing self-degradation and resentment in Part 2, Skura describes a pattern of change similar to the one she discusses in the transition from Launce's first soliloquy to his second. Her emphasis is on the corrosive manner in which Falstaff treats his relation to Shallow as a bitter parody of Harry's relation to him in Part 1:

> Even while participating in the tavern society, Hal had stepped aside to plot his strategy: "I know you all.". . . Now Falstaff stands back to manipulate Shallow. "I will fetch off these justices. I do see the bottom of justice Shallow." . . . Hal has "stolen" one thousand pounds from Falstaff; now Falstaff borrows the exact sum from Shallow with no more intent of returning it than hope of getting it back from Hal.[82]

Of the threat Falstaff directs at Shallow in 3.2, "it shall go hard but I'll make him a philosopher's two stones to me" (ll. 323-24)—in Skura's paraphrase, "I'll have his balls"—she remarks that "Falstaff is not promising to rape Shallow so much as 'to fuck him over,' but the scene comes as close to overt allusions to homoeroticism as any in the canon apart from Patroclus's scene with Achilles in *Troilus and Cressida*."[83] Her subsequent digression on Patroclus as "a version of the male friend who epitomizes (by exaggerating) Falstaff's combination of the roles of house jester and 'male varlet' " leads to the conclusion that although "Falstaff is not a Patroclus. . . . he is . . . pained by playing" such roles.[84]

I would qualify this powerful reading in only one respect: the pattern of change Skura traces is already discernible in Part 1. In the process of amusing and abusing Harry during their first scene together (1.2), Falstaff not only holds the mirror up to Harry's abuse of him but also invites a pay-back. By Being Bad, he seems perversely to invite the risk of Getting Had. In 4.2 he boasted of his abuses of the king's press but, as we saw, in a tone not free from self-contempt and in words that hinted at the complicity of his betters, that is, Harry. He concludes his first soliloquy in 5.3 with a reference to the outcome of his accomplishments as a recruiter, described in 4.2:

> Though I could scape shot-free at London, I fear the shot here, here's no scoring but upon the pate. Soft, who are you? Sir Walter Blunt. There's honor for you. Here's no vanity! I am as hot as molten lead, and as heavy too. God keep lead out of me! I need no more weight than mine own bowels. I have led my ragamuffins where they are peppered. There's not three of my hundred and fifty left alive, and they are for the town's end, to beg during life.
>
> (5.3.30-38)

As he confesses his battle fear, he insulates it with puns that convey the manliness of the witcracker and unrepentant artful dodger, more skilled in ducking bills than bullets. But the puns are heavyhanded; they embarrass his rationalizations with cynical bluster. He puffs up the prudential and "honest" cowardice by which he would avoid such vanity as Blunt's honorable death. Yet his taking responsibility for the casualties immediately after that move places the emphasis on the lethal consequences of his success as a profiteering recruiter and battle leader. "I have led my ragamuffins where they are peppered" is a bitter boast; he scores it on his own pate; the tone suggests that he despises his dishonorable cowardice no less than the honor he debunks. Thus the coward's rationalization modulates into the sinner's sardonic comment.

It isn't easy to catch either Falstaff's tones or their complex directional force if you station yourself in fantasy as a member of the theater audience being addressed by the hybridized figure composed of Falstaff and the actor playing Falstaff. In order to listen to Falstaff listening to himself, you have to imagine yourself as the eavesdropper *he* imagines and performs before. This requires an auditory station somewhere within the ear of the speaker, whom you make the subject of his speech when you premise that he gives himself to be heard—or, more reluctantly, to be overheard—by himself and not only presents but monitors and judges the representation of Falstaff that is the object of his speech.

From this station you may also intercept uncanny messages such as those that materialize in Part 2 under the spell of the idea that Falstaff not only vents his spleen at Shallow as a pathetic surrogate for the prince, he also treats him as a distorted mirror, an "old Double" (3.2.41), of himself.[85] As I have argued elsewhere,

> he does exactly what he accuses Shallow of doing . . . as if he enjoys reminding himself that his every third word is a lie, savors in himself what he contemns in others, takes perverse pleasure in imposing fictions on himself that he knows are fictions. . . . By the aggressive bravado of his soliloquy he likens his way of addressing the present to Shallow's way of addressing the past: to speak of making Shallow "a philosopher's two

stones to me" is not merely to acknowledge the folly of the alchemical dream of perpetual potency. Rather it is Falstaff's way of acknowledging, with a certain savage amusement, his relish for *imaginary* testicles, for the impotent bluster that will reduce him to "bait for the old pike."[86]

In his judiciary function Shallow is also an old Double of the Lord Chief Justice, an institutional relation emphasized by the latter's reappearance in 5.2 for the first time since his encounter with Falstaff in 1.2. Falstaff links them together in two other respects: by harping on their advanced age and by requesting from each a loan of a thousand pounds.[87] The Lord Chief Justice's principled and austere seniority is parodied by Shallow's lax and sycophantic senility. Nevertheless, the listener in Falstaff's ear, "swoln with some other grief," can hear something more than Shallow means when he picks up and remonstrates against the words "You must excuse me" with which Falstaff begs off from spending the night at Gloucestershire: "I will not excuse you, you shall not be excused, excuses shall not be admitted, there is no excuse shall serve, you shall not be excused" (5.1.3-6). He repeats the final phrase in his next utterance after summoning Davy (ll. 10-11). When, several lines later, he responds to Davy's inquiry about a bill with "Let it be cast and paid" and then again repeats his injunction to Falstaff, "Sir John, you shall not be excused" (ll. 19-20), the first part of the utterance bleeds into the second.

Through Justice Shallow's voice speaks the discourse of judgment and spiritual accountancy displaced from whatever greater authority he represents.[88] After the interchange that follows, Falstaff waves the others away so that he can listen to himself vent his bitter and disdainful opinion of the "semblable coherence" of "Master Shallow" and his servants: "It is certain that either wise bearing or ignorant carriage is caught, as men take diseases, one of another. Therefore take heed of their company" (ll. 64, 73-76). Yet in his very next words, when he goes on to represent to himself the pleasure his tales of Shallow will give to Harry, this advice is conspicuously ignored, for surely by now—having taken heed of the prince's company and intentions from the beginning, having taken their measure as recently as the soliloquy on sack in 4.3—he knows better, knows that the prospect of the prince exploding in Falstaffian laughter is one he might in his folly wish or hope for but will never see realized.

The soliloquy as a whole not only registers Falstaff's recognition that there is semblable coherence between his folly and the folly he criticizes; it also registers the turning of the speaker's anger from his rural targets toward himself. Skura's observation—"although he is forced to spend time with substitutes like Justice Shallow, Falstaff keeps thinking about the Prince as his absent audience"[89]—implies that this situation increases the anger and scorn he directs at Shallow. But the grotesque figure with which he concludes the soliloquy suggests to me that what angers him is his own persistent desire for the absent auditor. As he imagines Harry's mirth, he dresses it up in a mirthless similitude: "O, you shall see him laugh till his face be like a wet cloak ill laid up" (5.1.83-84)—"wrinkled," the Arden editor explains, "with innumerable creases" because "packed carelessly away."[90] It is as if Falstaff acknowledges this prospect as another "smooth comfort false" begotten on and resurrected from "the times deceas'd" by self-blinding desire—like the pathetic longing he had earlier condemned in Shallow's reminiscences. "Lord, Lord, how subject we old men are to this vice of lying" (3.2.302-3), and especially of lying to ourselves. His persistent longing to "curry with" the princely Thin Man he affects makes him no better than the pathetic Thin Man he despises. Thus at the end of 5.1, he shrinks from the contaminating embrace of Shallow's aggressive hospitality, responding reluctantly, impatiently, to his host's importunate summons: "Sir John! / FALSTAFF: "I come, Master Shallow, I come, Master Shallow" (ll. 86-87).

CODA: THE THIN MAN

"Then death rock me asleep, abridge my doleful days!" (2.4.194): Pistol is not the only speaker in this community who seeks to lay his head "in Furies' lap" (5.3.107). In Part 2, "death turns and stalks Falstaff . . . in the form of thinness,"[91] and the thinness Falstaff harps on ("This same starved justice" [3.2.303], "the very genius of famine" [ll. 312-13])[92] is a kind of memento mori calling the fat man to account. The Thin Man reappears in 5.4 in the form of the beadle whom Doll and Quickly later revile:

DOLL . . . you filthy famished correctioner . . .

BEADLE Come, come, you she knight-errant, come.

HOSTESS O God, that right should thus overcome might! Well, of sufferance comes ease.

DOLL Come, you rogue, come, bring me to a justice.

HOSTESS Ay, come, you starved bloodhound.

DOLL Goodman death, goodman bones!

HOSTESS Thou atomy, thou!

DOLL Come, you thin thing, come, you rascal!
(5.4.20-29)

Doll and the Hostess are speaking figuratively, and what they ask for is their day in court, perhaps with the intention of proving how society or its overmighty justiciars victimize them.[93] But if I shift my attention from what the speakers evidently mean to express to what their expressions can mean—if I take their figurative expressions seriously, "literally,"—they convey the complex desire of the ultimate peace, the punishment, the self-transcendence, that their transgressions cry out for: "Come, sweet death." The desire they fear and resist is the desire to be taken and consumed by old Double, the insatiable Thin Man, whose workings are mocked in such second bodies as those of the country justices of the peace, the Lord Chief Justice, and the king.

—*You must excuse me.*

—*I will not excuse you, you shall not be excused, excuses shall not be admitted, there is no excuse shall serve, you shall not be excused.*

—I come, Master Shallow, I come, Master Shallow.

*Notes*

[1] Unless otherwise noted, quotations from the Henriad follow the *Complete Works of Shakespeare,* ed. David Bevington, rev. 4th ed. (New York: Longman, 1997).

[2] The tone of these statements is affected by their being a replay of the parodic triumphant speech with which Falstaff greets Prince John and his companions in 4.3: "I have speeded hither with the very extremest inch of possibility; I have foundered nine score and odd posts; and here, travel-tainted as I am, have in my pure and immaculate valor taken Sir John Colevile of the Dale, a most furious knight and valorous enemy" (ll. 34-39).

[3] Here I follow William Empson, who in turn agrees (for once) with Dover Wilson "that Henry shows a good deal of forbearance in his conditions to Falstaff" (*Essays on Shakespeare,* ed. David B. Pirie [Cambridge: Cambridge UP, 1986], 68).

[4] Many of my observations in this account of Harry's relations to Henry and to Falstaff have their origins in my encounter with M. D. Faber's "Falstaff Behind the Arras," *American Imago* 27 (1970): 197-225; see especially 198-99, 206-7, and 209. Regardless of what I consider an unhelpful commitment to a kind of demotic Freudian lexicon—as in his attention to the struggle between Harry's consciousness and unconsciousness—I still, after all these years, find Faber's commentary the best guide to conflicts I prefer to approach in a more textual and more guardedly psychoanalytical manner, and I remain deeply indebted to it.

[5] See, for example, "Hydra and Rhizome" in *Shakespeare Reread: The Texts in New Contexts,* Russ McDonald, ed. (Ithaca, NY: Cornell UP, 1994), 79-104, esp. 94-95.

[6] David Bevington, ed., *Henry IV, Part 1* (Oxford: Clarendon Press, 1987), 166.

[7] See Philip C. McGuire, *Speechless Dialect: Shakespeare's Open Silences* (Berkeley: U of California P, 1985).

[8] For an account of these ethical discourses and their interaction, see my *Making Trifles of Terrors: Redistributing Complicities in Shakespeare* (Stanford: Stanford UP, 1997), xiii-xix, 222-46, 288-334, and passim.

[9] Bevington, ed., *Henry IV, Part 1* (1987), 102.

[10] Empson allows that "the actor could drag the words around to apply to the Prince" but finds a difficulty in the reference to the twenty-two years of companionship because it would imply that Falstaff has "forsworn" and been "bewitched" by Harry since the latter's birth (65-66).

[11] To avoid misleading implications, let me say that I use the term *subject* in this context to denote a site of agency or propriety, on the analogy, for example, of the locution "she is the subject of (her) desire and not merely the object of others'."

[12] Reasons for this decision are given on pp. 56-57, below.

[13] This illustrates what Bert O. States calls the "self-expressive mode," in which the actor relates to the audience, distinguished by States from the "collaborative" and "representational" modes; see *Great Reckonings in Little Rooms: On the Phenomenology of Theater* (Berkeley: U of California P, 1985), 120-206.

[14] Randall McLeod, "UN *Editing* Shak-speare," *SubStance* 33/34 (1981-82): 26-55, esp. 50.

[15] John Russell Brown, *Shakespeare's Plays in Performance* (New York: St. Martin's Press, 1971), 155.

[16] Morris Carnovsky with Peter Sander, "The Eye of the Storm: On Playing King Lear," *Shakespeare Quarterly* 28 (1977): 144-50, esp. 144.

[17] Robert Weimann, *Shakespeare and the Popular Tradition in the Theater: Studies in the Social Dimension of Dramatic Form and Function,* ed. Robert Schwartz (Baltimore and London: Johns Hopkins UP, 1978), 230.

[18] Weimann, 235.

[19] Weimann, 232-33.

[20] Weimann, 233. The final clause alludes to one of Weimann's more recent applications of the *locus/platea* distinction to conflicts of authority between

the represented and representing institutions; see "Bifold Authority in Shakespeare's Theatre," *SQ* 39 (1988): 401-17.

[21] I use the male pronoun for Elizabethan actors, who were either boys or men. Did a female character intermittently behave as if she knew she were a he? Elizabeth Pittenger has addressed this question in a brilliant unpublished study of Lyly's *Gallathea*.

[22] Again, my use of these terms loosely follows the discussion in States, 170-85.

[23] Legend for 2 through 4: 2) the actor presents himself to the theater audience in his role of actor-playing-character; 3) by addressing the theater audience, the character presents herself or himself as the actor playing that character; 4) the character behaves like an actor in his address to the onstage audience of other characters.

[24] Anne Righter [Barton], *Shakespeare and the Idea of the Play* (London: Chatto and Windus, 1962), 56-57.

[25] Righter, 60-61, emphasis added.

[26] Righter, 57. Righter quotes from *King Daryus*, ed. Alois Brandl, Il. 37-39.

[27] See Walter J. Ong, "The Writer's Audience Is Always a Fiction" in Ong, *Interfaces of the Word: Studies in the Evolution of Consciousness and Culture* (Ithaca, NY: Cornell UP, 1977), 53-81.

[28] Bert O. States, "The Dog on the Stage: Theater as Phenomenon," *New Literary History* 14 (1983): 373-88, esp. 373 and 380.

[29] The quoted phrase is from Lionel Abel, *Metatheatre: A New View of Dramatic Form* (New York: Hill and Wang, 1963), 60. Developing his notion of the "metaplay" in part as an apologia for the modernist drama of Brecht, Beckett, and Genet (among others), Abel valorizes this drama as the genre best suited to express the skeptical problematic Stanley Cavell would subsequently badger with notorious philosophical panache and persistence.

[30] Keir Elam, *Shakespeare's Universe of Discourse: Language Games in the Comedies* (Cambridge: Cambridge UP, 1984), 1.

[31] A. P. Rossiter, *Angel with Horns and Other Shakespeare Lectures*, ed. Graham Story (New York: Longmans, Green and Co., 1961), 53.

[32] Valerie Traub, *Desire and Anxiety: Circulations of sexuality in Shakespearean drama* (London: Routledge, 1992), 55.

[33] Traub, 56 and 66.

[34] Traub, 62ff.

[35] William Empson, *Some Versions of Pastoral* (London: Chatto and Windus, 1950), 104, emphasis added.

[36] Empson, *Essays on Shakespeare*, 72.

[37] Empson, *Essays on Shakespeare*, 65-66, emphasis added.

[38] Jonathan Goldberg, *Sodometries: Renaissance Texts, Modern Sexualities* (Stanford: Stanford UP, 1992), 153-54, emphasis added.

[39] Goldberg, 152.

[40] Goldberg suggests this in his convincing rebuttal of Gary Taylor's proposal to restore the latter in modern texts of *1 Henry IV*; see Jonathan Goldberg, "The Commodity of Names: 'Falstaff' and 'Oldcastle' in *1 Henry IV*" in *Reconfiguring the Renaissance: Essays in Critical Materialism*, Jonathan Crewe, ed. (Cranbury, NJ: Associated University Presses, 1992), 76-88, esp. 81. See also Gary Taylor, "The Fortunes of Oldcastle," *Shakespeare Survey* 38 (1985): 85-100. David Bevington's critique of the Taylor thesis in his Oxford edition of the play (106-10) has been questioned by Goldberg on philosophical grounds and defended by John W. Velz on the grounds criticized by Goldberg; see Goldberg, "The Commodity of Names," 87; and Velz, Review of Bevington's Oxford edition, *SQ* 43 (1992): 107-9, esp. 108. For a more recent attempt to work Oldcastle into the field of possible topical allusions around Falstaff, see Charles Whitney, "Festivity and Topicality in the Coventry Scene of *1 Henry IV*" *English Literary Renaissance* 24 (1994): 410-48.

[41] Taylor, 93-95, 98, 96, and 95.

[42] See my *Imaginary Audition: Shakespeare on Stage and Page* (Berkeley: U of California P, 1989), 25-42.

[43] Taylor, 98 and 99.

[44] For information on Oldcastle and the debate that swirled around him, see *The Oldcastle Controversy*, Peter Corbin and Douglas Sedge, eds. (Manchester, UK: Manchester UP, 1991). For this reference, and also for a wonderfully compact yet complete sketch of the Oldcastle question, I am grateful to the commentaries of Barbara A. Mowat and Paul Werstine in their New Folger Library edition of *Henry IV, Part 1* (New York: Washington Square Press, 1994) liv-lvii and 235-41.

[45] Kristen Poole, "Saints Alive! Falstaff, Martin Marprelate, and the Staging of Puritanism," *SQ* 46 (1995): 47-75, esp. 52n.

[46] Poole, 54.

⁴⁷ Poole, 71.

⁴⁸ Poole, 68 and 70-71.

⁴⁹ Poole, 67.

⁵⁰ Poole, 66.

⁵¹ See, for example, Poole's fine closing statement on page 75.

⁵² Empson, *Essays on Shakespeare,* 52. This chapter is a revised version of "Falstaff and Mr. Dover Wilson," which appeared in 1953 in *The Kenyon Review.* Because there is considerable evidence for the practice Empson mentions—getting soldiers killed to keep their pay—many editors and critics assume that this practice is implied in Falstaff's "I have led my ragamuffins where they are peppered" (5.3.35-36). It may be implied, but Empson's attribution of this motive to Falstaff is incorrect. Falstaff makes no such boast.

⁵³ Empson, *Essays on Shakespeare,* 52.

⁵⁴ Whitney, 424-25. In spite of the reservations I express here, Whitney's is the most enlightening study I have encountered both of Falstaff's performance in particular and of the differences and tense interactions between festivity and topicality in general. A lucid and comprehensive-yet-economic discussion of the way the titular concepts may be incorporated into a framework for speculating about the range of possible audience responses in a pluralistic theater may be found on pages 410-18.

⁵⁵ Whitney, 425. There is something wrong with the reference to Mikhail M. Bakhtin here. Whitney cites a passage from *Problems of Dostoevsky's Poetics* (ed. and trans. Caryl Emerson [Minneapolis: U of Minnesota P, 1984]), in which the word "double-voiced" appears just before a discussion of carnivalistic dialogism and seems to be applied to such phenomena as the mixing of styles ("multi-toned narration") and the use of such "inserted genres" as letters, manuscripts, citations, parodies, etc. (108-9). This doesn't seem as relevant to Falstaff's speech, or to the statement Whitney is trying make about it, as the following passage from *The Dialogic Imagination: Four Essays by M. M. Bakhtin* (ed. Michael Holquist, trans. Caryl Emerson and Michael Holquist [Austin: U of Texas P, 1981]):

> As a living, socio-ideological concrete thing, as heteroglot opinion, language, for the individual consciousness, lies on the borderline between oneself and the other. The word in language is half someone else's. It becomes "one's own" only when the speaker populates it with his own intention, his own accent, when he appropriates the word.... Prior to this moment of appropriation, the word ... exists in other people's mouths, in other people's contexts, serving other people's intentions: it is from there that one must take the word, and make it one's own.... Language ... is populated—overpopulated—with the intentions of others.
> 
> (293-94)

The description of the word prior to the moment of appropriation and thus "unhinged" from Falstaff as the subject of his speech fits Whitney's apparent purpose better than the passage he cites because it supports his thesis about the dispersal of interpretive authority among different sectors of the audience. But it is also a description of the way Falstaff's language is read by critics who don't explore the possibility that he populates it with his own intention, his own accent, and makes it his own.

⁵⁶ Whitney, 422.

⁵⁷ For different perspectives on Falstaff's performances as a self-mocking parodist and a self-proclaimed rogue, see Whitney, 429, 433, 438, 439, and 440.

⁵⁸ Whitney, 413-14.

⁵⁹ Whitney, 448.

⁶⁰ Weimann, 256-57.

⁶¹ Weimann, 258-60.

⁶² Weimann, 159.

⁶³ Meredith Anne Skura, *Shakespeare the Actor and the Purposes of Playing* (Chicago and London: U of Chicago P, 1993), 162.

⁶⁴ Skura, 160.

⁶⁵ Skura's discussion of this canine conundrum (160-61) follows that of States in "The Dog on the Stage" (379-81). See also Elam's astute and amusing account of Launce's troubles in this soliloquy (56).

⁶⁶ Skura, 161 and 163.

⁶⁷ Skura, 164-65.

⁶⁸ On the relation of conspicuous citation to the dominance of rhetoric over ethos, see Elam's stimulating discussions in *Shakespeare's Universe of Discourse* (223-26 and 287-89).

⁶⁹ Skura, 162-63.

⁷⁰ Skura, 116 and 120.

⁷¹ "[The prince] has given Falstaff charge of an infantry company because he knows Falstaff hates walking ... ; he can also guess, and take pleasure in behold-

⁷¹ ing, how Falstaff is likely to flout the regulations to exploit his position as captain" (Whitney, 424).

⁷² M. D. Faber's interesting suggestion that pocket-picking evokes the rifling of corpses on the battlefield (202) suggests the same overlap seen from the other side. Going to war, Harry will accentuate his dissociation from Falstaff—will "kill" what he represents—by continuing to put him down and keep him close to the ground.

⁷³ Harry's contrasting promise to Peto at 2.4.539-40 ("We must all to the wars, and thy place shall be honorable") seems included mainly to drive this home. In context it sounds like a reward for Peto's willingness to pick Falstaff's pocket.

⁷⁴ Empson is puzzled by the repetition of the number twenty-two (*Essays on Shakespeare*, 66), which Falstaff had also used in 2.2 ("I have forsworn his company hourly any time this two-and-twenty years" [ll. 15-16]). But the second reference contributes to a pattern of conspicuous backward references, and that may be explanation enough: it is one of several mnemonic triggers that keep 2.2 and 2.4 in full recall during the boundary crossing (from tavern to battlefield) of 3.3.

⁷⁵ Whitney, 424.

⁷⁶ Whitney, 422.

⁷⁷ The soliloquy is studded with terms that recall phrases and moments of 1.2 and the tavern scenes. Some examples: "a commodity of warm slaves" (4.2.17-18)—"a commodity of good names" (1.2.81-82); "Lazarus in the painted cloth" (4.2.25)—"hellfire and Dives" (3.3.31-32); "revolted tapsters, and hostlers trade-fallen" (4.2.28-29)—Francis and the Gadshill episode; "prodigals lately come from swine keeping" (4.2.34)—Harry and Falstaff.

⁷⁸ Whitney, 424.

⁷⁹ Empson, *Essays on Shakespeare*, 52.

⁸⁰ Whitney, 429.

⁸¹ Whitney, 440.

⁸² Skura, 121.

⁸³ Skura, 122. I see no evidence for the claim of "overt allusions to homoeroticism" in 3.2. Throughout this discussion Skura tends to run two separate scenes (3.2 and 5.3) together and treat them as one.

⁸⁴ Skura, 122-23.

⁸⁵ On this, see Skura, 121.

⁸⁶ Berger, *Making Trifles of Terrors*, 143-44.

⁸⁷ Compare 1.2.224-25 with 5.5.73-86. See also *1 Henry IV*, 2.4.156-57; 3.3.132-36; and 2.4.60-66. Empson notes that the reference to £1,000 "is kept echoing through both parts of the history; it seems to become a symbol of Falstaff's hopes and his betrayal" (*Some Versions of Pastoral*, 107). Though Empson ignores the exchange with the Lord Chief Justice, his comment applies to it.

⁸⁸ The scope and source of this authority are suggested by the still-echoing words that end the preceding scene. In these words the dying king recognizes the irony—but acknowledges the justice—of the misleading prophecy that he would die in Jerusalem: not, as "vainly I supposed the Holy Land" on a crusade to atone for the guilt of regicide and usurpation; the closest he would get would be the Jerusalem Chamber in Westminster Abbey: "Laud be to God! . . . bear me to that chamber; there I'll lie. / In that Jerusalem shall Harry die" (4.5.235-40). On this passage, see my *Making Trifles of Terrors*, 249-50.

⁸⁹ Skura, 120.

⁹⁰ A. R. Humphreys, ed., *The Second Part of King Henry IV* (London: Methuen, 1966), 161.

⁹¹ Skura, 123.

⁹² See also 3.2.309-12, 318, 323-25; and 5.1.61-63.

⁹³ "I pray God," the Hostess says of Doll, "that the fruit of her womb miscarry" (5.4.13-14). The statement is both a malapropism and a falsehood (since what swells Doll is not pregnancy but cushions), but it is nevertheless "true" on both counts. It expresses the general desire that all their schemes and hopes miscarry. But what they want to abort, to be delivered of, is the absence of the pregnancy and fulfillment whose workings they can only mock in an imaginary body composed of cushions and words. Their actual bodies, their persons and plots, are diminished by what the Hostess earlier miscalled "confirmities" (2.4.58), which I interpret to mean complicity with the male forces that victimize them—woman's acceptance of herself as "the weaker vessel, *as they say*, the emptier vessel" (2.4.60-61, emphasis added). They do not know what to make of a diminished thing, and thus "of sufferance comes ease."

---

Source: "The Prince's Dog: Falstaff and the Perils of Speech-Prefixity," in *Shakespeare Quarterly*, Vol. 49, No. 1, Spring, 1998, pp. 40-73.

# Sir John Oldcastle and the Construction of Shakespeare's Authorship

## Douglas A. Brooks, *Texas A&M University*

> Let vs returne vnto the Bench againe,
> And there examine further of this fray.
> —*Sir John Oldcastle*, 1.i.124-5

A decade ago the editors of the Oxford *William Shakespeare: The Complete Works* replaced the name of the character called Falstaff in *Henry IV Part I* with a hypothetically earlier version of the character's name, Sir John Oldcastle. The restoration of Oldcastle to the Oxford edition makes it the first authoritative text to undo an alteration which, as scholars have long suspected, Shakespeare himself must have made sometime between a non-extant 1596 performance text and the 1598 quarto of the play. The resulting scholarly debate over this editorial decision has touched on a number of significant issues linked to the authority and authenticity of "Shakespearean" texts, and it has raised important questions about how these texts were shaped by the material, religious, and political conditions in which they were produced.[1] In the case of *Henry IV Part I*, critics have struggled to reconstruct how an early version of the text with Oldcastle as the protagonist of the unworthy knight plot might have placed the play and its author in a complicated position between an individual's reputation and a nation's. Indeed, it is likely that a play featuring a fat rogue named Oldcastle would have insulted William Brooke, a titular descendent of the knight's Cobham Lordship who served briefly as Lord Chamberlain at about the time *Henry IV Part I* was first performed. Moreover, such a play certainly would have slurred the character's namesake, the Lord Cobham, a Lollard who was executed for treason and subsequently transformed by William Tyndale, John Bale, and John Foxe into one of England's greatest Protestant martyrs. Consequently, scholars have used the publication of the Oxford edition to speculate on Shakespeare's authorial intentions.

In this essay, I want to shift the discussion away from what Shakespeare might have intended by focusing instead on a significant aspect of the dramatist's authorship that has been under-examined in the recent debate over the Oxford *Henry IV Part I*. I argue that the initial deletion of Oldcastle from an early text of *Henry IV Part I* and its subsequent restoration to the Oxford edition constitute two important textual points in the history of Shakespeare's authorship; and I attempt to trace this history from the authorial attribution on the quarto title page of *Henry IV Part II* (1600) to the present moment in literary studies when Shakespeare's position as a canonical author faces reevaluation. Concomitantly, I try to account for the importance of Oldcastle's name to Shakespeare's authorial status by suggesting that the posthumous construction of Oldcastle's martyrdom has certain elements in common with the posthumous construction of Shakespeare's authorship.

I'd like to begin three years after Oldcastle became Falstaff. The title page of the 1600 edition of *Sir John Oldcastle Part I* indicates that the play was "Printed by V. S. for Thomas Pavier."[2] V. S. is one Valentine Simmes, a printer of some reputation who printed several Shakespeare quartos as well as plays staged by the Admiral's Men. As with many such quarto editions of plays, no author is mentioned, but we know from Philip Henslowe's diary that ten pounds were allotted "to pay mr monday mr drayton & mr wilsson & haythway for the first pte of the lyfe of Sr Jhon Ouldcastell . . ."[3] By the time of the 1619 reprint, however, "William Shakespeare" appears on the title page, and it is Pavier's turn to be abbreviated to "for T.P." The newfound importance bestowed on Shakespeare's authorial status underscores Pavier's efforts at that point to publish a collection of Shakespeare's plays three years after Ben Jonson's folio *WORKES* and four years before the First Folio appeared in print. Nevertheless, in the case of the *Sir John Oldcastle* reprint the author's name appears, oddly enough, on a title page that is falsely dated "1600" so Pavier can sidestep Stationers' restrictions by passing it off as the remnant of an earlier edition. Like the striking of the clock in *Julius Caesar*, the Shakespearean author-function is textually compelled to make an appearance before its time.

This brief but typical episode in the ongoing struggle between the early modern playhouse and printing house raises unsettling questions about the status of Shakespeare's authorship, especially when viewed from the perspective of current laws of intellectual property and Shakespeare's singular position in our culture. Pavier must have known in 1600 that the quarto he published was the collaboratively authored property of Henslowe. How could he republish it nineteen years later as a Shakespeare play? While it is impossible to answer with certainty, one thing seems clear: the proprietary status of printed drama in the period was so inconsequential that Pavier must have felt free to manipulate the identity of a given play's author(s) as the particular publishing circumstances required. In Shakespeare's case, there is ample textual evidence of such inconsequence if we consider the fact that nearly half of the plays that appeared in print before the 1623 Folio made no claims to Shakespeare's paternity. Only Nathaniel Butter's 1608 quarto edition of *King Lear*—printed for him by Nicholas Okes—accords top-of-the-title-page billing to "M. William Shak-speare": set in larger type than it had ever appeared before, the author's name is linked to the title of the play, "True Chronicle Historie of the life and / death of King LEAR and his three / daughters" with the possessive pronoun *"H I S"* set in italicized and widely spaced capital pica letters.[4] The only other place that Shakespeare could have seen his name set in comparably large type was blazoned across the title page of the 1609 *Sonnets* in capital letters.[5] In strictly typographic terms, Shakespeare, the poet, fared better as a "man in print"[6] during his lifetime than Shakespeare, the playwright.

Okes and Butter's title page announces rather loudly that here is an author and here is a play, and the correspondence between them is a typographically emphatic genitive. No doubt one likely motive for typographically fetishizing the possessive pronoun on *King Lear*'s 1608 title page was to differentiate Shakespeare's "True Chronicle Historie of the life and death of King LEAR and his three daughters" from a *non-Shakespearean* "True Chronicle History of King LEIR and his three daughters" published in 1603. In this sense, the typographic emergence of Shakespeare's authorial selfhood is fashioned for him, courtesy of Okes and Butter, according to an epistemological schema that has been influentially characterized by Stephen Greenblatt as "resolutely dialectical"[7]— although here the oppositionally charged moment of recognition takes place within the utterly commercial world of the London printing house. Indeed, so powerful is this publishing venture's urge to drag Shakespeare into authorhood that, strangely enough, the author's name is printed a second time in the same large type as a head-title on the first page of play text (B1ʳ), this time beneath a border ornament (9.5 by 1.25 centimeters);[8] and once again a genitive relation between author and play is emphasized: "M. William Shak-speare / *H I S* Historie, of King Lear."

Typographically speaking, however, things were not usually so spectacular for Shakespeare's status as an author in print. The first quarto of a Shakespeare play to mention the playwright, *Loves Labors Lost* (1598), merely indicates in small type near the middle of the title page that it has been "Newly corrected and augmented / By W. Shakespere" (A1ʳ). The logical assumption is that Shakespeare was newly correcting and augmenting what he himself had written, but the title page itself does not assert the play's authorship. Two years later, the title page of *Henry IV Part II* forecloses on the need to assume authorship by including for the first time the phrase, *"Written by William Shakespeare"* (A1ʳ). It bears repeating that this *"Written by William Shakespeare,"* which appears near the bottom in the smallest type on the page, is the first intance of an unambiguously authorial attribution to Shakespeare on the title page of an early modern play.

Authors correct, sometimes they augment, and frequently enough in early modern England they endeavored to correct and augment other authors' work.[9] Arguably, however, authors primarily write, and it is therefore significant that the first title page to attribute the *writing* of a play to Shakespeare belongs to a play that appears after its prequel, *Henry IV Part I*, had recently embroiled our playwright in something of a political—and perhaps religious—scandal. Here we find direct material evidence for Michael Foucault's claim that "[t]exts, books, and discourses really began to have authors (other than mythical, 'sacralized' and 'sacralizing' figures) to the extent that authors became subject to punishment, that is, to the extent that discourses could be transgressive."[10] Having presumably selected Sir John Oldcastle as the signifier for a fat rogue knight in an earlier (non-extant performance text) version of *Henry IV*, Shakespeare was compelled to give the character an alternative name in a subsequent printed version of the play. Sir John Oldcastle was, of course, the name of a proto-Protestant martyr and an ancestor, by marriage to Elizabeth Brooke, of William Brooke, the seventh Baron Cobham who was the Lord Chamberlain from August of 1596 until his death in March of 1597.[11]

Whether Shakespeare intended to travesty the House of Cobham or indifferently went with the name of the Lollard thorn in Henry V's side because it was already in his major source text, *The Famous Victories of Henry V,* has been the subject of much critical debate, especially since the recent critical controversy over restoring the name "Oldcastle" to the Oxford edition of *Henry IV Part I.* For now, however, I think it is important to try to see the restoration debate in the strictly material terms of Shakespeare's career in print. Viewed from this perspective, it seems extremely significant that the Oldcastle/Falstaff problem, which has generated a number of critical questions that go to the heart of authorial intention, is so closely linked to Shakespeare's typographic emergence as an author. Indeed, the printing history of Shakespeare's texts provides us with a remarkable convergence of the material evidence of his status as an author with the metaphysical grounds of authorship itself. And yet this convergence has gone unremarked in the recent discussion of the authorial/textual fate of the name Oldcastle in *Henry IV Part I*, perhaps because, as D. F. McKenzie observes, "[d]ialects of written language— graphic, algebraic, hieroglyphic and, most significantly for our purposes, typographic—have suffered an exclusion from critical debate about the interpretation of texts because they are not speech-related."[12]

As was the case with the spectacular typographic appearance of the playwright's name on the title page of

*King Lear, Henry IV Part I* is also "resolutely dialectical" in its relation to an earlier, anonymously authored *The Famous Victories of Henry V.* Sometime between 1596, when Shakespeare began his remake of *Famous Victories* for performance as *The History of Henry IV,* and 1598, when a quarto of *Henry IV* was first printed, the character of Sir John Oldcastle became Sir John Falstaff.[13] The 1598 quarto of *Famous Victories,* printed by Thomas Creede, lists "Sir John Oldcastle, alias Jockey" in the Dramatis Personae;[14] the 1598 quarto of *Henry IV* does not. In other words, the textual locus of the oppositionally constructed identity of *Henry IV Part I* is precisely the oppositional matter of Oldcastle vs. Falstaff, and Shakespeare must have removed the name Oldcastle from the performance text of *Henry IV Part I* and put Falstaff in its place in time for the change to be preserved in print.

Although the actual moment when matters of the world forced themselves on the materiality of Shakespeare's text can probably never be recovered, this much seems certain: by the time *Henry IV Part II* is published, the question of a character's name has given way to the initial attribution of Shakespeare's named authorship on the play's title page; and the play's epilogue specifically calls attention to the very oppositional construct that preempted the newly typographic status of the author's name: "for Olde-castle died a Martyre, and this is not the man" (L1ᵛ, 27-8). In short, Shakespeare's *Henry IV Part I* is not an earlier errant version of itself; the earlier version is not *Famous Victories;* and Falstaff is not Oldcastle. Furthermore, the publication of the authorially unattributed *Henry IV* quarto, cleansed of all but a punning reference to Oldcastle (I.ii.40-1) and a metrical irregularity haunted by the three syllables of his name (II.ii.102), anonymously constitutes Shakespeare's transition from the corrector/augmentor of *Loves Labor Lost* to the writer of *Henry IV Part II*. More than anything else, this brief two-year segment from the complicated printing history of Shakespeare's texts suggests that the playwright's newly typographic status as an author got forged in the smithy of adversity. Materially, this predicament receives vivid representation in the printed quarto text of *Henry IV Part II* which couples the title page's originary attribution of *written* authorship with the final page's notorious epilogue and "our humble Author['s]" (L1ᵛ, 23) attempt to clear up any misunderstandings that may have resulted from an early version of the first installment of *Henry IV*. Within a year or so of having written *Romeo and Juliet,* Shakespeare had learned firsthand what could be in a name.

Shakespeare's career in print seems to have been more erratic than we might expect of our greatest author, and it is possible, therefore, that Pavier's willingness to attribute *Sir John Oldcastle* to Shakespeare in 1619—when an authorized version of Shakespeare's plays was still a twinkling £ sign in the eye of John Heminge and Henry Condell—merely symptomized an emergent authorship that was still *in utero.* On the other hand, given the latent ontological density of authorship that typographically manifests itself in the scene of naming bounded by the publication of the two parts of *Henry IV,* it is equally conceivable that Pavier was counting on the Oldcastle/Falstaff controversy to lend his Shakespearean attribution some weight. Indeed, he may have even banked on a potential readership's capacity to relate, conflate, or confuse a play's title with a playwright's scandal over a lord's title.

Compelled to straddle the nominative and the titular, the signifier "Oldcastle" apparently had enough resonance to endure the two decades that separated the initial controversy from a subsequent publishing venture that may have sought to capitalize on it. There is, in fact, scattered evidence to suggest that some slippage did occur between the banished name of the Shakespeare character and the title of the Henslowe collaboration. Arguably, the first such mix-up—long noted by scholars—transpired two years after the initial scandal in the context of what seems to have been a performance of *Henry IV Part I* staged in London for the visiting Flemish ambassador. In a letter written March 6 of 1599/1600 by Rowland Whyte to Sir Robert Sidney, the governor of Flushing, Whyte informs his boss that "[a]ll this weeke the Lords have bene in Londen, and past away the tyme in feasting and plaies . . . on Thursday afternoon the Lord Chamberlain's players acted before Vereken *Sir John Old Castell,* to his great contentment."[15] Since Shakespeare began writing plays for the Chamberlain's Men in 1594, and the Henslowe play was very much the property of the Admiral's Men, most scholars believe that Whyte was referring to *Henry IV Part I* as *Sir John Oldcastle.*[16] Thus, in the mind of at least one of Pavier's contemporaries the name of the Lollard martyr was returned from Shakespearean textual exile long enough to greet a visiting dignitary. Within a few years of Whyte's error, the 1602 title page of *Merry Wives of Windsor* would restore the originary opposition of the epilogue of *Henry IV Part II* by putting the name of the character, Sir John Falstaff, in its title.

Approximately two years after Oldcastle was sent packing, both names appeared for the first time as the titles of plays: the martyr's name was appropriated for the title page of the Henslowe collaboration; the knight of the garter's name constituted the principal part of the title of Shakespeare's play, "A Most pleasant and excellent conceited Comedie, of Syr *Iohn Falstaffe,* and the merrie Wiues of *Winsor.*" According to an oft-repeated anecdote that surfaced for the first time exactly 100 years later in John Dennis's *The Comical Gallant: or The Amours of Sir John Falstaffe,*[17] the Falstaff play satisfied a command from Elizabeth I for another play about the fat knight.[18] Other anecdotal evidence indicates that Falstaff occupied a substantial amount of the queen's attention, for we learn from Nicholas Rowe that Elizabeth herself was behind the revision from Oldcastle to Falstaff as well. According to a tradition that Rowe seems to have founded, "this Part of Falstaff is said to have been written originally under the Name of Oldcastle; some of that Family being then remaining, the Queen was pleas'd to command [Shakespeare] to alter it; upon which he made use of Falstaff."[19] By dint of his status as Shakespeare's first scholarly editor, Rowe's account consigned the scandal of the Oldcastle/Falstaff name-change to the playwright's editorial legacy. Less obvious, however, is this account's contribution to the mythic development of Shakespeare's status as an author.

If we recall the significance of the Oldcastle/Falstaff controversy to the typographic coming-into-being of Shakespeare's authorhood on the title page of *Henry IV Part II,* then it makes an odd kind of sense that Rowe would attempt to stage a meeting between the bard and the queen on this issue. Writing in 1709, the same year that the statute of Anne, the world's first copyright act, had placed authorial rights on the juridical map by strictly limiting the term of copyright protection to fourteen years,[20] Rowe would have been hard-pressed to find much legal, political, or institutional support for his project to editorially bolster and enhance the status of Shakespeare's authorship. Yet, he seems to have sidestepped these inadequacies by linking Shakespeare to Elizabeth, by placing the still tremulous figure of the author in a direct encounter with a representative of institutionalized individuality.[21] Providing England's greatest queen with an opportunity to collaborate with its greatest author on the printed text of *Henry IV Part I,* Rowe may have suspected that the institution of monarchy, having suffered a number of setbacks of late, was poised to be eclipsed by strategies of subjectivity that lie dormant within the paradigm of the author. Such suspicions would not have been groundless.

There is some evidence that authorship and kingship were set to cross ascending and descending paths, respectively, at precisely the moment in which Rowe was preparing Shakespeare for his annotated authorial star turn. In 1694, the Licensing Act of 1637 that had augmented the English government's control over censorship was allowed to lapse, largely because it had become a restraint on trade.[22] Whatever legal foundation stationers had formerly relied upon to protect their interests lapsed with it. No longer required to register their publications, printers seem to have come into their own as unrestricted venture capitalists in the same year that the Bank of England was founded.[23] The roots of the copyright statute of 1709 and Rowe's editorial undertaking of the same year would no doubt have found fertile ground in the two decades that followed the 1688 revolution and the consequent supplanting of a "natural" monarch with a financial-military throne; but what seems less clear is how the tumultuous events of the post-1688 period prepared the way for the meeting that Rowe arranged between Shakespeare and Elizabeth on the textual fate of Sir John Oldcastle. At the level of anecdote, only Falstaff's future as a Shakespeare character hangs in the balance. The stakes get much higher when we recall the material/typographic link between the Oldcastle/Falstaff controversy and Shakespeare's authorial status.

Although Margreta de Grazia contends in her recent analysis of Shakespeare's "dynastic" editorship that the construction of the playwright's individualized status as an author is only fully realized by the textual apparatus of Edmund Malone's *Plays and Poems* of 1790, she also acknowledges that Malone's edition "is clearly indebted to a long line of eighteenth-century editors, beginning with Rowe in 1709."[24] There, at the beginning of one dynasty, meetings are arranged with the end of another dynasty. A few years before Rowe—in the case of John Dennis (1702)—and subsequently with Rowe himself, Falstaff's fate, first as a lover, then as a stand-in for Oldcastle, is anecdotally decided between Queen Elizabeth and Shakespeare. No such direct encounter between monarch and author had been previously envisioned by Richard James, the learned correspondent whom Gary Taylor characterizes as "our key witness for the intervention of the Cobhams."[25] If we accept Taylor's carefully argued conclusion that "MS James 35 probably dates from late 1634 or early 1635,"[26] then some twelve years after the First Folio authorized Shakespeare and two years before the Star Chamber decree of 1637 sought to reauthorize Charles I, James opts for a passive construction: "the poet was putt to make an ignorant shifte of abjusing Sr Jhon."[27] Only "the poet" and "Sr Jhon" get singled out in James' account where, in place of William Brooke as the offended party, we find a collective consisting of "personages descended from his [title]" and "manie others allso whoe ought to haue him in honourable memorie."[28] Presumably, the "manie others" are right-minded Protestants who have remained mindful of the earlier Lord Cobham's "constant and resolute martyrdom," as James put it.

Whether James's reluctance to make Elizabeth the agent of Oldcastle's displacement from *Henry IV Part I* indicates that no such royal directive was ever issued will probably remain a matter of speculation. There is, however, no precedent for James's reticence in the published accounts of Oldcastle's martyrdom that circulated in post-reformation England. On the contrary, treatments of royal agency in the life and death of the Lollard martyr are perhaps best characterized in the *Sir John Oldcastle* play by a judge who remarks of the knight's adherence to Wycliffe's doctrine, "This case concernes the Kings prerogative / And's dangerous to the state and common wealth" (A4ᵛ). Perhaps it was this concern that motivated a newly crowned Henry V to summon Oldcastle to Kensington in the summer of 1413. Upon his arrival, the king read to him aloud the more appalling passages from a few unbound quires of heretical writings that had been confiscated from a limner's shop in Paternoster Row and were said to be the Lord Cobham's property.[29] The basic plot elements for the subsequent drama of Shakespeare's authorship are already in place: an unpublished manuscript and a summons to its alleged proprietor from an annoyed monarch.

Among those chroniclers who were contemporaries of Oldcastle,[30] the knight was commonly viewed as "[a] strong man in bataile . . . but a grete heretik, and a gret enemye to the Cherch," as Capgrave put it.[31] A century later, writers began to raise the specter of Oldcastle's execution to exploit what G. R. Elton characterizes as "at least a superficial resemblance" between the remnants of Lollardy and the initial efforts by England to part ways with the Roman Catholic Church.[32] The first to recognize Oldcastle's potential for a history of English Protestantism was William Tyndale, who re-interpreted the Lollard's excommunication for heresy as an act of unjust persecution and published this reading as a brief appendix to the *Book of Thorpe,* an account of another fifteenth-century Lollard first printed in 1530. Responding quickly in his *Dialogue Concerning Tyndale,* Sir Thomas More did not hesitate to inform his readers that fire was used judiciously when "the Lorde Cobham [was] taken in Wales and burned in London."[33]

Yet it was precisely "thys terrible kynde of death with galowes, chaines, and fyre,"[34] in John Bale's phrase, that made the greatest impression on the architects of English Protestantism who were searching for the basement and first few stories of an edifice begun in mid-air.[35] Writing in 1544, Bale gathered together and re-shaped much of the chronicle material on the Oldcastle controversy into a form later incorporated directly into John Foxe's *Acts and Monuments.* Nevertheless, Bale's account was a substantive achievement in its own right, numbering some 112 pages and tracing its lineage directly to "a certen brefe examinacyon of the sayd Lorde Cobham" which "the true servaunt of God Willyam Tyndale put into the prent" (4$^r$). The bulk of Bale's account concerns the Church's efforts to persecute proto-reformers, its subsequent effort to minimize sympathy for Oldcastle's death, the betrayal of Lord Powis, the knight's martyrdom, and the oft-chronicled potential confrontation in St. Giles's field between the king and several of Oldcastle's fellow heretics. Nevertheless, on the subject of a meeting between a lord and his king, Bale's Oldcastle begins to stray from the well-beaten path of the chroniclers.

Whereas previous accounts only mention the initial session in Kensington, Bale provides Henry V with two opportunities to set the errant knight straight on matters of church and state. Being "a manne of great byrthe and in faver at that tyme with the kynge" (13$^r$), Lord Cobham is summoned to Kensington after the king has "gentyliye harde those bloud thurstye" (13$^r$) complaints against him by "these hygh Prelates with theyr pharysees and Scrybes" (12$^v$). No mention is made of the "certain erroneous bills" that earned the knight a hearing in the chronicles. When Oldcastle arrives, the King "call[s] him secretlye, admonyshyng him betwixt him and him / to submyt himselfe to his mother the holye churche / and, as an obedyent chyld, to acknowledge himselfe culpable" (14$^v$). Up to this point, Bale has followed the basic outline of his chronicle sources. Then, he suddenly veers off the chronicled path. Gone are the confiscated unbound quires of heretical writings read aloud by Henry, and in their place Bale gives Oldcastle the chance to voice his dangerous religious leanings directly to the king: " 'Unto you next my eternall lyuyinge God,' " he assures Henry, " 'owe I my whole obedience / and submytne thereunto . . . But as touchynng the Pope and his spiritualite / trulye I owe the~ neyther sute nor servyce / for so moche as I knowe him by the scriptures to be the great Antichrist / the sonne of perdicion / the open adversarye of God and the abhominacyon standynge in the holye place' " (14$^v$). Having shifted the material grounds of Oldcastle's Lollardy from his alleged writings to a transcription of his confessed beliefs, from *graphie* to *logos,* Bale has rather shrewdly upgraded a fifteenth-century heresy to the core doctrine of post-Reformation religious/nationalist propaganda under Henry VIII and later Elizabeth—a doctrine which Bale himself had helped to shape in plays like *King Johan.*[36]

Nevertheless, as often happens with such repressions, the *graphie* stages a return. By the second meeting with Henry V, Oldcastle has become an author, having intermittently written down an extended version of what he told the king during their first session. Bale gives it a centered title at the top of 16$^r$, "The Christen Beleue of / the lorde Cobham," and even narrates the conditions of its authorship. With the "furye of Antichrist thus kyndled agaynst him" and other "deadlye danngers" facing him "on everye syde," Bale tells us that Oldcastle "toke paper and penne in hande and so wrote a Christen confessyen or reckenyng of his fayth (which foloweth here after) and both signed and sealed it with his owne han-de" (16$^v$).[37] Hoping to bring together writing hand and royal hand, Oldcastle "toke the copye with him / and went therwith to the kynge trustinge to fynde mercye and faver at his hande" (16$^v$). Consistent with the early stages of authorhood, initially "the kynge wolde in no case receyue yt" (17$^r$). Subsequently, however, Henry summons the writer into his privy chamber, and this time he reads: "And hauyng his appele the-re at hande redye written / he shewed yt with all reverence to the kynge. Where-with the kynge was than moche more dyspleased than afore / and sayd angrily unto him / that he shuld not pursue his appele. But rather he shuld tarrye in holde, tyll soche tyme as yt were of the Pope allowed" (20ᵛ).

Thus, in both pre- and post-reformation accounts, the monarch is compelled to peruse a set of heretical writings linked to Oldcastle. However, in the gap that separates the historical Lord Cobham of the chronicles from the proto-Protestant figure of Bale's *Brefe Chronycle,* the authorial status of these writings has evolved from confiscated property attributed to an alleged Lollard to the self-authored, self-presented work of a proto-Protestant martyr. Whereas the former gets the knight an audience with the king, the latter lands him "in holde" at the Tower of London; this departure from the chronicle story line is consistent with Bale's larger concern to link proper name to intellectual property and to make sure that Oldcastle own his heresies in the presence of the monarch. As a narrative trope, the king's direct censure of Oldcastle's writings not only plays an important role in Bale's effort to fashion a posthumous career for the knight as England's great martyr, but also gets passed on to his successors, including John Foxe, Raphael Holinshed, and even Henslowe's team of playwrights.

First published in English two decades after Bale's account, the version of events included in Foxe's *Acts and Monuments* puts Oldcastle and his religious beliefs at center stage and casts the monarch as a supporting character in the plot trajectory that leads to the knight's denouement in St. Giles's field.[38] The role Foxe crafts for the king—hard upon the demise of the Marian government—is that of an ineffectual ruler manipulated by the clergy and dogma of the Catholic Church into going against "the moste noble knyght sir John Oldcastell the Lord Cobham."[39] It is not a flattering part for a king to play, but it enables Foxe to address the well-chronicled fact that Oldcastle had a problem with royal authority. Indeed the dilemma for Foxe must have been all too clear: having opted to follow in Bale's footsteps and retain Oldcastle as the type of the Protestant martyr, he also had to face the fact that the knight's involvement in treasonous activities against Henry V made him, in David Scott Kastan's apt phrase, "an uncomfortable hero of the Protestant nation."[40]

One of Foxe's solutions is to intimate that the king's problems with Oldcastle are really his problems with the papist church, and he gets the knight and the king together for their first meeting early on in the twenty-page section he devotes to Oldcastle's story; his account of both meetings[41] is taken verbatim from Bale.[42] In fact, the only change Foxe makes in Bale's version is to typographically enhance the status of Oldcastle's authorial debut. Bale's printer, we recall, breaks up the typographic flow of the narrative momentarily at the beginning of Oldcastle's written confession to give it a centered title of its own. At its conclusion, however, the text of the confession flows directly into the account of the second meeting with Henry. The only indication that the narrative has shifted from Oldcastle's written text back to the text that enframes it comes in a one-sentence segue that reminds the reader of the confession's author and indicates its intended audience: "This brefe confessyon of his fayth / the Lorde Cobham wrote (as is mencyned afore) and so toke yt with him to the court / offerynge yt with all mekensse unto the kynge to reade yt over" (19ʳ-19ᵛ). Alternatively, Foxe's printer sets off the title and text of Oldcastle's confession at its beginning and at its end, and he sets the body of the text in a smaller italic font.[43] As a text within a text within yet another text, the excessive typographic distinction accorded Oldcastle's writing not only accentuates his status as an author, but also inadvertently calls attention to the fact that the authorship of the frame text written by Bale has been silently incorporated by Foxe. Furthermore, the only other segment of Foxe's account that gets set in the same italic font is another text within a text, this time an equally set-off subsection attributed to Archbishop Arundel and entitled "The Diffinitiue sentence of / his condemnation."

The identical typographic distinction accorded Oldcastle's confession and condemnation strongly suggests that Foxe and his printer have relied on the press to enhance Bale's earlier effort to dislodge Oldcastle's martyrdom from the realm of the *logos* and relocate it under the sign of the *graphie.* Bale's account revises the story of Oldcastle's death from chronicle versions in which confiscated heretical writings lead to a confession, and that confession leads ultimately to the gallows, to a version in which a confession leads to a self-authored text, and that text leads ultimately to the gallows. Foxe takes the next logical step by marshalling the material of the printed text to establish a direct typographic link between Oldcastle's authorship and his martyrdom.[44] Foxe, a kind of proto-grammatologist, relies on the printing press to enable what Foucault termed "an insurrection of subjugated knowledge."[45]

By the time Raphael Holinshed turns his attention to Oldcastle, it is nearly half a century after the Act against Appeals to Rome (1533), and the primary concern of his brief and fragmented account—spread out over some twenty-five pages devoted to the reign of Henry V—is to situate the Lord Cobham and "all his deuises"[46] within the complex dealings that are needed to maintain a delicate balance between the crown's authority and the church's. Nevertheless, Bale has been so successful at instantiating his version of the wayward knight that when Holinshed addresses the topic of the meeting between lord and king, the grammatological trajectory of Bale's narrative reconstruction remains: "The lord Cobham not onely thanked [Henry V] of his most fa-uorable clemencie, but also declared first to him by mouth, and afterwards by writing, the foumdation of his faith, and the grounde of his beliefe, affirming his grace to be his supreme head, and competent iudge . . . The King understanding and persuaded by his Counsell . . . sent him to the Tower of London, there to abide the determination of the Cleargie."[47] But if Holinshed is willing to toe the Bale/Foxe story line that runs from speech to writing to Tower, he is unwilling to completely abandon the frequently chronicled element of confiscated heretical materials. Forced to reconcile two disparate traditions, he merely shifts the confiscation scene from its original place as the impetus for summoning Oldcastle to Kensington to a later point in the narrative after the knight has already escaped the Tower: "In the same place were found bookes written in english; & some of those bokes in times past had bin trimly gilte, & limned, beautified with Images, the heads wherof had bin scraped off, & in ye Litany, they had blotted forthe the name of our Lady, & of other saints, til they came to ye verse *payce nois Domine*. Diuers writings were founde there also, in derogation of suche honour as then was thought due to our Lady."[48] No longer unbound quires, Holinshed relies on a previous chronicler's account to render the evidence with the eye of a bibliophile. And while the heretical books "so disfigured with scrapings & / blotting out" (18-9) are still sent to the king, this time they are passed along directly to the Archbishop Arundel "to shewe the same in his ser- / mons at Paules crosse in Londo~."[49] No appalling passages are read nor confessions heard because Oldcastle—already a fugitive from the law— is unable to appear in the king's privy chambers.

Despite a number of important variables, what remains constant in all of these accounts of the meeting between Henry V and Lord Cobham is that, as individuals, each figure is compelled at some point to speak for and represent a larger collective body. For the pre-reformation version of the king, that body is the realm and the Roman Catholic church to which it has pledged its allegiance. For the post-reformation Henry, it is an evil and corrupt papist clergy that turns him into a kind of ventriloquist's dummy whose authority over the realm is limited to mouthing church policy. Alternatively, Oldcastle begins his career in the chronicles as the most notorious member of a shadowy assemblage of heretics who mutilate books and read in English. With the guidance and encouragement of post-reformation writers (Bale and Foxe), however, he comes to find his own individualized authorial voice; and, in doing so, he speaks and writes for the elect Protestant nation heralding the renaissance of the primitive church. The key determinant in these transformations is the particular collective or community with which the writer identifies.

It is likely that a comparable sense of community motivated Richard James to attribute the agency behind the Oldcastle/Falstaff name change to sanguinal descendants of the house of Cobham and spiritual descendants of a prominent Protestant martyr. Yet James's reluctance to single out, for example, Lord Chamberlain William Brooke or Queen Elizabeth as the agent of this emendation is already a nostalgic gesture because, once Shakespeare has written a version of *Henry IV* with Sir John Oldcastle in the *dramatis personae*, the legendary figure is essentially compelled to go it alone. As the next substantive treatment of Oldcastle's life and death after Foxe's, the Anthony Munday-Michael Drayton-Richard Hathway-Robert Wilson collaboration takes most of its cues not from an identification with a community, but from an individual playwright named Shakespeare. In the same way that Shakespeare's *King Lear* is resolutely dialectical with an earlier anonymous version, Henslowe's play constructs its identity and the identity of its eponymous hero throughout as a dialectic of genitives: our *Sir John Oldcastle*/Oldcastle vs. Shakespeare's. Indeed, this oppositional construction is already underway in the play's prologue when the reader is informed that "It is no pampered glutton we present, / Nor aged Councellor to youthfull sinne. / But one, whose vertue shone above the rest, / A valiant Martyr, and a vertuous peere" (A2$^r$). Here, it seems that prologue has followed hard upon epilogue, because the diction and sequence of these lines mirrors and inverts the disclaimer at the end of *Henry IV Part II*. Whereas Shakespeare maintains that "Oldcastle died a martyr, and this is not the [i.e., Tyndale, Bale, and Foxe's] man," Munday et al. respond by insisting that this is not Shakespeare's man because Oldcastle died a martyr. Thus, in a proto-Hegelian sense, this non-Shakespearean "one, whose vertue shone above the rest," is already rehearsing the singularity that will characterize Shakespeare's status as an author. If, as Annabel Patterson observes, "the story of Oldcastle was to assume a privileged position, as one of those cultural icons in which are epitomized a society's conflicting and shifting values,"[50] then the staging of his story by Henslowe's team of playwrights inadvertently prepared the way for Shakespeare to displace Oldcastle from that privileged position.

Singling out the Munday-Drayton-Hathway-Wilson collaboration as "a key document in any effort to see how the history play in this period changed and yet stayed the same," G. K. Hunter observes that "of the several (two-part) history plays that Henslowe's team produced in 1598-99 . . . [*Sir John Oldcastle*] is the one that seems to bear the most direct and specific relationship to its Shakespearean predecessor."[51] In Hunter's view, this close relationship is significant because it "show[s] us how far Shakespeare provided a starting point for the new-style history plays of the seventeenth century."[52] Accordingly, the two parts of

*Henry IV* represent a "turning point in the history of a genre,"[53] and Hunter not only locates a major shift in the generic history of the history play precisely "in the contrast between two transitional plays, *Henry IV* and *Oldcastle*,"[54] but also attributes the agency behind that shift to Shakespeare. Certainly Hunter gives Shakespeare more credit than an individual dramatist working in the highly collaborative environment of the early modern stage probably deserves, but it is nonetheless significant that he finds the playwright innovating precisely at the point that his authorship is established typographically. Half a century after Bale's Oldcastle first writes down his Christian beliefs, the historical figure finds himself mixed up in the emergence of Shakespeare's authorship in print. The transition glimpsed here from one author's confession to another's apology, from one innovator's controversial beliefs to another's controversy, corresponds closely to the parallel between Foxe's reliance on typography to link Oldcastle's written confession to his martyrdom and the typographic debut of Shakespeare as a writer on the title page of *Henry IV Part II* and his subsequent confession in that play's epilogue.

Given the ontological density of authorship generated from within the oppositional identity of *Henry IV Part I* and *Sir John Oldcastle*, it is perhaps not surprising that the latter is more directly and specifically preoccupied with Shakespeare than any other history play by Henslowe's collaborators. And Hunter inevitably stumbles onto this scene of individuation when he describes the main generic difference that constitutes the relationship between Shakespeare's *Henry IV* plays and the Henslowe collaboration. While Shakespeare's two plays are representative of historical drama which, according to Hunter, "defines the nation (implicitly) as a politico-military entity centered on the court," the collaboratively authored *Sir John Oldcastle* exemplifies "a historical drama that presents national consciousness as much more a matter of individual self awareness."[55] Having located the beginnings of the new history play in precisely the same oppositional interstice where Shakespeare's authorship typographically appears, Hunter also retraces the circumstances that prompt that appearance in the first place by selecting *Sir John Oldcastle* as the more individuated of the two dramas. In other words, Henslowe's Oldcastle can no longer speak for the Protestant nation because he has to defend himself against Shakespeare.

Not long after Oldcastle makes it on to the English stage—and subsequently into the printing house—under his own name, his legacy winds up impossibly entangled with the legacy of one of his chief detractors. Haunted through most of his brief career in drama by Shakespeare, Oldcastle never recovers from his brief stint as a Shakespeare character.[56] Two decades after he becomes Falstaff, even the one extant play that sought to rescue his reputation from the abuse it suffered in an early version of *Henry IV Part I* gets reprinted by its original publisher as a play written by Shakespeare. We recall that the typographic emergence of Shakespeare's authorship on the title page of *Henry IV Part II* followed hard upon the controversy that resulted from his alleged use of Oldcastle's name in an unpublished performance text of *Part I*. But what seems even more remarkable is that the decline of Oldcastle's fortunes as the founding father of the godly English nation also seems to coincide precisely with the printed debut of the author who, by the first half of the eighteenth century, will come to be promoted—according to Michael Dobson's apt characterization—as "both symbol and exemplar of British national identity."[57] It is tempting, therefore, to see the two *Henry IV* plays and *Sir John Oldcastle* as comprising an important transitional space in which Shakespeare's authorship replaces Oldcastle's martyrdom, in which the author function comes to lodge itself where previously the martyr function served to individualize and embody England's national consciousness. The representational trajectory of this displacement—ranging from the first post-Reformation accounts that transform Oldcastle into the Protestant nation's great martyr to those editorial and anecdotal accounts of the eighteenth century that transform Shakespeare into a national poet whose authority "exceed[s] the texts from which it supposedly derived"[58]—would seem to be linked to fluctuations in that other individualized embodiment of the nation, the monarch.

If the proto-form of Shakespeare's authorship can be glimpsed in Bale's and Foxe's representations of Lord Cobham's meeting with Henry V, and if the initial construction of Shakespeare's authorial identity appears to be grounded in the dialectic that characterizes the relation between his version of Oldcastle and the official proto-Protestant-martyr version represented by Bale, Foxe, and the Henslowe collaboration, then it follows that representations of Shakespeare would ultimately incorporate elements from the construction of Oldcastle's martyrological identity. One such element that becomes discernible just as Shakespeare begins to achieve a level of national importance comparable with Oldcastle's post-reformation career is the playwright's relationship with the monarch. John Dennis, we recall, is the first to suggest that such a relationship existed, and he indicates in the dedicatory epistle of his 1702 revision of *The Merry Wives of Windsor* that "[*Merry Wives*] pleas'd one of the greatest Queens that ever was in the world . . . This comedy was written at her Command, and by her direction, and she was so eager to see it Acted, that she commanded it to be finished in fourteen days."[59] Thus, Falstaff becomes the subject of a tradition in which Elizabeth's status as "one of the greatest Queens that was ever in the world" not only recalls Oldcastle's standing as "one, whose vertue shone above the rest," but also anticipates Shakespeare's promotion to the position of national poet and "patron of bourgeois morality" from the 1730s onward.[60]

Inadvertently cast as a place holder at the changing of the guard from a faded martyr to a shining author, the selection of Elizabeth for the executorship of Falstaff's destiny must be seen as a nostalgic response to a moment late in the seventeenth century when the monarchy as an institution was being dismantled by "ideologues of compromise"[61] in search of a pragmatic middle ground between royalists and parliamentarians. No doubt Portia's assertion that "A substitute shines brightly as a King / Until a king be by" was always something of a fantasy, but by the end of the seventeenth century the fantasy—dislodged from the remaining elements of its official reality—had become an illusion.[62] Nearly ready to emerge as England's master of illusion, Shakespeare is finally in the perfect position to take instructions from a monarch. Mere chronology, of course, dictates that Elizabeth be the monarch who intervenes on behalf of Falstaff; but it is significant nonetheless that Dennis arranges for a meeting between a figure who is on the verge of becoming "one of the greatest [authors] that ever was in the world" and a queen who, a century after her death, must have represented for him a privileged moment in the life cycle of the monarchy when it could still claim to be grounded in the reality of heredity and dynasty. Indeed, such a meeting underscores the extent to which authorship was poised in the final years of the seventeenth century to replace kingship as the paradigm for the individualized embodiment of the national consciousness.[63] If, as Hamlet asserts, "the king is a thing," then certainly the king can be some*thing* else.

As the "place-holder of the void," according to Slavoj Zizek's analysis of royal authority, the monarch is compelled to represent the "Master's sublime body" as "a pure 'reflective determination' " which "guarantees and personifies the *identity* of the State *qua* rational totality."[64] A sizable crack had already appeared in the mirror of this reflective determination by 1649, and the sudden escalation of editorial and scholarly scrutiny trained on Shakespeare's work in the first decades of the eighteenth century suggests that as the author was being prepared for the role of national poet, his sublime corpus was being prepared to displace the monarch's sublime body. In this context, Dennis's anecdotal account of Shakespeare and Elizabeth meeting to determine Falstaff's future marks an important spot in the trajectory of this displacement just as Bale's version of meetings between Oldcastle and Henry V captures and preserves an early moment in post-reformation England when a martyr temporarily displaced a monarch as the figure who personified the Protestant state. Once Oldcastle is displaced from Shakespeare's *Henry IV Part I* by Falstaff, only the "rational totality" of Zizek's Hegelian formulation remains, literally embodied in the character's obesity.

If the author's corpus is going to fill in for the monarch's body, that corpus must, of course, be authentic and authoritative. As the first person to produce a scholarly edition of Shakespeare's plays, it is significant that Nicholas Rowe worked back from Falstaff to Oldcastle seven years after the publication of Dennis's dedicatory anecdote. Thus Rowe attempted to do for Falstaff's textual past what Dennis had already done for the character's textual future: put the strings pulling Shakespeare's writing hand firmly in Elizabeth's hands. But there is more to it then just proffering—for the first time—the specific identity of the figure who stood behind the "ignorant shifte."

In their accounts of Oldcastle, Bale and Foxe had carefully subordinated royal authority to Oldcastle's authority by placing the martyr in a position—with reference to the Catholic Church—that was morally and spiritually superior to the monarch's. Following the lead of *Famous Victories'* anonymous author, Shakespeare essentially restored Henry V to his pre-reformation position of superiority by reducing Oldcastle to the status of a reprobate subsequently named Falstaff. A rigorous logic seems to be at work, therefore, when Rowe prepares Shakespeare to replace the monarch as the nation's individualized embodiment of bourgeois morality: now that Shakespeare is being readied to be morally superior to the monarch, the playwright's characterization of Oldcastle gets called upon to link Shakespeare and Elizabeth. Having set out to do for Shakespeare what Bale and Foxe had done for Oldcastle in their accounts of two meetings between the knight and his king, Rowe introduces a second meeting between the author and his queen in which Oldcastle's martyrdom is salvaged and secured.

Whether this transformation of Shakespeare's authorial status is linked—as I have suggested—to fluctuations in the status of the monarch, what seems indisputable is that the Restoration did for Shakespeare what the Reformation had done for Oldcastle. Promising from the scaffold that, like Christ, he would rise again on the third day, Oldcastle was compelled to wait more than a hundred years for Tyndale, Bale, and Fox to resurrect him. Similarly, when Colonel Joseph Hart looks back at what a few key Restoration figures contributed to Shakespeare's career, he also looks to Christ—this time with considerable irony—for a model: "Then comes the 'resurrection'—on speculation. Thomas Betterton the player, and Rowe the writer, make a selection from a promiscuous heap of plays found in a garret, nameless as to authorship . . . 'I want an author for this selection of plays!' said Rowe. 'I have it!' said Betterton; 'call them Shakespeare's!' "[65] What is remarkable about the Colonel's reconstruction of the posthumous Shakespeare is how it inadvertently aligns itself with the setting up of the posthumous Oldcastle in the chronicles. For the latter figure, it was a pile of unbound quires of heretical writings subsequently attributed to him that put Lord Cobham on the chronicled path to becoming first a Lollard nuisance, then post-Reformation England's greatest martyr. For Shakespeare, it turns out to be "a promiscuous heap of plays found in a garret, nameless as to authorship" that, subsequently attributed to him by his editors, enables the playwright to become first a nuisance to the Cobham legacy, then post-Restoration England's greatest author.

Given that Oldcastle shadowed the trajectory of Shakespeare's authorship from its typographic inception on the title page of *Henry IV Part II* to its scholarly reconstruction in Rowe's *Complete Works,* it should come as no surprise that the 1986 restoration of Oldcastle's name to the text of *Henry IV Part I* in the Oxford edition of *The Complete Works* comes hard upon the poststructuralist displacement of the author from its long-secure position as the guarantor and personification of humanist subjectivity.[66] Previously the construction of Oldcastle as a martyr (the figure who usurped the king's authority to exemplify the Protestant state) anticipated the construction of Shakespeare as an author (the figure who usurped the king's authority to exemplify the modern bourgeois state). Now Oldcastle's return coincides with the dismantling of Shakespeare's literary authority. Kastan has observed that "[t]he restoration of 'Oldcastle' [to *Henry IV Part I*] enacts a fantasy of unmediated authorship paradoxically mediated by the Oxford edition itself";[67] however, such mediation, along with its concomitant paradoxical fantasy of unmediation, has always been an essential component of Oldcastle's and Shakespeare's parallel posthumous careers. The former had Bale and Fox, the latter, Dennis and Rowe. My last task will be to show how this most recent act of mediation, this time by Stanley Wells and Taylor, further enhances the link between martyr and author.[68]

Taylor has argued that when Sir John Oldcastle/Falstaff's final speech (V.iv.162-6) is "put in the mouth of a fictional character called Falstaff, the words lose their historicity and ambiguity";[69] but his more radical position is that Shakespeare's portrayal of the Protestant martyr as a lying, cheating, thieving, and promiscuous scoundrel indicates that our greatest author "may have been popishly inclined."[70] If Shakespeare's status has faced serious challenges in the wake of what Roland Barthes famously referred to as "The Death of the Author,"[71] his Oxford editors seem primarily interested in damage control. Indeed, it is a rather nostalgic project that underwrites Taylor's final defense of restoring Oldcastle to the Oxford *Henry IV Part I*:[72] "I do not know," writes Taylor, "whether Shakespeare was ever a 'papist', though I rather suspect it. But I do know that Oldcastle is what Shakespeare wrote; that Oldcastle is what Shakespeare meant; and that Oldcastle is what his contemporaries understood."[73] Being the subject of knowledge about Shakespeare and his audience, Taylor believes that he has achieved what he terms "the recovery and restoration of the original authoritative *Logos*,"[74] a dubious achievement, perhaps, in the current critical climate. Jonathan Goldberg jumped at the chance to interrogate Taylor's logocentrism;[75] but what seems far more interesting about Taylor's position than his longing for *Logos* is the way in which his knowledge of Shakespeare's authorial intentions is linked to his suspicion that Shakespeare was Catholic.

Catholic writers in Shakespeare's day did ridicule Protestants for celebrating Oldcastle's martyrdom, so it makes some sense that Taylor might try to link Shakespeare's capable trashing of the martyr with, as Taylor puts it, "his willingness to exploit a point of view which many of his contemporaries would have regarded as 'papist.' "[76] Yet, Taylor never provides any substantive evidence of what Shakespeare's contemporaries would have regarded as papist. Instead, he searches through the plays for the playwright's religion: "In *Hamlet* Shakespeare exploited the Catholic belief in Purgatory; in *Richard III* he exploited Catholic beliefs about All Souls' Eve; in both *Twelfth Night* and *Measure for Measure* he mocked the hypocrisy of Puritans."[77] Surely, one didn't have to be "popish" in Elizabethan England to exploit Catholic beliefs or to mock Puritans.

In the end, however, all roads lead back to the author. Being a papist and exploiting a papist point of view must ultimately be the same thing for Taylor, because although he claims that knowledge of Falstaff's origins will reintroduce "historical resonances" to Shakespeare's play, what he has done is place the complex historical conditions of religious conflict in Shakespeare's England under erasure in order to proffer a radical view of the author's origins. Thus, Taylor begins his search through Shakespeare's plays for a Catholic world-view with another, more personal kind of history that Rowe and Betterton—the bard's first biographers—would have heartily applauded: "There is documentary evidence," Taylor asserts, "that both Shakespeare's father and one of his daughters may have been popishly inclined."[78] In short, all Taylor can really do to rehistoricize *Henry IV Part I* is either go back to Shakespeare's origins and speculate on his religious beliefs, or go on to other plays for biographical evidence. Stranded between the author's life and his life's work, it's hard to see how Taylor has reinserted history into the text.

What Taylor's defense of the Oxford *Henry IV Part I* makes abundantly clear is that if Oldcastle is going to be resurrected again, this time on Catholic grounds, then his old nemesis needs to be resurrected first. Shakespeare must be exhumed because Taylor and Wells inadvertently want, as Hart's scathing account puts it, "an author for this selection of plays!"[79] From a historical Restoration to a textual one, Oldcastle has remained a constant; but some things have changed. Whereas Rowe and Betterton's *Complete Plays* proclaimed "the King is dead! Long live Shakespeare!", Taylor and Well's *Complete Works* defiantly argues "the Author is dead. Long live Shakespeare."

And yet, if to restore Oldcastle is to reconstruct Shakespeare as a suspected recusant—that is, if banishing Falstaff from the authoritative texts of *Henry IV Part I* rehistoricizes the author as the most famous member of a marginalized and persecuted religious sect—then not only has Falstaff been turned back into Oldcastle, but so has Shakespeare. In short, Taylor can be confident that Oldcastle is what Shakespeare wrote and meant, because Taylor has reconstructed Shakespeare as Oldcastle—or to be more precise, as the notorious pre-martyrological Lord Cobham who lived in the shadowy margins of England's national religion. Thus, the figure who was for a time the godly nation's greatest martyr, has once again played a fundamental role in the construction of that nation's greatest author, from the religio-political controversy that preceded his debut as a writer on the title page of *Henry IV Part II*, to the controversy over the debut of Oldcastle as a character in the Oxford edition of *Henry IV Part I*. But didn't we already know all of this? Didn't we already know that banishing Falstaff meant dragging out the author to speak about Oldcastle? Isn't that exactly what happens in the epilogue of *Henry IV Part II* when the clown who played the fat knight reappears on stage speaking as the author about his Oldcastle problem?[80]

*Notes*

[1] The principal contributions to this debate are Gary Taylor, "The Fortunes of Oldcastle," *ShS* 38 (1985): 85-100; Taylor, "William Shakespeare, Richard James and the House of Cobham," *RES*, n.s. 38, 151 (August 1987): 334-54; E.A.J. Honigmann, "Sir John Oldcastle: Shakespeare's Martyr," in *"Fanned and Winnowed Opinions": Shakespearean Essays Presented to Harold Jenkins,* ed. John W. Mahon and Thomas A. Pendleton (London: Methuen, 1987), pp. 118-32; Pendleton, " 'This is not the man': On Calling Falstaff Falstaff," *AEB*, n.s. 4 (1990): 56-71; Jonathan Goldberg, "The Commodity of Names: 'Falstaff' and 'Oldcastle' in *I Henry IV*," *BuR* 35, 2 (1992): 76-88; Eric Sams, "Oldcastle and the Oxford Shakespeare," *N&Q*, n.s. 40, 2 (June 1993): 180-5; Kristen Poole, "Saints Alive! Falstaff, Martin Marprelate, and the Staging of Puritanism," *SQ* 46, 1 (Spring 1995): 47-75; and David Scott Kastan, " 'Killed With Hard Opinions': Oldcastle, Falstaff, and the Reformed Text of *I Henry IV*," forthcoming in *Textual Topography: Formations and Reformations.* ed. Thomas L. Berger and Laurie E. Maguire (Delaware: Univ. of Delaware Press). See also Peter Corbin and Douglas Sedge, eds., *The Oldcastle Controversy* (Manchester: Manchester Univ. Press, 1994), pp. 1-34; Robert J. Fehrenbach, "When Lord Cobham and Edmund Tilney 'were att odds': Oldcastle, Falstaff, and the Date of *I Henry IV*," *ShakeS* 18 (1986): 87-101; Rudolph Fiehler, "How Oldcastle Became Falstaff," *MLQ* 16, 1 (March 1955): 16-28; and George Walton Williams, "Second Thoughts on Falstaff's Name," *SQ* 30, 1 (Winter 1979): 82-4.

[2] *I Sir John Oldcastle,* Malone Society Reprint (London: Charles Whittingham and Co., 1908).

[3] Philip Henslowe, *Diary: Part I. Text,* ed. Walter W. Greg (Folcraft: Folcraft Press, 1904), p. 113.

[4] William Shakespeare, *King Lear,* in *Shakespeare's Plays in Quarto: A Facsimile Edition of Copies Primarily from the Henry E. Huntington Library,* ed. Michael J. B. Allen and Kenneth Muir (Berkeley: Univ. of California Press, 1981), 663-703, 663. Future references to Shakespeare's plays in quarto are from this source and will appear parenthetically in the text.

[5] Peter W. M. Blayney, *Nicholas Okes and the First Quarto, Volume 1: The Texts of "King Lear" and Their Origins* (Cambridge: Cambridge Univ. Press, 1982), p. 83.

[6] In 1604 Anthony Scoloker assures his readers that "He is A man in Print, and tis enough he hath undergone a Pressing" (Wendy Wall, *The Imprint of Gender: Authorship and Publication in the English Renaissance* [Ithaca: Cornell Univ. Press, 1993], p. 1).

[7] Stephen J. Greenblatt, *Renaissance Self-fashioning: From More to Shakespeare* (Chicago: Univ. of Chicago Press, 1980), p. 1.

[8] In fact, the type for the head-title was reimposed from the top of the title page (see Blayney, p. 97, fig. 6).

[9] Indeed, the first payment to a playwright recorded in *Henslowe's Diary* reads, "pd vnto Thomas dickers the 20 of desembr 1597 / for adycyons to fostus twentie shellinges and fyve / shellinges more for a prolog to Marloes tambelan / so in all J saye payde twentye five shellinges" (p. 38).

[10] Michel Foucault, "What Is an Author," in *Foucault Reader,* ed. Paul Rabinow (New York: Pantheon Books, 1984), p. 108. It is, of course, also true that by the time *Henry IV Part I* was published, Shakespeare had become popular and/or reputable enough as a playwright that the use of his name on a title page may have made good business sense to a publisher. The most famous evidence of Shakespeare's reputation at this point in his career comes from Francis Meres's *Palladis Tamia.* Meres writes, "As Plautus and Seneca are accounted the best for Comedy and Tragedy among the Latines: so Shakespeare among y' English

is the most excellent in both kinds for the stage; for Comedy, witnes his Ge'tleme' of Verona, his Errors, his Love labors lost, his Love labours wonne, his Midsummer night dreame, & his Merchant of Venice: for Tragedy his Richard the 2. Richard the 3. Henry the 4. King John, Titus Andronicus and his Romeo and Juliet" ([New York: Scholars' Facsimiles and Reprints, 1938], p. 282).

[11] In identifying William Brooke as the seventh Baron Cobham, most scholars follow the *Dictionary of National Biography*. However, David McKeen includes a genealogy of the Cobham Lordship indicating that Brooke was the tenth holder of the title (*A Memory of Honor: The Life of William Brooke, Lord Cobham*, 2 vols. [Salzburg, Austria: Universität Salzburg, 1986], 1:2; 2:700-2, appendix 2).

[12] D. F. McKenzie, *Bibliography and the Sociology of Texts* (London: British Library, 1985), p. 26.

[13] This is the chronology proposed by Giorgio Melchiori in *Shakespeare's Garter Plays: "Edward III" to "Merry Wives of Windsor"* (Newark: Univ. of Delaware Press, 1994), pp. 98-101.

[14] *Famous Victories* (London: Thomas Creede, 1598).

[15] Rowland Whyte, in Alice-Lyle Scoufos, *Shakespeare's Typological Satire: A Study of the Falstaff-Oldcastle Problem* (Athens: Ohio Univ. Press, 1979), p. 36. See Sams, "Oldcastle and the Oxford Shakespeare," pp. 181-2.

[16] See Taylor, "Fortunes," p. 90. Whyte's confusion may be explained in part by the fact that, as Andrew Gurr notes, "[t]he two approved companies [Admiral's and Chamberlain's] did get into the habit of matching their plays, Falstaff with Oldcastle, *Richard III* with *Richard Crookback*, *The Jew of Malta* with *The Merchant of Venice*, and others" (*The Shakespearean Playing Companies* [Oxford: Clarendon Press, 1996], p. 76).

[17] John Dennis, *The Comical Gallant: or The Amours of Sir John Falstaffe* (London: A. Baldwin, 1702), A2.

[18] It is worth noting that by the time Falstaff gets revived for *The Merry Wives of Windsor*, he, like his author, has come to be closely associated with printing. Indeed, as was the case with Shakespeare's indifference to publication, Falstaff "cares not what he puts in press" (*The Merry Wives of Windsor*, II.i.78 in *The Complete Works of Shakespeare*, 3d edn., ed. David Bevington [New York: Harper Collins, 1981]. All subsequent references to Shakespeare's plays are to this edition unless otherwise indicated.) See Margreta de Grazia, "Imprints: Shakespeare, Gutenberg, and Descartes," in *Alternative Shakespeares*, ed. Terence Hawkes (London and New York: Routledge, 1996), 2:63-94, esp. 76-7.

[19] Nicholas Rowe, in Scoufos, pp. 23-4.

[20] Mark Rose, "The Author as Proprietor: *Donaldson v. Becket* and the Genealogy of Modern Authorship," *Representations* 23 (Summer 1988): 51-85, 52.

[21] Shakespeare's authorship has been linked with Elizabeth recently by Leah S. Marcus. Taking seriously John Heminge and Henry Condell's claim in the reader's preface to the First Folio that "what [Shakespeare] thought he vttered with that easinesse, that wee haue scarse receiued from a blot in his papers," Marcus suggests that the playwright "may even have composed orally," and asserts that "Queen Elizabeth I apparently had the same skill" (*Unediting the Renaissance: Shakespeare, Marlowe, Milton* [London: Routledge, 1996], pp. 162, 163).

[22] Rose, p. 52.

[23] On these convergences see J. S. Peters, "The Bank, the Press, and the 'return of Nature': On Currency, Credit, and Literary Property in the 1690s," in *Early Modern Conceptions of Property*, ed. John Brewer and Susan Staves (London: Routledge, 1995), pp. 365-88, esp. 367-72.

[24] de Grazia, *Shakespeare Verbatim: The Reproduction of Authenticity and the 1790 Apparatus* (Oxford: Clarendon Press, 1991), p. 3.

[25] Taylor, "William Shakespeare," p. 335.

[26] Taylor, "William Shakespeare," p. 341.

[27] William James, in S. Schoenbaum, *William Shakespeare: A Documentary Life* (Oxford: Oxford Univ. Press, 1975), p. 143. See also Taylor, "William Shakespeare," pp. 335-6, and Taylor, "Fortunes," p. 86.

[28] James, p. 143.

[29] This is the account provided by John Capgrave, *The Chronicle of England* (London: Longman, Brown, Green, Longmans, and Roberts, 1858), pp. 303-4. In a subsequent chronicle, Capgrave returns to the session between Cobham and Henry, but abbreviates it considerably (*The Book of Illusstrious Henries*, trans. Francis Charles Hingeston [London: Longman, Brown, Green, Longmans, and Roberts, 1858], pp. 126-7).

[30] Substantiative chronicle accounts of Oldcastle are provided by Thomas Walsingham, Thomas Netter, Thomas Otterbourne, Thomas Eltham, and Thomas Hoccleve.

[31] Capgrave, p. 303.

32 G. R. Elton, *Policy and Police: The Enforcement of the Reformation in the Age of Thomas Cromwell* (Cambridge: Cambridge Univ. Press, 1972), p. 34.

33 Sir Thomas More, *The English Works of Sir Thomas More,* ed. W. E. Campbell and A. W. Reed, 2 vols. (London: Eyre and Spottiswoode, 1927), 2:274.

34 John Bale, *A Breif Chronicle concerning the Examination and Death of the Blessed Martyr of Christ, Sir John Oldcastle, the Lord Cobham* (1544) (STC 1276), 45$^r$.

35 See Patrick Collinson, *The Elizabethan Puritan Movement* (Berkeley: Univ. of California Press, 1967), p. 29.

36 See Kastan, " 'Holy Wurdes' and 'Slypper Wit': John Bale's King Johan and the Poetics of Propaganda," in *Rethinking the Henrician Era: Essays on Early Tudor Texts and Contexts,* ed. Peter C. Herman (Urbana: Univ. of Illinois Press, 1994), pp. 267-82, 269.

37 Annabel Patterson quotes these lines as a rebuttal of Archbishop Arundel's position that Oldcastle suffered from a "lack of learning" (*Reading Holinshed's Chronicle* [Chicago: Univ. of Chicago Press, 1994], p. 137).

38 John Foxe, *Acts and Monuments,* STC 11222.

39 Foxe, p. 261.

40 Kastan, "Killed," p. 9.

41 Foxe, pp. 261-2, 264.

42 Vindicating Oldcastle of treason becomes a major preoccupation of Foxe's in subsequent editions of *Acts.* For an astute analysis of how Foxe's book changes over successive editions, see Jesse Lander, "Foxe's *Book of Martyrs:* printing and popularizing the *Acts and Monuments,*" *Religion and Culture in Renaissance England,* ed. Claire McEachern and Debora Shuger (Cambridge: Cambridge Univ. Press, 1997), pp. 69-92.

43 Foxe, pp. 263, 264.

44 In *The Mirror of Martyrs or The life and death of that thrice valiant Captain and most godly Martyr Sir John Oldcastle Knight, Lord Cobham* (1601), John Weever condenses the link between author and martyr into a single couplet. Referring to the second meeting with Henry, Weever's Oldcastle states, "I come to Court and written with me bring / My swan's last funeral dirge to the King" (appendix D, *The Oldcastle Controversy,* pp. 223-53). The prominence of the typographic element in Foxe's attempt to aggrandize Oldcastle's status as a proto-Protestant martyr is entirely consistent with the role of the printing press in the reformation, a role that has received critical attention from Kastan, " 'The noyse of the new Bible':

McEachern and Shuger, pp. 46-68; John N. Wall, "The Reformation in England and the Typographical Revolution: 'By this printing . . . the doctrine of the Gospel soundeth to all nations,' " in *Print and Culture in the Renaissance: Essays on the Advent of Printing in Europe,* ed. Gerald P. Tyson and Sylvia S. Wagonheim (Newark: Univ. of Delaware Press, 1986), pp. 208-21; Jane O. Newman, "The World Made Print: Luther's 1522 *New Testament* in an Age of Mechanical Reproduction," *Representations* 11 (Summer 1985): 95-133; Greenblatt, "The Word of God in the Age of Mechanical Reproduction," in *Renaissance Self-fashioning,* pp. 75-114; Benedict Anderson, *Imagined Communities: Reflections on the Origin and Spread of Nationalism* (London: Verso, 1983), pp. 37-47; Elizabeth L. Eisenstein, *The Printing Press as an Agent of Change: Communications and Cultural Transformations in Early-Modern Europe,* 2 vols. (Cambridge: Cambridge Univ. Press, 1979), 1:302-440; Lucien Febvre and Henry-Jean Martin, *The Coming of the Book: The Impact of Printing 1450-1800,* trans. David Gerard (London: NLB, 1976), pp. 287-318.

45 Foucault, "Two lectures: Lecture One: 7 January 1976," in *Power/Knowledge: Selected Interviews and Other Writings, 1972-77,* ed. Colin Gordon (Brighton: Harvester Press, 1980), p. 81.

46 Raphael Holinshed, *The Firste volume of the Chronicles of England, Scotlande, and Irelande* (STC 13568) (London: John Harrison, 1577), p. 1189.

47 Holinshed, p. 1166. In fact, Holinshed seems to be quoting Edward Hall's 1548 account nearly verbatim. Hall writes, "The Lorde Cobham not onely thanked the kyng of his most favourable clemencye, but also declared firste hym by mouthe and afterwarde by writyng the foundacion of his faith, the ground of his belefe and the bottome of his stomacke" (*The Union of the Two Noble & Illustre Famelies of Lancasatre & Yorke,* ed. Henry Ellis [1548; rprt. London, 1809; New York, 1965], quoted in Patterson, p. 143). Nevertheless, as Patterson notes, Foxe argued in the 1570 edition of *Acts* that Hall's source was Bale's *Brief Chronicle* (Patterson, p. 144).

48 Holinshed, p. 1189. Holinshed's source for this passage, as Patterson notes, was Thomas Walsingham's *Historia Anglicana* (Patterson, p. 151). It is worth noting that when Heminge and Condell offer their mythic account of Shakespeare's authorship in the First Folio, the act of blotting figures significantly. They inform "the great Variety of Readers," that "[Shakespeare's] mind and hand went together: And what he thought, he vttered with that eafineffe, that wee have fcarfe received from him a blot in his papers" (*The First Folio of Shakespeare 1623,* ed. Doug Moston [New York: Applause, 1995], A3).

49 Holinshed, p. 1189.

⁵⁰ Patterson, p. 131.

⁵¹ G. K. Hunter, "Religious Nationalism in Later History Plays," in *Literature and Nationalism,* ed. Vincent Newey and Ann Thompson (Savage: Barnes and Noble Books, 1991), pp. 88-97, 92.

⁵² Ibid.

⁵³ Hunter, p. 95.

⁵⁴ Ibid.

⁵⁵ Ibid.

⁵⁶ Subsequent references to the knight in Thomas Fuller's *Church History of Britain* (1655) and Peter Heylyn's *Examen Historicum: Animadversions on the Church History of Britain* (1659) suggest that Oldcastle's reputation plummeted tremendously during the half-century that followed Shakespeare's play. See Taylor, "Fortunes," p. 91, and Corbin and Sledge, p. 32.

⁵⁷ Michael Dobson, *The Making of the National Poet: Shakespeare, Adaptation and Authorship, 1660-1769* (Oxford: Clarendon Press, 1992), p. 185.

⁵⁸ Ibid.

⁵⁹ John Dennis, quoted in Schoenbaum, *Shakespeare's Lives: New Edition* (Oxford: Clarendon Press, 1991), p. 51.

⁶⁰ Dobson, p. 184.

⁶¹ Taylor, *Reinventing Shakespeare: A Cultural History, from the Restoration to the Present* (Oxford: Oxford Univ. Press, 1989), p. 65.

⁶² Shakespeare, *The Merchant of Venice,* V.i.94-5. As Kastan notes, referring to Portia's remark and Shakespeare's account of the Battle of Shrewsbury (*Henry IV Part I,* V.iv.3-4), "[e]ven Henry can bear himself only '*like* the king'; he has no authentic royal identity prior to and untouched by representation" (" 'The King Hath Many Marchings in His Coats,' or, What did You Do in the War, Daddy?" in *Shakespeare Left and Right,* ed. Ivo Kamps [New York: Routledge, 1991], pp. 241-58, 253).

⁶³ Sharon Achinstein examines the relation between king and printer as it was reconfigured during the pamphlet wars of the English Revolution in her study, *Milton and the Revolutionary Reader* (Princeton: Princeton Univ. Press, 1994), pp. 78-101. Also of great relevance is Harold Love's analysis of the link between state authority and material practices of linguistic reproduction in *Scribal Publication in Seventeenth-Century England* (Oxford: Clarendon Press, 1993), pp. 157-76. Love locates this link in the relationship between "the relative status accorded to voice, script and print within the political structure" and the prominent social fiction that "located the origin of all secular power in the king's person" (p. 161). For Love, the Regicide of 1649 precluded royalty in the future from placing "any excessive trust in the power promised by legitimating fictions" (p. 176). Kevin Sharpe also examines the relation between Tudor-Stuart royal authorship and print culture, "The King's Writ: Royal Authors and Royal Authority in Early Modern England," in *Culture and Politics in Early Stuart England,* ed. Sharpe and Peter Lake (Stanford: Stanford Univ. Press, 1993), pp. 117-38. The relation between power and representation is given an excellent general treatment by Michael Taussig, "Maleficium: State Fetishism," *The Nervous System* (New York: Routledge, 1992), pp. 111-41.

⁶⁴ Slavoj Zizek, *For They Know Not What They Do: Enjoyment as a Political Factor* (London: Verso, 1991), p. 269.

⁶⁵ Joseph C. Hart, quoted in Dobson, p. 1.

⁶⁶ Foucault, for example, asserts that "[t]he coming into being of the notion of 'author' constitutes the privileged moment of *individualization* in the history of ideas, knowledge, literature, philosophy, and the sciences" (p. 101). For a useful overview of the critical assault on authorship see Sean Burke, *The Death and Return of the Author: Criticism and Subjectivity in Barthes, Foucault and Derrida* (Edinburgh: Edinburgh Univ. Press, 1992), pp. 8-19.

⁶⁷ Kastan, "Killed," p. 14.

⁶⁸ It is worth noting that although *The Norton Shakespeare* advertises itself as being "Based on the Oxford Edition," the Norton edition of *Henry IV Part I* returns Oldcastle to textual exile. Referring to the Oxford text, Greenblatt, the general editor of the Norton Edition writes, "But this decision [to restore Oldcastle] is a problem for several reasons. It draws perhaps too sharp a distinction between those things that Shakespeare did under social pressure and those he did of his own accord. More seriously, it pulls against the principle of a text that represents the latest performance version of a play during Shakespeare's lifetime: after all, even the earliest quarto title page advertises 'the humorous conceits of Sir John Falstaff' " ([New York: W. W. Norton and Company, 1997], p. 75).

⁶⁹ Taylor, "Fortunes," p. 95. Similarly, Stanley Wells writes of Oldcastle/Falstaff, "Awareness of the character's origins adds to the play's historical resonances" (*Shakespeare: A Life in Drama* [New York: W. W. Norton and Company, 1995], p. 140).

⁷⁰ Taylor, "Fortunes," p. 99.

[71] Roland Barthes, in *Theories of Authorship: A Reader*, ed. John Caughie (London: Routledge and Kegan Paul, 1981), pp. 208-13.

[72] Paul Werstine has persuasively argued a similar point in the context of the editorial tradition that underwrites Taylor and Michael Warren's work on the texts of *King Lear*. Noting that after the work of W. W. Greg, "it came to be assumed that editors already knew all they needed to about everything except the details," Werstine asserts that, "except for the printing house(s) that manufactured the particular book(s), the whole of early modern culture got consumed by an increasingly engorged author-function, which ate up the army of scribes, the theatrical industry (with its players, bookkeepers, costume-buyers, theater owners, and thousands of patrons), and the government with its censors" ("Editing after the End of Editing," *ShakeS* 24 [1996]: 47-54, 50).

[73] Taylor, "Fortunes," p. 100.

[74] Ibid.

[75] Goldberg, pp. 79-82.

[76] Taylor, "Fortunes," p. 99.

[77] Ibid.

[78] Ibid. See also Sams, who maintains that "[t]he young Shakespeare's earliest emotions and experiences were enshrined in the language and teaching of the old Catholic faith" (*The Real Shakespeare: Retrieving the Early Years, 1564-94* [New Haven: Yale Univ. Press, 1995], p. 11). Similarly, Honigman, who advises us to "brace ourselves, then, for howls of anguish about a Catholic Shakespeare," asserts that the playwright "started life as a Catholic and served for a while in the Catholic households of Alexander Hoghton and Sir Thomas Hesketh" (*Shakespeare: The Lost Years* [Manchester: Manchester Univ. Press, 1985], p. 126).

[79] Taylor himself compares Wells to Rowe in his discussion of the Oxford Shakespeare's publication. Noting that Wells "is a theatre historian as well as an editor, both a governor of the Royal Shakespeare Theatre and a Fellow of Balliol College," Taylor observes that, "Like Rowe, but in contrast to the subsequent editorial tradition initiated by Pope, Wells edits Shakespeare in the light of theatrical practice" (*Reinventing Shakespeare*, p. 311).

[80] I am grateful to David Scott Kastan for reading and significantly improving a draft of this essay. Anne Lake Prescott, Jean Howard, James Shapiro, and Peter Platt also read a draft and made a number of helpful suggestions. An early version of this essay, titled "'so disfigured with scrapings & blotting out': *I Henry IV* and the Making of an Author," was presented as part of the "Shakespeare and the Material Book" panel at the annual meeting of the Midwest Modern Language Association held in November 1996 in Minneapolis MN. I would like to thank Marcy North for inviting me to participate in the session and for raising important questions about my argument.

---

Source: "Sir John Oldcastle and the Construction of Shakespeare's Authorship," in *Studies in English Literature, 1500-1900,* Vol. 38, No. 2, Spring, 1998, pp. 333-61.

# "He Is But a Bastard to the Time": Status and Service in *The Troublesome Raigne of John* and Shakespeare's *King John*

## Edward Gieskes, *Boston University*

### INTRODUCTION

Shakespeare's *King John*, standing between the two tetralogies, marks a transition in his treatment of political and historical questions. This argument has been advanced by critics like Sigurd Burckhardt, Virginia Vaughan, Michael Manheim, and Marsha Robinson (among many others).[1] Vaughan, for example, writes that the play "demonstrates Shakespeare's experimentation with more sophisticated dramaturgical techniques to convey political complexities, techniques he perfected in the Henriad."[2] Most of the criticism focuses on Shakespeare's changing treatment of *political* questions to the exclusion of *social* considerations; but if *King John* marks a transition in Shakespeare's treatment of politics and history, it also marks a change in his depiction of the social issues attendant on that history and politics.[3] This essay will focus on the Bastard, arguably the central player in the action, as representative of the play's engagement with expressly social concerns: issues of class, rank, and vocation distinct from the explicitly political issues which have been discussed elsewhere.

Despite the limited historical records concerning the Bastard Faulconbridge, both Shakespeare and the author of *The Troublesome Raigne of John King of England* make him a major player in the "history" of King John's reign.[4] The different treatments of the same figure in these two plays represent different understandings of service to the crown. In the *Troublesome Raigne*, Philip Faulconbridge claims royal ancestry (after direct supernatural prompting) and proceeds to behave as a person of noble descent. He goes off to war in France, pursues and kills Austria, receives lands, and woos Blaunch, all as though he had always been a member of the aristocracy. By contrast, Shakespeare's Bastard Faulconbridge exhibits a very different relationship towards his own rise in status. His status as adopted Plantagenet is treated by the play as a vocation in our modern sense of employment. By the end of the play he administers the royal succession to the throne without any real opposition from the hereditary nobles around him. Shakespeare's Bastard actively chooses a career as a royal servant in choosing to acknowledge his bastardy while the Bastard of the *Troublesome Raigne* is forced to avow his ancestry, against his better judgment, and in this involuntary manner enters the aristocracy, and from thence comes to royal service. The two plays exhibit alternative conceptions of identity—one chosen, the other essential—which are linked to the ability of each character to serve his King.

### I.

Both *King John* and the *Troublesome Raigne* contain a recognition scene—each play's Bastard finds out the truth of his birth in the public and legal context of a land (or succession) dispute. In *King John*, the Bastard and his brother "come from the country" for judgment and in *Troublesome Raigne* they, having "committed a riot," appeal to the King on the issue.[5] In both plays, Robert Faulconbridge accuses his elder brother of being illegitimate and thus barred from inheriting the family estate.[6] The basic claim is identical but details of its presentation vary considerably.[7]

In the *Troublesome Raigne*, Philip (the Bastard) presents himself as the victim of his younger brother's slander and greed: "the wrong is mine; yet wil I abide all wrongs, before I once open my mouth to unrippe the shamefull slaunder of my parents, the dishonour of myself, & the wicked dealing of my brother in this princely assembly" (*T*, 86-90). He refuses even to address the "shamefull slaunder," in the best tradition of wounded honesty. Then Philip's younger brother Robert speaks, making his case in the face of his brother's silence. In the initial encounter the Bastard presents himself as slandered and offers no hint that he might know or believe his brother's accusation to be true. In the *Troublesome Raigne*, then, the Bastard believes he is the legitimate heir and desires his inheritance; it is only as a result of external intervention that he resigns his claim.[8]

Shakespeare's *King John* treats this scene differently. In the *Troublesome Raigne*, when King John demands who the brothers are and what their business is, only Robert makes reference to the Bastard's dubious parentage; in *King John* the Bastard himself raises the question. "What men are you?" asks the King, and Shakespeare's Bastard replies:

> Your faithful subject I, a gentleman,
> Born in Northamptonshire, and eldest son,
> *As I suppose,* to Robert Faulconbridge,
> A soldier, by the honour-giving hand
> Of Coeur-de-lion knighted in the field.
> (*K*, 1.1.50-54, my emphasis)

The "as I suppose" puts the matter into question from the very beginning of the encounter. The Bastard presents himself as uncertain of his parentage, immediately lending credence to his brother's accusation and eliciting wonder from the King and his attendants. Shakespeare's Bastard undercuts his own claim to the Faulconbridge land, suggesting that his actual desires run toward other goals. His specific desires can be inferred from his other speeches in this first scene. He noticeably fails to mention the inheritance in his first speech while making a point of referring to honor and status. His "supposed" father was "a soldier, by the honour-giving hand / Of Coeur-de-lion knighted in the field" and he himself is a "gentleman." Both these rank markers are discursively (if not actually) separate from direct dependence on land and inheritance. The Bastard thus appears to be more interested in status, soldierly virtue, and honor than in a regular annual income, however large and respectable.

The difference between the Bastards of the *Troublesome Raigne* and *King John* becomes even more clear in the actual recognition scenes. Both plays show the brothers submitting to royal arbitration, but the confrontation between the brothers in the *Troublesome Raigne* culminates with an appeal from the King to Philip (the Bastard) in order to settle the dispute:

> JOHN: Say who was thy father?
> PHILIP: Faith (my Lord) to answere you sure
>   he is my father that was neerest my mother
>   when I was gotten, & him I thinke to be
>   Sir *Robert Fauconbridge*.
> JOHN: *Essex,* for fashions sake demand agen,
>   And so an ende to this contention.
> ESSEX: *Philip* speake I say, who was thy
>   father?
> PHILIP: *Philippus atauis aedite regibus.*
>
> (*T,* 231-41)

In what appears to be an aside, Philip ventriloquizes Latin speech which is said to come from the air (and the river and the land and the trees), and this Latin reveals that he is the son of Richard I and thus of glorious birth:

> Birds in their flight make music with their
>   wings,
> Filling the ayre with glorie of my birth:
> Birds, bubbles, leaves and mountaines, Eccho,
>   all
> Ring in mine eares, that I am *Richards*
>   Sonne.
>
> (*T,* 252-55)

Despite this information, which he immediately accepts as fact, Philip still recalls his position among the country gentry:

> How are thy thoughts ywrapt in Honors
>   heaven?
> Forgetfull what thou art, and whence thou
>   camst.
> Thy fathers land cannot maintain these
>   thoughts,
> These thoughts are farre unfitting
>   *Fauconbridge:*
> And well they may; for why this mounting
>   minde
> Doth soare too high to stoupe to
>   *Fauconbridge.*
> Why how now? knowest thou where thou art?
> And knowest thou who expects thy answere
>   here
> Wilt thou upon a frantick madding vaine
> Goe loose thy land, and say thyself base
>   born?
> No, keepe thy land, though *Richard* were thy
>   Sire,
> What ere thou thinkst, say thou art
>   *Fauconbridge.*
>
> (*T,* 257-68)

Philip evinces a highly sensitive awareness of the order to which he belongs in this speech. Lines such as "Thy fathers land cannot maintaine these thoughts, / These thoughts are farre unfitting *Fauconbridge*" reveal his awareness of the economics of his position. He simply cannot support what Harrison calls the "port, charge, and countenance" of a Plantagenet on his income; and, more importantly, he recognizes the inappropriateness of a claim to royal blood by one born to his minor rank. Regardless of his having royal blood, he was not born a prince, but the son of a country gentleman, and that fact outweighs his being a royal bastard.[9] "Why how now? knowest thou where thou art? / And knowest thou who expects thy answer here?" he asks himself. Reminding himself of who he is (a country gentleman), where he stands (in what amounts to a court of law), and in whose presence (the King's), he claims Fauconbridge as his father and thus claims the land while denying his royal parentage.

Philip voices received notions of order and degree in this speech (an impression further reinforced by the denouement of the episode). He is born to one place in the hierarchy and will not *willfully* transgress the bounds of his ordained place: "Wilt thou on a frantic madding vaine / Goe loose thy land, and say thyself base born?" Obeying both economic and social pressures, the *Troublesome Raigne*'s Philip wisely chooses to abjure his royal father and claim a merely gentle one. The final lines of his speech—"keep thy land, though *Richard* were thy sire / What ere thou thinkst, say thou art *Fauconbridge*"—evidence this decision to remain, as he says, "what thou art, and whence thou camst." The voices of the wind, birds, and "bubbles" make him briefly "forgetfull" of his place "ywrapt in Honors heaven." However, he comes back to earth and, despite the fact that he now somehow knows himself to be Richard's son, he decides here to say he is "Fauconbridge" and keep his land rather than admit he is "base born" in bastardy. In essence, he chooses landed gentility over landless nobility.

Against his immediate inclinations, the decision predicated on his assessment of his position in the social structure, Philip is subsequently forced by what he calls "honors fire" to "sweare" that King Richard was his father, thus relinquishing his claim to the Fauconbridge land. Blood tells, and Philip's blood tells him to claim royal parentage despite his conscious intention. The intrusion of a force he recognizes as external to his will shapes his speech:

> Please it your Majestie, Sir *Robert Philip,*
>   that *Fauconbridge*
> cleaves to thy jawes: It will not out, I cannot
>   for my life
> Say I am Sonne unto a *Fauconbridge.*
> Let land and living goe, tis honors fire
> That makes me sweare King *Richard* was my
>   Sire.
>
>                              (*T,* 270-75)

In line 270 he begins to answer "Sir Robert Fauconbridge" but breaks off, unable to pronounce "Fauconbridge" and finishes the whole speech with "Please it your grace, I am King *Richards* Sonne." Philip is *physically* incapable of saying he is the son of a mere knight; his royal blood speaks for itself, claiming its royal nature. Philip's physical incapacity reaffirms the power of order and degree but in a different way than in lines 257-68 quoted above. Philip both is, and is not, born to gentry status: his blood is royal though his breeding is not. Sir Robert, his ostensible father, was a local gentleman and Philip would have been bred up in that rank; thus he feels as though he belongs among the local gentry. However, his blood is that of Richard I which places him in another rank altogether—at least in terms of the play. Philip's individual choice to remain on the land is transcended and obviated by this royal blood which forces him to claim "so greate a Sire" as Richard the Lion-hearted. His body refuses to speak the words that would deny its royal provenance; his "choice" of bastardy is determined for him by the powerful dictates of "honor" and facilitated by his body's refusal to be anything but what it is: Plantagenet.

In contrast to the *Troublesome Raigne*'s Philip, whose attempt to choose gentility over nobility fails before the power of his blood, the Bastard of *King John* chooses nobility over gentility, landlessness over landed status. Shakespeare's Bastard puts his legitimacy in question from the moment he first speaks, suggesting dissatisfaction with his social status from the very beginning. Unlike the *Troublesome Raigne*'s Bastard, who speaks and carries himself much as any of the other aristocratic characters, *King John*'s Bastard demonstrates his difference and distance from other characters. He is more clearly individuated from his first appearance onstage than the Bastard Fauconbridge ever is. He speaks familiarly with the King and Queen Eleanor, without the more elaborate honorific language used by his brother.[10] His decision to claim bastardy and relinquish the land and its considerable income thus appears motivated by his personal desire—not by the influence of some force recognized as external to his will. The Bastard's choice is his own.[11]

As in the *Troublesome Raigne,* the dispute is over the Faulconbridge land, and the claim made by Robert, the younger brother, is the same. When *King John* asks Robert who he is, after getting the Bastard's ambiguity-laden answer, Robert responds "the son and heir to that same Faulconbridge" (*K,* 1.1.56). The Bastard, like Philip in the *Troublesome Raigne,* describes Robert's claim that he is illegitimate as a slander having nothing to do with him.

> That [allegation of bastardy] is my brother's
>   plea, and none of mine;
> The which if he can prove, a pops me out
> At least from fair five hundred pounds a year:
> Heaven guard my mother's honour, and my
>   land!
>
>                              (*K,* 1.1.67-70)

The Bastard's attitude towards the debate is, however, far less serious than Philip's in the *Troublesome Raigne*. Robert's accusation becomes the source of a joke in the next few lines:

> Compare our faces and judge yourself.
> If old sir Robert did beget us both
> And were our father, and this son like him,
> O old sir Robert, father, on my knee
> I give heaven thanks I was not like to thee!
>                              (*K,* 1.1.79-83)

This joking tone pervades the Bastard's speeches in this scene, so much so that Queen Eleanor herself remarks, "why, what a madcap hath heaven lent us here!" (*K,* 1.1.84). The Bastard affects a devil-may-care attitude about the inheritance which contrasts to Philip's serious demeanor in the *Troublesome Raigne*. Where the *Troublesome Raigne*'s Philip wants (and tries) to claim legitimacy and thus keep title to the estate, Shakespeare's Bastard seems more or less uninterested in legitimacy and title. His jocular treatment of the dispute demonstrates his lack of serious interest in the land. He would, at this point, like to keep it but only because it provides him with a stable income. He could be said to be waiting for something better to come along, and it does in his "adoption" by Eleanor.

Robert, however, is interested in the land and makes his case to the King in that light. He argues, in basically the same terms used in the *Troublesome Raigne,* that his elder brother was conceived while Sir Robert was on an embassy for Richard I, an assertion proven by the fact that the Bastard "came into the world / Full fourteen weeks before the course of time" (*K,* 1.1.112-13). In addition to this proof of bastardy, Robert claims that Sir Robert made a death-bed will bequeathing the lands to him. However, all his arguments do no good because the law, as John presents it, clearly makes the Bastard the legal heir. Wills had no force in John's England, nor could any child be "bastardized" who was born in wedlock. Thus in Shakespeare's play, as in history, the Bastard's title is legal and unassailable. This legal situation is quite different from that in the *Troublesome Raigne* where at the moment Philip involuntarily claims Richard as his father his claim to the land evaporates—which further demonstrates that play's identification of position with blood. From the moment Philip asserts that his blood is Plantagenet, not Falconbridge, he loses any right to claim the Falconbridge land. In Shakespeare's play, the Bastard deliberately relinquishes his legal right to inherit.[12]

Robert responds petulantly to the fully legal succession King John mandates, objecting "Shall then my father's will be of no force / To dispossess this child which is not his?" (*K,* 1.1.130-31). This show of incredulity prompts a joking riposte from the Bastard: "Of no more force to dispossess me, sir, / Than was his will to get me, as I think" (*K,* 1.1.132-33). The Bastard's joke constitutes his most direct acknowledgment of his illegitimacy and leads Eleanor to pose a hypothetical question. She asks:

> Whether hadst thou rather be a
>   Faulconbridge,
> *And like thy brother,* to enjoy thy land,
> Or the reputed son of Coeur-de-lion,
> Lord of thy presence and no land beside?
>         (*K,* 1.1.134-37, my emphasis)

Essentially, she asks whether, if given the choice, he would stay on the land with the name and countenance of a Faulconbridge or leave it and take the name of Plantagenet.[13] Would he risk losing an income of five hundred pounds a year for the doubtful prospects of a landless royal bastard? The Bastard's incessant jokes about his brother's face (see *K,* 1.1.78-83, 92-94, 138-147), some of which lead to John and Eleanor's recognition of a resemblance to Richard I in the Bastard's "large composition" (*K,* 1.1.88), make the basis of his recognition external or physical, rather than internal or spiritual as it is in the *Troublesome Raigne.*[14] Shakespeare's Bastard responds by saying "I would give it [the land] every foot to have this face: / It would not be Sir Knob in any case" (*K,* 1.1.146-47). His response, like Eleanor's question, turns on the question of physical resemblance instead of innate abstract qualities. In other words, the Bastard claims a face, an appearance, rather than landed status. On the merit of the face alone, Eleanor offers to take him into her service.

The Bastard's acceptance of this proposed service represents several key shifts in his social position. First, by accepting Eleanor's offer the Bastard relinquishes the land that is legally his and takes up a much riskier calling as a courtier-soldier. "Brother," he says, finally resolving the dispute, "take you my land, I'll take my chance" (*K,* 1.1.151).[15] This act earns him a new name and rank: King John asks him to kneel and dubs him "Sir Richard, and Plantagenet" (*K,* 1.1.162). He enters the ranks of the nobility as a knight and also, more importantly, is acknowledged as royal kin. He kneels as a mere gentleman of Northamptonshire and arises, to use the King's words, "more great" (*K,* 1.1.161). This is radically different from the treatment of events in the *Troublesome Raigne,* where the Bastard *intends* to choose to retain his land but is forced to relinquish it by supernatural intervention. The *Troublesome Raigne*'s Bastard, upon rising to his feet after being dubbed Sir Richard prays "Graunt heavens that *Philip* once may shew himself / Worthie the honour of a *Plantaginet,* / Or basest glorie of a Bastard's name" (*T,* 302-5). He proclaims an essentialist idea of identity in which his acts will show the preexisting worth of his blood. *King John*'s Bastard, on the other hand, merely shakes his half-brother's hand in farewell and goes off to France in service to the king. "Well won is still well shot / And I am I, howe'er I was begot" (*K,* 1.1.174-75), he says, disregarding any essentialist concerns like those worries about acting in accordance with birth that are voiced by his counterpart in the *Troublesome Raigne.* In *King John,* the Bastard makes a conscious choice about his destiny rooted in his own well-articulated desires, making what might, however anachronistically, be called a career decision. He makes this more explicit in the famous speech which follows:

> this is worshipful society
> And fits the mounting spirit like myself;
> For he is but a bastard to the time
> That doth not smack of observation;
> And so am I, whether I smoke or no.
>         (*K,* 1.1.205-9)

His is a "mounting spirit," willing and eager to trade financial security and stability for a sixteenth-century version of upward mobility.

The dissatisfaction of Shakespeare's Bastard with his social status, apparent from the first, evidences his desire to move from a secure place in the local gentry to a more glorious position in the aristocracy. Despite the stigma of bastardy, he anticipates a gain in "honour" at the very least and, given the workings of the patronage system, might expect more tangible rewards. J. E. Neale, Conyers Read, and other historians of the Tudor era discuss this system and their analyses suggest that Eleanor's adoption of the Bastard promises access to her patronage—a potentially lucrative source of income. Furthermore, Shakespeare's depiction of the Bastard's subsequent progress suggests that the playwright had the contemporary political scene in mind rather than that of the twelfth century.[16]

In *The Troublesome Raigne,* the economic side of the Bastard Fauconbridge's "choice" is far more clearly defined. Elinor adopts him in these words: "I will not see thee want / As long as Elinor hath foote of land; / Henceforth thou shalt be taken for my sonne" (*T,* 294-96). In that play, the Bastard becomes Duke of Normandy—a further foregrounding of the "living and land" (*T,* 952) available to one of his rank. This never happens in Shakespeare's play. Shakespeare's Bastard becomes an important councilor of the King's but not a landed one; his rewards are those of office. The Bastard's "Brother, take you my land, I'll take my chance" gambles everything he possesses on this "chance." All the changes in his fortunes, his language, and his social position depend on this gamble, on his choice of royal service over his right to his "father's" land. A physical resemblance to Richard I makes this professional choice possible and thereby grants him access to higher rank—but his success in occupying that position has less to do with his birth than his talent.

II.

The Bastard's social trajectory can be traced through developments in his speech as he moves through *King John.* His choice of career, a choice made when he avows bastardy and thus enters the ranks of the attending nobility, takes him from a relatively low position in the hierarchy of rank—that of a country landholder resident on the land—to the much higher one of trusted royal servant. A crucial element in the Bastard's changing character is the fact that instead of being claimed by a mystical nobility, he claims (or professes) nobility and simultaneously acquires his rank and takes on the profession of servant to the crown. Eleanor does not merely recognize him as Richard the Lion-hearted's son, she offers him a job and the offer actually precedes formal recognition of his royal parentage: "I like thee well, wilt thou forsake thy fortune, / Bequeath thy land to him and follow me? / I am a soldier and bound to France" (*K,* 1.1.148-50). He accepts the job and only then does the king dub him "Sir Richard, and Plantagenet" (*K,* 1.1.162). His social rank, his rise to greater "honour," is contingent upon his choice of occupation.[17] It is in this spirit that he takes on his project of acquiring the noble linguistic habitus.[18]

In the first scene, the Bastard speaks in language more appropriate to Falstaff and Pistol in the Henriad than to the nobles who surround him in *King John.* In this initial scene the Bastard speaks in language appropriate to one of his status. He belongs, however tenuously, to the local gentry of Northamptonshire and his ostensible father, knighted on the field, was not born to the upper gentry but elevated to it. Keith Wrightson writes of this group in his *English Society 1580-1680,* arguing that the gentry stood between the yeomanry and the "titular nobility" in a hierarchy of rank which placed the nobility at the top, knights and esquires second, "mere gentlemen" (which is how the Bastard initially identifies himself), and all others below them.[19] Faulconbridge and his family historically belonged to the "mere gentlemen" level of this structure and had only recently risen to the next higher rung. Wrightson writes that gentility "derived from a degree of landed wealth sufficient to afford a certain life-style, which in turn gave rise to local recognition" which might, on rare occasions, grow into national recognition.[20] Gentlemen such as Faulconbridge (and by definition his sons) were locally recognized; their importance was limited to that local context and did not extend to the court or to the national political scene. Accordingly, the Bastard's language reveals a *lack* of urbanity and conventional "noble" rhetorical sophistication (a quality which marks all of the characters from the titular nobility in this scene) and thus his distance from the aristocracy.[21] Michael Manheim writes that "the Bastard we see and hear in the first act is an Elizabethan soldier-of-fortune. . . . He is a mixture of chivalry, intelligence, surface cynicism, brilliance, arrogance, egotism, personal charm, and almost total indifference to the uglier realities of the world around him."[22] Manheim goes on to characterize the Bastard's speech as "calculated to suggest that he . . . is of the blood royal."[23] While the Bastard is all the things Manheim suggests he is, his use of colloquial expressions, lurid images, and so on seems less a calculated attempt to prove an affinity with the "blood royal" than a sign of his difference. His "madcap" language and reliance on colloquialisms have more in common with the speech patterns of the country than with those of the court.[24]

The Bastard's long speech at line 182 hinges on questions of utterance and the kind of language available to him now that he is a member of the aristocracy. He shows himself to be aware of a change in the power of his words as well as its basis in his new rank:

A foot of honour better than I was
But many a foot of land the worse
Well, now can I make any Joan a lady.
'Good den, Sir Richard!'—'God a mercy fellow!'
And if his name be George, I'll call him
For new-made honour doth forget men's names

(*K,* 1.1.182-87)

His "foot of honour" enables him to change "any Joan"—any ordinary woman—into a "lady" as well as to change any George's name to Peter.[25] In other words, by virtue of his "new-made honour" the Bastard's language becomes performative, endowed with power he formerly lacked.[26] The change in his "honour" makes him "forget men's names" because " 'tis too respective and too sociable / For your conversion" (*K*, 1.1.188-89). He is too aware of the novelty of his nobility to recall the names (and thus share the society of) those who were formerly his peers. Interestingly, the Bastard seems to hypostatize his rank, to personify it, and locates the agency of forgetfulness in that hypostatized rank. What speaks and renames the people it encounters is not so much the Bastard himself but his "new-made honour." This is a crucial distinction; in these early scenes, the Bastard's consciousness is distanced from his rank, affording him the space from which to speak of "tickling Commodity," to discuss objectively the social practices of the class he has just entered (see the rest of this speech, especially lines 190-204), and to make other apparently critical utterances. What happens later, as his project not "to practice to deceive" but "to learn" progresses, is that his learning project effaces that distinction, erases the space of the Commodity speech, and produces a very different speaker and mode of speech.

The Bastard, in describing the operations of his "new-made honour," describes socially-dependent linguistic practices in ways that can be discussed further in light of Pierre Bourdieu's ideas about linguistic habitus, symbolic power, and their role in social relations. In the speech quoted above, the Bastard has just been made part of a class whose speech patterns he can describe with a measure of detachment and amusement. That he can do this at this point suggests that he is in possession of a different set of speech patterns, ones which are derived from a different class. These speech patterns are markers or spoken objectifications of what Bourdieu calls linguistic habitus:

> dispositions which are impalpably inculcated, through a long and slow process of acquistion, by the sanctions of the linguistic market, and which are therefore adjusted, without any cynical calculation or consciously experienced constraint, to the chances of material and symbolic profit which the laws of price formation characteristic of a given market objectively offer to the holders of a given linguistic capital.[27]

Shakespeare's Bastard, because he occupies a liminal position in the social order, has the capacity to articulate, if not a critique, at least an analysis of two sets of dispositions.[28] Implicitly, his speech up to and including this point has instantiated one habitus: that of Philip Faulconbridge, ambitious country gentleman. This habitus predisposes him to use colloquial expressions, what E. A. J. Honigmann might call "rustic proverbs" in addressing his social superiors—an attempt to play up his wit and thus what he would see as his "courtliness," a strategy designed to draw attention.[29] The Bastard characterizes the habitus he comments on, that of the courtier or minor noble (for lack of a better term), as excessively polite, "cultured" (in the sense of liberal learning), and, at least potentially, deceitful.

The Bastard's evocation of the courtier's "dialogue of compliment" serves two purposes: first, it ridicules that dialogue by caricature; but second, and more importantly, his speech shows the Bastard's awareness of and willingness to adopt the speech patterns he pokes fun at:

> Ere Answer knew what Question would
> Saving in dialogue of compliment,
> And talking of the Alps and Apennines,
> The Pyrenean and the river Po,
> It draws toward supper in conclusion so.
> But this is worshipful society,
> And fits the mounting spirit like myself;
> For he is but a bastard to the time
> That doth not smack of observation.
> (*K*, 1.1.200-208)

His caricature of the excessively polite conversation of "Question" and "Answer" closes with the interjection "but this is worshipful society, / And fits a mounting spirit like myself."[30] He halts the critique with a reminder that this is the kind of conversation that fits his "mounting spirit" now that he belongs to "worshipful society." He claims that "he is but bastard to the time / That doth not smack of observation." In other words, he is only a bastard (that is, outside the pale of society) insofar as he does not "observe" the demands of the time.[31]

The following lines offer a program for the inculcation of what amounts to both a new linguistic habitus and a new class habitus.[32] The Bastard's bastardy "to the time" only lasts so long as he "doth not smack of observation." To truly move beyond his bastardy he must suit not only his outward appearance but also his "inward motion" to the age's requirements. His theoretical knowledge of the practices of his new class must become practical reflexes:

> He is but a bastard to the time.
> That does not smack of observation.
> And so am I, whether I smoke or no.
> And not alone in habit and device,
> Exterior form, outward accoutrement,
> But from the inward motion to deliver
> Sweet, sweet, sweet poison for the age's tooth:
> Which though I will not practice to deceive,
> Yet, to avoid deceit I mean to learn;
> For it shall strew the footsteps of my rising.
> (*K*, 1.1.207-16)

What the Bastard is saying is that he must make the practices he has just carcatured his own, unconscious parts of his habitus, if he is to succeed in his rising and do so in good faith: "Yet, to avoid deceit, I mean to learn; / For it shall strew the footsteps of my rising." He "means to learn" in order to avoid deceit (and to avoid being deceitful) as he rises in rank and power—a rise in rank and power marked by increasing administrative responsibilities.

The Bastard's rise offers an instructive resemblance to the fortunes of the Cecil family. The Cecils grew from a cadet branch of an obscure family of minor gentry on the Welsh border under Henry VII to a family of great importance and honor under Elizabeth I. Their rise to prominence was dependent on their service to the crown. David Cecil, Burghley's grandfather, linked his family's fortunes to those of the Tudors. His small contribution as a yeoman of Henry VII's guard established a family connection that was the basis for Lord Burghley's service to Henry VII's granddaughter Elizabeth I.[33] Royal service, beginning with relatively minor posts, provided the Cecil family with what was eventually to be a vast income, elevation from the gentry to the peerage, and a position as chief advisers to the Queen.[34] The Bastard's service to the crown begins with mere soldiering for the Queen but ends with his role as sole determiner of King John's burial and young Henry's coronation. In the final scene all defer to his judgment; Salisbury and the Prince both wait on his ordering of the "business" (*K*, 5.7.94). His rise, from the countryside of Northamptonshire to the heights of the court, depends on his choice of job, which amounts to choosing the profession of nobility.

The play's final scene, which presents the king's death, the end of the French invasion, and the settling of the peace, also contains the Bastard's apotheosis as administrator. In the final lines the duty of disposing the "business" of state falls to him as King John wills it in one of his last speeches: "Have thou the ordering of this present time" (*K*, 5.7.77). And the Bastard does just that.

> SAL: Many carriages he hath dispatch'd
> To the sea-side, and put his cause and quarrel
> To the disposing of the cardinal:
> With whom yourself, myself and other lords,
> If you think meet, this afternoon will post
> To consummate this business happily.
> BAST: Let it be so: and you, my noble prince,
> With other princes that may best be spar'd
> *Shall* wait upon your father's funeral.
> P. HEN: At Worcester must his body be interr'd:
> For so he willed it.
> BAST: Thither *shall* it then:
> And happily *may* your sweet self put on
> The lineal state and glory of the land!
> To whom, with all submission, on my knee
> I do bequeath my faithful services
> And true subjection everlastingly.
> (*K*, 5.6.89-105, my emphasis)

Throughout most of the play, the Bastard's language has been couched in conditional phrases. This speech marks a dramatic shift. Someone whose origins are, as the first act reveals, at best ambiguous, now wields great rhetorical and actual authority. The Bastard's "let it be so," his "shall"s, and his odd "may" all demonstrate his authority, as does the fact that the prince and Salisbury, both of whom outrank him by birth, defer to his judgment.[35] He and the "other lords" will settle the terms of the peace while Prince Henry and "other princes that may best be spar'd" will "wait upon" King John's funeral.[36] The Bastard is clearly in charge here; he is in full control of the performative power of his language. The last lines quoted above demonstrate this control in that they cement the Bastard's position as royal servant and, implicitly, as trusted administrator: "With all submission, on my knee / I do bequeath my faithful services everlastingly."[37] His offer does not admit of refusal—one does not refuse a bequest of service—and thus in the act of making it he assures its acceptance.[38] This speech represents the fullness of his assimilation to the ranks of the nobility while it still bears the trace of his origins.[39]

The professionalism of the Bastard's choices, for lack of a better term, becomes clearer when juxtaposed to the "choices" made by *The Troublesome Raigne*'s Bastard. As shown above, Philip Fauconbridge chooses to acknowledge his parentage only because he is forced to do so by the burning of "honour's fire" within his veins. If given a free choice, he would remain on the land, secure in the possession of a landed income and some degree of local influence. Instead, his royal blood, of which he is apparently unconscious until his brother's accusations of bastardy, forces him to relinquish that land and take up a place in the court as bastard son of a king. The *Troublesome Raigne* gives the impression that this is what Philip was born to; his destiny is to become Sir Richard Plantagenet and accompany King John in his French wars regardless of his personal will. Among the indicators of this are the recognition scene itself, his rapid transformation into the glory-hungry soldier presented in the scenes where he chases and kills the Duke of Austria, his wooing of Blaunch (a detail absent in *King John*), and, most interestingly for my argument, the lack of change in his language from the beginning to the end of the play. Philip's diction remains relatively constant—unlike that of Shakespeare's Bastard. Where Shakespeare's Bastard's language is commented upon by Eleanor and the king, Philip's never is. Philip speaks with all the same pronouns, verb forms, and idioms as his royal kin, and the tone of his speech remains at an essentially constant level of seriousness. This makes him unlike

Shakespeare's Bastard whose tone shifts from satirically self-conscious to deadly serious by the end of *King John*. Philip is "to the manor born" even if he does not know it, while Shakespeare's Bastard can be seen as a parvenu seeking (with amazing success) to become such. This distinction reflects the difference between rank and career as preordained or destined, and rank and career as personal choice. The Bastard chooses his destiny rather than having it chosen for him. Because of his being born to his rank, Philip does not need to learn in the way that the Bastard does; he *is* what he is and the kind of service he provides expresses that essential being.

CONCLUSIONS

*King John* represents a changing understanding of service and of legitimacy in government.[40] This play presents the history of one character's movement up the social ladder and evokes the mechanisms of that rise. The Bastard's movement from rural landholder to the administrative voice that closes the play depends more on his personal choices and his talents than his birth. A comparison of the two plays suggests that the *Troublesome Raigne* holds to a more naturalized or traditional notion of noble status than *King John*. It is in Philip's *blood* to be royal while this status is more ambiguous in *King John*. *King John* seems to suspend two definitions of nobility: the Bastard does after all have royal blood even if it does not burn with "honour's fire" to make him speak, while inclining towards a less natural or inborn notion of nobility. In essence it is the Bastard's *talent*, not his blood, that ennobles him.[41] If the *Troublesome Raigne*'s Philip is not the strategist Shakespeare's Bastard is, it is because Philip, being essentially noble, has no need for conscious strategy, while the Bastard clearly does.

The Bastard initially sees language as a strategic tool, viewing the acquisition of a noble linguistic habitus as essential to the advancement of his career, an awareness wholly lacking in Philip. If the Bastard is to be an effective and successful member of the class he so suddenly joins, he must assimilate himself to its practices; he must, in a sense, become more noble than the nobles. This point is made clear by his battlefield speeches, which outdo any of the other nobles' speeches in the rhetoric of honorable war. This awareness points to another change in the understanding of the elements of social power: the Bastard's distinction derives from his linguistic mastery, and his power follows from that distinction. The play shows the operations of these elements in ways the *Troublesome Raigne*, with its ideological structure of a traditional honor culture, does not. In *King John*, power and social distinction are available to the capable few who choose to pursue them, and the play shows how the mastery of the aristocracy's social practices can lead to distinction, even if the mastering agent does not belong to the nobility by birth.

Where the *Troublesome Raigne* presents rank and distinction as inborn or pre-ordained by forces explicitly external to individual persons, *King John* presents them as available to those with the ability to take them. Personally chosen profession begins to succeed divinely ordained vocation, a succession also beginning to take place in early modern England. The Bastard remains, in a sense, born to the rank he accedes to, but his ability and his desire have more influence on his successful occupation of that rank than does his dubious birth.

*Notes*

[1] Sigurd Burckhardt, *Shakespearean Meanings,* (Princeton: Princeton Univ. Press, 1968); Virginia Mason Vaughan, "Between Tetralogies: *King John* as Transition," *Shakespeare Quarterly* 35 (1984): 407-20; Michael Manheim, *The Weak King Dilemma in the Shakespearean History Play* (Syracuse: Syracuse Univ. Press, 1973); Marsha Robinson, "The Historiographic Method of *King John*" in *King John: New Perspectives,* ed. Deborah T. Curren-Aquino (Newark: Univ. of Delaware Press, 1989), 29-40.

[2] Vaughan, 409.

[3] See Douglas Wixson, "'Calm Words Folded up in Smoke': Propaganda and Spectator Response in Shakespeare's *King John*," *Shakespeare Studies* 14 (1981): 111-27, which examines the play's dramaturgy in terms of contemporary political pamphleteering. See also John R. Elliott, "Shakespeare and the Double Image of King John," *Shakespeare Studies* 1 (1965): 64-84. Elliott discusses as politically motivated the conflict between two historical images of King John, as a proto-Protestant martyr king and as a weak, usurping, bad king.

[4] See Jacqeline Trace, "Shakespeare's Bastard Faulconbridge: An Early Tudor Hero," *Shakespeare Studies* 13 (1980): 59-69, for a genealogy of the character in *King John* as well as in *The Troublesome Raigne*. She finds no direct historical analog to the Bastard, and looks instead to such figures as Henry VIII's bastards, Wolsey's son Thomas Winter, and other Henrician and Elizabethan bastard adventurers as possible models for the character.

[5] William Shakespeare, *King John,* (1590/1), ed. E. A. J. Honigmann (London: Methuen, 1954), 1.1.44. Hereafter cited parenthetically by act, scene, and line and abbreviated *K*. *The Troublesome Raigne* is quoted from G. Bullough, *Narrative and Dramatic Sources of Shakespeare,* 8 vols. (London: Routledge Kegan Paul, 1975) vol. 4, ll.67-68. Hereafter cited parenthetically by line number and abbreviated *T*. I am not particularly interested here in questions of chronology (or authorship); it is more important for my argument that both were extant at roughly the same time, suggesting that the ideas presented in both were likewise contemporane-

ous. In both plays, the Bastard's family is only marginally historical and both authors use it to their own ends without much attention to what limited historical information exists about the Bastard, his brother, and their mother. In Shakespeare's play, the Bastard is consistently referred to as the Bastard and his name is spelled Faulconbridge. In *Troublesome Raigne,* the Bastard is usually referred to as Philip and his surname is spelled Fauconbridge. I have retained these and other spellings specific to each play in order to maintain the distance between two otherwise very similar plays.

[6] See Phyllis Rackin, *Stages of History: Shakespeare's English Chronicles* (Ithaca: Cornell Univ. Press, 1990), chap. 4, for a discussion of the similarity of this succession dispute to that between John and Arthur.

[7] As do the legalities of the claims: in the *Troublesome Raigne,* bastardy seems automatically to disqualify Philip from the inheritance, while in *King John* the fact that Philip is born in wedlock and is the elder gives him the right to the land regardless of who his father actually was.

[8] And he does not do even this: his claim evaporates when he is determined to be illegitimate. Volition is not an issue.

[9] Keith Wrightson's *English Society 1580-1680* (New Brunswick: Rutgers Univ. Press, 1982) demonstrates the complex and deeply ingrained awareness of rank and position in contemporary English society. He writes, "the most fundamental structural characteristic of English society was its high degree of stratification, its distinctive and pervasive system of social inequality" (17). The very bulk of contemporary writing on order and degree attests to a conscious awareness of the importance of attempting to maintain these distinctions. Philip is no exception.

[10] Where the Bastard says "my Liege" (*K,* 1.1.158), Robert says "my gracious Liege" (*K,* 1.1.95). Robert's speech is markedly more deferential and conventionally polite. Interestingly, Shakespeare's Bastard never reminds himself of his place or to whom he is speaking.

[11] In an article important to my thinking, David Scott Kastan writes that the Bastard "chooses his bastardy . . . He denies himself access to a lineal history that would grant and guarantee name and position in favor of a freedom in which he can create both" (" 'To Set a Form Upon That Indigest': Shakespeare's Fictions of History," *Comparative Drama* 17:1 [1983]: 14-15). I would suggest that the freedom to create "name and history" that Kastan alludes to is far smaller than he argues it is: the Bastard chooses a fairly conventional pattern for his new identity as a nobleman and, as I hope to demonstrate, works to assimilate himself ever more fully to that pattern as the play progresses.

[12] John himself acknowledges the Bastard's right to the land saying: "My mother's son did get your father's heir; / Your father's heir must have your father's land" (*K,* 1.1.128-129).

[13] Including the sense of face, the physical semblance. Eleanor asks if the Bastard wants to be like his brother, not just in terms of blood, but in a physical sense as well.

[14] Note that in the *Troublesome Raigne* Elinor discounts the physical resemblance's relevance to the question of Philip's bastardy, saying "Know you not, *Omne simile non est idem?*" (*T,* 197), going on to suggest that their mother thought of Richard as she lay with her husband, which thought caused the resemblance.

[15] It is important to note that the Bastard settles the squabble himself without reference to the King's judgment. The Bastard takes full charge of his affairs, as is fitting for one elevated to his status. John himself points to the Bastard's right to do this in his final lines to Robert: "Go, Faulconbridge: now hast thou thy desire; / A landless knight makes thee a landed squire" (*K,* 1.1.176-77). The authority is clearly the Bastard's and this is the first of many scenes where he summarily takes matters into his own hands.

[16] Wallace T. MacCaffery argues that "the Queen's service" was seen as a "career" for "the young man of good birth, poor estate, and average talents" (qualifications roughly matching those of Shakespeare's Bastard) with the possibility of "the solid respectability and substantial rewards of an official career" ("Place and Patronage in Elizabethan Politics" in *Elizabethan Government and Society,* ed. S. T. Bindoff and others [London: Univ. of London Press, 1961], 101). John Guy, Penry Williams, and the various biographers of the Cecil family attest to the role of talent in the selection of administrators.

[17] And this is not the case in the *Troublesome Raigne.* The Bastard is acknowledged as Plantagenet and offered the chance to "wait upon me and on thine Unckle heere, / Who shall give honour to thy noble mind" (*T,* 297-98). John knights him immediately—without waiting for a response—and the Bastard Fauconbridge is transformed.

[18] "Habitus" is defined by Pierre Bourdieu as "a disposition that generates meaningful practices and meaning-giving perceptions; it is a general transposable disposition which carries out a systematic, universal application—beyond the limits of what has been directly learnt—of the necessity inherent in the learning conditions" (*Distinction* [Cambridge: Harvard Univ. Press, 1984], 170). It is a structure of dispositions which structures an agent's responses to events. For further historical information,

see John Guy, *Tudor England* (Oxford: Oxford Univ. Press, 1988) and Penry Williams, *The Tudor Regime* (Oxford: Oxford Univ. Press, 1979).

[19] Wrightson, 19.

[20] Wrightson, 25. The Cecil family's fortunes might serve as a good example of this (infrequent) movement up the ladder of rank: from being minor courtiers and country landholders under Henry VII, the family grew in stature to become one of the most important and influential ones in Elizabeth's England.

[21] Rather than its presence. His rhetorical failures before the walls of Angiers in Act 2, Scene 1 can be seen as more evidence of incomplete mastery of "royal" rhetoric.

[22] Michael Manheim, "The Four Voices of the Bastard," in Curren-Aquino, 127.

[23] Manheim, "Four Voices," 128. Manheim's assertion that Old Faulconbridge was too dull to have been the Bastard's father, a "fact" that Manheim claims the Bastard's language demonstrates, ignores the fact that Faulconbridge was knighted on the field, presumably for valor, and that Richard I clearly valued him.

[24] Honigmann footnotes lines 169-175 (the Bastard's last speech before his "soliloquy" beginning at line 182): "'The proverbial sayings which follow are characteristic of the Bastard's rusticity of breeding' (Wright, comparing *Corinthians* 1.1.211)," underscoring the fact that despite his royal blood, he was raised with the manners of the country.

[25] "Joan" was apparently a common name for a "female rustic" (O.E.D. cited by Honigmann).

[26] Pierre Bourdieu discusses the ideal of performative language in *Language and Symbolic Power* (Cambridge: Harvard Univ. Press, 1991). See especially "Price Formation and the Anticipation of Profits."

[27] Bourdieu, *Language and Symbolic Power*, 51. Habitus is a multivalent word in Bourdieu's work; for now I am commenting only on the strictly linguistic aspect of the concept.

[28] Or perhaps three. The Bastard occupies a continuum of habitus that range from that of his brother to that of the King and the other nobles. Schematically: Robert— the Bastard—the King. The second term, of course, splits in the course of the play because the Bastard of the early part of the action metamorphoses into a dramatically different one by the end, but this schema serves well enough at this point.

[29] He engages in the same kind of wordplay that "noble" characters do in this and other Shakespearean plays. The difference lies in the vocabulary, the stock of linguistic capital, he has at his disposal. Structurally, the Bastard's speech approximates that of "madcap" noble figures such as, for example, *Romeo and Juliet*'s Mercutio or *Much Ado About Nothing*'s Don Benedick. This relation is, I think, what Manheim discusses in his article cited above.

[30] In which he is of course participating as "Question."

[31] Both our modern sense of observation as taking notice of or studying something and what Honigmann calls the "secondary sense" of obsequiousness are at work here (15, n. to line 208). The Bastard, in order to be fully integrated into his new rank, must observe the conventions of observation. Only then will he not be a "bastard to the time." In contrast to other scholars who see the Bastard as either remaining a "bastard to the time" and those who view his becoming a "son to the time," to use Ronald Stroud's phrase, as a kind of sell-out, a corruption of his critical virtue, I view his "conversion" as part and parcel of his ascent up the ladder of rank and not as an example of cynicism or deception ("The Bastard to the Time in *King John*," *Comparative Drama* 6:2 [1972]: 154-65). In the course of Acts 4 and 5, he does not lose the honesty most critics see him as possessing in Acts 1, 2, and 3, his honesty is simply of a different nature, one in keeping with the position to which he has assimilated himself.

[32] Linguistic habitus could be said to be a constitutive component of the class habitus which encompasses not only linguistic practice but what Bourdieu calls bodily hexis and the whole constellation of more or less conditioned responses that produce an agent's actions. See Bourdieu, *Language and Symbolic Power*, 83: "what expresses itself through the linguistic habitus is the whole class habitus of which it is one dimension."

[33] For the facts of the Cecil family's rise, see B. W. Beckingsale, *Burghley: Tudor Statesman 1520-1598* (London: MacMillan, 1967), to which this discussion is much indebted.

[34] Both Burghley and his son Robert Cecil were instrumental in shaping policy including (and this is a parallel to *King John*) the succession.

[35] The Bastard's "may" carries overtones both of a beneficent wish for the prince's happy coronation and the sense that he is somehow granting the prince permission.

[36] Note the contrast between this scene and the final scene of the *Troublesome Raigne*. The Bastard Philip of the *Troublesome Raigne* says, "Then Kings & Princes, let these broils have end, / And at more leasure talke upon the League. / Meanwhile to *Worster* let us beare the King, / And there interre his bodie, as beseemes. / But first, in sight of *Lewes*, Heire of *Fraunce*,

/ Lords take the crowne and set it on his head, / That by succession is our lawfull King" (*T,* 1178-84). He then shifts into a choric mode for the final patriotic speech of the play, losing his already tenuous individuation as he speaks the epilogue. This Bastard defers to the lords in a way Shakespeare's does not, and this speech carries far less of the assured and commanding tone conveyed by the end of Shakespeare's play.

[37] Compare with the succession of the Cecil family in the service of the Tudors. Burghley served Henry VIII, Edward VI, Mary (briefly), and Elizabeth I—rising in importance and trust with each successive monarch, a trust he passed on to his son Robert.

[38] Note also that *knights* pledge service to their lords; in pledging thus, he consolidates a position that might have remained ambiguous. The Bastard exercises his control over his future (and that of the kingdom insofar as he is authorized by John to "have the ordering of this present time") from a posture of submission, exemplifying his mastery of the symbolic practices of the aristocratic habitus.

[39] It is laden with "sweet, sweet, sweet poison for the age's tooth," "poison" which does indeed "strew the footsteps of [his] rising" (*K,* 1.1.213-15). It is also not deceptive. This is a sincere offer, even as it strategically ensures the continuance of his role in the court.

[40] Shakespeare's Bastard's power in the government is as legitimate as his birth is not, and his power's legitimacy has less to do with his birth than his ability and choice of profession.

[41] As the Bastard says, "Near or far off, well won is well shot, / And I am I, howe'er I was begot" (*K,* 1.1.174-75), as cited above. Regardless of his "base" birth, he is still who he is and that becomes "Sir Richard Plantagenet," the trusted adviser and half-brother to the King. Merit takes the place of birth but only, of course, to a limited extent.

---

Source: " 'He Is But a Bastard to the Time': Status and Services in *The Troublesome Raigne of John* and *Shakespeare's King John*," in *ELH,* Vol. 65, No. 4, 1998, pp. 779-98.

# History-Making in the Henriad

## Michael Goldman, *Princeton University*

Then and now are not so far apart, as my reader may confirm by trying to think back to when this sentence began. When did that *then* cease to be *now?* For that matter, when did the sentence really begin? Perhaps two weeks ago when I first drafted it, perhaps in kindergarten, perhaps as part of a gleam in my father's eye, perhaps in the Renaissance, to which we shall soon be going. Or perhaps the *then* we are seeking will not exist till a moment from now—or was it a moment ago?—when, troubled by some distracting twist in my argument, you looked back and began what I have called "this sentence" again.

I'm trying to evoke really two points in this riff on now and then. First, that the present moment is not a dimensionless point on the time line, but a temporal space of ambiguous duration. Second, that the past, even when, for all practical purposes, it may be clearly distinguished from the present—as when we speak of our childhood or the childhood of Prince Hal—the past is subject to a similar ambiguity. I am not referring to the familiar proposition, by now rather overworked, that we write and rewrite the past from the position of the present. Rather, I mean that the experience of the present, of living and acting in the present, involves a continual history-making activity. That is, it involves a redrawing, a reexperiencing of the borders between then and now, a beginning of the sentence again.

It's my notion, which I hope to explore in this essay, that for Shakespeare's audience in the *Henry IV* plays, the process of experiencing the drama—of undergoing, construing, fighting with, surrendering to the play as it unfolds—becomes in many ways the process of history-making itself. It creates a rhythm of instability, of perpetual realignment that we come to associate with the process of political action and decision-making we see on stage—a process that Shakespeare portrays as itself a process of representation, of struggling among and with representations like his and ours and those of people, past and present, in power over us. It is a process of aligning past and present, then and now, and one of the ways it works on us is by exposing us to many folds and wrinkles and ambiguities in our awareness of time.

I was led to notice this aspect of the *Henry IV* plays by the sense I'd had for some time of a certain recurrent texture, a complicating strangeness never adequately accounted for even among the wealth of wonderful criticism that the plays have elicited. Indeed, I first began to think along the lines I'll be following here when I found myself trying to make sense out of *1 Henry IV*'s own beginning, the address "So shaken as we are...." with which Henry opens the play.

> So shaken as we are, so wan with care,
> Find we a time for frighted peace to pant
> And breathe short-winded accents of new broils
> To be commenced in stronds afar remote.
> No more the thirsty entrance of this soil
> Shall daub her lips with her own children's blood,
> No more shall trenching war channel her fields,
> Nor bruise her flow'rets with the armed hoofs
> Of hostile paces. Those opposed eyes
> Which like the meteors of a troubled heaven
> Did lately meet in the intestine shock
> And furious close of civil butchery
> Shall now in mutual well-beseeming ranks
> March all one way and be no more opposed
> Against acquaintance, kindred, and allies.
> The edge of war, like an ill-sheathed knife
> No more shall cut his master. Therefore, friends,
> As far as to the sepulcher of Christ—
> Whose soldier now, under whose blessed cross
> We are impressed and engaged to fight—
> Forthwith a body of English shall we levy,
> Whose arms were molded in their mother's womb
> To chase these pagans in those holy fields
> Over whose acres walked those blessed feet
> Which fourteen hundred years ago were nailed
> For our advantage on the bitter cross.
> But this our purpose now is twelvemonth old,
> And bootless 'tie to tell you we will go.
> Therefore we meet not now.[1]
>
> (1.1.1-30)

The problem I faced was basic—how can this relatively long speech be performed effectively, and by that I simply mean interestingly. I had never heard it come across as anything but an inert block of oratory, and the reason seemed to be that performers had trouble sustaining a sense of purpose. What was the King doing here? Why was he telling his closest advisers—and at length—something that after twenty lines he admits they already know and in fact have known for a year?

Most actors treat the speech as a kind of extension of the familiar offstage music with which modern productions of the histories usually begin—a sort of prolonged trumpet blast meant to suggest regal pomp and ceremony. Unfortunately, dramatic interest doesn't thrive on anything so static. The problem is heightened because the speech is *about* purpose—Henry's purpose in calling his counselors together, Christ's purpose in walking the earth, the purpose of a strangely personified Peace in gasping out a promise of new war. The problem of understanding and dramatically correlating all these purposes is the same as that of finding a purpose the actor can latch onto in the speech itself. It's a problem about going back in time and aligning a lot of information about the past, more specifically about a variety of pasts, rather irregularly defined, into a coherent relation with the present.

The speech poses a problem about time even in its very first words. It begins with a curious disruption in the audience's sense of time, which is worth dwelling on, for a number of reasons.

> So shaken as we are, so wan with care,
> Find we a time for frighted peace to pant.

What does "find we a time" mean? Is this an order? A description of what is being done now? A pious hope? The phrase is rarely glossed, but most critics would seem to agree with Kittredge that it's an imperative of sorts—*let us find a time*. Yet if it's an imperative, it has a peculiar spin, especially if one thinks of it as an imperative issuing from a king speaking in public at the beginning of a play. It's not a very commanding command, and it suggests a questioning or entreating note very hard to omit in speaking, even if one wants to. It can be read, possibly, to suggest that *we have just found a time,* or, contrastingly, *by all means we must find a time.* As we shall see, neither of these, nor any paraphrasable reading on the spectrum between them, can make completely coherent sense in terms of the entire scene that follows. The speech keeps us vibrating between these possibilities, as if we couldn't decide what time it was. For there is an even greater problem: exactly *where* is this time that we—or is it he—are being urged to find?

Finding a time is different from, and more complex than, simply finding time. It means opening up a space in which certain things can happen, a certain kind of time. One of the things history does is to describe what kind of a time this time or that time was; one of the things politics does is to convert time into *a* time, an era, a period in which forces can be marshaled, the Era of Good Feeling, the hundred days, the Cold War. The time that Henry describes is a time shaken and ravaged by war, but it is a space in which peace can act. And yet the space is as imaginatively elusive as the description of peace itself, for it is a frightened, exhausted peace, which speaks of war. Or is it that it *will* speak of war as soon as it can catch its breath? Is this time that Henry invokes *now,* or rather, what kind of now is it? Are we—is Henry's England—in the midst of it or has it just begun; is it about to begin or are we searching, shaken as we are, for a way to make it happen—to realign its components, to make them, as Henry says "march all one way?" It is an opening, then, which, even as it plunges us into political planning and into an impassioned effort to sum up the past, immediately makes us feel uneasy about getting a purchase on time.

This uneasiness will be compounded twenty-odd lines later, when the audience receives a more violent disruption to its sense of time. Henry turns from contemplating Christ's divine purpose to rather more abruptly defining his own.

> But this our purpose now is twelvemonth old,
> And bootless 'tis to tell you we will go.
> Therefore we meet not now.

This is a surprise. Henry's purpose—his vision of a crusade—has seemed to open up directly from the finding of a time in line 2, open up with a manifest insistence on urgency and connectedness. Temporal and logical sequence have been almost pedantically emphasized ("lately . . . therefore . . . now . . . forthwith . . . therefore") It is an at least subliminal jolt to discover that Henry has been finding this time, if not actually repeating this speech, for a year.

These temporal disruptions work to establish a counterpoint with the problems Henry faces governing England and with those faced by Shakespeare and his audience in construing history. If we look more closely at the speech we notice that the sudden reference to a "twelvemonth-old" purpose is but one of several openings into the past that occur in it, evocations of distanced sources and origins of historical action. The first such source is the earth of England, a cruel mother who "daub[s] her lips with her own children's blood." There are also the English mothers in whose wombs the arms of English soldiers were moulded, specific ally for the purpose of chasing the pagans from Jerusalem. And there is Christ himself, described in terms that heighten our awareness of both sacred and secular action at a distance:

> Therefore friends,
> As far as to the sepulchre of Christ—
> Whose soldier now, under whose blessed cross
> We are impressed and engag'd to fight—
> Forthwith a power of English shall we levy,
> Whose arms were moulded in their mother's womb
> To chase these pagans in those holy fields

> Over whose acres walk'd those blessed feet
> Which fourteen hundred years ago were nail'd
> For our advantage on the bitter cross.
> But this our purpose now is twelvemonth old.
> . . .

The sepulchre is a point in space that is also a point in and out of time, a then that is eternally now, redefining the future. We are given the particular detail of Christ's feet, again at a particular location in space but also at a very specific distance (1400 years ago) in time. Christ's historical force has a traditionally apolitical dimension—it leaps over time to offer us individual access to eternal safety, but in the context of the scene and in the immediate context of the speech, we are urged to see it in its political dimension. "Our advantage" (a word Henry will later use in an urgently political sense: "Advantage feeds him fat while men delay," 3.2.180) suggests not only personal salvation but also the redemption of England and the consolidation of Lancastrian power.

To see what is unique about this opening scene we would do well to remember a point that has been very well made by David Kastan. Discussing *1 Henry VI*, he notes that in the opening scene of his first tetralogy, Shakespeare stresses the fact that we are in the midst of "an ongoing temporal process." A past exists, whose impact on the present requires our consideration.[2] Now, this is an important feature of all Shakespeare's histories, as it is, say, of the *Oresteia*, and it's certainly true of *1 Henry IV*. But in the latter play, something very different is happening as well. We are being forced to *find a time,* to wonder where in time we are coming from, to ask what is in fact anterior, what is present. How are we to situate ourselves in the face of the many ongoing thens out of which an uncertain now must be rescued? Yes, we are once more in the midst of a temporal process, but the midst is not easily located or described. *Finding* the midst is a political question, a history-making one, for it is a space from which to act.

Henry Bolingbroke is in the midst of a political situation that he is trying to control. He is attempting to align past and present, to project a purpose into the future. And now, as the scene moves on, we experience a further instability, related to those that have come before, about his control over the present—or is it the immediate or not so immediate past? Just as earlier we asked, where does Henry locate the time he is finding, we must now ask, what does he know and when did he know it? As Henry turns to Westmoreland and asks him to make his report, the audience faces mounting uncertainty about history and time.

Westmoreland brings news of civil war. Mortimer has been defeated by Glendower, and the crusade must be postponed. This is news to us, but is it news to Henry?

> It seems then that the tidings of this broil
> Brake off our business for the Holy Land.
>                                   (1.1.47-48)

Henry's response mimes surprise, but he casts it in the past tense of narrative ("brake") and introduces it by a phrase ("It seems") that suggests control, a presentation to his on-stage audience. But it is only after the news gets worse and more uncertain, that Henry suddenly seems to have known not only Westmoreland's news but even more recent facts:

> Here is a dear, a true-industrious friend,
> Sir Walter Blunt, new lighted from his horse.
> . . .
> And he has brought us smooth and welcome
>    news.
>                                   (62-66)

For the past thirty lines, Westmoreland's narrative has been invested with a feeling of present unfolding. Now it is abruptly placed in a superseded past.

We quickly realize, moreover, that the news Blunt brings is neither smooth nor entirely welcome. Once we think about past and future, as Henry soon forces us to do, we realize that the news only points to more trouble, which again Henry must struggle to control. Hotspur's victory raises the problem of Henry's son; would they had been exchanged at the point of origin! (*That* would have been a convenient realignment.) It also brings with it new signs of rebellion, over which Hotspur and Worcester must be confronted. And so the scene ends, with a heightened sense of busyness, of new purpose, and of greater urgency. Both time and the effort to organize time are speeding up. Rapid movement in time and space are insisted on:

> Cousin, on Wednesday next our council we
> Will hold at Windsor. So inform the lords;
> But come yourself with speed to us again. . .
>                                   (102-4)

It is important to notice that this has been a behind-the-scenes scene. Henry is setting up a meeting of the full council, into which much planning must go if it is to be manipulated properly. But it is also a public scene. Even with his inner circle Henry must always be shaping, controlling, and history-making. As we watch the news shifting from bad to good—as we watch the *same* news shifting from bad to good, to advantage or disadvantage, we too become involved in a constant realignment and redefinition of present and past. To take a final example from Henry's last words in the scene:

> For more is to be said and to be done
> Than out of anger can be uttered.
>                                   (105-6)

What is the source of Henry's anger—in both the temporal and logical sense? When and at what did he become angry? Logically, he has known of Hotspur's defiance since the scene began, but does he begin the scene showing this anger and at this cause?

My point in referring to the question of Henry's anger is not to discuss a particular performance solution, but to draw attention once more to the way in which the audience is being bombarded with unsettling invitations to temporal realignment. There are of course many different performance arcs that can be cut through this scene, but even if the actor plays something like anger in the opening lines, the anger shown at the end must be different both in tone and attribution than at the beginning. The effects are not crude, but they are numerous and have a cumulative destabilizing effect, no matter how the scene is performed. In this brilliant opening, we experience history-making by negotiating a series of subtle jolts in which origin and experience, purpose and event, past and present are continually, simultaneously realigned.

About the scene that follows, it might well be said that the transition to Falstaff and the tavern provides the most famous contrast in all Shakespeare—so famous that nothing more need be said about it. But the perspective we are pursuing here suggests a significant point that seems to have been ignored. For it's not only that in 1.2. we are projected into the antitemporal holiday world of the tavern, or that we begin an alternating rhythm of high and low, but that we first see the tavern world—which, remember, is from the Elizabethan audience's point of view, the *familiar* one of a popular historical play, *The Famous Victories*—that we come to what is apparently this more familiar version only after the historiographically charged treatment of the opening scene.

So the tavern scene is both new and old at once, and the more unexpected first scene has set up a context in which this new/old scene must be weighed and appreciated. Today we know Shakespeare's play so well that it may seem to tick along all too smoothly between court and tavern. But for Shakespeare's original audience—and, I would suggest, for us in an optimal production—the dive to the tavern is vertiginous. These worlds are not going to be neatly insulated and kept apart, anymore than the irresponsible Hal and the heroic Hal are to be the utterly distinct personae of *The Famous Victories*. And the leaking of one world and one characterization and one attitude to time into another will be reinforced by our felt concern with Shakespeare's own historiographical problem—how to keep these two worlds, with their very different relations to event and situation, simultaneously before us, how to hold onto both these conflicting truths about experience in the forward rush of time?

I want to continue scene by scene just once more, because the next scene, 1.3, is a very good example of how Shakespeare presents political struggles as contests in history-making, struggles over and with history. The King begins harshly:

> My blood hath been too cold and temperate
> Unapt to stir at these indignities
> And you have found me. . . .
>
> (1.3.1-3)

The anger—whose origin seemed curiously veiled when we encountered it in the first scene—is now produced or reproduced by Henry as a well-managed effect.

We watch not the King's anger but its use and political significance. Then we move on to a battle of historical descriptions (all versions of "how the quarrel between Hotspur and the King came about,") ending when Worcester redescribes Mortimer and Richard's history in order to convert Hotspur into a rebel. The most interesting description in the scene is of course Hotspur's brilliant narrative of the effeminate courtier who pestered him at the battlefront, but the key point about this narrative is that it has no political effect, except to make Hotspur attractive.

Here and elsewhere, Hotspur fails to grasp the difference between telling a good story and making history. All his narratives have a curiously *literary* quality, which I associate with their remoteness from the political; they tend to break off from the historical into the legendary. They do not carry their weight as parts of a sophisticated struggle for power, though they are exercises of personal charisma. That charisma of course has a political potential; Henry fears it and Worcester knows how to manipulate it. But Hotspur confuses history with what he calls "chronicle," which he sees as part of a permanent literary canon, a stable repository of truth:

> Shall it for shame be spoken in these days,
> Or fill up chronicles in time to come,
> That men of your nobility and power
> Did gage them both in an unjust behalf . . .
> To put down Richard, that sweet lovely rose,
> And plant this thorn, this canker,
>   Bolingbroke?
>
> (1.1.3.168-74)

This response of course has been cynically elicited by Worcester from his excitable nephew. Those in the audience who have been following Shakespeare's version of the story since *Richard II* know it is not so simple as that.

It's not easy to make historical drama feel like the reality of historical action, to organize a narrative and yet render the complexities of the uncertain political moment. But Shakespeare finds ways in *Henry IV* to make even this difficulty contribute to the destabilizing texture I've been discussing. Hal's famous "I know you all" soliloquy calls attention to Shakespeare's elegant solution of a narrative problem, keeping Hal's hands clean and his story clear, though at the possible expense of some verisimilitude. Similarly, Henry's "But this our purpose now is twelvemonth old" may suggest that he has yielded to the demands of exposition, again by sacrificing some probability. But the most interesting use of this tension has to do with the large-scale organization of Part One.

To explain this, one must first recognize that the most common oversimplification of historical analysis is the pattern most natural to drama. One might call it the "single-climax pattern." It views history as a version of the simplest private drama—the biorhythm of tension-climax-release. It's a story we like to tell about all kinds of life, including public life. It's what makes elections so satisfying to follow, at least when your side wins. Unlike, say, following the other events in the news, all the tensions go in one direction and are resolved thrillingly in a single day. This pattern also enjoys the advantage of being the simplest shape that will lend itself to the effective disposition of large theatrical forces. In *1 Henry IV* this pattern leads to Shrewsbury.

From the first, everything presses toward the climactic encounter on the battlefield. Shrewsbury offers the apperance of a simple test of political morality: is the character in question doing what's necessary to win? Hal yes, Falstaff no, Hotspur not enough. Characters are seen orienting their own sacrifices or self-indulgences toward that climax. The conduct of the play itself becomes a metaphor of government—the plot, like Harry, triumphs and orders all our feelings, however varied. We would like to linger with Falstaff and Hotspur, but we need to move on. Nevertheless, the variety and the profusion of slight slidings, delays, and doublings under the arc of the plot point to the truer complexity of history. The single-climax model, for all the pleasure we get out of it, is inadequate, except as a usefully deceptive metaphor, a politically inspired fiction.

The immense clarity of Hal's rescuing the king and defeating Hotspur in one prolonged *aristeia* is undercut, and not only by the figure of Falstaff, with his own narrative and parody of Hotspur's death. All the preparations for battle, with their emphasis on calculation, betrayal, and spin-doctoring, give us a different angle on the history we are watching from that of the "long hour by Shrewsbury clock"—Falstaff's phrase, we remember, for a fight that never happened in a time that never was. Behind the scenes in which the noble son articulately rescues the noble father, we are aware of the hidden drama of numbers in which, among other things, Hotspur's father silently betrays his son.

These slidings grow more pronounced in the Second Part. Remember I'm concerned here not with irony as such, with the puncturing of legends or propaganda, but with a kind of bifocalism, which takes many forms, including the play with and against the single-climax pattern. It's actually something between bifocalism and binocularism, since it produces neither unresolvable alternatives nor seamless depths. Its effect, in any case, is to reinforce the sense of what I've been calling "history-making." In *2 Henry IV*, one of the most notable examples of this bifocalism is the relation of the two parts themselves.

Much has been written about this relation, almost all of it in terms of an historical question about Shakespeare—what did he intend in writing a sequel and when, in the history of writing Part One, did he start to intend it? I would like to suggest that Part Two provokes such concerns because, in its relation to the first part, it fosters the impression of time being stopped and moving on at the same time.

Part Two continues narratively out of Part One, but in many ways it seems to be retelling the same story. Are we advancing or going over familiar territory? Are we moving ahead or marking time? We find ourselves in a curiously suspended moment, as if we had stepped back to Part One and were hanging there waiting for Henry to die, while at the same time the rebellions of Part One were being acted again. This of course is partly a requirement of the sequel genre, but this sequel seems to go further, to incorporate this aspect of sequelhood into its own texture, to make a dramatic point out of what today we would call its "belatedness."

Hal seems palpably to be marking time while he waits for the play to make its now familiar stops on his journey to legitimation. Playing a joke on Falstaff, Northumberland's defection, the reconciliation with the King—haven't we seen all this before, faster and younger and funnier? It's a virtuosic achievement, to give the audience what it has expected from Part One and yet to get on with the history—to fill up what seemed like a tiny space left over after Shrewsbury with an equally long historic narrative, and the resultant structure accomplishes many things. But one of them is to heighten our sense of history as a perpetual readjustment of the relation between now and then. Even the most important new character in Part II, who has no source either in the chronicle or in the structure of Part One—Justice Shallow—is most vivid as a narrator and re-narrator of the past, a past of inconsequential pastimes placed in a dim prepolitical backward before the crises of Richard II's reign, when Mowbray and Gaunt were merely names on the lips of would-be fashionable gentlemen.

One might remember, too, how scenes from the life of Richard II—scenes we never quite get to see in *his* play—are re-narrated in both parts of *Henry IV*. Especially dwelt on are moments when Bolingbroke and Richard appear in succession:

> Thou that threw'st dust upon his goodly head
> When through proud London he came sighing on
> After th'admired heels of Bolingbroke,
> Criest now, "O earth, yield us that king again."
>
> *(2 Henry IV,* 1.3.103-6)

And always the concern is with the realignment of present and past, with reinterpreting the past to gain political advantage in the present.

Probably the most striking reminder, however, of how the narrative relations between present and past can constitute the very material of political action comes at the beginning of *2 Henry IV:*

> Open your ears, for which of you will stop
> The vent of hearing when loud Rumour speaks?
>
> (Induction, 1-2)

I wonder if justice has been done to the boldness, the strangeness of this extraordinary choice on Shakespeare's part—to begin his sequel with Rumor. And there's perhaps no moment stranger, more puzzling than when Rumor suddenly interrupts himself:

> But what need I thus
> My well-known body to anatomize
> Among my household?
>
> (20-22)

We are addressed as rumor's household, a slightly aggressive note of intimacy. But why is the theater, in particular, the home of rumor? There are several possible answers, all important for Shakespeare's treatment of history. First, it may have to do with the appetite of any theatrical audience for intimate knowledge. Furthermore, rumor sets up a curious glancing relation with the factual information it purportedly conveys—it seems unusually close to the fact by virtue of its vividness and unofficial provenance, but distant from it by virtue of its unreliability. It reminds us of a gap even as it deceptively, pleasingly appears to leap it. It thrives on a gap of representation, which is also a gap of time.

There is also the matter of rumor's speed. Rumor spreads from an event with legendary rapidity, faster, it sometimes seems—and certainly seemed in Shakespeare's day—than any other mode of communication. Indeed in preelectric times, rumor had an exemplary metaphysical function rather like that of the speed of light since Einstein. It reminds us that even apparent instantaneity involves a gap. There is an event, a radiation of rumor from it, and out of that radiation, after an interval, needing interpretation, it reaches us.

We will return shortly to the specifically theatrical aspect of rumor, but first more needs to be said about rumor's historical and political significance. In *2 Henry IV,* rumor is acknowledged as a material fact of history, to be evaluated and wielded with care by the hopeful politician. Perhaps rumor is most emphatically connected both to high politics and historical narration at the beginning of act 3. There, Henry despondently imagines what it would be like to read "the book of fate" in which historical events could be seen before they happen. This reminds him of Richard's prophecy that has rung through the Henriad:

> "The time will come that foul sin gathering head
> Shall break into corruption"—so went on
> Foretelling this same time's condition
> And the division of our amity.
>
> (3.1.76-79)

Henry is haunted by Richard's uncanny prescience. Warwick, however, moves quickly to demystify this superstitious—and politically demoralizing—view by explaining Richard's prophecy in materialistic terms. Historical prediction, he says, is a form of rational political calculation:

> There is a history in all men's lives,
> Figuring the nature of the times deceased;
> The which observ'd a man may prophesy,
> With a near aim, of the main chance of things
> As yet not come to life. . . .
> King Richard might create a perfect guess
> That great Northumberland, then false to him,
> Would of that seed grow to a greater falseness. . . .
>
> (3.1.80-90)

With that, King Henry pulls himself together, and the discussion shifts into a practical mode—into an evaluation of rumor as a method of calculating rebel forces:

> *Henry.* They say the Bishop and Northumberland
> Are fifty thousand strong.
>    *Warwick.* It cannot be, my lord.
> Rumor doth double, like the voice and echo,
> The numbers of the fear'd. . . .
> To comfort you the more, I have receiv'd
> A certain instance that Glendower is dead.
>
> (95-103)

Glendower, who like Hotspur also confused legendary narration with history making, charisma with political effectiveness, is dead indeed. History is made by those who can grasp the real forces alive in the flux of the moment, who can swim, as Shakespeare will soon put it, in the tide that governs the affairs of men.

Warwick's rational analysis of rumor reminds us that the issue of representation as it is raised in these history plays is not merely an aesthetic or epistemological one. It goes to the root of politics itself, where understanding and action intersect. The serious political actor must fight to sift, control, manipulate a bundle of constantly changing representations. As Part Two draws to a close, Hal acts to take charge of his kingdom in an atmosphere that seethes with rumor, with a cynical understanding of the past that constitutes an expectation for his future. We watch him overcome rumor—he calls it "rotten opinion"—with his rejection of Falstaff.

Now, there is one more way in which the historico-political significance of rumor is connected to the phenomenology of theater and that is also foregrounded by *2 Henry IV*. This is the peculiar proximity that the play affords us to action as a source of rumor. In a number of places, but especially at the rejection of Falstaff, I think we feel—influenced as we are by busy preparations, public outcry, multiple audiences, crowds, and the general buzz around the rejection scene—that we're watching the propagation of rumor as if at the first microsecond after the big bang of an event. The play indeed makes us alert to an "event" as a letting loose of rumor in the world. Indeed, the release of rumor is itself an event, a political action, part of the fluid power-negotiation to which politicians must train themselves to respond and that history attempts to represent. Action becoming theater becoming action. The household of rumor, Shakespeare understands, has special though sobering access to the process of history.

Thinking about rumor brings home to us the intimate connection between history, action, and theater. Action always involves the representation of action, its performance, as it were, before an audience. Action in this sense requires an historical attention—an attempt at aligning then and now with an eye on the future. The historicizing attitude attempts to describe an event in vectored terms—what is the direction of this process? In this sense, the problem of history is entwined with the problem of action. And theater allows us peculiar access to this linkage of history and action, because in the theater we construe even the most entertaining moments into what we call the "action" of a play. If they don't construe—if we can't feel in some way that this activity is coming from somewhere and going someplace, they quickly bore.

Again, we must not confuse the issue here with the familiar poststructuralist critique of history. The point is not that, because representation involves a gap, history must involve one too, but rather that the existence of this gap means that we always live with one foot in the historical. Our experience is rooted in the ambiguous proximity of then, the "complex temporality" of now.[3] Every moment involves the construction of a past that gives the the present its momentary stability. *History,* in the usual sense of the term, magnifies the basic problems of representation, because it attempts to settle the past. But if we are, as we always are, shaken and wan with care, *getting* the past to settle is difficult and provisional. It involves finding a time, stabilizing a now from which to act. All action, but particularly what we think of as political action, involves a species of instantaneous critical historiography.

At this point, keeping the phenomenology of drama in mind helps with another problem, which might at first seem to blur the picture of history we have been developing. Isn't there, or at least wasn't there in Shakespeare's day, a concern with history as moral evaluation—not the vector of the scene, but its eternal valence? In the theater, however, all the moral revelations of a scene, interesting as they may be, are subject to the question: where does this new knowledge mean the action is going? Yes, in the prayer scene of *Hamlet* we are very interested to learn that Claudius is indeed guilty and would go to hell if killed at this moment, but above all we are aware that we must adjust to the fact that this confrontation, so appropriate to a fifth act, is being thrown at us in the third. Similarly, our inner debate about whether Henry IV is a good king is always involved with adjustments of the vector. We watch Prince John in Gaultree forest, and the instability of our response reflects our sense of the complexity, the bifocal/binocularity of the process that is unfolding—where does this mean England is going now? Not under the aspect of eternity, but contingently, as they all move on, rebels and rulers, winners and losers, schlemiels and schlemozzels, to further contingencies. The moral bouncing, like the temporal realignments, is something the play forces us not to sum up, but to live through. Not, that is, are the Lancasters in the right, or more right than wrong (though we are free to contemplate such questions) but, more pressingly, how are we to *grasp* this crosshatch of taint and virtue, of competing interests, of power and problem and maneuver? Grasping it is the truly *historical* activity, by which the reality of political action in the flux of time may be apprehended.

Where might we go from here? Is the texture I've been exploring an isolated feature of one pair of plays, or can we locate it in some larger Shakespearean universe? Let me conclude by suggesting, very briefly, a possible avenue for further exploration. The focus we have been observing—on rumor and realignment at the point of origin, the point somewhere beyond the shimmering border where *now* shades off into *then*—this focus may shed some light on one of Shakespeare's favorite motifs: let's call it "the theme of the Questionable Father."

Who is my father? Where and what is he? Is he, for instance, the self I must be true to, the absent judge who has deputized me, the forgiveness I must pray for, the law I must enforce, or is it escape, or is it rescue him from? Is he Father Christmas, our Father in Heaven, or more enigmatically, Father Time? From the ever-wandering Antipholus of Syracuse and his father Aegeon, to Hal and Henry IV, to Hamlet and Old Hamlet's ghost, to Angelo and the Duke of dark corners, we see young men (and young women, too, think of Viola and Portia) haunted, burdened and holding themselves back from action under the shadows of an obscurely fostering paternal or quasi-paternal imperative, a source of strength and weakness, of virtue and taint, a past that commands them but that they must uneasily redefine and re-present. Who are you, father? How did my sentence begin? Nay, answer me, stand and unfold yourself.

What we feel, then, on the scale of national history-making in *Henry IV* may have its counterpart, for Shakespeare, in the instabilities of personal life. Time, that pleases some, tries all, but not only because we grow old and die. It tests us because its structure is unfixed, depending on human action and negotiation. We move uneasily and irregularly within time, because time is the only dimension in which we can never locate ourselves with confidence. Which of . . . and here I want to conclude by quoting a phrase that brings my argument full circle by returning it to Shakespeare's method in the Henriad. It is the phrase he uses in his epilogue to close the circle at the end of the second tetralogy—to close, not with a smooth progression to a stable finish, but with yet another unexpected temporal disruption. For he concludes his chronicle of the rise of the House of Lancaster by making a bidirectional leap in time that, altering the meaning of its own sentence, abruptly cuts short the celebrations of Henry V's triumphs, harking back simultaneously to the promising theatrical past of Shakespeare's early days and to the tragic historical future of Henry's son, concentrating that movement into a surprising, bluntly impassive half-line:

> Small time: but in that small, most greatly
> lived
> This star of England. Fortune made his
> sword;
> By which, the world's best garden he
> achieved;
> And of it left his son imperial lord.
> Henry the Sixth, in infant bands crowned
> king
> Of France and England, did this king succeed;
> Whose state so many had the managing,
> That they lost France, and made his England
> bleed:
> Which oft our stage hath shown.
> (*Henry V,* epilogue, 5-13)

Very likely some of the original dramatic force of this passage came from flinging a late Elizabethan audience, which might well be concerned with the succession to an aging Queen, back to a bloody future. But certainly it continues to work, as so much in the Henriad does, by reminding us—forcing us to experience the fact—that to make history is to find oneself moving with dizzying, indeed frightening uncertainty in time. Which oft our stage hath shown.

*Notes*

[1] All Shakespearean citations are to *The Complete Signet Classic Shakespeare,* ed. Sylvan Barnet (New York: New American Library, 1972).

[2] David Kastan, *Shakespeare and the Shapes of Time* (Hanover: University Press of New England, 1982), 24.

[3] See Homi Bhabha, *The Location of Culture* (London: Methuen 1994).

---

Source: "History-Making in the Henriad," in *Shakespearean Illuminations: Essays in Honor of Marvin Rosenberg,* edited by Jay L. Halio and Hugh Richmond, University of Delaware Press, 1998, pp. 203-19.

# The Hybrid Reformations of Shakespeare's Second Henriad

## Maurice Hunt, *Baylor University*

Granted the late-medieval, early fifteenth-century settings of Shakespeare's *1* and *2 Henry IV* and *Henry V,* theater audiences are not surprised by the large number of references in these plays to Catholic practices and beliefs.[1] What has proved problematic for commentators is the coexistence of Catholic elements with explicitly Protestant traits in Shakespeare's characterizations of Falstaff, Henry IV, and Prince Hal/Henry V. In what follows, I argue that different forms of this mixture either impede or undermine these characters' attempts during the Second Henriad to reform themselves ethically and spiritually, at least until a noteworthy blend of Catholic and Protestant traits enables King Henry V in the aftermath of Agincourt to achieve a relatively successful transformation of character. Many plays of Shakespeare are syncretic in matters of religion: *Othello,* for example, reflects a mixture of Protestant predestinarian and Catholic voluntaristic theologies.[2] Having apparently committed himself in his portrait of Falstaff to satirizing the proto-Protestantism of his character's Lollard namesake Oldcastle, Shakespeare at the same time resolved to give the plays of the Second Henriad a late-medieval air, and hence perhaps found characterizations built upon a mixture of Catholic and Protestant components inevitable. What does not appear inevitable in the Second Henriad, however, is the sustained, thoughtful manner of the many critiques of Catholicism, Protestantism, and the Protestant Reformation entailed by the blend of antithetical religious traits within characters trying to reform themselves. Whether by accident or design, this dramatic phenomenon poses a question: how can individuals reform themselves in societies—like Shakespeare's—wherein Catholicism remained a strong threat to Protestantism by positing a contradictory route to reformation?[3] An answer to this question emerges from Henry's third and most successful attempt at reformation. Getting to that end involves starting with Falstaff.

Falstaff's name in original performances of *1 Henry IV* was Sir John Oldcastle, a conjuration of the Lollard martyr of the late fourteenth century. Shakespeare's apology concerning Falstaff in the Epilogue of *2 Henry IV*—"for Oldcastle died a martyr, and this is not the man" (29-30)—clinches the earlier proto-Protestant allusion in Hal's calling Falstaff "my old lad of the castle" in *1 Henry IV* (1.2.41).[4] Elizabethan godly Protestants thought of the Lollard Oldcastle, executed for his purported attempts to purify English Catholicism and make the Word of God more meaningful to the masses, as a saint.[5] Falstaff at one point tells Hal that the Prince is "indeed able to corrupt a saint" (1.2.90), ironically subverting the memory of the saint Oldcastle by reference to his namesake's tavern vices. Shakespeare's apology apparently grew out of objections that Oldcastle's Elizabethan heirs Sir William Brooke and his son Sir Henry Brooke raised over Falstaff's travesty of the Lollard's memory, including Falstaff's proto-Protestantism.[6] A detail strengthening Falstaff/Oldcastle's mock Protestantism involves his implication that men and women are to be saved by faith rather than merit (based on works): "O, if men were to be saved by merit," Falstaff comically says in an age when men *were* thought to be saved by merit, "what hole in hell were hot enough for [Gadshill]" (1.2.105-06). By Shakespeare's time, the dictum that Protestants primarily relied upon faith rather than merit acquired through spiritual good deeds had become a cliché;[7] Falstaff, skeptical about being saved by merit, seems to rely upon his self-serving belief—a Lutheran tenet attributed by Elizabethan Protestants to the Lollards—that undemonstrated faith alone can save him near the end of a hedonistic life void of good deeds.

This reading suggests that Falstaff's Protestantism occasionally mocks central tenets or practices of Reformation Protestants. Falstaff's Reformation Protestantism is implied by his pronouncement that " 'Tis for a man to labor in his vocation" (1.2.102-03). However, the "vocation" in which Falstaff "labors" is thievery. Falstaff misapplies Matthew 12:33 when he says of himself, during his playlet with Hal, "If then the tree may be known by the fruit, as the fruit by the tree, then peremptorily I speak it, there is virtue in that Falstaff" (2.4.423-25). If Falstaff were known by his fruits, he would be known by his deeds of theft. Gadshill tells the Chamberlain that the thieves, including Falstaff, "pray continually to their saint, the commonwealth, or rather not pray to her but prey on her, for they ride up and down on her and make her their boots [booty]" (2.1.80-83). Latent in this punning judgment lies a criticism of Reformation Protestants' rape of a sainted Catholic commonwealth, their plunder of its material wealth. The critique of Protestantism deepens when mention is made of these thieves' plan to waylay "pilgrims going to Canterbury with rich offerings" (1.2.123-24).

Finally, Falstaff could be any one of a number of Protestants walking the streets of Shakespeare's London when he says, "I would I were a weaver; I could sing psalms or anything" (2.4.130-31). (Concerning this utterance, David Bevington notes that "many psalm-singing Protestant immigrants from the Low Countries were weavers,"[8] and Clifford Davidson notes that the practice had caught on among craftsmen such as weavers in England.⁹) Falstaff's "Elizabethan" Protestantism unequivocally surfaces in his hypocritical condemnation of "whoreson smoothy-pates [who] do now wear nothing but high shoes and bunches of keys at their girdles" (*2 Henry IV* 1.2.37-39)—in other words, of short-haired Puritan tradesmen of the later sixteenth century who have bartered their faith for commercial success (something that Falstaff would doubtless be willing to do). Shakespeare's playing fast and loose with Falstaff's stage Protestantism, his making it of several ages and thus no age, makes it vaguely generic.[10] A combination of Oldcastle and the Elizabethan Puritan, Falstaff is both old-fashioned and progressive. On the one hand, the Falstaff constructed by Reformation allusions is too late to be a character actually involved in the events of Henry IV's late-medieval England. On the other, the Lollard Falstaff/Oldcastle comes too early to profit spiritually (even if he sincerely wanted to) from the godly Reformation of religion occurring in later Tudor times.

The paradox is evident in the play's dialogue. The first dialogue involving Falstaff that auditors hear in *1 Henry IV* stresses his out-of-dateness, his not knowing the time of day, his being out of sync with the natural sequence of day-night activities (1.2.1-12). He quotes the old-fashioned fustian tragedy, popular in the 1570s and 1580s but dated by the time of *Henry IV*'s production. And he styles himself as one of "Diana's foresters," a minion "of the moon" (1.2.25-26): epithets that link him with Queen Elizabeth, and thus tie him to an era which, in 1596-97, when *1 Henry IV* was first performed, was clearly drawing to a close. Told by Hal to hide behind the arras from the sheriff, Falstaff laments that he once had "a true face and good conscience . . . but their date is out" (2.4.496-98). All these lines emphasize Falstaff's belatedness, which will hinder his attempts to reform.[11]

Evidence exists that Falstaff's weak faith, usually deferred, at moments kindles a genuine desire to repent and reform himself. "Do I not bate? Do I not dwindle?" he asks Bardolph: "Why, my skin hangs about me like an old lady's loose gown. . . . Well, I'll repent, and that suddenly, while I am in some liking. I shall be out of heart shortly, and then I shall have no strength to repent. An I have not forgotten what the inside of a church is made of, I am a peppercorn, a brewer's horse" (3.3.2-9). These lines suggest that Falstaff's proto-Protestant faith is not nearly strong enough to overcome ignorance and vices that Elizabethan Protestants typically thought of as Catholic. Like any proto-Protestant before the advent of the sixteenth-century Reformation, which made the Bible available in national languages, Falstaff has imperfectly learned much of his religion from biblical tableaux woven into wall hangings hung in taverns and other buildings. Moreover, on the battlefield at Shrewsbury he mis-

uses the Catechism to rationalize cowardice, a dramatic fact made easier by the inability of late-medieval men to read it in English in an accessible book of devotions. Falstaff is a thief because he is idle, afflicted by a slothful, hedonistic temperament. If he in some minds represents Catholic England of Elizabethan Protestant imagination. Its dissolution is evident when Falstaff tells Prince Hal that "An old lord of the council rated me the other day in the street about you, sir, but I marked him not; and yet he talked very wisely, but I regarded him not; and yet he talked wisely, and in the street too" (1.2.82-86). Commentators on *1 Henry IV* have long recognized Shakespeare's ironic allusion here to Proverbs 1:20-24, to Wisdom which cries out in the streets but to deaf ears. If Falstaff is deaf to biblical wisdom, or if he misapplies it, the fault lies not wholly in his character but partly in his historical date. As a liar, thief, drunkard, and wencher, Falstaff stands in need of the personal spiritual reformation that Shakespeare's countrymen dated from the Protestant Reformation beginning in the first half of the sixteenth century. And yet, as noted above, Shakespeare problematically identifies Reformation Protestantism with thievery, with plundering the riches of a "sainted" commonwealth.[12] So portrayed, this flawed Protestantism does not promise his successful reformation of stereotypical Catholic vices, simply because it seems to participate in them.

It is difficult to overestimate Falstaff's need for spiritual reformation. The bankruptcy of Falstaff's saving faith symbolically reveals itself in *1 Henry IV* in the gross disproportion of his notorious debt—only "one halfpennyworth of bread" to two gallons of sack in the itemized tavern bill (2.4.529-36), only a symbolized bit of the transubstantiated body of Christ in relation to an excess of his blood. This grotesquerie underscores the enormity of Falstaff's addiction to pleasure at the expense of life-sustaining nourishment (that scrap of bread), an obsession that apparently keeps him from the true nourishment of the redemptive bread and wine served in church. By several devices, Shakespeare underscores Falstaff's great need of reformation for salvation. Falstaff perjures himself by claiming his lies about the Gadshill robbery are true, "or I am a Jew else, an Hebrew Jew" (2.4.177). Falstaff says that Bardolph's red nose constitutes his unconventional *memento mori:* "I never see thy face but I think upon hellfire and Dives that lived in purple; for there he is in his robes, burning, burning" (3.3.31-33). Yet in fact the postulated light in Bardolph's face serves Falstaff's vices, as a beacon at night between taverns (3.3.40-48). "God reward me for it!" (3.3.48), Falstaff blasphemously exclaims regarding the sack that he has bought Bardolph, and that he fancies fuels the nasal torch lighting his drunken way. "But thou art altogether given over," Falstaff pronounces of his crony, "and wert indeed, but for the light in thy face, the son of utter darkness" (3.3.35-38). A godly Protestant auditor, however, might object that the flame in Bardolph's face signifies that Bardolph is a "son of utter darkness."

Throughout the Second Henriad, Shakespeare offers no evidence for Falstaff's conclusive repentance and reformation. In *2 Henry IV,* Poins states that "the immortal part [of Falstaff] needs a physician, but that moves not him" (2.2.98-99). The Page touches on Falstaff's "Catholic" dissoluteness when with tongue-in-cheek he tells Hal that the company which Falstaff keeps in the tavern consists of members "of the old church" (2.2.142)—that is to say, "good fellows of the usual, disreputable fellowship."[13] Playgoers might think that the process of Falstaff's authentic reformation begins with his inclusion of himself in his condemnation of old men's addiction to the vice of lying, made as a preface to his clear-sighted correction of Shallow's history of his youth (*2 Henry IV* 3.2.302-26, esp. 302-03); but this apparently honest basis for personal reformation dissolves with his declaration that he will bilk Shallow out of his "land and beefs" (3.2.326-31). "If the young dace be a bait for the old pike, I see no reason in the law of nature but I may snap at him" (3.2.328-30), Falstaff concludes in proto-Darwinian fashion.[14]

The Hostess's memorable account of Falstaff's death confirms audiences' impression that this character never does get around to reforming himself until it is too late. On his deathbed, Falstaff may babble of green fields (*Henry V* 2.3.16-17), evidently his musings on Psalm 23; but the fact that he "babbles" suggests that his meditation is incoherent, directionless. He may cry out "'God, God, God!' three or four times" (2.3.18-19), but the Hostess urges him not to think on God (as though he will live). Falstaff may cry out against sack and women in his last hours (2.3.26-35), and, feverish ("rheumatic"), he may talk of the "Whore of Babylon" (2.3.37-38) (as though he seeks to die a proto-Protestant condemning a personification of the Church of Rome);[15] but all playgoers hear is evidence of his guilt, and nothing of his reformation. An upwardly progressive chill takes hold of Falstaff's body, and he dies before he can genuinely repent.[16] Thus the Hostess's blackly comic malapropism in her uttered conviction that dead Falstaff lies in "Arthur's bosom, if ever man went to Arthur's bosom" (2.3.9-10) aptly suggests the lack of Christian salvation in Falstaff's end.[17] Rather than to Abraham's salvific bosom, Falstaff in the Hostess's confused mind goes to that of a patron of secular chivalry.[18]

Shakespeare's characterizations of Prince Hal and later Henry V include and develop a critique of Protestant and Catholic traits working at cross purposes in the matter of personal reformation. As he formulates it, Hal's intended reformation appears mainly politico-ethical in nature. But Elizabethan playgoers would also have considered it spiritual, for Hal's misbehavior has consisted of those vices of the flesh that Reformers especially thought required amendment for the sinner's Christian salvation. This statement holds true even if a calculated Machiavellian program for personal political advancement wholly motivates Hal's performance of the sins of the tavern and brothel (a vexed question in the play), for the wages of sin are death, regardless of a person's reasons for sinning.[19]

Hal presents his calculated scheme for political advancement in *1 Henry IV* in his notorious soliloquy in act 1. In this speech, playgoers hear a stereotypical Protestant distrust of sloth, valuing of work, and curtailment of holiday.[20]

> I know you all, and will awhile uphold
> The unyoked humor of your idleness.
>
> . . . . .
>
> If all the year were playing holidays,
> To sport would be as tedious as to work;
> But when they seldom come, they wished-for come.
> (1.2.189-90, 198-201)

Hal's employment in his soliloquy of the pointedly Protestant word "reformation" (1.2.207) for his planned conversion strengthens the identification in his case of Protestantism and the distrust of sloth, valuing of work, and curtailment of holiday.[21] Hal intends his projected reformation of idleness and vice into a strict moral life to play its part in "Redeeming time" (1.2.211)—not simply the wasted time of the prince's life thus far but that of the exhausted, dissipated age of Henry IV's England as well.[22] Redeeming lost or wasted time by hours and days strictly regulated by religious meditation but mainly by serious productive work for the benefit of one's material life and soul as well as for the commonwealth became a hallmark of Tudor Protestantism.[23]

But even as stereotypical vices of Catholicism mingled with Falstaff's proto-Protestantism and could be said to undermine it, so a similar medley taints Hal's expression of his intention to reform and calls the authenticity of his resolution into question. "And like bright metal on a sullen ground," Hal states,

> My reformation, glittering o'er my fault,
> Shall show more goodly and attract more eyes
> Than that which hath no foil to set it off.
> (1.2.206-09)

With this language Hal conceives of his future reformation as mostly show with little substance, as something that, "glittering," superficially hides faults but dazzles beholders' eyes. Superficially, the metaphor makes Hal's purposed reformation a jewel glittering the better for the foil/fault set under it, enhancing it by contrast. But granted this primary meaning, playgoers can also hear the phrase "glittering o'er my fault," applied to Hal's intended reformation, as signifying that it will amount to golden, dazzling show deceptively covering his fault beneath it. Interpreted this way and considered within the matrix of the Second Henriad's Protestant critique of Catholicism, Hal's reformation conjures the image of those golden glittering icons of Catholicism, which by Elizabethan times had been smashed by reforming Protestants and condemned by their Elizabethan sons and daughters because their visual splendor once deceived gullible Christians.[24] Thus Shakespeare implicitly criticizes the idol worship latent in Hal's conception of his reformation. The taint of stereotypical Catholicism emanates as much from the articulated details of Hal's planned reformation as it does from the characterization of the degenerate idle holiday life that he expects to amend.

Shakespeare further undermines the Protestantism of Hal's intended reformation by involving him in Falstaff's and his cronies' thievery. Their robbery concerns—to repeat and slightly revise Gadshill's words—"pray[ing] continually to their saint, the commonwealth, or rather not pray[ing] to her but prey[ing] on her, for they ride up and down on her and make her their boots [booty]" (2.1.80-83). Hal joins the flawed Protestant Falstaff to pillage a "sainted" commonwealth, which was the later activity of Henry VIII, Cromwell, and their confederates, who sacked the Catholic monasteries.[25] The phrasing indicts Hal's projected reformation and its Protestant overtones.

As previously stated, Reformation Protestantism had by Elizabethan times made itself a religion of salvation by faith versus salvation by stereotypical Catholic deeds. Henry IV's planned medieval crusade against infidels in the Holy Land not only would divert armed aggression from himself to enemies outside England; leading troops there would also amount to a Catholic deed of penance for his part in Richard II's death. A different and more Protestant and modern kind of penitential deed constitutes Prince Hal's vehicle for his scripted reformation (at least in his account to his father of the projected process). Hal wishes that Hotspur's honors "were multitudes" (3.2.143), so that during calculated single combat with him he might

> make this northern youth exchange
> His glorious deeds for my indignities.
> Percy is but my factor, good my lord,
> To engross up glorious deeds on my behalf;
> And I will call him to so strict account
> That he shall render every glory up,
> Yea, even the slightest worship of his time,
> Or I will tear the reckoning from his heart.
> This in the name of God I promise here.[26]
> (3.2.145-53)

By means of these savage deeds, Prince Hal "will wear a garment all of blood / And stain [his] favors in a bloody mask, / Which, washed away, shall scour [his] shame with it" (3.2.135-37). Hal's words certainly ring with vindictive anger, traceable no doubt to his intense frustration over hearing his father and others praise Hotspur at his expense. But his notion that washing slain Hotspur's blood from his face shall scour shame from his countenance suggests that this deed of combat represents an act of personal penance.

But this method of redemption gets called into question by the negative overtones that it acquires in act 4 of *1 Henry IV*. Hal's chosen war-like vehicle of reformation possesses overtones of Catholic iconolatry. Vernon tells Hotspur that armed Hal and his comrades appear

> All plumed like estridges, that with the wind
> Bated like eagles having lately bathed,
> Glittering in golden coats, like images. . . .
> (4.1.98-100)

Resembling "gilded statues" (Bevington's gloss of "images"),[27] Prince Hal and his followers appear like those Catholic icons hated by Reformers, gilt images of all show and no worth that encourage idolatry.[28] Hal's pronouncement near the end of *1 Henry IV* firmly clinches the association in the Second Henriad between a glittering exterior and falsehood. "For my part," he tells Falstaff, who claims single-handedly to have killed Hotspur, "if a lie may do thee grace, / I'll gild it with the happiest terms I have" (5.4.155-56). The Chorus of *Henry V* makes explicit a pun latent in Shakespeare's use of the word "gilt" throughout *1* and *2 Henry IV*. Richard Earl of Cambridge, Henry Lord Scroop, and Sir Thomas Grey of Northumberland—all three traitors to Henry V—have, according to the Chorus, "for the gilt of France—O, guilt indeed!— / Confirmed conspiracy with fearful France" (2.Chorus.26-27). Playgoers can read this identification of guilty falsehood and glittering gold back into most of the distinctive appearances of the Catholic-icon imagery of the Henry IV plays.[29] Idol-worship, regarded from a Reformation Protestant viewpoint, convicted worshipers of guilt by misleading them into a false faith.[30]

In part 1, Hal's projected reformation of character becomes convincing for King Henry IV not through any evidence of his son's saving faith but through Hal's chivalric deed of rescuing the king from Douglas's assault (5.4.39-58), which becomes Hal's unlooked-for act of filial atonement. Furthermore, once Hal has killed Hotspur and captured Douglas, he sets his prisoner free, ransomless, rather than executing him because

> His valors shown upon our crests today,
> Have taught us how to cherish such high
>   deeds
> Even in the bosom of our adversaries.
>
> (5.5.29-31)

Bloody deeds rather than evidence of inner faith or morality save an ethically questionable man's life in a case of double-standard justice (other traitors such as Worcester and Vernon are quickly put to death). Hal perhaps favors Douglas out of gratitude for the effect that his capture has had on the Prince's relationship with his father.

Granted the several ways by which Shakespeare invites auditors to question the nature of Hal's reformation in *1 Henry IV,* theater audiences are not surprised by his lapsing in *2 Henry IV* into his former, dissolute life of the street and tavern.[31] Disguising himself as a tavern waiter, sneaking back to the Boar's Head (thus violating a promise made to his father) simply to observe Falstaff ridiculously in love, Hal is interrupted, once he discloses himself to argue with Falstaff, by Peto, who tells him that Henry IV needs the reputed slayer of Hotspur, Falstaff, to quell the remaining rebels. "By heavens, Poins, I feel me much to blame," Hal confesses,

> So idly to profane the precious time
> When tempest of commotion, like the south
> Borne with black vapor, doth begin to melt
> And drop upon our bare unarmèd heads.
> Give me my sword and cloak. Falstaff, good
>   night.
>
> (2.4.360-65)

Prince Hal has fallen into his former prodigal way of living partly because Falstaff cleverly wrested from him the credit for killing Hotspur, the deed upon which Hal's scripted reformation depended for its long-term credibility.

If early fifteenth-century England, rent by rebellion and relatively hard economic times, is ever to become a nation reformed, then the reformation of its monarch would seem to be a necessary precondition or corollary of the event.[32] This precondition initially concerns the character of Henry IV rather than that of his son. That Henry IV wants to be known as a reformer king becomes apparent in part 1 when Hotspur admits that this monarch "takes on him to reform / Some certain edicts and some strait decrees / That lie too heavy on the commonwealth" (4.3.80-82). The specter of a morally unreformed Henry VIII haunted Tudor Reformers in their efforts to purify their national religion.[33] Henry VIII's lapses were particularly egregious, since in himself he had married the pope and monarch into a prototype of the Reformer king. King Henry IV foreshadows this prototype when he says of his calculated absences from the public eye, "Thus did I keep my person fresh and new, / My presence, like a robe pontifical, / Ne'er seen but wondered at" (3.2.55-57). When Prince Hal begs pardon of his father for his prodigal youth, Henry IV's weighty response, "God pardon thee!" (3.2.29), is simultaneously a totalitarian monarch's pronouncement and a priestly absolution from God the Father.

Nevertheless, in Henry IV's case the blend of spiritual and secular power in the monarch proves unstable. This king vacillates between playing the parts of God's ordained agent and God's victim, the latter a wretched man who suspects that God has bred his scourge out of his own blood in the form of a prodigal son who indirectly punishes him for crimes against Richard II (3.2.4-11). The man who would be a priestly monarch yearns to atone for his sins by means of a pilgrimage to the holy city of Jerusalem, and yet he dies in the Jerusalem room of Westminster Abbey, as though a punster deity were mocking him.[34] Certain episodes of *1* and *2 Henry IV* predictively rehearse the Reformation scenario of the absolutist monarch and pontiff confronting each other. Act 4, scene 4, of *1 Henry IV* shows Richard Scroop, Archbishop of York, busily planning to muster allies to defend himself from Henry IV should the other rebels fail at Shrewsbury. Like Popes Clement VII and Paul III as they faced Henry VIII, Shakespeare's Archbishop of York becomes an adversary of the English nation so that he might purge the realm of the moral diseases incurred by the ambitions of an absolutist monarch who would appropriate pontifical roles for himself (*2 Henry IV* 4.1. 41-87).

Thus Shakespeare gives playgoers the impression that, if Prince Hal is to become in some sense a Reformation monarch, he ought not to follow his father's example. Hal's personal reformation seems to occur authentically when he becomes king and accepts the Lord Chief Justice as his father. "The tide of blood in me / Hath proudly flowed in vanity till now," newly crowned King Henry V announces:

> Now doth it turn and ebb back to the sea,
> Where it shall mingle with the state of floods
> And flow henceforth in formal majesty.
>
> (*2 Henry IV* 5.2.129-33)

When Henry V coolly rejects the bloated image of his own former vices, Falstaff, he does so in language that suggests a just-completed personal reformation. "Presume not that I am the thing I was," he tells Falstaff, "For God doth know, so shall the world perceive, / That I have turned away my former self" (*2 Henry IV* 5.5.56-58). In this reforming vein, Henry V has banished his tavern companions from his presence "till their conversations [their behavior] / Appear more wise and modest to the world" (*2 Henry IV* 5.5.101-02). This personal reformation of Henry V appears to be the basis for claims that he is "a Christian king, / Unto whose grace our passion is as subject / As is our wretches fettered in our prisons" (*Henry V* 1.2.241-43). He is a ruler who, in the Chorus's estimation, invites his subjects to imitate the actions of "the mirror of all Christian kings" (*Henry V* 2.Chorus. 6).[35]

A stereotyped Catholic foil accentuates the Protestant nature of Henry V's second reformation of character in an apparently conclusive way. Ely marvels that Henry V could have quickly developed integrity while living dissolutely, but he finds precedence for the possibility in Nature:

> The strawberry grows underneath the nettle,
> And wholesome berries thrive and ripen best
> Neighbored by fruit of baser quality;
> And so the Prince obscured his contemplation
> Under the veil of wildness, which, no doubt,
> Grew like the summer grass, fastest by night,
> Unseen, yet crescive in his faculty.
> (*Henry V* 1.1.61-67)

"It must be so," Canterbury agrees, "for miracles are ceased. And therefore we must needs admit the means / How things are perfected" (1.1.68-70).[36] It was a Reformation Protestant—not a late-medieval Catholic Archbishop—who believed that "no miracles occurred after the revelation of Christ."[37] By the late sixteenth-century, belief in the continued occurrences of religious miracles had, in Protestant opinion, become a stigmal badge of Catholicism. With the Protestant subscription to the ceasing of miracles came a corresponding opportunity for self-fashioning, for the godly life of relative self-perfection. That this is Henry V's new life is the burden of the Archbishop's slightly earlier speech:

> Consideration like an angel came
> And whipped th' offending Adam out of him,
> Leaving his body as a paradise
> T'envelop and contain celestial spirits.
> (1.1.29-32)

Archbishop Canterbury's memorable metaphor of the functioning beehive (1.2.183-206) is no metaphor if such self-fashioning is possible, but a likely reality, for this self-perfection, even if relative, among a large portion of the citizenry and their magistrates, including their "emperor," would realize obedience in a harmoniously working commonwealth.[38] According to the Archbishop, honeybees

> have a king, and officers of sorts,
> Where some, like magistrates, correct at home;
> Others, like merchants, venture trade abroad;
> Others, like soldiers, armèd in their stings,
> Make boot upon the summer's velvet buds,
> Which pillage they with merry march bring home
> To the tent royal of their emperor,
> Who, busied in his majesty, surveys
> The singing masons building roofs of gold,
> The civil citizens kneading up the honey,
> The poor mechanic porters crowding in
> Their heavy burdens at his narrow gate,
> The sad-eyed justice with his surly hum
> Delivering o'er to executors pale
> The lazy yawning drone.
> (1.2.190-204)

A Reformation Protestant commonwealth could identify with this society, mainly because it celebrates the individually and socially redemptive benefits of proper work. The soldiers' war-work finds its justification in the "singing masons' " and "civil citizens' " transformations of their plunder into the commonwealth's foodstuffs and architecture. And while auditors might feel sorry for the plight of the heavy-burdened porters, reconsideration suggests that even this painful work, necessary to society, saves the laborers, for those who do not work die. By framing his picture of a commonwealth with "magistrates, correct[ing] at home" and a sober judge ordering a drone's execution, Canterbury underscores the justice of this world of work, wherein the emperor especially is "busy" in his majesty. Elizabethan Protestants would thus have found understandable the efficiency of the Archbishop's ruler, Henry V, by means of the Archbishop's flattering implication.

Despite these positive portrayals of Henry V's second, more authoritative reformation, troubling undercurrents swirl through it. For one thing, it—as previously mentioned—is crafted partly on the rejection of his former Falstaffian self: the Prodigal within him (*2 Henry IV* 5.5.56-59). The father in the biblical parable of the prodigal son (Luke 15:11-32) accepts the formerly profligate but now reformed younger son and blesses him. Since the prodigal Falstaff and Prince Hal's low-life companions have not reformed themselves, King Henry cannot be blamed for rejecting them until they give evidence of character reformation (5.5.66-71). But he can be blamed for the hypocrisy of terming Falstaff and his cronies the "misleaders" of his youth (5.5.64), for audiences of the Second Henriad know that, from the beginning, Hal cleverly allowed himself to be "misled" by Falstaff so that his purposed reformation would look better. Traces of an old, ethically troubling duplicity in Henry V's rejection of Falstaff beg the question of the complete honesty (or authenticity) of his second reformation.[39] If as a "model" Christian king Henry V controls his passions, the effect produced occasionally suggests an unpleasantly cold man.

Moreover, Shakespeare evokes aspects of the Tudor Reformation at the beginning of *Henry V* in order ironically to show King Henry subverting one of the Reformation's principal benefits. Appreciating this claim involves initially grasping certain correspondences between the life and times of Henry VIII and those of Shakespeare's Henry V. Shakespeare's countrymen could consider these parallels stronger than those between Henry IV and the great Tudor monarch. Both Henry V and Henry VIII were fond of disguising themselves to trick others. In 1540, Henry VIII disguised himself, traveled to Rochester, met the newly arrived Anne of Cleves, embraced and kissed her, talked with her, and then later, undisguised, returned to her.[40] Both kings warred against the French. "In 1513, as part of the propaganda campaign to justify his invasion of France, Henry VIII commissioned an English translation of Tito Livio's *Vita Henrici Quinti*. . . . Henry VIII took his model sufficiently to heart to ride about his rain-drenched camp in France, encouraging his soldiers on the night before they set out to engage the French."[41] Both personally participated in the siege of a French city (Henry V at Harfleur, Henry VIII at Boulogne). Like Henry V, Henry VIII mercifully killed no one after the besieged city had surrendered (4,000 Boulognese departed unharmed). Like Henry V at Agincourt, Henry VIII at Boulogne achieved a miraculous victory. In the first French attempt to retake Boulogne, which pitted 14,000 Frenchmen against 5,000 Englishmen, many French troops died with little English loss of life. Like Shakespeare's Henry V, Henry VIII thanked God for this apparent martial miracle and ordered a *Te Deum* to be sung.[42] Both kings were reformers of religion who executed men for corrupting it (Shakespeare's Henry V executes Bardolph for stealing a *pax*). Both kings had to contend with northern rebels, including the Percies (Henry VIII was confronted by the Pilgrimage of Grace in 1536-37). Finally, both Henry VIII and Henry V shared the same name: "To his people [Henry VIII] remained to the end 'Bluff King Hal'."[43]

Dramatic similarities in Shakespeare's portraits of Henry V and Henry VIII suggest that the playwright intellectually linked these monarchs and their reigns. Even as Shakespeare shows Henry V disguising himself in false identities to his advantage, so in the playwright's later *King Henry VIII* he shows this monarch entering *"habited"* as a shepherd in a masque to dance with an unsuspecting Anne Bullen and with impunity savor her physical beauty (1.4.65-109 and s.d.). Like Shakespeare's King Henry VIII, Henry V enjoys the privilege of uncannily knowing his enemies' plots against him. Concerning the imminent treason of Scroop, Cambridge, and Grey, Bedford says that "The King hath note of all that they intend, / By interception which they dream not of" (*Henry V* 2.2.6-7). This mysterious political foresight anticipates and resembles Shakespeare's Henry VIII's, when the later ruler with the assistance of Dr. Butts, from a superior hidden vantage point, sees Gardiner and members of the Privy Council mistreating the king's agent, Cranmer. Even as Henry VIII later providentially detects his favorite Wolsey's treachery, so Henry V's prescience discovers the homicidal plot of Scroop, "the man that was his bedfellow, / Whom he hath dulled and cloyed with gracious favors" (2.2.8-9). The association of the two Henrys in Shakespeare's mind accounts for the resemblance between Henry V's formulation of Scroop's Judas-like betrayal and Henry VIII's angry conception of Wolsey's sin. "What shall I say to thee, Lord Scroop," Henry V begins,

> thou cruel,
> Ingrateful, savage, and inhuman creature?
> Thou that didst bear the key of all my
>   counsels,
> That knew'st the very bottom of my soul,
> That almost mightst have coined me into
>   gold,
> Wouldst thou have practiced on me for thy
>   use.
>                                   (2.2.94-99)

Nowhere else in the Shakespeare canon but in *King Henry VIII* 3.2 does the betrayal of the most trusted, rewarded inner counselor of a king acquire these archetypal Luciferian connotations. Having read Wolsey's missent inventory of his wealth secretly acquired, often at the king's expense, and the Cardinal's letters to the Pope, wherein he promotes his own ambition, a disillusioned Henry rejects the man he had "kept . . . next [to his] heart" and leaves Wolsey to— in his own words—fall "like Lucifer" (3.2. 158, 372).

The relevance of events in the reign of Henry VIII for those in Henry V's memorably materializes after the Archbishop of Canterbury actually uses the historically charged word "reformation" to convey Henry V's revolution of character:

> Never was such a sudden scholar made;
> Never came reformation in a flood
> With such a heady currance, scouring faults;
> Nor never Hydra-headed willfulness
> So soon did lose his seat, and all at once,
> As in this king.
>                                   (1.1.33-38)

In the dialogue that follows this reconstruction, Shakespeare begs the question of the relationship between Henry V's acknowledged reformation and the fifteenth-century analogue of a defining event of the English Protestant Reformation: Henry VIII's appropriation of the Catholic Church's immense, mainly dormant wealth. In the play, Canterbury refers to the fact that Parliament currently considers passing a bill originally introduced during Henry VI's reign. Under it, Henry V would become the beneficiary of the largest part of more than one-half of the Church's English possessions. In Canterbury's words,

> all the temporal lands which men devout
> By testament have given to the Church
> Would they strip from us, being valued thus:
> As much as would maintain, to the King's honor,
> Full fifteen earls and fifteen hundred knights,
> Six thousand and two hundred good esquires,
> And, to relief of lazars and weak age
> Of indigent faint souls past corporal toil,
> A hundred almshouses right well supplied;
> And to the coffers of the King besides
> A thousand pounds by th' year. Thus runs the bill.
>
> (1.1.9-19)

Henry V, like Henry VIII after him, would profit personally from the conversion of Catholic wealth into thousands of new aristocratic entitlements that he could bequeath to secure loyalty as well as into an additional one-thousand pounds annually for the royal coffers. More important, the proposed dispossession of the Church will be justly beneficial, for a hundred new almshouses will be built from the proceeds of the rechanneled wealth (as though the Church has hoarded riches uncharitably). By promoting passage of the bill, Henry V can genuinely be styled a Christian king.

But the Bishop of Ely expects that King Henry will block the legislation, simply because he is "a true lover of the holy Church" (1.1.24). Concerning "this bill / Urged by the Commons" (1.1.71-72), Canterbury asserts that the new king "seems indifferent, / Or rather swaying more upon our part / Than cherishing th'exhibiters against us" (1.1.73-75). Essentially Canterbury bribes Henry V by privately offering him a sum of money greater than the Church ever at one time gave an English monarch (but certainly less than the wealth diverted to the king by the provisions of the pending bill) if he will wage war in France to reestablish the English claim to that throne (which Canterbury attempts to justify through a murky explanation of the Salic law).[44] (Actually, embedded in the Archbishop's earlier allegory of the beehive is the subtle argument that the emperor wages "foreign" war to plunder the enemy ["velvet buds"] for domestic foodstuffs and building materials. Were Henry V to hear this veiled rationale and respond to it by pillaging the French, the Church would need to give even less money to the monarch for domestic use.) Whatever the case, both Henry and Canterbury tacitly understand that the king's acceptance of the Archbishop's private offer effectively kills the Parliament bill. Thus Henry V neglects a great spiritual good—the hundred new almshouses that his championing the parliamentary reform might accomplish. In this respect, his behavior does not testify to the profound spiritual dimension of his personal reformation as reported by Canterbury and others. Like Henry VIII after him, Henry V opens himself to the criticism that Catholic wealth redirected to his own and other noble strongboxes mainly serves the ends of militant personal glory and material gain, acquired under the jingoistic aegis of public good.[45]

Nevertheless, in the latter acts of *Henry V,* identifiably Reformation Protestant traits surface in the king that more than compensate for (or supersede) earlier troubling behavior. King Henry abandons his questionable practice of Machiavellian policy to tell the Dauphin's herald Montjoy humbly that he has resigned himself and his cause to God, and he does so in words that eschew bragging for a repentant plain idiom:

> For, to say the sooth,
> Though 'tis no wisdom to confess so much
> Unto an enemy of craft and vantage,
> My people are with sickness much enfeebled,
> My numbers lessened, and those few I have
> Almost no better than so many French,
> Who when they were in health, I tell thee, herald,
> I thought upon one pair of English legs
> Did march three Frenchmen. Yet, forgive me, God,
> That I do brag thus! This your air of France
> Hath blown that vice in me. I must repent.
> Go, therefore, tell thy master here I am;
> My ransom is this frail and worthless trunk,
> My army but a weak and sickly guard.
> Yet, God before, tell him we will come on,
> Though France himself and such another neighbor
> Stand in our way.
>
> (3.6.142-58)

A spirit of Protestant Calvinism informs King Henry's repentance of vain speech and his conception of his earthly being as a "frail and worthless trunk." Regarded in this context, the following utterance from his later St. Crispin's Day speech rings authentically:

> By Jove, I am not covetous for gold,
> Nor care I who doth feed upon my cost;
> It yearns me not if men my garments wear;
> Such outward things dwell not in my desires.
>
> (4.3.24-27)

The adversity of suffering hardships in France has begun to refine Henry's character into figurative gold.

Moreover, Henry V's conviction that "Every subject's duty is the King's; but every subject's soul is his own" (4.1.176-77) squares with the historically later Protestant greater emphasis upon the Christian's individual responsibility for confirming his or her salvation by daily charities and godly behavior unmediated by either a priest or religious ritual. (Catholic doctrine admitted some penitential deeds unmediated by a priest or ritual, such as penitential combat, but their number was far fewer than the total possible under Protestantism.) In a Protestant spirit, Henry implies that no outside authority such as a monarch or an institutionalized Church can vouch for the purity or sin of a person's soul. Henry V's non-Catholic notion of individual responsibility for the health of one's soul derives from his recently matured sense of personal accountability for his soldiers' lives and the welfare of English citizens. Henry disguised as a common soldier has told Bates that the king's "ceremonies laid by, in his nakedness he appears but a man" (4.1.105-06). When Henry thus vigorously forswears worship of the idol Ceremony, his denunciation acquires the value of a Protestant vilification of a stereotypical Catholic trait:

> And what have kings that privates have not too,
> Save ceremony, save general ceremony?
> And what art thou, thou idol ceremony?
> What kind of god art thou, that suffer'st more
> Of mortal griefs than do thy worshipers?
> What are thy rents? What are thy comings-in?
> O ceremony, show me but thy worth!
> (4.1.236-42)

Henry V goes on to say that the idol Ceremony is basically a hollow god, attractive only in its superficial trappings.

Still, Henry's proto-Protestant reformation of character does not satisfy his anxious belief that he stands in need of certain Catholic rituals of penance. The night before the Battle of Agincourt, a worried King Henry V prays,

> Not today, O Lord,
> O, not today, think not upon the fault
> My father made in compassing the crown!
> I Richard's body have interrèd new,
> And on it have bestowed more contrite tears
> Than from it issued forcèd drops of blood.
> Five hundred poor I have in yearly pay
> Who twice a day their withered hands hold
>   up
> Toward heaven, to pardon blood; and I have
>   built
> Two chantries, where the sad and solemn
>   priests
> Sing still for Richard's soul. More will I do;
> Though all that I can do is nothing worth,
> Since that my penitence comes after all,
> Imploring pardon.
> (4.1.290-303)

Despite this and one other vestige of Catholicism (see below), a distinctly Protestant spirit animates Henry V's St. Crispin's Day oration/sermon, inspiring his outnumbered troops to perform Herculean feats of arms at Agincourt. The inspiration of Christians chiefly by means of a central sermon-like speech became identified with Reformation Protestantism. Understanding the proto-Protestantism of Henry V's "sermon" to his soldiers involves appreciating its non-Catholic message of a democratic leveling of hierarchical privilege delivered via Christian language and ritual. His speech can be considered a sermon partly because it is delivered on the feast day of St. Crispin and is focused on the two saints Crispin and Crispinian. It amounts to a sermon designed, through brilliant rhetorical means, figuratively to put the spirit of Christian martyrs into enervated, apprehensive English soldiers. (By contrast "Saint" Oldcastle's spirit never did inhabit and purify the mountain of flesh, Falstaff.) In keeping with this day of martyrdom, Henry urges English survivors of Agincourt to show later generations their scars (as though they were those of near-martyrs). Superficially, this behavior resembles Catholic relic-veneration. Nevertheless, the names of the "host"—the English soldiers (4.3.34)—shall then be "Familiar in [their] mouth[s]" (4.3.52), as though they formed a symbolic rather than transubstantiated salvific body that auditors will ingest (through the story of Agincourt retold).[46] In this context, the Communion chalice is recalled by the "flowing cups" in which the "host"— "Harry the King, Bedford and Exeter, / Warwick and Talbot, Salisbury and Gloucester" (4.3.53-55)—is "freshly remembered." Like the regularly repeated Last Supper-Communion story of salvation through Christ, the immortalizing narrative of English St. Crispin's Day shall, according to Henry, recur "From this day to the ending of the world" (4.3.58).[47] And like the story of Christ's redemption commemorated by the Host and cup of wine, Henry's celebrated miracle of St. Crispin's Day gains its authority and transmits it through the original shedding of blood. "For he today that sheds his blood with me / Shall be my brother" (4.3.61-62), Henry V asserts: "be he ne'er so vile, / This day shall gentle his condition" (4.3.62-63). Henry's words vaguely evoke both the language of Christ to the thieves on either side of the cross and the details of the Last Supper. Imitating the life and death of Christ/Henry radically transforms and elevates a devotee's identity.[48]

Certainly Henry V's extravagant imitation of Christ puts him at risk for the charge of blasphemy.[49] In fact, he could be accused of inviting his troops to idolize him. Nevertheless, the Protestant insistence that the process of salvation applies equally to the foot soldier as to the king, if each is elect, surfaces in Henry's willingness to shed his royalty to stoop and join soldiers who spiritually distinguish themselves through their martyr-like willingness to shed their own blood for England. A warmth has replaced within Henry V a certain coldness he displayed during earlier moments of extreme self-control, such as that of Falstaff's banishment. The St. Crispin's Day's "sermon's" leveling of aristocrats to make all men plain brothers becomes a Protestant feature of *Henry V* when Shakespeare artfully makes its opposite a Catholic practice: the Catholic French warriors' blood in the Constable's words may be "spirited with wine" (3.5.21), but that wine never gets figuratively transformed into an immortal brotherhood of blood because the French embody an aristocratic hauteur. This icy attitude informs the King of France's battle oration, the complementary antithesis of Henry V's St. Crispin's Day exhortation. His oration fails to invigorate because it is little more than a mechanical, snobbish catalogue of pedigrees:

> Up, princes, and with spirit of honor edged
> More sharper than your swords, hie to the
>   field!
> Charles Delabreth, High Constable of France,
> You Dukes of Orleans, Bourbon, and of Berri,
> Alençon, Brabant, Bar, and Burgundy,
> Jaques Chatillion, Rambures, Vaudemont,
> Beaumont, Grandpré, Roussi, and
>   Faulconbridge,
> Foix, Lestrelles, Boucicault, and Charolais,
> High dukes, great princes, barons, lords, and
>   knights,
> For your great seats now quit you of great
>   shames.
> Bar Harry England, that sweeps through our
>   land
> With pennons painted in the blood of
>   Harfleur.
> Rush on his host, as doth the melted snow
> Upon the valleys, whose low vassal seat
> The Alps doth spit and void his rheum upon.
> Go down upon him—you have power
>   enough—
> And in a captive chariot into Rouen
> Bring him our prisoner.
>
>                                  (3.5.38-55)

One might object that King Henry, despite his rhetoric of brotherhood, reveals a trace of the French king's class-consciousness when he reads the Agincourt English casualty-list:

> Edward the Duke of York, the Earl of
>   Suffolk,
> Sir Richard Keighley, Davy Gam, esquire;
> None else of name, and of all other men
> But five-and-twenty.
>
>                                  (4.8.103-06)

But before we accuse him of hypocrisy, we need to realize that he is reading a list of English dead prepared formulaically by someone else. The fact that Henry just before he reads the English casualty-list recites a note of French dead (4.8.80-102)—a note which begins with princes and nobles and descends through "knights, esquires, and gallant gentlemen" and that includes a catalogue of most of the aristocrats chanted by the French King—reinforces the impression that too much should not be made of his manner of naming English dead.

Henry V's possession of two qualities the French king lacks further suggests his more generous attitude toward slain English troops. The French king's image of his aristocrat warriors hurtling down upon Henry's army like alpine snow, burying valleys beneath, betrays two characteristics of the speaker fatal to his cause—his lack of empathy with his common mercenaries and French gentry (much of that "melted snow") and an extreme disdain for simple folk (the French aristocratic avalanche will "spit and void [its] rheum upon" a "low vassal seat"). Never uniting with the rank and file of his army, the late-medieval, feudalistic Catholic King of France goes down to defeat.

Henry's St. Crispin's Day speech thus becomes more Protestant through comparison with its Catholic complement. Furthermore, Henry's address to his troops gets associated with Protestant labor in the implicit contrast of Protestant work with Catholic idleness when Westmorland prefaces the speech by exclaiming, "O, that we now had here / But one ten thousand of those men in England / That do no work today!" (4.3.16-18). For the English, Agincourt's "feats" of war (4.3.51) will amount to work of a kind far different from the Catholic saying of beads or lighting of candles. Henry V echoes Westmorland's word "work" in a proto-Protestant spirit when he says, "We are but warriors for the working day. / Our gayness and our gilt are all besmirched / With rainy marching in the painful field" (4.3.109-11). Once again Shakespeare evokes the stage Catholic imagery of a glittering ("gilt") outside only to deny it; Henry's troops are muddied, appropriate for a Protestant "working day." Beginning with his act 1 soliloquy in *1 Henry IV* (1.2.198-201), Henry has from time to time characterized fighting as a holiday game; but on the eve of Agincourt the odds against the English, their weakened, unreinforced state, and the monumental significance of the impending battle make work rather than game combat's appropriate referent. Finally, unlike the precious bones in an often-sold Catholic reliquary, Henry's bones, if he is killed in battle, shall in his estimation yield the French little if they try to sell them (4.3.123-25); for since he clearly intends to die fighting rather than risk capture (4.3.124), they will be shattered by warfare and unsuitable for enshrinement.

Henry V's St. Crispin's Day "sermon," charged with Protestant overtones, works a miracle, the English victory at Agincourt with only twenty-nine English dead (three of whom are noblemen) to ten-thousand French dead (of whom sixteen hundred are mercenaries and the rest French nobility, knights, and "gentlemen of blood and quality" [4.8.80-106]). This miraculous preservation of English lives prompts Henry to exclaim, "O God, thy arm was here! / And not to us, but to thy arm alone, / Ascribe we all" (4.8.106-08). "Take it, God," he concludes, "For it is none but thine" (4.8.111-12).[50] "For miracles are ceased," the Archbishop of Canterbury proclaimed at the beginning of the play, "And therefore we must needs admit the means / How things are perfected" (1.1.68-70). As noted earlier, the belief that miracles ceased after the revelation of Christ was a major tenet of Reformation Protestantism. The miniscule loss of English life at Agincourt, incredible to reason, suggests that the age of miracles extends to encompass the fifteenth century. The paradoxical implication in the play *Henry V* is that leading a proto-Protestant life of faith and service can result in a "Catholic" miracle. In typically syncretic fashion, Shakespeare melds aspects of two religious systems held to be antithetical during the later sixteenth century. In *All's Well That Ends Well,* Lafew, commenting on Helena's wondrous cure of the King of France's fistula, states, "They say miracles are past, and we have our philosophical persons to make modern and familiar things supernatural and causeless. Hence is it that we make trifles of terrors, ensconcing ourselves into seeming knowledge when we should submit ourselves to an unknown fear" (2.3.1-6). If we are to judge by this passage, Shakespeare, around the turn of the sixteenth century, became interested in a doctrine of miracle in which the hand of heaven could be seen, a doctrine that—by Lafew's logic—deserved admiration rather than intellectual inquiry into its causation.

Henry V's awareness that he has been the recipient of a divine miracle completes an arguably authentic personal reformation. The unprecedented difference between the English and French loss of life at Agincourt, rationally incomprehensible, by itself resolves Henry's long-harbored doubts about God's blessing upon him and his monarchy and completes the character revolution attempted previously but unsuccessfully. Concerning the English victory with so little loss of life, Henry commands,

> And be it death proclaimèd through our host
> To boast of this or take that praise from God
> Which is his only.
>
>             (4.8.114-16)

Henry's accomplished reformation can be detected in his humble response to his lords' desire "to have borne / His bruisèd helmet and his bended sword / Before him through" London:

> He forbids it,
> Being free from vainness and self-glorious pride,

> Giving full trophy, signal, and ostent
> Quite from himself to God.
>
>             (5.Chorus.17-22)

Nevertheless, playgoers must reconcile certain ungodly behaviors of Henry's during the Battle of Agincourt with his definitive reformation. Henry indicated then that at moments of group violence he could still become passion's slave. In the heat of conflict, he cruelly orders every English soldier to kill his prisoners because "the French have reinforced their scattered men" (4.6.36-38). Gower believes that Henry gives this savage order in retaliation for the French killing of the English boys guarding the luggage (4.7.1-10). But Henry in the text of the play gives his bloody order before he learns of this fact (thus making it appear prior), and he does so simply because French reinforcements suddenly threaten the English position. After Henry becomes aware of the slaughter of the helpless English boys, he snarls, "I was not angry since I came to France / Until this instant" (4.7.54-55). "Besides, we'll cut the throats of those we have," he ominously pronounces regarding the French prisoners in his entourage, "And not a man of them that we shall take / Shall taste our mercy" (4.7.62-64).[51] But in Shakespeare's staging these prisoners never are killed, for the French capitulate before the deed can be done.

Significantly, the above-described vestiges of the Old Adam surface in Henry *before* his learning of the miracle of Agincourt refines the remaining dross of sadism and pride into golden humility. King Henry V manifests this ultimately refined humility in his fifth-act wooing of Princess Katharine. An attractive directness and modest plainness of speech color his courtship.[52] "Thou wouldst find me such a plain king," he tells Katharine, "that thou wouldst think I had sold my farm to buy my crown. I know no ways to mince it in love, but directly to say, 'I love you' " (5.2.126-29). Henry forswears bragging (5.2.140); he at last admits to having a "saving faith" within him (5.2.204). Henry V's reformation is as complete as it could ever get in the short time remaining to this "star of England" (Epilogue, 6). One senses that Henry V will rarely—if ever—again be Machiavellian in quite the same cold way that he was, but rather will be a sincere, plain-speaking man who constitutes the implicit ideal of Elizabethan Shakespeare comedies such as *Love's Labor's Lost.*[53] Admittedly, a trace of the calculating Henry appears in his having made Katharine his "capital demand, comprised / Within the fore-rank of [the peace] articles" (5.2.96-97). Certainly the word "capital" carries economic overtones, the notion being that Henry has commodified his future queen. A political expediency, however, does not preclude, on the level of the heart, his sincere love-suit. The "good heart" (5.2.163) that Henry has purified within himself might be a model for Protestants sitting or standing in the Globe Theater. The Catholic "miracle" that at a decisive moment helps to cleanse this heart is Shakespeare's subtle argument for Protestant tolerance of Catholics and their dogma in a darkening world of religious division.[54]

*Notes*

[1] Shakespeare takes considerable pains to imbue the late medieval setting of *1 Henry IV* with the spirit of Catholicism. King Henry's reference to the Crucifixion "fourteen hundred years ago" (1.1.26) and his desire to be Christ's soldier in a crusade to wrest the Jerusalem sepulcher from pagan hands date the events of the play in the Catholic early fifteenth century. In this context, the speech's thirty-three verses evoke Christ's apocryphal age at his martyrdom, a fitting allusion in light of Henry's latent wish to atone for his guilt for Richard II's murder. The Catholic atmosphere of *1 Henry IV* thickens with Westmorland's mention of "Holy Rood Day" (1.1.52), references to pilgrims going to Canterbury, repeated oaths such as Prince Hal's "By'r Lady" (2.4.295), and Falstaff's phrase *"ecce signum!"* ("behold the proof!")—familiar words from the Mass—spoken with reference to the miracle of his claim of escape from a dozen enemies (2.4.162-67). The Catholic elements of *Henry V* are strongly emphasized by Stephen M. Buhler, " 'By the Mass, our hearts are in the trim': Catholicism and British Identity in Olivier's *Henry V*," *Cahiers Élisabéthains* 47 (April 1995): 55-70.

All quotations of Shakespeare's plays in the present article are from *The Complete Works of Shakespeare*, ed. David Bevington, 4th ed. (New York: Longman, 1997).

[2] See Maurice Hunt, "Predestination and the Heresy of Merit in *Othello*," *Comparative Drama* 30 (1996): 346-76, esp. 367-69.

[3] Huston Diehl, in *Staging Reform, Reforming the Stage: Protestantism and Popular Theater in Early Modern England* (Ithaca: Cornell University Press, 1997), demonstrates through a fine analysis of selected Shakespeare and early modern English plays (she omits the plays of the Second Henriad) that Elizabethan and Stuart playwrights subtly used "the theater to dramatize the divisive conflicts and explore the central religious controversies of the Reformation" (64).

[4] For an exhaustive study of the *Henry IV* plays as an exploration of the Oldcastle issue, see Alice-Lyle Scoufos, *Shakespeare's Typological Satire* (Athens: Ohio University Press, 1979). Also see Gary Taylor, "The Fortunes of Oldcastle," *Shakespeare Survey* 38 (1985): 85-100; E. A. J. Honigmann, "Sir John Oldcastle: Shakespeare's Martyr," *"Fanned and Winnowed Opinions": Shakespearean Essays Presented to Harold Jenkins*, ed. John W. Mahon and Thomas A. Pendleton (London: Methuen, 1987), 118-32; and Kristen Poole, "Saints Alive! Falstaff, Martin Marprelate, and the Staging of Puritanism," *Shakespeare Quarterly* 46 (1995): 47-75, esp. 48-53. Taylor's argument that editors ought to substitute Oldcastle's name for Falstaff's in the texts of the Second Henriad has been effectively rebutted by Jonathan Goldberg, "The Commodity of Names: 'Falstaff' and 'Oldcastle' in *1 Henry IV*," in *Reconfiguring the Renaissance: Essays in Critical Materialism*, ed. Jonathan Crewe (Lewisburg: Bucknell University Press, 1992), 76-88.

[5] For the story of Sir John Oldcastle as it was told and retold throughout the sixteenth century, "with different ideological emphases," see Annabel Patterson, *Reading Holinshed's "Chronicles"* (Chicago: University of Chicago Press, 1994), 130-53.

[6] Summaries of Falstaff's "Puritanical" traits of character and speech appear in J. Dover Wilson, *The Fortunes of Falstaff* (Cambridge: Cambridge University Press, 1943), 15-35; Poole, "Saints Alive! Falstaff, Martin Marprelate, and the Staging of Puritanism," 65-69; and especially in Grace Tiffany, "Puritanism in Comic History: Exposing Royalty in the Henry Plays," forthcoming in *Shakespeare Studies* 26 (1998). Generally critics such as Poole who notice these traits endorse the opinion that "the person of Falstaff is in and of himself a parody of the sixteenth-century puritan" (54). See, for example, Harold Bloom, *Ruin the Scared Truths: Poetry and Belief from the Bible to the Present* (Cambridge: Harvard University Press, 1989), 84. Usually critics regard this purported parody of Puritanism in Falstaff as Shakespeare's jibe at the Protestantism of the Lollard Oldcastle's late Elizabethan heirs William and Henry Brooke; See, for example, Robert J. Fehrenbach, "When Lord Cobham and Tilney 'were at odds': Oldcastle, Falstaff, and the Date of *1 Henry IV*," *Shakespeare Studies* 18 (1986): 87-101. Poole, however, regards the supposed Puritan satire generated by Falstaff's character as "perfectly in keeping with the tenor of the anti-Puritan literature of the late sixteenth century, especially the anti-Marprelate tracts and the burlesque stage performances of the Marprelate controversy, which frequently depicted Puritans as grotesque individuals living in carnivalesque communities" (54). Tiffany's article offers a stimulating alternative interpretation of the relevance of the Marprelate controversy to Falstaff's characterization.

[7] See Christopher Hill, "Protestantism and the Rise of Capitalism," *Change and Continuity in Seventeenth-Century England* (Cambridge: Harvard University Press, 1975), 81-102, esp. 82-83.

[8] Bevington, *The Complete Works of Shakespeare*, 779.

[9] Davidson made this comment in response to an earlier version of my present essay.

[10] Phyllis Rackin, in *Stages of History: Shakespeare's English Chronicles* (Ithaca: Cornell University Press, 1990), points out that "[t]he recognition of anachronism, in fact, was a basic premise of Reformation thought. No longer seen as an institution unchanged from its beginnings, the contemporary church was contrasted with the church as it had been before centuries of Roman Catholic corruption had polluted it" (10). Playgoers' recognition of anachronisms in Falstaff's stage Protestantism, by this logic, would betray the fact that they lived in the sixteenth century.

[11] This specific linkage of Falstaff and Queen Elizabeth has been noted by Barbara Hodgdon, *The End Crowns All: Closure and Contradiction in Shakespeare's History* (Princeton: Princeton University Press, 1991), 156.

[12] Despite Gadshill's claim that "There's money of the King's coming down the hill; 'tis going to the King's Exchequer" (*1 Henry IV* 2.2.53-54), Shakespeare nevertheless suggests that Falstaff and his cronies rob not the agents or officers of Henry IV's treasury but certain members of a commonwealth (one "sainted" because "preyed/prayed" upon). The persons plundered are termed "Travelers" (2.2.78 s.d.), apparently the Canterbury pilgrims and "traders riding to London with fat purses" (1.2.122-25) whom Poins first specified as the subjects of the robbery.

[13] Bevington, *The Complete Works of Shakespeare*, 819.

[14] This is essentially the interpretation of Edward I. Berry, "The Rejection Scene in *2 Henry IV*," *Studies in English Literature* 17 (1977): 201-18, esp. 202.

[15] This is the reading of both Roy Battenhouse, "Falstaff as Parodist and Perhaps Holy Fool," *PMLA* 90 (1975): 32-52, esp. 46-47; and Paul M. Cubeta, "Falstaff and the Art of Dying," *Studies in English Literature* 27 (1987): 197-211, esp. 206.

[16] By the logic of his symbolic role, Falstaff cannot reform himself. "I know thee not, old man," King Henry V says near the end of *2 Henry IV*, "Fall to thy prayers" (5.5.47). As the Old Man, the Old Adam, Falstaff's typology precludes his reformation. See D. J. Palmer, "Casting off the Old Man: History and St. Paul in *Henry V*," *Critical Quarterly* 12 (1970): 267-83, esp. 268-69.

[17] Falstaff's successful death-bed reformation is argued—unconvincingly, I believe—by J. Dover Wilson in his edition of *Henry V* (Cambridge: Cambridge University Press, 1947), 142; and by Christopher Baker, "The Christian Context of Falstaff's 'Finer End'," *Explorations in Renaissance Culture* 12 (1986): 68-86, esp. 81-83. Also see Michael Platt, "Falstaff in the Valley of the Shadow of Death," *Interpretations: Journal of Political Philosophy* 8, no. 1 (1979): 5-24.

[18] Concerning the Hostess's "Arthurian" judgment (2.3.9-10), Baker claims that Falstaff's "final end, resting in 'Arthur's bosom,' is the return of a comic prodigal to the father he sought to escape" ("The Christian Context of Falstaff's 'Finer End'," 70-71).

[19] For decades, a critical debate has focused upon the question of whether Prince Hal is truly debauched and thus genuinely in need of reformation or whether he play-acts the debauchee and so needs not actual reformation. An overview of the debate is provided by Kristian Smidt, *Unconformities in Shakespeare's History Plays* (Atlantic Highlands, N. J.: Humanities Press, 1982), 107-10, who joins those critics who think Hal is debauched and needs reformation (108). The critic to focus most recently the question of Hal's reformation, Jonathan Crewe ("Reforming Prince Hal: The Sovereign Inheritor in *2 Henry IV*," *Renaissance Drama* 21 [1990]: 225-42), concludes: "The most influential current arguments deny that there is any substantive reform of Prince Hal's character. These are the arguments, associated mainly with Stephen Greenblatt, which insist on Hal's role-playing, and hence on the theatricality of his madcap character and of the metamorphosis he effects in *1 Henry IV*" (225). (The reference to Greenblatt concerns "Invisible Bullets," *Shakespearean Negotiations: The Circulation of Social Energy in Renaissance England* [Berkeley and Los Angeles: University of California Press, 1988], 21-65, esp. 40-65.) My claim that accomplished vice taints the actor of it even when the sin is play-acted nevertheless entails some kind of true reformation of the subject. More important, my demonstration that Hal/Henry V possesses several faults that are not play-acted more conclusively argues for the refinement of his character and represents an alternative to Crewe's thesis concerning Hal's reformation of parricidal (oedipal) feelings.

[20] An excellent analysis of this soliloquy different from mine appears in Harold Toliver, "Workable Fictions in the Henry IV Plays," *University of Toronto Quarterly* 53 (1983): 53-71, esp. 59.

[21] Unquestionably Shakespeare's contemporaries used the modern term "reformation" for not only the Protestant revolution of purified manners but also for the cultural upheaval identified with King Henry VIII, his ministers, and the Church of England's displacement of Roman Catholicism. Subsection 3b under the noun 'Reformation' in the *OED* includes this illustrative usage taken from Fregeville's *Reformed Politicke*: "To the end to ship the Clergy in the League, they wer perswaded, that within six moneths the Reformation should be vtterly extinguished." In 1544, John Bale concluded that Sir John Oldcastle "dyed at the

importune sute of the clergye, for callynge vpon a Christen reformacyon in that Romyshe church of theyrs . . ." (*Brefe Chronycle concernynge the Examinacyon and death of the blessed martyr of Christ syr Johan Oldecastell the lorde Cobham* [Antwerp, 1544], fol. 53ʳ, as quoted in Poole, "Saints Alive! Falstaff, Martin Marprelate, and the Staging of Puritanism," 48).

[22] See J. A. Bryant, Jr., "Prince Hal and the Ephesians," *Sewanee Review* 67 (1959): 204-19; and Paul A. Jorgensen, " 'Redeeming Time' in Shakespeare's *Henry IV*," *Tennessee Studies in Literature* 5 (1960): 101-09.

[23] See Maurice Hunt, *Shakespeare's Labored Art* (New York: Peter Lang, 1995), 6.

[24] For excellent histories of the Protestant iconoclastic impulse during the English sixteenth century, see John Phillips, *The Reformation of Images: Destruction of Art in England, 1535-1660* (Berkeley and Los Angeles: University of California Press, 1973), 1-156; Margaret Aston, *England's Iconoclasts* (Oxford: Clarendon Press, 1988), vol. 1; *Iconoclasm vs. Art and Drama,* ed. Clifford Davidson and Ann Eljenholm Nichols, Early Drama, Art, and Music Monograph Series, 11 (Kalamazoo: Medieval Institute Publications, 1989); James R. Siemon, *Shakespearean Iconoclasm* (Berkeley and Los Angeles: University of California Press, 1985), 30-75; and Diehl, *Staging Reform, Reforming the Stage,* 9-39. Also see John N. King, *English Reformation Literature: The Tudor Origins of the Protestant Tradition* (Princeton: Princeton University Press, 1982), 144-60.

[25] See, for example, John Stow, *The Annales of England* (London: Ralph Newbery, 1592), 965-66. Stow, after composing the grim list of priests and citizens executed by Henry VIII in 1535 for resisting edicts of the Reformation, and after remarking that the king seized 376 religious houses, £32,000 worth of Church land, and more than £100,000 of church moveables in 1536 alone, indicts Henry VIII by writing: "It was (saith mine author) a pitifull thing to heare the lamentation that the people in the countrie made for [the expelled priests, monks, and nuns]: for there was great hospitalitie kept among them, and as it was thought more than ten thousand persons, masters and seruants had lost their liuings by the putting downe of those houses at that time" (966). For a commentary that applies to Henry VIII's and Edward VI's theft of moveable church property, see Eamon Duffy, *The Stripping of the Altars* (New Haven: Yale University Press, 1992), 379-503.

[26] Alexander Leggatt, in *Shakespeare's Political Drama: The History Plays and the Roman Plays* (London: Routledge, 1988), remarks that Prince Hal's language of commerce in this speech undercuts the honor he would win by killing Hotspur (94). It thus serves to suggest that this deed will ultimately fail as a vehicle for Hal's reformation.

[27] The idea of images "Glittering in golden coats" could possibly involve auditors' recollections of painted figures on tombs or even silhouettes in memorial brasses, which when polished look golden. Nevertheless, the next verse of the passage—"As full of spirit as the month of May" (4.1.101)—would discourage funereal evocations, a likelihood that would allow the play's late-medieval setting and its accumulating Catholic allusions to suggest to Elizabethans the notion of Catholic icons.

[28] Siemon demonstrates that "certain features of Shakespearean drama can be profitably understood as refracting the struggles over imagery and likeness that vexed post-Reformation England and found their most obvious expression in the various phenomena of iconoclasm" (*Shakespearean Iconoclasm,* 30). This critic posits in Shakespeare's *Henry V* "an iconic counterforce to the 'iconic tableaux' that the play repeatedly forms" (101).

[29] In a similar vein, David Scott Kastan makes this comment on *Richard II* 2.1.294 ("Wipe off the dust that hides our scepter's gilt"): "The homonymic pun on 'gilt' signals that the symbols of rule in Bolingbroke's usurping hand have been 'derogated,' we might say, tainted and diminished by the process of their attainment. 'Gilt' has been tarnished by Henry's guilt" ("Proud Majesty Made a Subject: Shakespeare and the Spectacle of Rule," *Shakespeare Quarterly* 37 [1986]: 471).

[30] The overtones of idol-worship inherent in Vernon's portrait of Hal and his comrades "Glittering in golden coats, like images" reappear more strongly when Falstaff at the end of *2 Henry IV* falls to his knees before recently crowned Henry V and exclaims, "My King! My Jove! I speak to thee, my heart" (5.5.46). Nevertheless, Falstaff's motives of flattering Hal at this moment to gain preferment render these overtones doubtful.

[31] A different explanation of Hal's backsliding, one that involves his progressively "wise" unlearning of certain of his own and other characters' ideas, is given by F. Nick Clary, "Reformation and Its Counterfeit: The Recovery of Meaning in *Henry IV, Part One*," *Ambiguities in Literature and Film,* ed. Hans P. Braendlin (Tallahassee: Florida State University Press, 1988), 76-94, esp. 80-84.

[32] The relatively hard economic times depicted at times in the Second Henriad (e.g., *1 Henry IV* 2.1.1-32) may have been a misleading fabrication of Shakespeare's. Fifteenth-century England appears to have been more prosperous than the preceding century and, in many

ways, more so than the following one. See Charles Phythian-Adams, *Desolation of a City: Coventry and the Urban Crisis of the Late Middle Ages* (Cambridge: Cambridge University Press, 1979).

[33] Stories of Henry VIII's repeated fornication and adultery, for example, accentuated the harshness of the 1539 Parliamentary enactment that priests were to have no wives and that priests with wives were to divorce them, or else they were to forfeit their goods and benefices and after a second warning suffer death (Charles Wriothesley, *A Chronicle of England During the Reigns of the Tudors,* 2 vols. [Westminster: J. B. Nichols, 1875], 1:102-03). Cf., however, Stephen Gardiner's treatise *On True Obedience* and Richard Rex's commentary on its portrait of a reformed Henry VIII in *Henry VIII and the English Reformation* (New York: St. Martin's Press, 1993), 24-25. Nevertheless, Henry VIII forfeited forever among European kings and princes his reputation of being a humane prince when he beheaded Sir Thomas More and Bishop John Fisher. His savagery during the spoilage of Thomas Becket's shrine—he had the saint's bones burnt, the ashes mingled with earth, and the composite shot from a cannon—shocked Europeans even more than his notorious beheadings (H. Maynard Smith, *Henry VIII and the Reformation* [London: Macmillan, 1962], 101-02).

[34] See Robert J. Fehrenbach, "The Characterization of the King in *1 Henry IV*," *Shakespeare Quarterly* 30 (1979): 43-50, esp. 44.

[35] Harold Jenkins, in *The Structural Problem in Shakespeare's "Henry the Fourth"* (London: Methuen, 1955), 24-25, set a precedent by maintaining that "in the two parts of *Henry IV* . . . there are not two princely reformations but two versions of a single reformation. And they are mutually exclusive." Jenkins resolved this contradiction by claiming that it is typical of folkloric narrative and that Shakespeare's method in this instance is theological allegory (and thus folkloric). Nevertheless, Edward I. Berry, in *Patterns of Decay: Shakespeare's Early Histories* (Charlottesville: University Press of Virginia, 1975), articulates "the inconsistencies in Hal's double reformation" (109). By positing three main attempts at personal reformation on Hal's part, I necessarily subscribe to Berry's qualifier.

[36] Moody E. Prior, in *The Drama of Power: Studies in Shakespeare's History Plays* (Evanston: Northwestern University Press, 1973), 321-24, understands King Henry V's apparent reformation as described by Ely and Canterbury as a doffing of the Old Man and a putting on of the New Man according to descriptions in Ephesians 4:22-24, John 3:6-7, and certain passages in the *Book of Common Prayer.*

[37] The quotation represents Bevington's gloss. For documentation of the idea, see Keith Thomas, *Religion and the Decline of Magic* (New York: Charles Scribner's Sons, 1971), 80, 107-8, 124-25, 128, 203, 256, 479, 485, 490, 577-78, 643. Samuel Harsnett's *A Declaration of Egregious Popish Impostures* (1603), a text informing Edgar's bogus miracle in act 4, scene 4, of Shakespeare's *King Lear,* amounts to a contemporary endorsement of the Protestant position concerning ceased miracles.

[38] Jonathan Dollimore and Alan Sinfield, however, argue for the metaphorical status of the notorious beehive of *Henry V* by asserting that it is the construct of a part of society claiming to be the whole ("History and Ideology: The Instance of *Henry V,*" in *Alternative Shakespeares,* ed. John Drakakis [London: Methuen, 1985], 212-13).

[39] Jonas A. Barish, in "The Turning Away of Prince Hal," *Shakespeare Studies* 1 (1965): 9-17, argues that Henry V's rejection of Falstaff amounts to a self-rejection, a turning away a more honest compassionate self. In the king's casting off Falstaff, "we find the exigencies of the history play leading to a 'reformation' that we can only feel as a dehumanization" (14).

[40] Wriothesley, *A Chronicle of England,* 1:109-10.

[41] Peter C. Herman, "'O 'tis a gallant king': Shakespeare's *Henry V* and the Crisis of the 1590s," in *Tudor Political Culture,* ed. Dale Hoak (Cambridge: Cambridge University Press, 1995), 204-25, esp. 220.

[42] Wriothesley, *A Chronicle of England,* 1:149-52.

[43] Smith, *Henry VIII and the Reformation,* 16.

[44] Dollimore and Sinfield note that during the latter part of Queen Elizabeth's reign, "[t]he Church resented the fact that it was expected to help finance foreign wars, but in 1588 Archbishop Whitgift encouraged his colleagues to contribute generously towards resistance to the Armada on the grounds—just as in *Henry V*—that it would head off criticism of the Church's wealth" ("History and Ideology: The Instance of *Henry V,*" 216). For the text of the Archbishop's opinion, see his May 1588 circular letter to England's Bishops quoted by John Strype, *The Life and Acts of John Whitgift,* 3 vols. (Oxford: Clarendon Press, 1822), 1:525.

[45] Jeffrey Knapp, in "Preachers and Players in Shakespeare's England," *Representations* 44 (Fall 1993): 29-59, places the conniving of the Bishop of Ely and the Archbishop of Canterbury at the beginning of *Henry V* within the context of Shakespeare's career-long negative depiction of episcopal militarism and claims that in this episode King Henry V disturbingly absorbs "both the bishops' money and their piety" (39).

⁴⁶ See Joel B. Altman, in " 'Vile Participation': The Amplification of Violence in the Theater of *Henry V*," *Shakespeare Quarterly* 42 (1991): 16, for the observation that "Shakespeare enables the audience of *Henry V* to participate Harry the King just as the drawers, companions, and—more distantly—the people of England participated the Prince in the two parts of *Henry IV*. Which is to say that now they share him in both a sacramental and a poetic—and most needfully, a political—way. In partaking him—to conflate Hooker and Jonson—in digesting him, turning him to nourishment, and growing 'very *Hee*'," Shakespeare's audience assimilates Henry's aggression, bravado, and savagery.

⁴⁷ Remarking that *Henry V* "has strong affinities with mainstream English Protestant conceptions of the eucharist" (33), Knapp investigates the broad symbolic function of the eucharistic *pax* in the play ("Preachers and Players in Shakespeare's England," 41).

⁴⁸ For other analyses of the St. Crispin's Day speech, see Norman Rabkin, *Shakespeare and the Problem of Meaning* (Chicago: University of Chicago Press, 1981), 45-46; and Lawrence Danson, "*Henry V*: King, Chorus, and Critics," *Shakespeare Quarterly* 34 (1983): 34-35, 42.

⁴⁹ Knapp comments that "Harry's gift to his soldiers . . . is to liberate a holy-seeming communion from the confines of the church to the open battlefield" ("Preachers and Players in Shakespeare's England," 41). There, physical violence and secular chivalry, rather than a godly ritual, become King Henry V's vehicle for his communion of brotherhood.

⁵⁰ Hodgdon states that "through Henry's pious insistence that God won the battle [of Agincourt], he reconnects himself to the mystifying force of divine right that was Richard II's special province" (*The End Crowns All*, 188).

⁵¹ The dramatic problem of King Henry V's double, apparently inconsistent order to cut French prisoners' throats has been well focused and analyzed by Joanne Altieri, "Romance in *Henry V*," *Studies in English Literature* 21 (1981): 223-40, esp. 223-24, 236; by Berry, *Patterns of Decay*, 109; and by John W. Blanpied, *Time and the Artist in Shakespeare's English Histories* (Newark: University of Delaware Press, 1983), 267.

⁵² Cf., however, Paola Pugliatti, "The Strange Tongues of *Henry V*," *The Yearbook of English Studies* 23 (1993): 235-53, esp. 243.

⁵³ Maintaining that all the aspects of Henry V's character form an integrated whole, Carol M. Sicherman, on the other hand, in " 'King Hal': The Integrity of Shakespeare's Portrait," *Texas Studies in Literature and Language* 21 (1979): 503-21, argues that Hal's maturation in the use of formal language, from prose to progressively more controlled and formal verse, charts his reformation (508).

⁵⁴ Knapp concludes that "the anticlericalism of the history plays may suggest Shakespeare's longing for a religion that would be inclusive and pacifist rather than elitist and bellicose; but the last of these plays [*Henry V*] seems to leave us with the image of a communion broadened from clergy to congregation, from paxes to peace, only when first sanctified by violence" ("Preachers and Players in Shakespeare's England," 41-42).

---

Source: "The Hybrid Reformations of Shakespeare's Second Henriad," in *Comparative Drama*, Vol. 32, No. 1, Spring, 1998, pp. 176-206.

# Shakespeare's Historicism: Visions and Revisions

## Paola Pugliatti, *University of Florence*

Paul Valéry said that history is "the most dangerous compound that the mind's chemistry has ever produced," because "it can justify whatever one wishes."[1] This article is an attempt to deal with several aspects of this dangerous compound: that of Shakespeare's historical plays themselves and the things they seem and have seemed to justify; that of the interpreters and their histories and the things they have justified through their readings of Shakespeare's historical plays; and finally the things that our revised perception of history, of historiography, and of historicism may still justify as regards Shakespeare's historical writings.

The debate about Shakespeare's English history plays has been in many ways peculiar. What makes the difference, of course, is the conviction that when dealing with political texts one has direct access to "reality"—indeed, to several levels of reality and even of "truth": on the one hand we have the impression—or conceive the illusion—that tackling Shakespeare's re-creation of English history may provide a key to "his" evaluation of both past and contemporary political issues, and that Shakespeare's reading of past events may shed light on the political "self-image" of Elizabethan England; on the other hand those texts have been used, more or less consciously and more or less explicitly, in order to extrapolate from them those "vibrations" that may serve as a comment on the interpreter's own historical and political context. The two perspectives are often inextricably entwined, for it is certainly impossible, and maybe not even desirable, for the interpreter to ignore those vibrations. But there is probably a feeling, looming behind all criticism of the history plays, that dealing with history means not merely interpreting but also restoring and reviving, a feeling deriving from the fact that history is not simply knowledge; for "memory," as Jacques Le Goff says, "is the locus of power."[2]

It is perhaps this sense of power that has marked the debate with rhetorical features that are not to be encountered in other areas of Shakespeare criticism. The debate has been cohesive, dialogic, and highly controversial. Refuting, confuting, disproving have been and still are its privileged procedures and have been employed throughout the century: initially to demolish the theories of the disintegrators; then, following this, but also as a consequence of it, to prove that those plays were worth the effort of reading and writing about; then to dismantle the prejudice that negated their political relevance; then to argue opposing views as regards Shakespeare's attitude toward a number of crucial political issues; and finally to challenge the "orthodox" representations established by the "old historicism."

The controversial character of the debate has also determined the need for frequent assessments: *Shakespeare Survey* published the first one, by Harold Jenkins, in 1953[3] and a sequel by Dennis Burden in 1987.[4] That the eighties was a decade in which the need was felt for new recapitulations of the "state of the art" is shown by at least two other essays: one by Graham Holderness, entitled "Agincourt 1944: Readings in the Shakespeare Myth," published in 1984,[5] and the other by Robin Headlam Wells, entitled "The Fortunes of Tillyard: Twentieth-Century Critical Debate on Shakespeare's History Plays," published in 1985.[6] Reading these assessments, one has the distinct impression that their aim is less that of reviewing a fragment of critical history than that of revising the various different contexts that determined those readings. The last link in the chain of recapitulations is, to my knowledge, a chapter entitled "Appropriations" in *Shakespeare Recycled* by Holderness, published in 1992.[7]

The liquidation of previous views established as "orthodoxies" led to the discovery of certain "prophet-critics," some of whom had long remained unheard. The most frequently quoted of those prophets is Richard Simpson who, as early as 1874, wrote an essay entitled "The Politics of Shakespeare's Historical Plays,"[8] confuting Pollard's view that Shakespeare's plays had nothing to do with politics thirty years before Pollard formulated it.[9] But not all of these prophets are universally recognized. Certain critics of the sixties and seventies, more or less organically connected with New Criticism, like Wilbur Sanders, Norman Rabkin, A. P. Rossiter,[10] and others, who formulated the first substantial corrective to Tillyard's vision, are considered anticipators by Headlam Wells, who argues that they were the first "to re-examine the dramaturgy of the histories in the light of the conflicts and paradoxes of Renaissance intellectual life",[11] while Holderness reads their rejection of Tillyard's *method* (which he believes was "in its cultural moment radical and controversial") as a backward step, in that it was founded on "a more traditional notion of art as free from the constructions of ideology or the determinants of history."[12] Their "prophetic" credentials are thus only in part recognized today, although their idea of "duplicity" and "ambivalence," which is, with variations, at the root of their cultural and textual readings, has been resumed in a number of essays[13] in the wake of Puttenham's definition of "Amphibology" as a figure conveying distinct political implications.

Another of the features that have characterized the debate is the fact that it has focused on the elaboration of a number of sharp oppositions that have been argued for or against in the light of new theses, of new historical inquiry, of new intertextual findings, of new critical attitudes, of new ideological requirements, of new sociological stipulations. These are the most important of these oppositions: Shakespeare did/did not celebrate the Tudor myth: he was/was not affirming the "natural" necessity of order and degree; his plays mirror the official political doctrines of his time/his plays, by showing contradictions and conflicts, undermine the official political doctrines of his time/his plays, albeit showing contradictions and conflicts, are functional to the diffusion of the official political doctrines of his time and therefore to a legitimation of power; Shakespeare's vision is providential/Shakespeare's vision is secular; the view of time represented is cyclical and recursive/the view of time represented is linear and progressive (this last statement has the advantage of a possible mediation in the following form: the view of time represented is both cyclical and linear, for it reproduces the Christian view, which is both liturgical and teleological). One or the other of the two poles of these oppositions is obviously argued for to support a more general prior conviction, namely: Shakespeare was a conservative/Shakespeare was a radical.

Despite the antithetical nature of the positions argued—or maybe precisely because of it and of the necessity to liquidate once and for all the contrasting position—one encounters in this area of Shakespeare criticism, with a frequency that is unequaled elsewhere, the use of certain simple rhetorical devices aimed at producing the impression that what the critic is saying is the very final word on the matter. Ironically, the ideas these expressions aim to naturalize are precisely those that have subsequently been most radically dismantled. It is possible to cite a whole series of such rhetorical gestures:

> *It is not likely that anyone will question my conclusion that* Shakespeare's Histories with their constant pictures of disorder cannot be understood without assuming a larger principle of order. (Tillyard, 1944)

> *Surely Shakespeare was voicing the prayer of the men of good will in all England* when he was writing the words with which Richmond closed [*Richard III*]. (Campbell, 1947)

> *What can be no longer doubted is that* . . . the history plays have a collective unity. (Jenkins, 1953)

> *There can be no doubt that* Shakespeare believed in this almost universally-accepted concept of degree, and that he accepted the Tudor doctrines of absolutism and passive obedience. (Ribner, 1957)

> *It is beyond doubt that* Shakespeare was acquainted with the "Tudor myth." (Riggs, 1971)

> *I find no compulsion to doubt that* Shakespeare intended to show his audience . . . the control of Providence . . . over the world of the plays. (Reed, 1984)[14]

The debate has also had some paradoxical aspects: these have concerned mainly the treatment of Tillyard's book. No work has been so vehemently confuted, none has been more radically demolished; nevertheless, all readings of the history plays take us back to Tillyard as a necessary starting point. As a consequence, the book's detractors have made its fortune much more than its admirers.

All those who have produced assessments of the debate have been aware of its epochal character; and it is obvious that, by reading their reconstructions, one may recover the views, urgencies, and interests that have prevailed in certain periods of our history. Writing in 1953, Harold Jenkins remarked that "the nineteenth century's conception [of the history plays] was in some measure the result of its predilections," and that "for an age of industrial and commercial progress, of growing nationalisms and imperialist expansion, the most obvious thing about Shakespeare's history plays was their expression of a national spirit." Jenkins was writing in a moment when the influence of Tillyard was still pervasive; he therefore does not remark what in due time would become a commonplace, namely, that although there are neither any open declarations of patriotism nor any explicit praise of the ideology of order, Tillyard's book is as much a creature of the postwar national spirit as Wilson Knight's drum-beating essay "The Olive and the Sword," which Jenkins defines as "an exploitation [of the history plays] to provide a 'gospel' for Britain at war."[15] More recently, Graham Holderness has brilliantly shown how, in the atmosphere of patriotism, national unity, and the pride deriving from victory—a post-Agincourt or maybe rather a post-Armada atmosphere—the Shakespeare myth coherently produced the apparently cool and historically detached study of Tillyard, Wilson Knight's "The Olive and the Sword," and Olivier's film *Henry V;* in other words, how "Shakespeare" was put, in those years, "at the service of the national war effort."[16]

There was no victory to celebrate in the sixties and in the seventies. In the cold war years the tendency was towards "duplicity," "ambivalence," "undecidability"; the politics of our readings were determined by the influence of the absurd, the methods of "New Criticism," and the "vertical" readings generated by various kinds of formalism, together with interest in the metatheatrical self-exposure of the dramatic mechanisms.[17] In sharp contrast to Tillyard's view, what Shakespeare communicated in those years to the critical mind was mainly his plays' recalcitrance, their unwillingness to fit into an imposed pattern, their resistance to one-sided interpretations. In the words of Graham Holderness, Shakespeare was, in those years, "a free-thinking liberal judiciously suspicious of all ideology."[18]

What follows is recent history. The suggestions of the last two decades have mainly concerned new ways in which the representation of the past should be constructed. The kind of image we now have of the English Renaissance is not, in itself, entirely new: as I said before, the monolithic image that had been constructed by the "old historicism" à la Tillyard had already been dismantled by certain books published in the sixties and in the seventies. What is comparatively new are the means and procedures we now opt for, the kind of broadly intertextual connections we establish, and, of course, the kind of standpoint from which all textual and contextual stipulations derive, which implies a redrawing of the boundaries between the literary and the nonliterary. But although the kind of negotiations we are now engaged in are certainly more fascinating and stimulating than those suggested either by the monologic visions imposed by the "old historicism" or by the self-explanatory and self-contained analyses of the new critics, the revised kind of historicism on which they are grounded is not necessarily or not always more convincing.

What has remained unchanged, however, is the (explicit or implicit) evaluation of Shakespeare's own political stance. As Annabel Patterson has remarked:

> Since the early nineteenth century, conservative critics from Coleridge to Tillyard, democrats like Hazlitt or Whitman, and even contemporary Marxist critics like Terry Eagleton, if they agree in nothing else, have converged in believing that Shakespeare accepted without question contemporary social hierarchy and its self-justification.[19]

The substance of Coleridge's and Tillyard's view has been repeated again and again, although in different, less straightforward, and therefore more intriguing and captivating ways. In order to account for the discrepancies or ambivalence that neither Coleridge nor Tillyard remarked—or wanted to remark—but that were one of the leitmotivs of the new critics, the recent evaluations provided by the neo-Marxist schools[20] tend to subsume all discrepancies and contradictions under the category of legitimating strategies, readable only as supportive of order. In short, as Holderness says,

> Old and new historicism, . . . despite their obvious antagonisms, appear to be in agreement that the relationship between dominant and subversive ideologies within the plays is implicitly an orthodox or conservative one.[21]

There are few exceptions to the tendency to argue, albeit in new ways, the traditional view of Shakespeare as conservative patriarch and as champion of the status quo. These have all been accompanied by a revival of interest in a series of traditional categories. The most important of these revivals is a return to various forms of author retrieval, which have been suggested in different contexts.[22] Writing in favor of a new form of biographism, Stanley Fish affirms that "we have not done away with intention and biography, but merely relocated them." He adds that reading is always biographical reading, and that only the "sources and agencies" may have different specifications.[23] Leah Marcus suggests that we should recuperate certain tools of the "old historicism," and primarily "an idea called the Author's intent or putative intentionality," although in the revised form of a construct.[24] Other critics have shown uneasiness regarding the disappearance of the author, although they reveal at the same time a certain embarrassment regarding a new definition of this encumbering substance. Graham Holderness declares that it would be unwise "completely to surrender . . . the genuine possibility that some kind of authorial 'mastery' shaped those texts and shaped them deliberately to particular ends."[25] More recently, Richard Wilson has affirmed that "the logical end of historicism is the nature of the author . . . as a cultural construct determined by the representational practices of a particular historical era."[26]

In some cases, although the issue of the author's opinions remains in the background, conclusions about some features of the plays' stance are drawn: the aspect which has most frequently been argued is the absence, in the history plays, of a providential design.[27] What is discussed in other cases are issues halfway between politics and historiography, such as Shakespeare's consciousness of the "pastness of the past" (Holderness) or his "perspectivism" (Hattaway).

In a few works, the return to the author has again led to an attempt to capture directly in the texts Shakespeare's personal political stance and opinions. Surprisingly, in this attempt "old" and "new" historicisms coincide. Patterson plainly states that she will ignore "the avant-garde proscriptions against talking about authors and intentions,"[28] and she develops arguments to redeem Shakespeare from the old charge of antipopulism. Patterson was writing in 1989, and she was then right in mentioning as "proscriptions" things that now seem to have regained a right of citizenship. Even more explicit is Michael Hattaway who, in an article entitled "Rebellion, Class-Consciousness, and

Shakespeare's *2 Henry VI*," has claimed that "at the beginning of his career Shakespeare was not a pillar of the establishment . . . but [was] himself a radical."[29] Both Patterson and Hattaway, in arguing their ideas of Shakespeare's populism, take as a test case the representation of Cade's rebellion, and both examine the Cade scenes on the basis of their "duplicity," thus revisiting in a political perspective the category of "purposeful ambiguity" that was one of the lines more intensely explored by critics in the sixties and seventies.

However, where the retrieval of the authorial principle can lead us is not clear; nor is there any agreement about what we mean when we speak of the author as "cultural construct," or about the way in which we should envisage the historicity of this construct and represent it. In theoretical statements, the author is "a locus of contingent intentions and desires" (Wilson); "a volatile, flexible, changing construction, engendered, and constantly reborn and rewritten, by the plays" (Holderness); it is "the product of collective exchange" (Greenblatt); it is "a writer whose intentions, if never fully recoverable, are certainly worth debating" (Patterson); it is a useful construct "when it is demoted from its traditionally privileged position as the overriding determinant of meaning" (Marcus); it is "a set of circumstances of enunciation" (Eco); and it is even William Shakespeare, a radical (Hattaway).[30]

One of the best argued and most captivating treatments of the issue of authorial intentions has come from Richard Wilson. Metaphorizing the long-fabled stories connected with the unearthing of Shakespeare's tomb, Wilson identifies the "illusions and discontents of old historicism" with the tourist's feeling when visiting Trinity Church that the Bard's material body is "unfathomable yet proximate, a tantalising presence-in-absence." He suggests that a new kind of historicism "can set to work on a different kind of excavation of the space occupied by the body beside the altar at Stratford, and like archaeology, it can start with the desire, if not to speak with the dead, at least to localise a subject in time and place."[31]

Wilson is a severe critic not only of "old historicism" but also of the American "new historicist" positions, and he discusses what he considers to be sharp differences between new historicism and cultural materialism, which he reduces to the formula that "where New Historicism aestheticises history, . . . Cultural Materialism historicizes the aesthetic." The "Death of the Author" and the "Intentional Fallacy" are read by Wilson as "the highest wall erected by modernism to defend the canon"; while the logical end of historicism is the revival of authorial intention as "the socially and legally sanctioned effect of a specific discursive formation."[32]

It seems to be a far cry from the idea of the author as "the socially and legally sanctioned effect of a specific discursive formation" to a view of Shakespeare, the man, as simply a "radical." However, when we examine the analytical fragments that follow the various theoretical statements explaining what a "cultural construct" should be, we find not only that the critical tools are more or less the same, whatever kind of historicism has been adopted or implicitly embraced; but also that the author as cultural construct is neither "volatile" nor "flexible," but is, in the final analysis, a "person" very much like the person of traditional biographism. Thus, Wilson's author as "a cultural construct determined by the representational practices of a particular historical era"[33] is described, at one point in his book, as "Shakespeare, who seems to have discriminated between even his own daughters, educating his favourite to write and leaving the other illiterate."[34]

Wilson then examines Jack Cade's insurrection in *2 Henry VI* to show that Shakespeare "used his professional debut to signal scorn for popular culture."[35] He therefore embraces the traditional view of a Shakespeare possessed by a deep loathing of the "populace" and the Bondean (fictional) view of Shakespeare as a tyrannical father and an unflinching capitalist oppressor; Hattaway uses the Cade scenes to pursue his idea of a "radical" Shakespeare; and Patterson, to argue for Shakespeare's consciousness of, and sympathy with, the cultural tradition of popular protest. There can be little doubt that from Wilson's perspective Patterson's (and even more Hattaway's) essay would appear as a specimen of "old style" historicism. For her part, Patterson explicitly criticizes Wilson's reading of the 1592 feltmakers' demonstration as "a summer solstice festival"[36] as an instance of suspicious historicism, based less on evidence than on bias. Despite their apparently irreconcilable differences, however, they both start from the same premises and the same correlation of events in constructing their hypotheses, and both rely on the kind of "local" reading that Wilson advocates as an essential tool of cultural materialism in his 1994 introduction to *Will Power*, where the essay on Cade was reprinted.[37] As for the relationship between Wilson and Hattaway, their main point of disagreement is in what Wilson sees as the "myth of a democratic Globe,"[38] which, on the contrary, Hattaway considers, albeit with many prudent question marks, a "popular" phenomenon. In this divergence, they simply rely on two different critical traditions, both arguable and both lacking conclusive evidence. Otherwise, their opposing claims evoke in equal measure the argument of source manipulation, although obviously to different ends. We might add a gloss to this dialogue. Wilson's argument that the Cade scenes are the immediate reaction to the feltmakers' revolt, which took place in June 1592, is based on the assumption that "the venomous fourth act of *Henry VI, Part Two*" was "written during July, 1592." The chain of reasoning is the following: in June 1592 the London clothiers rose against the expansion of the export of fabric dressed in the provinces; when the revolt broke out, Shakespeare was writing *2 Henry VI* (or he began to write it the following month), and he found a way to reflect in the Cade scenes his aversion toward the clothiers; Jack Cade himself is a clothier, and a number of clothing images are used in those scenes. Six years after the revolt, in 1598, Shakespeare invested £30 in a consignment of "knitted stockings" from the Cotswold wool manufacturers, thereby proving that he took part in these capitalist developments: he, therefore, could never have been in sympathy with the clothier Cade, whom he depicted six years before.[39] When Wilson republished his essay in 1994, the date of composition of *2 Henry VI* had been questioned by Hattaway in his New Cambridge edition of the play (Hattaway argues for an earlier dating, between 1589 and 1591, which, if accepted, would disrupt Wilson's argument). Wilson was thus obliged to add a footnote where he liquidates the problem, simply saying that the date of composition of *2 Henry VI* was "conclusively established by H. R. Born" in 1974, and that "though rival theories are sifted by M. Hattaway, . . . Born's dating remains unchallenged."[40]

I wish to make clear that the kind of historicism practiced by Wilson seems to me always to be suggestive and often revealing; I am not convinced, however, that it is the "definitive" kind of historicism, or that it is the most reliable kind of historicism, or even that it is the most progressive, or the only progressive, kind. Quite the opposite. Luckily, although the challenges it poses cannot be ignored, it leaves all the questions open: in particular, it does not invalidate the traditional view of historical reliability.

Going back to the author's intentionality seemed to be, only a few years ago, a crucial step; but while the theory elaborated convincingly on the "different kind of excavation" of the author's spoils we should be engaging in, the practice has not responded adequately. There is, I believe, no substantial difference between arguing that Shakespeare was a radical and arguing that he was a capitalist oppressor, or praising him as a supporter of order, no matter how those conclusions are reached: such statements are all suspicious because, however far we may have got away from any notions of objectivity, we must acknowledge that the plays—and the scanty extratextual evidence we have—are mute on the issue of the author's political opinions.[41]

But if any hypotheses about Shakespeare's evaluation of past and present political issues are bound to remain a matter for speculation, there are other things concerning their author that these plays can tell us, for they are explicit in revealing his methods of reading and writing and the various transactions he made with contemporary historical sources: in short, the intentions and directions of his historiographical practice.

Shakespeare may have subscribed to some of the political biases divulged by the chronicles, but all we can say is that he made some of his characters subscribe to them.[42] What we can say with more certainty, however, is that from the very start he abandoned the undifferentiated, monologic, chronological, cumulative, unmarked presentation of events, focusing in each play on a specific political problem; his main contribution to the historiography of his time may be seen in the way he practiced a problem-oriented, multivocal kind of historiography, creating a series of structures where history could be seen by a multiplicity of points of view and evaluated by a multiplicity of voices, in a number of languages and styles; constructing, in other words, an arena for social, political, and cultural conflict.[43]

Suggesting a more fertile version of the idea of "purposeful ambiguity," Leah Marcus has claimed that "if Shakespeare avoided the appearance of intentionality, it was at least part of the time by design. We must try to distinguish between a lack of intentionality and the avoidance of intentionality, which may be a radically different thing."[44] It is possible, I believe, to read the "avoidance of intentionality" in the history plays as the focal point of Shakespeare's historical discourse; and if we consider that one of the prescriptions for historians was that they should establish clear connections between past events and the present (Puttenham says that the moral value of history is in its "examining and comparing the times past with the present"[45]), then the refusal to make clear one's intentions becomes a much more critical and radical gesture than one might think at first. The plays' instability of meaning, their perspectivism, their irresolution, their dialogism, and their heteroglossia constitute, I believe, a significant breach with the orthodox practice of contemporary historians. They may be read as a mark of discontinuity, a break with tradition, and as a radical revision of the normal procedures of contemporary historical discourse. It is in his historiographical practice and only in it that Shakespeare's subversiveness is readable; and it is to his formal ruptures with the chronicle tradition (which are obviously not simply formal) that criticism engaged in the identification of dissonances should look in order to discuss his attitude toward dominant historiographical (and political) ideologies.

Introducing a fascinating "local" reading of *1 Henry VI*, in which there is an extremely plausible and convincing description of a cluster of disquieting analogies between Shakespeare's *pucelle* and Elizabeth, Marcus makes clear the limits of such a reading, going back to the issue of intentionality. Those elements that might generate subversive thoughts, Marcus says, are integrated into an unstable structure, so that in the end the play refuses to be read on the basis of a single set of political implications. The play, Marcus concludes, creates "such an open field for speculation that the audience response is scattered as a prism scatters colors. What might have been taken even at this early date as the Author's Intent is unreadable because it can be read in too many different ways."[46]

Marcus's self-undermining statement, coming at the end of a tightly argued topical reading, is, I believe, not simply a local comment on the undecidability and ambiguity of certain texts; rather, it signals the acknowledgment of the indirect, presumptive, and circumstantial nature of the historical paradigm.[47] By signaling the limits that even rigorous topical research should acknowledge, it tends to reinstate the strict discipline of doubt.

## Notes

[1] Paul Valéry, *Regards sur le monde actuel* (Paris: Gallimard, 1931), 63-64.

[2] Jacques Le Goff, "Storia," in *Enciclopedia* (Torino: Einaudi, 1981), 13: 576.

[3] "Shakespeare's History Plays: 1900-1951," *Shakespeare Survey* 6 (1953): 1-15.

[4] "Shakespeare's History Plays: 1952-1983," *Shakespeare Survey* 38 (1987): 1-18.

[5] *Literature and History* 10 (1984): 24-45.

[6] *English Studies* 66 (1985): 391-403.

[7] Graham Holderness, "Appropriations," in *Shakespeare Recycled* (London: Harvester, 1992), 21-50.

[8] In *The New Shakespeare Society Transactions* (1874): 396-441.

[9] A. F. Pollard, *The History of England from the Accession of Edward VI to the Death of Elizabeth, 1547-1603* (London: Longmans, Green and Co, 1905): 440.

[10] A. P. Rossiter, *Angel with Horns* (London: Longman, 1961); Ernest Talbert, *The Problem of Order: Elizabethan Political Commonplaces and an Example of Shakespeare's Art* (Chapel Hill: University of North Carolina Press, 1962); G. R. Elton, *"King Lear" and the Gods* (San Marino, Calif.: The Huntington Library, 1966); Norman Rabkin, *Shakespeare and the Common Understanding* (New York and London: The Free Press and Collier-Macmillan, 1967); Wilbur Sanders, *The Dramatist and the Received Idea* (Cambridge: Cambridge University Press, 1968); Robert Grudin, *Mighty Opposites: Shakespeare and Renaissance Contrariety* (Berkeley and Los Angeles: University of California Press, 1979).

[11] Wells, "The Fortunes of Tillyard," 398.

[12] Holderness, *Shakespeare Recycled*, 29.

[13] *See*, for example, Catherine Belsey, "Love in Venice," *Shakespeare Survey* 44 (1991): 41-53; Stephen Mullaney, "Lying Like Truth: Riddle, Representation and Treason in Renaissance England," *English Literary History* 47 (1980): 32-47.

[14] E. M. W. Tillyard, *Shakespeare's History Plays* (London: Chatto and Windus, 1944), 319; Lily B. Campbell, *Shakespeare's Histories: Mirrors of Elizabethan Policy* (San Marino, Calif.: The Huntington Library, 1947), 334; Irving Ribner, *The English History Play in the Age of Shakespeare* (Princeton: Princeton University Press, 1957), 154; David Riggs, *Shakespeare's Heroical Histories: "Henry VI" and its Literary Tradition* (Cambridge: Harvard University Press, 1971), 30; R. R. Reed, *Crime and God's Judgment in Shakespeare* (Lexington: University Press of Kentucky, 1984), 6. In all quotations, the italics are mine.

[15] Jenkins, "Shakespeare's History Plays," 1, 9.

[16] Holderness, "Agincourt 1944," 27.

[17] *See* J. L. Calderwood, *Shakespearean Metadrama: The Argument of the Play in "Titus Andronicus," "Love's Labour's Lost," "Romeo and Juliet," "A Midsummer Night's Dream" and "Richard II"* (Minneapolis: University of Minnesota Press, 1969).

[18] Holderness, *Shakespeare Recycled*, 30.

[19] Annabel Patterson, *Shakespeare and the Popular Voice* (Oxford: Blackwell, 1989), 5.

[20] *See*, in particular, Stephen Greenblatt, "Invisible Bullets: Renaissance Authority and Its Subversion," in *Political Shakespeare*, eds. Jonathan Dollimore and Alan Sinfield (Manchester: Manchester University Press, 1985), 18-47; "Murdering Peasants," in *Representing the English Renaissance*, ed. Stephen Greenblatt (Berkeley and Los Angeles: University of California Press, 1988), 1-29; Jonathan Dollimore and Alan Sinfield, "History and Ideology: The Instance of *Henry V*," in *Alternative Shakespeares*, ed. John Drakakis (London: Routledge, 1985), 206-27; Leonard Tennenhouse, *Power on Display: The Politics of Shakespeare's Genres* (New York and London: Methuen, 1986).

[21] Holderness, *Shakespeare Recycled*, 34.

[22] Even arguments concerning form have been revived: see the open-ended structure for D. S. Kastan, *Shakespeare and the Shapes of Time* (Hanover, N.H.: University Press of New England, 1982); the "variety of styles" and the device of the "interrupted ceremony" for Michael Hattaway, introduction to *The*

*Second Part of King Henry VI* (Cambridge: Cambridge University Press, 1991).

[23] Stanley Fish, "Biography and Intention," in *Contesting the Author,* ed. W. H. Epstein (West Lafayette, Ind.: Purdue University Press, 1991), 9-16; 13, 14.

[24] Leah Marcus, *Puzzling Shakespeare: Local Reading and Its Discontents* (Berkeley: University of California Press, 1988), 42.

[25] Graham Holderness, "Prologue: 'The Histories' and History," in Graham Holderness, Nick Potter and John Turner, *Shakespeare: The Play of History* (London: Macmillan, 1988), 16.

[26] Richard Wilson, *Will Power* (London: Harvester, 1994), 18.

[27] J. D. Cox, *Shakespeare and the Dramaturgy of Power* (Princeton: Princeton University Press, 1989); Kastan, *Shakespeare and the Shapes of Time;* Holderness, *Shakespeare Recycled;* Hattaway, introduction.

[28] Patterson, *Shakespeare and the Popular Voice,* 4.

[29] *Cahiers Elizabéthains* 33 (1988): 13-22, 15.

[30] Wilson, *Will Power,* ix; Holderness, "Prologue," 16; Greenblatt, "The Circulation of Social Energy," in *Shakespearean Negotiations* (Oxford: Clarendon Press, 1988), 1-20, 12; Patterson, *Shakespeare and the Popular Voice,* 4-5; Marcus, *Puzzling Shakespeare,* 42; Umberto Eco, *Lector in fabula* (Milano: Bompiani, 1979), trans. *The Role of the Reader* (Bloomington: Indiana University Press, 1979), chap. 3.5; Hattaway, "Rebellion," 15.

[31] Wilson, *Will Power,* 2.

[32] Ibid., 18.

[33] Ibid.

[34] Ibid., 29.

[35] Ibid.

[36] *Shakespeare and the Popular Voice,* 35.

[37] "A Mingled Yarn: Shakespeare and the Cloth Workers" was originally published in *Literature and History* 12 (1986): 164-84.

[38] Wilson, *Will Power,* 23.

[39] Wilson's reading seems to imply that hostility toward a popular protest means invariably to show scorn for popular culture, even though the motives of that protest are narrowly monopolistic and protectionist (or even xenophobic). Besides, the "documents" he quotes do not seem to bear evidence that "in 1598 [Shakespeare] invested £30 in a consignment of 'knitted stockings' at Evesham" (*Will Power,* 32), and cannot therefore support his interpretation of the Cade episode. It is perhaps worthwhile to spend a few words on those documents. The first is a letter dated 24 January 1598 from Abraham Sturley to Richard Quiney. Sturley says that he has heard from Richard's father "that our countriman, M$^r$ Shaksper, is willinge to disburse some monei vpon some od yardeland or other at Shottri or neare about vs." In the second, dated 25 October 1598, Richard Quiney is asking Shakespeare for £30 to help him "out of all the debettes I owe in London"; the third, dated ca. 30 October 1598, is a letter in which Adrian Quiney mentions to his son, Richard, the possibility of investing money in "knite stockynges" sold at Evesham. In this, Adrian simply hints at the possibility of getting money from Shakespeare to further this scheme ("Yff yow bargen with M$^r$ Sha . . or receve money therfor, brynge your money home yf yow maye, I see howe knite stockynges be sold, ther ys gret byinge of them at Evysshome."); the fourth, dated 24 November 1598, is again from Abraham Sturley to Richard Quiney. Here it is stated "that our countriman M$^r$ Wm. Shak. would procure vs monej," and the sum of £ "30 or 40" is mentioned as a help to make an investment "towardes sutch a match." The match was probably the buying of "knite stockynges" at Evesham, but on whose behalf the investment was being planned is not stated. Apart from the fact that there is no evidence that Shakespeare actually disbursed the money, what Richard Quiney's letter to him shows is that the sum of £30 was asked as a loan to the same Richard who, if he ever got it, may have used it for his own investment. Indeed, Richard's letter, if read in the context of the whole *dossier,* allows one to speculate that he insisted on his economic difficulties only to exert stronger pressure on the addressee. The letters are reproduced in E. K. Chambers, *William Shakespeare* (Oxford: Clarendon Press, 1930), 2: 101-3. William Carroll rightly argues that in those documents Shakespeare is mentioned only "as a possible source of money, but the investment ideas are all Quiney's," and concludes that Wilson misreads the documents conflating two different letters (*Fat King Lean Beggar* [Ithaca and London: Cornell University Press, 1966], 143). If read carefully, however, the sequence of letters does not seem to allow misunderstanding.

[40] Wilson, *Will Power,* 245.

[41] Again commenting on the treatment of Cade's rebellion, Derek Cohen unhistorically complains that Cade "is not given the chance to seem the revolution-

ary hero that many of his followers would have celebrated"; and above all he uses the fact that "At no time do the pretenders to the throne offer a redistribution of wealth" (!) as an argument which shows Shakespeare's antipopulist attitude (*The Politics of Shakespeare* [London: Macmillan, 1993], 60, 66).

[42] As Raymond Williams has observed, criticism often makes the mistake of isolating "speeches by particular characters as Shakespeare's essential beliefs" (afterword in Jonathan Dollimore and Alan Sinfield, eds., *Political Shakespeare*, 231-39, 231).

[43] When I say that Shakespeare's historiography is problem-oriented, I certainly consider, in the background of my assertion, the formula of *histoire-problème* versus *histoire-récit*, which was divulged and developed by the École des *Annales*. More realistically, however, I tend to refer to the fact that "classical" Western drama is always centered on a crisis (which is precisely the idea that, to a certain extent, was dispersed by the absurdists). It is therefore true to say that the problem-oriented effect of Shakespeare's texts was largely determined by the dramatic medium, its tradition and conventions. However, while the dramatic form is based on a crisis, history is conceptualized as a continuum. In the case of historical drama, therefore, the focalization on a crisis implies a segmentation and problematization of that continuum.

[44] Marcus, *Puzzling Shakespeare*, 42.

[45] George Puttenham, *The Arte of English Poesie*, ed. G. D. Willcock and Alice Walker (Cambridge: Cambridge University Press, 1936), 39.

[46] Marcus, *Puzzling Shakespeare,* 70. Discussing the instability of meaning in Shakespeare's plays, Angela Locatelli has interestingly developed the notion of "double enunciation" in an essay entitled "Shakespearean Enunciation and the Textual Subject of Ethics," forthcoming in *Mnema. Per Lino Falzon Santucci*, ed. P. Pugliatti (Messina: Armando Siciliano).

[47] *See,* on the circumstantial nature of the historiographical paradigm, Carlo Ginzburg, "Spie. Radici di un paradigma indiziario," in *Miti emblemi spie* (Torino: Einaudi, 1979); English trans., "Morelli, Freud and Sherlock Holmes," *History Workshop* 9 (1980): 5-36.

---

Source: "Shakespeare's Historicism: Visions and Revisions," in *Shakespeare and the Twentieth Century: The Selected Proceedings of the International Shakespeare Association World Congress, Los Angeles, 1996,* edited by Jonathan Bate, Jill L. Levenson, and Dieter Mehl, University of Delaware Press, 1998, pp. 336-49.

# Fearful Simile: Stealing the Breech in Shakespeare's Chronicle Plays

## Kathryn Schwarz, *Vanderbilt University*

> The quene perswaded and encoraged by these meanes, toke upon her and her husbande, the high power and aucthoritie ouer the people and subiectes. And although she ioyned her husbande with hir in name, for a countenaunce, yet she did all, she saied all, and she bare the whole swynge, as the strong oxe doth, when he is yoked in the plough with a pore silly asse.
>
> A domestick fury makes ill harmony in any family.[1]

Critically speaking, Shakespeare's *Henry VI* plays are always going to pieces. If the project of carving up these plays and giving only the best parts to Shakespeare has passed out of fashion, it has been replaced by various discussions of the plays as *self*-fragmenting—artifacts mirroring the disrupted state they describe. In this sense the logic of the plays might best be described in terms of repetition rather than linear progress: heroic flourishes, treacherous acts, the crowning, capturing, and killing of kings recur as patterns that all but eclipse the individuals concerned.[2] And the female characters of these plays, like the men and the battles and the vicissitudes of kingship, might be less distinct than they are variations on a theme.[3] Margaret is led onstage as Joan is dragged off; Joan's witchcraft anticipates that of the Countess; sexual excess is suspected about the virgin, suggested about the Countess, known about the queen; the woman warrior is reduced to ashes at the end of *Part 1* only to reappear as the "Captain Margaret" of *Part 3*. Yet the progress in the second Henriad toward a centralized image of power is not absent from these earlier plays, although it is differently gendered and certainly far different in its effects; images of female transgression come ever closer to home and, when they are inside, look rather different than they did when they were outside. As Jean Howard and Phyllis Rackin observe in *Engendering a Nation*, "The French women who threaten to subvert the English historical project in *Part 1* are unmarried; in *Part II*, the dangers they embody quite literally come home to England in the form of ambitious wives, married to the men who govern the land."[4] In the first, second, and third parts of *Henry VI*, the consolidation of power is marked by a movement of monstrous female agency from margin to center, a movement that begins with the claim that the enemy is an Amazon and ends in the recognition of something distinctly amazonian about the woman who is queen, mother, and wife.

Conventions of female excess distinguish between the domestic and the imported, between transgressions that radically oppose socialized femininity and those out of which it is formed. In *Still Harping on Daughters* Lisa Jardine draws such a distinction between viragoes and shrews: "The threat of the scold is local and *domestic;* that of the Amazon/virago is generalised 'rejection of her sex', a strangeness which travesties nature."[5] The amazonian references of Shakespeare's first tetralogy reflect early modern fascination with the possibility that the distinction might break down, that the two categories of transgression might, through the image of the amazonian wife, become one and the same. The result, I suggest, is an excursion into the uncanny, what Freud defines as "that class of the frightening which leads back to what is known of old and long familiar."[6] Images of Amazons in socially conventionalized roles locate the strange—and, indeed, the terrifying—within the familiar, resulting in the anxieties of conflation, displacement, and loss which Freud theorizes as the uncanny's effect; this is the effect of bringing Margaret home, of locating female power at the intersection of the alien and the domestic. That intersection, Freud argues, is an effect of rhetoric, a collapse of opposition into conflation at the level of language itself. In his reading, the term *heimlich* identifies not only the home, with its structures of familiarity, but the ways in which those structures produce the conditions of their own disruption: "Thus *heimlich* is a word the meaning of which develops in the direction of ambivalence, until it finally coincides with its opposite, *unheimlich. Unheimlich* is in some way or other a sub-species of *heimlich*."[7] With respect to Joan la Pucelle, rhetorically held at arm's length, the threat that the familiar might converge with the strange remains remote; but Queen Margaret, appropriating the *heimlich,* uncannily performs its conventions from within the terms of domesticity itself.

The shift inward is bracketed by the two kings' bodies: Henry V, who is mourned in his fallen presence and celebrated for his glorious past at the beginning of *1 Henry VI;* and Henry VI, whose corpse appears onstage in the far more muted procession that begins *Richard III*. These spectacular royal corpses anticipate and summarize the progressive threat to sovereign male authority, a threat played out in the actions of the tetralogy's women. Readers have always recognized that the women of these plays have an enervating effect on the men: they are "domineering females," "typically defined as opponents and subverters of the historical and historiographic enterprise," "associated with bloody rites of violence and 'misrule,' " known to be from hell because of the confusion of gender," representative of "illegitimate and therefore unnatural power," possessing "all the coded and recognizable ambiguities of the castrating woman."[8] Such vigorous consensus threatens to obscure the fact that its explanation is curiously doubled, conflating feminizing and effeminating processes that do not, upon consideration, add up to quite the same thing. Women, these readings suggest, destabilize male privilege through their appropriation of masculinity; at the same time, women sap male potency through their association with the feminized French. We might get around this rhetorical paradox by asserting that, in the Renaissance imagination, female masculinity is a sign of heterosexual excess, which is itself a conventionally feminine trait: "In life as on the stage," Rackin has argued, "masculine women were regarded as whores."[9] But I want to take seriously for a moment the sense in which explanations of Joan and, to a still greater extent, of Margaret call on notions of femininity and masculinity in the same breath. It is this simultaneity, I will argue, that constructs the specifically disruptive effect of female agency; by invoking a doubled set of conventions, the *Henry VI* plays complicate the hierarchical relationship not only of men to women but also of homosocial systems of power to heterosexual conventions and roles. In both their iconographic and their sexual functions, Joan and Margaret challenge rather than consolidate the naturalized referential assumptions of masculinity, and this tetralogy chronicles an increasingly acute failure to use women in order to negotiate the bonds among men.[10]

Judith Butler has described gender as "an identity tenuously constituted in time, instituted in an exterior space through a *stylized repetition of acts*."[11] For the female characters of the first tetralogy, gendered convention is not only highly and self-consciously stylized but doubled, presenting femininity and masculinity not as oppositional or mutually displacing terms but as simultaneous performative effects. It is a doubleness efficiently figured in the term *Amazon,* applied both to Joan and to Margaret; Amazon myth, with its paradoxical reference of masculine acts to female bodies, conflates the chivalric violence of encounters between men with the different violence of heterosexual conquest, with predictably disruptive effects. As objects of desire or items of exchange, Amazons do not consolidate male bonding; and if, as when Hercules "gives" the Amazon queen Hippolyta to Theseus, the attempt is made, the result is not comedy or confirmed masculine identity but parodic domestic roles and an inexorable progress toward tragic conclusions.[12] In the course of the *Henry VI* plays, the disruption defined through reference to Amazons changes; although readers have tended to equate Joan and Margaret as figures of the French, the feminine, or the theatrical, these plays stage a significant shift in the terms of gendered performance. That shift is articulated in the difference between *Amazon* and *amazonian,* a difference that mirrors as it theorizes the movement inward that structures the tetralogy.

In *1 Henry VI,* Joan is called an "Amazon" (1.2.104)[13] as an articulation of doubled identity; constantly forced on the awareness of spectators both onstage and off, her position as a manly woman generates a peculiarly essentializing rhetoric that traces her disruptive effect to the fact that she "is" a collection of contradictory things. Margaret, by contrast, is termed "amazonian" and subjectively described as "play[ing] the Amazon" (1.4.114; 4.1.106); doubled identity here gives way to doubled performance, to a rhetoric of identity as relentlessly contingent. Joan functions only problematically within an economy governed by men because her value, as a gendered commodity and as an iconographic figure, does not remain constant; described through extremes of masculinity and femininity, catalogued as a virgin and as a whore, she figures these structures of categorization themselves as constructing not a continuum but an unsocializable collection of opposites. Margaret, by contrast, manipulates the terms of the socialized continuum itself. The moments at which she is identified as a virgin or a whore—as Henry's bride, as Suffolk's mistress—serve not to identify her through unassimilable contradictions but precisely to assimilate her into the middle ground of domestic convention. And it is Margaret's revision of the roles of mother, wife, and queen that brings masculinity and femininity into their most acutely performative conflation.

The rhetorical strategy that distinguishes Joan from Margaret participates in a larger distinction among monitory texts. Joan is described in the language of exemplary catalogues, which impose gendered conventions through the reification of polarities; extravagances of good and bad, restrained and excessive, familiar and alien, are categorized against one another in order to suggest a socialized space between, and it is Joan's embodiment of extremes at the expense of this socialized space that makes her a threat. Margaret, by contrast, recalls the language of conduct manuals, in which conventions are rhetorically performed rather than iconographically framed: as she plays a series of self-consciously domestic roles, Margaret at once echoes and suggests the transgressive potential of the terms through which wives, mothers, and even queens are defined. Both systems rely heavily on the relationship of the body to sexual acts; but if the first reifies that relationship as a self-evidently referential structure, the second implies, often against its own declared ideological ends, that the body may be less accessibly material than the processes through which convention is performed. The shift between ways of theorizing, and thus controlling, identity recalls another theory of the relationship between the embodied and the performed. In

"The Signification of the Phallus" Lacan describes "the intervention of a 'to seem' that replaces the 'to have,' in order to protect it on the one side, and to mask its lack on the other."[14] In negotiating the various implications of being, having, and seeming, Lacan suggests a transition from the rhetoric of identity as difference to the rhetoric of seeming as masking or appropriating the place of difference. By invoking this structure in order to articulate the roles played by Joan and by Margaret, I do not wish to argue that the play's variously amazonian women occupy the place of the phallus—although, considering the fantastic materiality and infinite metonymic retreat of early modern Amazons, the association possesses a certain imaginative power. I suggest instead that the tetralogy's representational strategy mirrors Lacan's in representing the conventional signs of discrete sexual identity, first as embodied paradox and, more powerfully, as constructed through a performance that is also a veil.

The three parts of *Henry VI* complicate the naturalized connection between masculinity and men through the changing relationships not only between "masculine" and "female" but also between "amazonian" and "Amazon," relationships that range from equation and causality to paradox. Such complications of identity and referentiality are in a sense the inevitable result of theatricality itself, which, Barbara Freedman argues, is constituted through a strategy of misreading analogous to the events of the Lacanian mirror stage: "Both tragic and comic narratives stage misrecognition in the quest for recognition. Whereas Shakespeare's tragedies address the need and failure to find a place in another's eyes, the comedies are more concerned with dislocating perspective; they suggest that only a limited perspectival space defined by error constitutes identity."[15] In the *Henry VI* plays the theatrical effect itself is doubled, for, through its peculiar representation of women's place, Shakespeare's first tetralogy conflates the generic effects that Freedman describes. If Margaret's appearance as Henry's prospective bride at the end of *1 Henry VI* shifts that play's register from tragic to comic conclusions, and if the results of that marriage turn comedy back toward tragedy, the plays mix up the conventions of recognition and misrecognition as well. "A woman's general. What should we fear?" Richard asks in *3 Henry VI* (1.2.68), the false causality between statement and question marking the intersection of understanding and its failure. The attempt to relegate women to their place within masculinist hierarchies through the simple fact of recognizing them *as women* ignores another of the play's simple facts: that women may be masculine as well. "*Henry VI, Part III*, then, is spectacularly marked by the dissolution of every kind of male bond," write Howard and Rackin;[16] I want to argue here that the tetralogy's spectacles of female agency are less that dissolution's symptom than its cause.

To Be

*Henry VI, Part 1* defines Joan with relentless thoroughness as an outsider. Opposed to an English male aristocratic ideal, she is a woman, a peasant, a virgin, a whore, a saint, a witch, an Amazon, and French. Her threatened invasion, while it challenges English idealizations of heroic significance and physical space, could consolidate those ideals; if the English, at the end of *1 Henry VI*, return to a smaller England, they bring with them a clarified sense of what Englishness means. Such a process appears to reiterate a convention of subjectivity, a negotiation of the relationship between familiar and strange that produces identity through difference; the multiplication of Joan's alien identities not only reflects that which is not English but comes, through that opposition, to define Englishness itself. Recognition of Joan, and violent disassociation from her, construct the male heroic subject, or, in Rackin's historiographic terms, male heroic abstractions are opposed to the insistence of female bodies: "[T]he whole issue of physical presence vs. historical record, dramatized in *1 Henry VI* as a conflict between English men and French women, is central, not only to this particular play, but to the history play genre itself."[17] Joan's "femaleness," however theatrically contingent, is an ideologically absolute condition against which the play constructs its privileged terms. *Henry VI, Part 1* stages the processes of deliberately oppositional self-construction, what Butler, in her theory of "sex" as a function of sociality and power, describes as "a repudiation which produces a domain of abjection, a repudiation without which the subject cannot emerge." Butler goes on to argue, "This is a repudiation which creates the valence of 'abjection' and its status for the subject as a threatening spectre."[18] But if Joan is abject and her threatening otherness useful, I would argue that her utility is complicated by the relationship it sets up between who she is and what she does. The play most effectively equates identity to performance in a figure who is neither English nor male nor conventionally heroic; the essentializing rhetoric that surrounds Joan both mirrors and parodies the play's various representations of essential connections between maleness and masculinity, between kingship or heroism and authority. If the play's resolution, defined in terms of nationalism, gender, or individual subjectivity, depends on a return to naturalized causalities, that return is proleptically disrupted in the characterization of Joan herself. The threat posed by Joan is not simply her evident otherness—which might, after all, only tell the hero what he wants to know—but is also the sense in which that otherness produces a more efficient claim to embodied referentiality than that posed by English male heroic authority itself.

The representation of Joan is thus ideologically useful in that it clarifies categorical and hierarchical structures by defining her against them; at the same time, because her role draws together gendered conventions identifying both the powerful and the abject, it might call into question the discretion and the privileged position of defining structures themselves. *Henry VI, Part 1* insists on the verb of equation that links Joan to terms of description: Joan "is" a range of things, contradictory but always extreme, and in the spaces between them domesticity, as a nationalist and ultimately a familial ideology, is constituted. In her first encounter with the Dauphin, Joan offers a challenge and a warning: "My courage try by combat, if thou dar'st, / And thou shalt find that I exceed my sex" (1.2.89-90). That trial prompts the Dauphin's own statement of definition, the implications of which will follow Joan throughout the play. "Stay, stay thy hands! Thou art an Amazon, / And fightest with the sword of Deborah" (ll. 104-5). The Dauphin here conflates what Joan is, what she has, and what she does, suggesting an economy within which signification does not float but remains firmly anchored to the conditions of its production. Joan's body may not display the monomastic utility invoked by "Amazon," but it has been nonetheless modified for her purpose, transformed by her encounter with divine grace. She says, "And, whereas I was black and swart before, / With those clear rays which she infused on me / That beauty am I blessed with which you may see" (ll. 84-86). And her sword, if not actually the sword of Deborah, has been chosen by supernatural intervention, placed in her hands by a force that is not her own. The curious literalism of what should be metaphor gives Joan a singularity of function even as she is doubly read; throughout *1 Henry VI* her identity will be defined by equation, by the rhetoric of "I am" and "you are." "Assigned am I to be the English scourge" (l. 129), she says. For the admirers and the objects of this scourging, its outcome may be differently valued but its processes look much the same.

It is this gap—between the recognized efficiency of Joan's acts and the dispute over their value—that complicates negotiations of relationships among men. True to theatrical form, *1 Henry VI* privileges an almost exclusively homosocial universe; Howard and Rackin characterize the history play as "a specifically masculine genre" and argue that "its masculinity was identified with its function as an ideological apparatus for the construction of an emergent national consciousness."[19] Women in such a context are defined most logically as the matter from which homosocial bonds are built, and this function is as important in the consolidation of hostility as it is in the making of friendship. Figured as individual chivalric conflicts or as wars between nations, battles between men (like alliances) display women as prize, as motive, and as cause. More than anything else, such displays require that the task of defining women in terms of sexual value must rest with men; that value may shift—Helen of Troy may look different to the Trojans than she does to the Greeks—but women themselves are always excluded from its determination. Fighting for or through or because of women gives logic to a male homosocial universe only as long as the place of women themselves remains constant, and in *1 Henry VI* such constancy is an impossible fiction. Rather than being fought for, Joan la Pucelle is fought against, entering into the play's privileged masculine terms through the condition of masculinity itself. The resulting clash of conventions creates a kind of exemplary chaos, in which Joan is defined in terms that variously respond to evidence of her own agency rather than demonstrating the determinative power of men. When the French argue among themselves or with the English over her value, the terms of disagreement suggest that the relationship between her sexual and martial roles upsets the conditions through which the place of women is defined: is she given to the Dauphin as a gift or brought to him as an ally? Is she like the French in fighting for their cause, or are the French and the English, alike in being men, united against her? Are her grounds of battle those of nationalism, chivalric heroism, or some odd, early version of what we might now term women's rights? Responses to the play have suggested that Joan's presence onstage unites the English against the French, the men against the woman, the audience against the French, the audience and the English and arguably the French against Joan,[20] the multiple gestures toward some consolidation of alliances suggest that Joan la Pucelle has anything but a consolidating effect.

The shifting values attached to her produce a constellation of names that trace the failure of consensus: in his introduction to *Saint Joan* George Bernard Shaw writes, "She is the most notable Warrior Saint in the Christian calendar, and the queerest fish among the eccentric worthies of the Middle Ages."[21] The oddity of her iconography inflects Shakespeare's representation as well as those that precede and follow from it. In *1 Henry VI* she is "a holy maid" (1.2.51), "an Amazon" (l. 104), "Pucelle or pussel" (1.4.107), "a witch" (1.5.6), a "high-minded strumpet" (l. 12), "Divinest creature, Astraea's daughter" (1.6.4), "France's saint" (l. 29)—and this is only in Act 1. In the multiplicity of epithets and encomia, Shakespeare echoes his sources; for Hall, in particular, Joan requires an agility of description which, even as it condemns her as "monster" and "orgayne of the deuill," gives rhetorical space to her own claims. Speaking of "[t]his wytch or manly woman, (called the maide of GOD)," Hall ascribes her virginity (if it exists) simultaneously to her "foule face" and to her own agency, making her at once a sign of the depravity that is Frenchness and a deceiver of noble rulers, "wise men," and "lerned clarkes." He writes, "O Lorde, what dispraise is this to the nobilitie of Fraunce: What blotte is this to the Frenche nacion?"[22] The historical fact of Joan disrupts any rhetoric of analogy between Englishmen and

Frenchmen; France may, in Hall's reading as in Shakespeare's, be outside whatever is English, but Joan la Pucelle represents a clear threat not only to Englishness but also to anything redeemably male in that which is French. Joan disrupts the rhetoric that connects men to men; and if the French seem willing to privilege her utility over her threat to their own masculinity, it is nonetheless true that even their praise marks her difference. The sense in which that difference both separates her from men and divides men from one another becomes explicit when she persuades Burgundy to abandon the English cause for that of the French. "Done like a Frenchman—[*aside*] turn and turn again!" (3.3.85), she says, and suddenly Burgundy's relationship to national identity, whether French or English, is not connection and self-definition but treason.

"Amazon," perhaps the most imaginatively powerful of Joan's identities, might encompass all of her extremes; a mythological structure that accommodates Penthesilea, chaste hero of Troy, beside the sexually ravenous cannibals of the New World can surely find space for a saint who is also a high-minded strumpet. Indeed, martial chastity and sexual excess are often invoked simultaneously to *define* the Amazon, providing a logic for Joan's doubleness. Gabriele Bernhard Jackson reads such doubleness as the play's insistence on the shiftiness of iconographic value: "In my reading of *1 Henry VI*, the disjunctive presentation of Joan that shows her first as numinous, then as practically and subversively powerful, and finally as feminized and demonized is determined by Shakespeare's progressive exploitation of the varied ideological potential inherent in the topically relevant figure of the virago. . . . At no stage is the allocation of value clearcut."[23] Virgin and whore, saint and witch, ideal and debased, masculine and feminine, Joan makes inevitable the punning paradox of Talbot's "Pucelle or pussel." Readings of her iconography point to anxieties concerning women which range from demonic possession to Catholicism to martial violence to sexual excess to the presence of a queen on the throne; behind each of these readings is the recognition that Joan's conflation of sexual and martial agency, like that represented in stories about Amazons, interrupts the privileged system of homosocial masculinity, rather than being defined by its terms. In the constellation of terms attached to female martiality, the strategies of definition locating women in a particular social place are still in play; but their efficacy comes into question when women can also take the place of men.

Definitions of Joan do not converge even in the name of patriotism; if for Hall and for Holinshed her monstrosity is demonstrably un-English, for other contemporary writers the nationalist distinction is less simple. Agrippa, in *Female Pre-eminence,* writes, "The *English Nation* were most ungratefull, should they ever forget their Obligations to this Sex," but oddly follows this with a brief history of Joan, describing what she has done for the French: "taking *Arms* like an *Amazon,* [she] *arrested* their fortune, put a stop to the *torrent* of their victories, and by degrees restor'd the *withering de Luces* to their former lustre."[24] Christopher Newstead's *Apology for Women* follows Agrippa both in praising Joan and in invoking her in a context that fails to privilege nationalist agendas. He offers an exemplary catalogue of warlike women that places her in the company of Artemesia, Semiramis, Boadicea, and the Amazons of classical mythology.[25] And Thomas Heywood, again like Agrippa, brings her analogically close to Englishness, offering a chapter in his *Gynaikeion* titled "Of English Viragoes. And of *Ioan de Pucil.*"[26] Each of these accounts accepts the militant virginity that *1 Henry VI* places radically in question; each recognizes militance itself as a mode of nationalism not incongruously embodied in women. Still, though, such accounts suggest a certain ambivalence of their own: not everyone would agree with Newstead that Amazons make good exempla; not everyone would wish to return to the female heroic past celebrated by Agrippa, who himself calls Joan a "strange ridling Prodigy",[27] and Heywood mediates his praise of Joan through her claims and those of her chroniclers, giving her history few of his own words and little of his authority. Joan "would report to diuerse" concerning her divine visitation; "The French Chronicles affirme" her acts of heroism; "she was proclaimed a Virago" in a declaration from the pope.[28] Such gestures of ambivalence and mediation show that, while Joan's power to signify goes unchallenged, the question of *what* she signifies remains unclear. Both the accounts that praise her and those that deplore her do so in ways that allow the spectacle of female masculinity to rhetorically displace the importance of national boundaries. In *1 Henry VI,* whatever fighting against Joan does or does not prove about being masculine, it at least demonstrates the fact of being English; but her exemplary function in early modern texts suggests that even this process of consolidation may be obscured by the shifting terms in which she is read.

Rather than continuing to focus on the ways in which accounts of Joan differ, I would like to turn to the sense in which they seem always to produce the same effect. Whether we imagine the grammatical condition of *and* or *or*—whether Joan exists simultaneously through contradictory identities or moves through a range of registers or "is" one thing but is erroneously read as another—the extremes of characterization preclude what is in between. No matter what we accept or reject about her claims of virginity and pregnancy, Joan cannot function conventionally as chaste daughter, generative mother, or nurturing wife; she is dislocated throughout this play from the domestic universe in which the roles played by women materialize the connections among men.[29] Though her virginity is, according to her, absolute, it has no iconographic power to save her; Vives writes, "We haue redde of wome[n], that haue ben taken & let go agayne of the moste vnruly soudyours [soldiers], only for the reuerence of the name of virginitie, bicause they sayde that they were virgins,"[30] but such logic does not work for the soldiers who capture Joan. She has no recognized value on which men can agree; the representational force of her virginity is opposed to, without being mediated by, her own claims to sexuality and the English definition of her as a whore. The categories are less confused than insisted upon as separate but equal. The rhetoric that condemns her, recalling Talbot's pun on her name, reiterates the paradox rather than demanding a single "truth": "Now heaven forfend! The holy maid with child?" (5.4.65); "And yet, forsooth, she is a virgin pure! / Strumpet, thy words condemn thy brat and thee" (ll. 83-84). Joan's death, like her martial success and her iconographic effect, is a result of being at once neither and both. The space *between* virgin and whore, the complicated negotiation that produces the terms of the domestic, is precluded both by what others say about Joan and by what Joan says about herself; her ability to remain so relentlessly *outside*, however broadly the inside is defined, emerges from this sense in which she is never imaginably at home.

This becomes explicit when Joan tries to find some space within the *heimlich;* her final claim to be pregnant is an attempt to become recognizable as a commodity, a woman defined in terms of specific social value. Having witnessed the failure of her insistence on virginity and nobility, Joan performs what readers have always found to be a startling reversal, not only claiming pregnancy but revealing a disconcerting flexibility about the question of paternity. This, I would suggest, is a belated and doomed attempt to enter into the system of male bonds in conventionally feminine terms, to literally embody the condition that connects men to one another; and if her captors do not value the Dauphin's child, Joan is willing to change her story through the invention of a series of fathers until her body performs an acceptable role. But as the play makes clear, the attempt to rewrite this particular body as doing socially conventional work cannot succeed. What is perhaps most interesting here is that the men of the play do not *care* whether Joan's claims are true or false, whether she is indeed the mother of a child and, if so, whose child; in an ideological sense the question is not worth asking, for the literal fact of pregnancy could not, for Joan, be equated with the social value of maternity. Joan is defined by and as the frustration of the bonds that her final narrative attempts to form, and hers is not an identity that can be revised. Like the stories of amazonian maternity narrated by early modern authors, in which Amazons kill, cripple, or enslave their male children or return them to anonymous fathers, Joan's version of maternity cannot be translated into patriarchal terms. Her last desperate claim, and the death that follows, have been read as feminization, putting her body back into a recognizable social place; yet I think that this ending demonstrates more explicitly than any other element of Joan's story that for her such a place does not exist.[31]

Joan's threat to the male homosocial systems of the play rests on this dislocation; her identity as a woman is not socializable, and her martial performance threatens to make conventions of masculinity inscrutable as well. Battling each other, men affirm what masculinity is; battling Joan, whose doubleness is relentlessly legible, they have difficulty knowing what it means. When Bedford asks, "A maid? And be so martial?" he points to the fact that Joan's martial acts do not constitute a transvestite disguise plot; there is no moment of redeeming revelation and refeminization, for the female body is always visibly the referent of masculine acts.[32] "Where is my strength, my valor, and my force?" asks Talbot; "Our English troops retire; I cannot stay them. / A woman clad in armor chaseth them" (1.5.1-3). If Talbot conventionally marks the center of English male chivalric valor, he finds in Joan's female masculinity the potential unwriting of the referential structure that defines him; his statement "I know not where I am nor what I do" (l. 20) suggests that Joan's presence unravels the naturalized connection between masculinity and men. It is not Joan who kills him; indeed, they are not even opposites in the representational logic of *1 Henry VI* but are rather two objects that cannot occupy the same space at the same time. Rackin writes that "Talbot, the English champion, and Joan, his French antagonist, speak alternative languages."[33] When the English scourge speaks her deflating words over the English champion, she proves that he has come too far into her field of discourse.

Readers have theorized Joan's difference in many ways, from the mythological to the sexual to the economic to the theological, but her opposition to the play's martial, male, English center seems clear.[34] Indeed, in recalling her abortive battle with young Talbot, Joan herself sees it as a convention, a set of oppositions always already in quotation marks.

> Once I encountered him, and thus I said:
> "Thou maiden youth, be vanquished by a
>   maid."
> But with a proud, majestical high scorn
> He answered thus: "Young Talbot was not
>   born
> To be the pillage of a giglot wench."
> (4.7.37-41)

The maid is opposed to the "giglot wench," the French to the English, the Amazon to the would-be conqueror, the woman to the man. And yet such lines might be obscured by the image of Joan, and the distinction between outside and in threatens at times to disappear entirely; England itself is not safe from the effects of

Joan's iconography. Bedford articulates this vulnerability in one of the play's earliest speeches, while the body of Henry V still lies onstage: "Posterity, await for wretched years, / When at their mothers' moistened eyes babes shall suck, / Our isle be made a nourish of salt tears, / And none but women left to wail the dead" (1.1.48-51). England in this image becomes a place of women, a space defined by the loss of men; the land of Amazons is always, such rhetoric implies, closer than you think.

Or perhaps the *heimlich* is simply farther away. The moments at which the terms of the center are threatened suggest less an invasion than a dispersal; Joan la Pucelle, with all the strangeness she signifies, never comes close, but the various elements that converge to produce familiarity can always move apart. Leah Marcus takes this possibility to its logical extreme when she finds in Joan an image of Queen Elizabeth I:

> In *Henry VI, Part 1*, Joan La Pucelle functions in many ways as a distorted image of Queen Elizabeth I. She, like Elizabeth, is a woman who "acts like a man." She collects about her a markedly similar set of idealized symbolic identities. Yet she belongs to the enemy camp. The figure of Joan brings into the open a set of suppressed cultural anxieties about the Virgin Queen, her identity, and her capacity to provide continuing stability for the nation.[35]

If Joan looks like Elizabeth, if Elizabeth looks like Joan, this is not a domestication of the strange but an estrangement of the domestic; the metonymies that lead from queen to biblical heroine to classical goddess should never be pursued to the borders occupied by devils and witches and whores. Understood in the terms that define Joan la Pucelle, Queen Elizabeth I would figure a revision of royal iconography in which the sovereign, rather than embodying the bond that draws men together, makes monstrous the hierarchical connection of monarch to male subject and thus disrupts the lateral connections that define unified male subjectivity itself. Such disruption, *1 Henry VI* suggests, is the danger posed by female martiality; in the set of associations traced by Marcus, that danger is unimaginably escalated in the figure of a martial female queen.

*Henry VI, Part 1* ultimately resists the identification of Queen Elizabeth with Joan, or at least distorts the mirror image to the point of unrecognizability; there remains a powerful impulse to keep the figure of Joan la Pucelle outside the terms of the familiar. It is an impulse that has driven readings not only of dramatic structure but of canon: if Joan is definitively not English and in some sense not French, she is also sometimes not Shakespeare's. Tillyard, in *Shakespeare's History Plays*, describes this argument as he dismisses it:

> Apart from the queer reluctance to allow Shakespeare to have written ill or like other dramatists when he was immature, the chief reason why people have been hostile to Shakespeare's authorship [of *1 Henry VI*] is the way he treats Joan of Arc. That the gentle Shakespeare could have been so ungentlemanly as to make his Joan other than a saint was intolerable. This is precisely like arguing that Shakespeare could not have written *King John* because he does not mention Magna Carta.[36]

Not, perhaps, precisely. The gesture that defines Joan la Pucelle as "not Shakespeare's" is not merely a defense of chivalry or good historicism but a symptomatic reproduction of the play's own logic, logic that identifies the familiar through the power of the contrary example: if idealized Englishness is constructed against France's Joan, then the idealized Shakespeare, in controversies over the authorship of this play, has been constructed against a Joan who belongs to someone else entirely. By this logic, to allow Joan into the canon is to endanger the most important bond of all—that which links Shakespeare to his readers and thus to the "Shakespearean." In metatextual negotiations, as with those that take place onstage, the terms in which Joan is defined suggest the fragility of privileged systems of connection.

To Have

Possession may, as Lacan asserts, always be an illusion; it is also, however, a way of articulating the relationship between agency and desire that structures the representation of women in *Henry VI, Part 2*. As York speaks his last line to Joan—"Curse, miscreant, when thou com'st to the stake" (*1HVI*, 5.3.44)—the statement of finality, punctuated by the stage direction *"Exeunt,"* is immediately undermined by another stage direction: *"Enter Suffolk, with Margaret in his hand."* For Joan, being a Frenchwoman in the hands of the English is an experience of violence that demonizes sex; for Margaret, literally in the hand of Suffolk and metonymically in the hands of the king, the position is more conventionally eroticized, her body defined as a commodity well worth the effort expended to acquire it. "She's beautiful, and therefore to be wooed; / She is a woman, therefore to be won," says Suffolk (ll. 78-79); and where Joan's beuaty had been, like her sword, a weapon divinely bestowed, Margaret's is read as a commodity adding to her value and lending agency to the men who look at her. Immediately recognizable as an object of desire, Margaret is given a version of power which, like the power of all Petrarchan objects, returns itself to the man disempowered by her beauty. "Fie, de la Pole, disable not thyself," Suffolk says,

> Hast not a tongue? Is she not here?
> Wilt thou be daunted at a woman's sight?

> Ay, beauty's princely majesty is such
> Confounds the tongue and makes the senses rough.
>
> (ll. 67-71)

The hint that Margaret might possess the power to disable men—a hint to which the play will come back with, quite literally, a vengeance—is here transformed into a conventionally self-authored loss of speech analogous to that suffered by Sidney's Astrophil.[37]

The tropes that link sexual and political economies define Margaret's place onstage, making her at once a prize of war and a prisoner of love. "To be a queen in bondage is more vile / Than is a slave in base servility, / For princes should be free," she tells Suffolk, and he replies, "And so shall you, / If happy England's royal king be free" (ll. 112-15). The equation of sovereign privilege and erotic power will return to haunt the men who desire Margaret; for the moment, though, such shifts in agency and literalization are remote, and Suffolk constructs success from the familiar materials of Petrarchan language.

> Solicit Henry with her wondrous praise;
> Bethink thee on her virtues that surmount,
> And natural graces that extinguish art;
> Repeat their semblance often on the seas,
> That, when thou com'st to kneel at Henry's feet,
> Thou mayest bereave him of his wits with wonder.
>
> (ll. 190-95)

Agreeing to function as the connection between men, Margaret enables Suffolk to conquer his king, bringing Henry not only to desire but to dependence: "So am I driven by breath of her renown / Either to suffer shipwreck or arrive / Where I may have fruition of her love" (5.5.7-9). And yet, we should perhaps remember, triangles work in a number of directions; if Suffolk reads Margaret as a mediating term, for Margaret herself Suffolk mediates effectively—and briefly—between a position of disadvantage and one of extraordinary power. Margaret's body does not long remain a passive text, and Shakespeare's own text is governed less by Petrarchan conventions of desire than by the anxieties of a more material fragmentation. *Henry VI, Part 2* stages the shift from "Queen Margaret, England's happiness!" to the "blood-bespotted Neapolitan, / Outcast of Naples, England's bloody scourge!" of York's accusation (1.1.37; 5.1.117-18). Margaret, aggressively conventionalized as the matter of male bonds, becomes instead the cause of their most radical dissolution, precipitating the representational violence not of sonnets but of civil war.

Echoes of a familiar rhetoric attach themselves to Margaret long before York's reinvocation of the English scourge. "Such commendations as becomes a maid, / A virgin, and his servant, say to him," she instructs Suffolk at the end of *1 Henry VI* (5.3.177-78), immediately recalling that other maid who has scarcely left the stage.[38] But if Margaret's body—female, French, desirable, and of dubious lineage—recalls Joan la Pucelle, her performance is markedly different. She moves inward as decisively as Joan remains outside, her body focusing projections of the future as the body of Henry V had summoned nostalgia for the past. "Her valiant courage and undaunted spirit, / More than in women commonly is seen, / Will answer our hope in issue of a king" (*1HVI*, 5.5.70-72). Even here, in Suffolk's early words, Margaret is already both in and curiously out of place, her courage and spirit analogous to the conquests of Henry V, while Henry VI stands in a mediated relationship to both: "For Henry, son unto a conqueror, / Is likely to beget more conquerors, / If with a lady of so high resolve / As is fair Margaret he be linked in love" (ll. 73-76). The dynamics of this triangle, from the perspective of the living English male sovereign authority, have already gone wrong, as will those of the triangle formed by Margaret, Suffolk, and Henry VI. "She should have stayed in France and starved in France" (*2HVI*, 1.1.133), Gloucester says, but such literal marginalization, like the categoric strategy on which it relies, does not work for Margaret as it did for Joan. Identified as mother, queen, and wife, Margaret embodies a range of conventionally feminine obligations and transgressions that locate her in the midst of English nationalist negotiations, not despite but because of their aggressively domestic terms.

It is important to note that the disruptive effect of women in this play stems not from any rebellion against convention but from full participation in it. The Margaret of *2 Henry VI* plays out a woman's part: if the first play of this tetralogy presents the materiality of Joan's body iconographically, the second defines Margaret's body in terms of its utility, representing her first as an object and finally as an agent of acquisition. That shift in agency structures Margaret's appearances in the play, as the qualities that make her desirable to Suffolk and to Henry become the means through which she herself claims the agency of desire. Imagined as a royal accessory, she is acquired at a cost, gaining control of the English succession even as England loses control of France. The marriage, which Henry reads as a triumph of desire and Suffolk as a strategic climax, is for Margaret only the beginning. "Margaret shall now be Queen and rule the King; / But I will rule both her, the King, and realm" (5.5.107-8), Suffolk says at the end of *1 Henry VI*. It is a prophecy perhaps best answered by a stage direction from *2 Henry VI* that uncannily parallels Suffolk's entrance *"with Margaret in his hand"*: *"Enter the King with a supplication, and the Queen with Suffolk's head . . ."* (4.4, s.d.).

And *why,* we might briefly pause to wonder, is she carrying his head? Margaret does not directly cause Suffolk's death. But as she walks onstage, she has an odd effect on the doubled convention, erotic and political, of fragmentation-as-synthesis: the metaphor that presents the ruler as the head of the body politic, like the Petrarchan tropes that dissect the body of the mistress for the pleasure of other men, is displaced by this economy in which bodies, *men's* bodies, literally come apart. Margaret's mourning takes a darkly comic form— "Here may his head lie on my throbbing breast, / But where's the body that I should embrace?" (ll. 5-6)—as it materializes Suffolk's earlier conceit:

> If I depart from thee, I cannot live,
> And in thy sight to die, what were it else
> But like a pleasant slumber in thy lap?
> Here could I breathe my soul into the air,
> As mild and gentle as the cradle babe
> Dying with mother's dug between its lips. . .
>
> (3.2.388-93)

"Leaving you would kill me," the Petrarchan lover routinely tells his mistress, claiming her through her claim on him; but the dynamics of power look rather different if he is right. Objectified in such conventional terms, Margaret figures the ways in which conventions themselves might go wrong, reentering the representational space of *2 Henry VI* with the fragmented body of her object of desire.[39] And Suffolk's death marks the first explicit displacement of King Henry as well: "His body will I bear unto the King. / If he revenge it not, yet will his friends; / So will the Queen, that living held him dear," says the courtier who picks up the pieces (4.1.146-48). Imported to connect Suffolk to his king, Margaret transforms that connection into an image of violence and loss; in Margaret, Henry gets rather more than Suffolk had bargained for.

"These are no women's matters" (1.3.117), Glucester tells the queen as dissent threatens England, but the fragmentation central to *2 Henry VI* is precipitated first by male attempts to acquire Margaret and finally by Margaret's own strategies of acquisition, transforming passion into action, an object to an agent within explicitly feminine conditions of performance. Margaret effects disruption through adultery, envy, lust, shrewishness, extravagance, and conceit, her excesses conventionalized even as they are held responsible for the increasingly precarious state of England. Gloucester's wife Eleanor, who, like her husband, will fall victim to Margaret's revenge, recognizes her power of categorical upset, telling Henry: "Look to't in time. / She'll hamper thee and dandle thee like a baby. / Though in this place most master wear no breeches, / She shall not strike Dame Eleanor unrevenged" (ll. 144-47). But again, as in the Petrarchan fantasies of Suffolk and of King Henry himself, reading Margaret proves a dangerous business. The structures of power may be clear, but positions within them shift without warning; and Eleanor finds herself the object rather than the agent of revenge.

> Not all these lords do vex me half so much
> As that proud dame, the Lord Protector's wife.
> She sweeps it through the court with troops of ladies,
> More like an empress than Duke Humphrey's wife.
> Strangers in court do take her for the Queen.
>
> (ll. 75-79)

No one in Queen Margaret's court should look too much like Queen Margaret. But this is not the "Captain Margaret" of *3 Henry VI,* who emasculates her husband by taking command of his armies; this is instead a figure of specifically feminine pique, whose physical violence is limited to the stage direction *"She gives the Duchess a box on the ear"* (*2HVI,* 1.3.138, s.d.).

Margaret, in short, is dangerous in this play *because* she is conventional, because desire for her makes her husband an effeminate cuckold and because her own feminine vanity makes her a formidable political conspirator. The synthesis of desirability and agency disrupts the hierarchical relationship between homosocial privilege and the heterosexuality through which it is reproduced; Henry's marriage guarantees not the promised continuity of father and son but the intervention of women in the negotiations among men. Thus Gloucester falls as a consequence of both Margaret's ambition and his own conjugal indulgence, much as Henry falls to his own desire, for in the world of this play, men are victimized by Margaret's performance of femininity as effectively as York will be by her sword. Coppélia Kahn has argued that, in history plays, "liaisons with women are invariably disastrous because they subvert or destroy more valued alliances between men."[40] Such an effect, naturalized through repetition in the *Henry VI* plays, is in fact distinctly *un*-natural; it suggests that heterosexuality, rather than playing its proper part in the perpetuation of male homosocial systems of power, violates the hierarchical relationship on which that power is based, invading rather than delineating the space between men. Instead of the logic that draws men together through the processes of evaluation and exchange, these plays offer an alternative logic in which female agency disrupts male control over the significance of conventional roles. The terms of the *heimlich,* of domestic convention itself, thus become signs of disjunction rather than consolidation; in *2 Henry VI* the enemy is at home, and Henry's marriage, which Joyce Green MacDonald calls "a marriage contradicting in every particular the patriarchal mandate for the union of a prince," systematically strips him of the conditions of agency which, for the space of *3 Henry VI,* Margaret will take on.[41]

Henry's marriage to Margaret does not merely unman him but places him in a distinctly precarious relationship to the crown; echoing the chronicles, Gloucester holds that union responsible for the fragmentation of England itself.

> O peers of England, shameful is this league!
> Fatal this marriage, canceling your fame,
> Blotting your names from books of memory,
> Razing the characters of your renown,
> Defacing monuments of conquered France,
> Undoing all, as all had never been!
> 
> (1.1.96-101)

Margaret erases the glory of England as Joan la Pucelle had deflated posthumous Talbot's catalogue of glory—"Him that thou magnifi'st with all these titles / Stinking and fly-blown lies here at our feet" (4.7.75-76)—but here what Rackin has described as women's "anti-historical" effect is generated and articulated from within. Both Joan and Margaret threaten to obscure the terms through which men recognize one another and thus identify themselves, but in *2 Henry VI* history is obscured not by a battle but by a marriage. "My wife was wise and good had she bene rightly sought, / But our vnlawful getting it, may make a good thing nought," Henry says in *The Mirror for Magistrates.*[42] In *2 Henry VI,* Margaret, the "thing" to be "got," recoils upon the getter, turning the structures of acquisition and desire into her own narrative tools. Wanting to be queen, she marries Henry; wanting to be first in importance, she ousts Gloucester; simply, apparently, wanting, she acquires Suffolk, in whole and then in part. There is an insistently conventional femininity not only in the nature of these transgressions but in Margaret's mediated participation in them: as a desiring subject, she works indirectly, appropriating to her uses the structures and the desires of men. If Joan la Pucelle might consolidate an English male aristocratic ideal through opposition, Queen Margaret gets under its skin.

Domesticity, in this context, fails to reassure; there is no space, literal or mythological, between Margaret and England as there is between England and Joan, and Margaret's implication in nationalist and familial tropes fragments the political state even as she appropriates the rhetoric of statecraft. Margaret's presence is inescapably quotidian: where Joan's iconographic identities exist in synchronic contradiction, Margaret's have a diachronic utility. Chastity makes her a wife, sexuality makes her a queen, maternity makes her the mother of a prince, and, in *3 Henry VI,* martiality will make her an effective king. Because her roles begin in femininity and persist into usurpation, Margaret is difficult to put in her place; even Heywood, who places her among his "English Viragoes," prefers to say as little as possible, stating only that iconographic rhetoric lacks words to contain her.

> Of queene *Margaret* the wife of *Henrie* the sixt, her courage, resolution, and magnanimitie, to speake at large, would aske a Volume rather than a compendious discourse, to which I am strictly tyed. And therefore whosoever is desirous to be further instructed in the successe of those many battailes fought against the house of Yorke, in which she was personally present, I referre them to our English Chronicles, that are not sparing in commending her more than womanish spirit, to euerlasting memorie.[43]

As Heywood's catalogue of exempla directs the reader to the chronicles, diachronic action again displaces synchronic definition; Margaret must be read less according to what she is than to what she does. The privileging of action—or, in the context of Shakespeare's plays, of acting—is implicit in Margaret's adroit deployment of femininity in the second part of *Henry VI;* it will emerge fully in the aggressive seemings of the third.

To SEEM

As *3 Henry VI* begins, Margaret no longer stands in a mediated relationship to sovereign power. The king has become "Base, fearful, and despairing Henry!" (1.1.178), and Margaret claims the space of government. The claim, again, is based on an invasion that has already taken place. When Henry, yielding to York, disinherits his own son, Margaret first desires to disclaim her relationship to national and familial domesticity altogether: "Ah, wretched man! Would I had died a maid / And never seen thee, never borne thee son, / Seeing thou hast proved so unnatural a father!" (ll. 216-18). Margaret here wishes herself back in the position of Joan, the maid opposed to rather than implicated in the political and erotic terms of Englishness. But if for Joan that distance is always potentially an illusion, for Margaret it is not even that. Playing the roles of mother and wife, she chastises Henry for his own more tenuous connection to their son and by extension to kingship itself:

> Hadst thou but loved him half so well as I,
> Or felt that pain which I did for him once,
> Or nourished him as I did with my blood,
> Thou wouldst have left thy dearest heart-blood there,
> Rather than have made that savage duke thine heir
> And disinherited thine only son.
> 
> (ll. 220-25)

Constructing a causal relationship between maternity and good sovereignty, Margaret excludes the king, displacing him simultaneously in marital and martial terms: "I here divorce myself / Both from thy table, Henry, and thy bed. . . . The northern lords that have forsworn thy colors / Will follow mine, if once they see them spread" (ll. 247-48, 251-52). If generative heterosexuality identifies Margaret as the means through which Henry is connected to and reproduced in his son, here the means becomes an end; Margaret's declaration of agency, rather than her passively maternal body, reasserts the identity of Prince Edward as that identity is threatened by the king's paternal failure. Her martiality does not replace the conventional femininity of maternal obligation but emerges from it; with her claim to Henry's armies, Margaret makes violence itself domestic. Henry articulates the causality: "Poor Queen! How love to me and to her son / Hath made her break out into terms of rage!" (ll. 264-65), he says, revealing the sense in which the conventionalized femininity of *2 Henry VI* leads inexorably to the "ruthless queen" of *Part 3*. Margaret seems always to be between men in these plays, but as she shifts her investment from Suffolk to Henry, from Henry to his son, the dynamics of power implicit in that position become distinctly double-edged.

For the chroniclers Henry is "a ruler not Ruling," and Margaret, in consequence, becomes "quene Margarete his wyfe, in whom the whole rule of the realme consisted"; "The Quene, which bare the rule"; "the Quene, whiche then ruled the rost and bare the whole rule"; "Quene Margarete, whose breath ruled."[44] In such accounts Margaret's agency, however aggressively defined, results from the king's abdication; Hall writes, "[T]he Quene encouraged her frendes, and promised great rewardes to her helpers: for the kyng studied nothing but of peace, quyet and solitarie life."[45] Because there is no king, there must be Queen Margaret. Howard and Rackin suggest that this causality structures *3 Henry VI*: "Margaret's prominence in the action immediately suggests a weakness in the patriarchal structures that should have rendered her less visible and less powerful"; they conclude, "The scandal of *Henry VI, Part III* is not that a woman is a general, but that a man, and an anointed king to boot, can perform none of the actions expected of a father and a king."[46] But I think that for Shakespeare the construction of Queen Margaret is a more deliberate process: as it conflates claims to maternal and martial agency, her statement "I here divorce myself" takes on the force of a speech act, creating a role that exceeds the space left empty by the king. Accused of playing the Amazon, Queen Margaret figures an agency that is constructed without being contingent. Within the terms of amazonian logic, women may assume power through the absence of men, but in so doing, they alter the conditions of power itself, making it difficult if not impossible for the conventional relationships between agency and maleness to return. As she brings the spectacle of female martiality into England and into the play's national and familial structures, Margaret appropriates a kind of editorial control over what the roles of king and queen, husband and wife, man and woman can be understood to *mean,* closing down the imaginative possibility of a naturalized reinscription of hierarchy. The terms through which Margaret becomes amazonian are those of recognizing something already in place, not of discovering something new. Conventional domesticity does not provide a space of safety in *3 Henry VI,* for both Margaret's rhetoric and that which describes her suggest that martial women are not born but can be made.

"I would Your Highness would depart the field. / The Queen hath best success when you are absent," Clifford tells Henry, and Margaret adds, "Ay, good my lord, and leave us to our fortune" (2.2.73-75). This differs subtly but significantly from the account given by the chronicles, in which Margaret's success contextualizes Henry's failure: "Happy was the quene in her two battayls, but vnfortunate was the kyng in all his enterprises, for where his person was presente, ther victory fled euer from him to the other parte, & he commonly was subdued & vanqueshed."[47] In *3 Henry VI* Margaret's possessive—*our* fortune—exiles Henry from the condition of England; he does not lose the battle so much as vanish from its terms of representation, as when his son tells him, "When I return with victory from the field, / I'll see Your Grace. Till then I'll follow her" (1.1.261-62). The dyad of mother and son, like that of sovereign and subjects, excludes the king, for the Margaret of *3 Henry VI* is no longer constructed through triangles. Her roles draw substance from familial and political connections, but her relationship to agency is not contingent on third terms. Having consolidated the functions of domesticity, Margaret makes maternal and national obligation the same thing: to fight for her son is to fight for the integrity of England itself. "A woman's general. What should we fear?" Richard asks; but in the world of *3 Henry VI,* in which Margaret's synthesis of martiality and maternity intervenes in the connections and actions conventionally reserved for men, his question contains a differently self-evident answer than he imagines.

Where Joan la Pucelle embodies contradictory iconographic positions by literalizing a series of tropes, Margaret consolidates contradiction through the explicitness of playing, her masculine performance inseparable from the fictional female body she presents onstage. For Margaret's role-playing, even when referred to what seem the most essential of causes, is relentlessly performative; having appropriated the terms of Englishness, she disrupts them through a theatrical presence that confounds materiality and illusion. Butler writes, "[T]he regulatory norms of 'sex' work in a performative fashion to constitute the materiality of bodies and, more specifically, to materialize the body's sex, to materialize sexual difference in the service of the consolidation of the heterosexual imperative. . . . what constitutes the fixity of the body, its contours, its movements, will be fully material, but materiality will be rethought as the effect of power."[48] On the early modern stage such apparently counterintuitive causalities of embodiment reflect dramatic necessity, and for history plays the relationship between performative agency and political power poses questions that are particularly acute. For *3 Henry VI* those questions are at once focused and redoubled as the concerns of politics and sex converge in Queen Margaret. The connections among power, performance, and heterosexual imperatives produce a female sexual body that is not only a theatrical but a political intervention. And if, as Butler suggests, heterosexual sociality constructs and makes use of certain kinds of bodies, the manifestly constructed body of Margaret makes effective use of heterosexual sociality itself. A boy-actor in a woman's part, a Frenchwoman who becomes England's queen, a queen who acts as a king, a mother who defends the patrilineal rights of her son by standing in a father's place, Shakespeare's Queen Margaret constructs agency through a revision of the relationship of bodies to acts and of women to the systematic conventions of masculine identity.

Because these plays attempt to identify the center against what it is not—or, in the case of Queen Margaret, what it should not be—the space of English male subjectivity is defined by the performances of women. And, with Margaret's various deployments of domesticity, that space becomes ever more claustrophobic. As I have suggested, her domestic sphere is national as well as familial, a conflation that inflects the play more generally. Thus, having captured York, Margaret brings home the frustration of his political ambition through a death in the family: "Look, York, I stained this napkin with the blood / That valiant Clifford, with his rapier's point, / Made issue from the bosom of the boy" (1.4.79-81). Rutland's death, which is for Margaret a logical consequence of this kind of war, represents for his father a monstrous crossing of lines:

> O tiger's heart wrapped in a woman's hide!
> How couldst thou drain the lifeblood of the child,
> To bid the father wipe his eyes withal,
> And yet be seen to bear a woman's face?
> Women are soft, mild, pitiful, and flexible;
> Thou stern, obdurate, flinty, rough, remorseless.
>
> (ll. 137-42)

York here attempts to re-separate, to oppose "women" to "Margaret" and prove through her acts that she is not one; calling on conventions of femininity, he rhetorically returns women to their place. Yet Margaret's performance disrupts the masculine structures that give such conventions authority, denaturalizing the distinctions on which York insists; and even his own language mirrors Margaret's privileging of playing, of seeming over being seen to be. The verb of equation linking Margaret to the qualities she does or does not possess connects her to adjectives rather than to nouns; where Joan is Amazon, witch, strumpet, scourge, Margaret is stern, obdurate, flinty, rough, remorseless. Margaret does not *seem as, act as* she should, and York's metaphor of the "tiger's heart wrapped in a woman's hide," figuring the female body as a costume, implicates sexual essentialism itself in the rhetoric of performance.

According to York, Margaret epitomizes all that women and queens should not be: "But that thy face is, vizard-like, unchanging, / Made impudent with use of evil deeds, / I would assay, proud queen, to make thee blush" (ll. 116-18). According to early modern monitory texts, however, she acts precisely as women and queens always threaten to do; *The English Gentlewoman,* for example, describes predictable disillusion rather than monstrous wonders but echoes York's rhetoric closely nonetheless. "What prodegy fuller of wonder, then to see a woman thus transformed from nature?" Brathwait writes. "Her *face* is not her owne, note her *complexion;* her *eye* is not her owne, note her *straid motion;* her *habit* is not her owne, eye her *strange fashion.* Whilest *loose weares* imply *light workes;* and thin cobwebbe couers promise free admittance to all sensuall louers."[49] In such clichés, as in Shakespeare's first Henriad, female excess, inherently theatrical, is at once a snare for men and an appropriation of apparent maleness. Cosmetics and clothes produce a strangely masculine monster, and exposure of the essential woman holds as many unpleasant surprises as does the armor of feminine convention. Joan Riviere refers to "the conception of womanliness as a mask, behind which man suspects some hidden danger."[50] In *3 Henry VI* the danger is doubled: to interrogate one masquerade is to be confronted by another, and any attempt to see *either* the woman *or* the warrior results only in the reminder that Margaret, at any given moment, quite efficiently seems to be both. "Tell him my mourning weeds are laid aside / And I am ready to put armor on" (3.3.229-30), she says in response to Edward's challenge; her response, like Joan's encounter with young Talbot, is later mediated by quotation marks. The Post relays the message—"'Tell him,' quoth she, 'my mourning weeds are done, / And I am ready to put armor on'"—to which Edward replies, "Belike she minds to play the Amazon" (4.1.104-6).

The anxiety produced by such playing emerges fully in the only simile of York's great speech: "How ill-beseeming is it in thy sex / To triumph, like an Amazonian trull / Upon their woes whom fortune captivates!" (1.4.113-15). The term that finds a logical referent in Joan la Pucelle is attached only fearfully and contingently—"*like* an Amazonian trull"—to England's queen. If Margaret is "Amazonian," the adjective attaches itself uneasily; for if she marks the space "beyond"—beyond Englishness, maleness, a constant and referential understanding of power—she does so from so far inside the structures defining those terms that it is not clear where the English male aristocratic hero can safely go. "[Y]ou are more inhuman, more inexorable, / O, ten times more, than tigers of Hyrcania. / See, ruthless Queen, a hapless father's tears!" says York (ll. 154-56); the "inhumanity" of Margaret's performance lies in its exposure of the transgressive potential of women's roles, its playing out of the anxious possibility of literalization. Margaret gives York the blood of his son, identifying it by defining the paternal connection that he cannot recognize without her help. Metaphorically articulated, such an act precisely enables male bonding, using women to materialize fantasies of parthenogenesis. Literalizing the rhetoric of those fantasies in an act of violence, Margaret dismantles patrilineal systems of connection.

This is the threat posed by the amazonian in *3 Henry VI*: the play does not attack the conventions that define women's roles but performs them, demonstrating their vulnerability to revision from within. Margaret's transgressions gain force from their revelation that the logic of transgression is already in place, for in fact the terms of seeming—or, to take up York's term, ill-beseeming—that attend Margaret's performance are not alien but familiar. As John Knox's rhetoric in *The First Blast* suggests, female dominance might always shift from the political to the personal and back again; Knox's notorious observation that those seeing England under female rule "should judge the whole world to be transformed into Amazons" is followed by a detailed discussion of the Amazon at home.

> To the further declaration of the imperfections of women, of their natural weakness and inordinate appetites, I might adduce histories proving some women to have died for sudden joy, some for unpatience to have murdered themselves; some to have burned with such inordinate lust that, for the quenching of the same, they have betrayed to strangers their country and city; and some to have been so desirous of dominion that, for the obtaining of the same, they have murdered the children of their own sons. Yea, and some have killed with cruelty their own husbands and children.[51]

Women, Knox argues, are always potentially excessive, always potentially amazonian: women make bad enemies; women will betray their countries; women will become dangerous within the family, killing their children and their men. The Margaret of *3 Henry VI* emerges from this tradition of anxious polemics, in which the amazonian is linked to the domestic through terms of violence. The most logical victims of that violence are the husbands and children whose identity conventional femininity should work to mediate and define.

As Margaret's first victim, King Henry VI is identified in terms of his vulnerability to revision; in Warwick's words,

> The proud insulting Queen,
> With Clifford and the haught Northumberland,
> And of their feather many more proud birds,
> Have wrought the easy-melting King like wax.
>
> (2.1.168-71)

Describing himself as "the hapless male to one sweet bird" (5.6.15), Henry can be understood only in relation to the desires and intentions of his wife. Conquering her husband erotically and aesthetically, Margaret literalizes the fantasy of female power articulated by Suffolk and by Henry himself in conventionally Petrarchan terms; the revelation of *3 Henry VI* is that Petrarchan fictions have real consequences, leading as naturally to "Captain Margaret" as they do to the rhetoric of desire.[52] And Warwick, describing Henry as "My sovereign, with the loving citizens, / Like to his island girt in with the ocean, Or modest Dian circled with her nymphs" (4.8.19-21), suggests that a woman who appropriates the power ascribed to her by the language of courtship does so at the expense of men. Explicitly feminized, aestheticized, and made chaste, a Diana more modest than martial, Henry himself becomes a Petrarchan object, protected from the obligations of maleness and of kingship. As Diodorus writes of the Amazons, "Theire husbondes stonde in like condition as women and wives doo among vs in oure contrey, ordeyned of purpose to kepe the house at home, to be buxom and obedient vnto theire wives, clerely discharged from all maner of warre, beryng no rome nor office of worship in theire contrey."[53]

Richard wishes of Margaret "That you might still have worn the petticoat, / And ne'er have stol'n the breech from Lancaster" (5.5.23-24), but King Henry, mediating between memories of his father and hopes for his son, is always contingent—the significance of his death divided between foreshadowing and afterthought, the death itself a virtual aside. Prince Edward, too, represents a presence substantiated only through nostalgia and anticipation. Thus Oxford says of him, "O brave young prince! Thy famous grandfather / Doth live again in thee: long mayst thou live / To bear his image and renew his glories" (5.4.50-54). But for Prince Edward, as for his father, the connection to Henry V is displaced, his past and future defined and circumscribed by a body that is still onstage. Howard and Rackin argue that "the play also demystifies the idea that patriarchal blood lines, even ones unadulterated by bastardy, guarantee the valor or worth of the father's descendants. . . . Edward claims the throne in his father's name, but he does so in his mother's spirit."[54] Edward—the other Edward—calls Margaret "You, that are King, though he do wear the crown," and the crown prince is most recognizably his mother's son. In Richard's words, "Whoever got thee, there thy mother stands; / For well I wot thou hast thy mother's tongue" (2.2.90, 133-34).

The multiple representations of Margaret turn against her son even as they are turned to his cause; her role-playing itself precludes the return of kingship to any uncontested state. When Prince Edward appropriates the rhetoric of sovereignty, he does so through an essentialist logic that is newly fragile, his contested position as male heir figuring the play's detachment of referentiality from men. In response to Warwick's "Injurious Margaret!" Prince Edward asks, "And why not Queen?" Warwick's reply reveals that such signifiers are not firmly fixed: "Because they father Henry did usurp; / And thou no more art Prince than she is Queen" (3.3.78-80). Relying on primogeniture, Prince Edward is vulnerable to the failure of that term; and his connection to Henry V, like his father's, is ultimately a false trail, or at least one obscured by Margaret's intervention. The impossibility in this play of returning to an unproblematic condition of patrilineal logic results directly from her attempt to stage-manage such a return. When women cease to be objects proving a connection among men and become instead agents attempting to impose it, the register of the connection necessarily shifts from the natural to the constructed. This is the lesson that Prince Edward does not learn; where Margaret inverts sovereignty through a consolidation of roles, her son reads it as self-evident. And, in *3 Henry VI*, in the newly formed court of the rival King Edward IV, he reads it wrongly. His body recalls not a heroic past but the presence of his mother, and the terms of his death—Edward's "Take that, thou likeness of this railer here"—insist that his mother's body signifies as his father's name does not. This is a mirror game not between two King Edwards but between mother and son, and it is distinctly unhealthy to be the son of an Amazon.[55]

Margaret's rhetoric of mourning is at once conventionally maternal and a sharp reminder of another, earlier moment of violence. Comparing her son's death to that of Caesar, she says, "He was a man; this (in respect) a child, / And men ne'er spend their fury on a child" (5.5.51-57). Men may not; Margaret already has. And the death of Rutland reappears, not only as a linguistic ghost in a metatheatrical revenge plot but as a reminder that, through Margaret, domestic violence connects the fragmentation of families to that of England itself. *Henry VI, Part 3* does not present a dynamic in which essentialized femininity gives way to martial agency only to collapse back into maternal helplessness. Instead, the conditions of martiality are always those of maternity, and the female body is itself staged as performance.[56] Grieving mother, like grieving wife, is a role, neither more nor less genuine than the condition of being beautiful or amazonian or tiger-like. "Here sheathe thy sword. I'll pardon thee my death" (l. 70), Margaret tells her tormentors. Even physical vulnerability is a trope, a reminder of the fact that both rape and death here operate at the level of metaphor and that such metaphorical swords always cut both ways.

As it makes visible the constructedness of dramatic conventions and gender roles, Margaret's amazonian performance precipitates the disjoining of men from one another and from any essentialized condition of masculinity. By the play's conclusion, her presence seems necessary for masculinity to be connected to men at all. Before the final battle, it is not Prince Edward's presence or the king's name but Margaret's rhetoric that clothes men in the performativity of heroism, as the prince himself observes: "Methinks a woman of this valiant spirit / Should, if a coward heard her speak these words, / Infuse his breast with magnanimity, / And make him, naked, foil a man at arms" (5.4.39-42). This is only a local example of Margaret's larger implication in the structures of violence; from the beginning the play is explicit about her responsibility not only for individual performances of masculine martiality but for martial conflict itself. According to Edward, duke of York, it is her role-playing that brings England to irrecoverable self-fragmentation: "For what hath broached this tumult but thy pride? / Hadst thou been meek, our title still had slept; / And we, in pity of the gentle King, / Had slipped our claim until another age" (2.2.159-62). Having brought England to civil war, Margaret bears a responsibility that is theatrical as well as political and identifies her as the cause of the play: "Hadst thou been meek, our title still had slept"—or, in Edward's final condemnation, "No, wrangling woman, we'll no longer stay. / These words will cost ten thousand lives this day" (ll. 176-77). Margaret is thus conventionally feminized as a "wrangling woman" even as she plays her most martial role. Her own rhetoric of inspiration participates in the conflation of nationalist impulses with her position as a grieving wife: "Lords, knights, and gentlemen, what I should say / My tears gainsay; for every word I speak, / Ye see, I drink the water of mine eye" (5.4.73-75). Because her domestic chaos coincides with England's own, Margaret anticipates the state of disconnection toward which the tetralogy tends. Relationships defined in nationalist or familial terms are relentlessly denaturalized by her performative play. At the moment of victorious consolidation, Edward IV finds it difficult to banish this ghostly reminder of contingency and loss, as his proliferation of insistences suggests: "Away with her. Go, bear her hence perforce"; "Away, I say! I charge ye bear her hence"; "Away with her, and waft her hence to France." (5.5.68, 81; 5.7.41). The last question in this play full of questions—"What will Your Grace have done with Margaret?" (5.7.37)—suggests that disposing of an amazonian queen is a difficult speech act indeed.

The answer to this question is, I think, another question: as he contemplates the captive Margaret, Richard asks, "Why should she live, to fill the world with words?" (5.5.44). The image has a particularly historical—or perhaps, in Rackin's term, antihistorical—referent, for Margaret will indeed live on ahistorically into the England of *Richard III,* continuing to offer political forecasts long after she should have died in ignominious exile. Rather than disappearing in response to Edward's slightly hysterical orders, Margaret brings into the world of *Richard III* the economy of fragmentation and loss that had so distressed York, an economy in which kings are traded for kings, husbands for husbands, sons for sons:

> Though not by war, by surfeit die your
>   king,
> As ours by murder, to make him a king!
> Edward thy son, that now is Prince of Wales,
> For Edward our son, that was Prince of
>   Wales,
> Die in his youth by like untimely violence!
> Thyself a queen, for me that was a queen,
> Outlive thy glory, like my wretched self!
>                                    (1.3.197-203)

Through the anomalous presence of Queen Margaret, the language of reciprocity, which defines men as the tokens and the victims of exchange while women survive to count the costs, persists into *Richard III*.[57] Having survived the three parts of *Henry VI,* Margaret in this final play explicates the conflation of the political and the domestic that she has so disruptively performed, theorizing the narrative of loss that equates civil war and family feud.

To return to Clarence's question, what is to be done with Margaret? Edward's response at the end of *3 Henry VI* is a refusal of circles or mirrors, a statement that historical spectacles always move forward:

> And now what rests but that we spend the
>   time
> With stately triumphs, mirthful comic shows,
> Such as befits the pleasure of the court?
> Sound drums and trumpets! Farewell sour
>   annoy!
> For here, I hope, begins our lasting joy.
>                                    (5.7.42-46)

Edward is notoriously wrong here, and the failure to evade images and repetitions of the past, figured through the persistent presence of Queen Margaret, haunts not only *Richard III* but literary history itself. Robert Greene, in his notorious critique of Shakespearean originality, returns to what seems to have become a kind of historical primal scene:

> trust them not: for there is an vpstart Crow, beautified with our feathers, that with his *Tygers hart wrapt in a Players hyde,* supposes he is as well able to bombast out blanke verse as the best of you: and beeing an absolute *Iohannes fac totum,* is in his owne conceit the onely Shake-scene in a countery.[58]

Greene's misquotation is a near-quotation that replaces "woman" with "player" in a gesture that is no substitution at all. In playing, in seeming, in the ruthless appropriation of text, Shakespeare is equated with the Queen Margaret of his own reinvention.[59] If Joan la Pucelle has been taken to identify *1 Henry VI* as "not Shakespeare's," Margaret here becomes the sign that Shakespeare's text was never his to begin with—or perhaps such conventions of ownership, like Margaret's own paradoxical conventionality, produce only an infinite circularity, for what does it mean to attack Shakespeare for having no words of his own if the attack is formulated in Shakespeare's own words? Here again an attack from outside takes the form of that which is already inside; again the terms of alienation reproduce even as they invade the *heimlich;* and again Margaret, brought to England to articulate a relationship among men, becomes less the matter of that relationship than the sign of its radical failure.

*Notes*

[1] Edward Hall, *The Vnion of the two noble and illustrate fameliest of Lancastre and Yorke beeyng long in continual discension for the croune of this noble realme* (London, 1548), fol. Clj$^r$; and Richard Brathwait, *The English Gentlewoman, drawne out to the full Body: Expressing, What* Habilliments *doe best attire her, What* Ornaments *doe best adorne her, What* Complements *doe best accomplish her* (London, 1631), 40.

[2] Joseph Candido offers a useful overview of such structural readings in his essay "Getting Loose in the Henry VI Plays," *Shakespeare Quarterly* 35 (1984): 392-406, esp. 392n; see also Phyllis Rackin's description of the tetralogy in *Stages of History: Shakespeare's English Chronicles* (Ithaca, NY: Cornell UP, 1990), 62.

[3] For readings of the tetralogy's women as similar to one another, see David Bevington, "The Domineering Female in *1 Henry VI,*" *Shakespeare Studies* 2 (1966): 51-58, esp. 51; Leah Marcus, *Puzzling Shakespeare: Local Reading and its Discontents* (Berkeley: U of California P, 1988), 89-90; and Phyllis Rackin, "Anti-Historians: Women's Roles in Shakespeare's Histories," *Theatre Journal* 37 (1985): 329-44, esp. 332.

[4] Jean E. Howard and Phyllis Rackin, *Engendering a Nation: A feminist account of Shakespeare's English histories* (London and New York: Routledge, 1997), 65.

[5] Lisa Jardine, *Still Harping on Daughters: Women and Drama in the Age of Shakespeare* (Sussex, UK: Harvester Press, 1983), 105.

[6] Sigmund Freud, "The 'Uncanny'" (1919) in *The Standard Edition of the Complete Psychological Works*

*of Sigmund Freud,* ed. and trans. James Strachey, 24 vols. (London: The Hogarth Press, 1953), 17:220.

[7] Freud, 226. Freud reaches this claim by tracing the contradictory definitions of *heimlich;* for his extended analysis, see 220-26.

[8] Bevington, 51-58; Rackin, "Anti-Historians," 329; Marcus, 75; Nancy Gutierrez, "Gender and Value in *1 Henry VI:* The Role of Joan de Pucelle," *Theatre Journal* 42 (1990): 183-93, esp. 190; Patricia-Ann Lee, "Reflections of Power: Margaret of Anjou and the Dark Side of Queenship," *Renaissance Quarterly* 39 (1986): 183-217, esp. 214; and Christopher Pye, "The Theater, the Market, and the Subject of History," *English Literary History* 61 (1994): 501-22, esp. 511.

[9] Phyllis Rackin, "Historical Difference/Sexual Difference" in *Privileging Gender in Early Modern England,* Jean R. Brink, ed. (Kirksville, MO: Sixteenth Century Journal Publishers, 1993), 37-64, esp. 43.

[10] For an anthropological account of the processes through which women mediate and materialize connections among men, see Gayle Rubin, "The Traffic in Women: Notes on the 'Political Economy' of Sex" in *Toward an Anthropology of Women,* Rayna R. Reiter, ed. (New York: Monthly Review Press, 1975). For further theorization of women's roles in the construction of male homosocial bonds, see Eve Kosofsky Sedgwick, *Between Men: English Literature and Male Homosocial Desire* (New York: Columbia UP, 1985), esp. 1-20; and David M. Halperin, "Why is Diotima a Woman?" in *One Hundred Years of Homosexuality and Other Essays on Greek Love* (New York: Routledge, 1990).

[11] Judith Butler, *Gender Trouble: Feminism and the Subversion of Identity* (New York: Routledge, 1990), 140.

[12] Theseus's marriage to Hippolyta produces tragedy in a literal sense, resulting in the illicit desire of Phaedra for Hippolytus, staged by Seneca in *Hippolytus.*

[13] Quotations from the *Henry VI* plays follow *The Complete Works of Shakespeare,* ed. David Bevington, 4th ed. (New York: HarperCollins, 1992).

[14] Jacques Lacan, "The Signification of the Phallus" in *Écrits: A Selection,* trans. Alan Sheridan (New York: W. W. Norton, 1977), 281-91, esp. 289.

[15] Barbara Freedman, *Staging the Gaze: Postmodernism, Psychoanalysis, and Shakespearean Comedy* (Ithaca, NY: Cornell UP, 1991), 3.

[16] Howard and Rackin, *Engendering a Nation,* 93.

[17] Rackin, "Anti-Historians," 334. For an earlier version of this opposition of material to spiritual, see Bevington's claim that "Talbot triumphantly demonstrates the ascendancy of the truest sort of masculinity—not man's body but his mind and soul—over the trammels of the flesh" ("The Domineering Female," 55).

[18] Judith Butler, *Bodies That Matter: On the Discursive Limits of 'Sex'* (New York: Routledge, 1993), 3.

[19] Howard and Rackin, *Engendering a Nation,* 47.

[20] See for example Gutierrez's argument concerning Joan's effect on the audience: "The French soldiers and the contemporary English audience, normally 'natural' enemies, become allies when threatened by a woman" (190).

[21] George Bernard Shaw, *Saint Joan* (1924; rpt. New York: Random House, 1956), 3.

[22] Hall, fols. Cvii$^r$ and Cxiii$^v$. On the relationship between Shakespeare's portrayal of Joan and the chronicles', see Richard F. Hardin, "Chronicles and Mythmaking in Shakespeare's Joan of Arc," *Shakespeare Survey* 42 (1990): 25-35.

[23] Gabriele Bernhard Jackson, "Topical Ideology: Witches, Amazons, and Shakespeare's Joan of Arc," *English Literary Renaissance* 18 (1988): 40-65, esp. 64-65. See also Clayton G. MacKenzie, "Myth and Anti-Myth in the First Tetralogy," *Orbis Litterarum* 42 (1987): 1-26, esp. 2-3.

[24] Henry Cornelius Agrippa, *Female Pre-eminence: or the Dignity and Excellency of that Sex, above the Male* (1509), trans. H[enry] C[ase] (London, 1670), 66-67.

[25] See Christopher Newstead, *An Apology for Women: or, Womens Defence* (London, 1620), 17-18.

[26] See Thomas Heywood, *GYNAIKEION: or, Nine Bookes of Various History Concerninge Women* (London, 1624).

[27] Agrippa, 66.

[28] Heywood, 236. Christine de Pizan, whose *Le Ditié de Jeanne d'Arc* was the first poem praising Joan of Arc and the only one written during Joan's lifetime, celebrates her martial conquests without apparent ambivalence; for Christine de Pizan, of course, neither Joan's nationality nor her sex gave cause for concern. For one reading of this poem in the context of Christine's life and other writings, see Charity Cannon Willard, *Christine de Pizan: Her Life and Works* (New York: Persea Books, 1984), 204-7. For a discussion of the poem in the context of other early

literary representations of Joan of Arc, see Deborah Fraioli, "The Literary Image of Joan of Arc: Prior Influences," *Speculum* 56 (1981): 811-30.

[29] On the confusion of categories, see Jeanne Addison Roberts, "Birth Traumas in Shakespeare," *Renaissance Papers* (1990): 55-66, esp. 62.

[30] Johannes Ludovicus Vives, *A very Frutefull and pleasant boke called the Instruction of a Christen Woman,* trans. Richard Hyrde (London, 1541), G2$^r$.

[31] For a reading of Joan's feminization as a trope of woman-taming, see Jackson, 60.

[32] Shaw calls Joan "the pioneer of rational dressing for women" (3). On the visual doubleness of female body and masculine armor, see Marcus, 100; Gutierrez, 185; and Jackson, 54.

[33] Rackin, "Anti-Historians," 331. Catherine Belsey reads Joan in the context of such "extra-human" figures as Cleopatra and Lady Macbeth; see *The Subject of Tragedy: Identity and difference in Renaissance drama* (London: Methuen, 1985), 185.

[34] See, for example, Hardin, 35; Pye, 511; and John D. Cox, "Devils and Power in Marlowe and Shakespeare," *The Yearbook of English Studies: Early Shakespeare Special Number* 23 (1993): 46-64, esp. 61.

[35] Marcus, 53.

[36] E.M.W. Tillyard, *Shakespeare's History Plays* (London: Chatto and Windus, 1948), 162. Shaw suggests that even if the play is Shakespeare's, the intention is not, a possibility that displaces guilt while maintaining authority: "The impression left by it is that the playwright, having begun by an attempt to make Joan a beautiful and romantic figure, was told by his scandalized company that English patriotism would never stand a sympathetic representation of a French conquerer of English troops, and that unless he at once introduced all the old charges against Joan of being a sorceress and harlot, and assumed her to be guilty of all of them, his play could not be produced. As likely as not, this is what actually happened" (24).

[37] This conceit, that looking at the beloved object causes a loss of language which nonetheless produces poetry, runs throughout such sonnet sequences as *Astrophil and Stella*. See, for example, the famous concluding lines of Sonnet 1: "Thus great with child to speak, and helpless in my throes, / Biting my truant pen, beating myself for spite, / 'Fool,' said my Muse to me, 'look in thy heart and write' " (*Sir Philip Sidney: Selected Poems,* ed. Catherine Bates [New York: Penguin Books, 1994], ll. 12-14).

[38] Lee, in her account of the ways in which Margaret is iconographically connected to Joan, quotes Pius II: "They said that the spirit of the Maid, who had raised Charles to the throne, was renewed in the Queen" (199).

[39] For readings of this stage direction, see Janet Adelman, *Suffocating Mothers: Fantasies of Maternal Origin in Shakespeare's Plays,* Hamlet to The Tempest (New York: Routledge, 1992), 8; and Rackin, "Historical Difference," 42.

[40] Coppélia Kahn, *Man's Estate: Masculine Identity in Shakespeare* (Berkeley: U of California P, 1981), 55.

[41] Joyce Green MacDonald, " 'Hay for the Daughters!': Gender and Patriarchy in *The Miseries of Civil War* and *Henry VI*," *Comparative Drama* 24 (1990): 193-216, esp. 209.

[42] "How king Henry the syxt a vertuous prince, was after many other miseries cruelly murdered in the Tower of London" in *The Mirror for Magistrates* (1559), ed. Lily B. Campbell (Cambridge: Cambridge UP, 1938), 216.

[43] Heywood, 239-40. It is worth noting that reticence verging on disavowal characterizes the end of Hey—wood's list of viragoes: Joan la Pucelle, of whom he would prefer to say nothing that others have not already said, is followed by Emma, of whose slaughter of the Danes he says, "though it after prooued ominous, and was the cause of much miserie and mischiefe, yet it shewed in her a noble and notable resolution"; and Emma is followed by Margaret, the last item in his catalogue, of whom he would apparently prefer to say nothing at all. Here, as in the *Henry VI* plays, even the encomiasts show a certain ambivalence. For Heywood in particular this ambivalence appears to exercise its own fascination; in his 1640 catalogue of female worthies, *The Exemplary Lives and Memorable Acts of Nine the Most Worthy Women of the World,* he will return to Queen Margaret, making her his second Christian and his penultimate queen, to be followed only by Queen Elizabeth herself.

[44] Hall, fols. Clij$^r$, Cliiij$^r$, Clix$^{r-v}$, Clxvij$^v$, and Clxx$^v$. For readings of a possible connection between such descriptions of Margaret and representations of Queen Elizabeth I, see Lee, 214-17; and Marcus, 89-93.

[45] Hall, fol. Clxxvj$^v$.

[46] Howard and Rackin, *Engendering a Nation,* 84 and 85. See also Kahn's statement, "From this point on, it is Margaret who takes charge of the Lancastrian cause, a woman stepping into the vacuum of authority left by a weak man" (60-61).

[47] Hall, fol. Clxxxiiij$^r$.

[48] Butler, *Bodies That Matter,* 2.

[49] Brathwait, 123.

[50] Joan Riviere, "Womanliness as a Masquerade" (1929) in *The Inner World and Joan Riviere: Collected Papers 1920-1958,* ed. Athol Hughes (London: Karnac Books for the Melanie Klein Trust, 1991), 90-101, esp. 101.

[51] John Knox, *The First Blast of the Trumpet Against the Monstrous Regiment of Women* (1558) in *The Political Writings of John Knox,* ed. Marvin A. Breslow (Washington, DC: The Folger Shakespeare Library, 1985), 37-80, esp. 44-45.

[52] On the relationship between male tyranny and female sexual excess, see Rebecca Bushnell, "Tyranny and Effeminacy in Early Modern England" in *Reconsidering the Renaissance,* Mario A. di Cesare, ed. (Binghamton, NY: Medieval and Renaissance Texts and Studies, 1992), 335-54, esp. 343.

[53] Diodorus Siculus, *The Bibliotheca Historica,* trans. John Skelton, 2 vols. (London: Oxford UP, 1956), 1:287-88.

[54] Howard and Rackin, *Engendering a Nation,* 87.

[55] For accounts of Amazon violence against male children, see Diodorus Siculus, 200; and Strabo, *Geography of Strabo,* trans. Horace Leonard Jones, 8 vols. (London: William Heinemann, 1918), 5:235. Amazonian maternity is, in this sense, always about breaking the bonds among men.

[56] For readings of Margaret's grief as feminization, see Howard and Rackin, *Engendering a Nation,* 97; and Irene G. Dash, *Wooing, Wedding, and Power: Women in Shakespeare's Plays* (New York: Columbia UP, 1981), 191.

[57] For samples of the ongoing debate over Margaret's agency—do curses make history or merely take advantage of hindsight?—see Marcus, 95; and Rackin, "Anti-Historians," 337. For a historical view of the contingency of Margaret's power, see Lee, 192.

[58] Robert Greene, *Greenes Groatsworth of witte, bought with a million of Repentance* (London, 1592), F1$^v$.

[59] For readings of the relationship between Margaret and Shakespeare as suggested by Greene, see Howard and Rackin, *Engendering a Nation,* 96; see also Marcus, 96.

---

Source: "Fearful Simile: Stealing the Breech in Shakespeare's Chronicle Plays," in *Shakespeare Quarterly,* Vol. 49, No. 2, Summer, 1998, pp. 140-67.

# Tragedies

# Nobler in the Mind: The Dialect in *Hamlet*

## Geoffrey Aggeler, *University of Utah, Salt Lake City*

Let us imagine a Renaissance neostoic, such as Sir William Cornwallis the Younger, or Philippe de Mornay, or Joseph Hall, watching an early performance of *Hamlet* at the Globe sometime between 1599 and 1602. Mornay would be on an embassy from France, busy about promoting the interests of the Protestant cause and perhaps his Calvinist disposition would keep him away from the theater, but then again the memory of his good friend Sir Philip Sidney, who had a taste for Senecan tragedy, might influence him to attend. Joseph Hall, who had only recently given up the writing of Juvenalian formal verse satire and was about to enter the Anglican Church, might have had similar Calvinistic scruples. Sir William Cornwallis, whose essays are full of Shakespearean echoes, would have had no such scruples and probably did attend it, perhaps in company with his friend John Donne.

The Neostoic playgoer would certainly recognize the familiar outline of the model that emerges from Seneca's moral writings, the sage. He would perhaps discern part of it in the "To be, or not to be" (III. i. 55-88)[1] soliloquy as Hamlet considers the option of passively enduring the slings and arrows of outrageous fortune. He would certainly recognize it fully sketched out in the encomium on Horatio (III. ii. 63-72). It would, presumably, be gratifying to the moral sense of this playgoer to watch Hamlet progress from envy and admiration for the Stoic ideal to the Stoic faith he expresses in the final scene. Hearing "the readiness is all," he might reasonably conclude that Hamlet's *anagnorisis* has led him to Christian Stoic faith. Cornwallis might turn to Donne and quote from Seneca's *De Providentia* as a kind of summation: "What is the duty of a good man? To offer himself to Fate."

Donne might nod thoughtfully in reply, but it is doubtful whether he would agree that the tragedy's meaning could be reduced to this. For he would have been unable to miss the skepticism implicit in the dramatic contexts within which Hamlet utters Stoic commonplaces and expresses his admiration for the Stoic ideal. As the author of the skeptical *Satire III,* and one for whom the new philosophy put all in doubt, he would certainly perceive that Hamlet's expressions of Stoic faith in the last scene do not fully answer the questions he has raised in earlier meditations, especially in the "To be, or not to be" soliloquy. He might also point out that not all the spokesmen for Stoicism in the play are trustworthy.

Stoic perfectionism is first introduced in the play as a viable ideal by Claudius, who represents himself in his address to the court as a ruler-sage whose reason has enabled him to order his own passions and those of his queen and subjects with "discretion." He projects the Stoic ideal again moments later when he reproves Hamlet for exhibiting "unmanly grief" and failing to accept the will of heaven with a properly disposed heart and mind:

> Take it to heart? Fie! 'tis a fault to heaven,
> A fault against the dead, a fault to nature,
> To reason most absurd, . . .
> (I. ii. 100-2)

As Robert Miola points out, Claudius is a perversion of the Stoic model: "His reason serves his passion instead of checking it and degenerates into mere trickery. The Stoic watchwords—'reason', 'thinking', and 'judgement'—echo in various forms in his speech, ironic reminders of the ideal and witnesses to its perversion."[2]

The type of Stoicism Claudius enjoins is an avenue of retreat from political activism, emphasizing passivity, acceptance, and the cultivation of *apatheia*. Its defining quality is constancy, maintained by the practice of two of the cardinal virtues, temperance, and fortitude, and manifesting itself in heroic endurance rather than the performance of great deeds. In his *De Constantia Sapientis,* Seneca exalts Cato above more active heroes, defending his assertion "that in Cato the immortal gods had given us a truer exemplar of the wise man than earlier ages had in Ulysses and Hercules."[3] Renaissance Neostoics who rejected the active life could justify escaping its pressures and corrupting effects by maintaining a view of Stoic cosmopolitanism that relieved them of allegiance to governments or states and enjoined passive acceptance of the existing social order and whatever it imposed. Justus Lipsius is representative of this type of Neostoicism. His *De Constantia* urges the wise man to withdraw from courts and cities into rustic seclusion. Any attempt to change or reform society will destroy constancy.[4] Claudius compels Hamlet to remain in his court, but tries to persuade him to embrace a Stoic constancy that amounts to passivity.

A very different kind of Stoicism, enjoining participation and service, is set forth by Guillaume Du Vair in his *La Philosophie Morale des Stoiques*. Du Vair is in the activist tradition of Cicero and Marcus Aurelius, while Lipsius follows Seneca and Boethius in advocating withdrawal from the world to facilitate the rational practice of virtue. Activist Neostoicism was also represented in Shakespeare's time, as I noted earlier, by

Calvinists, such as Mornay, Hall, and La Primaudaye, who linked self-knowledge, knowledge of the divine, and duty to one's fellows. The concept of moral stewardship, generally regarded as a Calvinist notion with scriptural roots, could find support in the writings of the ancient Stoics, such as Epictetus, whose ideas in this regard are dramatized by Marston and Chapman. The emphasis on discipline and a sense of responsibility for the moral welfare of the community that gave Stoicism virtually the status of a state religion in ancient Rome also recommended it to Calvin and his followers. The point is relevant to a discussion of *Hamlet* because the prince himself progresses in the course of the play from a yearning to assume a passive Stoic stance to an activism that combines Stoic and Calvinist elements.

Shakespeare's treatments of Stoicism in other plays reveal both of these strains of the philosophy as potentially conducive to moral confusion. In *Julius Caesar,* he seems to be targeting Stoic activism, mainly, as I suggested earlier, the assumption, later dramatized by Chapman in *The Revenge of Bussy D'Ambois,* that a good man uncorrupted by passion can reconcile any task he perceives to be necessary with a correct moral purpose. In *Troilus and Cressida,* he represents the other type of Stoicism in Agamemnon. Addressing his lieutenants in the Greek council of war (I. iii.), Agamemnon enjoins "persistive constancy" and urges them to accept their frustrations as "naught else / But the protractive trials of great Jove" (I. iii. 19-20). By urging Stoic acceptance, he glosses over the fact that he really doesn't understand why the siege has failed. It remains for Ulysses, a politician and a realist, to exercise his *virtù* and, having identified the problem, to formulate a plan. What the activist *virtus* of Brutus and the passive *virtus* of Agamemnon have in common is a reliance upon reason that proves to be not merely unreliable but totally deceptive. One recalls Montaigne's definition of reason as man's capacity to delude himself:

> I alwaies call reason that apparance or shew of discourses which every man deviseth or forgeth in himselfe: that reason of whose condition there may be a hundred, one contrary to another, about one selfe same subject: it is an instrument of lead and wax, stretching, pliable, and that may be fitted to all byases and squared to all measures: there remaines nothing but the skill and sufficiency to know how to turne and winde the same.[5]

In an important recent article, Mark Matheson points out how Hamlet "passes beyond" a reliance on reason and relinquishes himself to the direction of his conscience, a transition which, Matheson argues, parallels that of contemporary Protestantism from the traditional Christian-humanist ideology, recently restated by Hooker, to "a new cultural paradigm, one in which a Protestant concept of conscience supplants reason as the crucial human faculty."[6] In Matheson's view, Stoicism and humanism are failing ideologies in the world of the play.

Matheson's argument is persuasive, but the play reflects as well Protestant, specifically Calvinist, adaptations of Stoicism. Hamlet's speeches in the final act express, to use Gordon Braden's words, "a Stoicism Christianized by an unclassically thorough humility before a greater power," a philosophical stance closer to Montaigne than Seneca.[7] Moreover, the skepticism as well as the fideism of Montaigne is clearly reflected in the last scenes. This does not really contradict Matheson's argument, or Braden's, because, as noted earlier, Montaigne and Calvin have much the same view of *recta ratio* and its limitations.

The attitude of Hamlet toward Stoicism and its embodiment in the sage is obviously ambivalent. On the one hand, he admires Horatio and envies his freedom from destructive passion, his *apatheia*. On the other, he is acutely aware of the limitations of Stoic rationalism. When he tells Horatio that there are more things in heaven and earth than are dreamt of in his philosophy, he is apparently referring to the limitations of natural philosophy in general and Horatio's Stoic rationalism in particular. Horatio's reputation as a "scholar" had prompted Bernardo and Marcellus to seek his verification of the apparition they saw on the battlements. With the confidence of an academic natural philosopher and a rationalist whose learning has not been tested beyond the confines of Wittenberg University, Horatio had "explained" the Ghost as a figment of their "fantasy" before he even saw it. The explanation is obviously inadequate but no more so than the numerous attempts by Shakespearean scholar-critics to "explain" the Ghost in terms of ideas and commonplace notions that were current in Shakespeare's time. Like the motives of Iago, the more it is explained the more elusive it becomes. Hamlet's remark to Horatio alerts the audience to the danger of relying on learning that is insufficiently based on experience in a world that challenges Stoic faith in its underlying all-permeating reason.

In his "To be, or not to be" soliloquy, Hamlet in effect juxtaposes Stoic *virtus* and Machiavellian *virtù*.[8] Passively enduring the blows of fortune and actively committing one's energies to mastering her are alternative responses that appear to be very different from each other. What they have in common is an adherence to purpose, the moral purpose of the sage and the political or military purpose of the man of action. Identifying the latter with Machiavellian *virtù,* rather than activist *virtus,* may not be wholly justified by the text but is, nonetheless, tempting because Shakespeare sets up the same juxtaposition, though in a different manner, in *Troilus and Cressida,* a play written soon after *Hamlet,* which exhibits some close affinities.

As noted earlier, Agamemnon is a Stoic sage, and his address to his lieutenants in the Greek council of war scene is a distillation of the main ideas in Seneca's *De Constantia Sapientis*. As a way of glossing over his own ignorance of the reasons why the Greek siege has failed, Agamemnon urges his lieutenants to manifest Stoic *virtus*. After Nestor attempts to "apply" Agamemnon's words, Ulysses utters his great speech on degree and order, whereby he attempts to draw Agamemnon out of his Stoic retreat into an assertion of leadership. His speech appeals to commonly held beliefs in the moral necessity of reverence for degree, but its purpose is thoroughly pragmatic. The obvious reason why he wants Agamemnon's authority reestablished is that Agamemnon is willing to let Ulysses do most of his thinking for him. Yet, in fact, Ulysses exerts no control whatever over the major events of the play. In terms of achieving concrete ends, he is as ineffectual as his commander, and the "policy" he practices, as Thersites remarks, "grows into an ill opinion" (V. iv. 8-16). Indeed the development of *Troilus and Cressida* as a whole illustrates Hamlet's point in the first five lines of "To be, or not to be," that Stoic resignation and commitment to action are equally futile courses. To take arms against a sea of troubles is to beat back the tide with a broom, yet, paradoxically, one may indeed "end them" for oneself if one could, by opposing them, achieve self-annihilation.

The key phrase in the soliloquy is "nobler in the mind." Even as he juxtaposes being and not-being and two opposed modes of adhering to purpose, Hamlet is also in effect juxtaposing subjective and objective reality and giving primacy to the former. The real question is not one of whether, in fact, passive endurance is a nobler course than active commitment but how the mind perceives the alternatives. Paradoxically, though his subjective stance appears to reduce Stoic *virtus* and *virtù* to the same level of futility, it is, in fact, in harmony with what Gordon Braden has called "the logic of Stoic retreat."[9] The external world is utterly devalued against the reality of the inner world, the judging self, the realm of *autarceia*, yet curiously this devaluing does not lead to any sort of affirmation of self-sufficiency. It leads instead, as Hamlet's soliloquy reveals, to a longing for the ultimate retreat—annihilation. Hamlet had expressed the same longing in an earlier soliloquy: "O that this too too sullied flesh would melt / Thaw, and resolve itself into a dew!" (I. ii. 129-30). In that soliloquy, too, he expresses Christian scruples about suicide, but as "To be, or not to be" reveals, they are based mainly on the fear that suicide will not lead to annihilation, that the burden of consciousness will continue in the next world.

Classical Stoic philosophy has little to say about "The undiscover'd country." Marcus Aurelius leaves open the question of whether or not there is an afterlife.[10] The Stoic eschatology presented in *The Aeneid* by Anchises (VI. 718-48) seems to express a belief that the divine spark lives on and presumably, after "nothing is left but pure / Ethereal sentience and the spirit's essential flame," it is destined for reunion with the *Logos spermatikos*.[11] Seneca is inconsistent on the subject, but Braden seems to be right in attaching greater significance to those passages in which he in effect denies the soul's immortality than those in which he seems to affirm it.[12] Again, Hamlet's sense of the limitations of Stoic natural philosophy is apparent. Among the things not dreamt of in natural philosophy is the whole realm of Christian eschatology, but the fact that Hamlet refers to this too as a "dream" emphasizes the extent of his own uncertainty. His superiority to the sage in understanding is, like the unmatched wisdom of Socrates, based on his superior awareness of what he does not know.

"To be, or not to be" may be fruitfully compared with Hieronimo's *"Vindicta mihi"* soliloquy in *The Spanish Tragedy* (III. xiii. 1-44) on which it may have been at least partly modeled. Like Hamlet, Hieronimo considers alternative responses to his situation—Christian patience or Stoic resignation versus active commitment against a sea of troubles. Like Hamlet's soliloquy, his speech reveals his growing awareness of the inadequacy of the conventional views of experience represented by these alternatives. By the end of *The Spanish Tragedy* Hieronimo is made to see what Hamlet intuits at the outset of his tragedy, that there are more things in heaven and earth than are dreamed of in anyone's "philosophy." Hieronimo, like Hamlet, is able to consider the alternatives critically, but, unlike Hamlet, he finds one acceptable and resolves to act: "And death's the worst of resolution" (III. xiii. 9). Hamlet's reflections are finally inconclusive and "resolution" is "sicklied o'er with the pale cast of thought." Hearing the soliloquy, Donne might remark to Cornwallis that a skeptic's meditations are always inconclusive.

For all his uncertainty, Hamlet is preoccupied with eschatology, mainly damnation, throughout much of the play, and he seems to have an unwavering emotional conviction of the reality of hell. The visitation of his father's spirit, contradicting his view that "no traveller returns" from the world beyond, evokes the literally unspeakable horrors of a purgatory that sounds more like Dante's infernal pit. Remembering this, he finds a ready excuse to put off killing Claudius at prayer. When he forges the letter dooming Rosencrantz and Guildenstern, he, in effect, wills their damnation as well by adding the phrase, "not shriving-time allow'd." He apparently maintains a Catholic belief in salvation *in articulo mortis,* which, along with purgatory itself, was denied by Protestant moral theology.[13]

His fear of being damned himself appears not merely in his scruples about suicide but in the meditation on corruption he utters just before his first encounter with the Ghost. Beginning with a discourse on Danish drunkenness and how it adds a "swinish phrase" to the name of Dane, he parallels the soiling of a national reputation with that of individuals by some inborn flaw or "mole of nature." No matter how virtuous or gifted an individual may be, he is doomed to disgrace by "the stamp of one defect":

> Being nature's livery or Fortune's star,
> His virtues else, be they as pure as grace,
> As infinite as man may undergo,
> Shall in the general censure take corruption
> From that particular fault. The dram of evil
> Doth all the noble substance often dout
> To his own scandal.
>
> (I. iv. 32-38)

The explicit concern is public opinion, as it affects both nations and individuals, identifying them with a single flaw.[14] But as is typical with Hamlet, such a meditation prompts introspection, and as Olivier sensed, he seems to be thinking of how not merely reputation but moral character, his own in particular, may be affected by a single inborn defect. Bearing in mind his preoccupation with eschatology, it is tempting to find in "the general censure" an ambiguous reference to both public judgment and the General Judgment.

If we choose to see an eschatological reference in these lines, we may see as well the beginning of a tension between the unambiguously Catholic eschatology shortly to be revealed in the Ghost's speeches, which stress the importance of the sacraments to salvation, and what appears to be an eschatology more in harmony with that of Luther and Calvin. Without referring specifically to predestination, Hamlet seems to be describing how some otherwise blameless individuals are damned, as well as disgraced, by a "vicious mole" that has been imposed on them by nature.

One should not, of course, make too much of a possible ambiguity, but it can't be denied that Hamlet feels victimized by providence:

> The time is out of joint. O cursed spite,
> That ever I was born to set it right.
>
> (I. v. 196-97)

> For this same lord
> I do repent; but heaven hath pleas'd it so,
> To punish me with this and this with me,
> That I must be their scourge and minister.
>
> (III. iv. 174-77)

The latter speech, uttered over the slain Polonius, can be read as a bitter acceptance of the damnable role of scourge that has been imposed on him. As conventionally conceived, the role of scourge and the role of minister are very different from each other and do not coexist in the same actor. A scourge is a damned instrument of divine justice whose fitness for a damnable role is due to a corruption for which providence is not to blame. A minister is a benevolent agent of divine justice who may complete the work begun by a scourge, but the two agents are very different in kind.[15] In seeing himself as one coerced into assuming both roles, Hamlet is clearly rejecting any Christian or Stoic notion of providence as benevolent design. It is perhaps his most profoundly skeptical moment in the play. In musing on the battlement, he had spoken of those who are victimized by nature, disgraced, and perhaps damned as a result of something "wherein they are not guilty." Now he describes himself as one victimized by heaven into assuming a role that will damn him.

Referring to eschatology in the world of the play, specifically what he sees as the "moral barbarism" of the premise that a good man unlucky enough to die without receiving the last sacraments must suffer hellish or purgatorial fires, Graham Bradshaw observes, "Divine justice would appear to have the morals of a fruit machine; but for much of the play this barbaric idea seems to function as a premise."[16] From a purely human standpoint, this would seem to be the case, even as it is clearly the case in *The Spanish Tragedy*. In that play, as I have argued, Kyd deliberately emphasizes the discrepancy between the orthodox Christian Stoic beliefs expressed by the living characters with regard to the process of divine justice and what is revealed in the judgment scenes that frame the main plot. The play begins and ends skeptically with eschatological revelations that in no way agree with or fulfill the orthodox Christian assumptions or expectations of the characters who live and die in the intervening acts. In *Hamlet*, too, divine justice seems to be at odds with human reason and morality. But Shakespeare's tragic design is more encompassing than is Kyd's. The tragic vision of *The Spanish Tragedy* is like that of *Job* without the theophany. *Hamlet* does not include a theophany as such, but it includes elements that must have been extremely suggestive to an audience consisting largely of Protestants attuned to religious discourse in which the mystery of divine justice was an awe-inspiring matter beyond the application, let alone comprehension, of such crude instruments as human reason and moral judgment.

In an essay cited earlier in this study, Paul R. Sellin begins his discussion of Reformation awe by focusing on *Everyman* as an expression of the medieval Catholic theology about to be displaced by the Reformation in the very countries in which the play was especially popular—Germany, the Low Countries, and England. As Sellin observes, "*Everyman* exhibits a great deal of sureness about how God relates to man. The benevolence of divine concern for all humankind is assumed, and the means by which man can ensure the certainty of enjoying grace are relatively precise, systematic, and reliable."[17] Everyman exercises all his faculties, including knowledge and free choice, in preparing himself for death. He receives the sacraments of Penance, the Eucharist, and Extreme Unction, the bountiful means provided by God Himself through His Church of obtaining grace.

In stark contrast to this dramatic representation of how God relates to man is the vision of the Reformers. For Luther, "God is a terrible and glorious, though to be sure an infinitely loving and bountiful, mystery whose omnipotence is eternal, incomprehensible, inscrutable, infallible, immense, awesome and above all hidden—*verè a Deus absconditus* (Isa. 45: 15)"[18] In the matter of His justice, Luther acknowledges that the palpable injustice in the world is a challenge to faith and that reason will lead man to impious conclusions:

> Behold! God governs the external affairs of the world in such a way that, if you regard and follow the judgment of human reason, you are forced to say, either that there is no God, or that God is unjust; as the poet said: "I am often tempted to think there are no gods." See the great prosperity of the wicked, and by contrast the great adversity of the good. . . . Is it not, pray, universally held to be most unjust that bad men should prosper, and good men afflicted? Yet that is the way of the world.[19]

. . . Luther condemned Skepticism, believing that conscience informed by the reading of Scripture would lead one to certainty in religious matters, but his extreme anti-rationalism, his utter contempt for reason as the malleable "whore of the devil," is essentially in harmony with Montaigne's Skeptical view of reason's unreliability. And Calvin, who adapts so much Stoicism into his moral philosophy, has no faith in *recta ratio* as a guide to righteousness. Like Luther, he takes Augustine's interpretations of Paul's teachings concerning the state of fallen man to deterministic extremes. While the natural faculties of fallen man—understanding, judgment, and will—have been corrupted, he possesses enough reason, a vestige of his prelapsarian state, to seek the truth. But unaided reason cannot overcome the debilitating effects of vanity and sin, and since the will is inseparable from reason, it too is in bondage to vanity and sin.[20] Like Luther, he stresses the inadequacy of human judgment applied to divine justice:

> First, therefore, this fact should occur to us: that our discourse is concerned with the justice not of a human court but of a heavenly tribunal, lest we measure by our own small measure the integrity of works needed to satisfy the divine judgment. Yet it is amazing with what great rashness and boldness this is commonly defined.[21]

When Hamlet sees himself as one victimized by heaven, he is following the judgment of his human reason to an impious conclusion. Only when he comes to realize the futility of applying his reason to apprehend the design of his fate will he be able to relinquish himself to the will of heaven. This realization comes about mainly as a result of his adventure at sea, during which he is preserved by a combination of rashness and what he sees as special providence, but that voyage is preceded by a meditation in which reason, as in *The Apology of Raymond Sebond,* completely discredits itself. Throughout the play, it has become progressively more apparent that introspection has led him not to the self-knowledge that should be the basis of virtuous activity but instead into a Montaignean *profond labyrinthe* in which he moves ever further from an understanding of his own motives and, therefore, ever further from commitment to action. He is paralyzed by self-awareness, and the Stoic commonplace that self-knowledge leads to virtuous activity is obviously thrown into question.

In his final soliloquy, shamed by the example of Fortinbras marching his troops to battle for a worthless piece of Polish territory, Hamlet castigates himself for his failure to act. His reason and his blood concur in urging him to revenge. Moreover, honor is at stake. What is remarkable about this speech is that it contains so many self-contradictions and yet is, as Graham Bradshaw remarks, "remarkably coherent."[22]

When the Norwegian captain tells Hamlet how worthless the prize is and yet how costly in potential casualties, Hamlet's initial response is amazement at the absurdity of such extravagant waste, yet he understands how such wars occur. They are the ulcerous results of extended peace and prosperity. They break out without any discernible cause, but the effects are, nonetheless, fatal. As Kittredge notes, he is restating an old theory that war is the natural exercise of the body politic, and without it the national character is subject to deterioration analogous to that which idleness and luxury cause in the human body.[23] Hamlet's restatement of this old theory does not, however, include any reference to the healthful effects of such exercise on the national character. As with the ulcer hidden within, the only discernible effect is that "the man dies." And what astonishes him is that such a terrible price will be paid for "this straw."

But having said this, he goes on to reflect upon how this piece of rash dreadful folly rebukes him personally for his inaction. Again he raises the great question, "What is a man . . . ?" He has no doubt that what sets man apart from beasts is the exercise of his godlike reason, and he rebukes himself for abusing his own reason to justify what he suspects is more cowardice than wisdom. But then he expresses his envy and admiration of Fortinbras, who has mindlessly committed himself and his army to mortal danger "even for an eggshell." According to the principle he has just stated, that man functions qua man when he exercises reason, Fortinbras is behaving in a subhuman fashion. But Hamlet is, nonetheless, compelled to admire this rash young adventurer because he is willing to risk everything for the sake of honor.

> Rightly to be great
> Is not to stir without great argument,
> But greatly to find quarrel in a straw
> When honour's at the stake.
>
> (IV. iv. 53-56)

Honor magnifies any cause, even a "straw." The idea that a great man will not stir without great cause goes back to the model of the great-spirited man in Aristotle's *Nichomachean Ethics,* as does the idea that honor compels action when it is threatened. But Hamlet is carrying this latter principle a step further to justify the kind of mindset represented by Hotspur or Troilus. Bradshaw relates this passage to the Trojan debate in *Troilus and Cressida,* specifically to Troilus's question, "What's aught but as 'tis valued?" and Hector's response that "value dwells not in particular will."[24] Indeed Hamlet articulates Troilus's whole view of honor, including his assumption that the involvement of national honor guarantees that any quarrel is honorable. Cassandra's

> . . . brain-sick raptures
> Cannot distaste the goodness of a quarrel
> Which hath our several honors all engaged
> To make it gracious.
>
> (II. ii. 123-26)

While Hamlet can sympathize with such a commitment to honor, he still maintains a full rational awareness of its insanity. Hesitating to take hostile action unless there is adequate cause implies rational deliberation, but if honor is involved the trivial becomes great and reason is irrelevant. Again the cause of Fortinbras is referred to as a "straw." But while honor can magnify a "straw" and make it, to use Troilus's phrase, a theme of honor and renown, honor itself is completely without substance, "a fantasy and trick of fame." Inspired by this illusion, thousands will fall, and their example shames him. He is shamed by his inability to act according to either the imperative of reason or the irrational imperative of honor, even though his cause, unlike that of Fortinbras, is sanctioned by reason as well as honor that is no illusion. And the precise cause of his paralysis eludes him.

Of course, at this particular moment he is hardly in a position to act. Guarded by Rosencrantz and Guildenstern and the rest of his escort, he no longer possesses either strength or means. He has forgone the perfect opportunity to take revenge and the likelihood of his having another seems remote. His final bloodthirsty flourish is an expression of frustrated impotence, as meaningless as the ranting for which he condemned himself in his second soliloquy. Once again he has unpacked his heart with words to no end.

As many have noted, Shakespeare seems to have been reading Montaigne when he wrote this play. Florio's translation had not yet appeared, but he could have been reading it in manuscript or in the original, and Anthony Burgess may be right in suggesting that he was writing about "a Montaigne-like man."[25] *Hamlet* is full of Montaignean echoes. The soliloquy I have been discussing, for instance, seems to echo Montaigne's contradictory views of war. On the one hand, he can speak of soldiering as a "profession or exercise, both noble in execution (for *the strongest, most generous and prowdest of all vertues, is true valour*) and noble in it's cause."[26] On the other, he can scoff at the stupidity of seeking glory in war: "So many names, so many victories, and so many conquests buried in darke oblivion, makes the hope to perpetuate our names but ridiculous, by the surprising of ten Argo-lettiers, or of a small cottage, which is knowne but by his fall."[27] And Hamlet's progress toward the Christian-Stoic fideism he expresses in the last act parallels *The Apology of Raymond Sebond* in many respects. Like Montaigne, Hamlet discovers the futility of relying on reason, which, as this soliloquy demonstrates, cannot refute the irrational imperative of a mindless appetite for military glory and is incapable by itself of moving one to take action in a just cause. In his first bitter soliloquy he condemns his mother's behavior as less seemly than that of "a beast that wants discourse of reason." His assumption, restated in the last soliloquy, is that it is reason that sets man above the beasts. But by exalting Fortinbras he is clearly jettisoning that assumption and putting the so-called rational and the irrational on a level, much as Montaigne does in *The Apology* when he presents his disturbingly persuasive argument that, viewed empirically, man is neither morally nor intellectually superior to other beasts. It is a profoundly humbling moment for Hamlet but essential to his progress toward a Montaignean recognition of man's need for God, without whom man is morally no better, is indeed worse, than a beast.

Though Montaigne was a devout Catholic who used Skepticism to support fideism and a complete submission to the teaching authority of the Catholic Church, he was, as noted earlier, in fundamental agreement with Luther and Calvin regarding the limitations of human reason and man's need for grace. What *Hamlet* reveals, among other things, is how Skepticism may prepare one for faith, contrary to the assumptions of the Reformers. Which is not to say that the play contradicts basic Protestant doctrine concerning the necessity of total submission to the divine will and the mysterious nature of the relationship between God and man. For Hamlet, as for Job, skeptical questioning that undercuts conventional assumptions and canned wisdom finally refutes itself and prepares the way for faith and acceptance.

Matheson rightly emphasizes "the emergence of a specifically Protestant discourse and of God's predestinating will" in the final act.[28] When Horatio expresses some shock at the fate of Rosencrantz and Guildenstern, Hamlet dismisses them as "not near my conscience." Since they had already damned themselves by willfully serving evil, he feels no guilt in having merely accelerated their inevitable progress into hell. His next speech to Horatio again emphasizes that he is at peace with his conscience and is indeed being directed by it in purging the state of Denmark. To refuse its mandate would be damnable:

> Does it not, think thee, stand me now upon—
> He that hath kill'd my king and whor'd my mother,
> Popp'd in between th' election and my hopes,
> Thrown out his angle for my proper life
> And with such coz'nage—is't not perfect conscience
> To quit him with this arm? And is't not to be damn'd
> To let this canker of our nature come
> In further evil?
> (V. ii. 63-70)

Thus Hamlet reveals that he has relinquished himself to the direction of God's voice within him. The Calvinist implications are unmistakable. As William Perkins wrote a few years before the play was first presented, conscience

> is (as it were) a little God setting in the middle of mens hearts, arraigning them in this life as they shall be arraigned for their offences at the Tribunal seat of the euerliving God in the day of iudgement. Wherefore the temporarie iudgement that is given by the conscience is nothing els but a beginning, or a fore-runner of the last iudgement.[29]

This is not to say that Hamlet has undergone a conversion to Calvinism during his adventure at sea. What he has discovered is the futility of opposing the divinity that shapes our ends and a consequent willingness to relinquish himself to it. As Jenkins and others have noted, his speech to Horatio assuring him of special providence echoes both Matthew x. 29 and Calvin, who emphasized special providence.[30] It also echoes the Stoic beliefs of Horatio.

Horatio does not utter Stoic precepts, like Chapman's Clermont D'Ambois or Marston's Pandulpho, but his self-characterization as more an antique Roman than a Dane and Hamlet's encomium defining him as an embodiment of Stoic perfection make clear the attitudes and beliefs he represents. When Hamlet says "There's a divinity that shapes our ends," Horatio recognizes an expression of his own faith as a Christian Stoic and responds, "That is most certain." Considering the extent to which Stoicism had been baptized by Calvinist Reformers, it is hardly surprising to find both Calvinist and Stoic resonances in a speech expressing total submission to providential design. While Calvin, in effect, replaced the Stoic concepts of *recta ratio* and the divine spark with his doctrine of Divine Illumination from within by the Holy Spirit, his followers in England, such as Perkins, maintained a view of the moral faculty as a divine agency within man, and the writings of other Protestant authors, such as Mornay and La Primaudaye, suggest that they incorporated the concept of the divine spark and identified it with the part of conscience dictating general principles.[31] The context of Hamlet's expressions of faith in the direction of his conscience must have been especially meaningful to an audience aware of the potential conflict between believers in the sovereignty of conscience and absolutist monarchs. The Protestant view of conscience as God within man, which found classical support in the doctrine of the spark, was an important doctrinal basis for resistance to absolutism and indeed tyranny in any form, and the tensions that would lead to the outbreak of civil war in the next century were already evident in the 1590s. Appropriately, Hamlet is being prompted by his conscience as he opposes a usurping tyrant.

Hamlet's acquired faith in special providence enables him to assume briefly the role of Stoic sage that he had idealized in his encomium on Horatio. It is not the role of passive Stoic that he had considered as an alternative in "To be, or not to be," but that of an activist ready to encounter evil and overcome it with guidance from within. A yearning for retreat from the pressures of the world into a subjective realm of reality has been replaced by an inner direction to change his world. Significantly, it is Horatio, not Hamlet, who exhibits anxiety about the impending duel with Laertes. Hamlet is perfectly resigned, in a state of "readiness," to encounter what can only be another murderous trap set by the plotting Claudius. To accept the challenge is rashness bordering on the suicidal, and understandably he feels "a kind of gaingiving as would perhaps trouble a woman." But, like Chapman's Stoic heroes Clermont and the Guise, he dismisses his well-grounded misgiving. Like Chapman, Shakespeare subtly undercuts the Stoic ideal of fortitude by having it prompt a denial of "unmanly" fear.

A Neostoic watching the final scene of the play might, nonetheless, be heartened by the spectacle of a man sustained by faith in providence carrying out the duty that his sense of moral purpose prescribes and having his faith vindicated as Claudius is destroyed by his own machinations. What a Skeptic might point out to him, however, is that Hamlet's performance in the role of the sage is dramatically undercut by the scenes that frame it. Moreover, if the ends of divine justice are being served, why is it that the process of serving it has paved the way for the emergence of a ruler probably less fit than Claudius?

In the scene immediately preceding the last one, Hamlet surrenders completely to his passions, and though his behavior toward Laertes is something he rightly repents, his exhibition of overwhelming grief over the death of Ophelia is clearly calculated to win him the sympathy of the audience that has been diminished by her suffering and the account of her miserable death. He is still clearly incapable of the *apatheia* he admires in the ideal of the sage. Nor are we likely to think less of him when he again surrenders completely to his passions as he kills Claudius. While he himself expresses a Stoic view of passion as evil and corrupting, his own actions imply a very different view of passion on the part of the playwright. For one thing, passion is shown to be the only means whereby Hamlet is ever able to overcome his inability to fuse thought with action. As long as he has even a moment to collect himself and reflect, he will refrain from acting on his resolutions, as he had clearly shown when he refrained from killing Claudius at prayer. Passion is potentially corrupting, but Shakespeare, like Marston in *Sophonisba,* reveals that a blend of passion with Stoic virtue is possible and even desirable. Complete *apatheia* is for the passive perfectionist who retreats from the world and objective reality itself.

If we can accept Horatio's hopeful prayer and farewell to Hamlet as reliable prophecy, the prince is not destined to suffer the hellish fires that afflict his father in purgatory, even though he too has died without the last sacraments. We probably shouldn't make much of Shakespeare's summary dismissal of the eschatology that was so prominently referred to earlier in the play. But the fact that Fortinbras will be inheriting the throne of Denmark can hardly be seen as part of a tragic affirmation. The glimpses and reports we have had of this young Norwegian adventurer throw into question his fitness to rule, and we are left to wonder when his boundless ambition will prompt him to risk even more lives for some straw or eggshell. The profound skepticism and pessimism implicit in this triumph of a ruthless appetite for power combined with a mindless commitment to glory seem to anticipate the darkness of *Troilus and Cressida.*

> Then everything includes itself in power,
> Power into will, will into appetite;
> And appetite, an universal wolf,
> So doubly seconded with will and power,
> Must make perforce an universal prey,
> And last eat up himself.
> (*Troilus and Cressida,* I. iii. 119-24)

Donne, always fascinated by the paradoxical, might point out this apparent contradiction to Cornwallis, but at the same time, as the future author of the Holy Sonnets, he might confess that he has been moved, perhaps to envy, by the spectacle of a good man raised from the anguish of skeptical despair to hope and certainty as he submits himself to a design beyond his comprehension and prepares to encounter death. He might also confess to being moved by a kind of wonder and fear as he ponders the great questions raised in the play, particularly those touching the nature of man and his relationship to God, whose mysterious designs for man according to His dreadful hidden will beget terror and mock the criteria of human judgment.

*Notes*

[1] Harold Jenkins, ed., *Hamlet,* New Arden edition (London: Methuen Press, 1982). All citations are from this edition.

[2] Robert Miola, *Shakespeare and Classical Tragedy The Influence of Seneca* (Oxford University Press, 1992), 59.

[3] Seneca, *De Constantia Sapientis,* Il. 2.

[4] This contradicts somewhat his early work, the *Politiques,* which is concerned with the theory of man and society and the concept of government. See Levi, *The French Moralists,* 55. See also Bement's excellent discussion of Lipsius and Du Vair as representative of the two types of Renaissance Neostoicism, *George Chapman,* 183-86.

[5] Montaigne, "An Apologie of Raymond Sebond," *Essayes,* trans. Florio, II, 314-15. . . .

[6] Mark Matheson, "*Hamlet* and 'A Matter Tender and Dangerous,'" *Shakespeare Quarterly* XLVI (1995): 383-97.

[7] Braden, *Renaissance Tragedy and the Senecan Tradition,* 221-22.

[8] For discussion of what these concepts have in common, see above chapter 3 [in *Nobler in the Mind: The Stoic-Skeptic Dialectic in English Renaissance Tragedy*], n. 61.

[9] Braden, *Renaissance Tragedy,* 23.

[10] Antoninus, Marcus Aurelius, *Communings with Himself,* XII. 5.

[11] *donec longa dies, perfecto temporis orbe, concretam exemit labem, purumque reliquit, aetherium sensum atque aurai simplicis ignem, has omnes, ubi mille rotam volvere per annos* trans. II. 747-48 C. Day Lewis, *The Aeneid of Virgil* (New York: Doubleday, 1953), 151. Cf. Diogenes Laertius, *Lives of the Eminent Philosophers,* VII. 148-49.

[12] Braden, *Renaissance Tragedy,* 23-24, 228, note 27.

[13] For discussion of the purgatorial context in the play and Protestant doctrine regarding purgatory, see Matheson, "*Hamlet* and 'A Matter Tender and Dangerous,'" 384-85.

[14] Harold Jenkins believes that the meaning is confined to this specific reference; "What the single fault corrupts is not, as so widely assumed, the man's character, but the opinion that is formed of it, his reputation, or 'image.'" Note to I. iv. 35 in his edition.

[15] See Bowers, "Hamlet as Minister and Scourge," 740-49.

[16] Graham Bradshaw, *Shakespeare's Scepticism* (New York: St. Martin's Press, 1987), 121.

[17] Sellin, "The Hidden God," 150.

[18] Ibid., 154.

[19] Martin Luther, "The Bondage of the Will," in *Martin Luther Selections from his Writings,* ed. John Dillenberger (New York: Anchor, 1961), 201.

[20] See chapter 1, notes 90 and 91.

[21] John Calvin, *Institutes* book 3, chap. 12, 1, ed. John T. McNeill (Philadelphia: Westminster Press, 1960).

[22] Bradshaw, *Shakespeare's Scepticism,* 10.

[23] *Hamlet,* ed. G. L. Kittredge (New York: Ginn, 1939), note to IV. iv. 27.

[24] Bradshaw, *Shakespeare's Scepticism,* 5-10.

[25] Burgess, *Shakespeare,* 119.

[26] Montaigne, *Essays,* III. xiii. 361, "On Experience," trans. Florio.

[27] Ibid., "Of the Institution and Education of Children," I. xxv, 179-80. M. A. Screech renders it, "So many names, so many victories and conquests lying buried in oblivion, make it ridiculous to hope that we shall immortalize our names by rounding up ten armed brigands or by storming some hen-house or other known only by its capture." *The Complete Essays* (New York: Penguin, 1987), 177.

[28] Matheson, "'A Matter Tender and Dangerous,'" 390.

[29] William Perkins, *A Discourse of Conscience* (London, 1596), 27. British Museum copy. See above, chapter 1.

[30] Jenkins, note to V. ii. 215-16, refers to Calvin, *Institutes,* I, esp. xvi. 1, xvii. 6.

[31] See Chapter 1 [in *Nobler in the Mind: The Stoic-Skeptic Dialectic in English Renaissance Tragedy*].

*Bibliography*

Chapman, George, *Bussy D'Ambois*. Edited by Robert J. Lordi. Lincoln: Nebraska University Press, 1964.

———. *The Revenge of Bussy D'Ambois*. Edited by Robert J. Lordi. In *The Plays of George Chapman, The Tragedies with Sir Gyles Goosecappe*. Edited by Allan Holladay. Cambridge: D. S. Brewer, 1987.

Kyd, Thomas. *The First Part of Hieronimo and The Spanish Tragedy*. Edited by Andrew S. Cairncross (Lincoln: University of Nebraska Press, 1967).

Marston, John. *Antonio and Mellida*. Edited by G. K. Hunter. Lincoln: University of Nebraska Press, 1965.

———. *Antonio's Revenge*. Edited by G. K. Hunter, Lincoln: University of Nebraska Press, 1965.

———. *The Malcontent*. Edited by M. L. Wine. Lincoln: University of Nebraska Press, 1964.

———. *The Dutch Courtesan*. Edited by M. L. Wine. Lincoln: University of Nebraska, 1965.

———. *The Wonder of Women or The Tragedy of Sophonisba,* a critical edition. Edited by William Kemp. New York: Garland, 1979.

———. *The Poems*. Edited by Arnold Davenport. Liverpool: Liverpool University Press, 1961.

Seneca. *Seneca His Tenne Tragedies*. Edited by Thomas Newton, introduced by T. S. Eliot. Bloomington: Indiana University Press, 1964.

Seneca, *Tragedies*. Translated by Frank Justus Miller, 2 vols. London: Heinemann, 1958.

Shakespeare, William. *Hamlet*. New Arden edition Harold Jenkins. London: Methuen Press, 1982.

Antoninus, Marcus Aurelius. *The Communings with Himself Together with His Speeches and Sayings*. Translated by C. R. Haines. London: Heinemann, 1961.

Aristotle, *The Nichomachean Ethics*. Translated by Sir David Ross. London: Oxford, 1961.

———. *The Politics*. Translated by T. A. Sinclair. Baltimore: Penguin, 1966.

———. *Poetics*. Translated by Kenneth A. Telford. Chicago: Henry Regnery, 1961.

———. *Rhetoric*. Translated by Edward M. Cope. New York: Arno Press, 1973.

Boethius, *Tractates Consolation*. Translated by H. E. Stewart and E. K. Rand (Cambridge, Mass.: Harvard University Press, 1956.

Calvin, John. *Commentary on Seneca's De Clementia*. Edited by Ford Lewis Battles and Andre Malan Hugo. Leiden: E. J. Brill, 1969.

———. *Institutes of the Christian Religion*. Edited by John T. McNeill. Philadelphia: Westminster Press, 1960.

Cicero. *De Officiis*. Translated by Walter Miller. London: Heinemann, 1961.

———. *De Finibus Bonorum et Malorum*. Translated by H. Rackham. Cambridge, Mass.: Harvard University Press, 1951.

Cornwallis, Sir William. *Essayes*. Edited by Don Cameron Allen. Baltimore: Johns Hopkins University Press, 1946.

DuVair, Guillaume. *The Moral Philosophie of the Stoicks*. Translated by Thomas James, edited by Rudolf Kirk. New Brunswick, N.J.: Rutgers University Press, 1951.

Hall, Joseph. *Heaven upon Earth and Characters of Vertues and Vices*. New Brunswick, N.J.: Rutgers University Press, 1948.

La Primaudaye, Peter de. *The French Academie*. Translated by T. B. London: Geor. Bishop, 1594.

Lipsius, Justus. *Two Books of Constancie*. Edited by Rudolf Kirk. New Brunswick, N.J.: Rutgers University Press, 1939.

Luther, Martin. *Lectures on Romans*. Translated by Wilhelm Pauck. Philadelphia: Library of Christian Classics XV, 1961.

———. "The Bondage of the Will," *Martin Luther Selections from His writings*. Edited by John Dillenberger, 166-203. New York: Anchor, 1961.

Montaigne, Michael de. *The Essayes*. Translated by John Florio, 3 vols. London: Henry Frowde, 1904.

———. *The Complete Essays*. Translated by M. A. Screech. New York: Penguin, 1987.

Mornay, Philippe de. *A Woorke Concerning the Trewnesse of the Christian Religion*. Translated by Sir Philip Sidney and Arthur Golding. London: Thomas Cadman, 1587.

———. *Discourse of Life and Death*. Translated by the Countess of Pembroke. London, 1592.

———. *The True Knowledge of Mans owne Selfe*. Translated by Anthony Munday. London, 1602.

———. *Lord of Plessis his Teares*. Translated by John Healey. London, 1609.

Perkins, William. *A Discourse of Conscience*. London, 1596.

Seneca, *Moral Essays*. Translated by J. W. Basore. 3 vols. London: Heinemann, 1963.

———. *Epistulae Morales*. Translated by Richard M. Gummere. London: Heinemann, 1970.

———. *The Stoic Philosophy of Seneca*. Translated by Moses Hadas. New York: Norton, 1958.

. . . . .

Bement, Peter. *George Chapman: Action and Contemplation in His Tragedies*. Salzburg Studies in English Literature: Jacobean Drama Studies, No. 8, Salzburg, 1974.

Braden, Gordon. *Renaissance Tragedy and the Senecan Tradition*. New Haven: Yale University Press, 1985.

Bradshaw, Graham. *Shakespeare's Scepticism*. New York: St. Martin's Press, 1987.

Burgess, Anthony, *Shakespeare*. New York: Knopf, 1970.

Levi, Anthony. *The French Moralists: The Theory of the Passions 1585 to 1649*. Oxford University Press, 1964.

Miola, Robert. *Shakespeare and Classical Tragedy: The Influence of Seneca*. Oxford University Press, 1992.

. . . . .

Bowers, Fredson. "Hamlet as Minister and Scourge." *PMLA* 70 (1955): 740-49.

Matheson, Mark. "*Hamlet* and 'A Matter Tender and Dangerous.'" *Shakespeare Quarterly* 46 (1995): 383-97.

Sellin, Paul R. "The Hidden God: Reformation Awe in Renaissance English Literature." *The Darker Vision of the Renaissance Beyond the Fields of Reason*. Edited by Robert S. Kinsman. Los Angeles: University of California Press 1974.

---

Source: "Nobler in the Mind: The Dialectic in *Hamlet*," in *Nobler in the Mind: The Stoic-Skeptic Dialectic in English Renaissance Tragedy,* University of Delaware Press, 1998, pp. 145-61.

# "The Luck of Caesar": Winning and Losing in *Antony and Cleopatra*

## Rick Bowers, *University of Alberta*

Those critics of *Antony and Cleopatra* who touch on the subject of Caesar's involvement are usually brief and disparaging before moving on to consider the principal love interest or to draw cultural comparisons between Egypt and Rome. Janet Adelman calls Caesar 'the exemplar of measure' in the play, while Dipak Nandy characterizes him as 'the epitome of the Renaissance "politique" '.[1] J. Leeds Barroll's lengthy characterization of Octavius reinforced the efficient but enigmatic nature of the character, while Lord David Cecil expressed guarded admiration in his study, describing Caesar as 'far-sighted, cool, self-controlled, and so single-mindedly intent on the achievement of his ambition, that nothing, neither the happiness of his sister nor a genuine feeling of pity for Antony in his fall, can turn him from it'.[2] More recently David Bevington, in his introduction to the New Cambridge Shakespeare, seems to have registered the last word on Caesar, calling him 'the voice inside the play for those male readers who cannot entertain the wholeness of Cleopatra and are threatened by the challenge she represents to a male desire for control'.[3]

Perhaps so. Those male readers thus described would benefit greatly from a quick perusal of an article by L.T. Fitz (better known as Linda Woodbridge), an article which Bevington cites, entitled 'Egyptian Queens and Male Reviewers: Sexist Attitudes in *Antony and Cleopatra* Criticism'.[4] Caesar is clearly an unsympathetic, rank misogynist. Indeed, 'Tis paltry to be Caesar' (5.2.2) as Cleopatra claims.[5] But such rejection out of hand nullifies learning anything about Caesar and his characteristic procedures, strategic procedures which, however detestable, are nonetheless effective within the play. These procedures mask personal power through civic piety, collapse military and political jurisdictions in populist fascism, subdue sensual representation, and proscriptively manipulate all opposition. Dispassionate information, plotting, and surveillance continually undermine romantic idealizations. In this essay I plan to argue that the play exploits romantic identification by inviting rejection of Caesar's attitude; and yet, at the same time, the play suggests that materialist survival is the most important single value.

Marilynn Williamson observes: 'We may never warm to Caesar (we seldom warm to effective rulers in Shakespeare), but we should not miss the fact that Shakespeare seems to have had some interest in stressing Octavius's control and responsibility'.[6] Such stress reinforces sympathy with Antony and Cleopatra at the same time as it intensifies the nature of Caesar's effect: win at all costs; losers die. The play generates crucial contradictory responses wherein identification with the romance of the title couple is also slanted towards uncomfortable complicity with the mandate of Caesar. Consequently, audience response is richer and more complex than the trimly paradoxical one suggested in Bevington's introduction to the play: 'Better to be Antony and lose than to be Caesar and win'.[7] Like Caesar, one might laugh at this sentimental rationalization about a story concerning power politics and personal notoriety.

Romantic critical associations, however, continue to thrive, as in the rhapsodic notions of Hélène Cixous: 'They have—from the moment Antony saw Cleopatra coming to him—abandoned the minuscule old world, the planet—the shell with its thrones and rattles, its intrigues, its wars, its rivalries, its tournaments of the phallus, so grotesquely represented by the game of penis-check played by the imperialist superpowers of the triumvirate, with the mean solemnity that makes history'.[8] This, as if history is made only retrospectively by such 'tournaments' and 'superpowers' and not lived in a moment-by-moment construction of meaning. Cultural historians and materialist critics alike posit constructions of love and emotional meaning that are inseparable from the specific material, historical, and political conditions which they constitute and which constitute them.[9] Thus, the love of Antony and Cleopatra does not transcend the politics of the play. As Linda Charnes puts it, their love does not represent an 'authoritative and sacralizing epistemology'.[10] Doubtless, Antony and Cleopatra are in love, but love for a Roman triumvir and an Egyptian queen can be neither transcendent nor private. Indeed Cleopatra's first question about love is as publicly bruited as it is quantitative: 'If it be love indeed, tell me how much' (1.1.14). Their love is as public as their every gesture, and hence political. Caesar's more solitary 'love' is the same.

I will analyze *Antony and Cleopatra* from the dual perspective of game/strategy theory and audience response, foregrounding Caesar as amoral exemplar, to explore the realist material nature of Shakespeare's play. Postwar materialist critics have usually seen *Antony and Cleopatra* in political terms, but not usually in terms of strategic analysis. The play, however, is rife with notions of positional strategy and tactical movement suggestive of an amoral godgame. Triumphant power is the object, and this power is inflected among the lines observed by Foucault in *Discipline and Punish:* 'Power is exercised rather than possessed; it is not the "privilege", acquired or preserved, of the dominant class, but the overall effect of its strategic positions—an effect that is manifested and sometimes extended by the position of those who are dominated'.[11] Power thus circulates in complex ways between and among characters in the play and within the shifting allegiances of audience response.

Novelist John Fowles originated the term; theorist R. Rawdon Wilson expands on its implications: '*Godgame* is John Fowles's term for the literary situation in which one character of superior intelligence and cunning creates a context of contrived bamboozlement that forces another character to struggle, as within a complex cognitive trap, to discover the godlike gamewright's hidden rules'.[12] At first glance, the Roman rules of engagement might seem clear and apparent to a successful military leader such as Antony. Antony's 'bamboozlement' is carried on within the wiles of Cleopatra's administration. But Cleopatra craves personal allegiance which she interprets as political, and her strategy of emotive reversal is simplistic: 'If you find him sad, / Say I am dancing; if in mirth, report / That I am sudden sick' (1.3.3-5). One can credit the power of her sexuality and her politics as 'infinite variety' (2.2.241) in Enobarbus's uncritical terms, and yet still question the place of love and political commitment in an individual's scale of values. Caesar certainly does. He demands more of Antony through Roman political catechism than Cleopatra can elicit through romantic exploration. After all, Caesar compels Antony's Roman obedience through deception, surprise, manipulation, sexual appeal, reverse psychology, false feeling, misinformation, sectarian prejudice, and personal plea—tactics contrived to gain total political dominance at the same time as they expose Antony's personal fears and inadequacies.

Again Foucault on the diversified nature of power relations: 'They define innumerable points of confrontation, focuses of instability, each of which has its own risks of conflict, of struggles, and of an at least temporary inversion of the power relations'.[13] In a sense, Caesar 'holds all the cards', forces the play, and manipulates the action. But Antony's allegiances and choices as well as Cleopatra's actions and understandings complicate audience commitments. Antony accepts the governing rule of Roman political preeminence, and engages with Caesar hoping to gain and consolidate power within the triumvirate through a separate peace in Egypt. But he is naive to the exclusive interconnections that Caesar both fosters and compels. Antony considers himself to be in a 'fight', the single object of which is to destroy the opponent. He thus leaves Cleopatra to 'engage' his competitor only to be cleverly aligned, engaged, and married to his competitor—a situation personally and politically intolerable to Cleopatra. Caesar, however, understands that he, Antony, Lepidus, Pompey, Cleopatra, and all other foreign potentates are involved in a dangerous 'game', a movable situation concerned with rules and involved with tactics that eventuate in testing, harming, and finally overcoming all opposition. 'Separate' peaces are disallowed. Antony and Cleopatra will learn this later, separately and to their individual chagrin. The emergent victor dictates the terms for all. And everything—military, political, personal, and symbolic—is implicated. 'All's fair in love and war', the cliché holds, and Cleopatra knows it just as Caesar does, even if Antony would rather not think about it. The simple fight of the soldier in Antony is buried by the complex game of the tactician in Caesar.

The main thrust of the play has to do with complexities of power at the end of an epoch, complexities more variable and historically consequential than Margot Heinemann suggests: 'Win or lose, the struggle between the triumvirs marks the end of the republic, so admired and idealised in the European Renaissance for its stern Roman virtues and the anti-absolutist principles of its aristocracy'.[14] In fact the play generates contradictory responses on emotional and political levels where romantic identification with Antony and Cleopatra (and in a pathetic lower key with Octavia), is slanted toward uncomfortable agreement with Caesar's sense of historical necessity. At one point, Caesar even ruminates with obvious self-satisfaction, 'The time of universal peace is near' (4.6.5), and although some like to consider this as an apprehension of the birth of Christ, it might better be conceived as an historicized, partisan statement of the *'Pax Romana'*. Under Caesar's new world order, dissent will dissolve as all opposition is eradicated. 'Universal peace' really means world peace as conceived, enforced, and policed by Caesar.

The play makes it clear that such a position is harrowing. And yet the drama takes its audience inside Caesar's complex youthful paternalism, a paternalism that integrates personality and power within a gamesphere where Caesar makes the rules and the only thing disallowed is losing. Indeed Caesar's 'powerful mandate' is present from the very first as performed in Cleopatra's insouciant mimicry: ' "Do this, or this; / Take in that kingdom, and enfranchise that. / Perform't, or else we damn thee" ' (1.1.22-4). The terms are unmistakable and exclusive. And yet Caesar enters scene 4, indulgent, but not 'too indulgent' (1.4.16) of his senior 'great competitor' (3) about whom he appears completely informed. Ironically, the youthful Caesar infantilizes Antony's conduct, 'As we rate boys who, being mature in knowledge, / Pawn their experience to their present pleasure' (1.4.31-2). Caesar, by contrast, takes no present pleasure in the military and political controversies of the day, foreign and domestic controversies about which his senior triumvirs are either ignorant or uninterested. And it is only when driven to the breaking point of administrative frustration that Caesar calls out Antony's name in a mixture of retrospective admiration and present disgust, narrating Antony's past accomplishments as Roman patriot, victor, and survivor in opposition to his present dissolute behavior in Egypt. As complex as he is resolved, Caesar patronizes Lepidus at the same time as he mobilizes action against Antony.

The dramatic action of the play, however, constantly registers a discrepancy between Antony's power (oddly passive, retrospective, and subject to idealization) and the fact that (as the Soothsayer says and the play by Shakespeare dramatizes) Caesar always prevails. Much of the dramatic texture of the play derives from this sense of doubleness, suggesting that tactical plot dominates romantic hope. Caesar offers invitations; Antony rationalizes and accepts. Caesar suggests tactical scenarios; Antony defies but complies. Caesar directly challenges; Antony, to his own disadvantage, responds. In response to Antony's question concerning outcomes—'whose fortunes shall rise higher, / Caesar's, or mine?'—the Soothsayer is unequivocal:

> Caesar's
> Therefore, O Antony, stay not by his side.
> Thy daemon—that thy spirit which keeps thee—
>   is
> Noble, courageous, high, unmatchable,
> Where Caesar's is not. But near him thy angel
> Becomes afeard, as being o'erpowered.
>   Therefore
> Make space enough between you.
>
> (2.3.18-24)

But Antony has spent nearly the whole of the preceding scene at Caesar's very side, the space between them metaphorically filled and conjugated through Caesar's sister in proposed marriage. And the Soothsayer's advice, 'Make space enough between you', (2.3.24) hearkens back to one of Antony's first assertions in the play: 'Here is my space' (1.1.34). *Here,* for Antony, denoted Egypt generally and Cleopatra's embrace specifically. He currently finds himself displaced when in place in his office as Roman triumvir.

It is significant that Antony has to hear these hard truths from the Egyptian soothsayer who has been mocked and patronised by Cleopatra's attendants. Consistently dignified and truthful, this third-world seer responds to Antony with a candor that no first-world Roman politico would dare to venture. He grasps the life-and-death nature of the stakes at play as he urges Antony, 'hie you to Egypt again' (2.3.15). And his final warning about Caesar is painfully direct: 'If thou dost play with him at any game / Thou art sure to lose' (2.3.26-7). But Antony, cynically manoeuvered into position as Caesar's brother-in-law, finds himself at play in the cutthroat world of Roman politics where he can neither dictate terms nor stop play. Antony is caught within a manipulative godgame, a contrived power-play wherein he is under observation and his usual tactics of direct confrontation are ineffective. The inextricable nature of his predicament is literalized jokingly in his absence by Cleopatra as she ponders catching fish:

> And as I draw them up,
> I'll think them every one an Antony,
> And say 'Ah, ha! Y'are caught!'
>
> (2.5.13-15)

Her fantasy is literalized in Rome. Antony is indeed 'caught', metaphorically reeled in and netted during his meeting with Caesar. But he thinks he is gaining politically. Caesar offers a sealing handshake to Antony, saying 'There's my hand' (2.2.155). But his offer is really an imperative, an order for Antony to shake hands at the same time as it represents a literalized, iron handclasp: 'Y'are caught'. Antony is indeed caught within Caesar's gamesphere, a gamesphere involving militarism, deceit, communication, and power politics.

At the same time, and with similar irony, Octavia is declared 'A blessed lottery to him' (2.2.248). But Antony has won nothing in his new Roman wife. The Penguin edition glosses 'prize' for 'lottery', but is thereby inadequate to the sense of chance signaled by the term. Indeed, the *OED* even uses the line from *Antony and Cleopatra* as an example of 'something which comes to a person by lot or fortune'. And yet even the *OED* is wrong in this instance. Octavia was deliberately thrust upon Antony in a manipulative move by Caesar. Nothing much was left to chance. Caesar mused aloud with a mixture of unctuousness and false rhetoric—

> It cannot be
> We shall remain in friendship, our conditions
> So diff'ring in their acts. Yet if I knew
> What hoop should hold us staunch, from edge
>   to edge
> O'th'world I would pursue it.
>
> (2.2.117-21)

—and Agrippa interceded with his rehearsed suggestion that Antony be wed to Caesar's sister. Antony then takes *Caesar's* hand in a grotesque literalization of the real marriage to take place, a political marriage of convenience fraught with mutual animosity and competition. Even the contiguity of their proper names—Octavia/Octavius—suggests confusion in the identity of Antony's spouse. And Caesar's concluding phrase—'from edge to edge / O'th'world'—chillingly suggests the wide-ranging extent to which he will pursue Antony's matrimonial obedience, a pursuit literalized in the remainder of the play.

Antony, even at this point, is as aware of Caesar's superior gamesmanship as he is himself uncertain of his own moves. Having heard and dismissed the Soothsayer, Antony ruminates as follows:

> Be it art or hap,
> He hath spoken true. The very dice obey him,
> And in our sports my better cunning faints
> Under his chance. If we draw lots, he speeds;
> His cocks do win the battle still of mine
> When it is all to nought, and his quails ever
> Beat mine, inhooped, at odds. I will to Egypt;
> And though I make this marriage for my peace,
> I'th'East my pleasure lies.
>
> (2.3.33-41)

He knows that Caesar is a winner, and he knows also that Caesar will play the game out to its final, painful, inevitable move. But Antony also harbors the romantic notion that he can acquiesce in Caesar's game, comply with Caesar's rules while retaining his own mental reservations concerning personal commitment in Egypt. Such reservations are deluded. The audience experiences the same compliant, romantic moves. And such compliance accentuates the painful irony of commitment and participation played out in the entire drama.

Antony withdraws even as he attempts to assert his position. Ruminating significantly, 'If we draw lots, he speeds' (2.3.36), Antony seems to be subconsciously aware that Caesar has already won the 'blessed lottery' (2.2.248) of Octavia's marriage which Maecenas attributed to Antony. Antony even picks up on and echoes Caesar's diction, his image of quails 'inhooped, at odds' (2.3.39) recalling Caesar's hypothetical 'What hoop should hold us staunch' (2.2.120). Later, as he departs with his new wife, Antony applies a staunch brotherly wrestling hold on Caesar, declaring,

> Come, sir, come,
> I'll wrestle with you in my strength of love.
> Look, here I have you; thus I let you go,
> And give you to the gods.
> (3.2.61-4)

But his bluff confidence is as superficial as it is misplaced. Antony is the one who has been 'caught'. Indeed, Caesar sees to it that the 'old ruffian' (4.1.4) never lays his hands on him again. The marriage ensures either Antony's fraternal obedience or, failing that, his correction and punishment. Caesar's admiration for Antony is decidedly in the past, rendering Barroll's postulation of Octavius's 'serious attempt at rapprochement with an esteemed but puzzling colleague'[15] a partial interpretation at best. The two triumvirs nervously calculate each other. Brotherly tussles escalate quickly into mistrust and full-scale war. And the gods, mentioned so often in this play, gravitate toward Caesar in support of his tactical, political, and military assertions, assertions which take on the form of a deeply strategic godgame.

Antony's ill-fitting yoke of marriage to Octavia is signaled in the imagery with which it is reported. The message to Cleopatra is as clipped as it is concise:

> MESSENGER He's bound unto Octavia.
> CLEOPATRA  For what good turn?
> MESSENGER For the best turn i'th'bed.
> (2.5.58-9)

Politics, as the saying goes, makes strange bedfellows, and Antony is bound to Caesar's sister's bed where he will receive a violent political pounding. The incestuousness of the imagery is as inescapable as is its violence and its sense of incapacity. Hence, Antony's early observation is rendered doubly ironic: he mused to himself, 'These strong Egyptian fetters I must break, / Or lose myself in dotage' (1.2.117-18), only to learn immediately that his first wife was conveniently dead and that leaving Egypt for Rome was relatively easy. The return trip will be infinitely more difficult, as understood by Menas who comments on Antony's marriage with politic discernment: 'Then is Caesar and he for ever knit together' (2.6.113). Inextricably so. Enobarbus, so often hailed for his bluff clarity, gets it all wrong, stating of Antony, 'He married but his occasion here' (2.6.129). Antony did nothing of the sort. He married *Caesar's* occasion in a tactical error which facilitates Caesar's strategy and governs the rest of the play.

Barroll thinks otherwise, de-emphasizing the politics of Antony's marriage to Octavia in an attempt to further characterize Caesar:

> This whole marriage-situation served Shakespeare not as a means of forwarding the political interaction between the two antagonists, but as a way of further characterizing Caesar himself. For what emerges here is the Roman leader's ability to subordinate what he calls his closest personal relationship to his acquisitive desires.[16]

Such subordination, however, *is* political. Octavia is subordinated to positional, political play. She represents a materialist literalization of her brother's position, a competitive position announced self-reflexively upon his first entrance: 'It is not Caesar's natural vice to hate / Our great competitor' (1.4.2-3). But a serious competition is underway even as he speaks. And strong feelings are involved. Consequently, Octavia's choric wishful thinking places her in an impossible neutral position as she declares,

> Husband win, win brother,
> Prays, and destroys the prayer; no midway
> 'Twixt these extremes at all.
> (3.4.18-20)

Her image of prayer is unavailing within the *realpolitik* of her situation. But Octavia realizes the instability of her middle ground at the same time as she unconsciously explicates the nature of the zero-sum game into which her husband and brother manoeuver themselves.

In *Fights, Games, and Debates,* conflict theorist Anatol Rapoport defines the situation succinctly: 'A zero-sum game is one in which A's gain is B's loss, and vice versa'.[17] Cleopatra recognizes these terms with the instinct of a hardened politico when she declares, 'In praising Antony I have dispraised Caesar' (2.5.107). But Antony still thinks he can have Rome and Egypt too, musing 'And though I make this marriage for my peace, / I'th'East my pleasure lies' (2.3.40-1). A couple of tactical assassinations begin to disabuse him of the notion, as Caesar has Lepidus rubbed out at the same time as Antony's subordinate liquidates Pompey. Antony has lost valuable potential allies as a result. But even Pompey subscribed to the old order of honor and decorum as he backhandedly reprimanded Menas for suggesting that the three triumvirs be assassinated in one stroke: 'Being done unknown, / I should have found it afterwards well done, / But must condemn it now' (2.7.78-80). Not so Caesar. He is already planning the demise of Lepidus, and would quietly endorse such a ruthless terrorist manoeuver. Then Menas would be conveniently disposed of, perhaps executed as a murderous madman or exposed as a traitor. Antony finds himself in a fight for his life, in a zero-sum game of political ascendancy. Herein audience sympathy and identification is also implicated. Like Antony, the audience must now face Caesar with romantic rules of honor suspended, with the ruthlessness of total war imposed.

Intelligence and delegation define the new terms for engagement. These are power terms which Antony never fully understands or utilizes. But Caesar has understood from the very first, as a messenger assures him,

> Thy biddings have been done; and every hour,
> Most noble Caesar, shalt thou have report
> How 'tis abroad.
>
> (1.4.34-6)

As imperialist outsider, Caesar requires constant information. Such knowledge implies power in Foucault's terms. According to Edward Said, knowledge directly reinforces power gains: 'Knowledge gives power, more power requires more knowledge, and so on in an increasingly profitable dialectic of information and control'.[18] Presumably this explains Caesar's complete information in Act 3, scene 6, as he informs Octavia of her husband's whereabouts with Cleopatra and includes a lengthy roll-call of Antony's foreign allies. But Antony can never fully 'know' Bocchus or Archelaus or any of the other disparate foreign kings with whom he is allied. His new allegiances are inconsistent, treasonous, un-Roman. That Antony has committed adultery against Octavia is maddening; that he has committed adultery against Caesar, against Rome, is unforgivable. Hence the scolding tone and barely concealed contempt of Caesar's final domestic word: 'Be ever known to patience. My dear'st sister!' (3.6.98). This, in the same lugubriously sarcastic tone as Caesar's later authoritative comment, 'Poor Antony!' (4.1.16). As he advances and consolidates his international power, Caesar both uss his siblings and, at the same time, loses personal respect for them.

Her tactical usefulness expired, Octavia is neither seen nor heard again in the play. But Caesar continues to delegate authority and move into striking position at the same time as he speeds up the action of his deadly game. Antony reacts with confusion and disbelief concerning Caesar's swift positional movements:

> Is it not strange, Canidius,
> That from Tarentum and Brundisium
> He could so quickly cut the Ionian sea
> And take in Toryne?
>
> (3.7.20-3)

And Cleopatra answers him in a tone of voice that combines bitchy remonstrance with the self-assurance of a political officer: 'Celerity is never more admired / Than by the negligent' (24-5). Earlier in the scene, Enobarbus warned the Queen of Egypt that 'Your presence needs must puzzle Antony' (10), but Caesar's presence puzzles and distracts him even more. Having learned that Caesar himself is with his troops in Toryne, Antony stammers, 'Can he be there in person? 'Tis impossible; / Strange that his power should be' (3.7.56-7). To Antony, Caesar's power is indeed strange, a power based on the indirection of tactics, movements, intelligence, strategy, and delegation. Indeed the many short and swift scene changes of Acts 3 and 4 take on the nature of positional play on a giant chess board. They suggest the provisional, mobile, and variable points of contact that are touched upon and explored in the exercise of power relations.

Antony would rather meet his competitor head-on. But his retrograde personal challenge is as desperate as it is ill-conceived. After his defeat in the first sea battle, Antony nostalgically compares procedures at the Battle of Philippi, declaring of Octavius,

> He at Philippi kept
> His sword e'en like a dancer, while I struck
> The lean and wrinkled Cassius; and 'twas I
> That the mad Brutus ended. He alone
> Dealt on lieutenantry, and no practice had
> In the brave squares of war.
>
> (3.11.35-40)

However, Antony's lieutenant Ventidius knows well that 'Caesar and Antony have ever won / More in their officer than person' (3.1.16-17). And the 'brave squares' of squadron-like military formation are currently being revised in Caesar's more innovative tactical approach. Thus Antony's desperate speculation rings hollow:

> His coin, ships, legions,
> May be a coward's, whose ministers would prevail
> Under the service of a child as soon
> As i'th'command of Caesar.
>
> (3.13.22-5)

Caesar *will* prevail through organization and delegation. And he responds to Antony's challenge of personal combat with undisguised levity: 'Let the old ruffian know / I have many other ways to die; meantime / Laugh at his challenge' (4.1.4-6). Antony has become an anachronistic joke. Caesar holds the main power position in their contest for ascendancy. Cleopatra even uses the approved political (and game theory) term in describing Caesar: 'He is a god, and knows / What is most right' (3.13.60-1).

Caesar's godgame has victimized Antony within deromanticized rules of engagement. Additionally, Caesar has brought formal strategy to bear upon his tactics. In standard game theory, such strategizing suggests a complete program governing what any opposing player will do in every conceivable situation within a game. Attack by sea and Antony will respond, although compromised, by sea. Laugh at his personal challenge and Antony will only be further enraged. Caesar confronts Antony with himself by ordering Antony's deserters to the front in order to emphasize the futility of his opposition:

> Plant those that have revolted in the vant,
> That Antony may seem to spend his fury
> Upon himself.
>
> (4.6.9-11)

Caesar's infiltration is extensive, operating at the power center of his opponent as he offers clemency to Cleopatra in return for her termination of Antony, seeks to destabilize her through Thidias's extravagant promises, and zeros in on Antony's reactions:

> Observe how Antony becomes his flaw,
> And what thou think'st his very action speaks
> In every power that moves.
>
> (3.12.34-6)

Caesar gains tactically from confirmation of Antony's reaction. Confused, Antony is both subject and object of his own destruction, as signalled earlier in Enobarbus's comment concerning Antony's rash personal challenge: 'Caesar, thou hast subdued / His judgement too' (3.13.36-7).

For Antony, opposition to Rome is opposition to oneself, is desertion and deposition. In her previously quoted article, 'The Political Context in *Antony and Cleopatra*', Marilynn Williamson notes the many desertions and depositions of the play as a distinct pattern of action leading to political tragedy: Menas deserts Pompey, Enobarbus deserts Antony, Antony deserts Octavia (having previously deserted Cleopatra), Octavius deposes Lepidus, Antony's officer deposes Pompey, Hercules deserts Antony, Cleopatra deserts Antony in battle, and Antony finally deserts himself for Cleopatra who eventually does the same for him. The series reads like a schematic, like a tactical endgame. Any audience is subject to and vicariously implicated in these many vacilations of commitment and loyalty. But while characters and audience alike constantly reassess political positions and degrees of support, Caesar, as the informed 'god' of the game strategizes and benefits from confused opposition.

True, Antony wins a further land skirmish, but this minor victory only delays and intensifies the nature of his ultimate loss. Moreover, Cleopatra's greeting to Antony after his land victory over Caesar is decidedly ironic:

> Lord of lords!
> O infinite virtue, com'st thou smiling from
> The world's great snare uncaught?
>
> (4.8.16-18)

Antony smiles in ignorant, intermediate satisfaction. He is caught within the exchanges of an all-out zero-sum game where only Caesar knows the cumulative score. Antony knows the extent of his disadvantage from the first, knows that his time of expert competition is over. Yet, throughout the play, he buries his sense of puniness and incapacity within retrospective grandeur:

> Now I must
> To the young man send humble treaties, dodge
> And palter in the shifts of lowness, who
> With half the bulk o'th'world played as I pleased.
>
> (3.11.61-4)

But he no longer dictates terms. Finally defeated outright, Antony lays blame elsewhere, refers to Caesar disparagingly as 'this novice' (4.12.14), 'the young Roman boy' (4.12.48), and 'boy Caesar' (3.13.17). His stunned exhortations of grandeur border on the delusional:

> Of late, when I cried 'Ho!',
> Like boys unto a muss, kings would start forth
> And cry 'Your will?'
>
> (3.13.90-2)

Such retrospective language is common among veteran players defeated at last by younger, sharply-skilled competitors.

Antony's self-confidence, however, continues toward desperation and exposes the extent of his uncertainty. He has already brutalized Caesar's envoy Thidias, has already inappropriately dispatched a schoolmaster to negotiate terms of withdrawal. Despite Antony's localized and romanticized overstatements to himself and his lover, Paul Yachnin hears the relative voices of command accurately: 'Antony's language of command grows weaker as Caesar's grows stronger'.[19] Such an observation relates directly to the zero-sum game in which the two have been involved. And Caesar sums up the situation accurately at news of Antony's death when he publicly addresses his vanquished rival:

> I must perforce
> Have shown to thee such a declining day
> Or look on thine. We could not stall together
> In the whole world.
>
> (5.1.37-40)

Throughout, Caesar has played for keeps. His technique involved calculated risk and dispassionate decision in line with a strategy. Antony, by contrast, made decisions passionately out of personal bias and then tried to rationalize his decisions. The superior gameplayer prevailed.

It is true that Cleopatra is a gameplayer too. But her games throughout are various and insouciant: billiards, angling, cross-dressing, dance, moral support, military gestures, the 'sport indeed!' (4.15.32) of physically power-lifting Antony toward her. Enraged in his defeat, Antony immediately suspects that she has 'packed cards with Caesar' (4.14.19). Cleopatra does indeed play for political advantage as seriously as Caesar does, but her methods are as passé as Antony's, involving romantic trust—'He's speaking now, / Or murmuring "Where's my serpent of old Nile?"' (1.5.24-5)—simple reversals—'If you find him sad, / Say I am dancing; if in mirth, report / That I am sudden sick' (1.3.3-5)—and wish-fulfilment: 'I dreamt there was an emperor Antony' (5.2.76). Her ruse with her treasurer Seleucus is easily seen through. Even *if* exposure of her deceit is calculated to dupe Caesar into believing that she wishes to live, she merely buys time to die. She contains the fabulous wealth of an ancient hereditary regime, and her proudest associations are, like Antony's, in the deific past tense, involving Isis and Julius Caesar and Pompey the Great. Her famous suicide rescues her from the shame of a new and unfeeling administration. Sadly, she plans afterward to 'play till doomsday' (5.2.232). It's all a lark. Within *Antony and Cleopatra,* Caesar's game is more logistical, more task-and-goal oriented in terms of consolidated ascendant power.

Moreover, Caesar plays for advantage in an eternal present tense wherein necessary conclusions are drawn 'on the move', are built upon in terms of complex and dispassionate strategy. His expertise suggests the advantage of gamewright. He alone knows the new rules fully, rules which subordinate military honor and magnanimous romance in the interests of political manoeuvering and imperialist domination. Romantic loyalty gives way to partisan support. Rationalizations are disallowed. Antony, by contrast, mourns the past, fixating on his own past glories and achievements while discrediting Caesar's newer and more tactical politico-military assertions. But Antony never fully understands that a new game is afoot. He competes, but competes at a terrible disadvantage within Caesar's strategizing gamesphere. Antony may indeed 'mock / The luck of Caesar' (5.2.284-5), as Cleopatra imagines, but Caesar's 'luck' might better be considered as a critical narrowing of possibility, a thoroughgoing sense of tactical advantage, a complete subordination of personal desire to political success. 'Luck' is the loser's word for it.

Antony and Cleopatra depended on luck. Caesar depended on strategy wherein Antony's behavior was observed, judged, and manipulated. Antony blustered impotently and desperately within a gamesphere where the rules were unfamiliar and his competitor stolidly unsentimental. Antony's consequent feelings of inadequacy and scorn for Caesar's youth are endemic to the nature of godgames, as explained by Wilson: 'Behind every godgame, there lies a situation that recalls, with full power to evoke the appropriate feelings, the common human intuition of being made a victim, a scapegoat, or a sacrifice and of being made puny or deluded by someone superior, a *they* set over and against oneself'.[20] Antony, with his Herculean associations and all-too-human weaknesses, experiences every situational possibility. Throughout, Caesar manipulates Antony with all the callousness of the gods in ancient myth.

In *Antony and Cleopatra,* the game of love has been a game of politics, has been a game of power. Within such a game, rules and objectives change with bewildering verve. Caesar alone anticipates, dictates, and stays informed of every instance. Steadfast consistency is a fiction of romantic love; tactical flexibility determines the politicized love of Shakespeare's play. The audience experiences uncomfortable material vacillations, vacillations such as those in the play, wherein romantic identification with Antony and Cleopatra is slanted toward political survival with Caesar. Necessary, even painful, choices must be made. Antony will never be a political winner. Neither will Cleopatra. True, Cleopatra cheats Caesar of her humiliation in Roman triumph, but such a victory is only victory by default. Besides, it too was anticipated. Caesar no doubt regrets the loss of public ostentation, but he wastes no time in bemoaning it. Instead, his last lines are conveyed, as Paul Yachnin puts it, 'in the form of a command so confident of obedience that it can slide casually toward a tone of solicitation'.[21] Just so. Such is power as underwritten by an expert whose very name is synonymous with ruthless imperialist domination. Admittedly, there are more things in life than politics. But one must survive in order to enjoy them. And in this play, it is Caesar who survives. Deromanticized performances of *Antony and Cleopatra* necessarily accentuate power politics along with the amoral basics of serious tactical gameplay. Caesar's godgame of political consolidation ensures Roman cultural survival and expansion.

*Notes*

[1] Janet Adelman, *The Common Liar: An Essay on 'Antony and Cleopatra'* (New Haven, 1973), p. 125. Dipak Nandy, 'The Realism of *Antony and Cleopatra*', in *Shakespeare in a Changing World,* ed. Arnold Kettle (London, 1964), p. 176.

[2] David Cecil, *Poets and Story-Tellers* (London, 1949), p. 14. See also J. Leeds Barroll, 'The Characterization of Octavius', *Shakespeare Studies* 6 (1970), 231-88.

[3] David Bevington, ed. *Antony and Cleopatra* (Cambridge, 1990), p. 22.

[4] See L.T. Fitz, 'Egyptian Queens and Male Reviewers: Sexist Attitudes in *Antony and Cleopatra* Criticism', *Shakespeare Quarterly* 28 (1977), 297-316.

[5] Throughout, I quote Shakespeare from the New Penguin *Antony and Cleopatra* edited by Emrys Jones (Harmondsworth, 1977).

[6] Marilynn Williamson, 'The Political Context in *Antony and Cleopatra*', *Shakespeare Quarterly* 21 (1970), 244.

[7] Bevington, ed. *Antony and Cleopatra,* p. 27.

[8] Hélène Cixous, 'Sorties: Out and Out: Attacks/Ways Out/Forays', in *The Newly Born Woman,* trans. Betsy Wing (Minneapolis, 1986), p. 128.

[9] For such positions see Catherine Belsey, *The Subject of Tragedy* (London, 1988); Jonathan Dollimore, *Radical Tragedy* (Chicago, 1984); Michel Foucault, *The History of Sexuality, Vol 1* trans., Robert Hurley (New York, 1978); and Lawrence Stone, *The Family, Sex and Marriage in England 1500-1800* (New York, 1977).

[10] Linda Charnes, 'What's love got to do with it? Reading the Liberal Humanist Romance in Shakespeare's *Antony and Cleopatra*', *Textual Practice* 6 (1992), 1. I depart, however, from Charnes's more dismissive readings of liberal humanist romance in *Antony and Cleopatra*. For example, I doubt that the standards of formulaic romance novels are uppermost in the minds of liberal humanist critics of the play.

[11] Foucault, *Discipline,* pp. 26-7.

[12] R. Rawdon Wilson, *In Palamedes' Shadow: Explorations in Play, Game, and Narrative Theory* (Boston, 1990), p. 251, n 6. In a Foreword to his revised edition of *The Magus* (London, 1977), Fowles mentions *The Godgame* as suggestive alternative title for the book, a title, he says, 'whose rejection I still sometimes regret' (p. 10).

[13] Foucault, *Discipline,* p. 27.

[14] Margot Heinemann, ' "Let Rome in Tiber melt!" Chaos and order in *Antony and Cleopatra*', *Shakespeare Jahrbuch* 128 (1992), 40.

[15] Barroll, 235.

[16] Ibid., 263.

[17] Anatol Rapoport, *Fights, Games, and Debates* (Ann Arbor, 1960), p. 133.

[18] Edward Said, *Orientalism* (New York, 1978), p. 36. Said focuses especially on Western colonial expansion and presumption in the last two centuries. But he is always historically suggestive, and one might easily substitute 'Rome' and 'Caesar' in the following assertion about British policy: '[Roman] knowledge of Egypt *is* Egypt for [Caesar]' (32).

[19] Paul Yachnin, 'Shakespeare's Politics of Loyalty: Sovereignty and Subjectivity in *Antony and Cleopatra*', *Studies in English Literature 1500-1900* 33 (1993): 348.

[20] Wilson, p. 142.

[21] Yachnin, 350. I see little significance, however, in Dollabella's putative 'secret loyalty' to Cleopatra as stressed by Yachnin. Such 'emotional defection' would be difficult to portray on stage and might better be considered as subversion contained within the authority of Caesar. That is, any scruples are permitted so long as Dollabella does as he is told.

---

Source: " 'The Luck of Caesar': Winning and Losing in *Antony and Cleopatra*," in *English Studies: A Journal of English Language and Literature,* Vol. 79, No. 6, November, 1998, pp. 522-35.

# Who "Has No Children" in *Macbeth?*

## Tom Clayton, *University of Minnesota*

> He has no children.
> *Macbeth* 4.3.216

> He that has no children knows not what love is.
> Tilley, Dent C341

The *Masks* of Shakespeare's plays demonstrate throughout that Shakespeare's ways make a settled view of his proceedings impossible to maintain unaltered so long as one continues to return to the scene of his playwrighting. The view I hold of Shakespeare's Macbeth at this writing is that he is a villain-hero—more than a mere protagonist—fatally ambitious but once full enough of the milk of human kindness to require letting by his wife in order to dare do more than may become a man, and so become none. He lives just long enough to know himself, too well, a regicide and worse, and to die in action by another's deed of the kind that made him a hero in the first place. He thus restores in a measure, however high his head upon a pole at play's end, something of the sometime man in place of the type and title of his reign, The Tyrant. He is throughout the observed of all observers, like Hamlet in this and in his vividness of imagination. His hope shattered in "success," he passes through security to desperation. The Weird Sisters gave him the first two, by his subjective piecing out of the first alone and taking the second too trustingly for granted—until he hears the word of promise of his ear broken to his hope in the word of Macduff's birth from his mother's womb untimely ripped. The better parts of even a desperate Macbeth are both there in the end, as traces of the man of milk as well as of defender's blood he was and fleetingly becomes again:

> Of all men else I have avoided thee
>   [Macduff].
> But get thee back, my soul is too much charg'd
> With blood of thine already.
>
> (5.8.4-6)[1]

His initial lack of fear is due to his "security," but even when that proves to have been a delusion he accepts Macduff's challenge with alacrity:

> Though Birnam wood be come to Dunsinane,
> And thou oppos'd, being of no woman born,
> Yet I will try the last. Before my body
> I throw my warlike shield. Lay on, Macduff,
> And damn'd be him that first cries, "Hold,
>   enough!"
>
> (5.8.30-34)

Famous last words, matter for an epitaph.

In 1.3 with fortune-teller's trifles like "hail to thee, Thane of Cawdor" (a transfer of title already declared by Duncan in 1.2.64-65 but news to Macbeth) and "hail to thee, that shall be King hereafter," the Weird Sisters marshalled Macbeth the way that he was going. When he goes of his own volition to visit *them* in 4.1, the dramatic (and literary) design, as foreshadowing, converges with motivation, mimetic action, and significance as prophetic truth itself, the power of which Macbeth seems to have conferred upon the Weird Sisters by killing Duncan and sealing his own fate. Each of their three prophesying caveats comes true—in reverse of the order in which they were given, and Macbeth dies to his deep damnation when he tries "the last"—that is, the first—of the Weird Sisters' caveats:

> Macbeth! Macbeth! Macbeth! Beware Macduff,
> Beware the Thane of Fife.
>
> (4.1.71-72)[2]

2

"He has no children." The half-line is declarative, metrical and limpid, and apparently without depth or guile on anyone's part—until one asks who "He" is. And thereby hangs a tale. More hangs on the answer than appears at first glance, and the question requires referring not to those two familiar, mild-mannered misleaders, preemptive paraphrase and tendentious description, but to the primary evidence of word and other action of the context, for an answer. There is an unwritten standing law that quotations should be few and brief; when this law is combined with the fact that readers seldom have a copy of the subject texts open at their side, a not uncommon result is some critical slippage between text and reader, occasionally including slippage between text and critic that is compounded in the reader. The pertinent local context follows, with my interpolations (of 1, 2, and 3) marked by {}. In 4.3, the first subscene consists in the long duologue between Macduff and Malcolm on the latter's fitness for rule that is terminated when the Doctor enters for the subscene concerned with the miracles of Edward the Confessor, which in turn gives way to the third subscene with Ross's entrance (at 160) and arrival from Scotland with news that he is understandably loath and slow to deliver.[3] Asked by Macduff, "Stands Scotland where it did?" he replies,

> Alas, poor country,
> Almost afraid to know itself! It cannot        165
> Be call'd our mother, but our grave; where
>   nothing,

But who knows nothing, is once seen to smile;
Where sighs, and groans, and shrieks that rent the air
Are made, not mark'd; where violent sorrow seems
A modern ecstasy. The dead man's knell    170
Is there scarce ask'd for who, and good men's lives
Expire before the flowers in their caps,
Dying or ere they sicken.
   *Macduff.*              O relation!
Too nice, and yet too true.
   *Malcolm.*   What's the newest grief?
   *Ross.*   That of an hour's age doth hiss the speaker;    175
Each minute teems a new one.
   *Macduff.*   How does my wife?
   *Ross.*   Why, well.
   *Macduff.*   And all my children?
   *Ross.*                   Well too.
   *Macduff.*   The tyrant has not batter'd at their peace?
   *Ross.*   No, they were well at peace when I did leave 'em.[4]    179

. . . . .

   *Ross.*   Your castle is surpris'd; your wife, and babes,    205
Savagely slaughter'd. To relate the manner,
Were on the quarry of these murther'd deer
To add the death of you.

{1} *Malcolm.*          Merciful heaven!
What, man, ne'er pull your hat upon your brows;
Give sorrow words. The grief that does not speak
Whispers the o'er-fraught heart, and bids it break.[5]    210
   *Macduff.* My children too? *(to Ross, ignoring Malcolm)*
   *Ross.*        Wife, children, servants, all
That could be found.
   *Macduff.* And I must be from thence!
My wife kill'd too? *(to Ross)*
   *Ross.*        I have said.
   {2} *Malcolm.*   Be comforted.
Let's make us med'cines of our great revenge
To cure this deadly grief.    215
   *Macduff.* He has no children. All my pretty ones? *(to Ross, ignoring Malcolm)*
Did you say all? O hell-kite! *(i.e., Macbeth)* All?
What, all my pretty chickens, and their dam
At one fell swoop?
   {3} *Malcolm.* Dispute it like a man.
   *Macduff.*   I shall do so; *(finally, to Malcolm)*    220
But I must also feel it as a man;
I cannot but remember such things were,
That were most precious to me. Did heaven look on,
And would not take their part? Sinful Macduff,
They were all strook for thee! naught that I am,    225
Not for their own demerits, but for mine,
Fell slaughter on their souls. Heaven rest them now!
   *Malcolm.* Be this the whetstone of your sword, let grief
Convert to anger; blunt not the heart, enrage it.
   *Macduff.* O, I could play the woman with mine eyes,    230
And braggart with my tongue! But, gentle heavens,
Cut short all intermission. Front to front
Bring thou this fiend of Scotland and myself;
Within my sword's length set him; if he scape,
Heaven forgive him too!
   *Malcolm.*   This [tune] goes manly.    235
Come go we to the King, our power is ready,
Our lack is nothing but our leave. Macbeth
Is ripe for shaking, and the pow'rs above
Put on their instruments. Receive what cheer you may,
The night is long that never finds the day.    240
   *Exeunt.*
                    (4.3-164-180, 205-40)

In this triologue, Malcolm is mostly silent but three times speaks briefly to Macduff as prompted by his verbal reactions to Ross's answers. Macduff does not respond to Malcolm, speaking only to Ross, formally and as much or more to himself, finally responding directly to Malcolm only the *third* time Malcolm speaks to him (4.3.219, 220).[6]

So who "has no children" in line 216? Malcolm, who is present, or Macbeth, who is not? The gloss in David Bevington's Bantam edition (1988) reads, "i.e., no father would do such a thing (?), or he (Malcolm) speaks comfort without knowing what such a loss feels like (?)" (4.3.217n). If "no father" is as presumably meant to be Macbeth, this note levels opposing solutions to the problem of ambiguity of reference— the "indeterminacy" or "indefinition" of a sort—and the differences of interpretation attending it. To my present way of thinking, the immediate context and the whole scene quite readily disambiguate by themselves, but the local reference in this case is also germane to *Macbeth* and Macbeth in relation to the meaning and significance of the whole play.[7]

When such critical questions arise—about the parental status of the Macbeths, for example—it is natural for students of all kinds to turn from the script itself to diverse authorities, such as current scholarly and reading editions; studies of the play in performance and performances themselves; perennials like A. C. Bradley's *Shakespearean Tragedy* (1904) and later discussions like Geoffrey Bullough's *Narrative and Dramatic Sources of Shakespeare* (1975); and classic essays on or near the subject, notably L. C. Knights's celebrated (and for its title notorious) "How Many Children Had Lady Macbeth?" and Cleanth Brooks's equally celebrated "Naked Babe and the Cloak of Manliness." The respective collections of their own essays reprinting these came out in the same year, 1947, two years after the end of World War II, appropriately enough, nearly half a century ago but still—or again—worth reading, along with Bradley and many studies now out of print.

For its comprehensiveness and circumspection the first of all resorted to—and also the last, often enough and for good reason—might well be Marvin Rosenberg's masterful *Masks of Macbeth* (1978), which makes a case both persuasive and (in an appendix) genially speculative for the Macbeths' parenthood. He sums up the critical position at the time as represented by the Variorum edition of 1901-3, which, "canvassing a spectrum of criticism, cites about as many who refer the *He* to Macbeth as to Malcolm" (554). Perhaps that is still the case at this end of the century, but it is not easy to tell, because when the half-line is not glossed in place or somewhere else it is impossible to know the editor or critic's view further than to suppose that he must have thought interpretation obvious and a gloss redundant.[8] And if obvious, then by implication Shakespeare's unambiguous intention. Editorial silence seems to mean that "He" is Macbeth. The lengthier the gloss, the more likely is identification of "He" as Malcolm, who is technically eligible as "yet / Unknown to woman" (126-27), if he is telling Macduff the truth at that point; but such a contrast suggests that his proponents may protest too much, Occam's razor-wise.

Perhaps the most self-assured recent case for Malcolm is given by Nicholas Brooke in his Oxford/World's Classics edition (1990, 4.3.216n):

> 1. Malcolm would *not offer such a simplistic cure* if he had children of his own; 2. Revenge on Macbeth's children is impossible because he has none; 3. If Macbeth had children, he would not have slaughtered others. The first sense seems to me *an inevitable snub to Malcolm's glib haste.* See proverb "he that has no children knows not what love is," Dent C341 (emphasis mine)

—which proverb applies as well—and better—to Macbeth.

The locus classicus of modern critical reasoning on the subject is Bradley's Note EE, beginning "Three interpretations have been offered of the words 'He has no children'" (399). Brooke (1990) naturally follows Bradley's exposition there with his own "spin," as does Kenneth Muir without spin in the New Arden edition (1962, 4.3.216n), whose neutral description reads,

> There are three explanations of this passage. (i) He [Macduff] refers to Malcolm, who if he had children of his own would *not suggest revenge as a cure* for grief. Cf. *John* III.iv.91: "He talks to me that never had a son." This was supported by Malone and Bradley. (ii) He refers to Macbeth, on whom he cannot take an appropriate revenge.... (iii) He refers to Macbeth, who would never have slaughtered Macduff's children if he had had any of his own. Cf. *3 Hen. VI* V. v. 63: "You have no children, butchers if you had, / The thought of them would have stirred up remorse." (Delius). *I adhere to (ii).* (emphasis mine)

Bradley had cited in more detail the parallels in *King John* and *Henry VI, Part Three* (5.5.63): in *King John,* "Pandulph says to Constance, 'You hold too heinous a respect of grief,' and Constance answers, 'He talks to me that never had a son'" (399), a parallel supporting Malcolm. In *3H6* "Margaret says to the murderers of Prince Edward, 'You have no children, butchers! if you had, / The thought of them would have stirred up remorse'" (400), a parallel supporting Macbeth; but Bradley "see[s] no argument except that the words of Macduff almost repeat those of Margaret; and this fact does not seem to have much weight. It shows only that Shakespeare might easily use the words in the sense of (*c*) if that sense were suitable to the occasion" (400).

Bradley's reasoning in favor of Malcolm is sound, as far as it goes, and I do not slight it here in quoting only his conclusions and primary reasons. Unlike Muir later, Bradley could not "think interpretation (*b* [= ii]) the most natural," partly because

> Macduff is not the man to conceive at any time the idea of killing children in retaliation; and that he contemplates it *here,* even as a suggestion, I find it hard to believe.... Macduff listens only to Ross.... When Malcolm interrupts, therefore, he puts aside his suggestion with four words spoken to himself, or (less probably) to Ross (his relative, who knew his wife and children), and continues his agonised questions and exclamations. (400)[9]

There are two main arguments *against* Macduff's referring to Malcolm. The first and most obvious is the immediate dramatic context itself. The difference between Bradley's neutral and Brooke's indignant characterizing of Malcolm's attempted interventions demonstrates the latitude and subjectivity of perception here, but the primary emphasis should be not on Malcolm's "glib haste" (or whatever it is) but on what Macduff's dialogue shows of himself: he is in shock, preoccupied with his loss and its causes, his guilty absence as he sees it and the murderer acting in his absence. He gives no hint that he even hears Malcolm until his third try; and, while an actor's delivery could easily effect a glancing reference to Malcolm, such reference is gratuitous, the more so in reproach of Malcolm. In the lines in question, 216-19, his concentration alternates between his murdered children and their murderer—*"He"* (Macbeth), all his children, "hell-kite" Macbeth, his children and their mother:

> *Macduff.* **He has no children.** All my pretty ones? *(to Ross, ignoring Malcolm)*
> Did you say all? O hell-kite! *(i.e., Macbeth)*
> All?
> What, all my pretty chickens and their dam
> At one fell swoop?

This intense concentration does not change direction until Malcolm's "Dispute it like a man." From there to the end of the scene Malcolm and the just retribution in prospect carry his attention and his animus, which includes his self-rebuke to "sinful Macduff" and his invoking "gentle heavens" to

> Cut short all intermission. Front to front
> Bring thou this fiend of Scotland and myself;
> Within my sword's length set him; if he scape,
> Heaven forgive him too!
>
> (4.3.231-35)

The scene ends on a stirring martial note that heralds the coming end of oppression and the Tyrant, advancing the "Western" aspect of *Macbeth* toward the showdown and the morality play that combines poetic justice with the tragic finale.

I should add that I think—not everyone does—that Malcolm's character in the entire play and in this scene as King-in-waiting is that of a worthy successor to Duncan very like his father, one whose attempted interventions with Macduff seem intended to be seen as sympathetic, and tentative and inexperienced in such cases rather than as gauche, callow, and deserving of rebuke.[10] Within the earlier part of the scene there is little enough to go on, however, which partly justifies Bradley and others' confining their attention to the immediate context alone: earlier Macduff was first shocked by Malcolm's confession of his vices of lust and avarice, and then stunned by his abrupt change when convinced of Macduff's integrity. Not surprisingly, to Malcolm's "Why are you silent?" then, he replies laconically, "Such welcome and unwelcome things at once / 'Tis hard to reconcile" (137-39).

3

The second argument and the more telling is the connection of him who "has no children" with the play as a whole. With Malcolm as "He," there is no connection of consequence, and the effect is local and the line an ephemeral throwaway. With Macbeth as "He," there is profound and reverberating resonance, and the line articulates a theme of the play and tacit motive of the protagonist hinted at elsewhere but made explicit—and succinctly so—here. As L. C. Knights describes one aspect of it (*Explorations* 40n), "The Macbeth-Banquo opposition is emphasized when we learn that Banquo's line will 'stretch out to the cracke of Doome' (4.1.117). Macbeth is cut off from the natural sequence, '*He has no children* (4.3.217), he is a 'Monster' (5.7.54). *Macbeth's isolation* is fully brought out in the last Act" (emphasis mine).

The ambiguous question of parental status is forced tantalizingly upon any interpreter's attention, critical or theatrical, at several points. Presumably we are meant to believe that Lady Macbeth has "given suck" (1.7.54), as she says she has;[11] and though Macbeth tells her to "Bring forth men-children only!" (1.7.72), there is no evidence in the received text of when she might have had this experience of breast-feeding (a Scottish practice not shared by upper-class English women), and no explicit reference made to a child or children dead or alive begotten by Macbeth *or* born to Lady Macbeth. In the sources Lady Macbeth had at least one son (Lulach) by an earlier marriage (to Gillecomgain, Bullough 433), and those may well explain the origin of "I have given suck"—but cannot explain its significance and effect in the play as we have it, where the details in context are

> I have given suck, and know
> How tender 'tis to love the babe that milks me;
> I would, while it was smiling in my face,
> Have pluck'd my nipple from his boneless gums,
> And dash'd the brains out, had I so sworn as you
> Have done to this.
>
> (1.7.54-59)

In a play in which others' children figure so prominently by themselves and in relation to their parents—Banquo's, Duncan's, Macduff's and Lady Macduff's, Old Siward's, and one might add the second and third Apparitions as well as Banquo's royal descendants—this is a curious oversight. Certain it is that Macbeth is haunted by his fear of Banquo, for "'Tis much he dares" (3.1.50), despite the fact that he might well find reason for security in Banquo's further strength, that "He hath a wisdom that doth guide his valor / To act in safety" (52-53), except that "under him / My genius is rebuked, as it is said / Mark Antony's was by Caesar" (54-56). He immediately recalls of the Weird Sisters that speaking to Banquo,

>                          prophet-like,
> They hail'd him father to a line of kings.
> Upon my head they plac'd a *fruitless crown,*
> And put a *barren sceptre* in my gripe,
> Thence to be wrench'd with an unlineal hand,
> No son of mine succeeding. If't be so,
> For Banquo's issue have I fil'd my mind,
> For them the gracious Duncan have I murther'd,
> Put rancors in the vessel of my peace
> Only for them, and mine eternal jewel
> Given to the common enemy of man,
> To make them kings—the seeds of Banquo kings!
> Rather than so, come fate into the list,
> And champion me to th' utterance!
>                          (58-71, emphasis mine)[12]

"No son of mine" stillborn or otherwise dead, or living now, or to be born hereafter. But one thing is very clear about the play as we have it, that we see no Macbeth child, son or daughter, and we hear no unequivocal reference to one. It would be reasonable (if idle) therefore to infer that Macbeth offspring were little if at all on Shakespeare's mind, as they well might not be, since he had none in the sources. "Following" sources in silence leaves ambiguous traces (propter hoc or only post hoc?), but the play as it is concentrated on Macbeth, the relationship between wife and husband, and to a lesser extent Lady Macbeth herself.[13]

It is surprising that in his classic essay on the play Cleanth Brooks says nothing at all about these matters, but as his title implies his interest was especially in the contrasting symbolism of pity, as with "the naked babe" of 1.7, and with the mere "cloak of manliness" of one who dressed but could not act the part ("Now does he feel his title / Hang loose about him, liked giant's robe / Upon a dwarfish thief," 5.2.20-22ff.)

It is not surprising that L. C. Knights in his ironically witty title did not address his own question, because his purpose in discussing "a re-orientation of Shakespeare criticism" (*Explorations* 15, "How Many" part 1) was to discourage the study of Shakespeare's characters as persons in their own right beyond the limits of the plays in which they are articulated.

> [T]he bulk of Shakespeare criticism is concerned with his characters, his heroines, his love of Nature or his "philosophy"—with everything, in short, except with the words on the page, which it is the main business of the critic to examine. I wish to consider . . . how this paradoxical state of affairs arose. To examine the historical development of the kind of criticism that is mainly concerned with "character" is to strengthen the case against it. (20)

Concluding, with the polemical exclusiveness usual to theoretical claim-staking, that "the only profitable approach to Shakespeare is a consideration of his plays as dramatic poems, of his use of language to obtain a total complex emotional response" (20), in part 2 he asks "How should we read Shakespeare?" and gives as example a detailed analysis of *Macbeth* (ii), beginning "*Macbeth* is a statement of evil" (32)—"but it is a statement not of a philosophy but of ordered emotion" (45). In keeping with his method, he says nothing of the "I have given suck" speech in relation to character or action, but finds it an instance of "the violence of the imagery" that complements "explicit references to the unnatural" (37).[14]

Both essays seem to me salutary for and beyond their day, and I see little enough to fault in either their orientation or their particular treatment, insofar as both were very much interested in the play as written, and attending to important aspects of the play previously neglected or ignored altogether. Because they are critical and text/script-centered, such addresses translate readily enough into the terms of theatrical performance and criticism.

4

The local (in 4.3) and the global (the whole play, its world and its action) reciprocally affect each other according to the reader's interpretation or the actor's expression of their relationship and may also be said to effect each other, according to how either is interpreted and given priority, entailing a correlative significance in the other. If the Macbeths have children, or at least a child, then it would be nonsense for Macduff to say Macbeth "has no children." If there is no evidence that the Macbeths at the time of the play's action have children, for all practical purposes they have not. And it matters especially that Macbeth "has no children."

Closest to his wife in our perception when she reads his letter aloud before we see them together and again when they plan and execute their regicidal plot, Macbeth is by degrees cut off first from her, as he becomes progressively more depressed, fearful, and finally desperate; and then from virtually all but Seyton, by which time he has

> . . . liv'd long enough: my way of life
> Is fall'n into the sere, the yellow leaf,
> And that which should accompany old age,
> As honor, love, obedience, troops of friends,
> I must not look to have; but in their stead,
> Curses, not loud but deep, mouth-honor, breath,
> Which the poor heart would fain deny, and dare not.
>                          (5.3.22-28)

There is no mention of the unique solace of children, here, and the prospect of living progeny, greater than the earlier greatest, is behind. Macbeth is alone to face his future—his death and his damnation.

Finally, Macbeth's barrenness is significant as an unspecified but implicit motive for his killing others and their children, and it is significant in another—perhaps more—important way as symbolizing a moral desiccation and a spiritual sterility contrasting with the symbolic green thumbs (or fingers) of the "gardener"-kings, both Duncan the unfortunate and too trusting, who in 1.4.28-29 says he has "begun to *plant* thee [Macbeth], and will labor / To make thee full of *growing*"; and his son and heir, Malcolm, who, summing up his immediate obligations and responsibilities at the end of the play, says,

> What's more to do
> Which would be *planted* newly with the time,
>
> . . . . .
>
> . . . This, and what needful else
> That calls upon us, by the grace of Grace,
> We will perform in measure, time, and place.
> (5.9.30-31, 37-39, emphasis added)

## 5

Although the play, scene, and dialogue require identification of "He" for performance and for audience (and reader) understanding, a stage direction so refined might well seem impossible, Shavian, or absurd: easy enough as "glances at Malcolm" or "he means Macbeth" (SDs no editor understandably has seen fit to supply), but inevitably somewhat Shavian, and therefore not Shakespearean, if meant to indicate Macbeth and, more, suggest an array of nuances in action and verbal expression scarcely to be scored. It seems doubtful whether many stage or screen Macbeths can have referred "He has no children" to Malcolm, and I can say with certainty that Colum Convey did not in the most recent *Macbeth* I have seen, not at least on the evening of 21 August 1996 at the Royal Shakespeare Theatre.[15]

I admire unabashedly a view that humanizes a protagonist increasingly desperate and cornered by entertaining as his motive his natural concern for his son's patrimony, and on that account I warmly applaud "Lady Macbeth's Indispensable Child" (Rosenberg, *Masks* 671-76), the more so when the author's witty caveat is over the entrance to qualify his generosity:

> Every Shakespearean is entitled to an imaginative speculation now and then, as long as he labels it speculation. This appendix speculates on an *extratextual* possibility in the staging of *Macbeth*. Anti-speculationists are warned. (671, author's emphasis)

No anti-speculationist I, just a pro-inferentialist, to whom 4.3 and the play say and show that Macbeth is the man of the hour in his play until he is out of time, a giant even as a "dwarfish thief," the Tyrant whose assassins have indeed battered at the peace of Macduff's wife and children (and also brought them the peace that passeth all understanding), and the King of fruitless crown and barren scepter accordingly on Macduff's distracted—hypothetical—mind as "He" who "has no children" and has been driven to desperation and libericide to try to prevent a future that comes upon him pari passu with his striving. That seems to be what makes *Macbeth* a tragedy, what made Macbeth Macbeth.

### Notes

[1] Quotations from *Macbeth* are from G. Blakemore Evans's *Riverside Shakespeare,* 2d ed. (1997).

Modern editions differ in the number of scenes in act 5. Hunter has six scenes. The Folio (followed by Brooke) has seven, occupying TLN 2395-2529 on a single opening at nn3$^v$-4$^r$ (758-59 of Charlton Hinman's *Facsimile*). Editions with eight scenes (e.g., Bevington, Foakes, Harbage) begin scene 8 at TLN 2435 ("Why should I play the Roman fool, and die"). Editions with nine scenes (e.g., Dent, Evans, Muir) begin 9 at TLN 2477 ("I would the friends we miss were safe arriv'd"). Wells and Taylor (and after them Greenblatt) have eleven scenes, distinguishing two scenes at TLN 2415 ("That way the noise is. Tyrant, show thy face!") and 2427 ("This way, my lord, the castle's gently render'd").

There are typographical and formal reasons (e.g., "Exeunt" and "Exit") in F itself for nine or eleven scenes, but the practical effects on the stage or in the reading are slight indeed; and, since fewer than 100 lines are involved, passages are easily located in any text.

[2] For "the last" as fulfilling *the first* of the Weird Sisters' caveats, see my note, "Macbeth's 'Yet I will try the last' What?" The *last* caveat given in 4.1 is the *first* to be realized in a moving Birnam wood in 5.5; the second ("none of woman born") remains second, leaving the first given as "the *last*" to be tried.

[3] Stephen Booth (106-11) gives detailed and witty attention both to 4.3 and "to Malcolm's behavior" as "the most perverse element in a perverse scene" (107), concluding that "Malcolm and Macduff are and remain our allies, but in the morally insignificant terms of our likes and dislikes as audience to an entertainment they are—because this scene is—irritating to us" (111). "Shakespeare develops the socially and emotionally awkward exchange between Ross and Macduff in such a way that it resembles the work of a clumsy playwright. Not only does Macduff have to prod Ross, he does so in lines that lack verisimilitude and seem prompted by the despair of a writer who does not

[4] Similar circumlocutory dialogue continues until Ross gives the awful news, beginning in line 204.

[5] Lines 208-9 may go some way to explain the apparent design of Lear's last speech—a single half-line—and death in the 1608 Quarto version of the play, "Breake hart, I prethe breake" (L3), *if* the line in Q is Lear's by design and not by misplaced speech-heading: it is Kent's line in the Folio.

[6] Evans and Muir make a single line of blank verse of the part-lines (220). Bevington, and Wells and Taylor (+ Greenblatt), treat both Malcolm's speech of three iambic feet and the two feet of the first line of Macduff's reply as short lines aligned with the left margin, like the ambiguous Folio (TLN 2069-70), in which part-lines of blank verse are all so aligned. Brooke leaves "I shall do so" as a short line, joining "Dispute it like a man" with "At one fell swoop?" (219). The distinction among the three would be lost in the theater and is of mainly editorial significance—there being some justification for all three—on the page.

[7] Most undergraduates, in my experience, infer without hesitation that "He" is Macbeth, which I accordingly take to be the natural, spontaneous reading and often assume without comment in discussing the play in the classroom—where in spring 1996 Oliver Thoenen, a history major originally from the United Kingdom, who had done *Macbeth* on his A levels, rightly drew me up short with the note in Bevington s Bantam edition (just quoted). The present essay germinated from class discussion of the matter.

[8] Among post-1950s editors silent on "He" are Dent, Evans, Harbage, Hunter, and Greenblatt. I sympathize with this exercise of editorial restraint.

[9] Noting that Bradley "strongly supported the view that this refers to Malcolm," R. A. Foakes (1968) continues that "it is more often taken as a reference to Macbeth" and that he "think[s] Macduff has Macbeth in mind" (4.3.216, 127).

[10] Garry Wills has recently expressed the view that

> Malcolm becomes a physician to Macduff's grief for his wife and children. . . . It is true that Malcolm is manipulative here, as in the testing scenes. He is fashioning Macduff into an instrument of his purpose. . . . The shrewd manipulator is far closer to James's image of himself than is the wimp or milksop Malcolm so often seen on the stage. Malcolm only takes his proper station in the play if we see him as the great counter-witch pitted against Macbeth. He has "purged" and strengthened Macduff. Now he launches him at the target, "devilish Macbeth." (123-24)

[11] There is in fact no way of knowing whether she remembers or fantasizes—as well as no reason to doubt her. Thus it is easy to see why some might argue that Shakespeare fulfilled his dramatic intentions in the contextual impact of this speech, without giving further thought to the child or children alluded to, presumably because not part of his envisioning and design. Stephen Booth writes that "Lady Macbeth's mysteriously missing children present an ominous, unknown, but undeniable time before the beginning" (94); and that's true, too.

[12] It is significant that while Macduff invokes "gentle heaven" to related purposes, Macbeth invokes "fate" and brings it on himself, not unassisted but of his own will in a special application of the idea that "character is fate" (Novelis), which George Eliot (*The Mill on the Floss,* 1860) thought "one of his questionable aphorisms" (6.5) but Thomas Hardy approved (*The Mayor of Casterbridge,* 1886, chap. 17). The idea is expressed first in the West by Heraclitus: ἠθῶs ἀυθρώπῳ δαίμωυ

[13] In round numbers supplied by Marvin Spevack's Character Concordance (in vol. 3, *Tragedies*) based on the first edition of Evans's *Riverside Shakespeare,* Macbeth has 32% of the dialogue to Lady Macbeth's 12%, ranking fifth in percentage of dialogue behind Hamlet (of course; 39%), Timon (36%), Henry V (33%), and Iago (33%—.02% less than Henry).

[14] It follows that his treatment of 4.3 looks beyond character: "the conversation between Macduff and Malcolm has never been adequately explained" (42). It has three functions, "but the main purpose of the scene is obscured unless we realize its function as choreic commentary. In alternating speeches the evil that Macbeth has caused is explicitly stated, without extenuation. And it is stated impersonally" (43)—and he quotes in illustration. Since in much of the scene "the impersonal function of the speaker is predominant, . . . [t]here are only two alternatives: either Shakespeare was a bad dramatist, or his critics have been badly misled by mistaking the *dramatis personae* for real persons in this scene" (44).

[15] Tim Albery, director; Roger Allam as Macbeth. Cf. Rosenberg:

> In the theatre some Macduffs have alluded to Macbeth, some to Malcolm. The *New Monthly Magazine,* in 1828, complaining about one stage Macduff's implication that Macbeth was meant, argued for Malcolm, "who is so forward with his counsel to a heartbroken father." . . . [Leigh] Hunt, too, saw Macduff turning away from Malcolm as "unable to understand a father's feelings," rather to Ross, for sympathy. When a Macduff of Kean's played it as Hunt suggested, the critic was impressed at the "deep and true effect . . . far beyond that which can be produced by any denunciation of impotent vengeance." (554)

## References

Booth, Stephen. 1983. *"King Lear," "Macbeth," Indefinition, and Tragedy.* New Haven: Yale University Press.

Bradley, A. C. 1904; reprints *Shakespearean Tragedy.* New York: Meridian, 1960.

Brooks, Cleanth. 1947. "The Naked Babe and the Cloak of Manliness. In *The Well-Wrought Urn: Studies in the Structure of Poetry.* New York: Reynal.

Bullough, Geoffrey. 1957-75. *Major Tragedies: "Hamlet," "Othello," "King Lear," "Macbeth."* Vol. 7, *Narrative and Dramatic Sources of Shakespeare.* New York: Columbia University Press. *Macbeth* 423-527.

Clayton, Tom. 1997. "Macbeth's 'Yet I will try the last' What? (*Macbeth* V. Viii. 32)." *N&Q* 247, no. 4 December.

Dent, R. W. 1981. *Shakespeare's Proverbial Language: An Index.* Berkeley: University of California Press.

Hinman, Charlton, prep. 1968. *Norton Facsimile: The First Folio of Shakespeare.* New York: Norton. *Macbeth* 739-59.

Knights, L. C. 1933; rev. ed., 1947; New York: New York University Press, 1964. "How Many Children Had Lady Macbeth?" In *Explorations: Essays in Criticism Mainly of the Literature of the Seventeenth Century.*

Rosenberg, Marvin. 1978. *The Masks of "Macbeth."* Berkeley: University of California Press.

Shakespeare, William. *Macbeth.* Edited by David Bevington, 1988. Bantam Shakespeare. New York: Bantam.

———. 1992. *The Complete Works of Shakespeare.* New York: Harper.

———. 1997. *The Complete Works of Shakespeare: Updated Fourth Edition.* New York: Longman.

———. Edited by Nicholas Brooke. 1990. Oxford Shakespeare/World's Classics. Oxford: Oxford University Press.

———. Edited by R. W. Dent. 1969. Blackfriars Shakespeare. Dubuque: Wm. C. Brown.

———. Edited by G. Blakemore Evans. 1997. *The Riverside Shakespeare.* 2d ed. Boston: Houghton. *Macbeth* 1355-90.

———. Edited by R. A. Foakes. 1968. Bobbs-Merrill Shakespeare Series. Indianapolis: Bobbs-Merrill.

———. Edited by Stephen Greenblatt. 1997. *The Norton Shakespeare Based on the Oxford Edition.* New York: Norton. *Macbeth* 2555-2618.

———. Edited by Alfred Harbage. 1956; rev. ed. 1971. Pelican Shakespeare. New York: Penguin.

———. Edited by G. K. Hunter. New Penguin Shakespeare. Harmondsworth: Penguin.

———. Edited by Kenneth Muir. 1962. New Arden Shakespeare. 9th ed. Cambridge: Harvard University Press.

———. Edited by Stanley Wells and Gary Taylor. 1986. *William Shakespeare: The Complete Works.* Oxford: Clarendon.

Spevack, Marvin. 1968. *A Complete and Systematic Concordance to the Works of Shakespeare.* Vol. 3, *Tragedies.* Hildesheim: Olms. *Macbeth* 663-750.

Tilley, Morris Palmer. 1950. *A Dictionary of the Proverbs in England in the Sixteenth and Seventeenth Centuries.* Ann Arbor: University of Michigan Press.

Wills, Garry. 1995. *Witches and Jesuits: Shakespeare's "Macbeth."* New York: Oxford University Press.

---

Source: "Who 'Has No Children' in *Macbeth*?," in *Shakespearean Illuminations: Essays in Honor of Marvin Rosenberg,* edited by Jay L. Halio and Hugh Richmond, University of Delaware Press, 1998, pp. 164-79.

# "An excellent thing in woman": Virgo and Viragos in *King Lear*

## Catherine S. Cox, *University of Pittsburgh at Johnstown*

Throughout *King Lear,* conventional interpretations of gender identity are challenged by ambiguously constructed female characters. The three women inhabiting Lear's world—his daughters Cordelia, Goneril, and Regan—supply the text with culturally and theoretically profound treatments of gender issues. The daughter figures, especially Cordelia, exhibit characteristics germane to Renaissance appropriations of early Christian and medieval (anti) feminist commonplaces, with the distinction between valorization and denigration rendered ambiguous by the subtle incorporation of competing motifs. I shall explicate the polysemous gender constructions of the daughters in *King Lear* in connection with literary and theological traditions in order to demonstrate that the play's ultimate sense of restoration and order is both contingent upon and betrayed by its rejection of "unnatural" gender.

Goneril and Regan, the two "unnatural hags" (2.4.278) as Lear will decry them, are negatively depicted as familiar *virago* types, but Cordelia is more complex: a figure of archetypal *virgo* goodness who simultaneously exhibits diverse characteristics of the virago.[1] Cordelia's embodiment of virgo and virago topoi, and indeed *Lear*'s representations of Woman in general, owe much to both Christian and secular intellectual traditions. Many of the prevalent characteristics attributed to the female sex and feminine gender in sixteenth- and seventeenth-century England derive from Aristotelian definitions expressed in scientific treatises such as *De generatione animalium, De partibus animalium,* and *De generatione et corruptione,* and from such commentaries as those of Albertus Magnus and Thomas Aquinas.[2] The more complex Christian tradition borrows the core positive/negative binarism from the Aristotelian masculine/feminine paradigm, but reframes the status of Woman by way of an additional, competing opposition: Mary, the epitome of the good woman and the archetypal virgo, versus Eve, instigator of sin yet mother of humankind, the original "virago," as she is named in the second Vulgate creation account.[3]

Patristic writers move uneasily between the two concepts, regarding the Virgin as the feminine ideal yet seeking to elide the problematic issues associated with gender. We might note in this regard the ambivalent declarations of no less a theologian than Saint Jerome, whose opinions on virginity, sexuality, and marriage have a profound and at times controversial influence upon Western Christian tradition. In his *Commentarii in epistolam ad Ephesios,* Jerome, otherwise known for such polemical treatises as *Adversus Jovinianum*—which fervently endorses the lauded status of the virgo—here describes a virago ideal: "Quandiu mulier partui servit et liberis, hanc habet ad virum differentiam, quam corpus ad animam. Sin autem Christo magis voluerit servire quam saeculo, mulier esse cessabit, et dicetur vir" (3.28). [As long as woman serves for birth and children, she has difference from man, as body from soul. But if she wishes to serve Christ more than the world, then she will cease to be woman and will be called man.][4] For Jerome as for Saint Paul, gender categories collapse in an ideal Christian environment of grace: "non est masculus neque femina" [there is no masculine nor feminine], Paul contends in his epistle to the Galatians (3.28).[5] But in an imperfect human world, the taint of gender persists; hence Paul's better-known assertion, "Mulieres viris suis subditae sint, sicut Domino" [Let women be subject to their men, as to the Lord] (Eph. 5.22), which promotes obedience and silence as appropriate feminine behavior, a point to which I shall return. The virgo ideal, based on centuries of devotional practice related to the Virgin Mary, represents redemption and life, the most lauded and desirable status for any woman to aspire to in order to transcend Eve's legacy of sin ("Mors per Evam: vita per Mariam" [Death through Eve: life through Mary], asserts Saint Jerome in his oft-cited *Epistola ad Eustochium*), while the virago elicits the ambivalent praise accorded the recipient of an honorary title ("dicetur vir") connected to an ambiguous ideal.[6]

Both 'virgo' and 'virago', then, categorize women in relatively positive patriarchal senses while never fully distancing them from the legacy of corruption and taint derived from the Genesis narrative. Both seek to recuperate woman's place in God's creation: the virgo by valorizing specific aspects of the feminine, the virago by negating femininity itself. As Barbara Newman comments in her recent analysis of the terms, "Although didactic writers liked to pun on these labels as if they were functionally equivalent, their affective connotations diverged widely. The virago was an honorary male, aspiring to the unisex ideal, while the virgin aspired to a highly gendered ideal embodied in the Virgin Mary."[7] Because the virgo represents a gendered ideal, the feminine at its best, women who choose to emulate the Virgin attempt to observe a code of behavior well defined within patristic tradition and its social applications. The virago, however, remains more ambiguous and troubling for the theologians, who simultaneously, and paradoxically, both denigrate and laud the same characteristics and behaviors.

Literary representations reflect the complexities and contradictions of the virgo/virago traditions. The depiction of women in early Christian treatises and in the narratives of those women who exemplify desired patriarchal virtues—hagiography, for instance, which describes in vivid detail both the chastity and martyrdom of its heroines—retains a sense of the underlying anxiety, inconsistency, and paradoxical ambivalence of their authors.[8] Virginal goodness frequently results in the heroine's torture and death, and viragos are contemptuously regarded for their purportedly unnatural expressions of cross-gendered identity. After centuries of popular interest, these types of heroines become attractive to Renaissance audiences as they are made accessible through both stage performance and written text—the archetypal figure of goodness and obedience, for example, is constructed in the virgo mode; though not purely hagiographic in the strict generic sense, the heroine embodies pseudohagiographic topoi as the subject of such well-known folktales and legends as the Griselda and Constance stories of Petrarch, Boccaccio, John Gower, and Chaucer.

We find reflected in these texts as well the ambivalent attitudes toward virgo and virago types found in the theological tradition: the virago qualities of the heroine, while valorized, are frequently misunderstood by those exposed to them, often provoking, at least indirectly, martyrdom for the otherwise laudably virginal heroine. And yet these very qualities—for example, assertiveness, courage, self-respect—are used concurrently to define female villains, whose manifest distortions of proper gender identity prove problematic or even disastrous for the heroine (e.g., the mothers-in-law of Chaucer's Custance). Indeed, categories of gender identity itself seem to collapse at times, as conventional characteristics and qualities of virgo and virago merge beyond differentiation, effectively challenging the very concept of gender identity and definition, and resisting any simple reduction to the masculine/feminine binarism and its underlying positive/negative valuation. Such are the patterns of ambiguous gender identity that characterize the daughters of *King Lear,* and it is to "these daughters and these sisters" (5.3.7) that we now return.

Although Cordelia appears in only four of the play's twenty-six scenes, the impact of her presence in the opening scene is perceptible throughout the entire play. Most significant in relation to the virgo/virago paradigms is Cordelia's silence, for her reluctant participation in Lear's flattery game is remarkable in its ambiguity. Her elusive and evasive speech is interpreted by some readers and viewers as a demonstration of love and goodness, by others as an assertive rejection of patriarchal authority, and by still others as an exhibition of arrogance, a kind of haughty naivete.[9] As Gayle Whittier asks in her provocative psychoanalytic study of gender in *King Lear,* "Is she recalcitrant daughter or wronged saint? Victim of patriarchy or proto-feminist?"[10] In any case Cordelia's response, "Nothing" (1.1.87), takes too literally her father's request, "what can you *say* to draw / A third more opulent than your sisters'? Speak" (85-87; my emphasis). When given an opportunity to revoke her words and replace them with language more compliant—"Nothing will come of nothing, speak again" (90)—her deviation from social and filial decorum becomes pointed, even brusque: "Unhappy that I am, I cannot heave / My heart into my mouth. I love your Majesty / According to my bond, no more nor less" (91-93). Earlier, Goneril, in her eloquent if platitudinous statement, has tellingly declared that her great love for Lear is "A love that makes breath poor, and speech unable" (62); Cordelia's legitimate inability to speak, then, would seem to correspond ironically to the inefficacy of language to convey true affection. If so, silence is Cordelia's only proper response, but it is compromised by her subsequent attempts at explanation and justification.

The play's closing directive will reiterate the ambivalence of both the characters and their author regarding the efficacy and propriety of speech: "The weight of this sad time we must obey, / Speak what we feel, not what we ought to say" (5.3.324-25).[11] While overtly connected to Cordelia's performance in the opening scene, Edgar's stated dichotomy between obligation and emotion, between decorum and truth, is a false one. Cordelia, in fact, manages neither: while her "nothing" appropriately articulates the silence befitting the virgo, it is followed by a sequence of scolding remarks that are neither truthful nor decorous, and her attempt at candor thus fails to communicate both "what [she] feel[s]" and "what [she] ought to say."[12] Paradoxically, Goneril and Regan succeed in accomplishing both; through their requisite praises, the sisters demonstrate what they feel—their desire to comply with Lear's wishes—and concomitantly what they ought to say, for their speeches are absolutely decorous as responses to Lear's stated request. Unlike the Cordeilla of the *Chronicles,* who attributes her terse performance to conscience and completely ignores the words of her sisters, Shakespeare's Cordelia takes her sisters' fluent, facile performances as valid indicators of what they wish to convey and chides them for setting such impossible, artificial standards for themselves and for her.

One of her more vexing rhetorical challenges—fraught with connotations of sexuality, language, and decorum—is therefore issued when Cordelia turns her attention toward the institution of marriage: "Why have my sisters husbands, if they say / They love you all?" (99-100). Her comments regarding marriage are not inconsistent with the concerns of the immediate situation, her intended betrothal, but they certainly reframe her "nothing" speech.[13] Cordelia compares the "love" she would have for a husband to the "love" she has for her father; yet, she is to be married off to the successful "rival," at Lear's choice. In both instances, Cordelia's relationship is defined not by eros or affection, but strictly by "bond," and she plans to divide her "love" in half—half her "care and duty" (102), that is. 'Husband' and 'father' are used interchangeably by Cordelia, who unnaturally collapses the distinction between them, framing each strictly in relation to her own requisite duty. When Cordelia speaks the truth to Lear, then, it would seem that the ill-received words are the result not necessarily of any inhering verbal inefficacy on Cordelia's part, but rather, of the fact that she speaks of the truth in all its blunt pragmatism. Here too her remarks compromise her gender status, for conventionally we would expect a young woman to evince an interest in romance and marriage; yet Cordelia reduces the mythic eros of the union to the strict economic and political particulars that an arranged marriage signifies. There is no hint of desire or anticipation, or even curiosity, for that matter. Yet her apparent resistance to marriage thematically befits a saintly heroine spiritually predisposed to embrace celibacy—for instance, in the (pseudo-)hagiographic tradition, Cecilia's *haire* or Custance's prayers. Whatever her motivation, Cordelia's scolding remarks trouble some critics who wonder at her belief that love is a fixed commodity, divisible in a zero-sum game.

More important is Cordelia's failure to recognize that the quality of love is not the issue here; what matters is the expression of love, the speech used to communicate emotion—or, more to the point, to construct the illusion of it. Lear, after all, has not asked which daughter loves him most, but rather which will provide the best public rhetorical performance: "*Tell me,* my daughters . . ." (48; my emphasis). Lear questions Cordelia's intentions only after she has failed to adhere to his directives: "But goes thy heart with this?" (105). Cordelia does not appreciate the distinction between public performance and private affect that Lear, perhaps without even quite realizing it himself, demands. Perhaps Cordelia challenges her father because Goneril is correct that true love defies the capacity of language to communicate it fully, that Cordelia's verbal inefficacy prevents her from practicing "that glib and oily art / To speak and purpose not" (224-25); perhaps her own sense of self-respect and pride, not inconsistent with that of conventional hagiographic heroines, precludes participation in such an ostentatious display of glibness.[14] In either case, in refusing to speak as expected she places herself in a twofold position of gendered otherness that reifies the virgo/virago paradigms: an excessively feminized and passive position owing to her initial silence, and, when she breaks her silence and challenges Lear's request, an inappropriately masculine voice.

In view of the governing metaphor of *King Lear*—Cordelia's speech, or lack thereof—it is significant that the treatment of gender in the canon of patristic writings and the literature influenced by those ideologies is connected, often cryptically and sometimes quite elaborately, to speech and language. With regard to Christian tradition, much has been written on the metaphor of silence and virginity in patristic writings and their commentators, particularly as both virginity and silence are valorized attributes for women.[15] The silent woman—virginal, enclosed, uncorrupted, and passive—is privileged as having attained a status closer to the Christian ideal than that of her loquacious counterpart. It is paradoxically through this virginal denial of voice that Woman, in Jerome's terms cited above, "dicetur vir."

Cordelia's saintly persona is called into question when she assumes a masculine voice, for, in speaking like a man she paradoxically compromises the honorary male status that her apparent conformity to Jerome's ideal would signify. Her feminine status is at least temporarily restored at the end of her appearance in this first scene, however, for her tears inscribe her character with the marks of laudable virgo femininity. As she simultaneously regrets her resistance to Lear and instructs her sisters to be kind—"The jewels of our father, with wash'd eyes / Cordelia leaves you" (268-69)—she recuperates her role as daughter and sister. Cordelia thus defies any attempt to limit her to a single gender category; her identity with regard to gender frequently and unpredictably shifts as she takes up and relinquishes a number of gender(ed) positions.

Cordelia's problematic performance aptly corresponds to her ambiguous status in Lear's family and court. She is at once both Lear's youngest daughter and, figuratively speaking, in the absence of male progeny, a stand-in for his eldest son; it is she to whom Lear had hoped to turn in his old age, she who had been designated heir, she to whom Lear had assigned "all cares and business" (1.1.39).[16] Lear himself reveals in his lament after banishing Cordelia, "I loved her most, and thought to set my rest / On her kind nursery" (122-23); she is simultaneously valorized as designated heir and demoted to nursemaid. In this respect Cordelia is coerced into inhabiting several competing gendered identities—daughter, son, wife, mother—resulting in her own ambiguously gendered status. The hint of incest (daughter as substitute wife?) further problematizes Cordelia's unresolved gender status, though Lear's impulsive decision to banish her suspends the issue until much later in the play. Lear, it seems, relies on his youngest daughter to assume the appropriate gender role when needed.

Cordelia's initial decision, "Love, and be silent" (62), appropriately adheres to the traditional patriarchal code of womanly silence discussed above; this is the passive, feminine behavior Lear admires. But when called upon to speak as a woman and as a daughter, her unwillingness to conform to established and expected codes incites Lear's rage. Her blunt words undermine her virgo image, for she speaks as a daughter but like a son: "I love your Majesty / According to my bond, no more nor less" (92-93); "You have begot me, bred me, lov'd me: I / Return those duties back as are right fit, / Obey you, love you, and most honor you" (96-98). When Cordelia betrays her own silence, she abandons her identity as daughter; apparently affronted at having to compete with her sisters in so ludicrous a game, she exhibits a masculine sense of entitlement, as if the "bond" she and Lear share should rightly ensure her place as Lear's successor and exempt her from public display.

Such forfeiture and substitution of gender identities call to mind the widespread early Christian, medieval, and Renaissance perceptions of the virgo and virago in relation to both silence and exile. Saint Bernard of Clairvaux's *Tractatus ad laudem gloriosae Virginis,* one of his Marian texts, refers to women who have chosen a life of virginity as exiles—specifically, "in exsilio filios Evae" [sons of Eve in exile].[17] The description is, on the surface, rather curious in its confusion of gender labels, for, as current representatives of Eve's legacy and lineage, women would presumably be "filiae," daughters, rather than "filii," sons. This discrepancy may be explained in part by the relative availability of labels for gender identity: by the twelfth century, when Bernard wrote, women are still bearing the misogynistic brunt of Eve's ascribed legacy of sin. As the embodiment of carnal concupiscence and subversive disobedience, or at least the potential for these, women are characterized with mistrust and apprehension as "filiae Evae," the daughters of Eve. Identifying good women—that is, those adhering to pastristic standards, especially with regard to virginity—in laudatory terms, while still acknowledging their physical attachment to Eve's legacy, then, is accomplished by way of Bernard's "filii Evae" label. That the women remain "Evae," "of Eve," is overt and inarguable; that they have somehow transcended her shameful legacy of sin is suggested, albeit cryptically, through their identification as "sons," "filii."

Like the banished Cordelia, women fulfilling the virgo ideal—"filii Evae" overtly committed to a life of spirituality—are in Bernard's words "in exsilio," in a state of exile. Literally, of course, men and women heeding the monastic call have chosen to separate themselves from the world at large and to occupy a cloistered environment in order to facilitate their devotion.[18] More important, however, the "exiled" status may be interpreted figuratively as the condition of any individual desiring to serve Christ: the devoted, spiritual individual is "exiled" in the sense of no longer being fully integrated into the secular world once the choice is made to serve a higher spiritual purpose. Such an individual may be socially, politically, and economically exiled as well by those with whom she or he must otherwise coexist, like family members. Ostracism may be imposed as a punishment or corrective measure if such an individual refuses to relinquish his or her chosen position—as in the case of the self-described "creature" of the eponymous *Book of Margery Kempe,* for instance.

An additional association of speech and exile that may prove enlightening with regard to *King Lear* also derives from Bernard, who uses an analogy of feminine otherness to guide monks in their interpretive and communicative activities. In his *Sermones super Cantica Canticorum,* he instructs, "Vobis, fratres, alia quam de aliis de saeculo, aut certe aliter dicenda sunt" [To you, brothers, one should speak of different things, or at least in a different way, than to those in the world].[19] As David Damrosch explains, Bernard is interested in images of women for "their otherness from men, and in particular for their ambiguous status as simultaneously essential members of society and second-class citizens, excluded from full participation in social life."[20] Thus while Bernard's concern with speech reflects his concern with the monastic life and its appropriate codes of behavior, he identifies a crucial connection between speech and otherness: to be excluded from a manner of speaking confirms one's place outside an established community. If Bernard's remarks are applied to the status of women as "other" in Christian writings and popular perception, we find that women's speech or lack of speech confirms their position with respect to an institutionally circumscribed environment—which, according to Bernard's logic, justifies their being ostracized as "other."

While it is Lear himself who renders Cordelia socially and legally "other" through his fiat of banishment, Cordelia's self-imposed figurative exile from cultural norms marks her as "other" even before Lear imposes his sentence. She is a marginalized outsider or, in the language of Bernard, an "exile," owing to her ambiguous gender status. In other words, Cordelia's banishment is already a given, even prior to the formal pronouncement by Lear; although secular in content, the character's chosen course of moral behavior satisfies traditional hagiographic conventions, and the reader or viewer can predict from the very start that Cordelia will ultimately be sacrificed for her moral principles. When she describes Goneril and Regan to Lear in detached terms—"Shall we not see these daughters and these sisters?" (5.3.7)—her preference for categories rather than names signifies her voluntary social and moral estrangement. And when Cordelia situates herself in relation to the tradition of those who have been marginalized, then persecuted—"We are not the first / Who with best meaning have incurr'd the worst" (5.3.3-4)—she confirms her identity and fulfills the destiny prepared for her at the play's outset.

But since Cordelia's conventional goodness must be both rewarded and punished by the standards set in virgo topoi, the play requires that Cordelia's suffering be forestalled, that banishment initiate but not wholly constitute her suffering until an even deeper and more profound spiritual commitment is revealed. Thus in the opening sequence, the process of betrothal merges with the process of division, and gender and politics become inextricably enmeshed. Making clear that she understands the economics of politics and matrimony—"Peace be with Burgundy! / Since that respects of fortune are his love, / I shall not be his wife" (1.1.247-49)—Cordelia prepares to suffer the consequences of her commitment to truth. But, as befits her inherent goodness, she will be assigned a spouse for whom Lear's land and power hold less interest than does Cordelia herself—hence France's intervention. While Cordelia's marriage will presumably require that she forfeit her physical, corporeal virgin status, the virgo identity so essential to Cordelia's character is nonetheless maintained, since she embodies a spiritual truth unaffected by physical status. Whether she undergoes legal banishment or sexual consummation, she remains "true" (107).

Once exiled, the virtuous Cordelia bears a striking similarity to the "sons of Eve in exile," remaining committed to the father for whom she was to fulfill the obligations of daughter and son. Just as Cordelia is exiled from her father (at his insistence), so too she is abandoned by her husband, which underscores her quasi-hagiographical status. The idyllic promise of marriage to France—"Be it lawful I take up what's cast away. . . . Thy dow'rless daughter, King, thrown to my chance, / Is queen of us, of ours, and our fair France" (1.1.253-57)—is short-lived, and Cordelia is left to face her fate alone. She is not to be ruled by any mortal man, it seems, whether father, husband, or king; exiled from spouse, father, and normal institutions, she is simultaneously excluded from the corresponding social roles of wife, daughter, and woman. Though curiously asexual in effect and behavior, Cordelia is nonetheless gendered—bigendered, we might say, since she embodies the characteristics of both masculine and feminine as formulated by Hélène Cixous, "the presence of both sexes, evident and insistent in different ways according to the individual, the nonexclusion of difference."[21]

Moreover, while *King Lear* cannot be described as an explicitly "Christian" play, set as it is in a pre-Christian era, the numerous Christian signs and symbols informing its characters and themes do justify an interpretation that takes into account the time and place of its creation as well as those of its textual antecedents. In connection with hagiographical conventions, Cordelia's poignant assertion, "O dear father, / It is thy business that I go about" (4.4.23-24), strongly suggests that her "business," like Christ's in Luke 2:49, transcends human affairs, and that her profession of loyalty to her "father" typologically testifies to her faith in and duty toward a power far greater than Lear's or her own. Here, as in the first scene of the play, Cordelia's tears mark her feminine identity and, in conjunction with residually hagiographic characterization, emphasize the emotional depth of her faith. Even before the episode of absolution, in which a tearful Cordelia selflessly grants Lear's request that she "forget, and forgive" (4.7.83), we see a Cordelia ready not only to disregard Lear's cruelty toward her but also to risk her own young life in an attempt to preserve her aged father's life and title. Though literally such a reversal seems an affront to nature—and contradicts her earlier evasion of Lear's imposed "nursery" duties—typologically it resonates with an emphatic endorsement of commitment and sacrifice. The saintly virgo respects a higher calling, and will exercise her virago strengths in an attempt to rectify the calamitous disintegration of Lear's world.[22] But this valiant virgo/virago, who exhibits the best aspects of the topoi, will necessarily be done to death by malign forces more powerful than her own.[23] Her ultimate martyrdom confirms the tradition from which Cordelia derives her place.

Contingent upon Cordelia's enactments of gender and gender identity, the play's resolution is strengthened in its rejection of the "unnatural" by the supporting roles of her two sisters. Though their significance to the play is obviously less than Cordelia's, their own embodiment of gendered stereotypes contributes to the establishment of Cordelia's ultimate identity as martyr. For once the tragic sequence is set in motion, the events leading to Lear's and Cordelia's deaths are facilitated by the malign behavior of Goneril and Regan, a pair of scheming viragos who demonstrate just about every negative stereotype of gender and gendered identity. Despite their many negative similarities, though, Goneril and Regan are obviously neither interchangeable nor redundant; each manifests "unnatural" gender in her own way, and each perpetrates evil in relation to her character's exhibition of gender status. It is fitting therefore that Regan, the least powerful and most socially proper of the daughters, should be the first of the three "unnatural" deaths, and that she should die by her elder sister Goneril's hand, the victim of "unnatural" evil more monstrous than her own. The comparative effect of the sisters' demonstrated stereotypical villainy is that Cordelia's positive feminine attributes are obviously enhanced.

But, as befits the virgo/virago conventions, Cordelia's polysemous gender identity is regarded with an uncomfortable ambivalence in the play. Shakespeare's own audience would, of course, hardly be unfamiliar with the concept of a female in power, given the recent reign of the *divina virago,* Elizabeth Tudor. As Leonard Tennenhouse observes in his cultural critique of Elizabethan political attitudes, "The female was no less female for possessing patriarchal powers.... The idea of a female patriarch appears to have posed no contradiction in terms of Elizabethan culture."[24] Despite Elizabeth's political position, her private sexual status and alleged behavior were targets of scrutiny and gossip; socially, the virago was regarded with apprehension and disdain.[25] Other works of literature in the Elizabethan era dramatize such a twofold valorization and denigration—for instance, Shakespeare's own reworking of the historical figure Joan of Arc in *1 Henry VI,* in which the female warrior is repeatedly impugned for sexual promiscuity and witchcraft.[26] These corrupted virago figures betray the culture's concern with the social consequences of inappropriate gender status, even if for political reasons disapproval is impossible.[27] It is quite telling, then, that images of witchcraft, monsters, demons, and vermin are frequently used by Lear, Albany, and others to describe the women's "unnatural" behavior; even Cordelia is impugned when Lear calls upon Hecate in banishing her and describes her to France as "a wretch whom Nature is asham'd / Almost t'acknowledge hers" (1.1.212-13).[28] Such images corroborate the audience's credence of the moral codes through which ambiguously or inappropriately gendered behavior is mediated and rejected.

It is with no little irony, then, that Lear praises the dead Cordelia by focusing on the correlation between her gender and her voice: "What is't thou say'st? Her voice was ever soft, / Gentle, and low, an excellent thing in woman" (5.3.273-74). His insistence here that her voice epitomized her most desirable feminine attributes has already been betrayed not only by his rejection of her words but also by the content of those words—there was nothing "gentle," "low," or "excellent" in Cordelia's blunt and assertive remarks about "honor" and "bond." Compounding the irony is the realization that this final image duplicates the opening scene; here again Lear requests speech from Cordelia, who offers "nothing." Having disowned and banished Cordelia precisely because of her voice, Lear now praises what angered him most, perhaps compromising some of the poignancy that this pietà might otherwise have produced. We find, too, an ironic reversal of Lear's formerly expressed interest in Cordelia's "kind nursery," for it is Lear who now cradles the body of Cordelia, temporarily inhabiting the maternal role that he had hoped to impose upon her. In death, then, Cordelia's virgo silence reinstates her position as Lear's favorite daughter; no one but Lear grieves for her, and no "voice" threatens to contradict or confront his nostalgic fantasy. "Gentle" silence is "excellent" in an ideal woman, even if the idealized status is contingent upon the death of the heroine.

Although the sisters' own polysemous gender identities reveal the potentially damaging consequences of gender run amok, Cordelia's behavior supplies a crucial balance, in that we realize that the sisters seem evil not solely because they are female but because they simply *are* evil. Even if gender alone does not account for their behavior, their treachery shows itself most overtly in connection with their "unnatural" gendered identities. Contextualized by a cultural history of ambivalence toward "good" women, Cordelia is the subject of both praise and contempt in Lear's world; despite her apparent goodness and virtue, as woman, wife, and daughter she can never fully free herself of Eve's legacy—at least not while she remains alive. Thus, while Cordelia's character exhibits a dimension of moral goodness, she nonetheless displays unnatural gender which poses a threat to natural order; her idealized virgo status is reified only in absence of any further speech. In a striking illustration of intersecting and paradoxical motifs of gender and representation, then, Goneril and Regan are necessarily killed off owing to their unwomanly evil, and Cordelia is killed off owing to both her womanly and unwomanly goodness.

Once the sisters' roles are reduced to what amounts to a fatal catfight and Cordelia succumbs to the ambivalence accorded a heroine of her type, the play can move toward the restoration of order promised by its established conformity to generic pattern. After the three daughters' bodies have been carried onstage—and the threat of "unnatural" women thus safely eliminated—*King Lear* is brought to a close with the changing of the guard, so to speak, as Edgar takes up the duties of rule and addresses his fellow male survivors:

> The weight of this sad time we must obey,
> Speak what we feel, not what we ought to say:
> The oldest hath borne most; we that are young
> Shall never see so much, nor live so long.
> (5.3.324-27)

The play's resolution is predicated upon the possibility and desirability of restoring "natural" order. In this regard the conventions of tragedy suit audience expectations and the gesture toward restoration appeals to our desire for closure.[29] But the absence of women/Woman in the closing lines should give us pause. For all the cathartic satisfaction we may experience at this palliating if not pat conclusion, we are compelled to acknowledge the constructedness of this world and this resolution, which have their being in the time and space of a text.

*Notes*

[1] All references to Shakespeare's plays are to *The Riverside Shakespeare,* ed. G. Blakemore Evans (Boston, 1974), with parenthetical citations in text.

[2] On the diverse origins of Western culture's understanding of sex and gender, see Thomas Laqueur, *Making Sex: Body and Gender from the Greeks to Freud* (Cambridge, Mass., 1990); Joan Cadden, *Meanings of Sex Difference in the Middle Ages* (Cambridge, 1993); Danielle Jacquart and Claude Thomasset, *Sexuality and Medicine in the Middle Ages,* trans. Matthew Adamson (Princeton, N.J., 1988); and Ian Maclean, *The Renaissance Notion of Woman: A Study in the Fortunes of Scholasticism and Medical Science in European Intellectual Life* (Cambridge, 1980), esp. pp. 2-9.

[3] Genesis 2.23: "Dixitque Adam: Hoc nunc, os ex ossibus meis, et caro de carne mea: haec vocabitur Virago, quoniam de viro sumpta est" [And Adam said: This now is bone from my bones, and flesh of my flesh: she shall be called Virago, because she was taken from man], *Biblia sacra iuxta vulgatam Clementinam,* ed. Alberto Colunga and Laurentio Turrado, 4th ed. (Madrid, 1965). All biblical citations are from this edition, with references noted; translations my own here and throughout unless otherwise indicated. On the "virago," see James Grantham Turner, *One Flesh: Paradisal Marriage and Sexual Relations in the Age of Milton* (Oxford, 1987), pp. 96-123.

[4] Saint Jerome, *Commentarii in epistolam ad Ephesios,* in *Patrologiae cursus completus, series latina,* ed. J. P. Migne (Paris, 1844-83, with reprints), vol. 26, col. 567; hereafter cited as *PL*.

[5] Compare Saint Ambrose, *Expositio in evangelii secundum Lucam,* ed. M. Adriaen, Corpus Christianorum Ecclesiasticarum, Series Latina 14 (Turnhout, 1957), 10.161. On early Christian, medieval, and early modern misogyny and its theological underpinnings, see Susanna Elm, *Virgins of God: The Making of Asceticism in Late Antiquity* (1994; Oxford, 1996), esp. pp. 120-21; R. Howard Bloch, *Medieval Misogyny and the Invention of Western Romantic Love* (Chicago, 1991), esp. pp. 37-91; Barbara Newman, *From Virile Woman to WomanChrist: Studies in Medieval Religion and Literature* (Philadelphia, 1995), pp. 1-45; and Caroline Walker Bynum, *Fragmentation and Redemption: Essays on Gender and the Human Body in Medieval Religion* (New York, 1991), esp. pp. 151-79.

[6] Saint Jerome, *Epistolae, PL,* vol. 22, col. 408.

[7] Newman, p. 5.

[8] A useful overview is provided by Thomas J. Heffernan, *Sacred Biography: Saints and Their Biographers in the Middle Ages* (Oxford, 1988).

[9] Derek Cohen (*Shakespeare's Culture of Violence* [New York, 1993]), e.g., argues that Cordelia "will not accept Lear's right to make her take the oath. Her famous 'Nothing' is a violently reductive challenge to Lear's and everyone else's conception of hierarchical authority" (p. 98).

[10] Gayle Whittier, "Cordelia as Prince: Gender and Language in *King Lear,*" *Exemplaria* 1 (1989): 367-99. Whittier describes *King Lear* as Shakespeare's "most misogynistic" tragedy (p. 367).

[11] Robert Matz ("Speaking What We Feel: Torture and Political Authority in *King Lear,*" *Exemplaria* 6 [1994]: 223-41) observes with regard to the opening sequence, "Lear's imposition of a lie believed as truth (his daughters' forced declarations of love) lacks the force to make that lie stick" (p. 233).

[12] I find a striking and instructive parallel to Cordelia's speech in the critique of Abraham's elusiveness by Jacques Derrida (*The Gift of Death,* trans. David Wills [Chicago, 1995]): "He speaks and doesn't speak. He responds without responding. He responds indirectly. He speaks in order not to say anything about the essential things that he must keep secret" (p. 59). In Cordelia's case, the "secret" would pertain to the fraudulence of Lear's plan. On Shakespearean secrecy see Patricia Parker, *Shakespeare from the Margins: Language, Culture, Context* (Chicago, 1996), esp. pp. 229-72.

[13] See Lynda E. Boose, "The Father and the Bride in Shakespeare," *PMLA* 97 (1982): 325-47, on the concerns of a betrothal in an aristocratic setting; and with regard to the connection between betrothal, sexuality, and language, William C. Carroll, "The Virgin Not: Language and Sexuality in Shakespeare," *Shakespeare Survey* 46 (1994): 107-19.

[14] Stanley Cavell ("The Avoidance of Love: A Reading of *King Lear,*" in his *Must We Mean What We Say?* [Cambridge, 1976], pp. 267-353) argues that Lear's torments cause Cordelia to "snap," though her words are "too calm, too cold" to convey the outrage she feels (p. 291).

[15] On the virgin/silence connection in early Christian and medieval theology, see Karma Lochrie, *Margery Kempe and Translations of the Flesh* (Philadelphia, 1991), pp. 13-53.

[16] Whittier describes Cordelia's "double indemnity of being both female and last-born" (p. 387). But see the challenge to primogeniture posited by Lisa Jardine, *Still Harping on Daughters: Women and Drama in the Age of Shakespeare* (Sussex, 1983), pp. 77-79.

[17] The image occurs in other medieval texts, most notably the *Salve Regina's* "exsules filii Hevae," the *Prymer's* "exiled sones of Eue," and the Prologue of Chaucer's *Second Nun's Tale,* "I, unworthy sone of Eve."

[18] On "otherness," "exile," and Christian commitment, see Julia Kristeva, *Strangers to Ourselves,* trans. Leon S. Roudiez (New York, 1991), pp. 77-93.

[19] Text and translation cited by David Damrosch, "*Non Alia Sed Aliter.* The Hermeneutics of Gender in Bernard of Clairvaux," in *Images of Sainthood in Medieval Europe,* ed. Renate Blumenfeld-Kosinski and Timea Szell (Ithaca, N.Y., 1991), pp. 181-95, at p. 182.

[20] Ibid., p. 183. On gender and the monastic orders, see also Jo Ann McNamara, "The *Herrenfrage:* The Restructuring of the Gender System, 1050-1150," in *Medieval Masculinities: Regarding Men in the Middle Ages,* ed. Clare A. Lees (Minneapolis, 1994), pp. 3-29.

[21] Hélène Cixous, "Sorties," in *The Newly Born Woman,* trans. Betsy Wing (Minneapolis, 1986), pp. 63-132, at p. 85.

[22] Valerie Traub, *Desire and Anxiety: Circulations of Sexuality in Shakespearean Drama* (London, 1992), finds that *King Lear* betrays fantasies and anxieties about women, particularly the virgin and the mother (pp. 64-65); see also the general overview provided by Ann Thompson, "Shakespeare and Sexuality," *Shakespeare Survey* 46 (1994): 1-8.

[23] In this capacity, Cordelia fulfills the symbolic function of sacrifice and preservation. The classic study of this "scapegoat" motif remains René Girard, *Violence and the Sacred* (Baltimore, 1979). Although Cordelia cannot die in place of Lear (he must inevitably experience his own death), she can forestall the demise of his kingdom. See Derrida (n. 12 above), whose analysis of sacrifice and death, motivated in part by Heidegger, seems particularly applicable to Cordelia and Lear: "The sameness of the self, what remains irreplaceable in dying, only becomes what it is, in the sense of an identity as a relation of the self to itself, by means of this idea of mortality as irreplaceability" (p. 45).

[24] Leonard Tennenhouse, *Power on Display: The Politics of Shakespeare's Genres* (New York, 1986), p. 103.

[25] See Carole Levin, *The Heart and Stomach of a King: Elizabeth I and the Politics of Sex and Power* (Philadelphia, 1994).

[26] See, e.g., *1 Henry VI* 1.2.104; 3.2.38, 52; *3 Henry VI* 1.4.111-14. On the representation of women in this tetralogy, see Marilyn L. Williamson, "'When Men Are Rul'd by Women': Shakespeare's First Tetralogy," *Shakespeare Studies* 19 (1987): 41-59.

[27] Lorna Hutson (*The Usurer's Daughter: Male Friendship and Fictions of Women in Sixteenth-Century England* [London, 1994]) considers the problem of alleged sexual transgression in Renaissance culture, including Shakespeare.

[28] See, e.g., 1.1.109-10; 1.4.259-61, 275-89; 2.4.160-64; 3.7.100-101; 4.3.39-49, 59-67.

[29] While the demands of the genre necessitate that some such speech be delivered, these lines are, as James Calderwood observes, "place[d] on the play like a band-aid on a gaping wound" ("Creative Uncreation in *King Lear,*" *Shakespeare Quarterly* 37 [1986]: 5-19, at 18); hence they leave many issues unresolved and expose the play's fiction. Bryan Crockett (*The Play of Paradox: Stage and Sermon in Renaissance England* [Philadelphia, 1995]) observes with regard to the "excruciating final scene" that the play's many paradoxes "can be resolved only in the communal experience of the audience" (p. 70).

---

Source: "'An Excellent Thing in Woman': Virgo and Viragos in *King Lear,*" in *Modern Philology,* Vol. 96, No. 2, November, 1998, pp. 143-57.

# *Coriolanus:* Punishment of the Civil Body

## William M. Hawley

A skilled practitioner of martial law, Coriolanus ultimately favors the emancipation of peace over war. Convicted of treason in disparate jurisdictions, though, he dies for having twice outlived his usefulness as a warrior. He remains unreflective about death and never questions or alters the hypotheticals leading to his destruction, unlike Hamlet or Macbeth. His hatred of theatrical shows only makes his performance all the more arresting. Because Rome and Antium mete out excessive punishments against him for imperfectly conceived reasons of social hygiene, social cohesion is maintained in two civil arenas without its *raison d'être* of achieving permanent reform or emancipation.

The play's Roman quality appears in Coriolanus's embrace of reform through martial law as against tribunal power, not in its imitation of Roman tragedy as such. Deuteronomy provides very broad outlines for the conduct of war, but the Romans codified their own detailed regulations on tactics and discipline in the work of Ruffus, among others. Of course, given the imperatives of warfare, slash and burn tactics have been the general order of battle throughout history. As years of painful experience have shown, even unconditional surrender is no guarantee of favorable treatment. In this play, Rome remains incapable of dividing its political labor, to borrow Durkheim's terms. It refuses to accommodate the warrior's code, just as Coriolanus will stubbornly resist political socialization.

Coke refers to Roman law and its Twelve Tables in his *Institutes,* but apart from capturing deserters he treats military affairs as existing outside the purview of the common law: "There is a Law Marshal for wars" (1 *Institutes* 10a).[1] The common law mixed ancient decrees, unwritten judicial decisions, and the Norman law brought to England after the Conquest. This intermingling resulted in legal statutes being written in French and Latin, though Coke used English whenever possible so that his countrymen might better understand the law.[2] Still, Shakespeare's audiences would have been moved by the rationale guiding Coriolanus's martial conduct because of the universally understood traditions of military discipline.

In section I, I examine the conflict between martial and civil law provoking Coriolanus's defection to the Volscian side in 491 BC. Rome's transition to tribunal power commenced two years earlier, so Shakespeare chose a historical period embroiled in wide-ranging political controversy. The English were alert to the political diversity of states, including those governed by "a monarch, or . . . aristocraticall, where few be in authority, or democraticall, where the people have the chief government without any superior, saving such as they elect and choose" (3 *Institutes* 80a). Military tactics are not an issue here; indeed, the subject was ridiculed as arcane in *Henry V* through Fluellen's pedantry. Shakespeare's audience would have been aware of the harsh ad hoc regulations enforcing discipline in their own ranks as well as those of Rome. They would have had a strong sense of the patriarchal nature of Roman civil law under the *patria potestas,* the power of a father over his son. The play elevates the role of women far beyond normal Roman standards, particularly in Volumnia's characterization as a sagacious political maneuverer. Coriolanus's role in tacitly enfranchising women opens him to vicious ad hominem attacks throughout the play. The common law nevertheless deviated sharply from its Roman predecessor, the adversarial trial system being but one of the primary distinctions.

In part II, I examine slander as the tortious act enabling treason charges to be leveled so effectively against Coriolanus. Slander at common law corresponds closely to its Roman counterpart. Next, I examine Coriolanus's punishment as a tragic spectacle, his body ravaged by wars, slander, and murderous swords. The elemental display of punishment overshadows the psychological and political issues in the play, however appealing they might be. The play reduces the outward show of tragedy to its essentials: the banishment, supplication, and slaughter of a hero too psychologically shallow in a modern sense to have an Oedipus conflict and too much the peacemaker to be played as a stage Nazi.

The criminal and tort law tradition is grounded in the concept that reason and justice lead us toward emancipation. Coke confirms this when he states that "every man desireth to be at naturall liberty" (2 *Institutes* 589). Coke's understanding of liberty differs from ours today, especially in the U.S., where individual rights are respected far more than the law would have allowed in Renaissance England. For Coke, it was natural that the subject should serve his king and the common good, while in return the law would prevent the king from annoying his industrious subjects with unjust levies and punishment. Aside from the new rights granted the plebes through their tribunes, the play's vision of reform or emancipation appears only through the lens of tragic waste in the form of the denunciation and murder of the hero.

*I. Civil vs. Martial Law*

A complicated division of civil and military codes gives their respective adherents—Coriolanus, the tribunes, the plebes—absolute confidence in the validity of their positions. The intensity of rage expressed derives from each party's belief in its political rectitude. In typical Shakespearean fashion, the plebes buffoonishly alter their opinions as the winds blow. The tribunes press for expansive, self-serving civil powers, which does not inherently invalidate them or their political ideas. Coriolanus aligns himself with the patricians to the extent that they share his sense of military discipline.

Martial law is a blanket set of regulations applicable to the civilian and military population in zones of active conflict. By contrast, military law is a code of conduct limited to military personnel. Coriolanus thrives in arenas of active warfare when pitted against a worthy opponent. He relishes the imposition of martial law in Corioles:

> Condemning some to death, and some to exile;
> Ransoming him, or pitying, threat'ning th' other;
> Holding Corioles in the name of Rome,
> Even like a fawning greyhound in the leash,
> To let him slip at will.
>
> (1.6.35-39)

He creates a military order outside the city that the Romans have themselves repudiated in favor of a republican state, yet whose existence serves their imperial aspirations.

Under martial law, Coriolanus can exercise autocratic power to enlarge the empire. He invokes the quintessential rule of battlefield discipline during the assault on Corioles: "He that retires, I'll take him for a Volsce, / And he shall feel mine edge" (1.4.28-29). Roman troops reject his orders, allowing him to be trapped alone within the besieged city. Under the Roman military law of Ruffus, their conduct would be actionable: "If any person, in war . . . fails to execute a command, he shall be punished with death" (Brand 159). Roman military law uses legal overkill to ensure that orders from above are obeyed and that individual soldiers are made responsible for the actions of their legion. Units that retreated unlawfully were "decimated," meaning that one-tenth of a legion would be randomly "run through with spears by the other legions for breaking the line of battle and causing the flight of others" (Brand 157).[3] The *Corpus Juris Civilis* echoes this command: "All disobedience of a general or the Governor of a province should be punished with death" (*Corpus* 11: 193). With a few minor variations, this theme of military discipline remained in force during the Renaissance and beyond, as for example in the British navy's 1661 Articles of War: "Every Person . . . who through Cowardice, Negligence, or Disaffection, shall in Time of Action withdraw, or keep back, or not come into the fight or engagement . . . shall suffer death" (Rodger 24). Partly because the heroic gesture is his *métier*, Coriolanus does not exact due punishment against his men, but their conduct explains his fury over corruption in Rome paralleling the breakdown of military discipline before Corioles. The play's first capital crime under military and civil law is committed by the plebes, not by Coriolanus.

The tribunes are newly privileged, mid-level politicians apt at manipulating public opinion to increase their influence. They represent plebeian rights in public trials and enforce their juridical power with ædiles. Sicinius seeks to thwart Coriolanus to the extent of denying that a valid consulship election ever occurred. Coriolanus's patrician backers are willing to "surety him," (3.1.177), or make his bail, as the banishment proceedings unfold. Older, consensus-seeking patricians like Cominius and Menenius appease the tribunes to retain their own authority. Thus, class relationships go far beyond the simple issue of plebeian versus patrician rights, as Kenneth Burke puts it in his elegant analysis of the play. True, Sicinius urges the crowd to cast Coriolanus from the Tarpeian rock, but Aufidius plots Coriolanus's death in Antium without the assistance of plebes. Burke thereby overstates the importance of plebeian class hatred in his formula whereby Coriolanus becomes a fit sacrifice for the tragedy. Burke's critique is influenced by cold war politics, evident when he remarks that pseudo-socialist dictators loot their impoverished nations' coffers while planning lavish retirements on the Riviera. Had he written the piece today, he might have added pseudo-democratic dictators to the list of rulers seeking golden parachutes. Burke's wit leads him to round off some legal and political edges that deserve closer scrutiny. Cominius's reference to Rome as a "falling fabric" legitimates martial law as one means to preserve the state from ruin through the misdeeds of various citizens (3.1.246).

Coriolanus conflates martial and civil law when he ponders the flight of his soldiers at Corioles: "This kind of service / Did not deserve corn gratis" (3.1.124-25). Linking acts of war with politics is inappropriate. Furthermore, having just been informed of a Volscian attack and the nullification of his election, he urges his colleagues to consider abrogating the rights of "the multitudinous tongue" (3.1.156). This request goes further than merely suggesting that free dispensation of corn nurtures sedition in Rome as it had in Greece. Such opinions align him with those whose intentions are dishonorable, including the nameless patricians who, in all probability, have been hoarding grain. Because Coriolanus refuses the spoils at Corioles, we can fairly assume he is not involved in monopolistic practices in Rome. Coriolanus's contempt for the plebes is mitigated by his attempt to reward a commoner who came to his aid at Corioles. He seems to adopt informally what IMT prosecutor Charles Dubost calls the "three precepts of the classical Roman jurists: 'Honeste vivere, alterum non lædere, suum ciuque tribuere.' (Live honorably, inflict no harm on another, give each his due)" (*IMT* 6: 425). The audience can of course weigh his failure to remember the almsman's name as it wishes.

Tribunes ratchet up the charge of usury as a way of poisoning the jury in advance of the time that they can arraign Coriolanus for treason. No evidence exists that Coriolanus sought tyrannical power, however rude his behavior may be toward those he considers deserters under martial law. The second charge leveled against him concerning the failure to distribute corn is a bootstrapping technique to make the treason accusation more palatable, a clever bit of lawyering designed to blind the populace to the real issues at stake. The tribunes seek to channel plebeian rage toward Coriolanus in order to make a conviction inevitable. Up to now, he has merely violated custom by refusing to display his scars; indeed, he remains thus far more innocent of felony than the cherubic Romeo. Coriolanus skirts the margins of political criminality with his expressions of ill-will toward the new order though he has always regarded Roman rule as immoral, not illegal. His emotional response to the verdict: "I banish you!" (3.3.123), constitutes a tactical failure; however, such invective is mild compared to the accusations made against him. One indication of the weakness of the tribunes' case is that they settle for the lesser punishment of banishment. Our faith in *Corpus Juris Civilis* is not strengthened when Cominius tries to convince Coriolanus that a repeal might be expected at some future date.

The 1607 Midlands corn uprisings are taken for granted in many circles as having directly influenced the play, but even if true they are not essential to its legal complexities. Andrew Gurr argues that Coke would have taken the commons' side in these disputes:

> 'Commons' here need mean no more than the plebeian faction, of course, but when the tribunes describe the citizens' statutory rights as
>
> Your liberties and the charters that you bear
> I'th'body of the weal
> (2.3.179-80)
>
> they are unequivocally echoing Coke, Chief Justice of the Common Pleas, who unheld Magna Charta as the great unwritten record of common rights.
> ("Body Politic" 68)

Gurr is right to find profound legal tensions in the play revolving around an expansive interpretation of the term, "commons." Coke certainly upheld the rule of common law based on Magna Carta, but he also argued on behalf of a powerful monarch. He defended the common law as the guarantor of a state order balancing the powers of the king, aristocracy, and commons.

Coriolanus seeks no such balance when he reiterates his allegiance to martial law upon entering Antium as an exile. He expects no quarter from Aufidius given their past enmity: "If he slay me, / He does fair justice" (4.4.24-25). His position in Roman military law is tricky because the regulations against desertion demand the death penalty, though he joins Aufidius only as a result of being unjustly banished himself. Shakespeare's work is filled with banished leaders returning home with foreign assistance to vie for power, but the Roman martial law to which Coriolanus adheres is categorical: "Those who flee from the Roman side to the enemy may be killed with impunity, as enemies" (Brand 167). Since the purpose of banishment is to neutralize rivals threatening the state from within, for Coriolanus to do the same from without would suffice to incriminate him in Rome. Such treason in Roman or common law makes intent a moot point.

During the *drôle de guerre,* the tribunes who engineered his banishment express delight that peace has apparently been restored. The populace cooperates by remaining silent about his fate, but upon hearing of his renewed assault, the plebes and tribunes who consented to his banishment forgive him with comical celerity. Class warfare, then, seems an almost entirely inessential component of the play's rising action. Burke finds Coriolanus to have been "appropriately punished" due to "excesses" which "lead necessarily to his downfall" ("Delights" 202, 195, 187). Burke's tactic of prophesying "after the event" in this instance falls short of explaining why Coriolanus dies (185). He sees equity, balance, and order in the tragic equation producing Coriolanus as the perfect victim bringing catastrophe down upon himself. From a legal perspective, though, we might find disorder, waste, and inequality marking the path of the hero's descent.

In preparing to leave Rome, Coriolanus consoles himself by noting: "There is a world elsewhere" (3.3.135), but unfortunately the political dynamics of Antium differ little from those of Rome. While the Roman charge of treason is plainly unfounded, Aufidius's accusation has legal merit because Coriolanus plans to give up present and future Volscian gains. Seen from the perspective of treason statutes in Renaissance England, Aufidius's charge lies midway in terms of seriousness between a direct threat to the safety of the king and his family and counterfeiting or altering English coins or importing base ones. Punishing evil figures prominently in the rationale of the death penalty, but Coke also argues that deterrence is a necessary component:

> By intendment of the law the execution of the offender is for example, ... but so it is not when a mad man is executed, but should be a miserable spectacle, both against law, and of extreame inhumanity and cruelty, and can be no example to others.
>
> (3 *Institutes* 6)

Shakespeare aligns himself with Coke's theory by proving the converse of this rule in having Coriolanus punished via Aufidius's rage. If Aufidius's evidence is more compelling than that of the tribunes, it is equally self-serving: "He sold the blood and labour / Of our great action; therefore shall he die, / And I'll renew me in his fall" (5.6.46-48). The Volscians cannot help but see merit in Aufidius's position, though a few urge that legal procedure be observed to stay the execution, if only for the sake of appearances. The Volscian conspiracy works its deadly effect because Coriolanus has become a political liability. Aufidius's passion and political maneuvering ironically confirm the link between Antium and Rome.

Retribution by conspiracy robs us of the wager of battle we might have expected between the principals. Coriolanus does not recognize Aufidius as his inferior until too late, though we have known it all along. Aufidius is a better administrator than warrior, having cleverly used Coriolanus as a stalking horse for his political ambitions: "When, Caius, Rome is thine, / Thou art poor'st of all; then shortly art thou mine" (4.7.56-57). Shakespeare regards Aufidius's subsequent demise as unworthy of report. The disaster befalling the Volscian camp and its leader the following year as reported by Plutarch might have appeared in the denouement of a Shakespearean history play. Here, we end by witnessing a cowardly act of stunning ferocity.

*II. Slander Law*

Punishment for slander has softened considerably over time, while the definition of the act itself has broadened in scope. Blackstone refers to the tyrant Dionysus ordering a subject executed for slander merely because he recounted a dream in which the ruler was slain. The *Corpus Juris Civilis* is almost as harsh: "When any one publicly abuses another in a loud voice, or writes a poem for the purpose of insulting him, or rendering him infamous, he shall be beaten with a rod until he dies" (1: 70). We define slander today as a personal tort based on false and defamatory declarations which may or may not have caused demonstrable harm. Slander is the oral version of libel, which is actionable language appearing in print. In some cases, words are prima facie slanderous; that is, action lies when the charge imputes criminality, horrible illness, or great immorality to another, notably when it results in loss of trade. Common law cases contain some key elements of the tort as it exists today, though certain concepts were defined in ways we would deem irrational.

Slander cases flourished in Coke's time, but to succeed they required that criminality be overtly alleged. As a matter of moral and public policy, Coke wished to prevent feuds of honor from erupting on the street:

> He who kills a man with his sword in fight is a great offender, but he is a greater offender who poisons another; for in the one case he, who is openly assaulted, may defend himself, and knows his adversary, and may endeavor to prevent it: but poisoning may be done so secretly that none can defend himself against it, for which cause the offence is the more dangerous, because the offender cannot easily be known; and of such nature is libelling, it is secret, and robs a man of his good name, which ought to be more precious to him than his life.
>
> (*Coke's Reports* 3: 255)

Blackstone refined Renaissance case law as to libel theory:

> The words scoundrel, rascal, villain, knave, miscreant, liar, fool, and such like general terms of scurrility, may be used with impunity, and are part of the rights and privileges of the vulgar. To constitute legal slander, the words must impute a precise crime; hence it is actionable to say a man is a highwayman, but it is not so, to say he is worse than a highwayman.
>
> (3 *Bl. Comm.* 125n)

Given how Renaissance law distinguished slanderous speech from other forms of invective, a reasonable Jacobean spectator would likely have viewed the tribunes' libelous remarks as both reprehensible and patently illegal.

Generalized references to mens rea absent a criminal act do not rise to the level of slander even though such speech might cause the hearer to fly into a rage. Two cases recounted by Sir George Croke, a renowned jurist under Charles I, illustrate the distinction in Renaissance law. In *Edward's Case* of 1582 (24 Eliz.), the slanderer describes an intent by the plaintiff, Edwards, to commit a crime: "Jo. Edwards did wrap Gunpowder in a piece of Tow, and laid it under my Window, and put fire to it, minding to burn my house" (1 *Croke* 6). The case for the slandered Edwards was upheld because his accuser links mens rea with the arson allegation. The 1599 (41 Eliz.) case of *Davies v. Taylor* demonstrates how slander would be actionable when inferences of mens rea or moral turpitude might reasonably be drawn. Suit was brought for these words: "*Thou art rotted with the pox,* And . . . adjudged, that the Words were actionable: For it is to be intended of the *French Pox*" (1 *Croke* 648). The slander found here does not suggest the commission of any crime, but it leaves the accused open to the public perception that he is a moral or physiological outcast.

Slander cases against women were forced to meet an unreasonably high test by today's standards. In the 1596-97 (38-39 Eliz.) case of *Pollard and his Wife v. Armshaw,* suit was brought for these words: *"Thou art a Whore, and J.S. hath the use of thy Body: The Cart is too good for thee"* (1 *Croke* 582). Surprisingly, the court held that no slander lay in the accusation. This apparent double standard given the outcome of *Davies v. Taylor* was nevertheless viewed as reasonable at the time. English common law privileged attacks on property over those against a woman's honor: "But, if one saith to a Woman, which keepeth an Inn, or a Tabling-House, *Thou keepest a house of bawdry.* It is Actionable; For thereby her house is slandered" (1 *Croke* 582-83). Such were the social lines drawn in English Renaissance common law on the use of hurtful speech.

Remedies for slander against women were held to a similarly high standard of proof in Coke's age. In the *Holwood v. Hopkins* case of 1600-01 (42-43 Eliz.), Holwood claimed that allegations of her being an "arrant whore" put an end to her marriage plans (1 *Croke* 787). Words like whore and heretic, being "spiritual Slander and Defamation" (1 *Croke* 787), generally remained safe from common law action; however, they could be punishable in the ecclesiastical courts, which had a vital interest in sustaining the institution of marriage. Legally speaking, loose talk about character is one thing, but if such charges were "purposely intended to hinder the marriage, the Action had been maintainable for the loss, which she sustained" (1 *Croke* 787). Holwood was unable to convince the court that Hopkins's vile remarks directly resulted in such a termination. A 1606 (4 Jac.) case, *Dame Morison v. Cade,* succeeded when innuendoes of moral turpitude were leveled against a widow. Cade reported to Morison's suitor that Askot *"had the use of her body"* (2 *Croke* 162). Upon hearing this, the suitor broke off his pursuit of Morison. Cade had argued successfully in a lower court that his accusation caused no direct harm on the rationale that a physician could literally be said to have use of a woman's body without imputing immorality. This lower court decision was reversed on appeal because the "usual and common sense" inference of the charge was found by the higher courts to be damaging (2 *Croke* 163). The initial lower court ruling against Dame Morison is less outrageous than it might appear to us because common law courts were scrupulous about circumscribing their decisions to the letter of the law. The lower court ruling confirms, however, that women held a lower status in the common law.

Coriolanus is vulnerable to slanders employed by his foes to validate their treason charges. Both Coke and Blackstone permit loopholes in speech acts of precisely the sort Shakespeare uses to advance his dramatic action. Any actor would understand Blackstone's remarks on oral interpretation:

> But now it seems clearly to be agreed that, by the common law and the statute of Edward III, words spoken amount only to a high misdemeanor, and no treason. For they may be spoken in head, without any intention, or be mistaken, perverted, or misremembered by the hearers; their meaning depends always on the connexion with other words, and things; they may signify differently even according to the tone of the voice, with which they are delivered; and sometimes silence itself is more expressive than any discourse. As therefore there can be nothing more equivocal and ambiguous than words, it would indeed be unreasonable to make them amount to high treason.
>
> (4 *Bl. Comm.* 79-80)

Words generally had to be linked with deeds to constitute treason, as with other felonies, though as we have seen there were important exceptions to the rule: "An overt act must be alleged and proved" (4 *Bl. Comm.* 79). Because Coriolanus's initial remarks decrying the tribunes' power constitute mere political opinion, not subversive intent, his foes set verbal snares to inflame the hero's passion.

The main slanders against the protagonist relate to usury, Volumnia's influence, and his political bias. Despite being warned about using slanderous speech, a citizen openly accuses Coriolanus of fixing corn prices in Rome.[4] Because the emotional charge is legally insubstantial, the mob soon shifts its focus to the question of Volumnia's influence on her son. During this extraordinarily well-ventilated debate on the character of one of Rome's leading figures, the citizen who made the usury charge now attacks Coriolanus as being motivated "to please his mother, and to be partly proud, which he is, even to the altitude of his virtue" (1.1.38-40). Besides foreshadowing the eventual success of Volumnia's supplication, this accusation permits Menenius to raise the issue of legally actionable words in the context of the *patria potestas:* "You slander / The helms o' th' state, who care for you like fathers" (1.1.76-77). Volumnia complicates psychological questions surrounding Coriolanus through her use of such innocent phrases as "if my son were my husband" (1.3.2-3). Psychological elements recur when Volumnia suggests that bleeding wounds are fairer than Hecuba's breasts and that Romans will "put our tongues into those wounds" (2.3.6-7). If Coriolanus has an Oedipal complex, so apparently does all of Rome.

Critics have turned to Freud to evaluate the effect of Volumnia's influence on her son. A. C. Bradley sees the final reconciliation as being good for Coriolanus's soul, but many psychological critics find neurotic implications in the relationship. Earlier Freudians assert that Volumnia dominates her son much as Gertrude haunts Hamlet. Critic Rufus Pitney calls the play a "tragedy ensuing from an oedipal mother-son relationship" and finds Volumnia to have structured her son's superego so that "his conscience compels him to choose his own death rather than his mother's" (380, 381). Psychiatrist Charles Hofling finds "morbid" elements in the mother-son relationship that affect Coriolanus's healthy marriage by causing a "phallic-narcissist" condition (427, 428). Critic Janet Adelman sees a "phallic aggressive pose" making Coriolanus a "rigid and cold" tragic hero (133, 141). The hero seems to me to be anything but frosty, nor does the play provide proof that a homoerotic "alliance" exists between Coriolanus and Aufidius, as Lisa Lowe suggests (87). Lowe uses psychological criticism while distancing herself from other Freudian feminist critics, including Coppélia Kahn, Janet Adelman, and Madelon Gohlke. Lowe suggests that Coriolanus has a "castration" complex brought about by patriarchal, not matriarchal, pressures (93). This observation might be more salient given a clearer historical context, for Lowe refers to "Elizabethan England" as the play's backdrop (89), when it is of the Jacobean period.

Shakespeare diminishes Volumnia's role in the supplication scene by having Coriolanus greet Virgilia first, contrary to Plutarch. Virgilia's humility is hardly a novelty in military marriages, but the presence of Valeria as a disinterested and unimpeachable presence along with Virgilia further reduces the mother's influence. Volumnia is a strict disciplinarian, though in light of the authoritarian standards of Rome she is not overly harsh. Roman wives had no more standing in the family than their children, but this patriarchal order did not mean that male offspring were necessarily well positioned. Many were cruelly mistreated by their fathers, and only after three extraordinarily harsh cases of abuse and disowning could a son wrest himself free of his father's grasp. Still, one of Coke's forerunners, Bracton, confirms an essential bias in the common law: "Women differ from men in many respects, for their position is inferior to men" (2: 31).[5] The Roman citizens, whose amateur psychological opinions count because they decide Coriolanus's fate, resign themselves to having ambivalent feelings about Volumnia's influence: "What he cannot help in his nature, you account a vice in him" (1.1.41-42). Aufidius makes the same psychological evaluation of his old nemesis after they have joined forces. The play consistently links psychological readings of the hero with the tactics of slander to divert our attention from issues of substantial public interest.

The slander that decisively shifts the play relates to Coriolanus's political leanings. Sicinius is a master at stage-managing baseless accusations of intentional criminal wrongdoing to strengthen his position:

> We charge you, that you have contriv'd to take
> From Rome all season'd office, and to wind
> Yourself into a power tyrannical,
> For which you are a traitor to the people.
> (3.3.63-66)

Sicinius leads the populace up to this accusation very carefully, perhaps more so than necessary given the discontent over poverty and starvation. Coriolanus, he says, demonstrates the requisite intention by words alone to be deemed a traitor, an argument so weak and overreaching that he pronounces the death sentence before the trial begins. Knowing that Coriolanus will be unable to restrain his fury upon hearing the illogical charges, Sicinius feels confident of his victory in the court of public opinion. Political speech operates here and elsewhere in a middle ground between slander and flattery, implying one whenever possible while engaging in the other. Coriolanus has already been blamed by one of his own soldiers for unnecessary vituperation: "Now, to seem to affect the malice and displeasure of the people is as bad as that which he dislikes, to flatter them for their love" (2.2.21-23). Without the tribunes' intervention, the reaction of the mob would have remained bifurcated, for when he is not being slandered, Coriolanus is hailed for his martial skill.

Coriolanus's opponents work themselves into a slanderous frenzy to blunt perceived threats to their personal and political well-being. Sicinius reveals the personal animosity he feels toward Coriolanus by insisting that the citizenry abuse the hero as he is led beyond the city walls. Further undercutting the tribunes' position is the vital Nicanor spy scene, in which a countryman is shown in fact to be working actively on behalf of the enemy: "I am a Roman, and my services are, as you are, against 'em" (4.3.4-5). Ruffus on military law is most explicit on this sort of demonstrable treachery: "Deserters to the enemy, and those who reveal our plans to the enemy shall be burned alive or hanged upon the gibbet" (Brand 60). This concept of law is identical to Coke's:

> If a subject joine with a foraine enemy, and come into England with him, he shall not be taken prisoner here and ransomed, or proceeded with as enemy shall, but he shall be taken as a traytor to the king.
>
> (3 *Institutes* 11)

For such overt disloyalty to go unsuspected or unreported while Coriolanus's bad manners are treated as treason is the kind of legal imbalance that a reasonable audience would regard as outrageous, ginning up the tragic effect through an inequitable distribution of justice.

By siding with the Volscians, Coriolanus becomes the traitor he was falsely alleged to be in Rome. He describes his motivation for revenge during the supplication scene, yet his rage is laced with a desire to reform Rome rather than seek its destruction. He is no stock revenger because he does not target old adversaries like Sicinius or Brutus. Perhaps this is the source of Aufidius's jealous awe of Coriolanus, a feeling shared by many of the play's characters. The virulence of the Volscian leader's final response is shocking: *"Draw the Conspirators, and kills Martius, who falls; Aufidius stands on him"* (5.6.130). This gross exhibition is pure desecration. We move beyond the legal realm of punishment to a tragic theatricality whereby a hero is insulted beyond all recognized bounds of decency. Shakespeare herein casts any legal impulse for reform into confusion.

*III. The Spectacle of Tragic Punishment*

Coriolanus's body is used as a metaphor for political life and its diseases, with his immune system breaking down entirely at the end in a violent spectacle of capital punishment. He demonstrates a special reluctance for political acting, which is theatrical acting writ small. Politics requires displays that strike Coriolanus as unbearable flattery. If Hamlet delays, Coriolanus refuses to act at all, which creates a tension endangering the forward action of the tragedy. Coriolanus despises ham acting much as Hamlet does dishonest shows, but he thinks his way through his dilemma as a military tactician. He leavens his flattery with contempt of those who desire it: "I will counterfeit the bewitchment of some popular man, and give it bountiful to the desirers" (2.3.101-02). Armed with a new ironic distance from his role, Coriolanus injects the bluster learned in his capacity as a military commander to hector his fellow Romans as he would his foes: "Your voices? For your voices I have fought!" (2.3.126). Receiving the approval of the crowd despite refusing to display his wounds, he overleaps the obstacle occasioned by his refusal to act by making a pretense of it, while Hamlet pretends in order to arrive at true action itself.

Coriolanus rejects ham acting on personal grounds, but the premise that honor and policy might join harmoniously—Durkheim's aim—is impossible given the political tensions. Norman Rabkin is thus correct to assert that "rational and humane order cannot really be restored because it cannot exist in society" to the extent that he means Roman or Volscian society (21). The contradiction is evident in Menenius, who praises the hero's nobility while chastising him for failing to soothe the populace. Coriolanus believes in cognitive behaviorism, fearing that unworthy practices will "teach my mind / A most inherent baseness" (3.2.122-23). The distanciation involved in the classical acting style he adopts enables him to stand for consulship once he realizes that he need not take his own political gestures seriously. When Cominius promises to stage-manage the action: "Come, come, we'll prompt you" (3.2.106), theatrical and legal issues begin to overtake the psychological and political aspects of the play.

For all his seeming superficiality or inflexibility, Coriolanus remains an irresistible figure in part because of his ironic attitude toward acting. Cominius is forced to admit that there is something admirable about Coriolanus even after the defection. The plebes' sense the loss of Coriolanus, though they express their remorse illogically: "And though we willingly consented to his banishment, yet it was against our will" (4.6.144-45). The Senators respond in kind when news of Coriolanus's peace offer reaches them, so Kenneth Burke is right to detect a catalytic quality in the hero's nature that affects Rome and Antium equally. But rather than revealing any fault or criminality within the hero, as Burke maintains, Coriolanus's non-performances constitute great acting that incites others to perform legal or illegal acts, as they will. His authoritarian streak accords with his military rank, though his contempt for the plebes as better suited for the gibbet than the battlefield is far too harsh. It is, nonetheless, a distinct curiosity in critical reaction to the play that a military man who proposes peace for the general good should be castigated so strongly as an unfit or emotionally crippled leader.

Coriolanus is not so much an absolutist as fully formed from the start, which cannot be said of Romeo, Hamlet, or Othello. His foes catalogue his defects in moral terms of "pride," "[defect] of judgment," or "nature" (4.7.37, 39, 41). Menenius refers to any alliance between Rome and Antium as unthinkable, a "violent'st contrariety" (4.6.73). Because she understands her son's martial disposition, Volumnia wins him back by arguing that reconciliation would constitute not a retreat but a double victory. The supplication scene creates theatrical metaphysics equal to the power of Greek tragedy, though without its supernatural dimensions. In this respect, too, the play differs from *Macbeth, Hamlet,* or *King Lear*. Coriolanus can no longer pretend to act as a public figure might. Reminded that the role of a conqueror is merely assumed, he responds with a theatrical analogy: "Like a dull actor now / I have forgot my part, and I am out, / Even to a full disgrace" (5.3.40-42). Silence reigns as Volumnia takes his hand in a restoration of the hero's private identity. In the theatre the silence is deafening, with many actors exploiting it for a minute or longer. The suppliants kneel before a theatrical hero, but he responds in a way that rejects the premise of the *patria potestas*. He finds their submission to be "unnatural" (5.3.184), which contradicts the patriarchal foundations of the *Corpus Juris Civilis*.

Coriolanus seeks an emancipation that is unknown in Roman law and scarcely visible in Renaissance law and tragedy. Shakespearean tragedy rejects the possibility of full emancipation here as it had in *Romeo and Juliet*. That Coriolanus should be asked for mercy by Rome is terribly ironic because he is in no position to dispense it. As one who has been exiled, it is he who should by rights be seeking pardon from those who banished him. Mercy of this sort must come from the leader, a point Coke emphasizes as essential to the common law: "Mercy and truth preserve the King, and by clemency is his throne strengthened. And hereupon is the law of England founded" (3 *Institutes* 233). Coriolanus appeals for peace, but he cannot overcome the legal and theatrical traps awaiting him.

The validity of the martial code guiding Coriolanus's civil behavior is established once and for all in contradistinction to the political discourse of Menenius, which can be pierced immediately by the military mind. When Menenius attempts to bluff his way past the Volscian guards, they quickly take him to be a "liar" and a "decay'd dotant" because he is incapable of distinguishing between the ranks of captain and general (5.2.31, 44). Coriolanus regards war and peace simply as the initiation and cessation of hostilities. For him, action constitutes eloquence in war, while eloquence is the less honorable action of civil peace. His peace proposal is rebuffed by Aufidius, who can speak both languages simultaneously and fluently. When Coriolanus weeps before him, he slanders this image of Mars with a devastating rejoinder: "Name not the god, thou boy of tears!" (5.6.100). By pleading for mercy, Coriolanus has threatened to breach his contract to serve Aufidius, but the Volscian leader violates a theatrical contract of his own in mixing the language of the politician and warrior. We, like Aufidius's giddy servingmen, rightly sense that Coriolanus could "thwack our general" (4.5.178-79). In view of Coriolanus's martial and theatrical superiority, the Volscian lords must search hard to find mitigating factors for the assassination: "His own impatience / Takes from Aufidius a great part of blame. / Let's make the best of it" (5.6.144-46). Aufidius's murderous premeditation is apparent to all, yet the Volscian lords seek to calm the political waters in precisely the same manner as their Roman counterparts.

The desecration of Coriolanus's body is a shameful and self-defeating act that is at once high theatre and an imitation of a primitive act of domination equivalent to Clytemnestra's treatment of Agamemnon. Aufidius senses his own disgrace: "My rage is gone, / And I am struck with sorrow" (5.6.146-47), but the solemnity that ensues cannot erase the horror of the act. Death is the only emancipation for the tragic hero, which is in reality a non-emancipation. At Stratford in 1959, the conspirators heaved Olivier over the balcony to hang by his heels. This *coup de théâtre* links the Roman punishment of throwing offenders off the Tarpeian Rock with the savage conspiracy engineered by Aufidius. That the prime conspirator receives no punishment is thoroughly unfair, but if the historians are correct, Aufidius has only one more year to live before he dies in a botched attempt to conquer Rome. In the play, though, Coriolanus's death never brings with it a believable promise of general peace, as Burke suggests it does.

## IV. The Ends of Civility

The body is killed by slander in civil law and by death in criminal law, both punishments being combined to form the basis of this tragedy. Coriolanus's demeanor ranges from tender to severe, like Othello's, but his actual theatrical role is put to the test far more than that of the Venetian general. Othello commits murder out of simple jealousy under English Renaissance law.[6] The slander suffered by Coriolanus under the body of Roman and Renaissance law is as plain as the criminality involved in his banishment and murder.

For a Shakespearean tragic protagonist to propose peace in his final moments is quite unusual. Generally, such heroes succumb after a prolonged state of excitement. Romeo, Hamlet, Macbeth, and Othello all reach heights of physical and emotional animation before they expire. Apart from a last minute argument with Aufidius, which merely marks a return to his old form, Coriolanus dies in a mood as forgiving as that of the Roman citizens and leaders who now desperately wish for his return. More successfully focused than *Julius Caesar* as to the fate of a singular hero, this play gives Coriolanus a theatrical bewitchment, some touch of the gods, that elevates him.[7] Hence the furtiveness of a slaughter that completes the destruction of his body begun over a multitude of military campaigns. The final vicious insult is inflicted by his inferiors, including vicariously the audience, which can contemplate its emancipation only in the most ironic fashion.

### Notes

[1] Coke distinguishes common law from military court procedure:

> And all matters done out of the Realm of England concerning warre, combate, or deeds of armes, shall

be tryed and termined before the Constable and Marshall of England, before whom the trial is by witnesses, or by combate; and their proceeding is according to the civil law, and not by the oath of twelve men.

(1 *Institutes* 261)

² Coke describes the mixture of Roman, Norman, and other laws in English common law:

For so many ancient Terms and words drawn from that legal French, are grown to be *Vocabula artis,* Vocables of Art, so apt and significant to express the true sense of the Laws, and are so woven in the Laws themselves, as it is in a manner impossible to change them, then if they were expressed in pure Latine.

(1 *Institutes* 9a, pref.)

Coke always favored strong parliamentary rule for reasons of national security: "The Romans vanquished our Ancestors the ancient Britains, for that they assembled not, they consulted not in common with them, nor Common Councels" (4 *Institutes* 9).

³ Desertion is a felony in the common law: "All idle and wandring souldiers or mariners, or idle persons wandring as souldiers or mariners, shall be reputed felons, and suffer as in case of felony" (3 *Institutes* 84).

⁴ Coke detests usury because it stifles normal human industry: "Usury is a contract upon the lone of money . . . directly against the Law of God . . . as a means either to exterminate, or to depauperate" (3 *Institutes* 151). He regards the practice as being "against the law of nature" (3 *Institutes* 152). The doubling of rent, for example, would qualify as a usurious practice (2 *Institutes* 89). He is by our standards entirely too sanguine about the mistreatment of Jews in English history, though to be fair it is he who records that English kings were the beneficiaries of supposed Jewish business practices between the reigns of Henry III and Edward I to the tune of £420,000. Coke admits gross hypocrisy in the annals of English legal history, which singled out Jews for deportation on charges of usury. The "Courts of the Justices assigned for the government of the Jewes" ended in 18 Ed. I when, by statute, the Jews were "utterly banished" from the realm (4 *Institutes* 254). A Chancery bureau continued through Coke's time: "The house annexed to his office, is called *domus Conversorum,* so called because H.3. founded this house to be a house of Jews as should be converted to the true religion of Jesus Christ, and there should have maintenance and allowance, which continueth to this day" (4 *Institutes* 95).

⁵ The second class status of women is obvious in Renaissance inheritance and property laws:

If a man give Lands to a man, To have and to hold, to him and the heirs Males of his body, and to him and to the heires Females of his body, the estate of the heirs Females is in remainder, and the daughters shall not inherit any part, so long as there is issue Male, for the estate to the heirs males is first limited, and shall be first served; and it is as much to say, and after to the heirs females, Males in construction of Law are to be preferred.

(1 *Institutes* 377)

⁶ Coke's definition of murder requires the element of malice aforethought, wording which today has been eliminated because it does not apply, for example, to a professional "hit":

Murder is when a man of sound memory, and of the age of discretion, unlawfully killeth within any county of the realm any reasonable creature *in rerum natura* under the king's peace, with malice fore-thought, either expressed by the party, or implied by law, so as the party wounded, or hurt, &c. die of the wound, or hurt, &c. within a year and a day after the same.

(3 *Institutes* 47)

⁷ Shakespeare's innocent intimation of the capital crime of witchcraft is an anachronism that would have interested James. Coke defines a witch as "a person that hath conference with the devill, to consult with him or to do some act" (3 *Institutes* 43). Also, minor Renaissance courts could prosecute scolding; thus, Coriolanus's incorrect assertion to Aufidius: "'tis the first time that ever / I was forc'd to scold" (5.6.104-05), had tangential legal implications.

*Works Cited*

Adelman, Janet. "'Anger's my Meat': Feeding, Dependency, and Aggression in *Coriolanus*." *Representing Shakespeare: New Psychoanalytic Essays*. Ed. Murray M. Schwartz and Coppélia Kahn. Baltimore: Johns Hopkins UP, 1980. 129-49.

Blackstone, Sir William. *Commentaries on the Laws of England*. Ed. Edward Christian. 4 vols. London: A. Strahan, 1803.

*Bracton on the Laws and Customs of England*. Ed. George W. Woodbine. Trans. Samuel E. Thorne. Vol. 2. Cambridge, MA: Belknap, 1968. 2 vols.

Bradley, A. C. *Shakespearean Tragedy*. London: Macmillan, 1937.

Bradwell, Stephen. *Mary Glovers Late Woeful Case. Witchcraft and Hysteria in Elizabethan England*. Ed. Michael MacDonald. London: Routledge, 1991. 1-150.

Brand, C. E. *Roman Military Law*. Austin: U of Texas P, 1968.

Burke, Kenneth. "*Coriolanus*—and the Delights of Faction." *Hudson Review* 19, 2 (1966): 185-202.

Coke, Sir Edward. *The First Part of the Institutes of the Laws of England; or, a Commentary upon Littleton.* London: Streater, 1670.

———. *The Second Part of the Institutes of the Laws of England.* London: Streater, 1671.

———. *The Third Part of the Institutes of the Laws of England.* London: W. Clarke, 1809.

———. *The Fourth Part of the Institutes of the Lawes of England.* London: Crooke, 1669.

———. *The Reports of Sir Edward Coke [Coke's K.B. Reports].* Ed. John Henry Thomas and John Farquahar Fraser. 6 vols. London: Butterworth, 1826.

Croke, Sir George. *The First Part of the Reports of Sir George Croke.* Ed. and trans. (from French to English) Sir Harbottle Grimston. London: A. Roper, 1669.

———. *The Second Part of the Reports of Sir George Croke.* Ed. and trans. Sir Harbottle Grimston. London: T. Newcomb, 1659.

Gurr, Andrew. "Coriolanus and the Body Politic." *Shakespeare Survey 28.* Cambridge: Cambridge UP, 1975. 63-69.

Hofling, Charles K., M.D. "An Interpretation of Shakespeare's *Coriolanus*." *American Imago* 14, 4 (1957): 407-35.

Justinian. *Corpus Juris Civilis.* Trans. S. P. Scott. Vols. 1-11. New York: AMS, 1973. 17 vols.

Lowe, Lisa. "'Say I play the man I am': Gender and Politics in *Coriolanus*." *Kenyon Review* 8, 4 (1986): 364-81.

Pitney, Rufus. "Coriolanus and his Mother." *Psychoanalytic Quarterly* 31, 3 (1962): 364-81.

Rabkin, Norman. "*Coriolanus:* The Tragedy of Politics." *Shakespeare Quarterly* 17, 3 (1966): 195-212.

Rodger, N. A. M., ed. *Articles of War: 1661, 1749, and 1866.* Emsworth, Eng.: Mason, 1982.

Shakespeare, William. *The Riverside Shakespeare.* Gen. ed. Blakemore Evans and J. J. M. Tobin. 2nd ed. Boston: Houghton, 1997.

---

Source: "*Coriolanus*: Punishment of the Civil Body," in *Shakespearean Tragedy and the Common Law: The Art of Punishment,* Peter Lang Publishing, Inc., 1998, pp. 105-21.

# *Julius Caesar* and the Properties of Shakespeare's Globe

## Dennis Kezar, *Vanderbilt University*

"The World makes many vntrue Constructions of these Speaches."[1]

For an antitheatricalist such as Stephen Gosson, the Renaissance stage travesties the courtroom, leaving the defendant with no voice and replacing a single judge with an injudicious jury: "At stage plays it is ridiculous, for the parties accused to reply, no indifference of judgment can be had, because the worst sort of people have the hearing of it, which in respect of their ignorance, of their fickleness, and of their fury, are not to be admitted in place of judgment. A judge must be grave, sober, discreet, wise, well exercised in cases of government, which qualities are never found in the baser sort."[2] In his indictment of drama Gosson charges poets and players with reducing the accused to a lifeless and common text, "openly blown into the ears of many and made a byword" (p. 167); and he charges the audience, "carried away with every rumor," with blind injustice: "they run together by heaps, they know not whither; and lay about with their clubs, they see not why. Which thing the ancient Philosophers considering called them a monster of many heads" (p. 164).

Conspicuously, few apologists for Renaissance theater directly engage Gosson's assertion that the stage is a law court perverted, that it submits false evidence to a biased, bacchant audience. Indeed, Thomas Heywood admits the malleability of this audience only when insisting upon the virtues of fictionalized exempla: "Lively and well spirited action . . . hath power to new mold the hearts of the spectators and fashion them to the shape of any noble and notable attempt."[3] Philip Sidney may obliquely concede the contingency of such modeling upon the audience's judgment when, for instance, he claims for the poet power "to bestow a Cyrus upon the world to make many Cyruses, *if they will learn aright why and how that maker made him.*"[4] But Sidney and the protheatricalists celebrate the bloodless "sweet violence"[5] of an exemplary and embellished drama that moves the spectator to virtuous and prescribed behavior; Gosson argues not only that this same transaction can promulgate vice—both intentionally and unintentionally[6]—but also that it commits felonious violence against the object of representation itself. Far from a "glass of behavior," Gosson's theater presents men as silent exteriors before a dangerously subjective audience, an inversion of the ideal courtroom: "For the place, no private man's life ought to be brought in question or accused, but where he may plead in his own defense and have indifferent judges to determine the case" (p. 163). Thus he approves of Roman theatrical censorship for restoring the judiciary to its rightful place: "[the Roman censors] would not have the life and behavior of the citizens, subject either to a poet's inkhorn, or a player's tongue, but to the seat of justice" (p. 165). In contrast to this fixed institution of judgment, he finds the Renaissance "common" stage an interpretively open-ended venue, where the inwardness of a "private man's life" becomes the property of a public both ductile and unpredictable.[7] At its most penetrating, Gosson's criticism of drama reveals the violence of what we might call "other-fashioning"—the coercion involved when a playwright silences a subject, appropriates that subject as spectacle, and displays it before the dubious construction of numberless judges.

Ironically, we find the most unflinching response to this definition of theatrical violence not in the prose of Gosson's opponents, but in the very public drama he seeks to censor. In my reading of *The Tragedy of Julius Caesar,* I claim that Shakespeare explores this same violence with acute self-consciousness; and that, more specifically, the dismemberment of Cinna the poet at the center of the dramatic action emblemizes the potentially ruinous energies of other-fashioning—focuses the anxieties about theatrical appropriation and audience response—that preside with thematic centrality over the play. Such a reading will involve an inversion of the paradigm typically imposed on the Renaissance stage when "self-fashioning" is the issue: rather than a cultural space that enables but ultimately contains a potentially subversive auto-poesis.[8] I argue that Shakespeare represents in this play a stage subversive for its incontinence, a theater in which self-presentation dissolves before the alterative gaze and indeterminate interpretation of the spectator. *Julius Caesar* will have a doubled part in this essay, however. While I seek to demonstrate that in his play Shakespeare metatheatrically considers the relation—as conceived by the antitheatricalists—between the playwright, his matter, and his audience, I also attempt to historicize this self-consciousness, arguing that the play appears in a time (1599) and a place (the Globe) at which the nature of this relation is being energetically redefined and debated. This reading of *Julius Caesar,* then, tries to present the play as a dramatic reading of a contentious contemporary issue, a critical representation of the public theater's epistemological economy. For it is through this critique that Shakespeare defines both the dramatist and his customers as roughhandlers of the representations they fashion and watch; it is through this critique that Shakespeare considers public drama's potential for irresponsibility. In so doing, he defines the playwright as implicated in a process of which many apologists for theater would absolve him: guilty by association with an untrustworthy audience, a corrupt jury, Shakespeare's dramatist knowingly violates the subjects he stages.

II

*"Fashion it thus"*

It might be objected that Gosson's view of theater as mistrial arises merely from his concern with a topical stage's potential for libel, a concern in fact shared by the state censors in Renaissance England.[9] But Gosson conceives the injury of theatrical misrepresentation much more broadly, so that even Roman history can be victimized by Elizabethan dramatic adaptations:

> If a true history be taken in hand . . . the poets drive it most commonly unto such points, as may best show the majesty of their pen . . . or wring in a show, to furnish the stage, when it is too bare; when the matter of itself comes short of this, they follow the practice of the cobbler, and set their teeth to the leather to pull it out.
>
> So was the history of Caesar and Pompey . . . when the history swelled, and ran too high for the number of the persons that should play it, the poet with Procrustes cut the same fit to his own measure; when it afforded no pomp at all, he brought it to the rack, to make it serve.
>
> (*Plays Confuted in Five Actions,* pp. 168-69)

Sidney's alchemy, whereby the brazen world of nature and history becomes golden, is here described as a violent and opportunistic craft. For Gosson does not seem to share Sidney's view of the inutile specificity of history; nor does he justify poetic fiction as the conversion of mundane fact into neoplatonic Truth. Rather, Gosson's "true history" exists as a prior authenticity endangered by subsequent authors who take it "in hand" and "make it serve" their own artistic designs—by playwrights who falsify historical evidence and "wring in" shows in order to construct compelling theatrical cases.

Something of this rhetoric of coercive and manipulative representation distinguishes Shakespeare's own metadramatic reflections upon the act of staging history. In the Prologue to *The Life of Henry the Fifth*, for instance, the Chorus admits the difficulty of dramatizing epic, and concedes the impossibility if not the impropriety of "cram[ming]" the play's historical subject "Within this wooden O"; and as the audience, we become accomplices to this constrictive, farcical force when we are invited to "Suppose within the girdle of these walls / Are now confined two mighty monarchies."[10] While Shakespeare's "Chorus to this history" grapples with the presentational problem of daring "to bring forth / So great an object . . . On this unworthy scaffold," however, it also introduces the interpretive consequences of treating an historical subject as a spectacular "object." By invoking the audience's "imaginary forces," this Chorus indicates that dramatist and spectator must collaborate in fashioning and evaluating the evidence before them, and implies that the ultimate meaning of dramatic representation resides in the subjective and constitutive response of the audience: "Linger your patience on, and we'll digest / Th' abuse of distance, force a play" (2.Chorus.31-32). If one subscribes to Gosson's dark view of the playwright and his "worst sort of" audience, moreover, this collaboration not only misrepresents "true history" through the dramatist's self-interested manipulation of the record, but also subjects the characters of that history to the equally suspect reception of spectators who—like an autonomous jury—follow their own ends in arriving at their verdict.

*Julius Caesar* dramatizes both sides of this exchange, demonstrating the potential violation of history and its subjects by theatrical representation and audience response. Replying skeptically to Casca's reading of the wonders and prodigies that herald the fifteenth of March, in fact, Cicero might be said to epigrammatize the open-ended process of other-fashioning: "Indeed it is a strange-disposed time. / But men may construe things after their fashion, / Clean from the purpose of the things themselves" (I.3.33-35). Primarily, of course, these lines warn against the inadvertent misprison central to tragedy—the defiance of augury, omens, and prophecy that generically signals Caesar's fall; the "hateful Error" that ruins Cassius, who dies having "misconstrued everything" (5.3.84). But in Shakespeare's history play Cicero's words resonate with a significance beyond the tragic myopia that can doom such interpreters. For the hermeneutic he describes—the subjective speculation and objectified spectacle that, for Gosson, corrupt the courtroom and reduce history to histrionics—also describes the theatrical mode by which men knowingly victimize others in *Julius Caesar*. Like the word "theater" itself (at once a place where one goes "to view" and a place where scenes are staged "to the view"), his verb "construe" blurs the distinction between the act of interpretation and the act of representation. Indeed, Cicero's insight becomes the conspirators' strategy as they construct their plot. Like the portents and soothsaying Caesar must ignore if this plot is to succeed, for instance, Calphurnia's dream has an internal validity and "purpose" that the conspirators must construe "after their fashion" if the show is to go on. Thus Decius claims that she has "all amiss interpreted" her vision (2.2.83), and he provides an alternative reading that effectively leads

Caesar to his slaughter. Similarly, although Brutus regrets "That every like is not the same" (2.2.128), he realizes the republicans must represent Caesar as a simulacrum of himself in order to alienate him in the people's eyes. In a soliloquy that rehearses the apology for tyrannicide he will soon deliver to the plebeians, he admits the expediency of construing Caesar after his own fashion, clean from the purpose of the thing himself:

> And since the quarrel
> Will bear no color for the thing he is,
> Fashion it thus: that what he is, augmented,
> Would run to these and these extremities.
> (2.1.28-31)

For Brutus, as for Gosson's violator of "true history," "the matter of itself comes short"; and the solution to the troublesome limitations of fact threatening to impede his plot and obstruct his case lies in theatricalized fiction, in fashioning the audience's perspective on the scene he is to perform by altering the evidence and ascribing to Caesar a new *telos*. Refusing the passive role of Sidney's historian—a pedant "so tied not to what should be but to what is, to the particular truth of things and not to the general reason of things"[11]—Brutus instead plays the poet and forces the awkwardly sui generis Caesar into the generic catastrophe of the de casibus tradition. He forces a play by "wringing in" a show.

This scene, however, draws blood, and herein lies the play's specific self-consciousness: men die in *Julius Caesar* not only from accidental misreading, not only from accepting the intentional misreadings of others, but also—much more unusually—from being consciously misread. As we shall see, Cinna the poet, dismembered for his name by an audience that has become actors, falls as the superlative victim of this last category, the archetypal sacrifice of a "private man's life" to the mistrial of public theater. For Cicero's words apply as much to the plebeian audience of this theater as they do to those who attempt to control their perspective on the evidence put before them. If representations can be manipulated after the politicians' fashion, so can they be misconstrued by the people's reception; if men can be appropriated by the political theater, so can they become the property of those who observe them.

And if men can be subjected to this estranging process, so can "true history"; if Cicero's observation pertains to those who inhabit Shakespeare's play, it also pertains to the playwright himself. On this metadramatic level, in fact, Cicero's acknowledgment of the construction to which omens and prognostications are susceptible attains further significance and irony. For by the late sixteenth century, a great deal of skepticism had arisen in England over an illusionistic strategy that *Julius Caesar,* like many Renaissance history plays, employs dramaturgically: the temporal sleight of hand whereby history is given a compelling predictive force and narrative shape.[12] The strong rhetoric with which such manipulations of omens and prophecy were attacked, moreover, suggestively resembles that of the antitheatricalists. Most shrill, perhaps, is Raphael Holinshed's condemnation of Peter of Pomfret, "a man in great reputation with the common people" whom Holinshed brands a "pseudoprophet or false foreteller of afterclaps . . . a deluder of the people."[13] Francis Bacon likewise regrets that "the nature of Man . . . coveteth divination." He approves of the "many severe laws made to suppress" such prophecies, "for they have done much mischief," and he claims "that almost all of them, being infinite in number, have been impostures, and by idle and crafty brains, merely contrived and feigned, after the event passed."[14] Holinshed and Bacon object to these anachronistic predictions for much the same reason that Gosson objects to the dramatization of history: in facilitating the "emplotment"[15] of history's chaos into an orderly story, they are the instruments of deceivers rather than decipherers.

There are obvious reasons for the author of *Julius Caesar* to consider his use of history so self-consciously. Shakespeare's principal source for the play—North's translation of Amyot's French version of a Latin translation of Plutarch's *Lives of the Noble Grecians and Romans*—already suggests the transformation of historical fact by collaborative human manufacture; as Sidney remarks, moreover, this poeticizing of history began with the first chronicler: "And who reads Plutarch's either history or philosophy, shall find he trimmeth both their garments with guards of poetry."[16] Shakespeare fashions his play, then, from a text already read and fashioned, moralized and translated. Significantly, the short scene of Cinna's apprehension occasions a disproportionate degree of poetic departure from this text. Shakespeare chooses to specify that this Cinna is "the poet"; chooses to subject this poet to a crowd that, realizing he is not Cinna the conspirator, nevertheless kills him because "his name's Cinna"; and chooses to suggest that Cinna's offstage fate will be dismemberment. In contrast, only one of the two accounts of "the murther of Cinna" in North's Plutarch describes the victim, in passing, as "a Poet." In this account, moreover, the crowd that kills Cinna genuinely confuses him with the conspirator, and tells us only that the plebeians "presently dispatched him" and "slue him outright."[17] In his first dramatic adaptation of a Plutarchan narrative the playwright thus freely alters his historical source.

Focusing on such authorial decisions, Gary Taylor has recently concluded the most extended discussion of Cinna's death with a judgment that would have pleased Gosson: "To tell the truth boldly, the more I think about Shakespeare's scene, the less I like it. It is wrong historically, it is wrong morally; it was wrong then, it is still wrong now."[18] Taylor does not, however, share Gosson's conception of the dramatist as an unabashed panderer to "the worst sort of people." Instead he indicts Shakespeare for both exaggerating the historical rabble's indiscriminate violence in this scene and depicting an apolitical poet's victimization at their hands, thereby creating a false opposition "between poet and plebeians, between poet and conspirator" (p. 338). The playwright, charges Taylor, creates a defense of poetry at the expense of truth. If we accept this argument, then Cinna's murder by the mob in 3.3 involves a program—a program extending to the camp poet's encounter with Cassius and Brutus in 4.3—whereby Shakespeare erects a false distinction between the poetic and political spheres. Far from a self-conscious exploration of the potential violence of the public theater, the scene appears on this reading a façade of false consciousness, a nefarious attempt to deny art's implication in the chaotic social world around it.

Is this the case? Taylor marshals strong evidence for his assertion that Shakespeare goes out of his way to enhance the fickleness of the rabble in this play. In North's Plutarch, for example, the funeral orations that precede Cinna's murder are separated by a day, and the crowd is constant in its disapproval of Caesar's assassination.[19] In Shakespeare's version, by contrast, the orations are juxtaposed, and "the popular voice" becomes a rhetorical barometer. Taylor also seems justified in arguing that the poets in this play conspicuously make nothing happen. Whereas in Plutarch it is a philosopher who intervenes in the quarrel between Brutus and Cassius, successfully reconciling them, in Shakespeare a poet enters after the reconciliation has already occurred, and his well-intended but untimely doggerel is subsequently ridiculed (4.2.187-91). But the distinction between the men of the word and the men of the world in *Julius Caesar* may not be as clear as this reading suggests. And if the nominal poets in this play seem to emphasize the division between art and politics, the politicians bridge this gulf in their representation as dramatists playing to an audience.

Taylor foists upon the author of *Julius Caesar* (1599) the conception of poetry expressed by the author of *Venus and Adonis* (1592-1593)—"a publicly intimate relationship between poet and patron" above history, ideology, and the *vulgus*.[20] A skeptic might object, of course, that intimacy is always a fictive pose for poets operating in a print culture, and that by submitting their words to fame's court such poets consciously (if surreptitiously) offer them as public property.[21] Whether or not this was Shakespeare's awareness when he composed his non-dramatic poetry for individual patrons, however, it must have become so in 1599, when a pirate divulged two of "his sugred Sonnets"—previously circulated only "among his priuate friends"—to the world.[22] Thus by 1599, if not before, there was irony, intentional or imposed, in the patronage poet's *occupatio*, as in Sonnet 102: "That love is merchandized whose rich esteeming / The owner's tongue doth publish everywhere." But the proto-romantic view of the poet Taylor ascribes to the author of *Julius Caesar* ignores more than the complex status of patronage poetry in the late sixteenth-century (and the significant body of recent criticism that has demonstrated this complexity).[23] It also ignores Shakespeare's awareness of the altogether different socioeconomic mise en scène that produced the play itself. Indeed, *Julius Caesar* dramatizes the irrelevance and obsolescence of the very mode of poetry Taylor accuses Shakespeare of perpetuating under false pretenses.

III

*"A strange-disposed time"*

Although *poet* remained both the popular and technical term for the playwright during Shakespeare's lifetime,[24] there are reasons both historical and textual to suppose that dramatists working in England's increasingly public theaters had occasion to reevaluate and revalue this term. As Elizabeth's court blurred the distinction between private courtship and public courtiership, so her elaborately theatricalized self-presentation erased the boundaries between stagecraft and statecraft. When political power can be dramatized, power itself devolves to a public where interpretive possibilities proliferate. On the Renaissance public stage, sovereign self-presentation is necessarily subjected to representation; the autonomous production of ideology (like selfhood) is rendered an object of the contingencies of reproduction. It was less theatrical self-assertion, therefore, than a complaint of theatrical vulnerability that underlay Elizabeth's remark to a deputation of Lords and Commons: "We princes are set upon stages in the sight and view of all the world."[25] Like Elizabeth, Hamlet realizes the danger of playing to the world. The collaborative social act of public theater, however, demands this economy, and Hamlet must finally submit to theatrical appropriation: "High on a stage . . . placed to the view"; reduced, like the court jester he has elegized, to a silent and portable synecdoche of the self; he becomes an erased mouth, a silence inviting spectators' glosses, the quietus ultimately required of the observed of all observers. For Hamlet and Elizabeth, the stage inexorably transforms the self into a passive spectacle fashioned for and by "the sight and view" of others.

In 1601 the Queen of England identified herself as the property of a public beyond her control: "I am Richard II. Know ye not that? . . . He that will forget God, will also forget his benefactors; this tragedy was played 40tie times in open streets and houses."[26] Stephen

Greenblatt has observed that Elizabeth responds here to the potential for iteration and indeterminacy[27] of a play construed after a subversive fashion, a play that seems to have broken the boundaries of its house and emerged into a world of limitless audience and multiple factions. To this we should add that her response is concomitant with a perceived disintegration of patronage assumptions ("He that will forget God, will also forget his benefactors"), and with her recognition that she has become a victim of other-fashioning. Whether referring to Shakespeare's play or to Hayward's tract, the anger and anxiety of Elizabeth's self-identification with Richard responds to the fact that it is an identification thrust upon her, an identification that threatens her identity. Like the commissioning viewer of an anamorphic painting, she looks to the story of Henry of Lancaster and Richard of Bordeaux for a familiar reflection of her self-image and finds instead—from another's perspective—a radically subversive alterity, a subrogated persona that troubles the semiotics of the whole composition.[28]

Two years before this dramatic alteration challenged Elizabeth's "Semper Eadem," the Chamberlain's Men had completed a metaphoric transition—from The Theatre, through The Curtain, to The Globe—[29] that seems appropriately responsive to a self-conscious shift, in England's public drama, from the aesthetically insulated to the politically fraught. It was on the Globe's stage, in 1599, that an actor playing the Chorus in *Henry V* anticipated a Caesar-like "general of our gracious Empress" returning triumphantly from Ireland (5.30-34); and it was earlier in this same year, many scholars agree, that *Julius Caesar* was first produced as the inaugural play in "this wooden O."[30] 1599, the year the "newly built" Globe became "the possession of William Shakespeare and others,"[31] would have been particularly unaccommodating for the vision of playwrighting "as a publicly intimate relationship between poet and patron." For the preceding year, the Privy Council responded to the annual letter of complaint from the Lord Mayor and the Court of Aldermen with a resolution that was unprecedented: it declared that all public playhouses were to be "plucked down" due to the "lewd matters that are handled on the stages" and the "very great disorders" resulting from the "resort and confluence of bad people." This order of the Privy Council (July 28, 1598), which might have given specific topical resonance to the antitheatrical and anticongregational Tribunes in the first scene of *Julius Caesar*, was of course never executed, but it marked the beginning of an intense period of legislation against London's public theaters. To gain "possession" of the Globe near the end of the sixteenth century was to enter a theater of contest in which private enterprise and state power were frequently at odds.

Indeed, the Globe itself was constructed of contested property. On December 28, 1598, James and Richard Burbage, together with a master carpenter and a dozen tradesmen, dismantled the deserted Theatre and transported its valuable timber to the Bankside, where it was erected as the new home of the Chamberlain's Men. Giles Allen, the increasingly antitheatrical landlord of the Theatre who had requested the departure of his thespian tenants earlier that year, seems to have desired to "convert the wood and timber thereof to some better use." In the subsequent lawsuit Allen's plaint is remarkable for its representation of the defendants as a mob run amok, threatening city and crown. The Burbages and their accessories, he charged,

> then and there armed themselves with divers and many unlawful and offensive weapons, as, namely, swords, daggers, bills, axes, and such like, and so armed did then repair unto the said Theatre. And then and there, armed as aforesaid, in very riotous, outrageous, and forcible manner, and contrary to the laws of your Highness' realm, attempted to pull down the said Theatre, whereupon divers of your subjects, servants, and farmers, then going about in peaceable manner to procure them to desist from that their unlawful enterprise, they (the said riotous persons aforesaid) notwithstanding procured then therein with great violence, not only then and there forcibly and riotously resisting your subjects, servants, and farmers, but also then and there pulling, breaking, and throwing down the said Theatre in very outrageous, violent, and riotous sort, to the great disturbance and terrifying not only of your subjects, said servants, and farmers, but of diverse others of your Majesty's loving subjects there near inhabiting.[32]

It is tempting to compare this riotous representation to the plebeians, "moved"—by Antony's promise of a new recreational park "On this side Tiber," fit for "common pleasures" (3.2.249-50)—to "Pluck down benches! Pluck down forms, windows, anything!" (3.2.258-59). Less conjecturally, we can observe that Allen's no doubt embellished account comes very near the energies that Shakespeare represents in the Globe's inaugural play. An intriguing insight into Shakespeare's complex response to this moment of artistic reassessment appears in Andrew Gurr's demonstration that, around the year 1600, he began to reconceive his customers as spectators rather than auditors.[33] Some of the epistemological and political implications of this transformation appear most clearly when we consider the altogether different response of a rival playwright to this same period of change.

For Ben Jonson, the recurrent metaphor of the "Poetomachia" is that of the trial or arraignment, so that the warring dramatists present, in Tibullus' phrase, competing "Law-cases in verse."[34] But Jonson's problem, even as he goes about defining the role of the socially relevant public poet, lies in determining that court in which he wishes to appeal his case. In *Poetaster* (1601), for instance, he legitimizes his ideal, politically and morally salutary poets (Horace and Vergil), by banishing the socially marginal (Ovid), and by purging the civically deleterious (Crispinus and Fannius). Jonson's poetic ideal proves less than efficacious on the public stage, however, where cases are tried not in Augustus' court, but by a corrupt jury. Jonson sends "An armed Prologue" to defend his play from rooms filled with "base detractors, and illiterate apes";[35] and in his "apologeticall Dialogue," addressing not a multitudinous spectatorship but an individual reader, he declares the world a "baud" and promises his next dramatic effort will seek a fit audience, however few: "Where, if I prove the pleasure but of one / So he judicious be; He shall b'alone / A Theatre unto me" (213-15). But in the public theater, such retreats into Stoic self-sufficiency are as impossible as imposing a fixed, textual meaning on a script intended for common consumption. In the Globe, to turn one's back on the world is inevitably to invite backstabbing. Thomas Dekker therefore prefaces his theatrical response to Jonson in terms perfectly pitched to elicit the latter's anxiety: "Horace hal'd his Poetasters to the barre, the Poetasters untruss'd Horace: how worthily eyther, or how wrongfully, (World) leave it to the jurie."[36] Before this jury, Dekker in *Satiro-Mastix* (1601) does with Horace much what the Essex party does with the story of Richard II in the same year: as a deposition scene appears subversive when placed in the contemporary political context, so does Horace look ridiculous when dropped "into the middle of a flamboyantly romantic tragi-comedy."[37] For Jonson, as for his Queen, the public theater submits one to an audience composed of *both* predatory rival playwrights and an injudicious tribunal.

Finding his case altered by 1603, then, Jonson replaces the Augustan court with the Tiberian to reflect the willful misreading and evidentiary misconstruction to which the public poet is vulnerable. In his dedicatory epistle to Lord Aubigny, he at once identifies *Sejanus'* reception with that of its dismembered "subject," and seeks to appeal the Globe's unjust verdict to a single patron: "It is a poem that—if I well remember—in your Lordship's sight, suffered no less violence from our people here than the subject of it did from the rage of the people of Rome, but with a different fate, as (I hope) merit."[38] Here, perhaps, is a case for Taylor's criticism of the dramatist disingenuously posing as an apolitical creature victimized by a world he claims the right to ignore, a playwright for whom "our people here" are indeed "vulgar interlopers" mangling the intimate artistic utterance of a play that has silently become "a poem."[39] For the Jonson of 1603, theatrical values ultimately prove corrosive to his conception of artistic integrity; the Globe, engaged in a bacchanalia of epistemological and evaluative indiscrimination, must either consume the Orphic poet or exile him to a private, meritocratic world elsewhere. What would later in Jonson's dramatic career become an effort to prevent this indiscrimination by seeking a poetic audience, not a theatrical spectatorship,[40] takes an early shape in his desire to place his literary evidence before homogeneous judges, not a heterogeneous jury. As late as 1611, in fact, he intermittently appeals to a higher evaluative court; his epistle to the Earl of Pembroke, published prefatorily to *Catiline,* reveals an attempt to convert drama into patronage poetry: "Now, it approcheth your censure cheerefully, and with the same assurance, that innocency would appeare before a magistrate." Like Milton after him, Jonson inhabits a "solitude" threatened by "evil tongues," a fragile kingdom of intentionality "with dangers compassed round," and he seeks to define his hermeneutically "fit audience" by insulating it from "the barbarous dissonance" of those inimical to his poetic meaning.

But this defiant, embattled stance must not be confused with Shakespeare's in the same period. If any Shakespearean dramatic text seems to invite such confusion, it is *Troilus and Cressida* (1601-03?), with its appended preface addressing an "eternal" reader in an ideal act of literary communication independent of history, the staling stage, and "the palmes of the vulger."[41] More substantially, however, the play represents a self-conscious departure from Jonson's conception of the theater poet; it may even be Shakespeare's fullest acknowledgment that the public playwright is not an innocent victim of the interpretive energies of a place such as The Globe.

*Troilus and Cressida*'s chiastic mock of *Poetaster*'s "armed Prologue," for instance, recognizes the permeability of authorial prophylactics against promiscuous interpretation. Rather than guarding his play from the audience's subjective misconstruction, Shakespeare's "prologue arm'd" (Prologue, 23) invites the audience to participate in this martial drama as autonomous, potentially combative judges: "Like or find fault, do as your pleasures are, / Now good or bad, 'tis but the chance of war" (30-31). If the preface contemptuously dismisses the clapper-clawing hands of the multitude, this prologue submits the play's reception to the multiple "pleasures" of a similarly arbitrary jury. And in his epilogue Pandarus suggests that all those who have participated in this sullying "performance" are not only infected by a venereal clap, but also equipped with a rapacious claw. The "traders in the flesh" (5.10.45) who fill "Pandar's hall" (47) figure a collaborative spectatorship that would hypocritically distance itself from the prurient and purveyant drama it has employed. In a rebuke that reminds us his name means nothing but "to go between," however, Pandarus refuses his customers such a voyeuristic withdrawal:

> O world, world, world! thus is the poor agent despis'd! O traders and bawds, how earnestly are you set a-work, and how ill requited! Why should

our endeavor be so lov'd and the performance so loath'd?

(36-39)

Pandarus' diction here, if not his sense, is that of the antitheatricalist excoriation of a Babylonian stage endeavoring to satisfy a devouring world—a pandering playwright vending his diseased images to an easily infected audience in the "market of bawdrie." His almost post-coital regret and eruptive self-aversion, in fact, seem to anticipate the contrition, as described in *A Refutation of the Apology for Actors,* of playgoers who "know the Histories before they see them acted [and] are very ashamed when they have heard what lyes the Players insert among them, and how greatly they deprave them."[42] Far from a defense of poetry, this epilogue incorporates the antitheatrical position in an unrepentant admission of dramatic guilt that finally indicts the audience as an accessory. To show, claims Pandarus, is to violate; to watch is to participate.

Such a conclusion is the caustic culmination of a play that metatheatrically considers its own role in the deflation and perversion of classical heroic characterology. The "strange fellow" whose argument Ulysses reiterates to lure Achilles to battle seems to articulate a benign version of this role when he claims that "[N]o man is the lord of any thing . . . Till he communicate his parts to others; / Nor doth he of himself know them for aught, / Till he behold them formed in th' applause / Where th' are extended" (3.3.115, 117-20). But James Calderwood's description of this communicative theory as involving "a generative intercourse between bearer and observer"[43] plays down Shakespeare's emphasis on the degenerative potentiality of such intercourse. In a drama that itself refracts the epics of Homer and Vergil through several different "recuyells" of the histories of Troy,[44] the fate of history and its subjects ultimately rests in the hands of the dramatist and his audience. Like Pandarus, the playwright can commodify the "parts" of historical subjects by assembling a textual pastiche for a predatory public; like Thersites, who is himself addressed as a "fragment,"[45] the playgoer can reduce all such representations to scabrous objects through dissective evaluation. The same hands that manufacture constitutive applause can serve as claws of misconstruction. By dramatizing such a transaction and transformation, *Troilus and Cressida* explores the darker possibilities of a theater that defines the dramatist not as a victim but as a conspirator. We can trace this exploration back to the Globe's inaugural play.

IV

*"Censuring Rome"*

*Julius Caesar* seems to know no other medium than the public stage, as critics have long demonstrated by pointing out its preference for the rhetorical mode over the lyrical, for public declamation and customary proverbs over private reflection and soliloquy.[46] As Brutus responds when asked if one can ever properly know one's self: "No, Cassius, for the eye sees not itself / But by reflection, by some other thing" (1.2.52-53). Frequently, this "other thing" proves to be the speculum of theater itself. In a marketplace reeking of the commoners' breath, Caesar is clapped and hissed for his political dumbshow "according as he pleas'd and displeas'd" his plebein audience, "as they use to do the players in the theatre" (1.3.259-61). Brutus urges his fellow conspirators to dissemble their purpose by bearing the staid countenance of "our Roman actors" (2.1.226). And Antony, the lover of plays who most successfully exploits political theater, drops a telling term as he urges Octavius to reevaluate Lepidus, the least consequential and most easily manipulated member of the triumvirate: "Do not talk of him / But as a property" (4.1.39-40). One of *Julius Caesar*'s central dramas is the appropriation of the private by the public, the denotation of "that within which passeth show" by "actions that a man might play," and the reduction of autonomous men to communicable parts and transferable stage properties. The play concedes the potential violence of this drama in the central, emblematic scene of Cinna's dismemberment. In *Julius Caesar*'s earlier consumption of its eponym, however, the play suggests that such physical violence can serve as a metaphor for the injury of theatrical other-fashioning.

Shakespeare's later Roman tragedies pluck out the heart of mystery with the ceremony of sacrifice and the savage coolness of an anatomy.[47] Cleopatra would prefer to be a "stark-nak'd" corpse rather than face her audience as a conscious property in the figurative dismemberment she imagines Octavius staging in his theatrical triumph, "pinion'd," "hoist," and displayed "to the shouting varlotry / Of censuring Rome." She ruins her mortal house unwilling to witness the "Mechanic slaves" who will expose Antony and herself "to the view," distorting their biographies through mannered theatricalism (5.2.49-62, 208-21). But while Cleopatra may resist theatrical appropriation by playing the Roman, the irony of this refuge is as inescapable as the theater that subsumes her. For the theater imagined in Shakespeare's Roman tragedies is populated by an intrusive public and exploitative actors; it tolerates no inscrutable inwardness, no self-sufficient independence from the theatrical economy; it sheds blood and breaks bodies to render the private public, to sacrifice individual subjectivity to theatrical viability and spectacle. Coriolanus may refuse to play to such a crowd, "turn[ing]" his "back" in a consummately antitheatrical gesture of introversion, standing instead "As if a man were author of himself," seeking to be "every man himself" and "not . . . other than one thing." But he is stabbed to death as the people shout "Tear him to pieces!"[48] And what is the public theater but the people? What are these people but Gosson's Hydra-like "monster"? As a proleptic and definitive answer to such questions, *Julius Caesar* digests its subject (who has proclaimed "always I am Caesar" [1.2.212] with the same self-consciousness, the same ironic untenability, and perhaps the same anxiety toward protean theatricality that underlies Elizabeth's *"Semper Eadem"*) early in the third act, when the conspirators decide that Caesar must die to be seen. Brutus tries and condemns his friend not for what he is, but for what he might be, for the undetermined and undisclosed subjunctive mood of his spirit:

> He would be crown'd
> How that might change his nature, there's the
>     question.
>                                             (2.1.12-13)
>
> . . . . .
>
> O that we then could come by Caesar's spirit,
> And not dismember Caesar! But, alas,
> Caesar must bleed for it!
>                                             (2.1.168-70)

Caesar must bleed because the conspiracy of *Caesar* can have no unscrutinized spirits. Caesar must bleed because the conspirators—no less than the plebeians who come to his funeral shouting "We will be satisfied! Let us be satisfied! (3.2.1)—wish to see his body opened before them like a text. Caesar must bleed for a theater whose liturgy is haruspication,[49] whose medium is synecdoche, and whose privileged jury is invariably comprised of multiple observers of a silenced object.

The constituents of this jury, however, proliferate wildly the moment the courtroom is confused with theater, the moment the accused is converted into evidentiary spectacle. A number of critics have demonstrated that Caesar's death coincides with his historicization and textualization.[50] His famous (*paene*) *ultima verba*, in fact, seem to function antithetically to the infamous anachronism that strikes in 2.1: as Sigurd Burckhardt has argued, the clock that punctuates the conspirators' plot resonates with the timelessness and interpretive indeterminacy of their action.[51] In an English stage-play, however, Caesar's marmoreal Latin appears to italicize the difference of history and its distance from the drama that relates it. Yet his last words are themselves the product of theatrical appropriation: although they live in the popular memory in Shakespeare's translation, they were originally delivered in Greek.[52] Caesar may die in his native tongue, but his speech is rendered alien by his maker. It is a fundamental irony of *Julius Caesar* that its most self-conscious presentation of the autonomous past of history proves inextricably bound to the eternal present of dramatic reenactment and reinterpretation.

While Caesar's blood is still warm, this metadramatic irony operates at the conspirators' expense as they celebrate the conclusion of their case and their authorship of a history play:

> *Cassius:*  Stoop then, and wash. How many
>     ages hence
> Shall this our lofty scene be acted over
> In states unborn and accents yet unknown.
>
> *Brutus:*  How many times shall Caesar bleed
>     in sport;
> That now on Pompey's basis lies along
> No worthier than the dust!
>                                             (3.1.111-16)

Cassius and Brutus assert the historical primacy of their action while anticipating the future stage history of this "lofty scene." They attempt to distinguish between a gory event and its aestheticized dramatization as "sport." But in *Julius Caesar* history is conceived a priori in theatrical terms, by actors who recognize its perspectival malleability. It is Brutus' presumed dramatic control over the action and evaluation of the history in which he participates that signals his hybris. Just as Brutus seeks to mold Caesar into a figure of deservingly punished *pleonexia*, for instance, so does he attempt to direct the roles of his fellow conspirators. Calling for Caius Ligarius, he prepares to convert a man with undetermined political allegiances into a character with an unambiguous part to play: "Send him but hither, and I'll fashion him" (2.1.220). And after assuming direction of an assassination rehearsed in "Pompey's Theatre" (1.3.152), Brutus insists on the conspirators' billing as sacrificers, not butchers, as purgers, not murderers. *Julius Caesar,* however, proves to be beyond Brutus' management; and his reversal from conspirator to conspired against coincides with the deposition of his self-presentation and an authorial usurpation of the play for which it was intended. Restaging the scene of tyrannicide around the property of Caesar's corpse, Antony in 3.2 assigns to the conspirators the very parts they had eschewed. Cassius and Brutus condemn themselves when they draw a false distinction between bloody history and bloodless drama, declaring the case closed while the jury is still out, and abandoning the public stage to Antony's constructions. Having reduced Caesar's body to a text with wounds that gape "like dumb mouths" (3.1.260), they forget the instability of this text. They fail to recognize that the ambiguous body of the condemned "may signify equally well the truth of the crime or the error of the judges, the goodness or evil of the criminal."[53] Thus, like their victim, the conspirators become objects of other-fashioning.

Shakespeare reveals his awareness that his own plotting of history is subject to the same interpretive energies it employs. Critics such as Taylor would deny this consciousness of contingency, reading Shakespeare's public drama as the literary "work" of an entrenched patronage poet rather than the "play" of an author willingly de-centered by the common theater.[54] An instructive corrective to this anachronism, however, appears in Samuel Johnson's editorial complaint:

> But of the works of Shakespeare the condition has been far different [from that of works published under the direct supervision of their authors]: he sold them, not to be printed, but to be played. They were immediately copied for the actors, and multiplied by transcript, vitiated by the blunders of the penmen, or changed by the affectation of the player; perhaps enlarged to introduce a jest, or mutilated to shorten the representation; and printed at last without the concurrence of the author, without the consent of the proprietor, from compilations made by chance or by stealth out of the separate parts written for the theatre.[55]

The original "condition" of Shakespeare's dramatic texts resembles Gosson's description of history adapted to the theater, a description that applies equally well to Caesar's body: "mutilated" as occasion demands; deconstructed into, and reconstituted from, the "separate parts" of different participatory perspectives; they exist less as intrinsic meaning than as material to be recreated in performance.

If this metaphor of a corporeal text subject to the unkindest cuts of all implies a distinction between victimhood and aggression, it is clear that Shakespeare identifies with the latter. To insist like a Jonsonian prologue upon a fixed, hermeneutically determined textualism is almost invariably to be a victim or a fool on Shakespeare's stage. Calling for a judgment consonant with his inflexible reading of a bond he has authored, Shylock becomes a victim of alternative interpretations; fashioning himself in a letter that seems to reflect the greatness of his own self-image, Malvolio becomes a "propertied" fool when he realizes his ridiculous part and cross-gartered fashion have been assigned by unseen witnesses.[56] Nobody's fool and never a self-proclaimed victim outside of the sonnets, Shakespeare recognizes the terms of the theatrical economy in which he operates. While the theater is open, no case is closed; when the jury is "the common eyes," a moment can transform plaintiff into defendant, text into pretext, the carefully wrought self into an appropriated other; when the price of admission buys the audience something as insubstantial as a play, the theater compensates by procuring all that it represents as the interpretive property of this audience.

There is evidence suggesting the special inevitability of this economy for the Renaissance author of *Julius Caesar*. By imagining "states unborn" and "accents yet unknown," Cassius prophesies the linguistic and cultural differences Shakespeare encounters as he recovers this "lofty scene" from history; simultaneously, then, this play looks back to an anterior future when the English state and language were "yet unknown" and forward to a present when those restaging the scene might have "Small Latine and Lesse Greek," a time when Cicero's linguistic inaccessibility to Casca might reflect Plutarch's to Shakespeare: it was Greek to both of them. But like the playwright's history, Cassius' prophecy is construed after a dramatic fashion: on a level we have already considered, this prophecy becomes for Shakespeare an opportunity for dramatic irony. We know what for Casca is tragically "unknown" and "unborn"—that the conspirators' "lofty scene" will be first "acted over" by Antony's accent, and that the play will conclude with the conspirators' deaths and the birth of the Second Triumvirate. From Shakespeare's literary and historical moment, however, the irony goes further. For by the end of the sixteenth century, Cassius' and Brutus' first performance had long been the stock of artists and the debated exemplum of moralists and political theorists, receiving different "accents" or evaluative emphases as monarchy and republic, tyrants and traitors, were viewed from different perspectives.[57] For a playwright capable of imagining an audience of "eyes not yet created,"[58] though, the shortest path to obsolescence and revisionary victimization is to deny the contingency of such emphasis upon the historical moment, to assume a unanimous and monological interpretive community, and to forget that his play is the property of the very history it represents—that his text (before the posthumous First Folio) has no status, only unforeseen "states." The political ambiguity of *Julius Caesar* is therefore the design of a survivor, not a victim. With Aufidius, Shakespeare acknowledges a truth fatally denied by Coriolanus: that in both history plays and history, "virtues / Lie in th' interpretation of the time" (4.7.49-50). Accordingly, if *Julius Caesar* has a central reference point, it is an audience at once constitutive and prone to metamorphosis.

The plebeians who comprise this audience, however, also embody the misconstructive jury, the bacchanalian rout, posited by the antitheatricalists in their indictment of the public stage as a courtroom travestied. In the central scene of Cinna's apprehension by this audience Shakespeare seems to concede many of the terms of the antitheatrical position as he looks critically at the economy in which he is implicated. This scene presents a mock treason trial, made disturbingly absurd by the fact that the accused withholds no interior allegiances to be revealed. If Caesar represented for the conspirators a mysterious "serpent's egg" of potentiality (2.1.32), Cinna discloses his innocence in direct, brief, wise, and true replies to his interrogators. The plebeians' response is to collapse the distinction between body and spirit that Brutus himself honored in the breach his dagger made; and the result is a savage farce, a brutal simplification of the theatrical appropriation that pervades the play.

As Cinna speaks his last vain words, he becomes what the plebeians wish him to be, a silent stage property to be fashioned as an insistent audience likes it:

> *Cinna:* I am not Cinna the conspirator.
> *4. Plebeian:* It is no matter, his name's Cinna. Pluck but his name out of his heart, and turn him going.
> *3. Plebeian:* Tear him, tear him!
> *Exeunt all the Plebeians dragging off Cinna.*
> (3.3.32-35).

We might follow Taylor's "Bardicide" in reading this passage as a self-conscious reference to Orpheus' dismemberment (pp. 334-38). But we must make a crucial distinction between Shakespeare's apparent allusion to the archetypal poet-victim here and the similarly oblique suggestion of Orpheus' fate we have seen in Jonson's dedication to *Sejanus*. Unlike Jonson, Shakespeare does not represent this figure—and the violence inflicted upon him by "the rage of the people of Rome"—in a moment of injured self-identification. Rather, Shakespeare seems to conjure the specter of Orpheus' *sparagmos* to demonstrate the fate of a *kind* of poet, a *kind* of voice, when subjected to the abattoir of public theater. Such a generic application, in fact, had precedent in the Renaissance: "the euhemeristic reading of the Orpheus myth as the displacement of Greek lyric poetry by Dionysiac ritual drama" might, for instance, have presented itself to the playwright in Golding's Ovid.[59] If Cinna serves as a figure for Orpheus, moreover, then we have in *Julius Caesar* an important early example of what Kenneth Gros Louis has described as a seventeenth-century poetic and iconographic development: the shift from representations of Orpheus triumphant to representations of Orpheus dismembered, reflecting an emergent skepticism toward poetry's ability to communicate clearly and to achieve its desired humanistic effects on its audience.[60] In the world of *Julius Caesar,* at any rate, to treat the nominal poets as Shakespeare's self-representations is to confuse the purpose of the play's conscious differentiation between victims and victimizers, between an obsolescent mode of poetic subjectivity and the drama that consumes it. Far from an insidious defense of drama's innocence and inconsequence, *Julius Caesar* enacts a farsighted, metatheatrical critique of the dramatist and his diverse clientele.

Cinna is no more Shakespeare than is the officious camp poet dismissed later in the play for his inutility and for his decidedly unheroic couplet:

> *Poet:* For shame, you generals! what do you mean?
> Love, and be friends, as two such men should be,
> For I have seen more years, I'm sure, than ye.
> *Cassius:* Ha, ha! how vildly does this cynic rhyme!

> *Brutus:* Get you hence, sirrah; saucy fellow, hence!
> *Cassius:* Bear with him, Brutus, 'tis his fashion.
> *Brutus:* I'll know his humor, when he knows his time.
> What should the wars do with these jigging fools?
> Companion, hence!
> (4.3.130-38)

Like Cinna, although by verbal rather than physical violence, this poet is removed from the stage because he is an anachronism, a "fashion" in the wrong place at the wrong time. Nearly ten years before *Julius Caesar* first appeared, Christopher Marlowe had introduced a revolutionary play with a prologue defining his theater in negative terms remarkably similar to Brutus':

> From jigging veins of rhyming mother wits,
> And such conceits as clownage keeps in pay,
> We'll lead you to the stately tent of war,
> Where you shall hear the Scythian Tamburlaine
> Threatening the world with his high astounding terms,
> And scourging kingdoms with his conquering sword.
> View but his picture in this tragic glass,
> And then applaud his fortunes as you please.[61]

For Shakespeare as for Marlowe, "the stately tent of war" offers little shelter for poets who do not know their time, exposing them instead to ridicule and to the ruinous energies of a theater that has overtaken them. For Shakespeare as for Marlowe, moreover, the "tragic glass" of this public theater confines mighty men in little room, represents historical figures through dramatic spectacle, and proffers this dramatized exterior to an uncertain reception. In such an economy, authorial intention can claim no more control over a text's consequences than Antony claims over the people he has "moved" through a carefully staged scene:

> Now let it work. Mischief, thou art afoot,
> Take thou what course thou wilt!
> (3.2.259-60)

In such an economy, a text's consequentiality consists in part of this predictability.

V

Significantly, every act of writing in *Julius Caesar* draws blood. In the broadsheets Cassius writes "in several hands," "wherein obscurely Caesar's ambition shall be glanced at" (1.2.316, 319-20); in the anonymous notes Cinna the conspirator throws in Brutus' way (1.3.145); and in the proscription list on which Antony damns lives with spots of ink (4.1.6), the injury textually inflicted seems to correspond with the author's intention. And yet the conspirators, as we have seen, involuntarily involve themselves in their own plot the moment they script it and declare it finished. Antony in turn loses sole authorship of his counterplot as it becomes the collaborative product of the other triumvirs. Having judged the proscription list complete, he is forced by Octavius to add the name of Lepidus' brother, a revision Lepidus makes contingent upon the inclusion of Antony's nephew. Similarly, once a text is composed in this play, it is subject to politicized readings beyond the author's control, and of this pervasive process the poet's death once again provides a central, emblematic image. Culminating a scene in which he amplifies the plebeians' outrage by gradually undressing Caesar's torn corpse, Antony publicly reads the dead man's will as a last incitement to riot (3.2.240-52). Just two scenes later, however, Caesar's will is figuratively dismembered as Antony determines "How to cut off some charge in legacies" (4.1.9). The intervening scene of Cinna's murder presents the literal dismemberment of an author whose will counts for nothing and whose audience chooses to misread him. In this scene Shakespeare schematizes the fate of all communication in the play. When the audience is both mobile and prone to action, when spectators become collaborators, when the jury arrogates the dual privilege of constituting meaning and executing its sentence, a speech-act's illocutionary intention dissolves into its perlocutionary effect. From the vantage point of 1601, such an awareness can only appear prophetic, for two years earlier Shakespeare claims for his drama the dangerous power to bestow an Exton on the world to make many Extons.[62]

But what justification have we for treating *Julius Caesar*'s plebeians as an unflattering, unmitigated representation of the Globe audience's potential? To what extent is Shakespeare's metadramatic antitheatricalism contained by Rome and the play that concerns it? A limited answer lies in recognizing the diachronic transformation of the crowd in *Julius Caesar*. The plebeians who make their final exit bearing Cinna at the end of Act 3 first took the stage preparing for Caesar's triumph at the beginning of Act 1, and we must include the facts of this metamorphosis in our assessment of Shakespeare's representation of the audience in this play. Instead of a pack of marauding plebeians pursuing a poet, we find in 1.1 "certain commoners" (*s.d.*) set upon by inquisitorial tribunes; instead of an indistinct rabble seeking blood we find a remarkably individuated cobbler able to pun with the best of Shakespeare's English tradesmen. The line distinguishing sixteenth-century England and ancient Rome in *Julius Caesar* is never more blurred than in this scene. The Tribunes alternately seem like London aldermen policing sumptuary laws and Puritan antitheatricalists censuring the license, social confusion, and spectacle of the public theater: Flavius and Murellus chastise the keepers of this shoemaker's holiday for doffing "the sign" of their profession and donning their "best attire" (4, 48); and having dispersed the crowd, they set out to "Disrobe the images" decked with Caesar's "ceremonies" (64-65). The "certain Commoners" who cross the stage in 1.1 would appear to have no more objectionable motive than the desire for spectacle, the wish "to see Caesar and rejoice in his triumph" (31). And yet the Tribunes' antitheatrical anxiety in this scene is justified (and, significantly, left unchallenged by a play that does not make them the conventional object of protheatrical satire). Not only do the masquerading commoners range about the liberties dislocated from their social station; they are also interpretive individuals, each capable of construing the meaning of words after his fashion, as the cobbler's relentless punning reveals. When the vulgar can divest themselves of their social signifiers, when the vernacular can be invested with paronomasial significance, the theatrical audience acquires interpretive agency and the theater itself thereby becomes epistemologically open-ended and politically consequential. In 1.1 the plebeians enter as political innocents, and Murellus reproves them for failing to realize that the triumph they yearn to watch "comes . . . over Pompey's blood" (51). In 3.3 the plebeians exit bloodied with the experience of political theater, having demonstrated that to watch in this play is also to act. While in 1.1 they observe a social carnival, in 3.3 they effect political carnage. In 1.1, the cobbler's playfulness with language, his witty misreading of the Tribunes' sense, appears innocuous, whereas in 3.3, the fourth plebeian's wordplay is fatal, his misreading of Cinna a literal pun that tears name from thing. In 1.1, finally, Shakespeare's audience might have recognized itself in the protheatrical image of a harmless, recreational spectatorship; in 3.3 this audience would have seen itself transformed into (or revealed as?) the misconstruing miscreation that elicited Roman theatrical censorship.

Such is the plebeians' metamorphosis from "stones" (1.1.36) to "men" (3.2.142),[63] from theatrical naïfs to initiates in the political theater. Like all metamorphoses, it involves less a break than a continuum: the difference between culling out a holiday and killing a man depends only on the degree of the spectators' participation. And like many initiations, it involves a ceremonial rite. If Caesar dies at the hands of republican fellow players unwilling to cede the theater to a single monarchical actor, Cinna dies as a sacrifice to an audience that has taken the stage. It may seem strange for Shakespeare to inaugurate his Globe in these terms, to baptize his audience with the blood of a poet, to figure its interpretive autonomy in a literal act of dismemberment. But dismemberment is his metaphor when, less than a year after *Julius Caesar*'s first performance, he invokes his audience's imaginative collaboration in *Henry V:* "Piece out our imperfections with your thoughts; / Into a thousand parts divide one man" (Prol. 24-25). In the theater of the world every character is subject to synecdochic reading, every act and representation imperfect and unfinished, every text submitted to the cutting room, the deceptively "little room" where spectators, no less than actors, conspire to "force a play." It is as an emblem of this theater's censurable energies and properties that Cinna is dragged offstage.[64]

## Notes

[1] Rowland Whyte, describing the interpretive frenzy provoked by a device displayed by Essex at an entertainment for the Queen in 1595, in *Letters and Memorials of State . . . Written and Collected by Sir Henry Sidney, Sir Philip Sidney, Robert Earl of Leicester, and Viscount Lisle,* ed. Arthur Collins (1746), I:362.

[2] Stephen Gosson, *Playes Confuted in Five Actions* (1582), sig. C8v. All references to Gosson's works in this essay appear in Arthur F. Kinney's edition (*Markets of Bawdrie: The Dramatic Criticism of Stephen Gosson* [Salzburg, 1974]). I have modernized the spelling but retained the punctuation of this edition. Unless otherwise noted, all references to Gosson appear in *Playes Confuted in Five Actions*.

[3] Thomas Heywood, *An Apology for Actors,* ed. Arthur Freeman (New York and London, 1973), sig. B4.

[4] Philip Sidney, *An Apology for Poetry,* in *Prose Works,* ed. Albert Feuillerat (Cambridge, Eng., 1963), p. 12 (my italics).

[5] *An Apology for Poetry,* p. 24.

[6] See *Playes Confuted in Five Actions,* p. 161.

[7] Gosson specifically objected to the recent arrival of the public stage, noting that even "modest" and "good" plays are "not fit for every man's diet: neither ought they commonly to be shown" (*The Schoole of Abuse,* p. 97).

[8] A (now besieged) formulation of Michel Foucault's subversion-containment model appearing most influentially in Stephen Greenblatt's *Shakespearean Negotiations: The Circulation of Social Energy in Renaissance England* (Berkeley, 1988), esp. pp. 21-65.

[9] For an excellent discussion of the state's attempts to control topical references on the Renaissance stage, see Paul Yachnin, "The Powerless Theater," *English Literary Renaissance,* 21.1 (Winter, 1991), 49-74.

[10] *The Life of Henry the Fifth,* Pro., 12, 19-20. References are to *The Riverside Shakespeare,* gen. ed. G. Blakemore Evans (Boston, 1974).

[11] *An Apology for Poetry,* p. 45.

[12] See Marjorie Garber, "'What's Past Is Prologue': Temporality and Prophecy in Shakespeare's History Plays," in *Renaissance Genres,* ed. Barbara Kiefer Lewalski (Cambridge, 1986), pp. 301-31. See also Sharon L. Jansen Jaech, "Political Prophecy and Macbeth's 'Sweet Bodements,'" *Shakespeare Quarterly,* 34 (1983), esp. p. 291.

[13] *Shakespeare's Holinshed,* ed. Richard Hosley (New York, 1968), p. 48 (*Chronicles,* 1587 ed., p. 180).

[14] Francis Bacon, "Of Prophecies," in *Essays,* ed. Edwin A. Abbott, 2 vols. (London, 1881), 2:20-21.

[15] Following Garber (p. 311, *n.* 15), I borrow this term from Hayden White's *Metahistory* (Baltimore, 1973), pp. 6-7.

[16] *An Apology for Poetry,* p. 68. Plutarch himself refused the title of "historian," choosing instead to relate and *evaluate* the "lives" and "minds" of his subjects.

[17] Plutarch's *Liues of the Noble Grecians and Romans,* trans. Sir Thomas North (1579), intro. George Wyndham, 6 vols. (New York, 1967), 6:69-70, 201.

[18] Gary Taylor, "Bardicide," in *Shakespeare and Cultural Traditions: The Selected Proceedings of the International Shakespeare Association World Congress, Tokyo, 1991,* ed. Tetsuo Kishi, Roger Pringle, and Stanley Wells (Newark, Del., 1991), p. 343. We must dismiss as specious Taylor's assertion that the scene also presents "a theatrically impossible dismemberment" (p. 334). The stage directions indicate Cinna is to be dragged offstage for his fate. Moreover, false limbs for such scenes appear in the few extant lists of Elizabethan stage properties, and the illusion of onstage dismemberment seems not to have been impossible in such plays as *Doctor Faustus* and *Titus Andronicus* (see Philip Henslowe's inventory of March, 1598, in C. Walter Hodges, *The Globe Restored* [New York, 1953], pp. 71-72. On pp. 73-74, Hodges demonstrates Elizabethan "stage machinery to produce the illusion of a beheading").

[19] See North's Plutarch, 6:15. In *The Life of Brutus* no mention is made of Brutus' oration; in *The Life of Caesar* no mention made of Antony's.

[20] Such is at least the ostensible authorial stance in *Venus and Adonis,* the epigram of which exhorts, *"Vilia miretur vulgus: mihi flavus Apollo / Pocula Castalia plena ministret aqua"* (from Ovid's *Amores,* 1.15.35-36). The subsequent dedicatory epistle to Henry Wriothesley also distinguishes between the unimportant censure of "the world" and the all-important pleasure of Shakespeare's patron.

[21] Arthur F. Marotti remains one of the more vocal proponents of this view. See his "Patronage, Poetry, and Print," *Yearbook of English Studies,* 21 (1991), pp. 1-26; and his "Shakespeare's Sonnets as Literary Property," in *Soliciting Interpretation: Literary Theory and Seventeenth-Century English Poetry,* ed. Elizabeth D. Harvey and Katharine Eisaman Maus (Chicago, 1990), pp. 143-73.

[22] Francis Meres, *Palladis Tamia, Wits Treasury* (1598), ed. D. C. Allen (Urbana, 1933), p. 283. William Jaggard printed the two sonnets (138 and 144) in *The Passionate Pilgrim* (1599).

[23] In "The Politics of *Astrophil and Stella,*" Ann Rosalind Jones and Peter Stallybrass reveal that the distinction between literary courtship and public courtiership was often blurred in late sixteenth-century England's "publicly intimate" poetry (*Studies in English Literature,* 24.1 [Winter, 1984], 53-68). For further demonstrations of the difficulty of maintaining privacy in the Elizabethan and Jacobean patronage systems, see Annabel M. Patterson, *Censorship and Interpretation: the Conditions of Writing and Reading in Early Modern England* (Madison, 1984); and David Norbrook, *Poetry and Politics in the English Renaissance* (London and Boston, 1984), esp. pp. 109-56, 195-234.

[24] Taylor observes this fact only to conflate what I am suggesting are the increasingly divergent roles of the patronage poet and the "theatre-poet" in late sixteenth-century England ("Bardicide," p. 345 *n.*8).

[25] Quoted in J. E. Neale, *Elizabeth I and her Parliaments, 1584-1601,* 2 vols. (London, 1965), 2:119.

[26] The Queen's comments were recorded by William Lambarde. See the Arden edition of Shakespeare's *King Richard II,* ed. Peter Ure (Cambridge, 1956), pp. lvii-lxii.

[27] *The Power of Forms in the English Renaissance,* ed. Stephen Greenblatt (Norman, Ok., 1982), p. 3.

[28] In one of the best recent readings of Hans Holbein's *The Ambassadors,* Charles Harrison describes its anamorphic effect as an intrusion of historicity upon essentiality: "the carefully achieved illusion of its instantaneity, its 'presentness,' damaged beyond repair by the representation of its contingency" ("On the Surface of Painting," *Critical Inquiry,* 15:2 [Winter, 1989], 324).

[29] Between 1597 and 1599 the Chamberlain's Men probably performed at The Curtain while The Theatre at Shoreditch was being razed and its timber used to build The Globe at Bankside. See Glynne Wickham, *Early English Stages, 1300-1660,* 2 vols. (Oxford 1972).

[30] See Gary Taylor, "Canon and Chronology," in *William Shakespeare: A Textual Companion* (Oxford, 1987), p. 121; and *Julius Caesar,* in *The New Cambridge Shakespeare,* ed. Marvin Spevack (Cambridge, Eng., 1988), pp. 1-5.

[31] From the postmortem inventory of Sir Thomas Brend (May 16, 1599). Cited by S. Schoenbaum, *Shakespeare: A Compact Documentary Life* (Oxford, 1977), p. 209.

[32] This and the preceding quotation of Allen appear in C. W. Wallace, *The First London Theatre: Materials for a History* (Lincoln, 1913), pp. 278-79.

[33] Andrew Gurr, *Playgoing in Shakespeare's London* (Cambridge, Eng., 1987), p. 93.

[34] *Poetaster,* 1.3.7. Citations are to *Ben Jonson,* ed. C. H. Herford, Percy and Evelyn Simpson, 11 vols. (Oxford, 1925-1952).

[35] *Poetaster,* "The Third Sounding," 6, 9. Like other playwrights in the War of the Theaters, Jonson imagines an audience that includes antagonistic playwrights and actors bent upon adulterating his text (see "The Third Sounding," 18-20, and Envy's speech, "After the Second Sounding"). John Michael Archer has shown that "the paranoid construction of Jonsonian authorship" was also a response to his fear of spies among his own actors and audience (*Sovereignty and Intelligence: Spying and Court Culture in the English Renaissance* [Stanford, 1993], pp. 94-120). One effect of the theatrical war, then, is to literalize the subjective and deliberately misconstruing audience—the audience-turned-actors—that I argue is a source of concern in *Julius Caesar.*

[36] Thomas Dekker, *Satiro-Mastix,* ed. Josiah H. Penniman (Boston and London, 1962), "To the World," 15-17.

[37] Katharine Maus, *Ben Jonson and The Roman Frame of Mind* (Princeton, 1984), p. 92.

[38] Jonson, "To The No Less Noble, By Virtue Than Blood: Esme, Lord Aubigny," 7-10.

[39] *Sejanus* provides many targets for Taylor's program of exposure. The indictment of Cremutius Cordus in Act 3, for instance, presents an untenable claim for the disinterestedness of historiography, a disingenuous denial of contemporary relevance, in a history play judged treasonously topical by the Privy Council in 1603.

[40] For Jonson's fully articulated desire for a "blind audience," see the Prologue to *The Staple of News.* For a discussion of the antagonism between spectacle and word that developed with some continuity throughout

Jonson's career, see D. J. Gordon, "Poet and Architect: The Intellectual Setting of the Quarrel Between Ben Jonson and Inigo Jones," in *The Renaissance Imagination,* ed. Stephen Orgel (Berkeley 1975), pp. 77-101.

[41] Just as the play's genre is an early topic of debate, so its earliest stage history is contested by the 1609 preface, which advertises *Troilus and Cressida* as "a new play, neuer stal'd with the stage, neuer clapper-clawd with the palmes of the vulger"; by the Stationers' Register, which records its existence in February, 1603; and by the quarto title-page (first state), which advertises the play "As it was acted by the Kings Maiesties seruants at the Globe."

[42] *A Refutation of the Apology for Actors,* by I.G. (1605). Quoted in Herschel Baker, *The Race of Time: Three Lectures on Renaissance Historiography* (Toronto, 1967), p. 80. For similar statements, see *The Schoole of Abuse,* pp. 92-93, and *Playes Confuted in Five Actions,* pp. 194-95.

[43] James L. Calderwood, *Shakespearean Metadrama* (Minneapolis, 1971), p. 136. See also his "Appalling Property in *Othello,*" *University of Toronto Quarterly,* 57:3 (Spring, 1988), 357.

[44] William Caxton's *Recuyell of the Histories of Troye* was just one of Shakespeare's available sources. See also Geoffrey Bullough, *Narrative and Dramatic Sources of Shakespeare* (London, 1966), 6:83-111.

[45] Carol Cook considers this same issue, though from a Lacanian perspective, in "Unbodied Figures of Desire," *Theatre Journal,* 38 (March, 1986), 44-46.

[46] See esp. Paul Cantor, *Shakespeare's Rome: Republic and Empire* (Ithaca, 1974), pp. 108-10.

[47] A similar claim has been made for the earlier *Titus Andronicus* (1593-1594), in which rape and dismemberment render Lavinia's body an annotated text, a silent emblem submitted to others' reconstructive reading. See Douglas E. Green, "Interpreting 'her martyr'd signs': Gender and Tragedy in *Titus Andronicus,*" *Shakespeare Quarterly,* 40 (1989), 317-26.

[48] *Coriolanus,* 3.3.134; 5.3.36; 4.7.42; 5.6.120; 5.2.65-66. Earlier Coriolanus seems to recognize that it is death that submits one to other-fashioning, life that grants the temporary privilege of maintaining one's self-conception: "While I remain above the ground you shall / Hear from me still, and never of me aught / But what is like me formerly" (4.1.51-53).

[49] David Kaula has found a pattern of eucharistic allusions in the ritual attending Caesar's murder in "'Let Us Be Sacrificers': Religious Motifs in *Julius Caesar,*" *Shakespeare Studies,* 14 (1981), 197-214.

[50] See Mark Rose, "Conjuring Caesar: Ceremony, History, and Authority in 1599," in *True Rites and Maimed Rites: Ritual and Anti-Ritual in Shakespeare and His Age,* ed. Linda Woodbridge and Edward Berry (Urbana and Chicago, 1992), p. 264.

[51] Sigurd Burckhardt, *Shakespearean Meanings* (Princeton, 1968), pp. 3-21.

[52] See Richard Macksey, "Last Words: The *Artes Moriendi* and a Transtextual Genre," *Genre,* 16 (Winter, 1983), 508. *"Et tu Brute?"* appears to have been a not uncommon theatrical tag before Shakespeare's play, and in *Every Man Out Of His Humour* (5.6.79) Jonson would parody it as a cliché.

[53] Michel Foucault, *Discipline and Punish: The Birth of the Prison,* trans. Alan Sheridan (New York, 1979), p. 46.

[54] See Alvin Kernan's *Shakespeare, The King's Playwright in the Stuart Court, 1603-1613* (New Haven, 1995). While Kernan demonstrates aspects of the patronage system in Shakespeare's Stuart drama, his case seems to me overstated and to ignore some of the performative issues considered here.

[55] Samuel Johnson, *Johnson on Shakespeare,* in *The Yale Edition of the Works of Samuel Johnson,* ed. Arthur Sherbo (New Haven, 1968), 7:51-52. Alexander Pope also speaks of Shakespeare's original manuscripts being "cut" and "divided" into the *"Piecemeal Parts"* of the *"Prompter's Book"* ("Preface to 'The Works of Shakespear,'" in *Eighteenth-Century Essays on Shakespeare,* ed. D. Nichol Smith [Oxford, 1963], p. 54).

[56] See *Twelfth Night,* 4.2.89. Like Shylock, Malvolio leaves his play less assimilated than "propertied" by the comedy's reestablished social order. Such coercion certainly appears elsewhere in Shakespeare's comedies and romances; but the appropriation of individuals as stage spectacle—as James Calderwood has argued—is essentially a tragic device, a problematic ethos that comedy and romance must finally transcend or absorb. See his "Appalling Property in *Othello,*" pp. 353-75.

[57] One need only consider the different assessments of Caesar's death in Plutarch, Appian, Dante, Michelangelo, Fulbecke, Sidney, and Milton for a sense of its interpretive possibilities. For a history of political interpretations of *Julius Caesar,* see John Ripley, *"Julius Caesar" on Stage in England and America, 1599-1973* (Cambridge, Eng., 1980).

[58] Sonnet 81, line 10. In the case of *Julius Caesar,* Shakespeare's prophecy of literary survival was especially appropriate: the committee established to erect his monument in Westminster Abbey initiated this

canonization with a commissioned performance of the play at Drury Lane, April 28, 1738 (see David Piper, *The Image of the Poet: British Poets and their Portraits* [Oxford, 1982], pp. 78-82).

[59] James Calderwood comes very close to ascribing such a reading to Shakespeare elsewhere, arguing that in *Titus Andronicus* Shakespeare explores a tension between lyric and dramatic genres suggested in the eleventh book of Golding's Ovid (*Shakespearean Metadrama,* pp. 28-30).

[60] Kenneth R. R. Gros Louis, "The Triumph and Death of Orpheus in the English Renaissance," *Studies in English Literature,* 9.1 (Winter, 1969), 63-80. Elizabeth Sewell has claimed that Shakespeare "trusts poetry, if Orpheus is undivided, if poetry and dreams and shadows and the theater are taken as a means toward learning and even toward science." See *The Orphic Voice: Poetry and Natural History* (New Haven, 1960), p. 110.

[61] *Tamburlaine the Great, Part I* (Prologue, 1-8), in *The Complete Works of Christopher Marlowe,* ed. Roma Gill (Oxford, 1987).

[62] In his reading of *Richard II* as a dramatization of "the interpretive efforts of the listener," Keir Elam considers Sir Pierce of Exton's construction of Bolingbroke's ambiguous utterance (5.4.1-2, 7-9) as the nexus between an undetermined illocutionary speech-act and perlocutionary action (*The Semiotics of Theatre and Drama* [London and New York, 1980], pp. 164-65).

[63] The plebeians' transformation from passive spectators to furious actors seems to evoke Ovid's account of the death of Orpheus (though, it should be noted, without tidy correspondence). Murellus calls them "blocks," "stones," "worse than senseless things" for their unreflective devotion to Caesar (1.1.34). In Ovid's account, Orpheus draws the trees, beasts, and stones to follow him, but these same stones become involuntarily "reddened with the blood of the singer" only when the Maenads hurl them at the poet (*Ovid's Metamorphoses,* trans. Rolfe Humphries [Bloomington, 1955], p. 259). Antony seems to contrast the plebeians to such passivity, however, when he declares in his funeral oration, "You are not wood, you are not stones" (3.2.142). Here the semi-autonomous plebeians resemble the bloodthirsty Maenads rather than their inanimate instruments. Nor does *Julius Caesar* clearly designate one particular character as a figure of Orpheus' victimization. The ominous "bird of night" that sits "Even at noon-day upon the market-place / Howting and shrieking" (1.3.26-28), for instance, may recall Ovid's description of the Maenads' attack on Orpheus: "they came thronging / Like birds who see an owl, wandering in daylight" (p. 260); thus the owl in 1.3 may represent an Orphic Caesar, soon to be set upon by the Furious conspirators. But if the conspirators are likened to the Maenads here, then reading the plebeians as "stones" turned against the conspirators by Antony's oration, or as Maenads themselves in the dismemberment of Cinna the poet, seems dubious. Nevertheless, both Caesar and Cinna die like Orpheus, "who stretched out / His hands in supplication, and whose voice / For the first time, moved no one" (p. 260). I would argue that Shakespeare's allusions to the death of Orpheus are in fact overdetermined in *Julius Caesar,* and that this reflects the play's bifurcation of the tragic victim (Orpheus) into Caesar and Brutus. This bifurcation pivots on the death of Cinna. Thus Antony, the conspirators, and the plebeians are described with reference to the Maenads.

[64] A version of this paper was presented at the 1996 International Shakespeare Association World Congress. I am grateful to Gordon Braden, Paul Cantor, James Nohrnberg, Herbert Tucker, and especially Katharine Maus for their help.

Source: "*Julius Caesar* and the Properties of Shakespeare's Globe," in *English Literary Renaissance,* Vol. 28, No. 1, Winter, 1998, pp. 18-46.

# Framing Ophelia: Representation and the Pictorial Tradition

## Kaara Peterson

In her far-ranging study *Over Her Dead Body: Death, Femininity and the Aesthetic,* Elisabeth Bronfen elucidates Western culture's fascination with depictions of dead, beautiful women in literature and the visual arts respectively, concluding that because such images are so omnipresent we are scarcely aware of their status as a resolute cultural tradition. Likening portraits of dead women to Poe's famous purloined letter—so numerous as to be invisible to the viewer's eye—Bronfen elaborates the aesthetic association between women and death, quoting Poe's notorious statement, "the death of a beautiful woman is, unquestionably, the most poetical topic in the world." Bronfen's study, of course, is part of a general concern these days with the implications of "representation," and her discussion can also be situated in the larger context of current interarts debates about whether traditions in one aesthetic mode affect and should be studied in conjunction with each other, or whether such approaches end up as a kind of ecphrastic iconology, wherein the verbal invariably becomes the interpreter of the visual.

Insofar as Ophelia is arguably Shakespeare's most recognizable female character, with a long and significant history of "purloining" in both verbal and visual media, she would seem to be an excellent focus for discussions of this kind. And indeed she is, albeit ironically so, for just as Bronfen's examples of dead women tend to remain distinct—generically categorizable as literary or visual bodies, either/or—so literary analysis rarely seeks to consider the ever-present visual interpretations and popular imaginings of Ophelia's character, and equally in discussing her representations art historians regularly prefer to concentrate on aspects of formal composition rather than explore her origins within the Shakespeare text. At the same time, in the case of Ophelia, we have an instance of a character whose portrait has been painted with such consistency that she has become something of a visual cliché, whereby the "typical" Ophelia of the plastic arts has so imprinted itself on our imaginations that we tend either to ignore how her death is reported in *Hamlet* or we tend to augment the text to include a drowning scene, which literalizes into a "seen," appearing in our mind's eye as we read.

My purpose in this essay is to bring together these previously disparate methodologies that split Ophelia's body up between disciplines. In addressing Shakespeare's character in this manner, however, I do not seek to establish an unequivocal "body" of work in which we can locate the "true" Ophelia, for my direction here will point out the reverse, that Ophelia is always elusive despite the fact that she is so "present" in artworks. She is an elusive figure because such artworks regularly take as their subject a literary fragment from *Hamlet* reporting Ophelia's death, a fragment in which it is doubly impossible for Ophelia's body to be present. The method I adopt is partially paradoxical, for I wish to unearth the "literary" body of Ophelia present in different visual representations at the same time that I want to utilize these same media to suggest the degree to which they have formed our understanding of the dramatic textual character.

In order to position Ophelia's dual representational history more precisely within both art-historical and dramatic-critical frameworks, I start by tracing the history of painted Ophelias as they first appear typically in the 18th century. My discussion of Gertrude's narrative of Ophelia's drowning next establishes the crucial context for understanding the important innovations of Arthur Hughes's 19th-century painting which I examine at length before returning to complete my catalogue of other important but more general examples of visual media from the 19th and 20th centuries; thus, I locate my literary investigation into Ophelia's origins in Shakespeare between visual arts contexts purposefully, hoping to elucidate Ophelia's extraordinary connection to both genres. In the final sections, I consider the broader implications of Ophelia's dual representational life for aspects of popular culture.

Prior to the mid-19th century, painted depictions of Shakespeare's Ophelia differ significantly from the image of the drowning, pathos-inspiring figure that typically haunts our imaginations today. When 18th-century illustrators of Shakespeare—e.g., Francis Hayman, Benjamin West, George Romney, and Nicholas Rowe—chose to depict Ophelia at all, they usually placed her in a larger, group context where her presence is not highlighted as a focal point. For example, as John Harvey has discussed with respect to two mid-18th-century plates of Hayman's *Mousetrap* scene, in these works other characters are the primary focus (5-6). West's *Ophelia* (1792) from the Boydell Shakespeare Gallery exhibition features her prominently in the mad scene, but with Laertes shown dismayed by her distributing flowers to the other characters. As William L. Pressly notes with respect to his collection of plates of paintings held by the Folger Library, "depictions of Ophelia did not become popular until the late eighteenth century" (49). The earliest exception to the presentation of Ophelia in a group context would seem to be Richard Westall's Boydell Gallery engraving (c. 1789) of an apprehensive-looking Ophelia heading with trepidation to the water's edge. Westall's engraving rapidly begins to look as though it could be the model for all future works, for as Pressly notes: "the episode most frequently chosen by artists [is] the moment just before Ophelia plunges to a watery death. Ophelia is typically shown adorned with flowers . . . loose tresses are also typical of Ophelia iconography" (50). However, rarely is she presented alone until the next century, when "character criticism" is on the rise in literary circles and when, more generally, Shakespeare reigns supreme in Romantic-era imaginations, as Jonathan Bate has noted.

It is to the mid-19th century that we must look for a substantial increase in the number of Ophelia-specific depictions: "Ophelia was the single most popular literary subject for artists, with more than fifty portrayals recorded in exhibition catalogues" (Pressly 49). Here the focus is regularly centered upon Ophelia, presented as a single subject, and usually in her drowning scene. As though we have been trained precisely by Poe to regard the death of a beautiful woman as a primarily aesthetic experience, we have come to expect seeing this scene if a painting bears the title "Ophelia." Ophelia's about-to-be-submerged or partially submerged body begins to seem clichéd, appearing most recently in the visual media in the form of director Kenneth Branagh's *Hamlet* (1997) as a flashback addendum to Gertrude's report. So where are we first persuaded that we "see" her drown?

> Queen: There is a willow grows askant the brook
> That shows his hoary leaves in the glassy stream.
> Therewith fantastic garlands did she make
> Of crow-flowers, nettles, daisies, and long purples,
> That liberal shepherds give a grosser name,
> But our cold maids do dead men's fingers call them.
> There on the pendent boughs her crownet weeds
> Clamb'ring to hang, an envious sliver broke,
> When down her weedy trophies and herself
> fell in the weeping brook. Her clothes spread wide,
> And mermaid-like awhile they bore her up,
> Which time she chanted snatches of old lauds,
> As one incapable of her own distress,
> Or like a creature native and indued
> Unto that element. But long it could not be
> Till that her garments, heavy with their drink,
> Pull'd the poor wretch from her melodious lay
> To muddy death.
>
> (4.7.165-82)

Gertrude's recital to the court of the events surrounding Ophelia's death is the only "evidence" we are given as the explanation for her drowning. While it is not new to observe that Gertrude cannot have been present during the drowning and thus reports what she has been told by someone else, it is significant to note that with the exception of Martha C. Ronk and Bridget Gellert Lyons, critics have neglected the import of this basic observation and glossed over the oddity of the aestheticized tone of the recital, choosing largely instead to fall in line with Harold Jenkins's opinion that Gertrude's "account of it, reaching chorus-like beyond the dialogue, the play expects us to accept" (546). I would argue, however, that rather than "expecting us to accept" the evidence, Shakespeare highlights its aestheticized quality. This passage is similar to the treatment of Lavinia in *Titus Andronicus,* where Shakespeare has Marcus use incongruous Petrarchan love poetry when he paradoxically and grotesquely praises her mutilated body.

Clearly, Shakespeare is not afraid to show his audience the on-stage spectacle of feminine death or suffering, as is amply illustrated by Cleopatra, Juliet, Desdemona, and by Gertrude herself. Thus, as Lyons has noted, "to accept" Gertrude's speech as if its discomfiting quality were merely accidental (deserving to be swept under the carpet) is to ignore an important issue in the characterization of Ophelia. Throughout the play, Ophelia has her opinions and statements recast for her by other characters—namely, Laertes, Hamlet, and Polonius—who wish her to behave in a manner they deem appropriate. To mention just one example, upon hearing from Ophelia that Hamlet has been courting her, Polonius recasts Ophelia's view of the relationship as one in which Hamlet ruthlessly exploits her naïveté so that he may conquer her sexually. Gertrude's speech is the epitome of such reconfigurings of Ophelia's realities, and it also should make us think twice about why her death need be so prettily recorded, and recorded unmistakably as an accident.

It is worthwhile to point out that the controversy within and without the play over whether Ophelia commits suicide or is drowned accidentally depends largely upon the discrepancy between what Gertrude says in this speech and the discussion that the gravediggers have in the subsequent scene. Although as Michael MacDonald has explained, Renaissance law was confusing and rather arbitrary about what determined whether one was "guilty of one's own murder," *felo de se,* or innocent by reason of insanity, the conversation of the gravediggers seems to indicate that Ophelia has committed suicide but is nevertheless being given some of the proper rites of a customary burial because she is of high social standing. Perhaps Gertrude is socially motivated to "portray"—hence the aesthetic inventory—Ophelia's suspicious death as an innocuous fall. Perhaps not.

While I will not solve the mystery of Gertrude's incongruous recital in the space of this essay, the incongruity is the relevant issue writ large. Unless we want to accuse him of extreme carelessness, Shakespeare intends to leave the circumstances of Ophelia's death—suicide or accident—inconclusive: he gives Gertrude this less than typical messenger performance (her only extended monologue in the play) and then provides for its immediate discrediting by the gravediggers. Whether we "side" with Gertrude's casting of the event as an accident attended by silvery, envious willows, whether we find surer ground with the gravediggers' opinion that she is a suicide being improperly well-buried, or whether we gloss over the speech's oddness and the identity of the particular agent of its delivery—all are equally to miss the very point: there is an epistemological gap in the text that cannot be filled in. We cannot explain away the difference between Gertrude's and the gravediggers' perception of what has happened to Ophelia's body. In fact, how conclusively does Shakespeare offer us the *corpus delicti* so to speak?

We are presented with a visually emblematic description of the event to which Gertrude was not a witness, which serves to make her an "unreliable narrator"; precisely because she is not a choric figure (only chorus-like, for some) here or elsewhere in the play, her remove from the progress of events and distance from a position of omniscience leaves her narrative without "authority," literally and metaphorically. Far from being the "authority"—the source of the information told from the perspective of a knowledgeable witness—she retells what someone else has told her about what has transpired, and she repeats it in self-conscious, mannered *literary* reportage. Her poetic figures, moreover, appear to borrow, at least partially, from Ovid's tale describing Arethusa's being changed into a river.

> The Poplar, and the hoary Willow, fed
> By bordring streames, their gratefull shadow
>   spred.
> In this coole Rivulet my foot I dipt;
> Then knee-deepe wade: nor so content,
>   unstript
> My self forth-with; upon a [willow] stud
> My robe I hung, and leapt into the flood.

. . . . .

> Where-ere I step, streames run; my haire now
>   fell
> In trickling deaw; and, sooner then I tell
> My destinie, into a Flood I grew.
>                                   (5.592-640)

Just as Shakespeare took Ovid's Philomela as the source for Lavinia's tragedy, so here the echoic quality of the vocabulary and situation suggests that again a tale by Ovid supplies Shakespeare with the source material for Gertrude's ventriloquization of Ophelia's story; the tale of Ophelia's drowning becomes a mannered, stylized, lyrical recital. According to J. Philip Brockbank's witty view: "the queen was too preoccupied with composing the felicitous verses she hoped to speak in court to spare time to take a grip on Ophelia's weedy trophies and haul her out" (111). But Gertrude, of course, was *not* present at the scene of drowning; thus, the poetic verse is occasioned rather by Gertrude's desire to perform for her audience. The oracular skill suggested by the "felicitous verse" has been mentioned by many critics—although it is only Jenkins's reference to her tone as "chorus like" that begins to sense the awkwardness and artificiality of Gertrude's new position as the historian of a tragedy to which she was not a witness.

Not being a witness to the drowning, Gertrude cannot be an "authority" about the event she relates. With respect to the question of how much she is an "author"—in the sense that she must make alterations to the unidentified messenger's "source material" in the process of refashioning it (much as Shakespeare refashions Ovid in penning the monologue)—this is of course indeterminable: we are unaware of what was told to her "before" (as if there were a before that exists beyond the play structure) she tells it in the fashion that she does. Nevertheless, the very impossibility of attributing any definable elements of authorship to Gertrude serves to make the point about the story's lacking authority.

Nor is Gertrude an "authority" in the very literal etymological sense of "originator" for the story she tells: the original report is authored by someone else whose identity is not known, a ghost author, a transparent originator in perhaps an endless series of deferred authorities. Indeed, careful examination of Gertrude's tale reveals the ghostly status or missing referent of the originating author/source, and it also reveals the missing authority for and of *this* history of Ophelia's body. After the report of the drowning, we have Ophelia's body directly in the funeral scene, but is the real history of the body—the story of the events that cause her death—identical to the body in Gertrude's story-telling of history? do we have the accurate account of a material body's history or a materializing history that has no body/nobody as the final, unequivocal referent? I think the point here is that there is no way to determine difference if it were to exist: the *history* becomes one and the same as the *story* once Gertrude "produces" her monologue—the French *histoire* (meaning both story and history) is a favorite of feminists for a reason. Ophelia's body, then, captured picturesquely, does not lack "reference" (or mention) by Gertrude, but as I have argued above, her body is still only the certain referent of a tale whose authority in all its senses must be understood to be lacking.

Interestingly, Gertrude's monologue is about witnessing the loss of a life to death, of a body that cannot be recouped from nature's grasp, much like Hamlet's ghostly father cannot recoup himself until he burns off his "purgatorial fires." But Gertrude's last chapter in the history of Ophelia also mimics or repeats the very circumstances that it purports to address; that is, her narrative describing the progressive loss of Ophelia's body also *enacts* that loss in the process of its telling, for the "unauthorized," finely-wrought tale that she tells always stands in for the missing original narrative, which is always a lost "body of work." Thus, Ophelia's body is lost once to death and once more to the very narrative about her death: this repetition suffers elision if the set-off speech is viewed merely as an uncomplicated extension of a "choric voice." We miss the implications of the artificiality and remove of its content and speaker.

In fact, to argue that Shakespeare intends us to gloss over Gertrude's performance is performative of the repetition of loss that I have described above, for if we pay no attention to the discomfort we feel for her language's artificial rhetoric—what makes critics resort to calling her voice "chorus-like"—and gloss over it, we actually reduplicate Ophelia's textual elision, the textual death in narrative. I suggest that we have become anaesthetized to the oddnesses attending the speech only because it has been augmented by a substantial catalogue of representations of a primarily visual nature: we have been trained to "read" this speech as a visual experience and fail to notice that Shakespeare leaves the event as reportage. For us, Ophelia's drowning scene has become a "seen" playing through our collective memory.

Gertrude "frames" Ophelia's story by making it as "pretty as a picture," and as such Gerturde's story becomes in turn the visual "history" of the body of Ophelia, more often than not, as is evidenced by the artistic repetitions of this particular scene. The variety of images produced reenacting the scene of Ophelia's drowning presents us, importantly, with the implicit statement that Gertrude's powerful rhetorical figures are not simply the tail-end to "Ophelia's story" in *Hamlet,* but that this one aspect of her life (death) has become essentially her entire story through a kind of synecdochic process—the part represents the whole.

A ventriloquized history becomes overwhelmingly the "story of Ophelia." This perhaps complicated movement finds a simple model if one notes that a whole series of paintings entitled "Ophelia" are all essentially thematic variations of *La Mort d'Ophélie* (Eugène Delacroix), because in portraying her death each implies that the story of "Ophelia" generally is that of her death. On the basis of such a large number of these paintings, one might think that she does nothing else in the play but fall into a brook and drown. Certainly, the main feature of Gertrude's monologue is also the desire to narrate Ophelia's progress to death: to borrow Peter Brooks's term, the "narrative desire" is to arrive finally at the beautiful, dying body of Ophelia, which is then reenacted and repeated by visual artists who perceive Ophelia as "a creature native and indued / Unto that element," as Gertrude describes it.

From the generations of paintings portraying Ophelia's death scene as narrated by Gertrude, Arthur Hughes's 1852 *Ophelia . . .* provides the most exemplary model. Hughes's canvas is a lunette shape with a remarkable frame: on it is reproduced, in excerpted form, the first half of Gertrude's lines from the text of *Hamlet.* Many reproductions of the painting (and engravings) do not feature the frame, and many critics do not mention this important detail. In Elaine Showalter's discussion, Hughes's *Ophelia* is primarily a representative of the iconography of madness: "In the Royal Academy show of 1852, Arthur Hughes's entry shows a tiny waif-like creature—a sort of Tinker Bell Ophelia—in a filmy white gown, perched on a tree trunk by the stream. The overall effect is softened, sexless, and hazy, although the straw in her hair resembles a crown of thorns. Hughe[s] juxtapos[es] childlike femininity and Christian martyrdom" (63). This painting, however, is less a painting of the "mad Ophelia" than it is another always-inscribed-in-the-death-moment Ophelia, her most repetitively invoked profile. As much as we might wish to see the Hughes canvas as a representation of feminine insanity, the painting's use of the textual excerpt asserts instead that the subject being depicted is Ophelia about to drown: we are looking at a moment just prior to her drowning and death, which is directed by the (con)text of the writing on the frame—it does not feature, for example, the earlier scene where she is actually present on stage in a state of madness.

Interestingly, Hughes's framing of Ophelia in this manner must also be understood to be a repetition of Gertrude's narrative framing of the story of Ophelia's drowning, for while the painting's framed/framing text refers to the visual subject it surrounds, this painted Ophelia can only rearticulate or repeat—but not refer back to—the text. In other words, the painting places Ophelia firmly in the context of Gertrude's story by literalizing what is already a "speaking picture" into a real picture. The painting articulates the progress of Ophelia's body to "muddy death" by repeating Gertrude's utterances: the word made painted flesh, so to speak, is truly re-presentational. Of course, it is possible that Hughes's painting and other like representations of Ophelia could be seeking to interrogate Gertrude's representation by making the odd pictorial quality of her speech a demonstrable, problematic reality, but as Elisabeth Bronfen's arguments suggest, the habit of art's preferring to portray dead beautiful women throughout history as aesthetic objects would seem to foreclose upon such an analytic response to the speech.

The way that the Hughes painting implicates the verbal text provides a particularly economical illustration of the way that painters replicate the framing strategy of Gertrude's speech, but all paintings of Ophelia depicting an earlier or later moment in her progress to death always already depict death, even if it is death-about-to-happen. Just as death has also already determined the teleology of Gertrude's story—the narrative end of which also desires precisely to portray an "end" aesthetically—so these canvases simply repeat one fraction of a continuous movement towards the end of the narrative. These paintings all feature the site of her death; i.e., watery landscapes and flora with or without other plant life, however abstract the representation.

Earlier contributions to the flood of images to which Hughes's 1852 *Ophelia* belongs include Richard Redgrave's *Ophelia Weaving Her Garlands,* (1842). Redgrave's sober, neoclassically-composed Ophelia sits on a bowing tree bough just above the flower-dotted water's edge; the scene's composition with the centrally-situated static woman is typical of formal portraiture of the era, as if Ophelia with her vaguely distracted features and corseted, heavy dress were sitting in a drawing room rather than about to experience a violent end.

This aspect is indeed captured in the pre-Hughes contributions of Delacroix, whose 1843 lithographs and the 1844 painting of *La Mort d'Ophélie* . . . strike the viewer with a scene of immediate peril: Ophelia's heavy body is about to fall into turbulent waters—a "brook" which looks more threatening than any of the rest of the watery depictions of Ophelia one encounters. The combination of the threateningly active river below and the suspended, about-to-fall Ophelia present her at a moment of imminent death; it is death in progress, in fact, moving along resolutely as she begins to lose her grip. In fact, Ophelia's death is a work in progress in a fuller sense, for Delacroix was apparently as fascinated with repainting and relimning the figure of Ophelia as he was with painting Hamlet. Similarly, as Leonard Roberts and Mary Virginia Evans have discussed, Arthur Hughes himself reworked several perspectives of the same scene.

By reason of a strange albeit pre-Raphaelite coincidence, in the same Royal Academy exhibition in which the Hughes *Ophelia* appeared, there was also featured Millais's 1852 *Ophelia* . . . , which soon became the most famously reproduced work illustrating Shakespeare's character. In this work, Elaine Showalter sees an interesting tension between the formalist detail and eroticism: "While Millais's Ophelia is sensuous siren as well as victim, the artist rather than the subject dominates the scene. The division of space between Ophelia and the natural details Millais had so painstakingly pursued reduces her to one more visual object; and the painting has such a hard surface, strangely flattened perspective, and brilliant light that it seems cruelly indifferent to the woman's death" (63). Death is indeed the central event being anticipated in the Millais painting, and Showalter's comments cannily zero in on the manner in which Ophelia's body is "reduced" and "flattened" into a "visual object" for purely aesthetic contemplation, for this making of a body into a work of art is analogous to Gertrude's original narration of the drowning, the "portrait" that threatens to reduce Ophelia's death to the status of only a verbal object.

The late 19th century saw moribund Ophelias multiplying in the art world, of which the anonymous "T. E. Monogrammist" *Ophelia* . . . in the Folger Shakespeare Library collection is in many ways representative. Mention should also be made of Henry Nelson O'Neil's *Ophelia* of 1874, followed shortly after by John William Waterhouse's 1889 *Ophelia,* one of several depictions of the same scene he repainted at least once in 1910. In all the aforementioned paintings, we have a case of the artist "following convention" (Pressly 50) by placing a crown of flowers in her loose hair and showing her in a white dress as she walks to the water's edge; the iconography or conventions of dress and landscape for depicting Ophelia's incipient death are firmly in place by this juncture.

At the beginning of the 20th century, the tradition continues with Odilon Rédon's 1908 *Ophélia,* which portrays in a more abstract manner an unidentifiable point in the drowning. For if the bright polychrome of the wash of flowers dominating the tableau does not make Ophelia look like she is being "drowned out" by them, an abstract body of water in an equally abstract landscape is still present in the upper right-hand region of the canvas: just as the *Hamlet* text on the frame defines what is about to happen at the edge of the brook in Hughes's painting, so Ophelia's watery context is always eerily proleptic for her death—is always referring to her imminent death. In Rédon's painting, Ophelia's face is tilted upwards, a garland of flowers is interwoven in her hair; and her eyes appear peacefully closed. Oddly, the painting is a twin of Rédon's depiction of Orpheus, another character with a long mythological history telling of his body's end in a watery grave.

Joseph Stella's *Ophelia* (c. 1926), while sharply limiting the viewer's perspective with a tight close-up of her face, nevertheless positions two waterlillies at the upper right and left-hand sides to convey the watery, floral context with remarkable economy.... Similarly, although Stanley William Hayter conceived of his 1936 *Ophelia* as a thorough abstraction—the plane of tangled, curvilinear geometric shapes is not representational—Hayter also confirms the existence of the traditional components of the Ophelian landscape: "*Ophelia* represents lines of flow in water, intense light, floating flower, insect, fragments of human form—held as with surface tensions of liquid" (Janis 121). Hayter's abstract "fragments of human form" connote a relatively anonymous body, but an *Ophelian* body nonetheless because of its placement in the floral, watery context of her death scene. In view of this dominant symbology, and although in some of these paintings there may indeed be some iconographical references to insanity of the type Showalter seeks, any "psychiatric" detail is ultimately secondary to the focus on death. The watery grave is a consistent feature of Ophelia's landscape, so much so that it is part and parcel of the standard Ophelian iconography.

At last count, Stephano Cusumano's quasi-cubist 1970 *Ophelia*... is the most recent entry in a still-growing catalogue. This perspective painting takes the progress toward death even one step closer than the Millais: featuring a mannequin-like figure with blocky, nearly androgynous facial planes, Cusumano depicts a body sinking below the water's surface, surrounded by air bubbles, obscured by and wrapped in weeds. Thus, despite the remarkable range of styles of Ophelia paintings reflected by the various schools and movements here—one might compare Millais to Cusumano for the similar placement of the body even if the manner of composition is vastly different—a discernible vocabulary of presentation articulates itself in all such works.

To put the painters themselves back into this text-painting relationship, one might describe them as being narrators of the (same) story and as continuing the process of elision that Ophelia has already undergone in the narrative. Reproducing Gertrude's speech, a painter reproduces it differently, in a different medium: artists make concrete an anatomical body that had no physicality in speech by "rearticulating" it, and this process is in itself a form of repetition, since Ophelia's painted body mimics the story of Ophelia's narrative body, altering in medium but not in content—there is no new tale to tell. That is, the painted body depicts its compliance with the textual, narrative body by presenting the same body in a different medium, progressing to death housed within new anatomical trappings. Yet the stability of the "real" body of Ophelia that we see in paintings is illusory precisely because the origin of the painted body *always* lies within the narrative body, and the *narrative* body's description by Gertrude, we must remember, has no "authority," no referent, no originator, pointing instead back to the epistemological gap in the text. This gap is also increasingly elided as we become used to seeing Ophelia depicted in this particular manner, so that painted Ophelias have come to influence our perceptions of the literary Ophelia as much as the literary has inaugurated painted Ophelias. In view of the great number of artists who paint this scene over and over again—with some like Hughes (see Roberts & Evans), Delacroix, and Waterhouse painting different approaches to Ophelia repetitively themselves—it would appear that the fascination lies in the extent to which Ophelia's image is already commonly a painterly subject but also because the scene remains unfamiliar, insofar as it stages the extra-dramatic moment of *Hamlet,* the moment where the text breaks down.

Not accidentally, the "hole" or non-signifying place in the text of *Hamlet* is also the feminine body's locus. As elaborated by Elisabeth Bronfen, the portrait of a dead woman reflects the instability of the feminine body and its symbolic connection to death more generally. Bronfen establishes her argument within Lacanian frameworks, locating the feminine body as both a sign of death and of the constant deferral of death; she theorizes that the dead feminine body is always being represented, apotropaically, as an intact, beautiful body: "The beauty of Woman and the beauty of the image both give the illusion of intactness and unity, cover the insupportable signs of lack, deficiency, transiency and promise their spectators the impossible—an obliteration of death's unique castrative threat to the subject" (64). According to this psychoanalytic model, in their being associated with "lacking" a phallus (and thus the ability to control "signification" or meaning), women are also uniquely connected to death, for death's awesome and threatening power is that it evacuates all meaning. Thus the struggle to make meaning, to make things signify, is always a battle against lack, or "non-meaning," or death. In this sense, the potential breakdown of signification that is threatened by a dead body gendered female becomes doubly threatening to the masculine subject, and this is why the *death of a woman* must therefore be constructed as the *death of a beautiful woman*—i.e., in order to foreclose upon the reality of death's leveling power, in order to reject the power of death to destroy a masculine identity that is grounded upon possession of the phallus. The dead and beautiful woman for Bronfen, therefore, indicates an excess of meaning—the dead feminine body is always being invested with a plethora of signification so as to ward off its radical instability, its potential to dissolve into nonmeaning and in turn, to divest the masculine subject of his identity.

To return to Ophelia and to *Hamlet,* since we cannot literally see Ophelia's body because it is only a figure evoked in Gertrude's speech in Shakespeare's text, we are left in turn with a body that does not signify, does not have an ultimate referent in narrative. According to Bronfen's model, it seems little coincidence that the death scene specifically is the scene constantly rearticulated by artists, who regularly present Ophelia in the scene contained in but denied visually by the text. For if Ophelia is not always being "dredged up" to begin her progress to death over and over again, the gap in the text might begin to evolve precisely as the site of instability where referentiality collapses, the site of the threatening correspondence of woman and death where meaning dissolves. Ophelia needs to be contained by a beautiful death and the stage of decomposition must only go so far. This may explain why there seem to be no paintings of a truly, unmistakably dead Ophelia, perhaps the closest approximation to this state being Millais's glassily blank or Stella's closed-eye, peaceful figure.

If paintings of Ophelia rearticulate the site where referentiality potentially collapses, paradoxically these representations also insure the ultimate referentiality of *Hamlet,* and by extension, of Shakespeare. Here it is helpful to return for a moment to the role of the textual frame in Hughes's *Ophelia.* The painting itself cannot refer to Ophelia with any concrete certainty, since the figure it depicts can only refer back to Gertrude's *speech* which is the only place that we can find her. Gertrude's speech, however, is of course part of Shakespeare's text proper, part of *Hamlet,* so that while paintings of Ophelia almost always take as their subject the place in the text *Hamlet* where the referentiality of Ophelia breaks down, nevertheless *Hamlet* still always serves as the final referent for Ophelia, gaps or no gaps. Lacan's oft-mentioned pronouncement that Ophelia is "linked forever, for centuries, to the figure of Hamlet" (20) is accurate, but as these artworks suggest, her link to the character Hamlet is less important than her more resolute link to the larger work, the play *Hamlet.* Insofar as *Hamlet* is, of course, in turn a play by Shakespeare, the additional twist here is that, ironically, the representations of Ophelia might turn out to be even less about her history than they might chronicle the continuing significance of Shakespeare for many cultures—European, American, and Japanese traditions at the very least. For over a century, it is precisely the dead, beautiful, painterly Ophelia that gets articulated over and over again in the "high" art tradition, coincident with the fairly regular ascendancy of Shakespeare as a figure of vast (multi) cultural importance.

As an extension of "high" culture production, moreover, Ophelia has also become a "low" or popular culture figure of sorts: her drowning is alluded to in the titles of psychology books (see Pipher), and her more-or-less placid body floats by our eyes periodically in media as varied as recently-televised episodes of the *X-Files,* resolutely reproducing and repeating visually the circumstances of Gertrude's narrative. In fact, the ever-popular depiction by Millais is frequently featured in postcard and calendar reproductions. Indeed, Portal Publications' 1995 calendar, *The Pre-Raphaelites,* includes not one, but two Ophelia paintings: Millais's becomes the pinup for "Miss May," while J. W. Waterhouse's *Ophelia* becomes "Miss November." In the space of one twelve-month calendar, these depictions of the about-to-drown Ophelia point to the consistent popularity with consumers of this theme of Ophelia's death.

Another example can be found in a 1996 Folger Library project entitled "Shakespeare's Heroines," a boxed set of notecards depicting esteemed female characters (including a 19th-century painting by Marcus Stone, featuring a dreamy, distracted Ophelia). What is so interesting about The Folger's marketing initiative and a patron's ability to purchase the Folger cards in a museum shop is the suggestion that "art-shop" products like the "Shakespeare's Heroines" notecards are more appealing to the targeted public than the experience of any real artwork that might be housed in the museum itself; revealingly, the patron of the Cleveland Museum of Art cannot buy a souvenir postcard of Stone's *Ophelia* because there is no concrete viewing experience possible in Cleveland of the work, located elsewhere in England, for which the notecards should be a reminder.

As this example makes clear, Ophelia—perhaps along with other less frequently invoked Shakespearean heroines—is a thoroughly marketable product, a Shakespeare-brand product. The impetus that leads patrons of art shops to purchase such items seems to be linked most concretely to efforts to commercialize the Bard, for it is to be on shaky ground to claim that consumers are necessarily familiar with either the paintings' specific literary context or even the text of *Hamlet* generally when they purchase a calendar with Ophelia gracing its interior. The Ophelia of the commercial and plastic arts seems to be in the odd position of saying less about "attitudes towards women and madness" (Showalter 69)—even when paintings such as Stone's *Ophelia* take madness as their explicit subject—and more about the success of "Shakespeare" as an adaptable commodity category, the success of the Shakespeare-products clearinghouse, so to speak. In this important sense, even Shakespeare's status as perhaps *the* literary marker of cultural importance, as a figure of immense cultural capital, appears to be losing ground rapidly to the market for "Shakespeare" products, regardless of whatever such products do (or do not) have to do with Shakespeare's texts. Depictions of Ophelia then, would seem to direct us unequivocally to Shakespeare's text, but do they? Instead, we appear to be faced with a free-floating reference to "Shakespeare" only most generally, a literally "free-floating" Ophelia severed from specific contexts.

Occasionally, however, pictorial repetitions of Gertrude's narrative go one step further into the representational quagmire which has developed around her "muddy death" and make the figure of Ophelia an issue precisely of *non-referentiality,* either accidentally or deliberately. For example, a postcard announcement and compact disc single by Australian artist Nick Cave features on its cover . . . an unmistakably Ophelia-styled drowning woman to promote a song that is not really about Ophelia at all. Cave's song "Where the Wild Roses Grow" does identify a woman as a "wild rose" (associated with Ophelia by the Victorians), but she has another name and is clearly not intended to *be* Ophelia. Making a reference to Ophelia, but only obliquely, the cover and advertisement enlist her and her watery landscape—the familiar iconographic vocabulary—to provide the image for a song of which she is not the subject. That each of the songs' lyrics in Cave's album tells the story of a murder suggests further that murder, and *not* Ophelia, is the specific thematic concern here. Thus, Ophelia is employed here to serve purely as an image, pointedly separated from her textual context or underpinnings; because the name "Ophelia" has come to mean reductively "a drowning woman scenario," this equivalence also works in reverse fashion, as is evidenced by Cave's cover, where drowned or drowning women become "Ophelias." Cave's cover photograph, however, is different from painted artworks that take Ophelia *as* their ostensible subject because Cave's "Ophelia" enacts (consciously or unconsciously) precisely that "unreferentiality," that separation between Shakespearean character and the established cultural modes of her representation.

Perhaps the best example of the separation discussed above can be found in Claude Chabrol's 1962 film *Ophélia.* The film, rather than being about Shakespeare's protagonist, instead focuses on the drama of a man who thinks he is Hamlet and includes the purely tangential story of a woman who must deny patiently and consistently, *"Je ne suis pas Ophélia. Je suis Lucy."* Oddly, the identity of the character is always in the position of *not* being Ophelia, as if Lacan had adapted his *"La femme n'éxiste pas"* (qtd. in Bronfen 211) for a screenplay. What happens to the woman in the film apparently has nothing to do with Shakespeare's character—there is no scene of drowning or anything significantly close to the scenes in which Ophelia appears in the play. Of course, neither is the "Hamlet" character really Hamlet: this character's significant deficiency is his trying to force his life into an artificial mold of Hamlet's. So finally, the film's title, *Ophélia,* does not even refer concretely to any Hamlet or Shakespeare's *Hamlet;* whether Chabrol intends it or not, "Ophelia" remains a free-floating apostrophe, an appellation misapplied to the story that unfolds in the film, significant only in that it refers always to "not Ophelias."

The "Ophelia" referenced and invoked by the titles of numerous paintings and other media sampled in this essay establishes a preliminary inventory that, taken as a whole, begins to look remarkably thematically consistent. Whether the example is from the 18th, 19th, or 20th century, more often than not, the artist has resolutely trained our gaze at one scene, one event. Yet unless we realize that the drowning Ophelia is a more complex figure than she may initially strike us, with two deeply intertwined histories of representation, our analysis remains partial. In many ways, Ophelia's floating body has become so great a part of our Shakespearean cultural history, that we seldom realize how little we—literary and cultural studies critics, editors, and art historians—have interrogated the deceptively too obvious Ophelia. The value of the interarts approach here is clear, helping us to reexamine a familiar, even excessively-canonical and clichéd landscape.

Ophelia has no history that is properly hers; rather the painted portraits of Ophelia are always already representations of Gertrude's first pictorial representation and must always be remembered to be so, or else we risk losing sight of Ophelia's progress through these complex layers of representation. Accordingly, because Showalter's study does not look deeply enough into the textual origins of Ophelia, her own directions for a more accurate study of her history are a bit wanting: "Ophelia does have a story of her own that feminist criticism can tell; it is neither her life story, nor her love story, nor Lacan's story, but rather the history of her representation" (59). Instead, the history of representation that we must evince is one that recognizes her as a site of the *convergence* of the literary body and the pictorial body. One might be persuaded to reimagine Cusumano's neo-cubist *Ophelia* of 1970 along the following lines: an anonymous-faced woman's body enshrouded by and wrapped in a thick veil of crownet weeds—leaves, in fact, of *Hamlet.* This reconfigured portrait might drive home the idea that Ophelia's complete story cannot be discerned without turning over those leaves, or pages, of the text that we must first find her in—or do we?

*Works Cited*

Bate, Jonathan. *Shakespeare and the English Romantic Imagination.* New York: Oxford UP, 1992.

Branagh, Kenneth, dir. *Hamlet.* Castle Rock Entertainment, 1997.

Brockbank, J. Philip. "Hamlet the Bonesetter." *Shakespeare Survey* 30 (1977): 103-15.

Bronfen, Elisabeth. *Over Her Dead Body: Death, Femininity and the Aesthetic.* New York: Routledge, 1992.

Brooks, Peter. *Reading for the Plot: Design and Intention in Narrative.* Cambridge: Harvard UP, 1992.

Cave, Nick. "Where the Wild Roses Grow." *Murder Ballads.* Mute Records Limited, 1995.

Chabrol, Claude, dir. *Ophélia.* Ind. dist., France, 1962.

Harvey, John. "Shakespeare and the Ends of Time: The Illustrations." *The Cambridge Review* (May 1996): 1-24.

Janis, Sidney. *Abstract and Surrealist Art in America.* New York: Reynal, 1944.

Lacan, Jacques. "Desire and the Interpretation of Desire in Hamlet." *Yale French Studies* 55-56 (1977): 11-52.

Lyons, Bridget Gellert. "The Iconography of Ophelia." *English Literary History* 44 (1977): 60-74.

MacDonald, Michael. "Ophelia's Maimed Rites." *Shakespeare Quarterly* 15 (1986): 309-17.

Ovid. *The Metamorphosis* [sic]. Englished, Mythologized, and Represented in Figures. 1621. Trans. George Sandys. Ed. Karl K. Hulley and Stanley T. Vandersall. Lincoln: U of Nebraska P, 1970.

Pipher, Mary. *Reviving Ophelia: Saving the Selves of Adolescent Girls.* New York: Putnam's, 1994.

Pressly, William L. *A Catalogue of Paintings in the Folger Shakespeare Library.* New Haven: Yale UP, 1993.

Roberts, Leonard, and Mary Virginia Evans. "'Sweets to the Sweet': Arthur Hughes's Versions of *Ophelia.*" *Journal of Pre-Raphaelite Studies* 1.2 (1988): 26-36.

Ronk, Martha C. "Representations of *Ophelia.*" *Criticism* 36.1 (1994): 21-43.

Shakespeare, William. *Hamlet.* Ed. Harold Jenkins. 1982. London: Methuen, 1994.

Showalter, Elaine. "Representing Ophelia: Women, Madness, and the Responsibilities of Feminist Criticism." *Shakespeare's Middle Tragedies.* Ed. David Young. Englewood Cliffs: Prentice-Hall, 1993. 56-69.

Stone, Marcus. *Ophelia.* 1896. "Shakespeare's Heroines." Notecards. The Folger Shakespeare Library. New York: te Neues Publishing, 1995.

*The X-Files.* "Emily." Created by Chris Carter. Perf. Gillian Anderson and David Duchovny. FOX. WFXT, Boston. 14 Dec., 1997.

---

Source: "Framing Ophelia: Representation and the Pictorial Tradition," in *Mosaic: A Journal for the Interdisciplinary Study of Literature,* Vol. 31, No. 3, September, 1998, pp. 1-24.

# "Rape, I fear, was root of thy annoy": The Politics of Consent in *Titus Andronicus*

## Sid Ray, *Pace University*

Scholars cannot resist the temptation to analyze the startling and eerie succession of hand severings in *Titus Andronicus*.[1] What distinguishes the current study from others is its focus not solely on the hands but on the combined impact of Lavinia's injuries—her rape and the amputation of her hands and tongue—and how they figure within the political context of the play and within early modern ideologies of marriage and monarchy. Only after Lavinia pages through Ovid's *Metamorphoses,* comparing herself to the raped Philomel, does Titus begin to grasp the range of meaning implied by her injuries. His statement to Lavinia, "rape, I fear, was root of thy annoy" (4.1.49), signals that the rape carries a metonymical significance at least as important as the severed hands and tongue.[2] Read collectively, the hand (the body part that demonstrates consent), the tongue (the body part that voices consent), and the rape (non-consensual intercourse) reflect profound anxiety over abrogated rights of consent. Lavinia's initial status as unmarried commodity suggests, more specifically, that her injuries address a bride's right to consent to marriage. If, however, we acknowledge Lavinia as a symbol of Rome and factor in her suitors' political motives, it becomes apparent that themes of political consent, the right of the people to consent to the authority of the monarch, find expression in the same ravished and mutilated body. Exploring both possibilities, this essay argues that in *Titus Andronicus* Shakespeare associates the right of a woman to consent to marriage with the ancient right of the social body to consent to the ruling power of the monarch. Because he figures the abrogation of those rights so violently, I contend that, in this early play, Shakespeare betrays republican leanings and sympathy for a constitutional form of government.

The assault on Lavinia, which occurs outside the city of Rome some time after Saturninus and Bassianus have articulated their competing philosophies of rulership, seems at first to bear little relevance to the issue of good governance. But an understanding of the analogy contemporary writers evoke between the household and the state and a close reading of Shakespeare's play of language indicate that Lavinia's injuries do, in fact, hold a great deal of political meaning. Before proceeding with an analysis of the play itself, I will therefore examine connections Renaissance theorists make between private and public policy, looking initially at an account of Elizabeth I's infamous directive for the amputation of the hands of two subjects, which took place during her marriage negotiations with the duke of Alençon. Although not the first to note this event's relevance, I hope to extend its significance by demonstrating how Lavinia's mutilated body dramatizes the people's right not only to consent to be ruled but also to advise their ruler. The interwoven marital and political ideologies revealed by this analysis and by a parallel between the Protestant marriage ceremony and the Tudor recognition ritual allow me to theorize a relationship between the domestic and the political in early modern treatises addressing consent.

The issue of consent was made a matter of public debate in 1579 when Elizabeth I demanded the amputation of the right hands of John Stubbs and William Page after they wrote and published a treatise decrying the queen's proposed marriage to the duke of Alençon. Outraged by the publication, Elizabeth "declared that she would rather lose a hand herself than mitigate . . . [the] punishment."[3] While the treatise in question, *The Discoverie of a Gaping Gulf,* brashly displays its author's presumption, particularly as Stubbs assumes a paternalistic view of the queen's marriage negotiations, it also reflects his deep concern for the welfare of the state. Stubbs feared that the queen's future husband would consider himself her ruler and head, "As the wife is subject to hir husband: so is her country to hys land."[4] Stubbs, and by all accounts the English people in general, dreaded that the queen's marriage would position her as inferior to the long-time enemy of England, and they thought that if Elizabeth gave her hand in marriage to an heir of France, she would be handing over the people of England as well. Unfortunately for Stubbs and Page, the queen did not care to be reminded that marriage entails a transfer of dominion involving the bride's submission to her husband's governance. Elizabeth's prenuptial situation, unusual in its implications for a female monarch, forced England to confront the incompatibility of Protestant marriage ideals with female governance. Besides troubling marital ideology, Stubbs and Page's pamphlet collapsed domestic concerns into political ones. In their publication, marital issues became a vehicle for the constitutionalist notion that subjects, or at least magistrates, have some responsibility to voice concern about governmental policy.[5]

Elizabeth's orders to cut off the hands of Stubbs and Page may seem a drastic way to ensure a woman's right to choose a spouse. But that was not the issue for the queen; she was angered primarily by the challenge to her royal authority. So while domestic reformers and defenders of women may have sympathized with Elizabeth's right to choose her own husband, the larger issue of her subjects' right to question such a serious decision was critical, especially in light of contemporary debates about advice and consent. Many of Elizabeth's judges, like many modern historians, considered the punishment excessive; and in his eyewitness account of the mutilation, William Camden offers three possible motives for the crowd's unusual silence:

> either out of horror at this new unwonted kind of punishment or out of commiseration towards the man, as being of an honest and unblemished repute; or else out of hatred of the marriage, which most men presaged would be the overthrow of religion.[6]

This violent event, confronting, as it did, issues of marital politics and political marriage in a significant, theatrical display of power, strikingly resembles the rape and dismemberments in *Titus Andronicus*.

Like *Titus*, which opens with a contested election and two disputed marriages, the Stubbs case raises important questions about the viability of marital ideals within lived political contexts, especially given shifting theories of authority's origins in the early modern period. When a woman "gives her hand in marriage," the metaphor implies, she consents to the marital transaction. In the hand-fasting tradition, the bride and groom display their mutual consent to the union and agree to carry out their respective marital duties.[7] Henry Smith notes: "As they are handfasted, so they must be heartfasted, for the eye, and the tongue, & the hand, will be her enimies, if the hart be not her friend."[8] But in sixteenth-century England the dynamic of the wedding ceremony, specifically the offering of hands, enacted rituals of exchange rather than rituals of mutuality. The bride's father, who owned his daughter during her premarital existence, transferred possession of her to the bridegroom, whereupon the groom became the bride's "head" and continued dominance over her. The coronation ritual enacted a similar process of exchange and consent. Analyzing that similarity is critical to understanding *Titus* because the father's tyrannical intervention in his daughter's marriage parallels his intervention in the election of the emperor.

While hand-fasting rituals emphasized mutual consent, the wedding ceremony of *The Book of Common Prayer, 1559* carefully stages the father's transfer of the daughter to the husband. Instead of a mutual giving of hands, the bride gives her hand and the groom takes it. This act of "taking" asserts the groom's ascendancy in the relationship, symbolizing the bride's sacrifice of a part of her body which the groom incorporates into his own. Thomas Gataker explains this yielding and incorporation in *A Good Wife God's Gift:* "She was at first *taken out of man;* and is therefore by *Creation as a limbe reaft from him.* And she was afterward ioyned againe in *Mariage* with *Man,* that by *Nuptiall coniunction* becoming *one flesh* with him, she might be as *a limbe restored* now and *fastened* againe *to him.*"[9] As a *"limbe restored,"* the bride becomes a part, or member, of the man, a person without autonomy, ruled by her protector. Renaissance divines preferred men and women to have their marriages consecrated in a church by a minister who would dictate the prescribed ritual in which the bride "gives her hand in marriage" to her father, who then gives it to the groom.[10] Though hand-fasting accompanied by the appropriate vows between a man and woman past a certain age constituted a valid marriage in Renaissance England, Protestants urged couples to consecrate the union in church because the church ceremony involved their parents. The bride's father would have to agree to the marriage, ensuring that the union was neither hasty nor illicit. Indeed, his presence would also ensure that the proper financial negotiations had been completed.

In spite of Protestant reformers' professed distaste for arranged marriage, the exchange between father and husband staged the private processes involved in arranged marriages, namely the transfer of ownership of the bride and her dowry. A wealthy father would engage a girl, often at a very young age, to an economically or politically suitable boy. Upon coming of age, the bride-to-be would or would not have the right of refusal, depending on her father's disposition. If the queen had married the duke of Alençon, her consent to the arrangement would have been a foregone conclusion; if the queen did not want to marry, she would simply have refused to do so because that was her prerogative as a supreme ruler. But the situation for all other aristocratic women was not comparable. In some cases a father would coerce his daughter into marriage, forcing her to extend her hand in a show of consent. This situation was not uncommon for aristocratic and even some of the poorer women in Renaissance England.[11] Indeed, "a system of arranged or enforced marriages was kept in existence until the abolition of wardship in the middle of the seventeenth century."[12] In domestic situations where property was at stake, parental consent or *consensus nuptialis* was profoundly important, especially given the financial instability of the aristocracy at the turn of the century.[13] Smith states, for example, "if a virgin make a vow, it should not be kept, vnlesse her father approue it, because she is not free: therefore if she did vow to marrie, yet the Father hath power by this law to break it."[14] Though Protestant marriage-tract writers argued for parental consent, they claimed that if the girl rejected a man her parents had chosen, she should not be forced into the marriage. But, as Margaret King records, "even with the advance of the notion of consent, many young women (and men) were compelled against their will or preference to marry persons chosen for them by their families."[15] Parents would often apply a great deal of pressure to gain their children's consent to a match and in some instances would resort to beating, abducting, or imprisoning the unwilling bride.[16] The history of such coercion may explain why Lavinia, already betrothed to Bassianus, remains silent in *Titus Andronicus* when her father agrees to marry her to Saturninus (1.1.244).

Officially the church required the bride's consent to the marriage and, by extension, her consent to be ruled by her husband—she did have a degree of agency in this regard. In *The Christen state of matrimoneye* Miles Coverdale writes: "Wedloke must be coupled togither with the good consent of both the parsonnes."[17] In a more overtly political treatise, *An Heptameron of Civill Discourses,* George Whetstone writes, "the office of Free choise, is the roote or foundation of Marriage."[18] During James's reign William Perkins writes, "The second thing required to the making of a [marriage] contract, is the free and full consent of the parties, which is indeed the very soule and life of the contract."[19] Adding a legal perspective, T. E.'s *The Lawes Resolvtions* notes that common and civil law in England dictate that both bride and groom consent to the match: "The full Contract of Matrimonie, is when it is made by words *de praesenti* in a lawfull consent, and thus two be made man and wife existing without lying together, yet Matrimonie is not accounted consummate until there goe with the consent of mind and will Coniunction of body."[20] While consent in theory was a primary concern, in practice it was often circumvented.

The importance of the bride's consent, even if it was coerced, suggests that its emphasis in early modern marital tracts had a purpose other than ensuring the bride's voice in her domestic arrangements. It is possible that, in their writings on domestic issues, sixteenth-century Protestant reformers were measuring how consent operates in the political paradigm in which the ruler is thought to be wedded to the kingdom. Through such debates regarding free choice in marriage, their constitutionalist contemporaries did find a subtle means of promoting political consent. They had a reason to do so; during the Tudor period the ritual of consent at the accession of a new monarch was altered dramatically. Changes in the coronation ceremony show that political consent was a heavily charged issue in Renaissance England, and one that could be more safely broached through its less-controversial marital analogue.

The transfer of daughter from father to husband that occurs in the marriage ceremony is similar to the transfer of power that occurs in the royal succession when the deceased monarch transfers governance to a younger version of him or herself as if that ruler were there. Thus the natural body of the ruler dies, but the mystical body lives in the successor. Indeed, the coronation ring represents the marriage of a ruler to the kingdom just as the wedding ring represents the marriage of husband and wife. To defend herself from those who wanted her to marry, Elizabeth I often raised her hand and displayed her coronation ring to indicate that she was already wedded to the people.[21] As the consent of the bride to be ruled by her husband is a critical element of the marriage ritual, so the consent of the people to accept their new ruler is also ceremonially significant. From the early reigns of Edward the Confessor and William the Conqueror up to the coronation of Edward VI, the "election" ritual in which the people were asked if they consented to the new ruler was vital to the coronation. But at the Tudor boy-king's accession the election ritual was changed into a simple "recognition" ritual in which the people of England, represented by the peers of the realm, were merely asked if they "recognized" the new ruler. The ritual was altered because "election" implied that the monarch had a profound obligation to the people, an implication that did not accord with the Tudor claim to absolute power. Historian Bertie Wilkinson writes that Edward VI "was not presented in the Abbey as elected by anybody: the people were asked only to give their good will and assent 'as by your duties of allegiance ye are bound to do.'"[22] At Edward's coronation, the election ritual had metamorphosed into a simple question put to the spectators: "Will you serve at this time, and give your good wills and assent to the same consecration, enunction, and coronation?"[23] This significant alteration of the ritual is, as William Jones observes, "a curious proof of the solicitude displayed by the Tudors, as it was much more by the next family, to suppress every recollection that could make their sovereignty appear to be of popular origin."[24] Such an alteration must have infuriated constitutionalists, Theodore Beza for one, who believed that "authority to rule is founded mostly on the consent of Parliament" rather than on the king's birthright.[25] Despite the alteration from "election" to "recognition," the ritual "preserved a tradition of voluntary allegiance by a free people to the new ruler."[26] In this way the recognition ritual mirrors the wedding ritual in which a woman "gives her hand in marriage" as a sign of her consent to be ruled. For Protestant marriage-tract writers and for anti-absolutist political theorists the right to consent to be ruled by anyone—a husband or a monarch—even if only ceremonial, is a critical component of social stability.

In regard to domestic politics, however, Protestantism "increased [the] authority of the husband and father" and "enhanced men's need to control women and power to do so."[27] If household governance is truly analogous to political governance, then such an argument would seem to contradict Protestant constitutionalist efforts to limit the monarch's absolute power. In reality, however, Protestant reformers did seek to limit absolute power in governance, even though their theories about marriage inflated paternal and husbandly power in the household. The reason for the discrepancy is that, in the sixteenth century, the access to and deployment of power by husbands and fathers (domestic patriarchalism) differed pointedly from the way monarchical power operated, despite the often-cited analogy between them.[28] Political theorist Richard Hooker, for example, believed that "patriarchal authority existed only within families; its political significance was limited to having predisposed men to monarchical government."[29] It was only later, in the seventeenth century, that King James and Robert Filmer fully promoted patriarchalism, a theory of governance in which the people are viewed as children to their ruler.[30] Protestant reformers recognized that children, as opposed to wives and subjects, are given no opportunity to consent to their "ruler's" authority, marking a fundamental difference between patriarchalism and monarchy. Indeed, the broadening of husbandly and paternal power in the household did not mean that Protestants advocated increased authority in the political arena. Queen Elizabeth considered radical Puritans to be threats to her power because they wanted to introduce reforms in the Anglican church even more substantial than those mandated by the crown. Members of Parliament were constitutionalist allies of the Protestant reformers in that both groups were seeking to impose limits on Tudor absolutism. John Ponet, a Puritan who fled England during Mary's reign, boldly declared that a prince should be resisted in the name of the true religion. He argued, along with John Knox, that the obligation to resist "extends not only to the people's magistrates but, if need be, to every individual."[31] Ponet was a close associate of Thomas Becon, who, in addition to writing the preface to Coverdale's *The Christen state of matrimonye,* was a political theorist. Like Ponet, Becon suggested that the people owe no obedience to a ruler if the ruler's laws and practices contravene God's laws. In his *Catechism,* Becon writes: "We must obey God more than men."[32]

Despite the significant differences between domestic and civil governance, marriage-tract writers did adopt various political paradigms to construct household hierarchies, just as political theorists adopted familial paradigms as models for monarchical rule.[33] Marriage theory was so malleable that political theorists could manipulate it to support their ideals. Susan Amussen writes, "Marriage was an accessible model for contract theorists. The political questions were obvious, if problematic: if there was an original contract between King and people, what were its terms?" Notably, the increased emphasis by humanist and Protestant writers in the sixteenth century on the bride's consent to be ruled by her husband coincides with writings by political radicals which insist that a monarch's power derives not from divine right but from the consent of the governed. In the mid-seventeenth century, Amussen notes, member of Parliament Henry Parker used the domestic model to argue *against* divine right. According to Amussen, Parker "reminded his readers that in cases of marital breakdown the ecclesiastical courts protected both partners, and argued that the wife could be almost equal to her husband. . . . 'And if men, for whose sake women were created, shall not lay hold upon the divine right of wedlock, to the disadvantage of women: much less shall Princes, who were created for the people's sake, challenge any thing, from the sanctity of their offices, that may derogate from the people.'"[34] But absolutists in the early seventeenth century claimed that husbands did not derive power from the consent of their wives to marry; they derived it instead from their position as husbands. In the same way, kings derived power from their position as heirs to past kings, with a power that in essence came directly from God instead of from the people. Because sixteenth-century marriage theorists had positioned women, children, and servants in descending order as the governed or subservient members of the household, the connection between female marital consent and the consent of the governed in the political spectrum may have been more than analogous for philosophers even before the turn of the seventeenth century.[35] Constance Jordan propounds this compelling theory: "it may be that the language of the rights of the subject derives from discussions concerning the limits of wifely obedience."[36] If writers could prove that husbands derived their ruling power from the consent of their wives, then a constitutionalist, limited monarchy would be easier to advocate. Thus Shakespeare, by demonstrating the ill effects on the individual female body of abrogated consent, subtly imparts the necessity of consent rituals for the collective social body.

Shakespeare was doubtless familiar with the writings of sixteenth-century political theorists such as Desiderius Erasmus, John Ponet, and George Buchanan, who drew on the writings of Sir John Fortescue. In *Governance of England,* Fortescue differentiates between governments in which the king rules by divine right and those in which he rules by the consent of the people. The former, *dominium regale,* is a form of government conducive to tyrants because it allows the ruler to make decisions without the consent of the people. The latter form of government, *dominium politicum et regale,* is one in which the ruler derives power from the people, and thus it requires him or her to act for the people's benefit. One hundred years after Fortescue's tract was published, Ponet and Buchanan reiterate the virtues of *dominium politicum et regale,* arguing from a basis in ancient law that kings have no absolute claim to governance but derive their power from the consent of the people. Even though many such constitutionalist treatises were considered radical, they were available to the English people, many of them in the English language—notably Ponet's

*Politike Power* and Smith's *De Republica Anglorvm*.[37] In 1591, two years prior to the first production of *Titus Andronicus,* Richard Hooker was writing *Laws of ecclesiastical polity,* which also articulated the theory that the queen ruled by consent of the commonwealth.[38] Likewise, Matthew Sutcliffe, Dean of Exeter, published the constitutionalist *De presbyterio,* noting that the monarch's power derived from the people's consent. Like these influential contemporary tracts, *Titus Andronicus* supports the analogy between marital consent in the little commonwealth of the household and political consent in the governance of states: the struggle for Lavinia's hand in marriage, the question of her consent to marriage, and her subsequent rape and mutilation by the Goths are bound up with issues of the emperor's access to power through the consent of the people.

At the beginning of the play, Lavinia resists her father's authority to bestow her on Saturninus and gives her hand instead to Bassianus, a man she had earlier consented to marry. Three short scenes later, the Goths return her to the stage, having amputated her hands, cut out her tongue, and raped her. Such a violent fate visually reinforces the sense that the underlying struggle for dominance in *Titus,* whether it be the struggle for Rome or the struggle for Lavinia, is played out through "maimed" rituals of consent. When Titus attempts to "give his daughter's hand in marriage" to Saturninus, his action both ignores Lavinia's desire to be Bassianus's wife and flouts the prior betrothal agreement. Titus's disregard for his daughter's betrothal contract parallels his disregard for the people's right to political consent. Playing the role of tyrannical father in both private and public realms, Titus chooses the emperor of Rome without heeding the voice of its subjects.

As "Rome's royal mistress" (1.1.241), Lavinia personifies the state, which implies that her consent ought to go to the man chosen as Rome's emperor. As Leonard Tennenhouse writes, "Rather than make Lavinia serve as the object of illicit lust, Shakespeare uses her body as the site for political rivalry among various families with competing claims to power over Rome. For one of them to possess Lavinia is for that family to display power over the rest—nothing more nor less than that."[39] Because Lavinia's body acts as an instrument of political power, the two candidates for emperor must not only deliver campaign speeches to the people of Rome but also fight for Lavinia's hand. The symmetry of the events encourages the audience to make an analogy between the struggle for power over Rome and the struggle for dominion over Lavinia.

In order to validate his claim on the empery, Saturninus enlists the law of primogeniture in his opening campaign speech: "I am his first born son that was the last / That ware the imperial diadem of Rome" (ll. 5-6). His claim is strong; in sixteenth-century England "the prime factor affecting all families which owned property was . . . the principle and practice of primogeniture, for the preservation and protection of which the entail was designed."[40] Primogeniture was also a rallying cry of absolutist monarchs who argued that their power derived from the mystical transference of power from the father-king to the heir, rather than from the consent of the people. J. P. Sommerville writes, "A number of claims to authority were commonly recognized as legitimate. These included original election by the people, victory in a just war, and gift from a sovereign ruler. It was widely agreed that the best form of government was a monarchy in which succession proceeded by primogeniture in the male line, but no one argued that this was the only valid type of government."[41] By invoking primogeniture, Saturninus demonstrates an absolutist's belief in divine right.

Bassianus has an equally persuasive platform—one that rests on a more democratic or constitutional principle. He states that succession should not be automatic, based on mystical traditions of first-blood but that the people themselves should choose their ruler: "But let desert in pure election shine; / And, Romans, fight for freedom in your choice" (ll. 16-17). His claim, however, results in a stand-off, since neither brother's cause is heeded by the people. Marcus explains:

> Know that the people of Rome, for whom we stand
> A special party, have by common voice,
> In election for the Roman empery,
> Chosen Andronicus, surnamed Pius
> For many good and great deserts to Rome.
> (ll. 20-24)

But Titus declines the empery—"What should I don this robe and trouble you?" (l. 189)—though he seems to invent the prerogative to do so. Instead of ruling, he adopts a paternalistic role and arranges a marriage for Rome by unilaterally choosing the new ruler. This breach of custom in the succession rings of tyranny in that it deprives the people of their voice in two ways: it prevents them from electing the emperor freely, and it prevents them from voicing their consent to his authority. An unorthodox representative of the people, Titus privileges patriarchal principles, heredity, and divine right over election and public opinion.[42] Once Titus favors hereditary right over the people's voices, the emperor is no longer obliged to satisfy the needs of the social body, to rule, in Fortescue's paradigm, according to *dominium politicum et regale,* with public consent. Instead he may interpret his authority as unlimited. According to the author of *Vindiciae contra tyrannos,* this situation imperils the state: "we should always remember that kings were created for the people's benefit, that rulers are called 'kings' when they promote the people's interest and are called 'tyrants', as Aristotle says, when they seek to promote their own."[43] Saturninus proves to be such a self-promoter, yet Titus plainly agrees with his claim: "Content thee, Prince, I will restore to thee / The people's hearts, and wean them from themselves" (ll. 210-11). These telling lines show Titus's tendency to see the people of Rome as children to be "weaned" from their choice of Bassianus and from their right to consent to another's power just as he later thinks to "wean" his daughter from her betrothal contract with him. Since Titus claims patriarchal prerogative in both the election and the marriage, the fate of Rome is the fate of the daughter in an arranged marriage.[44]

Titus, ignoring the people's desire for him to rule, unilaterally opts instead to *arrange* a match between the people of Rome and the man of his choosing. Indeed, both the structure and the language of the scene in which Titus names the emperor reflect the structure and language of contemporary marriage transactions. The choice of words in this electoral context recalls Ephesians, wherein St. Paul insists that "the husband is the head of the wife, even as Christ is the head of the church." Titus's words, "A better head her glorious body fits / Than his that shakes for age and feebleness" (ll. 187-88), deliberately evoke the analogy between marital and political models of governance. Thus his error in choosing Saturninus becomes apparent when Bassianus elopes with Lavinia.

Marriage and primogeniture were two of the most important and obvious ways in which wealth and power could be passed down in Renaissance England.[45] Because Saturninus's claim to Rome rests on primogeniture, Bassianus confounds that claim by enlisting marriage. He cannot have Rome, but he will have Lavinia; and the brothers who, a few moments earlier, were rivals for the empery now vie for the bride. Saturninus commands: "Lavinia will I make my empress, / Rome's royal mistress, mistress of my heart, / And in the sacred [Pantheon] her espouse" (ll. 240-42). Though Titus agrees to the match, Bassianus interjects, "Lord Titus, by your leave, this maid is mine" (l. 276) and whisks the silent Lavinia offstage. His actions, interpreted by Titus as traitorous, are justified by the betrothal contract—Bassianus "owns" Lavinia by virtue of a previous legal agreement. Despite the imperial prerogative, Lavinia does indeed belong to Bassianus, as Titus's sons bravely demonstrate: "That is another's lawful promis'd love" (l. 298). Importantly, Bassianus waits to enunciate his claim to his betrothed until after Saturninus *"courts Tamora in dumb show"* (l. 275 s.d.) and proves by his lechery to be unworthy.[46] Meanwhile the suddenness of Saturninus's desire for Tamora further forewarns of a reckless regime. According to contemporary constitutionalist writers, the lust of a ruler often signaled poor statecraft; a ruler who could not control his desires would perhaps elevate his own needs over the needs of the state and its people.[47] Thomas Smith defines a tyrant as "he, who is an euill king, & who hath no regard to the wealth of his people, but seeketh onely to magnifie himselfe and his, and to satisfie his vicious and cruell appetite, without respect of God."[48] Saturninus's sexual attraction to Tamora obscures his sense of duty to the Roman people and causes him foolishly to place the enemies of Rome too near the heart of its power.

Initially, of course, the audience suspects Saturninus of absolutism when he places the principle of primogeniture over that of the people's "voice." When he thinks Titus will take the throne, he impetuously begins to stage a rebellion: "Romans, do me right. / Patricians, draw your swords, and sheathe them not / Till Saturninus be Rome's emperor" (ll. 203-5). Once named emperor, Saturninus demands Lavinia as his wife without asking Lavinia herself and only flippantly acknowledges Titus's paternal jurisdiction over her. He says, "Lavinia will I make my emperess. . . . Tell me, Andronicus, doth this motion please thee?" (ll. 240-43). Saturninus adheres to what Smith calls the "verie daungerous" paradigm of absolute power "whereof the cause is the frailtie of mans nature, which (as Plato saith) cannot abide or beare long that absolute and uncontrowled authoritie, without swelling into too much pride and insolencie."[49]

If Smith's definition of tyranny applies to Saturninus, it also characterizes Titus, who is equally prideful and tyrannous; he and Saturninus prove to be doubles in their political philosophies. By having Titus unhesitatingly kill his own son Mutius when he assists the elopement of Bassianus and Lavinia, Shakespeare underscores the extent to which Titus is also invested in absolutism; his intertwined sense of patriarchalism and politics prefigure King Lear. Like Lear, the aged Titus shirks the responsibility of leading his people, yet hopes to retain his absolute power as father. Renaissance writers who argued that a ruler's power derives from divine right theorized that fathers were the original rulers in ancient communities. Fathers, like absolutists, receive their power not from their subjects—in this case, wives and children—but from God. As Sommerville writes,

> It was widely accepted that power over a family was in the hands of the father. But the father's power was often regarded as non-political, since it did not include the power to execute his wife or children. By claiming that fathers had at first possessed the right to inflict the death penalty upon members of their families, a number of authors tried to show that the earliest political societies were not self-governing democracies, but monarchies ruled over by a father and king.[50]

Titus adopts this ancient paradigm of father as absolute ruler with the right to inflict capital punishment on his family. His paternalism explains why he chooses Saturninus as emperor in the first place and why he deferentially consents to the new emperor's wishes to marry his daughter. He believes in divinely ordained succession of the first-born son, and the irony of that belief is unmistakable. During the remainder of the play, Titus becomes a victim of his own narrow philosophy of absolutist rule.

The consequences of Titus's choice of Rome's emperor and his choice of husband for Lavinia (which she rebels against) are displayed on Lavinia's body in the second act. Meanwhile the political and marital themes of the play become intertwined: Titus's disposition of the empery carries domestic resonances of a marriage negotiation, while his bestowal of Lavinia's hand carries political resonances of tyranny and insurrection. Such reciprocity only reflects the overlapping imperatives of political and marital consent in early modern treatises. Martin Luther himself believed that marriage and government operate in conjunction: "On the one hand, though not technically a sacrament, marriage is described as holy, a 'most spiritual' status, 'ordained and founded' by God himself. It is the source of domestic and public government, the foundation of human society, which without it would 'fall to pieces.'"[51] Luther's metaphor operates quite literally in *Titus Andronicus;* as a result of maimed consent rituals, both Rome and Lavinia fall to pieces, the former symbolically, the latter literally. Correspondingly, Saturninus and Bassianus's struggle to wed Lavinia and, later, Chiron and Demetrius's contest over who will rape her mirror the struggle between constitutionalists and absolutists in the early modern period.

As the site of contention, a "map of woe" (3.2.12), Lavinia endures radical disfigurement as the play unfolds. The ill-conceived nature of Saturninus's marriage manifests itself when the treacherous Tamora, now empress, announces plans to undo Titus, exploiting the instability of his family relations to do so. Chiron and Demetrius, as sons of the empress and newly empowered step-sons of the emperor, have broad claims to power. They project their political ambitions onto Lavinia's body, desiring her because they recognize her as the emblem of imperial power. Aaron, after all, lewdly encourages Chiron and Demetrius to "revel in Lavinia's treasury" (2.1.131). His terms forge an analogy between the rapist and the monarch who would raid the state coffers for his own indulgence rather than for the benefit of the people governed. In many ways, then, Chiron and Demetrius stand for the tyranny of an absolute monarch.

Like Bassianus in Act 1, Chiron stakes his right to Lavinia's body by challenging primogeniture, subordinating it to merit:

> Demetrius, thou dost overween in all, . . .
> 'Tis not the difference of a year or two
> Makes me less gracious, or thee more
>   fortunate;
> I am as able and as fit as thou
> To serve, and to deserve my mistress' grace,
> And that my sword upon thee shall approve,
> And plead my passions for Lavinia's love.
> (2.1.29-36)

Chiron takes the chance that Lavinia will desire him and choose him above his brother. His words "serve" and "deserve" underscore his younger-brother politics of merit. Meanwhile, Demetrius calls upon Saturninus's model, that of primogeniture: "Youngling, learn thou to make some meaner choice, / Lavinia is thine elder brother's hope" (2.1.73-74).

Replaying Titus's role as the interfering patriarch and arbiter of imperial power, Aaron intervenes in this moment of sibling rivalry. As Tamora's long-time lover, he acts as a father figure to the brothers, and his superior intelligence, cunning, and worldliness invest him with might and authority just as martial deeds grant Titus power when the play opens. Aaron, however, opts for an overtly abusive solution to this competition: "strike her home by force, if not by words" (l. 118). He encourages Chiron and Demetrius to combine strengths, overpower Lavinia, and rape her. Aaron effectively "hands" Lavinia over to two people she neither desires, nor gives consent to. Rape, from the Latin *rapere,* meaning "to seize," is a powerful figure for the repudiation and violation of consent. When Lavinia reappears, the stage directions read: *"Enter . . .* LAVINIA, *her hands cut off, and her tongue cut out, and ravish'd"* (2.4.0 s.d.). Thus Shakespeare dramatizes the horror of rape and political tyranny through the visual horror of Lavinia's disfigured body.

Besides the primary purpose of silencing Lavinia, the rape and mutilation grotesquely exaggerate the oppression of the aristocratic Elizabethan wife forced to consummate marriage with a man she does not desire. Lavinia's severed hands and tongue further dramatize the loss of consent, displacing internal and mental injuries onto conspicuous limbs. In combination, the injuries spectacularly figure absolute political power. Just as the people of Rome are rendered voiceless, in that the "common voice" (1.1.21 and 5.3.140) holds no sway in the accession of Saturninus, Lavinia is able neither to protest the Goths' tyranny nor to accuse them of their foul deeds. Where Rome figuratively falls to pieces and becomes a "wilderness of tigers" (3.1.54) at the hands of Saturninus, Lavinia's body is "lopp'd and hew'd" (2.4.17) because of her father's domestic tyranny.

Significantly, Chiron and Demetrius's glee when they rape and mutilate Lavinia is at odds with their initial protestations of love for her. Chiron's wish to "serve" and "deserve" Lavinia at the beginning of Act 2 contrasts dramatically with his fiendish delight at the sight of her maimed body, expressed in his cold-hearted taunt: "Write down thy mind, bewray thy meaning so, / And if thy stumps will let thee play the scribe" (ll. 3-4). The brothers' rapacity emerges only after Aaron patronizes them with his commanding presence and sexual energy, and when they discover Lavinia is not the demure, ideal woman they believed her to be. Despite the fact that Lavinia speaks only ten lines in all of Act 1, she proves quite vocal and even caustic in Act 2. When she surprises Tamora with Aaron, Lavinia sneers at her, "'Tis thought you have a goodly gift in horning" (2.3.67) and proceeds to insult her, in front of her sons, with the name Semiramis, a Babylonian goddess sometimes thought to be an oversexed woman, sometimes thought to have seduced her son.[52] Lavinia's efforts to resist the Goths only anger them, adding zeal to their subsequent abuse. Shown to be merely an object of exchange in Act 1, Lavinia now threatens Chiron and Demetrius as much as Aaron does, and for that she is brutally punished. What happens pleases the otherwise insatiable Tamora and helps Chiron and Demetrius to regain a sense of masculinity imperiled when they were "brought to yoke" (1.1.69) by Titus—"yoked" being a common metaphor for "wedded"—and utterly lost when they were mocked by Aaron. Part of their glee derives from their ability to turn Lavinia into the exaggeratedly passive, silent woman they took her for in Act 1. In a twisted parody of the marriage ceremony, they each take a hand, literalizing the marital metaphor and reestablishing their position as members of the dominant sex. Moreover, the injuries remind us that their brutality can be traced back to Saturninus's decision to free them and even further to Titus's abrogation of the people's consent.

Shakespeare reiterates the brutal consequences of Saturninus and Titus's absolutist philosophy when he adds another hand severing, this one staged in full view. Prior to this scene, Titus must confront the spectacle of Lavinia's mutilation and recognize his own impotence vis-à-vis Saturninus's tyranny. "Give me a sword, I'll chop off my hands too" (3.1.72) is his immediate reaction to the sight of his daughter's body. Only when he sees in graphic detail the devastating impact of tyranny on his daughter does he begin to grasp the perverted possibilities of a system of governance based on an exaggerated binary of authority and subordination which is figured in this play as tyrant and rape victim. Titus wonders: "Or shall we cut away our hands like thine? / Or shall we bite our tongues, and in dumb shows / Pass the remainder of our hateful days? / What shall we do?" (ll. 130-33). Expressing his desire to mirror Lavinia and become an emblem himself of abrogated consent, Titus offers to effect his own dismemberment. In doing so, he shows he misunderstands the significance of her mutilation. Unlike Lavinia, Titus is the willful agent of his own victimization whose self-mutilation parodies the actions of a woman *consenting* to marry; as such, he exempts himself from Lavinia's hidden injuries, the tongue severing and the rape.[53]

Ironically, the words Titus utters in the intimate moment shared with Aaron before the amputation lend themselves to a comparison with the marriage ceremony. After he tricks Lucius and Marcus into believing that one of them will give their hand to Aaron, Titus says, almost seductively, "Come hither, Aaron. I'll deceive them both; / Lend me thy hand, and I will give thee mine" (ll. 186-87). His language typifies consensual wedding vows exchanged between characters in a number of Shakespeare's plays.[54] Thus when Aaron amputates Titus's hand, he feminizes the once great warrior "train'd up in arms" (1.1.30) and plays the husband to Titus's bride.[55] In addition, Titus's severed hand ironically metonymizes his relationship to the people of Rome, whom he defended with arms on the battlefield but refused to protect as their chosen ruler. Titus recognizes that the hand remaining is a tyrannizing limb, not a protective one: "This poor right hand of mine / Is left to tyrannize upon my breast" (3.2.7-8), as it can no longer tyrannize his daughter or the people of Rome.

Literally dis-membered from the empire as a useless citizen, a warrior without a hand, Titus asks, "Then which way shall I find Revenge's cave?" (3.1.270), and the play proceeds through the stages of Senecan revenge drama. During the unfolding of the revenge plot, Shakespeare continually reminds the audience of Lavinia's and Titus's injuries through indecorous puns and repetitions. An allusion to the rapist Tarquin (l. 298) and repeated references to hands and severings indicate Shakespeare's investment in these tropes as an aural means of conveying his criticism of tyranny. Tyranny, we are reminded, can "dis-member" individuals figuratively; it strips them of their membership within the social realm and takes away their human rights. This suggests why Lavinia rarely leaves the stage; her disfigured body speaks volumes against political and domestic tyranny, and Titus's chastening of Marcus for a verbal pun on hands ironically sustains the similarly dis-figured word-play:

MARCUS Fie, brother, fie, teach her not thus to lay
Such violent hands upon her tender life.
TITUS How now! has sorrow made thee dote already?
Why, Marcus, no man should be mad but I.
What violent hands can she lay on her life?
Ah, wherefore dost thou urge the name of hands. . . .
O, handle not the theme, to talk of hands. . . .

As if we should forget we had no hands,
If Marcus did not name the word of hands!
(3.2.21-33)

The spectacle is unforgettable: Titus and Lavinia exiting the stage in Act 4, Titus carrying the severed head of one son, and Lavinia taking her father's severed hand in her mouth. Indeed, even when they have left the stage, other characters continue to pun cruelly on their tragedy. For example, Aaron confesses his evil deeds to Lucius and can't resist recounting the details:

'Twas her two sons that murdered Bassianus;
They cut thy sister's tongue, and ravish'd her,
And cut her hands, and trimm'd her as thou sawest.
(5.1.91-93)

Lucius replies, "O detestable villain! call'st thou that trimming?" To which Aaron answers, "Why, she was wash'd, and cut, and trimm'd, and 'twas / Trim sport for them which had the doing of it" (ll. 91-96). Punning on both rape and mutilation, "trim" focuses appropriate attention on the *cumulative* impact of Lavinia's injuries.

Such puns answer the purpose in the final scene when Marcus displaces Lavinia's mutilation onto the troubled city of Rome and, in the process, translates the literal injuries into figurative ones. He says to Lucius, "O, let me teach you how to knit again / This scattered corn into one mutual sheaf, / These broken limbs again into one body" (5.3.70-72). The puns escalate into tautologies; like Rome, Lavinia is a "map of woe"; her body is a raped country, voiceless, lacking hands to wash, feed, or defend itself. Lavinia's abused body, which has served as an overdetermined emblem of marital oppression, now figures the "civil wound" of Rome and its people "[b]y uproars sever'd" (ll. 87, 68).

At the same time, Marcus's choice of words to describe the rebirth of Rome, words such as "knit" and "these broken limbs," echo Renaissance marriage rhetoric like Gataker's: "one man and one woman are coupled and knit togeather in one fleshe and body," or an unattached woman is a *"limbe reaft"* from man, *"that by Nuptiall coniunction . . . might be as a limbe restored. . . ."*[56] Thus Lucius rehabilitates the dismembered body of Rome by proposing a consensual marriage between head and body, ruler and people. He even displaces Rome's ravishment onto himself when he claims to have "preserv'd her welfare in my blood, / And from her bosom took the enemy's point, / Sheathing the steel in my advent'rous body" (5.3.110-12). Using repetition to emphasize the connection between Lavinia and Rome, Marcus announces that the "new" Rome will be complete and strong with new tongues and hands: "*Speak,* Romans, *speak,* and if you say we shall, / Lo *hand* in *hand* Lucius and I will fall" (ll. 135-36, emphasis added). The true leader of the freshly rehabilitated Rome begins to right the wrongs committed in Act 1 by allowing the citizens their "voice" instead of investing himself with absolute authority. Aemilius sums up, "bring our emperor gently in thy *hand,* / Lucius our emperor, for well I know / The common *voice* do cry it shall be so" (ll. 138-40, emphasis added). In their descriptions of the new Rome, Aemilius and Marcus dare to "handle the theme"; they emphasize the body parts Lavinia has lost during the play. Ultimately, however, by recalling Lavinia's appalling fate and underscoring the legitimacy of the "common voice," they reject the precedent set by her father to abrogate the people's consent by unilaterally naming the emperor. Resolved with such didacticism, the play on the whole issues a clear warning: absolute monarchy abuses the people and causes the state to "fall to pieces."

Interpreted in this way, *Titus Andronicus* becomes less a clumsy and excessively gory first attempt at tragedy than a glimpse into the political consciousness of the young Shakespeare, perhaps not yet masterful enough to obscure his progressivism.[57] Though Shakespeare was himself the first-born son and heir to his father's assets, it appears that, as he explores the political dimensions of desire and marriage, he condemns rapacious, nonconsensual political rulership. When Shakespeare wrote this play, ten years after Stubbs and Page were punished for publishing *The Discoverie of a Gaping Gulf,* Queen Elizabeth had assured the English people that she would never compromise her position through marriage. Lavinia is not so circumspect. After resisting her father's authority "to give her hand in marriage," she is forced to yield her hands, tongue, and chastity, becoming a walking caricature of wifehood at the mercy of an unwanted husband and a personification of the state at the mercy of unchecked power.

*Notes*

[1] See Albert H. Tricomi's seminal article, "The Aesthetics of Mutilation in *Titus Andronicus,*" *Shakespeare Survey* 27 (1974): 11-20; David Willbern's enormously suggestive psychoanalytic reading, "Rape and Revenge in *Titus Andronicus,*" *English Literary Renaissance* 8 (1978): 159-82; Mary Laughlin Fawcett's erudite "Arms/Words/Tears: Language and the Body in *Titus Andronicus,*" *ELH* 50 (1983): 261-78; and Gillian Murray Kendall's instructive analysis of metaphor in "Lend me thy hand': Metaphor and Mayhem in *Titus Andronicus,*" *Shakespeare Quarterly* 40 (1989): 299-316. For more recent articles, see Katherine A. Rowe's "Dismembering and Forgetting in *Titus Andronicus,*" *SQ* 45 (1994): 269-303,

which argues compellingly that the severed hand acts as an emblem of disabled agency; and Michael Neill's edifying study of hands in Shakespeare's canon, "'Amphitheaters in the Body': Playing with Hands on the Shakespearian Stage," *SS* 48 (1995): 23-50.

[2] Quotations of *Titus Andronicus* follow the *Riverside Shakespeare,* ed. G. Blakemore Evans (Boston: Houghton Mifflin, 1974).

[3] Anne Somerset, *Elizabeth I* (New York: Alfred A. Knopf, 1991), 313; Wallace MacCaffrey, *Elizabeth I* (London: Edward Arnold, 1993), 200-204; J. B. Black, *Reign of Elizabeth 1558-1603,* 2d ed. (Oxford: Clarendon Press, 1959), 350. See also Neill's subtle reading of this event and its resonances (40-41).

[4] John Stubbs, *The Discoverie of a Gaping Gulf Whereinto England is Like to be Swallowed by another French mariage, if the Lord forbid not the banes, by letting her Maiestie see the sin and punishment thereof* (London, 1579), sig. D3$^v$.

[5] The tradition of advice and consent in the English monarchy has a long history; Parliament is meant to advise the monarch, and the people are supposed to consent to the new monarch's rulership before he or she officially accedes to the throne. In John Webster's *The Duchess of Malfi,* which has its own memorable scene featuring a severed hand, Antonio observes that kings need to be counselled and advised: "Though some o'th' court hold it presumption / To instruct princes what they ought to do, / It is a noble duty to inform them / What they ought to foresee" (quoted here from John Russell Brown's Revels edition [Manchester, UK, and New York: Manchester UP, 1974], 45).

[6] William Camden, *Annales* (1610), quoted here from MacCaffrey, 203. See also Black, 350.

[7] Man and woman were considered married in Renaissance England if both participants spoke their vows in the present tense. If, for example, a woman said to her lover, "I am your wife" and he said, "I am your husband," the legal system would have recognized the marriage as valid and binding, even if the vows were uttered in private. These *de praesenti* contracts often made for confusing situations. For instance, if the vows were spoken in the future tense, "I will have you," signifying a *de futuro* contract, the couple would be betrothed rather than married. Obviously *de praesenti* marriages foiled the arrangements of many an ambitious father. Sadly, there is evidence that some men would utter *de praesenti* vows to convince women to have intercourse with them and would later deny having made any promise; see George Eliot Howard, *A History of Matrimonial Institutions,* 3 vols. (Littleton, CO: Fred B. Rothman, 1994), 1:400.

[8] Henry Smith, *A Preparative to Mariage* (London, 1591), 49.

[9] Thomas Gataker, *A Good Wife Gods Gift: and, A Wife in Deed. Two Marriage Sermons* (London, 1623), 9.

[10] Josephine Roberts writes, "the church courts gradually became more reluctant to confirm disputed marriage contracts and moved towards recognition of a church wedding as the only satisfactory guarantee of a legally acceptable marriage"; see "'The Knott Never to Bee Untide': The Controversy Regarding Marriage in Mary Worth's *Urania*" in *Reading Mary Worth: Representing Alternatives in Early Modern England,* Naomi J. Miller and Gary Waller, eds. (Knoxville: The U of Tennessee P, 1991), 109-32, esp. 115.

[11] Margaret King elucidates: "Pressure to marry the parental candidate was surely most fierce in elite circles, where only the most determined and fortunate of heiresses could hope to choose her own marital destiny. Those completely free of property, and thus of any basis for negotiations in the marriage market, clearly had the most freedom to choose. But even among poorer families, family design and economic strictures dictated marriage partners" (*Women of the Renaissance* [Chicago: U of Chicago P, 1991], 34-35, esp. 35).

[12] David Atkinson, "Marriage under Compulsion in English Renaissance Drama," *English Studies: A Journal of English Language and Literature* 67 (1986): 483-504, esp. 484.

[13] Lynda E. Boose writes, "Until the thirteenth century, when the church at last managed to gain control of marriage law, marriage was considered primarily a private contract between two families concerning property exchange. The validity and legality of matrimony rested on the *consensus nuptialis* and the property contract, a situation that set up a potential for conflict by posing the mutual consent of the two children, who owed absolute obedience to their parents, against the desires of their families, who must agree beforehand to the contract governing property exchange" ("The Father and the Bride in Shakespeare," *PMLA* 97 [1982]: 325-47, esp. 326).

[14] Smith, 35.

[15] King, 34.

[16] See King, 34.

[17] Heinrich Bullinger, *The Christen state of matrimonye* . . . , trans. Miles Coverdale, preface by Thomas Becon (London, 1543), sig. El[v].

[18] George Whetstone, *An Heptameron of Civill Discourses* (London, 1582), sig. Y1[r].

[19] William Perkins, *Christian Economy: or, A Short Survey of the Right Manner of Erecting and Ordering a family According to the Scriptures,* trans. Thomas Pickering (London, 1609), 68.

[20] T. E., *The Lawes Resolvtions of Womens Rights: or, The Lawes Provision for Woemen* (London, 1632), 52.

[21] See Leah S. Marcus, "Erasing the Stigma of Daughterhood: Mary I, Elizabeth I, and Henry VIII" in *Daughters and Fathers,* Lynda E. Boose and Betty S. Flowers, eds. (Baltimore: Johns Hopkins UP, 1989), 400-417, esp. 413.

[22] Bertie Wilkinson, *The Coronation in History* (London: George Philip and Son, 1953), 20-21. See also William Jones, *Crowns and Coronations: A History of Regalia* (London: Chatto and Windus, 1902), 220-24.

[23] Jones, 223n.

[24] Jones, 222n.

[25] Theodore Beza, *Right of Magistrates* (1574), quoted here from *Constitutionalism and Resistance in the Sixteenth Century: Three Treatises by Hotman, Beza, & Mornay,* ed. Julian H. Franklin (New York: Pegasus Press, 1969), 100-135, esp. 118.

[26] Wilkinson, 17.

[27] Patricia Crawford, *Women and Religion in England 1500-1720* (New York and London: Routledge, 1993), 40 and 43.

[28] For an incisive discussion of the domestic analogy to political governance, see Constance Jordan, "The Household and the State: Transformations in the Representation of an Analogy from Aristotle to James I," *Modern Language Quarterly* 54 (1993): 307-26.

[29] Gordon Schochet, *Patriarchalism in Political Thought: The Authoritarian Family and Political Speculation and Attitudes Especially in Seventeenth-Century England* (Oxford: Basil Blackwell, 1975), 52.

[30] For a thorough analysis of the emergence of patriarchalism in Renaissance political thought, see Schochet, 37-84.

[31] Franklin, ed., 31.

[32] Thomas Becon, *The Catechism of Thomas Becon* . . . , ed. John Ayre (Cambridge: The University Press, 1844), 329.

[33] John Hayward, for example, writes, "the whole worlde is nothinge but a greate state; a state is no other then a greate familie; and a familie no other then a greate bodye. As one GOD ruleth the worlde, one maister the familie, as all the members of one bodye receiue both sense and motion from one heade. . . . So, . . . one state should be gouerned by one commaunder" (*An Answer to the First Part of a Certaine Conference, Concerning Svccession* [London, 1603], sig. B4[r]).

[34] Susan Dwyer Amussen, *An Ordered Society: Gender and Class in Early Modern England* (New York: B. Blackwell, 1988), 58. See also Henry Parker, *Jus Populi* (London, 1644).

[35] See, for example, Robert Cleaver's statement "The gouernours of families, if (as it is in marriage) there be more then one, vpon whom the charge of government lyeth, though vnequally, are, first the *Cheefe gouernour,* which is the *Husband,* secondly *a fellow helper,* which is the *Wife*" (*A Godlie Forme of Hovseholde Government: for the Ordering of Private Families, according to the direction of God's Word* [London, 1598], sig. B2[r]). No matter how marriage-tract writers entitle the wife, she must obey the *"Cheefe gouernour,"* just as for absolutists, the people must obey their monarch.

[36] Constance Jordan, *Renaissance Feminism: Literary Texts and Political Models* (Ithaca, NY: Cornell UP, 1990), 5.

[37] Many anti-absolutist tracts were written during this period. *Vindiciae contra Tyrannos* and Buchanan's *Powers of the Crown of Scotland,* published in Latin as *De Juri Regni,* were bestsellers; Sir John Fortescue's treatises, Erasmus's *Education of a Prince,* Theodore Beza's *Right of Magistrates,* Thomas Smith's *De Republica Anglorum: The Maner of Gouernment or policie of the Realme of England* (London, 1583), and Ponet's *Politike Power* were also well known. Further, John Aylmer's *Harborowe for Faithful and True Subjects* argued that the queen was not an absolute ruler, and, in the early 1590s, Matthew Sutcliff's *De presbyterio* expressed anti-absolutist sentiments, as did Hooker's *Laws of ecclesiastical polity.* For a more thorough discussion of these tracts, see J. P. Sommerville, *Politics and Ideology in England, 1603-1640* (London and New York: Longman, 1986), 10-11.

[38] See Sommerville, 11. See also Jordan, "The Household and the State," 323-24. Jordan observes

that "Hooker locates the origins of a father's subjection not in sovereignty itself, as [Jean] Bodin had done, but in an act of deliberate agreement on the part of the people to be ruled by a king, much like the consent a woman gives when she becomes a wife and agrees to be ruled by her husband" (324). This consent differs from marital consent only in that the people, having consented, must then fully submit to their ruler; the consent cannot be revoked.

[39] Leonard Tennenhouse, *Power on Display: The politics of Shakespeare's genres* (New York and London: Methuen, 1986), 108.

[40] Lawrence Stone, *The Family, Sex and Marriage In England, 1500-1800* (New York: Harper and Row, 1977), 87.

[41] Sommerville, 26.

[42] As Wilkinson notes, Titus's abrogation of any recognition ritual "not only reflects the evolution of the community's assent to the coronation of its rulers, it also shows, beneath the formal expressions of assent, the interaction of two dominant factors in any succession, 'election' and hereditary right. These were the main elements, in harmony or conflict, which determined the people's voice in the accession of a ruler and which, indeed, went far to determine the nature of the monarchy itself" (17).

[43] *Vindiciae contra tyrannos, sive de principis in populum, populique in principem, legitima potestate*, quoted in Franklin, ed., 172.

[44] For a discussion of Rome as a feminized city-state, see Linda Woodbridge, "Palisading the Body Politic" in *True Rites and Maimed Rites: Ritual and Anti-Ritual in Shakespeare and His Age*, Linda Woodbridge and Edward Berry, eds. (Urbana: U of Illinois P, 1992), 270-98, esp. 272-74.

[45] On the importance of primogeniture and marriage in the transmission of wealth, see Stone, 88.

[46] This stage direction was apparently invented by Nicholas Rowe in his 1709 edition of the *Works*. Though he strikes it from the new Arden edition of the play, Jonathan Bate agrees that Saturninus must pay some courtesy to Tamora during this scene to warrant his missing the elopement; see Jonathan Bate, ed., *Titus Andronicus* (New York and London: Routledge, 1995), 145n.

[47] Rebecca Bushnell persuasively argues that lust accompanies tyranny and effeminates the ruler to his lustful desires. Bushnell writes, "The association between femininity and tyranny thus is to be perceived in two related images: the lustful and shrewish woman as the mirror images of tyrannical rule, and the 'effeminated' prince subjected to his lust while he rules others tyrannically. The latter image occurs more frequently in the literature of the period, especially in the parade of Renaissance stage tyrants whose only vulnerability is their lust for women or their uxoriousness, recalling the 'effeminate' Hercules and Omphale Tragedies . . ." (*Tragedies of Tyrants: Political Thought and Theater in the English Renaissance* [Ithaca, NY: Cornell UP, 1990], 68).

[48] Thomas Smith, 9.

[49] Thomas Smith, 7-8.

[50] Sommerville, 22.

[51] Martin Luther, "Das siebend Capitel St. Paul zu den Corinthern ausgelegt" (1532), quoted here from Howard, 387.

[52] The various versions of the Semiramis story are fascinating; see *Brewer's Book of Myth and Legend*, ed. J. C. Cooper (London: Cassell, 1992). For evidence that Semiramis seduced her son, see Lisa Jardine, *Still Harping on Daughters: Women and Drama in the Age of Shakespeare* (Sussex, UK: Harvester Press, 1983), 76.

[53] Michael Neill sees Titus's sacrifice in a subtly different light. He reads Titus's consent to the amputation as "recall[ing] one of the most celebrated demonstrations of Roman *virtus*—the sacrifice of his right hand by the captured warrior Gaius Mucius Scaevola. . . . Just as Scaevola's mutilation of his right hand expresses his contempt for Rome's royal enemy, so Titus sacrifices his left as a defiant offering to his own tyrannic emperor, Saturninus" (39). Neill, too, reads Titus's offering as an outward recognition that tyranny reigns.

[54] Shakespeare often uses the metaphor of "giving one's hand in marriage" to enact betrothal agreements. In *King Lear*, for example, when Burgundy begs Lear to reconsider disowning Cordelia, he says, "Royal King, / Give but that portion which yourself propos'd, / And here I take Cordelia by the hand, / Duchess of Burgundy" (1.1.242-44). Likewise Claudio says to Hero in *Much Ado About Nothing*, "Give me your hand before this holy friar—/ I am your husband if you like of me" (5.4.58-59). In *Romeo and Juliet*, Romeo implores Friar Lawrence, "Do thou but close our hands with holy words, / Then love-devouring death do what he dare, / It is enough I may but call her mine" (2.6.6-8).

[55] Katherine Rowe locates this scene within both the heroic tradition and the marital one. She ar-

gues that it "grotesquely parodies the ritual gesture of handclasping that often accompanies gift-exchange in the heroic tradition" and that it tropes on "the image of two hands clasped in marriage" (291 and 293).

[56] Hermann of Wied, *The Glasse of godly Loue* in Thomas Pritchard, *The Schoole of honest and vertuous Lyfe* (London, 1579), 77; and Gataker, 9.

[57] I am not alone in detecting Shakespeare's progressive politics in this play. Bate, for one, remarks in his introduction to the Arden *Titus* that "Shakespeare's earliest tragedy may be shot through with an unexpected vein of republicanism" (21).

---

Source: " 'Rape, I Fear, Was Root of Thy Annoy': The Politics of Consent in *Titus Andronicus*," in *Shakespeare Quarterly,* Vol. 49, No. 1, Spring, 1998, pp. 22-39.

# Shakespeare and *Clarissa*: 'General Nature', Genre and Sexuality

## Martin Scofield, *University of Kent*

*I. Universality and Difference*

Most critics in the eighteenth century, unlike academic critics today, were confident of at least one assumption about great literature: that the truths it embodied were universal and that, in the words of Dr Johnson in his Preface to Shakespeare, 'Nothing can please many and please long but just representations of general nature.' It is a view which depends of course on even more basic assumptions—that there is such an entity as 'general nature' (or at least that the category is useful); and that in turn there is such an entity (or meaningful category) as 'human nature'—a certain intrinsic 'humanness' which remains in some way constant despite variations from country to country and race to race, and despite the changes in behaviour over time. But while it might be agreed that there are some constant factors in human behaviour (without which it is difficult to see how we could respond to the literature of the past at all), the notion of a 'human nature' (whether as an essence, a useful category or some kind of shadowy ideal), has become (notoriously) in recent years almost impossible to use. It is probably fair to say that some such view lay behind nearly all literary criticism from Johnson's time (and indeed before) to our own. Questioned or rejected as these ideas have been by the various forms of deconstruction, post-structuralism, new historicism and the like, literary criticism has, again notoriously, become uncertain of its foundations and has looked about for new ones. The stress has been put on relativism, on the notion that cultural values change, and on the idea that every age reads past works of literature not just differently (this was always conceded) but radically differently, not even always in 'the spirit that the author writ' (another eighteenth-century maxim, this time Pope's) but sometimes against that spirit, in readings that dissect, analyse, recreate in the image of the critic's own time. The stress has been put not on an 'unchanging human nature' but rather on the idea that human nature does change, and that literature is important above all because it both records and contributes to that process of change.

In the case of Richardson, eighteenth-century admirers were virtually united in the kind of praise they accorded him, and this praise had two main formulations: that he embodied universal truths, and that he was like Shakespeare. 'Of Nature born, by Shakespeare got' was the first line of a poem on Richardson by David Garrick; Dr Johnson for his part described Richardson as 'a writer similar in genius to Shakespeare, being acquainted with the innermost recesses of the heart' ('the heart' being a kind of constant, like 'human nature') and as having 'an absolute command of the passions, so as to be able to affect his readers as himself is affected';[1] and he also asserted that there were 'few sentiments [in the sense of thoughts or reflections] that may not be traced up to Homer, Shakespeare or Richardson'.[2] The trio of great names, widely separated by history, is itself a good example of the universalizing and trans-historical view of literary value. In 1813, again, *The Monthly Magazine* called Richardson 'the Shakespeare of Romance'.[3]

The tradition of comparing Richardson and Shakespeare has continued into our own day. There are a few dissenting voices like that of Walter Allen who compared Fielding with Shakespeare, and Richardson with Milton. But Mark Kinkead-Weekes put the comparison strongly when he wrote: 'The great invention of *Clarissa* can indeed be seen as the discovery of how to use comedy to probe tragedy . . . What is significant is that the probing of tragedy by comedy is as centrally "Shakespeare" as the depth of characterization and the mastery of human nature that were the distinguishing features of Shakespeare for the eighteenth century.'[4] This introduces the idea of mixing the genres; and Kinkead-Weekes's whole book, entitled *Samuel Richardson: Dramatic Novelist,* puts its emphasis (as in Henry James's famous advice to the novelist, 'Dramatize, dramatize!') on Richardson's dramatic powers of immediacy of presentation, dialogue, and of writing 'to the moment' (the feature of epistolary convention where the character is writing of events immediately after they have happened or even as they happen). He also emphasized the Shakespearian quality of Richardson's exploration of character and his overall moral vision: 'Richardson was, I think, the first novelist to merit comparison with Shakespeare in both the power to explore "free" characters, and the struggle to comprehend and make the centre hold against the strongest challenge he could mount.'[5] ('Centre' here has a Jamesian sense of 'central moral view').

I shall return to these questions of moral vision in relation to the two writers; but I want also to consider the possibility of other kinds of comparisons than the ones illustrated above. What of the differences of genre between a novel of several volumes and over a million words and a play of some two to three thousand lines which lasts three hours on the stage? What of the differences between an art of immediate presentation designed to be embodied by actors, and an art of drama mediated through the epistolary convention and the convention of an 'editorial' author who arranges this correspondence and who guides the reader through it? What, above all, of the differences between a self-confessedly didactic novelist and an 'invisible' playwright who, as Johnson said, 'seems to write without any moral purpose'?

*II. Genre: Tragedy Versus Comedy*

*Clarissa* is a tragedy that might have been made a comedy. There is of course a great deal of wit and humour in the novel, and the situation and tone are not so very different, at least in its earlier stages, from Richardson's earlier novel *Pamela* where the heroine resists the seductive wiles of Mr B and the novel moves to the comic conclusion of marriage. Some contemporary readers of the earlier parts of *Clarissa* expressed to Richardson their hopes that the novel would end happily. Richardson's most energetic correspondent, Lady Bradshaig, wrote with earnest entreaties that he would not be so hard-hearted as to let Clarissa die. Richardson replied: 'I would not think of leaving my heroine short of Heaven.'[6] The reply reinforces the idea that Richardson's religious and didactic intention was a large part of the pressure that led the novel towards tragedy. He clearly developed a conception in which Clarissa would remain true to an absolute principle of integrity and virtue despite an emotional attraction to Lovelace, and Lovelace would remain true to a principle of Nature as opposed to morality (rather like Shakespeare's Edmund), to the principle of male sexual licence and domination, in spite of the sensitivity and intelligence which could see and admire Clarissa's own moral intelligence and virtue. 'Thou Nature art my goddess', says Edmund, and Lovelace speaks of his hopes of the Triumph of Nature over Principle. But Lovelace can feel intense remorse, and even Edmund tries to countermand the order for Cordelia's murder.

Richardson's drama of male sexuality, female virtue and parental and social prohibition suggests comparisons with Shakespeare, but not so much in the realm of tragedy as in comedy. It is not an exaggeration to say that Shakespeare characteristically treats sexuality (particularly if we confine ourselves to the subject of love before marriage) in terms of comedy rather than tragedy, and in ways which question assumptions (as in Richardson) of sexual polarity. In *As You Like It* Rosalind is banished by her wicked uncle with only Celia for an ally (as Anna Howe is to Clarissa), and teaches Orlando how to woo her by adopting a male disguise that seems to suggest a playing down of the absolute differences of male and female roles and of the absolute opposition of male and female sexuality. This mitigation of absolute sexual polarity also occurs in *Twelfth Night* where Orsino falls in love with Viola by way of being initially attracted to her as a young man; whereas his possessive and fantastical passion for Olivia evaporates into an absurd destructiveness parodic of Othello's (and close to Lovelace's) in his lines at Act 5.1.115-17:

Why should I not, had I the heart to do it,
Like to th' Egyptian thief, at point of death
Kill what I love;

and Olivia comes to love Sebastian by way of her love for his disguised twin sister. (The convections of disguise and mistaken identity are simply used as compressions or figurations of these processes). In *Much Ado About Nothing* one half of the plot turns on the question of Hero's chastity, but Don John's plot is exposed, and the brutality and arrogance of Claudio's violent spurning of his bride is also exposed and repented of (an arrogant moralism not unlike that of James Harlowe at his sister's supposed 'fall').

Shakespeare, then, tends to view the problems of premarital love and sexuality in a comic rather than tragic light, as amenable to the human and reconciling conventions of the genre. His 'sexual' tragedies tend to focus on marital relations: in *Othello* the jealous rage of the supposedly wronged husband; in *Antony and Cleopatra* the confusions and conflicting and self-destroying aims and ambitions of a mature man and woman both thwarted and exalted by their relationship. None of Shakespeare's tragedies centres, as Richardson's does, on the chastity, or more exclusively the virginity, of an unmarried woman. The tragedy of *Romeo and Juliet* arises from the 'fate' enjoined on them by their feuding families and an additional element of chance or accident. The question of Juliet's 'virtue' hardly arises. In this and in the ways we have already noted, it is of all Shakespeare's tragedies the one closest to comedy (although several other tragedies are intensified and made complex by their comic elements and even by the sense that they often seem to arise out of 'a comic matrix').[7] It is the lightness, the volatility, the youthfulness of *Romeo and Juliet* that gives the tragedy its unique romanticism and sadness.

But it is in *Measure for Measure,* a Shakespearian comedy which comes perhaps closest to tragedy, that we find the most suggestive parallels and contrasts with *Clarissa*. Angelo's character is of course very different to Lovelace's: the icily repressed puritan governor as opposed to the irresponsible aristocratic rake. But in his sudden passion for Isabella, in particular his sexual attraction to her virtue, he shows responses akin to Lovelace's. Perhaps too, as has been suggested, Richardson half recalls some of Angelo's phrases in the language he gives to Lovelace.[8] When, for example, Lovelace is writing to Belford about the maid-servant Dorcas's fidelity to his 'bad cause', he notes: 'The vicious are as bad as they can be; and do the devil's work without looking after; while he is continually spreading snares for the others; and, like a skilful angler, suiting his baits to the fish he angles for.' (III, 247);[9] which recalls Angelo: 'O cunning enemy, that, to catch a saint, / With saints dost bait thy hook!' (*Measure for Measure* 2.2.185-6). Again, when Belford is meditating (to Lovelace) on his own and Lovelace's past follies he uses language which recalls Isabella's rebukes to Angelo:

> Lords of the creation! Who can forbear indignant laughter! When we see not one of the individuals of that creation (his perpetual eccentric self excepted) but acts within his own natural and original appointments: and all the time, proud and vain as the conceited wretch is of fancied and self-dependent excellence, he is obliged not only for the ornaments, but for the necessaries of life . . . to all the other creatures; strutting with his blood and spirit in his veins, and with their plumage on his back: for what has he of his own, but his very mischievous, monkey-like, bad nature?
>
> (IV, 8)

Isabella is terser and more concentratedly metaphoric (as we would expect of Shakespeare's creation) but has the same combination of scorn for man's godlike pretensions, with the imagery of dress and animals:

> But man, proud man,
> Dressed in a little brief authority,
> Most ignorant of what he's most assured,
> His glassy essence, like an angry ape
> Plays such fantastic tricks before high heaven
> As makes the angels weep . . .
>
> (2.2.120-5)

It is perhaps characteristic of Shakespeare that his most serious study of a man who is, in effect, a would-be rapist, is the study of a repressed puritan rather than of a rake. There are very few rapists in Shakespeare's plays: the only other obvious examples are Cloten in *Cymbeline,* who is a spoilt fool, and Demetrius and Chiron in *Titus Andronicus,* who are just princely thugs. There are also few or no brilliantly rakish seducer-villains in Shakespeare (perhaps surprisingly). Iachimo in *Cymbeline* comes closest to Lovelace in his wit and style and command of language, and an unscrupulous viciousness which does not even have the mitigating elements of Lovelace's genuine recognition and admiration of virtue. He also has Lovelace's witty but cynical assumption that women always have a simpering sexual awareness beneath a show of modesty: 'No need but of the most delicate hints to *them* . . . Like so many musical instruments, touch but a single wire, and the dear souls are sensible all over' (III, 63)—(reminiscent of Pope in its combination of 'Every woman is at heart a rake' with 'The spider's touch, how infinitely fine! / Feels in each thread and lives along the line': Richardson has among his powers a vividly poetic feeling for language). It is also like Iachimo's sly observation (invention?) of Imogen's reading of 'the tale of Tereus': 'Here the leaf's turned down / Where Philomel gave up' (*Cymbeline,* 2.2.45-5). Mercutio might, in a story other than *Romeo and Juliet,* have fulfilled Lovelace's role—he has the wit, the passion, the crude but virile sexual language. It has of course been suggested that one reason (apart from plot) he is killed half way through the play may be that his presence would have been fatal to the atmosphere of high romantic love. But Mercutio as we know him never shows the final sexual ruthlessness of a Lovelace, and we feel he would have too much honour and honesty to stoop to Lovelace's underhand violence and deception (and perhaps too much self-knowledge to be lured by a Clarissa's virtue).

A more apt and suggestive comparison with Lovelace, from Shakespeare's plays, is Lucio in *Measure for Measure.* Lucio is a gentleman (if not an aristocrat like Lovelace), and proud of his class status. He also has the sensitivity to recognize, even be awed by, Isabella's virtue ('I hold thee as a thing enskied and sainted'). At the same time he is sexually loose in his habits, frequenting prostitutes and despising them at the same time, so that his finally having to marry Kate Keepdown is to him as bad as 'pressing to death, whipping and hanging'. He has less wit and passion than Lovelace, but Lovelace shares his combination of snobbish hauteur towards and complicity with the low-life characters he exploits. In reflecting to Belford on women's love of praise he recalls a 'well-dressed, handsome girl' laughing at and enjoying the praises of a chimney sweep in the streets: 'Egad, girl, thought I, I despise thee as a Lovelace: but were I the chimney sweeper, and could only contrive to get into thy presence, my life to my virtue, I would have thee.' Lovelace has not, it appears, habitually gone with prostitutes in the past, but part of his degradation in the novel is his increasingly being drawn into the world of Mrs Sinclair and her women, a world which he has (perhaps) for a long time inhabited in a moral sense.

But for a full sense of Lovelace's 'Shakespearian' qualities we have to turn to more impressive figures than Lucio—or rather, figures at once more impressive and more disturbing. There is something of Hamlet in Lovelace's love of plotting: 'Had I been a military hero, I should have made gunpowder useless; for I should have blown up all my adversaries by dint of stratagem, turning their own devices upon them' (II, 55). Compare Hamlet's ''tis the sport to have the enginer / Hoist with his own petard'. There is something of Iago in his sophistries ('She did deceive her father, marrying you' *Othello* 3.3.209') and in his basic attitude to female sexual virtue (Iago: 'Blessed fig's end! The wine she drinks is made of grapes'); and his subtle self-justifications, almost self-deceptions (Iago:

'And what's he then that says I play the villain, / When this advice to Cassio is free, I give, and honest'; Lovelace: 'But ingenuousness was ever a signal part of my character'). This last is less of a perversion of the truth than in Iago's case, but there is something of the same sophistry or self-deception of claiming frankness or sincerity because an action *could* be construed as a good one and also because they both admit their true motives to themselves. Finally there is something of Edmund in Lovelace's sexual virility, wit and courage. The vigour of Edmund's first soliloquy in which he proclaims himself one of those

> Who in the lusty stealth of nature take
> More composition and fierce quality
> Than doth within a dull, stale, tirèd bed
> Go to th' creating a whole tribe of fops
> Got 'tween a sleep and wake.
> (*The Tragedy of King Lear* 1.2.11-15)

—and the sexual punning of his dialogue with Goneril ('Yours in the ranks of death') find a parallel in the vividness of Lovelace's language: 'Now fire, now ice, my soul is continually *upon the hiss,* as I may say' (II, 432) and in the sometimes fantastic inventiveness of his metaphors, which also have a touch of Hotspur in them, of Ben Jonson's characters, and of Milton's Satan 'snuffing the wide air':

> This it is to have leisure on my hands! What a matchless plotter thy friend! Stand by and let me swell!—I am already as big as an elephant, and ten times wiser!—mightier too by far! Have I not reason to snuff the moon with my proboscis?
>
> (II, 114)

That the poetic force of Lovelace's language can call up so many Shakespearian and other echoes suggests something of the extraordinary complexity of his character. But because he is a character in an eighteenth-century epistolary novel with a didactic and religious intention, he cannot become either a tragic hero like Hamlet, or a tragic villain like Iago or Edmund.[10] Rather he is degraded from his full potential and complexity rather as Milton's Satan is degraded from great heroic individualist to a shape-changer and finally a hissing serpent. Nor, because Richardson is determined to avoid a comic resolution, and determined not to 'think of leaving my heroine short of heaven', is Lovelace allowed the chance to reform of the sexual sinner of comedy, like Lucio in *Measure for Measure,* or (closer to Lovelace's own crime—and strength of character) Angelo in the same play.

> They say best men are moulded out of faults,
> And, for the most, become much more the better
> For being a little bad. So may my husband.
> (5.1.436-8)

So says Mariana, pleading for Angelo's life: but the charities possible in tragi-comedy are not possible either in tragedy (which *Clarissa* almost is) or in the religiously didactic epistolary novel. Even Caliban, who tried to rape Miranda, is pardoned at the end of *The Tempest,* and allowed to 'sue for grace'. And in *Pericles* the young lord (close in class and type to Lovelace) is allowed to be abashed and chastened by Mariana's innocence: such is the benevolent vision of Shakespeare's late romances.[11]

A dramatic and even Shakespearian inspiration, but also the constraints of genre and of history, are felt too in the creation of the character of Clarissa. Clarissa is not a pallid Victorian heroine: she has an intelligence and moral strength which put her in a class apart from either the pathos of the 'fallen woman' like George Eliot's Hetty Sorel or the wilful egoism of the nearly erring Rosamund Vincy. And her moral reasoning and prolonged effort at virtue and sincerity is allowed fuller play than that of a more substantial woman than either of the above, who dies tragically for love, Maggie Tulliver in *Mill on the Floss*. She also has a power of speech and repartee which one critic has likened to that of the Restoration female wits: her snubbing of Solmes has been compared with Millamant's snubbing of Sir Wilful (in *The Way of the World*) and she has been seen as combining the innocence of Margery Pinchwife with the trenchancy of Mrs Alithea (in *The Country Wife*).[12] Her retorts to her brother, though of course more serious and painful, are reminiscent of Ophelia's lively resistance to Laertes's possessive warnings about her honour.

But we cannot imagine Clarissa talking and joking with the freedom of a Rosalind with Orlando or still less of a Helena with Parolles. Gentlemen and ladies of the early seventeenth century (if we can see Shakespeare as the ideal representative of it) found it much easier to be liberal in matters of talk about sex than Richardson and the post-puritan eighteenth century, with its tension-producing combination of aristocratic and gentlemanly licence and middle-class respectability. At the dinner at Mrs Sinclair's with Lovelace and his three friends (as Belford reports it) Clarissa shames the company by quoting Cowley against 'florid talk' and showing her displeasure by her eye, 'Not poorly, like the generality of her sex affecting ignorance of meanings too obvious to be concealed; but so resenting, as to show each impudent laugher the offence given to, and taken by, a purity, that had mistaken its way, when it fell into such a company' (II, 486). Clarissa is not prudish here but she is stern: as a figure intended to be exemplary she has to be so. The novel, as a great representative work of the mid-eighteenth century, carries the burden of new sexual and social anxieties.

On a more tragic level, Clarissa can echo Hamlet's language, as when she writes of how her doubts, perplexities and hopes 'each getting the victory by turns, harrow up my soul between them' (II, 9). On another occasion, after learning that her father has said he would 'kneel for her, if nothing else will do, to prevail upon her to oblige me', she reacts with the poignant compassion of Cordelia before the broken figure of her father in Act 4 Scene 6 of *King Lear* ('O look upon me, sir,/ And hold your hands in benediction o'er me. / You must not kneel.')

> A father to KNEEL to his child! There would not have been any bearing of that! What I should have done in such a case I know not. Death would have been much more welcome to me than such a sight, on such an occasion, in behalf of a man so very, very disgustful to me! But I had deserved annihilation had I suffered my father to kneel in vain.
>
> (II, 166)

But again the pathos is at one remove in the novel, a matter of the heroine's inward reflection. Clarissa's father never kneels, either in emotional blackmail or in Lear's pathetic contrition; and Clarissa never risks the step of fully resisting her father and of giving herself to Lovelace, which would have led either to marriage, or to a different kind of tragedy. *Clarissa*, showing a restraint characteristic of the more refined and polite eighteenth century, is about the refraining from action and the turning away from life, as opposed to the Shakespearian commitment which risks all and suffers the full sharpness of tragedy as a result. And while it might seem at first glance grudging to deny Clarissa the courage of risk-taking (since, after all, someone might say, she did run away with Lovelace), Richardson's punctilious care in pointing out that she was *tricked* into running away almost takes this particular moment of courage away from her as he endeavours to guard her against the criticisms of his most prudent and censorious (and largely female) readers.

### III. The Uses of Quotation

One measure both of the responsiveness of Richardson to Shakespearian suggestions and of the gap between the two authors' imaginations and between their two historical periods can be seen in Richardson's use of Shakespearian quotation. In the case of Lovelace the use is generally ironic (ironic and critical on the part of Richardson), in a way that points to the potentially tragic division in Lovelace's nature. There is the case for instance of his famous quotation of Ferdinand's speech about Miranda (*The Tempest*, 3.1.39-48):

> Full many a lady
> I've eyed with best regard; and many a time
> Th'harmony of their tongues hath into bondage
> Brought my too diligent ear. For *sev'ral* virtues
> Have I liked *sev'ral* women. Never any
> With so full a soul, but some defect in her
> Did quarrel with the noblest grace she ow'd,
> And put it to the *foil*. But SHE!—O SHE!
> So perfect and so peerless is created,
> Of every creature's best.

(Quotation as in Richardson, 1.150). The irony arises from the way this shows Lovelace's sensitivity and genuine wonder at Clarissa, qualities that are nevertheless, as we know, not held with complete sincerity. Even the emphasis on *'sev'ral'* may suggest Lovelace's complacent self-regard for his own conquests. The idealizing love of Ferdinand is quickly seen in Lovelace's case to involve a dangerous temptation: 'All that's excellent in her sex is in this lady! Until by MATRIMONIAL or EQUAL intimacies, I have found her *less than angel,* it is impossible to think any other's' (which is rather like the temptation Isabella's purity presents to Angelo). There is a different kind of irony, again, in Lovelace's quotation from *Othello* a few pages earlier: 'Thou wilt say I rave. And so I do: "Perdition catch my soul, but I *do* love her." *Else* could I bear the implacable revilings of her implacable family? *Else* could I basely creep about—not her proud father's house—but his paddock and garden walls?' There is not only irony (potentially tragic, as it is tragic in Othello's case) in the fact that perdition *does* catch his soul, but also in the contrast of his scheming and calculating desire to dominate and the half-posturing of his epistolary style, with Othello's genuine rapture.

At other times Lovelace's Shakespearian quotations simply give an added depth and subtlety to his character. In vol. IV letter X, estimating the possibility of Clarissa committing suicide he imagines that she must reason with herself in the terms of Claudio's great speech on death ('Ay but to die and go we know not where') which he quotes in full. It gives an added sense of his cultivation and poetic judgement, but it may also register the irony of his lack of reflection that Clarissa would hardly have been content with such a non-Christian objection and fear of death (though we might also recall how the pious Dr Johnson would be heard muttering the lines to himself in his later years). In vol. II letter CX (425-6) there is a subtler and more chilling use of Shakespearian quotation when Lovelace, writing to Belford about how he gloats over the idea of conquering Clarissa, adapts Hector's speech to Achilles in *Troilus and Cressida* (4.7.137-40)

> Henceforth, O watchful fair one, guard thee well:
> For I'll not kill thee There! nor There! nor There!
> But, by the zone that circles Venus' waist,
> I'll kill thee everywhere.

The arrogant brutality of Hector, already in Shakespeare a deeply ironic and sceptical treatment of Trojan heroism, is evoked to show the arrogant destructiveness, the almost self-confessed misogyny of Lovelace's obsession with Clarissa, and its self-dramatizing panache.

Clarissa alludes less to Shakespeare, but her memories of the poet's words are still significant, and what is more are less calculated, more spontaneous and, as one would expect, reflect both her taste and her virtue. We have already seen how she uses Hamlet's phrase 'harrow up my soul' (II.9),—though as if inadvertently, and without explicit self-conscious quotation in the pressure of rendering her feelings about her loss of her reputation and her 'cruel doubts and perplexities' after fleeing with Lovelace. But the most notable instance of her (again 'involuntary') quotation of Shakespeare comes in her delirious jottings when she regains consciousness after her rape. Richardson uses Clarissa's derangement to explore the hidden elements in her mind, and the episode has been described as 'the first honest attempt to deal with the unconscious since Lear and Ophelia'.[13] But while it is doubtless honest, one wonders if it succeeds artistically. The episode seems to me, indeed, to mark one of the limits of Richardson's imagination and to suggest a dimension that, unlike Shakespeare, he cannot fully achieve.

In letter XXXIII in volume III, Lovelace writes to Belford, transcribing some papers, some torn or scratched through, which Clarissa has written as soon as she has recovered enough physically from the rape. This itself might seem a rather awkward aspect of the epistolary technique which Richardson is forced to use: it is difficult to imagine Lovelace copying out these indictments of himself; and the only reasons he gives are that he does it for 'the novelty of the thing', and to 'show thee how her mind works now that she is in this whimsical way.' Paper VII takes a more oblique, even 'literary' form: it is a kind of poetic declamation against Lovelace, with echoes of *Twelfth Night* and the Sonnets ('Thou eating canker worm, that preyest upon the opening bud, and turnest the damask rose into livid yellowness'). In all this the device of the papers seems especially awkward, the rhetoric is formal in a limiting way, and the literary echoes only increase our sense of artificiality. In paper X Clarissa has written down (and Lovelace transcribes) a collection of quotations, including two from *Hamlet*: the Ghost's 'I could a tale unfold / Would harrow up thy soul', and Hamlet's (in adapted form)

> —Oh! you have done an act
> That blots the face and blush of modesty;
>     Takes off the rose
> From the fair forehead of an innocent Love
> And makes a blister there.

It is notable that Clarissa (and Richardson) takes a speech directed against female lust to apply to Lovelace: a Freudian might doubtless say it suggests an unconscious guilt on Clarissa's part. But this would be straining the meaning: it hardly has that effect. And the main reaction I think we have to this passage, on reflection, is to feel the awkwardness of the stratagem for revealing Clarissa's inner life. And it calls up comparisons—the power of the direct Shakespearian presentation of passion and madness in Hamlet, or Ophelia or Lear—which can only make Richardson's attempt look extremely limited.

Much more telling is letter XXXV, where Lovelace describes the first meeting with Clarissa after the rape, where a genuinely novelistic drama is again possible. Clarissa's dignity and scathing contempt of Lovelace, and the latter's vain, stammered attempts at self-excuse are powerfully done, and the rhetoric seems justified by the intensity of the dramatic situation. Where Richardson can present the dramatic but formal and always 'polite' exchanges of protagonists, he can achieve considerable power. But the inner revelation of real soliloquy and the poetry of madness or derangement eludes him. And this is surely a measure of the limitation of the age: the tensions produced by a considerable permissiveness of sexual behaviour among the aristocratic classes on one hand and an anxiety about sexual licence, a middle-class propriety which inherits many of the puritan traits of repressiveness, give rise to a novel which explores just this theme, but whose technique is limited precisely by the constraints and anxieties it explores.

Richardson's concern to avoid what he called 'the horrid' also betrays this inhibition. Writing to Lady Bradshaigh, and in the course of defending himself against charges of hardheartedness and cruelty and defending his decision not to give the novel a happy ending, he distinguishes between 'Acts of Terror and Warning' and 'Acts of Horror', and says that 'the catastrophe of Shakespeare's *Romeo and Juliet* may truly be called "horrid" '.[14] He quotes in particular Juliet's speech before taking the potion, with its fears of waking in the burial vault of the Capulets 'Where bloody Tybalt, yet but green in earth, / Lies festering in his shroud' etc. Richardson seems to disparage this, for he calls this 'truly horrid', and says he hopes he has avoided all Rant, Horror, indecent images and inflaming descriptions. Again it can be said that his fear of offending his genteel lady readers constitutes a limitation.

## IV. Letters and Sexuality

Despite its capacity for drama in Richardson's hands, the epistolary novel suffers from the limitation of presenting action at two removes: it is mediated both through the mind of the author and through the imagined mind of the letter-writer. The former mediation is that of any literature, though drama, and particularly drama seen on the stage, gives the greatest illusion of its absence. Performed drama presents, as it were, the living, suffering body; whereas the epistolary novel presents that body mediated through two levels of reflection. And what both Richardson and his protagonist Lovelace say about letters confirms this sense that the letter (at least as a means of communication rather than as a novelistic technique) denies the body. Richardson suggests that communication through letters is purer, less interrupted by accident, than ordinary conversation:

> This correspondence is, indeed, the cement of friendship; it is friendship avowed under hand and seal: friendship upon bond, as I may say; more pure, yet more ardent, and less broken in upon, than personal conversation can be even amongst the most pure, because of the deliberation it allows, from the very preparation to, and action of writing.

The phrase 'even amongst the most pure' suggests particularly an element of puritanism behind this. And he goes on a few lines later:

> Who then shall decline the converse of the pen? The pen that makes distance, presence; and brings back to sweet remembrance all the delights of presence; which makes even presence but body, while absence becomes the soul;[15]

The spiritualizing tendency of this, the sense of an escape from the physical, receives a more explicitly sexual connotation in a later remark in the same letter when the young lady to whom Richardson is writing is advised to write principally to her own sex 'since ours is hardly ever void of design, and makes correspondence dangerous'. Even at the safe physical distance implied by letter-writing the designs of men had to be closely watched.

This suggestion makes even more pointed the connection between the above letter and one of Lovelace's. He is telling Belford of a conversation with Clarissa about letter-writing, where he is trying to get Clarissa to let him read letters between her and Miss Howe:

> I proceeded therefore—That I loved letter-writing, as I had more than once told her, above all species of writing; it was writing from the heart (without the fetters prescribed by method or study), as the very word *correspondence* implied. Not the heart only; the soul was in it. Nothing of body, when friend writes to friend; the mind impelling sovereignly the vassal fingers. It was, in short, friendship recorded; friendship given under hand and seal; demonstrating that the parties were under no apprehension of changing from time or accident, when they so liberally gave testimonies, which would always be ready, on failure or infidelity, to be turned against them.
>
> (II.431)

The phrase 'The mind impelling sovereignly the vassal fingers' suggests the domination of body by the will, the (male) intellect, the exact opposite of Eliot's phrase about 'the intellect at the tips of the senses'.[16] Here the senses are at the tip of the manipulating intellect. The 'design' of men's letters, which Richardson talks about in his own letter, is of course preeminently the quality of many of Lovelace's *reported* letters (though not, as I shall argue below, many of his *printed* letters), particularly those at the end of volume 1 where he is persuading Clarissa to agree to meet him in the summer house and elope with him (an agreement she subsequently tries in a further letter to revoke, but he deliberately fails to collect the letter); or where he persuades her to go to Mrs Sinclair's.

Letters in Shakespeare's plays also (doubtless partly because of the demands of the genre, and their use generally as part of the plot where they are items on which action will turn) have more often the character of agents of design than that of free disinterested communications of friendship. Indeed, letters in Shakespeare are more often than not extremely untrustworthy or at least problematic—either because they are intended to trick or deceive, or because they are self-deceiving, or because they give bad advice or advice which the recipient is unwilling to take. (It has been said that nowhere in Shakespeare's plays is advice shown as doing any good: bad advice is followed and good advice is ignored.) In the comedies letters are used to show the affectation or pretension of the sender (Don Armado to Jaquenetta in *Love's Labour's Lost* or Orlando in *As You Like It*); or (as forged letters) to deceive and expose a recipient (Malvolio in *Twelfth Night*). The letter as a statement 'avowed under hand and seal' or 'upon hand' (to use Richardson's terms) is in Shakespeare something that is more often than not turned against the writer, either because it is intercepted by a hostile party (as the Duke intercepts Valentine's letter in *The Two Gentlemen of Verona*), or because it is read in a way that mocks the sender (as Rosalind does with Phoebe's letter in *As You Like It*).

In the history plays and tragedies letters often have a malign or negative part to play in the plot. The letter in 2.4 of *1 Henry IV* which warns Hotspur against his undertaking against the King is condemned as that of a 'frosty-spirited rogue', and the advice is (fatally) not taken. The cool reasoning of a letter is not suited to Hotspur's fiery spirit. The letters to Brutus (as if coming from Rome itself) lead Brutus to promise an action which results in failure and death. The letter of Cressida to Troilus in Act 5 comes after Troilus has seen Cressida's infidelity with Diomedes, and is condemned as 'Words, words, mere words, no matter from the heart.' Edmund's forged letter in *King Lear* brings about Edgar's alienation from his father: Goneril's to Edmund, intercepted by Edgar, reveals a further dimension of her corruption. Macbeth first tells Lady Macbeth of the witches' prophecies in a letter which does not state any criminal intention, but which might darkly seem to prompt Lady Macbeth's more ready ruthlessness ('Lay it to thy heart'). Letters are also vulnerable to delay (a turning point in the tragedy of Romeo and Juliet), crucial ambiguity (as in the order by Edmund of Edward II's death in Marlowe's play), destruction (as in Julia's tearing up of Proteus's letter in *The Two Gentlemen of Verona*) and ambiguity of author or addressee (as in Valentine's writing a letter as if from Julia, which she then gives to him, in the same play). Letters can be torn up into their constituent letters, as Julia does, and the names detached out of anger (Julia's towards her own name) or a kind of sentimental fetishism (as Julia does with the phrase 'love-wounded Proteus': 'my bosom as a bed / Shall lodge thee'.) In short, letters in Shakespeare's plays are distinctly slippery and malleable entities, more often the cause of misunderstandings and failures of communication than 'pure' or 'ardent' or displaying 'the force of friendship'.

Might one not suggest that Shakespeare's use of letters is symptomatic of an age more sceptical about writing and written correspondence than was the mid eighteenth century (when, too, writers first began to write private letters with an eye to eventual publication)? At any rate, Shakespeare's most articulate hero, Hamlet, is awkward in his letter to Ophelia; and, partly perhaps because 'presence' is such a vital matter for drama (the presence of a speaking subject), one cannot imagine any of Shakespeare's characters expressing the view of letters that Lovelace does. For in Shakespeare's plays, indeed, the general fate of letters suggests rather the pressures of 'time and accident', the vulnerability or unreliability of epistolary 'friendship given under hand and seal', and the proneness of letters 'to be turned against' their senders or recipients. They are rarely the embodiments of sincerity.[17]

Returning to Richardson we can say that a paradoxical feature of most of Lovelace's letters is that they *are* sincere. None of his 'designing' letters to Clarissa (with the exception of four letters after the rape, urging her to marry him (vol. III letters LIV, LV, LVI and LX are given directly, but are reported to Anna Howe and others by Clarissa herself, with her comments and criticisms, and sometimes of course her innocent credulities. So Lovelace as an *epistolary* plotter is not given predominance. Rather we see him most fully in his open and undesigning letters to Belford, where paradoxically we see his sincerity, and his powers of description. And in *these* letters,

physicality, the 'body' that he tells Clarissa is excluded from letters can be allowed fully through Lovelace's powers, as it were, of a novelist, so we get something like the marvellously grotesque description of Mrs Sinclair (vol. III, pp. 194-5): or the vivid Lawrentian (and Chaucerian) sense of animal life in letter XIX of vol. II (pp. 67-8) where Lovelace describes a farmyard scene as an illustration of lovers' conferring and receiving obligations:

> A strutting rascal of a cock have I beheld chuck, chuck, chuck, chucking his mistress to him, when he has found a single barley-corn, taking it up with his bill, and letting it drop five or six times, still repeating his chucking invitation; and when two or three of his feathered ladies strive who shall be the first for it [*O Jack! a cock is a grand signor of a bird*] he directs the bill of the foremost to it; and, when she has got the dirty pearl, he struts over her with an erected crest, and with an exulting chuck—a chuck-aw-aw-w, circling round her with dropped wings, sweeping the dust in humble courtship; while the obliged she, half-shy, half-willing, by her cowering tail, prepared wings, yet seemingly affrighted eyes, and contracted neck, lets one see that she knows the barley-corn was not all he called her for.

The life of the novel lies in its narrative drama and physical presentation (of which this is a small but vivid instance). But the moral message of the novel is the denial of this kind of life. Clarissa's letters only possess this dramatic power in volume I, before her elopement with Lovelace (particularly in those letters where she recounts the struggle with her family and the drama of her resistance to Solmes). In resisting her father and resisting Solmes's overtures she is resisting in the name of life, in the name of her own nature as a woman, and her letters have a corresponding passion. After her elopement with Lovelace she is forced to deny passion in the name of her sense of honour, and her letters become correspondingly a matter of moral and religious reflection, where they are not simply recounting facts. And the epistolary convention becomes in these instances a means of reflecting on moral questions rather than presenting drama. As a result, for the modern reader, the closing volume becomes the most difficult to read: the capacity of the epistolary form for moral disquisition takes over and quenches the drama.

It is difficult not to feel, in fact, that Richardson *the artist* is of Lovelace's party without knowing it; and that it is Richardson the moralist who takes over after the rape has been committed, and who has to take over then. One can go further, and say that after her elopement with Lovelace it is impossible not to feel that a certain over-delicacy and concern with mere reputation marks Clarissa's responses after her 'elopement'. In saying this I am aware that I am in the end running in the face of Richardson's whole intention—which is that Clarissa should stand for a moral principle, and stand for it in as human, self-doubting and passionate a way as possible. Lovelace is presented ultimately as tyrannical and ruthless. Had Clarissa submitted to him, the result might have been a different kind of tragedy. It might in fact have been more genuinely tragic in a Shakespearian sense—where tragedy means the following through of passionate impulse and meeting the consequences. The analogies in Shakespeare are not very close, but *Romeo and Juliet* or *Antony and Cleopatra* would I suppose be the closest. Tolstoy's *Anna Karenina* would be closer still: Anna is married, of course; and Vronsky is not a rake. But Anna's defiance of respectability is almost as great as Clarissa's might have been; and a certain destructiveness in Vronsky is brought out in the horse-racing scene. In Shakespeare, as I've suggested, *Measure for Measure* is in some ways a closer parallel of the resistance of virtuous virginity to brutal compulsion: but, with great significance for the Shakespearian vision, Shakespeare allows the problem to be explored via the genre of comedy. Angelo is allowed to avoid the worst consequences of his acts, and Isabella is allowed to learn a more human virtue.

*V. Rape, Writing and Morality*

Shakespeare treats the subject of rape in any full way only in two works, and his way of doing so is significant both in relation to letters and genre and to the broader moral and historical questions I am exploring. When, in *The Rape of Lucrece,* the heroine has to communicate the news of her shame to her husband Collatine, she simply writes asking him to come to her. She dares not write down the cause of her grief in case he does not believe in her innocence, and waits until she can 'prove' it by suicide. She also feels that she can make her sincerity more apparent if she tells him what has happened to his face: 'she would not blot the letter / With words, till action might become them better.' And the poet comments:

> To see sad sights moves more than hear them told,
> For then the eye interprets to the ear
> The heavy motion that it doth behold,
> When every part a part of woe doth bear.
> 'Tis but a part of sorrow that we hear;
>   Deep sounds make lesser noise than shallow fords,
>   And sorrow ebbs, being blown with wind of words.
>
>                                         (1324-30)

It is, one might say, almost a statement of the dramatist's credo, a belief in the greater emotional power of live drama as against the drama of reflective prose—or the novel. Where in any novel, one might ask, is the force of *grief* so powerfully rendered as it is, say, in the rendering of Lear's grief at the death of Cordelia, with its poignant physical touches, and the added effect, only possible on the stage, of the silent anguish and helplessness of the onlookers, Kent, Albany and Edgar?

It may be, too, that the horror of rape is especially incommunicable in written or even spoken words. At the climax of her narration to Collatine Lucrece cannot bring herself to complete her story. She manages to 'throw forth Tarquin's name', and then

> 'He, he,' she says—
> But more than he her poor tongue could not speak,
> Till after many accents and delays,
> Untimely breathings, sick and short essays,
>   She utters this: 'He, he, fair lords, 'tis he
>   That guides this hand to give this wound to me.'
>
>                                         (1717-22)

And her final statement (like Othello's) is completed not by words alone but by an action: 'Even here she sheathèd in her harmless breast / A harmful knife, that thence her soul unsheathed', (where the language suggests paradoxically sexual overtones). The final revelation of her 'confession' is also the action of her suicide, and she does not have to live to face the shame of her husband's response to her words. Richardson, by contrast, is hard put to find a mode in which to render Clarissa's narration of her ordeal, and her reaction to it. The moral difference between the two heroines is of course that Lucrece kills herself and Clarissa explicitly rejects this course of action. Lovelace makes the contrast with Lucrece himself in III.220 ('no Lucretia-like vengeance upon herself in her thought'); and Clarissa herself in her rambling letter to Lovelace after the rape begins to make a vengeful comparison of Lovelace and Tarquin but suppresses it: 'A less complicated villainy cost a Tarquin—but I forget what I would say again—.' (II.212).[18]

Shakespeare's poem, though, is not one of the finest examples of his art. The harsh story is treated with a kind of brittle rhetorical distancing, with several set pieces of declamation. One feels that Shakespeare is happier artistically speaking, with the resolutions of comedy (in *Measure for Measure* or *Cymbeline* or *Pericles*) in dealing with this particular crime—resolutions which of course allow its avoidance. His only other tragic treatment of rape is in *Titus Andronicus,* that example of Senecan horror-mongering, where the violence is so extreme and the verbal response to it so coldly rhetorical, that one feels that it is an exercise in the stylization of horror, rather than a profound attempt to understand it humanely and morally.

But in terms of what one might call the iconography of rape *Titus Andronicus* has some very significant features. Like her mythological prototype Philomel, Lavinia is horribly dismembered by having her tongue cut out. The victim of rape is deprived of a voice with which to speak of her crime. But Philomel tells her story by way of art—by weaving it into a tapestry which she can show to her sister Procne. Lavinia, in a horrific variation, is deprived of hands as well as tongue: she cannot weave her story—nor can she write. She can only indicate what has happened to her by turning to the classic story of Philomel herself, in Ovid's *Metamorphoses:* she turns to the art of the past. There is a structural similarity here to the way in which Clarissa, in her first distracted writings after her violation turns partly to quotation (from *Hamlet,* among other sources) to render her deepest feelings. Beyond that Lavinia, to indicate the culprits, has to take Marcus's staff in her mouth and write in the sand 'Stuprum—Chiron—Demetrius.' This agonizing moment is perhaps too appalling for an aesthetic response: but structurally one can again see a significance which has its parallels in *Clarissa* (parallels which would of course have been far from the mind of Richardson, with his expressed distaste for the 'horrid'): the painfully hampered writing, and the recourse to Latin to make bearable the writing of the crime, are symbolically akin to Clarissa's less dreadful predicament, her fragmented and distorted writing and her inability to do more than hint at the crime that she has suffered. Despite the vast differences in degree of horror, circumstance, tone and decorum, the two writers' treatments of the crime show marked structural and symbolic similarities. But Shakespeare, perhaps ultimately without the deepest artistic conviction, chooses the mode of Senecan horror, while Richardson in a politer eighteenth century not only avoids the 'horrid' but has chosen a genre where the still horrifying facts can be—as far as possible—de-sensationalized and controlled, mediated through the triple screen of letter within letter within 'editorial' (or authorial) overview. Despite (or perhaps because of) its lack of sensationalistic power his is, in this instance, the more humane rendering.

There are two further points of comparison between *Clarissa* and *The Rape of Lucrece,* which relate to social history and politics. By submitting to her rape to avoid death with dishonour—Tarquin threatens that he will kill her and then say he found her sleeping with her servant—Lucrece is able then to tell her kinsmen of the crime, and the result is that Tarquin is overthrown and with him the institution of Roman kingship. The real Lucretia therefore became a type of republican heroine, although Shakespeare only mentions the change 'from kings to consuls' in his 'Argument'. *Clarissa,* while not concerned with national politics, is also part of a profound shift of values in which a more morally sensitive and responsible middle class asserted its morality against an aristocratic code. (Beaumarchais' *The Marriage of Figaro* 1784, translated in 1785, is another manifestation of the same shift.)

But an even more significant moral difference lies in the fact that in these great representative stories of the struggle between female chastity and male will, Lucrece is protecting her chastity as a married woman and (as importantly) her husband's honour, whereas Clarissa is defending her virgin chastity and her own honour. Lucrece, in a way difficult to understand for a modern reader, laments the fact that she can no longer be regarded as a 'loyal wife': 'Of that type hath Tarquin rifled me'. She also talks of 'The stainèd taste of violated troth', which raises some complex moral questions: if she was forced to submit to Tarquin to save her own life and honour, *and* her husband's honour, how can this be seen as the violation of her troth? Shakespeare is following a Roman ethic, which was presumably felt to have some validity for his own time, where a wife's chastity was important above all because of her husband's honour rather than her own, and where any sexual violation involves some sense of guilt on the part of the woman. Lucrece can even speak of 'My life's foul deed'. Clarissa on the other hand has become a more independent moral agent, whose own honour and, more than this, whose Christian salvation, are paramount. In her case too it is virtually sexuality itself which is the great threat. She has to guard herself against her attraction to Lovelace. The preservation of the unmarried woman's virginity has become the central moral and social question of what is perhaps the greatest and most representative of eighteenth-century novels. In Shakespeare, the story of Lucrece is not one of the great achievements of his oeuvre, but he follows the Roman story and emphasis and its concern with married chastity. Elsewhere (as we have seen) his treatment of sexual morality is more various, less a matter of stark moral contrasts, and virgin chastity (while being taken very seriously in *The Tempest* and elsewhere) is never the focus of tragic conflict.

*VI. Conclusions*

Social and cultural historians differ markedly in their interpretations of the changes in moral attitude towards sex and marriage that took place between Shakespeare's age and Richardson's, depending partly on what kind of evidence they choose to look at. Lawrence Stone, drawing on a very wide range of social documents (though less on literary sources, apart from diaries) comes to the conclusion that sexual attitudes among the upper classes between 1500 and 1800 passed through four approximate stages: a phase of moderate toleration until the end of the sixteenth century; a phase of repressiveness that began around 1570 and lasted until about 1660; a phase of 'permissiveness, even licence' from 1660 to around 1770; and from 1770 for the next century and more a new wave of repression that coincided with the growth of evangelicalism. This would put Shakespeare at a point of transition between a phase of toleration and one of repressiveness, and Richardson, similarly, at a point towards the end of a phase of licence and before the beginnings of a new phase of repression. Both writers appear to be located at particular points of tension which provide a dynamic for their art.[19]

At the same time each writer drew, of course, on traditions which preceded their own ages: Shakespeare on a rich and complex mixture of classical literature and history, Tudor historiography, sophisticated literary predecessors, popular dramatic tradition, folk festival; Richardson more narrowly on late seventeenth- and early eighteenth-century puritan writing, Restoration drama, predecessors in the novel like Defoe, and, as I have tried to show, Shakespeare himself.

Out of these pressures and influences—in conjunction with what one has to recognize as the ultimately mysterious element of unique creativity in the writers themselves—come the distinctively different visions of sexuality. Both writers are, of course, preoccupied with the conflict of licence and law, body and spirit, as, probably, are the writers of any age. But Shakespeare puts the emphasis either on tolerant comic resolution (as in *Measure for Measure*, or *The Winter's Tale*) or tragedy in which there is no element of religious martyrdom or consolation.[20] Richardson in contrast either writes a comedy like *Pamela* in which the emphasis is didactically on Virtue Rewarded, or a type of tragedy like *Clarissa* where again the issue is presented as a stark confrontation of opposites (predatory masculine will against a religious virtue intensely concerned with propriety) and in which a clear religious didactic intention is stronger than a more Shakespearian sense of tragedy which emphasizes the essentially human intractability, waste and loss.

It is also notable how exclusively in his two major novels Richardson focuses on sexuality, and sexuality as a moral struggle; whereas for Shakespeare it is part (albeit an often dark and agonized part) of a wider vision. Rita Goldberg sees *Clarissa* as centrally representative of eighteenth-century sexual morality:

> It is almost as if the exertion of the will against an immovable identity in each individual woman provides the moral energy for a whole social world.[21]

Later she comments: 'Of the seven deadly sins the eighteenth century finds lust the deadliest.' In the light of Stone's accounts of the permissiveness of the eighteenth century up to about 1770 and indeed in the light of Boswell's diaries and even *Tom Jones* this may seem a sweeping and questionable statement. But if applied to the kind of moral and intellectual world and tradition in which Richardson moved it does not seem inapposite. Richardson's major novels, especially *Clarissa*, are posited on the central idea that sexual desire is a great threat to society and civilization, and must be tamed by rigorous social and religious laws. Shakespeare's world is less anxious, more various, with a greater sense of the varieties of sexuality and its mysterious metamorphoses and resolutions as well as its tragic intractabilities. Against Goldberg's comment on the eighteenth-century moralists' view of lust we may set Claudio's 'Sure, it is no sin; / Or of the deadly seven it is the least.' It is not that Shakespeare is more 'permissive' than Richardson: his plays are full of the darkest sense of the destructiveness of uncontrolled sexuality; and in the last plays (*The Tempest* and *The Winter's Tale* in particular) there is a strong emphasis on the importance of marriage in rendering sexual relations moral and chaste. But his plays as a whole give us a complexity which is beyond Richardson's, a breadth of view far richer than the moral simplicities of *Pamela* or even the acute polarities of *Clarissa* with its 'dark and sometimes luxuriant dallyings with the beauties of death'.[22] Richardson may have rightly been seen by eighteenth-century readers as the modern writer who came closest in art and understanding to Shakespeare. Today we are more aware of the differences. But the thrill of recognition that we can get from reading writers as differently constituted, historically, as Richardson and Shakespeare, suggests that their work is more than just a record of change and difference. If we can only see where we differ from the past, and where past periods differ from each other, those differences lose their power to provoke and challenge us.

## Notes

[1] Sir John Hawkins, *Life of Samuel Johnson* (2nd edn) (London, 1787), p. 214n., quoted in *Samuel Richardson: a Biography,* T. C. Duncan Eaves and Ben D. Kimpel (Oxford, 1971), p. 388.

[2] *Ibid.*, p. 588.

[3] Cited in Mark Kinkead-Weekes, *Samuel Richardson, Dramatic Novelist* (London, 1973), p. 396.

[4] *Ibid.*, p. 451.

[5] *Ibid.*, p. 456.

[6] *The Selected Letters of Samuel Richardson,* ed. J. Carroll (Oxford, 1964), p. 104.

[7] See Susan Snyder, *The Comic Matrix of Shakespeare's Tragedies* (Princeton, 1979).

[8] E.g. by Valerie Grosvenor Myer, *Samuel Richardson: Passion and Prudence* (London, 1986), chapter 7.

[9] Quotations from *Clarissa* are taken from the Everyman edition (London, 1967, vol. 1, 1976 vols. II-IV).

[10] In the striking BBC Television adaptation of 1991 the tragic possibilities of Lovelace's role were interestingly and effectively increased by intensifying his remorse and by having him die in a duel with his friend Belford, rather than challenged abroad by Clarissa's cousin Col. Mordern. Given the elements of moral sensitivity in Lovelace and Belford's persistent championing of Clarissa in the novel, this was a convincing adaptation. But it moved the story away from its status as an exemplary hagiography of Clarissa and towards something more like a Shakespearian tragedy.

[11] Shakespeare nowhere, however, essays the difficult dramatic situation of having an actual seducer, still less a rapist, marry his victim. Other dramatists in the period 1594-1625 were more daring (or foolhardy). In *The Queen of Corinth* by John Fletcher, the rapist marries the victim, who has also subsequently taken the place of a second potential victim (a version of the 'bed-trick'). The two women face the rapist at the end of the play (in some ways like Mariana and Isabella) one asking for leniency and marriage and the other for his death. When the second case is revealed as a substitution, the way is free to allow the heroine to marry him. There was an indication in the first Act that the heroine/victim was originally in love with the rapist, and he with her. And the rapist is urged on by friends against his better judgement at the beginning and is bitterly repentant and (like Angelo) begs for death at the end. But the psychology of the heroine is difficult to credit, especially when she begs for marriage immediately after the rape, when the rapist is masked and therefore at that point unknown to her, and when he has also used accomplices. Nor is there any exploration of general moral issues as in *Measure for Measure*. For a discussion of this and other examples from the period, see Suzanne Gossett, ' "Best men are moulded out of faults": Marrying the Rapist in Jacobean Drama', *English Language Review,* 14 (1984), 305-27.

[12] James Grantham Turner, 'Lovelace and the Paradoxes of Liberation', in *Samuel Richardson: Tercentenary Essays,* ed. M. A. Doody and P. Sabor (Cambridge, 1989), 70-88.

[13] Mark Kinkead-Weekes, *Samuel Richardson, Dramatic Novelist* (London, 1973), p. 231.

[14] *Selected Letters,* p. 104.

[15] *Ibid.* p. 65; quoted in Terry Eagleton, *The Rape of Clarissa* (Oxford, 1982), pp. 43-4.

[16] 'Philip Massinger', *Selected Essays* (London, 1966), pp. 209-10. Laura Fasick points out that Richardson exemplifies in Clarissa a sense of the moral sensibility of the body itself as opposed to Lovelace's cold detached manipulation of the body by the mind, 'Sentiment, authority and the female body in the novels of Samuel Richardson', *Essays in Literature,* 5: 19 (Fall, 1992), 193-203.

[17] It should be pointed out, however, that this function of letters in Shakespeare's plays contrasts with the humanist tradition of letter-writing, as in Erasmus, where the potential authenticity of letters is stressed, together with—in terms very similar to Richardson's quoted above—their ability to make the absent present. See Lisa Jardine, 'Reading and the technology of textual affect: Erasmus's familar letters and Shakespeare's *King Lear',* in *Reading Shakespeare Historically* (London, 1996), pp. 78-97.

[18] Ian Donaldson in *The Rapes of Lucretia: a Myth and its Transformations* (Oxford, 1982), also points out that Lovelace cites Lucretia again towards the end of the novel in conversation with Lord M and his cousins, saying that if a lady destroys herself by grief or by the dagger as Lucretia did, 'Is there more than one fault the man's and is not the other hers?' Lovelace's tone is insufferable, but Donaldson does come to the conclusion that 'it would be possible also to say that Clarissa loses the will to live' and that Richardson 'may seem too easily to accept the notion . . . that rape "is a fate worse than death".'

[19] Lawrence Stone, *The Family, Sex and Marriage in England, 1500-1800* (London, 1977). More recent research also suggests that attitudes to sexual morality (e.g. in the Church Courts) became stricter in the first decades of the seventeenth century. See Martin Ingram, *Church Courts, Sex and Marriage in England 1570-1640* (Cambridge, 1987), which throws an interesting light on *Measure for Measure.*

[20] Recent, particularly feminist, criticism and theoretical practice has, of course, questioned the degree of resolution in the comedies, particularly *Measure for Measure:* see e.g. Carol T. Neely, *Broken Nuptials in Shakespeare's Plays* (New Haven and London, 1985), pp. 101-2. The comedy of *Measure for Measure* certainly leaves a lot of problems unanswered, but a 'reconciling' reading or production still seems to me possible to make convincing, particularly in the light of the expectations of the genre.

[21] Rita Goldberg, *Sex and Englightenment: Women in Richardson and Diderot* (Cambridge, 1984), pp. 68-9.

[22] Donaldson, *The Rapes of Lucretia,* p. 82.

---

Source: "Shakespeare and Clarissa: 'General Nature', Genre and Sexuality," in *Shakespeare Survey: An Annual Survey of Shakespearian Study and Production,* Vol. 51, 1998, pp. 27-43.

# Romances and Poems

# Subjectivity, Exemplarity, and the Establishing of Characterization in Lucrece

## A. D. Cousins, *Macquarie University*

As might be expected, much of the more recent commentary on *Lucrece* has focused on the interrelated matters of politics, gender, and subjectivity. The poem's representation of the Roman world and its politics, especially its sexual/gender politics, has been studied; how *Lucrece* emerges from the variously political discourses of later Elizabethan society, and its negotiations with them, have been considered; the poem's representations of subjectivity in relation to patriarchy and rape have been widely discussed.[1] In focusing on such matters, most commentary has inevitably centered on the characterization of Lucrece herself. But as a result, the mutually constitutive nature of the characterizations of Tarquin, Collatine, and Lucrece has received insufficient attention.[2] Here I want to propose that by examining the reciprocal formation of consciousness and role among Tarquin, Collatine, and Lucrece as far as the beginning of the poem's rape scene,[3] one sees that the characterizations established early in *Lucrece* are more complex in their discursive relations than has been previously acknowledged. Recognition of their being so helps to illuminate not only subsequent happenings in the poem such as Lucrece's insistent denial of her own innocence and her decision to suicide, but also crucial concerns of the poem such as its skeptical interrogation of exemplarity, and the interaction between exemplarity and historical process.

In particular, I shall argue here that while Tarquin is a tyrant figure—and distinctly a Platonic type of the tyrant—he is also a demonic parody of the Petrarchan lover, insofar as he pursues a lady, Lucrece, who is portrayed as at once an exemplar of the chaste Roman matron and an incarnation of the Petrarchan mistress. Violating her, Shakespeare's Tarquin sexually heightens and violates the Petrarchan discourse of love. Yet it is not Lucrece's primary misfortune that, in her guise as Petrarchan mistress, she attracts a tyrant figure (in fact, a proto-tyrant) who defines himself specifically as tyrant in relation to her via the role of grimly parodic Petrarchan lover. Rather, as is argued here, it seems that Lucrece's primary misfortune lies in the hubris of her husband, Collatine. When part of the Roman army besieging Ardea, Collatine tries to gain a personal victory over the king's son, his superior and kinsman: Collatine's boastful vying with the proto-tyrant redirects Tarquin's violence and desire from the enemy/foreign/public to the kindred/Roman/private. The poem registers that redirection of Tarquin's violence and desire not only in terms of Petrarchan discourse, but also in terms of the myths of the Golden Age and of Eden. Tarquin becomes an analog to Satan; Lucrece, indicated as embodying both Tarquin's and Collatine's notions of the absolute good on earth, becomes an analog to the earthly paradise and (an *incorruptible*) Eve; and Collatine thus figures as a self-betraying Adam who tempts the serpent into—and into violating—his earthly paradise, his (unwilling) Eve.

Perceived in light of these Platonic, Petrarchan, and Golden Age/Edenic discourses, the intricate interactions among Tarquin, Collatine, and Lucrece in the early part of Shakespeare's poem are elucidated as follows. Tarquin's mutually reinforcing, interconnected roles, read in conjunction with Lucrece's mutually reinforcing and interconnected roles, antithetic to Tarquin's, explain Lucrece's comprehensive sense of violation, of contamination, and also her deep sense of defacement, of her innermost self's having been stolen. This reading, in turn, illuminates her decision to commit suicide and, moreover, sheds light on the skeptical questioning of exemplarity in *Lucrece*, both discrediting and validating the poem's reliability as a means of interpreting history.

The most expedient way to undertake the reading I have outlined in the preceding paragraph is probably to begin, as the poem begins, with the narrator's characterization of Tarquin. Tarquin's historical role as proto-tyrant seems to be his basic one in the poem. Shakespeare's narrator may also picture Tarquin in the roles of parodic Petrarchan lover and of Satan, but it is indicated that they are Tarquin's expressions of his tyrannical role in relation to Lucrece. At the beginning of the "Argument," the narrator indicates that Tarquin's immediate role model is his father, whose pride, treachery, violence, and violations (of custom, laws, and family bonds) manifest his will to power, his will to tyranny (lines 1-6). The poem reveals, of course more thoroughly than does the "Argument," that Tarquin is certainly his father's son (likewise implicit in Ovid's narrative)—and that he is not merely in his father's image.

The opening of *Lucrece* predominantly characterizes Tarquin in terms of desire. The "Argument" emphasizes his underlying role to be that of proto-tyrant (lines 1-8),[4] and the opening stanzas do so as well (lines 20-1 and 36-42); but as proto-tyrant he is initially and chiefly characterized in the poem by the "desire" (line 2) that informs the expressions of his tyrannical role in relation to Lucrece (lines 3-7). The narrator implies several things about the nature of that desire: its treachery ("trustless" and "false," in line 2, suggest that it betrays Tarquin while impelling him to betray Collatine and Lucrece); its possession of Tarquin (he becomes "[l]ust-breathed," the narrator says in line 3); its sinister, even demonic, energy (lines 4-7)—its violence which displaces the military violence directed by Tarquin against Ardea. Desire, treachery, and violence are, according to Plato's *Republic,* marks of the tyrannical character. In fact, desire and the need to gratify it tyrannize over the tyrant: he becomes driven by a "master passion" in whose service he will violate even domestic sanctities.[5] The characterization of Tarquin as proto-tyrant accords in these respects, then, with Plato's characterization of the tyrant in his *Republic.*[6] And it does so in others as well. According to Plato's text, desire possesses the tyrant, but the tyrant is also vulnerable to fears: "He is naturally a prey to fears and passions of every sort."[7] Tarquin's soliloquy in his chamber dramatizes the compelling force of his desire in conflict with the constraining power of his fears (lines 190-280).[8] Plato also describes the tyrant as bestial and, more specifically, as a wolf to his fellow citizens.[9] Shakespeare's narrator compares Tarquin, just before the rape of Lucrece, to a "cockatrice" (line 540), a "gripe" (line 543; that is, to a vulture or an eagle), and a "foul night-waking cat" (line 554). Tarquin is thereafter compared to a "wolf" when he rapes Lucrece (line 677).[10] Subsequently he is figured as a "full-fed hound or gorged hawk" (line 694), and as a "thievish dog" (line 736). In his primary role as proto-tyrant, Tarquin seems deliberately represented in accord with Plato's account of the tyrannical character: he may be, as Ovid had indicated and as Shakespeare apparently accepted from Ovid, truly his father's son; but he is also more than a reincarnation of his tyrannical father.

The extent to which the proto-tyrant is more than simply an imitation of his father is evident in his relation to Lucrece. The ways in which Tarquin perceives Lucrece and defines himself in response to his understanding of her express, of course, his desire for her and thus his role as Platonic tyrant figure in relation to her. As I have suggested previously, one such expression of his role as tyrant in relation to her is his role as parodic Petrarchan lover. When first the narrator describes Tarquin, characterizing him predominantly in terms of desire, it seems that "[l]ust-breathed" Tarquin (line 3) is as a man possessed. What tyrannizes over the proto-tyrant is desire for a woman depicted to him, by her husband, in a way that anachronistically celebrates her as a type of the Petrarchan lady: "Collatine unwisely did not let / To praise the clear unmatched red and white / Which triumph'd in that sky of his delight" (lines 10-2). The narrator confirms that image of Lucrece by adding to his report of Collatine's imprudent eulogy. He praises Lucrece's eyes, identifying them with the stars. They are, he says, "[M]ortal stars as bright as heaven's beauties" (line 13). Reworking the Petrarchan motif of the lady's eyes being, or resembling, stars, Shakespeare's narrator confirms what his report of Lucrece's public celebration by Collatine has previously, and likewise metonymically, indicated through Petrarchan allusion ("red and white," line 11): Lucrece's role as Petrarchan object of desire. So Tarquin, the Platonic tyrant figure tyrannized by desire for a woman delineated to him as virtually prefiguring Laura, becomes in relation to her a counterpart to the Petrarchan lover. But the differences between Tarquin and, say, Petrarch's speaker in *"Passa la nave mia colma d'oblio"* are more important than the similarities. In particular, the latter's desire for his lady seems ambiguous, alternating between the erotic and the spiritual. Tarquin's desire for Lucrece is, however, solely unspiritual, a "lightless fire" (line 4) concerned only with the body and with violation: "lurk[ing] to aspire, / And girdle with embracing flames the waist / Of Collatine's fair love, Lucrece the chaste" (lines 5-7). Expressing his will to tyranny, his proto-tyrannic role, Tarquin's desire makes him a brutal parody of the Petrarchan lover as a species and his pursuit of Lucrece a sexual heightening/violation of the Petrarchan discourse of love. As might be expected, this parodic characterization of Tarquin is implied very distinctly and emphatically in the narrator's account of Lucrece's rape.

The interaction between this parodic role and Tarquin's other main roles in relation to Lucrece is intriguing; but before it can be examined those roles through which her subjectivity is chiefly fashioned in the poem must be considered. Lucrece's primary role in the poem is, almost inevitably, that of chaste Roman matron: the narrator first identifies her as "Collatine's fair love, Lucrece the chaste" (line 7). Her subsequent guise of Petrarchan lady complements her initial one by heightening the reader's sense of both her chastity and her beauty (lines 12-4). The two roles also have a less obvious harmony, for they can be seen—though in different ways—as culturally imposed. Lucrece's initial role gives her selfhood in terms of a conventional category of the female in her society. In that sense the basic role given to her in the poem, a role that concurs with her own self-image, appears to be socially constructed. Lucrece not only recognizes the role of chaste Roman matron as essential to her self-image, but also acknowledges her feeling or consciousness of its being imposed from without (by implication, socially). Her most explicit acknowledgment occurs just after her three long complaints, when she is pondering suicide: "I was a loyal wife: / So am I now,—O no, that cannot be! / Of that true type hath Tarquin rifled me" (lines 1048-50).[11] The reader may not agree with Lucrece's refusal to accept her own innocence but, that aside, it is clear that Lucrece thinks of herself primarily as a chaste Roman matron and as having received that role from without.

Lucrece's externalized self-image thus appears to be inseparable from, and explanatory of, both her profound consciousness of herself as an exemplar of chastity and her profound fear of becoming an exemplar of unchastity. She recognizes that others have established her as the former and that they can turn her into the latter: she recognizes her vulnerability as an exemplar, and how indifferent to her inner life and beyond her control that aspect of her existence is (lines 519-39 and 806-40). Her consciousness of herself as exemplar clarifies, in turn, her sense of being immersed in historical process. Rape impels Lucrece to look anxiously to the future and also anxiously to the past, as well it might.[12] But for her, as exemplar, there is a special reason for its doing so. Exemplarity in her world, as of course in Shakespeare's, is a means of illuminating and stabilizing historical process, of defining subjectivity within it. Anticipating misrepresentation of her role as exemplar, its unjustly parodic inversion, Lucrece concurrently anticipates the falsification of history (lines 813-26). To preserve her existence as an exemplar of chastity is likewise, for Lucrece, significantly if partly to save the present from future misinterpretation, to protect history from false tradition. The case is similar yet interestingly different when she turns to the past. Looking to a picture of the Trojan past for comfort, Lucrece seeks consolation in discovering an exemplar of misery (lines 1443-56), not only to find a companion in her distress but also to find another self—one whom she may vindicate and so, through whom, amend history (lines 1457-98).

In order to further explore the subject of Lucrece's preoccupation with her exemplarity and with control of meaning and subjectivity in interpretation of the past, it is necessary to address what seem to be her other main roles in the poem. These other roles are, much like the ones previously considered, imposed from without. That is to say, while the narrator reveals them to be consonant with personal appearance and impulse in Lucrece, they are also shown to derive from Collatine's devotion to her and from Tarquin's perception of her via the celebratory picture drawn by her husband. They connect with and complement her roles as chaste Roman matron and Petrarchan lady, just as they evoke from Tarquin roles linked to his guises of Platonic tyrant figure and parodic Petrarchan lover. They are, moreover, syncretic and in part anachronistic: as was indicated earlier, they figure Lucrece as a type of the earthly paradise and as an innocent, incorruptible Eve; Tarquin therefore comes to figure as a type of Satan (and later, of course, he becomes an analog to Sinon); and Collatine thence comes to figure as a self-betraying Adam who unwittingly tempts the serpent to violate, to steal. It is a powerful mingling of discourses—Platonic, Petrarchan, Golden Age/Edenic—that combines with what is chiefly an Ovidian historical discourse to characterize the three main actors in Shakespeare's narrative and thereby re-present the rape of Lucrece.

The representation of Lucrece in terms of Golden Age/Edenic discourse begins with the narrator's initial depiction of her as an ideal Petrarchan lady. When the narrator first mentions Collatine's unwary celebration of Lucrece, he affirms her husband's reported and summarized speech by describing her face as the "sky of [Collatine's] delight; / Where mortal stars as bright as heaven's beauties, / With pure aspects did him peculiar duties" (lines 12-4). The Petrarchan allusions in these lines have already been discussed; what I wish to emphasize here is that the Petrarchan imagery suggests Lucrece to be Collatine's heaven on earth ("lent" to him by "the heavens," as the narrator subsequently remarks in another context [line 17]). With the initial use of Petrarchan discourse in the poem, then, another discourse also emerges, the Golden Age/Edenic: from that signifying of Lucrece to be Collatine's heaven on earth follows imaging of her as the earthly paradise and as Eve. In fact Lucrece's face, "that sky of [Collatine's] delight" (line 12), is soon after described twice by the narrator as a "fair field" (lines 58 and 72). The elaborate, conventional trope seems important for several reasons. First, it suggests that Lucrece's face is an ideal landscape and so it complements the preceding image of her face as Collatine's "sky of . . . delight" (line 12). Further, the trope forms part of a compressed allegory that, in emphasizing the fusion of beauty and virtue in Lucrece, indicates her to be a Golden Age innocent living in a world far removed from the "world's minority" (line 67).[13] Moreover, it pictures Lucrece so attractively (and as so vulnerable) at the moment when she is welcoming Tarquin into her home. Finally, the trope derives from Petrarchan tradition—as lines 71-2 signal—and thus hints at the extent to which Golden Age/Edenic discourse in the poem is generated by Petrarchan discourse. The latter also initiates the former, as it happens, in what is the last identification of Lucrece as an earthly paradise before she is raped.

That moment of identification, which deserves closer attention than it is often given, occurs in the report of Tarquin's long, intense gazing on the sleeping Lucrece (lines 365-71 and 386-420), the visual assault that precedes his more directly physical one. The narrator starts his account as follows:

> Her lily hand her rosy cheek lies under,
> Coz'ning the pillow of a lawful kiss;
> Who therefore angry, seems to part in sunder,
> Swelling on either side to want his bliss:
> Between whose hills her head entombed is,
> Where like a virtuous monument she lies,
> To be admir'd of lewd unhallowed eyes.
>
> Without the bed her other fair hand was,
> On the green coverlet; whose perfect white
> Show'd like an April daisy on the grass,
> With pearly sweat resembling dew of night.
> Her eyes like marigolds had sheath'd their light,
> And canopied in darkness sweetly lay,
> Till they might open to adorn the day.
>
> (lines 386-99)

Petrarchan images of "lily" and of "ros[e]" (line 386), used recurrently to describe Lucrece, introduce the passage. They serve immediately to eroticize the picture of the sleeping woman in terms of propriety and of impropriety ("Coz'ning," "lawful," line 387). The "[c]oz'ning"/"lawful" conceits, in themselves, obliquely contrast with the playfully imagined, innocent, frustrated desire of the "pillow" which may rightfully "kiss" Lucrece, to Tarquin's unlawful, violent, and as yet unfulfilled desire to possess her physically. However, insofar as these conceits are at once suggestive of conflict (the mock conflict between "hand" and "pillow") and linked to Petrarchan imagery, they serve also to remind the reader that it is especially the Petrarchan images used to describe Lucrece throughout the poem that identify her as a site of conflict. The first instance of Petrarchan imagery, for example, identifies her as the embodiment of perfect beauty through whom Collatine can vaunt his superiority over Tarquin, but through whom, likewise, Tarquin will assert his tyrannical will, and his tyrannical role, over Collatine (lines 7-14). According to the narrator, moreover, a struggle between "beauty and virtue" (line 52) as to which "should underprop [Lucrece's] fame" (line 53) can be seen in the "silent war of lilies and of roses" (line 71) occurring "in her fair face's field" (line 72). If is interesting and significant, too, that the Petrarchan images beginning the passage lead subsequently to the notion of Lucrece as monument, a notion connecting with her sense of herself as an exemplar of chastity (lines 390-2). But it seems most interesting and most significant that then, only after associating her with conflict and emphasizing her role as exemplar (an emphasis with overtones of death), the Petrarchan images introduce the picture of her as an earthly paradise.

There is a striking contrast between the playful, ominous, reverential prelude to that picture and the picture itself. An unspoiled, tranquil, natural richness is suggested by the picture's vivid detail: the "perfect[ly] white" hand (line 394) lying on "the green coverlet" (line 394), which is likened to an "April daisy on the grass" (line 395); the "pearly sweat resembling dew of night" (line 396); the "eyes like marigolds" that have "sheath'd their light" (line 397). Metonymically that detail associates the inviolate, perfectly beautiful Lucrece with an inviolate, perfectly beautiful nature. And one sees Petrarchan images both introducing that picture of Lucrece and helping to create it. Lucrece's "other fair hand," like the one beneath her head, is of "perfect" whiteness; further, the narrator celebrates the splendor of her eyes (lines 397-9) in terms that form a counterpart to those used by him near the poem's beginning (lines 13-4). Lucrece thus appears as both an earthly paradise and a Golden Age innocent; but such representations alone do not establish her role as a type of Eve. Her husband and Tarquin chiefly impose that role on her.

In his account of Collatine's "boast of Lucrece' sov'reignty" (line 36), the narrator tells of him

> [r]eck'ning his fortune at such high proud rate
> That kings might be espoused to more fame,
> But king nor peer to such a peerless dame.
> (lines 19-21)

In a moment when military conflict with a foreign enemy is deferred, Collatine uses his wife as a means of seeking personal victory over his superior and kinsman; the result of his hubris (line 19) is that he redirects Tarquin's violence and desire from the enemy/foreign/public to the kindred/Roman/private. His overreaching pride—an aggressive, patriarchal vanity that firmly links him with the otherwise dissimilar Tarquin—leads him to flaunt the wife who is his heaven on earth, his earthly paradise, and, in effect, an innocent from the Golden Age, before the proto-tyrant who, then perceiving her as "the heaven of his [own] thought" (line 338), quickly resolves to disposses him. So, as I have suggested earlier, Collatine unknowingly tempts Tarquin (lines 36-8) to violate and thus to steal the woman represented by the narrator as an embodiment of Golden Age/Edenic discourses. In doing that, he also unwittingly refigures both himself as a self-betraying Adam (an Adam who falls through pride) and Lucrece as an innocent, unfallen Eve. Simultaneously and appropriately, of course, he thereby helps to refigure Tarquin as a type of Satan, Tarquin's subsequent actions reinforcing his own role and that imposed on Lucrece.

The process of characterization I have outlined is not merely the result of some simple, male rivalry. It derives from Collatine's attempt to impose over Tarquin's will to illegitimate power—as proto-tyrant and son of a tyrant—Collatine's own will to illicit power, functioning within and expressed through the notionally unthreatening and not-to-be-threatened sphere of the domestic (functioning and expressed safely, as he is apparently to be taken as thinking, if he is to be taken as thinking at all). In that attempt, of course, Lucrece is objectified and so Tarquin perceives her; on the other hand, the end of the poem suggests that Lucrece has always been objectified by her husband and by her father (see especially lines 1751-806). Tarquin, moreover, could arguably never have perceived her except as "an *object* of consciousness,"[14] although he may not have seen or particularly considered her at all had not Collatine set her image compellingly before him. The end of that struggle between wills to illicit power, between domestic and public regimes (respectively Collatine's and Tarquin's), seems immediately to be the mutual constitution of the subjectivities of its participants, including Lucrece as an unknowing participant. The struggle of wills generates, in short, refigured subjectivities for each participant and thence a comprehensively refigured myth of the Fall.

One can now consider, I suggest, Tarquin's role as Satan. That role seems implicit from virtually the moment he enters Lucrece's home. The narrator says, referring initially to Lucrece and subsequently to Tarquin:

> This earthly saint adored by this devil,
> Little suspecteth the false worshipper;
> For unstain'd thoughts do seldom dream on evil,
> Birds never lim'd no secret bushes fear:
> So guiltless she securely gives good cheer
> And reverend welcome to her princely guest,
> Whose inward ill no outward harm express'd.
>
> For that he colour'd with his high estate,
> Hiding base sin in pleats of majesty,
> That nothing in him seem'd inordinate,
> Save sometime too much wonder of his eye . . .
> (lines 85-95)

The allusion to Lucrece as "[t]his earthly saint" (line 85) evokes her connected roles as chastity's exemplar and Petrarchan lady; it harmonizes, too, with the notion that she is Collatine's heaven on earth. More to the point, however, the trope allows the narrator to characterize Tarquin antithetically to her as a "devil" (line 85), a "false worshipper" (line 86), and agent of "evil" (line 87), who conceals from her his "inward ill" (line 91), his "base sin" (line 93). That insistently demonic representation of Tarquin is elaborated upon by the narrator's subsequent references to his "parling looks" (line 100), which are likened to "baits" and "hooks" (line 103). But it is specifically an emphasis on innocence in the characterization of Lucrece—and allusion to her as an embodiment of the earthly paradise—that indicate Tarquin to be Satanic rather than merely demonic, here and subsequently in the narrative.

As I have argued, the opening description of Lucrece as "[t]his earthly saint" develops into a representation of her as someone naturally innocent. "[U]nstain'd thoughts do seldom dream on evil, / Birds never lim'd no secret bushes fear," the narrator says (lines 87-8),[15] explaining her "guiltless" (line 89) and unsuspecting reception of her visitor. The images initiating the perception of Lucrece as naturally innocent point back to the image of "her fair face's field" (line 72),[16] with its connotations of an ideal landscape and of Golden Age virtue, and forward to the description of her, just prior to Tarquin's assault, as a type of the earthly paradise, of uncontaminated nature (lines 386-99). And it is precisely her natural innocence which the narrator proceeds to emphasize in describing how she responds to the intense, erotic gaze of Tarquin—the "inordinate" (line 94) stare that she necessarily notices but cannot decipher. According to the narrator:

> [S]he that never cop'd with stranger eyes,
> Could pick no meaning from their parling looks,
> Nor read the subtle shining secrecies
> Writ in the glassy margents of such books;
> She touch'd no unknown baits, nor fear'd no hooks:
> Nor could she moralize his wanton sight,
> More than his eyes were open'd to the light.
> (lines 99-105)

Unable to read, much less to interpret, the language of seduction in Tarquin's eyes, Lucrece perceives no harm in his gaze. In being unaware of the artifice of seduction, she is like a fish that neither recognizes enticement nor fears to be snared (line 103; an allusion to the familiar Petrarchan motif of hooks and ensnarement). Thus Lucrece, represented predominantly in terms that both suggest her natural innocence and evoke her recurrent presentation as a type of the earthly paradise (which thereby refigures her as Eve), is unwittingly betrayed by her husband (in effect, an overreaching Adam) to temptation by the demonized (Satanized) Tarquin. He, moreover, disguised as his apparent self (lines 90-4), knowingly falls from high estate in pursuing her (lines 190-301, 491-504; in lines 362-4 he is compared to a "serpent"). The poem's narrator puts before the reader a Romanized, Petrarchized, re-visioned story of the Fall—and in doing so arguably generates much of the intellectual intricacy, as well as emotive power, in Shakespeare's version of the Lucretia story.

Lucrece seems to be no simple Eve figure; certainly, she becomes a quite complex one as the poem progresses. Lucrece/Eve fights back, so to speak, and makes Tarquin/Satan experience not just a fall from the dignity of high estate, from the honor code of the Roman aristocracy, but a fall from high estate itself in Rome. Tarquin, likewise, appears not to be simply refigured as, and refiguring of, Satan. To begin with, his nocturnal soliloquy on whether or not to rape Lucrece shows him pondering in effect whether to abandon or to deepen his Satanic role (lines 127-301, especially lines 181-2, 190-245, 253-80). What seems particularly relevant at this point, however, is that the Petrarchan discourse used recurrently throughout the earlier part of the poem to construct Tarquin's subjectivity appears strikingly at the end of his speech to signal his consciously imperfect resolution of his inner conflict. Near the very end of his soliloquy, he declares:

> Affection is my captain, and he leadeth;
> And when his gaudy banner is display'd,
> The coward fights, and will not be dismay'd.
> (lines 271-3)

And the final words of his speech are:

> Desire my pilot is, beauty my prize;
> Then who fears sinking where such treasure lies?
> (lines 279-80)

The lines first quoted evoke Petrarch's sonnet *"Amor, che nel penser mio vive et regna,"* translated by Wyatt and Surrey; Tarquin's words offer a desperately pugnacious reworking of the love-as-warfare allegory in Petrarch's poem.[17] Tarquin's concluding words perhaps likewise evoke Petrarch's *"Passa la nave";* if so, they offer an aggressive reworking of the love-as-a-perilous-sea-voyage allegory in that poem. There is a Petrarchan finale, as it were, to Tarquin's soliloquy—and appropriately so. Tarquin's acute self-consciousness in his soliloquy can be seen in his sensitivity to history: paradoxically enough, like Lucrece he is all too aware of how he may be officially represented, of how his existence may be constructed (but not in his case misconstrued), in years to come (lines 202-10, 223-4). Exemplarity is a concern for him as it is for Lucrece. His acute self-consciousness can also be seen in his sensitivity to his own speechmaking, in his politician's sense of the rhetorical nature, the theatricality, of his moment of decision (lines 225-7, 267-8).[18] A Petrarchan finale certainly befits such a speech, but it seems especially suitable because Petrarchan discourse acknowledges, notionally with regret, reason's incapacity to govern desire (as in the reference to passion's defeat of reason in *"Passa la nave"*).[19] Petrarchan discourse can be used, therefore, to legitimize one's denial of constraint by reason. So, in effect, it is used here by Tarquin. The proto-tyrant making up his mind to commit rape is shown *de facto* to misappropriate and, likewise, desperately to rework Petrarchan discourse (lines 248-52).[20] He is thus represented in order for the reader to perceive the dishonesty of his characterizing himself as the warrior compelled now to fight in the service of passion, as the lover overwhelmed by desire.[21] The Petrarchan ending to the soliloquy signals his consciously specious resolution of his dilemma.

That ending signals, of course, other things as well. It confirms how thoroughly parodic a Petrarchan lover Tarquin is. Yet arguably, too, it confirms something about Tarquin as a Platonic tyrant/Satanic figure: he can possess—and then momentarily—"the heaven of his thought" (line 338) only by violation (line 348), which he knows to be also self-violation because it is a violation of the aristocratic Roman code of conduct by which he, at any rate, thinks his existence primarily defined (lines 197-224). Moreover, Tarquin's final, mock-Petrarchan characterization of himself as love's warrior leads to what can be perceived, after his piously inaccurate remark about the gods' abhorrence of rape (lines 349-50), as his committing a rape which distantly parodies the myth of Mars's rape of Rhea Silvia. Certainly, the rape of Lucrece does seem an ironic counterpart to that myth. The ancient myth tells of a rape which is an originary event for Rome—the chaste Rhea Silvia, raped by the god of war, conceives Romulus and Remus. The rape of Lucrece is, likewise, an originary event for Rome, but in a significantly different way: the Roman Republic is unwittingly and indirectly engendered by a warrior/parodic "warrior of love," a self-confessed enemy to the gods (lines 344-57), who in doing so initiates the overthrow of the monarchy and hence his own downfall.

From the discussion of Tarquin as concurrently a type of Satan and an antithesis to *Pater Mavors,* one might consider what a study of the reciprocal formation of consciousness and role among Tarquin, Lucrece, and Collatine would reveal about the establishing of characterization in Shakespeare's second narrative poem. To begin with, such an analysis strongly suggests that the characterizations established early in *Lucrece* are more complex in their discursive relations than has been previously acknowledged. The three main figures in the poem are not merely translated from the pages of Ovid: they are at once Ovidian and comprehensively transformed. In particular, they become actors in a Romanized, Petrarchized, re-visioned myth of the Fall—a version in which the Eve figure is innocent and betrayed, not betraying (and in which she ultimately gains her revenge on the counterpart to Satan).

Moreover, thus perceiving the characterizations of Tarquin, Lucrece, and Collatine early in the poem illuminates not only the subsequent happenings in it, but some of its main concerns as well. When one recognizes that Tarquin's sexual assault involves his forcing on Lucrece his mutually reinforcing, interconnected roles, antithetic to hers, then the scope of his violence is elucidated: his assault appears to involve unusually comprehensive psychic violence in conjunction with extreme physical violence.[22] Lucrece's profound sense of contamination seems, therefore, even more understandable. So too does her decision to commit suicide. Yet this reading illuminates not only these later occurrences in the poem, but also the issues that are arguably its main concerns. The mutually constitutive nature of characterization early in the poem indicates that Lucrece's interactive roles are *variously* imposed on her from without and, further, that she knows her basic role as chaste Roman matron to have been externally imposed and to be removable. The externality of Lucrece's selfhood, and her awareness of its being so, explains her feeling of contamination and her decision to commit suicide, for it becomes apparent that she thinks of Tarquin's assault as having stolen her main role in her world. And Lucrece's sense that her role as chaste Roman matron derives from without also sheds light on her insistent denial of her innocence. In her mind, apparently, Tarquin's assault has erased her basic self and thus she is no longer chaste and hence not completely innocent.[23]

More important, Lucrece's awareness of the externally imposed nature of her basic role is linked to her consciousness of herself as an exemplar of chastity, a connection that raises questions about exemplarity in, and beyond, the poem. Well aware that her role of exemplar, like her role as chaste Roman matron, derives from without, Lucrece believes that her rape immediately deletes the latter and will subsequently make ambiguous or cancel out the former. To regain the one, and to preserve the other, she resolves upon suicide. Her perception of who she ultimately is, and the self-negating decision that results from it (to lose herself in order to save herself), raises several major questions about exemplarity. First, if one's role as exemplar is imposed from without, in light of external circumstance and with no—or little—precise knowledge of one's inner life, then how reliable can exemplarity be as a means of defining subjectivity, of identifying an incarnation of an ideal? Further, how can exemplarity therefore be regarded as a reliable means of interpreting history, of clarifying and stabilizing it? This question has a special relevance, I think, because the intertextual relations of Shakespeare's narrative suggest how often and how variously Lucrece's role as exemplar has been reconstructed: continuity, variation, and contradiction all mark its descent. Moreover, what does it indicate about exemplarity if Lucrece has to kill herself to preserve its/her integrity and hence the integrity of historical tradition? Lucrece successfully preserves her exemplarity, preserves historical tradition, and seemingly reveals the hermeneutic limitations or incapacity of exemplarity. There are of course other questions implicitly raised; but my primary concern here is to emphasize that exemplarity is not merely subverted in the poem, though aspects of it certainly are—such as what some sixteenth-century writers considered to be its unquestionable interpretative authority; rather, it is subjected to close and skeptical examination. Shakespeare's narrative suggests that exemplarity is both reliable and unreliable as a means of defining subjectivity and interpreting history. In Tarquin's case, for instance, exemplarity is more or less simply accurate; but because of its contingency upon externals and hearsay, it has to be made accurate in the case of Lucrece (by means of her suicide). Hence, *Lucrece* shows exemplarity to be concurrently efficient and deficient—a skeptical approach towards exemplarity that might lead one to find *Lucrece* more akin to the essays of Montaigne than to the writings of Shakespeare's English contemporaries.[24] Ultimately, examining the intricately interactive establishing of characterization in *Lucrece* leads one to encounter a transformation of myth, and an examination of exemplarity and its interpretative function, that make one reconsider the poem as a whole.

## Notes

[1] For examples of the critical approaches and concerns mentioned, see: Coppélia Kahn, "The Rape in Shakespeare's *Lucrece*," *ShakS* 9 (1976): 45-72; Robert S. Miola, *Shakespeare's Rome* (Cambridge: Cambridge Univ. Press, 1983), pp. 18-41; Nancy J. Vickers, "'This Heraldry in Lucrece' Face,'" *PoT* 6 (1985): 171-84; Heather Dubrow, *Captive Victors: Shakespeare's Narrative Poems and Sonnets* (Ithaca: Cornell Univ. Press, 1987), pp. 80-168; Georgina Ziegler, "My lady's chamber: female space, female chastity in Shakespeare," *TexP* 4,1 (Spring 1990): 73-90; Linda Woodbridge, "Palisading the Elizabethan Body Politic," *TSLL* 33, 3 (Fall 1991): 327-54; and Annabel Patterson, *Reading Between the Lines* (London: Routledge, 1993), pp. 297-312. I am grateful to one of *SEL*'s readers for some astute and helpful comments on an earlier form of this essay.

[2] In fact, none as far as I am aware.

[3] That is, approximately lines 1-441 (William Shakespeare, *Lucrece*, in *The Poems*, ed. F. T. Prince [London: Methuen, 1976]). Further references to *Lucrece* will appear parenthetically in the text by line number.

[4] Cf. lines 30-4.

[5] Plato, *The Republic*, trans. David Lee (Harmondsworth: Penguin, 1979), 9.572-5. On the genre of tyrant tragedies, see Rebecca W. Bushnell, *Tragedies of Tyrants: Political Thought and Theater in the English Renaissance* (Ithaca: Cornell Univ. Press, 1990).

[6] See also lines 652-65, spoken by Lucrece.

[7] Plato, 9.579b.

[8] Cf. lines 120-89.

[9] Plato, 8.569b and 565d-6a.

[10] Cf. line 676.

[11] Cf. lines 519-39, 806-40, 1184-211, and so on.

[12] On the Renaissance discourse of exemplarity, see Timothy Hampton, *Writing from History: The Rhetoric of Exemplarity in Renaissance Literature* (Ithaca: Cornell Univ. Press, 1990). See also Larry Scanlon, *Narrative, Authority, and Power: The Medieval Exemplum and the Chaucerian Tradition* (Cambridge: Cambridge Univ. Press, 1994), pp. 27-54.

[13] See also lines 52-73. "Field" is also, of course, a heraldic reference.

[14] The phrase is Mikhail Bakhtin's (from the appendix of *Problems of Dostoevsky's Poetics,* ed. and trans. Caryl Emerson [Manchester: Manchester Univ. Press, 1984], p. 293).

[15] Cf. lines 386-99.

[16] Cf. line 58.

[17] See lines 9-14 of "*Amor, che nel penser mio vive et regna*" (in *Petrarch's Lyric Poems: The Rime Sparse*

and Other Lyrics, ed. and trans. Robert M. Durling [Cambridge: Harvard Univ. Press, 1976], p. 285); and lines 13-4 of *"Passa la nave mia colma d'oblio,"* (in *Petrarch's Lyric Poems,* p. 335).

[18] Cf. line 278.

[19] Petrarch, *"Passa la nave,"* line 13.

[20] Cf. lines 271-3 and 279-80.

[21] Cf. lines 197-201 and 271-3.

[22] Lucrece clearly does not understand the full extent of Tarquin's imposition of psychic violence; she understands, however, that he is forcing his antithetic role(s) on her.

[23] See lines 1048-50, 519-39, 806-40, and 1184-211.

[24] See "Of Cruelty," for example, and Hampton's interesting discussion of it and other of Montaigne's essays in *Writing from History,* pp. 134-97.

---

Source: "Subjectivity, Exemplarity, and the Establishing of Characterization in Lucrece," in *Studies in English Literature, 1500-1900,* Vol. 38, No. 1, Spring, 1998, pp. 45-60.

# On the Symbolism of *The Tempest*

## John G. Demaray, *Rutgers University*

A profound and continuing wonder stirred in characters by visionary dreams, reveries and magical spectacles is at the deepest core of *The Tempest*. This deep experience of wonder, which transforms corrupt characters and inspires the virtuous, distinguishes this late masque-like drama from comedies and tragedies more dependent upon traditional, unfolding, confrontational dramatic conflict.

"O, it is monstrous: monstrous:" calls out the terrified Alonso upon seeing Ariel disguised as a Harpy. The man of "sin," Alonso stands transfixed as his more insightful companion Gonzalo says, "I' th name of something holy, Sir, why stand you/In this strange stare?" (D. 13).

"Let me liue here euer," Ferdinand joyfully remarks upon seeing the visionary betrothal masque, "So rare a wondered Father and a wise/Makes this place Paradise" (D. 15).

"These are not naturall euents, they strengthen/From strange to stranger," says Alonso in awe when meeting seamen whom he thought dead (D. 18).

In the final scene Gonzalo conveys some sense of the total experience of the island's magic and the strange events that have gone before:

> All torment, trouble, wonder, and amazement
> Inhabits heere. Some heauenly power guide vs
> (D. 17)

The narrative contains relatively little action, but those characters who wander, dream, stare and listen in awestruck horror or amazement are changed and metaphorically reborn through the strangeness of things experienced but rarely understood. In this way, fancies and symbolic magical spectacles underlie and in large measure motivate action. Thematically, the play moves from a range of subjective and fanciful utopian reveries and visions interspersed, as has been seen, with jolting and equally fanciful "antic" countervailing spectacles, on to a revelation of true identities and of external reality.

Contrasting virtuous and corrupted dreams of a Golden Age, a coming millennium, haunt the imaginations of central characters. In the manner of a host of utopian and millenarian writers of the late Renaissance, the characters speculate, with differing degrees of casualness, seriousness, selfishness, or moral rectitude, on some personal variant of an ideal future time, a period when their sometimes wildly imaginative reveries on power, wealth, possessions, or natural plentitude may be fulfilled. External "reality" is placed in ever-changing perspectives as it is cast against the characters' imagined visions, and these visions are constantly tested against that reality.

The idle, irresponsible fancies of Gonzalo on the creation of an ideal commonwealth; the vicious speculations of Caliban, Trinculo and Stephano on riches and rule gained by murder; the parallel brutal, thwarted reveries and acts of Sebastian and Alonso aimed at seizing political power also through murder; and the ideal dreams of Prospero on fecundity and blessedness in marriage—all are presented through spectacle imagery and allusion. But in each case the reveries projected in spectacle, whether good or ill, are shattered or qualified by a rational awakening to earthly realities. Thematically, the play is a sharp but not cynical corrective to then-prevalent dreams of a Golden Age or a "new world" of perfect harmony, dreams given theatrical form in the main masques of court spectacles and suggested too, in very different ways, in the fictions of both utopian literature and the literature of exploration.

As symbolically represented by unique characters and action on a magical Mediterranean island, this awakening to earthly realities—to deceit and moral ambiguity in politics and social life and, in the case of Prospero, to the fact of human mortality—has been observed to contain oblique reflections of the "brave" new, but troubled, colonial world. Yet the drama's varied political, social and religious motifs are absorbed within a sweeping symbolism suggesting that all imagined ideal societies—whether those that might exist in some "brave new world" of total innocence, or those seriously or mockingly envisaged in the dreamlike fantasy of utopian literature, or those wondrously represented in the fleeting Golden Age theatrical Triumphs of aristocrats—all are uniformly subject to the coils of an imperfect, mortal social life.

Before *The Tempest* was first staged in 1611, the ideal aristocratic social visions that climaxed court masquing spectacles, though diverse in their "hinges," were notable in not directly representing the New World or colonial enterprises. When the New World finally did make its appearance on the Whitehall stage in a masque presented on 15 February 1613, the year of the second and last recorded performance of Shakespeare's play, this New World proved yet another fantastical variation of that golden world carried over from masque to masque. George Chapman's *The Memorable Maske of the two Honorable Houses of Inns of Court: the Middle Temple and Lyncolns Inne* featuring twelve Virginian Indians as triumphant main masquers, is a staged aristocratic dream vision rather than any recognizable depiction of native American life.[1]

The action of Chapman's masque unfolds between a stage set representing a New World island controlled by Indians of the Virginian "continent," and island from which the Indians come, and the British seat of state of King James at the hall's rear-center, the place to which the Indians triumphantly proceed. The featured performers, however, are neither the innocent, noble savages nor the monstrous primitives who, according to much political criticism, served as types of the strange "Other" and so prompted European acts of colonial control and repression. As New World rulers and worshippers of the sun, they are courtly aristocratic types who are identified as "Princes" and "Knights" and who perform as the social equals of the British aristocratic audience. The main masquers' courtly "habits," made from "cloath of siluer, richly embroidered, with golden Sunns," show only a touch of court-style "native" decoration in that there "ran a traile of gold, imitating Indian worke" about "euery Sunne"—an appropriate design gesture in otherwise traditional sumptuous masquing costumes (A2 verso). And they act as independent noble characters in a masquing world that, while abundant in natural wealth depicted in the main masque stage set, is conspicuously free of the colonial tyranny, sexual subjugation, drunkenness, slavery, oppression, cruelty and ethnic conflict that are the hallmark subjects of much recent political-literary criticism.

Even the New World antic performers who enter in a brief opening antimasque, though bizarre types suggestive of courtly Neapolitan intrigue, lack the evil malignancy of antiestablishment figures such as the witches in *The Masque of Queenes*. These New World antic figures are outlandish baboons "attir'd like fantasticall Trauailers, in Neopolitane sutes, and great ruffes." When their single "Anticke, and delightful" and seemingly gratuitous dance is over, they simply return to "their Tree" at the side of the stage (A).

The main masque that follows places the New World Virginian Indians "close to nature" in an unexpected way—a way doubtless longed for by James and members of his court, though certainly not anticipated by modern historians of the actual Virginia plantation. In an elaborate main masque stage spectacle, a rock transforms into a cloud. The cloud then "opens"; and to swelling music played by court musicians dressed as Priests of the Sun, the stately Indians are "discovered" within a radiant gold mine that glitters beneath a low, red sun.

Action is now "hinged," in the words of the masquing figure Honor, on the Virginian "Princes" coming to "Britan" to do "due homage" to the "*Lawe* and Vertue, celebrated" in the "sacred Nuptials" of the Princess Elizabeth and Frederick, and to pay homage in particular to the king who presides over both the marriage and the masque (D. 2). The work thus proceeds with the pacing of the masquers across the stage, their descent to the central hall for their main dances, and their triumphant presentation to and unmasking before the king.

The character Honor also debates with other figures over whether the hovering stage sun is rising or setting. The character "Eunomia," the "presenter" of the masquers and the personification of Law, prescriptively states the masque's thematic resolution, with which the featured performers through their symbolic movements show themselves in accord. In a speech using conventional masque sun iconography, Eunomia suggests that the stage sun will be seen rising when the ruling Virginian princes turn from past superstitions and, in a masquing triumph that implies a new political and religious allegiance, give their devotion to the personified true British sun which is "Enlightened with a Christian Piety."

> Virginian Princes, ye must now renounce
> Your superstitious worship of these Sunnes,
> Subject to cloudy darknings and descents,
> And of your sweet deuotions, turne the euents
> To this our Britain Phoebus
>
> (E)

Much could be said theoretically of Honor's admonition about what the Indians "must renounce" and to what they must "turn." It could be asserted, following the example of some recent critical approaches to *The Tempest* that "explain away" the work's internal contexts in order to give weight to external materials, that the masque's subterranean but now uncovered meaning and subtexts provide a central ideological statement on the power and politics of European colonialism. The masque would then point, in the light of wider historical "intertextualities," to the European subjugation of native Americans, destruction of the natives' religion and culture, and appropriation and exploitation of the natives' wealth and natural resources. And the masque could be seen to deny the very cultural existence of native Americans by making them nearly identical to Europeans.

But such claims, however meaningful as wide and general moral and political observations, would in turn unduly "suppress" the work's full contexts and its idealized main masque representation. In the golden world of Chapman's work, the island of the masque is *not* colonized. It is under the control of the aristocratic Indians, with personified gods and allegorical figures present but without the presence of colonizers. The Indians, in the manner of aristocratic performers in masque after masque, willingly and in festive triumph give their devotion of their own free will to the "state" identified with the sun. Their transfer of the object of their devotion from a lesser sun to a more glorious "Phoebus," another iconographic convention of main masques, is a festive act of free will. And after their choreographic compliment to the state—represented as a classical "Phoebus" Apollo imbued with inner "Christian Piety"—the masquers—Virginian Princes and Knights—can be assumed, as an inferred element of the masque fiction, to continue exercising local authority over their uncolonized homeland, but now under the aegis of the British sun king. Just how much the sun king would extract from their gold mine is open to question; here the masque indeed hints, by its graphic association of the Indians with gold, at the sun king's hopes of possibly obtaining native wealth. Finally, the typal "disguisings" of the main masque figures—Honor, Eunomia, the Indians, and the King as Phoebus—are all conventional generic fictions rather than realistic indexes to actual personal and social identities; and the Indians might well be regarded as receiving a compliment (rather than a dismissal) in being depicted as foreign, native aristocrats.

If the masque's dreamlike utopian political arrangements *were* compared to some form of actual government, then these arrangements might be seen as more reminiscent of an international commonwealth, in which native "Virginians" freely choose to recognize a foreign king while retaining local political authority, than of a colony in which natives are ruled by foreign occupying officials subject to a foreign monarch.

Considered as a masque written to flatter the king and court, the work is an imaginatively flamboyant and at times amusing construct of the new "open" court symbolism. Its romance elements are so phantasmagorical—mixing baboons dressed with ruffs, a gold mine, aristocratic Indians, and the king as the classical god Apollo—as to be surrealistic. Yet in directing attention to a New World so exotic it is historically unrecognizable, this late masque, mounted in the same year as *The Tempest*, might have caused persons familiar with that world and with voyage and colonial issues—possibly Shakespeare among them—to reflect upon actual New World problems involving the treatment of natives, the imposition of political power, and the expropriation of New World gold and natural resources. But it is also likely that at Whitehall in 1613, the masque would generally have been received as a stylized, celebratory, and ideologically conventional representation of how even aristocratic foreigners are drawn by honor and virtue to pay homage to and make bounty available to the glorious English king. What Chapman's masque most lucidly captures is a very special generic quality in main masque spectacles to which Shakespeare responded: an unrestrained and illusionary aristocratic utopianism that clearly called out for some kind of realistic modulation.

In *The Tempest*, Prospero seeks to control an imperfect world through his magic. Although critics, impressed and somewhat misdirected by Prospero's rhetoric, regularly lapse into the assumption that the Magus actually gives up the exercise of his powers at the beginning of the final scene, Prospero in fact has it both ways. He theatrically states in the present tense that he "abjures" his magic. But with his powers at their apex, he continues to use them, manipulating both events and characters to the very end of the dramatic action. He then promises, at the conclusion of scene 9, to employ his magic in the future to ensure clear sailing weather, though in the Epilogue immediately following he declares, in seeking the empathy of the audience, that his spells are *"ore-throwne"* (D. 19).

Before the final reconciliations that constitute a metaphoric rebirth, characters in the imperfect world of the play indulge themselves with social "imaginings." The essentially good counselor Gonzalo fancies an "antic" commonwealth of political and personal lassitude fortuitously supplied by a superabundant Nature. "I would with such perfection gouerne Sir," he remarks to Antonio, "T'Excell the Golden Age" (D. 7). Gonzalo's idle-man's commonwealth grows out of a cultural milieu of utopian works including Thomas More's communal *Utopia*, Robert Burton's agricultural commonwealth in the "Democritus" section of *The Anatomy of Melancholy*, tall tales of voyage authors about noble "primitive" societies; and polemical religious tracts predicting a coming millennium.[2] Gonzalo's reverie can also be seen more directly as a court counselor's satiric comment on the supposedly "perfect" hierarchical society revealed at the climax of familiar court theatricals such as Daniel's *The Vision of the 12. Goddesses* and Jonson's *Hymenaei* and *The Haddington Masque,* and in particular Jonson's later masque *The Golden Age Restored.*"[3]

Stimulated by the word play of Antonio, Sebastian and Alonso, by talk of the lushness of the grass, and by the magical freshness of recently drenched garments, Gonzalo's casual social reveries on inaction and superabundance are rendered, as were court spectacles, "to minister occasion to these Gentlemen." His remarks are sharply antic. With his imagination amusingly active but his intellect seemingly at rest, Gonzalo announces that in his commonwealth he will "(by contraries)/Execute all things" (D. 7). The counselor would have "all men idle, all:/And Women too" (D. 7):

All things in common Nature should produce
Without sweat or endeuour: Treason, fellony,
Sword, Pike, Knife, Gun, or neede of any Engine,
Would I not haue: but Nature should bring forth
Of it owne kinde, all foyzon, all abundance
To feed my innocent people.

(D. 7)

Despite Gonzalo's fanciful insistence that Nature should supply all in his imagined commonwealth, his past actions rationally contradict his fancy. Prospero has said earlier that Gonzalo humanely placed food in the small boat in which the Magus and Miranda had been set dangerously adrift by their enemies. The counselor took action to preserve their lives precisely because Nature could not be depended upon to do so.

Gonzalo's society of idleness, supposedly excelling the Golden Age, is eventually disclosed as a construction of negatives on an empty dream of "nothingness," a dream produced for the occasion with amusing but stinging overtones:

> . . . no kinde of Trafficke
> Would I admit: No name of Magistrate:
> Letters should not be knowne: Riches,
>   poverty,
> And use of seruice, none; Contract,
>   Succession,
> Borne, bound of Land, Tilth, Vineyard, none:
> No use of Mettall, Corne, or Wine, or Oyle:
> No occupation . . .
>
> (D. 7)

When Antonio mocks the counselor saying that he "dost talke nothing" (D. 7), Gonzalo in turn mocks the "sensible and nimble Lungs" of the gentlemen who "laugh at nothing" (D. 7). "'Twas you we laugh'd at," Antonio replies (D. 7). Gonzalo then strikes back, emphasizing the "nothingness" of the gentlemen's concerns, and implying that the men are fools associated with the moon, the source of madness.

Gonzalo's comments, with their ironic edge and their implication of egalitarian "leveling," are an original and mocking contrary to traditional iconography exalting an industrious, cultured and structured aristocratic-royalist state. But the "nothingness" of the words confirms that neither the imagined commonwealth nor its ideal contrary reflect actual social existence. The counselor's remarks thus satirically criticize even as they wittily entertain. They also hint at Gonzalo's inclination toward moral weakness: an excessive passivity in speaking against yet accepting corrupt nobles as masters. Here, central motifs—the emptiness of certain reveries, and the lunacy of those attending to them—foreshadow allusions to the emptiness of Caliban's vision and the comparative fullness of Prospero's.

In vivid contrast to Gonzalo's program for the mutual sharing of Nature's bounty, Caliban and his companions Trinculo and Stephano, ignoring others, basely and selfishly dream of hoarding the bounty of nature and mankind for themselves. Caliban gives vent to his earthly desires by paradoxically speaking of heavenly dreams. During a drunken conversation with Trinculo and Stephano, Caliban awkwardly describes the imagined descent of antic fools and virtuous figures from the changeable realm of the moon, the lowest and most material body in the Ptolemaic cosmos. Caliban's moon references thematically derive in part from traditional, exotic moon allusions in masques such as Jonson's *Masque of Blackness* (1605) and Thomas Campion's *Lord Hayes Masque;* and they anticipate those in Jonson's *News from the New World Discovered in the Moon* (1620).[4] In this last work, virtuous main masque moon people, the harbingers of an ideal Golden Age society, float down to earth and "shake off" their glittering silver "Isicles." Left behind on the moon, according to a Herald in the antimasque, are "two or three Moon-*Calves!*" (ll. 233-34). A character designated as Factor asks, "O, I, *Moone-Calves!* what Monster is that, I pray you?" To which the Herald replies, "Monster? none at all; a very familiar thing like our foole here on earth" (ll. 235-38).

In *The Tempest* Trinculo and Stephano, who are too gross even to "cut" the clouds in an abrupt descent, are imagined by an ignorant and foolish Caliban as gods who have directly descended by falling from above.

> Cal.: Ha'st thou not dropt from heauen?
>
> Ste. Out o'th Moon, I doe assure thee. I was the Man ith' Moone, when time was.
>
> Cal. I haue seene thee in her: and I doe adore thee. . . .
>
> (D. 10)

Caliban's foolish adoration of this spurious Man in the Moon is the antithesis of the monster's detestation of Prospero, who is seen as aided by the sun. Caliban curses the sun's brilliant light, and calls down upon Prospero those harmful "infections that the Sunne suckes vp" (D. 9). On the other hand, Caliban views Stephano as "a braue God" (D. 10), a figure who bears an all-too-earthly "liquor" that the monster in confusion says is "Celestiall." Caliban, in turn, is given an established "antic" lunar nickname by Stephano:

> How now, Moone-Calfe, how do's thine Ague?
>
> (D. 10)

Awkward, subhuman, earthly Caliban, adoring the base seamen and drinking their liquor, crassly imagines a Golden World of physical possessions and wealth—an island that he will own. And following the creature's reminiscence on the gradual "opening" of the heavens to instrumental music and voices as in a staged masque spectacle, he dreams of clouds dividing to reveal the mundane object of his desires:

> Cal. Be not affeard, the Isle is full of noyses, Sounds, and sweet aires, that giue delight and hurt not:

> Sometimes a thousand twangling Instruments
> Will hum about mine eares; and sometime voices,
> That if I then had wak'd after long sleepe,
> Will make me sleepe againe, and then, in dreaming,
> The clouds methought would open, and shew riches
> Ready to drop vpon me, that, when I wak'd,
> I cri'd to dreame again.
>
> (D. 12)

A comparable yet thematically different depiction of the masque-like opening of the heavens before shepherds occurs in Milton's *On the Morning of Christ's Nativity*. There, the "music sweet" of "Divinely warbled voice/Answering the stringed noise" is said by the poetic narrator to help the "fancy" envisage an "Age of Gold,"[5] an age that in this case is represented as spiritually transcendent. The music in Milton's poem introduces the "discovery" of heavenly cherubim and seraphim within a "globe of circular light"; and this discovery is followed by the appearance in the scenic heavens of the theological figures Faith, Hope, and Mercy who then descend to earth on "tissued clouds down steering" (ll. 146-47).

Although critics seeking to show empathetic qualities in Caliban rightly suggest that the monster reacts with humane delight to "sounds and sweet airs," they overlook the fact that Caliban's allusions to instrumental and vocal music are but the matrix for the culminating masque-like depiction of the monster's flawed ideal. The noisy "twangling" and the "hum" of stringed instruments, followed by the sound of voices, stir in Caliban dreams of clouds opening, not upon virtuous figures ready gracefully to descend to an honored viewer, but rather upon material riches ready to "drop" on a dreamer. And, too, they overlook a remark by Stephano on the music in Caliban's fanciful "brave kingdom," that echoes again the theme of "nothingness."

> Ste. This will proue a braue kingdome to me,
> Where I shall haue my Musicke for nothing.
>
> (D. 12)

In the later betrothal masque—the antitype of Caliban's antic dream and Gonzalo's antic reveries—Prospero's representation of a Golden Age marriage can be seen in tune with a virtuous conception of nature and society.

Before the masque begins, Prospero warns Ferdinand to beware of brutish lust engendered by "th' fire ith' blood" (D. 14). Ferdinand states and subsequently demonstrates that he can indeed suppress burning passion by restraining "the ardour of my Liuer" (D. 14), one of the supposed "seats" of fiery desire. However, passion and lust have flamed in other characters earlier. In scene 2, Prospero wrathfully condemns the monster for attempting to rape Miranda. Later, Caliban, Trinculo and Stephano plot sedition and murder after becoming, in the words of Ariel, "red-hot with drinking" (D. 15).

By contrast, the betrothal masque features iconography suggestive of a cool, restrained, chaste love appropriate to the honored couple, and antithetical to the fiery passions that in earlier scenes spurred Caliban's lust and desire for riches and power. An aristocratic vision of peace, harmony and plenitude centered on a new theme—the bearing of children—now briefly supplants and suppresses Prospero's awareness of the reality of Caliban's sedition and obsessions. In the masque it is the mother goddess Juno who, in gracefully descending and then in blessing the betrothed couple, gives rich expression to ideals of honor, prosperity, joy and, most important, human and earthly plenitude.

> *Iu. Honor, riches, marriage, blessing,*
> *Long continuance, and encreasing,*
> *Hourly yes, be still upon you,*
> *Juno sings her blessings on you*
> *Earth's increase, poison plenty*
> *Barrens, and Garners, near empty.*
> *Vines, with clustering bunches growing,*
> *Plants, with goodly berthed bowing:*
> *Spring come to you at the farthest,*
> *In the very end of Hairiest.*
> *Scarcity and want shall shun you,*
> *Ceres blessing so is on you.*
>
> (D. 15)

In *Anthony and Cleopatra*, the passionate and moody Cleopatra, at the moment of her death, identifies with the element that was thought to burn with varying intensity in human beings. "I am Fire and Ayre," she declares, "my other Elements/I giue to baser life" (D. 367). Throughout *The Tempest*, it is precisely the element of fire, with its power to cause the heat of burning desire, that Prospero seeks to keep at a distance from cool and chaste Miranda. In conjuring up the masque, the Magus thus banishes from the stage—while allowing their names to be mentioned—two other characters associated with fiery passion: "*Marses* hot Minion" (D. 14), that is, the goddess Venus; and her son Cupid. Prospero features Iris, Ceres and Juno as main masquers, each of them associated with an element other than fire. Iris with her "refreshing showers" and "watry Arch" carries iconographic allusions to water; Ceres, with her "Medes" "bankes" and "Turfie-Mountaines," the earth; and Juno, the "Queene o'th Skie" who descends, the air (D. 14).

Although Iris and Ceres are distinctive in the betrothal masque in speaking slightingly of Venus and Cupid, they are otherwise presented as traditional iconographic figures of, respectively, the rainbow and earthly fertility, in consonance with their established roles in works as varied as Virgil's *Aeneid*, Ovid's *Metamorphosis*, and in Daniel's *The Vision of the 12. Goddesses* and *Tethys Festival,* and Ben Jonson's *Hymenaei.* Shakespeare's Juno appears most indebted to Jonson. In the text of Daniel's *Vision of the 12. Goddesses,* Juno was represented primarily as a figure of divine power without specific attributes, but in Jonson's marriage masque *Hymenaei,* the goddess directly signifies those meanings prominent in *The Tempest:* "ayre" and, through an anagram, "union." In the words of the figure Reason in Jonson's masque,

> And see where IVNO, whose great name
> Is VNIO, in the *anagram,*
> Displays her glistering state, and chaire,
> As she enlightened all the ayre!
>
> (ll. 232-35)

Jonson may well have induced Shakespeare to develop long-recognized anagrams of his own. It seems likely that Shakespeare introduced the name Caliban as an anagram for "Canibal," in the seventeenth century usage of the word, a "sauage" (D. 5) living close to the earth. The contrasting name Prospero appears to be an anagram for "Prosperity." It is the name *"Prosper"* that Alonso thinks he hears echoing within the sound of thunder when Ariel, disguised as a harpy, vanishes in scene 7 (D. 13). In the next scene, when the betrothal masque is interrupted by Prospero's thought of the seditious Caliban, thematic oppositions in the play are further underlined by the roles and names of these two figures.

The idealized but interrupted betrothal masque briefly but memorably highlights Prospero's unattainable, evanescent dream of social harmony. Shakespeare, here and earlier, artfully chooses and intermingles masque-like hieroglyphics to insure social meanings adjusted to his own theatrical purposes.

Prospero's movement from fury to reconciliation in the play's last scene is not powerful drama. A passing comment by Ariel about the sadness of the wandering nobles spurs the Magus to follow his human feelings.

> Ar. . . . your charm so strongly works 'em
> That if you now beheld them, your affections
> Would become tender
>
> (D. 16)

The Magus's reply is surprisingly casual: "Dost thou thinke so Spirit?" To which Ariel says, "Mine would, Sir, were I humane" (D. 16). Prospero suddenly declares, "And mine shall." Yet before rationally deciding on the "sole drift" of his "purpose," the Magus, as if out of a need to convince himself of his own "affections," asks a self-reflective rhetorical question:

> Hast thou (which art but aire) a touch, a
>   feeling
> Of their afflictions, and shall not my selfe,
> One of their kinde, that relish all as sharpely,
> Passion as they, be kindlier mou'd then thou art?
>
> (D. 16)

The question proves decisive. Prospero avows in only five lines that he is "strook to th' quick" by fury but will now take action relying upon his "nobler reason" (D. 16). The change is introduced, not as a deeply felt dramatized experience, but as a quick and rather matter-of-fact reasoned decision that leads into a series of dominating, ritualistic, magical actions.

On the private stage at Blackfriars or the public stage at the Globe, actors with only these few lines to work with might imaginatively improvise and act out an emotional change that is only haltingly suggested by Prospero's brief, flat questions and remarks. But at Whitehall on the uplifted royal stage, and particularly on the green rug of the center-hall performing space, performers in close proximity to the audience could have emphasized the change memorably through the magical rituals, "presentations" and "unmaskings" that were a climactic part of Whitehall Spectacle Triumphs.

In the opening lines of the play's final scene, the Magus, in full magical regalia, proclaims that his zenith of power has at last arrived. He now turns to the magical resolution of his "Project" at the evensong hour of Vespers as day fades into night.

> Now do's my Proiect gather to a head:
> My charms cracke not; my Spirits obey, and
>   Time
> Goes vpright with his carriage: how's the day?
> Ar. On the sixt hower; at which time, my Lord,
> You said our worke should cease.
>
> (D. 16)

This resolution begins with rituals of "robing" and empowerment. Ariel had earlier been ordered to Prospero's Cell to obtain the magical robes that Prospero called "trumpery" and that Trinculo subsequently called "wardrobe" (D. 15), a term often used for theatrical costumes. The garments were donned by the comic conspirators in an antic mockery of true kingship. But now in this final scene of the play, the robes are most seriously assumed by Prospero in his role as Magus as he apparently displays his instruments of power: a magical wand and an occultist book.

Even Caliban had recognized the force of Prospero's magic; the monster had insisted that the overthrow of the Magus depended upon the destruction of his occult books. "Braine him," the monster declared, "Having first seiz'd his bookes." Caliban twice repeated this admonition. "Remember/First to possesse his Bookes; for without them/He's but a Sot"; "Burne but his Bookes" (D. 12).

In the final scene, after having donned his magical robes, Prospero, stepping forward from his Cell, makes his great declamation on the terrible strength of his occult power. Echoing the "Chief Dame's" magical claims in the *Masque of Queenes* (ll. 218-43) and the sorceress Medea's praise of magical art in the *Metamorphosis* (7.197-219), Prospero announces that his "rough Magicke" has "bedymm'd" the sun, called forth "windes" that stirred the seas, and even raised the shades of the dead.

> . . . Graues at my command
> Haue wak'd their sleepers, op'd, and let 'em forth
> By my so potent Art.
>
> (D. 16)

For many in court and public audiences and very possibly for James I himself, Prospero's necromantic recalling the dead to life would have been viewed as blasphemously mirroring Christ's raising of Lazarus as recorded in Scripture. Earlier in the scene, Prospero had been addressed by Ariel as "my Lord," the title applied to Christ in Patristic commentary.

> . . . how's the day?
> Ar. On the sixt hower; at which time, my Lord,
> You said our worke should cease.
>
> (D. 16)

According to all four Gospel accounts, it was at the sixth hour that, as Christ hung crucified on the Cross, darkness came over the earth and the graves gave up their dead. In the words of the Gospel of Matthew, which are echoed in the Gospels of Mark and Luke,

> Now from the sixth hour there was darkness over all the land unto the ninth hour.
>
> (27.45)

> And the graves were opened; and many bodies of the saints which slept arose.
>
> (27.52)[6]

Yet Prospero's actions are the reverse of those of the crucified Christ of Scripture—and the reverse of those of the changeable figure Medea in Ovid's Latin poem the *Metamorphosis*. In the Bible, Christ's Passion ultimately results in a disclosure of divinity that overcomes death and reveals an eternal kingdom. In Ovid's poem, Medea exercises her demonic magical powers to restore the youth of aging Aeson, the father of her husband Jason. Overtones of these scriptural and poetic allusions resonate in the play. But in actions that are the antithesis of Christ's scriptural victory over death and revelation of a heavenly kingdom, and of Medea's restoration of Aeson's youth in Ovid's work, Prospero, like a main masquer removing a visor and disclosing a human face, strips away his screening weeds as Magus, "abjures" and so renounces occult necromantic and other magical powers, and comes forward in his social role as Duke of Milan and as a frail and aging human being. Prospero ultimately acts out of virtue rather than fury, but there remains about the Magus and his magic a moral ambivalence. Prospero has performed virtuous works of reconciliation while admitting to the raising of tempests and the dead. These last actions would have been recognized as blasphemous deeds of black and necromantic magic in violation of God's natural law, deeds that certainly would have been condemned by King James and officials of his court.[7]

And Prospero, having verbally "abjured" his rough magic, continues to promote virtuous results through dubious occult means. When Prospero confronts his enemies, the confused nobles are reconciled to the Magus not through dramatic acted-out demonstrations of anguish or love, but rather through the jolting experience of Prospero's magic. The Magus confirms that Alonso is still under a spell and so subject to the "subtilties" or illusions of the island. In this state Alonso asks "pardon" for his "wrongs" and thereupon directly resigns the falsely gained Dukedom of Milan in favor of the rightful Duke Prospero. But in telling his "strange story," Alonso confesses that the affliction of his mind and his past madness have been overcome by the astonishing magical reappearance of Prospero, referred to here as an apparent phantom or "inchanted trifle" (D. 17). When Alonso asks for forgiveness, the Magus actually intervenes to prevent him from delving introspectively into memories of past evil.

> Alo. I Must aske my child forgiuenesse;
>
> Pro. There, Sir, stop,
> Let vs not burthen our remembrances, with
> A heauiness that's gon.
>
> (D. 18)

A sense of the miraculous pervades the scene. Prospero's magic so awes the nobles that, in the words of the Magus, "they deuoure their reason and scarse thinke." And Prospero, in a comment recalling the paramount role Inigo Jones gave to the "eyes" in achieving spiritual enlightenment, repeats a truism of court iconographic stagecraft: "Their eies doe offices of Truth" (D. 17). The enchanter then inspires amazement by producing "a wonder": magically presenting Miranda and Ferdinand playing chess. "A most high miracle," Sebastian cries upon seeing the seemingly drowned Ferdinand resurrected and in the company of this unknown young maid (D. 17).

This unexpected "wonder" appealing for its "Truth" to the eyes rather than the other senses would very likely have been mounted at Whitehall at a central rear-stage position as a sudden "discovery." If traditional staging techniques were followed at court, backflats or perhaps a curtain would have been quickly drawn to disclose the betrothed couple in an iconographic tableau. Lambent light cast by oil lamps or candles may well have illumined Ferdinand and Miranda, now perhaps dressed in conventional sparkling outer garments covered with reflecting metal "orbs" or "spangs," as they revealed their inner virtue through gracious movements even while playing at the battle game of chess. Some years later in Thomas Middleton's allegorical *A Game of Chess* (1624), a play satirizing the machinations of the English and Spanish courts' marriage negotiations, performers acted out the roles of belligerent chess pieces. At Whitehall, the iconographic "speaking picture" would have signified the spiritual chastity of Miranda in her reactions to the seemingly playful deceptions of her betrothed at the gaming board.

> Mir. Sweet Lord, you play me false.
>
> Fer. No my dearest loue,
> I would not for the world.
>
> Mir. Yes, for a score of Kingdomes, you
> should wrangle,
> And I would call it faire play.
>
> (D. 17)

Together, the iconography and dialogue demonstrate that in earthly play at chess, even as in earthly love, there resides the potential for mortal corruption.

Not long afterward, Miranda, looking upon mortals other than her father for the first time, experiences astonishment. "O wonder!" she exclaims (D. 17). Alonso, stunned by the visionary appearance of his son Ferdinand whom he thought drowned, desires deep oracular understanding of the events. But again Prospero prevents immediate introspective knowledge, directing Alonso's sensibility away from intellectual comprehension and toward magical experience.

> Alo. . . . there is in this busnesse, more
> than nature
> Was euer conduct of: some Oracle
> Must rectifie our knowledge.
>
> Pro. Sir, my Liege,
> Doe not infest your minde, with beating on
> The strangenesse of this businesse; at pickt
> leisure
> (Which shall be shortly single) I'le resolue
> you,
> (Which to you shall seeme probable) of euery
> These happend accidents: till when, be
> cheerful
> And thinke each thing well
>
> (D. 18)

Even the last entrance of Caliban inspires amazement. "This is a strange thing," Alonso remarks, "as eer I look'd on" (D. 18).

In *The Winter's Tale,* King Leontes of Sicilia, by seeking and receiving a message from the Delphic Oracle, obtains deep prophetic knowledge of his own misdeeds. But in *The Tempest* such deep knowledge is deferred. Rather, the immediate experience of wondrous events followed by the gradual emergence of amazed characters from spells and illusions to a recognition of true identities, provides a gradual dawning, but not a full illumination, of intellectual insight. Shakespeare, playing upon spectacle traditions of magical transformation, uses the "unmasking" of identities as a metaphor for spiritual rebirth. He thus gives to his drama the general theme of human regeneration familiar to ancient mystery plays, but not by making explicit allusions to such dramas. He relies instead upon immediately known masque forms, devices and ceremonial actions.

In this way, Alonso slowly begins to recognize the true identities of Miranda and Prospero as they symbolically "unmask." Having witnessed the astonishing "discovery" of Miranda playing at chess, Alonso is puzzled. "What is this Maid," he asks his son, "with whom thou wasn't at play?"

> Is she the goddesse that hath seuer'd vs,
> And brought vs thus together?
>
> (D. 18)

Miranda's magical "discovery" has indeed been like that of a virtuous goddess in a masque, one whose absence has allowed for past antic action, but one whose surprise entry and power restore social harmony. Ferdinand, speaking as someone spiritually reborn through his "second father" Prospero, now strips the screening disguise from Miranda and presents her in her underlying human reality:

> Sir, she is mortall;
> But by immortall prouidence, she's mine:
> I chose her when I could not aske my Father
> For his aduice, nor thought I had one: She
> Is daughter to this famous Duke of Millaine,
> Of whom, so often I have heard renowne,
> But neuer saw before: of whom I haue
> Receiu'd a second life; and second Father
>
> (D. 18)

Gonzalo joins in underscoring the play's theme of discovery and unmasking by adding that "In one voyage" many persons and things were found, among them, "all of vs our selues/When no man was his owne" (D. 18). With the final visionary entrance of Miranda at the end of the nobles' wanderings, "all" of the aristocrats are symbolically "unmasked" to themselves and restored to their own identities. The confused seamen who also now appear, having been aroused by Ariel from enchanted sleep, experience a wondrous re-awakening to themselves and to all around them. And when a distracted Caliban wearing the Magus's stolen clothing is driven on stage together with Stephano and Trinculo, the monster is at first verbally chastised by Prospero. But then, as the Magus again assumes the role of a "second Father," Caliban is greeted by Prospero as "mine" and promised pardon. Caliban, seeing the figure he now calls his "fine . . . Master" transformed in appearance by state robes, is himself astonishingly transformed. Caliban alone among the play's characters announces, with possible religious undertones, that he will "be wise hereafter,/And seeke for grace" (D. 18-19).

An air of uncertainty nonetheless remains, for much has been left unexplained. Prospero has promised Alonso growing revelations in times to come; in addition, the Magus promises ever-expanding knowledge from his personal tale.

> Alo. I long
> To hear the story of your life; which must
> Take the eare strangely.
>
> Pro. I'le deliuer all.
>
> (D. 19)

Prospero's wondrous magic will continue too, for the Magus announces that he will engage in one more extraordinary exercise of his art before he breaks his staff and drowns his book. He will, with the help of Ariel, give Alonso

> calm Seas, auspicious gales
> And saile so expeditious, that shall catch
> Your Royall fleete farre off. My *Ariel,* chicke,
> That is thy charge; Then to the Elements
> Be free, and fare thou well:
>
> (D. 19)

In the magical calm that follows the tempest, charmed winds will waft Prospero and the reconciled nobles from the Mediterranean island of utopian dreams. Ariel will be free to return to the elements; and Caliban, to occupy the island that the creature coveted. The strange, revealing tale that Prospero promises to tell, as he breaks from the realm of illusion to reenter the mainland world, is left mysteriously unspoken at the end of the play.

The play's Epilogue, even more than the "entries" and "unmaskings" of characters in the drama's last scene, shows the tensions Shakespeare faced in adapting the social forms of the masquing Triumph to a staged drama. The Triumph forms produced a pressure to create plays in which there was an actual break from the theatrical world of romance and dream into the actual social world of the audience in the hall. In turn, the counterpressures of dramatic form required a certain aesthetic distance between audience and performers, even in the Epilogue.

Shakespeare responded by composing a play in which the "release" of performers into the actual society of spectators in the hall is never complete. There are no revels in which the commoners who were actors totally unmask—that is, fully cast off the screen of their make-believe identities and enter into the court as known persons in an existing social hierarchy. The actors remain theatrical character-types whose entry into the social world essentially takes place in the context of the drama. It is Prospero alone who, having disclosed himself as the "true" Duke of Milan, unmasks sufficiently to reveal, beneath the theatrical guise of the Duke, an elder actor pointedly appealing to an audience for applause and prayers. In the Epilogue, when Prospero briefly reappears alone to ask that the "good hands" of the audience release him from the magical "bands" still confining him, his request is more than an emotive appeal for applause (D. 19). It is an appeal for permission to break further from the constraining illusions of the play. And at Whitehall, the actor would very likely have made this personal plea, not from a raised stage as is often assumed, but close to the audience from the central green rug bordering the tiers or degrees on which the aristocrats were seated. The performer then would have been in a position to make a final step that was in fact barred to him as an actor and a commoner—the troubling step at the root of tensions in applying the masque to dramatic form—the step over the carpet's edge and into an actual aristocratic society.

Such tensions are echoed in the social world within the play. The innocent Miranda may believe in seeming harbingers of a "braue new world" into which she is about to enter; but Prospero dryly remarks, "'Tis new to thee" (D. 17-18). And in the Epilogue, when the Magus asks for the prayers of the audience, he is sadly considering the possibility of his own future despair. For in *The Tempest,* the social realm now contained within the play allows for the continuing existence of ideals of innocence and virtuous union; but it is a social realm with a potential for war and sedition mirroring that of the external world, and it is a social realm in which divine providence is invoked by Prospero in recognition of human mortality.

*Notes*

[1] *The Memorable Masque . . . As it was performed before the king, at White-Hall on Shroue Munday at night; being the 15 of February, 1613. At the Princely celebration of the most Royall Nuptialls of the* Palsgraue, *and his trice graious Princess* Elizabeth. &c (London: Printed by G. Eld, for George Norton, 1613).

² Thomas More, *Utopia,* ed. Edward Surtz (New Haven, 1964); and the utopian comments in the "Democritus Junior to the Reader" segment of Robert Burton's *The Anatomy of Melancholy* eds. Floyd Dell and Paul Jordan-Smith (New York, 1955), 83-93.

³ See Jonson's masques *Hymenaei* and *The Golden Age Restored* in *Ben Jonson,* 7.208-41, 419-29. The theme of the return of a Golden Age appeared also in Thomas Heywood's pageant play *The Golden Age* (1611). The repeated and very popular representation of ideal Arcadian and Golden Age themes in Stuart and Caroline court theatricals has been treated in Erica Veevers, *Images of Love and Religion: Queen Henrietta Maria and Court Entertainments* (Cambridge, England, 1989); and in the citing of Arcadian figures and iconography by John Harris, Stephen Orgel, and Roy Strong, *The King's Arcadia: Inigo Jones and the Stuart Court* [a printed catalogue for a 1973 exhibition at the Masquing House] (London, 1973). See also the discussion of seventeenth century millenarian tracts in E. V. Tuveson, *Millennium and Utopia* (Berkeley and Los Angeles, 1949).

⁴ See *The Masque of Blacknesse* and *News From the New World Discover'd in the Moon* in *Ben Jonson,* 7.167-89, 512-25. See also Thomas Campion, "The Description of a Maske, Presented before the Kinge Maiestie *at White-Hall, on Twelfth Night* last, in honour of the Lord Hayes, and his Bride, Daughter and Heire to the Honourable the Lord Dennye" (London: Imprinted by John Wilndet for John Brown, 1607).

⁵ *John Milton,* 45-46, ll. 93-105.

⁶ See the passages in Matthew, together with Mark 15.33 and Luke 23.44, in Bibles popular in England during the period; namely, the *Geneva Bible* (London: Rouland Hall, 1560); *The holy Byble, conteynying the olde and newe Testament Set foorth by authoritie,* Bishop's Version (London: Richard Jugge, 1575); and *The Bible: Holy Scripture,* Geneva Version (London: Christopher Barker, 1576).

⁷ See King James's comments on magicians in league with the devil in *Daemonologie in forme of a Dialogue,* xii. In this text, the figure Epistemon, a spokesman for the king's views, does admit that some persons have simply studied magic without entering "themselues in Sathans seruice," but he immediately adds that such persons are nevertheless dangerously exposed to the devil's "baites" and so may fall into his hands. In a central statement that would appear unmistakably to reflect what is known of the king's own opinions, Epistemon then condemns the actual "practise" of magic as an "offense" against God (15). In *Daemonologie* James even denounced the conjurer-diplomat Girolamo Scotto who had performed card tricks for Queene Elizabeth and who had occasionally served as an ambassabor for the occultist Holy Roman Emperor Rudolf II, the ruler with whom Frederick was consulting in 1611 at the approximate time the English marriage was announced. The king also dismissed from court and did not patronize the Queen's former advisor, Dr. John Dee, who was part occultist, part mathematician, part navigational expert, and part charlatan.

See also Frances Yates's studies of occult influences in England and in the English court in *Giordano Bruno and the Hermetic Tradition* (Chicago, 1969); *The Occult Philosophy in the Elizabethan Age* (London, 1979); and *The Rosicrucian Enlightenment* (London, 1972). See also Colin Still, *Shakespeare's Mystery Play,* revised as *The Timeless Theme;* Michael Srigley, *Images of Regeneration;* and Christopher McIntosh, *The Rosy Cross Unveiled: The History, Mythology and Rituals of an Occult Order* (Wellingborough, 1980). R. W. Rowse in *Sex and Society in Shakespeare's Age: Simon Forman the Astrologer* (New York, 1974) examines the relationship between Forman, the astrologer and magician, and the French Huguenot couple, the Montjoies, in whose house on Silver Street Shakespeare lived in 1602, and probably before and after that year.

---

Source: "On the Symbolism of *The Tempest,*" in *Shakespeare and the Spectacles of Strangeness: The Tempest and the Transformation of Renaissance Theatrical Forms,* Duquesne University Press, 1998, pp. 110-34.

# Ganymedes and Kings: Staging Male Homosexual Desire in *The Winter's Tale*

## Nora Johnson, *Swarthmore College*

When historians discuss the relation between homosexual practice and homosexual identity in England before the eighteenth century, they often note that male same-sex behaviors coincided with neither a set of psychosocial characteristics nor a clear sexual preference. Alan Bray, for instance, describes satirical portrayals of the courtier who engaged in sodomy, arguing that these portrayals were striking from a twentieth-century perspective because of their failure to represent a specifically homosexual identity: "on this point [the satirists] are remarkably consistent: the sodomite is a young man-about-town, with his mistress on one arm and his 'catamite' on the other."[1] Following, as he says, "broadly" in the traditions of Mary McIntosh, Jeffrey Weeks, and Michael Foucault, Bray argues that representations of sodomy before the late-seventeenth century reveal the historical contingency of the modern homosexual. He cites Donne's first *Satire*, for example, which accuses one man-about-town of enjoying the "nakedness and bareness" of a "plump muddy whore or prostitute boy," and he notes that Johnson's Sir Voluptuous Beast makes his wife listen to tales about his sexual exploits, recounting to her "the motions of each petticoat / And how his Ganymede moved and how his goat."[2]

The evidence that Bray culls from sources other than satire is equally telling and equally resistant to identifying an exclusively homosexual "type." He describes the reputation of Sir Anthony Ashley, one of James I's courtiers known for his love of boys, who was also known to be a married man and the father of a daughter. He similarly reports Lucy Hutchinson's description of court life under James:

> The face of the Court was much changed in the change of the king, for King Charles was temperate, chaste, and serious; so that the fools and bawds, mimics and catamites of the former court grew out of fashion and the nobility and courtiers, who did not quite abandon their debaucheries, yet so reverenced the king as to retire into corners to practice them.[3]

What emerges from Bray's study is more than simply the absence of what twentieth-century historians would call "homosexuality." These accounts suggest that homosexual practice was part of an aristocratic sexual esthetic, a "fashion," in which the courtier sampled at will from an array of erotic practices, none of which could impose itself upon him as a rigid identity. Even Ashley's apparent preference for boys seems to have been compatible with his role as a husband and father. To reiterate the point that has become associated especially with the work of Foucault, sodomy in early modern England is an act, not an identity.

Certainly homosexual desire as imagined by James himself seems to have involved no sense of sexual nature. On the contrary, his letters to his favorite George Villiers enact almost an escape from identity, a sense that one of the pleasures of illicit sexuality was its license to undo the categories of self-definition. James addresses one such letter to "My only sweet and dear child," for instance, and he prays

> That we may make at this Christmas a new marriage ever to be kept hereafter; for, God so love me, as I desire only to live in this world for your sake, and that I had rather live banished in any part of the earth with you than live a sorrowful widow's life without you. And so god bless you, my sweet child and wife, and grant that ye may ever be a comfort to your dear dad and husband.[4]

James thinks of this relationship as if it were a marriage in which both partners are wives at the same time that James is father and husband and Villiers is child and wife. Far from being identified by his desire for another man, James imagines homoeroticism as an undoing of identity itself. In fact, James's words to Villiers resonate strongly with Bray's contention, developed further by Jonathan Goldberg, that sodomy in this period belongs not so much to a system of sexual taxonomy as to a system of unintelligibility, a social order in which sexual contact between men signifies only when it can be associated with chaos, anarchy, heresy, or sorcery.[5] In this reading, the scandal James risks is not a revelation of personal identity so much as an unleashing of ideological forces that could threaten to undo his own kingship.

Neither James nor the early modern courtier who employs a ganymede, then, is a homosexual in any modern sense of the word. But what are we to assume about the ganymede or catamite himself? The terms in which we are accustomed to explaining the invention of sexual identity—the molly house subcultures in Bray's account, the discursive subject in Foucault's analysis—are inadequate to explain the status of the passive "boy" whose presence gurantees homoerotic content in the accounts of debauchery mentioned above. The ganymede is emphatically not the homosexual subject Foucault teaches us to associate with modernity; among other disqualifying factors, his participation in the homoerotic is taken to be a function of his youth, rather than some expression of essence or nature. In some accounts the ganymede himself desires a woman, while an adult male desires him. But the early modern representations I will examine below suggest that the ganymede's role as an object of homosexual desire extends beyond mere passivity in important ways, that he is imagined as intrinsically fit to be such an object, even, at times, in spite of his own professed desires. Moreover, although we know little or nothing about the relation between actual boys and literary representations of ganymedes, the employment of boys as erotic objects in early modern theater makes the ganymede an integral part of a theater company's reputation. In this light, the eroticized boy is more than a literary strategy for representing aristocratic sexual license. Because *The Winter's Tale* is centrally concerned, in my reading, with legitimating theatrical practice, its meditations on boyhood similarly become more than nostalgia for the lost past of the two kings whose relationship dominates the play. Representing boyhood becomes instead a way of negotiating the homoerotic, both for Leontes and Polixenes and for the institution of theater itself. In both cases, the reputation for sodomy means more than "acts."

I will argue, then, that even in the absence of a totalizing rhetoric of homosexual identity, the ganymede's participation in the homoerotic identifies him powerfully, so much so that his presence onstage works to stigmatize the theatrical profession. Such an argument is offered not to counter the notion that homosexuality is a historically contingent construct; especially as formulated by Foucault, that insight has powerfully altered perceptions both of sexuality and of early modern Europe. Instead, I want to add this study to the growing body of work that moves beyond the potential reductiveness of a Foucaultian paradigm.[6] We can surely emphasize the radical newness of homosexuality "as we know it" without ignoring the multiple and complex ways that sodomy could interact with notions of self before the modern era. As Gregory Bredbeck argues,

> if [essentialist critics begin] with the assumption that we can trace an atemporal conception of homosexuality throughout history, the other alternative has been to say that because we *cannot* trace this particular concept through history, nothing can be traced. In each instance "the homosexual" is essentialized as the absolute standard of adjudication. "It" is what we must find if we are to find anything at all.[7]

This essay explores what might be traced, and examines the interactions between theatrical self-consciousness and illicit desire in *The Winter's Tale*.

II

Ganymedes were, of course, not the only group of individuals to be categorized by their participation in sexual acts. On the contrary, the typecasting of women is a familiar part of the early modern sexual terrain, and one that Foucault more or less ignores. One of the factors that makes women such fascinating additions to the sexual taxonomy of this period, though, and that makes them important for a discussion of ganymedes is their paradoxical relation to sexual subjectivity. Women could be characterized absolutely by their sexual acts, without really being imagined to possess agency, or even desire.

Early modern women were sometimes represented as a kind of sexual fixed point in an otherwise chaotic staging of eroticized identities. When Ben Johnson wants to portray debauchery at its worst, for instance, he has his master cozener Volpone engage in an elaborate fantasy of sexual license. "Inviting" the chaste and married Celia to be his mistress, Volpone promises her participation in an extended erotic stage play:

> my dwarfe shall dance,
> My eunuch sing, my foole make vp the
>     antique.
> Whil'st, we, in changed shapes, act *Ovids*
>     tales,
> Thou, like *Evropa* now, and I like *Iove,*
> Then I like *Mars,* and thou like *Erycine.*
>
> . . . . .
>
> Then will I have thee in more moderne formes,
>
> . . . . .
>
> And I will meet thee, in as many shapes:[8]

It is a mark of Celia's perfect adherence to the role of the virtuous woman that she refuses to participate in Volpone's theatrical production, that she maintains her personal integrity by declining to play the adulterous role that both her husband and her would-be lover have scripted for her. In spite of the bewildering transformations of the men around her (her husband reverses in minutes his initial decision to lock his wife up in a chastity belt, deciding instead to prostitute her in hopes of winning Volpone's money; Volpone himself leaps up from his pretended deathbed to inform her that he had appeared just the day before as a mountebank at her window), Celia remains constant to her own and her husband's honor. In fact, her character requires no development beyond the demonstration that she will never swerve from the course of chastity.

To repeat a point made often by feminist critics, a reputation for participating in or resisting participation in a particular sexual act had the power to characterize a woman absolutely—onstage, at least—in the English Renaissance.[9] For all that Jonson apparently delights in the possibilities of the ever-changing theatrical self, made manifest in the play's nearly endless recourse to disguise and deception, *Volpone* also exploits the notion of a woman's constancy, the possibility that a woman's sexual fidelity and, by extension, her infidelity, could stand for everything about her. Such a notion is possible, of course, only when women are considered as objects of greater or lesser use to the system of family and marriage, only in an essentially male erotic economy. To the Volpone who stages a theater of erotic pleasure, Celia matters because she either will or will not take up the adulterous part assigned her. Moreover, the conjunction of theatricality and sexuality in an endless exchange of erotic roles, so highly prized by Volpone, depends implicitly upon Celia's unwillingness to play those roles. Her absolute stillness and chastity make her appealing as a sexual object, after all, at the same time that her resistance to Volpone's role-playing provides him with a kind of foil for his sexual improvisations. The erotic fluidity of the self that characterizes Volpone's fantasy includes the deployment of a fixed sexual self, a feminine locus to which sexuality can attach as an identity, rather than a masculine escape from identity through sexual play. Celia inhabits this identity not so much because of her own desires as because of her perfect adherence to the desire of her husband.

I mention Celia here because I want to make the case that the ganymede, the effeminate boy who was stereotypically the object of male homosexual desire in early modern England, was similarly imagined to be defined by his sexual availability to mature men and similarly deployed as a locus of sexuality's power to stigmatize or characterize. When the dangerously powerful male favorite Gaveston plans to entertain his king in Marlowe's *Edward II,* for instance, he gives elaborate stage directions:

> Sometime a lovely boy in Dian's shape,
> With hair that gilds the water as it glides,
> Crownets of pearl about his naked arms,
> And in his sportful hands an olive-tree,
> To hide those parts which men delight to see,
> Shall bathe him in a spring.[10]

As many critics have noted, this passage is erotic in part because of the fantasy that the lovely boy is "in Dian's shape," that he impersonates a goddess.[11] Oddly, though, Gaveston expresses the fantasy that a boy wearing only bracelets and an olive branch could convincingly represent Diana. The erotic opportunity offered the viewer here is not in fact the deliberate impersonation of a goddess. The boy impersonates nothing. He simply has, always, "naturally," the body of a Dian; he entertains merely by displaying himself at opportune moments. In order, in other words, to do justice both to the passage's obvious homoerotic content and to its claims to represent a tale out of Ovid, an audience would have to imagine the boy's profound physical androgyny, a kind of ocular proof of his femininity that goes beyond the use of long gowns and chopines to emphasize the ambiguous "parts men love to see." This lovely boy is almost impossibly effeminate. In Gaveston's staging of erotic transformations, the boy's part is to register an ineluctable physical androgyny; what was free erotic play for James and Villiers becomes ontology for the lovely boy, his physical nature. The celebration of an eroticized fluidity of self relies implicitly upon the fixity of the boy as an androgynous erotic object, giving him a sexuality that has little or no relation to any desires he might be imagined to express. His body is, thus, paradoxically both fluid and fixed: fluid in its failure to adhere to any one gender and fixed in its permanent ambiguity.

Even when theatrical staging and physicality are not at issue, literary representations of the beloved boy tend to emphasize the inevitability of the boy's sexual objectification, the sense that this particular boy is made for this particular kind of love. When Richard Barnfield writes his *Affectionate Shepheard,* he imagines a ganymede whose appearance "intangled" the speaker Daphnis's will: "Cursing the Time, the Place, the sense, the sin; / I came, I saw, I viewed, I slipped in."[12] Even though Ganimede is in love with Queen Gwendolen and unlikely to respond to Daphnis's advances, Ganimede is imagined to be the cause of the older man's desires by virtue of his physical beauty. As the poem's second stanza indicates by its syntax, Ganimede's physical attributes insert themselves into the middle of Daphnis's (admittedly peremptory) self-examination, where they intrude upon the speaker's power to resist him:

> If it be sinne to loue a sweet-fac'd Boy,
> (Whose amber locks trust vp in golden tramels
> Dangle adowne his louely cheekes with ioy,
> When pearle and flowers his faire haire enamels)
> If it be sinne to loue a louely Lad;
> Oh then sinne I, for whom my soule is sad.

Instead of penetrating the boy, this sentence structure suggests, Daphnis is physically penetrated by Ganimede's beauty. Into the middle of his mediation on sin is inserted a picture of Ganimede's amber locks and lovely cheeks. Daphnis's expressions move well beyond a statement of personal preference, here. Instead of noting simply that Ganimede's beauty pleases him, Daphnis implies that Ganimede's beauty acts upon him, virtually against the speaker's will. Even when the boy himself is imagined to love a woman, he is figured as the locus of homosexual desire; Ganimede's physical appeal is as absolute as the androgyny of Gaveston's boy. In each case, the speaker projects desire onto the body of the ganymede figure, making the boy a physical embodiment of homoeroticism.[13]

What the example of the ganymede suggests is that our current understanding of sodomy as lacking the power to inscribe early modern subjects is only a partial understanding. Representations of the subject who does the desiring, figured here as the courtly sodomite, do in fact imply that sodomy is merely one in a range of sexual behaviors with no particular signifying force. If we shift our focus to the object of desire, however, it becomes clear that the signifying force of sexuality has simply been deflected away from the sodomite. It registers instead in the body of the ganymede, the partner who, like a woman in a heterosexual coupling, might be said to lack power. The sodomite has the ability to change shapes at will; the ganymede, like the woman, is shaped by the sodomite's gaze into a static embodiment of that fluid will.

It is this imagined physical inevitability of the ganymede's participation in homosexual attraction that makes him, I think, an important figure in discussions of the relation between theatrical practice and homosexual identity. To the extent that "real-life" catamites were employed as boy actors, these boys would bring with them a reputation for sodomy that included a larger cultural willingness to attribute homosexual desire to them as physical types.[14] Thus the theater itself, as an institution, negotiates a complicated set of attitudes about desire and the fixity of identity. Obviously theatrical performance gave great pleasure to the majority of Londoners in the period, and certain players became well known and much admired.[15] At the same time, players as a class remained heavily stigmatized. Rather like the courtly sodomite, players were imagined to shift identities at will and to partake of illicit sexuality. On the other hand, resembling the literary figure of the ganymede more than the aristocratic man-about-town, they were not well shielded from the social consequences of their erotic performances. In documents I will explore below, the Renaissance version of a long antitheatrical tradition identified players as immoral and dangerous, not least because of their willingness to engage in sexualized display in general and to employ cross-dressed boys in particular. Further complicating the player's status in this period, city officials struggled to minimize or abolish professional playing in London for reasons both economic and moral, while the court officially acted as patrons of the theater companies, even asserting that it was necessary to maintain professional players in town so that Elizabeth could be properly entertained when she so desired. As a result, players might be particularly familiar with the discrepancies between aristocrats and citizens. Playing companies entertained most of London's population, but their official legitimacy came from their ability to entertain the court, while a less exalted group of officials stigmatized playing for their own complex reasons.

As an economic enterprise, then, the stage can be thought of as trafficking in sexual identity, negotiating a form of exchange between its wealthy patrons—the courtiers (and sovereign) whose sexual behaviors pointed toward no particular sexual identification—and the boys apparently desired by those courtiers, whose sexual and economic employment inscribed homosexual desire upon them. If free erotic play is the prerogative of the aristocratic sodomite, it is the actor's profession and an important source of his reputation. Like the ganymede, the player's body is given a kind of heaviness that balances the weightless erotic play of the courtly sodomite.

### III

I am drawn to this depiction of theater—as place in which sexual determinism negotiates with courtly erotic play—in part because it accords with my sense of late-Shakespearean romance. The romances seem to me preoccupied with two of the more prominent features of antitheatrical discourse: the suggestion that stage practice is inherently associated with illicit sexuality and the suggestion that play acting is an assault upon the stability of the individual self. Using the example of *The Winter's Tale,* I want to argue that the romances locate theatrical practice in close relation to illicit desire, acknowledging sodomy as a characteristic mode of being for the players and playwrights implicated in theatrical practice, incorporating both the erotic play of selfhood that typifies James's letters and the sense of sexual identity that characterizes the ganymede. While the ganymede and the courtier are not the only figures one can imagine participating in sodomy in the period—much of Bray's work, for instance, documents the prevalence of homosexual behaviors in households and villages, noting that there, as at court, the perpetrator of sodomy was in no way identified as "homosexual"—the ganymede and courtier represent two poles of sodomy's power to characterize. These two poles, moreover, figure prominently in the erotic imagination of *The Winter's Tale,* which juxtaposes questions of sexual stigma with questions of theatrical practice. What *The Winter's Tale* comes to associate with theater, finally, is not only the erotic indeterminancy that Valerie Traub has identified,[16] but also a dependance upon the notion of sexual fixity, a deployment of the ganymede as a figure for sodomy's power to characterize participants in theatrical practice. Furthermore, I will argue, the play uses these very stigmatized features of theatrical practice to legitimate playing. As a kind of defense of the institution, *The Winter's Tale* reinscribes theater as a force both sexual and moral.

The theater was, after all, the source of seemingly endless sexual allegations in early modern England. Anthony Munday notes the power of playgoing to corrupt women:

Some citizens wives, upon whom the Lord for ensample to others hath laide his hands, have even on their death beds with tears confessed, that they have received at those spectacles such filthie infections as have turned their minds from chast cogitations, and made them of honest women light huswives.[17]

Jonson himself, in *Poetaster,* has his stage version of the historical Ovid assume an automatic connection between playing and sodomy: "What? shall I have my son a stager now? an enghle for players?"[18] In "A Common Player" J. Cocke claims that an actor "If hee marries, hee mistakes the Woman for the Boy in Woman's attire, by not respecting a difference in the mischiefe."[19] Phillip Stubbes complains that after a stage play "every mate sorts to his mate, every one bringes another homeward of their way verye freendly, and in their secret conclaves (covertly) they play the *Sodomits,* or worse."[20] Cocke also notes that these sexually undiscriminating actors participate in an unacceptably protean selfhood because of the many roles they play and the costumes they wear: "Take him at the best, he is but a shifting companion; for he lives effectually by putting on, and putting off.... His own [profession] ... is compounded of all Natures, all humours, all professions" (257). The net effect of this sexual and ontological impurity is for Thomas White a scandal of self-loss: "Wherefore if thou be a father, thou losest thy child: if thou be a maister, thou losest thy servaunt; and thou be what thou canst be, thou losest thy selfe that hauntest those scholes of vice, dennes of theeves, and Theaters of all lewdness."[21] The chaotic play of identity and desire that the aristocratic sodomite is imagined to enjoy freely becomes in these descriptions a sinister aspect of theatrical practice, a cause for the player's notoriety.

Moreover, as the title of one of these antitheatrical tracts, *A Very Fruitful Exposition of The Commandements,* suggests, those who protested theater's alleged sexual excess tended to position themselves on the side of fertility and nature, condemning plays for their failure to bear moral fruit.[22] John Northbrooke refers to plays as "unfruitfull and barren trees [that] shall be cut down" (75), while the author of the *Refutation of the Apology for Actors* refers to plays as "fruitless," and Henry Crosse says of the attraction to earthly pleasures that it "yeeld[s] no fruite at all."[23] Standing in opposition to the reaping of both orthodox spiritual profits and all-important economic profits, theater, with its alleged enticements to nonprocreative sexuality, seemed to fly in the face of God's great commandment to be fruitful and multiply. Ultimately, as *The Winter's Tale* figures and refigures theatrical practice, it will reappropriate this notion of fertility and claim it for the stage.

I begin my discussion of *The Winter's Tale,* however, by asking why the play's many descriptions of boyhood sound so like these early modern descriptions of theatrical practice. Like theater, it seems, boyhood is figured as a realm of sexual and ontological instability, as Leontes makes clear in a paranoid aside to Mamillius: "Go, play, boy, play: thy mother plays, and I / Play too; but so disgrac'd a part, whose issue / Will hiss me to my grave."[24] Child's play, sexual play, theatrical play—boyhood, illicit sexuality, theatrical stigma—are what come to mind when Leontes looks at his son. Childhood has become one repository for the scandal of the undifferentiated theatrical self. In a later passage, in fact, Polixenes describes youth in terms that again bring theater to mind. Leontes asks him, "Are you so fond of your young prince, as we / Do seem to be of ours?" and Polixenes describes his own son:

> Now my sworn friend, and then mine enemy;
> My parasite, my soldier, statesman, all.
> He makes a July's day short as December;
> And with his varying childness cures in me
> Thoughts that would thick my blood.
> (1.2.167-71)

To be free to cast off one's identity and assume another as boyhood does here is a pleasure—and a threat—associated with theatrical practice.[25] As the ganymede does for the sodomite, the child does for the institution of the theater in these passages. Talking about boys becomes an implicit way of talking about men.

Leontes also associated boyhood with an ambiguity of gender that is again a familiar component of attacks upon the theater:

> Looking on the lines
> Of my boy's face, methoughts I did recoil
> Twenty-three years, and saw myself unbreech'd,
> In my green velvet coat; my dagger muzzl'd
> Lest it should bite its master, and so prove,
> As ornaments oft do, too dangerous.
> (1.2.153-58)

To be "unbreech'd" is to be dressed in gender-neutral clothing; for a boy this implies a less than absolute separation from the female gender.[26] Mamillius (or, really, Leontes' fantasy of his own past, occasioned by Mamillius) wears his dagger muzzled, as if to indicate that he has not reached phallic manhood. There is, furthermore, the implication that Mamillius's relative ambiguity of gender is imperiled by mature masculinity. Rather than imagine the harm that an unsheathed dagger might do to others, Leontes focuses upon the danger to the dagger's wearer. Sexual maturity, according to Leontes' fantasy, must mean an end to a fluidity of gender that has much in common with the fluidity of the theatrical self. At the heart of the play's anxious reminiscences about boyhood, then, is a larger cultural uneasiness about the theater.

At the same time, however, Polixenes sanitizes boyhood, idealizing the instability of self that characterizes both boyhood and the stage:

> *Herm.*                              Was not my lord
> The verier wag o' th' two?
> *Pol.* We were as twinn'd lambs that did frisk
>     i' th' sun,
> And bleat the one at th' other: what we
>     chang'd
> Was innocence for innocence: we knew not
> The doctrine of ill-doing, nor dream'd
> That any did. Had we pursu'd that life,
> And our weak spirits ne'er been higher rear'd
> With stronger blood, we should have answer'd
>     heaven
> Boldly "not guilty," the imposition clear'd
> Hereditary ours.
> *Herm.*                          By this we gather
> You have tripp'd since.
> *Pol*                    O my most sacred lady,
> Temptations have since then been born to's: for
> In those unfledg'd days was my wife a girl;
> Your precious self had then not cross'd the
>     eyes
> Of my young play-fellow.
>
>                               (1.2.65-80)

The absence of the individual self in this passage, the impossibility of distinguishing Leontes from Polixenes, has, ironically, become a sign of Edenic purity, a pastoral opposite to the ungodly crisis of self-definition provoked for tract writers by the scandal of theatrical role playing.[27] Polixenes has also managed in this passage to refigure fertility, the marital sexuality that culminates in Hermione's pregnancy, as the interruption of that Eden.[28] In much the same way that Polixenes makes the stigma of theatrical practice into an Eden, *The Winter's Tale* works to make that stigma into a more fertile pastoral, a realm that welcomes and ultimately makes use of heterosexual fertility as a way of legitimating the scandalous stage.[29] In its reflection upon the relationships between theatrical practice and illicit desire, moreover, the play negotiates a position for the theater that incorporates elements both of courtly erotic play and of the erotic fixity of the ganymede.

Polixenes' articulation of an all-male pastoral, and its interruption by Hermione, effects a double movement away from the realm of scandalous theatrical sexuality. First, the idealization of boyhood moves toward erasing any trace of the relation between youth and the stigmatized elements of theater embodied in the boy actor, a relation hinted at several times in the passages I have cited. Second, Polixenes posits Hermione's arrival as an absolute end to his union with Leontes, and as Camillo implies in the play's opening scene, that union is bound up both with theater and with homosexual desire. Camillo tells the courtier Archidamus:

> Sicilia cannot show himself over-kind to Bohemia. They were trained together in their childhoods, and there rooted betwixt them then such an affection which cannot choose but branch now. Since their more mature dignities and royal necessities made separation of their society, their encounters, though not personal, have been royally attorneyed with interchange of gifts, letters, loving embassies, that they have seemed to be together, though absent; shook hands, as over a vast; and embraced, as it were, from the ends of opposed winds. The heavens continue their loves! (1.1.21-32)

According to the logic of Camillo's narration, Leontes and Polixenes want to be together but must be separated. As Leontes and Polixenes abandon physical immediacy for "mature dignity," they begin to employ others as go-betweens, as expressions of their relationship. What is at stake here is the public representation of relationship between men, an interchange of loving embassies and letters that will ultimately come to seem at least partially defensive, an assurance that the contact between Leontes and Polixenes is "not personal."

Furthermore, their very identity as mature men, as kings, demands that they be kept apart. The literal import of these lines is that Leontes and Polixenes want to touch, but the lines also reveal that these men owe their mature dignities to the fact that they cannot embrace. As they move apart they grow in stature, so that by the end of this speech they seem larger than life, reaching out across a vast, from the opposite ends of the earth. The extent to which these men avoid touching one another, finally, is the extent to which they tower over other men. Their affection for one another, associated with boyhood, stands in opposition to their kingly stature. If boys could embody the homoerotic in the cultural imagination of early modern England, and if in doing so they allowed adult men to avoid the possible consequences of homosexual desire, that potential of boyhood, as Camillo's speech asserts, comes down to a more personal level; however wistfully, he narrates the all important distance here between men and sexualized, undifferentiated youth. It was a sign of the sodomite's power that he could play with desire and identity and not get caught, but players, outside the circle of privilege that supported courtly indiscretions, are much more likely to require a justification for their participation in sexual play. *The Winter's Tale*, concerned as it is with legitimating theatrical practice, voices at least initially an anxious desire to separate mature men from the scandal of the playing boy.

Camillo has implied that go-betweens and a narrative of maturation are the tools through which Leontes and Polixenes will be distanced from the sexual and ontological threats of boyhood. Important as boys are in this staging of kings, however, it is Hermione who symbolically continues their loves. If Hermione comes between Leontes and Polixenes, then she is also the most obvious of their intermediaries, the chief actor in the theater of their relationship. In act 1 Leontes calls her in to speak for him when he wants Polixenes to extend his visit ("Tongue-tied our queen? speak you" 1.2.27), an act she performs, to her peril, all too enthusiastically.[30] As she fulfills this function, Polixenes begins to cast her in the part I have described above: "O my most sacred lady, / Temptations have . . . been born to's." Part sacred and part temptation, Hermione is placed by both men in the position of go-between, and imagined by both of them to be sexually compromised. Leontes and Polixenes collaborate in the staging of Hermione as a necessary expression of their relationship, as a means of imagining that their "affections" have been replaced by "mature dignities." At the same time, their shared willingness to imagine her sexual impurity hints at the instability of their erotic compromise with what the play at this point posits as maturity, as a kingly distance from the desire they associate with boyhood. For all the play's work to distance the king from the ganymede, it ultimately recuperates both figures, both in its representation of these men and in its exploration of theatrical practice.

Of course Hermione is not impure, in spite of Polixenes' fantasy that she has corrupted the men's youth and Leontes' mad conviction that she poisons their friendship in the present moment. Such an admission, moreover, creeps into the very language that Leontes uses to imagine her as an adulteress:

> Affection! thy intention stabs the centre:
> Thou dost make possible things not so held,
> Communicat'st with dreams;—how can this
>   be?—
> With what's unreal thou coactive art,
> And fellow'st nothing: then 'tis very credent
> Thou may'st co-join with something; and thou
>   dost,
> (And that beyond commission) and I find it,
> (And that to the infection of my brains
> And hard'ning of my brows).
>           (1.2.138-46)

The speech is echoed at the moment Leontes sentences his wife, meant as a statement of confidence in his own suspicions, but expressed as a tacit admission that he has projected his own desires onto her: "Your actions are my dreams."[31] Leontes' own mind is engaging in the actions he attributes to Hermione. Affection—perhaps Leontes' own emotions and imaginings—"stabs the centre." For all the obscurity of the image, its sexual referent is clear, and the rest of the language used to describe Leontes' mental processes furthers the sexual implications. Moreover, Leontes' own thinking in this passage is fellowing, cojoining, coactive, both promiscuous and fertile, culminating in a kind of mental pregnancy, a swelling of horns upon Leontes' brow that parallels the swelling of Hermione's womb. Not only does his deranged creativity imply an admission that there is no reason to condemn his wife; it suggests further a strategy that the play as a whole takes up: the recuperation of sexual scandal as a fertile power. Leontes' individual use of Hermione as an expression of his imaginings is accompanied, ultimately, by the play's use of her as an expression and even a celebration of the imaginative power of a sexually stigmatized male theatrical community.

IV

The early scenes of *The Winter's Tale* enforce an anxious distinction between boys and men, letting boys stand in for the scandal of theatrical practice. Included in that effort is an attempt to use Hermione as a sign both of the distance between Leontes and Polixenes and of the loves they bear one another. The shared fantasy that she is impure suggests that the easy version of that story is inadequate, that desire and the implicit destabilization of identity cannot be dismissed or idealized as the province of boys. In addition, the language Leontes uses to describe that fantasy—as a promiscuous and fertile mental cojoining—resonates profoundly with what I believe to be a central part of the play's legitimation of theatrical playing.

Leontes' equation of his wife's fertility with his own mental processes—and his clear preference for the product of his own mind—recalls Plato's grounding of poetry in what Renaissance moralists would have regarded as a scandalous erotic context. In the *Symposium*, Socrates speaks of a lesson he has learned from the wise Diotima:

> Men whose bodies only are creative, betake themselves to women and beget children. . . . But creative souls—for there are men who are more creative in their souls than in their bodies—conceive that which is proper for the soul to conceive or retain. . . . And he who in youth has the seed of [virtue and wisdom] implanted in him and is himself inspired, when he comes to maturity desires to beget and generate. . . . and when he finds a fair and noble and well-nurtured soul, and there is union of the two in one person, he gladly embraces him, and to such an one he is full of fair speech about virtue and the nature and pursuits of a good man . . . and at the touch and presence of the beautiful he brings forth the beautiful which he conceived long before . . . and in company they tend that which he brings forth, and they are bound together by a far nearer tie and have a closer friendship than those who beget mortal children, for the children who are their common offspring are fairer and more immortal. Who when he thinks of Homer and Hesiod and other great poets, would not rather have their children than any ordinary human ones?[32]

These sentiments are, according to Diotima, among the lesser teachings of love, and although Socrates emphasizes that the love of one beautiful man should lead to an appreciation of the beautiful in general, many early modern readers identified the *Symposium* with homosexuality.³³

The *Symposium* represents one way of legitimating the literary productions of an implicitly homosexual male culture, and it bears more than a passing resemblance to Polixenes' idealized male pastoral and Leontes' tormented and fertile imagination. Although the play will move to punish Leontes for his fantasy, and will reconfigure his attachment to Polixenes by way of the heterosexual marriage of their children, I emphasize Plato's idealization of a male homosexual poetics because a similar ideal is active throughout *The Winter's Tale*. The play works with considerable ardor to establish a convincing affiliation between the playwright's craft and "great creating nature," and while that affiliation can function as a heterosexual imperative—Hermione's pregnancy and the family bonds that guarantee an heir to the throne can be seen as the ultimate sources of truth, the play's ultimate wisdom—the affiliation between poetry and pregnancy can also serve as a platonic boast about the superiority of male poetic production. Indeed, *The Winter's Tale* and *The Symposium* employ women and fertility in ways that are, initially at least, remarkably similar. In "Why Is Diotima a Woman?" David Halperin analyzes Plato's adoption of Diotima as the mouthpiece for his erotic teachings, including, I would add, his eroticization of poetic production.³⁴ Referring to Diotima as "a version of pastoral," Halperin notes that her presence in *The Symposium* allows Plato simultaneously to "invest Diotima with an erotic and prophetic authority" and to evacuate that feminine authority, to use Diotima as a figure for "The male imaginary, the specular poetics of male identity and self-definition" (145). I will return to Halperin's reading of *The Symposium* in the final section of this essay, but I want first to trace the ways in which *The Winter's Tale's* pastoral celebration and recuperation of Hermione lend themselves, like Diotima, to the preoccupations of an eroticized male poetic community. If the play's first half registers an anxious awareness of contemporary antitheatrical tracts and their complaints about the fruitlessness of the literary, its second half incorporates women and nature into a declaration of the procreative power of sexually stigmatized male theatrical production. In fact, the play goes to great lengths to emphasize the independence of women as part of a strategy, I will argue, that, like Plato's, will ultimately serve to highlight the powers and desires of men. Especially through the figures of Camillo and Hermione, *The Winter's Tale* legitimates its own erotic practice while simultaneously obeying the injunction to be fruitful and multiply.

In many ways, the sheep-shearing feast in act 4 is a clear vote for the kinds of fertility that are associated with spring and pregnancy and agriculture rather than with men and poetry. As in the Shepherd's reminiscences about his "old wife" and as in Perdita's preference for the flowers that nature makes, Perdita's frankly sexual remarks to Florizel indicate that this is a new pastoral to which women and heterosexual desire are most emphatically invited.³⁵

> *Per.* O, these [flowers] I lack
> To make you garlands of; and my sweet friend,
> To strew him o'er and o'er!
> *Flo.* What, like a corpse?
> *Per.* No, like a bank, for love to lie and play on:
> Not like a corpse; or if—not to be buried,
> But quick, and in mine arms.
> (4.4.127-32)

Perdita's next remarks indicate as well that there is a new theater in action here, charming even in its mild sexual scandal:

> *Per.* Methinks I play as I have seen them do
> In Whitsun pastorals: sure this robe of mine
> Does change my disposition.
> *Flo.* What you do,
> Still betters what is done.
> (4.4.133-36)

That Camillo and Polixenes should intrude upon this heterosexual pastoral suggests that this "natural" sheep-shearing feast is in some way anathema to the earlier male Eden in which twinned lambs never had to face the shearer. Their intrusion says, I think, a great deal about the uses of nature in a sexually stigmatized artistic endeavor.

Camillo is established early on as an accessory to the erotic bond between Leontes and Polixenes; he is the narrator of the opening scene's story of the two kings' affections, and he keeps Leontes from harming Polixenes. In addition, Leontes' exchange with him in act 1 casts Camillo in a role that strongly recalls a well-known icon of Renaissance homosexuality:

> . . . ay, and thou
> [*Polixenes'*] cupbearer,—whom I from meaner form
> Have bench'd and rear'd to worship, who may'st see
> Plainly as heaven sees earth and earth sees heaven,
> How I am gall'd,—might'st bespice a cup,
> To give mine enemy a lasting wink;
> Which draught to me were cordial.
> (1.2.312-18)

In his address to Camillo, Leontes reenacts the story of Jove's Ganymede, the cup bearer to the god who raised him from earth to heaven and who kept him as his lover. The language of raising up an inferior, combined with the sense that Camillo's vision now spans the gap between heaven and earth, recalls both the erotic myth and its allegorical implications for the merging of the divine with the physical.[36]

Moreover, Leontes' chain of allusions implies that Camillo is, as Hermione has been imagined, somehow the favorite of both kings. Camillo is cup bearer to Polixenes, but his draught would nourish Leontes; he has been raised up by Leontes, but he attends Polixenes during his stay in Sicilia. The implied eroticism of Camillo's position is shared between the two kings, and the implication is that Camillo in some sense shares Hermione's role as erotic go-between and as actor in the theater of their affections. One of Leontes' most vivid declarations of certainty about Hermione's infidelity, after all, implies a symmetry between that infidelity and Camillo's promised poisoning of Bohemia: "I have drunk, and seen the spider" (2.1.45). As Leontes sees it, both Hermione and Camillo are objects of exchange between himself and Polixenes, and Camillo's associations with Ganymede make him a secondary player in the staging of the erotic bond between the two kings.

Camillo and Polixenes make their entrance in the play's second half negotiating once again the conflict between a man's duty to his homeland and his affection for another man. Although Polixenes stresses that he needs Camillo present for business reasons, his request that Camillo not leave is strongly reminiscent of the earlier exchange between Leontes and Polixenes: "I pray thee, good Camillo, be no more importunate: 'tis a sickness denying thee anything; a death to grant this" (4.2.1-3). That the business at hand should be Polixenes' interruption of a heterosexual pastoral (and that Florizel should apparently have no mother on hand, even in Bohemia), suggests that the concerns that shaped the earlier Edenic realm of twinned lambs have resurfaced in the relation between Camillo and Polixenes.

As mentioned above, Florizel claims that he is "heir" to his own "affections" as he makes plans to elope with Perdita. Camillo, however, who is more profoundly committed to the affections of his two masters, effects a reworking of Florizel's and Perdita's scheme for his own purposes:

> Now were I happy, if
> His going I could frame to serve my turn,
> Save him from danger, do him love and honour,
> Purchase the sight again of dear Sicilia
> And that unhappy king, my master, whom
> I so much thirst to see.
> (4.4.509-14)

As Camillo puts it, he has "a woman's longing" to see his home and his king, and his employment here as an assistant to the young couple is a means toward the end of uniting himself and Polixenes with the object of their affections. The implication is that Camillo's participation in the staging of male affection stands in an opportunistic relation to the spectacle of heterosexual affection and to the natural pastoral upon which it intrudes. Perdita's comment upon her own participation in the elopement ("I see the play so lies / That I must bear a part," 4.4.655-66) is more apt than she realizes; she is being made to play act not only her own marriage, but also the reunion of the men whose desires are a powerful shaping force in the play.[37]

If the play legitimates its own theatrical practice in part by staging a celebration of the "natural"—only to refigure that pastoral as implicitly in the service of the homoerotic—it moves similarly toward legitimation in the staging of Hermione's return. *The Winter's Tale* takes great pains to establish this source of moral veracity as having come from outside the realm of male control and male fantasy. Paulina has disciplined Leontes thoroughly, calling his imaginings "Fancies too weak for boys, too green and idle / For girls of nine," and speaking out of turn repeatedly to remind him of his former tyrannies (3.2.181-82). Paulina speaks in direct opposition to male authority, and her disclaimers as she reveals the statue to be alive, protecting her from the possibility that she might be "assisted / by wicked powers" or that her "unlawful business" might be "hooted at / Like an old tale," actually serve to emphasize the power of her artistic deception, the fact that it transcends the laws that govern acceptable stagecraft.

We learn too that backstage, as it were, during the sheep-shearing celebration, Hermione and Paulina have quietly been staging their own spectacle. While Paulina has engineered Leontes' sixteen years of mourning, Hermione has "preserved / [Herself] to see the issue," with "issue" here meaning both the daughter she has lost and the outcome of a play—in this case, a play partly of her making. Given that Hermione began *The Winter's Tale* with the burden of representing Leontes' esteem for Polixenes, as a player in the theater of male affection, it is remarkable that in the second half of the play she and Paulina have taken control of the plot, have planned their own theatrical strategy. Even though the ultimate result of this female theater is to reward Leontes for his conversion and to prove Hermione's fidelity to her husband and his lineage, the play's ending looks like it is authorized by women, largely because of the way that Paulina stages her power over Leontes and her power over the "statue" of Hermione.[38] Like Diotima—in fact, much more emphatically than Diotima—Paulina speaks in a voice that insists upon its own difference, its distance from the erotic preoccupations of men.

The return of Hermione, then, looks like a kind of triumph for the feminine, an artistic coup that, like the sheep-shearing feast, seems to proclaim its independence from the all-male community that produces sexually stigmatized theatrical spectacles. As metatheater, this apparent female power could be thought to represent a final distancing from the stigmatized theatricality that marked the play's opening scenes. Hermione's coming to life as a statue seems, moreover, to be a final elision of the spectacle of the boy actor, the figure who, more than any other, represents the sexual dangers of the theater; the emphasis in the play's last scene is upon the reality of Hermione's womanhood, after all, and not upon the androgyny of the boy who represents her. Hermione appears to step forward from out of the staged representation of "woman" and to assert her living reality, a reality made more convincing by her status throughout the play as the embodiment of truth. In this sense she continues the motion begun by Polixenes in the "twinn'd lamb" pastoral, the motion to erase the figure of the boy actor.

Furthermore, Paulina makes a brief remark that raises the question of lesbian desire, apparently marking an absolute distinction between the erotic possibilities of her own stagecraft and that of the two kings. In act 5, when Florizel and the unrecognized Perdita arrive in Sicilia, a servant describes Perdita to Leontes and Paulina with a sense of wonder:

> This is a creature,
> Would she begin a sect, might quench the zeal
> Of all professors else; make proselytes
> Of who she but bid follow
>
> (5.1.106-9)

Paulina responds with mock horror, "How! not women?" (5.1.109). By underlining for us the sexual potential of this description of Perdita, Paulina takes us into new erotic territory. She implies at least an awareness of a desire that is outside male control, either for the purposes of progeny or poetry. In fact, her joke seems to emphasize the hiddenness and unrepresentability of lesbian desire, and by extension its distance from traditional models of the literary.[39]

However, this heightened sense of the reality of the female at the end of *The Winter's Tale* also works paradoxically as a boast about the fecundity of the male community that produced the play. Like the gestures made in act 4 toward a heterosexual pastoral, the efforts that act 5 has made toward establishing the independence of women are simultaneously available as part of a male homosexual stagecraft. Paulina's passing joke about lesbian desire, for instance, is answered in a manner that suggests that the scandalous boy actor has not been as thoroughly removed from the play's erotic economy as my earlier argument implied: "Women will love her, that she is a woman / More worth than any man; men, that she is / The rarest of all women" (5.1.110-12). The servant's response highlights a different erotic possibility than Paulina's joke, emphasizing not the lesbian but the bisexual possibilities of Perdita's attractiveness. His rather elaborate explanation for her ubiquitous appeal sounds a bit like Sonnet 20 ("A man in hue all hues in his controlling, / Which steals men's eyes and women's souls amazeth," 7-8), or like the kinds of erotic play that characterize *Twelfth Night;* the play's response to the possibility of an independent lesbian desire is to return to the terrain of the boy actor, to reassert the fundamental androgyny of a Perdita who is played by a boy in women's clothes, and thus to remind its audience of the ganymede's participation in the broader range of theatrical eroticisms. Rather than figuring the ganymede as a sign of stigmatized sexual identity from which mature and powerful men can distance themselves, *The Winter's Tale* implicates the ganymede, finally, in every aspect of the stage's erotic practice. We are prepared by the play's boasts about the power and appeal of the ganymede to regard Hermione's return not so much as the elision of the boy actor but as his triumph. The boy who impersonates the "real" Hermione, along with the theatrical company that engineers his impersonation, asserts power so absolute that it dares to stage its own exclusion.

That exclusion goes beyond boasting that a boy can convincingly play a mature woman with miraculous powers, however. On a deeper level, the play uses this final moment to register in silent eloquence the cost of the effort to distance boys from men. Mamillius, identified repeatedly in the play's first half with his father's past, has died at the end of act 2 and is thus hauntingly absent in this scene of miraculous reunion. Leontes' family has in a sense acquired a son through Perdita's marriage to Florizel, but the effort to substitute Polixenes' son for Leontes' through the institution of marriage is, in light of the initial failure of Leontes' and Hermione's union to erase the past, a particularly hollow theatrical convenience. Paulina herself critiques it just before the newly wedded couple arrives in Sicilia:

> Had our prince,
> (Jewel of children) seen this hour, he had pair'd
> Well with this lord; there was not full a month
> Between their births.
>
> (5.1.115-18)

In her wonderful sadistic way, Paulina emphasizes the fatality of Leontes' former paranoia, keeping alive the memory of the past if not in this case the actual victim of it. In addition, she speaks uncharacteristically here for the union of men, subtly replacing the image of Perdita's marriage to Florizel with a different masculine pairing. Even the most independent voice of female power in this play speaks up to long for the past of the twinned lambs.

The play's final scene of miraculous heterosexual restoration, then, is claimed by the power of the sexually stigmatized boy in at least two ways. On the one hand, the very reality of the statue's femaleness is a boast about theater, about the power of a cross-dressed boy to fool an audience, even an onstage audience. On the other hand, the legitimate claim of Mamillius to be present at this family reunion ensures that the marriage of Florizel and Perdita and the miraculous rebirth of Hermione will on some level acquire their poignancy because they are compensation for another loss, for the jewel of children who cannot be replaced by stagings of even the most forgiving and fertile heterosexual embrace.

## V

I return, finally, to Halperin's discussion of *The Symposium* in order to clarify the relation between *The Winter's Tale's* assumption of female procreativity and the problem with which I began this essay: the difference in signifying power between the participation of boys and the participation of men in homosexual and homoerotic acts. Halperin argues that Diotima functions as a mimetic device through which Plato appropriates a putatively "feminine" erotics as the cornerstone of his own teachings, his own articulation of what *The Symposium* calls "right pederasty." Concerned as she is with the erotics of pedagogy, Diotima aligns herself, in Halperin's account, with the symbolic appropriations of female procreativity that typify male rites of passage in ancient and modern patriarchal cultures. Like the couvade, like ritual scarrings that symbolize menstruation in men, like pederastic rites that initiate boys into manhood and employ procreative imagery, Diotima gives witness to "the determination of men to acquire the powers they ascribe (whether correctly or incorrectly) to women," which Halperin calls "a remarkably persistent and widespread feature of male culture."[40]

Importantly, according to Halperin, these appropriations of female procreativity inevitably depend upon the failure of men to represent women:

> Even in the midst of mimicking menstruation, pregnancy, giving birth, and breastfeeding, the male actors must share with their audience the understanding that their procreative performances are symbolic, not real—that nose-bleeding is *not* menstruating, that oral insemination is *not* breastfeeding. The point of all those rites, after all, is to turn boys into men, not into women: for the cultural construction of masculinity to succeed it is necessary that the process intended to turn boys into men be genuinely efficacious, no less "generative" than female procreativity itself, but it is also necessary that the men who do the initiating retain their identity as men—something they can only do if their assumption of "feminine" capacities and powers is understood to be an impersonation, a cultural fiction, or (at the very least) a mere analogy. (146)

Thus Halperin accounts for *The Symposium*'s relative lack of concern for Diotima's authenticity, its willingness to let readers suspect that Socrates merely uses her as a voice through which to speak his own erotic doctrines.

*The Symposium*, then, lets the mask of female impersonation slip for the purposes of bolstering the power of men and bolstering the power of "masculine" and "feminine" as categories of definition. Its efforts to do so are, as Halperin points out, fully appropriate to a treatise on the pederastic initiation of Greek boys. *The Winter's Tale,* on the other hand, while similarly preoccupied with the transition from boyhood to "more mature dignities"—and with the erotic significance of that transition—performs its version of what Halperin calls "mimetic transvestism" to what is ultimately a much more unsettling effect. Leontes and Polixenes portray themselves, and others portray them, as having outgrown their childish proximity to one another and to the implicit homoeroticism of boyhood. Because the ganymede repeatedly intrudes, however, upon the terrain of heterosexual reconciliation and procreation, the play finally dramatizes the difficulty of distancing men from boys, of marking any absolute passage through time from one erotic mode to another. As I have argued in the early portions of this essay, the implied narrative of masculine development that relegates something like homosexual identity to boyhood (while allotting to mature men a literally insignificant or uninscriptive range of sexual choices) is finally unsustainable in the erotic context of English Renaissance theater. Because all players could share in the sexual stigma of the ganymede, because everyone on the Shakespearean stage was implicated in the boy actor's sexual display, no real rite of passage is finally possible. When *The Winter's Tale* allows the ganymede to peek out from behind its display of natural and female fecundity, it reveals, finally, not the supreme confidence of Platonic distinctions between male and female, but instead a peculiarly theatrical breakdown of the distinctions between ganymede and king. In so doing, it claims for the theater not only the free play of sexual desire, but also the power of that desire to adhere to subjects.

## Notes

[1] Alan Bray, *Homosexuality in Renaissance England* (London: Gay Men's Press, 1982), 34.

[2] John Donne, *Satire I* 1.39-40, *The Satires, Epigrams, and Verse Letters,* ed. W. Milgate (Oxford: Clarendon, 1967), quoted in Bray, *Renaissance England,* 53; Epigramme 25, "On Sir Voluptuous Beast," in *Ben Jonson,*

ed. C. H. Herford and Percy Simpson (Oxford: Clarendon, 1937), 8:34, quoted in Bray, *Renaissance England,* 16.

[3] Bray, *Renaissance England,* 70; *Memoirs of the life of Colonel Hutchinson,* ed. J. Hutchinson, rev. C. H. Firth, (London, 1906), 84, quoted in Bray, *Renaissance England,* 55.

[4] [December 1623?] Letter 218 in G. P. V. Akrigg, ed., *Letters of King James VI and I* (Berkeley: University of California Press, 1984), 431.

[5] See Jonathan Goldberg, *Sodometries: Renaissance Texts, Modern Sexualities* (Stanford, Calif.: Stanford University Press 1992), 17 and throughout. In *James I and the Politics of Literature: Jonson, Shakespeare, Donne, and Their Contemporaries,* Goldberg discusses at some length the difficult relationship between James's kingship and his relations with his favorites (Stanford, Calif.: Stanford University Press, 1983), see esp. 143-46.

[6] See for example Bredbeck's introduction, to *Sodomy and Interpretation: Marlowe to Milton* (Ithaca: Cornell University Press, 1991), quoted in text. Goldberg argues that "the invocation of historical difference . . . cannot be used as a way of cordoning off the past from the present' (*Sodometries,* 6). Louise O. Fradenburg and Carla Freccero present a series of articles that complicate the "acts vs. identities" debate, including their own introduction, which asks whether "alterism functions within current historicist practice precisely to *stabilize* the identity of 'the modern'" ("Premodern Sexualities in Europe," *Gay and Lesbian Quarterly* 1 [1995]:378). See also Lorraine Daston and Katherine Park, who challenge "the conventional binary periodization of sexuality into 'modern' and 'pre-modern'" ("The Hermaphrodite and the Orders of Nature: Sexual Ambiguity in Early Modern France" *Gay and Lesbian Quarterly* 1 [1995]:419). Alan Sinfield's speculations are particularly helpful in their readjustment of the notion of historical difference:

> I have a suspicion that the quest for the moment at which the modern homosexual subject is constituted is misguided. I suspect that what we call gay identity has, for a long time, been always in the process of getting constituted—as the middle classes have been always rising, or, more pertinently, as the modern bourgeois subject has for a long time been in the process of getting constituted. Theorists of poststructuralism . . . sometimes write as if they were showing that Shakespeare and his contemporaries did not envisage full or even coherent subjectivities in anything like the modern way. But actually these scholars tend to discover ambivalent or partial signs of subjectivity; they catch not the absence of the modern subject, but its emergence. . . . Of course, the human subject is never full, and hence may, at any moment, appear unformed. And so with gay subjectivity, which because of its precarious social position is anyway more fragile and inconstant: it is on-going, we are still discovering it" (*Cultural Politics—Queer Reading* [Philadelphia: University of Pennsylvania Press, 1994] 14).

[7] Bredbeck, *Sodomy and Interpretation,* xi.

[8] Ben Jonson, *Volpone,* in *Ben Jonson,* 5, ed. C. H. Herford and Percy Simpson (Oxford: Clarendon Press, 1937) 3.7.219-33.

[9] This observation is too widespread to be cataloged, but the following examples are instructive. Madelon (Sprengnether) Gohlke notes that "Once Othello is convinced of Desdemona's infidelity . . . he regards her not as a woman who has committed a single transgression but as a whore, one whose entire behavior may be explained in terms of lust" ("'I Wooed Thee with My Sword': Shakespeare's Tragic Paradigms," in *Representing Shakespeare: New Psychoanalytic Essays,* ed. Murray M. Schwartz and Coppelia Kahn, 174 [Baltimore: Johns Hopkins University Press, 1980]). Similarly, Coppelia Kahn points out that "the cuckold may take revenge against either his wife or her lover, or against both. According to the double standard, however, she has become a whore, irrevocably degraded by even one sexual transgression" (*Man's Estate: Masculine Identity in Shakespeare* [Berkeley: University of California Press, 1981], 121). Janet Adelman's reading of, for instance, *Hamlet,* speaks powerfully of the importance of sexuality in the characterization of a Gertrude or an Ophelia, and the play becomes for her a paradigm for the anxieties about women's sexuality that resonate throughout the Shakespearean canon: "as they enter into sexuality, the virgins—Cressida, Desdemona, Imogen—will be transformed into whores, their whoredom acted out in the imaginations of their nearest and dearest; and the primary antidote to their power will be the excision of their sexual bodies, the terrible revirginations that Othello performs on Desdemona, and Shakespeare on Cordelia" (*Suffocating Mothers: Fantasies of Maternal Origin in Shakespeare's Plays, "Hamlet" to "The Tempest"* [New York: Routledge, 1992], 36). Speaking not so much of adultery but simply of marriage, Carol Thomas Neely argues that the loss of virginity signals for Shakespeare's heroines the loss of "their position as idealized beloveds" (*Broken Nuptials in Shakespeare's Plays* [New Haven: Yale University Press, 1985], 63). Critics who focus more primarily upon the inscription of women's bodies also locate sexuality—perhaps necessarily—at the center of the idea of woman. Susan J. Wiseman, writing about *'Tis Pity She's a Whore,* notes that "it is . . . Anabella's body rather than Giovanni's which comes to bear the meaning" of the incest they commit together ("*'Tis Pity She's a Whore:* Representing the Incestuous Body," in *Renaissance Bodies: The*

*Human Figure in English Culture,* c. 1540-1660, ed. Lucy Grant and Nigel Llewellyn [London: Reaktion Books, 1990] 188). Peter Stallybrass analyzes contradictory cultural assumptions about women's sexuality that are expressed as actual features of women's bodies, be they figured as "grotesque" or "classical" ("Patriarchal Territories: The Body Enclosed," in *Rewriting the Renaissance: The Discourses of Sexual Difference in Early Modern Europe,* ed. Margaret W. Ferguson, Maureen Quilligan, and Nancy J. Vickers [Chicago: University of Chicago Press, 1986]).

[10] H. B. Charlton and R. D. Waller, eds., *Works and Life of Christopher Marlowe,* 2d. ed. (London: Methuen, 1933), 1.1.61-66.

[11] For a variety of approaches to this scene and the play as a whole, see Alan Bray, "Homosexuality and the Signs of Male Friendship in Elizabethan England," in *Queering the Renaissance,* ed. Jonathan Goldberg 40-61 (Durham, N.C.: Duke University Press, 1994); Bredbeck, *Sodomy and Interpretation,* 56-86; Goldberg, *Sodometries,* 105-43; Lisa Jardine, *Still Harping on Daughters: Women and Drama in the Age of Shakespeare* (New York: Columbia University Press, 1983), 22-24; Bruce R. Smith, *Homosexual Desire in Shakespeare's England: A Cultural Poetics* (Chicago: University of Chicago Press, 1991), 209-23. These critics all note the boy's androgyny, but stop short of emphasizing the extent to which his appearance here really is not a cross-dressed performance. The boy is more or less naked. His body, not his costume, is in Dian's shape.

[12] *The Poems of Richard Barnfield,* ed. Montague Summers (London: Fortune Press, 1936), 1-24. See Bray, *Renaissance England,* 60-61, Bredbeck, *Sodomy and Interpretation,* 149-60, Goldberg, *Sodometries,* 68-9, and Smith, *Homosexual Desire,* 99-115 for more extensive readings of Barfield.

[13] There is the further suggestion that Ganimede is physically inscribed even by heterosexual desire when Daphnis describes him as a beloved "Vpon whose forehead you may plainely reade / Loues Pleasure, grau'd in yuorie Tables bright" (15.4). Again, it is not the desire of the boy himself that is at stake here, so much as his susceptibility to being inscribed by pleasure.

[14] Among the many critics who discuss the erotic significance of the boy actor see especially Laura Levine, *Men in Women's Clothing: Anti-Theatricality and Effeminization, 1579-1642* (Cambridge: Cambridge University Press, 1996); and Stephen Orgel, *Impersonations: The Performance of Gender in Shakespeare's England* (Cambridge: Cambridge University Press, 1996). See also Valerie Traub's challenge to the notion that pederasty and effeminacy were primary modes of male homosexual expression in this period (*Desire and Anxiety: Circulations of Sexuality in Shakespearean Drama* [New York: Routledge, 1992], 94). My own intention is not to conflate pederasty with sodomy, so much as to explore the signifying power of this one form of sodomitical desire. There is, of course, merit to Stephen Orgel's claim that early modern England evinced no "morbid fear of homoeroticism as such" (36). While recognizing the culture's investment in homoerotic patronage and friendship, and in transvestite theater, I want nevertheless to give antisodomitical discourse its due. As Louis Montrose has recently argued, to accept antitheatricalism as an authentic cultural expression rather than a negligible pathology is "to respect the intelligence and sincerity of contemporary opponents, and also to appreciate that the Elizabethan theater may have exercised a considerable but unauthorized and therefore deeply suspect affective power upon those Elizabethan subjects who experienced it" (*The Purpose of Playing: Shakespeare and the Cultural Politics of the Elizabethan Theatre* [Chicago: University of Chicago Press, 1996], 45). It seems unlikely to me, given the importance of Puritan belief in this period, that the pleasure of theater was unaccompanied by a genuine awareness of its controversial sexuality.

[15] The two books that most powerfully influence my understanding of theater as an instituion in this period are Andrew Gurr, *Playgoing in Shakespeare's London* (Cambridge: Cambridge University Press, 1987); and Leeds Barroll, *Politics, Plague, and Shakespeare's Theater* (Ithaca: Cornell University Press, 1991). Both stress the dangers of overstating the connections between the theaters and the aristocracy, Gurr by critiquing the notion that it was predominantly the wealthy and powerful who frequented the theaters, and Barroll by arguing persuasively that James I did not in fact regard the stage as an extension of his own monarchy, as some new historicists have implied. Nevertheless, their own works imply a complex interaction between patronage and regulation of the theaters, not because the court understood the greatness of art and the city officials were moralistic puritans, but because both governing bodies knew the stage could be defended or attacked for strategic reasons. See Montrose, *Purpose of Playing,* chapter 5, for a careful study of the relation between court patronage and city regulation in Elizabeth's reign. I am also grateful to A. R. Braunmuller and the members of his Folger Institute seminar, 1996, for many rich discussions of the position of the stage in early modern England, and to Susan Zimmerman's colloquium at the Folger, 1996-97, for very helpful feedback on this essay. This work and the larger project from which it was taken would have been impossible, moreover, without the help of Janet Adelman and Joel Altman.

[16] Traub, *Desire and Anxiety,* 16.

[17] *A second and third blast of retreat from plaies and Theaters* (London, 1580) 3-4.

[18] Ben Jonson, *Poetaster,* in *Ben Jonson,* 4, ed. C. H. Herford and Percy Simpson (Oxford: Clarendon Press, 1932) 1.2.15-16.

[19] "But so long as he lives unmarried, hee mistakes the Boy, or a Whore for the Woman; by courting the first on the stage, or visiting the second at her devotions" (E. K. Chambers, *The Elizabethan Stage* [Oxford: Clarendon Press, 1923], 257). *A Common Player* is attributed to Cocke by Chambers, who reproduces the text from two variant editions included among the essays of John Stephens (255).

[20] *The Anatomie of Abuses: contayning a Discoverie, or briefe Summarie, of such Notable Vices and Imperfections, as now raigne in many Christian Countreyes of the Worlde, but (especiallie) in a verie famous Llande called Ailgna,* 1583. Ed. F. J. Furnivall (London: New Shakespeare Society, 1877-79) 144-45.

[21] White argues that "the cause of plagues is sinne . . . and the cause of sinne are playes: therefore the cause of plagues are playes." For White, the devastation caused by the plague joins with the moral destructiveness of theater, making tangible the self-loss associated with theatrical practice (*A Sermon preached at Pawles Crosse on Sunday the thirde of November 1577 in the time of the Plague,* [London, 1578], 48).

[22] Noted in Russell Fraser, *The War against Poetry* (Princeton: Princeton University Press, 1970), 26. Fraser outlines early modern objections to the poetic, noting that the attribution of sterility to poetry was related to a growing capitalist emphasis upon productivity. See especially 4-6.

[23] John Northbrooke, *A Treatise Wherein Dicing, Dauncing, Vaine playes, or Enterluds . . . are Reproved,* London, 1577-75; Henry Crosse, *Vertues Commonwealth: Or the Highway to Honour* (London, 1603), V4. In *Refutation,* I.G. charges that "men have deuised many unlawful artificiall Pleasures, whereby they might passe away (as their name *Pastimes* signifie) the most precious time of their life . . . idlely and fruitlesse, without any profit to the Church, or Common-wealth wherein they lieu, or to their owne soules . . . choking up the good Seed of the Word, which should dwell plentifully in their heartes, and in sted thereof, sowing the Tares reaped from ungodly and obscaene Stage-playes" (1615, introduction and bibliographical notes by Richard H. Perkinson [New York: Scholars' Facsimiles and Reprints, 1941] A3-4).

[24] *A Winter's Tale,* ed. J. H. P. Pafford (London: Methuen, 1963) 1.2.187-89. All further references are to this edition.

[25] Like the catamite who seems intrinsically homoerotic, boys seem here by their nature to be theatrical beings. Their "varying childness" makes them paradoxically static, full-time occupants of a state of undifferentiatedness that others visit only in memories of childhood, or onstage. The pleasure of changing identities was also associated with homosexual practice in early modern England. Discussing romance in chapter 4 and satire in chapter 5 of *Homosexual Desire,* Bruce Smith argues persuasively that homosexual behavior in this period, along with its literary representation, could include extensive play with gender identity. See also Smith's discussion of "boy" as a term that inscribes "a distinction in power vis-à-vis a social or moral superior" (195).

[26] For a discussion of breeching, see Adelman, *Suffocating Mothers,* 7. Adelman discusses breeching in relation to the maternal in *The Winter's Tale* on 228.

[27] Although Virgil's eclogues are the Renaissance's source for pastoral convention, early modern writers also knew a version of pastoral that downplayed the political import of Virgil's poetry in favor of a more sentimentalized nostalgia for the rustic life, figured as an Eden or a Golden Age. To the extent that Polixenes' description of childhood can be compared with the pastoral at all (admittedly, among more important differences, most pastoral poetry was not written from the perspective of the sheep), it must be as an echo of this latter nostalgic pastoral rather than as a Virgilian treatment of social problems. The play's later sheep-shearing scenes, however, are much more strongly Virgilian in their use of pastoral landscape and song to discuss what are clearly not utopian concerns. For extended treatments of both Polixenes' nostalgia and the sheep-shearing scene, see Peter Lindenbaum, *Changing Landscapes: Anti-Pastoral Sentiment in the English Renaissance* (Athens: University of Georgia Press, 1986), 111-27; and Paul Alpers, *What Is Pastoral?* (Chicago: University of Chicago Press, 1996), 204-22.

[28] Bruce Smith discusses Polixenes' version of the pastoral in the context of the all-male educational institutions in which Elizabethan men spent their childhood and adolescence, noting the likelihood that these institutions fostered homosexual behavior (*Homosexual Desire,* 98-99).

[29] Jonathan Dollimore explores the contradictions of the "natural" in relation to the perverse, meaning by *perverse* a category of oppositions to the dominant order (disguising itself as natural) that come increasingly to be identified with sexual difference. I see some such relation working itself out in *The Winter's Tale,* with Puritan assumptions about the natural order of heterosexual fertility and economic productivity standing in opposition to the imagined unnatural behaviors of theatrical practicers and patrons. Like Dollimore's work, *The Winter's Tale* explores the contradictions inherent in the category of the natural, and it further embarks

upon a reappropriation of nature as a function of a homoeroticized artistic endeavor (*Sexual Dissidence: Augustine to Wilde, Freud to Foucault* (Oxford: Clarendon Press, 1991]).

[30] Stanley Cavell writes compellingly of the necessity for Polixenes to leave Sicilia (*Disowning Knowledge in Six Plays of Shakespeare* [Cambridge: Cambridge University Press, 1987], 212-14. Charles Frey identifies with a particular poignancy Hermione's success at bridging the gap over which the two kings shake hands, noting that just after Leontes has described his initial sexual conquest of her as a sour and crabbed opening of her white hand, Hermione turns and offers that hand to Polixenes: "Why lo you now; I have spoke to th' purpose twice: / The one, for ever earn'd a royal husband; / Th'other, for some while a friend *[Giving her hand to Pol.]*" (1.2.106-8). (*Shakespeare's Vast Romance: A Study of "The Winter Tale"* [Columbia: University of Missouri Press 1980], 122).

[31] The classic source for this observation is C. L. Barber ("'Thou That Beget'st Him That Did Thee Beget': Transformation in *Pericles* and *The Winter's Tale*," *Shakespeare Survey* 22 [1969], 59-67). For a reading of Shakespeare's sonnets that locates male-female relationships within an economy of male bonds, see Eve Sedgwick, *Between Men: English Literature and Male Homosocial Desire* (New York: Columbia University Press, 1983), 24-48.

[32] Plato, *The Symposium*, in *The Republic and Other Works by Plato*, trans. B. Jowett (New York: Anchor Press, 1973) 352. All further references are to this edition.

[33] Sidney, for instance, remarks that philosophers "do authorize abominable filthiness" more than poets do, and he offers the *Phaedrus* and *Symposium* as evidence (*The Defense of Poesie*, (1583), in *Literary Criticism: Plato to Dryden,* ed. Allan H. Gilbert, 406-61 [Detroit: Wayne State University Press, 1940]). See also Gilbert 444 n. 94, which cites Scaliger's condemnation of the *Symposium* "and other monsters." I am indebted to Heather Weidemann for her suggestion that the *Symposium* was central to my reading of *The Winter's Tale*. I am not, however, suggesting that the *Symposium* is a source for the play or that Shakespeare knew it. The parallels between these two texts seem to me attributable to the persistence of certain strategies for legitimating male writing.

[34] David Halperin, "Why Is Diotima a Woman," in *One Hundred Years of Homosexuality and Other Essays on Greek Love* (New York: Routledge, 1990). I am grateful to Gregory Bredbeck for suggesting the parallels between Halperin's reading of Plato and my own work with this play, and for additional suggestions beyond the scope of individual citation.

[35] A long line of critics associate the play's pastoral with the female; see especially Adelman's discussion: "Through its association with the female and its structural position in the play—outside Leontes's control, outside his knowledge—the pastoral can figure this [maternal] body, the unknown place outside the self where good things come from" (*Suffocating Mothers,* 231). Peter Erickson agrees that *The Winter's Tale* associates this pastoral with women, while he emphasizes the extent to which such a female power serves patriarchy (*Patriarchal Structures in Shakespeare's Drama* [Berkeley: University of California Press, 1985] 158-62).

[36] Leonard Barkan discusses the importance of Ganymede as an image of homosexual desire in the Renaissance in *Transuming Passion: Ganymede and the Erotics of Humanism* (Stanford, Calif.: Stanford University Press, 1991).

[37] Frey argues that one of the great purposes of *The Winter's Tale's* second half is to recuperate the notion of "play" that Leontes' jealousy had made suspect in the play's first half. He sees Perdita's and Florizel's use of costumes as an important motion toward the restoration of faith in drama (*Shakespeare's Vast Romance,* 143-47). I would argue, however, that an early modern audience's faith in drama would require awakening for cultural reasons that go beyond Leontes' personal expressions of mistrust, including the complex of sexual allegations made about theatrical practice in the period.

[38] Many critics have noted that the play's resolution depends upon Leontes' ability to rely upon female powers. See, for example, Kahn, *Man's Estate,* 216-19, and Marianne L. Novy, *Love's Argument: Gender Relations in Shakespeare* (Chapel Hill: University of North Carolina Press, 1984), 176-77. Neely argues that the romances make possible an intertwining of "sexual/marital anxieties" with "political conflicts," in part because the frightening power of female sexuality has been displaced onto the father-daughter bond as a result of the mother's real or imagined death. She finds in *The Winter's Tale* the most powerful transformation of incestuous desire into an acceptance of heterosexual fertility, a transformation brought about through the agency of Hermione, Paulina, and Perdita (chap. 5). Although Adelman claims that the romances aim collectively to restore "the ideal parental couple lost at the beginning of *Hamlet*" (*Suffocating Mothers,* 193), in her reading paternal authority is the play's ultimate concern, and she would agree that paternal authority manages at best a momentary compromise with the sexual mother in *The Winter's Tale* (220-38). In Erickson's reading, Paulina is "less of an exception to the general rule of female obedience than she appears to be" (*Patriarchal Structures,* 162), since, like the play's other women, she exerts her efforts on behalf, ultimately, of male power (148-70).

[39] In characterizing lesbian desire as an unrepresentable realm potentially outside of male control, I am building on the sense of its remoteness articulated in Donne's "Sapho to Philaenis":

> Men leave behinde them that which their sin showes
> And are as theeves trac'd, which rob when it snows.
> But of our dallyance no more signes there are,
> Then fishes leave in streames, or Birds in aire.
> And betweene us all sweetnesse may be had;
> All, all that Nature yields, or Art can adde.
> (39-44)

The poem itself belies the separateness of lesbian sex—which after all serves Donne's purposes, not Sappho's—but nevertheless invests in a fantasy of its utopian isolation. I am of course using the term "lesbian" here and throughout with a consciousness of its historical anachronism. See Valerie Traub, "The (In)Significance of 'Lesbian' Desire in Early Modern England," in Goldberg, *Queering the Renaissance*.

[40] Halperin, "Why Is Diotima a Woman?" 143.

---

Source: "Ganymedes and Kings: Staging Male Homosexual Desire in *The Winter's Tale*," in *Shakespeare Studies: An Annual Gathering of Research, Criticism, and Reviews*, Vol. 26, 1998, pp. 187-217.

# Shakespeare's Queer *Sonnets* and the Forgeries of William Henry Ireland

## Michael Keevak, **National Taiwan University**

In 1795 a young man named William Henry Ireland, then about eighteen years of age, fabricated a series of Shakespearean forgeries that, for the space of few months at least, were enthusiastically believed by both the educated English public and some of the leading scholars and critics of the day. By the end of his meteoric career, Ireland's portfolio of impostures included legal deeds, promissory notes, receipts, letters both to and from Shakespeare, a portrait sketch, and even a "lost" tragedy, *Vortigern,* written in the bard's own hand. After his exposure Ireland tried to defend his actions first in a pamphlet, and then in an elaborated and rather "improved" version in his *Confessions,* and the story was reiterated many times until his death thirty years later.[1] In each instance we are presented with a teenager driven mainly by a desire to please his unresponsive and greedy father, Samuel Ireland—antiquarian, book publisher, fervent bardolator—who often reminded his son that he would gladly give away his entire collection in return for just one authentic example of Shakespeare's handwriting.[2] The story becomes more and more incredible as it unfolds, and it becomes increasingly clear that Ireland's eventual aim, which failed disastrously, was to put himself forward as a new young bard. The few pieces of modern criticism devoted to him give us a fuller picture of the scandal, both of the moral and psychological character of the perpetrator(s), and of the cultural and literary climate in which so many men and women willingly believed in the impostures.[3] In some sense the papers are interesting wish-fulfillments, late eighteenth-century versions of what the poet "should" have been like—not, in other words, the rather uncomplimentary legends that had already grown up around him: poacher, holder of horses, Stratford yokel, and so forth. Ireland thus furnishes a more Protestant Profession of Faith to counteract the disturbingly Catholic or "papist" one purportedly left by the poet's father; a gushing and protoRomantic love letter to "Anna Hatherrewaye" (including an effusive poem and even a lock of his hair); Deeds of Gift which sound much more generous and intelligent than Shakespeare's actual will; and very informal letters from Southampton and even the Queen herself, which, in the words of one enthusiast, proved once and for all that Shakespeare was "the Garrick of his age."[4]

The documents make a certain kind of sense in the context of 1795, in other words, but as is often the case with such forgeries it seems surprising in hindsight that anybody could actually have been fooled. For the papers are ridiculously suspect on too many counts, with their dubious source in the house of an invented Mr. H., who freely gave them, one by one, to the worshipful young man (and who even began to correspond with the elder Ireland without the latter recognizing his son's own handwriting); their errors of diction and historical anachronism (a promissory note mentioning the Globe theater ten years before it was built); their laughably exaggerated "Elizabethan" spelling (in the words of Edmond Malone, "the orthography of no age whatsoever");[5] and their often preposterous subject matter (a Deed of Gift in which the poet professes his undying gratitude to a contemporary William Henry Ireland who saved him from drowning in the Thames!). By the same token, however, the very speed with which the discoveries had been made—within the space of a couple of months only—was probably the most convincing proof for Ireland's contemporaries that the documents were real (or that they must be the work of more than one person). Actually, the praise which the papers received and the ease with which each new item had been accepted astonished even their maker—despite his own self-perception as a neglected poetic genius—particularly since he had produced them so quickly, and since in many cases one document often necessitated the composition of another in order to explain or correct it.

For instance, the Deed of Gift to Ireland's Elizabethan namesake included all the profits from several plays (an anachronism, since playwrights did not own their work in this way),[6] including *King Lear,* a phony manuscript version of which had just been "discovered"—a ploy clearly designed both to authenticate the play itself and to provide a justification for the fact that Ireland should be able to publish or produce the treasure once it had been unearthed. An impossible coincidence, perhaps, but it was nonetheless believed, just as it was not necessarily too good to be true that this same sixteenth-century W. H. might be the same as the W. H. addressed in Thomas Thorpe's mysterious dedication of the *Sonnets!* Similarly, Ireland's climactic imposture, another Deed of Gift, conveniently referred to other unauthenticated finds, such as the love letter and *Vortigern,* the latter not coincidentally being in preparation for production at the Drury Lane theater. But evenmore audaciously, the rights to this play were (again anachronistically) granted to an unnamed and presumably illegitimate child of Shakespeare left in the care of John Heminge, fellow actor and coeditor of the First Folio, thus making a number of enticing insinuations about possible family ties between Heminge and Ireland's Mr. H., or a possible connection between this child, "of whome wee have spokenn butt who muste nott be named here," and Ireland's fictive namesake.[7]

In some way, in other words, the forger seems to be attempting to fashion himself as a true descendant of Shakespeare, both genealogically and artistically.

Such a plethora of lies, however, inevitably caught up with their prevaricator, and despite the care Ireland employed to use authentic paper from the period, an ink that looked old when the documents were held before a flame, and seals cleverly remade from Elizabethan ones, Malone had little trouble demonstrating the documents' many inconsistencies and inaccuracies in his scrupulously thorough *Inquiry into the Authenticity of Certain Miscellaneous Papers* of 1796, one of the first examples of "professional" Shakespeare criticism and the chief force behind Ireland's exposure. As Malone concludes, those involved in the forgery "know nothing of the history of Shakespeare, nothing of the history of the Stage, or the history of the English Language."[8] Within the space of a few days, *Vortigern* was laughed off the stage, and there was nothing left to do but for young William Henry to confess. The elder Ireland, however, stubbornly refused to believe that his son was capable of such acts, nor of such elevated artistic creations, and continued to insist on the papers' authenticity until his death four years later.[9] William Henry went on to write many more books, sometimes pseudonymously, but he was never again to rise from obscurity.

The whole case remains, in a word, a fascinating and important piece of evidence relating to the history of Shakespeare-worship, which at this time was just beginning to take shape,[10] as well as a family drama which ultimately becomes, in the words of Samuel Schoenbaum, "invested with an almost unendurable pathos."[11] But it is rather more difficult to concur with Brian Vickers that the Ireland episode, other than the fact it managed to fool so many people for a time, "has no significance for the history of the interpretation of Shakespeare."[12] I will argue that the Ireland forgeries indicate a great deal not only about the way that Shakespeare—actor, playwright, poet, cultural icon—was regarded by the late eighteenth century, but also about how more modern preoccupations have grown out of the very same debates. The center of our obsession, then as now, is the Shakespeare biography, or rather lack thereof. It is something of a cliché to be reminded that we know next to nothing about Shakespeare's life, that our knowledge is confined mainly to dry legal records or unsatisfying contemporary references, and that so little about him is "revealed" in his works. Readers are thus forced to find their own answers for understanding the national poet, and the *Sonnets* have predictably become a favorite site for those searching after more intimate details—since the poems are written in the first person and they tempt us to read in them a very provocative "story." In fact the sheer number of controversies which have grown up around the poems is itself no less than spectacular—to name a few, whether they were pirated; why so few copies remain; why contemporaries don't mention them; whether they were withdrawn from publication; what their correct order is; when they were written; whether they are autobiographical; who are Mr. W. H., the young man, the rival poet, and the dark lady; whether the poems are homosexual or adulterous; and, worst of all, whether "William Shakespeare" is merely a pseudonym for another author who wished to remain unknown.[13]

Each of these debates has inspired its own veritable industry of subsequent comment. A number of them are of course rather hollow and irrelevant, and it has often been lamented how many false questions and crackpot theories have grown up around the poems; as E. K. Chambers famously put it, "[m]ore folly has been written about the sonnets than about any other Shakespearean topic."[14] But the extent to which these debates depend on conjectures about Shakespeare's "real life" is extraordinary, and it is no accident that the *Sonnets* stand in the center of this sort of biographical game. The problem hinges on the extent to which the poems can serve as "evidence" for the life of Shakespeare (or somebody else), and it is in precisely the same way that the Ireland forgeries—and the supposed letter from Queen Elizabeth in particular, which will be our focus here—relate to these discussions. For both the impetus and the result of the documents was their presumed ability to fill in some of the large gaps that existed in the Shakespeare biography, and indeed Ireland himself describes a similar motivation for his creations. We have already mentioned the Profession of Faith, the letter to Anne Hathaway, and the Deeds of Gift as representative of this sort of biographical fantasy, but it is the Queen's letter which had unwittingly produced the most telling "story"—and the most telling response from one former believer, George Chalmers.[15] "Wee didde receive youre prettye Verses goode Masterre William through the hands off oure Lorde Chambelayne," Elizabeth is made to write, "ande wee doe Complemente thee onne theyre greate excellence." She continues:

> Wee shalle departe fromme Londonne toe Hamptowne forre the holy-dayes where wee Shalle expecte thee withe thye beste Actorres thatte thou mayste playe before oureselfe toe amuse usse bee notte slowwe butte comme toe usse bye Tuesdaye nexte asse the lorde Leycesterre will bee withe usse.
>
> Elizabeth. R.

The letter is also addressed: "For Master William Shakespeare atte the Globe bye Thames." Finally, on an attached piece of paper the poet was made to add, obviously to provide an explanation for the fact that the letter itself has survived:

> Thys Letterre I dydde receyve fromme mye moste gracyouse Ladye Elyzabethe ande I doe requeste itte maye be kepte withe all care possyble.
>
> Wm. Shakespeare.[16]

William Henry's chaotic spelling and seeming disinterest in punctuation are just two of the more noticeable features in the forgeries, but here the chattiness of the Queen is positively astonishing. Malone had many other objections, however: would Elizabeth have misspelled Leicester's name in such a way (even if standard orthography did not yet exist), not to mention London or Hampton Court? Why should the letter have survived when so many other documents, not to mention the "prettye Verses" themselves, have not? Perhaps the reference to Leicester was designed to give the note an added air of authenticity, but since he had died in 1588 it would have to be written when Shakespeare was at most twenty-four years old, and (unluckily) in that year the Globe did not yet exist either.[17] According to Ireland's subsequent account, the idea of a letter from the Queen was suggested to him by a legendary missive from James I, which (it was hoped) might turn up with the other papers; "[m]y principal object in the production of this letter was to make our bard appear of so much consequence in his own time as to be personally noticed by so great and politic a princess as our Elizabeth," but "[a]s to the verses alluded to in my gracious epistle, they certainly never had existence, to the best of my knowledge."[18] But the letter had already worked its intended effect, to herald Shakespeare as "the Garrick of his age," and it was the chief piece of evidence which in 1797 led Chalmers to posit his own theory, in his *Apology for the Believers in the Shakspeare-Papers,* that the "prettye Verses" were none other than Shakespeare's *Sonnets,* and that all of them were in fact addressed to the Queen![19]

To be fair, when Chalmers's hypothesis is placed beside the vast legion of fantastic, ridiculous, and lunatic theories in the long and varied history of Shakespeare criticism, and that of the *Sonnets* in particular, his conclusion might seem rather tame and perhaps even arguable.[20] It certainly ranks higher than George Elliott Sweet's contention that Elizabeth *was* "Shakespeare,"[21] but even Sweet's position could be said to grow out of the very same set of biographical problems that have plagued all readers. Chalmers simply offers another version of the "story" behind the poems' composition: essentially that Shakespeare was attempting to praise his monarch after the example of Spenser (who was quite successful in obtaining preferment in this way), and that one should read the first seventeen poems—the "pro-creation sonnets" which urge a young man to marry and reproduce—as in fact rhetorical proposals to the Virgin Queen. So far so good, perhaps, but Chalmers will have to perform a lot of verbal gymnastics in order to prove that all the poems are addressed to only one person, and that the rest of the sequence, especially the markedly denigrating poems in the "dark lady" group, are also designed to appeal to the Queen.[22] As a matter of fact Chalmers has little to say about these final poems.

But it is vital to understand that Chalmers does *not* claim that the Ireland forgeries are authentic; rather, he offers an "Apology for the Believers" in the documents, which is to say an attempt to explain why he and others *had* been fooled, and why the documents had made sense as new evidence relating to the life of the bard. Chalmers's real target is not the forger at all but Malone's recently published *Inquiry,* which in Chalmers's view was too sarcastic and snobbish in its demonstrations. "If Mr. Malone had written, instead of his *Inquiry,* a pamphlet in plain prose," writes Chalmers in his preface, "stating his objections without irony, and submitting his documents without scoffs; . . . no one would have answered what few would have read; since a cheat exploded is a cheat no more" (*A* iii). Chalmers endeavors to show just how many times this (as he felt) self-proclaimed authority was misleading or mistaken. Perhaps he does manage to correct Malone on a few occasions, but there is also an overwhelming pointlessness to most of Chalmers's 628 pages, since, although he begins by admitting his own gullibility, he has to spend so much time proving how it might have been possible, and the tedious legalistic paragraphs which open the book concerning the distinctions between possibility and probability are hardly enlivened by the bitter attack on "the public accuser" that follows. What is really the difference if Malone's detection has turned out to be "right by chance" rather than "convincing by argument" (*A* 123)?[23]

Let us recall that the monarch's letter is actually rather modest when compared with some of Ireland's more reckless creations to come. Moreover Chalmers's treatment fills only the first ninety or so pages of his book, and his theory regarding the *Sonnets* soon gives way to other considerations. But this does not lessen the importance of that theory for the history of Shakespeare criticism, despite the fact that ridicule was both immediate and potent. For Chalmers continued to assert that the poems were addressed to the Queen *even after* he admits that her letter itself is spurious. In some sense, then, his reading of the *Sonnets* must have existed before the letter was even forged. At first glance this might seem far-fetched or illogical, since is it really likely that Chalmers could have "guessed" beforehand that Elizabeth is the poems' true addressee? Isn't it clear, in other words, that the forged letter produced the theory rather than the other way around? Perhaps his reading had not been fully or even explicitly formulated before the letter actually appeared, but there were undoubtedly certain "problems" regarding the meaning of the poems that had been bothering readers ever since the 1609 text was restored (also by Malone) in 1780. Ireland's letter, that is, merely served as a convenient means (or an excuse or a justification) to explain or unravel a particular mystery *already* in place, and we have begun to see that many of the forgeries themselves represent similar kinds of "solutions." Chalmers's theory, in a word, is really a response to something other than the debate over Elizabeth's letter; the main issue, then as now, is the (apparently undeniable) fact that most of the 154 poems are addressed to a man. This has always been the Sphinx's riddle of *Sonnet* criticism. Was Shakespeare really a sodomite, the term regularly used before the invention of "homosexual" identities in the nineteenth century?[24] On these grounds George Steevens had refused to publish the *Sonnets* at all, stating that "the strongest act of Parliament that could be framed would fail to compel readers into their service."[25]

When other early authorities broached the subject of the poems' sexuality it was only in order to render it somehow innocent—which is to say normative, "heterosexual" (this term did not exist yet either): for the *Sonnets*, we are told, describe not a love affair between men but only an idealized friendship (Coleridge), their praise of a young man merely represents a tradition and is not really sexual (Malone), and they are not autobiographical poems anyway (John Boswell, Jr.). Peter Stallybrass has acutely noted how in all of these comments the possibility, or reality, of sodomy is always central but never explicitly named,[26] and Chalmers's theory is clearly one more attempt to circumvent this same unnamed danger—that the bard is guilty of sodomy—simply by showing that the addressee is really a woman. If the poems are addressed to someone of the opposite sex, in other words, then all their problems can be made to disappear, just as one would have nothing more to worry about if Shakespeare "himself" were really a woman in disguise. Chalmers is also neither the first nor the last to change the gender of the addressee to suit contemporary tastes; Coleridge succumbed to the same tendency,[27] and it had also occurred in what is arguably the first "reading" of the *Sonnets* we possess, John Benson's bowdlerized edition of 1640, which, in addition to combining and rearranging the poems and giving them titles, actually alters some masculine references to make them more "properly" feminine. Hardly a marginal phenomenon or an isolated publication, however, Benson's edition was the basis for all new versions of the *Sonnets* for nearly a century and a half—until, that is, Malone.[28]

Chalmers's book is thus responding not only to Malone's *Inquiry* but also to prevailing tastes and contemporary judgments regarding Shakespeare's poems. In his *Inquiry* Malone announced that a definitive *Life of Shakespeare* was forthcoming, and his recent edition of the poems had included a biographical sketch which was probably the first to plumb the depths of the *Sonnets* for biographical evidence.[29] But utilizing the *Sonnets* in this way also carried with it certain anxieties—namely, about sodomy—and it is in this very area that Malone disagreed most violently with Steevens. The infamous sonnet 20 was the main source of contention even then, for while here the poet seems to say that his "passion" for the male "Master Mistress" is purely platonic (since the speaker relinquishes the "pricked ... out" friend to the "use" or sexual pleasure of women only), this rhetorical act is achieved via the most titillating and suggestive sexual language of the entire sequence.[30] Steevens had grumbled that "[i]t is impossible to read this fulsome panegyrick, addressed to a male object, without an equal mixture of disgust and indignation," and Malone replied with the now familiar defense that "such addresses to men, however indelicate, were customary in our author's time, and neither imported criminality nor were esteemed indecorous."[31] Implicitly, then, Chalmers is arguing not merely that the great Shakespeareans had not found the correct "solution" to the *Sonnets,* but also that the poems could be rescued from "fulsome," "disgusting," "indignant," "indelicate," "indecorous," or indeed "criminal" readings. For if the addressee of all the poems is really the Queen, Chalmers says, would it not be appropriate for Shakespeare to refer to her as his "Master Mistress," since she was both his "love" and his sovereign, both a woman and a prince (*A* 51-52, 58)? Malone, he says, faulted the poems for "professing too much love . . . to a man," but when readers realize the truth "they will be happy to find that the poet was incapable of such grossness." "Ought we to wonder," he concludes, "that in performing this great operation [of praise], he should confound the sexes?" (*A* 60-61).[32]

This seems at best a rather thick-headed reading, but at the same time Chalmers is fantasizing a biography for Shakespeare built up around the poems' newly understood "story" (*A* 51):

> The fact is that Shakespeare had not leisure to write one hundred and twenty such sonnets to any man; being wholly occupied in providing for the day, which was passing over him; that the poet had no love, but a teeming wife to whom he was strongly attached by early ties; and for whom he could hardly provide by any means: Add to these circumstances that in another sonnet, Shakspeare maintains the unity of his object by saying to his idol, Elizabeth:
>
> For to no other pass my verses tend,
> Than of your graces and your gifts to tell;
> And more, much more than in my verse can sit,
> Your own glass shows you, when you look in it.
>
> (103.10-13)

The only thing remarkable about this (remarkably bad) reading is that it is arguably the first of its kind, the first fully autobiographical reading of the *Sonnets* in the history of Shakespeare criticism—despite the fact that Malone had already initiated the trend in his 1780 and 1790 editions.[33] Moreover, Chalmers can now make any of the poems contribute to this same "story," which, circularly, the poems are said to describe. In this sense he is also setting a precedent that will (unfortunately) be followed by so many other critics, both scholarly and otherwise. Only eleven years later the *Sonnets* were already being described as "paint[ing] most unequivocally the actual situation and sentiments of the poet," and by 1838 there was no turning back after the appearance of a volume titled *Shakespeare's Autobiographical Poems*.[34]

But the debate between Chalmers and Malone did not end here, even though Malone, probably wisely, declined to respond. For Chalmers refused to let matters stand as they were. Rather than simply allowing the fuss over the Ireland case to run its due course and be forgotten, in the way that many such controversies soon die away, two years later Chalmers produced another volume, *A Supplemental Apology for the Believers in the Shakspeare-Papers,* also more than six hundred pages, which is surely one of the oddest things about this whole rather odd affair. For the title page tells us that the volume was written in "reply to Mr. Malone's answer, which was early announced, but never published."[35] If the first *Apology* was more about Malone than about the Ireland forgeries themselves, even though they were the book's ostensible subject, the second volume does not even need a response from Malone to keep the debate alive. Chalmers now has only "newspaper paragraphs, magazine essays, and monthly criticisms" to contend with (*SA* vi), but it hardly seems to make any difference. Moreover, having had two years to work out his initial theory in more detail, Chalmers now needs the space for his "supplemental" proofs: that since, as he now argues, Spenser's *Amoretti* were addressed to Queen Elizabeth as well (an equally surprising claim), and since Shakespeare was influenced by Spenser (as was also argued in the first *Apology*), one must reread Shakespeare's poems in the light of Spenser's, which were both Shakespeare's chief model and the best evidence that Shakespeare's were also addressed to the Queen (*SA* 21). There is more than just a little circularity in this reasoning, for the main proof that Shakespeare addresses the Queen is the fact that Spenser does so as well, and the main evidence that Spenser does so is his similarity to Shakespeare—not to mention the fact that the female addressee of the *Amoretti* is also idealized. As in Chalmers's first book we are rhetorically asked to consider who else but Elizabeth could possibly fit the kind of exaggerated description found in Spenser's poems. Like Shakespeare, "[i]t is . . . extremely improbable that Spenser, living with his Wife and family at Kilcolman . . . should have addressed such a body of Amatory Sonnets to a private Woman, whom to address in such encomiastic strains would have been dangerous in him and unsafe in her" (*SA* 31). The shadow of sex between men may be absent here but the biographical reading techniques are unchanged.

And yet this is not all, for once Chalmers attempts to flesh out his theory by actually examining individual poems, it is evident that such a demonstration is by no means easy to accomplish. It is all well and good to claim that the poems' many references to "he" or "him" could also refer to Elizabeth as a prince (even if this already seems a bit far-fetched), but what about the poems' many erotic or bawdy details, which would seem to lose much of their rhetorical force if they were not really directed toward another man? In sonnet 20 how could the Queen be "pricked . . . out for women's pleasure" even if it were possible that she qualified as "the Master Mistress" of the speaker's "passion" (unless of course the poems are lesbian, a possibility which Chalmers certainly does not entertain either)? Or when sonnet 16 suggests to the addressee that "many maiden gardens yet unset, / With virtuous wish would bear your living flowers," how would this apply to a proposed marriage for the Queen? Or in another vein, in sonnet 69 how could Shakespeare have gotten away with claiming that Elizabeth's "fair flower" had been given "the rank smell of weeds," and that she therefore "dost common grow"? We could extend these questions indefinitely, but these three poems are actually used by Chalmers to prove his point (*SA* 58-59, 70, 77). This struggle against sodomy becomes panicky and even hysterical, and Chalmers is forced to resort to ever more remote interpretive claims to make his theory work.

But the real meat and substance of the argument concerns the definition of "normal" gender designations, and a rather complicated problem of what we could call gender crossing. For a great many of the *Sonnets* refer to the addressee—and sometimes the speaker himself—"as" a woman. For instance the friend has a woman's face, heart, and eye in sonnet 20, he is compared to both Adonis and Helen in 53, and to Eve in 93 (where the speaker is also "a deceived husband"). The speaker likens himself to an unwed mother in 36, to a widowed one in 97, to Philomela in 102, and to "a careful housewife" in 143. But more generally, in terms of the whole genre of the Petrarchan sonnet sequence, one of the most interesting and unusual things about Shakespeare's poems is precisely the fact that the speaker's "mistress" is really (or at the same time) a "master," and that this male addressee is an *object* of beauty and indeed "passion."[36] But this is also what bothers readers like Chalmers so much, and what seems to compel him to prove that all the "feminine" references to the male beloved are in fact references to a woman—or rather the Queen. This last distinction is important, for if the poems already cross gender lines by associating the male addressee with a mistress, Chalmers's reading takes the addressee's "feminine" position literally by (as it were) crossing back to make the poems refer not only to a real woman, but also to someone who is "more than a woman." If the "Master Mistress" is the Queen, we have crossed class lines as well as those of gender. A related idea is read back onto the addressee of the *Amoretti* as well, since both poets, "in their situations as married men and in their circumstances as to wealth," certainly would not have "addressed such Sonnets to ordinary Women (and much more to ordinary Men)" (*SA* 51). The proof (in Shakespeare) is that one cannot "apply to [a] man the feminine epithet 'tender churl,' and the womanish epithets 'unthriftyloveliness' and 'beauteous niggard'" (*SA* 53n). Indeed it is neither fit nor proper "to apply such sentiments . . . to a man, or indeed to any woman, except Elizabeth" (*SA* 54n). In which gender category, then, is the Queen said to reside?

Chalmers's reading of sonnet 20, however, is predictably the most revealing. A number of critics have remarked how often this poem, the bawdiest and (apparently) most sodomitical of the entire sequence, has ironically become the center of interpretations in precisely the opposite direction: most commonly, that the speaker and his addressee are "just friends."[37] But if the addressee is a woman, and indeed the Queen herself, the problems intensify. "Master Mistress" only means "chiefest" mistress, Chalmers says; this is perhaps fair enough. "A man in hue" may also refer to Elizabeth's "masculine" quality of "lofty pride," but how likely is it that the obviously bawdy phrase "pricked thee out" merely means "marked" (*SA* 59n)? In this reading Elizabeth is merely "marked" as a woman, and therefore she is "pricked . . . out for women's pleasure" in the sense that she is "marked" with "the pleasure which *belongs to* woman" (*SA* 60n; my emphasis). The "love" which the speaker gets is supposedly only that of virtue,[38] but why would the "use" of the Queen in this sense be appropriate for other women? Chalmers says that "thy love's use" is the "treasure" of other women in the sense that "chastity is the appropriate treasure of women." If this already seems a bit hard to follow, we will wonder what the Queen is "pricked out" with. "It will after all be asked, what additional circumstance was it which nature, in her doting, superadded, and which defeated the poet from possessing his master-mistress. I will not shrink from the question. . . . Elizabeth was sprung of heavenly race" (and he cites Spenser to prove it). The "one thing" added by nature is her "divine origin, or high birth"; this was "the additional circumstance that dashed all his hopes: For she was only a man in hue; and she was more than a woman, by addition" (*SA* 60-61n). Although this reading, he claims, has the advantage of "clearing obscurities by the context" (*SA* 61), such a tortuous theory has understandably won little support. For all of the poem's dynamic eroticism—and especially the "one thing" with which the friend is "pricked . . . out for women's pleasure"—has been deflated or distilled into simplistic praise of the Virgin Queen. Like the friend she may also be "more than a woman," but his/her "love's use" has been primly de-eroticized, and the bawdy jest in which the friend's "one thing" is called a "nothing"—an unmistakable sexual pun—is quietly expurgated.

It is only in this way that Shakespeare can be saved from the charge which had already been leveled against him by one of Chalmers's contemporaries: that he was "a miscreant, who could address amatory Verses to a man, 'with a romantic platonism of affection'" (cited in *SA* 73). But now, having been "freed . . . from this stain," "darkness brightens into light, order springs out of confusion, and contradiction settles into sense" (*SA* 73-74). Never mind that pronouns are changed from his to her and back again (e.g., *SA* 68-69), or that Chalmers's only proof is a list of "feminine" labels which "cannot be properly applied to a man": "unthrifty loveliness," "beauteous niggard," "dear my love," "outward fair," "grace of person," "beauty of eye," and so on (*SA* 72n, 76n, 78n, 79). And how, he blindly asks, could a man possibly "be exhibited as an object for the eyes of men" in sonnet 16 (*SA* 78)? Shakespeare must be saved at any cost from "the odious imputation of platonism" (*SA* 89n), much as the fictive William Henry Ireland had been made to rescue him from the Thames. And as for the twelve-line sonnet 126, with its seemingly irrefutable male invocation ("thou, my lovely boy"), Chalmers remarks that since the poem lacks its final two lines "the printer had before him a very imperfect Manuscript" (*SA* 86). This is no doubt a last resort, and from this point on the argument abruptly dies away, if it ever had any life to begin with, by apologizing for the fact that it is not possible to treat every poem in the sequence with the same level of attentiveness (*SA* 81). This is hardly surprising, since the break occurs just when we come to the "dark lady" poems, even though it might seem necessary to "rescue" the poet from them (and her) as well.

One may wonder why we should even bother with Chalmers's theories after two hundred years. Do they reside merely in "the by-ways of eighteenth-century letters,"[39] or is it possible to argue that these big books are more than just an effect of an antique milieu in which bardolatrous forgeries were so readily accepted? Although the Ireland case has received its share of analysis, far too little attention has been paid to Chalmers's involvement in the controversy, and to the manner in which his books have much to teach us about larger critical questions—and about the effects of sodomy in particular. In this sense we must orient our understanding of Chalmers's response to contemporary queer studies debates, which not accidentally have as one of their main points of focus the early modern period. One reason for this is that in the sixteenth and early seventeenth centuries the term "sodomy" could be used to refer not only to sexual acts between men or between women, but also to any non-normative form of sexual behavior (extramarital intercourse, non-vaginal sex, masturbation, bestiality, rape, and so on), and many contemporary queer theorists have adopted a similar designation for "queer" in order to make it more inclusive, or less exclusionary, than a term like "gay and lesbian studies."[40] In this sense the

*Sonnets* are unquestionably queer or sodomitical poems, either in terms of their (supposed) relationship with the young man or the dark lady, but clearly it is much more urgent for Chalmers to free Shakespeare from the possibility of same-sex desire than from an adulterous affair. Just as the forged letter from Elizabeth may simply have given Chalmers an opportunity to relieve Shakespeare from the graver charge of "platonism," the whole theory about a female addressee is a belated rescue operation whose "solution" stems from a cultural anxiety about sodomy just as much as from the letter itself. Even in the first *Apology* the forgeries had already moved into the background. But Chalmers also looks "backward" in the way in which he endeavors to define a normatively sexual Shakespeare which will counteract an anxiety about sodomy already being felt. As Stallybrass writes, "[t]he justification of Shakespeare is always subsequent to the charge of deviation—just as the concept of the 'heterosexual' is a belated response to the *prior* concept of the 'homosexual.'"[41] This is one reason why the Ireland affair is such a valuable and instructive piece of evidence for queer studies. But let us also recall that Chalmers's reading is also the first predominantly autobiographical one of Shakespeare's poems, and we should pause to ask why the initial foray into this sort of criticism should have taken this particular form rather than any other. Is it important, in other words, that the *first* autobiographical reading should have the avoidance of sodomy at its center?

In terms of queer studies I am reminded of the opening of Eve Kosofsky Sedgwick's *Epistemology of the Closet,* where we are told that "an understanding of virtually any aspect of modern Western culture must be, not merely incomplete, but damaged in its central substance to the degree that it does not incorporate a critical analysis of modern homo/heterosexual definition."[42] This statement seems to apply equally well to Chalmers's own form of definitional crisis, for we cannot understand what is really at stake in the eighteenth-century imaginary of (a "normal") Shakespeare without also understanding the sodomy that bardolatry had to work against even as it was being fashioned. Moreover, one of the consequences of the lack of biographical information relating to the poet was the amount that one had to rely on the works for an understanding of the author "himself," and of course a group of first-person poems like the *Sonnets* were inevitably the most alluring treasure trove of all. But this also meant that one had to account for (or deny) what the poems appeared to say—namely, that the speaker had addressed "amatory verses" to another man. It was only in the eighteenth century that this process was beginning to take shape, the main reason being that Thorpe's text had only just been restored. But once the sodomitical Shakespearean text had been rediscovered, it also had to be integrated into the bard's official biography. Thus the issue of bardolatry itself, and the question of biographical criticism in general, cannot be entirely separated from the (newly formed) definition of an explicitly "heterosexual" Shakespeare. The homo/hetero definition was also at work in 1795—even if the terms themselves had not yet been invented—in the ostensibly desexualized terrains of bardolatry and autobiography.

Yet what of our own readings? Can we really be said to fare any better? One of the most enlightening things about Chalmers's theory, in fact, is just how representative it is as a moral vindication of Shakespeare based on his sexual "orientation," and many (if not most) readers have also concentrated on the homo/hetero distinction (especially Joel Fineman) despite the fact that the poems can be read or divided in other ways, and indeed that the real "scandal" of the *Sonnets* might lie more in their description of the dark lady's "promiscuous womb" than in some form of pederasty.[43] Joseph Pequigney has provided the most detailed review of the way in which the sexuality in the *Sonnets* has been consistently whitewashed throughout their modern critical history—up to and including Stephen Booth's currently standard edition.[44] Such bowdlerization can even be accomplished under the aegis of historical or cultural difference, since if one misreads or oversimplifies Alan Bray's arguments (especially), that male "friendship" took on particular and to us surprising forms in Renaissance society,[45] or that an individual sodomite would not have conceived of him/herself in a way that would correspond to a modern "gay" (or even queer) identity,[46] wouldn't it be possible to say that the *Sonnets* are not "gay" poems" at all but something which we no longer understand or recognize? This is part of the message of Pequigney's book, for critics' longstanding refusal to read what is "really there" in the poems blinds them to a narrative which is not only homoerotic but "sexual in both orientation and practice"—even if Pequigney's version comes close to reducing the poems merely to another, alternative story.[47] Or is it, in Chalmers's words, "for impure minds only to be continually finding something obscene in objects that convey nothing obscene, or offensive, to the chastest hearts" (*SA* 63)? Put another way, at what point do our own "dirty minds" pursue sexual puns or innuendoes which are no longer appropriate for a Renaissance poem, as if at some point such readings had crossed over into distinctly modern (not to mention Elizabethan) sexual slang? The terms of the problem are well encapsulated in the subtitle of Jonathan Goldberg's *Sodometries: Renaissance Texts, Modern Sexualities,* for how are these two categories to be connected?

We have already examined the speaker's preoccupation with the "one thing" (or "nothing") which the male "Master Mistress" is "pricked . . . out" with in sonnet 20, but this is by no means our only example. The male body is also provocatively described as a "sweet up-locked treasure" in sonnet 52, its value being continually renewed by the "unfolding" of phallic "pride":

> So is the time that keeps you as my chest,
> Or as the wardrobe which the robe doth hide
> To make some special instant special blest,
> By new unfolding his imprisoned pride.
> (52.9-12)

Or sonnet 56, which is an expression of the fulfillment and reawakening of sexual desire, seems (contextually speaking, at least) to refer only to male bodies:

> Sweet love renew thy force, be it not said
> Thy edge should blunter be than appetite,
> Which but today by feeding is allayed,
> Tomorrow sharp'ned in his former might.
> (56.1-4)

Or the bawdy language of sonnet 80 (one of the "rival poet" group) likewise seems to be an all-male affair:

> My saucy bark, inferior far to his,
> On your broad main doth wilfully appear,
> Your shallowest help will hold me up afloat,
> Whilst he upon your soundless deep doth ride;
> Or, being wracked, I am a worthless boat,
> He of tall building and of goodly pride.
> (80.7-12)

Lastly, Pequigney points out that a number of words in sonnet 33 suggest references to fellatio,[48] even though the opening of the poem is also a rather conventional periphrasis of the dawn:

> Full many a glorious morning have I seen
> Flatter the mountain tops with sovereign eye,
> Kissing with golden face the meadows green,
> Gilding pale streams with heav'nly alchemy,
> Anon permit the basest clouds to ride
> With ugly rack on his celestial face[.]
> (33.1-6)

But can we really account for this sort of erotic playfulness merely by saying that these are examples of premodern male "friendship," or that praise of a young man is merely a well-worn tradition? Does it matter if a paradigmatic marriage poem like sonnet 116 ("Let me not to the marriage of true minds / Admit impediments") is in context not only addressed to another man, but has rhetorical force only when its homoeroticism is set against the less idealized sexuality of the "dark lady" poems? Or is it merely our modern "impure minds" that lead us astray into the dangerous and heretical world of sodomy? Where shall we *stop* reading?

It is also remarkable how many of the controversies that surround the *Sonnets* are inextricably bound up with the issue of sodomy. Again, why should this be so? Arguably, any of the points of debate outlined above is affected by the question of the poems' queerness, precisely because of the scandalous "story"—whatever its specifics—that the speaker appears to tell. Are we not tempted to say that the *Sonnets* were unauthorized largely because of the sodomitical relationships which they appear to trace, and therefore that the poems must not have been intended for publication? Similar fantasies seem to lie behind our claims that they might have been suppressed soon after their publication. Or to what extent is the search for the identity of the young man, Mr. W. H., the rival poet, or the dark lady really more interested in the fact that any or all of them could have been the speaker's sexual partner(s)?[49] The point is that we too are titillated or disturbed—culturally speaking—by the poems' queer suggestiveness, and in this sense our own "apologetic" theories, although they may be couched in very different-sounding terms, really take their cue from Chalmers.

Hardly an issue for the *Sonnets* only, critics have begun to examine similar blind spots relating to other sodomitical moments in the Shakespeare canon.[50] Even more, queer theorists have taught us that the question of sodomy is startlingly central to English Renaissance culture as a whole, since in addition to the traditional and familiar ways in which the period was both patriarchal and homosocial with regard to women, there is also ample contemporary evidence of (for example) a fashionable homoeroticism in Elizabethan and Jacobean court life; "homosexual" literary models revived from the ancients and perpetuated as the western tradition; institutionalized pederasty in Renaissance humanism, higher education, church practices, and master/servant relations; cross-dressing and gender masquerade in the popular theater; the discovery and colonization of the "sodomites" of the New World; and such documented sodomites as Christopher Marlowe, Francis Bacon, and King James I. In some sense, then, the culture of the English Renaissance *is* a queer culture, and from this perspective the idea of a "gay Shakespeare" may indeed be a kind of tautology.[51]

Whether or not the period could be said to have had any sort of self-identified sodomitical (sub)culture,[52] or whether or not Shakespeare "himself" was (or should have been) "gay," the *Sonnets* are nonetheless queer, and perhaps a lot queerer than most critics have been willing to allow. But more importantly, the poems have served as a particular kind of cultural pretext for our own readings as well. For we too do not escape the need—perhaps even the necessity—to define what is "heterosexual," since even though it may be "normal" it is strangely not a given, and the only way we can determine its normality is by circumscribing what seem to be its "opposites": in this case, same-sex "amatory verses." The point is that it really makes little difference if the *Sonnets* "really are" "gay" poems, since our culture also regularly responds to them—or apologizes for them—as if they were. The poems present us with a certain burden or a challenge that must be answered or defended, forcing us once again to define them as "normal" in spite of the possibility or the fear that they might be the contrary. And the fact that their author is the great and immortal Shakespeare only partly explains this sort of preoccupation. Perhaps the poems tell us less about any Renaissance "homosexual" identity than about what has come to be defined as normative and heterosexual in our own time. It is the roots of this kind of *production* of heterosexual normality that queer theory seeks to analyze; it represents a challenge to not only the sexual subject (in both senses) of Shakespeare's *Sonnets,* but to normative sexuality as well, and one hopes that such analysis, much like other forms of cultural study, is capable of producing—at the very least—a less exclusionary mode of criticism.

## Notes

[1] William Henry Ireland, *An Authentic Account of the Shakspearian Mss.* (London, 1796); Ireland, *Confessions* (London, 1805); Ireland, *Vortigern* (London, 1832).

[2] Ireland, *Confessions,* 45.

[3] The basic works on the Ireland case are Derk Bodde, *Shakespere and the Ireland Forgeries* (Cambridge: Harvard University Press, 1930); John Mair, *The Fourth Forger: William Ireland and the Shakespeare Papers* (London: Cobden-Sanderson, 1938); Bernard Grebanier, *The Great Shakespeare Forgery: A New Look at the Career of William Henry Ireland* (London: Heinemann, 1966); and S. Schoenbaum, *Shakespeare's Lives,* 2d ed. (Oxford: Oxford University Press, 1993, 135-68). These are supplemented by Sidney Lee, "Samuel Ireland," *Dictionary of National Biography,* 1921 ed., 10:468-73; Philip W. Sergeant, "Young Ireland: An Unappreciated Jester," in *Liars and Fakers* (London: Hutchinson, 1925), 237-93; Zoltán Haraszti, "Ireland's Shakespeare Forgeries," in *More Books: The Bulletin of the Boston Public Library* 9 (1934): 333-50; Schoenbaum, "The Ireland Forgeries: An Unpublished Contemporary Account," in *Shakespeare and Others* (Washington: Folger, 1985), 144-53; and Schoenbaum, *William Shakespeare: Records and Images* (London: Scolar Press, 1981), 117-36.

[4] Cited in Ireland, *Confessions,* 280.

[5] Malone, *An Inquiry into the Authenticity of Certain Miscellaneous Papers and Legal Instruments* (London, 1796; rep. New York: Kelley, 1970), 33.

[6] Even Malone brings up this objection (234, 290-91). See also Arthur F. Marotti, "Shakespeare's Sonnets as Literary Property," in *Soliciting Interpretation: Literary Theory and Seventeenth-Century English Poetry,* ed. Elizabeth D. Harvey and Katharine Eisaman Maus (Chicago: University of Chicago Press, 1990), 143-73.

[7] Cited in Grebanier, 170.

[8] Malone, 352-53.

[9] See Samuel Ireland, *Mr. Ireland's Vindication of His Conduct Respecting the Publication of the Supposed Shakespeare Mss.* (London, 1796; rep. New York: Kelley, 1970); and Grebanier, 273-84.

[10] See for instance Arthur Sherbo, *The Birth of Shakespeare Studies: Commentators from Rowe (1709) to Boswell-Malone (1821)* (East Lansing, MI: Colleagues Press, 1986).

[11] *Shakespeare's Lives,* 165.

[12] *Shakespeare: The Critical Heritage,* 6 vols. (London: Routledge, 1974-81), 6:65.

[13] The most valuable source for reviews of these (and other) debates remains the monumental edition of the *Sonnets* by Hyder E. Rollins, Variorum ed., 2 vols. (Philadelphia: Lippincott, 1944). Useful summaries can also be found in Robert Giroux, *The Book Known as Q: A Consideration of Shakespeare's Sonnets* (New York: Atheneum, 1982); and the editions of W. G. Ingram and Theodore Redpath (New York: Barnes & Noble, 1965), and John Kerrigan (Harmondsworth: Penguin, 1985).

[14] *William Shakespeare: A Study of Facts and Problems,* 2 vols. (Oxford: Clarendon Press, 1930), 1:561.

[15] For a short account of Chalmers, "almost the last of the extinct race of authors who were antiquarians rather than historians," and his "indefatigable industry . . . during the last fifty years of his long life," see Aeneas James George Mackay, "George Chalmers," *Dictionary of National Biography,* 1921 ed., 3:1354-55.

[16] Reprinted in Malone, 25-26.

[17] Malone, 70-73, 83-84, 88-95, 97-98.

[18] *Confessions,* 76.

[19] (London, 1797; rep. New York: Kelley, 1971). Further citations, abbreviated *A,* will appear in the text. When citing Chalmers I have occasionally repunctuated and removed italics for the sake of clarity.

[20] See by way of comparison the theories discussed in Rollins's edition; Schoenbaum, *Shakespeare's Lives;* and Frank W. Wadsworth, *The Poacher from Stratford: A Partial Account of the Controversy over the Authorship of Shakespeare's Plays* (Berkeley: University of California Press, 1958).

[21] *Shake-Speare: The Mystery* (Stanford: Stanford University Press, 1956).

[22] Cf. a contemporary remark from the *Monthly Review* cited in Schoenbaum, *Shakespeare's Lives:* "When a writer has once determined that all Shakespeare's Sonnets must relate to the same subject, and must be addressed to the same person, he will violate every rule of language in order to maintain his position" (168).

[23] According to Schoenbaum, when Malone's volume appeared Chalmers had already been planning a book arguing for the authenticity of the papers, and he was "understandably reluctant to lose the fruits of his industry. . . . [and] salvaged his demonstration by converting it into a defense of his credulity and an onslaught against the scholar who had embarrassed him" (*Shakespeare's Lives,* 167).

[24] The standard source for an analysis of the invention of a "homosexual species" is Michel Foucault, *The History of Sexuality,* trans. Robert Hurley, 3 vols. (New York: Pantheon, 1978-1986), vol. 1. For further elaborations of the construction of "homosexual" identity see Diana Fuss, *Essentially Speaking: Feminism, Nature, and Difference* (New York: Routledge, 1989); David F. Greenberg, *The Construction of Homosexuality* (Chicago: University of Chicago Press, 1988); Jonathan Ned Katz, "The Invention of Heterosexuality," *Socialist Review* 20 (1990): 7-34; and Celia Kitzinger, *The Social Construction of Lesbianism* (London: Sage, 1987).

[25] Cited in Peter Stallybrass, "Editing as Cultural Formation: The Sexing of Shakespeare's Sonnets," *Modern Language Quarterly* 54 (1993): 95.

[26] Ibid., 94-95.

[27] Ibid., 99.

[28] There was one edition in 1711 which used Thorpe's text, but its title page identifies the poems as "One Hundred and Fifty Four Sonnets, all of them in Praise of his Mistress" (cited in Ingram and Redpath, xxi). Margreta de Grazia points out, in "The Scandal of Shakespeare's Sonnets," *Shakespeare Survey* 46 (1994): 35-36, that Benson did not change every reference to another man, as is sometimes implied in the criticism. The notorious sonnet 20 for example remains intact, with the exception of a new title: "The Exchange."

[29] Malone, 3-4; de Grazia, *Shakespeare Verbatim: The Reproduction of Authenticity and the 1790 Apparatus* (Oxford: Clarendon Press, 1991), 152-62.

[30] Quotations from the *Sonnets* are taken from Stephen Booth's edition (New Haven: Yale University Press, 1977), with occasional modifications.

[31] Cited in Joseph Pequigney, *Such Is My Love: A Study of Shakespeare's Sonnets* (Chicago: University of Chicago Press, 1985), 30.

[32] Cf. Coleridge's remark that Shakespeare's gender confusion (particularly in sonnet 20) must have been "a purposed blind" (cited in Stallybrass, 99), and Sweet's idea that the "dark lady" poems were written "as part of his [i.e., Elizabeth's] disguise" (62).

[33] See Rollins, 2:248; Schoenbaum, *Shakespeare's Lives,* 168; and de Grazia, *Shakespeare Verbatim,* 173.

[34] Cited in Schoenbaum, *Shakespeare's Lives,* 182, 186.

[35] (London, 1799; rep. New York: Kelley, 1971). Further citations, abbreviated *SA,* will appear in the text. According to Mackay, Chalmers returned to the controversy yet once more in 1800 with an *Appendix to the "Supplemental Apology,"* which judging by its full title no longer has any connection with the Ireland forgeries at all.

[36] Cf. Eve Kosofsky Sedgwick, *Between Men: English Literature and Male Homosocial Desire* (New York: Columbia University Press, 1985), 28-48.

[37] See Rollins, 2:239; Schoenbaum, *Shakespeare's Lives,* 168; and Pequigney, who comments: "This poem seems a curiously inappropriate one for annotators and critics to single out as the principal prop of their contention that the friendship treated in the Sonnets is innocent of erotic content. But . . . [the poem] confronts so openly the question of eroticism in the relations between the friends that until, or unless, it can somehow be rendered innocuous, their efforts are doomed to failure" (40).

[38] At this point (*SA* 60n) Chalmers inexplicably quotes *3 Henry 6* 3.2.63—"That love which virtue begs and virtue grants"—in order to prove that sonnet 20 describes only an innocent love for the friend (who in this reading is the Queen anyway).

[39] Schoenbaum, *William Shakespeare: Records and Images,* 136.

[40] On Renaissance sodomy see Alan Bray, *Homosexuality in Renaissance England* (London: Gay Men's Press, 1982); Gregory W. Bredbeck, *Sodomy and Interpretation: Marlowe to Milton* (Ithaca: Cornell University Press, 1991); Bruce R. Smith, *Homosexual Desire in Shakespeare's England: A Cultural Poetics* (Chicago: University of Chicago Press, 1991); Jonathan Goldberg, *Sodometries: Renaissance Texts, Modern Sexualities* (Stanford: Stanford University Press, 1992); and Goldberg, ed., *Queering the Renaissance* (Durham: Duke University Press, 1994). On "queer" and its problematic designations see Judith Butler, *Bodies That Matter: On the Discursive Limits of "Sex"* (New York: Routledge, 1993); Donald Morton, "The Politics of Queer Theory in the (Post)Modern Moment," *Genders* 17 (1993): 121-50; Sheila Jeffreys, "The Queer Dis-

appearance of Lesbians: Sexuality in the Academy," *Women's Studies International Forum* 17 (1994): 459-72; and Biddy Martin, "Sexualities without Genders and Other Queer Utopias," *Diacritics* 24 (1994): 104-21.

[41] Stallybrass, 102.

[42] (Berkeley: University of California Press, 1990), 1.

[43] Fineman, *Shakespeare's Perjured Eve: The Invention of Poetic Subjectivity in the Sonnets* (Berkeley: University of California Press, 1986); de Grazia, "The Scandal of Shakespeare's Sonnets," 47. Cf. Stephen Orgel, "Nobody's Perfect: Or Why Did the English Stage Take Boys for Women?" in *Displacing Homophobia: Gay Male Perspectives in Literature and Culture,* ed. Ronald R. Butters, et al. (Durham: Duke University Press, 1989), 26: "Homosexuality in this culture appears to have been less threatening than heterosexuality, and only in part because it had fewer consequences and was easier to desexualize." See also Orgel's updated discussion in *Impersonations: The Performance of Gender in Shakespeare's England* (Cambridge: Cambridge University Press, 1996).

[44] Despite the undeniably great value of Booth's edition he disappointingly concludes that "William Shakespeare was almost certainly homosexual, bisexual, or heterosexual. The sonnets provide no evidence on the matter" (548)—as if in the end the poems had nothing to offer for the question of sexuality, or even the question of the question.

[45] Bray, "Homosexuality and the Signs of Male Friendship in Elizabethan England," in Goldberg, ed., *Queering the Renaissance,* 40-61.

[46] Bray, *Homosexuality in Renaissance England,* 58-80.

[47] Pequigney, 1.

[48] Ibid., 104-8.

[49] I would not however subscribe to Rollins's contention that "[t]he subject of homosexuality would never have been discussed in the first place if Shakespeare's readers had not been so eager to prove the friend a real man" (2:239).

[50] For instance *1 Henry 4* (Goldberg, *Sodometries,* 145-75); *Romeo and Juliet* (Goldberg, ed., *Queering the Renaissance,* 218-35); *Troilus and Cressida* (Bredbeck, 33-48); *The Merchant of Venice* (Michael Shapiro, *Gender in Play on the Shakespearean Stage: Boy Heroines and Female Pages* [Ann Arbor: University of Michigan Press, 1994], 93-117); *As You Like it* and *Twelfth Night* (Valerie Traub, *Desire and Anxiety: Circulations of Sexuality in Shakespearean Drama* [London: Routledge, 1992], 117-44).

[51] See Sedgwick, *Epistemology of the Closet* (Berkeley: University of California Press, 1990), 52.

[52] See Bray, *Homosexuality in Renaissance England,* 81-114; Joseph Cady, "'Masculine Love,' Renaissance Writing, and the 'New Invention' of Homosexuality," *Journal of Homosexuality* 23 (1992): 9-40.

---

Source: "Shakespeare's Queer Sonnets and the Forgeries of William Henry Ireland," in *Criticism,* Vol. XL, No. 2, Spring, 1998, pp. 167-89.

# The Generic Complexities of *A Lover's Complaint* and Its Relationship to the Sonnets in Shakespeare's 1609 Volume

## Jennifer Laws, *University of Otago*

From being largely ignored by early readers and critics, Shakespeare's *A Lover's Complaint* has in recent years attracted some attention. Questions of authorship and approximate dating may have been exhaustively worked through, but many other problems remain, not the least being the poem's generic status and its relationship (if any) to the sonnets in the 1609 volume.[1] These last two aspects are, I believe, intimately connected, for an appreciation of the generic complexities inherent in the narrative poem can illuminate its function within the volume as a whole.

The importance of genre in the interpretation of texts has become a commonplace of Renaissance literary criticism. Many scholars have pointed out that in all periods the various genres are distinguished from one another not only by form and subject matter but by the values and attitudes that accrue to specific groupings; and so the choice of genre and the way it is handled can become a potent contribution to the meaning of the text.[2] In the Renaissance, however, genre became a particularly significant concept, for writers looked back to classical models and based much of their 'imitation' on the various 'kinds', as Sidney and Puttenham testify.[3] Not that generic theory necessarily constrained them; rather, the most creative poets extended or challenged generic conventions and frequently mixed two or more kinds in the one text. This occurred not only in large works, such as Sidney's *New Arcadia* and Spenser's *The Faerie Queene,* with their blending of romance and epic and their inclusion of many other kinds, but also in smaller texts. A recent collection of essays by various scholars explores this propensity to play with genre and emphasises, in the words of the editor, the 'mixture of genres and the transformations of kinds' that occurred in many different sorts of poems, including pastoral and complaint.[4]

Much has been written on Shakespeare's proclivity to experiment with genre. Rosalie Colie explains the mingling of the *sal, acetum,* or even *fel* epigram with the *mel* sonnet in Shakespeare's sequence, with the result that the poet is able to 'preserve the mixed bitter and sweet experience of loving, in a solution entirely his own' (pp. 68-75);[5] and Heather Dubrow suggests that Shakespeare both adopts and criticises Petrarch's genre, for 'in using Petrarchan conceits to describe behavior that hardly conforms to Petrarchan codes, he [Shakespeare] raises the disturbing possibility that perhaps even poets who write more conventional sonnets are lying about the nature of love.'[6] Dubrow also discusses at length the way Shakespeare both extends and subverts generic traditions in his narrative poems. She links *Venus and Adonis* to the problem comedies, for it raises 'ethical issues that trouble the reader because they do not admit of clear solutions, and, again like those comedies, it calls many of the assumptions of its own genre into question.'[7] Similarly, Dubrow argues that *The Rape of Lucrece* can be seen as a 'complaint against the complaint' largely because, unlike other poems in that genre, it explores character and motive behind the action and, in particular, renders 'the concept of guilt problematical'.[8] While some of what both these critics say can be considered open to debate,[9] the main conclusion that Shakespeare extends or subverts generic expectations seems incontravertible.

Given this sophisticated playing with genre, we might well expect Shakespeare to show equal skill in manipulating different traditions in *A Lover's Complaint,* a poem written several years after *The Rape* when he was a more experienced writer. But recent criticism has failed to appreciate the fact that the poem might not be all that its title proclaims. Two editors have placed the poem firmly within the woman's complaint tradition: John Kerrigan argues for the similarity of *A Lover's Complaint* to Daniel's *Rosamond,* 'which, more than any other in the kind, was to prompt Shakespeare to emulation'; and John Roe, while rightly pointing to some of the differences between Shakespeare's narrative poem and Daniel's, still sees *A Lover's Complaint* primarily within the woman's complaint tradition.[10]

My contention in this essay is that, although Shakespeare's poem clearly owes something to the woman's complaint tradition, it differs fundamentally from other narratives written in that genre at the end of the sixteenth century. In the way that it raises questions about female sexuality and guilt and presents convincing human behaviour, *A Lover's Complaint* may be seen as following in the footsteps of its predecessor, *The Rape of Lucrece;* but it also differs greatly from that poem in that it combines complaint not with Ovidian narrative but with pastoral lyric, especially of the kind found in *Englands Helicon,* though once again there are considerable differences.[11] These two genres of complaint and pastoral lyric do, of course, have something in common, for many of the lyrics take the form of a woman lamenting her fate; but, while they may share this topos, their attitudes and values do not coincide. A consideration of the two traditions, with particular attention to the women and the way they are presented, will show that *A Lover's Complaint* does not belong wholly to either of them, but forms a hybrid genre of its own which enables Shakespeare implicitly to criticise the values of both these kinds, substituting a much more realistic view of human life than either complaint or pastoral lyric usually allows. Furthermore, I shall argue in the last section of this essay that, looked at in this light, the poem is able to provide a fitting end to *The Sonnets*, a function that is denied it if we persist in seeing it solely in the tradition of *Rosamond*.

. . . . .

The immediate predecessor of the woman's complaint genre which became so popular in the 1590s is the collection of tales published first in 1559 under the title of *The Mirror for Magistrates*. In later editions of this work, two complaints in the voice of women were added, one spoken by Jane Shore and the other by Eleanor Cobham. There is little to distinguish these two stories from the rest of the tragedies in the volume, the women's demise merely serving to illustrate how Fortune deals with the excessively ambitious.[12] However, *Shore's Wife* in particular proved an inspiration to later writers who began to stress not the blind workings of Fortune in the story but retribution for unchastity—a theme which barely exists in the original. By the 1590s the woman's complaint had developed into a recognisable genre of its own, characterised by a very narrow range of topics and attitudes towards sexuality. The writers of these poems were conscious of working within a well-defined tradition, as they often refer to previous examples: Daniel's Rosamond mentions '*Shores* wife' (l. 25); and Drayton's Matilda compares herself favourably in the first few stanzas to Rosamond, Lucrece, Shore's wife, and Lodge's Elstred.[13]

Hallett Smith in his account of this group of poems points to Daniel's *Rosamond* as the prototype of the new woman's complaint, which brought a 'softening and sweetening of the effects of the old warning against pride and other sins of princes'.[14] But such a statement needs carefully qualifying. It is true that Rosamond in Daniel's complaint stresses the need for pity—from the poet himself, who should be moved by a 'wofull womans case' as his happiness depends on 'a womans grace' (41-2) and from his Delia so that her sighs might bring the wretched Rosamond to 'sweet Elisean rest' (9), for in one night she found herself 'unparadis'd' (449). But as the poem proceeds, we find that judgement rather than pity is being passed on Rosamond. In place of the tirades against Fate in the more political complaints, we are shown no less graphically the horrors of unchastity; and this is in spite of the fact that Rosamond can hardly be held accountable for her transgressions. The poem shows a strange inconsistency about apportioning blame. On the one hand, everything and everybody conspires to almost force Rosamond into fornicating with the king: she is sent to court ill-prepared for the sophistication of that life and badly advised by an older woman, as well as being harrassed by the king himself; and she herself at one point sees the hand of Fate in her downfall: 'for that must hap decreed by heavenly powers / Who work our fall, yet make the fault still ours' (412-3). On the other hand, for the most part she accepts that the 'fault' lies with herself and her own lack of moral strength. She fails to take account of the dreadful examples of lost maidenhood on the casket, and so declares:

> I sawe the sinne wherein my foote was entring,
> I sawe how that dishonour did attend it
> I sawe the shame whereon my flesh was ventring,
> Yet had I not the powre for to defende it;
> So weake is sence when error hath condemn'd it:
> We see what's good, and thereto we consent us;
> But yet we choose the worst, and soone repent us.
> (421-7)

She, as the woman, must take all the blame. The throwaway line, '''Tis shame that men should use poore maydens so' (385), spoken when she is contemplating the exploits of Jupiter with Amymone and Io, is not applied to herself. In fact, all our sympathy at the end is directed towards the king, who is, after all, the cause of her predicament. For several stanzas we are regaled with a description of his grief and suffering as he embraces his dead mistress (617-700), whereas Rosamond herself is despatched quite quickly and, it should be noted, forced to administer her own poison, as a sort of poetic justice:

> Those handes that beauties ministers had bin,
> Must now gyve death, that me adorn'd of late:
> That mouth that newly gave consent to sin,
> Must now receive destruction in there-at.
> That body which my lusts did violate,
> Must sacrifice it selfe t'appease the wrong,
> So short is pleasure, glory lasts not long.
> (596-602)

As if the original 1592 version did not make her guilt abundantly clear, 20 stanzas were added in the 1594 edition, all on the theme of Rosamond's sin and the sin of wicked women who aid and abet such behaviour.

Exactly what 'pleasure' Rosamond experiences is never revealed, as she seems to suffer from the day she loses her virtue and she certainly never enjoys any sexual pleasure. In line 600 she refers to her 'lusts', but in the light of the rest of the poem these seem to be general desires rather than anything sexual. The king himself is unattractive and old; in fact, there is an insistence that her first experience with him is distasteful, and she comes merely to tolerate his love-making: 'For nature checks a new offence with lothing: / But use of sinne doth make it seeme as nothing' (454-5). Sin here is allowing her body to be used in order to gain worldly riches (but even this, of course, she is denied as she is immured in a labyrinth). It is as though the poet is so set on showing us the awful fate attendant on unchastity that no hint of pleasure for the woman is allowed, even though she is blamed for 'sin'.

In Lodge's *Elstred,* we find the same insistence on the sins of the woman. In spite of all the moans and tears calling for our sympathy (with water literally dripping off the bodies of mother and daughter as they rise from their river grave to tell their story), the heroine excuses 'Fortune fickle', and places the blame for her downfall squarely on herself:[15]

> It was not thou, my conscience doth excuse thee,
> It was my sinne that wrought myne overturning.
> It was but justice, from the heavens inflicted
> On lustfull life, defamed and convicted.
>
> (pp. 74-5)

Even Cassandra, in her lament at the end of Barnfield's narrative poem, sees her own guilty relationship with Agamemnon as the prime cause of her unhappy fate, cautioning all young maids to 'example take by me, / To keepe their oathes, and spotlesse chastity', and claiming that happiness is dying at birth before being able to sin.[16]

In other complaints the situation is reversed, and we are treated to extravagant praise for the woman's defence of her chastity. The insufferable Matilda defies all bounds of modesty by proclaiming that her 'Vertue made beauty more angelicall' (line 91); and in the face of the most extreme temptations and threats, finally takes her own life to avoid King John's dishonourable intentions, rejoicing in her martyrdom:

> My glorious life, my spotlesse Chastity,
> Now at this hower bee all the joyes I have,
> These be the wings by which my name shall flye,
> In memorie, these shall my Name engrave;
> These, from oblivion shall mine honour save.
> With Laurell, these my browes shall coronize,
> And make mee live to all posterities.
>
> (ll. 925-31)

Under happier circumstances, the humble innkeeper's wife defends her honour in *Willobie His Avisa,* where page after page celebrates the inviolable virtue of the heroine.[17]

The point I wish to establish is that, although these complaints are in the voice of the female victim, they are not sympathetic towards the woman and there is little attempt to understand her viewpoint. Her 'sins' are stressed and yet she is denied any sexual pleasure. Moreover, her character becomes unnecessarily limited as she projects herself in one dimension only— chaste or unchaste—the only other quality she possesses being the predictable one of beauty. The poems are unremittingly moralistic and didactic, with ruin and death for the woman as the inevitable outcome of failing to guard her chastity or at least preferable to losing that virtue.

Such is not the case with Shakespeare's maid. She may be in a state of deep distress, but she is not a totally ruined woman who returns as a ghost to tell her story. In fact, she is very much alive and retains some of her good looks:

> Time had not scythèd all that youth begun,
> Nor youth all quit, but spite of heaven's fell rage
> Some beauty peeped through lattice of seared age.[18]
>
> (12-14)

She still presents a charming spectacle as she sits under her bonnet with her hair slightly dishevelled, symbolic of a life that has not been properly restrained, but which yet retains some semblance of order:

> Her hair, nor loose nor tied in formal plat,
> Proclaimed in her a careless hand of pride:
> For some, untucked, descended her sheaved hat,
> Hanging her pale and pinèd cheek beside;
> Some in her threaden fillet still did bide,
> And, true to bondage, would not break from thence,
> Though slackly braided in loose negligence.
>
> (29-35)

The phrase 'careless hand of pride' is particularly revealing. We can read it as 'the hand that does not care about pride in appearance'; but we can also interpret it as 'the hand of pride that does not care about appearances'.[19] In both interpretations there is a sense of defiance, a lack of concern for the opinion of others, which is quite contrary to the abject penitence expected of a fallen woman. 'Pride' and 'loose' also carry sexual connotations; the maid, it seems, is not just a victim.

This 'pride' of flesh and spirit is reflected in the movement of her eyes: they are not fixed submissively to the earth all the time, but sometimes raised to the heavens or even allowed to 'extend their view right on' (24). In fact, unlike the usual wretched complaint lady, her fury is turned not upon herself, but upon her heartless seducer. First she is seen in a fit of anger throwing away his gifts and then we hear her denouncing his 'false blood' and 'lies', while she tears up his letters in 'top of rage' (52-56).

The sorrow she expresses has more to do with giving away her affections than losing her virginity:

> I might as yet have been a spreading flower,
> Fresh to myself, if I had self-applied
> Love to myself, and to no love beside.
> (75-7)

The word 'flower' hints at her lost maidenhood, but it is 'love' she is chiefly regretting. Later she uses the same image of a flower to denote the 'affections' she gave to the young man *before* she yielded to him, reserving for herself just the 'stalk' (146-7). And when she is finally conned into taking off her 'white stole of chastity', she is hurt most by the fact that her honest giving has not been matched by his, that she has exposed her nakedness, while he has remained 'veiled' (312), covering his duplicity with 'the garment of a grace' (316). Most telling of all, the final lines of the poem end not with the expected warning to other young women, but with a frank acknowledgement that she would probably act in exactly the same way again, and that the charms of the young man 'Would yet again betray the fore-betrayed, / And new pervert a reconcilèd maid.' Many a complaint lady has compounded her guilt by not taking any notice of the dire warnings of others, as we saw with Rosamond, but at least in the end she upholds the claims of chastity. Not so the maid, who realises that her own feelings will always have priority.

The maid's feelings include a response to the sensuous appeal of the young man. We feel the lure that the young man has for her in the descriptions of his beauty which call on the sense of touch as well as sight:

> His browny locks did hang in crookèd curls,
> And every light occasion of the wind
> Upon his lips their silken parcels hurls.
> (85-7)

As Kerrigan notes, the young man is given just the same irresistible charm usually accorded by a lover to his lady when he sees her containing all the attributes of love, for 'Love lacked a dwelling and made him her place' (82).[20] In fact, as the title of the poem implies, the lady here *is* the 'lover';[21] she has become not just the passive recipient of another's love or lust, but the very active participant in a relationship.

In spite of the maid's complicity in her seduction, the blame is felt to lie almost entirely on the young man, for he is the one who deceives and betrays his lover. He damns himself out of his own mouth as he relates the cold and callous way he has treated his former mistresses, seeming to think that a lack of affection for his victims excuses his behaviour. Whatever the effect of these declarations on the maid, we cannot miss the irony in his statement, 'Harm have I done to them, but ne'er was harmèd' (194). His avowed lack of love appears to be morally far worse than the too loving, if misguided, passion of the maid and the other female victims.

Thus, although Shakespeare follows the complaint tradition in his choice of the basic situation with a male seducer and a female victim, the maid is very far from a typical lamenting lady: her privileging of love over chastity, her frank recognition of her own sexuality, her pride and assertiveness, with the consequent refusal to blame herself, and her exemption from the narrator's censure place her outside the generic conventions. And yet, if she defies one set of expectations, there is something very familiar about the maid sitting on the hillside under her straw bonnet telling the world about her lost love. We are reminded of the forlorn shepherdess of pastoral poetry, or even the maiden of a folk-song heard singing in the valley below, 'O don't deceive me, O never leave me,/How could you use a poor maiden so?'

In *Englands Helicon,* first published at about the same time as *A Lover's Complaint* was composed, there are several complaints in the voice of a woman.[22] They are, of course much shorter than Shakespeare's poem, but one in particular strikes a familiar chord. *An excellent Pastoral Dittie* (pp. 66-7) begins with a 'nimph' speaking here to another woman, bemoaning her abandoned state and the general miseries of love with its 'guilefull promises'. The narrative frame which gives rise to the woman's lament is clearly analogous to the situation in Shakespeare's poem when the old man comes to listen to the maid in silent sympathy. A lack of particularity is also another characteristic which both poems have in common and which they share with other pastoral lyrics, for unlike lamenting ladies, who are usually identifiable historical persons associated with life at court,[23] nymphs and shepherds either remain anonymous or are given traditional rustic names which distinguish them little as individuals.[24] The maid and nymph are both unnamed country girls telling their troubles to an unnamed listener in an unspecified place. They thus become not so much egregious examples, but representatives of humanity with whom we can sympathise or identify.

Equally cogent in establishing a parallel between Shakespeare's poem and those in *Englands Helicon* are the attitudes and values expressed. In the first place, there is no emphasis on lost chastity and therefore no didactic message with dire consequences for the woman. *An excellent Pastoral Dittie* is about lost love and the 'nimph' is no more ruined than Shakespeare's maid, when in the last lines she says farewell to love and all its pains and even to weeping as she 'can wail no more'. She may lack the fire and energy of the maid's fury, but she does not seem destined for an early death like the lamenting ladies who return from the grave to tell their stories. Instead, the song appears to act as some kind of catharsis and the implication is that life will continue. Secondly, the woman is a self-confessed lover, not the passive recipient of another's desire, as the last but one stanza reveals:

> My life was light, my blood did spirt and
> spring,
> my body quicke, my hart began to leape:
> And every thornie thought did prick and sting,
> the fruite of my desired joyes to reape.

Shakespeare's maid has obviously much more in common with this young woman than with Daniel's reluctant Rosamond.

But, if *A Lover's Complaint* demonstrates similarities with the pastoral lyric tradition, it does not fit wholly into that kind. One important difference is that in pastoral the physical manifestation of love is largely ignored. We might infer from *An excellent Pastorall Dittie* that sexual desire was present in the nymph, for she wanted the 'fruite' of her 'desired joyes', but such joy would seem to be a vision for the future and there is no mention of lost virginity. This is typical of other shepherdesses; in fact, most leave out any reference to their sexuality. In all the poems with a female speaking persona in *Englands Helicon,* not one mentions chastity or improper sexual behaviour. They may moan at the torments of love, like Rosalind (p. 139); or mock their lover, like Cardenia (p. 156); or simply mourn for past love, like Lycoris (p. 163); but they never suggest that they have been taken advantage of sexually.[25] On the other hand, we are in no doubt about the sexual experience of Shakespeare's maid. She may stress the primacy of love, but she has unquestionably been seduced. This lends a more serious and tragic note to the poem, which contrasts with the often trivial and sentimental nature of much pastoral verse apparent even in such title words as 'dittie'.

The other main difference between *A Lover's Complaint* and the poems in *Englands Helicon* is that it is not pastoral in the restricted sense established by Theocritus and Virgil who depicted in idealistic terms the lives of shepherds and shepherdesses. The maid is just a country girl who apparently is not looking after sheep and the young man with his 'silken' locks (87) and his riding skills (106-12) would seem to belong more to the aristocracy than the peasant class. Even the animals that the old man is grazing are cattle (57) and there is not a sheep in sight. In contrast *Englands Helicon* deals almost exclusively with shepherds and shepherdesses (or nymphs, as they are frequently called). So concerned was the editor or publisher to establish the pastoral character of the volume that slight changes were made to a few poems that were not specifically pastoral to bring them into line.[26] The failure of *A Lover's Complaint* to join this popular cult might seem a trifling matter but, in the light of recent scholarship, it gains considerable significance. Louis Montrose offers a nice explanation for the extraordinary popularity of classical pastoral in Elizabethan times by suggesting that its artificial rural life was a way of reaffirming the values of the privileged classes: even to write pastoral poetry was to make a bid for belonging to an inner coterie. This sociopolitical reading of pastoral depends, as Montrose says, upon the activity of shepherding: georgic with its emphasis on husbandry and hard work is excluded; only the depiction of the gentlemanly pursuit of sitting under the trees with time for love and poetry, while ostensibly 'working' at looking after sheep, yields itself to this kind of interpretation.[27] *A Lover's Complaint* clearly resists this kind of reading, just as it resists any political reading based on classical pastoral with the kind of Virgilian echoes that Annabel Patterson convincingly investigates in such poems as the *Shepheardes Calender*.[28] By refusing the form of classical pastoral, *A Lover's Complaint* signals that its interest does *not* lie in sociopolitical matters, that it is *not* the kind of poetry which, in Puttenham's words, sets out

> ... under the vaile of homely persons and in rude speeches to insinuate and glaunce at greater matters, and such as perchance had not bene safe to have beene disclosed in any other sort, which may be perceived by the Eglogues of *Virgill,* in which are treated by figure matters of greater importance then the loves of *Titirus* and *Corydon*.[29]

In other words, Shakespeare is not writing allegorically of rural life but asking us to take seriously the literal surface of the poem; the 'greater matters' he is considering are no less than those of the human heart.

This does not mean, however, that Shakespeare's poem falls into the category of primitive pastoral which Puttenham contrasts with the classical eclogue and which he sees as just reflecting 'the rusticall manners of loves and communication'. For, by drawing on the archetypal characteristics and images associated with pastoral, Shakespeare makes complex use of the rural background to further his ideas on human love and sexuality. On the one hand, the poem sets up the notion of the innocence of the countryside as opposed to a harsher life elswhere: we hear of the old man who in past days had been 'a blusterer that the ruffle knew/Of court, of city' (58-9), but who now is described as 'reverend' or worthy of respect (57), while his courteous behaviour reflects the simple goodness attributed to rural living; in addition, the maid, as we have already seen, reminds us of many an innocent country girl of folk-tale or pastoral. On the other hand, from the very beginning, this idyllic way of life is compromised. In the first stanza, we are offered not only a 'plaintful story' but one that, with more sinister overtones, is told in a double voice' and which shatters the peace of the hillside 'storming' the maid's world 'with sorrow's wind and rain'. Even the maid herself is described ambiguously as 'fickle', a word which in the context can be read as 'agitated' or in a 'changeable' mood, but which inevitably carries connotations of inconstancy.[30] As the story unfolds we learn that the treachery which invades this retired place is not limited to the young man, but involves the maid as well; for, although she is not the one to be unfaithful in love, she rebels against her own better judgement, admitting in the last lines of the poem that she would succumb again and allow the young man to 'yet again betray the fore-betrayed, / And new pervert a reconcilèd maid.' The innocence of the pastoral world has been evoked only to be subverted: nowhere, however humble or retired, can escape the deception that threatens us not just from the outside but from deep within ourselves.

The particular images used to describe the landscape also serve to enhance the sense of the all-pervasiveness of treachery. In the first few lines we hear the story reverberating through the hills as it comes in a 'double voice' from a 'sist'ring vale'; 'double', as we have seen, may appropriately evoke the idea of duplicity but, like 'sist'ring', it also suggests the notion of repetition. Moreover, the story echoes through time as well as space; it is as old as life itself, for the sound comes from a 'concave womb'. The river, too, with its 'weeping margin' (39) seems to mourn for the maid as she throws the remnants of her past life into it. All creation from the beginning of time is implicated in the 'sad-tuned tale'.

Thus, by a complex intermingling of complaint and pastoral lyric, Shakespeare creates a poem that treats without didactic moralising the plight of a betrayed woman and accepts without flinching the existence of female desire; in addition, by rejecting the classical form of pastoral while using its archetypal symbols, he is able to widen the significance of his love story to indicate that all life, however innocent it seems, is subject to betrayal and deception. It is precisely these characteristics that make *A Lover's Complaint* a fitting tail-piece to the sonnets; for, whereas the traditional sonnet sequence and the traditional complaint fit well together—as two sides of the same coin, both concerned with chastity—Shakespeare's sonnets, as we shall see, demand quite a different sort of companion poem.

. . . . .

In some senses, it must be admitted, the narrative poem appears to be just tacked on as an afterthought for, in contrast to Daniel's 1592 volume, there is no reference to the complaint on the main title page of Shakespeare's volume and no reference back to the sonnets within the narrative poem. Certainly any attempt to make the emotional situation of the complaint into an exact parallel or contrast with that in the sonnets breaks down very quickly, in spite of Kerrigan's declaration that 'there are two emotional triangles, and the poet is in both.'[31] The fact is that there is no 'emotional triangle' in the complaint, for the poet/narrator is not emotionally involved. Instead, he is remarkably distanced from the story, merely overhearing what is being narrated for the benefit of the old man (and he too is equally silent and uninvolved). The only emotion is between the victim and her seducer.

However, rejecting a relationship built on plot or bibliographical detail does not mean rejecting any connection between the two parts of the volume; nor does it mean limiting the relationship to the sort of 'echoes and resemblances' which, as Roe reminds us, exist throughout all Shakespeare's work.[32] Instead, although I dispute the particular relationship he proposes, I believe Kerrigan is right in assuming there is likely to be some connection between the sonnets and the complaint. The chief reason given for this is the structure of the 1609 volume, which follows an expected tripartite pattern. So far I have only mentioned the two main parts of Shakespeare's sequence, but in fact it can be divided into three, if we take the last two anacreontic sonnets (153 and 154) as a unit on their own.[33] Seen as a collection of sonnets, followed by anacreontics and then a longer poem, Shakespeare's 1609 volume begins to look remarkably like other contemporary sequences so that, in Kerrigan's words, 'Shakespeare's audience had a framework for reading it'.[34] Such a common external structure does not, of course, prove that there is a significant connection between the parts, but the likelihood of its being a volume that is deliberately, rather than haphazardly, put together is convincing; and, as the parts of other sequences are frequently closely linked, the likelihood of a significant relationship between the parts in Shakespeare's volume cannot be dismissed. The way in which the sonnets and the longer poem are linked in other sequences varies greatly; clearly the relationship of Daniel's *Rosamond* to his *Delia* is entirely different from Spenser's *Epithalamion* to his *Amoretti*. Thus, while largely conforming to contemporary expectations in its structure, the opportunity is there for Shakespeare to experiment further by creating a volume with its own internal patterning.

This patterning is one of parallelism and difference. The parallels are most obvious in the common thematic concerns; for, although the sonnets range widely over many topics, such as the effects of time and the various ways of defeating its ravages, they also foreshadow the attitudes to love which we have already noticed in *A Lover's Complaint*. One of these is the irresistible power of beauty and love. This can be a source of pleasure: numerous sonnets in the first part of the sequence tell of the happiness that comes from even thinking of the beloved friend or looking at his picture (for instance, 29 and 30, 46 and 47), just as the maid revels at first in the beauty of her young man. But in both sonnets and complaint, love becomes tainted with treachery and turns into a source of anguish; and yet its power remains undiminished. Even in her extreme anger and hurt, the maid declares at the end that she would act in the same way again; and in the sonnets we witness a growing awareness of the friend's faults and yet a continual return to declarations of love. The poet fears he must live 'Like a deceivèd husband', still bound to the relationship by the 'sweet love' of the friend's face, suspecting, but never sure of deception (93). In the sonnets to the dark lady, the lover's sense of powerlessness is even more extreme: the poet is 'frantic-mad' and suffering as though in a fever, but he can do nothing to escape his emotional entrapment, continuing to feed 'on that which doth preserve the ill' (147). On another occasion, in an image that is both pathetic and absurd, he is reduced to a crying baby begging for the attention of its mother, who is busy chasing after an escaped chicken (143). All reason and self-respect have deserted him.

It is this sense of degradation with the consequent loss of the poet's true self that seems to be the greatest cause of anguish, at least in the sonnets to the dark lady: 'In things right true my heart and eyes have erred' (137), he exclaims; and although in the following sonnet there is an apparently more light-hearted approach to the question of telling lies, there is a chilling irony in the statement that 'love's best habit is in seeming trust', especially when we have already learnt from past sonnets that a pun on 'lies' (with others as well as the poet) is justified. The full force of the poet's self-disgust, however, is felt in the last two sonnets before the anacreontics. Here love is acknowledged, and there is clearly an element of tenderness in the 'gentle cheater' and the 'sweet self', but the overwhelming tone is one of bitter self-accusation: 'For, thou betraying me, I do betray / My nobler part to my gross body's treason' (151). This bitterness becomes even more intense in 152 when he sees himself as his own greatest betrayer; for, in believing the false lady to be true, he is 'perjured most' and becomes the 'more perjured eye,/To swear against the truth so foul a lie'. This same sense of self-betrayal also permeates *A Lover's Complaint*. From the very beginning the maid was aware of the young man's reputation and knew 'the patterns of his foul beguiling' (170), but her own desires betrayed her as much as her lover's pleadings. As she herself exclaims:

> O appetite, from judgement stand aloof!
> The one a palate hath that needs will taste,
> Though Reason weep, and cry 'It is thy last!
> (166-8)

And, of course, she recognises at the end of the poem that she would still be quite unable to resist any further temptation of a similar kind. The fate of the nun also illustrates how love can make us betray our most determined intentions; for she enters a convent to escape secular love only to leave the religious life for the young man, 'All vows and consecrations giving place' (263).

But what links the sonnets and complaint together even more closely is their extraordinary lack of any focus on chastity. We have already seen how the maid escapes the usual tirades against unchaste behaviour that are heaped on all other fallen lamenting ladies. The sonnets, too, elude generic expectations; for, unlike the usual Petrarchan poet/lover bemoaning the cruel chastity of his lady, Shakespeare's narrator seeks the friendship and love of a male friend and rails against the treachery of his mistress, with whom he already has a sexual relationship. In spite of the homoerotic and deeply emotional tone of the sonnets to or about the young man, any overt sexual behaviour is explicitly denied in Sonnet 20 and nowhere is there even the suggestion of the usual sonnet kiss, so that the issue of chastity does not arise in that relationship. In the last part of the sequence, the dark lady's promiscuity and lack of faithfulness is scorned—she is indeed 'the wide world's common place' (137)—but sexual behaviour in itself is not castigated. Similarly, the relationship between the friend and the lady is bitterly resented, but for reasons of broken trust and the unworthiness of the lady rather than any ideological notion of the need for sexual purity. Just as the poet blames himself for his own treachery in loving what is not worthy, so he berates his friend for allowing himself to be deceived and for acting against his better judgement: 'But yet be blamed, if thou thyself deceivest / By wilful taste of what thyself refusest' (40). Throughout the whole sequence, chastity is not an issue, except as it forms a part of the wider interests of love and loyalty. Instead, the concerns that bind sonnets and complaint together are those of the human heart: what it means to be in love with someone not worthy of that love, to suffer the anguish of betrayal and of a divided self that is powerless to resist.

But as well as these thematic similarities between the sonnets and the complaint, there is one obvious difference, which concerns gender; for the complaint challenges the misogynistic attitude in the sonnets by removing the chief blame for treachery from the female sex to the male. Although the whole question of gender is extremely complex in Shakespeare's sonnet sequence and difficult to untangle (partly because of the androgynous nature of the young man), it is clear that there is a misogynistic streak not only in the poems to the dark lady but also at times in references to the friend. The young man may share some good female qualities—beauty and a 'gentle heart'—but he is also praised for lacking women's deceit; he has an eye 'less false in rolling' (20) and he is no 'painted beauty' (21). When his more sinister characteristics are acknowledged, then he is linked to the archetypal deceptive woman, for his beauty grows like 'Eve's apple' (93). Moreover, in spite of the fact that both friend and lady act treacherously towards the poet, making love behind his back, it is the lady who attracts all the blame. The poet constantly excuses his male friend, seeking for reconciliation and pleading that they 'must not be foes' (40); the friend remains a 'better angel', whereas the lady is the 'worser spirit' (144), and upon her head fall bitter accusations not only for her 'foul faults' (148) but for the poet's own lack of integrity, his 'perjured' self (152). This gender bias is inverted in the complaint, the prime blame being now placed on the man, while the maid, like the poet of the sonnets, becomes the victim. The effect of this is to extend the sense of treachery in love to all humanity, both male and female sharing the tendency to deceive and be deceived.

*A Lover's Complaint,* however, does more than endorse and extend the thematic concerns of love and betrayal in the sonnets; for it presents a very different perspective on these issues. In the sonnets, the single, uninterrupted voice of the poet draws us inexorably into his world so that we share the ecstasies and degradations of his plight; the bizarre triangular situation may be unique, but we identify closely with the states of mind experienced by the speaker. As we have seen, the opposite is true of the complaint, for the situation here is not unique: the maid is the unnamed, archetypal abandoned woman heard so often before in folksong or lyric, lamenting her lost love against a timeless pastoral background—her story is, as we say, as old as the hills; and even within this poem, we soon learn that she is just the most recent in a long line of seductions by the young man. Moreover, although we feel a certain sympathy for the weeping woman, we are encouraged to view her plight objectively by the narrative technique. First there is an elaborate frame to the lament, for the story begins by inviting us to view the maid from the outside through the eyes of the poet (who may or may not be the same as the poet of the sonnets); and then we become doubly distanced from her, for she talks to the old man so that the poet merely overhears the tale; and even then what he hears is further removed because it is an echo of the original, bouncing off a nearby hillside. Later the maid incorporates the voice of her seducer in her narrative so that we never become exclusively drawn into her consciousness. Sorry as we are for her, there is nothing approaching the intense experience of reading the sonnets. In fact, we might find ourselves giving a wry smile at the last stanza with its exclamatory 'O' at the beginning of each line as the maid remembers her lover's irresistible charms, followed by the anti-climactic declaration that she would do it all again.

This change of perspective affects our response not only to the maid's story, but also to the sonnets. After their personal anguish, the relative calm and detached viewpoint of the complaint acts like the conclusion to a play, helping us to come to terms with the previous suffering. The poet's experience in the sonnets is not invalidated, but it is put in a wider context: love and the betrayal of love come to be seen as a part of a never-ending cycle which we have to learn to live with.

In one sense the 1609 volume can be read as a bleak indictment of humanity—the irredeemable propensity for treachery and weakness in both male and female, with the implication in *A Lover's Complaint* that this is a universal phenomenon to be constantly repeated. The maid would fall again, and there is nothing for the old man to say, for if she cannot learn from experience, she would not benefit from advice. In another sense, however, the peculiar qualities of Shakespeare's complaint give some hope or at least relief from this gloomy picture. The very lack of closure or moral judgement suggests a tolerance of human weakness that is rare in itself but all the more remarkable when the weakness in question is female unchastity, a sin calculated to arouse the fiercest condemnation in any literature of the period, but particularly in the woman's complaint genre.[35] In place of the expected didactic moralising, we have a kindly humanity expressed in the courtesy of the old man as he sits down at a 'comely distance' (65) to listen in silent sympathy to the maid's story. He himself has been acquainted with the 'ruffle' of life (58) and now in the 'charity of age' he offers to try to help her 'suffering ecstasy' (69-70). Such kindness is a small glimmer of light in a benighted world and darkness soon overwhelms it as the maid reveals the treachery of her seducer and her own inability to withstand him. Nevertheless, the old man's courtesy at the beginning of the poem, together with the absence of any harsh judgement on the maid at the end, is a plea, however muted, for understanding and love in its widest sense. If erotic love so frequently fails us, charity remains. From this vantage-point, we can look back at the sonnets and see not only their anguish but the possibility of some amelioration. *A Lover's Complaint,* as well as adding to the sense of treachery in the world, indicates that not all human existence is irrevocably bleak.

## Notes

[1] It is now generally accepted that *A Lover's Complaint* is by Shakespeare and that, although the exact date of composition is not known, it was written around the turn of the century. For a summary of the linguistic scholarship dealing with authenticity and dating, see *William Shakespeare: The Sonnets and A Lover's Complaint,* edited by John Kerrigan (Harmondsworth: Penguin Books, 1986), pp. 389-90. For a defence of Thorpe as a reliable publisher, see Katherine Duncan-

Jones, 'Was the 1609 *Shake-speares Sonnets* Really Unauthorised?', *Review of English Studies,* New Series, 34 (May 1983), pp. 151-71.

² See, for instance, Heather Dubrow, *Genre,* The Critical Idiom (London: Methuen, 1982); and Alastair Fowler, *Kinds of Literature: An Introduction to the Theory of Genres and Modes* (Cambridge, Mass.: Harvard University Press, 1982).

³ Sidney divides literature into many 'kindes', but acknowledges that they may be mixed, 'for, if severed they be good, the conjunction cannot be hurtfull'. See Sir Philip Sidney, 'An Apologie for Poetrie', in *Elizabethan Critical Essays,* edited with an Introduction by G. Gregory Smith, vol. 1 (London: Oxford University Press, 1904), pp. 150-207 (p. 175); and in Book 1 of 'The Arte of English Poesie', George Puttenham devotes Chapters xi-xxx to the various poetic 'formes' (*Elizabethan Critical Essays,* Vol. 11, pp. 3-193).

⁴ Barbara K. Lewalski, editor, *Renaissance Genres: Essays on Theory, History and Interpretation* (Cambridge, Mass.: Harvard University Press, 1986), p. 7.

⁵ See Rosalie Colie, *The Resources of Kind: Genre-Theory in the Renaissance,* edited by Barbara K. Lewalski (Berkeley: University of California Press, 1973), pp. 68-75.

⁶ Heather Dubrow, *Genres,* p.15.

⁷ Heather Dubrow, *Captive Victors: Shakespeare's Narrative Poems and Sonnets* (Ithaca and London: Cornell University Press, 1987), p. 78.

⁸ Heather Dubrow, *Captive Victors,* pp. 143 and 146.

⁹ See, for instance, my paper, 'Paradoxes of Possession in Shakespeare's *Lucrece*', *Parergon,* New Series, 13: 1 (July 1995), pp. 53-68, in which I argue for a much more sympathetic treatment of Lucrece by the narrator and for a more confused concept of chastity within the mind of the narrator, not just within the mind of Lucrece.

¹⁰ See Kerrigan, p. 13; and John Roe, editor, *Shakespeare: The Poems,* The New Cambridge Shakespeare (Cambridge: Cambridge University Press, 1992), pp. 62-5. In Roe's edition *A Lover's Complaint* is published alongside Shakespeare's other poems but not with the sonnets. While Roe questions the likelihood of any significant relationship between sonnets and complaint, he admits the case is 'far from being closed' (p. 64).

¹¹ A. C. Partridge, *A Substantive Grammar of Shakespeare's Nondramatic Texts* (Charlottesville: The University Press of Virginia, 1976), categorises the poem as a 'belated experiment in Spenserian pastoral' (p. 176).

While this comes close to my emphasis on the pastoral element in the poem, it differs from my perspective in that it looks to the more specific literary influence of Spenser, rather than to the genre of pastoral.

¹² In *Shore's Wife,* the woman prospers for some time after her loss of chastity. She becomes the power behind the throne, and we are told a great deal about her just use of authority (ll. 197-210). Her sufferings only begin after the death of King Edward and are not seen as a direct result of her unchastity. The reference here is from *The Mirror for Magistrates,* edited by Lily B. Campbell (New York: Barnes and Noble, 1960).

¹³ All quotations from and references to Daniel's *Rosamond* are from *Samuel Daniel: Poems and A Defence of Ryme,* edited by Arthur Colby Sprague (London: Routledge and Kegan Paul, 1930). References to and quotations from Drayton's *Matilda* are from *The Works of Michael Drayton,* edited by J. William Hebel, 5 vols (Oxford: Basil Blackwell, 1931-3), Vol. I.

¹⁴ Hallett Smith, *Elizabethan Poetry* (Cambridge, Mass.: Harvard University Press, 1952), p. 106.

¹⁵ The quotations from *Elstred* are taken from *The Complete Works of Thomas Lodge,* revised edition, 4 vols (New York: Russell and Russell, 1963), Vol. II.

¹⁶ *The Poems of Richard Barnfield,* edited by The Rev. Montague Summers, limited edition (London: The Fortune Press, 1936), p. 84.

¹⁷ For the text of this poem, see *The Queen Declined: An Interpretation of 'Willobie His Avisa',* edited by B. N. De Luna (Oxford: Clarendon Press, 1970).

¹⁸ Quotations from and references to Shakespeare's 1609 volume, both sonnets and complaint, are from the edition by John Kerrigan (see note 1 above).

¹⁹ See Kerrigan's note to line 30 (p. 399) for these two interpretations.

²⁰ See Kerrigan's note to line 82 (p. 405).

²¹ See Roe's note to the title of the poem, in which he states that 'in the sixteenth century, 'lover', in the erotic sense, more often than not denoted a woman' (p. 264). I argue that the term is unexpected here in that it is collocated with 'complaint', most complaint ladies being solely *victims* of love, rather than lovers.

²² All quotations from and references to this collection are to *Englands Helicon,* edited by Hugh MacDonald (London: Routledge and Kegan Paul, 1949).

²³ *Willobie His Avisa* (1594) is one of the first complaints to have a countrywoman as the heroine. It illus

trates, as Hallet Smith points out, 'the process of democratization of the complaint form' (p. 121-2). Shakespeare's poem can be seen as part of this process, although the effect of Avisa's humble birth is quite different from that of Shakespeare's maid; for Avisa's poor status is used to contrast with the high-born treachery of her would-be seducers to show that virtue is more likely to exist amongst the unpretentious, whereas Shakespeare's point is the ubiquity of treachery.

[24] Peter V. Marinelli, *Pastoral* (London: Methuen, 1971) draws attention to the universal quality inherent in pre-Romantic pastoral, in which 'the shepherd remains first and foremost an emblem of humanity, a general rather than a specific type, and his afflictions and joys are universal' (p. 6).

[25] It may be noted that, even in the poems with a male speaking persona, chastity is seldom mentioned. The poem *The Sheepheard* Delicius *his Dittie* (p. 125) stands out as an exception with its emphasis on the 'cruell chastitie' of the beloved. Hallett Smith notes the tendency in English pastoral literature 'to subdue the sexual element and make the love scenes romantic and innocent' (p. 16).

[26] See Hallett Smith, p. 25.

[27] Louis Adrian Montrose. 'Of Gentlemen and Shepherds: The Politics of Elizabethan Pastoral Form,' *ELH*, 50 (1983), pp. 415-59, especially pp. 415-33.

[28] Annabel Patterson, *Pastoral and Ideology: Virgil to Valéry* (Oxford: Clarendon Press, 1988). For a discussion of the *Shepheardes Calender,* see pp. 118-31.

[29] *Elizabethan Critical Essays,* Vol. II, p. 40.

[30] For a discussion of the meanings of the word 'fickle' and the possibility of it being a mistranscription of 'fitful', see Roe, p. 264. I see no reason to doubt the authenticity of 'fickle' as its ambiguity continues the moral doubt already established by the use of the word 'double'.

[31] Kerrigan, p. 17.

[32] Roe, p. 63.

[33] There are good reasons for considering the last two sonnets (153 and 154) as a separate unit, for they show a change in tone and subject matter, turning from the bitter personal experience of the preceding sonnets to the mythic antics of Cupid. The poet is still present in the 'I' of both 153 and 154, but the emotion is given a general significance: all love now is seen as past cure, unable to be cooled by water. Thus, thematically, these anacreontic sonnets look back to the previous sonnets and forward to *A Lover's Complaint,* providing a kind of bridge between the two but maintaining a distinct character of their own.

[34] For a discussion of various tripartite volumes containing sonnets, lyrics and a long poem, see Kerrigan, pp. 13-14.

[35] Joan Rees, 'Sidney and *A Lover's Complaint',* *Review of English Studies,* New Series, 42 (May 1991), pp. 157-67, has drawn attention to the moral ambiguities of Shakespeare's complaint compared to the greater moral certainties in Sidney's story of Dido in the *New Arcadia* and in Daniel's *Rosamond*. She argues that, in spite of Sidney's 'capacity to enter sympathetically into female experience', both he and Daniel 'give a defined end to their stories and clarify the moral issues. Shakespeare does neither' (p. 166).

---

Source: "The Generic Complexities of A Lover's Complaint and its Relationship to the Sonnets in Shakespeare's 1609 Volume," in *AUMLA*, No. 89, May, 1998, pp. 79-97.

# The Magic of Shakespeare's Sonnets

## Malabika Sarkar, *Jadavpur University*

All readers of Renaissance poetry are unanimous in regarding the sonnets of Shakespeare as constituting the greatest love poetry in the language. Elegant, moving tributes to Shakespeare's handling of the themes of love and time, clever and often sensational investigations of the possible identities of the friend and the dark lady, scholarly and intelligent debates regarding the dates of composition and possible sequence of the sonnets fill many library shelves. This paper seeks not to offer any fresh insights on dating or identities but to draw attention to one dimension of the predominant themes of love and time in the sonnets that, to my knowledge, has never been examined. It is my submission that one of the most fascinating areas of Renaissance thought, occult philosophy or magic, provides a context within which the sonnets need to be read and that such a reading would simplify and organize our perception of the activity of meaning within the sonnet sequence by providing us with a graph to help us map the implications of thoughts and images in the sonnets. Simultaneously, it would add new dimensions of meaning to familiar passages and enhance our awareness of the richness and complexity of the sonnets.

Renaissance magic[1] was made up of various strands, including cabalism and hermeticism. The great flowering of occult philosophy in the Italian Renaissance was the result of the work of Marsilio Ficino and Pico della Mirandola, later to be systematized and tabulated by Henry Cornelius Agrippa.[2] Many of these ideas were imported into Britain by Giordano Bruno in the 1580s and were assimilated and popularized by England's own magus John Dee, who may have been the model for Shakespeare's Prospero.[3] There were two characteristics fundamental to the various kinds of magic: first, a belief in the correspondence between the different cosmic levels of the natural, the celestial, and the supercelestial, and secondly, a belief in the possibility of manipulating one of the higher worlds in order to bring down influences or enlightenment to the lower. Magic or occult philosophy, therefore, was a philosophy of power.

Although Shakespeare's interest in magic and occult philosophy is generally admitted, with the exception of Frances Yates too often has this been discussed simply with reference to the ghosts, fairies, and witches that people Shakespeare's plays. Yet Shakespeare's interest in magic went far deeper than this and in play after play he explored the question of the relation of power to magic. Nowhere is the power of magic so apparent as in *A Midsummer Night's Dream* and *The Tempest:* both are plays which, for many, end with uneasy questions about the effects of magic. In the graph of Shakespeare's changing perceptions of the power of magic, an early instance might be *Love's Labour's Lost,* with its possible sceptical reference to occult philosophy as 'the school of night'.[4] But *A Midsummer Night's Dream,* possibly written around 1595-6, and thus probably immediately after the sonnets, marks a new belief in the efficacy of magic. The play's ending may seem unsatisfactory, with Demetrius in love with Helena only as a result of the external application of the juice of the magical flower in his eyes. Yet Shakespeare probably intended to indicate that magic has transformed the very essence of Demetrius's character. In sharp contrast, in *The Tempest* Shakespeare rejects magic, with Prospero renouncing magic at the end, precisely because he feels that magic can affect appearances but cannot substantially alter the essence of things.[5] His magic is quite unable to bring about any change in the character of his brother Antonio. It is this debate about the power of magic in Shakespeare that provides a frame of reference for the sonnets, and the polarities and obsessions of the sonnets become clear once they are placed in the context of Shakespeare's overall interest in magic.

Any enquiry into the presence of magic in the sonnets must begin with an examination of the relationship between love and magic in the Renaissance. This is indeed a vast subject but it is essential to consider briefly some of its main features. In the Platonic philosophy of love, the tremendous emotional power of Eros is manifested through the ability of Eros to be a link between the existence and the essence of beings. Even profane (i.e. psycho-physical) love is a step towards intellectual contemplation. Love, in a sense, involves the same hierarchized ascent that is fundamental to magic. Indeed, the concept of 'spiritús' that is central to Ficino's occult philosophy is also a major factor in the philosophy of love since love, as in Ficino's *Commentary on Plato's Symposium,*[6] involves a radiation of energy through the eyes which transforms the object and, interacting with the 'spiritus', creates an image or impression of the beloved on the mind of the lover. That is why—in the context of the notion of love being both mortal (i.e. changeable) and immortal (i.e. never extinguished)—Ficino brings together love and memory in an equation that is echoed in a number of Shakespeare sonnets:

> Whenever we meet that person whom we formerly loved, we are shaken, our hearts jump or quiver, or our livers melt and our eyes tremble, and our faces

turn many colours (like the rainbow when the sun shines opposite the misty air). For his presence suggests to the eyes of the soul in his presence, the form lying dormant in the mind, as though rousing the fire slumbering under the ashes by blowing on it.[7]

Repeatedly, in Ficino, love is presented as magic or enchantment.

> In love there is all the power of enchantment. The work of enchantment is the attraction of one thing by another because of a certain similarity of their nature.[8]

Love is an enchanter and 'the work of love is effected by bewitchment, magic spells and potions'.

Giordano Bruno extended the Ficinian concept of love as magic from its essentially philosophical and physiological bias to a more practical psychological theory of magic. In *Eros and Magic in the Renaissance*,[9] Ioan P. Couliano has analysed Bruno's *De vinculis in genere, 'Of Enchantment in General'*, as an important and entire thesis on erotic magic which carries to its logical conclusion the Ficinian position on the subject showing erotic magic to be a method that the accomplished magus can use to manipulate not only another individual but entire masses.

In spite of this obvious line of development, there is one very major difference between Ficino and Bruno—one which has a direct bearing on the treatment of love in Shakespeare's sonnets. In the *Eroici Furori* Bruno distinguishes between the heroic Eros whose object is God and the natural Eros whose object is a woman. In a bitter attack on Petrarch, whom he calls 'this vernacular poet who sighed for a girl of Valchiusa . . . lacking the intelligence to apply himself to better things', he exclaims

> Here we find, written down, bound in books, displayed to the eyes, intoned to the ears, a noise, a bawling, a buzzing of charades, of tales, of puns, insinuations, epistles, sonnets, epigrams, books, prolix documents, violent sweats, lives wasted away with gnashings of teeth to deafen the stars, lamentations resounding in the caverns of hell, woes that stun the souls of the living, sighs to cause the merciful gods to faint, all that for the sake of these eyes, these ears, this blush, . . . this sun in eclipse, this crazy person, this slut . . . which, by means of a superficial appearance, a shadow, a phantasm, a dream, a Circe-like charm in the service of procreation, deceives us by taking the form of beauty.[10]

In Bruno, this undeserving woman is replaced by a divine being, goddess-like, identified with Diana and often interpreted as Queen Elizabeth herself. But, in general terms, this anti-Petrarchism and denigration of woman is strikingly reminiscent of Shakespeare's dark lady sonnets.

Shakespeare's sonnets are predominantly poems about power—the power of love and the power of time. Reading them as love poems, one is struck by their passionate intensity—the searing experience of guilt, revulsion, shame, self-analysis, and despair, combined with desire, pride, joy, comfort, and triumph—that make them such compelling reading. Perhaps the one feeling that is wholly absent in the sonnets is any sense of peace. The speaker of the sonnets is on a continuous 'high', whether the feeling be one of frustration and despair or of buoyancy and triumph. In Shakespeare's relationship with both the friend and the dark lady there is a continuous sense of tension and urgency generated by his perception of the power of time in the sonnets to the young friend and his consciousness of the power of a unique experience of love in the dark lady sonnets.

Shakespeare's sonnets are addressed to two persons: a young man who is fair and socially and morally superior, and a woman who is dark, dishonest, and downright damnable. Both these persons exercise an emotional power over him. The essence of these two relationships is summed up in Sonnet CXLIV ('Two loves I have, of comfort and despair'[11]) which, with its paradigm of angel and devil, invites us to relate it to Renaissance occult philosophy, a philosophy of power. At first sight, the basic situation appears to be that of everyman with two spirits, a good angel and a devil, fighting for his soul. On closer scrutiny the position turns out to be more complex. True, the 'man right fair' is a 'better angel', a 'saint', and the 'woman coloured ill' 'the worser spirit', a 'female evil', the man's purity contrasting with the woman's 'foul pride'. The difference from the everyman situation is that the two spirits are not fighting for possession of the poet's soul. They are, in fact, supremely uninterested in him and are engaged in a relationship of their own which causes him obvious anxiety.

This situation is not unique to this sonnet, for what is evident in the entire sonnet sequence is the poet's vulnerability and his sense of bondage to both the young man and the dark lady. They are like spirits who exercise their power and full control over him. But, given this obvious common denominator, there is a fundamental difference in Shakespeare's relationship to the two characters. If the nature of the two relationships is best explained with reference to the framework of magic, then the relationship with the dark lady is a relationship of enchantment and enchainment of a soul-destroying intensity that is a form of black magic and the relationship with the friend expectedly demonstrates signs of white magic. This is not an oversimplification, as a closer examination reveals.

Sonnets CXXVII to CLII are generally regarded as the sonnets to the dark lady. These sonnets present her as 'black as hell' (CXLVII), with black eyes and brow (CXXXII), and 'black wires' (CXXX) in place of hair on her head. Yet this dark colouring is insignificant in comparison with the blackness within her, for in nothing is she as black as in her deeds (CXXXI). Even her playing the virginals has a diabolical effect as it makes 'dead wood more blest than living lips' (CXXVIII). Her heart is full of hatred and lies, and yet the torment of it is that both the friend and the poet are prisoners of this dark lady (CXXXIII). If the bond between this woman and the poet is love, then this is a kind of love whose natural comparisons are with fever (CXLVII), plague (CXXXVII, CXLI), and madness (CXL).

The sense of despair and bondage that characterizes this relationship results in one of the most violent sonnets of the entire sonnet sequence, Sonnet CXXIX, 'The expense of spirit in a waste of shame'. Its images of war, murder, savagery, cruelty, hunting, and baiting, all culminate in the hopelessness of the concluding lines

> All this the world well knows; yet none knows well
> To shun the heaven that leads men to this hell.

The mesmerizing, enslaving, corrupting power of the dark lady is indeed acknowledged in sonnet after sonnet. One such example is Sonnet CXLVII ('My love is as a fever, longing still'), which ends a contemplation of its own sickness and absence of sanity with the admission

> For I have sworn thee fair, and thought thee bright
> Who art as black as hell, as dark as night.

Shakespeare's dark lady appears to be the archetypal 'belle dame sans merci', the literary precursor of Keat's 'Belle Dame' and Coleridge's Geraldine, with power to captivate and to corrupt.

This throws further light on Sonnets CXXXV and CXXXVI, with their play on 'will'. The erotic implications of 'will' in these sonnets have often been pointed out and are undeniably there. In fact their presence is quite consistent with the sonnets' involvement with magic, as sexuality was a common adjunct of Renaissance magic. But the play on 'will', the subjugation or absorption of the poet's will—in its straightforward sense—by the dark lady, also implies the domination of any power of volition of the poet's by the powerful evil spirit who now rules over him.

Power, indeed, is a concept that is recurrent in the dark lady sonnets, culminating in Sonnet CL:

> O! from what power hast thou this powerful might
> With insufficiency my heart to sway?
> To make me give the lie to my true sight
> And swear that brightness doth not grace the day?
> Whence hast thou this becoming of things ill,
> That in the very refuse of thy deeds
> There is such strength and warrantise of skill
> That in my mind thy worst all best exceeds?

The sonnets explore the concept of magic as power and the dark lady sonnets present a Brunian woman who, in a typical instance of magic gone awry, assumes total control over the poet rather than appearing as a spirit over whom the poet-magus can exercise control and give commands.

That there is nothing trivial or frivolous about such a situation is clear from the suffering, despair, and violence expressed in the sonnets together with an admission of obsession. Repeatedly this love is seen as disfiguring and defiling. At one level we are back at the medieval world of demons and witches, and the dark lady is the natural companion of the witches of *Macbeth* or of Sycorax in *The Tempest*.

In the sonnets addressed to the friend the situation is very different. The young man is not only fair without but also inwardly fair. As sonnet LIV records:

> O! how much more doth beauty beauteous seem
> By that sweet ornament that truth doth give:
> The rose looks fair, but fairer we it deem
> For that sweet odour which doth in it live.

The sonnets to the friend begin with an impassioned plea to the young man to marry and replicate his beauty. Later, Shakespeare takes it upon himself to preserve that beauty in his sonnets. Conscious of the destructiveness of time, he declares

> And all in war with Time for love of you,
> As he takes from you I engraft you new.

There are distinct metaphors that Shakespeare uses in his quest for immortalization. These range from the metaphor of grafting to distilling essences to the creation of a memorial in verse. Like the Pyramids or the Taj Mahal, the verbal construct, Shakespeare's sonnets, will immortalize his friend. This theme of immortalization has, however, two curious facets. First, the eternity of the sonnets is itself earth-bound and time-bound

> So long as men can breathe or eyes can see,
> So long lives this, and this gives life to thee.

In these entirely secular poems there is no consciousness of the eternity of heaven as, for instance, in Donne's 'The Anniversary' which speaks of 'this or a love increased there above'. Secondly, repeatedly Shakespeare refers to the creation of a memory image of his friend in language that is strongly suggestive of another aspect of Renaissance magic, the art of memory.

The art of memory was a technique for exploiting the imagistic nature of that faculty by associating ideas to images systematically ordered for ease of recall. This was originally a mnemotechnical classical art referred to by Cicero and Quintilian which consisted of the technique whereby Roman orators associated different images with different parts of a building and stored these associations in the memory. They would be thus accessible to recall as soon as the eye passed over these places. This art was recommended in the Middle Ages by Albertus Magnus and Thomas Aquinas. This mnemotechnical system was incorporated in the Renaissance into its occult philosophy. Renaissance Neoplatonism, with its Hermetic core, transformed the art of memory into a branch of magic. Frances Yates, in her book *The Art of Memory*,[12] has discussed in detail the memory theatre of Giulio Camillo and the much later memory theatre of Robert Fludd, and has suggested connections with the Globe Theatre. But there is also another aspect of the art of memory that Yates has discussed—memory as a magical system of reform.

Central to the Renaissance art of memory was its creation of ideal figures and images which, when impressed upon the memory, would reform, renovate, inspire, and instil good influences into the whole being of the person receiving these impressions. Such was the influence of Ficino's *figura mundi,* or image of the world, Giulio Camillo's memory theatre, or the magic circles of Bruno's memory treatises. In *De vita coelitus comparanda,* Ficino speaks of a figure of the world which could be a painting on the ceiling of one's bedroom, or a pendent or other piece of jewellery to be worn, which had places associated with good magical or astral influences and which, when memorized, would renovate the individual, making him a better adjusted person able to receive good influences and protect him from harmful ones. This magical art of memory provides a frame of reference for an understanding of the full implications of the sonnets immortalizing the young man.

While the dark lady sonnets explore the darker side of magic as power, the sonnets to the young man examine the power of magical memory. In its handling of the theme of immortalization, the sequence presents remarkable instances of the creation of memory images. Such figures or constructs are distinct from a dwelling on remembrance of things past, as in Sonnet XXX ('When to the sessions of sweet silent thought'), where memory is random and unorganized while the creation of memory images involves a deliberate act of judicious selection and a careful imprinting of image. One example of this is Sonnet XXIV:

> Mine hath play'd the painter and hath stell'd
> Thy beauty's form in table of my heart;
> My body is the frame wherein 'tis held,
> And perspective it is best painter's art—
> For through the painter must you see his skill
> To find where your true image pictur'd lies,
> Which in my bosom's shop is hanging still,
> That hath his windows glazed with mine eyes:
> Now see what good turns eyes for eyes have done:
> Mine eyes have drawn thy shape, and thine for me
> Are windows to my breast, where-through the sun
> Delights to peep, to gaze therein on thee:
> Yet eyes this cunning want to grace their art,
> They draw but what they see, know not the heart.

Not only the depiction of the friend's 'beauty's form' on the tablet of his heart, the recreation of the 'true image' of his friend, but, even more important, the ability of that image to draw down the good influence of the sun indicates a clear relationship with Renaissance magical memory. The final couplet's distinction between an actual painting drawn by a painter and this memory image in the heart completes a conceit that gradually evolves through the sonnets which ultimately depicts the text itself as such a tablet or ornament that serves as a memory image.

> Not marble, nor the gilded monuments
> Of princes shall outlive this powerful rime;
> But you shall shine more bright in these contents . . .
> Nor Mars his sword nor war's quick fire shall burn
> The living record of your memory.
>
> (LV)

Image, form, shape—these are recurrent terms in the sonnets to the friend in their repeated attempts to anchor the young man's worth in the mind of the poet. The text is the externalization of that mental image. In Sonnet CXXII he writes

> Thy gift, thy tables, are within my brain
> Full character'd with lasting memory,
> Which shall above that idle rank remain,
> Beyond all date even to eternity:
> Or at the least so long as brain and heart
> Have faculty by nature to subsist;
> Till each to raz'd oblivion yield his part
> Of thee, thy record never can be miss'd.
> That poor retention could not so much hold,

> Nor need I tallies thy dear love to score;
> Therefore to give them from me was I bold,
> To trust those tables that receive thee more:
> To keep an adjunct to remember thee
> Were to import forgetfulness in me.

The young man's memory image has been imprinted on the poet's mind, and the depth and corresponding value of this impression is much greater than any external record can be.

It is remarkable with what consistency the sonnet sequence presents two concurrent sets of metaphors. In one, the friend's immortality is ensured through a memory image inscribed or painted in the poet's heart. In the other, the friend's image is preserved in the sonnet (LX, LXIII, LXV), where, like a jewel, it shines bright. There is a striking resemblance in this to Ficino's magical memory images—a painting on the ceiling or a pendent or jewel. For the poet, the friend's memory image, like a Ficinian painting or a Brunian seal, has been absorbed and impressed on his heart. Renovated by the effect of such absorption, he has created for the world at large and for all lovers in particular a jewel in black ink, the sonnet sequence.

Taken as a whole, the sequence of Shakespeare's sonnets can be seen to explore two vital areas of magic, erotic magic and the art of memory. Shakespeare's sonnets are unique in having two different persons holding centre stage, a man and a woman, although the sequence is dedicated to one 'onlie begetter'. It has of course been traditional to regard woman as nature and man as culture, and this could to an extent explain Shakespeare's attitude to his two loves. But in an age which saw the humble adoration of poets to an assortment of Stellas, Delias, even Ideas, let alone the full flowering of the cult of the Queen, the extent of Shakespeare's anti-Petrarchist attitude to woman in the dark lady sonnets can be explained only with reference to a Brunian view of erotic magic. Since, although recognized as inferior, she still remains powerful and irresistible, she is seen also as a demon, a devil. She needs to be exorcized and it is precisely that awareness that fills the tortured sonnets that follow Sonnet CXLIV.

The friend, on the other hand, as recognizably handsome, good, and virtuous, is presented in configurations strongly reminiscent of good white magic. The repeated solar imagery in the sonnets to the friend, the constant interplay on the 'eye of heaven', the sun, and the young man's eyes[13]—such strategies are strongly reminiscent of Ficinian magic. That this is so is clear from Sonnet XIV, which declares

> But from thine eyes my knowledge I derive,
> And, constant stars, in them I read such art
> As truth and beauty shall together thrive,
> If from thy self to store thou would'st convert;

In the sonnets magic does not merely provide metaphors and conceits. It dominates the three central characters—the poet, the young man, and the dark lady—and conditions their relationships. It is also true to say, I think, that the intertexture of magic thrives on the anonymity of the young man and the dark lady, making the sonnets explorations of the Renaissance mind. Fixing of identities would have led to debate and provoked interest of a more specifically biographical nature. The anonymity of the young man and the dark lady, on the other hand, permits a more open approach and sustains the philosophical dimensions of these poems.

Finally, the magic of the sonnets is ultimately related to Shakespeare's sustained exploration of magic in his plays, including *Love's Labour's Lost, A Midsummer Night's Dream, Hamlet, The Tempest,* and *A Winter's Tale.* Shakespeare's view of magic in these plays spans the polarities of magic as an evil corrupting power, and magic as good and renovative. The known dichotomies of the two romances *The Tempest* and *A Winter's Tale* include the dichotomy of the two kinds of magic—*A Winter's Tale* ends with an assertion of the possibilities of good magic while Shakespeare's questioning of the power of magic in *The Tempest* includes not only Sycorax but also Prospero, who ultimately renounces magic. These deeply troubling polarities of magic provide a frame of reference for Shakespeare's exploration of magic in relation to the themes of love and time in his sonnets.

*Notes*

[1] There is by now fairly extensive scholarly work on Renaissance magic. Particular reference should be made, however, to the many books by Frances A. Yates, especially *Giordano Bruno and the Hermetic Tradition* (London, 1964) and *The Occult Philosophy in the Elizabethan Age* (London, 1979).

[2] For a general survey of the subject in relation to Shakespeare see John S. Mebane, *Renaissance Magic and the Return of the Golden Age: The Occult Tradition and Marlowe, Jonson and Shakespeare* (Lincoln and London, 1989).

[3] See Frances A. Yates, *Shakespeare's Last Plays: A New Approach* (London, 1975).

[4] For detailed discussions of this aspect of the play and its background see M. C. Bradbrook, *The School of Night: A Study in the Literary Relationships of Sir Walter Raleigh* (Cambridge, 1936) and Frances A. Yates, *A Study of 'Love's Labour's Lost'* (Cambridge, 1936).

[5] On this aspect of magic, see Paul Stevens, 'Magic structures: *Comus* and the illusions of fancy', *Milton Quarterly.* 17/3 (1983), 84-90.

[6] See *Commentary of Marsilio Ficino on the Symposium of Plato on the Subject of Love,* trans. Sears Reynolds Jayne (Columbia, 1944).

[7] *Ibid.* p. 201.

[8] *Ibid.* p. 199.

[9] Ioan P. Couliano, *Eros and Magic in the Renaissance* (Chicago, 1987).

[10] *Ibid.* p. 68.

[11] All quotations from Shakespeare's sonnets are from *Shakespeare, Complete Works,* ed. W. J. Craig (London, 1905).

[12] Frances A. Yates, *The Art of Memory* (London, 1966).

[13] See, for example, Sonnets VII, XVIII, XXIV, XXXIII.

---

Source: "The Magic of Shakespeare's Sonnets," in *Renaissance Studies,* Vol. 12, No. 2, June, 1998, pp. 251-60.

# What May Words Do? The Performative of Praise in Shakespeare's Sonnets

## David Schalkwyk, *University of Cape Town*

In a previous essay on Shakespeare's sonnets and their relation to performance, I have suggested that it may not be especially fruitful to approach these sonnets in particular, and early modern Petrarchan poetry in general, by assuming that their linguistic aims are primarily epistemological.[1] I argue in that essay that commentators' mistaken assumptions about what the language of the sonnets is doing lead them to overlook the ways in which a sonnet's conditions of address are embodied in particular social and political contexts of performance. To pursue the fact of embodiment as the condition of a sonnet's address, I claim,

> is to problematize the relationship between the signified and the referent—that is, between the embodied addressee and addressor on the one hand and the actual circumstances of the address, including a material context of uneven social relations, on the other—and to leaven the concept of subjectivity with the public reality of an audience.[2]

In the present essay I wish to take this argument further, this time by shifting attention from the generally theatrical notion of performance to the more philosophically technical concept of the *performative* as a particular use of language not confined to any genre. I shall argue that Shakespeare's sonnets use language as neither epistemology nor description but as a form of social action: in a series of performatives in which the power relations between "you" and "I" are negotiated.

The concept of the performative comes from J. L. Austin, who made explicit in philosophical terms what users of language have always known intuitively: that a form which at first glance looks like a description may in fact be doing something quite different.[3] When Astrophil cries out "What may words say, or what may words not say, / Where truth itself must speak like flattery?"[4] his invocation of the limits of words overlooks their power to transform, rather than merely to reflect, a situation. Better to have asked what words may *do,* for then Astrophil might have negotiated more successfully, as Shakespeare does, the dilemma between truth and flattery.

Many of Shakespeare's sonnets to the young man attempt to negotiate the unequal political and social relationship between actor-poet and aristocratic patron via performative uses of language. The actor-poet seeks, sometimes in vain, not so much to persuade careless nobility as to bring about something *in* the saying of it. Thus I hope to demonstrate that in the sonnets negotiations between power and weakness, authority and subordination, are bound up with performative rather than descriptive uses of language, and that such performatives are the means by which the actor-poet negotiates a politics of self-authorization. The illocutionary force of the performative constitutes a major part of that "dynamic, unending slippage between power and powerlessness and between one of their principle sources, success and failure," which Heather Dubrow has characterized as being typically Petrarchan.[5] Even if Shakespeare was not acquainted with Austin, his poetic practice reveals a subtle understanding of the ways in which the necessary logic of the illocutionary act, as opposed to the merely contingent force of a perlocutionary or rhetorical utterance, may transform the relationship between addressor and addressee. In Shakespeare's sonnets language is mobilized not merely to say that things are so descriptively, or to move an audience through rhetorical skill merely *by* saying something, but to transform a situation, to make it so of conventional necessity *in* saying something.[6]

My analysis of Shakespeare's illocutionary logic is divided into three sections, each of which explores an aspect of the performative in Shakespeare's sonnets: 1) the ways in which the actor-poet attempts to negate the rhetoric of his rival through what I call the quasi-performative; 2) the illocutionary logic of tautology in the poems; and 3) the use of performative language to avoid the question of truthfulness altogether through the powers of illocutionary transformation. I shall follow the method of my 1994 *SQ* essay by reading the poetry in conjunction with similar moments or uses in the drama, particularly *Antony and Cleopatra.* Through its overt staging of the performative—its *performance* of the performative—the play renders more explicit the nature of speech acts in the poems. Austin reminds us that such speech acts are apt to disguise their actual nature by masquerading in the guise of constative or descriptive *forms.*[7] Such formal masquerading has led to their actual force being overlooked in the first place. I shall thus begin with a well-known scene from *Antony and Cleopatra,* before going on to discuss the sonnets concerned with the rival poet, in order to show how a concern with theatricality and performativity in the play might illuminate the antitheatrical performatives of Sonnet 23.

I

Recall the moment, in Act 5 of *Antony and Cleopatra*, when both the historical queen of Egypt and the boy-actor representing her appear as a duck/rabbit figure glimpsed for a moment, impossibly, in *both* aspects at the same time:

> CLEOPATRA Nay, 'tis most certain, Iras. Saucy lictors
> Will catch at us like strumpets, and scald rhymers
> Ballad us out o'tune. The quick comedians
> Extemporally will stage us and present
> Our Alexandrian revels; Antony
> Shall be brought drunken forth, and I shall see
> Some squeaking Cleopatra boy my greatness
> I' the posture of a whore.
>
> IRAS    O the good gods!
>
> CLEOPATRA Nay, that's certain.
>
> (5.2.214-22)[8]

The "impossible" perception of both aspects, queen and actor, at the same time is, in contrast to two-dimensional figures like the duck-rabbit drawing, made possible by the bifold nature of theatrical performance. Here embodied action and spoken verse provide a double perspective, by which Gorgon and Mars can be presented simultaneously.[9] In a moment of almost vertiginous self-reflexivity, we observe a figure, representing a historical character, entertaining the horrible thought of being the spectator of the unflattering representation of herself. The horror lies both in its inevitability ("Nay, 'tis certain") and in its reflection of the powerlessness of the represented subject before the authority of representation and performance embodied in the transformative shape of the actor. This force is particularly well conveyed by the poetic transformation of the noun *boy* into a verb. But the self-reflexivity that enables us to entertain at once the double aspect of Cleopatra as boy-actor and historical figure, as "queen" *and* "whore," is itself the re-mark of its own powerful effect. This capacity of representation to reflect upon both itself and the conditions of its own possibility, thereby displaying its limitations and precariousness, is precisely the sign of its massive authority. The scene calls attention to what Robert Weimann terms the "bifold authority" of theatrical performance: the authority of the actor to represent, transform, and limit the authority of a class that was the patron of and the most influential and powerful audience of the Jacobean theater.[10]

Shakespeare's Sonnet 23 is equally concerned with the anxiety of representation through performance, although it expresses the other side of the "bifold authority" exemplified in Cleopatra's speech. It presents the perspective of an actor overwhelmed by the feeling of impotent vulnerability before an audience made powerful both by its social and political position and by its *formal* capacity merely as audience to take offense:

> As an unperfect actor on the stage,
> Who with his fear is put besides his part,
> Or some fierce thing replete with too much rage,
> Whose strength's abundance weakens his own heart;
> So I for fear of trust forget to say
> The perfect ceremony of love's rite,
> And in mine own love's strength seem to decay,
> O'ercharged with burthen of mine own love's might.
> O let my books be then the eloquence
> And dumb presagers of my speaking breast,
> Who plead for love and look for recompense
> More than that tongue that more hath more expressed.
>  O learn to read what silent love hath writ.
>  To hear with eyes belongs to love's fine writ.[11]

Sharing the double aspect of Cleopatra's speech, this sonnet displays the imbrication of theatrical and political differences of situation and power. It is one of the key poems in the subsequence addressed to the young man, since it conveys more powerfully than any other the inarticulateness of the actor before an aristocratic audience and views the silence of that audience as a source of power rather than as a sign of repression.[12]

The political and cultural inequality of the relationship between addressor and addressee is reflected in the asymmetrical distribution of silence and speech across actor and audience. The stage-fright expressed in the opening line arises from the poet's acute sense of vulnerability and inadequacy, both as "unperfect actor" and on account of the socially inappropriate strength of his passion for that distant patron. Whereas the silence of stage fright signifies the actor-poet's social inadequacy, the absence of the patron's voice from the poem mutely expresses the patron's overwhelming authority. The sonnet owes its existence to the fact that, as a poet, the actor, however "unperfect," can make that silence speak through the written word. By urging the patron to withdraw to the more private space of the page, and by enacting such a withdrawal through the poem itself, the actor-poet hopes to create a place in which the "Injurious distance" (44.2), imposed by both his inappropriate theatricality and his status in the theater as social institution, may be diminished.[13] Eloquence is, unusually, here the reflection of impotence rather than a sign of accomplishment, and the poem itself is a paradoxically eloquent plea to be allowed to leave out difference (105.8) by moving into a private sphere with the beloved as poet rather than as tongue-tied actor. Only via the eloquent silence of writing, which matches the powerfully significant silence of the patron, will the actor-poet be able to assume a less abject position. It is in order to achieve this transformation that the speaker (who in the world of the poem does not [yet] abandon the exposure of the actor) resorts rather desperately to a series of performatives: "O let my books.... O learn to read." Through these illocutionary acts, the beloved is urged to negate the differences in rank and love—differences historically represented by the public distance between stage and spectator—in the supposedly socially undifferentiated exchange of written texts.

Sonnet 23 is only a moment in a sequence of negotiations and renegotiations between actor-poet and aristocratic youth, and the failure of the negotiations is made clear by the number of sonnets that continue to be informed by the actor-poet's acute awareness of his status as performer. He finally embraces this condition at the end of the narrative—"my nature is subdued / To what it works in, like the dyer's hand" (111.6-7)—but not before he has used the illocutionary force of his verse to transform the conventions of praise. In other sonnets Shakespeare's actor-poet does attempt to resolve differences of social rank and patronage via conventional arguments comparing the plain truth of his own style with the false persuasive force of ornament used by other poets. But here the actor-poet's appeals to what Joel Fineman calls a Cratylitic "poetics of a unified and unifying eye"[14] are a cover for a much more forceful, performative dimension. In the last analysis such appeals do not seek an epistemological correspondence among sight, word, and object but rather negotiate a series of pragmatically determined social and erotic consummations through the force of illocutionary or quasi-illocutionary speech acts.

The claim in Sonnet 23 that the poet's silent appeal via the ear can say "more than that tongue that more hath more expressed" is probably an early reference to the rivalry with the unknown poet, which is dealt with explicitly in the sonnets following 76. If so, it shows that one cannot simply avoid the "bifold authority" of performance and representation by abandoning the eloquence of the theater for the unstaged, private muteness of the book. The performative power of verse can be imitated, even superseded, and the private space that binds poet and reader invaded by others more authoritative, more favored, or more persuasive. It is thus the dynamic power of the rival poet's writing—"the proud full said of his great verse, / Bound of the prize of all too precious you" (86.1-2)—that the actor-poet fears in the relationship between his rival and his patron. This relationship is itself the silent expression of a "silent love," feared not for its power to mirror its addressee but rather to make its way into his heart.

Like Puttenham, Shakespeare deals with the problem of similitude in an unmetaphysical, flexibly strategic way, as different forms of social action impress themselves upon him in his drive to achieve a kind of self-authorization through verse.[15] Take Sonnet 21:

> So is it not with me as with that muse,
> Stirred by a painted beauty to his verse,
> Who heav'n itself for ornament doth use,
> And every fair with his fair doth rehearse—
> Making a couplement of proud compare
> With sun and moon, with earth and sea's rich gems,
> With April's first-born flow'rs, and all things rare
> That heaven's air in this huge rondure hems.
> O let me true in love but truly write,
> And then believe me, my love is as fair
> As any mother's child, though not so bright
> As those gold candles fixed in heaven's air.
>   Let them say more that like of hearsay well;
>   I will not praise that purpose not to sell.

Ostensibly an attack on mere ornament, the poem is in fact an excuse for a kind of inaction. Its persuasive force lies precisely in its argument that both "painted beauty" and painted verse must be false because of their persuasiveness. Ostensibly, too, a rejection of the "couplement of proud compare" that marks both conventional love and conventional verse, it pushes its own rehearsal of such a comparison as far as it will go without actually becoming the thing it apparently rejects. Furthermore, through its own "couplement of proud compare" between the lavishness of others and its own truth, the sonnet attempts to engineer the belief upon which it depends and towards which it moves. The point is not simply that the poem itself indulges in the very ornament that it sets out to denigrate but that such denigration is a form of deliberate action. The poem attempts to change the unequal power relations that subtend it, conditioning both the writing and its perceived truth: "O let me true in love but truly write, / And then believe me, my love is as fair / As any mother's child." The young man is enjoined to *allow* the actor-poet to write in a particular style (in which its self-proclaimed lack of rhetoricity constitutes its most powerful rhetoric) as the condition of allowing himself to be persuaded both of his own exemplary human beauty and of the fairness of the poet's love.

Sonnet 21 is, however, more than an appeal to be allowed to write without the ornament of similitude (a possibility that the very writing of the poem contradicts); it is a *quasi-performative,* by which the actor-poet strives to create the conditions that will ensure belief as the result of an illocutionary rather than a merely perlocutionary act. I say "quasi-performative" because the appeal rests on no clear-cut conventional form such as promising, warning, crowning, or declaring war. At the same time, the poet does not wish to leave the effect of his utterance to the caprices of a merely rhetorical, notoriously unpredictable force. The appeal "O let me true in love but truly write" is less a political request to be allowed to do something than a conditional one to make belief its necessary (and not contingent) consequence: "if true in love I could manage to write truly (i.e., without ornament), then you would *have* to believe as a matter of logical necessity."

Many of the sonnets to the young man, I am arguing, attempt to negotiate the unequal political and social relationship between actor-poet and aristocratic patron by means of such quasi-performatives. A poem seeks, not always successfully, to bring about something *in* the saying of it rather than (as in rhetoric) *by* the saying of it. This use of quasi-performatives may account for the sonnets that have often been viewed as unsatisfactory because the couplet, in a strikingly artificial way, runs counter to the thrust of the first twelve lines, often attenuating blame by means of acceptance or banishing suspicion with what appears to be groundless affirmation of the beloved's truth. Such turns may not be mirrors of the "speaker's vain attempts to resolve the conflicts in his own mind" but rather attempts, from a position of social and erotic vulnerability, to transform the beloved into truth through the self-proclaiming power of the quasi-performative.[16]

If we take Sonnet 84 as an illustration of the argument of this subsequence regarding the "true-telling" of "true plain words" (82.12), we can see how strongly such "true-telling" is nonetheless conceived as a strategy of rhetorical accountancy, of borrowing and lending "glory," of reckoning the profit and loss of admiration and fame:[17]

> Who is it that says most, which can say more
> Than this rich praise, that you alone are you—
> In whose confine immurèd is the store
> Which should example where your equal grew?
> Lean penury within that pen doth dwell,
> That to his subject lends not some small glory,
> But he that writes of you, if he can tell
> That you are you, so dignifies his story.
> Let him but copy what in you is writ,
> Not making worse what nature made so clear,
> And such a counterpart shall fame his wit,
> Making his style admired everywhere.
>   You to your beauteous blessings add a curse,
>   Being fond on praise, which makes your praises worse.

The sonnet argues against the notion that, since the patron may "ever live young" (19.4) in the poet's "gentle verse," the "monument" (81.9) that such poetry creates is worthy of the recompense that comes of patronage: in other words, that poetry indeed offers a world-without-end bargain. But if this is true of the actor-poet's sonnets, then it must also be true of sonnets written by others. In contrast to claims that it is only through the power of his poetry that Time shall "never cut from memory / My sweet love's beauty" (63.11-12), this sonnet tries to diminish the "store" contained within the poet's pen by suggesting that the exchange operates in the opposite direction. That the expenditure is in fact the patron's is stated most clearly in Sonnet 79, lines 7-14:

> Yet what of thee thy poet doth invent
> He robs thee of and pays it thee again.
> He lends thee virtue, and he stole that word
> From thy behaviour; beauty doth he give
> And found it in thy cheek; he can afford
> No praise to thee but what in thee doth live.
>   Then thank him not for that which he doth say,
>   Since what he owes thee thou thyself dost pay.

The use of the third person and the past tense directs attention away from this present writing toward another text, already written, and so suppresses any question regarding its own *present* theft. The tautological formulation *you alone are you* is the culmination of a complex series of social actions that, despite being conceived in economic terms, rather seek to obliterate free exchange with the settled values of feudal relations. The mere "copy" that Sonnet 84 prescribes as the proper business of the poetry of praise, by a curious inversion of the usual economy governing the relationship between poet and patron, finally serves to praise and glorify the poet himself: it is the patron who expends himself by glorifying the wit and style of a poet, here, crucially, the actor-poet's poetic, social, and sexual competitor. Within the context of such materially located rivalry, the sophistry of this argument should be apparent, warning us against taking at face value the poet's appeal to his own epistemological purity or rigor. His "rich praise," both epideictically and logically empty, is no less an exercise of social force than the good words that others write.

In the early sonnets at least, the actor-poet, overwhelmed and fearful of the public space that imposes differences of rank, blood, and social power, hopes to persuade the young man to retreat to a private world in which the speech acts of promising faithfulness, declaring love, and commanding trust will not be informed and distorted by the exigencies of material difference and unequal power. The paradox—that only when perfectly silent can the actor-poet's breast speak truly—is understandable given the uncertainties that accompany public declarations of this kind. As we have seen, however, the retreat from stage to page implored in Sonnet 23 is not good enough, since even the page is invaded by the words of others, competing for favor. The actor-poet makes the painful, Derridean discovery that language itself—in whatever form, including silence—is always already marked by the material space and spacing of the stage, by the always-present possibility of intrusion and citation.[18]

Austin, however, reminds us that praise, like greeting, performatively constitutes a reciprocal relationship which obtains no matter what the intentions of either party may be. In other words, one can refuse the basic consensus that underlies even our disagreements by refusing to greet someone; one can also refuse to accept praise. Accepting such praise, however, constitutes an ethical obligation that is part of the performative situation. Such an obligation is not as clearly marked as it would be in the case of a promise or a bet, but this makes it no less binding than the implicit obligations undertaken in those cases. To accept praise from someone is implicitly also to allow them to judge, criticize, or condemn. And it is from this conventionally incurred obligation that the peculiarly ethical power of Shakespeare's sonnets derives, despite the social weakness of the actor-poet. Like a promise, such an obligation lies, publicly, "in eyes of men" (16.12), not in the eyes of the one who promises.[19] The readers of the sonnets have the authority to weigh up the obligations that they enact: it is not in the power of either the maker of a promise or the recipient of praise to declare a promise null and void. This asymmetry is the logical condition of promising as performative.

Shakespeare's sonnets thus hold an ethical power purely by virtue of the performative situation of praise, even when the poet declares himself most abjectly slavelike in his relation to the more powerful beloved. It is in relation to such implied obligation that the actor-poet seeks, through the institutionalized, conventional performative or quasi-performative, to create what he calls a "marriage of true minds" (116.1). And as Lars Engle argues so convincingly, such a marriage is shown by the sonnets to be part of the context-bound pragmatics of social existence and change.[20]

The right to blame, which is implied in the illocutionary logic of praise, may be what imbues the poetry with a gathering self-confidence as the subsequence progresses. This culminates in the poet's recourse to tautology, which he had up to then reserved for the ineffable subject of praise. The denigration, via the somewhat obsequious argument that "you are you," of rival attempts to ornament the beloved, is turned in the final stages of the subsequence into an almost magisterial assertion of self via the same tautology, now converted into the divine: "I am that I am" (121.9). If the declaration could have seemed a kind of description (the ultimate, unornamented, description of praise), the first-person form can only be a self-authorizing elevation of oneself above the vagaries of descriptive praise or blame. This is a pure performative: a self-proclaimed declaration of independence very like that declared by Antony and Cleopatra when, "[c]ontemning Rome" (3.6.1), they crown themselves in the Alexandrian marketplace.[21] It is certainly quite different from the protestations of abject dependence and servitude that we encounter earlier in the subsequence (Sonnets 26, 29, 49, and 57).

The early poems bewail not only the beloved's untrustworthiness and social and erotic distance, but also the actor-poet's powerlessness to invoke the conventional, public authority of performatives. He can neither forge the kind of public performative space that marks the Alexandrian self-coronation nor invoke the public and conventional obligations incurred by promises of love or trust because his "own love's strength" puts him in "fear of trust" (23.7,5). He thus resorts, on the one hand, to contradictory claims about the power of "these black lines" to make the beloved still "live" (63.13-14) and, on the other, to the argument that only he can recognize the extent to which his poetry is in fact empowered by the young man's incomparable beauty: "There lives more life in one of your fair eyes / Than both your poets can in praise devise" (83.13-14).

We should now be able to see that the performative thrust of Sonnet 84 ("Who is it that says most which can say more / Than this rich praise, that you alone are you") is directed not toward the accurate description of a unique external object but rather toward the discovery and enactment of a rhetoric that will render an appropriate account of the *social* rather than the *epistemological* relationship between the praiser and the praised. In 84, the quasi-performative noted above in Sonnet 21 is presented generally in the third person, where its conditional logic is shown more clearly: "But he that writes of you, if he can tell / That you are you, so dignifies his story. / Let him but copy what in you is writ, / . . . And such a counterpart shall fame his wit, / Making his style admired everywhere." Description, here in the form of the tautology "you are you," masquerades as the epitome of truthfulness. It is in fact a double performative: it performs both a sophisticated form of definition and a remarkably audacious self-authorization operating under the guise of humility. It marks a decisive move away from the epistemological argument that continues to inform the other sonnets.[22]

II

When Shakespeare's actor-poet claims that tautology is the highest form of praise, this is a performative utterance which does not describe the young man but rather instantiates him as the paradigm from which beauty gets its name. As such a paradigm, the young man is beyond description. He is the standard from which words such as *fair, kind,* and *true* derive their meanings. It is logically and socially inappropriate to apply those concepts *to* him, since they are derived *from* him. We can see the logic of this argument more clearly by looking at an example from Wittgenstein: to say that the standard meter is a meter long is not to describe it but rather to institute it as a rule for the concept "one meter."[23] Since the standard meter *is* the standard, it is inappropriate to describe it as being one meter long. Such a proposition is either true or false. But if the standard meter is the length that settles just what a meter *is,* then it lies beyond truth or falsity. As the rule by which other lengths are to be judged, it cannot itself be said to be one meter long, for what standard should we use to establish this? To describe the standard as a meter would be as tautologically empty as the statement "you alone are you." One can say that the standard meter is the measure by which we decide what a meter is, but one cannot say that it is one meter long.

Shakespeare's declaration that "you alone are you" is thus declaring: "you are the standard by which we measure what beauty is, by which beauty gets its name." The argument against the rival poet claims that if the young man is not an object which may be described (truly or falsely) as beautiful but in fact the standard by which the concepts of fairness, truth, and beauty are established, then it makes no sense to *describe* him as such. All one can do is proclaim him, over and over again, as the *paradigmatic* instance of beauty: "I never saw that you did painting need, / And therefore to your fair no painting set" (83.1-2).

Shakespeare's sonnets show that the ornamental descriptions of other poets are not only logically vacuous or redundant; they also denigrate the paradigm as paradigm, reducing it from timeless rule to just another object among others. To praise the young man by a standard of beauty taken from some other paradigm or standard of reference is either to empty the words of all meaning (like using a tailor's tape-measure to judge the standard meter) or, by subordinating the young man to a higher standard, to diminish his status, to insult him.

This argument is remarkable for its capacity to deprecate the "ornament" of normal forms of praise on logical rather than rhetorical grounds. Such forms of praise can be dismissed for committing what Gilbert Ryle calls a "category-mistake," which has both social and logical aspects:[24] rival poets make the logical mistake of assuming that the young man is merely one more object among others to be praised (it matters not that they regard him as the best). In doing so, they commit a social and political error of denigrating him. It thus becomes clear why Shakespeare's verse should be "so barren of new pride, / So far from variation or quick change" (76.1-2). It deals in definitions rather than descriptions, in the reiterated instantiation of concepts—"fair, kind, and true" (105.9)—with reference to a paradigm case that by definition is "Still constant in a wondrous excellence" (105.6), rather than in the syntactical elaborations of mere description. Such barrenness is what is best about it: it marks its true understanding of its object of praise.

Sonnet 79 exemplifies the logical economy by which the meanings of the words used in descriptions of the young man are neither bestowed on him nor used in propositions that could be true or false, but are derived from the young man himself:

> Yet what of thee thy poet doth invent
> He robs thee of and pays it thee again.
> He lends thee virtue, and he stole that word
> From thy behaviour; beauty doth he give
> And found it in thy cheek. . . .

Although the young man's admirer writes as if his beloved were intrinsically constituted as a paradigm by the authoring and authorizing power of Nature (see 20), it is the writer's own aesthetic, rhetorical, and political project to authorize the power of his own verse over its subject: first, by elevating him to this position; then, by proclaiming himself to be the only one to have recognized this incomparability. We should note the sleight of hand here, since the self-authorizing performative of the first is performed under the guise of the humble descriptiveness of the second. It is the young man who must be persuaded that he is indeed the universal standard of beauty; once dazzled by his own status, he will fail to notice that it is the actor-poet's verse, not Nature, that institutionalizes him, retrospectively, as such: "And him as for a map doth nature store, / To show false art what beauty was of yore" (68.13-14). Replace "nature" with "Will," and you have the properly secularized agent of such conceptual mapping. Thus the poet attains a self-authorizing independence in the final sonnets of the subsequence, achieved by distancing himself both from the theatrical community in which his "dyer's hand" is "subdued" and the courtly society of informers and hack poets that threatens him.

The logic of paradigmatic instantiation signalled by tautology does not make the object the meaning of the word in a Cratylitic sense but rather allows objects in the world to be appropriated in different ways as rules for the use of words. In doing so, it closes the gap between words and the world and, most important for this discussion, avoids Sidney's dilemma mentioned in the opening above. But the appropriation of objects as paradigmatic instances is a performative speech act with far-reaching social implications, since it raises the question of authorization: who has the right, or the power, to decide the standards by which words get their meanings? After witnessing the power of the self-authorizing performative in the poems that deal with court rivalry, we therefore need to explore the actor-poet's authoritative relationship to a broader community when the object of his affections is neither male nor fair but female and black. If Shakespeare's actor-poet can declare his independence of "suborned informer[s]" (125.13) and "frailer spies" (121.7) by magisterially invoking the divine tautology "I am that I am" in his own person, the later subsequence shows a persona much less assured about the power of the performative to forge a "world elsewhere" (*Coriolanus*, 3.3.139).

The opening poem of the subsequence, Sonnet 127, begins with a confident elaboration of the argument sketched above regarding "beauty's name" and its exemplification by some chosen standard, a confidence that the rest of the sequence almost immediately belies. The opening lines—"In the old age black was not counted fair, / Or if it were it bore not beauty's name"—are a variation on the theme that the meaning of words is open to change as and when new paradigms are authorized. In days gone by, the poem suggests, even if beauty had included blackness, blackness would certainly not have counted as a paradigm. No one would have dreamed of teaching a novice Petrarchan poet the meaning of the word *beauty* by pointing to a dark woman. But Will reminds us that all this has changed. Since "each hand hath put on nature's pow'r, / Fairing the foul with Art's false borrowed face / *Sweet beauty hath no name*" (ll. 5-7). In other words, the concept of beauty has been emptied of content, since there are no longer indubitable paradigm cases by which to exemplify it and its relation to truth. Such apparent paradigms of fairness as there are are untrustworthy, for one can no longer tell whether they have "profaned" (l. 8) or not. To exemplify the concept of beauty via a woman who appears to be fair would nowadays be like trying to settle the length of a meter with a piece of elastic.

The crux of this poem's subtle argument lies in the logical operative "therefore," which marks the transition from octave to sestet. For, taken as the reason why he has chosen a dark mistress, the word confirms the poet's self-authorizing power to revive the name of beauty by instantiating a new paradigm, the now-exemplary "Dark Lady of the Sonnets." In this subtly self-aggrandizing poem, the poet no longer opposes language users who persist in their own perverse usage by following their own paradigmatic samples. Rather (so he implies) he effects a sea-change in the very concept through his choice of mistress: "Yet so they mourn becoming of their woe, / That every tongue says beauty should look so" (ll. 13-14).

The agreement conveyed by "every tongue" is unusual in a sequence that is frequently at odds with the world at large and with itself. This agreement does not last long, however. Within a sonnet or two, the poet is not only at odds with common opinion but is also unwilling to oppose it in any public way: "Yet in good faith some say that thee behold / Thy face hath not the pow'r to make love groan; / To say they err I dare not be so bold, / Although I swear it to myself alone" (131.5-8). And as the subsequence progresses, the poet internalizes the difference between his unauthorized judgment of the mistress and a world that now stands "hugely politic" (124.11) against the madness of his private discourse. This difference is powerfully registered by the device, extensively analyzed in *Shakespeare's Perjured Eye,* of the contest between his heart and eyes, indeed, all his senses, which now draw back in horrified disgust from a perversely persistent perversity: "My thoughts and my discourse as madmen's are, / At random from the truth vainly expressed; / For I have sworn thee fair, and thought thee bright, / Who art as black as hell, as dark as night" (147.11-14).

"At random from the truth vainly expressed": this is, of course, one aspect of "lust in action" (129.2). But it could also be applied to one of the most intriguing moments in *Antony and Cleopatra,* when, in a surprising Petrarchan moment, the defeated queen subjects Antony to a lover's extravagant blazon:

> CLEOPATRA His face was as the heavens, and therein stuck
> A sun and moon, which kept their course and lighted
> The little O, the earth.
> DOLABELLA            Most sovereign creature—
> CLEOPATRA His legs bestrid the ocean; his reared arm
> Crested the world; his voice was propertied
> As all the tunèd spheres, and that to friends;
> But when he meant to quail and shake the orb,
> He was as rattling thunder. For his bounty,
> There was no winter in 't; an autumn 'twas
> That grew the more by reaping. His delights
> Were dolphinlike; they showed his back above
> The element they lived in. In his livery
> Walked crowns and crownets; realms and islands were
> As plates dropped from his pocket.
> (5.2.78-91)

Dolabella cries out, "Cleopatra—" surprised and horrified at what he perceives to be the madness, the eccentricity and excessiveness of her "thoughts and . . . discourse." The felicity of such discourse depends on the willingness of the audience to concur in both its truth and force. Dispassionately rejecting the falsity of Cleopatra's praise but also horrified by its exorbitant power, Dolabella responds with a pitying but firm "no" to her question: "Think you there was, or might be such a man / As this I dreamt of?" (ll. 92-93). As many critics have pointed out, the question, with its subjunctive modification, is concerned as much with the powers of poetry as with the truth of history. It returns us to, or rather, anticipates, Cleopatra's later concern with the power of fiction to represent and transform her own historically specific figure into the stuff either of myth or political propaganda. Reading Cleopatra's praise of Antony in the way that the actor-poet reads the "full proud sail" of rival poet's verse, Dolabella flatly denies the veracity of her dream. Being false to its object, a product of projection rather than truthful description, it is "At random from the truth" and because it is so, it is "vainly expressed."[25]

But as so often happens in this play, with its Chinese-box effect of audiences nested within wider audiences, we are free to answer Cleopatra's question otherwise, just as we were able, in the opening scene, to accept Philo's invitation to "behold and see" by judging his judgment:

> Look, where they come.
> Take but good note, and you shall see in him
> The triple pillar of the world transformed
> Into a strumpet's fool. Behold and see.
> (1.1.10-13)

What we, watching Philo and Demetrius watching Antony and Cleopatra, behold is a remarkable scene which gives full rein to the performative as a way of attempting to transform, successfully or not, a situation through the power of merely saying so. The scene is too long and complex to analyze in full here. We should merely note the way in which Antony instantiates himself and Cleopatra as a paradigm of the "nobleness of life" itself: "The nobleness of life / Is to do thus; when such a mutual pair / And such a twain can do 't, in which I bind, / On pain of punishment, the world to weet / We stand up peerless" (ll. 38-42). But it is one thing to make such a declaration in the private world of a lyric poem—as Donne, for example does—quite another to stage it publicly in one's capacity as the "triple pillar of the world." Antony's theatrical declaration betrays precisely the difficulty of such self-fashioning and self-authorizing public show: if Antony and Cleopatra can turn their sensuality into a paradigm of nobleness only by binding "the world" to accept it "On pain of punishment," if they must resort to physical force in order to effect it, then it fails as a performative. On the other hand, as I have argued elsewhere, if our own involvement in what we have communally instituted as the "literary" stems at least in part from its capacity to show us the instantiations and relationships between the concepts of our language, it also opens the space for the constitution, however brief and unstable, of an imaginary consensus whereby paradigms may be shifted, concepts renegotiated.[26] If it is Cleopatra rather than Philo who publicly refuses Antony's extravagant gesture, she does so in a powerfully ambiguous phrase: "Excellent falsehood!" (l. 42). This is to part-reject, part-deny, part-admire a claim that, if it is ostensibly "at random from the truth" and "vainly expressed," may indeed, from the imaginary perspective of the theater audience, fall beyond the limits of truth altogether. As many critics have noted, an ambivalence about truth and lying, deceit and trust, marks Antony and Cleopatra's relationship throughout the play, and it is never finally settled one way or the other, just as it is never settled whether Antony is a "strumpet's fool" or a Colossus whose "legs bestrid the ocean."

I do not mean by this that we are each left to decide for ourselves, for that would mean that we would finally settle on a truth, one way or another. Rather, I want to suggest that, just as performatives are logically independent of truth or falsity—of correspondence with an entity that already exists in the world—but rather transform the world or bring about a situation merely in their saying, *Antony and Cleopatra* and the sonnets both represent and perform this transformative power of language in the imaginary space of theatrical and poetic production. If Cleopatra fears this process in her reflection upon what she will become at the hands of "quick comedians" in Rome, she fully indulges in it in her "dream" of Antony—a dream, we must recall, that is not simply or merely a fiction:

> But if there be nor ever were one such,
> It's past the size of dreaming. Nature wants stuff
> To vie strange forms with fancy; yet t'
>   imagine
> An Antony were nature's piece 'gainst fancy,
> Condemning shadows quite.
> (5.2.95-99)

Such an Antony is not a product of fancy, because, like the young man of the sonnets, he is "nature's piece 'gainst fancy." On the other hand, he is not a mere empirical object of description. Rather, to "*imagine* / An Antony" is to see both how paltry are mere fictions, and how dull mere men. Cleopatra speaks here of *an* Antony: not merely the man called Antony but the historical figure turned into generic type or paradigm, just as the poet of the sonnets turns its young man into "beauty's name."

### III

*Antony and Cleopatra* is imbued with a philosophy of language and the imaginary that transcends classical oppositions between fact and fiction. Lying between truth and fancy, history and fiction—"dolphinlike" as Antony's desires—the figure that Cleopatra imagines is the object of a performative use of language that is neither true nor false but, rather, enacts or brings into being the figure of which it speaks. To read Cleopatra's utterance as the object of a truth-claim is, like Dolabella, to deny that it does or ever could exist. But to see it for what it is—a different language-game, as Wittgenstein would say, and one that could be said to constitute epideixis as such—is to find "new heaven, new earth" (1.1.17).

This is not a transcendentalizing reading of either the sonnets or *Antony and Cleopatra*. Such a language-game is still very much of this earth, even if it extends it beyond the limits dreamed of by positivist philosophy. We can see its mundane operation in one final moment of Act 5 when, re-enacting the self-authorizing moment in the Alexandrian marketplace when she appeared "in th' habiliments of the goddess Isis" (3.6.17), Cleopatra proclaims herself not whore or mistress but Antony's wife: "Husband, I come!" (5.2.287). Again, this is not a constative or descriptive act but a performative one. Is Cleopatra's urgent vocative—which names Antony as he is called by Egypt—not a condensed form of the marriage ceremony: a unilateral declarative that transforms in the saying her relationship with Antony and thereby changes our judgment of it? Furthermore, it is neither an "Excellent falsehood" nor a gesture of pure transcendence. It constitutes an acceptance that the title involves publicly accessible standards of behavior which are an independent measure of her condition rather than Antony's self-authorized show of pride in 1.2. "Now to that name my courage prove my title!" (5.2.288): Cleopatra's death is a kind of performative by which she lives up to that transforming "title" and, at the same time, effects a transformation of its values.

If through the performative power of her suicide Cleopatra does not transcend the mundane world but rather subjects herself to its transformative institutions, of which the concepts "husband" and "wife" are a signal part, she nonetheless transforms the ideological thrust of the patriarchal institution in which they have their life. No theoretician of speech acts would accept Cleopatra's vocative as an instance of the felicitous performance of the marriage ceremony. But the play invites us to do so: it asks us to accept the authority of a figure who is "No more but e'en a woman, and commanded / By such poor passion as the maid that milks" (4.15.78-79) and who, in the absence of consenting husband or presiding officer, claims for herself the right not only to chose but also to *make* her own husband.[27] Shakespeare's play thus effects a transformation exactly the reverse of that which Cleopatra fears at the hands of comedians, imbuing her through its own power with the capacity to transfigure herself from whore to queen, self-fashioned/self-fashioning, not abjectly made, wife.

The power of certain speech acts in *Antony and Cleopatra*, either to transcend questions of truth and falsity or to transform a situation, should enable us to see more clearly how poems such as Sonnet 138 enact their own kinds of transformative force. In his reading of this sonnet, Edward Snow both draws parallels with *Antony and Cleopatra* and also sees in it "a moment of repose" and a "subtle realignment of values."[28] Against this, Nona Feinberg proposes a feminist argument that such repose is achieved through the silencing of the woman, so that in the end "the sonnet celebrates the speaker's verbal power at the cost of the loss of the Dark Lady's voice."[29]

In "'She never told her love'" I suggest that the silencing or scattering of the beloved is complicated, if not contradicted, when the blazon is embodied in the theater, especially when silence makes itself heard through the irreducible presence of a mute body on the stage. It could be argued that the sonnet is the poetic form least able to accommodate another's voice in anything but the most cursory or indirect way.[30] But this is to ignore a possibility that the theater makes palpable, namely an original context of address and reception in which the response of the beloved, though not recorded in the poem itself, would have been not only possible but inevitable. It is, we recall, precisely to avoid the unwelcome consequences and circumstances of such an address that the actor-poet urges his patron audience to "hear with eyes" in Sonnet 23. The presence, and intrinsic power, of an audience to shape the poet's own voice and stance should not be overlooked in a discussion of whether Sonnet 138 achieves a tone of repose, smugness, or grim seriousness.

Few critics who accept the notion that Petrarchan sonnets in general necessarily exclude, silence, or disembody the beloved-as-woman comment on the silence—almost always icily aloof, to be sure—of the young man. With this in mind it might be useful to compare Sonnet 93 with the much more famous 138, since they share distinctive subject matter, even if they diverge in their final treatment of a common predicament:[31]

> So shall I live, supposing thou art true,
> Like a deceivèd husband—so love's face
> May still seem love to me, though altered new:
> Thy looks with me, thy heart in other place.
> For there can live no hatred in thine eye,
> Therefore in that I cannot know thy change.
> In many's looks, the false heart's history
> Is writ in moods and frowns and wrinkles strange,
> But heav'n in thy creation did decree,
> That in thy face sweet love should ever dwell,
> Whate'er thy thoughts or thy heart's workings be,
> Thy looks should nothing thence but sweetness tell.

> How like Eve's apple doth thy beauty grow,
> If thy sweet virtue answer not thy show.

We should note first that while Sonnet 138 is addressed to an audience from which the woman is implicitly excluded, Sonnet 93 has the young man himself as its direct and primary audience. One would expect this to make it more intimate, achieving the "mutual render, only me for thee" (125.12) that Sonnets 23 and 125 attempt to effect. But this is not so: 93 conveys as much alienation and uncertainty, distance and obeisance, as we find in the more overt poems of estrangement. The proximity of 93 to the much better known 94 allows us to recognize, in the beloved whose face shows neither "thy thoughts" nor "thy heart's workings," the enigmatic and discomfiting "lords and owners of their faces" of Sonnet 94 (l. 7). Furthermore, the silence of the beloved is here and in 94—indeed, throughout the subsequence—a source of the young man's strength: the aloof, judgmental, and mute power of the spectator.

It is across this distance, then, of both social power and inscrutable enigma that the poet declares his decision to do what Sonnet 138 announces in such a different mode: to "live, supposing thou art true, / Like a deceivèd husband." This in fact paraphrases the famous opening line of 138. Sonnet 138 lacks the conventional flattery of lines like "For there can live no hatred in thine eye" and "But heav'n in thy creation did decree, / That in thy face sweet love should ever dwell." But such flattery is quickly undercut in 93 by the implication that this apparently gracious gift of nature may be both what "puts fair truth upon so foul a face" (137.12) by hiding the "false heart's history" and a sign of promiscuity, since the beloved is said to be unable or unwilling to "frown" on anyone. That this inscrutably beautiful beloved is given no opportunity to speak, even indirectly, is indicative of an almost total asymmetry of power which works in favor of the beloved rather than the poet. The decision by the poet to "live, supposing thou art true" is thus made entirely unilaterally in an exasperated and fearful attempt to adapt to an intolerable situation, in which all "mutual render" is excluded *a priori* both by the beloved's implacable silence and the double-edged argument that his heart may be in another place precisely because "there can live no hatred in [his] eye."

Directed as a monologue to the beloved, Sonnet 93 engages less in a description than in what I have called a quasi-performative: the attempt to effect a situation simply in saying something. Appearances to the contrary, there is no perlocutionary force in the argument, for what would this achieve? By the poem's own argument, to persuade the beloved to a change of heart would be pointless, for how would the writer know that such a change has taken place? So the poet simply has to console himself in the belief that the poem itself will bring into being the state of "homogeny" that it so longs for. It enacts the adoption of a belief, a way of living. But such an enactment can be no more than a lonely tactic as long as the lie is lived and believed entirely unilaterally: "So shall *I* live, supposing *thou* art true."

In contrast, as Edward Snow shows, Sonnet 138 at least reports, and perhaps also enacts, in a variety of nuanced ways that I need not rehearse here, a kind of mutual rather than unilateral transformation of a relationship through the acceptance of a lie. The difference between 138 and 93 lies in the fact that the beloved shares the decision to live in terms of a pair of fictions that finally constitute the relationship and its undoubted, if imperfect, consummations. In other words, the disempowering Petrarchan distance, constituted in part by the absence of an answering voice and marking not only 93 but the whole of the subsequence to the young man, is closed by the "mutual render" of the heterosexual couple's lying with and to each other. To agree to engage in this relationship through the powers of the lie is neither to harp on what is nor to accept the shadows of mere fancy but to bring forth a situation in the mode of what, following Cleopatra, we may call an "Excellent falsehood." It is to abandon the idea of a "simple truth"—one to which 93 still clings and from which it derives its pain—in favor of the power of the performative, by which saying makes things so.

*Notes*

[1] David Schalkwyk, "'She never told her love': Embodiment, Textuality, and Silence in Shakespeare's Sonnets and Plays," *Shakespeare Quarterly* 45 (1994): 381-407.

[2] Schalkwyk, 382.

[3] See J. L. Austin, *How To Do Things With Words,* ed. J. O. Urmson and Marina Sbisà, 2d ed. (Cambridge, MA: Harvard UP, 1975).

[4] Philip Sidney, "Astrophil and Stella" in *Sir Philip Sidney,* ed. Katherine Duncan-Jones (Oxford and New York: Oxford UP, 1989), Sonnet 35.

[5] Heather Dubrow, *Echoes of Desire: English Petrarchism and its Counterdiscourses* (Ithaca, NY, and London: Cornell UP, 1995), 10.

[6] Illocutionary acts are those by which, in terms of agreed and institutionalized convention, to say something is at one and the same time to do it. To say "I promise you I shall love you forever" is not to describe anything in the world but *in* the saying of it to perform the act of promising, and to place oneself

under an undeniable ethical obligation. Perlocutionary acts, on the other hand, are rhetorical acts: there is no direct, conventional, or internal link between the speech act and its consequences. By performing the illocutionary act of promising I shall love you forever, I may perform perlocutionary acts as divergent as winning your love in return, provoking your eternal scorn, or evoking critical admiration from an audience who read my sonnets. I may equally be able to achieve any of these perlocutionary effects through a constative utterance like "My mistress' eyes are nothing like the sun." Whereas there is no gap between saying and performance in the case of illocutionary acts, perlocutionary acts are mediated by every kind of contingent, material circumstance, and their effects may range from the intentional to the purely accidental. Such effects, however, are never enacted by convention *in the making of the utterance*. See Austin, 7-11.

[7] Austin, 4.

[8] Quotations of Shakespeare's plays follow *The Complete Works of Shakespeare*, ed. David Bevington, 4th ed. (New York: HarperCollins, 1992). For a discussion of "seeing as" in terms of the duck/rabbit figure, see Ludwig Wittgenstein, *Philosophical Investigations*, trans. G.E.M. Anscombe, 2 vols. (New York: Macmillan, 1958), 2:193$^e$-229$^e$.

[9] For an application of Wittgenstein's discussion of aspect perception to *Henry V*, see Norman Rabkin, "Rabbits, Ducks, and *Henry V*," *SQ* 28 (1977): 279-96.

[10] See Robert Weimann, "Bifold Authority in Shakespeare's Theatre," *SQ* 39 (1988): 401-17. See also the tendency of the Chorus in *Henry V* and of Father Time in *The Winter's Tale* to address the spectators as "gentles all."

[11] Quotations of the sonnets follow *Shakespeare's Sonnets*, ed. Stephen Booth (New Haven, CT, and London: Yale UP, 1977).

[12] For a discussion of the ways in which silence can be a source of empowerment, see my "'She never told her love'" and Dubrow, 82-94.

[13] I explore the relationship between privacy and theatricality in the sonnets in "'As an unperfect actor on a stage': Theatricality and Privacy in the Sonnets of William Shakespeare and Mary Wroth," an unpublished paper presented at the 1998 annual meeting of the Shakespeare Association of America, Cleveland, Ohio.

[14] Joel Fineman, *Shakespeare's Perjured Eye: The Invention of Poetic Subjectivity in the Sonnets* (Berkeley, Los Angeles, and London: U of California P, 1986), 15.

[15] See George Puttenham, *The Arte of English Poesie* (London, 1584), Ddiij$^r$. Cf. Fineman, who argues that "ornament" is a "discourse of special vividness" which nonetheless remains subservient to the ideal of similitude:

> praise is conventionally understood to be a referential discourse that amplifies its referent by means of ornamental trope.... traditional poetic and epideictic theory tend regularly to describe both mimesis and metaphor in terms of the same notion of likeness: verisimilar likeness or resemblance in the first case, the likeness of figural comparison and similitude in the second.

[16] Heather Dubrow, *Captive Victors: Shakespeare's Narrative Poems and Sonnets* (Ithaca, NY, and London: Cornell UP, 1987), 222.

[17] Thomas M. Greene, "Pitiful thrivers: failed husbandry in the Sonnets" in *Shakespeare and the Question of Theory*, Patricia Parker and Geoffrey Hartman, eds. (London and New York: Methuen, 1986), 230-44.

[18] This is in fact the philosophical lesson that Derrida draws in his encounter with so-called "Speech Act Theory"; see Jacques Derrida, *Limited Inc*, ed. Gerald Graff (Evanston, IL: Northwestern UP, 1988).

[19] For a discussion of the public nature of performatives, see Austin, 9-11.

[20] See Lars Engle, *Shakespearean Pragmatism: Market of His Time* (Chicago: U of Chicago P, 1993).

[21] What affronts the "Romans" is the public, performative nature of these declaratives, which both assume and display their own self-enacted authority in "the public eye," "the marketplace," and "the common showplace" (3.6.11, 3, 12). Caesar's indignant account not only reflects a plethora of performatives, such as crowning, proclaiming, bestowing and dividing kingdoms; it also draws attention to such performatives' own reflexive, and for Caesar extremely vexing, self-constituting authority. Antony and Cleopatra engage in the self-proclaimed constitution of the very public institutions that make such performatives possible; the enactment is a simultaneous refusal of Roman authority, jurisdiction, and legal and political claims—"Contemning Rome, he has done all this" (1.1)—enacting in concrete terms what is earlier little more than a gesture of impatience and insult: "Let Rome in Tiber melt and the wide arch / Of the ranged empire fall" (1.1.35-36).

[22] We are reminded here of Antony's account of the Egyptian crocodile: "It is shaped, sir, like itself, and it is as broad as it hath breadth. It is just so high as it is,

and moves with its own organs. It lives by that which nourisheth it, and the elements once out of it, it transmigrates" (2.7.43-46). "Will this description satisfy him?" Caesar asks mockingly and incredulously (l. 51); but logically speaking, Antony's joke is no different from the description "you are you" (84.8) that the actor-poet of the sonnets—he who "purpose[s] not to sell" (21.14)—peddles to the young man as the only *truly* "rich praise" he deserves and should expect.

[23] Wittgenstein, 1:25ᵉ.

[24] Gilbert Ryle, *The Concept of Mind* (Chicago: U of Chicago P, 1949), 18-23, esp. 18.

[25] For a fine extended analysis of this speech in Wittgensteinian terms, see Brian Cheadle, "'His legs bestrid the ocean' as a 'form of life'" in *Drama and Philosophy*, James Redmond, ed. (Cambridge: Cambridge UP, 1990), 87-106.

[26] David Schalkwyk, "Fiction as 'Grammatical' Investigation: A Wittgensteinian Account," *The Journal of Aesthetics and Art Criticism* 53 (1995): 287-98.

[27] See Mary Hamer, "Cleopatra: housewife," *Textual Practice* 2 (1988): 159-79. Hamer points out that one of the cultural threats posed by Cleopatra lies in her exemplification of the fact that Egyptian women "enjoyed one freedom that made them a scandal to the men of Rome: they were free to choose their own husbands" (163).

[28] Edward A. Snow, "Loves of Comfort and Despair: A Reading of Shakespeare's Sonnet 138," *ELH* 47 (1980): 462-83, esp. 462 and 479.

[29] Nona Feinberg, "Erasing the Dark Lady: Sonnet 138 in the Sequence," *Assays: Critical Approaches to Medieval and Renaissance Texts* 4 (1987): 97-108, esp. 108.

[30] But see Dubrow's counter to this argument in *Echoes of Desire,* 82-94.

[31] One should not lose sight of the fact that these two sonnets might have been addressed to the same person. See Heather Dubrow, "'Incertainties now crown themselves assur'd': The Politics of Plotting Shakespeare's Sonnets," *SQ* 47 (1996): 291-305. Although Dubrow's argument is compelling in its own way, I am following tradition by assuming that 93 has the young man and 138 the woman as their respective addressees.

---

Source: "What May Words Do? The Performative of Praise in Shakespeare's Sonnets," in *Shakespeare Quarterly,* Vol. 49, No. 3, Fall, 1998, pp. 251-68.

# *Pericles* Deconstructed

## David Skeele, *Slippery Rock University Theatre*

*"I do not fear the flaw."*
(act III, scene i)

One of the more pervasive images in current popular culture is that of the "channel surfer." In this image, a person (for some reason, usually a male)[1] sits in the dark, staring glassily at a flickering television screen, while his hand clutches a remote control. As his finger presses down on the channel button, rhythmically, every two or three seconds, he is confronted by a quick succession of disconnected snapshots: "gangster-rap" video, wildlife documentary, sexy beer commercial, "real-life" police drama, Barney the Dinosaur, Australianrules football—the world as a bewildering array of incongruous images.[2] Though it lies outside the bounds of the cliché, it would not be difficult to imagine our hypothetical channel surfer wearying of this electronic collage and attempting to focus on one program for a length of time. However, on a number of these programs—fashion shows, music videos, advertisements—he would find the same rapid-fire barrage of images being consciously employed. He would find that his restless search for instant, momentary gratification had actually become an *aesthetic*.

To expand the boundaries even further, let us follow our attention-deficient subject into the realm of the extremely unlikely. Let us imagine that he decided, in a fit of self-improvement, to escape the mind-numbing influence of his television by attending a live performance: a live performance scripted, of course, by the world's most recognizable icon of high culture, William Shakespeare. To his surprise, when he enters the theater, he finds that the jumbled scrap heap of images and associations that he thought he had left safely in his den has followed him into the Renaissance. Anachronistic bits of costuming and setting blend in bizarre combinations. Different scenes are played in completely different styles, as though they belonged in separate plays. Scenes are transposed, cut into smaller fragments, and scattered throughout the play. Abstract, metaphorical visual images take precedence over (and even displace) the coherence of the words and the continuity of the plot.

Now let us become truly ridiculous and suppose that our channel surfer, enraged at this perceived degradation of his aesthetic experience, consults a stack of the latest criticism in order to find the "true" meaning of the play he has just seen—to find the coherent and unified pattern that has just been so egregiously violated. What does he find instead? In one book, he finds that Shakespeare's texts consist merely of the "free play of language," isolated word fragments floating in random configurations through the void. In another, he finds that all previously discovered patterns of meaning were simply tools of a patriarchal, elitist ruling body: "cultural constructions" which must now be "deconstructed" and replaced with alternative political agendas. Thumbing through the rest of the pile, he encounters a maze of related ideas, all of which seem to come down to one basic idea: there is no pattern, there is no central meaning. Shakespeare's plays, finally, consist of jumbles of dissociated ideas and images. With a sigh, he turns on the T.V.

This account is, of course, somewhat absurd, yet it does indeed seem that our present age is characterized by a feeling of fragmentation and that this feeling permeates everything from popular culture to the most complex levels of Shakespeare interpretation. This is not to suggest, however, that fragmentation is unique to current Shakespeare study and performance—it has been lurking in the Western psyche for a long time. Early in the century, modernist interpreters of Shakespeare were clearly aware of a growing sense of dislocation, yet their response was to fight against it by continuing to search for new unifying patterns. Many contemporary Shakespeareans, on the other hand, show a contrasting tendency to embrace the fragmentation and (while not entirely free from the anxiety that attends being adrift in a void) to revel in the freedom of being more disconnected than ever before from old biases and assumptions. It is this particular paradigm shift, perhaps more than any other, that has convinced many cultural commentators that we have entered a new age: the age of postmodernism.

With the newfound dominance of this paradigm of fragmentation, the present would seem to be a propitious time indeed for the most fractured of Shakespeare's plays. One could reasonably expect that this chapter might form the happy ending to this narrative, in which *Pericles* suddenly vaults to the forefront of the canon: the once "miserable" fragment now reigning supreme in a postmodern kingdom of fragments. While such a drastic change of status is still possible for *Pericles*—one could at least say that the idea is less ridiculous now than at any other point in the play's history—the actual situation is far more ambiguous. This ambiguity is due in part to the very contemporaneity of postmodernism. Because the present is always in a state of transition, of flux, it is impossible to know whether an essay on or production of *Pericles* (or any other play) represents the fruits of a coherent movement or is simply a wobbly indicator of some future trend. In the case of *Pericles,* the situation is complicated by the fact that few critics and directors who might be considered post-modern have yet to turn their full attention to the play. Consequently, this chapter offers hints, not certainties; not a resolution, but the suggestion of a postmodern *Pericles* in progress.

Literary criticism has been particularly neglectful of *Pericles,* though the critic's attack on textual unity significantly predated the director's. The main wellspring of the new attitude toward fragmentation is a critical philosophy, introduced by Jacques Derrida, that was unveiled in America as early as the late 1960s. Known as "deconstruction," this philosophy was originally presented as a critique of the limitations of structuralism—in fact, deconstruction is considered the first "post-structuralist" movement. Though any attempt to describe deconstruction within a space appropriate to this study will inevitably result in gross oversimplification, it is possible to elucidate several of the ways in which Derrida stretched or transcended these limitations. One of Derrida's main objections to the structuralists' method was that in attempting to fit the text into their predetermined structures, they were not really dealing with the works in their totality. Parts of the text that did not fit the model—flaws, gaps, ruptures—were being glossed over, mended, or pushed into the margins. It is precisely these flaws, Derrida suggested, that should be the focus of critical analysis, for they are the keys to the text's disunity, the refusal of its language to conform to any externally imposed framework of meaning. It was this rejection of meaning that formed the centerpiece of Derrida's argument. For while he applauded the work of structuralists in helping to destroy the myth of realizable authorial intention, he felt that they were far too timid in their liberation of the text. By replacing the imposed unity of the author with the imposed unity of "structure," he maintained, they were simply trading in one set of chains for another. Rather, he argued that one must eradicate the notion of a "presence" of *any* kind behind the words. One must embrace the "absolute danger"[3] of breaking free from the idea of inherited meaning altogether and celebrate in its place the "free play of language."

What, then, does deconstructive criticism seek to reveal in a particular text, if it is not some inherent meaning? Answer: it usually seeks simply to reflect itself. In other words, in always seeking to prove its basic credo—that no text has inherent meaning—deconstructive criticism, at least in its purest form, ends up being primarily *about* deconstructive criticism.

By completely freeing texts from the authority of inherited meaning and dismissing the need for unified structure, deconstruction opened up new vistas of possibility for Shakespearean criticism. Yet, as Hugh Grady points out, the *direct* impact of deconstruction proper on Shakespeare studies has been minimal. For several reasons, the theorists whom Howard Felperin calls "textual" deconstructionists[4]—those who use the text primarily as a proving ground for deconstruction—have mostly (though not completely) avoided Shakespeare.[5] Of the "textual" critics that have chosen to deconstruct Shakespeare, virtually none have evinced interest in *Pericles.*

There are a couple of possible reasons for this neglect. Deconstruction is essentially a subversive act, one that takes a certain glee in dissecting the sacred cows of Western Civilization. While critical opinion of *Pericles* has certainly improved over the years, there is little shock value to be gained in dismantling it, as it is still one of the least sacred cows in the Shakespearean pasture. Also, a major tactic of deconstructive criticism is to attack the idea of textual unity. Here again, *Pericles* makes a rather unattractive target: the unity established for it by modernist critics is still so fresh, so fragile, so debatable, that the play would be a straw man to even a novice deconstructionist. Compared to a tightly structured work like *Othello,* whose unity has remained beyond reproach for centuries, *Pericles* seems to deconstruct itself.

Deconstruction's greatest impact on Shakespeare interpretation has been indirect, as its influence has rippled outward into several schools of criticism that were already deeply involved in the study of Shakespeare. Such schools, represented most notably by feminism and new historicism/cultural materialism, have adopted the critical license afforded by deconstruction without necessarily accepting the extremity of its assault on meaning or its ideological barrenness. The critics allied with these schools have been referred to by Felperin as "contextual" deconstructionists, meaning that their interpretations, no matter how radically liberated from the constraints of inherited meaning, are not left floating in a moral void but are placed within the context of a particular ideology.

Still, while *contextual* poststructuralists have had a profound effect on the state of Shakespeare studies, even they have yet to contribute much to the interpretation of *Pericles.* In fact, Steven Mullaney's cultural materialist reading—in *The Place of the Stage* (1988)[6]—constitutes one of the few significant poststructuralist considerations of the play. Cultural materialism and new historicism are highly contextual—both of them being based to one degree or another in Marxist analysis of the mechanics of cultural dominance and subjugation—and their relationship to deconstruction is somewhat complex. If most poststructuralist literary criticism can be said to have sprung in part from the writings of Derrida, historically inflected poststructuralism owes more of a debt to Michel Foucault. Where

Derrida had held up the literary text as the site of discontinuity and disjuncture, Foucault, in such works as *Discipline and Punish* (1975) and *The History of Sexuality* (1978),[7] did the same for the great "text" of history. Foucault thoroughly attacked the notion that the denizens of a historical period can be characterized by some unified worldview or central cultural attitude—a notion championed by such "old" historicists as E. M. W. Tillyard in his *The Elizabethan World Picture*. Foucault looked for the contradictions, the cracks in the world picture, the margins surrounding the center, and rather than seeing a single dominant outlook shaping a given culture, he found a multiplicity of voices, a babble of discourses fighting for political and cultural dominance.

New historicist and cultural materialist critics of Shakespeare examine Elizabethan England through the same fractured lens, and in doing so, they do not so much shatter textual unity as render the whole question quite irrelevant. For these critics, the Shakespeare text is not a self-contained structure; it is not an isolated body that can be "privileged" over other written material of the period. Rather, it is simply one text among many historical "texts" competing for pride of place with diaries, theological tracts, royal proclamations, and writs of deed. In other words, a play like *Pericles* should not be analyzed as a self-contained soliloquy but as part of a dialogue: a text in conversation with other texts. As Mullaney writes:

> I have sought . . . to view the popular stage not only or primarily as a literary phenomenon, but as one of a diverse body of cultural practices. . . . In *The Place of the Stage*, literary analysis is conceived not as an end in itself but as a vehicle, a means of gaining access to tensions and contradictions.[8]

The particular tensions and contradictions he identified with regard to *Pericles* were those endemic to an age moving rapidly into capitalism. He begins his argument by citing Frederic Jameson's theory that the genre of Shakespearean romance is a nostalgic, Utopian response to the growing power of the marketplace, as Shakespeare "opposes the phantasmagoria of imagination to the bustling commercial activity at work all around it."[9] After noting one major contradiction inherent in the theory—that the play which exhibits this "phantasmagoria" is itself part of the "bustling commercial activity"—Mullaney found several scenes in which Shakespeare, nonetheless, seems in his text to demonstrate anxiety over the capitalistic implications of parts of his story. For his first example, Mullaney used one of the least remarked-upon scenes in the play: act I, scene iv, in which Pericles brings grain to relieve the starving citizenry of Tharsus. As Mullaney noted, in one of Shakespeare's prime sources, Lawrence Twine's *Pattern of Painfull Adventures* (1579), the hero Apollonius (Twine's version of Pericles) displays a Machiavellian side that Shakespeare takes great pains to suppress. Unloading his wheat in the Tharsian marketplace, Apollonius demands that the Tharsians pay "eight peeces of brasse for every bushel." Though he quickly decides to return the money, this only serves to redouble the populace's debt to him. As Mullaney observes, "a gift marks the beginning of a coercive system of exchange, one that comes into play . . . in cultural situations where more overt systems of obligation or domination are unavailable" (139). In significant contrast to this display of mercantile greed and cunning, the scene penned by Shakespeare (Mullaney was not concerned with questions of authorship) takes place not in a marketplace, but in a neutral area somewhere near the harbor, and his Pericles simply asks for "love" and "harbourage" in return for his gift.

Mullaney's observation that Shakespeare seems to have cleaned up the less spiritual aspects of his story is even more interesting when applied to one of the play's most notorious gaps in logic: the scene in which Pericles inexplicably decides to leave his infant daughter in the care of Cleon and Dionyza for fourteen years. This is a plot twist that has proven resistant even to most myth-criticism (which relies little on realistic logic), and though Mullaney did not attempt to fill in the gap, he did give it significance. In Twine's version, Apollonius "leaves his daughter to embark on a voyage around the Mediterranean, 'meaning . . . to exercise the trade of merchandize'" (139).

Next, Mullaney tackled the brothel scenes. After pointing out that these scenes represent the only time in the play in which Shakespeare allows the marketplace onto the stage (perhaps because of the unflattering picture of commerce that they paint), Mullaney again used discrepancies between Twine and Shakespeare to suggest the latter's anxiety over a changing cultural climate. Twine's daughter-figure, here named Tharsia, escapes degradation and ruin through a markedly different strategy than her Shakespearean counterpart: she repeatedly enthralls would-be customers so much with her tale of woe that they forget about sex and agree to pay merely for the privilege of listening. As Mullaney observed, what Tharsia does is essentially to create a theater within the brothel. Because sexual assignations were rumored to be frequent amid the anonymity of the theater-crowd and because "Shakespeare's audience was lured into the theatre at least in part by the promise of illicit liaisons," this is a combination that would have made great sense to an Elizabethan audience. However, where Tharsia's actions baldly affirm the economic interdependency of playhouse and whorehouse, Marina's proselytizing revealed Shakespeare practicing "an evasion of the economic and cultural roots of the popular stage" (145).

Clinching Mullaney's argument was the figure of Gower. By bringing the "moral Gower" onstage to narrate the play, Shakespeare is essentially championing one source over the other, using Gower's powerful authorial, authoritative presence to "obscure the discomfiting significance of Twine's *Painfull Adventures.*" Because Gower is a distinctly medieval presence, he is able to "introduce *Pericles* as a tale of universal significance, ancient but unaging, forever timely and uncontaminated by historical and cultural contexts" (148). Because Mullaney regarded the use of such an onstage authorial voice to be an unprecedented theatrical innovation, *Pericles* achieves a new importance, representing the Elizabethan-Jacobean theater's first "radical effort to dissociate the popular stage from its cultural contexts." It was a harbinger of the tradition—eventually practiced by generations of playwrights (and, it is implicit, literary critics)—of imagining "that popular drama could be a purely aesthetic phenomenon, free from history and historical determination" (147).

Mullaney's criticism aside, it is interesting to note that the postmodern *stage* seems to have provided a slightly more hospitable home for the disunified *Pericles* than has the poststructuralist publication. Though in the modernist era, new interpretations of the play tended to appear on the page decades before they found their way to the stage, it seems clear that deconstructive, postmodern productions of *Pericles* have preceded poststructuralist critiques: that it is the director who has seized the initiative.

Peter Sellars has frequently been referred to as a "deconstructionist," and perhaps no director has worn the mantle so deservedly. Since his first professional productions in the early 1980s (such as *Pericles* in 1983), he has brought to bear an interpretive method that flies in the face of orthodox directorial objectives, such as unity of concept, clarity of plot, and historical consistency. Loosely paralleling the doctrines of Derrida and Foucault, Sellar's is a methodology that favors multiplicity over unity, the excitement of the individual moment over the cogency of the whole, the clash of competing discourses over the search for a central meaning. He has declared that "we live in a world that is about simultaneity and contradiction,"[10] and the jarring juxtaposition of disparate elements is apparent in virtually every aspect of his production work.

For instance, his productions almost invariably contain a mixed bag of often contradictory historical references, as he tries to incorporate into them a "deliberate notion that time is circular, which we lost in the early nineteenth century with the invention of photography."[11] Acting styles may differ radically from character to character. The production's tone may fluctuate wildly. Moments of high drama are undercut by juvenile humor, and comedy often contains deep pain. Sellars even fragments the audience's viewpoint. In an attempt to keep the audience from merely sitting and absorbing "predigested culture,"[12] Sellars often intentionally fashions visual imagery that clashes with the action or environment of the play. He calls this "visual counterpoint,"[13] and uses it to call the audience's attention to the choices he is making, to encourage them "to shift focus between the simultaneous worlds of the author and the director"[14] (a clear echo of the self-referentiality of deconstructive criticism—the production is not simply about the text, but about the *production* of the text).

In his interpretation of Shakespeare, Sellars reveals another strong affinity with deconstruction: a special fascination with the flaws in the pattern, the places where unified understanding begins to unravel. As he says:

> My recipe is . . . [to] go through and find the repetitions and obscure passages . . . I also find where Shakespeare has taken a detour . . . I isolate those repetitions, the obscure passages and the detours—and I make *these* the base of the production, because these are the things I first resisted.[15]

Because *Pericles* is still generally held to be one of Shakespeare's main repositories of repetitions, obscure passages, and detours, it is not entirely surprising that Sellars gravitated toward it, nor even that he chose it to be the inaugural production of his reign as artistic director of Boston Shakespeare Company. Not only did *Pericles* seem promisingly flawed, but it epitomized Sellars's view of contemporary life as an "image glut, a series of rapid, moving images from every period of civilization."[16] Noting that *Pericles* consists of a conglomeration of diverse influences and styles, Sellars compared the play to a wonderfully eclectic piece of architecture:

> Architecture is one living link we have with a play like *Pericles,* which contains classical, Christian and Egyptian references. Down where I live, near Wall Street, there is a hilarious . . . building with classical, Christian and early Egyptian elements. We're surrounded by this incredible web of references that we never notice.[17]

In his characteristically anachronistic production of *Pericles,* Sellars managed to incorporate all of these references. For instance, he brought a trace of Egypt (or at least the African continent) into the production by casting black actor Ben Halley, Jr. as Pericles and having him played as a "richly-clad African."[18] In the set design (a collaboration between Sellars and Michael Nishball), the play's classical references were reinforced through a series of perspective drawings from Serlio's *Five Books of Architecture* that were projected on the walls (a device which also served to give the already-impressive stage space a startling sense of depth). Perhaps the most important historical reference was the one he seems to downplay in his description of the building: Wall Street itself.

Sellars is not merely a "textual" deconstructionist. Like Mullaney, he is intensely interested in the workings of class and power—specifically in the parallels between the seats of economic power in the play or opera text and the "oppressive class structure that . . . is alive and well . . . in the United States of America."[19] In *Figaro,* he made the parallel clear by placing the Count's abode in the Trump Tower, in *Job* he flanked God with corporate sponsors Mickey Mouse and Donald Duck, and in *Pericles* he made use of the same kinds of analogies. The court of Tyre became a stuffy board of directors (making Pericles' lust for travel and adventure that much more understandable), Simonides was a tuxedoed clown, and the Knights at Pentapolis translated into demonic businessmen. When Pericles suffers his greatest fall from fortune, it too was communicated in present-day economic terms. Upon learning of Marina's supposed death, he signified his catatonic despair by "becom[ing] a kind of imperial wino, snoozing his misery away under a cardboard carton."[20]

It was not only the historical references that clashed. The acting showed similar signs of deliberate fragmentation. Terry Hands had made the observation that the minor characters are sketched in broad strokes and that "Shakespeare's method appears to avoid peripheral involvement in order to focus on Pericles himself." Sellars apparently agreed, using a distinct and separate acting style to highlight Pericles' difference from the people surrounding him. Ben Halley, Jr. was a hugely romantic, almost bombastic figure, sharply contrasting his powerfully resonant voice and razor-sharp articulation to the more prosaic comic mannerisms of most of the other characters. The resulting impression, as Elizabeth Hageman elegantly phrased it, was of Pericles as "a man of glorious rhetoric in a landscape of unreason, of triviality."[21]

Costuming increased the gulf between Pericles and these characters, particularly the device (drawn, perhaps, from Sellar's experience in puppetry and Asian theater) of outfitting all of the evildoers in a variety of plastic masks ranging from the comic to the frighteningly grotesque.

The journey through the "landscape of unreason" began in the court of Antioch (Sellars kept the order of scenes largely intact), and here masks and costuming combined to create an atmosphere at once sinister and sensual. Antiochus, naked except for a series of studded leather bands (and studded leather jockstrap), wore a bearded, bold-headed mask which froze his expression into a perpetual snarl. Played by Henry Woronicz, he stalked the stage aggressively, brandishing a giant sword. His daughter, though unmasked, was in a similar state of undress, wearing only a skimpy white bikini. Jack Kroll of *Newsweek* remarked on the eerie sexuality of the scene, as well as on its connections to contemporary pop culture: "The daughter in her skivvies is as sexy as a Hustler layout; the father looks like Conan the Barbarian. The scene is truly erotic."[22]

From barbarian Antioch, Pericles traveled (equipped with a modern suitcase) to Tharsus, where Tom Foley and Sindri Anderson played a Cleon and Dionyza who were chillingly indifferent to their starving populace. Wearing cartoonish old-age masks, the royal couple "discussed the famine raging in their midst while eating small wedges of food from their forks."[23]

On the shores of Pentapolis, Pericles encountered clownish Fishermen. Wearing colorful ragtag outfits, funny hats, and Pinocchio noses, they ice fished into a trap in the stage and counseled Pericles in broad Gloucester accents. In the court of Simonides, however, the roles were reversed. Though Simonides wore a comic rubber nose to go with his elegant evening wear (a surreal coming-out party was the intended look),[24] in this aristocratic household it was "the mean Knight" Pericles who was the clown. For this scene, costume designer Craig Sonnenberg placed Pericles in a bushy, preposterous crown of laurels and made his "rusty armor" into a torso-length fat-suit (suggesting, perhaps, that he has inherited his father's middle-aged gut?). Dressed in this manner, clutching his emblematic twig, he made a touchingly pathetic suitor, particularly in contrast to the svelte, business-suited Knights. The Knights were both comic and threatening. Wearing red hockey masks and moving in herky-jerky unison, they presented a bizarre picture of deadly corporate conformity. The tournament was staged as a dance contest, with the stiffly stylized disco movements of the Knights eventually giving way before the superior skills of Pericles, who swept Thaisa off her feet with an energetic jitterbugging number. As described by Kevin Kelly, the end of the tournament played "like a sharp satire on chivalry" as "the Knights run offstage in disgrace and are heard hotfooting it through the basement."[25]

The play's most disturbing scenes—as well as its funniest—were probably those set in Mytilene. Here the corporate world once again reared its ugly head, as the major set piece indicating the brothel was a large onstage television set to which its employees sat glued, its flickering light a constant reminder that white slavery was a logical extreme in a world so crassly commercial. The costumes were also disturbing. Pandar sported tennis shoes, schoolboy shorts and blazer, and a pig mask. Boult looked like a syphilitic Dickens villain, dressed in a long frock coat and a pockmarked mask that elongated his nose and twisted his mouth into an evil sneer. The Bawd's faintly ravaged plastic face (fringed by a cheap blong wig) was the most "realistic" in the play, which made it the most chilling, creating the look of a woman whose demeanor had been paralyzed by one too many bad facelifts.

Lysimachus journeyed to the brothel in a business suit, funny glasses, and a bulbous red nose. Webster A. Stone of the *Harvard Crimson,* who had mixed feelings about Sellars's masks, felt that in this scene they helped solve one of the trickiest moments in the play: "When Lysimachus removes his mask repenting of his past ways, the easy gimmick becomes a tour-de-force."[26]

Stone (along with most of the other critics) was less positive about the production in general. One of the main problem areas cited by critics was the acting. Coming into Boston Shakespeare, Sellars inherited what was essentially a semiprofessional pick-up company, with a few veteran performers sprinkled among a corps largely made up of Harvard undergraduates and recent graduates. Unable to afford very many guest actors of Halley's caliber, Sellars was guaranteed an uneven level of performance—undoubtedly the one type of fragmentation he did *not* intend. Sandra Shipley's "lovely"[27] Thaisa emerged unscathed, and Halley was generally admired—though Stone called him "a stiff, operatic James Earl Jones" whose "manner is too rigidly classical and neither dramatic nor human." From there it generally went downhill. Sellars had the inspired notion of casting Boston street performer Brother Blue in the role of Gower, but the result was, in the words of Kevin Kelly, "a good idea gone slightly awry." "Brother Blue speaks the lines in his own disjointed manner, and with gestures of a certain arthritic grace," Kelly wrote, "unfortunately, he garbles most of his speeches." An even bigger problem, it seems, was Jeannie Affelder's Marina. Hageman attributed the production's failure (in her eyes) to Affelder's "wooden" performance, while Stone wrote that she "moves and speaks with soulless uniformity."

It was not only the acting that turned off some of the critics—a general distrust of Sellars's methods was apparent in the reviews. "Postmodern" was barely in the vocabulary of the average reviewer in 1983, and at least two critics viewed Sellars's fragmentation of the play as the result of simple lack of vision or avant-garde pretentiousness rather than as something that might possibly be a valid aesthetic in its own right. Hageman felt that "[the play's] lack of success should be attributed to Sellars's failure to pattern the moods of the play." Stone wrote that "though this production has some innovation, drama and wit, more often it is confused, contrived, disjointed and dull." Only Kroll fully appreciated Sellars's efforts, writing that "the lesser-known Shakespeare plays are a Pandora's box crammed full of surprises. Sellars dives into this box like a child discovering all sorts of treasures." Citing the great diversity of the Elizabethan audience[28] (consisting at once of "'groundings' having fun" and "more 'refined' types being turned on the deepest profundities of art"), Kroll astutely ascribed the director's electicism to a desire to make the play accessible on different levels simultaneously. Kroll found this "double-dip Shakespearean power" in evidence throughout the production: the scene at Antioch "mixes melodrama and poetry in just the right fizzing proportions"; the brothel scenes "mix bawdiness and chastity in a blend of Mel Brooks vulgarity and John Keats romanticism"; "from the skid-row imagery" of Pericles' despair "Sellars moves with tremendous emotional force to the great reunion scene."

For Kroll, then, this fragmented, disunified *Pericles* was not ultimately incoherent. Sellars, like many critics influenced by deconstruction, does not follow a Derridean party line, eschewing the possibility of meaning altogether. Rather, he aims at a clash of multiple meanings, at what Amy S. Green calls postmodernism's "new model of coherence, a coherence based on tensions, oppositions and flux,"[29] and Kroll's reaction suggests that he may have achieved it.

Of course, not everyone found coherence in this *Pericles,* but it is a testament to Sellars's skill in blending elements of humor into the production (and perhaps to the relative sophistication of his jokes) that there was little misreading of his efforts as mere pandering to the masses or simple parody of the play. Kevin Kelly remarked that "this just may be the funniest *Pericles* of all time," but he never saw fit to question Sellars's seriousness of intent.

Michael Greif, who directed *Pericles* at the New York Shakespeare Festival in 1991, was not quite so fortunate. Sellars may have benefitted somewhat from the respect and tolerance that a small city could be expected to bestow on a resident nascent hero of the avant-garde. The New York critics, on the other hand, showed no such reticence, having already sharpened their teeth on postmodern Shakespeare by the time of Greif's production. In 1989, the Festival had produced *Cymbeline,* staged by new artistic director JoAnne Akalaitis as a "Romantic fantasy set in Victorian England" and presented as a collage of discordant images and viewpoints drawn from the vivid, overheated nineteenth-century imagination. This production has become almost legendary for the loud and vicious media shouting match it incited between most of the city's newspaper reviewers, who excoriated it, and a group of scholars, who rallied to its defense in the pages of *American Theatre.*[30] To the critics, the show's fractured, anachronistic perspective marked it as pure cartoon parody, a director indulging in a series of what Frank Rich called "sniggling music-hall gags at the play's expense."[31] Clive Barnes labeled it a "misreading so ignorant as to be effectively beneath consideration,"[32] and John Simon called it "staggeringly, unremittingly, unconscionably absurd."[33] In return, scholar Elinor Fuchs ridiculed the New York press at length for their own ignorance of this new aesthetic of fragmentation, one which consciously sought to give the audience "a multiple and decentered way of understanding the world and our own subjectivity . . . [and to] demand that [they] respond to many 'texts' at once."[34] In the same issue, James Leverett mocked the critics for their devotion to the "shrine of unity," which he defined as "the narrow set of aesthetic criteria that ultimately serve to mask the pernicious operations of social power and privelege."[35]

Not quite the same firestorm was ignited by Greif's *Pericles*. Yet in its wildly anachronistic settings and costumes and its violent changes of mood and tone, it was a production every bit as fragmented and decentered as Akalaitis' *Cymbeline*. In some ways, his visual framework was even more eclectic than Akalaitis's, blending historical references drawn from a period spanning over a thousand years. Greif did, however, pattern his history slightly more formally than did Akalaitis her crazy quilt Victoriana. If there was any ruling visual concept for Greif, it was the idea of Pericles' journey as a trip through time as well as space. Beginning in a primitive Antioch (circa 200 B.C.), he moved the story through the ages in a not-quite-linear fashion until he reached a Mytilene, which closely resembled contemporary Miami Beach. Mirroring this progression even as he guided the audience through it was Gower, who began the night draped in a robelike piece of canvas and ended it looking like a "suave, sport-jacketed Harry von Zell."[36]

Throughout all of these radical shifts place and time, the stage space remained remarkably simple. Giving the play a seashore motif, designer John Arnone placed the action in a pit of sand backed by a series of sliding screens, which could be changed to indicate each new setting. It was, however, a distinctly artificial seashore, for like Sellars, Greif lost no opportunity to call attention to his artistic process, to expose the theatrical underpinnings. The offstage characters sat on folding chairs, clearly visible to the audience ("in hallowed avantgarde cliché fashion,"[37] sneered John Simon). Stagehands moved props and scenery in clear view, even openly operating a thunder sheet and sprinkler during the storm scene.

Within this spare theatrical frame, however, the combination of Arnone's assorted properties and backdrops and the "style-jumping flair"[38] of costume designer Gabriel Berry made each setting thoroughly unique. In Antioch, the characters were "swathed in Roman-era cloths and drapings,"[39] as hooded corpses hung behind them and an ominous jet of flame periodically blasted out of the floor. Tharsus appeared to be a French North African protectorate, with Steve Mellor's Cleon in a fez and black actress Saundra MacLain sporting a leopard-skin leotard (a combination that simultaneously managed to suggest a contemporary American Shriner and his tacky suburban wife). Pentapolis was played in the broadest comic fashion. It featured a medieval "jousting tournament à la Monty Python,"[40] hosted by a goofball Simonides in a blonde Prince Valiant wig. The six knights were represented by a cardboard cutout (with one actor sticking his head through different neckholes to play the different characters), which knocked over furniture and other actors as it was clumsily manipulated by stagehands. The brothel was people with "seedy beach rats" with Brooklyn accents and decorated with a sign announcing "We welcome only guests using condoms." Like Sellars, Greif supplied his brothel with a television, but the statement it made was somewhat less subtle, as it continually broadcast the Clarence Thomas hearings.

In general, the critical response to Greif's postmodern treatment was harsh. Interestingly, it was not quite as caustic as the venom to which Akalaitis had been subjected. Perhaps the critics who had pilloried *Cymbeline* had been chastened by the unexpected counterattack in *American Theatre*, but more likely a "travesty" of *Pericles* seemed less of a call to arms (Frank Rich opened his review by saying: "People may not hold their noses at the mere mention of . . . *Pericles,* but at the very least they shrug their shoulders"[41]). Otherwise, much of the critical reaction was nearly identical: a somewhat muted version of the same antipostmodern rhetoric. The primary objects of scorn, predictably, were the production's apparent lack of coherence and its apparent lack of seriousness, two qualities that seemed to the critics to go hand in hand. As Rich wrote:

> Since *Pericles* is a hodgepodge, there is nothing wrong in principle with Greif's own leapfrogging, or if you will, post-modern approach. But the . . . constant about-faces in tone tell the audience early on that there is no blazing passion underlying the director's conceits, no personal vision that might weave the loose threads into a magical, dreamy tapestry.

John Simon also made the facile equation that anachronism and change of tone equal parody (he called the former "the easiest theatrical jape") and complained that "you do not save a romantic yet serious play, flawed as it may be, by camping it up." Howard Kissel, whose *New York Post* review was entitled "More Parody Than *Pericles*," attacked both director and audience by declaring that Greif's discordant style "is probably a logical choice for the T.V. generation, for whom coherence is not a priority. Accustomed to the disjointed style of sitcom, they are contented to settle for a few yocks and not worry too much about how it all fits together."[42] Even some of the show's supporters proceeded on the assumption that Greif's approach was intentionally tongue in cheek. Michael Feingold, after spending several paragraphs mocking the kind of academic solemnity that could have produced the *Pericles* of Terry Hands, congratulated Greif for taking "this overladen tale in the playful spirit in which it was intended." David Sheward opined that "director Michael Greif has wisely decided that the only way to go with material like this is to stage it as a joke, since it is impossible to perform with a straight face."[43]

Greif, who felt he was taking the play very seriously, was surprised by the charges that he had directed a parody. And he was equally puzzled by the notion that he had intentionally rendered *Pericles* incoherent. In a recent interview, he said, "I didn't set out to create a 'postmodern' *Pericles*. I was simply trying to bring out what I saw in the play."[44] What he saw in the play, deep down, was something vaguely approaching unity: "My approach was to take each scene at its own face value and play it for all it was worth, but at the same time the whole play represents the journey of Pericles. It is an *oblique* journey—it doesn't move in a straight line—but there is a mythic journey which runs through all of the scenes." Greif's invocation of the word "myth" is surprising, but his preparatory reading included large doses of Carl Jung and Joseph Campbell, and several of the conclusions he reached regarding the play were not much different than those of his modernist predecessors. For instance, Greif saw woven into the play the same counterpoint of contrasting characters that Daniels had identified, and like him, he chose to accentuate this pattern with the use of thematic doubling. Greif had followed Daniels in casting the same actress (Martha Plimpton) as both Marina and the Daughter of Antiochus, but he even came up with some interesting new combinations, with Bobo Lewis playing both the Lychorida and the Bawd, and Byron Nelson doubling as Antiochus and Simonides.

This last contrast was especially important to Greif. Like a number of structuralist critics, he saw the "bad father" Antiochus and the "good father" Simonides as perfect reverse reflections of each other, polar opposite guideposts on Pericles' journey, and he tried to emphasize that both in his casting and his staging. It was perhaps the slapstick "tomfoolery"[45] at Pentapolis that had been seized on most frequently by detractors, but Greif argued that the broad comedy of the scene was not intended as diversion but was in fact thematically essential. It is not uncommon to hold up Pentapolis as the counterreflection of Antioch. In this scene, both Hands and Daniels played up the sense of chivalry, honor, and human kindness that were so noticeably absent in the opening scene. But Greif went much farther. Taking the idea that the tournament the audience sees could be one that is totally colored by Pericles' imagination, Greif presented it as an *idealized* vision of the tournament. In other words, in order to banish the shadows of the first scene, his Pericles conjured up "an adolescent cartoon fantasy,"[46] a Pentapolis which in its total buffoonery, its complete lack of seriousness, existed as the ultimate remedy for the gloom of Antioch.

In Greif's judgment, however, this concept was only partially successful. Just as many people had a hard time adjusting to the multiple viewpoints and subjectivity of Akaliatis's Victorian kaleidoscope, many of the audience and critics of *Pericles* were thrown by the farcical treatment of the scene. "I don't think the audience really got the connection [to the earlier scene]," admitted Greif. Part of the problem, he felt, was the fact that Antioch had not been made nearly sinister enough to justify the extremity of its antidote—its menace was no competition for the delirious comedy that followed a few scenes later. The other problem was that the scene at Pentapolis was "*too* funny—it kind of overwhelmed the production. The audience thought they'd caught the tone of the whole production, and they just *expected* to laugh after that scene." Such a reaction from the audience then made it difficult to lure them back into the scenes that he wished to treat more seriously. Rich agreed with Greif's assessment, blaming the "unmoving" reconciliation scene on "the jokey tone of the sequences preceding this reunion," which "make it impossible for the actors to raise the production's emotional temperature at that late juncture, no matter how hard they try."

Greif's use of film clips during the latter portions of the play also provoked controversy. During Marina's kidnapping, an old black-and-white movie showing pirates swarming onto a galleon was projected onto the back wall, and the dumb show in which Pericles reacts to the news of his daughter's death was treated as a silent film, with an overly made-up Campbell Scott (the actor who played Pericles) shown soundlessly wailing and tearing his hair. Greif conceded that the first clip was unnecessary and "gimmicky" but defended the dumb show as an integral part of another throughline in the production. Like Sellars, Greif endowed his production with a certain postmodern self-referentiality, asserting that "*Pericles* is a story that is partly about the act of storytelling, and I was interested in looking at the different ways we have of doing that." To that end, he had Don R. McManus, as Gower, explore a variety of different styles of delivery as he moved through the ages. "When we got to this particular dumbshow," said Greif, "we realized that we were at the point in history—early Hollywood—where we really *had* dumbshows. [The silent movie] was one of the most important ways we told stories."

Though some of Greif's throughlines remained obscure—either through audience misperception of his ideas or uncertain execution of them—for many the journey of Pericles did seem to chart a coherent course through the rapidly changing styles, settings, and periods, thanks largely to the performance of Campbell Scott. Scott (the son of George C. Scott and Colleen Dewhurst) brought a combination of gentle intelligence and boyish charm that was admired by nearly all the reviewers. For Feingold, he was the production's "constant still center of virtue and integrity." Robert Simonson wrote that "Scott's steady-as-he-goes performance provides the center that holds this capricious dramatic universe together."[47] David Richards echoed these sentiments, noting that "without Mr. Scott's solid and reliable performance, the production would be doomed by its determination to go off in a dozen different directions."[48]

Not all of the actors fared as well with the critics, most of whom found the general performance level to be as diverse as the rest of the production. Richards declared that "in keeping with Pericles' peregrinations, the acting is all over the place," while Clive Barnes complained that the performances "veered narrowly between the painlessly mediocre and the painfully inadequate."[49] The most intense criticism was saved for the Marina of Martha Plimpton. Greif consciously chose "to defy the cliché that says she is a passive, demure creature." Instead, he and Plimpton strove to find the edge to Marina, "the anger and spirit of an adolescent who has just been deprived of the closest thing to a parent she has ever known."[50] The choice was a risky one, and not many critics were pleased to lose the traditional angel of innocence. Jan Stuart noted that "the bullish Plimpton tends to browbeat others into virtuosity [sic] rather than win them over to it," though she did, he added, "save the character from blandness."[51] Richards called her "a frightful scold, for a creature whose purity is supposed to speak for itself," while Feingold was harsher still: "Martha Plimpton's Marina is nothing but a shrill, streetwise tramp—unfortunate, since the script spends so much time praising her demure behavior and silver-voiced musicality." Plimpton did have at least two defenders in John Michael Koroly, who felt that her "gutsy, fiercely confident interpretation of her character saves it from becoming just another virtuous maiden,"[52] and Mimi Kramer, who welcomed the idea of "a beautifully pissed-off Marina."[53]

Kramer was one the production's few wholehearted advocates, one of the few who fully approved of both the play and Greif's treatment of it. Fascinatingly, she identified this *Pericles* as a rare example of *unobtrusive* directorial handling. In Kramer's view, it was the director of *unified* Shakespeare who was guilty of the "sledgehammer" approach, as he tried to straitjacket all the parts of a play into a "self-serving conceit." Contrastingly, Greif's "idea seems to have been to direct each scene in whatever style or with whatever conceit would serve it best." For Kramer, Greif had managed to create a *Pericles* that was anachronistic yet serious, fragmented yet ultimately coherent:

> The current production swings between broad comedy and wild histrionics without ever descending into . . . camp . . . Mr. Greif, who clearly knows what's poignant, what's witty, what's melodramatic, keeps us entertained while never letting us forget the darker strands of the play's fabric.

Gerald Weales of *Commonweal* was equally enthusiastic. Having attended the play with *Theatre Week* critic Elizabeth Osborn, Weales wrote that "the production confirmed both Osborn's faith in the play's essential coherence and my sense of its grand incoherence, and at the same time delighted both of us . . . with no mandatory tone to violate, it vacillates between excessive broadness and touching lyricism."[54] After making note of the thread provided by the play's father/daughter theme (a theme pointed up for Weales by Greif's casting), he closed his review by saying, "Thematic coherence, after all, but that seems of much less importance than the theatrical vigor that Shakespeare and Greif gave to scene after scene."

In the eyes of a few commentators, at least, Greif's postmodern *Pericles,* like that of Sellars, achieved a "coherence of tensions, oppositions and flux."[55] Though the success attained by both directors was mixed, their productions heralded the arrival of a new kind of *Pericles:* one that values the fragmentation of the text, not just as a problem to be "fixed" but as something that is interesting and exciting in itself.

It is, of course, difficult to predict the future of the postmodern *Pericles,* or the poststructural one. It seems fairly safe to say, however, that we have not seen the last of this kind of approach to the play, both on the page and on the stage. The various methodologies that comprise poststructuralism continue to thrive in the academy, and it is almost inevitable that more of its critics will eventually turn their attention to *Pericles*—perhaps when there are no more dominant traditions left to subvert or central plays left to decenter. The road is somewhat harder for postmodern Shakespeare performance. In the theater—particularly the *classical* theater—the grip of tradition tends to unclench more slowly. However, as the information age continues to exacerbate our sense of a fragmented world and as talented young postmodern directors continue to unveil their unique visions of that world, it is not hard to imagine that fractured, fragmented Shakespeare productions will proliferate, and even that fractured, fragmented *Pericles* will continue to assume a more prominent place among them.

Even though it is unclear what lies immediately over the horizon for *Pericles,* the distance it has traveled since the nineteenth century and the perils it has navigated along the way provide an intriguing narrative. It is a voyage filled with fierce battles, with wildly fluctuating fortunes, and at the beginning, even a bit of suspense. The late eighteenth century, where it re-emerged into the public consciousness after over a hundred years of neglect, proved an unfortunate launching point, running the play immediately afoul of the influential George Steevens. During its tumultuous passage through the nineteenth century, where it was generally blasted for its refusal to conform to either Victorian morality or the realist aesthetic, it looked as though it might founder and sink before its journey had truly begun. Fortunately, in the closing years of the century, a hasty inclusion among Shakespeare's "Romances" provided *Pericles* with the hint of a reprieve, as did the miraculously successful stage production of Samuel Phelps.

In the twentieth century, however, the sailing has been considerably smoother, as *Pericles* has seen a remarkable reversal of earlier judgments. In the modern age, with the rise of a new breed of professional, "problem-solving" Shakespeareans capable of unifying absolutely anything (and resultingly, a new critical paradigm which stressed unity at all costs), the most challenging of Shakespeare's "problems" began to take on a new value. Eventually, the stage director (who has always been a problem-solving critic), inspired in part by critical reappraisals, began to fashion powerful and innovative productions that heightened profoundly the esteem of the play.

In recent years, the paradigm of unity and seamless construction has weakened its hold, usurped to an extent by a new interest in fragmentation and deconstruction. Whether this trend holds great promise for *Pericles* is still uncertain. Critical consideration of the play has temporarily (one can only assume) slowed to a trickle, though a couple of recent productions have suggested that a deliberately fragmented approach can be a fruitful one. And alongside these "postmodern" stagings, more traditional productions continue to proliferate. During the winter of 1991-92, no less than four American regional theaters were offering nearly simultaneous productions of the play (Greif's was one), prompting Maggie Kramm of *American Theatre* to write an article on the phenomenon. "This convergence of *Pericleses* isn't really a coincidence," she ventured, "*Pericles* is seemingly a play whose time has come round."[56] Whether this is true remains to be seen, but it is clear that the play has reached a level of importance and esteem that would have once been unthinkable. Not a bad achievement for a miserable fragment.

## Notes

[1] Channel surfing is one of the favorite time-wasting activities of MTV's Beavis and Butthead. Female comedians regularly lampoon the adult male's obsessive attachment to the television remote. I am unaware of any popular references to female channel surfers, although there is probably very little basis for ascribing the trait exclusively to males.

[2] Channel surfing as a metaphor for and influence on postmodernism is, of course, not an entirely original concept. For instance, Raymond Williams makes a similar point in *Television, Technology and Cultural Form* (New York: Schocken Books, 1975), 87. Cited in Amy S. Green, *The Revisionist Stage: American Directors Reinvent the Classics* (Cambridge: Cambridge University Press, 1994), 174.

[3] Jacques Derrida, *Of Grammatology,* trans. Gayatri Chakravorty Spivak (Baltimore: Johns Hopkins University Press, 1976), 5. Quoted in Vincent B. Leitch, *Deconstructive Criticism: An Advanced Introduction* (New York: Columbia University Press, 1983), 24.

[4] Howard Felperin, *Beyond Deconstruction: The Uses and Abuses of Literary Theory* (Oxford: Oxford University Press, 1985). Cited in Grady, *The Modernist Shakespeare,* (Oxford: Oxford University Press, 1991) 214.

[5] As Hugh Grady writes, " . . . because Derrida has directed his primary attention to philosophical texts and issues, and because the Yale deconstructors had begun their carexers as specialists in the nineteenth century who had early been concerned with reversing New Criticism's valorization of the Renaissance over Romanticism, deconstructive close readings of Shakespeare are among the most prominent texts of neither deconstruction in general nor of contemporary Shakespeare criticism." In Grady, *The Modernist Shakespeare,* 214.

[6] Mullaney prefers the term "cultural materialist" to "new historicist" (xi), and I am not one to question his preference. Grady, in *Modernist Shakespeare,* makes a reasonable distinction between the two schools, stating that new historicism, as typified by the work of Stephen Greenblatt, tends to be fairly apolitical, while cultural materialism is more Marxist inflected. Mullaney's work does seem to focus more on economic power structures than the more generic patterns of "subversion and containment" which characterize new historicism.

[7] Dates given are those of English editions.

[8] Steven Mullaney, *The Place of the Stage* (Chicago and London: University of Chicago Press, 1988), x.

[9] Frederic Jameson, *The Political Unconscious: Narrative as a Socially Symbolic Act* (Ithaca: Cornell University Press, 1981), 148. Cited in Mullaney, *The Place of the Stage,* 140.

[10] In Richard Trousdell, "Peter Sellars Rehearses *Figaro,*" *The Drama Review* 35, no. 1 (Spring 1991): 83.

[11] In Arthur Bartow, *The Director's Voice* (New York: TCG, 1988), 279.

[12] Bartow, *Director's Voice,* 284.

[13] Peter Sellars, quoted in Don Shewey, "I Hate Decoration Onstage': Peter Sellars Talks About Design," *Theatre Crafts* (January 1984): 24.

[14] Amy S. Green, *The Revisionist Stage: American Directors Reinvent the Classics* (Cambridge: Cambridge University Press, 1994), 149.

[15] Bartow, *Director's Voice*, 277.

[16] Shewey, "I Hate Decoration," 27.

[17] Shewey, "I Hate Decoration," 27.

[18] Elizabeth Hageman, "Shakespeare in Massachusetts, 1983," *Shakespeare Quarterly* 35 (1984): 224.

[19] Quoted in Green, *Revisionist Stage*, 154.

[20] Jack Kroll, "Daring to be Different," *Newsweek*, 14 November 1983, 83.

[21] Hageman, "Shakespeare in Massachusetts, 1983," 224.

[22] Kroll, "Daring to be Different," 83.

[23] Kevin Kelly, "*Pericles* with Great Feeling," *Boston Globe*, 13 October 1983.

[24] According to Sandra Shipley, the actress who played Thaisa, in telephone interview, 22 June 1995.

[25] Kelly, "Great Feeling."

[26] Webster A. Stone, "Beyond Interpretation," *Harvard Crimson*, 21 October 1983.

[27] Kelly, "*Pericles* with Great Feeling."

[28] *Pericles* is, of course, Jacobean, if the most commonly held date of composition (1608) is correct, but it was performed in an "Elizabethan" manner: publicly, at the Globe.

[29] Amy S. Green, *The Revisionist Stage: American Directors Reinvent the Classics* (Cambridge: Cambridge University Press, 1994), 177.

[30] December 1989. The response came in the form of two full-length articles—Elinor Fuchs's "Misunderstanding Postmodernism" (pp. 24-31) and James Leverett's, "Why the Critics Turned Savage" (pp. 25, 63-65)—and two shorter commentaries—David Norbrook's "The Cold War Revisited" (27) and Nancy Graves's "Did Frank Rich Really Look?" (29).

[31] *New York Times*, cited in Fuchs, "Misunderstanding Postmodernism," 28.

[32] Clive Barnes, *New York Post*, cited in Fuchs, "Misunderstanding Postmodernism," 28.

[33] John Simon, *New York*, cited in Fuchs, "Misunderstanding Postmodernism," 28.

[34] Fuchs, "Misunderstanding Postmodernism," 25.

[35] Leverett, "Why the Critics Turned Savage," 63.

[36] Michael Feingold, "By Fire and Water," *Village Voice*, 3 December 1991.

[37] John Simon, "Prince of Tiresome," *New York*, 9 December 1991.

[38] Feingold, "Fire and Water."

[39] Ibid.

[40] L. C. Cole, "The Prince and the Snooper," *New York Native*, 16 December 1991.

[41] Frank Rich, "*Pericles* Hints at Shakespearean Things to Come," *New York Times*, 25 November 1991.

[42] Howard Kissel, "More Parody Than *Pericles*," New York Post, 25 November 1991.

[43] David Sheward, "*Pericles*," *Back Stage*, 29 November 1991.

[44] Telephone interview, 19 June 1995.

[45] Simon, "Prince of Tiresome."

[46] Telephone interview, 19 June 1995.

[47] Robert Simonson, "*Pericles, Prince of Tyre*," *Theatre Week*, 30 December 1991.

[48] David Richards, "The Perils of Pericles, a Serial Adventure," *New York Times*, 1 December 1991.

[49] Clive Barnes, "The Perils of the Public's *Pericles*," *New York Post*, 25 November 1991.

[50] Telephone interview, 19 June 1995.

[51] Jan Stuart, "*Pericles* with Postmodern Spice," *New York Newsday*, 25 November 1991.

[52] John Michael Koroly, "*Pericles, Prince of Tyre*," radio review for WRSU-FM, New Brunswick, New Jersey, aired 15-21 December 1991. Transcripts in the archives of the Public Theater.

[53] Mimi Kramer, "Mirabile Dictu," *New Yorker*, 9 December 1991.

[54] Gerald Weales, "The Bard Lives: *Pericles & Night's Dream*," *Commonweal*, 14 February 1992.

[55] Green, *The Revisionist Stage*, 177.

[56] Maggie Kramm, "The Hero Nobody Knows: Five Actors Playing Pericles," *American Theatre*, (June 1992): 10-17.

## Works Cited

Feingold, Michael. "By Fire and Water." *Village Voice*, 3 December 1991.

Fuchs, Elinor. "Misunderstanding Postmodernism." *American Theatre* (December 1989): 24-31.

Green, Amy S. *The Revisionist Stage: American Directors Reinvent the Classics.* Cambridge: Cambridge University Press, 1994.

Hageman, Elizabeth H. "Shakespeare in Massachusetts, 1983." *Shakespeare Quarterly* 35 (1984): 224-25.

Kelly, Kevin. "*Pericles* With Great Feeling." *Boston Globe*, 13 October 1983.

Leverett, James. "Why the Critics Turned Savage." *American Theatre* (December 1989): 25, 63-65.

Shewey, Don. "'I Hate Decoration Onstage': Peter Sellars Talks About Design." *Theatre Crafts* (January 1984): 24-27.

Simon, John. "Prince of Tiresome." *New York*, 9 December 1991, pp. 97-98.

---

Source: "*Pericles* Deconstructed," in *Thwarting the Wayward Seas: A Critical and Theatrical History of Shakespeare's Pericles in the Nineteenth and Twentieth Centuries,* University of Delaware Press, 1998, pp. 126-45.

# Guide to *Shakespearean Criticism* Series

| | |
|---|---|
| **VOLUMES 1-10** | Provides an historical overview of the critical response to each Shakespearean work. Includes criticism from the seventeenth century to the present. |
| **VOLUMES 11, 12, 14, 15, 17, 18, 20, 21, 23, 24, 26** | Examines the performance history of Shakespeare's plays on the stage and screen through eyewitness reviews and retrospective evaluations of individual productions. Also provides comparisons of major interpretations and discusses staging issues. |
| **VOLUMES 27, 29-31, 33-36, 38-41, 43-47** | Focuses on criticism published after 1960. Each volume is ordered around a theme, such as politics, religion, or sexuality, with a topic entry that introduces the volume and several entries devoted to individual works. |
| *Yearbooks:* **VOLUMES 13, 16, 19, 22, 25, 28, 32, 37, 42, 48** | Compiled annually beginning in 1989. Includes the most noteworthy essays of the year published on Shakespeare as recommended by an international advisory board of distinguished Shakespearean scholars. |

# Cumulative Character Index

The Cumulative Character Index identifies the principal characters of discussion in the criticism of each play and non-dramatic poem. The characters are arranged alphabetically. Page references indicate the beginning page number of each essay containing substantial commentary on that character.

**Aaron**
*Titus Andronicus* **4**: 632, 637, 650, 651, 653, 668, 672, 675; **27**: 255; **28**: 249, 330; **43**: 176

**Adonis**
*Venus and Adonis* **10**: 411, 420, 424, 427, 429, 434, 439, 442, 451, 454, 459, 466, 473, 489; **25**: 305, 328; **28**: 355; **33**: 309, 321, 330, 347, 352, 357, 363, 370, 377

**Adriana**
*The Comedy of Errors* **16**: 3; **34**: 211, 220, 238

**Albany**
*King Lear* **32**: 308

**Alcibiades**
*Timon of Athens* **25**: 198; **27**: 191

**Angelo**
*Measure for Measure*
anxiety **16**: 114
authoritarian portrayal of **23**: 307
characterization **2**: 388, 390, 397, 402, 418, 427, 432, 434, 463, 484, 495, 503, 511; **13**: 84; **23**: 297; **32**: 81; **33**: 77
hypocrisy **2**: 396, 399, 402, 406, 414, 421; **23**: 345, 358, 362
repentance or pardon **2**: 388, 390, 397, 402, 434, 463, 511, 524

**Anne (Anne Boleyn)**
*Henry VIII* See **Boleyn**

**Anne (Anne Page)**
*The Merry Wives of Windsor* See **Page**

**Antigonus**
*The Winter's Tale*
characterization **7**: 394, 451, 464
death (Act III, scene iii) **7**: 377, 414, 464, 483; **15**: 518, 532; **19**: 366

**Antonio**
*The Merchant of Venice*
excessive or destructive love **4**: 279, 284, 336, 344; **12**: 54; **37**: 86
love for Bassanio **40**: 156
melancholy **4**: 221, 238, 279, 284, 300, 321, 328; **22**: 69; **25**: 22
pitiless **4**: 254
as pivotal figure **12**: 25, 129
*Twelfth Night* **22**: 69

**Antonio and Sebastian**
*The Tempest* **8**: 295, 299, 304, 328, 370, 396, 429, 454; **13**: 440; **29**: 278, 297, 343, 362, 368, 377; **45**: 200

**Antony**
*Antony and Cleopatra*
characterization **6**: 22, 23, 24, 31, 38, 41, 172, 181, 211; **16**: 342; **19**: 270; **22**: 217; **27**: 117; **47**: 77, 124, 142
Caesar, relationship with **48**: 206
Cleopatra, relationship with **6**: 25, 27, 37, 39, 48, 52, 53, 62, 67, 71, 76, 85, 100, 125, 131, 133, 136, 142, 151, 161, 163, 165, 180, 192; **27**: 82; **47**: 107, 124, 165, 174
death scene **25**: 245; **47**: 142
dotage **6**: 22, 23, 38, 41, 48, 52, 62, 107, 136, 146, 175; **17**: 28
nobility **6**: 22, 24, 33, 48, 94, 103, 136, 142, 159, 172, 202; **25**: 245
political conduct **6**: 33, 38, 53, 107, 111, 146, 181
public vs. private personae **6**: 165; **47**: 107
self-knowledge **6**: 120, 131, 175, 181, 192; **47**: 77
as superhuman figure **6**: 37, 51, 71, 92, 94, 178, 192; **27**: 110; **47**: 71
as tragic hero **6**: 38, 39, 52, 53, 60, 104, 120, 151, 155, 165, 178, 192, 202, 211; **22**: 217; **27**: 90
*Julius Caesar*
characterization **7**: 160, 179, 189, 221, 233, 284, 320, 333; **17**: 269, 271, 272, 284, 298, 306, 313, 315, 358, 398; **25**: 272; **30**: 316
funeral oration **7**: 148, 154, 159, 204, 210, 221, 238, 259, 350; **25**: 280; **30**: 316, 333, 362

**Apemantus**
*Timon of Athens* **1**: 453, 467, 483; **20**: 476, 493; **25**: 198; **27**: 166, 223, 235

**Arcite**
*The Two Noble Kinsmen* See **Palamon and Arcite**

**Ariel**
*The Tempest* **8**: 289, 293, 294, 295, 297, 304, 307, 315, 320, 326, 328, 336, 340, 345, 356,

379

364, 420, 458; **22:** 302; **29:** 278, 297, 362, 368, 377

**Armado**
*Love's Labour's Lost* **23:** 207

**Arthur**
*King John* **9:** 215, 216, 218, 219, 229, 240, 267, 275; **22:** 120; **25:** 98; **41:** 251, 277

**Arviragus**
*Cymbeline* See **Guiderius and Arviragus**

**Audrey**
*As You Like It* **46:** 122

**Aufidius**
*Coriolanus* **9:** 9, 12, 17, 19, 53, 121, 148, 153, 157, 169, 180, 193; **19:** 287; **25:** 263, 296; **30:** 58, 67, 89, 96, 133

**Autolycus**
*The Winter's Tale* **7:** 375, 380, 382, 387, 389, 395, 396, 414; **15:** 524; **22:** 302; **37:** 31; **45:** 333; **46:** 14, 33

**Banquo**
*Macbeth* **3:** 183, 199, 208, 213, 278, 289; **20:** 279, 283, 406, 413; **25:** 235; **28:** 339

**Baptista**
*The Taming of the Shrew* **9:** 325, 344, 345, 375, 386, 393, 413

**Barnardine**
*Measure for Measure* **13:** 112

**Bassanio**
*The Merchant of Venice* **25:** 257; **37:** 86; **40:** 156

**the Bastard**
*King John* See **Faulconbridge (Philip) the Bastard**

**Beatrice and Benedick**
*Much Ado about Nothing*
Beatrice's femininity **8:** 14, 16, 17, 24, 29, 38, 41, 91; **31:** 222, 245
Beatrice's request to "kill Claudio" (Act IV, scene i) **8:** 14, 17, 33, 41, 55, 63, 75, 79, 91, 108, 115; **18:** 119, 120, 136, 161, 245, 257
Benedick's challenge of Claudio (Act V, scene i) **8:** 48, 63, 79, 91; **31:** 231
Claudio and Hero, compared with **8:** 19, 28, 29, 75, 82, 115; **31:** 171, 216
marriage and the opposite sex, attitudes toward **8:** 9, 13, 14, 16, 19, 29, 36, 48, 63, 77, 91, 95, 115, 121; **16:** 45; **31:** 216; **48:** 14
mutual attraction **8:** 13, 14, 19, 24, 29, 33, 41, 75; **48:** 14
nobility **8:** 13, 19, 24, 29, 36, 39, 41, 47, 82, 91, 108
popularity **8:** 13, 38, 41, 53, 79
transformed by love **8:** 19, 29, 36, 48, 75, 91, 95, 115; **31:** 209, 216
unconventionality **8:** 48, 91, 95, 108, 115, 121
vulgarity **8:** 11, 12, 33, 38, 41, 47
wit and charm **8:** 9, 12, 13, 14, 19, 24, 27, 28, 29, 33, 36, 38, 41, 47, 55, 69, 95, 108, 115; **31:** 241

**Belarius**
*Cymbeline* **4:** 48, 89, 141

**Benedick**
*Much Ado about Nothing* See **Beatrice and Benedick**

**Berowne**
*Love's Labour's Lost* **2:** 308, 324, 327; **22:** 12; **23:** 184, 187; **38:** 194; **47:** 35

**Bertram**
*All's Well That Ends Well*
characterization **7:** 15, 27, 29, 32, 39, 41, 43, 98, 113; **26:** 48; **26:** 117; **48:** 65
conduct **7:** 9, 10, 12, 16, 19, 21, 51, 62, 104
physical desire **22:** 78
transformation or redemption **7:** 10, 19, 21, 26, 29, 32, 54, 62, 81, 90, 93, 98, 109, 113, 116, 126; **13:** 84

**Bianca**
*The Taming of the Shrew* **9:** 325, 342, 344, 345, 360, 362, 370, 375
Bianca-Lucentio subplot **9:** 365, 370, 375, 390, 393, 401, 407, 413, 430; **16:** 13; **31:** 339

**the boar**
*Venus and Adonis* **10:** 416, 451, 454, 466, 473; **33:** 339, 347, 370

**Boleyn (Anne Boleyn)**
*Henry VIII* **2:** 21, 24, 31; **41:** 180

**Bolingbroke**
*Richard II* See **Henry (King Henry IV, previously known as Bolingbroke)**

**Borachio and Conrade**
*Much Ado about Nothing* **8:** 24, 69, 82, 88, 111, 115

**Bottom**
*A Midsummer Night's Dream*
awakening speech (Act IV, scene i) **3:** 406, 412, 450, 457, 486, 516; **16:** 34
folly of **46:** 1, 14, 29, 60
imagination **3:** 376, 393, 406, 432, 486; **29:** 175, 190; **45:** 147
self-possession **3:** 365, 376, 395, 402, 406, 480; **45:** 158
Titania, relationship with **3:** 377, 406, 441, 445, 450, 457, 491, 497; **16:** 34; **19:** 21; **22:** 93; **29:** 216; **45:** 160
transformation **3:** 365, 377, 432; **13:** 27; **22:** 93; **29:** 216; **45:** 147, 160

**Brabantio**
*Othello* **25:** 189

**Brutus**
*Coriolanus* See **the tribunes**

*Julius Caesar*
arrogance **7:** 160, 169, 204, 207, 264, 277, 292, 350; **25:** 280; **30:** 351
as chief protagonist or tragic hero **7:** 152, 159, 189, 191, 200, 204, 242, 250, 253, 264, 268, 279, 284, 298, 333; **17:** 272, 372, 387
citizenship **25:** 272
funeral oration **7:** 154, 155, 204, 210, 350
motives **7:** 150, 156, 161, 179, 191, 200, 221, 227, 233, 245, 292, 303, 310, 320, 333, 350; **25:** 272; **30:** 321, 358
nobility or idealism **7:** 150, 152, 156, 159, 161, 179, 189, 191, 200, 221, 242, 250, 253, 259, 264, 277, 303, 320; **17:** 269, 271, 273, 279, 280, 284, 306, 308, 321, 323, 324, 345, 358; **25:** 272, 280; **30:** 351, 362
political ineptitude or lack of judgment **7:** 169, 188, 200, 205, 221, 245, 252, 264, 277, 282, 310, 316, 331, 333, 343; **17:** 323, 358, 375, 380
self-knowledge or self-deception **7:** 191, 200, 221, 242, 259, 264, 268, 279, 310, 333, 336, 350; **25:** 272; **30:** 316
soliloquy (Act II, scene i) **7:** 156, 160, 161, 191, 221, 245, 250, 253, 264, 268, 279, 282, 292, 303, 343, 350; **25:** 280; **30:** 333
*The Rape of Lucrece* **10:** 96, 106, 109, 116, 121, 125, 128, 135

**Buckingham**
*Henry VIII* **22:** 182; **24:** 129, 140; **37:** 109

**Cade (Jack [John] Cade)**
*Henry VI, Parts 1, 2, and 3* **3:** 35, 67, 92, 97, 109; **16:** 183; **22:** 156; **25:** 102; **28:** 112; **37:** 97; **39:** 160, 196, 205

**Caesar**
*Antony and Cleopatra*
Antony, relationship with as leader **48:** 206
*Julius Caesar*
ambiguous nature **7:** 191, 233, 242, 250, 272, 298, 316, 320
arrogance **7:** 160, 207, 218, 253, 272, 279, 298; **25:** 280
idolatry **22:** 137
leadership qualities **7:** 161, 179, 189, 191, 200, 207, 233, 245, 253, 257, 264, 272, 279, 284, 298, 310, 333; **17:** 317, 358; **22:** 280; **30:** 316, 326
as tragic hero **7:** 152, 200, 221, 279; **17:** 321, 377, 384
weakness **7:** 161, 167, 169, 179, 187, 188, 191, 207, 218, 221, 233, 250, 253, 298; **17:** 358; **25:** 280

**Caius, Doctor**
*The Merry Wives of Windsor* **47:** 354

**Caliban**
*The Tempest* **8:** 286, 287, 289, 292, 294, 295, 297, 302, 304, 307, 309, 315, 326, 328, 336, 353, 364, 370, 380, 390, 396, 401, 414, 420, 423, 429, 435, 454; **13:** 424, 440; **15:** 189, 312, 322, 374, 379; **22:** 302; **25:** 382; **28:** 249; **29:** 278, 292, 297, 343, 368, 377, 396; **32:** 367; **45:** 211, 219, 226, 259; **48:** 299

**Calphurnia**
*Julius Caesar*
Calphurnia's dream **45:** 10

**Cambridge**
*Henry V* See **traitors**

**Canterbury and the churchmen**
*Henry V* **5:** 193, 203, 205, 213, 219, 225, 252, 260; **22:** 137; **30:** 215, 262

**Cardinal Wolsey**
*Henry VIII* See **Wolsey**

**Cassio**
*Othello* **25:** 189

**Cassius**
*Julius Caesar* **7:** 156, 159, 160, 161, 169, 179, 189, 221, 233, 303, 310, 320, 333, 343; **17:** 272, 282, 284, 344, 345, 358; **25:** 272, 280; **30:** 351; **37:** 203

**Celia**
*As You Like It* **46:** 94

**Chorus**
*Henry V*
role of **5:** 186, 192, 226, 228, 230, 252, 264, 269, 281, 293; **14:** 301, 319, 336; **19:** 133; **25:** 116, 131; **30:** 163, 202, 220

**the churchmen**
*Henry V* See **Canterbury and the churchmen**

**Cinna**
*Julius Caesar*
as poet **48:** 240

**Claudio**
*Much Ado about Nothing*
boorish behavior **8:** 9, 24, 33, 36, 39, 44, 48, 63, 79, 82, 95, 100, 111, 115; **31:** 209
credulity **8:** 9, 17, 19, 24, 29, 36, 41, 47, 58, 63, 75, 77, 82, 95, 100, 104, 111, 115, 121; **31:** 241; **47:** 25
mercenary traits **8:** 24, 44, 58, 82, 91, 95
noble qualities **8:** 17, 19, 29, 41, 44, 58, 75
reconciliation with Hero **8:** 33, 36, 39, 44, 47, 82, 95, 100, 111, 115, 121
repentance **8:** 33, 63, 82, 95, 100, 111, 115, 121; **31:** 245
sexual insecurities **8:** 75, 100, 111, 115, 121

**Claudius**
*Hamlet* **13:** 502; **16:** 246; **21:** 259, 347, 361, 371; **28:** 232, 290; **35:** 104, 182; **44:** 119, 241

**Cleopatra**
*Antony and Cleopatra*
Antony, relationship with **6:** 25, 27, 37, 39, 48, 52, 53, 62, 67, 71, 76, 85, 100, 125, 131, 133, 136, 142, 151, 161, 163, 165, 180, 192; **25:** 257; **27:** 82; **47:** 107, 124, 165, 174
characterization **47:** 77, 96, 113, 124
contradictory or inconsistent nature **6:** 23, 24, 27, 67, 76, 100, 104, 115, 136, 151, 159, 202; **17:** 94, 113; **27:** 135
costume **17:** 94
creativity **6:** 197; **47:** 96, 113
death **6:** 23, 25, 27, 41, 43, 52, 60, 64, 76, 94, 100, 103, 120, 131, 133, 136, 140, 146, 161, 165, 180, 181, 192, 197, 208; **13:** 383; **17:** 48, 94; **25:** 245; **27:** 135; **47:** 71
personal attraction of **6:** 24, 38, 40, 43, 48, 53, 76, 104, 115, 155; **17:** 113
self-knowledge **47:** 77, 96
staging issues **17:** 94, 113
as subverter of social order **6:** 146, 165; **47:** 113
as superhuman figure **6:** 37, 51, 71, 92, 94, 178, 192; **27:** 110; **47:** 71, 174, 192,
as tragic heroine **6:** 53, 120, 151, 192, 208; **27:** 144
as voluptuary or courtesan **6:** 21, 22, 25, 41, 43, 52, 53, 62, 64, 67, 76, 146, 161; **47:** 107, 174

**Cloten**
*Cymbeline* **4:** 20, 116, 127, 155; **22:** 302, 365; **25:** 245; **36:** 99, 125, 142, 155; **47:** 228

**Collatine**
*The Rape of Lucrece* **10:** 98, 131; **43:** 102; **48:** 291

**Cominius**
*Coriolanus* **25:** 245

**Conrade**
*Much Ado about Nothing* See **Borachio and Conrade**

**Constance**
*King John* **9:** 208, 210, 211, 215, 219, 220, 224, 229, 240, 251, 254; **16:** 161; **24:** 177, 184, 196

**Cordelia**
*King Lear*
attack on Britain **25:** 202
characterization **2:** 110, 116, 125, 170; **16:** 311; **25:** 218; **28:** 223, 325; **31:** 117, 149, 155, 162; **46:** 218, 225, 231, 242
as Christ figure **2:** 116, 170, 179, 188, 222, 286
gender identity **48:** 222
rebelliousness **13:** 352; **25:** 202
on stage **11:** 158
transcendent power **2:** 137, 207, 218, 265, 269, 273
women, the Christian ideal of **48:** 222

**Corin**
*As You Like It* See **pastoral characters**

**Coriolanus**
*Coriolanus*
anger or passion **9:** 19, 26, 45, 80, 92, 157, 164, 177, 189; **30:** 79, 96
as complementary figure to Aufidius **19:** 287
death scene (Act V, scene vi) **9:** 12, 80, 100, 117, 125, 144, 164, 198; **25:** 245, 263
as epic hero **9:** 130, 164, 177; **25:** 245
immaturity **9:** 62, 80, 84, 110, 117, 142; **30:** 140
inhuman attributes **9:** 65, 73, 139, 157, 164, 169, 189, 198; **25:** 263
internal struggle **9:** 31, 43, 45, 53, 72, 117, 121, 130; **44:** 93
introspection or self-knowledge, lack of **9:** 53, 80, 84, 112, 117, 130; **25:** 296; **30:** 133
isolation or autonomy **9:** 53, 65, 142, 144, 153, 157, 164, 180, 183, 189, 198; **30:** 58, 89, 111
manipulation by others **9:** 33, 45, 62, 80; **25:** 296
as military leader **48:** 230
modesty **9:** 8, 12, 19, 26, 53, 78, 92, 117, 121, 144, 183; **25:** 296; **30:** 79, 96, 129, 133, 149
narcissism **30:** 111
noble or aristocratic attributes **9:** 15, 18, 19, 26, 31, 33, 52, 53, 62, 65, 84, 92, 100, 121, 148, 157, 169; **25:** 263; **30:** 67, 74, 96
pride or arrogance **9:** 8, 11, 12, 19, 26, 31, 33, 43, 45, 65, 78, 92, 121, 148, 153, 177; **30:** 58, 67, 74, 89, 96, 129
punishment of **48:** 230
reconciliation with society **9:** 33, 43, 45, 65, 139, 169; **25:** 296
as socially destructive force **9:** 62, 65, 73, 78, 110, 142, 144, 153; **25:** 296
soliloquy (Act IV, scene iv) **9:** 84, 112, 117, 130
as tragic figure **9:** 8, 12, 13, 18, 25, 45, 52, 53, 72, 80, 92, 106, 112, 117, 130, 148, 164, 169, 177; **25:** 296; **30:** 67, 74, 79, 96, 111, 129; **37:** 283
traitorous actions **9:** 9, 12, 19, 45, 84, 92, 148; **25:** 296; **30:** 133
as unsympathetic character **9:** 12, 13, 62, 78, 80, 84, 112, 130, 157

**the courser and the jennet**
*Venus and Adonis* **10:** 418, 439, 466; **33:** 309, 339, 347, 352

**Cranmer**
*Henry VIII*
prophesy of **2:** 25, 31, 46, 56, 64, 68, 72; **24:** 146; **32:** 148; **41:** 120, 190

**Cressida**
*Troilus and Cressida*
as ambiguous figure **43:** 305
inconsistency **3:** 538; **13:** 53; **16:** 70; **22:** 339; **27:** 362
individual will vs. social values **3:** 549, 561, 571, 590, 604, 617, 626; **13:** 53; **27:** 396
infidelity **3:** 536, 537, 544, 554, 555; **18:** 277, 284, 286; **22:** 58, 339; **27:** 400; **43:** 298
lack of punishment **3:** 536, 537
as mother figure **22:** 339
objectification of **43:** 329
as sympathetic figure **3:** 557, 560, 604, 609; **18:** 284, 423; **22:** 58; **27:** 396, 400; **43:** 305

**Dark Lady**
*Sonnets* **10:** 161, 167, 176, 216, 217, 218, 226, 240, 302, 342, 377, 394; **25:** 374; **37:** 374; **40:** 273; **48:** 346

**the Dauphin**
*Henry V* See **French aristocrats and the Dauphin**

**Desdemona**
*Othello*
as Christ figure **4**: 506, 525, 573; **35**: 360
culpability **4**: 408, 415, 422, 427; **13**: 313; **19**: 253, 276; **35**: 265, 352, 380
innocence **35**: 360; **43**: 32; **47**: 25
as mother figure **22**: 339; **35**: 282
passivity **4**: 402, 406, 421, 440, 457, 470, 582, 587; **25**: 189; **35**: 380
spiritual nature of her love **4**: 462, 530, 559
staging issues **11**: 350, 354, 359; **13**: 327; **32**: 201

**Diana**
*Pericles*
as symbol of nature **22**: 315; **36**: 233

**Dogberry and the Watch**
*Much Ado about Nothing* **8**: 9, 12, 13, 17, 24, 28, 29, 33, 39, 48, 55, 69, 79, 82, 88, 95, 104, 108, 115; **18**: 138, 152, 205, 208, 210, 213, 231; **22**: 85; **31**: 171, 229; **46**: 60

**Don John**
*Much Ado about Nothing* See **John (Don John)**

**Don Pedro**
*Much Ado about Nothing* See **Pedro (Don Pedro)**

**Dromio Brothers**
*Comedy of Errors* **42**: 80

**Duke**
*Measure for Measure*
as authoritarian figure **23**: 314, 317, 347; **33**: 85
characterization **2**: 388, 395, 402, 406, 411, 421, 429, 456, 466, 470, 498, 511; **13**: 84, 94, 104; **23**: 363, 416; **32**: 81; **42**: 1; **44**: 89
as dramatic failure **2**: 420, 429, 441, 479, 495, 505, 514, 522
godlike portrayal of **23**: 320
noble portrayal of **23**: 301
speech on death (Act III, scene i) **2**: 390, 391, 395
*Othello* **25**: 189

**Edgar**
*King Lear* **28**: 223; **32**: 212; **32**: 308; **37**: 295; **47**: 9
Edgar-Edmund duel **22**: 365

**Edmund**
*King Lear* **25**: 218; **28**: 223
Edmund's forged letter **16**: 372

**Edmund of Langley, Duke of York**
*Richard II* See **York**

**Elbow**
*Measure for Measure* **22**: 85; **25**: 12

**Elbow (Mistress Elbow)**
*Measure for Measure* **33**: 90

**elder characters**
*All's Well That Ends Well* **7**: 9, 37, 39, 43, 45, 54, 62, 104

**Elizabeth I**
*Love's Labour's Lost* **38**: 239

**Emilia**
*Othello* **4**: 386, 391, 392, 415, 587; **35**: 352, 380; **43**: 32
*The Two Noble Kinsmen* **9**: 460, 470, 471, 479, 481; **19**: 394; **41**: 372, 385; **42**: 361

**Enobarbus**
*Antony and Cleopatra* **6**: 22, 23, 27, 43, 94, 120, 142; **16**: 342; **17**: 36; **22**: 217; **27**: 135

**Evans, Sir Hugh**
*The Merry Wives of Windsor* **47**: 354

**fairies**
*A Midsummer Night's Dream* **3**: 361, 362, 372, 377, 395, 400, 423, 450, 459, 486; **12**: 287, 291, 294, 295; **19**: 21; **29**: 183, 190; **45**: 147

**Falstaff**
*Henry IV, Parts 1 and 2*
characterization **1**: 287, 298, 312, 333; **25**: 245; **28**: 203; **39**: 72, 134, 137, 143; **48**: 117, 151
as comic figure **1**: 287, 311, 327, 344, 351, 354, 357, 410, 434; **39**: 89; **46**: 1, 48, 52
as coward or rogue **1**: 285, 290, 296, 298, 306, 307, 313, 317, 323, 336, 337, 338, 342, 354, 366, 374, 391, 396, 401, 433; **14**: 7, 111, 125, 130, 133; **32**: 166
as deceiver deceived **47**: 308
diminishing powers of **47**: 363
dual personality **1**: 397, 401, 406, 434
female attributes **13**: 183; **44**: 44; **47**: 325
Iago, compared with **1**: 341, 351
as Jack-a-Lent **47**: 363
Marxist interpretation **1**: 358, 361
as parody of the historical plot **1**: 314, 354, 359; **39**: 143
as positive character **1**: 286, 287, 290, 296, 298, 311, 312, 321, 325, 333, 344, 355, 357, 389, 401, 408, 434
rejection by Hal **1**: 286, 287, 290, 312, 314, 317, 324, 333, 338, 344, 357, 366, 372, 374, 379, 380, 389, 414; **13**: 183; **25**: 109; **39**: 72, 89; **48**: 95
as satire of feudal society **1**: 314, 328, 361; **32**: 103
as scapegoat **1**: 389, 414; **47**: 358, 363, 375
stage interpretations **14**: 4, 6, 7, 9, 15, 116, 130, 146; **47**: 1
as subversive figure **16**: 183; **25**: 109
*Henry V* **5**: 185, 186, 187, 189, 192, 195, 198, 210, 226, 257, 269, 271, 276, 293, 299; **28**: 146; **46**: 48
*The Merry Wives of Windsor*
characterization in *1* and *2 Henry IV*, compared with **5**: 333, 335, 336, 337, 339, 346, 347, 348, 350, 373, 400, **18**: 5, 7, 75, 86; **22**: 93

diminishing powers **5**: 337, 339, 343, 347, 350, 351, 392
as Herne the Hunter **38**: 256, 286; **47**: 358
incapability of love **5**: 335, 336, 339, 346, 348; **22**: 93
personification of comic principle or as Vice figure **1**: 342, 361, 366, 374; **5**: 332, 338, 369, 400; **38**: 273
recognition and repentance of follies **5**: 338, 341, 343, 348, 369, 374, 376, 397
sensuality **5**: 339, 343, 353, 369, 392
shrewdness **5**: 332, 336, 346, 355
threat to community **5**: 343, 369, 379, 392, 395, 400; **38**: 297
as unifying force **47**: 358
vanity **5**: 332, 339
victimization **5**: 336, 338, 341, 347, 348, 353, 355, 360, 369, 373, 374, 376, 392, 397, 400
as villain **47**: 358

**Faulconbridge, (Philip) the Bastard**
*King John* **41**: 205, 228, 251, 260, 277; **48**: 132
as chorus or commentator **9**: 212, 218, 229, 248, 251, 260, 271, 284, 297, 300; **22**: 120
as comic figure **9**: 219, 271, 297
development **9**: 216, 224, 229, 248, 263, 271, 275, 280, 297; **13**: 158, 163
as embodiment of England **9**: 222, 224, 240, 244, 248, 271
heroic qualities **9**: 208, 245, 248, 254, 263, 271, 275; **25**: 98
political conduct **9**: 224, 240, 250, 260, 280, 297; **13**: 147, 158; **22**: 120

**Fenton**
*The Merry Wives of Windsor*
Anne Page-Fenton plot **5**: 334, 336, 343, 353, 376, 390, 395, 402; **22**: 93

**Ferdinand**
*The Tempest* **8**: 328, 336, 359, 454; **19**: 357; **22**: 302; **29**: 362, 339, 377

**Feste**
*Twelfth Night*
characterization **1**: 558, 655, 658; **26**: 233, 364; **46**: 1, 14, 18, 33, 52, 60, 303, 310
role in play **1**: 546, 551, 553, 566, 570, 571, 579, 635, 658; **46**: 297, 303, 310
song **1**: 543, 548, 561, 563, 566, 570, 572, 603, 620, 642; **46**: 297
gender issues **19**: 78; **34**: 344; **37**: 59

**Fluellen**
*Henry V* **30**: 278; **37**: 105

**Fool**
*King Lear* **2**: 108, 112, 125, 156, 162, 245, 278, 284; **11**: 17, 158, 169; **22**: 227; **25**: 202; **28**: 223; **46**: 1, 14, 18, 24, 33, 52, 191, 205, 210, 218, 225

**Ford, Francis**
*The Merry Wives of Windsor* **5**: 332, 334, 343, 355, 363, 374, 379, 390; **38**: 273; **47**: 321

**Ford, Mistress Alice**
*The Merry Wives of Windsor* **47**: 321

**Fortinbras**
*Hamlet* **21**: 136, 347; **28**: 290

**French aristocrats and the Dauphin**
*Henry V* **5**: 188, 191, 199, 205, 213, 281; **22**: 137; **28**: 121

**Friar**
*Much Ado about Nothing* **8**: 24, 29, 41, 55, 63, 79, 111

**Friar John**
*Romeo and Juliet* See **John (Friar John)**

**Friar Lawrence**
*Romeo and Juliet* See **Lawrence (Friar Lawrence)**

**the Friend**
*Sonnets* **10**: 279, 302, 309, 379, 385, 391, 394

**Ganymede**
*A Winter's Tale* **48**: 309

**Gardiner (Stephen Gardiner)**
*Henry VIII* **24**: 129

**Gaunt**
*Richard II* **6**: 255, 287, 374, 388, 402, 414; **24**: 274, 322, 325, 414, 423; **39**: 263, 279

**Gertrude**
*Hamlet* **21**: 259, 347, 392; **28**: 311; **32**: 238; **35**: 182, 204, 229; **43**: 12; **44**: 119, 160, 189, 195, 237, 247
  death monologue **48**: 255

**Ghost**
*Hamlet* **1**: 75, 76, 84, 85, 128, 134, 138, 154, 171, 218, 231, 254; **16**: 246; **21**: 17, 44, 112, 151, 334, 371, 377, 392; **25**: 288; **35**: 152, 157, 174, 237; **44**: 119

**Gloucester**
*King Lear* **46**: 254

**Gobbo, Launcelot**
*The Merchant of Venice* **46**: 24, 60

**Goneril**
*King Lear* **31**: 151; **46**: 231, 242

**Gonzalo**
*The Tempest* **22**: 302; **29**: 278, 343, 362, 368; **45**: 280; **48**: 299

**Gower chorus**
*Pericles* **2**: 548, 575; **15**: 134, 141, 143, 145, 149, 152, 177; **36**: 279; **42**: 352

**Grey**
*Henry V* See **traitors**

**Guiderius and Arviragus**
*Cymbeline* **4**: 21, 22, 89, 129, 141, 148; **25**: 319; **36**: 125, 158

**Hal**
See **Henry (King Henry V, formerly known as Prince Henry [Hal] of Wales)**

**Hamlet**
*Hamlet*
  as a fool **46**: 1, 29, 52, 74
  delay **1**: 76, 83, 88, 90, 94, 98, 102, 103, 106, 114, 115, 116, 119, 120, 148, 151, 166, 171, 179, 188, 191, 194, 198, 221, 268; **13**: 296, 502; **21**: 81; **25**: 209, 288; **28**: 223; **35**: 82, 174, 212, 215, 237; **44**: 180, 209, 219, 229
  divided nature **16**: 246; **28**: 223; **32**: 288; **35**: 182, 215; **37**: 241
  elocution of the character's speeches **21**: 96, 104, 112, 127, 132, 172, 177, 179, 194, 245, 254, 257
  madness **1**: 76, 81, 83, 95, 102, 106, 128, 144, 154, 160, 234; **21**: 35, 50, 72, 81, 99, 112, 311, 339, 355, 361, 371, 377, 384; **35**: 117, 132, 134, 140, 144, 212; **44**: 107, 119, 152, 209, 219, 229
  melancholy **21**: 99, 112, 177, 194; **35**: 82, 95, 117; **44**: 209, 219
  as negative character **1**: 86, 92, 111, 171, 218; **21**: 386; **25**: 209; **35**: 167
  reaction to his father's death **22**: 339; **35**: 104, 174; **44**: 133, 160, 180, 189
  reaction to Gertrude's marriage **1**: 74, 120, 154, 179; **16**: 259; **21**: 371; **22**: 339; **35**: 104, 117; **44**: 133, 160, 189, 195
  religion **48**: 195
  romantic aspects of the character **21**: 96; **44**: 198
  as scourge or purifying figure **1**: 144, 209, 242; **25**: 288; **35**: 157
  sentimentality vs. intellectuality **1**: 75, 83, 88, 91, 93, 94, 96, 102, 103, 115, 116, 120, 166, 191; **13**: 296; **21**: 35, 41, 44, 72, 81, 89, 99, 129, 132, 136, 172, 213, 225, 339, 355, 361, 371, 377, 379, 381, 386; **25**: 209; **44**: 198
  soliloquies **1**: 76, 82, 83, 148, 166, 169, 176, 191; **21**: 17, 31, 44, 53, 89, 112, 268, 311, 334, 347, 361, 384, 392; **25**: 209; **28**: 223; **44**: 107, 119, 229
  theatrical interpretations **21**: 11, 31, 78, 101, 104, 107, 160, 177, 179, 182, 183, 192, 194, 197, 202, 203, 208, 213, 225, 232, 237, 249, 253, 254, 257, 259, 274, 311, 339, 347, 355, 361, 371, 377, 380; **44**: 198
  virility **21**: 213, 301, 355

**Helena**
*All's Well That Ends Well*
  as agent of reconciliation, renewal, or grace **7**: 67, 76, 81, 90, 93, 98, 109, 116
  as dualistic or enigmatic character **7**: 15, 27, 29, 39, 54, 58, 62, 67, 76, 81, 98, 113, 126; **13**: 66; **22**: 78; **26**: 117; **48**: 65
  as "female achiever" **19**: 113; **38**: 89
  desire **38**: 96; **44**: 35
  pursuit of Bertram **7**: 9, 12, 15, 16, 19, 21, 26, 27, 29, 32, 43, 54, 76, 116; **13**: 77; **22**: 78
  virginity **38**: 65
  virtue and nobility **7**: 9, 10, 12, 16, 19, 21, 27, 32, 41, 51, 58, 67, 76, 86, 126; **13**: 77
*A Midsummer Night's Dream* **29**: 269

**Henry (King Henry IV, previously known as Bolingbroke)**
*Henry IV, Parts 1 and 2* **39**: 123, 137
*Richard II*
  Bolingbroke and Richard as opposites **24**: 423
  Bolingbroke-Mowbray dispute **22**: 137
  comic elements **28**: 134
  guilt **24**: 423; **39**: 279
  language and imagery **6**: 310, 315, 331, 347, 374, 381, 397; **32**: 189
  as Machiavellian figure **6**: 305, 307, 315, 331, 347, 388, 393, 397; **24**: 428
  as politician **6**: 255, 263, 264, 272, 277, 294, 364, 368, 391; **24**: 330, 333, 405, 414, 423, 428; **39**: 256
  Richard, compared with **6**: 307, 315, 347, 374, 391, 393, 409; **24**: 346, 349, 351, 352, 356, 395, 419, 423, 428
  his silence **24**: 423
  structure, compared with **39**: 235
  usurpation of crown, nature of **6**: 255, 272, 289, 307, 310, 347, 354, 359, 381, 385, 393; **13**: 172; **24**: 322, 356, 383, 419; **28**: 178

**Henry (King Henry V, formerly known as Prince Henry [Hal] of Wales)**
*Henry IV, Parts 1 and 2*
  as the central character **1**: 286, 290, 314, 317, 326, 338, 354, 366, 374, 396; **39**: 72, 100
  dual personality **1**: 397, 406; **25**: 109, 151; **48**: 95
  as Everyman **1**: 342, 366, 374
  fall from humanity **1**: 379, 380, 383
  general assessment **1**: 286, 287, 289, 290, 314, 317, 326, 327, 332, 357, 397; **25**: 245; **32**: 212; **39**: 134; **48**: 151
  as ideal ruler **1**: 289, 309, 317, 321, 326, 337, 342, 344, 374, 389, 391, 434; **25**: 109; **39**: 123; **47**: 60
  as Machiavellian ruler **47**: 60
  as negative character **1**: 312, 332, 333, 357; **32**: 212
  Richard II, compared with **1**: 332, 337; **39**: 72
*Henry V*
  brutality and cunning **5**: 193, 203, 209, 210, 213, 219, 233, 239, 252, 260, 271, 287, 293, 302, 304; **30**: 159; **43**: 24
  characterization in *1* and *2 Henry IV* contrasted **5**: 189, 190, 241, 304, 310; **19**: 133; **25**: 131; **32**: 157
  chivalry **37**: 187
  courage **5**: 191, 195, 210, 213, 228, 246, 257, 267
  disguise **30**: 169, 259
  education **5**: 246, 267, 271, 289; **14**: 297, 328, 342; **30**: 259
  emotion, lack of **5**: 209, 212, 233, 244, 264, 267, 287, 293, 310
  as heroic figure **5**: 192, 205, 209, 223, 244, 252, 257, 260, 269, 271, 299, 304; **28**: 121,

146; **30:** 237, 244, 252; **37:** 187
humor **5:** 189, 191, 212, 217, 239, 240, 276
intellectual and social limitations **5:** 189, 191, 203, 209, 210, 225, 226, 230, 293; **30:** 220
interpersonal relations **5:** 209, 233, 267, 269, 276, 287, 293, 302, 318; **19:** 133; **28:** 146
mercy **5:** 213, 267, 289, 293
mixture of good and bad qualities **5:** 199, 205, 209, 210, 213, 244, 260, 304, 314; **30:** 262, 273
piety **5:** 191, 199, 209, 217, 223, 239, 257, 260, 271, 289, 310, 318; **30:** 244; **32:** 126
public vs. private selves **22:** 137; **30:** 169, 207
self-doubt **5:** 281, 310
slaughter of prisoners **5:** 189, 205, 246, 293, 318; **28:** 146
speech **5:** 212, 230, 233, 246, 264, 276, 287, 302; **28:** 146; **30:** 163, 227

**Henry (King Henry VI)**
*Henry VI, Parts 1, 2, and 3*
characterization **3:** 64, 77, 151; **39:** 160, 177; **47:** 32
source of social disorder **3:** 25, 31, 41, 115; **39:** 154, 187
as sympathetic figure **3:** 73, 143, 154; **24:** 32

**Henry (King Henry VIII)**
*Henry VIII*
as agent of divine retribution **2:** 49
characterization **2:** 23, 39, 51, 58, 60, 65, 66, 75; **28:** 184; **37:** 109
incomplete portrait **2:** 15, 16, 19, 35; **41:** 120
as realistic figure **2:** 21, 22, 23, 25, 32

**Henry (Prince Henry)**
*King John* **41:** 277

**Hermia**
*A Midsummer Night's Dream* **29:** 225, 269; **45:** 117

**Hermione**
*The Winter's Tale*
characterization **7:** 385, 395, 402, 412, 414, 506; **15:** 495, 532; **22:** 302, 324; **25:** 347; **32:** 388; **36:** 311; **47:** 25
restoration (Act V, scene iii) **7:** 377, 379, 384, 385, 387, 389, 394, 396, 412, 425, 436, 451, 452, 456, 464, 483, 501; **15:** 411, 412, 413, 518, 528, 532
sex as identity **48:** 309
supposed death **25:** 339; **47:** 25

**Hero**
*Much Ado about Nothing* **8:** 13, 14, 16, 19, 28, 29, 44, 48, 53, 55, 82, 95, 104, 111, 115, 121; **31:** 231, 245; **47:** 25

**Hippolyta**
*A Midsummer Night's Dream* **48:** 23

**Holofernes**
*Love's Labour's Lost* **23:** 207

**Horatio**
*Hamlet* **44:** 189
stoic perfection, example of **48:** 195

**Hotspur**
*Henry IV, Parts 1 and 2* **25:** 151; **28:** 101; **39:** 72, 134, 137; **42:** 99
*Henry V* **5:** 189, 199, 228, 271, 302

**Humphrey**
*Henry VI, Parts 1, 2, and 3* **13:** 131

**Iachimo**
*Cymbeline* **25:** 245, 319; **36:** 166; **47:** 274

**Iago**
*Othello*
affinity with Othello **4:** 400, 427, 468, 470, 477, 500, 506; **25:** 189; **44:** 57
as conventional dramatic villain **4:** 440, 527, 545, 582
as homosexual **4:** 503
Machiavellian elements **4:** 440, 455, 457, 517, 545; **35:** 336, 347
motives **4:** 389, 390, 397, 399, 402, 409, 423, 424, 427, 434, 451, 462, 545, 564; **13:** 304; **25:** 189; **28:** 344; **32:** 201; **35:** 265, 276, 310, 336, 347; **42:** 273
revenge scheme **4:** 392, 409, 424, 451
as scapegoat **4:** 506
as victim **4:** 402, 409, 434, 451, 457, 470

**Imogen**
*Cymbeline* **4:** 21, 22, 24, 29, 37, 45, 46, 52, 56, 78, 89, 108; **15:** 23, 32, 105, 121; **19:** 411; **25:** 245, 319; **28:** 398; **32:** 373; **36:** 129, 142, 148; **47:** 25, 205, 228, 245, 274, 277
reawakening of (Act IV, scene ii) **4:** 37, 56, 89, 103, 108, 116, 150; **15:** 23; **25:** 245; **47:** 252

**Isabella**
*Measure for Measure* **2:** 388, 390, 395, 396, 397, 401, 402, 406, 409, 410, 411, 418, 420, 421, 432, 437, 441, 466, 475, 491, 495, 524; **16:** 114; **23:** 278, 279, 280, 281, 282, 296, 344, 357, 363, 405; **28:** 102; **33:** 77, 85

**Jack [John] Cade**
*Henry VI, Parts 1, 2, and 3* See **Cade**

**the jailer's daughter**
*The Two Noble Kinsmen* **9:** 457, 460, 479, 481, 486, 502; **41:** 340

**Jaques**
*As You Like It*
love-theme, relation to **5:** 103; **23:** 7, 37, 118, 128
as malcontent **5:** 59, 70, 84
melancholy **5:** 20, 28, 32, 36, 39, 43, 50, 59, 63, 68, 77, 82, 86, 135; **23:** 20, 26, 103, 104, 107, 109; **34:** 85; **46:** 88, 94
pastoral convention, relation to **5:** 61, 63, 65, 79, 93, 98, 114, 118
Seven Ages of Man speech (Act II, scene vii) **5:** 28, 52, 156; **23:** 48, 103, 105, 126, 138, 152; **46:** 88, 156, 164, 169

Shakespeare, relation to **5:** 35, 50, 154; **48:** 42
as superficial critic **5:** 28, 30, 43, 54, 55, 63, 65, 68, 75, 77, 82, 86, 88, 98, 138; **34:** 85

**the jennet**
*Venus and Adonis* See **the courser and the jennet**

**Jessica**
*The Merchant of Venice* **4:** 196, 200, 228, 293, 342; **48:** 54, 77

**Joan of Arc**
*Henry VI, Parts 1, 2, and 3* **16:** 131; **32:** 212

**John (Don John)**
*Much Ado about Nothing* **8:** 9, 12, 16, 17, 19, 28, 29, 36, 39, 41, 47, 48, 55, 58, 63, 82, 104, 108, 111, 121

**John (Friar John)**
*Romeo and Juliet*
detention of **5:** 448, 467, 470

**John (King John)**
*King John* **41:** 205, 260
death **9:** 212, 215, 216, 240
decline **9:** 224, 235, 240, 263, 275
Hubert, scene with (Act III, scene iii) **9:** 210, 212, 216, 218, 219, 280
moral insensibility **13:** 147, 163
negative qualities **9:** 209, 212, 218, 219, 229, 234, 235, 244, 245, 246, 250, 254, 275, 280, 297
positive qualities **9:** 209, 224, 235, 240, 244, 245, 263

**Julia**
*The Two Gentlemen of Verona* **6:** 450, 453, 458, 476, 494, 499, 516, 519, 549, 564; **40:** 312, 327, 374

**Juliet**
*Romeo and Juliet* See **Romeo and Juliet**

**Launcelot Gobbo**
*The Merchant of Venice* See **Gobbo**

**Kate**
*The Taming of the Shrew*
characterization **32:** 1; **43:** 61
final speech (Act V, scene ii) **9:** 318, 319, 329, 330, 338, 340, 341, 345, 347, 353, 355, 360, 365, 381, 386, 401, 404, 413, 426, 430; **19:** 3; **22:** 48
love for Petruchio **9:** 338, 340, 353, 430; **12:** 435
portrayals of **31:** 282
shrewishness **9:** 322, 323, 325, 332, 344, 345, 360, 365, 370, 375, 386, 393, 398, 404, 413
transformation **9:** 323, 341, 355, 370, 386, 393, 401, 404, 407, 419, 424, 426, 430; **16:** 13; **19:** 34; **22:** 48; **31:** 288, 295, 339, 351

**Katherine**
*Henry V* **5:** 186, 188, 189, 190, 192, 260, 269, 299, 302; **13:** 183; **19:** 217; **30:** 278; **44:** 44

*Henry VIII*
    characterization **2:** 18, 19, 23, 24, 38; **24:** 129; **37:** 109; **41:** 180
    Hermione, compared with **2:** 24, 51, 58, 76
    politeness strategies **22:** 182
    religious discourse **22:** 182
    as tragic figure **2:** 16, 18

Kent
    *King Lear* **25:** 202; **28:** 223; **32:** 212; **47:** 9

King
    *All's Well That Ends Well* **38:** 150

King Richard II
    *Richard II* See **Richard**

King Richard III, formerly Richard, Duke of Gloucester
    *Richard III* See **Richard**

Lady Macbeth
    *Macbeth* See **Macbeth (Lady Macbeth)**

Laertes
    *Hamlet* **21:** 347, 386; **28:** 290; **35:** 182

Launce and Speed
    *The Two Gentlemen of Verona*
        comic function of **6:** 438, 439, 442, 456, 458, 460, 462, 472, 476, 478, 484, 502, 504, 507, 509, 516, 519, 549; **40:** 312, 320

Lavatch
    *All's Well That Ends Well* **26:** 64; **46:** 33, 52, 68

Lavinia
    *Titus Andronicus* **27:** 266; **28:** 249; **32:** 212; **43:** 1, 170, 239, 247, 255, 262

Lawrence (Friar Lawrence)
    *Romeo and Juliet*
        contribution to catastrophe **5:** 437, 444, 470; **33:** 300
        philosophy of moderation **5:** 427, 431, 437, 438, 443, 444, 445, 458, 467, 479, 505, 538
        as Shakespeare's spokesman **5:** 427, 431, 437, 458, 467

Lear
    *King Lear*
        curse on Goneril **11:** 5, 7, 12, 114, 116
        love-test and division of kingdom **2:** 100, 106, 111, 124, 131, 137, 147, 149, 151, 168, 186, 208, 216, 281; **16:** 351; **25:** 202; **31:** 84, 92, 107, 117, 149, 155; **46:** 231, 242
        madness **2:** 94, 95, 98, 99, 100, 101, 102, 103, 111, 116, 120, 124, 125, 149, 156, 191, 208, 216, 281; **46:** 264
        as scapegoat **2:** 241, 253
        self-knowledge **2:** 103, 151, 188, 191, 213, 218, 222, 241, 249, 262; **25:** 218; **37:** 213; **46:** 191, 205, 225, 254, 264

Leontes
    *The Winter's Tale*
        characterization **19:** 431; **43:** 39; **45:** 366

        jealousy **7:** 377, 379, 382, 383, 384, 387, 389, 394, 395, 402, 407, 412, 414, 425, 429, 432, 436, 464, 480, 483, 497; **15:** 514, 518, 532; **22:** 324; **25:** 339; **36:** 334, 344, 349; **44:** 66; **45:** 295, 297, 344, 358; **47:** 25
        Othello, compared with **7:** 383, 390, 412; **15:** 514; **36:** 334; **44:** 66; **47:** 25
        repentance **7:** 381, 389, 394, 396, 402, 414, 497; **36:** 318, 362; **44:** 66

Lucentio
    *The Taming of the Shrew* **9:** 325, 342, 362, 375, 393

Lucio
    *Measure for Measure* **13:** 104

Lucrece
    *The Rape of Lucrece*
        chastity **33:** 131, 138; **43:** 92
        as example of Renaissance *virtù* **22:** 289; **43:** 148
        heroic **10:** 84, 93, 109, 121, 128
        patriarchal woman, model of **10:** 109, 131; **33:** 169, 200
        self-perception **48:** 291
        self-responsibility **10:** 89, 96, 98, 106, 125; **33:** 195; **43:** 85, 92, 158
        unrealistic **10:** 64, 65, 66, 121
        verbose **10:** 64, 81, 116; **25:** 305; **33:** 169
        as victim **22:** 294; **25:** 305; **32:** 321; **33:** 131, 195; **43:** 102, 158

Macbeth
    *Macbeth*
        ambition **44:** 284, 324
        characterization **20:** 20, 42, 73, 107, 113, 130, 146, 151, 279, 283, 312, 338, 343, 379, 406, 413; **29:** 139, 152, 155, 165; **44:** 289
        courage **3:** 172, 177, 181, 182, 183, 186, 234, 312, 333; **20:** 107; **44:** 315
        disposition **3:** 173, 175, 177, 182, 186; **20:** 245, 376
        imagination **3:** 196, 208, 213, 250, 312, 345; **20:** 245, 376; **44:** 351
        as "inauthentic" king **3:** 245, 302, 321, 345
        inconsistencies **3:** 202
        as Machiavellian villain **3:** 280
        manliness **20:** 113; **29:** 127, 133; **44:** 315
        psychoanalytic interpretations **20:** 42, 73, 238, 376; **44:** 284, 289, 297, 324; **45:** 48, 58
        Richard III, compared with **3:** 177, 182, 186, 345; **20:** 86, 92; **22:** 365; **44:** 269
        as Satan figure **3:** 229, 269, 275, 289, 318
        self-awareness **3:** 312, 329, 338; **16:** 317; **44:** 361
        as sympathetic figure **3:** 229, 306, 314, 338; **29:** 139, 152; **44:** 269, 306, 337
        as tragic hero **44:** 269, 306, 315, 324, 337

Macbeth (Lady Macbeth)
    *Macbeth*
        ambition **3:** 185, 219; **20:** 279, 345
        characterization **20:** 56, 60, 65, 73, 140, 148, 151, 241, 279, 283, 338, 350, 406, 413; **29:** 109, 146

        childlessness **3:** 219, 223; **48:** 214
        good and evil, combined traits of **3:** 173, 191, 213; **20:** 60, 107
        inconsistencies **3:** 202; **20:** 54, 137
        influence on Macbeth **3:** 171, 185, 191, 193, 199, 262, 289, 312, 318; **13:** 502; **20:** 345; **25:** 235; **29:** 133
        psychoanalytic interpretations **20:** 345; **44:** 289, 297; **45:** 58
        sleepwalking scene **44:** 261
        as sympathetic figure **3:** 191, 193, 203

Macduff
    *Macbeth* **3:** 226, 231, 253, 262,; **25:** 235; **29:** 127, 133, 155

MacMorris
    *Henry V* **22:** 103; **28:** 159; **30:** 278

Malcolm
    *Macbeth* **25:** 235
    fatherhood **48:** 214

Malvolio
    *Twelfth Night*
        characterization **1:** 540, 544, 545, 548, 550, 554, 558, 567, 575, 577, 615; **26:** 207, 233, 273; **46:** 286
        forged letter **16:** 372; **28:** 1
        punishment **1:** 539, 544, 548, 549, 554, 555, 558, 563, 577, 590, 632, 645; **46:** 291, 297, 338
        as Puritan **1:** 549, 551, 555, 558, 561, 563; **25:** 47
        role in play **1:** 545, 548, 549, 553, 555, 563, 567, 575, 577, 588, 610, 615, 632, 645; **26:** 337, 374; **46:** 347

Mamillius
    *The Winter's Tale* **7:** 394, 396, 451; **22:** 324

Margaret
    *Henry VI, Parts 1, 2, and 3*
        characterization **3:** 18, 26, 35, 51, 103, 109, 140, 157; **24:** 48
        Suffolk, relationship with **3:** 18, 24, 26, 157; **39:** 213
    *Richard III* **8:** 153, 154, 159, 162, 163, 170, 193, 201, 206, 210, 218, 223, 228, 243, 248, 262; **39:** 345

Marina
    *Pericles* **37:** 361

Menenius
    *Coriolanus* **9:** 8, 9, 11, 14, 19, 26, 78, 80, 106, 148, 157; **25:** 263, 296; **30:** 67, 79, 89, 96, 111, 133

Mercutio
    *Romeo and Juliet*
        bawdy **5:** 463, 525, 550, 575
        death **5:** 415, 418, 419, 547; **33:** 290
        as worldly counterpart to Romeo **5:** 425, 464, 542; **33:** 290

minor characters
    *Richard III* **8:** 154, 159, 162, 163, 168, 170,

177, 184, 186, 201, 206, 210, 218, 223, 228, 232, 239, 248, 262, 267

**Miranda**
*The Tempest* **8:** 289, 301, 304, 328, 336, 370, 454; **19:** 357; **22:** 302; **28:** 249; **29:** 278, 297, 362, 368, 377, 396

**Mistress Elbow**
*Measure for Measure* See **Elbow (Mistress Elbow)**

**Mistress Quickly**
*Henry V* See **Quickly**

**Mortimer**
*Henry IV, Parts 1 and 2* **25:** 151

**Norfolk**
*Henry VIII* **22:** 182

**Northumberland**
*Richard II* **24:** 423

**Nurse**
*Romeo and Juliet* **5:** 419, 425, 463, 464, 575; **33:** 294

**Oberon**
*A Midsummer Night's Dream*
as controlling force **3:** 434, 459, 477, 502; **29:** 175

**Octavius**
*Antony and Cleopatra* **6:** 22, 24, 31, 38, 43, 53, 62, 107, 125, 146, 178, 181, 219; **25:** 257
*Julius Caesar* **30:** 316

**Olivia**
*Twelfth Night* **1:** 540, 543, 545; **46:** 286, 324, 369; **47:** 45

**Ophelia**
*Hamlet* **1:** 73, 76, 81, 82, 91, 96, 97, 154, 166, 169, 171, 218, 270; **13:** 268; **16:** 246; **19:** 330; **21:** 17, 41, 44, 72, 81, 101, 104, 107, 112, 136, 203, 259, 347, 381, 386, 392, 416; **28:** 232, 325; **35:** 104, 126, 140, 144, 182, 238; **44:** 189, 195, 248
in art **48:** 255
death **48:** 255
as icon **48:** 255
influence on popular culture **48:** 255

**Orlando**
*As You Like It*
as ideal man **5:** 32, 36, 39, 162; **34:** 161; **46:** 94
as younger brother **5:** 66, 158; **46:** 94

**Orsino**
*Twelfth Night* **46:** 286, 333; **47:** 45

**Othello**
*Othello*
affinity with Iago **4:** 400, 427, 468, 470, 477, 500, 506; **25:** 189; **35:** 276, 320, 327
as conventional "blameless hero" **4:** 445, 486, 500

credulity **4:** 384, 385, 388, 390, 396, 402, 434, 440, 455; **13:** 327; **32:** 302; **47:** 25, 51
Desdemona, relationship with **22:** 339; **35:** 301, 317; **37:** 269; **43:** 32
divided nature **4:** 400, 412, 462, 470, 477, 493, 500, 582, 592; **16:** 293; **19:** 276; **25:** 189; **35:** 320
egotism **4:** 427, 470, 477, 493, 522, 536, 541, 573, 597; **13:** 304; **35:** 247, 253
self-destructive anger **16:** 283
self-dramatizing or self-deluding **4:** 454, 457, 477, 592; **13:** 313; **16:** 293; **35:** 317
self-knowledge **4:** 462, 470, 477, 483, 508, 522, 530, 564, 580, 591, 596; **13:** 304, 313; **16:** 283; **28:** 243; **35:** 253, 317
spiritual state **4:** 483, 488, 517, 525, 527, 544, 559, 564, 573; **28:** 243; **35:** 253

**Page, Anne**
*The Merry Wives of Windsor* **47:** 321
Anne Page-Fenton plot **5:** 334, 336, 343, 353, 376, 390, 395, 402; **22:** 93; **47:** 308

**Page, Mistress Margaret**
*The Merry Wives of Windsor* **47:** 321

**Painter**
*Timon of Athens* See **Poet and Painter**

**Palamon and Arcite**
*The Two Noble Kinsmen* **9:** 474, 481, 490, 492, 502

**Parolles**
*All's Well That Ends Well*
characterization **7:** 8, 9, 43, 76, 81, 98, 109, 113, 116, 126; **22:** 78; **26:** 48, 73, 97; **26:** 117; **46:** 68
exposure **7:** 9, 27, 81, 98, 109, 113, 116, 121, 126
Falstaff, compared with **7:** 8, 9, 16

**pastoral characters (Silvius, Phebe, and Corin)**
*As You Like It* **23:** 37, 97, 98, 99, 108, 110, 118, 122, 138; **34:** 147

**Paulina**
*The Winter's Tale* **7:** 385, 412, 506; **15:** 528; **22:** 324; **25:** 339; **36:** 311

**Pedro (Don Pedro)**
*Much Ado about Nothing* **8:** 17, 19, 48, 58, 63, 82, 111, 121

**Perdita**
*The Winter's Tale*
characterization **7:** 395, 412, 414, 419, 429, 432, 452, 506; **22:** 324; **25:** 339; **36:** 328; **43:** 39
reunion with Leontes (Act V, scene ii) **7:** 377, 379, 381, 390, 432, 464, 480

**Pericles**
*Pericles*
characterization **36:** 251; **37:** 361
patience **2:** 572, 573, 578, 579
suit of Antiochus's daughter **2:** 547, 565, 578, 579
Ulysses, compared with **2:** 551

**Petruchio**
*The Taming of the Shrew*
admirable qualities **9:** 320, 332, 341, 344, 345, 370, 375, 386
audacity or vigor **9:** 325, 337, 355, 375, 386, 404
characterization **32:** 1
coarseness or brutality **9:** 325, 329, 365, 390, 393, 398, 407; **19:** 122; **43:** 61
as lord of misrule **9:** 393
love for Kate **9:** 338, 340, 343, 344, 386; **12:** 435
portrayals of **31:** 282
pragmatism **9:** 329, 334, 375, 398, 424; **13:** 3; **31:** 345, 351
taming method **9:** 320, 323, 329, 340, 341, 343, 345, 355, 369, 370, 375, 390, 398, 407, 413, 419, 424; **19:** 3, 12, 21 **31:** 269, 295, 326, 335, 339

**Phebe**
*As You Like It* See **pastoral characters**

**Pistol**
*Henry V* **28:** 146

**plebeians**
*Coriolanus* **9:** 8, 9, 11, 12, 15, 18, 19, 26, 33, 39, 53, 92, 125, 153, 183, 189; **25:** 296; **30:** 58, 79, 96, 111

**Poet and Painter**
*Timon of Athens* **25:** 198

**the poets**
*Julius Caesar* **7:** 179, 320, 350

**Polixenes**
*The Winter's Tale*
Leontes, relationship with **48:** 309

**Polonius**
*Hamlet* **21:** 259, 334, 347, 386, 416; **35:** 182

**Porter**
*Henry VIII* **24:** 155
*Macbeth* **3:** 173, 175, 184, 190, 196, 203, 205, 225, 260, 271, 297, 300; **20:** 283

**Portia**
*The Merchant of Venice* **4:** 194, 195, 196, 215, 254, 263, 336, 356; **12:** 104, 107, 114; **13:** 37; **22:** 3, 69; **25:** 22; **32:** 294; **37:** 86; **40:** 142, 156, 197, 208

**Posthumus**
*Cymbeline* **4:** 24, 30, 53, 78, 116, 127, 141, 155, 159, 167; **15:** 89; **19:** 411; **25:** 245, 319; **36:** 142; **44:** 28; **45:** 67, 75; **47:** 25, 205, 228

**Prince Henry**
*King John* See **Henry (Prince Henry)**

**Prospero**
*The Tempest*

characterization **8:** 312, 348, 370, 458; **16:** 442; **22:** 302; **45:** 188, 272
as God or Providence **8:** 311, 328, 364, 380, 429, 435
magic, nature of **8:** 301, 340, 356, 396, 414, 423, 458; **25:** 382; **28:** 391; **29:** 278, 292, 368, 377, 396; **32:** 338, 343
psychoanalytic interpretation **45:** 259
redemptive powers **8:** 302, 320, 353, 370, 390, 429, 439, 447; **29:** 297
as ruler **8:** 304, 308, 309, 420, 423; **13:** 424; **22:** 302; **29:** 278, 362, 377, 396
self-control **8:** 312, 414, 420; **22:** 302; **44:** 11
self-knowledge **16:** 442; **22:** 302; **29:** 278, 292, 362, 377, 396
as Shakespeare or creative artist **8:** 299, 302, 308, 312, 320, 324, 353, 364, 435, 447
as tragic hero **8:** 359, 370, 464; **29:** 292

**Proteus**
*The Two Gentlemen of Verona* **6:** 439, 450, 458, 480, 490, 511; **40:** 312, 327, 330, 335, 359; **42:** 18

**Puck**
*A Midsummer Night's Dream* **45:** 96, 158

**Quickly (Mistress Quickly)**
*Henry V* **5:** 186, 187, 210, 276, 293; **30:** 278

**Regan**
*King Lear* **31:** 151; **46:** 231, 242

**Richard (King Richard II)**
*Richard II*
artistic temperament **6:** 264, 267, 270, 272, 277, 292, 294, 298, 315, 331, 334, 347, 368, 374, 393, 409; **24:** 298, 301, 304, 315, 322, 390, 405, 408, 411, 414, 419; **39:** 289
Bolingbroke, compared with **24:** 346, 349, 351, 352, 356, 419; **39:** 289
characterization **6:** 250, 252, 253, 254, 255, 258, 262, 263, 267, 270, 272, 282, 283, 304, 343, 347, 364, 368; **24:** 262, 263, 267, 269, 270, 271, 272, 273, 274, 278, 280, 315, 322, 325, 330, 333, 390, 395, 402, 405, 423; **28:** 134; **39:** 279, 289
dangerous aspects **24:** 405
delusion **6:** 267, 298, 334, 368, 409; **24:** 329, 336, 405
homosexuality **24:** 405
kingship **6:** 253, 254, 263, 272, 327, 331, 334, 338, 364, 402, 414; **24:** 278, 295, 336, 337, 339, 356, 419; **28:** 134, 178; **39:** 256, 263
loss of identity **6:** 267, 338, 368, 374, 381, 388, 391, 409; **24:** 298, 414, 428
as martyr-king **6:** 289, 307, 321; **19:** 209; **24:** 289, 291; **28:** 134
nobility **6:** 255, 258, 259, 262, 263, 391; **24:** 260, 263, 274, 280, 289, 291, 402, 408, 411
political acumen **6:** 263, 264, 272, 292, 310, 327, 334, 364, 368, 374, 388, 391, 397, 402, 409; **24:** 405; **39:** 256
private vs. public persona **6:** 317, 327, 364, 368, 391, 409; **24:** 428

role-playing **24:** 419, 423; **28:** 178
seizure of Gaunt's estate **6:** 250, 338, 388
self-dramatization **6:** 264, 267, 307, 310, 315, 317, 331, 334, 368, 393, 409; **24:** 339; **28:** 178
self-hatred **13:** 172; **24:** 383; **39:** 289
self-knowledge **6:** 255, 267, 331, 334, 338, 352, 354, 368, 388, 391; **24:** 273, 289, 411, 414; **39:** 263, 289
spiritual redemption **6:** 255, 267, 331, 334, 338, 352, 354, 368, 388, 391; **24:** 273, 289, 411, 414

**Richard (King Richard III, formerly Richard, Duke of Gloucester)**
*Henry VI, Parts 1, 2, and 3*
characterization **3:** 35, 48, 57, 64, 77, 143, 151; **22:** 193; **39:** 160, 177
as revenger **22:** 193
soliloquy (*3 Henry VI*, Act III, scene ii) **3:** 17, 48
*Richard III*
ambition **8:** 148, 154, 165, 168, 170, 177, 182, 213, 218, 228, 232, 239, 252, 258, 267; **39:** 308, 341, 360, 370, 383
attractive qualities **8:** 145, 148, 152, 154, 159, 161, 162, 165, 168, 170, 181, 182, 184, 185, 197, 201, 206, 213, 228, 243, 252, 256; **16:** 150; **39:** 370, 383
credibility, question of **8:** 145, 147, 154, 159, 165, 193; **13:** 142
death **8:** 145, 148, 154, 159, 165, 168, 170, 177, 182, 197, 210, 223, 228, 232, 243, 248, 252, 258, 267
deformity as symbol **8:** 146, 147, 148, 152, 154, 159, 161, 165, 170, 177, 184, 185, 193, 218, 248, 252, 267; **19:** 164
inversion of moral order **8:** 159, 168, 177, 182, 184, 185, 197, 201, 213, 218, 223, 232, 239, 243, 248, 252, 258, 262, 267; **39:** 360
as Machiavellian villain **8:** 165, 182, 190, 201, 218, 232, 239, 243, 248; **39:** 308, 326, 360, 387
as monster or symbol of diabolic **8:** 145, 147, 159, 162, 168, 170, 177, 182, 193, 197, 201, 228, 239, 248, 258; **13:** 142; **37:** 144; **39:** 326, 349
other literary villains, compared with **8:** 148, 161, 162, 165, 181, 182, 206, 213, 239, 267
role-playing, hypocrisy, and dissimulation **8:** 145, 148, 154, 159, 162, 165, 168, 170, 182, 190, 206, 213, 218, 228, 239, 243, 252, 258, 267; **25:** 141, 164, 245; **39:** 335, 341, 387
as scourge or instrument of God **8:** 163, 177, 193, 201, 218, 228, 248, 267; **39:** 308
as Vice figure **8:** 190, 201, 213, 228, 243, 248, 252; **16:** 150; **39:** 383, 387

**Richard Plantagenet, Duke of York**
*Henry VI, Parts 1, 2, and 3* See **York**

**Richmond**
*Richard III* **8:** 154, 158, 163, 168, 177, 182, 193, 210, 218, 223, 228, 243, 248, 252; **13:** 142; **25:** 141; **39:** 349

the **Rival Poet**
*Sonnets* **10:** 169, 233, 334, 337, 385; **48:** 352

**Roman citizenry**
*Julius Caesar*
portrayal of **7:** 169, 179, 210, 221, 245, 279, 282, 310, 320, 333; **17:** 271, 279, 288, 291, 292, 298, 323, 334, 351, 367, 374, 375, 378; **22:** 280; **30:** 285, 297, 316, 321, 374, 379; **37:** 229

**Romeo and Juliet**
*Romeo and Juliet*
death-wish **5:** 431, 489, 505, 528, 530, 538, 542, 550, 566, 571, 575; **32:** 212
immortality **5:** 536
Juliet's epithalamium speech (Act III, scene ii) **5:** 431, 477, 492
Juliet's innocence **5:** 421, 423, 450, 454; **33:** 257
maturation **5:** 437, 454, 467, 493, 498, 509, 520, 565; **33:** 249, 257
rebellion **25:** 257
reckless passion **5:** 419, 427, 431, 438, 443, 444, 448, 467, 479, 485, 505, 533, 538, 542; **33:** 241
Romeo's dream (Act V, scene i) **5:** 513, 536, 556; **45:** 40
Rosaline, Romeo's relationship with **5:** 419, 423, 425, 427, 438, 498, 542, 575

**Rosalind**
*As You Like It* **46:** 94, 122
Beatrice, compared with **5:** 26, 36, 50, 75
charm **5:** 55, 75; **23:** 17, 18, 20, 41, 89, 111
disguise, role of **5:** 75, 107, 118, 122, 128, 130, 133, 138, 141, 146, 148, 164, 168; **13:** 502; **23:** 35, 42, 106, 119, 123, 146; **34:** 130; **46:** 127, 134, 142
femininity **5:** 26, 36, 52, 75; **23:** 24, 29, 46, 54, 103, 108, 121, 146
love-theme, relation to **5:** 79, 88, 103, 116, 122, 138, 141; **23:** 114, 115; **34:** 85, 177

**rustic characters**
*As You Like It* **5:** 24, 60, 72, 84; **23:** 127; **34:** 78, 161
*A Midsummer Night's Dream* **3:** 376, 397, 432; **12:** 291, 293; **45:** 147, 160

**Scroop**
*Henry V* See **traitors**

**Sebastian**
*The Tempest* See **Antonio and Sebastian**

**Shylock**
*The Merchant of Venice*
alienation **4:** 279, 312; **40:** 175; **48:** 77
ambiguity **4:** 247, 254, 315, 319, 331; **12:** 31, 35, 36, 50, 51, 52, 56, 81, 124; **40:** 175
forced conversion **4:** 209, 252, 268, 282, 289, 321
Jewishness **4:** 193, 194, 195, 200, 201, 213, 214, 279; **22:** 69; **25:** 257; **40:** 142, 175, 181; **48:** 65, 77
motives in making the bond **4:** 252, 263, 266, 268; **22:** 69; **25:** 22

as Puritan **40:** 127, 166
as scapegoat figure **4:** 254, 300; **40:** 166
as traditional comic villain **4:** 230, 243, 261, 263, 315; **12:** 40, 62, 124; **40:** 175
as tragic figure **12:** 6, 9, 10, 16, 21, 23, 25, 40, 44, 66, 67, 81, 97; **40:** 175

**Sicinius**
*Coriolanus* See **the tribunes**

**Silvia**
*The Two Gentlemen of Verona* **6:** 450, 453, 458, 476, 494, 499, 516, 519, 549, 564; **40:** 312, 327, 374

**Silvius**
*As You Like It* See **pastoral characters**

**Sly**
*The Taming of the Shrew* **9:** 320, 322, 350, 370, 381, 390, 398, 430; **12:** 316, 335, 416, 427, 441; **16:** 13; **19:** 34, 122; **22:** 48; **37:** 31

**soldiers**
*Henry V* **5:** 203, 239, 267, 276, 281, 287, 293, 318; **28:** 146; **30:** 169,

**Speed**
*The Two Gentlemen of Verona* See **Launce and Speed**

**Stephano and Trinculo**
*The Tempest*
comic subplot of **8:** 292, 297, 299, 304, 309, 324, 328, 353, 370; **25:** 382; **29:** 377; **46:** 14, 33

**Stephen Gardiner**
*Henry VIII* See **Gardiner**

**Talbot**
*Henry VI, Parts 1, 2, and 3* **39:** 160, 213, 222

**Tamora**
*Titus Andronicus* **4:** 632, 662, 672, 675; **27:** 266; **43:** 170

**Tarquin**
*The Rape of Lucrece* **10:** 80, 93, 98, 116, 125; **22:** 294; **25:** 305; **32:** 321; **33:** 190; **43:** 102
Petrarchan lover **48:** 291
platonic tyrant **48:** 291
Satan role **48:** 291

**Thersites**
*Troilus and Cressida* **13:** 53; **25:** 56; **27:** 381

**Theseus**
*A Midsummer Night's Dream*
characterization **3:** 363
Hippolyta, relationship with **3:** 381, 412, 421, 423, 450, 468, 520; **29:** 175, 216, 243, 256; **45:** 84
as ideal **3:** 379, 391
"lovers, lunatics, and poets" speech (Act V, scene i) **3:** 365, 371, 379, 381, 391, 402, 411, 412, 421, 423, 441, 498, 506; **29:** 175
as representative of institutional life **3:** 381, 403

**Time-Chorus**
*The Winter's Tale* **7:** 377, 380, 412, 464, 476, 501; **15:** 518

**Timon**
*Timon of Athens*
comic traits **25:** 198
as flawed hero **1:** 456, 459, 462, 472, 495, 503, 507, 515; **16:** 351; **20:** 429, 433, 476; **25:** 198; **27:** 157, 161
misanthropy **13:** 392; **20:** 431, 464, 476, 481, 491, 492, 493; **27:** 161, 175, 184, 196; **37:** 222
as noble figure **1:** 467, 473, 483, 499; **20:** 493; **27:** 212

**Titania**
*A Midsummer Night's Dream* **29:** 243

**Titus**
*Titus Andronicus* **4:** 632, 637, 640, 644, 647, 653, 656, 662; **25:** 245; **27:** 255

**Touchstone**
*As You Like It*
callousness **5:** 88
comic and farcical elements **46:** 117
as philosopher-fool **5:** 24, 28, 30, 32, 36, 63, 75, 98; **23:** 152; **34:** 85; **46:** 1, 14, 18, 24, 33, 52, 60, 88, 105
relation to pastoral convention **5:** 54, 61, 63, 72, 75, 77, 79, 84, 86, 93, 98, 114, 118, 135, 138, 166; **34:** 72, 147, 161
satire or parody of pastoral conventions **46:** 122
selflessness **5:** 30, 36, 39, 76

**traitors (Scroop, Grey, and Cambridge)**
*Henry V* **16:** 202; **30:** 220, 278

**the tribunes (Brutus and Sicinius)**
*Coriolanus* **9:** 9, 11, 14, 19, 33, 169, 180

**Trinculo**
*The Tempest* See **Stephano and Trinculo**

**Troilus**
*Troilus and Cressida*
contradictory behavior **3:** 596, 602, 635; **27:** 362
Cressida, relationship with **3:** 594, 596, 606; **22:** 58
integrity **3:** 617
opposition to Ulysses **3:** 561, 584, 590
as unsympathetic figure **18:** 423; **22:** 58, 339; **43:** 317
as warrior **3:** 596; **22:** 339

**Ulysses**
*Troilus and Cressida*
speech on degree (Act I, scene iii) **3:** 549, 599, 609, 642; **27:** 396

**Venetians**
*The Merchant of Venice* **4:** 195, 200, 228, 254, 273, 300, 321, 331

**Venus**
*Venus and Adonis* **10:** 427, 429, 434, 439, 442, 448, 449, 451, 454, 466, 473, 480, 486, 489; **16:** 452; **25:** 305, 328; **28:** 355; **33:** 309, 321, 330, 347, 352, 357, 363, 370, 377

**Viola**
*Twelfth Night* **26:** 308; **46:** 286, 324, 347, 369

**Virgilia**
*Coriolanus* **9:** 11, 19, 26, 33, 58, 100, 121, 125; **25:** 263; **30:** 79, 96, 133

**Volumnia**
*Coriolanus*
Coriolanus's subservience to **9:** 16, 26, 33, 53, 62, 80, 92, 100, 117, 125, 142, 177, 183; **30:** 140, 149; **44:** 79
influence on Coriolanus **9:** 45, 62, 65, 78, 92, 100, 110, 117, 121, 125, 130, 148, 157, 183, 189, 193; **25:** 263, 296; **30:** 79, 96, 125, 133, 140, 142, 149; **44:** 93
as noble Roman matron **9:** 16, 19, 26, 31, 33
personification of Rome **9:** 125, 183

**Wat the hare**
*Venus and Adonis* **10:** 424, 451

**the Watch**
*Much Ado about Nothing* See **Dogberry and the Watch**

**Williams**
*Henry V* **13:** 502; **16:** 183; **28:** 146; **30:** 169, 259, 278

**witches**
*Macbeth*
and supernaturalism **3:** 171, 172, 173, 175, 177, 182, 183, 184, 185, 194, 196, 198, 202, 207, 208, 213, 219, 229, 239; **16:** 317; **19:** 245; **20:** 92, 175, 213, 279, 283, 374, 387, 406, 413; **25:** 235; **28:** 339; **29:** 91, 101, 109, 120

**Wolsey (Cardinal Wolsey)**
*Henry VIII* **2:** 15, 18, 19, 23, 24, 38; **22:** 182; **24:** 80, 91, 112, 113, 129, 140; **37:** 109; **41:** 129

**York (Edmund of Langley, Duke of York)**
*Richard II* **6:** 287, 364, 368, 388, 402, 414; **24:** 263, 320, 322, 364, 395, 414; **39:** 243, 279

**York (Richard Plantagenet, Duke of York)**
*Henry VI, Parts 1, 2, and 3*
death of **13:** 131

# Cumulative Critic Index

**Abel, Lionel**
*Hamlet* **1**: 237

**Abrams, Richard**
Authorship Controversy (topic entry) **41**: 98
*King Lear* **46**: 218
*The Two Noble Kinsmen* **41**: 385

**Adams, Howard C.**
*Troilus and Cressida* **27**: 400

**Adams, John C.**
*Romeo and Juliet* **11**: 507
*The Tempest* **15**: 346

**Adams, John F.**
*All's Well That Ends Well* **7**: 86

**Adams, John Quincy**
*Othello* **4**: 408
*Romeo and Juliet* **5**: 426

**Adams, Joseph Quincy**
*The Phoenix and Turtle* **10**: 16

**Adams, Robert M.**
*The Tempest* **29**: 303

**Adamson, Jane**
*Othello* **4**: 591

**Adamson, W. D.**
*Othello* **35**: 360

**Addenbrooke, David**
*Macbeth* **20**: 263

**Addison, Joseph**
*Hamlet* **1**: 75
*Henry IV, 1 and 2* **1**: 287
*King Lear* **2**: 93

**Adelman, Janet**
*All's Well That Ends Well* **13**: 84
*Antony and Cleopatra* **6**: 211; **27**: 110; **47**: 77
*Coriolanus* **9**: 183
*Hamlet* **44**: 160
*Measure for Measure* **13**: 84
*Othello* **22**: 339; **42**: 198
Psychoanalytic Interpretations (topic entry) **44**: 79
*Troilus and Cressida* **22**: 339

**Adler, Doris**
*Antony and Cleopatra* **17**: 94

**Agate, James**
*Coriolanus* **17**: 157
*Hamlet* **21**: 155, 167, 169, 177, 194
*Henry IV, 1 and 2* **14**: 25
*King Lear* **11**: 46, 51
*Macbeth* **20**: 182, 184
*Othello* **11**: 262, 266
*Richard II* **24**: 298
*Romeo and Juliet* **11**: 444
*Troilus and Cressida* **18**: 300
*The Two Noble Kinsmen* **9**: 462

**Agee, James**
*Henry V* **14**: 213, 214

**Aggeler, Geoffrey**
*Hamlet* **48**: 195

**Aichinger, C. P.**
*Hamlet* **35**: 212

**Aire, Sally**
*As You Like It* **23**: 131
*The Merry Wives of Windsor* **18**: 56
*A Midsummer Night's Dream* **12**: 271
*Pericles* **15**: 165
*Twelfth Night* **26**: 294

**Akrigg, G. P. V.**
*Henry V* **30**: 252

**Alden, Barbara**
*Othello* **11**: 212

**Alden, Raymond Macdonald**
*Sonnets* **10**: 247

**Aldus, P. J.**
*Hamlet* **35**: 134

**Alexander, Bill**
*The Merry Wives of Windsor* **18**: 64

**Alexander, Peter**
*Henry VIII* **2**: 43

**Alger, William Rounseville**
*Othello* **11**: 208

**Allen, Don Cameron**
*The Rape of Lucrece* **10**: 89
*Venus and Adonis* **10**: 451

**Allen, John A.**
*A Midsummer Night's Dream* **3**: 457

**Allen, Shirley**
*Pericles* **15**: 135

**Allen, Shirley S.**
*Antony and Cleopatra* **17**: 20
*A Midsummer Night's Dream* **12**: 175
*The Winter's Tale* **15**: 419

**Alleva, Richard**
*Hamlet* **21**: 321

**Alleyn, Henry**
*Cymbeline* **15**: 50

**Almeida, Barbara Heliodora C. de M. F. de**
*Troilus and Cressida* **3**: 604

**Alpert, Hollis**
*Hamlet* **21**: 160

**Altemus, Jameson Torr**
*As You Like It* **23**: 41

**Altick, Richard D.**
*Richard II* **6**: 298

**Altieri, Joanne**
*Henry V* **5**: 314

**Altman, Joel B.**
*Henry V* **19**: 133

**Alulis, Joseph**
*As You Like It* **46**: 94

**Alvarez, A.**
*All's Well That Ends Well* **26**: 26
*Coriolanus* **17**: 166
*Hamlet* **21**: 268
*King Lear* **11**: 74

*The Merchant of Venice* **12**: 66
*Othello* **11**: 286
*The Phoenix and Turtle* **10**: 31
*The Taming of the Shrew* **12**: 356
*Troilus and Cressida* **18**: 322
*Twelfth Night* **26**: 253
*The Two Gentlemen of Verona* **12**: 473

Alvis, John
Politics and Power (topic entry) **30**: 11

Amhurst, Nicholas
*Henry VIII* **2**: 15

Amory, Mark
*All's Well That Ends Well* **26**: 58
*Macbeth* **20**: 309

Anderson, Linda
*The Merry Wives of Windsor* **38**: 264

Anderson, Mary
*The Winter's Tale* **15**: 443

Andreasen, Nancy J. C.
Madness (topic entry) **35**: 34

Andres, Michael Cameron
*Hamlet* **35**: 167

Andrews, Nigel
*The Tempest* **15**: 294

Anson, John
*Julius Caesar* **7**: 324

Ansorge, Peter
*All's Well That Ends Well* **26**: 46
*Coriolanus* **17**: 193
*Cymbeline* **15**: 75
*Julius Caesar* **17**: 382
*The Merchant of Venice* **12**: 74
*A Midsummer Night's Dream* **12**: 259
*Richard II* **24**: 349
*The Tempest* **15**: 280

Anstey, Edgar
*Henry V* **14**: 202

Anthony, Earl of Shaftesbury
*Hamlet* **1**: 75

Appleton, William W.
*Macbeth* **20**: 48

Archer, William
*All's Well That Ends Well* **26**: 8
*Henry IV, 1 and 2* **14**: 16, 20, 21
*Measure for Measure* **23**: 284
*A Midsummer Night's Dream* **12**: 196
*Richard III* **14**: 400
*The Tempest* **15**: 222
*Twelfth Night* **1**: 558; **26**: 201, 216
*The Winter's Tale* **15**: 437

Arden, John
*Henry V* **14**: 336

Arditti, Michael
*Macbeth* **20**: 315

Armstrong, William A.
*Hamlet* **21**: 136

Arnold, Aerol
*Richard III* **8**: 210

Aronson, Alex
Appearance vs. Reality (topic entry) **34**: 12

Arthos, John
*All's Well That Ends Well* **7**: 58
*Macbeth* **3**: 250
*Othello* **4**: 541
*The Phoenix and Turtle* **10**: 50
Shakespeare and Classical Civilization (topic entry) **27**: 1
*The Two Gentlemen of Verona* **6**: 532
*The Tempest* **45**: 247

Ashcroft, Peggy
*Antony and Cleopatra* **17**: 113
*Romeo and Juliet* **11**: 516

Asnani, Shyam M.
Clowns and Fools (topic entry) **46**: 14

Asp, Carolyn
*Love's Labour's Lost* **38**: 200
*Macbeth* **29**: 133
Psychoanalytic Interpretations (topic entry) **44**: 35
*Troilus and Cressida* **27**: 396

Asquith, Ros
*Richard III* **14**: 490
*Troilus and Cressida* **18**: 382

Astington, John
*Twelfth Night* **28**: 1; **46**: 338

Aston, Anthony
*Hamlet* **21**: 10

Atkinson, Brooks
*As You Like It* **23**: 72, 75
*Hamlet* **21**: 219
*Henry IV, 1 and 2* **14**: 60, 63, 64
*Julius Caesar* **17**: 318
*King John* **24**: 209
*King Lear* **11**: 58
*Macbeth* **20**: 200, 224, 232, 240
*The Merchant of Venice* **12**: 53
*A Midsummer Night's Dream* **12**: 209, 239
*Much Ado about Nothing* **18**: 171, 172, 175
*The Taming of the Shrew* **12**: 341, 345, 348
*Troilus and Cressida* **18**: 313
*Twelfth Night* **26**: 246

Auberlen, Eckhard
*Henry VIII* **2**: 78

Auden, W. H.
*Henry IV, 1 and 2* **1**: 410
*Much Ado about Nothing* **8**: 77

*Sonnets* **10**: 325
*Twelfth Night* **1**: 599

Austin, L. F.
*The Merry Wives of Windsor* **18**: 26

Axton, Marie
*The Phoenix and Turtle* **38**: 378

Bache, William B.
Fathers and Daughters (topic entry) **36**: 51

Bacon, Lord Francis
*Richard II* **6**: 250

Baddeley, V. C. Clinton
*Troilus and Cressida* **18**: 394

Badeau, Adam
*Hamlet* **21**: 62

Bagebot, Walter
*Measure for Measure* **2**: 406

Baildon, H. Bellyse
*Titus Andronicus* **4**: 632

Baines, Barbara J.
*Henry IV, 1 and 2* **39**: 123

Baker, David J.
*Henry V* **22**: 103

Baker, Donald
*As You Like It* **23**: 132

Baker, Felix
*Antony and Cleopatra* **17**: 26

Baker, George Pierce
*Romeo and Juliet* **5**: 448

Baker, H. Barton
*Romeo and Juliet* **11**: 378, 399, 422

Baker, Harry T.
*Henry IV, 1 and 2* **1**: 347

Baker, Herschel
*Macbeth* **20**: 64

Baker, Nick
*Pericles* **15**: 173

Baker, Susan
Appearance vs. Reality (topic entry) **34**: 45

Baldwin, Thomas Whitfield
*The Comedy of Errors* **1**: 21; **34**: 215

Balk, Wes
*The Taming of the Shrew* **12**: 366

Bamber, Linda
Gender Identity (topic entry) **40**: 15

Bamford, Karen
*Cymbeline* **36**: 148

Banks-Smith, Nancy
*Richard II* **24**: 364

Barber, C. L.
*As You Like It* **5**: 79
*The Comedy of Errors* **34**: 190
*Hamlet* **44**: 152
*Henry IV, 1 and 2* **1**: 414
*Love's Labour's Lost* **2**: 335
*The Merchant of Venice* **4**: 273
*A Midsummer Night's Dream* **3**: 427
*Pericles* **2**: 582
*Sonnets* **10**: 302
*Twelfth Night* **1**: 620
*The Winter's Tale* **7**: 480

Barish, Jonas
*As You Like It* **28**: 9
*Measure for Measure* **28**: 9
*The Merchant of Venice* **28**: 9
*The Merry Wives of Windsor* **28**: 9
*A Midsummer Night's Dream* **28**: 9
Violence in Shakespeare's Works (topic entry) **43**: 1

Barkan, Leonard
*Titus Andronicus* **43**: 203

Barker, Frank Granville
*Coriolanus* **17**: 168
*Hamlet* **21**: 216

Barker, Kathleen M. D.
*Richard II* **24**: 402

Barker, Ronald
*Twelfth Night* **26**: 245

Barnaby, Andrew
*As You Like It* **34**: 120; **37**: 1

Barnes, Clive
*As You Like It* **23**: 101
*The Comedy of Errors* **26**: 154
*Hamlet* **21**: 231, 269
*Measure for Measure* **23**: 330
*The Merchant of Venice* **12**: 80
*A Midsummer Night's Dream* **12**: 252
*Pericles* **15**: 158
*Twelfth Night* **26**: 290
*The Winter's Tale* **15**: 482

Barnes, Howard
*King Lear* **11**: 56

Barnes, Thomas
*Hamlet* **21**: 40

Barnet, Sylvan
*As You Like It* **5**: 125
*Twelfth Night* **1**: 588

Barnfield, Richard
*Venus and Adonis* **10**: 410

Barnstorff, D.
*Sonnets* **10**: 190

Barry, Gerald
*A Midsummer Night's Dream* **12**: 249

**Bartels, Emily C.**
 Hamlet **28:** 223
 King Lear **28:** 223
 Titus Andronicus **43:** 176

**Bartholomeusz, Dennis**
 The Winter's Tale **15:** 401, 465, 503, 507

**Barton, Anne**
 Antony and Cleopatra **6:** 208
 The Comedy of Errors **1:** 61
 Henry V **30:** 169
 The Merry Wives of Windsor **5:** 400
 Twelfth Night **1:** 656

**Barton, John**
 All's Well That Ends Well **26:** 48
 Troilus and Cressida **18:** 403

**Baskervill, Charles Read**
 The Merchant of Venice **4:** 226

**Bate, Jonathan**
 Shakespeare and Classical Civilization (topic entry) **27:** 46
 Sonnets **16:** 472
 Venus and Adonis **25:** 305

**Bates, Ronald**
 The Phoenix and Turtle **10:** 27

**Bateson, F. W.**
 Sonnets **10:** 277

**Battenhouse, Roy W.**
 Antony and Cleopatra **6:** 192
 Henry IV, 1 and 2 **1:** 434
 Henry V **5:** 260
 King Lear **31:** 149
 Macbeth **3:** 269
 Measure for Measure **2:** 466
 Othello **4:** 573
 The Rape of Lucrece **10:** 98
 Richard II **6:** 402
 Romeo and Juliet **5:** 542

**Baumlin, Tita French**
 Venus and Adonis **16:** 452

**Bawcutt, N. W.**
 Measure for Measure **23:** 400
 The Two Noble Kinsmen **9:** 492

**Baxter, John**
 Cymbeline **25:** 319

**Bayley, John**
 Coriolanus **30:** 133
 King Lear **31:** 162
 Othello **4:** 552
 Timon of Athens **27:** 175
 Troilus and Cressida **3:** 634; **27:** 381

**Bayley, P. C.**
 Henry VI, 1, 2, and 3 **24:** 25

**Bean, John C.**
 The Taming of the Shrew **9:** 426

**Beauchamp, Gorman**
 Henry V **14:** 242

**Beaufort, John**
 As You Like It **23:** 73
 Measure for Measure **23:** 352
 Much Ado about Nothing **18:** 219
 Richard III **14:** 480
 The Taming of the Shrew **12:** 347
 Twelfth Night **26:** 313

**Beauman, Sally**
 As You Like It **23:** 66
 Henry V **14:** 287, 295, 297, 301
 Love's Labour's Lost **23:** 186
 Macbeth **20:** 197
 Pericles **15:** 138
 Titus Andronicus **17:** 459
 Troilus and Cressida **18:** 292

**Beaurline, L. A.**
 King John **41:** 228

**Beckman, Margaret Boerner**
 As You Like It **34:** 172

**Beckwith, Sarah**
 Macbeth **19:** 245

**Beerbohm, Max**
 Hamlet **21:** 140
 King John **24:** 201
 Macbeth **20:** 164
 A Midsummer Night's Dream **12:** 203
 Much Ado about Nothing **18:** 145

**Belsey, Catherine**
 Desire (topic entry) **38:** 19
 The Merchant of Venice **22:** 3
 A Midsummer Night's Dream **28:** 15
 Romeo and Juliet **25:** 181
 Shakespeare's Representation of Women (topic entry) **31:** 43

**Bennett, H. S.**
 Pericles **15:** 139
 Romeo and Juliet **11:** 458

**Bennett, Josephine Waters**
 All's Well That Ends Well **7:** 104

**Bennetts, Leslie**
 Much Ado about Nothing **18:** 223

**Benson, Frank**
 Twelfth Night **26:** 207

**Benson, John**
 Sonnets **10:** 153

**Benston, Alice N.**
 The Merchant of Venice **4:** 336

**Bentley, Eric**
 Julius Caesar **17:** 350

**Berek, Peter**
 The Taming of the Shrew **31:** 276

**Berge, Mark**
 King Lear **46:** 225

**Berger, Harry, Jr.**
 General Commentary **13:** 457
 Henry IV, 1 and 2 **28:** 101; **42:** 99; **48:** 95
 King Lear **46:** 242
 Macbeth **3:** 340
 Much Ado about Nothing **8:** 121
 Othello **35:** 380
 Richard II **13:** 172
 The Tempest **29:** 278

**Berger, Thomas L.**
 Henry V **13:** 183

**Bergeron, David M.**
 Cymbeline **4:** 170
 Henry IV, 1 and 2 **19:** 157; **39:** 143
 Henry VI, 1, 2, and 3 **3:** 149
 Richard II **19:** 151

**Berggren, Paula S.**
 Gender Identity (topic entry) **40:** 1
 The Two Noble Kinsmen **9:** 502

**Berkeley, David S.**
 All's Well That Ends Well **38:** 155

**Berkowitz, Gerald M.**
 Antony and Cleopatra **17:** 82
 Hamlet **21:** 301
 Much Ado about Nothing **18:** 211

**Berlin, Normand**
 Macbeth **20:** 279

**Berman, Ronald**
 Henry VI, 1, 2, and 3 **3:** 89
 Love's Labour's Lost **2:** 348
 Measure for Measure **33:** 52

**Bermann, Sandra L.**
 Sonnets **40:** 303

**Bernard, John**
 Othello **11:** 190; **32:** 201

**Berry, Edward**
 Othello **16:** 293

**Berry, Edward I.**
 Henry V **30:** 220
 Henry VI, 1, 2, and 3 **39:** 177
 Henry VIII **41:** 120

**Berry, Philippa**
 Hamlet **42:** 212
 The Rape of Lucrece **22:** 289

**Berry, Ralph**
 All's Well That Ends Well **26:** 114
 As You Like It **23:** 118; **34:** 72
 Coriolanus **9:** 174; **17:** 248
 Hamlet **21:** 361
 Henry V **14:** 328
 Julius Caesar **7:** 356; **17:** 317, 421
 Love's Labour's Lost **2:** 348
 Measure for Measure **23:** 335, 375; **33:** 69
 The Merchant of Venice **12:** 48
 The Merry Wives of Windsor **5:** 373; **18:** 52, 64
 A Midsummer Night's Dream **12:** 207
 Much Ado about Nothing **31:** 184
 The Taming of the Shrew **9:** 401
 The Tempest **15:** 338
 Timon of Athens **20:** 470
 Titus Andronicus **17:** 472
 Troilus and Cressida **18:** 406
 Twelfth Night **26:** 342, 374
 The Two Gentlemen of Verona **6:** 529; **12:** 488

**Bertin, Michael**
 Twelfth Night **26:** 299

**Bertram, Joseph L.**
 King Lear **11:** 93
 Much Ado about Nothing **18:** 182

**Bertram, Paul**
 Henry VIII **2:** 60

**Bethell, S. L.**
 Antony and Cleopatra **6:** 115
 Henry VI, 1, 2, and 3 **3:** 67
 Othello **4:** 517
 The Winter's Tale **7:** 446

**Bethell, Tom**
 Authorship Controversy (topic entry) **41:** 48, 61

**Bevington, David**
 Antony and Cleopatra **17:** 101
 Love's Labour's Lost **16:** 17; **38:** 209
 The Merry Wives of Windsor **18:** 71
 Politics and Power (topic entry) **30:** 29
 The Winter's Tale **45:** 295

**Bevington, David M.**
 Henry VI, 1, 2, and 3 **3:** 103
 A Midsummer Night's Dream **3:** 491

**Bickerstaff, Isaac**
 See also Steele, Sir Richard
 Julius Caesar **7:** 152

**Bickersteth, Geoffrey L.**
 King Lear **2:** 179

**Billington, Michael**
 All's Well That Ends Well **26:** 57
 Antony and Cleopatra **17:** 40, 54
 As You Like It **23:** 103, 120, 145
 The Comedy of Errors **26:** 149, 157, 158
 Cymbeline **15:** 60
 Hamlet **21:** 323, 329
 Henry V **14:** 307
 Julius Caesar **17:** 372, 382
 King John **24:** 215, 221, 236
 Love's Labour's Lost **23:** 207, 231
 Macbeth **20:** 298, 317
 The Merchant of Venice **12:** 82
 The Merry Wives of Windsor **18:** 49, 54
 Pericles **15:** 174, 176
 Richard II **24:** 336, 337, 380
 The Tempest **15:** 271
 Titus Andronicus **17:** 465

*Twelfth Night* **26**: 282, 346
*The Winter's Tale* **15**: 474

**Bingham, Madeleine**
*Julius Caesar* **17**: 315

**Bishop, T. G.**
*The Comedy of Errors* **37**: 12
*The Winter's Tale* **45**: 297

**Black, James**
*Henry IV, 1 and 2* **14**: 150; **39**: 89
*Measure for Measure* **2**: 519
*The Tempest* **19**: 357

**Blackmur, R. P.**
*Sonnets* **10**: 315

**Paula Blank**
*Richard II* **42**: 118

**Blau, Herbert**
*King Lear* **11**: 154

**Bliss, Lee**
*Henry VIII* **2**: 72

**Bloom, Allan**
*Julius Caesar* **7**: 310
Politics and Power (topic entry) **30**: 1

**Bloom, Harold**
*A Midsummer Night's Dream* **45**: 158

**Bluestone, Max**
*Henry IV, 1 and 2* **14**: 67
*Troilus and Cressida* **18**: 338

**Blumenthal, Eileen**
*Antony and Cleopatra* **17**: 67

**Bly, Mary**
*All's Well That Ends Well* **38**: 118

**Boaden, James**
*Hamlet* **21**: 31
*Henry V* **14**: 180
*Henry VIII* **24**: 68
*King John* **24**: 175, 176
*Macbeth* **20**: 59
*Sonnets* **10**: 169

**Boas, Frederick S.**
*As You Like It* **5**: 54
*King John* **9**: 240
*Measure for Measure* **2**: 416
*The Merry Wives of Windsor* **5**: 347
*A Midsummer Night's Dream* **3**: 391
*The Phoenix and Turtle* **10**: 8
*The Rape of Lucrece* **10**: 68
*Romeo and Juliet* **5**: 443
*Timon of Athens* **1**: 476
*Titus Andronicus* **4**: 631
*Troilus and Cressida* **3**: 555
*The Two Gentlemen of Verona* **6**: 451

**Bodenstedt, Friedrich**
*Othello* **4**: 422

**Bodkin, Maud**
*Othello* **4**: 468

**Bogard, Travis**
*Richard II* **6**: 317

**Bolton, Joseph S. G.**
*Titus Andronicus* **4**: 635

**Bonaventure, Sister Mary**
*The Phoenix and Turtle* **38**: 326

**Bonazza, Blaze Odell**
*The Comedy of Errors* **1**: 50

**Bond, R. Warwick**
*Cymbeline* **15**: 36
*The Two Gentlemen of Verona* **6**: 46

**Bond, Ronald B.**
*Romeo and Juliet* **33**: 241

**Bonheim, Helmut**
*Richard II* **6**: 385

**Bonheim, Jean**
*Richard II* **6**: 385

**Bonjour, Adrien**
*Julius Caesar* **7**: 284
*King John* **9**: 263; **41**: 260
*The Winter's Tale* **7**: 456

**Bonnard, George A.**
*A Midsummer Night's Dream* **3**: 42
*The Phoenix and Turtle* **10**: 17
*Richard II* **6**: 310

**Bono, Barbara J.**
Gender Identity (topic entry) **40**: 90

**Boose, Lynda E.**
*As You Like It* **19**: 3
*The Comedy of Errors* **19**: 3
Fathers and Daughters (topic entry) **36**: 78
*The Merchant of Venice* **13**: 37
*The Merry Wives of Windsor* **19**: 3
*The Taming of the Shrew* **19**: 3; **28**: 24; **31**: 351

**Booth, Michael R.**
*Henry VIII* **24**: 91

**Booth, Stephen**
*Hamlet* **44**: 107
*Macbeth* **3**: 349
*Sonnets* **10**: 349

**Booth, Wayne**
*Macbeth* **3**: 306

**Boothroyd, Basil**
*Richard II* **24**: 331
*Troilus and Cressida* **18**: 346, 347

**Boothroyd, J. B.**
*Measure for Measure* **23**: 309
*The Tempest* **15**: 258
*Titus Andronicus* **17**: 440

**Borot, Luc**
*Titus Andronicus* **17**: 481

**Bost, James S.**
*The Taming of the Shrew* **12**: 396

**Boswell, James**
*King Lear* **11**: 6
*Sonnets* **10**: 166

**Bowers, A. Robin**
*Rape of Lucrece* **43**: 148

**Bowers, Fredson Thayer**
*Hamlet* **1**: 209
*Titus Andronicus* **4**: 637

**Bowers, Rick**
*Antony and Cleopatra* **48**: 206

**Bowman, James**
*Hamlet* **21**: 322

**Boxer, Setphen**
*Julius Caesar* **17**: 407

**Boxill, Roger**
<lv*All's Well That Ends Well* **26**: 62
*Richard III* **14**: 484

**Boyd, Brian**
*King John* **32**: 93; **41**: 251

**Bradbrook, M. C.**
Appearance vs. Reality (topic entry) **34**: 1
*Timon of Athens* **20**: 492; **27**: 203

**Bradbrook, Muriel C.**
*All's Well That Ends Well* **7**: 51
*Henry IV, 1 and 2* **1**: 418
*Henry VI, 1, 2, and 3* **3**: 75
*Love's Labour's Lost* **2**: 321, 330
*Measure for Measure* **2**: 443
*The Merchant of Venice* **4**: 261
*The Merry Wives of Windsor* **5**: 366; **18**: 44
*The Rape of Lucrece* **10**: 78
*Romeo and Juliet* **5**: 479; **11**: 488
*The Taming of the Shrew* **9**: 355
*Titus Andronicus* **4**: 646
*Twelfth Night* **1**: 655
*The Two Gentlemen of Verona* **6**: 486
*The Two Noble Kinsmen* **9**: 490

**Bradby, G. F.**
*As You Like It* **5**: 65

**Braddock, M. C.**
*Romeo and Juliet* **11**: 488

**Bradley, A. C.**
*Antony and Cleopatra* **6**: 53
*Coriolanus* **9**: 43, 53
*Hamlet* **1**: 120
*Henry IV, 1 and 2* **1**: 333
*Henry V* **5**: 209
*Julius Caesar* **7**: 188
*King Lear* **2**: 137; **11**: 137
*Macbeth* **3**: 213
*The Merry Wives of Windsor* **5**: 348

*Othello* **4**: 434
*Sonnets* **10**: 238
*Twelfth Night* **1**: 566

**Bradshaw, Graham**
*Othello* **22**: 207; **25**: 189
*Sonnets* **25**: 189

**Brady, Owen E.**
*Macbeth* **20**: 308
*The Merry Wives of Windsor* **18**: 35

**Brahms, Caryl**
*Julius Caesar* **17**: 368
*King Lear* **11**: 76
*Measure for Measure* **23**: 317
*Othello* **11**: 292
*The Taming of the Shrew* **12**: 361
*The Tempest* **15**: 263
*Timon of Athens* **20**: 448
*Titus Andronicus* **17**: 447
*Troilus and Cressida* **18**: 325
*Twelfth Night* **26**: 254
*The Two Gentlemen of Verona* **12**: 463, 475

**Brandes, George**
*As You Like It* **5**: 50
*Coriolanus* **9**: 39
*Hamlet* **1**: 116
*Henry IV, 1 and 2* **1**: 329
*King Lear* **2**: 136
*Love's Labour's Lost* **2**: 315
*Measure for Measure* **2**: 414
*The Merry Wives of Windsor* **5**: 346
*A Midsummer Night's Dream* **3**: 389
*Much Ado about Nothing* **8**: 36
*Pericles* **2**: 551
*Timon of Athens* **1**: 474
*Troilus and Cressida* **3**: 554
*The Two Gentlemen of Verona* **6**: 456
*The Two Noble Kinsmen* **9**: 460

**Brathwait, Richard**
*Venus and Adonis* **10**: 411

**Braunmuller, A. R.**
*King John* **24**: 245; **41**: 243

**Bredbeck, Gregory W.**
*Sonnets* **40**: 268

**Breight, Curt**
*The Tempest* **16**: 426

**Breitenberg, Mark**
*Love's Labour's Lost* **22**: 12

**Brewer, Derek**
*The Merry Wives of Windsor* **38**: 278

**Brennan, Anthony S.**
*Antony and Cleopatra* **47**: 107

**Brewster, Dorothy**
*Henry V* **14**: 177

**Bridie, James**
*Othello* **11**: 268

**Brien, Alan**
  *All's Well That Ends Well* **26**: 25
  *Coriolanus* **17**: 165
  *Hamlet* **21**: 223
  *King Lear* **11**: 73, 91
  *The Merchant of Venice* **12**: 65
  *Much Ado about Nothing* **18**: 184
  *Othello* **11**: 283
  *Pericles* **15**: 141
  *The Taming of the Shrew* **12**: 356
  *Troilus and Cressida* **18**: 320
  *Twelfth Night* **26**: 250
  *The Two Gentlemen of Verona* **12**: 472

**Briggs, Julia**
  *All's Well That Ends Well* **28**: 38
  *Measure for Measure* **28**: 38

**Brigham, A.**
  *King Lear* **2**: 116

**Brill, Lesley W.**
  *Timon of Athens* **1**: 526

**Brink, Bernhard Ten**
  *Antony and Cleopatra* **6**: 52

**Brink, Jean R.**
  Shakespeare's Representation of Women (topic entry) **31**: 53

**Brissenden, Alan**
  *A Midsummer Night's Dream* **3**: 513

**Bristol, Michael D.**
  *The Winter's Tale* **19**: 366

**Brittin, Norman A.**
  *Twelfth Night* **1**: 594

**Broadbent, J. B.**
  *Sonnets* **10**: 322

**Brockbank, Philip**
  *All's Well That Ends Well* **26**: 87
  *Coriolanus* **17**: 227
  General Commentary **13**: 476
  *Henry VIII* **24**: 118
  *Julius Caesar* **13**: 252
  *Troilus and Cressida* **13**: 53

**Brodwin, Leonora Leet**
  *Romeo and Juliet* **33**: 233

**Bromley, John C.**
  *Richard III* **39**: 341

**Bromley, Laura G.**
  *Rape of Lucrece* **43**: 85

**Bronson, Bertrand H.**
  *Love's Labour's Lost* **2**: 326

**Brook, Peter**
  *Antony and Cleopatra* **17**: 65
  *As You Like It* **23**: 173
  *King Lear* **11**: 84
  *A Midsummer Night's Dream* **12**: 254, 259
  *Romeo and Juliet* **11**: 459
  *The Winter's Tale* **15**: 528

**Brooke, C. F. Tucker**
  *Henry IV, 1 and 2* **1**: 337, 341
  *Othello* **4**: 451
  *Troilus and Cressida* **3**: 560
  *The Two Noble Kinsmen* **9**: 461

**Brooke, Nicholas**
  *All's Well That Ends Well* **7**: 121
  *Richard III* **8**: 243
  *Romeo and Juliet* **5**: 528
  *Titus Andronicus* **27**: 246

**Brooke, Stopford A.**
  *As You Like It* **5**: 57
  *Henry V* **5**: 213
  *Julius Caesar* **7**: 205
  *King Lear* **2**: 149
  *Othello* **4**: 444
  *Romeo and Juliet* **5**: 447

**Brooks, Charles**
  *The Taming of the Shrew* **9**: 360

**Brooks, Cleanth**
  *Henry IV, 1 and 2* **1**: 380
  *Macbeth* **3**: 253

**Brooks, Douglas A.**
  *Henry IV, 1 and 2* **48**: 117

**Brooks, Harold F.**
  *The Comedy of Errors* **1**: 40
  *The Two Gentlemen of Verona* **6**: 504

**Brooks, Jeremy**
  *Romeo and Juliet* **11**: 462
  *The Winter's Tale* **15**: 470

**Broude, Ronald**
  *Titus Andronicus* **4**: 680; **27**: 282

**Broun, Heywood**
  *Julius Caesar* **17**: 324

**Brower, Reuben Arthur**
  *Coriolanus* **9**: 164
  *Hamlet* **1**: 259
  *The Tempest* **8**: 384

**Brown, Carolyn E.**
  *The Taming of the Shrew* **32**: 1
  *Measure for Measure* **42**: 1

**Brown, Charles Armitage**
  *Sonnets* **10**: 176
  *The Two Gentlemen of Verona* **6**: 439

**Brown, Constance A.**
  *Richard III* **14**: 435

**Brown, Ivor**
  *All's Well That Ends Well* **26**: 13
  *As You Like It* **23**: 78, 87
  *Hamlet* **21**: 156, 178, 196, 218
  *Henry IV, 1 and 2* **14**: 29
  *King John* **24**: 203
  *King Lear* **11**: 48
  *Macbeth* **20**: 232, 244
  *The Merchant of Venice* **12**: 47, 52
  *Much Ado about Nothing* **18**: 159
  *Richard III* **14**: 409
  *Romeo and Juliet* **11**: 443
  *The Taming of the Shrew* **12**: 351
  *Titus Andronicus* **17**: 445
  *The Two Gentlemen of Verona* **12**: 459

**Brown, Jane K.**
  *A Midsummer Night's Dream* **45**: 126

**Brown, Jeffrey**
  *Othello* **35**: 276

**Brown, John Mason**
  *As You Like It* **23**: 76
  *Julius Caesar* **17**: 319
  *Macbeth* **20**: 227
  *The Tempest* **15**: 242

**Brown, John Russell**
  *All's Well That Ends Well* **26**: 34
  *As You Like It* **5**: 103
  *The Comedy of Errors* **1**: 36
  *Cymbeline* **4**: 113; **15**: 70, 122
  *Hamlet* **21**: 217
  *Macbeth* **20**: 254, 265
  *Measure for Measure* **23**: 312
  *The Merchant of Venice* **4**: 270; **12**: 67
  *The Merry Wives of Windsor* **5**: 354
  *A Midsummer Night's Dream* **3**: 425 **12**: 244, 262
  *Much Ado about Nothing* **8**: 75; **18**: 261
  *Othello* **11**: 305
  *Richard II* **24**: 414
  *Romeo and Juliet* **11**: 466
  *The Taming of the Shrew* **9**: 353; **12**: 363
  *The Tempest* **15**: 193
  *Troilus and Cressida* **18**: 329
  *Twelfth Night* **1**: 600; **26**: 366, 371
  *The Two Gentlemen of Verona* **12**: 478
  *The Winter's Tale* **7**: 469; **15**: 524

**Browne, Junius Henri**
  *Othello* **11**: 323

**Browne, Martin E.**
  *Coriolanus* **17**: 182

**Brownell, Arthur**
  *Measure for Measure* **23**: 280

**Browning, I. R.**
  *Coriolanus* **9**: 117

**Browning, Robert**
  *Sonnets* **10**: 213

**Brownlow, F. W.**
  *The Two Noble Kinsmen* **9**: 498

**Brubaker, Edward S.**
  *King John* **24**: 249

**Bruce, Brenda**
  *Romeo and Juliet* **11**: 519

**Brucher, Richard T.**
  *Titus Andronicus* **27**: 255

**Brustein, Robert**
  *The Comedy of Errors* **26**: 176
  *Coriolanus* **17**: 180, 221
  *Henry IV, 1 and 2* **14**: 66
  *Much Ado about Nothing* **18**: 228
  *Othello* **11**: 321

**Bruster, Douglas**
  *The Two Noble Kinsmen* **41**: 340

**Bryan, George B.**
  *Richard II* **24**: 291

**Bryant, J. A., Jr.**
  *Cymbeline* **4**: 105
  *The Merry Wives of Windsor* **5**: 376
  *Twelfth Night* **46**: 291
  *Richard II* **6**: 323

**Bryant, James C.**
  *Romeo and Juliet* **33**: 300

**Bryden, Ronald**
  *Hamlet* **21**: 253
  *Henry IV, 1 and 2* **14**: 72, 81
  *Henry V* **14**: 277
  *King John* **24**: 221
  *The Merry Wives of Windsor* **18**: 38
  *Othello* **11**: 296

**Buckle, Richard**
  *King Lear* **11**: 63
  *The Merry Wives of Windsor* **18**: 33
  *Much Ado about Nothing* **18**: 162

**Buckmann-de Villegas, Sabine**
  *Julius Caesar* **17**: 411

**Bucknill, John Charles**
  *King Lear* **2**: 120

**Buhler, Stephen M.**
  *Julius Caesar* **37**: 203

**Bullen, A. H.**
  *Titus Andronicus* **4**: 631

**Bullogh, Geoffrey**
  *King John* **41**: 234

**Bulthaupt, Heinrich**
  *The Winter's Tale* **7**: 396

**Burckhardt, Sigurd**
  *Henry IV, 1 and 2* **1**: 421
  *Julius Caesar* **7**: 331
  *King John* **9**: 284
  *King Lear* **2**: 257
  *The Merchant of Venice* **4**: 293

**Burke, Kenneth**
  *Coriolanus* **9**: 148; **30**: 67
  *Julius Caesar* **7**: 238
  *Othello* **4**: 506

**Burkhardt, Louis**
  *Measure for Measure* **32**: 16

**Burnett, Mark Thornton**
*Hamlet* **28**: 232
*Love's Labour's Lost* **25**: 1

**Burnim, Kalman**
*Macbeth* **20**: 32

**Burrows, Jill**
*The Comedy of Errors* **26**: 164
*Measure for Measure* **23**: 347

**Burt, Richard A.**
*The Taming of the Shrew* **31**: 269

**Burton, Richard**
*Hamlet* **21**: 245

**Bush, Douglas**
*The Rape of Lucrece* **10**: 73
*Venus and Adonis* **10**: 424

**Bush, Geoffrey**
*As You Like It* **5**: 102
*King Lear* **2**: 207

**Bushnell, Nelson Sherwin**
*The Tempest* **8**: 340

**Butler, Francelia**
*Timon of Athens* **20**: 433

**Butler, Guy**
*As You Like It* **46**: 117

**Buxton, John**
*The Phoenix and Turtle* **38**: 329

**Byles, Joanna Montgomery**
*Hamlet* **44**: 180

**Byrne, Muriel St. Clare**
*All's Well That Ends Well* **26**: 28
*As You Like It* **23**: 85
*Cymbeline* **15**: 100
*Henry VIII* **24**: 106
*Othello* **11**: 287
*Pericles* **15**: 145
*The Tempest* **15**: 261
*Timon of Athens* **20**: 449
*The Two Gentlemen of Verona* **12**: 464

**Calderwood, James L.**
*All's Well That Ends Well* **7**: 93; **38**: 65
*Coriolanus* **9**: 144, 198
*Hamlet* **35**: 215
*Henry IV, 1 and 2* **39**: 117; **47**: 1
*Henry V* **5**: 310; **30**: 181
*Henry VI, 1, 2, and 3* **3**: 105
*King John* **9**: 275; **41**: 269
*Love's Labour's Lost* **2**: 356; **38**: 219
*A Midsummer Night's Dream* **3**: 477; **19**: 21; **22**: 23
*Othello* **13**: 304
*Romeo and Juliet* **5**: 550
*Titus Andronicus* **4**: 664

**Callaghan, Dympna**
*Henry IV, 1 and 2* **25**: 89
*Richard II* **25**: 89

**Camden, Carroll**
*Hamlet* **35**: 126

**Campbell, K. T. S.**
*The Phoenix and Turtle* **10**: 42

**Campbell, Mrs. Patrick**
*Macbeth* **20**: 165

**Campbell, Oscar James**
*As You Like It* **5**: 70
*Coriolanus* **9**: 80
*King Lear* **2**: 188
*Measure for Measure* **2**: 456
*The Tempest* **15**: 247
*Troilus and Cressida* **3**: 574
*Twelfth Night* **1**: 577
*The Two Gentlemen of Verona* **6**: 468

**Campbell, Thomas**
*Coriolanus* **17**: 131
*Hamlet* **1**: 97
*King John* **24**: 177
*Much Ado about Nothing* **8**: 16
*The Tempest* **8**: 302
*The Winter's Tale* **7**: 387; **15**: 400

**Candido, Joseph**
*The Comedy of Errors* **16**: 3; **34**: 220
*Henry VI, 1, 2, and 3* **39**: 213
*King John* **13**: 147

**Cantor, Paul A.**
*King Lear* **37**: 213

**Capell, Edward**
*Henry VI, 1, 2, and 3* **3**: 20
*Henry VIII* **2**: 21
*Love's Labour's Lost* **2**: 300
*Measure for Measure* **2**: 394
*Richard III* **8**: 153
*The Taming of the Shrew* **9**: 318
*Titus Andronicus* **4**: 614

**Carducci, Jane S.**
*Titus Andronicus* **43**: 222

**Carlisle, Carol J.**
*As You Like It* **23**: 28
*Cymbeline* **15**: 11
*King Lear* **11**: 158
*Romeo and Juliet* **11**: 407
*Two Gentlemen of Verona* **42**: 18

**Carlson, Harry**
*Coriolanus* **17**: 183

**Carlson, Marvin**
*Othello* **11**: 235

**Carlson, Susan**
*As You Like It* **34**: 177

**Carlyle, Thomas**
*Henry V* **5**: 197

**Carr, Joan**
*Cymbeline* **36**: 142

**Carroll, Lewis**
*Henry VIII* **24**: 76
*The Tempest* **15**: 205

**Carroll, William C.**
*Love's Labour's Lost* **2**: 367
*The Merry Wives of Windsor* **5**: 379; **47**: 314
*Richard III* **19**: 164
*Sexuality (topic entry)* **33**: 28
*The Taming of the Shrew* **9**: 430; **37**: 31
*The Winter's Tale* **37**: 31

**Cartelli, Thomas**
*All's Well That Ends Well* **38**: 142
*Henry VI, 1, 2, and 3* **28**: 112
*Macbeth* **20**: 406

**Carter, Albert Howard**
*All's Well That Ends Well* **7**: 62

**Carter, Stephen**
*The Rape of Lucrece* **32**: 321

**Case, Arthur E.**
*All's Well That Ends Well* **26**: 94

**Case, R. H.**
*Antony and Cleopatra* **6**: 60

**Cavell, Stanley**
*Coriolanus* **30**: 111
*King Lear* **31**: 155
*Macbeth* **29**: 91

**Cazemian, Louis**
*Henry IV, 1 and 2* **1**: 355

**Cecil, David**
*Antony and Cleopatra* **6**: 111

**Cerasano, S. P.**
*Richard III* **14**: 490

**Cespedes, Frank V.**
*Henry VIII* **2**: 81

**Chaillet, Ned**
*The Comedy of Errors* **26**: 158
*Hamlet* **21**: 308
*Richard III* **14**: 474
*The Two Gentlemen of Verona* **12**: 490

**Challinor, A. M.**
Authorship Controversy (topic entry) **41**: 42

**Chalmers, George**
*Measure for Measure* **2**: 394
*Sonnets* **10**: 156, 158

**Chambers, Colin**
*Richard III* **14**: 475

**Chambers, E. K.**
*All's Well That Ends Well* **7**: 27
*Antony and Cleopatra* **6**: 64
*As You Like It* **5**: 55
*The Comedy of Errors* **1**: 16
*Coriolanus* **9**: 43
*Cymbeline* **4**: 46
*Henry IV, 1 and 2* **1**: 336
*Henry V* **5**: 210
*Henry VIII* **2**: 42
*Julius Caesar* **7**: 189
*King John* **9**: 244
*King Lear* **2**: 143
*Love's Labour's Lost* **2**: 316
*The Merchant of Venice* **4**: 221
*The Merry Wives of Windsor* **5**: 350
*A Midsummer Night's Dream* **3**: 395
*Much Ado about Nothing* **8**: 39
*Othello* **4**: 440
*Pericles* **2**: 554
*Richard II* **6**: 277
*Richard III* **8**: 182
*Romeo and Juliet* **5**: 445
*The Taming of the Shrew* **9**: 330
*The Tempest* **8**: 326
*Timon of Athens* **1**: 478
*Troilus and Cressida* **3**: 557
*Twelfth Night* **1**: 561
*The Two Gentlemen of Verona* **6**: 460
*The Winter's Tale* **7**: 410

**Chambers, R. W.**
*King Lear* **2**: 170
*Measure for Measure* **2**: 437

**Champion, Larry S.**
*The Comedy of Errors* **1**: 56
*Henry V* **30**: 227
*Henry VI, 1, 2, and 3* **3**: 154; **39**: 187
*King John* **13**: 152
*Much Ado about Nothing* **31**: 216
*Othello* **35**: 253
*Titus Andronicus* **4**: 662

**Chaney, Joseph**
*Love's Labour's Lost* **38**: 172

**Chapman, John**
*King Lear* **11**: 55

**Charles, Casey**
*Twelfth Night* **42**: 32

**Charlton, H. B.**
*All's Well That Ends Well* **7**: 37
*The Comedy of Errors* **1**: 23
*Hamlet* **1**: 166
*Henry IV, 1 and 2* **1**: 357
*Henry V* **5**: 225
*Julius Caesar* **7**: 218
*Love's Labour's Lost* **2**: 322
*Measure for Measure* **2**: 434
*The Merry Wives of Windsor* **5**: 350
*A Midsummer Night's Dream* **3**: 402
*Richard II* **6**: 304
*Richard III* **8**: 197
*Romeo and Juliet* **5**: 464
*The Taming of the Shrew* **9**: 334
*Titus Andronicus* **4**: 640
*Troilus and Cressida* **3**: 571
*Twelfth Night* **1**: 573
*The Two Gentlemen of Verona* **6**: 472

**Charnes, Linda**
*Troilus and Cressida* **43**: 340

**Charney, Hanna**
Madness (topic entry) **35:** 49

**Charney, Maurice**
Antony and Cleopatra **6:** 155, 161
Coriolanus **9:** 136
Henry V **14:** 303
Julius Caesar **7:** 296
King John **25:** 98
Madness (topic entry) **35:** 49
Timon of Athens **25:** 198
Titus Andronicus **16:** 225
Troilus and Cressida **27:** 366

**Chateaubriand**
Romeo and Juliet **5:** 420

**Chaudhuri, Sukanta**
Kingship (topic entry) **39:** 20

**Cheney, Donald**
The Rape of Lucrece **10:** 125

**Chesterton, C. K.**
A Midsummer Night's Dream **3:** 393

**Child, Harold**
All's Well That Ends Well **26:** 72
The Comedy of Errors **26:** 182
Coriolanus **17:** 34
Henry IV, 1 and 2 **14:** 120
The Merry Wives of Windsor **18:** 67
A Midsummer Night's Dream **12:** 282
Much Ado about Nothing **18:** 232
Richard II **24:** 390
The Winter's Tale **15:** 500

**Chillington, Carol A.**
Coriolanus **17:** 194
Henry VI, 1, 2, and 3 **24:** 38

**Chinoy, Helen Krich**
The Merchant of Venice **12:** 91

**Christensen, Ann C.**
Coriolanus **42:** 218

**Church, Tony**
Hamlet **21:** 416

**Cibber, Colley**
Hamlet **21:** 19
King John **9:** 209

**Cibber, Theophilus**
King Lear **11:** 114
Romeo and Juliet **11:** 379

**Cirillo, Albert R.**
As You Like It **5:** 130
Romeo and Juliet **11:** 475

**Clapp, Henry A.**
As You Like It **5:** 44
A Midsummer Night's Dream **3:** 380

**Clark, Cumberland**
A Midsummer Night's Dream **3:** 400

**Clarke, Asia Booth**
Hamlet **21:** 70

**Clarke, Charles Cowden**
As You Like It **5:** 36
Henry IV, 1 and 2 **1:** 321
King John **9:** 229; **24:** 186
A Midsummer Night's Dream **3:** 376
Much Ado about Nothing **8:** 24
Romeo and Juliet **11:** 400
The Tempest **8:** 308

**Clarke, Mary**
All's Well That Ends Well **26:** 37
Cymbeline **15:** 51
Henry V **14:** 260
King John **24:** 203
Othello **11:** 280
Timon of Athens **20:** 450
Troilus and Cressida **18:** 314
The Two Gentlemen of Verona **12:** 465

**Clarke, Mary Cowden**
Romeo and Juliet **11:** 400

**Clayton, Thomas**
Macbeth **48:** 214
Othello **28:** 243

**Clemen, Wolfgang H.**
Hamlet **1:** 188
Henry VI, 1, 2, and 3 **3:** 71
King Lear **2:** 199
Richard III **8:** 206
Romeo and Juliet **5:** 477
Titus Andronicus **4:** 644

**Clements, John**
The Tempest **15:** 366

**Clurman, Harold**
All's Well That Ends Well **26:** 27
King Lear **11:** 92, 103
The Merchant of Venice **12:** 78
A Midsummer Night's Dream **12:** 240
The Two Gentlemen of Verona **12:** 471

**Coates, John**
Antony and Cleopatra **27:** 117

**Cochrane, Claire**
Timon of Athens **20:** 475

**Coddon, Karin S.**
Madness (topic entry) **35:** 68
Macbeth **13:** 361
Twelfth Night **34:** 330

**Coffey, Denise**
Much Ado about Nothing **18:** 254

**Coghill, Nevill**
Measure for Measure **2:** 491
The Merchant of Venice **4:** 250
The Taming of the Shrew **9:** 344
The Winter's Tale **7:** 464; **15:** 518

**Cohen, D. M.**
The Merchant of Venice **40:** 175

**Cohen, Derek**
Henry VI, 1, 2, and 3 **25:** 102, 109
King Lear **25:** 202
Titus Andronicus **43:** 255
Violence in Shakespeare's Works (topic entry) **43:** 24

**Cohn, Ruby**
Coriolanus **17:** 188

**Cole, Douglas**
Troilus and Cressida **27:** 376

**Cole, John William**
Henry V **14:** 186
King John **24:** 196
A Midsummer Night's Dream **12:** 185
Richard II **24:** 280
The Tempest **15:** 210

**Coleman, John**
As You Like It **23:** 18
Hamlet **21:** 59
Macbeth **20:** 105
The Taming of the Shrew **12:** 371

**Coleman, Robert**
The Two Gentlemen of Verona **12:** 467

**Coleridge, Hartley**
Antony and Cleopatra **6:** 32
The Merry Wives of Windsor **5:** 339
Much Ado about Nothing **8:** 19
The Two Noble Kinsmen **9:** 455
The Winter's Tale **7:** 389

**Coleridge, Samuel Taylor**
All's Well That Ends Well **7:** 15
Antony and Cleopatra **6:** 25
As You Like It **5:** 23
The Comedy of Errors **1:** 14
Coriolanus **9:** 17
Hamlet **1:** 94, 95
Henry IV, 1 and 2 **1:** 310, 311
Henry VI, 1, 2, and 3 **3:** 27
Julius Caesar **7:** 160
King Lear **2:** 106
Love's Labour's Lost **2:** 302
Macbeth **3:** 184
Measure for Measure **2:** 397
A Midsummer Night's Dream **3:** 365
Much Ado about Nothing **8:** 16
Othello **4:** 399, 402, 405, 406
Pericles **2:** 544
Richard II **6:** 255, 262
Richard III **8:** 161
Romeo and Juliet **5:** 425
Sonnets **10:** 159, 173
The Tempest **8:** 295, 299
Timon of Athens **1:** 459
Titus Andronicus **4:** 617
Troilus and Cressida **3:** 541
The Two Noble Kinsmen **9:** 447
Venus and Adonis **10:** 414
The Winter's Tale **7:** 383, 387

**Colie, Rosalie L.**
As You Like It **34:** 147

**Cymbeline 4:** 148
**King Lear 31:** 92
**Romeo and Juliet 5:** 559
**Sonnets 40:** 247
**Troilus and Cressida 43:** 293

**Colley, John Scott**
Cymbeline **47:** 228

**Collier, Jeremy**
See also Steevens, George; Hic et Ubique; Longinus; and Lorenzo
Hamlet **1:** 73
Henry IV, 1 and 2 **1:** 286
Henry V **5:** 185
Timon of Athens **1:** 456

**Collins, A. S.**
Timon of Athens **1:** 492

**Collins, Glenn**
The Comedy of Errors **26:** 172
Julius Caesar **17:** 398

**Colman, E. A. M.**
Cymbeline **36:** 155
Sexuality (topic entry) **33:** 1

**Colman, George**
King Lear **2:** 102
The Merchant of Venice **4:** 192

**Colvin, Clare**
Julius Caesar **17:** 394
Richard III **14:** 473

**Conklin, Paul**
Hamlet **21:** 339

**Conrad, Hermann**
Sonnets **10:** 214

**Cook, Ann Jennalie**
The Merchant of Venice **12:** 95

**Cook, Carol**
Much Ado about Nothing **31:** 245
Troilus and Cressida **43:** 329

**Cook, Dorothy**
Henry V **5:** 289

**Cook, Dutton**
The Merchant of Venice **12:** 16
Othello **11:** 244
Richard III **14:** 397
The Tempest **15:** 217

**Cook, Judith**
Antony and Cleopatra **17:** 113
Julius Caesar **17:** 387
Macbeth **20:** 294
Much Ado about Nothing **18:** 235, 236
Richard III **14:** 511

**Cooke, William**
The Merchant of Venice **12:** 4
Othello **11:** 189

**Cookman, A. V.**
Romeo and Juliet **11:** 447

Cope, Walter
  Love's Labour's Lost 2: 299

Copland, Murray
  The Phoenix and Turtle 10: 40

Corballis, Richard
  Madness (topic entry) 35: 7

Corbet, Richard
  Richard III 8: 144

Corfield, Coano
  The Tempest 8: 458

Coriat, Isador H.
  Macbeth 3: 219
  Romeo and Juliet 5: 425

Corliss, Richard
  Much Ado about Nothing 18: 221

Cornwallis, Sir William
  Richard III 8: 144

Cotton, Nancy
  The Merry Wives of Windsor 47: 321

Cottrell, John
  Coriolanus 17: 161
  Hamlet 21: 203
  Henry V 14: 232
  The Merchant of Venice 12: 90
  Othello 11: 311

Coursen, H. R.
  Hamlet 44: 133
  Macbeth 44: 289
  Much Ado about Nothing 18: 201

Coursen, Herbert R., Jr.
  Macbeth 3: 318
  The Tempest 8: 429

Courthope, W. J.
  The Two Gentlemen of Verona 6: 460

Courtney, W. L.
  A Midsummer Night's Dream 12: 206

Cousins, A. D.
  The Rape of Lucrece 48: 291
  Venus and Adonis 28: 355

Coveney, Michael
  All's Well That Ends Well 26: 71
  As You Like It 23: 139, 146
  Hamlet 21: 292, 326
  Henry IV, 1 and 2 14: 88
  <lHenry VIII 24: 126
  King Lear 11: 111
  Love's Labour's Lost 23: 230
  Macbeth 20: 291
  Much Ado about Nothing 18: 208
  Twelfth Night 26: 285, 329, 337
  The Winter's Tale 15: 488

Cox, Catherine I.
  Clowns and Fools (topic entry) 46: 78

Cox, Catherine S.
  King Lear 48: 222

Cox, Francis
  Troilus and Cressida 18: 353

Cox, Frank
  Henry VI, 1, 2, and 3 24: 27

Cox, J. F.
  Much Ado about Nothing 18: 257

Cox, John D.
  All's Well That Ends Well 13: 66
  Henry V 30: 215
  Henry VI, 1, 2, and 3 3: 151; 13: 131
  Richard III 13: 131

Cox, Majore Kolb
  Romeo and Juliet 33: 249

Cox, Roger L.
  The Comedy of Errors 19: 34
  Henry IV, 1 and 2 1: 438
  The Taming of the Shrew 19: 34
  The Two Gentlemen of Verona 19: 34

Craig, Edward
  Much Ado about Nothing 18: 147

Craig, H. A. L.
  Much Ado about Nothing 18: 178

Craig, Hardin
  The Comedy of Errors 1: 31
  Coriolanus 30: 74
  Pericles 2: 564
  The Taming of the Shrew 9: 341

Craik, T. W.
  Much Ado about Nothing 8: 63
  Twelfth Night 26: 337

Cran, Mrs. George
  The Merry Wives of Windsor 18: 26
  Much Ado about Nothing 18: 156

Crane, Milton
  As You Like It 5: 92
  Twelfth Night 1: 590

Crewe, Jonathan
  Rape of Lucrece 43: 158

Crick, Bernard
  Antony and Cleopatra 17: 61
  Twelfth Night 26: 286

Crist, Judith
  The Merchant of Venice 12: 69

Crockett, Bryan
  The Tempest 45: 211

Crosman, Robert
  Sonnets 16: 461

Crowley, Richard C.
  Coriolanus 9: 177

Crowne, John
  Henry VI, 1, 2, and 3 3: 16

Crowther, Bosley
  Henry V 14: 209, 211
  Macbeth 20: 199

Cruttwell, Patrick
  Hamlet 1: 234

Csengeri, Karen
  Pericles 16: 391

Cumberland, Richard
  Henry IV, 1 and 2 1: 305
  Henry V 5: 192

Cummings, Peter
  Sexuality (topic entry) 33: 12

Cunliffe, John William
  Henry V 5: 217

Cunningham, James
  Hamlet 42: 229
  King Lear 42: 229
  Macbeth 42: 229
  Othello 42: 229

Cunningham, John
  Macbeth 44: 337

Cunningham, J. V.
  The Phoenix and Turtle 10: 24

Cunningham, Karen
  Titus Andronicus 43: 247

Curry, Walter Clyde
  Macbeth 3: 239
  The Tempest 8: 356

Curtis, Anthony
  The Comedy of Errors 26: 160
  The Winter's Tale 15: 484

Curtis, Jared R.
  Othello 4: 580

Curtis, Nick
  Macbeth 20: 315

Cusack, Sinead
  The Merchant of Venice 12: 104

Cushman, Robert
  The Comedy of Errors 26: 162
  Henry IV, 1 and 2 14: 101
  Macbeth 20: 301
  Measure for Measure 23: 344
  A Midsummer Night's Dream 12: 269, 274
  Twelfth Night 26: 268
  The Two Gentlemen of Verona 12: 481

Cutts, John P.
  The Comedy of Errors 34: 211
  Cymbeline 47: 205
  The Two Gentlemen of Verona 40: 327

Daigle, Lennett J.
  Venus and Adonis 33: 330

Daly, Joseph Francis
  As You Like It 23: 52
  The Merry Wives of Windsor 18: 19

D'Amico, Jack
  Madness (topic entry) 35: 62
  Politics and Power (topic entry) 30: 49

Danby, David
  Hamlet 21: 319

Danby, John F.
  Antony and Cleopatra 6: 125
  Henry IV, 1 and 2 1: 391
  Pericles 2: 573
  The Two Gentlemen of Verona 6: 492

Daniel, George
  As You Like It 5: 25

Daniell, David
  Coriolanus 17: 201

Danson, Lawrence
  Desire (topic entry) 38: 48
  Hamlet 44: 198
  The Merchant of Venice 4: 328
  Titus Andronicus 27: 318

Darlington, W. A.
  Cymbeline 15: 59
  King Lear 11: 53
  The Merchant of Venice 12: 65
  Othello 11: 284
  The Taming of the Shrew 12: 354

Dash, Irene G.
  A Midsummer Night's Dream 42: 46
  Othello 35: 369
  Romeo and Juliet 33: 257
  Shakespeare's Representation of Women (topic entry) 31: 1
  Twelfth Night 46: 369

David, Richard
  All's Well That Ends Well 26: 40
  As You Like It 23: 109
  Cymbeline 15: 83
  Hamlet 21: 355
  Henry IV, 1 and 2 14: 49
  Henry V 14: 259
  Julius Caesar 17: 384
  King John 24: 206, 228
  Love's Labour's Lost 23: 191, 207
  Macbeth 20: 302, 318
  Measure for Measure 23: 299
  Richard II 24: 325, 419
  The Taming of the Shrew 12: 352
  Titus Andronicus 17: 448
  Troilus and Cressida 18: 307, 314
  Twelfth Night 26: 231
  The Winter's Tale 15: 490

Davidson, Clifford
  Timon of Athens 27: 196

**Davidson, Frank**
*The Tempest* **8**: 420

**Davies, John**
*Henry VIII* **24**: 127
*Venus and Adonis* **10**: 411

**Davies, Robertson**
*Henry V* **14**: 263
*The Merchant of Venice* **12**: 56

**Davies, Thomas**
*All's Well That Ends Well* **26**: 92
*Antony and Cleopatra* **6**: 23; **17**: 5
*Hamlet* **21**: 21, 29, 334
*Henry IV, 1 and 2* **14**: 111
*Julius Caesar* **7**: 159
*King John* **9**: 216; **24**: 162, 167, 168
*King Lear* **11**: 116
*Macbeth* **3**: 181; **20**: 12, 25, 22
*Richard III* **14**: 365
*Romeo and Juliet* **11**: 377
*The Taming of the Shrew* **12**: 309
*Troilus and Cressida* **18**: 278
*The Winter's Tale* **15**: 396

**Davis, Lloyd**
Appearance vs. Reality (topic entry) **34**: 23
Desire (topic entry) **38**: 31

**Davis, Michael**
*Macbeth* **44**: 315

**Dawes, James**
*Sonnets* **32**: 327

**Dawson, Anthony B.**
*As You Like It* **23**: 162
*Hamlet* **21**: 371
*Henry IV, 1 and 2* **14**: 160
*Henry V* **14**: 342
*Julius Caesar* **17**: 426
*Macbeth* **20**: 413
*Measure for Measure* **23**: 395
*Richard II* **24**: 428
*The Tempest* **15**: 385
*The Winter's Tale* **15**: 532

**Dawson, Helen**
*Love's Labour's Lost* **23**: 201
*A Midsummer Night's Dream* **12**: 256

**de Grazia, Margareta**
General Commentary **13**: 487
*Sonnets* **28**: 363; **40**: 273

**de Jongh, Nicholas**
*As You Like It* **23**: 141, 148
*King John* **24**: 239
*Twelfth Night* **26**: 334

**de Sousa, Geraldo U.**
*Henry VI, 1, 2, and 3* **37**: 97

**De Quincey, Thomas**
*Macbeth* **3**: 190
*The Two Noble Kinsmen* **9**: 447

**Dean, Leonard F.**
*Henry IV, 1 and 2* **1**: 370
*Richard II* **6**: 315

**Dean, Paul**
General Commentary **13**: 481

**Deats, Sara Munson**
Violence in Shakespeare's Works (topic entry) **43**: 32

**Deighton, K.**
*Pericles* **2**: 553

**Demaray, John G.**
*The Tempest* **48**: 299

**Dench, Judi**
*Antony and Cleopatra* **17**: 82

**Dennis, Carl**
*Twelfth Night* **47**: 45

**Dennis, John**
*Coriolanus* **9**: 9
*Julius Caesar* **7**: 151
*The Merry Wives of Windsor* **5**: 333; **18**: 5, 7

**Dent, Alan**
*All's Well That Ends Well* **26**: 13
*As You Like It* **23**: 69
*Julius Caesar* **17**: 370
*Macbeth* **20**: 166
*Richard II* **24**: 329

**Dent, R. W.**
*A Midsummer Night's Dream* **3**: 441

**Derrick, Patty S.**
*Two Gentlemen of Verona* **42**: 18

**Desai, R. W.**
*The Winter's Tale* **37**: 305

**Desmet, Christy**
Appearance vs. Reality (topic entry) **34**: 54
*Cymbeline* **47**: 286

**Dessen, Allan C.**
*As You Like It* **32**: 212
*Henry IV, 1 and 2* **32**: 212
*King Lear* **32**: 212
*Macbeth* **32**: 212
*Romeo and Juliet* **32**: 212
*Titus Andronicus* **17**: 483, 492

**Detmer, Emily**
Violence in Shakespeare's Works (topic entry) **43**: 61

**DeVine, Lawrence**
*Titus Andronicus* **17**: 473

**DeWilde, G. J.**
*Macbeth* **20**: 89

**Dexter, John**
*As You Like It* **23**: 124

**Di Biase, Carmine**
*Cymbeline* **28**: 373

**Dibdin, Charles**
*Richard II* **6**: 255

*Romeo and Juliet* **5**: 419
*The Two Gentlemen of Verona* **6**: 438

**DiGangi, Mario**
*As You Like It* **46**: 142

**Dick Bernard F.**
*Julius Caesar* **17**: 364

**Dickey, Franklin M.**
*Romeo and Juliet* **5**: 485
*Troilus and Cressida* **3**: 594
*Venus and Adonis* **10**: 449

**Dickey, Stephen**
*Pericles* **36**: 279
*Twelfth Night* **19**: 42

**Dickinson, Hugh**
*Henry VI, Parts 1, 2, and 3* **47**: 32

**Diehl, Huston**
*Measure for Measure* **48**: 1

**DiGangi, Mario**
*Measure for Measure* **25**: 12; **33**: 90

**Digges, Leonard**
*Julius Caesar* **7**: 149
*Twelfth Night* **1**: 539

**Dillon, Janette**
*Sonnets* **10**: 372

**Disch, Thomas M.**
*Julius Caesar* **17**: 403
*Love's Labour's Lost* **23**: 228

**Dithmar, E. A.**
*The Merry Wives of Windsor* **18**: 16
*Twelfth Night* **26**: 214

**Dobranski, Stephen B.**
*Much Ado about Nothing* **48**: 14

**Dodds, W. M. T.**
*Measure for Measure* **2**: 463

**Dodsworth, Martin**
*All's Well That Ends Well* **26**: 72
*Hamlet* **21**: 334
*Julius Caesar* **17**: 389
*Love's Labour's Lost* **23**: 215

**Doebler, John**
*Venus and Adonis* **10**: 486

**Dolan, Frances E.**
Violence in Shakespeare's Works (topic entry) **43**: 39

**Donaldson, E. Talbot**
*Troilus and Cressida* **43**: 305

**Donaldson, Ian**
*All's Well That Ends Well* **38**: 123
*The Rape of Lucrece* **33**: 131

**Donnellan, Declan**
*The Tempest* **15**: 338

**Donno, Elizabeth Story**
*Twelfth Night* **46**: 286

**Donohue, Joseph**
*Macbeth* **20**: 376

**Donohue, Joseph W., Jr.**
*Macbeth* **20**: 32, 70, 73

**Doone, Rupert**
*Richard III* **14**: 420

**Doran, John**
*The Merchant of Venice* **12**: 6

**Doran, Madeleine**
*Antony and Cleopatra* **27**: 96

**Dorsch, T. S.**
*The Comedy of Errors* **26**: 142, 186
*Julius Caesar* **7**: 277

**Dowden, Edward**
*All's Well That Ends Well* **7**: 26
*Antony and Cleopatra* **6**: 41
*As You Like It* **5**: 43
*The Comedy of Errors* **1**: 16
*Coriolanus* **9**: 31
*Hamlet* **1**: 115
*Henry IV, 1 and 2* **1**: 326
*Henry VI, 1, 2, and 3* **3**: 41
*Julius Caesar* **7**: 174
*King John* **9**: 234
*King Lear* **2**: 131
*Love's Labour's Lost* **2**: 308
*Macbeth* **3**: 207
*Measure for Measure* **2**: 410
*A Midsummer Night's Dream* **3**: 379
*Much Ado about Nothing* **8**: 28
*Pericles* **2**: 549
*The Phoenix and Turtle* **10**: 9
*The Rape of Lucrece* **10**: 68
*Richard II* **6**: 267
*Richard III* **8**: 168
*Romeo and Juliet* **5**: 437
*Sonnets* **10**: 215
*The Taming of the Shrew* **9**: 325
*The Tempest* **8**: 312
*Timon of Athens* **1**: 470
*Titus Andronicus* **4**: 625
*Troilus and Cressida* **3**: 548
*Twelfth Night* **1**: 561
*The Two Gentlemen of Verona* **6**: 449
*The Two Noble Kinsmen* **9**: 456
*Venus and Adonis* **10**: 419
*The Winter's Tale* **7**: 395

**Dowling, Ellen**
*The Taming of the Shrew* **12**: 441

**Downer, Alan S.**
*Macbeth* **20**: 107
*Romeo and Juliet* **11**: 463

**Downes, John**
*Hamlet* **21**: 9
*Macbeth* **20**: 12
*A Midsummer Night's Dream* **12**: 144
*Romeo and Juliet* **11**: 377
*The Tempest* **15**: 195

**Downs-Gamble, Margaret**
  *The Taming of the Shrew* **31:** 339

**Drake, James**
  *Hamlet* **1:** 73

**Drake, Nathan**
  *Richard II* **6:** 259
  *Richard III* **8:** 162
  *Sonnets* **10:** 158, 161
  *Venus and Adonis* **10:** 416

**Draper, John W.**
  *As You Like It* **5:** 66
  *King Lear* **2:** 168
  Shakespeare's Representation of Women (topic entry) **31:** 12
  *Timon of Athens* **1:** 487, 489
  *Twelfth Night* **1:** 581

**Draper, R. P.**
  *Richard II* **39:** 289

**Dreher, Diane Elizabeth**
  Fathers and Daughters (topic entry) **36:** 12

**Drew, John**
  *Richard II* **24:** 291
  *The Taming of the Shrew* **12:** 330

**Driver, Tom F.**
  *King Lear* **11:** 97
  *Macbeth* **3:** 293
  *Richard III* **8:** 223
  *Romeo and Juliet* **5:** 518

**Dromey, Mary Jane Scholtes**
  *Coriolanus* **17:** 148

**Dronke, Peter**
  *The Phoenix and Turtle* **38:** 367

**Drury, Alan**
  *As You Like It* **23:** 129
  *The Merry Wives of Windsor* **18:** 54
  *Pericles* **15:** 164

**Dryden, John**
  *Henry IV, 1 and 2* **1:** 285
  *Julius Caesar* **7:** 149
  *Macbeth* **3:** 170
  *The Merry Wives of Windsor* **5:** 332
  *A Midsummer Night's Dream* **3:** 361
  *Pericles* **2:** 537
  *Richard II* **6:** 250
  *Romeo and Juliet* **5:** 415
  *The Tempest* **8:** 286; **15:** 189, 343
  *Troilus and Cressida* **3:** 536; **18:** 276, 277
  *The Winter's Tale* **7:** 376

**Dubrow, Heather**
  *The Rape of Lucrece* **10:** 135
  *Sonnets* **10:** 367; **40:** 238

**Duff, William**
  *A Midsummer Night's Dream* **3:** 362

**Dukes, Ashley**
  *Richard II* **24:** 302
  *Romeo and Juliet* **11:** 447

**Dunbar, Mary Judith**
  *Pericles* **36:** 251

**Duncan-Jones, Katherine**
  Authorship Controversy (topic entry) **41:** 110
  *Richard II* **24:** 382
  *Sonnets* **42:** 296
  *Venus and Adonis* **25:** 328

**Dundas, Judith**
  *Rape of Lucrece* **10:** 128

**Dunkel, Wilbur**
  *Henry VIII* **24:** 80

**Dunkley, Chris**
  *The Taming of the Shrew* **12:** 397

**Dunn, Allen**
  *A Midsummer Night's Dream* **13:** 19

**Dunn, Esther Cloudman**
  *The Rape of Lucrece* **10:** 74

**Dusinberre, Juliet**
  *As You Like It* **28:** 46
  Gender Identity (topic entry) **40:** 51
  *King John* **16:** 161
  *The Taming of the Shrew* **31:** 307

**Duthie, George Ian**
  *Romeo and Juliet* **5:** 480
  *The Taming of the Shrew* **9:** 347

**Dyboski, Roman**
  *Coriolanus* **9:** 62

**Dyson, H. V. D.**
  *Henry VI, 1, 2, and 3* **3:** 64

**Dyson, J. P.**
  *Macbeth* **3:** 302

**Eagleton, Terence**
  *Coriolanus* **9:** 153
  *Macbeth* **3:** 321
  *Measure for Measure* **2:** 507
  *Troilus and Cressida* **3:** 617
  *Twelfth Night* **34:** 293

**Edelman, Charles**
  *Cymbeline* **22:** 365
  *King Lear* **22:** 365
  *Macbeth* **22:** 365

**Eder, Richard**
  *Antony and Cleopatra* **17:** 71
  *As You Like It* **23:** 119
  *Henry V* **14:** 325
  *Macbeth* **20:** 306
  *Richard III* **14:** 468

**Edinborough, Arnold**
  *Antony and Cleopatra* **17:** 47
  *Hamlet* **21:** 222
  *Henry V* **14:** 265, 269
  *Much Ado about Nothing* **18:** 176
  *The Taming of the Shrew* **12:** 368
  *Timon of Athens* **20:** 458
  *Twelfth Night* **26:** 248

**Edwards, Christopher**
  *As You Like It* **23:** 138
  *Coriolanus* **17:** 212
  *Hamlet* **21:** 314, 315
  *Henry VI, 1, 2, and 3* **24:** 48
  *Love's Labour's Lost* **23:** 216
  *The Taming of the Shrew* **12:** 409
  *Troilus and Cressida* **18:** 385, 390
  *Twelfth Night* **26:** 305, 330
  *The Two Gentlemen of Verona* **12:** 493

**Edwards, Philip**
  *Hamlet* **44:** 119
  *Pericles* **2:** 586
  *Romeo and Juliet* **33:** 272
  *Sonnets* **10:** 342
  *Twelfth Night* **1:** 654
  *The Two Noble Kinsmen* **9:** 481

**Egan, Robert**
  *The Tempest* **8:** 435

**Eggert, Katherine**
  *Henry V* **28:** 121

**Eliot, T. S.**
  *Coriolanus* **9:** 58
  *Hamlet* **1:** 142
  *Othello* **4:** 454

**Ellen, Terry**
  *Henry VIII* **24:** 82
  *Much Ado about Nothing* **18:** 133

**Elliot, John R., Jr.**
  *Richard II* **39:** 235

**Elliott, G. R.**
  *The Comedy of Errors* **1:** 27
  *Macbeth* **3:** 286
  *Othello* **4:** 470, 522

**Elliott, Michael**
  *The Winter's Tale* **15:** 449

**Ellis, David**
  Clowns and Fools (topic entry) **46:** 68

**Ellis, Roger**
  Clowns and Fools (topic entry) **46:** 1

**Ellis-Fermor, Una**
  *Coriolanus* **9:** 121
  *Henry IV, 1 and 2* **1:** 379

  *Henry V* **5:** 244
  *Julius Caesar* **7:** 252
  *Measure for Measure* **2:** 432
  *Timon of Athens* **1:** 490
  *Troilus and Cressida* **3:** 578; **18:** 412

**Ellrodt, Robert**
  *The Phoenix and Turtle* **38:** 350
  *Sonnets* **28:** 380

**Elsom, John**
  *All's Well That Ends Well* **26:** 54
  *Antony and Cleopatra* **17:** 66
  *As You Like It* **23:** 112, 122
  *Henry IV, 1 and 2* **14:** 86
  *King John* **24:** 220
  *Measure for Measure* **23:** 338
  *A Midsummer Night's Dream* **12:** 271
  *Pericles* **15:** 159
  *Richard II* **24:** 345, 371
  *The Taming of the Shrew* **12:** 389
  *The Tempest* **15:** 279
  *Troilus and Cressida* **18:** 357
  *The Two Gentlemen of Verona* **12:** 491

**Elze, Karl**
  *All's Well That Ends Well* **7:** 21
  *Henry VIII* **2:** 35
  *The Merchant of Venice* **4:** 209

**Emerson, Ralph Waldo**
  *The Phoenix and Turtle* **10:** 7

**Emerson, Sally**
  *The Comedy of Errors* **26:** 157
  *Henry VI, 1, 2, and 3* **24:** 34

**Empson, William**
  *Hamlet* **1:** 202
  *Henry IV, 1 and 2* **1:** 359
  *Measure for Measure* **2:** 486
  *The Rape of Lucrece* **10:** 96
  *Sonnets* **10:** 256
  *Troilus and Cressida* **3:** 569

**Engle, Lars**
  *The Merchant of Venice* **25:** 22; **40:** 197
  *Sonnets* **13:** 445

**Enright, D. J.**
  *Coriolanus* **9:** 112

**Enterline, Lynn**
  *The Winter's Tale* **42:** 301

**Erickson, Peter**
  *As You Like It* **5:** 168
  *Hamlet* **44:** 189
  *King Lear* **31:** 137
  *Love's Labour's Lost* **38:** 232
  *The Merry Wives of Windsor* **5:** 402

**Erskine, John**
  *Romeo and Juliet* **5:** 450

**Ervine, St. John**
  *The Two Gentlemen of Verona* **12:** 459

**Esslin, Martin**
  *As You Like It* **23:** 98
  *The Winter's Tale* **15:** 480

**Ettin, Andrew V.**
  *Titus Andronicus* **27:** 275

**Evans, B. Ifor**
  *The Merchant of Venice* **4:** 267
  *A Midsummer Night's Dream* **3:** 415

**Evans, Bertrand**
  *All's Well That Ends Well* **7:** 81
  *As You Like It* **5:** 107
  *The Comedy of Errors* **1:** 37
  *Love's Labour's Lost* **2:** 338
  *Macbeth* **3:** 338
  *Measure for Measure* **2:** 498
  *The Merry Wives of Windsor* **5:** 355
  *A Midsummer Night's Dream* **3:** 434
  *Much Ado about Nothing* **8:** 82
  *Pericles* **2:** 575
  *Romeo and Juliet* **5:** 470
  *Twelfth Night* **1:** 625
  *The Two Gentlemen of Verona* **6:** 499

**Evans, G. Blakemore**
  *Romeo and Juliet* **11:** 517; **33:** 210

**Evans, Gareth Lloyd**
  *All's Well That Ends Well* **26:** 48
  *As You Like It* **23:** 132
  Clowns and Fools (topic entry) **46:** 52
  *Henry IV, 1 and 2* **14:** 81
  *King Lear* **11:** 112
  *Macbeth* **20:** 262, 296, 329, 379
  *The Merry Wives of Windsor* **18:** 46
  *A Midsummer Night's Dream* **12:** 276
  *Richard III* **14:** 490
  *The Taming of the Shrew* **12:** 358
  *Troilus and Cressida* **18:** 349, 403
  *Twelfth Night* **26:** 272
  *The Two Gentlemen of Verona* **12:** 480

**Evans, Malcolm**
  *Love's Labour's Lost* **2:** 365

**Evans, Peter**
  *The Merry Wives of Windsor* **18:** 90

**Evans, Robert O.**
  *Romeo and Juliet* **5:** 530

**Everett, Barbara**
  *Antony and Cleopatra* **17:** 79
  *Hamlet* **1:** 268
  *King Lear* **2:** 229
  *Much Ado about Nothing* **8:** 91; **28:** 56
  *Romeo and Juliet* **33:** 294
  *Sonnets* **28:** 385
  *Troilus and Cressida* **27:** 347

**Ewbank, Inga-Stina**
  *Hamlet* **1:** 270
  *The Tempest* **19:** 379
  *The Two Gentlemen of Verona* **6:** 541
  *The Winter's Tale* **7:** 476; **13:** 409

**Eyres, Harry**
  *Richard II* **24:** 385

**Faber, M. D.**
  *A Midsummer Night's Dream* **3:** 483
  *Othello* **35:** 282
  *Romeo and Juliet* **5:** 556

**Fairchild, Arthur H. R.**
  *The Phoenix and Turtle* **10:** 9

**Fairchild, Hoxie N.**
  *Measure for Measure* **2:** 427

**Falk, Florence**
  *A Midsummer Night's Dream* **3:** 502

**Farber, Manny**
  *Henry V* **14:** 212

**Farber, Stephen**
  *The Taming of the Shrew* **12:** 373

**Farjeon, Herbert**
  *All's Well That Ends Well* **26:** 14
  *As You Like It* **23:** 68
  *Henry IV, 1 and 2* **14:** 28
  *King Lear* **11:** 47, 52
  *A Midsummer Night's Dream* **12:** 235, 294
  *Othello* **11:** 264
  *Richard II* **24:** 300, 303
  *Richard III* **14:** 410
  *The Tempest* **15:** 233
  *Twelfth Night* **26:** 359

**Farley-Hills, David**
  *The Taming of the Shrew* **31:** 261
  *Timon of Athens* **16:** 351

**Farmer, Richard**
  *Henry V* **5:** 190
  *Pericles* **2:** 538

**Farnham, Willard**
  *Antony and Cleopatra* **6:** 136
  *Coriolanus* **9:** 92

**Farrah**
  *Henry V* **14:** 295

**Farrell, Kirby**
  Fathers and Daughters (topic entry) **36:** 25
  *Romeo and Juliet* **13:** 235
  *Venus and Adonis* **33:** 370

**Faucit, Helena (Lady Martin)**
  *As You Like It* **5:** 44
  *Cymbeline* **4:** 37
  *Hamlet* **21:** 386
  *Othello* **11:** 334
  *The Winter's Tale* **15:** 413

**Fawcett, Mary Laughlin**
  *Titus Andronicus* **43:** 239

**Fehrenbach, Robert J.**
  *Henry IV, 1 and 2* **39:** 137

**Feingold, Michael**
  *Measure for Measure* **23:** 353
  *Much Ado about Nothing* **18:** 222
  *Richard III* **14:** 483

**Felheim, Marvin**
  *The Merry Wives of Windsor* **18:** 21; **38:** 313
  *A Midsummer Night's Dream* **12:** 198
  *The Taming of the Shrew* **12:** 331
  *The Two Gentlemen of Verona* **12:** 456; **40:** 330

**Felperin, Howard**
  *Henry VIII* **2:** 66
  *Macbeth* **44:** 341
  *Pericles* **2:** 581

**Feltham, Owen**
  *Pericles* **2:** 537

**Felton, Felix**
  *A Midsummer Night's Dream* **12:** 213

**Felver, Charles**
  Clowns and Fools (topic entry) **46:** 33

**Fender, Stephen**
  *A Midsummer Night's Dream* **3:** 459

**Fenton, James**
  *The Comedy of Errors* **26:** 162
  *Much Ado about Nothing* **18:** 211
  *Twelfth Night* **26:** 302

**Fenwick, Henry**
  *Richard II* **24:** 364

**Ferber, Michael**
  *The Merchant of Venice* **40:** 127

**Ferguson, Otis**
  *A Midsummer Night's Dream* **12:** 212

**Fergusson, Francis**
  *The Comedy of Errors* **1:** 35
  *Hamlet* **1:** 184
  *Macbeth* **3:** 267
  *Richard III* **39:** 305
  *Troilus and Cressida* **18:** 298

**Ferry, Anne**
  *Sonnets* **40:** 292

**Fichter, Andrew**
  *Antony and Cleopatra* **6:** 224

**Fiedler, Leslie A.**
  *Henry VI, 1, 2, and 3* **3:** 140

**Field, Kate**
  *Hamlet* **21:** 81

**Fielding, Henry**
  *Hamlet* **21:** 15

**Fienberg, Nona**
  *Pericles* **2:** 590; **36:** 274

**Figes, Eva**
  Kingship (topic entry) **39:** 62

**Findlater, Richard**
  *Antony and Cleopatra* **17:** 37
  *The Comedy of Errors* **26:** 164
  *Henry IV, 1 and 2* **14:** 37
  *A Midsummer Night's Dream* **12:** 198
  *The Taming of the Shrew* **12:** 358
  *Twelfth Night* **26:** 304
  *The Two Gentlemen of Verona* **12:** 476
  *The Winter's Tale* **15:** 469

**Findlay, Alison**
  *Hamlet* **35:** 144

**Fineman, Joel**
  *Rape of Lucrece* **43:** 113

**Fink, Joel G.**
  *The Comedy of Errors* **26:** 171

**Fink, Z. S.**
  *As You Like It* **5:** 68

**Finkelpearl, Philip J.**
  *The Two Noble Kinsmen* **37:** 312

**Fisch, Harold**
  *Antony and Cleopatra* **47:** 71

**Fisher, James E.**
  *Othello* **11:** 306

**Fisher, Sandra K.**
  *Henry IV, 1 and 2* **13:** 213
  *Henry V* **13:** 213
  *Richard II* **13:** 213

**Fitz, L. T.**
  *Antony and Cleopatra* **27:** 144

**Fitzgerald, Percy**
  *Henry VIII* **24:** 70
  *A Midsummer Night's Dream* **12:** 287
  *Othello* **11:** 253
  *The Tempest* **15:** 343

**Fitzpatrick, Thomas**
  *King Lear* **2:** 99

**Fitzsimons, Raymond**
  *The Merchant of Venice* **12:** 14

**Flathe, J. L. F.**
  *Macbeth* **3:** 199

**Fleming, Peter**
  *Antony and Cleopatra* **17:** 30
  *As You Like It* **23:** 79, 83
  *Macbeth* **20:** 188
  *Measure for Measure* **23:** 297
  *The Merchant of Venice* **12:** 52
  *Othello* **11:** 275
  *Richard II* **24:** 319
  *Romeo and Juliet* **11:** 446
  *Twelfth Night* **26:** 243
  *The Winter's Tale* **15:** 461

**Flesy, F. G.**
  *Measure for Measure* **2:** 548
  *Timon of Athens* **1:** 469

**Fletcher, George**
  *King John* **24:** 184

**Flint, Stella**
  *The Taming of the Shrew* **12:** 408

**Fly, Richard D.**
  *King Lear* **2:** 271
  *Timon of Athens* **1:** 522
  *Troilus and Cressida* **3:** 630; **27:** 354

**Foakes, R. A.**
  *The Comedy of Errors* **26:** 183; **34:** 208
  *Cymbeline* **4:** 134
  *Hamlet* **25:** 209
  *Henry VIII* **2:** 51
  *King Lear* **25:** 218
  *Measure for Measure* **2:** 516
  *The Tempest* **45:** 188
  *Troilus and Cressida* **27:** 341

**Folland, Harold F.**
  *Richard II* **6:** 393

**Foote, Samuel**
  *King Lear* **11:** 5

**Forbes-Robinson, John**
  *King Lear* **11:** 21

**Ford-Davies, Oliver**
  *Coriolanus* **17:** 195

**Forker, Charles R.**
  *Henry VI, 1, 2, and 3* **3:** 97

**Forman, Simon**
  *Cymbeline* **4:** 17
  *The Winter's Tale* **7:** 375

**Forster, John**
  *Hamlet* **21:** 22, 51
  *King Lear* **11:** 17
  *Macbeth* **20:** 98

**Fortin, Rene E.**
  *Julius Caesar* **7:** 336
  *King Lear* **2:** 286
  *The Merchant of Venice* **4:** 324

**Foster, Charles J.**
  *Henry IV, 1 and 2* **14:** 4
  *The Merry Wives of Windsor* **18:** 12

**Foster, Donald W.**
  Authorship Controversy (topic entry) **41:** 85

**Foster, Verna A.**
  *The Winter's Tale* **25:** 339

**Foulkes, Richard**
  *The Merchant of Venice* **12:** 43, 107
  *A Midsummer Night's Dream* **12:** 172
  *Richard II* **24:** 283

**Fowler, Alastair**
  *The Winter's Tale* **36:** 362

**Fowler, William Warde**
  *Julius Caesar* **7:** 200

**Fox-Good, Jacquelyn**
  *The Tempest* **37:** 320

**Frail, David**
  *As You Like It* **46:** 105

**France, Richard**
  *Julius Caesar* **17:** 334
  *Macbeth* **20:** 213

**Fraser, Russell**
  *All's Well That Ends Well* **26:** 87

**Freedman, Barbara**
  *The Comedy of Errors* **19:** 54
  *The Merry Wives of Windsor* **5:** 392

**Freedman, Gerald**
  *Titus Andronicus* **17:** 463

**Freer, Coburn**
  *Cymbeline* **36:** 166

**French, A. L.**
  *Antony and Cleopatra* **6:** 202
  *Richard II* **6:** 359

**French, Marilyn**
  *Henry VI, 1, 2, and 3* **3:** 157
  *Macbeth* **3:** 333
  *The Merry Wives of Windsor* **5:** 395
  *Othello* **35:** 327

**French, Philip**
  *Henry V* **14:** 308
  *Julius Caesar* **17:** 372
  *The Merry Wives of Windsor* **18:** 41
  *Romeo and Juliet* **11:** 473

**Frenzel, Karl**
  *Antony and Cleopatra* **6:** 39

**Freud, Sigmund**
  *Hamlet* **1:** 119
  *King Lear* **2:** 147
  *Macbeth* **3:** 223
  *Richard III* **8:** 185

**Frey, Charles**
  Fathers and Daughters (topic entry) **36:** 37
  *The Tempest* **29:** 373
  *The Two Gentlemen of Verona* **12:** 488
  *The Winter's Tale* **7:** 497

**Friedman, Michael D.**
  *Much Ado about Nothing* **16:** 45; **31:** 222

**Fripp, Edgar I.**
  *Henry VIII* **2:** 46

**Frost, William**
  *King Lear* **2:** 216

**Frye, Northrop**
  *Antony and Cleopatra* **6:** 178
  *The Comedy of Errors* **1:** 32
  *Coriolanus* **9:** 142
  *Cymbeline* **4:** 115
  *Henry V* **5:** 269
  *Henry VIII* **2:** 65

*King Lear* **2:** 253
  *The Merry Wives of Windsor* **5:** 353
  *Pericles* **2:** 580
  *Romeo and Juliet* **5:** 575
  *Sonnets* **10:** 309
  *The Tempest* **8:** 401
  *Timon of Athens* **1:** 512
  *Troilus and Cressida* **3:** 642
  *The Winter's Tale* **7:** 479; **36:** 289

**Fuchs, Barbara**
  *The Tempest* **42:** 320

**Fujimura, Thomas H.**
  *The Merchant of Venice* **4:** 308

**Fuller, Edward**
  *Measure for Measure* **23:** 279

**Fuller, Thomas**
  *Henry IV, 1 and 2* **1:** 285

**Funke, Lewis**
  *The Two Gentlemen of Verona* **12:** 470

**Furness, Horace Howard**
  *Antony and Cleopatra* **6:** 62
  *As You Like It* **5:** 45
  *Cymbeline* **4:** 48
  *A Midsummer Night's Dream* **3:** 386

**Furness, Horace Howard, Jr.**
  *Hamlet* **21:** 151

**Furnivall, F. J.**
  *Sonnets* **10:** 213
  *Twelfth Night* **1:** 557

**Furse, Roger**
  *Richard III* **14:** 515

**Fuxier, J.**
  *A Midsummer Night's Dream* **12:** 272
  *Much Ado about Nothing* **18:** 215
  *Richard III* **14:** 489

**Gajowski, Evelyn**
  *Othello* **19:** 253
  *Antony and Cleopatra* **47:** 174

**Gallenca, Christiane**
  *The Merry Wives of Windsor* **38:** 256

**Ganz, Arthur**
  *All's Well That Ends Well* **26:** 62
  *Richard III* **14:** 484

**Garber, Marjorie**
  *Antony and Cleopatra* **45:** 28
  *Hamlet* **45:** 28
  *A Midsummer Night's Dream* **45:** 96
  *Romeo and Juliet* **33:** 246
  *The Tempest* **45:** 236
  *The Winter's Tale* **45:** 366

**Gardiner, Judith Kegan**
  *Sonnets* **10:** 379

**Gardner, Helen**
  *As You Like It* **5:** 98
  *Hamlet* **1:** 224

**Gardner, Lyn**
  *Antony and Cleopatra* **17:** 82

**Garebian, Keith**
  *Macbeth* **20:** 307
  *The Merry Wives of Windsor* **18:** 51

**Garland, Robert**
  *King Lear* **11:** 56

**Garner, Shirley Nelson**
  *Cymbeline* **47:** 25
  *Much Ado about Nothing* **47:** 25
  *Othello* **47:** 25
  *The Winter's Tale* **47:** 25

**Garner, Stanton B., Jr.**
  *The Tempest* **8:** 454
  *The Winter's Tale* **36:** 301; **45:** 374

**Garnett, Edward**
  *Troilus and Cressida* **18:** 286

**Garnett, Richard**
  *The Two Gentlemen of Verona* **6:** 464

**Garrick, David**
  *Romeo and Juliet* **5:** 378; **11:** 382

**Gascoigne, Bamber**
  *As You Like It* **23:** 89
  *Cymbeline* **15:** 65
  *King Lear* **11:** 87
  *Macbeth* **20:** 251
  *Measure for Measure* **23:** 316
  *Much Ado about Nothing* **18:** 179
  *Othello* **11:** 290
  *Richard III* **14:** 454
  *The Taming of the Shrew* **12:** 360

**Gaw, Allison**
  *The Comedy of Errors* **1:** 19

**Geduld, Harry M.**
  *Henry V* **14:** 225

**Gelb, Arthur**
  *The Merchant of Venice* **12:** 70

**Gelb, Hal**
  *Measure for Measure* **2:** 514

**Geller, Lila**
  *Cymbeline* **36:** 158

**Gellert, Roger**
  *Hamlet* **21:** 229
  *Henry VI, 1, 2, and 3* **24:** 20
  *Julius Caesar* **17:** 368
  *King Lear* **11:** 87
  *Measure for Measure* **23:** 315
  *A Midsummer Night's Dream* **12:** 248

**Genster, Julia**
  *Othello* **16:** 272**

**Gent, Lucy**
  *Venus and Adonis* **33**: 357

**Gentleman, Francis**
  *Antony and Cleopatra* **6**: 22
  *As You Like It* **5**: 19
  *Coriolanus* **9**: 12
  *Cymbeline* **15**: 94
  *Hamlet* **21**: 16
  *Henry IV, 1 and 2* **1**: 295
  *Henry V* **5**: 190
  *Henry VI, 1, 2, and 3* **3**: 21
  *Julius Caesar* **7**: 158
  *King John* **9**: 212; **24**: 167
  *Love's Labour's Lost* **2**: 301
  *Macbeth* **3**: 175; **20**: 21
  *The Merchant of Venice* **12**: 4
  *A Midsummer Night's Dream* **3**: 363
  *Much Ado about Nothing* **18**: 230
  *Richard II* **6**: 253
  *Romeo and Juliet* **11**: 384, 495
  *Titus Andronicus* **4**: 615
  *Troilus and Cressida* **3**: 538

**Gerard, Albert**
  *Troilus and Cressida* **3**: 596
  *Twelfth Night* **1**: 638

**Gerard, Alexander**
  *Measure for Measure* **2**: 394

**Gervinus, G. G.**
  *All's Well That Ends Well* **7**: 19; **26**: 93
  *Antony and Cleopatra* **6**: 33
  *As You Like It* **5**: 32
  *Coriolanus* **9**: 19
  *Cymbeline* **4**: 29
  *Hamlet* **1**: 103
  *Henry IV, 1 and 2* **1**: 317
  *Henry V* **5**: 199
  *Henry VI, 1, 2, and 3* **3**: 31
  *Henry VIII* **2**: 31
  *Julius Caesar* **7**: 161
  *King John* **9**: 224
  *King Lear* **2**: 116
  *Love's Labour's Lost* **2**: 305
  *Macbeth* **3**: 196
  *Measure for Measure* **2**: 402
  *The Merchant of Venice* **4**: 204
  *The Merry Wives of Windsor* **5**: 339
  *A Midsummer Night's Dream* **3**: 372
  *Much Ado about Nothing* **8**: 19
  *Othello* **4**: 415
  *Pericles* **2**: 546
  *The Rape of Lucrece* **10**: 66
  *Richard II* **6**: 264
  *Richard III* **8**: 165
  *Romeo and Juliet* **5**: 431
  *Sonnets* **10**: 185
  *The Taming of the Shrew* **9**: 323
  *The Tempest* **8**: 304
  *Timon of Athens* **1**: 467
  *Titus Andronicus* **4**: 623
  *Troilus and Cressida* **3**: 544
  *Twelfth Night* **1**: 551
  *The Two Gentlemen of Verona* **6**: 445
  *The Two Noble Kinsmen* **9**: 455
  *Venus and Adonis* **10**: 418
  *The Winter's Tale* **7**: 390

**Ghose, Zulfikar**
  *Macbeth* **25**: 235

**Gibbons, Brian**
  *Coriolanus* **25**: 245
  *Henry VI, 1, 2, and 3* **25**: 245
  *Richard III* **25**: 245
  *Romeo and Juliet* **25**: 245
  *The Tempest* **28**: 391
  *Titus Andronicus* **25**: 245

**Gibson, H. N.**
  Authorship Controversy (topic entry) **41**: 66

**Gibbs, Patrick**
  *All's Well That Ends Well* **26**: 24

**Gibbs, Wolcott**
  *As You Like It* **23**: 73
  *King Lear* **11**: 71
  *Macbeth* **20**: 225, 226
  *The Tempest* **15**: 240

**Gibson, Joy Leslie**
  *Richard II* **24**: 339

**Gielgud, John**
  *Hamlet* **21**: 182, 192, 237
  *Julius Caesar* **17**: 344, 356
  *King Lear* **11**: 50
  *Much Ado about Nothing* **18**: 168, 170
  *Othello* **11**: 295
  *Richard II* **24**: 411
  *Romeo and Juliet* **11**: 448
  *The Tempest* **15**: 311

**Gieskes, Edward**
  *King John* **48**: 132

**Gilbert, Miriam**
  *Richard II* **24**: 423

**Gilbert, W. Stephen**
  *Henry IV, 1 and 2* **14**: 85
  *Henry V* **14**: 283

**Gilder, Jeanette**
  *As You Like It* **23**: 40, 46
  *Twelfth Night* **26**: 215

**Gilder, Rosamond**
  *Hamlet* **21**: 172
  *Macbeth* **20**: 230
  *Othello* **11**: 272
  *Richard III* **14**: 413
  *The Tempest* **15**: 246
  *Twelfth Night* **26**: 226

**Gildon, Charles**
  *All's Well That Ends Well* **7**: 8
  *Antony and Cleopatra* **6**: 20
  *As You Like It* **5**: 18
  *The Comedy of Errors* **1**: 13
  *Coriolanus* **9**: 8
  *Cymbeline* **4**: 17
  *Hamlet* **1**: 75, 76
  *Henry IV, 1 and 2* **1**: 286
  *Henry V* **5**: 186
  *Henry VI, 1, 2, and 3* **3**: 17
  *Julius Caesar* **7**: 152
  *King John* **9**: 208
  *King Lear* **2**: 93
  *Love's Labour's Lost* **2**: 299
  *Macbeth* **3**: 171
  *Measure for Measure* **2**: 387
  *The Merchant of Venice* **4**: 192
  *The Merry Wives of Windsor* **5**: 334
  *A Midsummer Night's Dream* **3**: 362
  *Much Ado about Nothing* **8**: 9
  *Othello* **4**: 380, 384
  *The Rape of Lucrece* **10**: 64
  *Richard II* **6**: 252
  *Richard III* **8**: 145
  *Romeo and Juliet* **5**: 416
  *Sonnets* **10**: 153
  *The Taming of the Shrew* **9**: 318
  *The Tempest* **8**: 287
  *Timon of Athens* **1**: 454
  *Titus Andronicus* **4**: 613
  *Troilus and Cressida* **18**: 277
  *Twelfth Night* **1**: 539
  *The Two Gentlemen of Verona* **6**: 435
  *The Winter's Tale* **7**: 377

**Gilliatt, Penelope**
  *Much Ado about Nothing* **18**: 188

**Gillies, John**
  *Antony and Cleopatra* **28**: 249
  *Othello* **28**: 249
  *The Tempest* **29**: 343
  *Titus Andronicus* **28**: 249

**Girard, René**
  *The Merchant of Venice* **4**: 331
  *A Midsummer Night's Dream* **29**: 234; **45**: 147
  *Troilus and Cressida* **43**: 317
  *Twelfth Night* **46**: 333
  *The Two Gentlemen of Verona* **13**: 12; **40**: 335
  *The Winter's Tale* **36**: 334

**Giroux, Robert**
  *Love's Labour's Lost* **23**: 224

**Glavin, John**
  *Romeo and Juliet* **19**: 261

**Glaz, A. Andre**
  *Othello* **35**: 265

**Glazov-Corrigan, Elena**
  *Cymbeline* **28**: 398; **36**: 186; **47**: 296
  *Pericles* **19**: 387

**Glick, Claris**
  *Hamlet* **21**: 347

**Glover, Julian**
  *Coriolanus* **17**: 195

**Goddard, Harold C.**
  *As You Like It* **5**: 88
  *Coriolanus* **9**: 100
  *Cymbeline* **4**: 89
  *Hamlet* **1**: 194
  *Henry IV, 1 and 2* **1**: 397
  *Henry V* **5**: 252

  *Henry VI, 1, 2, and 3* **3**: 73
  *The Merchant of Venice* **4**: 254
  *A Midsummer Night's Dream* **3**: 412
  *Much Ado about Nothing* **8**: 55
  *The Taming of the Shrew* **9**: 345
  *The Two Gentlemen of Verona* **6**: 484

**Godfrey, D. R.**
  *Othello* **35**: 310

**Godshalk, William Leigh**
  *All's Well That Ends Well* **7**: 113
  *Henry V* **30**: 273
  *Measure for Measure* **33**: 61
  *The Merry Wives of Windsor* **5**: 374
  *The Two Gentlemen of Verona* **6**: 526

**Godwin, William**
  *Troilus and Cressida* **3**: 539

**Goethe, Johann Wolfgang von**
  *Hamlet* **1**: 91; **21**: 379
  *Henry IV, 1 and 2* **1**: 311
  *Troilus and Cressida* **3**: 541

**Goldberg, Jonathan**
  *Henry IV, 1 and 2* **22**: 114

**Goldman, Michael**
  *Henry IV, 1 and 2* **48**: 143
  *Henry V* **30**: 163
  *Othello* **11**: 362

**Goldstein, Neal L.**
  *Love's Labour's Lost* **38**: 185

**Gollanez, Sir Israel**
  *The Merchant of Venice* **4**: 224

**Gomme, Andor**
  *Timon of Athens* **1**: 503

**Gordon, D. J.**
  *Coriolanus* **30**: 58

**Gordon, Giles**
  *Julius Caesar* **17**: 390
  *Measure for Measure* **23**: 344
  *Pericles* **15**: 173
  *Richard III* **14**: 487, 488

**Gorfain, Phyllis**
  *Pericles* **2**: 588

**Gottfried, Martin**
  *As You Like It* **23**: 101
  *Love's Labour's Lost* **23**: 206

**Gould, Gerald**
  *Henry V* **5**: 219

**Gould, Robert**
  *Timon of Athens* **1**: 453

**Gourlay, Patricia Southard**
  *The Winter's Tale* **36**: 311

**Gow, Gordon**
  *As You Like It* **23**: 124

**Goy-Blanquet, Dominique**
*Henry VI, 1, 2, and 3* **24:** 48
*Julius Caesar* **17:** 393

**Grady, Hugh**
*As You Like It* **37:** 43

**Graham, Virginia**
*Richard III* **14:** 422

**Grangier, Derek**
*Measure for Measure* **23:** 307

**Granville-Barker, F.**
*As You Like It* **23:** 84

**Granville-Barker, Harley**
*Antony and Cleopatra* **6:** 80; **17:** 104
*Coriolanus* **9:** 84
*Cymbeline* **4:** 56; **15:** 111
*Hamlet* **1:** 160
*Henry V* **5:** 226
*Julius Caesar* **7:** 210; **17:** 416
*King Lear* **2:** 154; **11:** 145
*Love's Labour's Lost* **2:** 317; **23:** 237
*Macbeth* **20:** 353
*The Merchant of Venice* **4:** 232; **12:** 115
*A Midsummer Night's Dream* **12:** 291
*Othello* **4:** 488
*Richard II* **24:** 301
*Romeo and Juliet* **5:** 454; **11:** 505
*Twelfth Night* **1:** 562; **26:** 357
*The Winter's Tale* **7:** 412; **15:** 514

**Gray, Henry David**
*Pericles* **2:** 558

**Gray, Simon**
*Twelfth Night* **26:** 265

**Grebanier, Bernard**
*Hamlet* **35:** 182

**Green, Andrew J.**
*Hamlet* **1:** 207

**Green, Brian**
*The Phoenix and Turtle* **38:** 345

**Green, Douglas E.**
*Twelfth Night* **46:** 362
*Titus Andronicus* **43:** 170

**Green, Harris**
*Much Ado about Nothing* **18:** 197

**Green, Janet M.**
*King Lear* **46:** 276

**Green, London**
*Richard III* **14:** 383, 390

**Greenblatt, Stephen**
*King Lear* **31:** 107

**Greene, Gayle**
*Julius Caesar* **7:** 350; **30:** 333
*Othello* **4:** 587
*Troilus and Cressida* **43:** 298

**Greene, Robert**
*Henry VI, 1, 2, and 3* **3:** 16

**Greene, Thomas M.**
*Love's Labour's Lost* **2:** 351
*Sonnets* **10:** 385

**Greenfield, Thelma Nelson**
*The Taming of the Shrew* **9:** 350

**Greg, Walter W.**
*As You Like It* **5:** 60
*Hamlet* **1:** 134

**Greif, Karen**
*Twelfth Night* **34:** 316; **46:** 310

**Grene, Nicholas**
*Antony and Cleopatra* **22:** 217
*Coriolanus* **30:** 79

**Grennan, Eamon**
*As You Like It* **34:** 155
*The Comedy of Errors* **34:** 238
*Henry V* **30:** 202

**Grey, Zachary**
*The Tempest* **8:** 292

**Griffin, Alice**
*Macbeth* **20:** 234
*The Merchant of Venice* **12:** 55, 64, 72
*Richard III* **14:** 426

**Griffith, Elizabeth**
*Antony and Cleopatra* **6:** 22
*As You Like It* **5:** 20
*Coriolanus* **9:** 12
*Henry IV, 1 and 2* **1:** 296
*Henry V* **5:** 191
*Henry VIII* **2:** 19
*Richard II* **6:** 254
*Richard III* **8:** 152
*Romeo and Juliet* **5:** 418
*The Taming of the Shrew* **9:** 319
*Titus Andronicus* **4:** 615
*Troilus and Cressida* **3:** 538
*The Two Gentlemen of Verona* **6:** 438
*The Winter's Tale* **7:** 381

**Griffiths, G. S.**
*Antony and Cleopatra* **6:** 120

**Griffiths, L. M.**
*Titus Andronicus* **4:** 626

**Griffiths, Trevor R.**
*The Tempest* **15:** 312

**Grindon, Mrs. Rosa Leo**
*The Merry Wives of Windsor* **5:** 349

**Gross, Gerard J.**
*All's Well That Ends Well* **38:** 132

**Gross, John**
*Henry VIII* **24:** 126

**Gross, Kenneth**
*Othello* **13:** 313

**Guinness, Alec**
*Richard II* **24:** 318

**Guizot, M.**
*Romeo and Juliet* **5:** 436

**Gunderode, Freiherr von**
*Hamlet* **21:** 17

**Gurr, Andrew**
General Commentary **13:** 494
*Hamlet* **44:** 241
*Henry V* **30:** 234
*Sonnets* **10:** 358

**Gussow, Mel**
*Henry IV, 1 and 2* **14:** 87
*King John* **24:** 237
*Love's Labour's Lost* **23:** 226
*Macbeth* **20:** 312
*Much Ado about Nothing* **18:** 191, 214
*Pericles* **15:** 162
*Timon of Athens* **20:** 468
*Titus Andronicus* **17:** 473, 480
*Twelfth Night* **26:** 297, 313

**Guthrie, Tyrone**
*All's Well That Ends Well* **26:** 15, 19
*The Merchant of Venice* **12:** 129
*The Tempest* **15:** 364

**Guthrie, William**
*Hamlet* **1:** 79

**Gutierrez, Nancy A.**
*Henry VI, 1, 2, and 3* **16:** 131

**Hackett, James Henry**
*Hamlet* **21:** 53
*Henry IV, 1 and 2* **14:** 4

**Hager, Alan**
*The Taming of the Shrew* **16:** 13

**Hale, David George**
*Coriolanus* **30:** 105

**Hale, Lionel**
*Love's Labour's Lost* **23:** 187

**Hales, John W.**
*Macbeth* **3:** 205

**Halio, Jay L.**
*As You Like It* **5:** 112
*Coriolanus* **9:** 169
*A Midsummer Night's Dream* **29:** 263; **45:** 169

**Hall, Joan Lord**
*Antony and Cleopatra* **19:** 270

**Hall, Jonathan**
Desire (topic entry) **38:** 56
*Henry IV, 1 and 2* **32:** 103

**Hall, Peter**
*Hamlet* **21:** 251
*Macbeth* **20:** 265
*The Tempest* **15:** 274, 338
*Twelfth Night* **26:** 257

**Hallam, Henry**
*Hamlet* **1:** 98
*King Lear* **2:** 111
*Romeo and Juliet* **5:** 426
*Sonnets* **10:** 175

**Hallinan, Tim**
*The Taming of the Shrew* **12:** 400

**Halliwell-Phillipps, J. O.**
*Love's Labour's Lost* **2:** 307
*A Midsummer Night's Dream* **3:** 370
*The Phoenix and Turtle* **10:** 7
*Sonnets* **10:** 217

**Halmstrom, John**
*Othello* **11:** 300

**Halpern, Richard**
*The Tempest* **45:** 280

**Halverson, John**
*Richard II* **28:** 134; **39:** 243

**Hamilton, A. C.**
*Henry VI, 1, 2, and 3* **3:** 83
*Titus Andronicus* **4:** 659; **43:** 195
*Venus and Adonis* **10:** 454

**Hamilton, Donna B.**
*King John* **22:** 120
*The Winter's Tale* **25:** 347

**Hamlin, William M.**
*The Tempest* **45:** 226

**Hammersmith, James P.**
*Richard III* **13:** 142

**Hammond, Gerald**
*Sonnets* **40:** 228

**Handelman, Susan**
*Timon of Athens* **1:** 529

**Hands, Terry**
*Coriolanus* **17:** 190
*Henry V* **14:** 293

**Hankey, Julie**
*Richard II* **24:** 371

**Hankin, St. John**
*Julius Caesar* **17:** 308

**Hanmer, Sir Thomas**
*Hamlet* **1:** 76
*Henry V* **5:** 188

**Hapgood, Norman**
*Henry V* **14:** 199

**Hapgood, Robert**
General Commentary **13:** 502
*King Lear* **13:** 343
*Othello* **11:** 332; **35:** 247

**Harbage, Alfred**
*King Lear* **11:** 101

**Harcourt, John B.**
*Macbeth* **3:** 297

**Hardin, Richard F.**
  *Henry V* **22**: 137
  *Julius Caesar* **22**: 137
  Kingship (topic entry) **39**: 45
  *The Merry Wives of Windsor* **5**: 390
  *Richard II* **22**: 137

**Harding, D. W.**
  Shakespeare's Representation of Women (topic entry) **31**: 16

**Haring-Smith, Tori**
  *The Taming of the Shrew* **12**: 416

**Harrier, Richard C.**
  *Troilus and Cressida* **3**: 602

**Harris, Anthony**
  Magic and the Supernatural (topic entry) **29**: 65

**Harris, Arthur J.**
  *Measure for Measure* **23**: 291

**Harris, Bernard**
  *Henry VIII* **2**: 67

Harris, Diana
  *The Tempest* **42**: 332

**Harris, Frank**
  *The Comedy of Errors* **1**: 18
  *Pericles* **2**: 555
  *Richard II* **6**: 279
  *Sonnets* **10**: 240
  *Timon of Athens* **1**: 480

**Harris, Jonathan Gil**
  *Antony and Cleopatra* **47**: 192

**Harrison, Carey**
  *The Taming of the Shrew* **12**: 372

**Harrison, G. B.**
  *Timon of Athens* **1**: 499

**Harrison, W. A.**
  *Sonnets* **10**: 216

**Harron, Mary**
  *Titus Andronicus* **17**: 477

**Hart, John**
  *The Tempest* **37**: 335

**Hart, John A.**
  *As You Like It* **34**: 78
  Clowns and Fools (topic entry) **46**: 60
  Fathers and Daughters (topic entry) **36**: 32

**Hart, Jonathan**
  *The Rape of Lucrece* **22**: 294
  *Venus and Adonis* **33**: 363

**Hart, Lynda**
  *Henry IV, 1 and 2* **14**: 109

**Hart-Davis, Rupert**
  *A Midsummer Night's Dream* **12**: 210

**Hartley, Anthony**
  *King Lear* **11**: 64

**Hartsock, Mildred E.**
  *Julius Caesar* **7**: 320

**Hartwig, Joan**
  *Cymbeline* **36**: 99
  *The Taming of the Shrew* **31**: 335
  *Twelfth Night* **1**: 658; **46**: 297

**Harvey, Gabriel**
  *The Rape of Lucrece* **10**: 63
  *Venus and Adonis* **10**: 410

**Harvey, John Martin**
  *The Taming of the Shrew* **12**: 335

**Harwood, Ellen Aprill**
  *Venus and Adonis* **33**: 339

**Hassel, R. Chris**
  *As You Like It* **34**: 85

**Hassel, R. Chris, Jr.**
  *The Merchant of Venice* **4**: 321
  *A Midsummer Night's Dream* **3**: 506
  *Richard III* **14**: 497

**Hassell, Graham**
  *Hamlet* **21**: 328

**Hatch, Robert**
  *Hamlet* **21**: 200
  *The Merchant of Venice* **12**: 70
  *Richard III* **14**: 424

**Hatlen, Burton**
  *Coriolanus* **42**: 243

**Hattaway, Michael**
  *Henry VI, 1, 2, and 3* **39**: 222
  Sexuality (topic entry) **33**: 39

**Hatton, Joseph**
  *The Merchant of Venice* **12**: 31

**Hawkes, Terence**
  *Love's Labour's Lost* **2**: 359
  *Richard II* **6**: 374

**Hawkins, C. Halford**
  *Julius Caesar* **17**: 289

**Hawkins, F. W.**
  *King John* **24**: 179
  *Macbeth* **20**: 92
  *Richard II* **24**: 267
  *Romeo and Juliet* **11**: 397

**Hawkins, Harriet**
  *Antony and Cleopatra* **25**: 257
  *Othello* **25**: 257
  *Romeo and Juliet* **25**: 257

**Hawkins, Sherman H.**
  *Henry IV, 1 and 2* **39**: 100

**Hawkins, William**
  *Cymbeline* **4**: 19

**Hawley, William M.**
  *Coriolanus* **48**: 230

**Hayes, Richard**
  *Much Ado about Nothing* **18**: 166

**Hayles, Nancy K.**
  Appearance vs. Reality (topic entry) **34**: 5
  *As You Like It* **5**: 146
  *Cymbeline* **4**: 162

**Hayman, Ronald**
  *Hamlet* **21**: 183
  *Julius Caesar* **17**: 357
  *King Lear* **11**: 67
  *A Midsummer Night's Dream* **12**: 254
  *Othello* **11**: 295
  *Romeo and Juliet* **11**: 474

**Hays, Janice**
  *Much Ado about Nothing* **8**: 111

**Hazlitt, William**
  *All's Well That Ends Well* **7**: 9
  *Antony and Cleopatra* **6**: 25
  *As You Like It* **5**: 24
  *The Comedy of Errors* **1**: 14
  *Coriolanus* **9**: 15; **17**: 129
  *Cymbeline* **4**: 22
  *Hamlet* **1**: 96; **21**: 30, 41
  *Henry IV, 1 and 2* **1**: 312
  *Henry V* **5**: 193
  *Henry VI, 1, 2, and 3* **3**: 25
  *Henry VIII* **2**: 23
  *Julius Caesar* **17**: 273
  *King John* **9**: 219; **24**: 174
  *King Lear* **2**: 108; **11**: 12, 16
  *Love's Labour's Lost* **2**: 303
  *Macbeth* **3**: 185; **20**: 58, 59, 86
  *Measure for Measure* **2**: 396
  *The Merchant of Venice* **4**: 195; **12**: 9, 10, 11
  *The Merry Wives of Windsor* **5**: 337
  *A Midsummer Night's Dream* **3**: 364; **12**: 152
  *Much Ado about Nothing* **8**: 13
  *Othello* **4**: 402; **11**: 191, 195, 196, 197, 198
  *Pericles* **2**: 544
  *The Rape of Lucrece* **10**: 65
  *Richard II* **6**: 258; **24**: 267
  *Richard III* **8**: 161, **14**: 376, 377, 380
  *Romeo and Juliet* **5**: 421; **11**: 393, 395
  *Sonnets* **10**: 160
  *The Taming of the Shrew* **9**: 320
  *The Tempest* **8**: 297
  *Timon of Athens* **1**: 460
  *Titus Andronicus* **4**: 617
  *Troilus and Cressida* **3**: 540
  *Twelfth Night* **1**: 544
  *The Two Gentlemen of Verona* **6**: 439
  *Venus and Adonis* **10**: 415
  *The Winter's Tale* **7**: 384

**Heath, Benjamin**
  *The Tempest* **8**: 292
  *Titus Andronicus* **4**: 614

**Hecht, Anthony**
  *Sonnets* **37**: 346

**Hecht, Anthony B.**
  *The Tempest* **25**: 357

**Heffernan, Carol F.**
  *The Taming of the Shrew* **31**: 345

**Heilbrun, Carolyn G.**
  *Hamlet* **44**: 237

**Heilman, Robert**
  Politics and Power (topic entry) **30**: 22

**Heilman, Robert Bechtold**
  *Antony and Cleopatra* **6**: 175
  *Henry IV, 1 and 2* **1**: 380
  *King Lear* **2**: 191
  *Macbeth* **3**: 312, 314; **29**: 139; **44**: 306
  *Othello* **4**: 508, 530
  *Richard III* **8**: 239
  *The Taming of the Shrew* **9**: 386

**Heine, Heinrich**
  *The Merchant of Venice* **4**: 200
  *Richard III* **8**: 164
  *Troilus and Cressida* **3**: 542

**Heinemann, Margot**
  *King Lear* **22**: 227; **46**: 269

**Helgerson, Richard**
  *Henry VI, 1, 2, and 3* **22**: 156

**Helms, Lorraine**
  Gender Identity (topic entry) **40**: 27
  Shakespeare's Representation of Women (topic entry) **31**: 68
  *Troilus and Cressida* **43**: 357

**Hemingway, Samuel B.**
  *Henry IV, 1 and 2* **1**: 401; **14**: 130
  *A Midsummer Night's Dream* **3**: 396

**Henneman, John Bell**
  *Henry VI, 1, 2, and 3* **3**: 46

**Henze, Richard**
  *The Comedy of Errors* **1**: 57
  *Julius Caesar* **30**: 321
  *The Taming of the Shrew* **9**: 398
  *Twelfth Night* **34**: 287

**Heraud, J. A.**
  *Antony and Cleopatra* **6**: 37
  *Othello* **4**: 421
  *Sonnets* **10**: 191

**Herbert, T. Walter**
  *A Midsummer Night's Dream* **3**: 447

**Herford, C. H.**
  *Antony and Cleopatra* **6**: 76
  *The Phoenix and Turtle* **10**: 16

**Herring, Robert**
  *Cymbeline* **15**: 46
  *Henry VIII* **24**: 105

**Hethmon, Robert H.**
*Measure for Measure* **23:** 407

**Hewes, Henry**
*Antony and Cleopatra* **17:** 43
*Hamlet* **21:** 232, 239, 288
*King John* **24:** 210
*King Lear* **11:** 72, 89, 103
*The Merchant of Venice* **12:** 54, 62, 71, 79
*A Midsummer Night's Dream* **12:** 240
*Much Ado about Nothing* **18:** 173
*Othello* **11:** 314
*The Taming of the Shrew* **12:** 365
*Timon of Athens* **20:** 456
*Troilus and Cressida* **18:** 337
*Twelfth Night* **26:** 247

**Hewison, Robert**
*Coriolanus* **17:** 208
*A Midsummer Night's Dream* **12:** 274
*Twelfth Night* **26:** 316

**Heyse, Paul**
*Antony and Cleopatra* **6:** 38

**Hibbard, George R.**
*Antony and Cleopatra* **27:** 105
*Love's Labour's Lost* **23:** 233
*Othello* **4:** 569
*The Taming of the Shrew* **9:** 375

**Hic et Ubique**
See also Steevens, George; Collier, Jeremy; Longinus, and Lorenzo
*Hamlet* **1:** 87
*Twelfth Night* **1:** 542

**Hieatt, A. Kent**
*Cymbeline* **13:** 401

**Hieatt, Charles W.**
*The Winter's Tale* **36:** 374

**Higgins, John**
*Antony and Cleopatra* **17:** 65
*Coriolanus* **17:** 190
*The Merry Wives of Windsor* **18:** 42
*The Taming of the Shrew* **12:** 386
*The Two Gentlemen of Verona* **12:** 490

**Hignett, Sean**
*Richard III* **14:** 473

**Hill, Aaron**
*Hamlet* **1:** 76; **21:** 377

**Hill, Errol G.**
*The Tempest* **15:** 322

**Hill, R. F.**
*Richard II* **6:** 347
*Romeo and Juliet* **5:** 492

**Hill, Sir John**
*Antony and Cleopatra* **6:** 21
*Romeo and Juliet* **11:** 494

**Hill, William**
*Henry V* **14:** 174

**Hillebrand, Harold Newcomb**
*Richard II* **24:** 272

**Hillman, David**
*Troilus and Cressida* **42:** 66

**Hillman, Richard**
*Hamlet* **44:** 219
*Henry IV, 1 and 2* **19:** 170
*Henry V* **19:** 170
*Measure for Measure* **22:** 302
*Richard II* **19:** 170
*The Tempest* **8:** 464; **22:** 302
*The Two Noble Kinsmen* **19:** 394; **41:** 301
*The Winter's Tale* **22:** 302

**Hinely, Jan Lawson**
*The Merry Wives of Windsor* **5:** 397
*A Midsummer Night's Dream* **45:** 107

**Hinman, Chariton**
*Timon of Athens* **1:** 518

**Hirsch, Foster**
*Richard III* **14:** 447

**Hirsh, James**
*Othello* **19:** 276

**Hirst, David L.**
*The Tempest* **15:** 327

**Hirvela, David P.**
*King John* **24:** 241

**Hobday, C. H.**
*Henry V* **30:** 159
*The Two Noble Kinsmen* **41:** 317

**Hobson, Harold**
*Antony and Cleopatra* **17:** 33
*Henry IV, 1 and 2* **14:** 54, 84
*Henry V* **14:** 281
*Much Ado about Nothing* **18:** 205
*Troilus and Cressida* **18:** 362
*The Winter's Tale* **15:** 486

**Hoby, Sir Edward**
*Richard II* **6:** 249

**Hockey, Dorothy C.**
*Much Ado about Nothing* **8:** 73

**Hodgdon, Barbara**
*King John* **19:** 182
*Romeo and Juliet* **13:** 243
*Troilus and Cressida* **16:** 70

**Hodgson, Moira**
*Measure for Measure* **23:** 354

**Hoeniger, F. David**
*Cymbeline* **4:** 103
*Pericles* **2:** 576, 578
*The Winter's Tale* **7:** 452

**Hofling, Charles K.**
*Coriolanus* **9:** 125
*Cymbeline* **36:** 134

**Holden, Anthony**
*Coriolanus* **17:** 163
*Hamlet* **21:** 213

**Holden, Stephen**
*The Tempest* **15:** 288

**Holderness, Graham**
*Henry V* **14:** 247
*King Lear* **31:** 84
*Richard II* **6:** 414
*The Taming of the Shrew* **12:** 404
*The Winter's Tale* **16:** 410

**Holding, Edith**
*As You Like It* **23:** 10

**Hole, Richard**
*Othello* **4:** 397

**Holland, Norman N.**
*A Midsummer Night's Dream* **29:** 225
Psychoanalytic Interpretations (topic entry) **44:** 11
*Romeo and Juliet* **5:** 513, 525

**Holland, Peter**
*As You Like It* **23:** 151
*Measure for Measure* **23:** 362
*A Midsummer Night's Dream* **29:** 216; **45:** 117
*The Tempest* **32:** 334

**Hollander, John**
*Twelfth Night* **1:** 596, 615

**Holleran, James V.**
*Hamlet* **13:** 268

**Holloway, John**
*Coriolanus* **9:** 139
*King Lear* **2:** 241

**Holmer, Joan Ozark**
*Romeo and Juliet* **32:** 222; **45:** 40

**Holmes, Martin**
*Henry IV, 1 and 2* **14:** 146
*The Merry Wives of Windsor* **18:** 86

**Holmstrom, John**
*Othello* **11:** 300

**Holt, John**
*The Comedy of Errors* **1:** 13

**Homan, Sidney**
*Antony and Cleopatra* **47:** 103
*Henry V* **30:** 207
*The Merry Wives of Windsor* **18:** 95

**Homan, Sidney R.**
*The Comedy of Errors* **34:** 194
*A Midsummer Night's Dream* **3:** 466; **48:** 23
*Richard II* **6:** 391

**Home, Henry, Lord Kames**
*Romeo and Juliet* **5:** 418

**Honigmann, E. A. J.**
*All's Well That Ends Well* **13:** 77; **38:** 89
*Julius Caesar* **30:** 342
*Macbeth* **29:** 146
*Timon of Athens* **1:** 507

**Hope, John Francis**
*All's Well That Ends Well* **26:** 11

**Hope-Wallace, Philip**
*As You Like It* **23:** 80, 81
*Cymbeline* **15:** 47
*Hamlet* **21:** 181
*Henry VI, 1, 2, and 3* **24:** 16
*Julius Caesar* **17:** 343
*King John* **24:** 214
*Macbeth* **20:** 221
*Richard III* **14:** 461
*Troilus and Cressida* **18:** 305
*The Two Gentlemen of Verona* **12:** 462

**Hopkins, Lisa**
*As You Like It* **48:** 32
*Henry V* **37:** 105
*Macbeth* **42:** 258
*A Midsummer Night's Dream* **48:** 32
*The Two Gentlemen of Verona* **48:** 32

**Horn, Franz**
*Coriolanus* **9:** 16
*Macbeth* **3:** 190
*Romeo and Juliet* **5:** 423

**Hornby, Richard**
*Julius Caesar* **17:** 403

**Horwich, Richard**
*The Merchant of Venice* **4:** 326

**Hosley, Richard**
*Othello* **11:** 359

**Hotson, Leslie**
*Sonnets* **10:** 270

**Houseman, John**
*Julius Caesar* **17:** 326, 347, 348
*King John* **24:** 211

**Houston, Penelope**
*Romeo and Juliet* **11:** 472
*The Taming of the Shrew* **12:** 372

**Howard, Alan**
*Coriolanus* **17:** 195
*Henry V* **14:** 297

**Howard, Jean E.**
Gender Identity (topic entry) **40:** 61

**Howard, Skiles**
*A Midsummer Night's Dream* **25:** 36

**Hoy, Cyrus**
Fathers and Daughters (topic entry) **36:** 45
*Timon of Athens* **1:** 523

*The Two Noble Kinsmen* **41:** 308
*Love's Labour's Lost* **47:** 35

**Hoyle, Martin**
*The Comedy of Errors* **26:** 168
*Julius Caesar* **17:** 391
*Troilus and Cressida* **18:** 389
*Twelfth Night* **26:** 322

**Hubert, Judd D.**
*Much Ado about Nothing* **19:** 68

**Hubler, Edward**
*Othello* **4:** 544
*Sonnets* **10:** 279

**Hudson, Rev. H. N.**
*As You Like It* **5:** 39
*Coriolanus* **9:** 26
*Henry VI, I and 2* **1:** 323, 324
*Henry VI, 1, 2, and 3* **3:** 35
*Henry VIII* **2:** 32
*Julius Caesar* **7:** 167
*King Lear* **2:** 125
*Macbeth* **3:** 203
*Measure for Measure* **2:** 406
*The Merry Wives of Windsor* **5:** 341
*A Midsummer Night's Dream* **3:** 377
*Twelfth Night* **1:** 555

**Huebert, Ronald**
*The Merry Wives of Windsor* **5:** 385

**Hughes, Alan**
*Coriolanus* **17:** 144
*Hamlet* **21:** 112
*Macbeth* **20:** 151
*Much Ado about Nothing* **18:** 138
*Othello* **11:** 259
*Richard III* **14:** 405

**Hughes, John**
*Othello* **4:** 384

**Hugo, Francois-Victor**
*Coriolanus* **9:** 25

**Hugo, Victor**
*Antony and Cleopatra* **6:** 37
*Henry IV, 1 and 2* **1:** 323
*King Lear* **2:** 124
*Othello* **4:** 421
*The Winter's Tale* **7:** 394

**Hulse, Clark**
*The Rape of Lucrece* **10:** 121
*Venus and Adonis* **10:** 480

**Hulse, S. Clark**
*Titus Andronicus* **27:** 325

**Humphreys, A. R.**
*Henry IV, 1 and 2* **1:** 419

**Humphreys, Arthur**
*Julius Caesar* **30:** 297

**Hunt, Hugh**
*Julius Caesar* **17:** 418
*The Merchant of Venice* **12:** 119

*The Merry Wives of Windsor* **18:** 75
*Twelfth Night* **26:** 233

**Hunt, Leigh**
*Hamlet* **21:** 50
*Julius Caesar* **17:** 272
*King John* **24:** 180
*King Lear* **11:** 10, 136
*Much Ado about Nothing* **18:** 231
*Othello* **11:** 198
*Richard III* **14:** 379, 389
*Timon of Athens* **1:** 460; **20:** 439

**Hunt, Maurice**
*Comedy of Errors* **42:** 80
*Coriolanus* **19:** 287
*Cymbeline* **36:** 115
*Henry IV, 1 and 2* **48:** 151
*Henry VIII* **41:** 190
*Love's Labour's Lost* **38:** 239
*A Midsummer Night's Dream* **22:** 39
*Richard III* **39:** 349; **42:** 130
*Titus Andronicus* **27:** 299
*Twelfth Night* **25:** 47
*The Two Gentlemen of Verona* **6:** 564

**Hunter, G. K.**
*All's Well That Ends Well* **7:** 76; **26:** 52
*As You Like It* **5:** 116
*Henry IV, 1 and 2* **1:** 402
*Henry V* **16:** 217
*Henry VI, 1, 2, and 3* **16:** 217; **24:** 55
*King Lear* **16:** 217
Politics and Power (topic entry) **30:** 39
*Richard II* **16:** 217
*Richard III* **16:** 217
Shakespeare and Classical Civilization (topic entry) **27:** 21
*Sonnets* **10:** 283
*The Taming of the Shrew* **16:** 217
*Troilus and Cressida* **16:** 217
*Twelfth Night* **1:** 635

**Hunter, Joseph**
*Twelfth Night* **1:** 549

**Hunter, Mark**
*Julius Caesar* **7:** 221

**Hunter, Robert Grams**
*All's Well That Ends Well* **7:** 98
*Cymbeline* **4:** 116
*Macbeth* **44:** 351
*Othello* **4:** 582
*The Two Gentlemen of Verona* **6:** 514

**Hurd, Richard**
*As You Like It* **5:** 18

**Hurdis, James**
*Coriolanus* **9:** 13

**Hurrell, John D.**
*The Merchant of Venice* **4:** 284

**Hurren, Kenneth**
*Antony and Cleopatra* **17:** 56

*As You Like It* **23:** 106
*Hamlet* **21:** 298
*Love's Labour's Lost* **23:** 204
*A Midsummer Night's Dream* **12:** 251
*Much Ado about Nothing* **18:** 206
*Titus Andronicus* **17:** 467
*Troilus and Cressida* **18:** 357
*Twelfth Night* **26:** 326
*The Winter's Tale* **15:** 487

**Huston, J. Dennis**
*Love's Labour's Lost* **2:** 375
*A Midsummer Night's Dream* **3:** 516
*The Taming of the Shrew* **9:** 419

**Hutchings, Geoffrey**
*All's Well That Ends Well* **26:** 64

**Hutson, Lorna**
*Twelfth Night* **34:** 344; **37:** 59

**Hyde, Mary Crapo**
*As You Like It* **23:** 71

**Hyland, Peter**
*As You Like It* **34:** 130
*Troilus and Cressida* **25:** 56

**Hyman, Lawrence W.**
*Measure for Measure* **2:** 524

**Hynes, Sam**
*The Rape of Lucrece* **10:** 80

**Ide, Richard S.**
*Measure for Measure* **13:** 94

**Ihering, Rudolf von**
*The Merchant of Venice* **4:** 213

**Inchbald, Elizabeth**
*Henry IV, 1 and 2* **1:** 309
*Much Ado about Nothing* **8:** 12

**Inglis, Brian**
*Troilus and Cressida* **18:** 311

**Irving, Henry**
*Hamlet* **21:** 381

**Irving, Laurence**
*Henry VIII* **24:** 87
*Much Ado about Nothing* **18:** 136
*Othello* **11:** 255
*Twelfth Night* **26:** 210

**Isaacs, Edith J. R.**
*Richard II* **24:** 308

**Isaacs, Hermine Rich**
*The Taming of the Shrew* **12:** 346
*The Tempest* **15:** 237

**Iser, Wolfgang**
*As You Like It* **34:** 131

**Itzin, Catherine**
*Macbeth* **20:** 17

**Jackson, Barry**
*Henry VI, 1, 2, and 3* **24:** 12

**Jackson, Berners W.**
*Pericles* **15:** 155, 158
*The Taming of the Shrew* **12:** 485
*Twelfth Night* **26:** 292

**Jackson, Glenda**
*Antony and Cleopatra* **17:** 113

**Jackson, MacDonald**
*The Tempest* **42:** 332

**Jackson, Russell**
*All's Well That Ends Well* **26:** 58
*As You Like It* **23:** 158
*Love's Labour's Lost* **23:** 217
*Richard II* **24:** 373

**Jackson, T. A.**
*Henry IV, 1 and 2* **1:** 361

**Jacobson, Gerald F.**
*A Midsummer Night's Dream* **3:** 44

**Jaffa, Harry V.**
*King Lear* **2:** 208
*Measure for Measure* **33:** 101

**Jahn, J. D.**
*Venus and Adonis* **10:** 466

**James, D. G.**
*Hamlet* **1:** 191
*King Lear* **2:** 201
*Pericles* **2:** 561
*The Tempest* **8:** 423

**James, Emrys**
*Henry IV, 1 and 2* **14:** 92
*Henry V* **14:** 301

**James, Heather**
*Titus Andronicus* **27:** 306

**James, Henry**
*Cymbeline* **15:** 41
*Henry V* **14:** 194
*Henry VIII* **24:** 77
*King Lear* **11:** 27
*Macbeth* **20:** 135
*The Merchant of Venice* **12:** 29
*The Merry Wives of Windsor* **18:** 25
*Othello* **11:** 225
*Richard III* **14:** 405
*Romeo and Juliet* **11:** 424, 426

**James, John**
*Antony and Cleopatra* **17:** 80
*The Comedy of Errors* **26:** 161

**Jameson, Anna Brownell**
*All's Well That Ends Well* **7:** 12
*Antony and Cleopatra* **6:** 27
*As You Like It* **5:** 26
*Coriolanus* **9:** 16
*Cymbeline* **4:** 24
*Henry VI, 1, 2, and 3* **3:** 26
*Henry VIII* **2:** 24
*King John* **9:** 220
*King Lear* **2:** 110
*Macbeth* **3:** 191
*Measure for Measure* **2:** 397

*The Merchant of Venice* **4**: 196
*Much Ado about Nothing* **8**: 14
*Othello* **4**: 406
*Romeo and Juliet* **5**: 423
*Sonnets* **10**: 167
*The Tempest* **8**: 301
*Twelfth Night* **1**: 545
*The Winter's Tale* **7**: 385

**Jamieson, Michael**
*As You Like It* **23**: 176
Shakespeare's Representation of Women (topic entry) **31**: 60

**Janakiram, A.**
*The Rape of Lucrece* **33**: 195

**Jarman, Derik**
*The Tempest* **15**: 299

**Jayne, Sears**
*The Taming of the Shrew* **9**: 381

**Jefford, Barbara**
*Antony and Cleopatra* **17**: 113

**Jekels, Ludwig**
*Macbeth* **3**: 226

**Jenkins, Harold**
*As You Like It* **5**: 93
*Hamlet* **44**: 229
*Henry VI, 1 and 2* **1**: 404
*Twelfth Night* **1**: 610

**Jenkins, Peter**
*The Taming of the Shrew* **12**: 394

**Jennings, H. J.**
*King Lear* **11**: 39

**Jennings, Richard**
*Othello* **11**: 264

**Jensen, Ejner J.**
*Love's Labour's Lost* **28**: 63
*The Merchant of Venice* **28**: 63
*The Merry Wives of Windsor* **28**: 63
*Much Ado about Nothing* **28**: 63

**Joffee, Linda**
*Henry V* **14**: 312

**John, Lord Chedworth**
*Measure for Measure* **2**: 395

**Johnson, Nora**
*The Winter's Tale* **48**: 309

**Johnson, Robert Carl**
*Romeo and Juliet* **33**: 290

**Johnson, Samuel**
*All's Well That Ends Well* **7**: 8
*Antony and Cleopatra* **6**: 21
*As You Like It* **5**: 19
*Coriolanus* **9**: 11
*Cymbeline* **4**: 20
*Hamlet* **1**: 83
*Henry IV, 1 and 2* **1**: 290
*Henry V* **5**: 189
*Henry VI, 1, 2, and 3* **3**: 19

*Henry VIII* **2**: 18
*Julius Caesar* **7**: 156
*King John* **9**: 211
*King Lear* **2**: 101
*Love's Labour's Lost* **2**: 300
*Macbeth* **3**: 171, 172
*Measure for Measure* **2**: 390
*The Merchant of Venice* **4**: 193
*The Merry Wives of Windsor* **5**: 335
*Othello* **4**: 390
*Richard II* **6**: 253
*Richard III* **8**: 146
*Romeo and Juliet* **5**: 418
*The Taming of the Shrew* **9**: 318
*The Tempest* **8**: 292
*Timon of Athens* **1**: 454
*Titus Andronicus* **4**: 614
*Troilus and Cressida* **3**: 538
*Twelfth Night* **1**: 542
*The Two Gentlemen of Verona* **6**: 437
*The Winter's Tale* **7**: 380

**Jonassen, Frederick B.**
*The Merry Wives of Windsor* **47**: 363

**Jones, D. A. N.**
*King John* **24**: 216
*Macbeth* **20**: 258
*Measure for Measure* **23**: 320
*The Merry Wives of Windsor* **18**: 43
*Pericles* **15**: 151
*Richard III* **14**: 463
*Troilus and Cressida* **18**: 342

**Jones, David E.**
*Henry IV, 1 and 2* **14**: 78
*Timon of Athens* **20**: 458

**Jones, Emrys**
*Measure for Measure* **23**: 345
*Much Ado about Nothing* **18**: 212
*Titus Andronicus* **27**: 285

**Jones, Ernest**
*Hamlet* **1**: 179

**Jones, Gemma**
*The Winter's Tale* **15**: 495

**Jones, Gordon P.**
*Love's Labour's Lost* **23**: 223

**Jones, James Earl**
*Othello* **11**: 319

**Jones, Robert C.**
*Richard II* **39**: 263

**Jonson, Ben**
*Julius Caesar* **7**: 148
*Pericles* **2**: 536
*Titus Andronicus* **4**: 612
*The Winter's Tale* **7**: 376

**Jorgens, Jack**
*Richard II* **24**: 379

**Jorgens, Jack J.**
*Hamlet* **21**: 208

*Henry V* **14**: 238
*Julius Caesar* **17**: 358
*Macbeth* **20**: 283
*Pericles* **15**: 163
*Richard III* **14**: 443
*The Taming of the Shrew* **12**: 374

**Jorgensen, Paul A.**
*The Comedy of Errors* **1**: 55
*Hamlet* **35**: 117
*King Lear* **2**: 262; **31**: 133
*Macbeth* **3**: 327

**Joseph, Bertram L.**
*Cymbeline* **15**: 67

**Joseph, Sister Miriam, C.S.C.**
*Hamlet* **1**: 231

**Jump, John**
*Julius Caesar* **30**: 369

**Kael, Pauline**
*Macbeth* **20**: 276

**Kahn, Coppelia**
*Coriolanus* **30**: 149
Gender Identity (topic entry) **40**: 33
*The Merchant of Venice* **40**: 151
*The Rape of Lucrece* **10**: 109; **33**: 200
*Romeo and Juliet* **5**: 566
*The Taming of the Shrew* **9**: 413
*Timon of Athens* **27**: 212
*Venus and Adonis* **10**: 473

**Kaison, Albert E.**
*Richard III* **14**: 358

**Kaiser, Walter**
Clowns and Fools (topic entry) **46**: 48

**Kalem, T. E.**
*Richard III* **14**: 482

**Kalson, Albert E.**
*The Comedy of Errors* **26**: 170

**Kaminsky, Judith**
*Rape of Lucrece* **43**: 141

**Kamps, Ivo**
*Henry VIII* **37**: 109

**Kantorowicz, Ernst H.**
*Richard II* **6**: 327

**Karhl, George M.**
*Much Ado about Nothing* **18**: 116
*Richard III* **14**: 366

**Kastan, David Scott**
*Antony and Cleopatra* **17**: 101
*Henry IV, 1 and 2* **19**: 195
*The Merry Wives of Windsor* **18**: 71

**Katz, Leslie S.**
*The Merry Wives of Windsor* **32**: 31; **47**: 344

**Kauffman, Stanley**
*Hamlet* **21**: 321
*Henry V* **14**: 291, 313
*Much Ado about Nothing* **18**: 195
*Othello* **11**: 322

**Kaufman, Gerald**
*The Taming of the Shrew* **12**: 371

**Kaufmann, R. J.**
*Troilus and Cressida* **3**: 611

**Kautsky, Karl**
*The Merry Wives of Windsor* **5**: 343

**Kay, Carol McGinnis**
*Henry VI, 1, 2, and 3* **3**: 131
*Othello* **4**: 596

**Keach, William**
Desire (topic entry) **38**: 1

**Kean, Charles**
*A Midsummer Night's Dream* **12**: 184
*Richard II* **24**: 279

**Keatman, Martin**
Authorship Controversy (topic entry) **41**: 76

**Keats, John**
*King Lear* **2**: 109
*Sonnets* **10**: 160

**Kee, Robert**
*Henry VI, 1, 2, and 3* **24**: 29

**Keesee, Donald**
*All's Well That Ends Well* **38**: 155

**Keevak, Michael**
*Sonnets* **48**: 325

**Kegl, Rosemary**
*The Merry Wives of Windsor* **28**: 69; **47**: 331

**Kehler, Dorothea**
*The Comedy of Errors* **34**: 251
*Hamlet* **32**: 238

**Keith, W. J.**
*Henry V* **14**: 270

**Kellaway, Kate**
*Twelfth Night* **26**: 324

**Kelly, Henry Ansgar**
*Henry IV, 1 and 2* **1**: 429

**Kelly, Hugh**
*Richard III* **14**: 364

**Kelly, Katherine E.**
*The Two Gentlemen of Verona* **16**: 122

**Kemble, Frances Anne**
*Henry VIII* **2**: 38
*Othello* **11**: 227
*Romeo and Juliet* **11**: 401

**Kemble, John Philip**
*Macbeth* **3:** 186

**Kemp, Peter**
*As You Like It* **23:** 147
*King John* **24:** 231
*Love's Labour's Lost* **23:** 221
*Twelfth Night* **26:** 323

**Kemp, T. C.**
*Henry V* **14:** 259
*Henry VI, 1, 2, and 3* **24:** 15
*Henry VIII* **24:** 112
*Julius Caesar* **17:** 344
*The Taming of the Shrew* **12:** 350

**Kendall, Gillian Murray**
*Titus Andronicus* **13:** 225

**Kendall, Paul M.**
*Troilus and Cressida* **3:** 587

**Kennedy, Dennis**
*Antony and Cleopatra* **17:** 73
*A Midsummer Night's Dream* **12:** 231
*The Winter's Tale* **15:** 454

**Kenny, Thomas**
*Cymbeline* **4:** 35
*Hamlet* **1:** 113
*Twelfth Night* **1:** 554

**Kenrick, William**
*Measure for Measure* **2:** 391
*Much Ado about Nothing* **8:** 11
*Othello* **4:** 392
*The Winter's Tale* **7:** 380

**Keown, Eric**
*Antony and Cleopatra* **17:** 32, 36
*As You Like It* **23:** 80, 89
*Cymbeline* **15:** 55, 65
*Henry IV, 1 and 2* **14:** 58
*King John* **24:** 215
*Macbeth* **20:** 189, 222, 251
*Measure for Measure* **23:** 315
*The Merry Wives of Windsor* **18:** 34
*Much Ado about Nothing* **18:** 160, 163, 179, 185
*Othello* **11:** 277
*The Taming of the Shrew* **12:** 355
*Troilus and Cressida* **18:** 305, 324, 331
*Twelfth Night* **26:** 242, 253
*The Two Gentlemen of Verona* **12:** 474

**Keown, Roger**
*All's Well That Ends Well* **26:** 37

**Kermode, Frank**
*Cymbeline* **15:** 75
*Henry VIII* **2:** 49
*King Lear* **11:** 104
*The Tempest* **8:** 396; **15:** 295
*The Two Noble Kinsmen* **9:** 480

**Kernan, Alvin**
*Measure for Measure* **33:** 58
*The Tempest* **32:** 343
*Timon of Athens* **27:** 155

**Kernan, Alvin B.**
*Henry IV, 1 and 2* **1:** 427
*Henry V* **5:** 287
*Henry VI, 1, 2, and 3* **3:** 76
*King Lear* **2:** 255
*The Taming of the Shrew* **9:** 424

**Kernodle, George R.**
*King Lear* **2:** 177

**Kerr, Heather B.**
*Titus Andronicus* **43:** 186

**Kerr, Walter**
*Antony and Cleopatra* **17:** 23, 45
*The Merchant of Venice* **12:** 124
*Much Ado about Nothing* **18:** 192; 219
*Othello* **11:** 315
*Richard III* **14:** 469
*The Taming of the Shrew* **12:** 364
*The Two Gentlemen of Verona* **12:** 469

**Kerrigan, John**
*Henry IV, 1 and 2* **16:** 161
*Sonnets* **10:** 394; **28:** 407

**Kerrigan, William**
*As You Like It* **34:** 109
*General Commentary* **13:** 523
*Hamlet* **28:** 280

**Keyishian, Harry**
*Hamlet* **35:** 174
*Othello* **35:** 261

**Kezar, Dennis**
*Julius Caesar* **48:** 240

**Kiasashvili, Nico**
*Richard III* **14:** 477

**Kiberd, Declan**
Shakespeare's Representation of Women (topic entry) **31:** 8

**Kiefer, Frederick**
*Pericles* **22:** 315; **36:** 233
*Romeo and Juliet* **5:** 573

**Kierkegaard, Soren**
See Taciturnus, Frater

**Kiernan, Pauline**
*Sonnets* **32:** 352
*Venus and Adonis* **32:** 352; **33:** 377

**Kiernan, Thomas**
*Coriolanus* **17:** 162

**Kiernan, Victor**
*Timon of Athens* **37:** 222

**Kilbourne, Frederick W.**
*As You Like It* **23:** 6
*Henry VI, 1, 2, and 3* **24:** 3
*King John* **24:** 163
*Measure for Measure* **23:** 267, 274
*The Merry Wives of Windsor* **18:** 8
*Much Ado about Nothing* **18:** 112

*Pericles* **15:** 129
*Richard II* **24:** 261
*The Tempest* **15:** 190
*Troilus and Cressida* **18:** 278

**Kimbrough, Robert**
*As You Like It* **5:** 164
*Cymbeline* **16:** 442
*Macbeth* **29:** 127
*Pericles* **16:** 442
*The Tempest* **16:** 442
*Troilus and Cressida* **27:** 374
*The Winter's Tale* **16:** 442

**King, Bruce**
*Coriolanus* **30:** 140

**King, Walter N.**
*Much Ado about Nothing* **8:** 95
*Twelfth Night* **34:** 301

**Kingston, Jeremy**
*As You Like It* **23:** 105
*The Comedy of Errors* **26:** 149, 150
*Cymbeline* **15:** 18
*Hamlet* **21:** 281, 324
*Henry VI, 1, 2, and 3* **24:** 50
*Julius Caesar* **17:** 375
*Macbeth* **20:** 257
*The Merry Wives of Windsor* **18:** 37, 41, 61
*Pericles* **15:** 150
*Richard III* **14:** 463
*The Taming of the Shrew* **12:** 384
*Timon of Athens* **20:** 474
*Titus Andronicus* **17:** 469
*Troilus and Cressida* **18:** 392
*Twelfth Night* **26:** 262, 267
*The Two Gentlemen of Verona* **12:** 482
*The Winter's Tale* **15:** 479

**Kinney, Arthur F.**
*The Comedy of Errors* **34:** 258

**Kirk, John Foster**
*Hamlet* **21:** 58

**Kirkman, Francis**
*A Midsummer Night's Dream* **3:** 361

**Kirkman, Rev. J.**
*King Lear* **2:** 129

**Kirsch, Arthur**
*Hamlet* **16:** 381; **35:** 85; **44:** 209
*Macbeth* **16:** 381
*Othello* **16:** 381
*The Tempest* **42:** 339

**Kirsch, Arthur C.**
*All's Well That Ends Well* **7:** 109
*Cymbeline* **4:** 138
*Macbeth* **44:** 324
*Much Ado about Nothing* **8:** 115

**Kirschbaum, Leo**
*Julius Caesar* **7:** 255
*Macbeth* **3:** 278
*The Merchant of Venice* **40:** 166

**Kirstein, Lincoln**
*A Midsummer Night's Dream* **12:** 295

**Kitchin, Laurence**
*Coriolanus* **17:** 169

**Kitto, H. D. F.**
*Hamlet* **1:** 212

**Kittredge, George Lyman**
*Macbeth* **3:** 225

**Kleinstuck, Johannes**
*Troilus and Cressida* **3:** 599

**Kliman, Bernice W.**
*Hamlet* **21:** 311

**Kline, Herbert W.**
*The Merchant of Venice* **12:** 40

**Knapp, Jeffrey**
*Henry V* **25:** 116
*Henry VI, 1, 2, and 3* **25:** 116

**Knapp, Margaret**
*The Comedy of Errors* **26:** 138

**Knight, Charles**
*All's Well That Ends Well* **7:** 16
*Henry V* **5:** 198
*Henry VI, 1, 2 and 3* **3:** 29
*Henry VIII* **2:** 27
*Love's Labour's Lost* **2:** 304
*Measure for Measure* **2:** 401
*A Midsummer Night's Dream* **3:** 371
*Sonnets* **10:** 182
*Timon of Athens* **1:** 464
*Titus Andronicus* **4:** 619
*Twelfth Night* **1:** 548
*The Two Gentlemen of Verona* **6:** 442

**Knight, G. Wilson**
*All's Well That Ends Well* **7:** 67
*Antony and Cleopatra* **6:** 85
*The Comedy of Errors* **1:** 25
*Coriolanus* **9:** 65
*Cymbeline* **4:** 78
*Hamlet* **1:** 144
*Henry VIII* **2:** 51
*Julius Caesar* **7:** 227, 233
*King Lear* **2:** 156; **11:** 127, 130, 150
*Macbeth* **3:** 231, 234
*Measure for Measure* **2:** 421
*The Merchant of Venice* **12:** 117
*A Midsummer Night's Dream* **3:** 401
*Much Ado about Nothing* **8:** 43
*Othello* **4:** 462; **11:** 339
*Pericles* **2:** 559, 565
*Romeo and Juliet* **11:** 509
*Sonnets* **10:** 290
*The Tempest* **8:** 364
*Timon of Athens* **1:** 483, 499
*Troilus and Cressida* **3:** 561
*Twelfth Night* **1:** 570
*Venus and Adonis* **10:** 428
*The Winter's Tale* **7:** 417, 436

**Knight, Joseph**
*The Merchant of Venice* **12:** 21

*Othello* **11:** 223, 245
*Richard III* **14:** 398
*Romeo and Juliet* **11:** 421, 422

**Knights, L. C.**
*Antony and Cleopatra* **6:** 131
*Coriolanus* **9:** 110
*Hamlet* **1:** 221
*Henry IV, 1 and 2* **1:** 354, 411
*Julius Caesar* **7:** 262
*King Lear* **2:** 222
*Macbeth* **3:** 241
*Measure for Measure* **2:** 446
*Sonnets* **10:** 251
*The Tempest* **29:** 292
*Timon of Athens* **1:** 515
*Troilus and Cressida* **3:** 584
*The Winter's Tale* **7:** 493

**Knoepflmacher, U. C.**
*Henry IV, 1 and 2* **1:** 413

**Knowles, James Sheridan**
*Romeo and Juliet* **11:** 413

**Kobialka, Michael**
*The Comedy of Errors* **26:** 138

**Kolin, Philip C.**
*Titus Andronicus* **32:** 249

**Koller, Ann Marie**
*Julius Caesar* **17:** 302

**Komisarjevsky, Theodore**
*Macbeth* **20:** 192

**Kott, Jan**
*As You Like It* **5:** 118
Gender Identity (topic entry) **40:** 65
*Hamlet* **1:** 247
*Henry IV, 1 and 2* **1:** 418
*King Lear* **2:** 245; **11:** 151
*Macbeth* **3:** 309
*A Midsummer Night's Dream* **3:** 445
*Richard II* **6:** 354
*Richard III* **8:** 232; **39:** 308
*The Tempest* **8:** 408; **15:** 361; **29:** 368
*Titus Andronicus* **17:** 449
*Troilus and Cressida* **3:** 609
*Twelfth Night* **1:** 639

**Kowsar, Mohammad**
*Richard III* **14:** 477

**Kramer, Jerome A.**
*Rape of Lucrece* **43:** 141

**Kramer, Mimi**
*Coriolanus* **17:** 220
*Much Ado about Nothing* **18:** 227

**Kreider, P. V.**
*As You Like It* **5:** 72

**Krempel, Daniel**
*Henry V* **14:** 222

**Kreyssig, Friedrich**
*King Lear* **2:** 124

*The Merchant of Venice* **4:** 208
*Twelfth Night* **1:** 553

**Krieger, Elliot**
*As You Like It* **5:** 148
*Much Ado about Nothing* **31:** 191

**Krieger, Murray**
*Measure for Measure* **2:** 482
*Richard III* **8:** 218
*Sonnets* **10:** 329; **40:** 284

**Kroll, Jack**
*Antony and Cleopatra* **17:** 68
*As You Like It* **23:** 121
*Othello* **11:** 316
*Richard III* **14:** 471

**Kronenfeld, Judy**
*King Lear* **22:** 233

**Kronenfeld, Judy Z.**
*As You Like It* **34:** 161

**Krutch, Joseph Wood**
*Hamlet* **21:** 171
*Julius Caesar* **17:** 321
*Macbeth* **20:** 229
*Richard III* **14:** 411
*The Taming of the Shrew* **12:** 344
*The Tempest* **15:** 241
*Troilus and Cressida* **18:** 297
*Twelfth Night* **26:** 223

**Kuhl, Ernest P.**
*The Taming of the Shrew* **12:** 427

**Kuner, Mildred C.**
*Titus Andronicus* **17:** 462

**Kurland, Stuart M.**
*Hamlet* **28:** 290
*Pericles* **37:** 360
*The Winter's Tale* **19:** 401

**Kurtz, Martha**
*Henry IV, 1 and 2* **37:** 122
*Henry V* **37:** 122
*Henry VI, 1, 2, and 3* **37:** 122
*Richard II* **37:** 122
*Richard III* **37:** 122

**Kyle, Howard**
*Henry VIII* **24:** 85

**Lady Martin**
See Faucit, Helena

**LaGuardia, Eric**
*All's Well That Ends Well* **7:** 90

**Laird, David**
*Romeo and Juliet* **5:** 520

**Lamb, Charles**
*Hamlet* **1:** 93
*King Lear* **2:** 106; **11:** 136
*Macbeth* **3:** 184
*Othello* **4:** 401; **11:** 334
*Richard III* **8:** 159; **14:** 368, 369
*Timon of Athens* **1:** 459
*Twelfth Night* **1:** 545
*The Two Noble Kinsmen* **9:** 446

**Lamb, Margaret**
*Antony and Cleopatra* **17:** 12, 84

**Lamb, Mary Ellen**
*Measure for Measure* **13:** 104
*A Midsummer Night's Dream* **3:** 498

**Lambert, J. W.**
*Antony and Cleopatra* **17:** 58
*As You Like It* **23:** 99, 105
*Hamlet* **21:** 293
*Love's Labour's Lost* **23:** 202, 210
*Macbeth* **20:** 293
*The Merchant of Venice* **12:** 93
*Richard II* **24:** 355
*The Taming of the Shrew* **12:** 393
*The Tempest* **15:** 272
*Troilus and Cressida* **18:** 356
*Twelfth Night* **26:** 283

**Lamont, Rosette**
*The Tempest* **15:** 292

**Lamont, Rosette C.**
*The Tempest* **15:** 287

**Lancashire, Anne**
*Timon of Athens* **1:** 518

**Lancaster, Osbert**
*All's Well That Ends Well* **26:** 95

**Landor, Walter Savage**
*Sonnets* **10:** 167

**Landry, D. E.**
*Cymbeline* **4:** 167; **45:** 67

**Landstone, Charles**
*King Lear* **11:** 124

**Lane, John Francis**
*The Tempest* **15:** 285

**Lane, Robert**
*Henry V* **28:** 146
*King John* **32:** 114

**Lang, Andrew**
*Much Ado about Nothing* **8:** 33

**Lang, David Marshall**
*Richard III* **14:** 476

**Langbaine, Gerard**
*Antony and Cleopatra* **6:** 20
*Cymbeline* **4:** 17
*Henry V* **5:** 185
*Henry VI, 1, 2, and 3* **3:** 17
*The Merry Wives of Windsor* **5:** 332
*Much Ado about Nothing* **8:** 9
*Pericles* **2:** 538

**Langbaum, Robert**
*Henry IV, 1 and 2* **1:** 408

**Langham, Michael**
*Antony and Cleopatra* **17:** 48

**Langton, Robert Gore**
*Antony and Cleopatra* **17:** 74

**Lanham, Richard A.**
*The Rape of Lucrece* **10:** 116; **33:** 190
*Sonnets* **40:** 221

**Lanier, Douglas**
*The Comedy of Errors* **25:** 63; **34:** 201

**Lanier, Sidney**
*The Phoenix and Turtle* **10:** 7

**Lardner, James**
*Hamlet* **21:** 309

**Laroque, Francois**
*Henry VI, 1, 2, and 3* **39:** 205
*Macbeth* **29:** 109
*The Merry Wives of Windsor* **18:** 56
*Romeo and Juliet* **32:** 256
*Titus Andronicus* **17:** 481
*Twelfth Night* **26:** 318

**Larson, Orville K.**
*Richard III* **14:** 516

**Latham, Grace**
*The Two Gentlemen of Verona* **6:** 453

**Laver, James**
*Macbeth* **20:** 52

**Law, Robert Adger**
*Henry IV, 1 and 2* **1:** 348

**Lawlor, John**
*Romeo and Juliet* **5:** 509

**Lawrence, W. J.**
*Henry VIII* **24:** 150
*The Tempest* **15:** 196

**Lawrence, William Witherle**
*All's Well That Ends Well* **7:** 32
*Cymbeline* **4:** 53
*Measure for Measure* **2:** 429
*Troilus and Cressida* **3:** 566

**Laws, Jennifer**
*Sonnets* **48:** 336

**Leavis, F. R.**
*Cymbeline* **4:** 77
*Measure for Measure* **2:** 449
*Othello* **4:** 477
*The Winter's Tale* **7:** 436

**Lecter-Siegal Amy**
*Measure for Measure* **33:** 85

**Lee, Jane**
*Henry VI, 1, 2, and 3* **3:** 39

**Lee, Sidney**
*Henry V* **14:** 334
*Pericles* **2:** 553
*The Phoenix and Turtle* **10:** 8
*The Rape of Lucrece* **10:** 69
*Sonnets* **10:** 233

**Leech, Clifford**
*All's Well That Ends Well* **7:** 54

*Antony and Cleopatra* **17:** 34
*Henry IV, 1 and 2* **1:** 393
*Henry VIII* **2:** 64
*Macbeth* **29:** 152
*Measure for Measure* **2:** 479
*Pericles* **2:** 571
*Romeo and Juliet* **5:** 562
Shakespeare and Classical Civilization (topic entry) **27:** 60
*The Taming of the Shrew* **12:** 350
*The Tempest* **8:** 380
*Twelfth Night* **1:** 645
*The Two Noble Kinsmen* **9:** 479, 486

Leggatt, Alexander
*As You Like It* **5:** 141; **46:** 254
*The Comedy of Errors* **1:** 63
*Cymbeline* **4:** 159
*Henry VI, 1, 2, and 3* **39:** 160
*King John* **41:** 205
*Love's Labour's Lost* **2:** 362
*Pericles* **36:** 257
*The Taming of the Shrew* **9:** 407
*Twelfth Night* **1:** 660
*The Two Gentlemen of Verona* **6:** 549

Lejeune, C. A.
*Henry V* **14:** 204

Lelyveld, Toby
*The Merchant of Venice* **12:** 6

Lemmon, Jeremy
*Macbeth* **20:** 382

Lennox, Charlotte
*Cymbeline* **4:** 18
*Hamlet* **1:** 81
*Henry IV, 1 and 2* **1:** 289
*Henry V* **5:** 188
*Henry VI, 1, 2, and 3* **3:** 18
*Henry VIII* **2:** 16
*King Lear* **2:** 100
*Macbeth* **3:** 172
*Measure for Measure* **2:** 388
*Much Ado about Nothing* **8:** 9
*Othello* **4:** 386
*Richard II* **6:** 252
*Richard III* **8:** 145
*Romeo and Juliet* **5:** 416
*Troilus and Cressida* **3:** 537
*Twelfth Night* **1:** 540
*The Two Gentlemen of Verona* **6:** 436
*The Winter's Tale* **7:** 377

Lenz, Joseph M.
*The Winter's Tale* **36:** 380

Leonard, Hugh
*Henry V* **14:** 278
*Twelfth Night* **26:** 262

Lesser, Simon O.
*Macbeth* **45:** 48

Lessing, Gotthold Ephraim
*Hamlet* **1:** 84

Levenson, Jill L.
*Romeo and Juliet* **11:** 451

Lever, J. W.
*Measure for Measure* **2:** 505
*The Merchant of Venice* **4:** 263
*Sonnets* **10:** 293

Levett, Karl
*Much Ado about Nothing* **18:** 229

Levin, Bernard
*As You Like It* **23:** 89, 115, 120
*Cymbeline* **15:** 62
*Henry VI, 1, 2, and 3* **24:** 31
*King Lear* **11:** 110
*A Midsummer Night's Dream* **12:** 270
*Twelfth Night* **26:** 330

Levin, Harry
*Hamlet* **1:** 227
*Macbeth* **44:** 261
*Othello* **4:** 562
*Romeo and Juliet* **5:** 496
*Timon of Athens* **1:** 520

Levin, Richard A.
*Julius Caesar* **30:** 362
*The Rape of Lucrece* **33:** 138
*Twelfth Night* **46:** 324

Levine, Nina S.
*Richard III* **39:** 345

Lewalski, B. K.
*Much Ado about Nothing* **31:** 209

Lewalski, Barbara K.
*The Merchant of Venice* **4:** 289
*Twelfth Night* **1:** 642

Lewes, George Henry
*Hamlet* **21:** 384
*Othello* **11:** 201, 219

Lewis, Anthony J.
*Pericles* **36:** 264

Lewis, C. S.
*The Phoenix and Turtle* **10:** 20
*The Rape of Lucrece* **10:** 77
*Sonnets* **10:** 287
*Venus and Adonis* **10:** 448

Lewis, Chariton M.
*Hamlet* **1:** 125

Lewis, Cynthia
*Cymbeline* **19:** 411

Lewis, Majorie Dunlavy
*The Merry Wives of Windsor* **47:** 354

Lewis, Wyndham
*Coriolanus* **9:** 62
*Henry VI, 1 and 2* **1:** 351
*Othello* **4:** 455
*Timon of Athens* **1:** 481

Lewsen, Charles
*Antony and Cleopatra* **17:** 55
*Henry V* **14:** 280
*Pericles* **15:** 161

Lezra, Jacques
*Measure for Measure* **13:** 112

Lictenberg, Georg Christoph
*Hamlet* **21:** 17

Lidz, Theodore
*Hamlet* **35:** 132

Lieber, Naomi Conn
*Titus Andronicus* **32:** 265

Lief, Madelon
*The Two Noble Kinsmen* **41:** 326

Lillo, George
*Pericles* **2:** 538

Lindenbaum, Peter
*The Two Gentlemen of Verona* **6:** 555

Lindheim, Nancy
*Venus and Adonis* **10:** 489

Linville, Susan E.
*King Lear* **16:** 311

Liston, William T.
*A Midsummer Night's Dream* **45:** 143

Littledale, Harold
*The Two Noble Kinsmen* **9:** 457

Lloyd, William Watkiss
*Henry V* **5:** 203
*Pericles* **2:** 547
*The Two Gentlemen of Verona* **6:** 447

Lockridge, Richard
*Romeo and Juliet* **11:** 418

Loewenstein, Joseph
*Hamlet* **13:** 282

Loggins, Vernon P.
*Troilus and Cressida* **43:** 377

Lolleran, James V.
<*Hamlet* **13: 268**

Londre, Felicia Hardison
*Coriolanus* **17:** 151

Loney, Glenn
*As You Like It* **23:** 117

Long, John H.
*A Midsummer Night's Dream* **3:** 418

Long, Michael
*Antony and Cleopatra* **6:** 219

Longinus
See also Steevens, George; Collier, Jeremy; Hic et Ubique; Lorenzo
*Hamlet* **1:** 86

Longstaffe, Steve
*King John* **37:** 132

Lorenzo
See also Steevens, George; Collier, Jeremy; Hic et Ubique; Longinus
*Othello* **4:** 391
*Richard III* **8:** 147

Lowe, Lisa
*Coriolanus* **30:** 125

Lowell, James Russell
*The Tempest* **8:** 308

Lowenthal, David
*King Lear* **46:** 177

Lubbock, Tom
*Pericles* **15:** 174

Lucas, Walter
*The Taming of the Shrew* **12:** 369

Lucking, David
*The Merchant of Venice* **13:** 43
*Romeo and Juliet* **32:** 276; **42:** 266

Luders, Charles Henry
*The Winter's Tale* **15:** 440

Lusardi, James P.
*King Lear* **19:** 295

Lustig, Vera
*Julius Caesar* **17:** 406

Lyons, Charles R.
*A Midsummer Night's Dream* **3:** 474

Mabie, Hamilton Wright
*Antony and Cleopatra* **6:** 53

Mac Liammoir, Micheal
*Othello* **11:** 285

Macauly, Alastair
*Twelfth Night* **26:** 335

MacCallum, M. W.
*Coriolanus* **9:** 45
*Julius Caesar* **7:** 191

MacCarthy, Desmond
*Hamlet* **21:** 157, 179
*A Midsummer Night's Dream* **12:** 223
*Richard III* **14:** 416
*Troilus and Cressida* **18:** 302

MacCary, W. Thomas
*Love's Labour's Lost* **38:** 194
*Much Ado about Nothing* **31:** 241
*The Two Gentlemen of Verona* **40:** 365

Macdonald, Dwight
*Hamlet* **21:** 242

MacDonald, Jan
*The Taming of the Shrew* **12:** 338

MacDonald, Joyce Green
*The Rape of Lucrece* **33:** 155

**MacDonald, Ronald R.**
*Antony and Cleopatra* **6:** 228
*Measure for Measure* **16:** 114
*A Midsummer Night's Dream* **29:** 210

**MacIntyre, Jean**
*King Lear* **47:** 9

**Mack, Maynard**
*Antony and Cleopatra* **6:** 163; **27:** 90
*Hamlet* **1:** 198
*Julius Caesar* **7:** 298
*King Lear* **2:** 249; **11:** 132
*The Taming of the Shrew* **9:** 369

**Mack, Maynard, Jr.**
*Hamlet* **1:** 264
*Macbeth* **29:** 155

**Mackail, J. W.**
*Sonnets* **10:** 243

**Mackenzie, Henry**
*Hamlet* **1:** 88
*Henry IV, 1 and 2* **1:** 304

**Mackenzie, Suzie**
*As You Like It* **23:** 142

**Macklin, Charles**
*Othello* **11:** 185

**MacLeish, Archibald**
*Julius Caesar* **17:** 323

**Macready, William Charles**
*King John* **24:** 181
*King Lear* **11:** 15
*Macbeth* **20:** 100, 101, 103
*Romeo and Juliet* **11:** 398

**Madariaga, Salvador de**
*Hamlet* **1:** 171

**Maginn, William**
*As You Like It* **5:** 28
*Macbeth* **3:** 193
*A Midsummer Night's Dream* **3:** 365
*Othello* **4:** 409

**Magnusson, Lynne A.**
*Henry VIII* **22:** 182
*Othello* **42:** 273

**Maguin, J. M.**
*Henry V* **14:** 284
*Henry VI, 1, 2, and 3* **24:** 36
*Julius Caesar* **17:** 396
*King John* **24:** 238
*Much Ado about Nothing* **18:** 215
*Pericles* **15:** 166
*The Taming of the Shrew* **12:** 410
*Titus Andronicus* **17:** 481

**Maguin, Jean Marie**
*Julius Caesar* **30:** 293
*The Merry Wives of Windsor* **18:** 60
*The Tempest* **32:** 367

**Mahood, M. M.**
*Macbeth* **3:** 283
*Richard II* **6:** 331
*Romeo and Juliet* **5:** 489
*Sonnets* **10:** 296
*The Winter's Tale* **7:** 460

**Mairowitz, David Zane**
*Troilus and Cressida* **18:** 359

**Majors, G. W.**
*The Rape of Lucrece* **10:** 106

**Malcolm, Donald**
*Henry IV, 1 and 2* **14:** 62, 65

**Malcolmson, Cristina**
*Twelfth Night* **19:** 78; **46:** 347

**Mallett, Phillip**
*Richard III* **39:** 387

**Mallin, Eric S.**
*Troilus and Cressida* **16:** 84; **43:** 365

**Malone, Edmond**
*Henry VI, 1, 2, and 3* **3:** 21
*Henry VIII* **2:** 19
*King John* **9:** 218
*A Midsummer Night's Dream* **3:** 363
*Pericles* **2:** 538, 543
*The Rape of Lucrece* **10:** 64
*Richard III* **8:** 158
*Sonnets* **10:** 155, 156
*Titus Andronicus* **4:** 616
*Venus and Adonis* **10:** 412

**Manheim, Leonard F.**
*Twelfth Night* **34:** 338

**Manheim, Michael**
*Henry VI, 1, 2, and 3* **3:** 143
*King John* **9:** 297; **13:** 158

**Manningham, John**
*Richard III* **8:** 144
*Twelfth Night* **1:** 539

**Mantel, Hilary**
*Henry V* **14:** 309

**Manvell, Roger**
*Henry V* **14:** 203
*Macbeth* **20:** 148, 203
*A Midsummer Night's Dream* **12:** 214
*Richard III* **14:** 442

**Manzoni, Alessandro**
*Richard II* **6:** 260

**Marchitello, Howard**
*The Merchant of Venice* **32:** 41

**Marcus, Frank**
*As You Like It* **23:** 99
*The Taming of the Shrew* **12:** 387

**Marcus, Leah**
*The Taming of the Shrew* **22:** 48

**Marcus, Mordecai**
*A Midsummer Night's Dream* **3:** 511

**Marder, Louis**
Authorship Controversy (topic entry) **41:** 5

**Mares, F. H.**
*Much Ado about Nothing* **18:** 239

**Margeson, John**
*Henry VIII* **24:** 146; **41:** 129

**Markels, Julian**
*Antony and Cleopatra* **6:** 181; **27:** 121

**Marowitz, Charles**
*Hamlet* **21:** 256
*King Lear* **11:** 78
*Love's Labour's Lost* **23:** 200

**Marriott, J. A. R.**
*Henry VI, 1, 2, and 3* **3:** 51

**Marsh, Derick R. C.**
*Romeo and Juliet* **5:** 565

**Marsh, Henry**
*A Midsummer Night's Dream* **3:** 361

**Marsh, Ngaio**
*Twelfth Night* **26:** 364

**Marshall, Cynthia**
*As You Like It* **48:** 42

**Marshall, David**
*A Midsummer Night's Dream* **3:** 520

**Marshall, Margaret**
*Hamlet* **21:** 201
*Othello* **11:** 268

**Marston, Westland**
*King Lear* **11:** 18
*Romeo and Juliet* **11:** 404

**Martin, Theodore**
*As You Like It* **23:** 47
*The Merchant of Venice* **12:** 25

**Martindale, Charles**
Shakespeare and Classical Civilization (topic entry) **27:** 67

**Martindale, Michelle**
Shakespeare and Classical Civilization (topic entry) **27:** 67

**Marx, Joan C.**
*Cymbeline* **36:** 125

**Marx, Karl**
*Timon of Athens* **1:** 466

**Marx, Leo**
*The Tempest* **8:** 404

**Marx, Steven**
*Henry V* **32:** 126

**Masefield, John**
*Coriolanus* **9:** 52
*Henry V* **5:** 212
*King John* **9:** 245
*Macbeth* **20:** 363
*The Phoenix and Turtle* **10:** 14
*Richard III* **8:** 184

**Mason, John Monck**
*Sonnets* **10:** 156

**Massey, Daniel**
*Measure for Measure* **23:** 416

**Massey, Gerald**
*Sonnets* **10:** 196
*Titus Andronicus* **4:** 624

**Masters, Anthony**
*A Midsummer Night's Dream* **12:** 277
*Timon of Athens* **20:** 471

**Matchett, William H.**
*King John* **41:** 277
*The Phoenix and Turtle* **38:** 357
*The Winter's Tale* **7:** 483

**Matheson, Mark**
*Hamlet* **32:** 284
*Othello* **32:** 294

**Matthews, Brander**
*Cymbeline* **4:** 52
*Henry V* **5:** 213
*Julius Caesar* **7:** 204; **17:** 296
*Romeo and Juliet* **5:** 448

**Matthews, C. M.**
*Othello* **4:** 564

**Matthews, Harold**
*As You Like It* **23:** 85
*Coriolanus* **17:** 167
*Henry VI, 1, 2, and 3* **24:** 24
*King Lear* **11:** 75
*Love's Labour's Lost* **23:** 197
*Measure for Measure* **23:** 311, 317
*Much Ado about Nothing* **18:** 180
*Othello* **11:** 294
*Richard III* **14:** 460

**Matthews, Harold G.**
*Troilus and Cressida* **18:** 307, 323

**Matthews, William**
*Love's Labour's Lost* **2:** 345

**Matus, Irvin**
Authorship Controversy (topic entry) **41:** 57, 63

**Maus, Katharine Eisaman**
*Love's Labour's Lost* **19:** 92
*Measure for Measure* **33:** 112
*The Rape of Lucrece* **33:** 144

**Maxwell, Baldwin**
*Hamlet* **35:** 204

**Maxwell, J. C.**
*Timon of Athens* **1:** 495

**Mayer, Jean-Christophe**
*Henry IV, Parts 1 and 2* **42**: 141
*Henry V* **42**: 141

**Mazer, Cary M.**
*Much Ado about Nothing* **18**: 148
*The Taming of the Shrew* **12**: 337

**McAleer, John J.**
*Henry IV, and 1 and 2* **14**: 13

**McAlindon, T.**
*Hamlet* **1**: 249
*Richard II* **6**: 397
*Troilus and Cressida* **3**: 624

**McAlindon, Tom**
*Antony and Cleopatra* **19**: 304
*Coriolanus* **25**: 263
*Henry IV, 1 and 2* **32**: 136

**McBride, Tom**
*Henry VIII* **2**: 75
*Measure for Measure* **2**: 522

**McCarten, John**
*Hamlet* **21**: 199
*Henry V* **14**: 210

**McClain, John**
*The Two Gentlemen of Verona* **12**: 469

**McCloskey, John C.**
*Henry V* **5**: 239

**McCollom, William G.**
*Much Ado about Nothing* **31**: 178

**McConnell, Stanlie**
*Henry V* **14**: 219

**McCourt, James**
*The Tempest* **15**: 298

**McCoy, Richard C.**
Kingship (topic entry) **39**: 34

**McCreadie, Marsha**
*Henry V* **14**: 326

**McDonald, Jan**
*The Taming of the Shrew* **12**: 317

**McDonald, Russ**
*The Tempest* **19**: 421
*Richard III* **47**: 15

**McElroy, Bernard**
*King Lear* **2**: 273
*Macbeth* **3**: 329

**McEwan, Ian**
*As You Like It* **23**: 123

**McFarland, Thomas**
*King Lear* **46**: 231

**McGlinchee, Claire**
*The Merchant of Venice* **12**: 63
*A Midsummer Night's Dream* **12**: 241

*Much Ado about Nothing* **18**: 174
*Troilus and Cressida* **18**: 338

**McGrath, John**
*Macbeth* **20**: 259

**McGuire, Philip C.**
*A Midsummer Night's Dream* **29**: 256
*The Tempest* **45**: 200

**McKellan, Ian**
*Richard II* **24**: 337

**McKenzie, Stanley D.**
*Coriolanus* **9**: 193

**McLaughlin, John J.**
*Richard III* **39**: 383

**McLaughlin, John**
*Hamlet* **21**: 249

**McLuhan, Herbert Marshall**
*Henry IV, 1 and 2* **1**: 385

**McLuskie, Kathleen**
*King Lear* **31**: 123
Shakespeare's Representation of Women (topic entry) **31**: 35

**McMullan, Gordon**
*Henry VIII* **32**: 148

**McMullen, Glenys**
Clowns and Fools (topic entry) **46**: 18

**McNeely, Trevor**
*Othello* **47**: 51

**McPeek, James A. S.**
*Much Ado about Nothing* **8**: 88
*Richard II* **6**: 334

**Meadowcroft, J. R. W.**
*King Lear* **11**: 165

**Mebane, John S.**
Magic and the Supernatural (topic entry) **29**: 12

**Mehl, Dieter**
*Macbeth* **44**: 269

**Merchant, Moelwyn W.**
*Henry VIII* **24**: 71

**Merchant, W. M.**
*Timon of Athens* **1**: 500

**Meres, Francis**
*The Rape of Lucrece* **10**: 63
*Sonnets* **10**: 153
*Venus and Adonis* **10**: 410

**Merryn, Anthony**
*Measure for Measure* **23**: 312

**Meryman, Richard**
*Othello* **11**: 297

**Meszaros, Patricia K.**
*Coriolanus* **9**: 180

**Metzger, Mary Jane**
*The Merchant of Venice* **48**: 54

**Mezieres, Alfred J. F.**
*Macbeth* **3**: 198
*Romeo and Juliet* **5**: 437

**Micheli, Linda McJ.**
*Henry VIII* **24**: 101; **41**: 180

**Michell, John**
Authorship Controversy (topic entry) **41**: 2

**Michener, Charles**
*Othello* **11**: 321
*Pericles* **15**: 162

**Midgley, Graham**
*The Merchant of Venice* **4**: 279

**Mikalachki, Jodi**
*Cymbeline* **32**: 373

**Miko, Stephen J.**
*The Tempest* **29**: 297
*The Winter's Tale* **13**: 417

**Miles, Geoffrey**
*Julius Caesar* **37**: 229

**Millard, Barbara C.**
Fathers and Daughters (topic entry) **36**: 60
*King Lear* **13**: 352

**Miller, J. Hillis**
*Troilus and Cressida* **3**: 635

**Miller, Jonathan**
*The Merchant of Venice* **12**: 92
*The Taming of the Shrew* **12**: 400, 402
*The Tempest* **15**: 338

**Miller, Robert P.**
*Venus and Adonis* **10**: 439

**Miller, Ronald F.**
*King Lear* **2**: 278
*A Midsummer Night's Dream* **3**: 486

**Miller, Tice L.**
*The Taming of the Shrew* **12**: 425

**Mills, John A.**
*Hamlet* **21**: 89, 44, 274

**Milne, Tom**
*The Taming of the Shrew* **12**: 359

**Miola, Robert S.**
*Othello* **16**: 283
*Julius Caesar* **30**: 326
Shakespeare and Classical Civilization (topic entry) **27**: 39
*Titus Andronicus* **43**: 206

**Milton, John**
*Richard III* **8**: 145

**Mincoff, M.**
*The Two Noble Kinsmen* **9**: 471

**Mincoff, Marco**
*Henry VIII* **41**: 158

**Miner, Madonne M.**
*Richard III* **8**: 262

**Mizener, Arthur**
*Sonnets* **10**: 265

**Modjeska, Helena**
*As You Like It* **23**: 42

**Moffet, Robin**
*Cymbeline* **4**: 108

**Moglen, Helene**
*Twelfth Night* **34**: 311

**Moisan, Thomas**
*The Taming of the Shrew* **32**: 56

**Monsey, Derek**
*All's Well That Ends Well* **26**: 36

**Montagu, Elizabeth**
*Hamlet* **1**: 85
*Henry IV, 1 and 2* **1**: 293
*Julius Caesar* **7**: 156
*Macbeth* **3**: 173

**Montague, C. E.**
*Measure for Measure* **23**: 286
*Richard II* **24**: 408

**Montegut, Emile**
*Love's Labour's Lost* **2**: 306
*Twelfth Night* **1**: 554
*The Winter's Tale* **7**: 394

**Montrose, Louis Adrian**
*As You Like It* **5**: 158
*Love's Labour's Lost* **2**: 371
*A Midsummer Night's Dream* **29**: 243; **45**: 84

**Moody, A. D.**
*The Merchant of Venice* **4**: 300

**Mooney, Michael E.**
*Antony and Cleopatra* **16**: 342
*Julius Caesar* **19**: 321
*Richard III* **16**: 150

**Moore, Dan**
*The Merchant of Venice* **12**: 80

**Moore, Don D.**
*Much Ado about Nothing* **18**: 216

**Moore, Edward M.**
*Measure for Measure* **23**: 293
*The Merchant of Venice* **12**: 44

**Moore, Hannah**
*Hamlet* **21**: 20

**Moore, Jeanie Grant**
*Richard II* **39**: 295

**Morgann, Maurice**
*Henry IV, 1 and 2* **1:** 298
*The Tempest* **8:** 293

**Morley, Henry**
*As You Like It* **23:** 26
*Cymbeline* **15:** 19, 20
*Henry IV, 1 and 2* **14:** 15
*King John* **24:** 194
*King Lear* **11:** 20
*Macbeth* **20:** 121
*A Midsummer Night's Dream* **12:** 169, 183
*Othello* **11:** 217
*Richard II* **24:** 273
*The Taming of the Shrew* **12:** 323
*Timon of Athens* **20:** 444

**Morley, Sheridan**
*All's Well That Ends Well* **26:** 57
*Coriolanus* **17:** 213
*Cymbeline* **15:** 86
*Hamlet* **21:** 314, 333
*Henry V* **14:** 282
*Henry VIII* **24:** 123
*Julius Caesar* **17:** 388
*The Merry Wives of Windsor* **18:** 62
*Much Ado about Nothing* **18:** 207
*Romeo and Juliet* **11:** 483
*The Taming of the Shrew* **12:** 410
*Titus Andronicus* **17:** 485
*Troilus and Cressida* **18:** 363
*Twelfth Night* **26:** 293, 306, 317, 325
*The Two Gentlemen of Verona* **12:** 492
*The Winter's Tale* **15:** 488

**Morris, Brian**
*Macbeth* **3:** 345

**Morris, Corbyn**
*Henry IV, 1 and 2* **1:** 287

**Morris, Harry**
*As You Like It* **46:** 164

**Morris, Mowbray**
*Othello* **11:** 249

**Morrisey, LeRoy J.**
*As You Like It* **23:** 9

**Morse, Ruth**
*The Two Gentlemen of Verona* **40:** 359

**Morse, William R.**
*The Winter's Tale* **19:** 431

**Mortimer, Anthony**
*Venus and Adonis* **42:** 347

**Mortimer, Raymond**
*Hamlet* **21:** 197
*Othello* **11:** 267

**Morton, Richard**
*Timon of Athens* **20:** 431

**Mosdell, D.**
*Henry V* **14:** 215

**Moseley, Charles**
*Macbeth* **44:** 361

**Moss, Roger**
*The Merry Wives of Windsor* **47:** 325

**Moulton, Ian Frederick**
*Richard III* **37:** 144

**Moulton, Richard G.**
*Henry VI, 1, 2, and 3* **3:** 48
*Julius Caesar* **7:** 179
*Richard III* **8:** 170
*Romeo and Juliet* **5:** 444
*The Tempest* **8:** 315
*The Winter's Tale* **7:** 407

**Mowat, Barbara A.**
*Cymbeline* **4:** 124
Shakespeare's Representation of Women (topic entry) **31:** 29
*The Winter's Tale* **45:** 333

**Mueller, Martin**
*King Lear* **28:** 301

**Muir, Edwin**
*King Lear* **2:** 183

**Muir, Kenneth**
*As You Like It* **5:** 154
*Macbeth* **3:** 300; **29:** 76
*The Merchant of Venice* **12:** 81
*Pericles* **2:** 568; **36:** 199
*The Phoenix and Turtle* **10:** 18
Shakespeare and Classical Civilization (topic entry) **27:** 15
*Timon of Athens* **1:** 495; **27:** 161
*Troilus and Cressida* **3:** 589
*The Two Noble Kinsmen* **9:** 474
*Venus and Adonis* **10:** 459

**Mullaney, Steven**
*Hamlet* **28:** 311

**Muller, Wolfgang G.**
*Richard III* **39:** 360

**Mullin, Michael**
*Hamlet* **21:** 270
*Henry IV, 1 and 2* **14:** 92
*Macbeth* **20:** 175, 192, 210, 245, 324
*A Midsummer Night's Dream* **12:** 250

**Mullini, Roberta**
Clowns and Fools (topic entry) **46:** 24

**Mulryne, J. R.**
*Coriolanus* **17:** 195
*Much Ado about Nothing* **18:** 252
*Pericles* **15:** 167

**Munoz, Marie-Christine**
*The Comedy of Errors* **26:** 178

**Murphy, Arthur**
*All's Well That Ends Well* **7:** 8
*Hamlet* **1:** 82; **21:** 21
*Henry IV, 1 and 2* **1:** 290
*Henry VIII* **2:** 17
*King Lear* **2:** 98
*Macbeth* **3:** 172; **20:** 23
*Measure for Measure* **2:** 390
*Much Ado about Nothing* **18:** 114
*Richard III* **14:** 364
*Romeo and Juliet* **11:** 382, 385
*The Tempest* **15:** 200
*The Winter's Tale* **7:** 379; **15:** 397

**Murphy, Gerard**
*Henry IV, 1 and 2* **14:** 98

**Murray, Gilbert**
*Hamlet* **1:** 130

**Murray, Peter B.**
*Hamlet* **37:** 241

**Murry, John Middleton**
*Antony and Cleopatra* **6:** 94
*Coriolanus* **9:** 58
*Henry IV, 1 and 2* **1:** 365
*Henry VI, 1, 2, and 3* **3:** 55
*King John* **9:** 248
*King Lear* **2:** 165
*The Merchant of Venice* **4:** 247
*The Phoenix and Turtle* **10:** 14
*Richard II* **6:** 287
*The Tempest* **8:** 353
*Twelfth Night* **1:** 572
*The Winter's Tale* **7:** 419

**Myrick, Kenneth O.**
*Othello* **4:** 483

**Nagarajan, S.**
*Twelfth Night* **1:** 609

**Nagler, A. M.**
*Romeo and Juliet* **11:** 514
*The Tempest* **15:** 303

**Nardo, Anna K.**
*Hamlet* **35:** 104
*Romeo and Juliet* **33:** 255

**Naremore, James**
*Macbeth* **20:** 206

**Nashe, Thomas**
*Henry VI, 1, 2, and 3* **3:** 16

**Nathan, George Jean**
*Henry VIII* **24:** 100
*Macbeth* **20:** 222
*Richard III* **14:** 414
*The Tempest* **15:** 251

**Nathan, Norman**
*The Merchant of Venice* **4:** 252, 266

**Nechkina, M.**
*Henry IV, 1 and 2* **1:** 358

**Neely, Carol Thomas**
*All's Well That Ends Well* **38:** 99
Gender Identity (topic entry) **40:** 75
*Hamlet* **19:** 330
*King Lear* **19:** 330
*Macbeth* **19:** 330

Madness (topic entry) **35:** 8
*Much Ado about Nothing* **31:** 231
*The Winter's Tale* **7:** 506

**Neill, Kerby**
*Much Ado about Nothing* **8:** 58

**Neill, Michael**
*Henry IV, 1 and 2* **28:** 159
*Henry V* **28:** 159
*Henry VI, 1, 2, and 3* **28:** 159
*Othello* **13:** 327
*Richard II* **28:** 159

**Nemerov, Howard**
*A Midsummer Night's Dream* **3:** 421
*The Two Gentlemen of Verona* **6:** 509

**Nemirovich-Danchenko, V. I.**
*Julius Caesar* **17:** 295

**Nesbitt, Cathleen**
*The Winter's Tale* **15:** 449

**Nevo, Ruth**
*All's Well That Ends Well* **48:** 65
*The Comedy of Errors* **34:** 245
*Pericles* **36:** 214
*The Two Gentlemen of Verona* **6:** 560
*The Winter's Tale* **45:** 344

**Newlin, Jeanne T.**
*Troilus and Cressida* **18:** 395, 437

**Newman, Karen**
*Henry V* **19:** 203
*The Merchant of Venice* **40:** 208

**Nice, David**
*Troilus and Cressida* **18:** 387

**Nicholls, Graham**
*Measure for Measure* **23:** 379

**Nichols, Lewis**
*The Tempest* **15:** 237, 240

**Nicoll, Allardyce**
*Othello* **4:** 457

**Nietzsche, Friedrich**
*Hamlet* **1:** 114
*Julius Caesar* **7:** 179

**Nightingale, Benedict**
*All's Well That Ends Well* **26:** 55, 71
*Antony and Cleopatra* **17:** 57
*As You Like It* **23:** 128, 148
*The Comedy of Errors* **26:** 150
*Coriolanus* **17:** 192, 207
*Cymbeline* **15:** 73
*Hamlet* **21:** 267, 297, 330
*Henry IV, 1 and 2* **14:** 90
*Henry V* **14:** 282
*Henry VI, 1, 2, and 3* **24:** 32
*Henry VIII* **24:** 115, 124
*Julius Caesar* **17:** 380
*King John* **24:** 216
*King Lear* **11:** 109

*Macbeth* **20:** 289, 314
*Measure for Measure* **23:** 321, 327, 339, 355
*The Merchant of Venice* **12:** 95
*The Merry Wives of Windsor* **18:** 55
*A Midsummer Night's Dream* **12:** 257, 275
*Much Ado about Nothing* **18:** 205
*Pericles* **15:** 148, 160, 175
*Richard II* **24:** 345, 374, 381
*Richard III* **14:** 464
*Romeo and Juliet* **11:** 485
*The Taming of the Shrew* **12:** 389
*The Tempest* **15:** 269, 289
*Titus Andronicus* **17:** 466
*Troilus and Cressida* **18:** 343, 389
*Twelfth Night* **26:** 270, 327, 336
*The Winter's Tale* **15:** 477, 485, 486

**Nilan, Mary M.**
*The Tempest* **15:** 215, 305

**Noble, James Ashcroft**
*Sonnets* **10:** 214

**Noble, Richmond**
<lv*Love's Labour's Lost* **2:** 316

**Nokes, David**
*Troilus and Cressida* **18:** 364

**North, Richard**
*Much Ado about Nothing* **18:** 200

**Norton, Elliot**
*Antony and Cleopatra* **17:** 52

**Novick, Julius**
*Hamlet* **21:** 287
*Henry V* **14:** 304
*Measure for Measure* **23:** 331
*Titus Andronicus* **17:** 461, 474

**Novy, Marianne**
Fathers and Daughters (topic entry) **36:** 54
Gender Identity (topic entry) **40:** 9
*King Lear* **31:** 117
*The Merchant of Venice* **40:** 142
Shakespeare's Representation of Women (topic entry) **31:** 3
*Troilus and Cressida* **27:** 362; **43:** 351

**Novy, Marianne L.**
*The Taming of the Shrew* **31:** 288

**Nowottny, Winifred M. T.**
*King Lear* **2:** 213, 235
*Othello* **4:** 512
*Romeo and Juliet* **5:** 522
*Timon of Athens* **1:** 505
*Troilus and Cressida* **3:** 590

**Nunn, Trevor**
*Julius Caesar* **17:** 421

**Nuttail, A. D.**
*Measure for Measure* **2:** 511
*The Tempest* **29:** 313
*Timon of Athens* **13:** 392; **27:** 184

**O'Loughlin, Sean**
*The Phoenix and Turtle* **10:** 18

**Odell, George C. D.**
*Antony and Cleopatra* **17:** 5
*As You Like It* **23:** 8, 19
*Henry V* **14:** 178, 182, 188, 189, 194, 195
*Henry VI, 1, 2, and 3* **24:** 4
*Henry VIII* **24:** 70, 77, 84
*King John* **24:** 165
*Measure for Measure* **23:** 267
*The Merry Wives of Windsor* **18:** 9
*A Midsummer Night's Dream* **12:** 144, 146, 155, 180
*Much Ado about Nothing* **18:** 113
*Pericles* **15:** 130
*Richard II* **24:** 262, 271
*The Tempest* **15:** 199, 201
*Timon of Athens* **20:** 428, 442, 445
*Troilus and Cressida* **18:** 280
*The Winter's Tale* **15:** 397, 431, 444

**Ogawa, Yasuhiro**
*Hamlet* **42:** 279

**Ogburn, Charlton**
Authorship Controversy (topic entry) **41:** 32

**Ogden, Dunbar H.**
*The Comedy of Errors* **26:** 154

**Oliver, Edith**
*The Comedy of Errors* **26:** 175
*Hamlet* **21:** 288
*Julius Caesar* **17:** 401
*Othello* **11:** 314
*Twelfth Night* **26:** 299

**Oliver, H. J.**
*Coriolanus* **30:** 129
*Timon of Athens* **27:** 157

**Olivier, Laurence**
*Antony and Cleopatra* **17:** 28
*Hamlet* **21:** 202
*Henry V* **14:** 252
*Othello* **11:** 297

**Ong, Walter J.**
*The Phoenix and Turtle* **10:** 31

**Orgel, Stephen**
Sexuality (topic entry) **33:** 18
*The Tempest* **29:** 396
*The Winter's Tale* **19:** 441; **45:** 329

**Orgel, Stephen Kitay**
*The Tempest* **8:** 414

**Ormerod, David**
*A Midsummer Night's Dream* **3:** 497

**Ornstein, Robert**
*Antony and Cleopatra* **47:** 96
*Hamlet* **1:** 230
*Henry IV, 1 and 2* **1:** 431

*Henry V* **5:** 293
*Henry VI, 1, 2, and 3* **3:** 136
*Henry VIII* **2:** 68
*Julius Caesar* **7:** 282
*King John* **9:** 292
*King Lear* **2:** 238
*Measure for Measure* **2:** 495
*A Midsummer Night's Dream* **29:** 175
*Troilus and Cressida* **27:** 370
*The Two Gentlemen of Verona* **40:** 312

**Orwell, George**
*King Lear* **2:** 186

**Osborne, Laurie**
*Twelfth Night* **37:** 78

**Osborne, Laurie E.**
*The Merry Wives of Windsor* **38:** 273

**Over, William**
*Coriolanus* **17:** 225

**Overholser, Winfred**
Madness (topic entry) **35:** 24

**Owens, Margaret E.**
*Henry VI, 1, 2, and 3* **37:** 157

**O'Connor, Garry**
*Julius Caesar* **17:** 394
*King John* **24:** 223
*Love's Labour's Lost* **23:** 204
*Richard II* **24:** 383
*Titus Andronicus* **17:** 479
*Twelfth Night* **26:** 318

**O'Connor, John J.**
*Hamlet* **21:** 310
*King John* **24:** 232
*Richard II* **24:** 368
*Troilus and Cressida* **18:** 370

**O'Dair, Sharon**
*Julius Caesar* **25:** 272

**O'Rourke, James**
*Macbeth* **44:** 366
*Troilus and Cressida* **22:** 58

**Pack, Robert**
*Macbeth* **3:** 275

**Page, Malcolm**
*Richard II* **24:** 405

**Page, Nadine**
*Much Ado about Nothing* **8:** 44

**Palmer, D. J.**
*As You Like It* **5:** 128; **46:** 88
*Julius Caesar* **7:** 343
*Macbeth* **20:** 400
*The Merchant of Venice* **40:** 106
*Titus Andronicus* **4:** 668
*Twelfth Night* **1:** 648

**Palmer, Daryl W.**
*The Winter's Tale* **32:** 388

**Palmer, John**
*Coriolanus* **17:** 147
*King John* **9:** 260
*Love's Labour's Lost* **2:** 324
*A Midsummer Night's Dream* **3:** 406; **12:** 220
*The Taming of the Shrew* **12:** 333
*Troilus and Cressida* **18:** 284
*The Winter's Tale* **15:** 446

**Pansinetti, P. M.**
*Julius Caesar* **17:** 354

**Panter-Downes, Mollie**
*Richard II* **24:** 331

**Paolucci, Anne**
*A Midsummer Night's Dream* **3:** 494

**Papp, Joseph**
*Troilus and Cressida* **18:** 423

**Paris, Bernard J.**
Psychoanalytic Interpretations (topic entry) **44:** 89
*Richard II* **19:** 209

**Parker, A. A.**
*Henry VIII* **2:** 56

**Parker, Barbara L.**
*Julius Caesar* **25:** 280
*Macbeth* **47:** 41

**Parker, Brian**
*Richard III* **14:** 523

**Parker, David**
*Sonnets* **10:** 346

**Parker, Patricia**
*Cymbeline* **47:** 265
General Commentary **22:** 378

**Parker, R. B.**
*All's Well That Ends Well* **7:** 126
*King Lear* **19:** 344

**Parr, Wolstenholme**
*Coriolanus* **9:** 13
*Othello* **4:** 396

**Parrott, Thomas Marc**
*As You Like It* **5:** 84
*Love's Labour's Lost* **2:** 327
*A Midsummer Night's Dream* **3:** 410
*Timon of Athens* **1:** 481
*The Two Gentlemen of Verona* **6:** 476

**Parsons, Philip**
*Love's Labour's Lost* **2:** 344

**Parten, Anne**
*The Merchant of Venice* **4:** 356
*The Merry Wives of Windsor* **38:** 300

**Pasco, Richard**
*Richard II* **24:** 346
*Timon of Athens* **20:** 494

**Paster, Gail Kern**
*Julius Caesar* **13**: 260

**Pater, Walter**
*Love's Labour's Lost* **2**: 308
*Measure for Measure* **2**: 409
*Richard II* **6**: 270

**Patterson, Annabel**
*Henry V* **13**: 194
*A Midsummer Night's Dream* **13**: 27

**Paulin, Bernard**
*Timon of Athens* **1**: 510

**Payne, Ben Iden**
*Measure for Measure* **23**: 294
*The Merchant of Venice* **12**: 131

**Payne, Michael**
*The Tempest* **45**: 272

**Pearce, Edward**
*Twelfth Night* **26**: 320

**Pearce, Frances M.**
*All's Well That Ends Well* **7**: 116

**Pearce, G. M.**
*All's Well That Ends Well* **26**: 51
*Antony and Cleopatra* **17**: 73
*As You Like It* **23**: 116, 124
*Henry IV, 1 and 2* **14**: 104
*King John* **24**: 233
*Love's Labour's Lost* **23**: 222
*Richard II* **24**: 370
*The Taming of the Shrew* **12**: 395
*Timon of Athens* **20**: 473
*Troilus and Cressida* **18**: 365, 369

**Pearce, Jill**
*Troilus and Cressida* **18**: 388
*Twelfth Night* **26**: 326

**Pearlman, E.**
*Henry V* **32**: 157
*Henry VI, 1, 2, and 3* **22**: 193; **37**: 165; **42**: 153
*Richard III* **22**: 193; **39**: 370
*Romeo and Juliet* **33**: 287

**Pearson, Lu Emily**
*Venus and Adonis* **10**: 427

**Pearson, Norman Holmes**
*Antony and Cleopatra* **6**: 142

**Pechter, Edward**
*Henry IV, 1 and 2* **1**: 441
*Othello* **37**: 269

**Pedicord, Harry William**
*King John* **24**: 171

**Pepys, Samuel**
*Hamlet* **21**: 9
*Henry VIII* **2**: 15
*Macbeth* **3**: 170; **20**: 11
*Measure for Measure* **23**: 267
*The Merry Wives of Windsor* **5**: 332
*A Midsummer Night's Dream* **3**: 361; **12**: 144

*Romeo and Juliet* **5**: 415; **11**: 377
*The Tempest* **15**: 189

**Pequigney, Joseph**
Desire (topic entry) **38**: 40
*The Merchant of Venice* **22**: 69
*Sonnets* **10**: 391
*Twelfth Night* **22**: 69

**Percival, John**
*A Midsummer Night's Dream* **12**: 250

**Perret, Marion D.**
*The Taming of the Shrew* **31**: 295

**Perry, Ruth**
Madness (topic entry) **35**: 1

**Perry, Thomas A.**
*The Two Gentlemen of Verona* **6**: 490

**Peter, John**
*All's Well That Ends Well* **26**: 44
*Antony and Cleopatra* **17**: 76
*As You Like It* **23**: 112
*The Comedy of Errors* **26**: 177
*Hamlet* **21**: 327
*Henry VI, 1, 2, and 3* **24**: 47
*Henry VIII* **24**: 122
*Julius Caesar* **17**: 392, 406
*King John* **24**: 235
*Measure for Measure* **23**: 356
*The Merry Wives of Windsor* **18**: 58
*Much Ado about Nothing* **18**: 209
*Richard III* **14**: 486
*The Taming of the Shrew* **12**: 387
*Titus Andronicus* **17**: 477
*Troilus and Cressida* **18**: 361, 382
*Twelfth Night* **26**: 329

**Peterson, Douglas L.**
*Cymbeline* **4**: 141
*Romeo and Juliet* **5**: 533
*The Tempest* **8**: 439

**Peterson, Kaara**
*Hamlet* **48**: 255

**Petronella, Vincent**
*The Comedy of Errors* **34**: 233
*The Phoenix and Turtle* **10**: 45

**Pettet, E. C.**
*All's Well That Ends Well* **7**: 43
*King John* **9**: 267
*Measure for Measure* **2**: 474
*A Midsummer Night's Dream* **3**: 408
*Much Ado about Nothing* **8**: 53
*Romeo and Juliet* **5**: 467
*The Taming of the Shrew* **9**: 342
*Twelfth Night* **1**: 580
*The Two Gentlemen of Verona* **6**: 478
*The Two Noble Kinsmen* **9**: 470

**Pettigrew, John**
*The Comedy of Errors* **26**: 155
*Henry V* **14**: 267
*Measure for Measure* **23**: 333

*Pericles* **15**: 156
*Timon of Athens* **20**: 459
*Twelfth Night* **26**: 290
*The Two Gentlemen of Verona* **12**: 486

**Phelps, Samuel**
*As You Like It* **23**: 18

**Phelps, W. May**
*King Lear* **11**: 21

**Phialas, Peter G.**
*As You Like It* **5**: 122
*The Comedy of Errors* **1**: 53
*Henry V* **5**: 267
*Love's Labour's Lost* **38**: 163
*The Merchant of Venice* **4**: 312
*A Midsummer Night's Dream* **3**: 450
*Much Ado about Nothing* **31**: 198
*Richard II* **6**: 352
*Twelfth Night* **34**: 270
*The Two Gentlemen of Verona* **6**: 516

**Philip, Duke of Wharton**
*Henry V* **14**: 175

**Phillabaum, Corliss E.**
*Timon of Athens* **20**: 446

**Phillipps, Augustine**
*Richard II* **6**: 249

**Phillips, Graham**
Authorship Controversy (topic entry) **41**: 76

**Phillips, James E.**
*Julius Caesar* **17**: 351

**Phillips, James Emerson, Jr.**
*Antony and Cleopatra* **6**: 107
*Henry V* **14**: 216
*Julius Caesar* **7**: 245
*Richard III* **14**: 429

**Phillips, Robin**
*Measure for Measure* **23**: 335

**Pierce, Robert B.**
*Henry VI, 1, 2, and 3* **3**: 126
*Richard II* **6**: 388
*Richard III* **8**: 248

**Pietscher, A.**
*The Merchant of Venice* **4**: 214

**Pilkington, Ace G.**
*Henry V* **19**: 217

**Piper, William Bowman**
*Sonnets* **10**: 360

**Pitcher, John**
*The Tempest* **29**: 355

**Pittenger, Elizabeth**
*The Merry Wives of Windsor* **19**: 101

**Planche, James Robinson**
*The Taming of the Shrew* **12**: 316

**Platt, Peter G.**
*Cymbeline* **47**: 252
*Pericles* **42**: 352

**Playfair, Giles**
*Macbeth* **20**: 95

**Playfair, Nigel**
*As You Like It* **23**: 60

**Plotz, John**
*Coriolanus* **37**: 283

**Poel, William**
*Henry V* **14**: 336
*King Lear* **11**: 142
*Macbeth* **20**: 350
*Measure for Measure* **23**: 405
*The Merchant of Venice* **12**: 111
*Romeo and Juliet* **11**: 499

**Pollock, Lady**
*As You Like It* **23**: 17
*Hamlet* **21**: 58

**Poole, Adrian**
*Richard II* **28**: 178

**Poole, Kristen**
*Henry IV, 1 and 2* **32**: 166

**Pope, Alexander**
*Cymbeline* **4**: 17
*Henry V* **5**: 187
*Richard II* **6**: 252
*Troilus and Cressida* **3**: 536
*The Two Gentlemen of Verona* **6**: 435
*The Two Noble Kinsmen* **9**: 444
*The Winter's Tale* **7**: 377

**Pope, Elizabeth Marie**
*Measure for Measure* **2**: 470

**Popkin, Henry**
*All's Well That Ends Well* **26**: 48
*Measure for Measure* **23**: 332
*Richard II* **24**: 378
*Timon of Athens* **20**: 469

**Porter, Joseph A.**
*Henry IV, 1 and 2* **1**: 439

**Potter, John**
*Cymbeline* **4**: 20
*The Merchant of Venice* **4**: 193
*The Merry Wives of Windsor* **5**: 335
*Othello* **4**: 390
*Timon of Athens* **1**: 455
*Twelfth Night* **1**: 543

**Potter, Lois**
*Julius Caesar* **17**: 405
*Love's Labour's Lost* **23**: 230
*Timon of Athens* **20**: 474

**Potter, Nick**
*As You Like It* **16**: 53
*King Lear* **31**: 84
*Twelfth Night* **16**: 53

**Potter, Stephen**
  *Henry IV, 1 and 2* **14**: 30, 36
  *Richard II* **24**: 314

**Powell, Raymond**
  *Othello* **32**: 302

**Preston, Dennis R.**
  *Twelfth Night* **34**: 281

**Price, Hereward T.**
  *Henry VI, 1, 2, and 3* **3**: 69
  *Venus and Adonis* **10**: 434

**Price, Jonathan Reeve**
  *King John* **9**: 290

**Price, Joseph G.**
  *All's Well That Ends Well* **26**: 73, 97; **38**: 72

**Price, Thomas R.**
  *Love's Labour's Lost* **2**: 310
  *The Winter's Tale* **7**: 399

**Priestley, J. B.**
  *As You Like It* **5**: 63
  *Henry IV, 1 and 2* **1**: 344
  *Twelfth Night* **1**: 567

**Priestley, Joseph**
  *King John* **9**: 215

**Prince, F. T.**
  *The Phoenix and Turtle* **10**: 35
  *The Rape of Lucrece* **10**: 81

**Prior, Moody E.**
  *Henry V* **5**: 299
  *Henry VI, 1, 2, and 3* **39**: 154

**Pritchett, V. S.**
  *Much Ado about Nothing* **18**: 184
  *Richard III* **14**: 453
  *The Taming of the Shrew* **12**: 360

**Procter, Bryan Waller**
  *Hamlet* **21**: 44
  *Macbeth* **20**: 91
  *The Merchant of Venice* **12**: 13
  *Othello* **11**: 199
  *Romeo and Juliet* **11**: 396

**Prosser, Eleanor**
  *Hamlet* **1**: 254; **35**: 152

**Proudfoot, Richard**
  *A Midsummer Night's Dream* **12**: 268

**Prouse, Derek**
  *Richard III* **14**: 423

**Prouty, Charles Tyler**
  *Twelfth Night* **34**: 323

**Pryce-Jones, Alan**
  *The Comedy of Errors* **26**: 153
  *The Two Gentlemen of Verona* **12**: 473

**Pryce-Jones, David**
  *Henry VI, 1, 2, and 3* **24**: 21
  *Othello* **11**: 298

**Puckler-Muskau, Prince**
  *Macbeth* **20**: 96

**Pugliatti, Paolo**
  *Henry IV, 1 and 2* **48**: 167
  *Henry V* **25**: 131

**Puknat, Elisabeth M.**
  *Romeo and Juliet* **11**: 414

**Purdom, C. B.**
  *Henry VIII* **2**: 65

**Pursell, Michael**
  *The Taming of the Shrew* **12**: 378

**Pushkin, A. S.**
  *Henry VI, 1 and 2* **1**: 313
  *Measure for Measure* **2**: 399

**Putney, Rufus**
  *Venus and Adonis* **10**: 442

**Pye, Christopher**
  *Henry V* **16**: 202
  *King Lear* **16**: 202
  *Macbeth* **16**: 328
  *Richard II* **16**: 202

**Quayle, Anthony**
  *Henry IV, 1 and 2* **14**: 38

**Quiller-Couch, Sir Arthur**
  *All's Well That Ends Well* **7**: 29
  *Antony and Cleopatra* **6**: 71
  *As You Like It* **5**: 61
  *The Comedy of Errors* **1**: 19
  *Cymbeline* **15**: 105
  *Macbeth* **3**: 229
  *Measure for Measure* **2**: 420
  *The Merchant of Venice* **4**: 228
  *Much Ado about Nothing* **8**: 41
  *The Taming of the Shrew* **9**: 332
  *The Tempest* **8**: 334
  *Twelfth Night* **1**: 569
  *The Two Gentlemen of Verona* **6**: 466
  *The Winter's Tale* **7**: 414

**Quinn, Michael**
  *Richard II* **6**: 338

**Rabkin, Leslie Y.**
  *Othello* **35**: 276

**Rabkin, Norman**
  *Antony and Cleopatra* **6**: 180
  *Coriolanus* **30**: 96
  *Henry V* **5**: 304
  *Julius Caesar* **7**: 316
  *The Merchant of Venice* **4**: 350
  *Richard II* **6**: 364
  *Romeo and Juliet* **5**: 538
  *Troilus and Cressida* **3**: 613
  *Venus and Adonis* **10**: 462

**Rackin, Phyllis**
  *Antony and Cleopatra* **6**: 197; **27**: 135
  *Coriolanus* **9**: 189
  *Henry IV, 1 and 2* **16**: 183
  *Henry V* **16**: 183
  *Henry VI, 1, 2, and 3* **16**: 183; **39**: 196
  *King John* **9**: 303; **41**: 215
  *King Lear* **2**: 269
  Politics and Power (topic entry) **30**: 46
  *Richard III* **25**: 141
  Shakespeare's Representation of Women (topic entry) **31**: 48

**Radel, Nicholas F.**
  *The Two Noble Kinsmen* **41**: 326

**Raleigh, Walter**
  *Cymbeline* **4**: 48
  *Measure for Measure* **2**: 417
  *Pericles* **2**: 554
  *Rape of Lucrece* **10**: 70
  *Timon of Athens* **1**: 477
  *Venus and Adonis* **10**: 423

**Ramsey, Jarold W.**
  *Timon of Athens* **1**: 513

**Ranald, Margaret Loftus**
  *The Comedy of Errors* **26**: 180
  *The Taming of the Shrew* **31**: 282, 326

**Ransley, Peter**
  *Twelfth Night* **26**: 284

**Ransom, John Crowe**
  *Sonnets* **10**: 260

**Ratcliffe, Michael**
  *Antony and Cleopatra* **17**: 78
  *As You Like It* **23**: 138
  *Coriolanus* **17**: 209
  *Henry VI, 1, 2, and 3* **24**: 45
  *Julius Caesar* **17**: 392, 405
  *King John* **24**: 235
  *Love's Labour's Lost* **23**: 214
  *Pericles* **15**: 175
  *Richard III* **14**: 485
  *Romeo and Juliet* **11**: 483
  *The Taming of the Shrew* **12**: 398
  *Titus Andronicus* **17**: 485
  *Twelfth Night* **26**: 315

**Ravenscroft, Edward**
  *Titus Andronicus* **4**: 613

**Ravich, Robert A.**
  Psychoanalytic Interpretations (topic entry) **44**: 1

**Ray, Robin**
  *Antony and Cleopatra* **17**: 78

**Ray, Sid**
  *Titus Andronicus* **48**: 264

**Read, David**
  *Henry IV, Parts 1 and 2* **42**: 162
  *Henry V* **42**: 162

**Rebhorn, Wayne A.**
  *Henry IV, 1 and 2* **39**: 130
  *Julius Caesar* **16**: 231; **30**: 379
  *Venus and Adonis* **33**: 321

**Rede, W. L.**
  *The Merchant of Venice* **12**: 12

**Redfern, James**
  *Hamlet* **21**: 181

**Redfern, Stephen**
  *Henry IV, 1 and 2* **14**: 31

**Redgrave, Michael**
  *Antony and Cleopatra* **17**: 38

**Reed, Robert Rentoul, Jr.**
  Magic and the Supernatural (topic entry) **29**: 53

**Rees, Roger**
  *Cymbeline* **15**: 88

**Reese, Jack E.**
  *Titus Andronicus* **17**: 501

**Reese, M. M.**
  *Henry IV, 1 and 2* **39**: 134
  *Henry V* **30**: 237
  *Henry VI, 1, 2, and 3* **3**: 77
  *King John* **9**: 280
  *Richard III* **8**: 228

**Reibetanz, John**
  *King Lear* **2**: 281

**Reid, B. L.**
  *Hamlet* **1**: 242

**Reid, Stephen**
  *Othello* **35**: 301

**Reik, Theodor**
  *The Merchant of Venice* **4**: 268

**Reynolds, Frederick**
  *Much Ado about Nothing* **18**: 115

**Reynolds, George F.**
  *Hamlet* **21**: 407

**Reynolds, Sir Joshua**
  *Macbeth* **3**: 181

**Ribner, Irving**
  *Henry VI, 1, 2, and 3* **3**: 100
  *Julius Caesar* **7**: 279
  *King Lear* **2**: 218
  *Macbeth* **3**: 289
  *Othello* **4**: 527, 559
  *Richard II* **6**: 305
  *Romeo and Juliet* **5**: 493
  *The Taming of the Shrew* **9**: 390
  *Titus Andronicus* **4**: 656

**Rice, Julian**
  *Othello* **35**: 352

**Rich, Alan**
  *Henry V* **14**: 290

**Rich, Frank**
  *Coriolanus* **17**: 217
  *Julius Caesar* **17**: 401

*Measure for Measure* **23:** 351
*Much Ado about Nothing* **18:** 217
*Othello* **11:** 319
*Richard II* **24:** 375
*Richard III* **14:** 479

**Richard, David**
*Henry V* **14:** 337
*Othello* **11:** 317

**Richardson, D. L.**
*Sonnets* **10:** 174

**Richardson, Ian**
*Richard II* **24:** 346

**Richardson, Jack**
*Richard III* **14:** 471

**Richardson, Ralph**
*A Midsummer Night's Dream* **12:** 284

**Richardson, William**
*As You Like It* **5:** 20
*Hamlet* **1:** 88
*Henry IV, 1 and 2* **1:** 307
*King Lear* **2:** 103
*Richard III* **8:** 154
*Timon of Athens* **1:** 456

**Richman, David**
*Much Ado about Nothing* **18:** 264

**Richmond, H. M.**
*Henry VIII* **41:** 171

**Richmond, Hugh M.**
*As You Like It* **5:** 133
*Cymbeline* **47:** 260
*Henry V* **5:** 271
*Henry VI, 1, 2, and 3* **3:** 109
*Henry VIII* **2:** 76; **28:** 184
*Julius Caesar* **7:** 333
*A Midsummer Night's Dream* **3:** 480
*Richard II* **39:** 256
*Richard III* **16:** 137

**Ridley, M. R.**
*Antony and Cleopatra* **6:** 140
*King John* **9:** 250
*The Taming of the Shrew* **9:** 337

**Riemer, A. P.**
*Antony and Cleopatra* **6:** 189
*As You Like It* **5:** 156
*Love's Labour's Lost* **2:** 374
*Much Ado about Nothing* **8:** 108

**Riggs, David**
*Henry VI, 1, 2, and 3* **3:** 119
<l*Richard III* **39:** 335

**Ripley, John**
*Coriolanus* **17:** 232, 248
*Julius Caesar* **17:** 345

**Riss, Arthur**
*Coriolanus* **22:** 248

**Rissik, Andrew**
*Antony and Cleopatra* **17:** 80

**Ristori, Adelaide**
*Macbeth* **20:** 345

**Ritchey, David**
*Richard III* **14:** 527

**Ritson, Joseph**
*Hamlet* **1:** 90
*Julius Caesar* **7:** 158

**Rives, Amelie**
*The Taming of the Shrew* **12:** 325

**Roberts, Jeanne Addison**
*The Merry Wives of Windsor* **5:** 369; **38:** 297; **47:** 358, 375

**Roberts, Josephine A.**
*Sonnets* **37:** 373

**Roberts, Peter**
*The Comedy of Errors* **26:** 147
*Cymbeline* **15:** 60
*Hamlet* **21:** 283
*Henry IV, 1 and 2* **14:** 74
*Henry V* **14:** 273
*Henry VI, 1, 2, and 3* **24:** 22
*Julius Caesar* **17:** 375
*King Lear* **11:** 84, 97
*Measure for Measure* **23:** 347
*The Merchant of Venice* **12:** 67
*The Merry Wives of Windsor* **18:** 43
*Much Ado about Nothing* **18:** 179, 189, 213, 216
*Othello* **11:** 304
*Pericles* **15:** 152
*Richard II* **24:** 332, 338
*Richard III* **14:** 459, 465
*The Taming of the Shrew* **12:** 385
*Troilus and Cressida* **18:** 332
*Twelfth Night* **26:** 271
*The Two Gentlemen of Verona* **12:** 483
*The Winter's Tale* **15:** 473, 480

**Robertson, John M.**
*The Rape of Lucrece* **10:** 70

**Robertson, W. Graham**
*The Merchant of Venice* **12:** 35

**Robinson, David**
*The Taming of the Shrew* **12:** 370
*The Tempest* **15:** 294

**Robinson, Henry Crabb**
*Hamlet* **21:** 43
*King Lear* **11:** 12, 18
*A Midsummer Night's Dream* **12:** 153
*Othello* **11:** 193
*Pericles* **15:** 135
*Richard II* **24:** 269
*The Taming of the Shrew* **12:** 316
*The Tempest* **15:** 210
*The Two Gentlemen of Verona* **12:** 452

**Robson, Flora**
*The Winter's Tale* **15:** 528

**Roche, Thomas P.**
*Sonnets* **10:** 353

**Roderick, Richard**
*Henry VIII* **2:** 16

**Roe, John**
*The Phoenix and Turtle* **38:** 334
*Rape of Lucrece* **43:** 92

**Roesen, Bobbyann**
*Love's Labour's Lost* **2:** 331

**Rogers, Paul**
*A Midsummer Night's Dream* **12:** 238

**Rogers, Robert**
*Othello* **35:** 320

**Rogoff, Gordon**
*Hamlet* **21:** 240
*Julius Caesar* **17:** 402
*Richard II* **24:** 377

**Ronk, Martha**
*Hamlet* **44:** 248
Psychoanalytic Interpretations (topic entry) **44:** 66
*The Winter's Tale* **36:** 349

**Rose, Mark**
*Julius Caesar* **30:** 374

**Rosen, William**
*Antony and Cleopatra* **6:** 165

**Rosenberg, Marvin**
*King Lear* **11:** 161
*Macbeth* **20:** 297, 338, 387
*Othello* **11:** 344

**Rosenfeld, Megan**
*Love's Labour's Lost* **23:** 221

**Rosenfeld, Sybil**
*Coriolanus* **17:** 140
*The Two Gentlemen of Verona* **12:** 453

**Ross, Daniel W.**
*Hamlet* **13:** 296

**Ross, Lawrence J.**
*Othello* **11:** 354

**Ross, T. A.**
*The Merchant of Venice* **4:** 238

**Rossi, Alfred**
*A Midsummer Night's Dream* **12:** 238

**Rossiter, A. P.**
*Coriolanus* **9:** 106; **30:** 89
*Henry V* **30:** 193
*Much Ado about Nothing* **8:** 69
*Richard II* **6:** 343
*Richard III* **8:** 201

**Rossky, William**
*The Two Gentlemen of Verona* **40:** 354

**Rostron, David**
*Henry V* **14:** 180

*Henry VIII* **24:** 74
*Julius Caesar* **17:** 274

**Rothschild, Herbert B., Jr.**
*Henry IV, 1 and 2* **1:** 433
*Richard II* **6:** 381

**Rothwell, Kenneth**
*Henry V* **14:** 315
*The Taming of the Shrew* **12:** 402

**Rothwell, Kenneth S.**
*All's Well That Ends Well* **26:** 51
*Macbeth* **20:** 277

**Rougement, Denis de**
*Romeo and Juliet* **5:** 484

**Rowe, Katherine A.**
*Titus Andronicus* **43:** 262

**Rowe, Nicholas**
*Hamlet* **1:** 74; **21:** 9
*Henry IV, 1 and 2* **1:** 286
*Henry V* **5:** 186
*Henry VI, 1, 2, and 3* **3:** 17
*Henry VIII* **2:** 15
*The Merchant of Venice* **4:** 191
*The Merry Wives of Windsor* **5:** 334
*Romeo and Juliet* **5:** 415
*The Tempest* **8:** 287
*Timon of Athens* **1:** 453
*The Winter's Tale* **7:** 376

**Rowse, A. L.**
*Sonnets* **10:** 377

**Roy, Emil**
*Troilus and Cressida* **43:** 287

**Rozett, Martha Tuck**
*Antony and Cleopatra* **47:** 165

**Rozmovits, Linda**
*The Merchant of Venice* **48:** 77

**Rubenstein, Frankie**
Dreams in Shakespeare (topic entry) **45:** 1

**Rudnytsky, Peter L.**
*Henry VIII* **41:** 146

**Ruskin, John**
*The Tempest* **8:** 307

**Russell, Edward R.**
*King Lear* **11:** 42
*The Tempest* **8:** 311

**Russell, Robert**
*The Taming of the Shrew* **12:** 365

**Rustin, Michael**
*Romeo and Juliet* **33:** 225

**Rutherford, Malcolm**
*All's Well That Ends Well* **26:** 70
*Hamlet* **21:** 324, 331
*Julius Caesar* **17:** 369
*Macbeth* **20:** 314
*Troilus and Cressida* **18:** 391
*Twelfth Night* **26:** 328

Rutter, Carol
  All's Well That Ends Well 19: 113

Rylands, George
  Antony and Cleopatra 17: 24
  Othello 11: 295
  Pericles 15: 139
  Romeo and Juliet 11: 458

Rylands, George H. W.
  The Rape of Lucrece 10: 71
  Sonnets 10: 255

Rymer, Thomas
  Julius Caesar 7: 150
  Othello 4: 370

Sacharoff, Mark
  Julius Caesar 30: 358

Sage, Lorna
  The Taming of the Shrew 12: 390

Salgaudo, Gaumini
  Magic and the Supernatural (topic entry) 29: 46

Salingar, L. G.
  Twelfth Night 1: 603

Salinger, Leo
  King Lear 31: 77
  The Merry Wives of Windsor 47: 308

Salkeld, Duncan
  Hamlet 35: 140

Salomon, Patricia P.
  Henry V 32: 185

Salvini, Tommaso
  King Lear 11: 29
  Othello 11: 229

Sampson, Martin W.
  The Two Gentlemen of Verona 6: 465

Sams, Eric
  Twelfth Night 26: 332

Sanders, Norman
  Julius Caesar 30: 316
  The Two Gentlemen of Verona 6: 519

Sanderson, James L.
  The Comedy of Errors 1: 66

Sanfield, Keith
  Macbeth 20: 315

Santayana, George
  Hamlet 1: 128

Sargent, Ralph M.
  The Two Gentlemen of Verona 6: 480

Sarkar, Malabika
  Sonnets 48: 346

Sasayama, Takashi
  Hamlet 28: 325
  King Lear 28: 325

Saunders, J. G.
  King Lear 37: 295

Saunders, J. W.
  Antony and Cleopatra 17: 110
  Henry VIII 24: 155

Schalkwyk, David
  Sonnets 48: 352
  The Winter's Tale 22: 324

Schanzer, Ernest
  Antony and Cleopatra 27: 32
  Julius Caesar 7: 268, 272
  Measure for Measure 2: 503
  A Midsummer Night's Dream 3: 411
  Pericles 2: 579
  The Winter's Tale 7: 473

Schein, Harry
  Richard III 14: 432

Scheye, Thomas E.
  The Two Gentlemen of Verona 6: 547

Schiffhorst, Gerald J.
  Pericles 36: 244

Schlegel, August Wilhelm
  All's Well That Ends Well 7: 9
  Antony and Cleopatra 6: 24
  As You Like It 5: 24
  The Comedy of Errors 1: 13
  Coriolanus 9: 14
  Cymbeline 4: 21
  Hamlet 1: 92
  Henry IV, 1 and 2 1: 309
  Henry V 5: 192
  Henry VI, 1, 2, and 3 3: 24
  Henry VIII 2: 22
  Julius Caesar 7: 159
  King John 9: 218
  King Lear 2: 104
  Love's Labour's Lost 2: 301
  Macbeth 3: 183
  Measure for Measure 2: 395
  The Merchant of Venice 4: 194
  The Merry Wives of Windsor 5: 336
  A Midsummer Night's Dream 3: 364
  Much Ado about Nothing 8: 13
  Othello 4: 400
  Richard II 6: 255
  Richard III 8: 159
  Romeo and Juliet 5: 421
  Sonnets 10: 159
  The Taming of the Shrew 9: 320
  The Tempest 8: 294
  Timon of Athens 1: 459
  Titus Andronicus 4: 616
  Troilus and Cressida 3: 539
  Twelfth Night 1: 543
  The Two Gentlemen of Verona 6: 439
  The Two Noble Kinsmen 9: 446
  The Winter's Tale 7: 382

Schlegel, Frederick
  Sonnets 10: 160

Schlueter, June
  King Lear 19: 295

Schlueter, Kurt
  The Two Gentlemen of Verona 40: 320

Schmidt, Dana Adams
  As You Like It 23: 96

Schneider, Michael
  A Midsummer Night's Dream 45: 160

Schneider, Pierre
  Timon of Athens 20: 466

Schoen, Elin
  Othello 11: 319

Schoenbaum, S.
  Authorship Controversy (topic entry) 41: 18
  Love's Labour's Lost 23: 211
  The Merchant of Venice 12: 94
  The Taming of the Shrew 12: 393

Schork, R. J.
  Cymbeline 47: 274

Schucking, Levin L.
  Antony and Cleopatra 6: 67
  Julius Caesar 7: 207
  King Lear 2: 151
  The Tempest 8: 336

Schwartz, Elias
  The Phoenix and Turtle 38: 342

Schwartz, Kathryn
  Henry IV, 1 and 2 48: 175

Scofield, Martin
  King Lear 48: 277
  Measure for Measure 48: 277
  Othello 48: 277
  Titus Andronicus 48: 277

Scofield, Paul
  Timon of Athens 20: 464

Scott, Clement
  Hamlet 21: 96, 132
  King Lear 11: 34
  Macbeth 20: 130
  The Merchant of Venice 12: 17
  Much Ado about Nothing 18: 120
  Othello 11: 243
  Romeo and Juliet 11: 427

Scott, William O.
  The Two Gentlemen of Verona 6: 511

Scuro, Daniel
  Titus Andronicus 17: 452

Sedgwick, Eve Kosofsky
  Sonnets 40: 254

Sedulus
  Much Ado about Nothing 18: 198

Seelig, Sharon Cadman
  Richard II 32: 189; 39: 279

Seiden, Melvin
  King Lear 2: 284
  Twelfth Night 1: 632

Seltzer, Daniel
  Othello 11: 350
  The Phoenix and Turtle 10: 37

Sen Gupta, S. C.
  As You Like It 5: 86
  The Comedy of Errors 1: 34
  Henry VI, 1, 2, and 3 3: 92
  Love's Labour's Lost 2: 328
  Troilus and Cressida 3: 583

Sen, Sailendra Kumar
  Coriolanus 9: 130

Seoufos, Alice-Lyle
  As You Like It 5: 162

Seronsy, Cecil C.
  The Taming of the Shrew 9: 370

Sewall, Richard B.
  King Lear 2: 226

Seward, Thomas
  Antony and Cleopatra 6: 21

Sewell, Arthur
  Henry IV, 1 and 2 1: 396
  King Lear 2: 197
  Measure for Measure 2: 484

Sewell, Elizabeth
  A Midsummer Night's Dream 3: 432

Sewell, George
  Sonnets 10: 154

Sexton, Joyce H.
  Cymbeline 47: 277
  Shakespeare's Representation of Women (topic entry) 31: 34

Sexton, Joyce Hengerer
  Much Ado about Nothing 8: 104

Seymour, Alan
  Othello 11: 301

Shaaber, M. A.
  Henry IV, 1 and 2 1: 387

Shabani, Ranjee G.
  The Phoenix and Turtle 10: 21

Shakespeare, William
  Venus and Adonis 10: 409

Shannon, Laurie J.
  The Two Noble Kinsmen 41: 372; 42: 361

Shapiro, James
  Henry IV, 1 and 2 19: 233

Shapiro, Michael
- Cymbeline **47**: 245
- The Merchant of Venice **40**: 156
- The Taming of the Shrew **31**: 315
- The Two Gentlemen of Verona **40**: 374

Shapiro, Stephen A.
- Othello **35**: 317
- Romeo and Juliet **5**: 516

Sharp, Cecil
- A Midsummer Night's Dream **12**: 289

Shattuck, Charles H.
- Julius Caesar **17**: 277, 287
- As You Like It **23**: 20, 54
- Hamlet **21**: 72, 145
- Henry V **14**: 200
- King John **24**: 187
- Measure for Measure **23**: 282
- A Midsummer Night's Dream **12**: 199
- The Merry Wives of Windsor **18**: 15, 22, 31
- Othello **11**: 327
- Twelfth Night **26**: 211, 219

Shaw, Bernard
- Antony and Cleopatra **6**: 52
- All's Well That Ends Well **26**: 9
- As You Like It **5**: 52; **23**: 51
- Coriolanus **9**: 42
- Cymbeline **4**: 45; **15**: 23, 32
- Hamlet **21**: 129, 154
- Henry IV, 1 and 2 **1**: 328, 332; **14**: 24
- Henry V **5**: 209
- Julius Caesar **7**: 187, 188; **17**: 306
- The Merchant of Venice **12**: 33
- A Midsummer Night's Dream **12**: 194
- Much Ado about Nothing **8**: 38; **18**: 146, 152
- Othello **4**: 433, 442; **11**: 335
- Richard III **8**: 181, 182; **14**: 402
- Romeo and Juliet **11**: 438
- The Taming of the Shrew **9**: 329
- The Tempest **15**: 223
- The Two Gentlemen of Verona **12**: 454

Shaw, Glen Byam
- Julius Caesar **17**: 419
- Macbeth **20**: 242

Shaw, William P.
- Troilus and Cressida **18**: 332

Shebbeare, John
- Othello **4**: 388

Shelley, Percy Bysshe
- King Lear **2**: 110
- The Two Noble Kinsmen **9**: 447

Sheppard, Samuel
- Pericles **2**: 537

Henry V **19**: 233
The Merchant of Venice **32**: 66
Richard II **19**: 233

Sher, Antony
- King Lear **11**: 169

Sheridan, Thomas
- Hamlet **1**: 83

Shewey, Don
- Coriolanus **17**: 238

Shickman, Allan R.
- King Lear **46**: 205

Shindler, Robert
- Sonnets **10**: 230

Shorter, Eric
- As You Like It **23**: 141
- Timon of Athens **20**: 466

Showalter, Elaine
- Madness (topic entry) **35**: 54

Shrimpton, Nicholas
- All's Well That Ends Well **26**: 63
- As You Like It **23**: 143
- The Comedy of Errors **26**: 169
- Coriolanus **17**: 215
- Hamlet **21**: 317
- Henry IV, 1 and 2 **14**: 110
- Henry VIII **24**: 124
- King John **24**: 230
- Love's Labour's Lost **23**: 220
- Macbeth **20**: 312
- Measure for Measure **23**: 350
- The Merry Wives of Windsor **18**: 63
- A Midsummer Night's Dream **12**: 275
- Richard III **14**: 488
- Romeo and Juliet **11**: 486
- The Tempest **15**: 368
- Troilus and Cressida **18**: 383
- Twelfth Night **26**: 307

Shulman, Jeffrey
- A Midsummer Night's Dream **45**: 136

Shumaker, Wayne
- Magic and the Supernatural (topic entry) **29**: 28

Shurgot, Michael W.
- The Taming of the Shrew **12**: 435
- Troilus and Cressida **18**: 451

Shuttleworth, Betram
- Macbeth **20**: 146

Siddons, Sarah
- Macbeth **20**: 60
- The Winter's Tale **15**: 400

Siegel, Paul N.
- Hamlet **25**: 288
- Macbeth **3**: 280
- A Midsummer Night's Dream **3**: 417
- Othello **4**: 525
- Romeo and Juliet **5**: 505

Siemon, James Edward
- Cymbeline **4**: 155
- The Merchant of Venice **4**: 319

Sierz, Alex
- Macbeth **20**: 318

Simeon, James R.
- Richard II **28**: 188

Simmons, J. L.
- Henry IV, 1 and 2 **25**: 151
- Henry V **25**: 151
- Henry VI, 1, 2, and 3 **25**: 151
- The Two Gentlemen of Verona **40**: 343

Simon, Francesca
- Henry IV, 1 and 2 **14**: 98

Simon, John
- All's Well That Ends Well **26**: 59
- The Comedy of Errors **26**: 175, 182
- Coriolanus **17**: 219
- Hamlet **21**: 243, 290
- Henry V **14**: 292, 305
- King Lear **11**: 106
- Love's Labour's Lost **23**: 227
- Measure for Measure **23**: 353
- A Midsummer Night's Dream **12**: 298
- Much Ado about Nothing **18**: 193, 221, 225
- Richard II **24**: 354, 376
- Richard III **14**: 480, **14**: 470
- Twelfth Night **26**: 314

Simpson, Percy
- Julius Caesar **17**: 311

Simpson, Richard
- Sonnets **10**: 205

Sinclair, Andrew
- The Taming of the Shrew **12**: 398

Sinden, Donald
- King Lear **11**: 165
- Twelfth Night **26**: 273

Sinfield, Alan
- The Merchant of Venice **37**: 86

Singh, Jyotsna
- Antony and Cleopatra **47**: 113

Singleton, Mary
- King Lear **11**: 8

Sirluck, Katherine A.
- The Taming of the Shrew **19**: 122

Sisk, John P.
- The Merchant of Venice **4**: 317

Sisson, C. J.
- <The Taming of the Shrew **12**: **430**

Sitwell, Edith
- Macbeth **3**: 256

Skeele, David
- Pericles **48**: 364

Skinner, Richard Dana
- Troilus and Cressida **18**: 296

Skura, Meredith Anne
- Clowns and Fools (topic entry) **46**: 29
- Psychoanalytic Interpretations (topic entry) **44**: 28
- Richard II **42**: 173
- Richard III **25**: 164
- The Tempest **13**: 425

Slater, Ann Pasternak
- Twelfth Night **26**: 303

Slights, Camille Wells
- The Merchant of Venice **4**: 342
- Much Ado about Nothing **25**: 77
- The Taming of the Shrew **13**: 3
- The Two Gentlemen of Verona **6**: 568

Slights, William W. E.
- Timon of Athens **1**: 525

Slulsky, Harold
- Hamlet **35**: 157

Small, S. Asa
- Henry IV, 1 and 2 **1**: 353

Smallwood, R. L.
- Henry IV, 1 and 2 **14**: 105

Smallwood, Robert
- As You Like It **23**: 149
- Love's Labour's Lost **23**: 232
- Measure for Measure **23**: 359
- Pericles **15**: 177
- Richard II **24**: 383
- Troilus and Cressida **18**: 392

Smidt, Kristian
- Hamlet **16**: 259
- Pericles **25**: 365

Smith, Bruce R.
- Sonnets **40**: 264

Smith, Gordon Ross
- Henry V **30**: 262
- Julius Caesar **7**: 292; **30**: 351

Smith, James
- Much Ado about Nothing **8**: 48; **31**: 229

Smith, Lisa Gordon
- The Taming of the Shrew **12**: 357

Smith, Marion Bodwell
- The Comedy of Errors **1**: 49

Smith, Peter D.
- The Taming of the Shrew **12**: 367

Smith, Peter J.
- Twelfth Night **26**: 332

Smith, Rebecca
- Hamlet **35**: 229

Smith, Warren D.
- Romeo and Juliet **5**: 536

Smith, William
- Julius Caesar **7**: 155

**Smollett, Tobias**
*Hamlet* **1:** 82

**Snider, Denton J.**
*Antony and Cleopatra* **6:** 43
*As You Like It* **5:** 46
*Coriolanus* **9:** 33
*Cymbeline* **4:** 38
*Henry V* **5:** 205
*Henry VI, 1, 2, and 3* **3:** 42
*Henry VIII* **2:** 39
*King John* **9:** 235
*King Lear* **2:** 133
*Love's Labour's Lost* **2:** 312
*Macbeth* **3:** 208
*Measure for Measure* **2:** 411
*The Merchant of Venice* **4:** 215
*The Merry Wives of Windsor* **5:** 343
*A Midsummer Night's Dream* **3:** 381
*Much Ado about Nothing* **8:** 29
*Othello* **4:** 427
*Richard II* **6:** 272
*Richard III* **8:** 177
*Romeo and Juliet* **5:** 438
*The Taming of the Shrew* **9:** 325
*The Tempest* **8:** 320
*Timon of Athens* **1:** 472
*Troilus and Cressida* **3:** 549
*The Two Gentlemen of Verona* **6:** 450
*The Winter's Tale* **7:** 402

**Snyder, Susan**
*All's Well That Ends Well* **22:** 78
*Macbeth* **44:** 373
*Othello* **4:** 575
*Romeo and Juliet* **5:** 547

**Soellner, Rolf**
*Timon of Athens* **1:** 531; **27:** 191

**Solomon, Alisa**
*Love's Labour's Lost* **23:** 228
*Much Ado about Nothing* **18:** 226
*The Tempest* **15:** 290

**Solway, Diane**
*Twelfth Night* **26:** 312

**Sommers, Alan**
*Titus Andronicus* **4:** 653

**Southall, Raymond**
*Troilus and Cressida* **3:** 606

**Spalding, William**
*The Two Noble Kinsmen* **9:** 448

**Spanabel, Robert R.**
*Henry V* **14:** 189

**Spargo, John Webster**
*Henry IV, 1 and 2* **1:** 342

**Speaight, Robert**
*All's Well That Ends Well* **26:** 47
*Antony and Cleopatra* **17:** 60
*As You Like It* **23:** 92, 107
*The Comedy of Errors* **26:** 148
*Cymbeline* **15:** 79
*Hamlet* **21:** 254, 257, 284
*Henry IV, 1 and 2* **14:** 75, 79, 88
*Henry V* **14:** 274
*Henry VIII* **24:** 117
*Julius Caesar* **17:** 370, 378, 383
*King Lear* **11:** 77, 99
*Love's Labour's Lost* **23:** 198, 202
*Macbeth* **20:** 260, 294
*Measure for Measure* **23:** 287, 324, 328
*Much Ado about Nothing* **18:** 181, 190
*Othello* **11:** 304
*Richard II* **24:** 296, 333, 351
*Richard III* **14:** 455, 466
*Romeo and Juliet* **11:** 463
*The Taming of the Shrew* **12:** 357
*The Tempest* **8:** 390; **15:** 224, 273, 283
*Timon of Athens* **20:** 463
*Troilus and Cressida* **18:** 289, 327, 347
*Twelfth Night* **26:** 255, 263, 269, 284
*The Two Gentlemen of Verona* **12:** 457, 478, 484
*The Winter's Tale* **15:** 427, 482, 489

**Speaight, Robert W.**
*Pericles* **15:** 154

**Spedding, James**
*Henry VIII* **2:** 28

**Spencer, Anthony**
*Richard III* **14:** 357

**Spencer, Benjamin T.**
*Antony and Cleopatra* **6:** 159
*Henry IV, 1 and 2* **1:** 372

**Spencer, Hazelton**
*Henry IV, 1 and 2* **14:** 116
*Henry VI, 1, 2, and 3* **24:** 6
*Macbeth* **20:** 12
*Measure for Measure* **23:** 269, 276
*The Merry Wives of Windsor* **18:** 10
*Much Ado about Nothing* **8:** 47
*Richard II* **24:** 263
*Timon of Athens* **20:** 429
*Troilus and Cressida* **18:** 281

**Spencer, Janet M.**
*Henry V* **37:** 175

**Spencer, T. J. B.**
*Julius Caesar* **30:** 285
Shakespeare and Classical Civilization (topic entry) **27:** 56

**Spencer, Theodore**
*Hamlet* **1:** 169
*Henry IV, 1 and 2* **1:** 366
*King Lear* **2:** 174
*Macbeth* **3:** 248
*Pericles* **2:** 564
*The Two Noble Kinsmen* **9:** 463

**Spender, Stephen**
*Macbeth* **3:** 246

**Spinrad, Phoebe S.**
*King Lear* **46:** 264
*Measure for Measure* **22:** 85
*Much Ado about Nothing* **22:** 85

**Spivack, Bernard**
*Othello* **4:** 545
*Richard III* **8:** 213
*Titus Andronicus* **4:** 650

**Sprague, Arthur Colby**
*Hamlet* **21:** 11, 35, 392
*Henry IV, 1 and 2* **14:** 10, 133
*Henry V* **14:** 319
*Henry VI, 1, 2, and 3* **24:** 51
*Henry VIII* **24:** 140, 152
*Macbeth* **20:** 65, 113
*The Merchant of Venice* **12:** 36
*The Merry Wives of Windsor* **18:** 68
*Othello* **11:** 202, 257
*Richard II* **24:** 395
*Richard III* **14:** 517
*Twelfth Night* **26:** 360
*The Winter's Tale* **15:** 517

**Sprengnether, Madelon**
*Antony and Cleopatra* **13:** 368
*Coriolanus* **30:** 142
Psychoanalytic Interpretations (topic entry) **44:** 93

**Sprigg, Douglas C.**
*Troilus and Cressida* **18:** 442

**Spurgeon, Caroline F. E.**
*Antony and Cleopatra* **6:** 92
*Coriolanus* **9:** 64
*Cymbeline* **4:** 61
*Hamlet* **1:** 153
*Henry IV, 1 and 2* **1:** 358
*Henry VI, 1, 2, and 3* **3:** 52
*Henry VIII* **2:** 45
*Julius Caesar* **7:** 242
*King John* **9:** 246
*King Lear* **2:** 161
*Love's Labour's Lost* **2:** 320
*Macbeth* **3:** 245
*Measure for Measure* **2:** 431
*The Merchant of Venice* **4:** 241
*Much Ado about Nothing* **8:** 46
*Pericles* **2:** 560
*Richard II* **6:** 283
*Richard III* **8:** 186
*Romeo and Juliet* **5:** 456
*The Taming of the Shrew* **9:** 336
*Timon of Athens* **1:** 488
*The Winter's Tale* **7:** 418

**Spurling, Hilary**
*All's Well That Ends Well* **26:** 45
*As You Like It* **23:** 97
*Hamlet* **21:** 281
*Henry VIII* **24:** 116
*Julius Caesar* **17:** 372, 377
*King John* **24:** 217
*Macbeth* **20:** 259
*Measure for Measure* **23:** 323
*The Merry Wives of Windsor* **18:** 38
*Pericles* **15:** 149
*The Tempest* **15:** 270
*Troilus and Cressida* **18:** 344, 351

*Twelfth Night* **26:** 260, 267
*The Winter's Tale* **15:** 478

**Squire, Jack Collings**
*Macbeth* **20:** 172

**Squire, Sir John**
*Henry VIII* **2:** 44

**St. George, Andrew**
*Love's Labour's Lost* **23:** 229
*Measure for Measure* **23:** 356
*Richard II* **24:** 379

**St. John, Christopher**
*The Merry Wives of Windsor* **18:** 27

**Stack, Rev. Richard**
*Henry IV, 1 and 2* **1:** 306

**Staebler, Warren**
*As You Like It* **5:** 82

**Stallybrass, Peter**
*Macbeth* **29:** 120

**Stampfer, Judah**
*Julius Caesar* **7:** 339
*King Lear* **2:** 231

**Stanhope, Lord**
*Much Ado about Nothing* **8:** 8

**Stanislavski, Constantin**
*Othello* **11:** 233

**Stapfer, Paul**
*Julius Caesar* **7:** 169

**Stapleton, M. L.**
*Sonnets* **25:** 374

**Starkey, David**
*Henry VIII* **24:** 120

**Stauffer, Donald A.**
*Cymbeline* **4:** 87
*Julius Caesar* **7:** 257
*The Merry Wives of Windsor* **5:** 353
*Pericles* **2:** 569
*Romeo and Juliet* **5:** 469
*The Taming of the Shrew* **9:** 343
*The Two Gentlemen of Verona* **6:** 479

**Steadman, John M.**
*The Merry Wives of Windsor* **38:** 286

**Stedman, Jane W.**
*Pericles* **15:** 161
*The Tempest* **15:** 283

**Steele, Richard**
*Hamlet* **21:** 9

**Steele, Sir Richard**
See also Bickerstaff, Isaac
*Hamlet* **1:** 74
*Twelfth Night* **1:** 540

**Steevens, George**
See also Collier, Jeremy; Hic et

**Ubique; Longinus; Lorenzo**
  *Antony and Cleopatra* **6:** 24
  *The Comedy of Errors* **1:** 13
  *Cymbeline* **4:** 20, 21
  *King Lear* **11:** 7, 8
  *Macbeth* **3:** 182
  *Measure for Measure* **2:** 393
  *Much Ado about Nothing* **8:** 12
  *Pericles* **2:** 540
  *Richard III* **8:** 159
  *Sonnets* **10:** 155, 156
  *Titus Andronicus* **4:** 616
  *Troilus and Cressida* **3:** 538
  *Twelfth Night* **1:** 543
  *The Two Noble Kinsmen* **9:** 445
  *Venus and Adonis* **10:** 411

**Stein, Arnold**
  *Macbeth* **3:** 263
  *Troilus and Cressida* **43:** 277

**Stein, Rita**
  *Richard II* **24:** 353

**Steinberg, Theodore L.**
  *Venus and Adonis* **33:** 352

**Stempel, Daniel**
  *Antony and Cleopatra* **6:** 146
  *Othello* **35:** 336

**Stephenson, A. A., S.J.**
  *Cymbeline* **4:** 73

**Stephenson, William E.**
  *The Two Gentlemen of Verona* **6:** 514

**Sterne, Richard L.**
  *Hamlet* **21:** 237, 245

**Sternroyd, Vincent**
  *Much Ado about Nothing* **18:** 134

**Sterrit, David**
  *The Taming of the Shrew* **12:** 399

**Stewart, J. I. M.**
  *Henry IV, 1 and 2* **1:** 389
  *Julius Caesar* **7:** 250
  *Othello* **4:** 500

**Stewart, Patrick**
  *The Merchant of Venice* **12:** 97

**Still, Colin**
  *The Tempest* **8:** 328

**Stirling, Brents**
  *Antony and Cleopatra* **6:** 151
  *Julius Caesar* **7:** 259
  *Macbeth* **3:** 271
  *Othello* **4:** 486, 536
  *Richard II* **6:** 307

**Stockard, Emily E.**
  *Sonnets* **42:** 375

**Stockholder, Kay**
  *Macbeth* **44:** 297; **45:** 58
  *The Merchant of Venice* **45:** 17
  *The Winter's Tale* **45:** 358

**Stoker, Bram**
  *Much Ado about Nothing* **18:** 132
  *Romeo and Juliet* **11:** 433

**Stokes, Margaret**
  *As You Like It* **23:** 26
  *Romeo and Juliet* **11:** 406

**Stokes, Sewell**
  *King Lear* **11:** 53

**Stoll, Elmer Edgar**
  *All's Well That Ends Well* **7:** 41
  *Antony and Cleopatra* **6:** 76
  *As You Like It* **5:** 59, 75
  *Coriolanus* **9:** 72
  *Hamlet* **1:** 151
  *Henry IV, 1 and 2* **1:** 338
  *Henry V* **5:** 223
  *Measure for Measure* **2:** 460
  *The Merchant of Venice* **4:** 230, 445
  *Romeo and Juliet* **5:** 458
  *The Tempest* **8:** 345

**Stone, George Winchester, Jr.**
  *Antony and Cleopatra* **17:** 6
  *Cymbeline* **15:** 6
  *Hamlet* **21:** 23
  *Macbeth* **20:** 25
  *A Midsummer Night's Dream* **12:** 147
  *Much Ado about Nothing* **18:** 116
  *Othello* **11:** 183
  *Richard III* **14:** 366
  *Romeo and Juliet* **11:** 386
  *The Tempest* **15:** 203

**Storey, Graham**
  *Much Ado about Nothing* **8:** 79

**Strachey, Edward**
  *Hamlet* **1:** 102

**Strachey, Lytton**
  *The Tempest* **8:** 324

**Straumann, Heinrich**
  *The Phoenix and Turtle* **10:** 48

**Strehler, Giorgio**
  *The Tempest* **15:** 338

**Stribrny, Zdenek**
  *Henry V* **30:** 244

**Stubbes, George**
  *Hamlet* **1:** 76

**Styan, J. L.**
  *All's Well That Ends Well* **26:** 85, 117
  *As You Like It* **23:** 64, 118
  *A Midsummer Night's Dream* **12:** 215, 228, 264
  *The Winter's Tale* **15:** 451

**Suchet, David**
  *The Tempest* **15:** 374

**Suddard, Mary, S.J.**
  *Measure for Measure* **2:** 418

**Suhamy, Henri**
  *Hamlet* **35:** 241

**Sullivan, Dan**
  *Antony and Cleopatra* **17:** 43
  *Titus Andronicus* **17:** 460

**Sullivan, Patrick**
  *The Merchant of Venice* **12:** 83

**Summers, Joseph H.**
  *Twelfth Night* **1:** 591

**Summers, Montague**
  *Troilus and Cressida* **18:** 283

**Sundelson, David**
  *Measure for Measure* **2:** 528
  *The Tempest* **29:** 377

**Suzman, Janet**
  *Antony and Cleopatra* **17:** 113

**Swan, Christopher**
  *King John* **24:** 232

**Swander, Homer**
  *A Midsummer Night's Dream* **16:** 34

**Swander, Homer D.**
  *Cymbeline* **4:** 127

**Sweeney, Louise**
  *Macbeth* **20:** 273

**Swinarski, Konrad**
  *All's Well That Ends Well* **26:** 114

**Swinburne, Algernon Charles**
  *Antony and Cleopatra* **6:** 40
  *As You Like It* **5:** 42
  *The Comedy of Errors* **1:** 16
  *Coriolanus* **9:** 31
  *Cymbeline* **4:** 37
  *Henry IV, 1 and 2* **1:** 325
  *Henry V* **5:** 205
  *Henry VIII* **2:** 36
  *King Lear* **2:** 129
  *Love's Labour's Lost* **2:** 307
  *Much Ado about Nothing* **8:** 28
  *Othello* **4:** 423
  *Pericles* **2:** 550
  *The Rape of Lucrece* **10:** 69
  *Richard II* **6:** 282
  *Richard III* **8:** 167
  *Romeo and Juliet* **5:** 437
  *Troilus and Cressida* **3:** 548
  *The Two Gentlemen of Verona* **6:** 449
  *The Two Noble Kinsmen* **9:** 456
  *Venus and Adonis* **10:** 419
  *The Winter's Tale* **7:** 396

**Swinden, Patrick**
  *As You Like It* **5:** 138

**Sykes, H. Dugdale**
  *Pericles* **2:** 556

**Sylvester, Bickford**
  *The Rape of Lucrece* **10:** 93

**Symonds, John Addington**
  *Titus Andronicus* **4:** 627

**Symons, Arthur**
  *Antony and Cleopatra* **6:** 48
  *Coriolanus* **17:** 140
  *Titus Andronicus* **4:** 628

**Taciturnus, Frater (Kierkegaard, Seren)**
  *Hamlet* **1:** 102

**Taine, Nippolyte A.**
  *As You Like It* **5:** 35
  *Much Ado about Nothing* **8:** 27

**Talbert, Ernest William**
  *The Comedy of Errors* **1:** 43

**Tate, Nahum**
  *Julius Caesar* **7:** 149
  *King Lear* **2:** 92
  *Richard II* **6:** 250; **24:** 260

**Tatham, John**
  *Pericles* **2:** 537

**Tatlock, John S. P.**
  *Troilus and Cressida* **3:** 558

**Taubman, Howard**
  *The Comedy of Errors* **26:** 153
  *Cymbeline* **15:** 62
  *Hamlet* **21:** 236
  *Othello* **11:** 313
  *Timon of Athens* **20:** 455
  *Troilus and Cressida* **18:** 336

**Tave, Stuart M.**
  *A Midsummer Night's Dream* **45:** 175

**Tayler, Edward W.**
  *King Lear* **16:** 301

**Taylor, Anthony Brian**
  *A Midsummer Night's Dream* **16:** 25

**Taylor, Donn Ervin**
  *As You Like It* **34:** 102

**Taylor, Gary**
  *Henry V* **30:** 278
  Authorship Controversy (topic entry) **41:** 81

**Taylor, John Russell**
  *Macbeth* **20:** 272
  *Romeo and Juliet* **11:** 471
  *The Taming of the Shrew* **12:** 369

**Taylor, Mark**
  *Cymbeline* **15:** 66
  Fathers and Daughters (topic entry) **36:** 1
  *King Lear* **16:** 372
  *Macbeth* **16:** 372
  *A Midsummer Night's Dream* **29:** 269
  *The Tempest* **25:** 382
  *Twelfth Night* **16:** 372

**Taylor, Michael**
  *Cymbeline* **4**: 172
  *Pericles* **36**: 226

**Taylor, Paul**
  *Hamlet* **21**: 325, 332
  *Macbeth* **20**: 316
  *Richard II* **24**: 381
  *Twelfth Night* **26**: 335

**Teague, Frances**
  *Love's Labour's Lost* **23**: 222

**Tennenhouse, Leonard**
  Kingship (topic entry) **39**: 1
  Violence in Shakespeare's Works (topic entry) **43**: 12

**Tenschert, Joachim**
  *Coriolanus* **17**: 185

**Terry, Ellen**
  *Cymbeline* **15**: 23
  *Hamlet* **21**: 107
  *King John* **24**: 198
  *Macbeth* **20**: 144
  *The Merchant of Venice* **12**: 34, 114
  *The Merry Wives of Windsor* **18**: 27
  *A Midsummer Night's Dream* **12**: 187
  *Much Ado about Nothing* **18**: 245
  *Othello* **11**: 336
  *Romeo and Juliet* **11**: 434
  *The Winter's Tale* **15**: 429

**Thaler, Alwin**
  *The Two Gentlemen of Verona* **6**: 471

**Thatcher, David**
  *Measure for Measure* **32**: 81; **33**: 117

**Thayer, C. G.**
  *Henry V* **5**: 318

**Theobald, Lewis**
  *Henry V* **5**: 187
  *Henry VI, 1, 2, and 3* **3**: 18
  *Julius Caesar* **7**: 153
  *King John* **9**: 209
  *King Lear* **2**: 94
  *Love's Labour's Lost* **2**: 299
  *Measure for Measure* **2**: 388
  *Othello* **4**: 385
  *Timon of Athens* **1**: 454
  *Titus Andronicus* **4**: 613
  *Troilus and Cressida* **3**: 537
  *Twelfth Night* **1**: 540

**Thomas, Brook**
  *Cymbeline* **47**: 237

**Thomas, Ceridwen**
  *Measure for Measure* **23**: 358

**Thomas, Moy**
  *Hamlet* **21**: 101

**Thomas, Sidney**
  *King Lear* **32**: 308
  *Richard III* **8**: 190

**Thompson, Ann**
  *Comedy of Errors* **42**: 93
  *Cymbeline* **36**: 129
  *Love's Labour's Lost* **42**: 93

**Thompson, Karl F.**
  *Richard II* **6**: 321
  *Twelfth Night* **1**: 587
  *The Two Gentlemen of Verona* **6**: 488

**Thomson, Leslie**
  *Antony and Cleopatra* **13**: 374

**Thomson, Patricia**
  *Troilus and Cressida* **27**: 332

**Thomson, Peter**
  *Antony and Cleopatra* **17**: 62
  *As You Like It* **23**: 108
  *Cymbeline* **15**: 81
  *Hamlet* **21**: 294
  *Henry IV, 1 and 2* **14**: 91
  *King John* **24**: 218, 225
  *Measure for Measure* **23**: 328
  *A Midsummer Night's Dream* **12**: 260
  *Richard III* **14**: 467
  *The Taming of the Shrew* **12**: 484
  *Twelfth Night* **26**: 288

**Thomson, Richard**
  *Richard II* **24**: 352

**Thomson, Virgil**
  *Much Ado about Nothing* **18**: 249

**Thorne, W. B.**
  *Cymbeline* **4**: 129
  *Pericles* **2**: 584
  *The Taming of the Shrew* **9**: 393

**Thorp, Joseph**
  *Macbeth* **20**: 191

**Thorpe, Thomas**
  *Sonnets* **10**: 153

**Tice, Terrence N.**
  *Julius Caesar* **45**: 10

**Tieck, Ludwig**
  *Hamlet* **21**: 30

**Tierney, Margaret**
  *Antony and Cleopatra* **17**: 58

**Tiffany, Grace**
  *The Merry Wives of Windsor* **22**: 93; **38**: 319

**Tilley, Morris P.**
  *Twelfth Night* **1**: 563

**Tillyard, E. M. W.**
  *All's Well That Ends Well* **7**: 45
  *Antony and Cleopatra* **6**: 103
  *The Comedy of Errors* **1**: 46
  *Cymbeline* **4**: 68
  *Hamlet* **1**: 176
  *Henry IV, 1 and 2* **1**: 378
  *Henry V* **5**: 241
  *Henry VI, 1, 2, and 3* **3**: 59
  *King John* **9**: 254
  *Love's Labour's Lost* **2**: 340
  *Measure for Measure* **2**: 475
  *The Merchant of Venice* **4**: 282
  *Othello* **4**: 483
  *Pericles* **2**: 563
  *Richard II* **6**: 294
  *Richard III* **8**: 193
  *The Taming of the Shrew* **9**: 365
  *The Tempest* **8**: 359
  *Titus Andronicus* **4**: 639
  *The Winter's Tale* **7**: 429

**Tinker, Jack**
  *As You Like It* **23**: 140

**Tinkler, F. C.**
  *Cymbeline* **4**: 64
  *The Winter's Tale* **7**: 420

**Tofte, Robert**
  *Love's Labour's Lost* **2**: 299

**Toliver, Harold**
  *Antony and Cleopatra* **13**: 383

**Tolstoy, Leo**
  *Henry IV, 1 and 2* **1**: 337
  *King Lear* **2**: 145

**Tompkins, J. M. S.**
  *Pericles* **2**: 572

**Toole, William B.**
  *Richard III* **8**: 252

**Totten, Eileen**
  *Richard II* **24**: 346

**Tovey, Barbara**
  *The Merchant of Venice* **4**: 344

**Towse, John Ranken**
  *Hamlet* **21**: 107
  *Henry VIII* **24**: 83
  *King Lear* **11**: 26, 31
  *Measure for Measure* **23**: 281
  *The Merry Wives of Windsor* **18**: 28
  *Othello* **11**: 231
  *Richard II* **24**: 291

**Traci, Philip**
  *Antony and Cleopatra* **47**: 124
  *As You Like It* **46**: 127
  *The Merry Wives of Windsor* **38**: 313
  *The Two Gentlemen of Verona* **40**: 330

**Tracy, Robert**
  *Hamlet* **35**: 163

**Traister, Barbara Howard**
  Kingship (topic entry) **39**: 16
  Magic and the Supernatural (topic entry) **29**: 1

**Traub, Valerie**
  *Hamlet* **44**: 195
  *Henry IV, 1 and 2* **13**: 183
  *Henry V* **13**: 183
  Psychoanalytic Interpretations (topic entry) **44**: 44

**Traversi, Derek A.**
  *Antony and Cleopatra* **6**: 100
  *The Comedy of Errors* **1**: 39
  *Coriolanus* **9**: 73, 157
  *Cymbeline* **4**: 93
  *Henry IV, 1 and 2* **1**: 383
  *Henry V* **5**: 233
  *Julius Caesar* **7**: 303
  *Macbeth* **3**: 323
  *Measure for Measure* **2**: 452
  *The Merchant of Venice* **4**: 315
  *Othello* **4**: 493
  *The Taming of the Shrew* **9**: 362
  *The Tempest* **8**: 370
  *Troilus and Cressida* **3**: 621
  *The Two Gentlemen of Verona* **6**: 502
  *The Winter's Tale* **7**: 425

**Tree, Herbert Beerbohm**
  *Henry IV, 1 and 2* **14**: 19
  *Henry VIII* **24**: 89
  *Julius Caesar* **17**: 310
  *The Tempest* **15**: 228

**Tree, Maud**
  *Julius Caesar* **17**: 313
  *The Merry Wives of Windsor* **18**: 30

**Treglown, Jeremy**
  *All's Well That Ends Well* **26**: 50
  *Antony and Cleopatra* **17**: 69
  *As You Like It* **23**: 129
  *Cymbeline* **15**: 87

**Trench, Richard Chenevix**
  *Antony and Cleopatra* **6**: 39

**Trewin, J. C.**
  *All's Well That Ends Well* **26**: 46
  *Antony and Cleopatra* **17**: 33, 70
  *As You Like It* **23**: 20, 70, 82, 91, 95, 114, 126, 135
  *The Comedy of Errors* **26**: 146
  *Coriolanus* **17**: 160
  *Cymbeline* **15**: 48, 57, 68, 77, 87
  *Hamlet* **21**: 216, 224, 230, 293, 300
  *Henry IV, 1 and 2* **14**: 28, 58, 73
  *Henry V* **14**: 77, 318
  *Henry VI, 1, 2, and 3* **24**: 11, 21, 41
  *Henry VIII* **24**: 91, 118
  *Julius Caesar* **17**: 374
  *King Lear* **11**: 61, 66, 88, 110
  *Love's Labour's Lost* **23**: 184, 212
  *Macbeth* **20**: 187, 241, 252, 292, 311
  *Measure for Measure* **23**: 301, 309, 316, 322
  *A Midsummer Night's Dream* **12**: 236, 242, 248, 258
  *The Merry Wives of Windsor* **18**: 34, 47, 70
  *Much Ado about Nothing* **18**: 160, 163
  *Othello* **11**: 285, 291, 300
  *Pericles* **15**: 136, 142, 152, 160
  *Richard II* **24**: 335, 372
  *Richard III* **14**: 416, 419, 455, 457

*Romeo and Juliet* 11: 441
*The Taming of the Shrew* 12: 355, 385
*The Tempest* 15: 259, 266, 267, 282
*Timon of Athens* 20: 462
*Titus Andronicus* 17: 442, 456, 469
*Troilus and Cressida* 18: 306, 331, 345, 352, 358
*Twelfth Night* 26: 230, 244, 261, 295
*The Two Gentlemen of Verona* 12: 461, 474, 482
*The Winter's Tale* 15: 462, 464, 471

**Tricomi, Albert H.**
*Titus Andronicus* 4: 672; 27: 313

**Trotter, Stewart**
*The Comedy of Errors* 26: 151

**Truax, Elizabeth**
*Rape of Lucrece* 43: 77

**Turgenieff, Ivan**
*Hamlet* 1: 111

**Turner, Frederick**
*As You Like It* 46: 156
*The Tempest* 15: 335

**Turner, John**
*Hamlet* 16: 246
*King Lear* 31: 84

**Tyler, Thomas**
*Sonnets* 10: 226

**Tynan, Kenneth**
*King John* 24: 213
*Measure for Measure* 23: 298
*The Merchant of Venice* 12: 50
*A Midsummer Night's Dream* 12: 247
*Othello* 11: 278, 288, 289
*Pericles* 15: 141
*Richard II* 24: 317
*Richard III* 14: 420
*Romeo and Juliet* 11: 460
*The Taming of the Shrew* 12: 354
*The Tempest* 15: 257
*Titus Andronicus* 17: 439

**Ulrici, Hermann**
*All's Well That Ends Well* 7: 15
*Antony and Cleopatra* 6: 31
*As You Like It* 5: 30
*The Comedy of Errors* 1: 14
*Coriolanus* 9: 18
*Cymbeline* 4: 28
*Hamlet* 1: 98
*Henry IV, 1 and 2* 1: 314
*Henry V* 5: 195
*Henry VI, 1, 2, and 3* 3: 27
*Henry VIII* 2: 25
*Julius Caesar* 7: 160
*King John* 9: 222
*King Lear* 2: 112
*Love's Labour's Lost* 2: 303
*Macbeth* 3: 194
*Measure for Measure* 2: 399
*The Merchant of Venice* 4: 201
*The Merry Wives of Windsor* 5: 338
*A Midsummer Night's Dream* 3: 368
*Much Ado about Nothing* 8: 17
*Othello* 4: 412
*Pericles* 2: 544
*Richard II* 6: 263
*Richard III* 8: 163
*Romeo and Juliet* 5: 427
*Sonnets* 10: 182
*The Taming of the Shrew* 9: 322
*The Tempest* 8: 302
*Timon of Athens* 1: 462
*Titus Andronicus* 4: 618
*Troilus and Cressida* 3: 543
*Twelfth Night* 1: 546
*The Two Gentlemen of Verona* 6: 442
*The Winter's Tale* 7: 387

**Unger, Leonard**
*Henry IV, 1 and 2* 1: 406

**Uphaus, Robert W.**
*The Winter's Tale* 7: 501

**Upton, John**
*Coriolanus* 9: 11
*Henry IV, 1 and 2* 1: 289
*Julius Caesar* 7: 155
*Titus Andronicus* 4: 613
*The Two Gentlemen of Verona* 6: 436

**Ure, Peter**
*Timon of Athens* 1: 511

**Vache, Jean**
*Coriolanus* 17: 201

**Valesio, Paolo**
Madness (topic entry) 35: 40

**Van de Water, Julia C.**
*King John* 9: 271

**Van Doren, Mark**
*All's Well That Ends Well* 7: 39
*Antony and Cleopatra* 6: 104
*As You Like It* 5: 77
*The Comedy of Errors* 1: 30
*Coriolanus* 9: 78
*Cymbeline* 4: 70
*Henry IV, 1 and 2* 1: 365
*Henry V* 5: 230
*Henry VI, 1, 2, and 3* 3: 57
*Henry VIII* 2: 48
*Julius Caesar* 7: 242
*King John* 9: 251
*Measure for Measure* 2: 441
*The Merry Wives of Windsor* 5: 351
*Richard II* 6: 292
*Richard III* 8: 187
*Romeo and Juliet* 5: 463
*The Taming of the Shrew* 9: 338
*Timon of Athens* 1: 489
*Twelfth Night* 1: 575
*The Two Noble Kinsmen* 9: 469
*The Winter's Tale* 7: 432

**Van Laan, Thomas F.**
*Richard II* 6: 409
*Richard III* 8: 258

**Vandenbroucke, Russell**
*Cymbeline* 15: 78
*King John* 24: 224

**Vandenhoff, George**
*Romeo and Juliet* 11: 413

**Vaughan, Alden T.**
*The Tempest* 45: 219

**Vaughan, James N.**
*Richard III* 14: 411

**Vaughan, Virgina Mason**
*King John* 41: 221
*Othello* 28: 330
*The Tempest* 15: 379; 45: 219

**Velie, Alan R.**
*Pericles* 2: 585

**Velz, John W.**
*Julius Caesar* 7: 346
Shakespeare and Classical Civilization (topic entry) 27: 9

**Venezky, Alice**
*Henry VIII* 24: 112
*King Lear* 11: 62
*Much Ado about Nothing* 18: 157
*The Winter's Tale* 15: 463

**Vernon, Grenville**
*Julius Caesar* 17: 323
*Richard II* 24: 306, 309
*Twelfth Night* 26: 225

**Verplanck, Gulian C.**
*Pericles* 2: 545
*Timon of Athens* 1: 466
*Twelfth Night* 1: 550

**Vickers, Brian**
*Henry V* 5: 276
*The Merry Wives of Windsor* 5: 363
*Twelfth Night* 1: 650

**Vickers, Nancy J.**
*The Rape of Lucrece* 10: 131; 43: 102

**Victor, Benjamin**
*The Two Gentlemen of Verona* 6: 437; 12: 450

**Vidal, Gore**
*Much Ado about Nothing* 18: 164

**Videbaek, Bente A.**
*As You Like It* 46: 122, 210

**Vincent, Barbara C.**
*Antony and Cleopatra* 47: 149

**Voltaire, François-Marie Arouet de**
*Hamlet* 1: 80
*Julius Caesar* 7: 154

**Von Rumelin, Gustav**
*Macbeth* 3: 202

**Vyvyan, John**
*A Midsummer Night's Dream* 3: 437
*Romeo and Juliet* 5: 498
*The Two Gentlemen of Verona* 6: 494

**Waddington, Raymond B.**
*The Merchant of Venice* 40: 117

**Wade, Nicholas**
*Henry V* 14: 314

**Wain, John**
*Much Ado about Nothing* 8: 100
*Romeo and Juliet* 5: 524
*Twelfth Night* 26: 249

**Waith, Eugene M.**
*Antony and Cleopatra* 6: 172
*Macbeth* 3: 262; 20: 367
*Titus Andronicus* 4: 647; 17: 487; 27: 261
*The Two Noble Kinsmen* 41: 355

**Walcutt, Charles C.**
*Hamlet* 35: 82

**Waldock, A. J. A.**
*Hamlet* 1: 148

**Walker, Roy**
*As You Like It* 23: 87
*Henry V* 14: 266
*King John* 24: 215
*Macbeth* 3: 260
*The Merchant of Venice* 12: 51
*Timon of Athens* 20: 452
*Twelfth Night* 26: 251

**Walkley, A. B.**
*As You Like It* 23: 46
*Much Ado about Nothing* 18: 151
*The Two Gentlemen of Verona* 12: 457
*The Winter's Tale* 15: 445

**Wall, Stephen**
*Coriolanus* 17: 210
*Henry IV, 1 and 2* 14: 102
*Macbeth* 20: 310
*Measure for Measure* 23: 340, 357
*Troilus and Cressida* 18: 384
*The Winter's Tale* 15: 493

**Wallace, John M.**
*Coriolanus* 25: 296
*Timon of Athens* 27: 235

**Walley, Harold R.**
*The Merchant of Venice* 4: 243
*The Rape of Lucrece* 10: 84

**Walpole, Horace**
*The Winter's Tale* 7: 381

**Walter, J. H.**
*Henry V* 5: 257

**Walwyn, B.**
*The Merchant of Venice* **4**: 193

**Wanamaker, Zoe**
*Twelfth Night* **26**: 308

**Wangh, Martin**
*Othello* **4**: 503

**Wapshott, Nicholas**
*Hamlet* **21**: 232

**Warburton, William**
*As You Like It* **5**: 18
*Henry IV, 1 and 2* **1**: 287
*Julius Caesar* **7**: 155
*Love's Labour's Lost* **2**: 300
*Othello* **4**: 386
*The Tempest* **8**: 289
*The Two Noble Kinsmen* **9**: 445

**Ward, Adolphus William**
*Henry VI, 1, 2, and 3* **3**: 50

**Ward, David**
*Hamlet* **22**: 258

**Ward, John Paul**
*As You Like It* **46**: 134

**Warde, Frederick**
*Henry V* **14**: 195

**Wardle, Irving**
*Antony and Cleopatra* **17**: 76
*As You Like It* **23**: 96, 110, 114, 128, 137
*The Comedy of Errors* **26**: 157
*Coriolanus* **17**: 191
*Cymbeline* **15**: 72, 80
*Hamlet* **21**: 267, 280, 291, 296, 328, 330
*Henry IV, 1 and 2* **14**: 84, 89, 101
*Henry V* **14**: 286
*Henry VI, 1, 2, and 3* **24**: 45
*Henry VIII* **24**: 125
*Julius Caesar* **17**: 379, 405
*King John* **24**: 219, 234
*King Lear* **11**: 90, 108
*Love's Labour's Lost* **23**: 200, 203
*Macbeth* **20**: 256, 289, 299, 317
*Measure for Measure* **23**: 319, 326, 343
*The Merchant of Venice* **12**: 72
*The Merry Wives of Windsor* **18**: 48, 49
*A Midsummer Night's Dream* **12**: 253, 277
*Much Ado about Nothing* **18**: 177, 204
*Richard II* **24**: 335
*Richard III* **14**: 452, 462, 475
*The Taming of the Shrew* **12**: 384, 389, 409
*The Tempest* **15**: 269, 278
*Titus Andronicus* **17**: 465
*Troilus and Cressida* **18**: 341, 355, 350, 363, 381
*Twelfth Night* **26**: 265, 282, 301, 321, 336
*The Two Gentlemen of Verona* **12**: 481
*The Winter's Tale* **15**: 475, 492

**Warner, Beverley E.**
*Henry IV, 1 and 2* **1**: 328

**Warren, Roger**
*All's Well That Ends Well* **26**: 61; **38**: 80
*Antony and Cleopatra* **17**: 81
*As You Like It* **23**: 115, 126, 136, 143
*The Comedy of Errors* **26**: 161, 167
*Coriolanus* **17**: 214
*Cymbeline* **4**: 150; **15**: 88
*Hamlet* **21**: 316
*Henry IV, 1 and 2* **14**: 108
*Henry VI, 1, 2, and 3* **24**: 42
*Henry VIII* **24**: 121
*Julius Caesar* **17**: 390
*Love's Labour's Lost* **23**: 212
*Macbeth* **20**: 299, 312
*Measure for Measure* **23**: 342, 348
*The Merchant of Venice* **12**: 96
*The Merry Wives of Windsor* **18**: 62
*A Midsummer Night's Dream* **12**: 273, 285
*Much Ado about Nothing* **18**: 210
*Pericles* **15**: 172, 180; **16**: 399
*Romeo and Juliet* **11**: 485
*The Taming of the Shrew* **12**: 396
*Titus Andronicus* **17**: 475
*Troilus and Cressida* **18**: 366, 386
*Twelfth Night* **26**: 295, 305
*The Two Gentlemen of Verona* **12**: 495
*The Winter's Tale* **15**: 494

**Warton, Joseph**
*King Lear* **2**: 95
*The Tempest* **8**: 289

**Warton, Thomas**
*Romeo and Juliet* **5**: 419

**Wasson, John**
*Measure for Measure* **23**: 413

**Watkins, Ronald**
*Macbeth* **20**: 382

**Watkins, W. B. C.**
*Venus and Adonis* **10**: 429

**Watson, Donald G.**
*Venus and Adonis* **33**: 309

**Watson, Robert N.**
*Measure for Measure* **16**: 102
*Richard III* **8**: 267
*The Winter's Tale* **36**: 318

**Watt, David**
*Henry VI, 1, 2, and 3* **24**: 16
*The Tempest* **15**: 265

**Watters, Tammie**
*Antony and Cleopatra* **17**: 67

**Watts, Richard, Jr.**
*As You Like It* **23**: 72
*King Lear* **11**: 57

**Waugh, Evelyn**
*Titus Andronicus* **17**: 443

**Weales, Gerald**
*The Comedy of Errors* **26**: 177

**Webster, Margaret**
*Cymbeline* **15**: 121
*Henry IV, 1 and 2* **14**: 118
*Love's Labour's Lost* **23**: 250
*Macbeth* **20**: 374
*The Merry Wives of Windsor* **18**: 74
*A Midsummer Night's Dream* **12**: 293
*Much Ado about Nothing* **18**: 247
*Othello* **11**: 273, 342
*Richard II* **24**: 310
*Romeo and Juliet* **11**: 512
*The Taming of the Shrew* **9**: 340
*The Tempest* **15**: 253
*Timon of Athens* **20**: 491

**Wedmore, Frederick**
*King Lear* **11**: 33
*Macbeth* **20**: 142
*Othello* **11**: 222
*Romeo and Juliet* **11**: 425

**Weever, John**
*Julius Caesar* **7**: 148
*Venus and Adonis* **10**: 410

**Wehl, Feodor**
*A Midsummer Night's Dream* **12**: 167

**Weightman, J. G.**
*Henry V* **14**: 264

**Weightman, John**
*The Merchant of Venice* **12**: 76

**Weil, Herbert S.**
*Measure for Measure* **23**: 301

**Weimann, Robert**
*The Two Gentlemen of Verona* **6**: 524

**Weiner, Albert B.**
*Macbeth* **20**: 123

**Weinraub, Bernard**
*Macbeth* **20**: 273

**Weinstein, Philip M.**
*The Winter's Tale* **7**: 490

**Weiss, Theodore**
*The Comedy of Errors* **1**: 59

**Wekwerth, Manfred**
*Coriolanus* **17**: 185

**Weller, Barry**
*The Two Noble Kinsmen* **41**: 363

**Wells, Charles**
*Antony and Cleopatra* **27**: 126
Shakespeare and Classical Civilization (topic entry) **27**: 35

**Wells, Robert Headlam**
*Henry V* **37**: 187
Politics and Power (topic entry) **30**: 42

**Wells, Stanley**
*All's Well That Ends Well* **26**: 56
*Antony and Cleopatra* **17**: 83
*The Comedy of Errors* **26**: 163; 179
*Coriolanus* **17**: 172
*Hamlet* **21**: 259
*Julius Caesar* **17**: 397
*King John* **24**: 235; 240
*Macbeth* **29**: 101
*Measure for Measure* **23**: 372
*The Merry Wives of Windsor* **18**: 59
*A Midsummer Night's Dream* **12**: 188; **29**: 183
*Richard II* **24**: 356
*Richard III* **14**: 486
*The Taming of the Shrew* **12**: 398
*Timon of Athens* **20**: 472
*Titus Andronicus* **17**: 486
*Troilus and Cressida* **18**: 368
*Twelfth Night* **26**: 317
*The Two Gentlemen of Verona* **6**: 507; **12**: 492

**Wells, Stanley W.**
*The Tempest* **28**: 415

**Welsford, Enid**
*As You Like It* **5**: 75
*King Lear* **2**: 162
*A Midsummer Night's Dream* **3**: 397
*Twelfth Night* **1**: 571

**Welsh, Andrew**
*Pericles* **36**: 205

**Wendell, Barrett**
*Cymbeline* **4**: 43
*Twelfth Night* **1**: 560

**Wendlandt, Wilhelm**
*Timon of Athens* **1**: 473

**Wentersdorf, Karl P.**
*The Taming of the Shrew* **12**: 431

**Werder, Karl**
*Hamlet* **1**: 106

**Wesley, Samuel**
*Antony and Cleopatra* **6**: 20

**West, E. J.**
*Twelfth Night* **1**: 579

**West, Fred**
*Othello* **35**: 347

**West, Grace Starry**
*Titus Andronicus* **27**: 293

**West, Michael**
*The Taming of the Shrew* **9**: 404

**West, Rebecca**
*Hamlet* **1**: 218

**West, Robert H.**
  *King Lear* **2:** 265; **31:** 129

**West, Thomas G.**
  *Troilus and Cressida* **3:** 638

**Westlund, Joseph**
  *All's Well That Ends Well* **38:** 96
  *Cymbeline* **45:** 75
  *The Tempest* **32:** 400

**Whately, Thomas**
  *Macbeth* **3:** 177
  *Richard III* **8:** 148

**Wheeler, Richard P.**
  Fathers and Daughters (topic entry) **36:** 70
  *Hamlet* **44:** 152
  Psychoanalytic Interpretations (topic entry) **44:** 18
  *Richard III* **39:** 326
  *The Tempest* **45:** 259

**Whitaker, Virgil K.**
  *Julius Caesar* **7:** 264

**White, Antonia**
  *The Taming of the Shrew* **12:** 349

**White, Howard B.**
  *Timon of Athens* **27:** 223

**White, R. S.**
  *The Merry Wives of Windsor* **38:** 307

**White, Richard Grant**
  *As You Like It* **23:** 167
  *Henry IV, 1 and 2* **1:** 327
  *Much Ado about Nothing* **8:** 23
  *Othello* **4:** 424

**Whitebait, William**
  *Hamlet* **21:** 198
  *Richard III* **14:** 422

**Whitehead, Frank**
  *King Lear* **22:** 271

**Whitehead, Ted**
  *Hamlet* **21:** 308

**Whiter, Walter**
  *As You Like It* **5:** 21

**Whitney, Charles**
  *Henry VIII* **28:** 203

**Whittaker, Herbert**
  *All's Well That Ends Well* **26:** 22
  *A Midsummer Night's Dream* **12:** 239

**Whittier, Gayle**
  General Commentary **13:** 530

**Whitworth, C. W.**
  *The Comedy of Errors* **26:** 165

**Wickham, Glynn**
  *The Tempest* **29:** 339
  *The Two Noble Kinsmen* **41:** 289

**Wiess, Theodore**
  *Henry IV, 1 and 2* **39:** 72

**Wigston, W. F. C.**
  *The Phoenix and Turtle* **10:** 7
  *The Winter's Tale* **7:** 397

**Wilcher, Robert**
  *Twelfth Night* **46:** 303

**Willbern, David**
  *The Rape of Lucrece* **33:** 179

**Willems, Michèle**
  *Henry IV, Parts 1 and 2* **47:** 60

**Wilcher, Robert**
  *As You Like It* **5:** 166

**Wilcox, Helen**
  Gender Identity (topic entry) **40:** 99

**Wilde, Oscar**
  *Sonnets* **10:** 218

**Wilkes, Thomas**
  *Macbeth* **20:** 20
  *Othello* **4:** 389
  *Richard III* **14:** 363

**Willbern, David**
  *Henry IV, Parts 1 and 2* **42:** 185
  <*Titus Andronicus* **4:** 675

**Willcock, Gladys Doidge**
  *Love's Labour's Lost* **2:** 319

**Willeford, William**
  Clowns and Fools (topic entry) **46:** 74

**William, David**
  *The Merry Wives of Windsor* **18:** 84
  *The Tempest* **15:** 352

**Williams, Charles**
  *Henry V* **5:** 228
  *Troilus and Cressida* **3:** 568

**Williams, Clifford**
  *The Comedy of Errors* **26:** 188

**Williams, Gary Jay**
  *A Midsummer Night's Dream* **12:** 153, 161, 278
  *Timon of Athens* **20:** 481

**Williams, George Walton**
  *Macbeth* **28:** 339

**Williams, Gordon**
  *Macbeth* **20:** 343
  *Venus and Adonis* **33:** 347

**Williams, Gwyn**
  *The Comedy of Errors* **1:** 45; **34:** 229

**Williams, Harcourt**
  *Macbeth* **20:** 186
  *Much Ado about Nothing* **18:** 134

**Williams, John T.**
  *Richard III* **14:** 528
  *The Tempest* **15:** 371

**Williams, Mary C.**
  *Much Ado about Nothing* **8:** 125

**Williams, Simon**
  *A Midsummer Night's Dream* **12:** 168

**Williams, Stanley T.**
  *Timon of Athens* **20:** 476

**Williamson, Audrey**
  *All's Well That Ends Well* **26:** 41
  *Coriolanus* **17:** 159
  *Henry IV, 1 and 2* **14:** 35
  *Henry VIII* **24:** 113
  *King John* **24:** 206
  *Macbeth* **20:** 186, 234
  *Othello* **11:** 279
  *Richard II* **24:** 304, 315
  *The Tempest* **15:** 234
  *Troilus and Cressida* **18:** 318

**Williamson, Jane**
  *Measure for Measure* **23:** 363

**Williamson, Marilyn L.**
  *All's Well That Ends Well* **38:** 99
  *Henry V* **5:** 302; **30:** 259
  *Romeo and Juliet* **5:** 571

**Williamson, Nicol**
  *Hamlet* **21:** 268

**Willis, Deborah**
  *The Tempest* **13:** 440

**Willis, Susan**
  *Troilus and Cressida* **18:** 371

**Wills, Garry**
  *Coriolanus* **17:** 223
  *Hamlet* **21:** 244

**Wilmeth, Don B.**
  *Richard III* **14:** 370

**Wilson, Daniel**
  *The Tempest* **8:** 309

**Wilson, Edmund**
  *Henry IV, 1 and 2* **1:** 393

**Wilson, Harold S.**
  *Measure for Measure* **2:** 490
  *Romeo and Juliet* **5:** 487

**Wilson, John Dover**
  *Antony and Cleopatra* **6:** 133
  *As You Like It* **5:** 114
  *Hamlet* **1:** 138, 154
  *Henry IV, 1 and 2* **1:** 125, 366, 373
  *Henry V* **5:** 246
  *Henry VI, 1, 2, and 3* **3:** 66
  *Julius Caesar* **7:** 253
  *King Lear* **2:** 160
  *Love's Labour's Lost* **2:** 342; **23:** 252
  *The Merry Wives of Windsor* **5:** 360
  *Much Ado about Nothing* **31:** 171

  *Richard II* **6:** 289
  *Sonnets* **10:** 334
  *The Tempest* **8:** 348
  *Titus Andronicus* **4:** 642
  *Venus and Adonis* **10:** 427

**Wilson, Milton**
  *Hamlet* **21:** 220

**Wilson, Rawdon R.**
  *As You Like It* **46:** 169
  *The Rape of Lucrece* **33:** 169

**Wilson, Richard**
  *Julius Caesar* **22:** 280

**Wilson, Rob**
  Psychoanalytic Interpretations (topic entry) **44:** 57

**Wincor, Richard**
  *Pericles* **2:** 570
  *The Winter's Tale* **7:** 451

**Wingate, Charles E. L.**
  *King Lear* **11:** 119
  *Macbeth* **20:** 103
  *Much Ado about Nothing* **18:** 115
  *The Taming of the Shrew* **12:** 411

**Winny, James**
  *Henry IV, 1 and 2* **1:** 424
  *Henry V* **5:** 281
  *Henry VI, 1, 2, and 3* **3:** 115
  *Richard II* **6:** 368
  *Sonnets* **10:** 337

**Winstanley, William**
  *Richard III* **8:** 145

**Winter, Jack**
  *The Taming of the Shrew* **12:** 366

**Winter, William**
  *Antony and Cleopatra* **6:** 51
  *As You Like It* **23:** 27
  *Coriolanus* **17:** 132
  *Cymbeline* **15:** 21, 43, 96
  *Hamlet* **21:** 64, 143
  *Henry IV, 1 and 2* **14:** 9
  *Henry VIII* **24:** 129
  *Julius Caesar* **17:** 284, 286
  *King Lear* **11:** 25
  *Measure for Measure* **23:** 281
  *The Merry Wives of Windsor* **18:** 14, 17, 18, 29, 66, 126
  *A Midsummer Night's Dream* **12:** 192, 225, 280
  *Richard II* **24:** 289
  *Richard III* **14:** 503
  *Romeo and Juliet* **11:** 416, 423
  *The Taming of the Shrew* **12:** 414
  *Twelfth Night* **26:** 207, 212
  *The Winter's Tale* **15:** 442

**Winton, Calhoun**
  *Henry V* **14:** 178

**Wittenburg, Robert**
  *The Tempest* **29:** 362

**Witts, Noel**
  *As You Like It* **23:** 113

**Wixson, Douglas C.**
*King John* **9**: 300

**Wofford, Susanne L.**
*As You Like It* **28**: 82

**Wolf, Matt**
*Antony and Cleopatra* **17**: 81

**Womersley, David**
*King John* **13**: 163

**Wood, Glena D.**
*King Lear* **46**: 191

**Wood, James O.**
*Pericles* **2**: 583

**Wood, Robert E.**
*The Comedy of Errors* **26**: 190

**Wood, Roger**
*All's Well That Ends Well* **26**: 37
*Henry V* **14**: 260
*King John* **24**: 203
*Othello* **11**: 280
*Troilus and Cressida* **18**: 314

**Woodbridge, Linda**
Shakespeare's Representation of Women (topic entry) **31**: 41

**Woods, George B.**
*Hamlet* **21**: 78

**Woollcott, Alexander**
*A Midsummer Night's Dream* **12**: 224

**Worden, Blair**
General Commentary **22**: 395

**Wordsworth, William**
*Sonnets* **10**: 159, 160, 167

**Worsley, T. C.**
*Antony and Cleopatra* **17**: 31
*As You Like It* **23**: 94
*The Comedy of Errors* **26**: 145
*Cymbeline* **15**: 45, 58, 64
*Hamlet* **21**: 225
*Henry IV, 1 and 2* **14**: 38, 39, 56
*Henry V* **14**: 256
*Henry VI, 1, 2, and 3* **24**: 17
*Julius Caesar* **17**: 366
*King Lear* **11**: 58, 60, 65
*Macbeth* **20**: 188, 221, 239
*Measure for Measure* **23**: 297, 311, 313
*The Merchant of Venice* **12**: 52
*The Merry Wives of Windsor* **18**: 36
*Much Ado about Nothing* **18**: 157, 177
*Othello* **11**: 276
*Pericles* **15**: 143
*Richard II* **24**: 305, 320, 322
*The Taming of the Shrew* **12**: 353
*Titus Andronicus* **17**: 441
*Troilus and Cressida* **18**: 313, 319, 330
*Twelfth Night* **26**: 229, 245, 256

**Worthen W. B.**
*Antony and Cleopatra* **47**: 142

**Wotton, Sir Henry**
*Henry VIII* **2**: 14

**Woudhuysen, H. R.**
*Titus Andronicus* **17**: 478
*Twelfth Night* **26**: 325

**Wright, Abraham**
*Othello* **4**: 370

**Wright, Laurence**
*The Winter's Tale* **36**: 344

**Wright, Neil H.**
*The Tempest* **8**: 447

**Wyatt, Euphemia Van Rensselaer**
*Julius Caesar* **17**: 325
*Macbeth* **20**: 201, 230, 233
*The Merchant of Venice* **12**: 63
*Much Ado about Nothing* **18**: 174
*The Tempest* **15**: 245
*Twelfth Night* **26**: 228
*The Two Gentlemen of Verona* **12**: 471

**Wylie, Betty Jane**
*Pericles* **15**: 181

**Wyndham, George**
*Sonnets* **10**: 236
*Venus and Adonis* **10**: 420

**Wynne-David, Marion**
*Titus Andronicus* **27**: 266

**Yates, Frances A.**
*Henry VIII* **2**: 71
*Cymbeline* **47**: 219

**Yearling, Elizabeth M.**
*Twelfth Night* **1**: 664

**Yeats, W. B.**
*Henry IV, 1 and 2* **1**: 332
*Henry V* **5**: 210
*Richard II* **6**: 277

**Yoder, R. A.**
*Troilus and Cressida* **3**: 626

**Young, B. A.**
*All's Well That Ends Well* **26**: 43
*Antony and Cleopatra* **17**: 55
*As You Like It* **23**: 104, 112, 121
*Hamlet* **21**: 252
*Henry V* **14**: 271, 275, 279
*Henry VI, 1, 2, and 3* **24**: 19, 30
*Julius Caesar* **17**: 377, 379
*King John* **24**: 220
*Love's Labour's Lost* **23**: 196, 203, 207
*Macbeth* **20**: 256, 292, 307
*Measure for Measure* **23**: 319, 326
*The Merry Wives of Windsor* **18**: 40, 46, 47
*Much Ado about Nothing* **18**: 187, 203, 209
*Pericles* **15**: 147
*Richard III* **14**: 462
*The Taming of the Shrew* **12**: 382, 388
*The Tempest* **15**: 268
*Timon of Athens* **20**: 461
*Titus Andronicus* **17**: 464
*Troilus and Cressida* **18**: 340, 354
*Twelfth Night* **26**: 281

**Young, Bruce W.**
*The Winter's Tale* **36**: 328

**Young, C. B.**
*Cymbeline* **15**: 102
*Henry VIII* **24**: 136
*Julius Caesar* **17**: 408
*Pericles* **15**: 178
*Richard III* **14**: 507

**Young, David**
*As You Like It* **23**: 102
*Macbeth* **16**: 317
*The Tempest* **29**: 323

**Young, David P.**
*As You Like It* **5**: 135
*A Midsummer Night's Dream* **3**: 453; **29**: 190

**Young, Julian Charles**
*Coriolanus* **17**: 132
*Julius Caesar* **17**: 273

**Young, Stark**
*Hamlet* **21**: 148
*Julius Caesar* **17**: 321
*Othello* **11**: 270
*Richard II* **24**: 307
*Richard III* **14**: 412
*The Taming of the Shrew* **12**: 344
*Troilus and Cressida* **18**: 295
*Twelfth Night* **26**: 224

**Zarkin, Robert**
*The Tempest* **15**: 297

**Zender, Karl F.**
*Macbeth* **3**: 336
*Measure for Measure* **28**: 92; **33**: 77
*Othello* **28**: 344

**Zimbardo, Rose A.**
*Henry V* **5**: 264
*A Midsummer Night's Dream* **3**: 468

**Zinter, Sheldon P.**
*All's Well That Ends Well* **26**: 91, 128; **38**: 150
*Henry IV, 1 and 2* **14**: 156

# Cumulative Topic Index

The Cumulative Topic Index identifies the principal topics of discussion in the criticism of each play and non-dramatic poem. The topics are arranged alphabetically. Page references indicate the beginning page number of each essay containing substantial commentary on that topic. A parenthetical reference after a topic indicates that the topic is extensively discussed in that volume.

**absurdities, inconsistencies, and shortcomings**
*The Two Gentlemen of Verona* **6:** 435, 436, 437, 439, 464, 507, 541, 560

**accident or chance**
*Romeo and Juliet* **5:** 418, 444, 448, 467, 470, 487, 573

**acting and dissimulation**
*Richard II* **6:** 264, 267, 307, 310, 315, 368, 393, 409; **24:** 339, 345, 346, 349, 352, 356

**adolescence**
*Romeo and Juliet* **33:** 249, 255, 257

**adultery**
*The Comedy of Errors* **34:** 215

**aggression**
*Coriolanus* **9:** 112, 142, 174, 183, 189, 198; **30:** 79, 111, 125, 142; **44:** 11, 79

**alienation**
*Timon of Athens* **1:** 523; **27:** 161

**allegorical elements**
*King Lear* **16:** 311
*The Merchant of Venice* **4:** 224, 250, 261, 268, 270, 273, 282, 289, 324, 336, 344, 350
*The Phoenix and Turtle* **10:** 7, 8, 9, 16, 17, 48; **38:** 334, 378
*The Rape of Lucrece* **10:** 89, 93
*Richard II* **6:** 264, 283, 323, 385
*The Tempest* **8:** 294, 295, 302, 307, 308, 312, 326, 328, 336, 345, 364; **42:** 320
*Venus and Adonis* **10:** 427, 434, 439, 449, 454, 462, 480; **28:** 355; **33:** 309, 330

**ambiguity**
*Antony and Cleopatra* **6:** 53, 111, 161, 163, 180, 189, 208, 211, 228; **13:** 368
*Hamlet* **1:** 92, 160, 198, 227, 230, 234, 247, 249; **21:** 72; **35:** 241
*King John* **13:** 152; **41:** 243
*Measure for Measure* **2:** 417, 420, 432, 446, 449, 452, 474, 479, 482, 486, 495, 505
*A Midsummer Night's Dream* **3:** 401, 459, 486; **45:** 169
*Richard III* **44:** 11; **47:** 15
*Sonnets* **10:** 251, 256; **28:** 385; **40:** 221, 228, 268
*Troilus and Cressida* **3:** 544, 568, 583, 587, 589, 599, 611, 621; **27:** 400; **43:** 305
*Twelfth Night* **1:** 554, 639; **34:** 287, 316
*Venus and Adonis* **10:** 434, 454, 459, 462, 466, 473, 480, 486, 489; **33:** 352

**ambition or pride**
*Henry VIII* **2:** 15, 38, 67
*Macbeth* **44:** 284, 324

**ambivalent or ironic elements**
*Henry VI, Parts 1, 2, and 3* **3:** 69, 151, 154; **39:** 160
*Richard III* **44:** 11
*Troilus and Cressida* **43:** 340

**amorality, question of**
*The Two Noble Kinsmen* **9:** 447, 460, 492

**amour-passion or *Liebestod* myth**
*Romeo and Juliet* **5:** 484, 489, 528, 530, 542, 550, 575; **32:** 256

**amputations, significance of**
*Titus Andronicus* **48:** 264

**anachronisms**
*Julius Caesar* **7:** 331

**androgyny**
*Antony and Cleopatra* **13:** 530
*As You Like It* **23:** 98, 100, 122, 138, 143, 144; **34:** 172, 177; **46:** 134
*Romeo and Juliet* **13:** 530

**anti-Catholic rhetoric**
*King John* **22:** 120; **25:** 98

**anti-romantic elements**
*As You Like It* **34:** 72

**antithetical or contradictory elements**
*Macbeth* **3:** 185, 213, 271, 302; **25:** 235; **29:** 76, 127; **47:** 41

**anxiety**
*Romeo and Juliet* **13:** 235

**appearance, perception, and illusion**
*A Midsummer Night's Dream* **3:** 368, 411, 425, 427, 434, 447, 459, 466, 474, 477, 486, 497, 516; **19:** 21; **22:** 39; **28:** 15; **29:** 175, 190; **45:** 136

**Appearance versus Reality** (Volume **34**: 1, 5, 12, 23, 45, 54)
   *All's Well That Ends Well* **7**: 37, 76, 93; **26**: 117
   *As You Like It* **34**: 130, 131; **46**: 105
   *The Comedy of Errors* **34**: 194, 201
   *Coriolanus* **30**: 142
   *Cymbeline* **4**: 87, 93, 103, 162; **36**: 99; **47**: 228, 286
   *Hamlet* **1**: 95, 116, 166, 169, 198; **35**: 82, 126, 132, 144, 238; **44**: 248; **45**: 28
   *Macbeth* **3**: 241, 248; **25**: 235
   *The Merchant of Venice* **4**: 209, 261, 344; **12**: 65; **22**: 69
   *Much Ado about Nothing* **8**: 17, 18, 48, 63, 69, 73, 75, 79, 88, 95, 115; **31**: 198, 209
   *The Taming of the Shrew* **9**: 343, 350, 353, 365, 369, 370, 381, 390, 430; **12**: 416; **31**: 326
   *Timon of Athens* **1**: 495, 500, 515, 523
   *The Two Gentlemen of Verona* **6**: 494, 502, 511, 519, 529, 532, 549, 560
   *Twelfth Night* **34**: 293, 301, 311, 316
   *The Winter's Tale* **7**: 429, 446, 479

**appetite**
   *Twelfth Night* **1**: 563, 596, 609, 615

**archetypal or mythic elements**
   *Macbeth* **16**: 317

**archetypal structure**
   *Pericles* **2**: 570, 580, 582, 584, 588; **25**: 365

**aristocracy and aristocratic values**
   *As You Like It* **34**: 120
   *Hamlet* **42**: 212
   *Julius Caesar* **16**: 231; **22**: 280; **30**: 379

**art and nature**
   See also **nature**
   *Pericles* **22**: 315; **36**: 233
   *The Phoenix and Turtle* **10**: 7, 42

**art versus nature**
   See also **nature**
   *As You Like It* **5**: 128, 130, 148; **34**: 147
   *The Tempest* **8**: 396, 404; **29**: 278, 297, 362
   *The Winter's Tale* **7**: 377, 381, 397, 419, 452; **36**: 289, 318; **45**: 329

**artificial nature**
   *Love's Labour's Lost* **2**: 315, 317, 324, 330; **23**: 207, 233

**Athens**
   *Timon of Athens* **27**: 223, 230

**Athens and the forest, contrast between**
   *A Midsummer Night's Dream* **3**: 381, 427, 459, 466, 497, 502; **29**: 175

**assassination**
   *Julius Caesar* **7**: 156, 161, 179, 191, 200, 221, 264, 272, 279, 284, 350; **25**: 272; **30**: 326

**audience interpretation**
   *Julius Caesar* **48**: 240

**audience perception**
   *The Comedy of Errors* **1**: 37, 50, 56; **19**: 54; **34**: 258
   *King Lear* **19**: 295; **28**: 325
   *Richard II* **24**: 414, 423; **39**: 295
   *Pericles* **42**: 352; **48**: 364

**audience perception, Shakespeare's manipulation of**
   *The Winter's Tale* **7**: 394, 429, 456, 483, 501; **13**: 417; **19**: 401, 431, 441; **25**: 339; **45**: 374

**audience perspective**
   *All's Well That Ends Well* **7**: 81, 104, 109, 116, 121

**audience response**
   *Antony and Cleopatra* **48**: 206
   *Hamlet* **28**: 325; **32**: 238; **35**: 167; **44**: 107
   *Julius Caesar* **7**: 179, 238, 253, 255, 272, 316, 320, 336, 350; **19**: 321; **48**: 240
   *Macbeth* **20**: 17, 400, 406; **29**: 139, 146, 155, 165; **44**: 306
   *Measure for Measure* **48**: 1

**audience versus character perceptions**
   *The Two Gentlemen of Verona* **6**: 499, 519, 524

**authenticity**
   *The Phoenix and Turtle* **10**: 7, 8, 16
   *Sonnets* **10**: 153, 154, 230, 243; **48**: 325

**Authorship Controversy** (Volume **41**: 2, 5, 18, 32, 42, 48, 57, 61, 63, 66, 76, 81, 85, 98, 110)
   *Cymbeline* **4**: 17, 21, 35, 48, 56, 78
   *Henry VI, Parts 1, 2, and 3* **3**: 16, 18, 19, 20, 21, 26, 27, 29, 31, 35, 39, 41, 55, 66; **24**: 51
   *Henry VIII* **2**: 16, 18, 19, 22, 23, 27, 28, 31, 35, 36, 42, 43, 44, 46, 48, 51, 58, 64, 68; **41**: 129, 146, 158, 171
   *Love's Labour's Lost* **2**: 299, 300; **32**: 308
   *Pericles* **2**: 538, 540, 543, 544, 545, 546, 548, 550, 551, 553, 556, 558, 564, 565, 568, 576, 586; **15**: 132, 141, 148, 152; **16**: 391, 399; **25**: 365; **36**: 198, 244
   *Timon of Athens* **1**: 464, 466, 467, 469, 474, 477, 478, 480, 490, 499, 507, 518; **16**: 351; **20**: 433
   *Titus Andronicus* **4**: 613, 614, 615, 616, 617, 619, 623, 624, 625, 626, 628, 631, 632, 635, 642
   *The Two Gentlemen of Verona* **6**: 435, 436, 437, 438, 439, 449, 466, 476
   *The Two Noble Kinsmen*
     Shakespeare not a co-author **9**: 445, 447, 455, 461
     Shakespearean portions of the text **9**: 446, 447, 448, 455, 456, 457, 460, 462, 463, 471, 479, 486; **41**: 308, 317, 355
     Shakespeare's part in the overall conception or design **9**: 444, 446, 448, 456, 457, 460, 480, 481, 486, 490; **37**: 313; **41**: 326

**autobiographical elements**
   *As You Like It* **5**: 25, 35, 43, 50, 55, 61
   *The Comedy of Errors* **1**: 16, 18
   *Cymbeline* **4**: 43, 46; **36**: 134
   *Hamlet* **1**: 98, 115, 119; **13**: 487

*Henry VI, Parts 1, 2, and 3* **3**: 41, 55
*King John* **9**: 209, 218, 245, 248, 260, 292
*King Lear* **2**: 131, 136, 149, 165
*Measure for Measure* **2**: 406, 410, 414, 431, 434, 437
*A Midsummer Night's Dream* **3**: 365, 371, 379, 381, 389, 391, 396, 402, 432
*Othello* **4**: 440, 444
*Pericles* **2**: 551, 554, 555, 563, 581
*The Phoenix and Turtle* **10**: 14, 18, 42, 48
*Sonnets* **10**: 159, 160, 166, 167, 175, 176, 182, 196, 205, 213, 215, 226, 233, 238, 240, 251, 279, 283, 302, 309, 325, 337, 377; **13**: 487; **16**: 461; **28**: 363, 385; **42**: 296; **48**: 325
*The Tempest* **8**: 302, 308, 312, 324, 326, 345, 348, 353, 364, 380
*Timon of Athens* **1**: 462, 467, 470, 473, 474, 478, 480; **27**: 166, 175
*Titus Andronicus* **4**: 619, 624, 625, 664
*Troilus and Cressida* **3**: 548, 554, 557, 558, 574, 606, 630
*Twelfth Night* **1**: 557, 561, 599; **34**: 338
*The Winter's Tale* **7**: 395, 397, 410, 419

**avarice**
   *The Merry Wives of Windsor* **5**: 335, 353, 369, 376, 390, 395, 402

**battle of Agincourt**
   *Henry V* **5**: 197, 199, 213, 246, 257, 281, 287, 289, 293, 310, 318; **19**: 217; **30**: 181

**battle of the sexes**
   *Much Ado about Nothing* **8**: 14, 16, 19, 48, 91, 95, 111, 121, 125; **31**: 231, 245

**bawdy elements**
   *As You Like It* **46**: 122
   *Cymbeline* **36**: 155

**bear-baiting**
   *Twelfth Night* **19**: 42

**beauty**
   *Sonnets* **10**: 247
   *Venus and Adonis* **10**: 420, 423, 427, 434, 454, 480; **33**: 330, 352

**bed-trick**
   *All's Well That Ends Well* **7**: 8, 26, 27, 29, 32, 41, 86, 93, 98, 113, 116, 126; **13**: 84; **26**: 117; **28**: 38; **38**: 65, 118
   *Measure for Measure* **13**: 84

**bird imagery**
   *The Phoenix and Turtle* **10**: 21, 27; **38**: 329, 350, 367

**body, role of**
   *Troilus and Cressida* **42**: 66

**body politic, metaphor of**
   *Coriolanus* **22**: 248; **30**: 67, 96, 105, 125

**bonding**
   *The Merchant of Venice* **4**: 293, 317, 336; **13**: 37

**British nationalism**
See also **nationalism and patriotism**
Cymbeline **4:** 19, 78, 89, 93, 129, 141, 159, 167; **32:** 373; **36:** 129; **45:** 6; **47:** 219, 265

**brutal elements**
A Midsummer Night's Dream **3:** 445, 491, 497, 511; **12:** 259, 262, 298; **16:** 34; **19:** 21; **29:** 183, 225, 263, 269; **45:** 169

**Caesarism**
Julius Caesar **7:** 159, 160, 161, 167, 169, 174, 191, 205, 218, 253, 310; **30:** 316, 321

**Calvinist implications**
Hamlet **48:** 195

**capriciousness of the young lovers**
A Midsummer Night's Dream **3:** 372, 395, 402, 411, 423, 437, 441, 450, 497, 498; **29:** 175, 269; **45:** 107

**caricature**
The Merry Wives of Windsor **5:** 343, 347, 348, 350, 385, 397

**carnival elements**
Henry IV, Parts 1 and 2 **28:** 203; **32:** 103
Henry VI, Parts 1, 2, and 3 **22:** 156
Richard II **19:** 151; **39:** 273

**censorship**
Richard II **24:** 260, 261, 262, 263, 386; **42:** 118

**ceremonies, rites, and rituals, importance of**
See also **pageantry**
Coriolanus **9:** 139, 148, 169
Hamlet **13:** 268; **28:** 232
Julius Caesar **7:** 150, 210, 255, 259, 268, 284, 316, 331, 339, 356; **13:** 260; **22:** 137; **30:** 374
Richard II **6:** 270, 294, 315, 368, 381, 397, 409, 414; **24:** 274, 356, 411, 414, 419
Titus Andronicus **27:** 261; **32:** 265; **48:** 264
The Two Noble Kinsmen **9:** 492, 498

**change**
Henry VIII **2:** 27, 65, 72, 81

**characterization**
As You Like It **5:** 19, 24, 25, 36, 39, 54, 82, 86, 116, 148; **34:** 72; **48:** 42
The Comedy of Errors **1:** 13, 21, 31, 34, 46, 49, 50, 55, 56; **19:** 54; **25:** 63; **34:** 194, 201, 208, 245
Henry IV, Parts 1 and 2 **1:** 321, 328, 332, 333, 336, 344, 365, 383, 385, 389, 391, 397, 401; **19:** 195; **39:** 123, 137; **42:** 99, 162
Henry V **5:** 186, 189, 192, 193, 199, 219, 230, 233, 252, 276, 293; **30:** 227, 278; **42:** 162
Henry VI, Parts 1, 2, and 3 **3:** 18, 20, 24, 25, 31, 57, 64, 73, 77, 109, 119, 151; **24:** 22, 28, 38, 42, 45, 47; **39:** 160; **47:** 32
Henry VIII **2:** 17, 23, 25, 32, 35, 39; **24:** 106
King John **9:** 222, 224, 229, 240, 250, 292; **41:** 205, 215
King Lear **2:** 108, 125, 145, 162, 191; **16:** 311; **28:** 223; **46:** 177, 210

Love's Labour's Lost **2:** 303, 310, 317, 322, 328, 342; **23:** 237, 250, 252; **38:** 232; **47:** 35
Macbeth **20:** 12, 318, 324, 329, 353, 363, 367, 374, 387; **28:** 339; **29:** 101, 109, 146, 155, 165; **45:** 67; **47:** 41
Measure for Measure **2:** 388, 390, 391, 396, 406, 420, 421, 446, 466, 475, 484, 505, 516, 524; **23:** 299, 405; **33:**
The Merry Wives of Windsor **5:** 332, 334, 335, 337, 338, 351, 360, 363, 366, 374, 379, 392; **18:** 74, 75; **38:** 264, 273, 313, 319
The Tempest **8:** 287, 289, 292, 294, 295, 308, 326, 334, 336; **28:** 415; **42:** 332; **45:** 219; **48:** 299
Titus Andronicus **4:** 613, 628, 632, 635, 640, 644, 647, 650, 675; **27:** 293; **43:** 170, 176,
Troilus and Cressida **3:** 538, 539, 540, 541, 548, 566, 571, 604, 611, 621; **27:** 381, 391
Twelfth Night **1:** 539, 540, 543, 545, 550, 554, 581, 594; **26:** 257, 337, 342, 346, 364, 366, 371, 374; **34:** 281, 293, 311, 338; **46:** 286, 324
The Two Gentlemen of Verona **6:** 438, 442, 445, 447, 449, 458, 462, 560; **12:** 458; **40:** 312, 327, 330, 365
The Two Noble Kinsmen **9:** 457, 461, 471, 474; **41:** 340, 385
The Winter's Tale **47:** 25

**chastity**
A Midsummer Night's Dream **45:** 143

**Chaucer's Criseyde, compared with**
Troilus and Cressida **43:** 305

**chivalry, decline of**
Troilus and Cressida **16:** 84; **27:** 370, 374

**Christian elements**
See also **religious, mythic, or spiritual content**
As You Like It **5:** 39, 98, 162
Coriolanus **30:** 111
King Lear **2:** 137, 170, 179, 188, 191, 197, 207, 218, 222, 226, 229, 238, 249, 265, 286; **22:** 233, 271; **25:** 218; **46:** 276
Macbeth **3:** 194, 239, 260, 269, 275, 286, 293, 297, 318; **20:** 203, 206, 210, 256, 262, 289, 291, 294; **44:** 341, 366; **47:** 41
Measure for Measure **2:** 391, 394, 399, 421, 437, 449, 466, 479, 491, 511, 522; **48:** 1
Much Ado about Nothing **8:** 17, 19, 29, 55, 95, 104, 111, 115; **31:** 209
The Phoenix and Turtle **10:** 21, 24, 31; **38:** 326
The Rape of Lucrece **10:** 77, 80, 89, 96, 98, 109
Sonnets **10:** 191, 256
Titus Andronicus **4:** 656, 680
Twelfth Night **46:** 338
The Two Gentlemen of Verona **6:** 438, 494, 514, 532, 555, 564
The Winter's Tale **7:** 381, 387, 402, 410, 417, 419, 425, 429, 436, 452, 460, 501; **36:** 318

**as Christian play**
King Lear **48:** 222

**church versus state**
King John **9:** 209, 212, 222, 235, 240; **22:** 120

**civilization versus barbarism**
Titus Andronicus **4:** 653; **27:** 293; **28:** 249; **32:** 265

**Clarissa, (Samuel Richardson), compared with**
King Lear **48:** 277
Measure for Measure **48:** 277
Othello **48:** 277
Titus Andronicus **48:** 277

**class distinctions, conflict, and relations**
Henry V **28:** 146
Henry VI, Parts 1, 2, and 3 **37:** 97; **39:** 187
The Merry Wives of Windsor **5:** 338, 343, 346, 347, 366, 390, 395, 400, 402; **22:** 93; **28:** 69
A Midsummer Night's Dream **22:** 23; **25:** 36; **45:** 160
The Taming of the Shrew **31:** 300, 351

**classical influence and sources**
The Comedy of Errors **1:** 13, 14, 16, 31, 32, 43, 61
The Tempest **29:** 278, 343, 362, 368

**Clowns and Fools (Volume 46:** 1, 14, 18, 24, 29, 33, 48, 52, 60)
As You Like It **5:** 24, 28, 30, 32, 36, 39, 54, 61, 63, 72, 75, 76, 77, 79, 84, 86, 93, 98, 114, 118, 135, 138, 166; **23:** 152; **34:** 72, 85, 147, 161; **46:** 88, 105, 117, 122
King Lear **2:** 108, 112, 125, 156, 162, 245, 278, 284; **11:** 17, 158, 169; **22:** 227; **25:** 202; **28:** 223; **46:** 191, 205, 210, 218, 225
Twelfth Night **1:** 543, 548, 558, 561, 563, 566, 570, 572, 603, 620, 642, 655, 658; **26:** 233, 364; **46:** 297, 303, 310

**colonialism**
Henry V **22:** 103
The Tempest **13:** 424, 440; **15:** 228, 268, 269, 270, 271, 272, 273; **19:** 421; **25:** 357, 382; **28:** 249; **29:** 343, 368; **32:** 338, 367, 400; **42:** 320; **45:** 200, 280

**combat**
King Lear **22:** 365
Macbeth **22:** 365

**comedy of affectation**
Love's Labour's Lost **2:** 302, 303, 304; **23:** 191, 224, 226, 228, 233

**comic and tragic elements, combination of**
King Lear **2:** 108, 110, 112, 125, 156, 162, 245, 278, 284; **46:** 191
Measure for Measure **16:** 102
Romeo and Juliet **5:** 496, 524, 528, 547, 559; **46:** 78
Troilus and Cressida **43:** 351

**comic and farcical elements**
All's Well That Ends Well **26:** 97, 114; **48:** 65
Antony and Cleopatra **6:** 52, 85, 104, 125, 131, 151, 192, 202, 219; **47:** 77, 124, 149, 165
The Comedy of Errors **1:** 14, 16, 19, 23, 30,

34, 35, 43, 46, 50, 55, 56, 59, 61; **19:** 54; **26:** 183, 186, 188, 190; **34:** 190, 245
*Coriolanus* **9:** 8, 9, 14, 53, 80, 106
*Cymbeline* **4:** 35, 56, 113, 141; **15:** 111, 122; **47:** 296
*Henry IV, Parts 1 and 2* **1:** 286, 290, 314, 327, 328, 336, 353; **19:** 195; **25:** 109; **39:** 72
*Henry V* **5:** 185, 188, 191, 192, 217, 230, 233, 241, 252, 260, 276; **19:** 217; **28:** 121; **30:** 193, 202
*The Merry Wives of Windsor* **5:** 336, 338, 346, 350, 360, 369, 373; **18:** 74, 75, 84
*Richard II* **24:** 262, 263, 395; **39:** 243
*Twelfth Night* **26:** 233, 257, 337, 342, 371
*Venus and Adonis* **10:** 429, 434, 439, 442, 459, 462, 489; **33:** 352

**comic form**
*As You Like It* **46:** 105
*Measure for Measure* **2:** 456, 460, 479, 482, 491, 514, 516; **13:** 94, 104; **23:** 309, 326, 327

**comic resolution**
*Love's Labour's Lost* **2:** 335, 340; **16:** 17; **19:** 92; **38:** 209

**comic, tragic, and romantic elements, fusion of**
*The Winter's Tale* **7:** 390, 394, 396, 399, 410, 412, 414, 429, 436, 479, 483, 490, 501; **13:** 417; **15:** 514, 524, 532; **25:** 339; **36:** 295, 380

**commodity**
*King John* **9:** 224, 229, 245, 260, 275, 280, 297; **19:** 182; **25:** 98; **41:** 228, 269

**communication, failure of**
*Troilus and Cressida* **43:** 277

**compassion, theme of**
*The Tempest* **42:** 339

**complex or enigmatic nature**
*The Phoenix and Turtle* **10:** 7, 14, 35, 42; **38:** 326, 357

**composition date**
*The Comedy of Errors* **1:** 18, 23, 34, 55
*Henry VIII* **2:** 19, 22, 35; **24:** 129
*Pericles* **2:** 537, 544
*Sonnets* **10:** 153, 154, 161, 166, 196, 217, 226, 270, 277; **28:** 363, 385
*Twelfth Night* **37:** 78

**conclusion**
*All's Well That Ends Well* **38:** 123, 132, 142
*Love's Labour's Lost* **38:** 172
*Troilus and Cressida* **3:** 538, 549, 558, 566, 574, 583, 594
   comedy vs. tragedy **43:** 351

**conflict between Christianity and Judaism**
*The Merchant of Venice* **4:** 224, 250, 268, 289, 324, 344; **12:** 67, 70, 72, 76; **22:** 69; **25:** 257 **40:** 117, 127, 166, 181; **48:** 54, 77

**conscience**
*Richard III* **8:** 148, 152, 162, 165, 190, 197,
201, 206, 210, 228, 232, 239, 243, 252, 258; **39:** 341

**as consciously philosophical**
*The Phoenix and Turtle* **10:** 7, 21, 24, 31, 48; **38:** 342, 378

**conspiracy or treason**
*The Tempest* **16:** 426; **19:** 357; **25:** 382; **29:** 377

**constancy and faithfulness**
*The Phoenix and Turtle* **10:** 18, 20, 21, 48; **38:** 329

**construing the truth**
*Julius Caesar* **7:** 320, 336, 343, 350; **37:** 229

**consummation of marriage**
*Othello* **22:** 207

**contemptus mundi**
*Antony and Cleopatra* **6:** 85, 133

**contractual and economic relations**
*Henry IV, Parts 1 and 2* **13:** 213
*Richard II* **13:** 213

**contradiction, paradox, and opposition**
*As You Like It* **46:** 105
*Romeo and Juliet* **5:** 421, 427, 431, 496, 509, 513, 516, 520, 525, 528, 538; **33:** 287; **44:** 11
*Troilus and Cressida* **43:** 377

**contrasting dramatic worlds**
*Henry IV, Parts 1 and 2* **14:** 56, 60, 61, 84, 105; **48:** 95
*The Merchant of Venice* **44:** 11

**contrasts and oppositions**
*Othello* **4:** 421, 455, 457, 462, 508; **25:** 189

**corruption in society**
*As You Like It* **46:** 94
*King John* **9:** 222, 234, 280, 297

**costume**
*As You Like It* **46:** 117
*Hamlet* **21:** 81
*Henry VIII* **24:** 82, 87; **28:** 184
*Richard II* **24:** 274, 278, 291, 304, 325, 356, 364, 423
*Romeo and Juliet* **11:** 505, 509
*Troilus and Cressida* **18:** 289, 371, 406, 419

**counsel**
*The Winter's Tale* **19:** 401

**Court of Love**
*The Phoenix and Turtle* **10:** 9, 24, 50

**court society**
*The Winter's Tale* **16:** 410

**courtly love**
*Troilus and Cressida* **22:** 58

**courtly love tradition, influence of**
*Romeo and Juliet* **5:** 505, 542, 575; **33:** 233

**courtship and marriage**
See also **marriage**
*As You Like It* **34:** 109, 177; **48:** 32
*Much Ado about Nothing* **8:** 29, 44, 48, 95, 115, 121, 125; **31:** 191, 231

**credibility**
*Twelfth Night* **1:** 540, 542, 543, 554, 562, 581, 587

**critical history**
*Henry IV, Parts 1 and 2* **42:** 185; **48:** 167

**cynicism**
*Troilus and Cressida* **43:** 298

**dance**
*Henry VI, Parts 1, 2, and 3* **22:** 156

**dance and patterned action**
*Love's Labour's Lost* **2:** 308, 342; **23:** 191, 237

**dark elements**
*All's Well That Ends Well* **7:** 27, 37, 39, 43, 54, 109, 113, 116; **26:** 85; **48:** 65
*Twelfth Night* **46:** 310

**death, decay, nature's destructiveness**
*Antony and Cleopatra* **47:** 71
*As You Like It* **46:** 169
*Hamlet* **1:** 144, 153, 188, 198, 221, 242; **13:** 502; **28:** 280, 311; **35:** 241; **42:** 279
*King Lear* **2:** 93, 94, 101, 104, 106, 109, 112, 116, 129, 131, 137, 143, 147, 149, 156, 160, 170, 179, 188, 197, 207, 218, 222, 226, 231, 238, 241, 245, 249, 253, 265, 269, 273; **16:** 301; **25:** 202, 218; **31:** 77, 117, 137, 142; **46:** 264
*Love's Labour's Lost* **2:** 305, 331, 344, 348
*Measure for Measure* **2:** 394, 452, 516; **25:** 12
*Venus and Adonis* **10:** 419, 427, 434, 451, 454, 462, 466, 473, 480, 489; **25:** 305; **33:** 309, 321, 347, 352, 363, 370

**decay of heroic ideals**
*Henry VI, Parts 1, 2, and 3* **3:** 119, 126

**deception, disguise, and duplicity**
*As You Like It* **46:** 134
*Henry IV, Parts 1 and 2* **1:** 397, 406, 425; **42:** 99; **47:** 1, 60; **48:** 95
*The Merry Wives of Windsor* **5:** 332, 334, 336, 354, 355, 379; **22:** 93; **47:** 308, 314, 321, 325, 344
*Much Ado about Nothing* **8:** 29, 55, 63, 69, 79, 82, 88, 108, 115; **31:** 191, 198
*Sonnets* **25:** 374; **40:** 221
*The Taming of the Shrew* **12:** 416

**Deconstructionist interpretation of**
*Pericles* **48:** 364

**deposition scene**
*Richard II* **42:** 118

**Desire (Volume 38: 1, 19, 31, 40, 48, 56)**
*All's Well That Ends Well* **38:** 96, 99, 109, 118
*As You Like It* **37:** 43

*Love's Labour's Lost* **38:** 185, 194, 200, 209
*The Merchant of Venice* **22:** 3; **40:** 142; **45:** 17
*The Merry Wives of Windsor* **38:** 286, 297, 300
*Troilus and Cressida* **43:** 317, 329, 340,

**discrepancy between prophetic ending and preceding action**
*Henry VIII* **2:** 22, 25, 31, 46, 49, 56, 60, 65, 68, 75, 81; **32:** 148; **41:** 190

**disillusioned or cynical tone**
*Troilus and Cressida* **3:** 544, 548, 554, 557, 558, 571, 574, 630, 642; **18:** 284, 332, 403, 406, 423; **27:** 376

**disorder**
*Troilus and Cressida* **3:** 578, 589, 599, 604, 609; **18:** 332, 406, 412, 423; **27:** 366

**disorder and civil dissension**
*Henry VI, Parts 1, 2, and 3* **3:** 59, 67, 76, 92, 103, 126; **13:** 131; **16:** 183; **24:** 11, 17, 28, 31, 47; **25:** 102; **28:** 112; **39:** 154, 177, 187, 196, 205

**displacement**
*All's Well That Ends Well* **22:** 78
*Measure for Measure* **22:** 78

**divine will, role of**
*Romeo and Juliet* **5:** 485, 493, 505, 533, 573

**domestic elements**
*As You Like It* **46:** 142
*Coriolanus* **42:** 218

**double-plot**
*King Lear* **2:** 94, 95, 100, 101, 104, 112, 116, 124, 131, 133, 156, 253, 257; **46:** 254
*Troilus and Cressida* **3:** 569, 613

**doubling of roles**
*Pericles* **15:** 150, 152, 167, 173, 180

**dramatic elements**
*Sonnets* **10:** 155, 182, 240, 251, 283, 367
*Venus and Adonis* **10:** 459, 462, 486

**dramatic shortcomings or failure**
*As You Like It* **5:** 19, 42, 52, 61, 65
*Love's Labour's Lost* **2:** 299, 301, 303, 322
*Romeo and Juliet* **5:** 416, 418, 420, 426, 436, 437, 448, 464, 467, 469, 480, 487, 524, 562

**dramatic structure**
*The Comedy of Errors* **1:** 19, 27, 40, 43, 46, 50; **26:** 186, 190; **34:** 190, 229, 233; **37:** 12
*Cymbeline* **4:** 17, 18, 19, 20, 21, 22, 24, 38, 43, 48, 53, 64, 68, 89, 116, 129, 141; **22:** 302, 365; **25:** 319; **36:** 115, 125
*Othello* **4:** 370, 390, 399, 427, 488, 506, 517, 569; **22:** 207; **28:** 243
*The Winter's Tale* **7:** 382, 390, 396, 399, 402, 407, 414, 429, 432, 473, 479, 493, 497, 501; **15:** 528; **25:** 339; **36:** 289, 295, 362, 380; **45:** 297, 344, 358, 366

**as dream-play**
*A Midsummer Night's Dream* **3:** 365, 370, 372, 377, 389, 391; **29:** 190; **45:** 117

**Dreams in Shakespeare (Volume 45:** 1, 10, 17, 28, 40, 48, 58, 67, 75)
*Antony and Cleopatra* **45:** 28
*Cymbeline* **4:** 162, 167; **44:** 28; **45:** 67, 75
*Hamlet* **45:** 28
*Julius Caesar* **45:** 10
*A Midsummer Night's Dream* **45:** 96, 107, 117
*Romeo and Juliet* **45:** 40
*The Tempest* **45:** 236, 247, 259

**dualisms**
*Antony and Cleopatra* **19:** 304; **27:** 82
*Cymbeline* **4:** 29, 64, 73

**duration of time**
*As You Like It* **5:** 44, 45
*A Midsummer Night's Dream* **3:** 362, 370, 380, 386, 494; **45:** 175

**economic relations**
*Henry V* **13:** 213

**economics and exchange**
*The Merchant of Venice* **40:** 197, 208

**editorial and textual issues**
*Sonnets* **28:** 363; **40:** 273; **42:** 296

**education**
*All's Well That Ends Well* **7:** 62, 86, 90, 93, 98, 104, 116, 126
*The Two Gentlemen of Verona* **6:** 490, 494, 504, 526, 532, 555, 568

**education or nurturing**
*The Tempest* **8:** 353, 370, 384, 396; **29:** 292, 368, 377

**egotism or narcissism**
*Much Ado about Nothing* **8:** 19, 24, 28, 29, 55, 69, 95, 115

**Elizabeth, audience of**
*Sonnets* **48:** 325

**Elizabeth's influence**
*The Merry Wives of Windsor* **5:** 333, 334, 335, 336, 339, 346, 355, 366, 402; **18:** 5, 86; **38:** 278; **47:** 344

**Elizabethan and Jacobean politics, relation to**
*Hamlet* **28:** 232; **28:** 290, 311; **35:** 140

**Elizabethan attitudes, influence of**
*Richard II* **6:** 287, 292, 294, 305, 321, 327, 364, 402, 414; **13:** 494; **24:** 325; **28:** 188; **39:** 273; **42:** 118

**Elizabethan betrothal and marriage customs**
*Measure for Measure* **2:** 429, 437, 443, 503

**Elizabethan culture, relation to**
*Antony and Cleopatra* **47:** 103

*As You Like It* **5:** 21, 59, 66, 68, 70, 158; **16:** 53; **28:** 46; **34:** 120; **37:** 1; **46:** 142
*The Comedy of Errors* **26:** 138, 142; **34:** 201, 215, 233, 238, 258; **42:** 80
*Hamlet* **1:** 76, 148, 151, 154, 160, 166, 169, 171, 176, 184, 202, 209, 254; **13:** 282, 494; **19:** 330; **21:** 407, 416; **22:** 258
*Henry IV, Parts 1 and 2* **19:** 195; **48:** 117, 143, 151, 175
*Henry V* **5:** 210, 213, 217, 223, 257, 299, 310; **16:** 202; **19:** 133, 233; **28:** 121, 159; **30:** 215, 262; **37:** 187
*Julius Caesar* **16:** 231; **30:** 342, 379
*King Lear* **2:** 168, 174, 177, 183, 226, 241; **19:** 330; **22:** 227, 233, 365; **25:** 218; **46:** 276; **47:** 9
*Measure for Measure* **2:** 394, 418, 429, 432, 437, 460, 470, 482, 503
*The Merchant of Venice* **32:** 66; **40:** 117, 127, 142, 166, 181, 197, 208; **48:** 54, 77
*Much Ado about Nothing* **8:** 23, 33, 44, 55, 58, 79, 88, 104, 111, 115
*The Rape of Lucrece* **33:** 195; **43:** 77
*The Taming of the Shrew* **31:** 288, 295, 300, 315, 326, 345, 351
*Timon of Athens* **1:** 487, 489, 495, 500; **20:** 433; **27:** 203, 212, 230
*Titus Andronicus* **27:** 282
*Troilus and Cressida* **3:** 560, 574, 606; **25:** 56
*Twelfth Night* **1:** 549, 553, 555, 563, 581, 587, 620; **16:** 53; **19:** 42, 78; **26:** 357; **28:** 1; **34:** 323, 330; **46:** 291

**Elizabethan dramatic conventions**
*Cymbeline* **4:** 53, 124
*Henry VIII* **24:** 155

**Elizabethan literary influences**
*Henry VI, Parts 1, 2, and 3* **3:** 75, 97, 100, 119, 143; **22:** 156; **28:** 112; **37:** 97

**Elizabethan love poetry**
*Love's Labour's Lost* **38:** 232

**Elizabethan poetics, influence of**
*Romeo and Juliet* **5:** 416, 520, 522, 528, 550, 559, 575

**Elizabethan politics, relation to**
*Henry IV, Parts 1 and 2* **22:** 395; **28:** 203; **47:** 60; **48:** 117, 143, 167, 175
*Henry VIII* **22:** 395; **24:** 115, 129, 140; **32:** 148
*King John* **48:** 132
*Richard III* **22:** 395; **25:** 141; **37:** 144; **39:** 345, 349; **42:** 130

**Elizabethan setting**
*The Two Gentlemen of Verona* **12:** 463, 485

**Elizabethan society**
*The Merry Wives of Windsor* **47:** 331

**emulation or rivalry**
*Julius Caesar* **16:** 231

**England and Rome, parallels between**
*Coriolanus* **9:** 39, 43, 106, 148, 180, 193; **25:** 296; **30:** 67, 105

**English language and colonialism**
  Henry V **22**: 103; **28**: 159

**English Reformation, influence of**
  Henry VIII **2**: 25, 35, 39, 51, 67; **24**: 89

**epic elements**
  Henry V **5**: 192, 197, 246, 257, 314; **30**: 181, 220, 237, 252

**erotic elements**
  A Midsummer Night's Dream **3**: 445, 491, 497, 511; **12**: 259, 262, 298; **16**: 34; **19**: 21; **29**: 183, 225, 269
  Venus and Adonis **10**: 410, 411, 418, 419, 427, 428, 429, 442, 448, 454, 459, 466, 473; **25**: 305, 328; **28**: 355; **33**: 321, 339, 347, 352, 363, 370

**as experimental play**
  Romeo and Juliet **5**: 464, 509, 528

**Essex Rebellion, relation to**
  Richard II **6**: 249, 250; **24**: 356

**ethical or moral issues**
  King John **9**: 212, 222, 224, 229, 235, 240, 263, 275, 280

**ethnicity**
  The Winter's Tale **37**: 306

**Euripides, influence of**
  Titus Andronicus **27**: 285

**evil**
  See also good versus evil
  Macbeth **3**: 194, 208, 231, 234, 239, 241, 267, 289; **20**: 203, 206, 210, 374
  Romeo and Juliet **5**: 485, 493, 505

**excess**
  King John **9**: 251

**fame**
  Coriolanus **30**: 58

**family honor, structure, and inheritance**
  Richard II **6**: 338, 368, 388, 397, 414; **39**: 263, 279
  Richard III **8**: 177, 248, 252, 263, 267; **25**: 141; **39**: 335, 341, 349, 370

**family, theme of**
  Cymbeline **44**: 28

**fancy**
  Twelfth Night **1**: 543, 546

**as farce**
  The Taming of the Shrew **9**: 330, 337, 338, 341, 342, 365, 381, 386, 413, 426

**farcical elements**
  See comic and farcical elements

**fate**
  Richard II **6**: 289, 294, 304, 352, 354, 385

Romeo and Juliet **5**: 431, 444, 464, 469, 470, 479, 480, 485, 487, 493, 509, 530, 533, 562, 565, 571, 573; **33**: 249

**Fathers and Daughters** (Volume 36: 1, 12, 25, 32, 37, 45, 70, 78)
  As You Like It **46**: 94
  Cymbeline **34**: 134
  King Lear **34**: 51, 54, 60
    cruelty of daughters **2**: 101, 102, 106; **31**: 84, 123, 137, 142
  Pericles **34**: 226, 233
  The Winter's Tale **34**: 311, 318, 328

**feminist criticism**
  As You Like It **23**: 107, 108
  Comedy of Errors **42**: 93
  Love's Labour's Lost **42**: 93
  Measure for Measure **23**: 320

**feminist interpretation**
  A Midsummer Night's Dream **48**: 23

**festive or folklore elements**
  Twelfth Night **46**: 338

**feud**
  Romeo and Juliet **5**: 415, 419, 425, 447, 458, 464, 469, 479, 480, 493, 509, 522, 556, 565, 566, 571, 575; **25**: 181

**fire and water**
  Coriolanus **25**: 263

**flattery**
  Coriolanus **9**: 26, 45, 92, 100, 110, 121, 130, 144, 157, 183, 193; **25**: 296
  Henry IV, Parts 1 and 2 **22**: 395
  Henry VIII **22**: 395
  Richard III **22**: 395

**folk drama, relation to**
  The Winter's Tale **7**: 420, 451

**folk elements**
  The Taming of the Shrew **9**: 381, 393, 404, 426

**folk rituals, elements and influence of**
  Henry VI, Parts 1, 2, and 3 **39**: 205
  The Merry Wives of Windsor **5**: 353, 369, 376, 392, 397, 400; **38**: 256, 300

**food, meaning of**
  The Comedy of Errors **34**: 220
  Troilus and Cressida **43**: 298

**forest**
  The Two Gentlemen of Verona **6**: 450, 456, 492, 514, 547, 555, 564, 568

**Forest of Arden**
  As You Like It
    as "bitter" Arcadia **5**: 98, 118, 162; **23**: 97, 98, 99, 100, 122, 139
    Duke Frederick's court, contrast with **5**: 46, 102, 103, 112, 130, 156; **16**: 53; **23**: 126, 128, 129, 131, 134; **34**: 78, 102, 131; **46**: 164

    pastoral elements **5**: 18, 20, 24, 32, 35, 47, 50, 54, 55, 57, 60, 77, 128, 135, 156; **23**: 17, 20, 27, 46, 137; **34**: 78, 147; **46**: 88
    as patriarchal society **5**: 168; **23**: 150; **34**: 177
    as source of self-knowledge **5**: 98, 102, 103, 128, 130, 135, 148, 158, 162; **23**: 17; **34**: 102
    as timeless, mythical world **5**: 112, 130, 141; **23**: 132; **34**: 78; **37**: 43; **46**: 88
    theme of play **46**: 88

**forgiveness or redemption**
  The Winter's Tale **7**: 381, 389, 395, 402, 407, 436, 456, 460, 483; **36**: 318

**free will versus fate**
  Macbeth **3**: 177, 183, 184, 190, 196, 198, 202, 207, 208, 213; **13**: 361; **44**: 351, 361, , 366, 373
  The Two Noble Kinsmen **9**: 474, 481, 486, 492, 498

**freedom and servitude**
  The Tempest **8**: 304, 307, 312, 429; **22**: 302; **29**: 278, 368, 377; **37**: 336

**French language, Shakespeare's use of**
  Henry V **5**: 186, 188, 190; **25**: 131

**Freudian analysis**
  A Midsummer Night's Dream **44**: 1

**friendship**
  See also **love and friendship** and **love versus friendship**
  Coriolanus **30**: 125, 142
  Sonnets **10**: 185, 279; **28**: 380
  The Two Noble Kinsmen **9**: 448, 463, 470, 474, 479, 481, 486, 490; **19**: 394; **41**: 363, 372; **42**: 361

**Gender Identity and Issues** (Volume 40: 1, 9, 15, 27, 33, 51, 61, 65, 75, 90, 99)
  All's Well That Ends Well **7**: 9, 10, 67, 126; **13**: 77, 84; **19**: 113; **26**: 128; **38**: 89, 99, 118; **44**: 35
  Antony and Cleopatra **13**: 368; **25**: 257; **27**: 144; **47**: 174, 192
  As You Like It **46**: 127, 134
  The Comedy of Errors **34**: 215, 220
  Coriolanus **30**: 79, 125, 142; **44**: 93
  Hamlet **35**: 144; **44**: 189, 195, 198
  Henry IV, Parts 1 and 2 **13**: 183; **25**: 151; **44**: 44; **48**: 175
  Henry V **13**: 183; **28**: 121, 146, 159; **44**: 44
  Julius Caesar **13**: 260
  The Merchant of Venice **40**: 142, 151, 156
  Othello **32**: 294; **35**: 327
  Richard II **25**: 89; **39**: 295
  Richard III **25**: 141; **37**: 144; **39**: 345
  Romeo and Juliet **32**: 256
  Sonnets **37**: 374; **40**: 238, 247, 254, 264, 268, 273
  The Taming of the Shrew **28**: 24 **31**: 261, 268, 276, 282, 288, 295, 300, 335, 351
  Twelfth Night **19**: 78; **34**: 344; **37**: 59; **42**: 32; **46**: 347, 362, 369

*The Two Gentlemen of Verona* **40:** 374
*The Two Noble Kinsmen* **42:** 361

genre
  *All's Well That Ends Well* **48:** 65
  *As You Like It* **5:** 46, 55, 79
  *The Comedy of Errors* **34:** 251, 258
  *Coriolanus* **9:** 42, 43, 53, 80, 106, 112, 117, 130, 164, 177; **30:** 67, 74, 79, 89, 111, 125
  *Hamlet* **1:** 176, 212, 237
  *Love's Labour's Lost* **38:** 163
  *The Merchant of Venice* **4:** 191, 200, 201, 209, 215, 221, 232, 238, 247; **12:** 48, 54, 62
  *Much Ado about Nothing* **8:** 9, 18, 19, 28, 29, 39, 41, 44, 53, 63, 69, 73, 79, 82, 95, 100, 104; **48:** 14
  *Richard III* **8:** 181, 182, 197, 206, 218, 228, 239, 243, 252, 258; **13:** 142; **39:** 383
  *The Taming of the Shrew* **9:** 329, 334, 362, 375; **22:** 48; **31:** 261, 269, 276
  *Timon of Athens* **1:** 454, 456, 459, 460, 462, 483, 492, 499, 503, 509, 511, 512, 515, 518, 525, 531; **27:** 203
  *Troilus and Cressida* **3:** 541, 542, 549, 558, 566, 571, 574, 587, 594, 604, 630, 642; **27:** 366
  *The Two Gentlemen of Verona* **6:** 460, 468, 472, 516; **40:** 320

genres, mixture of
  *Timon of Athens* **16:** 351; **25:** 198

gift exchange
  *Love's Labour's Lost* **25:** 1

good versus evil
  *See also* **evil**
  *Measure for Measure* **2:** 432, 452, 524; **33:** 52, 61
  *The Tempest* **8:** 302, 311, 315, 370, 423, 439; **29:** 278; 297

grace
  *The Winter's Tale* **7:** 420, 425, 460, 493; **36:** 328

grace and civility
  *Love's Labour's Lost* **2:** 351

Greece
  *Troilus and Cressida* **43:** 287

grotesque or absurd elements
  *Hamlet* **42:** 279
  *King Lear* **2:** 136, 156, 245; **13:** 343

handkerchief, significance of
  *Othello* **4:** 370, 384, 385, 396, 503, 530, 562; **35:** 265, 282, 380

*Hercules Furens* (Seneca) as source
  *Othello* **16:** 283

Hippolytus, myth of
  *A Midsummer Night's Dream* **29:** 216; **45:** 84

historical accuracy
  *Henry VI, Parts 1, 2, and 3* **3:** 18, 21, 35, 46, 51; **16:** 217; **24:** 16, 18, 25, 31, 45, 48

*Richard III* **8:** 144, 145, 153, 159, 163, 165, 168, 213, 223, 228, 232; **39:** 305, 308, 326, 383

historical allegory
  *The Winter's Tale* **7:** 381; **15:** 528

historical elements
  *Cymbeline* **47:** 260

historical and romantic elements, combination of
  *Henry VIII* **2:** 46, 49, 51, 75, 76, 78; **24:** 71, 80, 146; **41:** 129, 146, 180

historical content
  *Henry IV, Parts 1 and 2* **1:** 310, 328, 365, 366, 370, 374, 380, 387, 421, 424, 427, 431; **16:** 172; **19:** 157; **25:** 151; **32:** 136; **39:** 143; **48:** 143, 167
  *Henry V* **5:** 185, 188, 190, 192, 193, 198, 246, 314; **13:** 201; **19:** 133; **25:** 131; **30:** 193, 202, 207, 215, 252
  *King John* **9:** 216, 219, 220, 222, 235, 240, 254, 284, 290, 292, 297, 300, 303; **13:** 163; **32:** 93, 114; **41:** 234; 243
  *The Tempest* **8:** 364, 408, 420; **16:** 426; **25:** 382; **29:** 278, 339, 343, 368; **45:** 226

historical determinism versus free will
  *Julius Caesar* **7:** 160, 298, 316, 333, 346, 356; **13:** 252

historical epic, as epilogue to Shakespeare's
  *Henry VIII* **2:** 22, 25, 27, 39, 51, 60, 65

historical epic, place in or relation to Shakespeare's
  *Henry IV, Parts 1 and 2* **1:** 309, 314, 328, 374, 379, 424, 427
  *Henry V* **5:** 195, 198, 205, 212, 225, 241, 244, 287, 304, 310; **14:** 337, 342; **30:** 215
  *Henry VI, Parts 1, 2, and 3* **3:** 24, 59; **24:** 51; **48:** 167

historical principles
  *Richard III* **39:** 308, 326, 387

historical relativity, theme of **41:** 146

historical sources, compared with
  *Richard II* **6:** 252, 279, 343; **28:** 134; **39:** 235

historiography
  *Henry VIII* **37:** 109

homoerotic elements
  *As You Like It* **46:** 127, 142
  *Henry V* **16:** 202
  *Sonnets* **10:** 155, 156, 159, 161, 175, 213, 391; **16:** 461; **28:** 363, 380; **37:** 347; **40:** 254, 264, 273

homosexuality
  *As You Like It* **46:** 127, 142
  *Measure for Measure* **42:** 1
  *The Merchant of Venice* **22:** 3, 69; **37:** 86; **40:** 142, 156, 197

*Twelfth Night* **22:** 69; **42:** 32; **46:** 362
*The Winter's Tale* **48:** 309

honor or integrity
  *Coriolanus* **9:** 43, 65, 73, 92, 106, 110, 121, 144, 153, 157, 164, 177, 183, 189; **30:** 89, 96, 133

hospitality
  *The Winter's Tale* **19:** 366

as humanistic play
  *Henry VI, Parts 1, 2, and 3* **3:** 83, 92, 109, 115, 119, 131, 136, 143

hunt motif
  *Venus and Adonis* **10:** 434, 451, 466, 473; **33:** 357, 370

hypocrisy
  *Henry V* **5:** 203, 213, 219, 223, 233, 260, 271, 302

ideal love
  *See also* **love**
  *Romeo and Juliet* **5:** 421, 427, 431, 436, 437, 450, 463, 469, 498, 505, 575; **25:** 257; **33:** 210, 225, 272

idealism versus pragmatism
  *Hamlet* **16:** 246; **28:** 325

idealism versus realism
  *See also* **realism**
  *Love's Labour's Lost* **38:** 163
  *Othello* **4:** 457, 508, 517; **13:** 313; **25:** 189

identities of persons
  *Sonnets* **10:** 154, 155, 156, 161, 166, 167, 169, 173, 174, 175, 185, 190, 191, 196, 218, 226, 230, 233, 240; **40:** 238

identity
  *The Comedy of Errors* **34:** 201, 208, 211
  *Coriolanus* **42:** 243
  *A Midsummer Night's Dream* **29:** 269
  *The Two Gentlemen of Verona* **6:** 494, 511, 529, 532, 547, 560, 564, 568; **19:** 34

illusion
  *The Comedy of Errors* **1:** 13, 14, 27, 37, 40, 45, 59, 63; **26:** 188; **34:** 194, 211

illusion versus reality
  *Love's Labour's Lost* **2:** 303, 308, 331, 340, 344, 348, 356, 359, 367, 371, 375; **23:** 230, 231

imagery
  *Venus and Adonis* **10:** 414, 415, 416, 420, 429, 434, 449, 459, 466, 473, 480; **25:** 328; **28:** 355; **33:** 321, 339, 352, 363, 370, 377; **42:** 347

imagination and art
  *A Midsummer Night's Dream* **3:** 365, 371, 381, 402, 412, 417, 421, 423, 441, 459, 468, 506, 516, 520; **22:** 39; **45:** 96, 126, 136, 147

**immortality**
  *Measure for Measure* **16**: 102

**imperialism**
  *Henry V* **22**: 103; **28**: 159

**implausibility of plot, characters, or events**
  *All's Well That Ends Well* **7**: 8, 45
  *King Lear* **2**: 100, 136, 145, 278; **13**: 343
  *The Merchant of Venice* **4**: 191, 192, 193; **12**: 52, 56, 76, 119
  *Much Ado about Nothing* **8**: 9, 12, 16, 19, 33, 36, 39, 44, 53, 100, 104
  *Othello* **4**: 370, 380, 391, 442, 444; **47**: 51

**inaction**
  *Troilus and Cressida* **3**: 587, 621; **27**: 347

**incest, motif of**
  *Pericles* **2**: 582, 588; **22**: 315; **36**: 257, 264

**inconsistencies**
  *Henry VIII* **2**: 16, 27, 28, 31, 60

**inconsistency between first and second halves**
  *Measure for Measure* **2**: 474, 475, 505, 514, 524

**induction**
  *The Taming of the Shrew* **9**: 320, 322, 332, 337, 345, 350, 362, 365, 369, 370, 381, 390, 393, 407, 419, 424, 430; **12**: 416, 427, 430, 431, 441; **19**: 34, 122; **22**: 48; **31**: 269, 315, 351

**as inferior or flawed play**
  *Henry VI, Parts 1, 2, and 3* **3**: 20, 21, 25, 26, 35
  *Pericles* **2**: 537, 546, 553, 563, 564; **15**: 139, 143, 156, 167, 176; **36**: 198
  *Timon of Athens* **1**: 476, 481, 489, 499, 520; **20**: 433, 439, 491; **25**: 198; **27**: 157, 175

**infidelity**
  *Troilus and Cressida* **43**: 298

**innocence**
  *Macbeth* **3**: 234, 241, 327
  *Othello* **47**: 25
  *Pericles* **36**: 226, 274

**innocence to experience**
  *The Two Noble Kinsmen* **9**: 481, 502; **19**: 394

**Ireland, William Henry, forgeries of**
  *Sonnets* **48**: 325

**Irish affairs**
  *Henry V* **22**: 103; **28**: 159

**ironic or parodic elements**
  *The Two Gentlemen of Verona* **6**: 447, 472, 478, 484, 502, 504, 509, 516, 529, 549; **13**: 12
  *Henry VIII* **41**: 129

**irony**
  *All's Well That Ends Well* **7**: 27, 32, 58, 62, 67, 81, 86, 109, 116
  *Antony and Cleopatra* **6**: 53, 136, 146, 151, 159, 161, 189, 192, 211, 224

  *As You Like It* **5**: 30, 32, 154
  *Coriolanus* **9**: 65, 73, 80, 92, 106, 153, 157, 164, 193; **30**: 67, 89, 133
  *Cymbeline* **4**: 64, 77, 103
  *Henry V* **5**: 192, 210, 213, 219, 223, 226, 233, 252, 260, 269, 281, 299, 304; **14**: 336; **30**: 159, 193
  *Julius Caesar* **7**: 167, 257, 259, 262, 268, 282, 316, 320, 333, 336, 346, 350
  *The Merchant of Venice* **4**: 254, 300, 321, 331, 350; **28**: 63
  *Much Ado about Nothing* **8**: 14, 63, 79, 82; **28**: 63
  *The Rape of Lucrece* **10**: 93, 98, 128
  *Richard II* **6**: 270, 307, 364, 368, 391; **24**: 383; **28**: 188
  *Sonnets* **10**: 256, 293, 334, 337, 346
  *The Taming of the Shrew* **9**: 340, 375, 398, 407, 413; **13**: 3; **19**: 122
  *The Two Noble Kinsmen* **9**: 463, 481, 486; **41**: 301
  *The Winter's Tale* **7**: 419, 420

**the island**
  *The Tempest* **8**: 308, 315, 447; **25**: 357, 382; **29**: 278, 343

**Italian influences**
  *Sonnets* **28**: 407

**Jacobean culture, relation to**
  *Coriolanus* **22**: 248
  *Macbeth* **19**: 330; **22**: 365
  *Pericles* **37**: 361
  *The Winter's Tale* **19**: 366, 401, 431; **25**: 347; **32**: 388; **37**: 306

**jealousy**
  *The Merry Wives of Windsor* **5**: 334, 339, 343, 353, 355, 363; **22**: 93; **38**: 273, 307
  *Othello* **4**: 384, 488, 527; **35**: 253, 265, 282, 301, 310; **44**: 57, 66
  *The Winter's Tale* **44**: 66; **47**: 25

**Jonsonian humors comedy, influence of**
  *The Merry Wives of Windsor* **38**: 319

**judicial versus natural law**
  *Measure for Measure* **2**: 446, 507, 516, 519; **22**: 85; **33**: 58, 117

**justice**
  *As You Like It* **46**: 94
  *Othello* **35**: 247

**justice and mercy**
  *Measure for Measure* **2**: 391, 395, 399, 402, 406, 409, 411, 416, 421, 437, 443, 463, 466, 470, 491, 495, 522, 524; **22**: 85; **33**: 52, 61, 101
  *The Merchant of Venice* **4**: 213, 214, 224, 250, 261, 273, 282, 289, 336; **12**: 80, 129; **40**: 127
  *Much Ado about Nothing* **22**: 85

**juxtaposition of opposing perspectives**
  *As You Like It* **5**: 86, 93, 98, 141; **16**: 53; **23**: 119; **34**: 72, 78, 131

**Kingship (Volume 39: 1, 16, 20, 34, 45, 62)**
  *Henry IV, Parts 1 and 2* **1**: 314, 318, 337, 366, 370, 374, 379, 380, 383, 424; **16**: 172; **19**: 195; **28**: 101; **39**: 100, 116, 123, 130; **42**: 141; **48**: 143
  *Henry V* **5**: 205, 223, 225, 233, 239, 244, 257, 264, 267, 271, 287, 289, 299, 302, 304, 314, 318; **16**: 202; **22**: 137; **30**: 169, 202, 259, 273; **42**: 141
  *Henry VI, Parts 1, 2, and 3* **3**: 69, 73, 77, 109, 115, 136, 143; **24**: 32; **39**: 154, 177, 187; **47**: 32
  *Henry VIII* **2**: 49, 58, 60, 65, 75, 78; **24**: 113; **41**: 129, 171
  *King John* **9**: 235, 254, 263, 275, 297; **13**: 158; **19**: 182; **22**: 120
  *Richard II* **6**: 263, 264, 272, 277, 289, 294, 327, 354, 364, 381, 388, 391, 402, 409, 414; **19**: 151, 209; **24**: 260, 289, 291, 322, 325, 333, 339, 345, 346, 349, 351, 352, 356, 395, 408, 419, 428; **28**: 134; **39**: 235, 243, 256, 263, 273, 279, 289; **42**: 173
  *Richard III* **39**: 335, 341, 345, 349

**knighthood**
  *The Merry Wives of Windsor* **5**: 338, 343, 390, 397, 402; **47**: 354

**knowledge**
  *Love's Labour's Lost* **22**: 12; **47**: 35

**language and imagery**
  *All's Well That Ends Well* **7**: 12, 29, 45, 104, 109, 121; **38**: 132, 65
  *Antony and Cleopatra* **6**: 21, 25, 39, 64, 80, 85, 92, 94, 100, 104, 142, 146, 155, 159, 161, 165, 189, 192, 202, 211; **13**: 374, 383; **25**: 245, 257; **27**: 96, 105, 135
  *As You Like It* **5**: 19, 21, 35, 52, 75, 82, 92, 138; **23**: 15, 21, 26; **28**: 9; **34**: 131; **37**: 43; **48**: 42
  *The Comedy of Errors* **1**: 16, 25, 39, 40, 43, 57, 59; **34**: 233
  *Coriolanus* **9**: 8, 9, 13, 53, 64, 65, 73, 78, 84, 100, 112, 121, 136, 139, 142, 144, 153, 157, 174, 183, 193, 198; **22**: 248; **25**: 245, 263; **30**: 111, 125, 142; **37**: 283; **44**: 79
  *Cymbeline* **4**: 43, 48, 61, 64, 70, 73, 93, 108; **13**: 401; **25**: 245; **28**: 373, 398; **36**: 115, 158, 166, 186; **47**: 205, 286, 296
  *Hamlet* **1**: 95, 144, 153, 154, 160, 188, 198, 221, 227, 249, 259, 270; **22**: 258, 378; **28**: 311; **35**: 144, 152, 238, 241; **42**: 212; **44**: 248
  *Henry IV, Parts 1 and 2* **13**: 213; **16**: 172; **25**: 245; **28**: 101; **39**: 116, 130; **42**: 153; **47**: 1
  *Henry V* **5**: 188, 230, 233, 241, 264, 276; **9**: 203; **19**: 203; **25**: 131; **30**: 159, 181, 207, 234; **30**: 159, 181, 207, 234
  *Henry VI, Parts 1, 2, and 3* **3**: 21, 50, 52, 55, 57, 66, 67, 71, 75, 76, 97, 105, 109, 119, 126, 131; **24**: 28; **37**: 157; **39**: 213, 222
  *Henry VIII* **41**: 180, 190
  *Julius Caesar* **7**: 148, 155, 159, 188, 204, 207, 227, 242, 250, 277, 296, 303, 324, 346, 350; **13**: 260; **17**: 347, 348, 350, 356, 358; **19**: 321; **22**: 280; **25**: 280; **30**: 333, 342
  *King Lear* **2**: 129, 137, 161, 191, 199, 237, 257, 271; **16**: 301; **19**: 344; **22**: 233; **46**: 177

*King John* **9**: 212, 215, 220, 246, 251, 254, 267, 280, 284, 292, 297, 300; **13**: 147, 158; **22**: 120; **37**: 132; **48**: 132
*Love's Labour's Lost* **2**: 301, 302, 303, 306, 307, 308, 315, 319, 320, 330, 335, 344, 345, 348, 356, 359, 362, 365, 371, 374, 375; **19**: 92; **22**: 12, 378; **23**: 184, 187, 196, 197, 202, 207, 211, 221, 227, 231, 233, 237, 252; **28**: 9, 63; **38**: 219, 226
*Macbeth* **3**: 170, 193, 213, 231, 234, 241, 245, 250, 253, 256, 263, 271, 283, 300, 302, 306, 323, 327, 338, 340, 349; **13**: 476; **16**: 317; **20**: 241, 279, 283, 367, 379, 400; **25**: 235; **28**: 339; **29**: 76, 91; **42**: 258; **44**: 366; **45**: 58
*Measure for Measure* **2**: 394, 421, 431, 466, 486, 505; **13**: 112; **28**: 9; **33**: 69
*The Merry Wives of Windsor* **5**: 335, 337, 343, 347, 351, 363, 374, 379; **19**: 101; **22**: 93, 378; **28**: 9, 69; **38**: 313, 319
*The Merchant of Venice* **4**: 241, 267, 293; **22**: 3; **25**: 257; **28**: 9, 63; **32**: 41; **40**: 106
*A Midsummer Night's Dream* **3**: 397, 401, 410, 412, 415, 432, 453, 459, 468, 494; **22**: 23, 39, 93, 378; **28**: 9; **29**: 263; **45**: 143, 169, 175; **48**: 23, 32
*Much Ado about Nothing* **8**: 9, 38, 43, 46, 55, 69, 73, 88, 95, 100, 115, 125; **19**: 68; **25**: 77; **28**: 63; **31**: 178, 184, 222, 241, 245; **48**: 14
*Othello* **4**: 433, 442, 445, 462, 493, 508, 517, 552, 587, 596; **13**: 304; **16**: 272; **22**: 378; **25**: 189, 257; **28**: 243, 344; **42**: 273; **47**: 51
*Pericles* **2**: 559, 560, 565, 583; **16**: 391; **19**: 387; **22**: 315; **36**: 198, 214, 233, 244, 251, 264
*The Rape of Lucrece* **10**: 64, 65, 66, 71, 78, 80, 89, 93, 116, 109, 125, 131; **22**: 289, 294; **25**: 305; **32**: 321; **33**: 144, 155, 179, 200; **43**: 102, 113, 141
*Richard II* **6**: 252, 282, 283, 294, 298, 315, 323, 331, 347, 368, 374, 381, 385, 397, 409; **13**: 213, 494; **24**: 269, 270, 298, 301, 304, 315, 325, 329, 333, 339, 356, 364, 395, 405, 408, 411, 414, 419; **28**: 134, 188; **39**: 243, 273, 289, 295; **42**: 173
*Richard III* **8**: 159, 161, 165, 167, 168, 170, 177, 182, 184, 186, 193, 197, 201, 206, 218, 223, 243, 248, 252, 258, 262, 267; **16**: 150; **25**: 141, 245; **39**: 360, 370, 383; **47**: 15
*Romeo and Juliet* **5**: 420, 426, 431, 436, 437, 456, 477, 479, 489, 492, 496, 509, 520, 522, 528, 538, 542, 550, 559; **25**: 181, 245, 257; **32**: 276; **33**: 210, 272, 274, 287; **42**: 266
*Sonnets* **10**: 247, 251, 255, 256, 290, 353, 372, 385; **13**: 445; **28**: 380, 385; **32**: 327, 352; **40**: 228, 247, 284, 292, 303
*The Taming of the Shrew* **9**: 336, 338, 393, 401, 404, 407, 413; **22**: 378; **28**: 9; **31**: 261, 288, 300, 326, 335, 339; **32**: 56
*The Tempest* **8**: 324, 348, 384, 390, 404, 454; **19**: 421; **29**: 278; **29**: 297, 343, 368, 377
*Timon of Athens* **1**: 488; **13**: 392; **25**: 198; **27**: 166, 184, 235
*Titus Andronicus* **4**: 617, 624, 635, 642, 644, 646, 659, 664, 668, 672, 675; **13**: 225; **16**: 225; **25**: 245; **27**: 246, 293, 313, 318, 325; **43**: 186, 222, 227, 239, 247, 262
*Troilus and Cressida* **3**: 561, 569, 596, 599, 606, 624, 630, 635; **22**: 58, 339; **27**: 332; 366; **42**: 66

*Twelfth Night* **1**: 570, 650, 664; **22**: 12; **28**: 9; **34**: 293; **37**: 59
*The Two Gentlemen of Verona* **6**: 437, 438, 439, 445, 449, 490, 504, 519, 529, 541; **28**: 9; **40**: 343
*The Two Noble Kinsmen* **9**: 445, 446, 447, 448, 456, 461, 462, 463, 469, 471, 498, 502; **41**: 289, 301, 308, 317, 326
*The Winter's Tale* **7**: 382, 384, 417, 418, 420, 425, 460, 506; **13**: 409; **19**: 431; **22**: 324; **25**: 347; **36**: 295; **42**: 301; **45**: 297, 344, 333

**language versus action**
*Titus Andronicus* **4**: 642, 644, 647, 664, 668; **13**: 225; **27**: 293, 313, 325; **43**: 186

**law versus passion for freedom**
*Much Ado about Nothing* **22**: 85

**laws of nature, violation of**
*Macbeth* **3**: 234, 241, 280, 323; **29**: 120

**legal issues**
*King Lear* **46**: 276

**legitimacy**
*Henry VI, Parts 1, 2, and 3* **3**: 89, 157; **39**: 154,
*Henry VIII* **37**: 109

**legitimacy or inheritance**
*King John* **9**: 224, 235, 254, 303; **13**: 147; **19**: 182; **37**: 132; **41**: 215

**liberty versus tyranny**
*Julius Caesar* **7**: 158, 179, 189, 205, 221, 253; **25**: 272

**love**
See also **ideal love**
*All's Well That Ends Well* **7**: 12, 15, 16, 51, 58, 67, 90, 93, 116; **38**: 80
*As You Like It* **5**: 24, 44, 46, 57, 79, 88, 103, 116, 122, 138, 141, 162; **28**: 46, 82; **34**: 85
*King Lear* **2**: 109, 112, 131, 160, 162, 170, 179, 188, 197, 218, 222, 238, 265; **25**: 202; **31**: 77, 149, 151, 155, 162
*Love's Labour's Lost* **2**: 312, 315, 340, 344; **22**: 12; **23**: 252; **38**: 194
*The Merchant of Venice* **4**: 221, 226, 270, 284, 312, 344; **22**: 3, 69; **25**: 257; **40**: 156
sacrificial love **13**: 43; **22**: 69; **40**: 142
*A Midsummer Night's Dream*
passionate or romantic love **3**: 372, 389, 395, 396, 402, 408, 411, 423, 441, 450, 480, 497, 498, 511; **29**: 175, 225, 263, 269; **45**: 126, 136
*Much Ado about Nothing* **8**: 24, 55, 75, 95, 111, 115; **28**: 56
*Othello* **4**: 412, 493, 506, 512, 530, 545, 552, 569, 570, 575, 580, 591; **19**: 253; **22**: 207; **25**: 257; **28**: 243, 344; **32**: 201; **35**: 261, 317
*The Phoenix and Turtle* **10**: 31, 37, 40, 50; **38**: 342, 345, 367
*Sonnets* **10**: 173, 247, 287, 290, 293, 302, 309, 322, 325, 329, 394; **28**: 380; **37**: 347
*The Tempest* **8**: 435, 439; **29**: 297, 339, 377, 396

*Twelfth Night* **1**: 543, 546, 573, 580, 587, 595, 600, 603, 610, 660; **19**: 78; **26**: 257, 364; **34**: 270, 293, 323; **46**: 291, 333, 347, 362
*The Two Gentlemen of Verona* **6**: 442, 445, 456, 479, 488, 492, 494, 502, 509, 516, 519, 549; **13**: 12; **40**: 327, 335, 343, 354, 365
*The Two Noble Kinsmen* **9**: 479, 481, 490, 498; **41**: 289, 301, 355, 363, 372, 385
*The Winter's Tale* **7**: 417, 425, 469, 490

**love and friendship**
See also **friendship**
*Julius Caesar* **7**: 233, 262, 268; **25**: 272

**love and honor**
*Troilus and Cressida* **3**: 555, 604; **27**: 370, 374

**love and passion**
*Antony and Cleopatra* **6**: 51, 64, 71, 80, 85, 100, 115, 159, 165, 180; **25**: 257; **27**: 126; **47**: 71, 124,, 174, 192

**love and reason**
See also **reason**
*Othello* **4**: 512, 530, 580; **19**: 253

**love, lechery, or rape**
*Troilus and Cressida* **43**: 357

**love versus fate**
*Romeo and Juliet* **5**: 421, 437, 438, 443, 445, 458; **33**: 249

**love versus friendship**
See also **friendship**
*The Two Gentlemen of Verona* **6**: 439, 449, 450, 458, 460, 465, 468, 471, 476, 480; **40**: 354, 365

**love versus lust**
*Venus and Adonis* **10**: 418, 420, 427, 434, 439, 448, 449, 454, 462, 466, 473, 480, 489; **25**: 305; **28**: 355; **33**: 309, 330, 339, 347, 357, 363, 370

**love versus reason**
See also **reason**
*Sonnets* **10**: 329

**love versus war**
*Troilus and Cressida* **18**: 332, 371, 406, 423; **22**: 339; **27**: 376

**Machiavellianism**
*Henry V* **5**: 203, 225, 233, 252, 287, 304; **25**: 131; **30**: 273
*Henry VI, Parts 1, 2, and 3* **22**: 193

**Madness (Volume 35**: 1, 7, 8, 24, 34, 49, 54, 62, 68)
*Hamlet* **19**: 330; **35**: 104, 117, 126, 132, 134, 140, 144
*King Lear* **19**: 330
*Macbeth* **19**: 330
*Othello* **35**: 265, 276, 282
*Twelfth Night* **1**: 554, 639, 656; **26**: 371

**Magic and the Supernatural (Volume 29**: 1, 12, 28, 46, 53, 65)

*The Comedy of Errors* **1**: 27, 30
*Macbeth*
    supernatural grace versus evil or chaos **3**: 241, 286, 323
    witchcraft and supernaturalism **3**: 171, 172, 173, 175, 177, 182, 183, 184, 185, 194, 196, 198, 202, 207, 208, 213, 219, 229, 239; **16**: 317; **19**: 245; **20**: 92, 175, 213, 279, 283, 374, 387, 406, 413; **25**: 235; **28**: 339; **29**: 91, 101, 109, 120; **44**: 351, 373
*A Midsummer Night's Dream* **29**: 190, 201, 210, 216
*The Tempest* **8**: 287, 293, 304, 315, 340, 356, 396, 401, 404, 408, 435, 458; **28**: 391, 415; **29**: 297, 343, 377; **45**: 272; **48**: 299
*Sonnets*
    occult **48**: 346
*The Winter's Tale*
    witchcraft **22**: 324

**male discontent**
*The Merry Wives of Windsor* **5**: 392, 402

**male domination**
*Love's Labour's Lost* **22**: 12
*A Midsummer Night's Dream* **3**: 483, 520; **13**: 19; **25**: 36; **29**: 216, 225, 243, 256, 269; **42**: 46; **45**: 84

**male/female relationships**
*As You Like It* **46**: 134
*The Comedy of Errors* **16**: 3
*The Rape of Lucrece* **10**: 109, 121, 131; **22**: 289; **25**: 305; **43**: 113, 141,
*Troilus and Cressida* **16**: 70; **22**: 339; **27**: 362

**male sexual anxiety**
*Love's Labour's Lost* **16**: 17

**manhood**
*Macbeth* **3**: 262, 309, 333; **29**: 127, 133

**Marlowe's works, compared with**
*Richard II* **42**: 173

**marriage**
    See also **courtship and marriage**
*The Comedy of Errors* **34**: 251
*Hamlet* **22**: 339
*Love's Labour's Lost* **2**: 335, 340; **19**: 92; **38**: 209, 232
*Measure for Measure* **2**: 443, 507, 516, 519, 524, 528; **25**: 12; **33**: 61, 90
*The Merry Wives of Windsor* **5**: 343, 369, 376, 390, 392, 400; **22**: 93; **38**: 297
*A Midsummer Night's Dream* **3**: 402, 423, 450, 483, 520; **29**: 243, 256; **45**: 136, 143; **48**: 32
*Othello* **35**: 369
*The Taming of the Shrew* **9**: 322, 325, 329, 332, 329, 332, 334, 341, 342, 343, 344, 345, 347, 353, 360, 362, 375, 381, 390, 398, 401, 404, 413, 426, 430; **13**: 3; **19**: 3; **28**: 24; **31**: 288
*Titus Andronicus*
    marriage as political tyranny **48**: 264
*Troilus and Cressida* **22**: 339
*The Two Gentlemen of Verona* **48**: 32

**martial vs. civil law**
*Coriolanus* **48**: 230

**Marxist criticism**
*Hamlet* **42**: 229
*King Lear* **42**: 229
*Macbeth* **42**: 229
*Othello* **42**: 229

**masque elements**
*The Two Noble Kinsmen* **9**: 490
*The Tempest* **42**: 332

**master-slave relationship**
*Troilus and Cressida* **22**: 58

**mediation**
***The Merry Wives of Windsor*** **5**: 343, 392

**as medieval allegory or morality play**
*Henry IV, Parts 1 and 2* **1**: 323, 324, 342, 361, 366, 373, 374; **32**: 166; **39**: 89; **47**: 60
*Measure for Measure* **2**: 409, 421, 443, 466, 475, 491, 505, 511, 522; **13**: 94
*Timon of Athens* **1**: 492, 511, 518; **27**: 155

**medieval chivalry**
*Richard II* **6**: 258, 277, 294, 327, 338, 388, 397, 414; **24**: 274, 278, 279, 280, 283; **39**: 256
*Troilus and Cressida* **3**: 539, 543, 544, 555, 606; **27**: 376

**medieval dramatic influence**
*All's Well That Ends Well* **7**: 29, 41, 51, 98, 113; **13**: 66
*King Lear* **2**: 177, 188, 201; **25**: 218
*Othello* **4**: 440, 527, 545, 559, 582

**medieval homilies, influence of**
*The Merchant of Venice* **4**: 224, 250, 289

**medieval influence**
*Romeo and Juliet* **5**: 480, 505, 509, 573

**medieval literary influence**
*Henry VI, Parts 1, 2, and 3* **3**: 59, 67, 75, 100, 109, 136, 151; **13**: 131
*Titus Andronicus* **4**: 646, 650; **27**: 299

**medieval mystery plays, relation to**
*Macbeth* **44**: 341

**medieval physiology**
*Julius Caesar* **13**: 260

**mercantilism and feudalism**
*Richard II* **13**: 213

**merit versus rank**
*All's Well That Ends Well* **7**: 9, 10, 19, 37, 51, 76; **38**: 155

**Messina**
*Much Ado about Nothing* **8**: 19, 29, 48, 69, 82, 91, 95, 108, 111, 121, 125; **31**: 191, 209, 229, 241, 245

**metadramatic elements**
*As You Like It* **5**: 128, 130, 146; **34**: 130
*Henry V* **13**: 194; **30**: 181
*Love's Labour's Lost* **2**: 356, 359, 362
*Measure for Measure* **13**: 104
*A Midsummer Night's Dream* **3**: 427, 468, 477, 516, 520; **29**: 190, 225, 243
*The Taming of the Shrew* **9**: 350, 419, 424; **31**: 300, 315
*The Winter's Tale* **16**: 410

**metamorphosis or transformation**
*The Merry Wives of Windsor* **47**: 314
*Much Ado about Nothing* **8**: 88, 104, 111, 115
*The Taming of the Shrew* **9**: 370, 430

**metaphysical poem**
*The Phoenix and Turtle* **10**: 7, 8, 9, 20, 31, 35, 37, 40, 45, 50

**Midlands Revolt, influence of**
*Coriolanus* **22**: 248; **30**: 79

**military and sexual hierarchies**
*Othello* **16**: 272

**mimetic rivalry**
*The Two Gentlemen of Verona* **13**: 12; **40**: 335

**as "mingled yarn"**
*All's Well That Ends Well* **7**: 62, 93, 109, 126; **38**: 65

**Minotaur, myth of**
*A Midsummer Night's Dream* **3**: 497, 498; **29**: 216

**as miracle play**
*Pericles* **2**: 569, 581; **36**: 205

**misgovernment**
*Measure for Measure* **2**: 401, 432, 511; **22**: 85
*Much Ado about Nothing* **22**: 85

**misogyny**
*King Lear* **31**: 123
*Measure for Measure* **23**: 358

**misperception**
*Cymbeline* **19**: 411; **36**: 99, 115; **47**: 228, 237, 252, 277, 286, 296

**mistaken identity**
*The Comedy of Errors* **1**: 13, 14, 27, 37, 40, 45, 49, 55, 57, 61, 63; **19**: 34, 54; **25**: 63; **34**: 194

**modernization**
*Richard III* **14**: 523

**Montaigne's *Essais*, relation to**
*Sonnets* **42**: 375
*The Tempest* **42**: 339

**moral choice**
*Julius Caesar* **7**: 179, 264, 279, 343

**moral corruption**
*Troilus and Cressida* **3**: 578, 589, 599, 604, 609; **18**: 332, 406, 412, 423; **27**: 366

**moral corruption of English society**
 Richard III **8:** 154, 163, 165, 177, 193, 201, 218, 228, 232, 243, 248, 252, 267; **39:** 308

**moral inheritance**
 Henry VI, Parts 1, 2, and 3 **3:** 89, 126

**moral intent**
 Henry VIII **2:** 15, 19, 25; **24:** 140

**moral lesson**
 Macbeth **20:** 23

**moral relativism**
 Antony and Cleopatra **22:** 217; **27:** 121

**moral seriousness, question of**
 Measure for Measure **2:** 387, 388, 396, 409, 417, 421, 452, 460, 495; **23:** 316, 321

**morality**
 Henry V **5:** 195, 203, 213, 223, 225, 239, 246, 260, 271, 293
 The Merry Wives of Windsor **5:** 335, 339, 347, 349, 353, 397
 The Two Gentlemen of Verona **6:** 438, 492, 494, 514, 532, 555, 564
 Venus and Adonis **10:** 411, 412, 414, 416, 418, 419, 420, 423, 427, 428, 439, 442, 448, 449, 454, 459, 466; **33:** 330

**multiple perspectives of characters**
 Henry VI, Parts 1, 2, and 3 **3:** 69, 154

**music**
 The Tempest **8:** 390, 404; **29:** 292; **37:** 321; **42:** 332
 Twelfth Night **1:** 543, 566, 596

**music and dance**
 A Midsummer Night's Dream **3:** 397, 400, 418, 513; **12:** 287, 289; **25:** 36
 Much Ado about Nothing **19:** 68; **31:** 222

**mutability, theme of**
 Sonnets **42:** 375

**mythic elements**
 See religious, mythic, or spiritual content

**mythological allusions**
 As You Like It **46:** 142
 Antony and Cleopatra **16:** 342; **19:** 304; **27:** 110, 117; **47:** 71, 192

**naming, significance of**
 Coriolanus **30:** 58, 96, 111, 125

**narrative strategies**
 The Rape of Lucrece **22:** 294

**nationalism and patriotism**
 See also **British nationalism**
 Henry V **5:** 198, 205, 209, 210, 213, 219, 223, 233, 246, 252, 257, 269, 299; **19:** 133, 217; **30:** 227, 262
 Henry VI, Parts 1, 2, and 3 **24:** 25, 45, 47

 King John **9:** 209, 218, 222, 224, 235, 240, 244, 275; **25:** 98; **37:** 132
 The Merry Wives of Windsor **47:** 344
 The Winter's Tale **32:** 388

**nature**
 See also **art and nature** and **art versus nature**
 As You Like It **46:** 94
 The Tempest **8:** 315, 370, 390, 408, 414; **29:** 343, 362, 368, 377
 The Winter's Tale **7:** 397, 418, 419, 420, 425, 432, 436, 451, 452, 473, 479; **19:** 366; **45:** 329

**nature as book**
 Pericles **22:** 315; **36:** 233

**nature, philosophy of**
 Coriolanus **30:** 74

**negative appraisals**
 Cymbeline **4:** 20, 35, 43, 45, 48, 53, 56, 68; **15:** 32, 105, 121
 Richard II **6:** 250, 252, 253, 255, 282, 307, 317, 343, 359
 Venus and Adonis **10:** 410, 411, 415, 418, 419, 424, 429

**Neoclassical rules**
 As You Like It **5:** 19, 20
 Henry IV, Parts 1 and 2 **1:** 286, 287, 290, 293
 Henry VI, Parts 1, 2, and 3 **3:** 17, 18
 King John **9:** 208, 209, 210, 212
 Love's Labour's Lost **2:** 299, 300
 Macbeth **3:** 170, 171, 173, 175; **20:** 17
 Measure for Measure **2:** 387, 388, 390, 394; **23:** 269
 The Merry Wives of Windsor **5:** 332, 334
 Romeo and Juliet **5:** 416, 418, 426
 The Tempest **8:** 287, 292, 293, 334; **25:** 357; **29:** 292; **45:** 200
 Troilus and Cressida **3:** 537, 538; **18:** 276, 278, 281
 The Winter's Tale **7:** 376, 377, 379, 380, 383, 410; **15:** 397

**Neoplatonism**
 The Phoenix and Turtle **10:** 7, 9, 21, 24, 40, 45, 50; **38:** 345, 350, 367
 Sonnets **10:** 191, 205

**nightmarish quality**
 Macbeth **3:** 231, 309; **20:** 210, 242; **44:** 261

**nihilistic elements**
 King Lear **2:** 130, 143, 149, 156, 165, 231, 238, 245, 253; **22:** 271; **25:** 218; **28:** 325
 Timon of Athens **1:** 481, 513, 529; **13:** 392; **20:** 481
 Troilus and Cressida **27:** 354

**"nothing," significance of**
 Much Ado about Nothing **8:** 17, 18, 23, 55, 73, 95; **19:** 68

**nurturing or feeding**
 Coriolanus **9:** 65, 73, 136, 183, 189; **30:** 111; **44:** 79

**oaths, importance of**
 Pericles **19:** 387

**obscenity**
 Henry V **5:** 188, 190, 260

**Oldcastle, references to**
 Henry IV, Parts 1 and 2 **48:** 117

**omens**
 Julius Caesar **22:** 137; **45:** 10

**oppositions or dualisms**
 King John **9:** 224, 240, 263, 275, 284, 290, 300

**order**
 Henry V **5:** 205, 257, 264, 310, 314; **30:** 193
 Twelfth Night **1:** 563, 596; **34:** 330; **46:** 291, 347

**order versus disintegration**
 Titus Andronicus **4:** 618, 647; **43:** 186, 195

**other sonnet writers, Shakespeare compared with**
 Sonnets **42:** 296

**Ovid, influence of**
 A Midsummer Night's Dream **3:** 362, 427, 497, 498; **22:** 23; **29:** 175, 190, 216
 Titus Andronicus **4:** 647, 659, 664, 668; **13:** 225; **27:** 246, 275, 285, 293, 299, 306; **28:** 249; **43:** 195, 203, 206

**Ovid's *Metamorphoses*, relation to**
 The Winter's Tale ,**42:** 301
 Venus and Adonis **42:** 347

**pagan elements**
 King Lear **25:** 218

**pageantry**
 See also **ceremonies, rites, and rituals, importance of**
 Henry VIII **2:** 14, 15, 18, 51, 58; **24:** 77, 83, 84, 85, 89, 91, 106, 113, 118, 120, 126, 127, 140, 146, 150; **41:** 120, 129, 190

**paradoxical elements**
 Coriolanus **9:** 73, 92, 106, 121, 153, 157, 164, 169, 193

**parent-child relations**
 A Midsummer Night's Dream **13:** 19; **29:** 216, 225, 243

**pastoral convention, parodies of**
 As You Like It **5:** 54, 57, 72

**pastoral convention, relation to**
 As You Like It **5:** 72, 77, 122; **34:** 161; **37:** 1

**pastoral tradition, compared with**
 A Lover's Complaint **48:** 336

**patience**
 Henry VIII **2:** 58, 76, 78
 Pericles **2:** 572, 573, 578, 579; **36:** 251

**patriarchal claims**
*Henry VI, Parts 1, 2, and 3* **16:** 131 **25:** 102

**patriarchal or monarchical order**
*King Lear* **13:** 353, 457; **16:** 351; **22:** 227, 233; **25:** 218; **31:** 84, 92, 107, 117, 123, 137, 142; **46:** 269

**patriarchy**
*Cymbeline* **32:** 373; **36:** 134; **47:** 237
*Henry V* **37:** 105; **44:** 44
*Troilus and Cressida* **22:** 58

**patriotism**
See **nationalism and patriotism**

*Pattern of Painful Adventures* (Lawrence Twine), compared with
*Pericles* **48:** 364

**Pauline doctrine**
*A Midsummer Night's Dream* **3:** 457, 486, 506

**pedagogy**
*Sonnets* **37:** 374
*The Taming of the Shrew* **19:** 122

**perception**
*Othello* **19:** 276; **25:** 189, 257

**performance history**
*The Taming of the Shrew* **31:** 282

**performance issues**
See also **staging issues**
*King Lear* **2:** 106, 137, 154, 160; **11:** 10, 20, 27, 56, 57, 132, 136, 137, 145, 150, 154; **19:** 295, 344; **25:** 218
*Much Ado about Nothing* **18:** 173, 174, 183, 184, 185, 186, 187, 188, 189, 190, 191, 192, 193, 195, 197, 199, 201, 204, 206, 207, 208, 209, 210, 254
*Sonnets* **48:** 352
*The Taming of the Shrew* **12:** 313, 314, 316, 317, 337, 338; **31:** 315

**pessimistic elements**
*Timon of Athens* **1:** 462, 467, 470, 473, 478, 480; **20:** 433, 481; **27:** 155, 191

**Petrarchan poetics, influence of**
*Romeo and Juliet* **5:** 416, 520, 522, 528, 550, 559, 575; **32:** 276

**philosophical elements**
*Julius Caesar* **7:** 310, 324; **37:** 203
*Twelfth Night* **1:** 560, 563, 596; **34:** 301, 316; **46:** 297

**physical versus intellectual world**
*Love's Labour's Lost* **2:** 331, 348, 367

**pictorial elements**
*Venus and Adonis* **10:** 414, 415, 419, 420, 423, 480; **33:** 339

**Platonic elements**

*A Midsummer Night's Dream* **3:** 368, 437, 450, 497; **45:** 126

**play-within-the-play, convention of**
*Henry VI, Parts 1, 2, and 3* **3:** 75, 149
*The Merry Wives of Windsor* **5:** 354, 355, 369, 402
*The Taming of the Shrew* **12:** 416; **22:** 48

**plot**
*The Winter's Tale* **7:** 376, 377, 379, 382, 387, 390, 396, 452; **13:** 417; **15:** 518; **45:** 374

**plot and incident**
*Richard III* **8:** 146, 152, 159; **25:** 164

**Plutarch and historical sources**
*Coriolanus* **9:** 8, 9, 13, 14, 16, 26, 39, 92, 106, 130, 142, 164; **30:** 74, 79, 105

**poet-patron relationship**
*Sonnets* **48:** 352

**poetic justice, question of**
*King Lear* **2:** 92, 93, 94, 101, 129, 137, 231, 245
*Othello* **4:** 370, 412, 415, 427

**poetic style**
*Sonnets* **10:** 153, 155, 156, 158, 159, 160, 161, 173, 175, 182, 214, 247, 251, 255, 260, 265, 283, 287, 296, 302, 315, 322, 325, 337, 346, 349, 360, 367, 385; **16:** 472; **40:** 221, 228,

**political and social disintegration**
*Antony and Cleopatra* **6:** 31, 43, 53, 60, 71, 80, 100, 107, 111, 146, 180, 197, 219; **22:** 217; **25:** 257; **27:** 121

**political content**
*Titus Andronicus* **43:** 262

**Politics (Volume 30:** 1, 4, 11, 22, 29, 39, 42, 46, 49)
*Coriolanus* **9:** 15, 17, 18, 19, 26, 33, 43, 53, 62, 65, 73, 80, 92, 106, 110, 112, 121, 144, 153, 157, 164, 180; **22:** 248; **25:** 296; **30:** 58, 67, 79, 89, 96, 105, 111, 125; **37:** 283; **42:** 218; **48:** 230
*Hamlet* **44:** 241
*Henry IV, Parts 1 and 2* **28:** 101; **39:** 130; **42:** 141; **48:** 143, 175
*Henry VIII* **2:** 39, 49, 51, 58, 60, 65, 67, 71, 72, 75, 78, 81; **24:** 74, 121, 124; **41:** 146
*Julius Caesar* **7:** 161, 169, 191, 205, 218, 221, 245, 262, 264, 279, 282, 310, 324, 333, 346; **17:** 317, 318, 321, 323, 334, 350, 351, 358, 378, 382, 394, 406; **22:** 137, 280; **25:** 272, 280; **30:** 285, 297, 316, 321, 342, 374, 379; **37:** 203
*King John* **9:** 218, 224, 260, 280; **13:** 163; **22:** 120; **37:** 132; **41:** 221, 228
*King Lear* **46:** 269
*Measure for Measure* **23:** 379
*A Midsummer Night's Dream* **29:** 243
*Pericles* **37:** 361
*The Tempest* **8:** 304, 307, 315, 353, 359, 364, 401, 408; **16:** 426; **19:** 421; **29:** 339; **37:** 336; **42:** 320; **45:** 272, 280

*Timon of Athens* **27:** 223, 230
*Titus Andronicus* **27:** 282; **48:** 264
*Troilus and Cressida* **3:** 536, 560, 606; **16:** 84

**popularity**
*Pericles* **2:** 536, 538, 546; **37:** 361
*Richard III* **8:** 144, 146, 154, 158, 159, 162, 181, 228; **39:** 383
*The Taming of the Shrew* **9:** 318, 338, 404
*Venus and Adonis* **10:** 410, 412, 418, 427; **25:** 328

**power**
*Henry V* **37:** 175
*Measure for Measure* **13:** 112; **22:** 85; **23:** 327, 330, 339, 352; **33:** 85
*A Midsummer Night's Dream* **42:** 46; **45:** 84
*Much Ado about Nothing* **22:** 85; **25:** 77; **31:** 231, 245

**pride and rightful self-esteem**
*Othello* **4:** 522, 536, 541; **35:** 352

**primitivism**
*Macbeth* **20:** 206, 213; **45:** 48

**primogeniture**
*As You Like It* **5:** 66, 158; **34:** 109, 120

**as "problem" plays**
*The Comedy of Errors* **34:** 251
*Julius Caesar* **7:** 272, 320
*Measure for Measure* **2:** 416, 429, 434, 474, 475, 503, 514, 519; **16:** 102; **23:** 313, 328, 351
*Troilus and Cressida* **3:** 555, 566
lack of resolution **43:** 277

**procreation**
*Sonnets* **10:** 379, 385; **16:** 461
*Venus and Adonis* **10:** 439, 449, 466; **33:** 321, 377

**providential order**
*King Lear* **2:** 112, 116, 137, 168, 170, 174, 177, 218, 226, 241, 253; **22:** 271
*Macbeth* **3:** 208, 289, 329, 336
*Measure for Measure* **48:** 1

**Psychoanalytic Interpretations of Shakespeare's Works (Volume 44:** 1, 11, 18, 28, 35, 44, 57, 66, 79, 89, 93)
*As You Like It* **5:** 146, 158; **23:** 141, 142; **34:** 109; **48:** 42
*Coriolanus* **44:** 93
*Cymbeline* **45:** 67, 75
*Hamlet* **1:** 119, 148, 154, 179, 202; **21:** 197, 213, 361; **25:** 209; **28:** 223; **35:** 95, 104, 134, 237; **37:** 241; **44:** 133, 152, 160, 180, 209, 219
*Henry IV, Parts 1 and 2* **13:** 457; **28:** 101; **42:** 185; **44:** 44
*Henry V* **13:** 457; **44:** 44
*Julius Caesar* **45:** 10
*Macbeth* **3:** 219, 223, 226; **44:** 11, 284, 289, 297; **45:** 48, 58
*Measure for Measure* **23:** 331, 332, 333, 334, 335, 340, 355, 356, 359, 379, 395; **44:** 89

*Merchant of Venice* **45:** 17
*A Midsummer Night's Dream* **3:** 440, 483; **28:** 15; **29:** 225; **44:** 1; **45:** 107, 117
*Othello* **4:** 468, 503; **35:** 265, 276, 282, 301, 317, 320, 347; **42:** 198; **44:** 57
*Romeo and Juliet* **5:** 513, 556
*The Tempest* **45:** 259
*Troilus and Cressida* **43:** 287
*Twelfth Night* **46:** 333

**psychological elements**
*Cymbeline* **36:** 134; **44:** 28

**public versus private principles**
*Julius Caesar* **7:** 161, 179, 252, 262, 268, 284, 298; **13:** 252

**public versus private speech**
*Love's Labour's Lost* **2:** 356, 362, 371

**public versus private worlds**
*As You Like It* **46:** 164
*Coriolanus* **37:** 283; **42:** 218
*Romeo and Juliet* **5:** 520, 550; **25:** 181; **33:** 274

**as "pure" poetry**
*The Phoenix and Turtle* **10:** 14, 31, 35; **38:** 329

**Puritanism**
*Measure for Measure* **2:** 414, 418, 434
*Twelfth Night* **1:** 549, 553, 555, 632; **16:** 53; **25:** 47; **46:** 338

**racial issues**
*Othello* **4:** 370, 380, 384, 385, 392, 399, 401, 402, 408, 427, 564; **13:** 327; **16:** 293; **25:** 189, 257; **28:** 249, 330; **35:** 369; **42:** 198

**rape**
*Titus Andronicus* **43:** 227, 255; **48:** 277

**realism**
See also **idealism versus realism**
*The Merry Wives of Windsor* **38:** 313
*The Tempest* **8:** 340, 359, 464
*Troilus and Cressida* **43:** 357

**reality and illusion**
*The Tempest* **8:** 287, 315, 359, 401, 435, 439, 447, 454; **22:** 302; **45:** 236, 247

**reason**
See also **love and reason** *and* **love versus reason**
*Venus and Adonis* **10:** 427, 439, 449, 459, 462, 466; **28:** 355; **33:** 309, 330

**reason versus imagination**
*Antony and Cleopatra* **6:** 107, 115, 142, 197, 228; **45:** 28
*A Midsummer Night's Dream* **3:** 381, 389, 423, 441, 466, 506; **22:** 23; **29:** 190; **45:** 96

**rebellion**
See also **usurpation**
*Henry IV, Parts 1 and 2* **22:** 395; **28:** 101
*Henry VIII* **22:** 395

*King John* **9:** 218, 254, 263, 280, 297
*Richard III* **22:** 395

**rebirth, regeneration, resurrection, or immortality**
*All's Well That Ends Well* **7:** 90, 93, 98
*Antony and Cleopatra* **6:** 100, 103, 125, 131, 159, 181
*Cymbeline* **4:** 38, 64, 73, 93, 105, 113, 116, 129, 138, 141, 162, 170
*Measure for Measure* **13:** 84; **16:** 102, 114; **23:** 321, 327, 335, 340, 352; **25:** 12
*Pericles* **2:** 555, 564, 584, 586, 588; **36:** 205
*The Tempest* **8:** 302, 312, 320, 334, 348, 359, 370, 384, 401, 404, 414, 429, 439, 447, 454; **16:** 442; **22:** 302; **29:** 297; **37:** 336
*The Winter's Tale* **7:** 397, 414, 417, 419, 429, 436, 451, 452, 456, 480, 490, 497, 506; **25:** 339 452, 480, 490, 497, 506; **45:** 366

**reconciliation**
*As You Like It* **46:** 156
*All's Well That Ends Well* **7:** 90, 93, 98
*Antony and Cleopatra* **6:** 100, 103, 125, 131, 159, 181
*Cymbeline* **4:** 38, 64, 73, 93, 105, 113, 116, 129, 138, 141, 162, 170
*The Merry Wives of Windsor* **5:** 343, 369, 374, 397, 402
*A Midsummer Night's Dream* **3:** 412, 418, 437, 459, 468, 491, 497, 502, 513; **13:** 27; **29:** 190
*Romeo and Juliet* **5:** 415, 419, 427, 439, 447, 480, 487, 493, 505, 533, 536, 562
*The Tempest* **8:** 302, 312, 320, 334, 348, 359, 370, 384, 401, 404, 414, 429, 439, 447, 454; **16:** 442; **22:** 302; **29:** 297; **37:** 336; **45:** 236

**reconciliation of opposites**
*As You Like It* **5:** 79, 88, 103, 116, 122, 138; **23:** 127, 143; **34:** 161, 172; **46:** 156

**redemption**
*The Comedy of Errors* **19:** 54; **26:** 188

**regicide**
*Macbeth* **3:** 248, 275, 312; **16:** 317, 328

**relationship to other Shakespearean plays**
*Twelfth Night* **46:** 303
*Henry IV, Parts 1 and 2* **42:** 99, 153; **48:** 167

**relationship between Parts 1 and 2**
*Henry IV, Parts 1 and 2* **32:** 136; **39:** 100

**religious and theological issues**
*Macbeth* **44:** 324, 341, 351, 361, 366, 373
*Measure for Measure* **48:** 1

**religious, mythic, or spiritual content**
See also **Christian elements**
*All's Well That Ends Well* **7:** 15, 45, 54, 67, 76, 98, 109, 116
*Antony and Cleopatra* **6:** 53, 94, 111, 115, 178, 192, 224; **47:** 71
*Cymbeline* **4:** 22, 29, 78, 93, 105, 108, 115, 116, 127, 134, 138, 141, 159; **28:** 373; **36:** 142, 158, 186; **47:** 219, 260, 274
*Hamlet* **1:** 98, 102, 130, 184, 191, 209, 212, 231, 234, 254; **21:** 361; **22:** 258; **28:** 280; **32:** 238; **35:** 134
*Henry IV, Parts 1 and 2* **1:** 314, 374, 414, 421, 429, 431, 434; **32:** 103; **48:** 151
*Henry V* **25:** 116; **32:** 126
*Macbeth* **3:** 208, 269, 275, 318; **29:** 109
*Measure for Measure* **48:** 1
*Othello* **4:** 483, 517, 522, 525, 559, 573; **22:** 207; **28:** 330
*Pericles* **2:** 559, 561, 565, 570, 580, 584, 588; **22:** 315; **25:** 365
*The Tempest* **8:** 328, 390, 423, 429, 435; **45:** 211, 247
*Timon of Athens* **1:** 505, 512, 513, 523; **20:** 493

**repentance and forgiveness**
*Much Ado about Nothing* **8:** 24, 29, 111
*The Two Gentlemen of Verona* **6:** 450, 514, 516, 555, 564
*The Winter's Tale* **44:** 66

**resolution**
*Measure for Measure* **2:** 449, 475, 495, 514, 516; **16:** 102, 114
*The Merchant of Venice* **4:** 263, 266, 300, 319, 321; **13:** 37
*The Two Gentlemen of Verona* **6:** 435, 436, 439, 445, 449, 453, 458, 460, 462, 465, 466, 468, 471, 476, 480, 486, 494, 509, 514, 516, 519, 529, 532, 541, 549; **19:** 34

**retribution**
*Henry VI, Parts 1, 2, and 3* **3:** 27, 42, 51, 59, 77, 83, 92, 100, 109, 115, 119, 131, 136, 151
*Julius Caesar* **7:** 160, 167, 200
*Macbeth* **3:** 194, 208, 318; **48:** 214
*Richard III* **8:** 163, 170, 177, 182, 184, 193, 197, 201, 206, 210, 218, 223, 228, 243, 248, 267

**revenge**
*Hamlet* **1:** 74, 194, 209, 224, 234, 254; **16:** 246; **22:** 258; **25:** 288; **28:** 280; **35:** 152, 157, 167, 174, 212; **44:** 180, 209, 219, 229
*The Merry Wives of Windsor* **5:** 349, 350, 392; **38:** 264, 307
*Othello* **35:** 261

**revenge tragedy elements**
*Julius Caesar* **7:** 316
*Titus Andronicus* **4:** 618, 627, 628, 636, 639, 644, 646, 664, 672, 680; **16:** 225; **27:** 275, 318

**reversal**
*A Midsummer Night's Dream* **29:** 225

**rhetoric**
*Venus and Adonis* **33:** 377
*Romeo and Juliet* **42:** 266

**rhetoric of consolation**
*Sonnets* **42:** 375

**rhetoric of politeness**
*Henry VIII* **22:** 182

**rhetorical style**
*King Lear* **16**: 301; **47**: 9

**riddle motif**
*Pericles* **22**: 315; **36**: 205, 214

**rightful succession**
*Titus Andronicus* **4**: 638

**rings episode**
*The Merchant of Venice* **22**: 3; **40**: 106, 151, 156

**role-playing**
*Julius Caesar* **7**: 356; **37**: 229
*The Taming of the Shrew* **9**: 322, 353, 355, 360, 369, 370, 398, 401, 407, 413, 419, 424; **13**: 3; **31**: 288, 295, 315

**as romance play**
*As You Like It* **5**: 55, 79; **23**: 27, 28, 40, 43

**romance or chivalric tradition, influence of**
*Much Ado about Nothing* **8**: 53, 125

**romance or folktale elements**
*All's Well That Ends Well* **7**: 32, 41, 43, 45, 54, 76, 104, 116, 121; **26**: 117

**romance or pastoral tradition, influence of**
*The Tempest* **8**: 336, 348, 396, 404; **37**: 336

**romantic and courtly conventions**
*The Two Gentlemen of Verona* **6**: 438, 460, 472, 478, 484, 486, 488, 502, 507, 509, 529, 541, 549, 560, 568; **12**: 460, 462; **40**: 354, 374

**romantic elements**
*The Comedy of Errors* **1**: 13, 16, 19, 23, 25, 30, 31, 36, 39, 53
*Cymbeline* **4**: 17, 20, 46, 68, 77, 141, 148, 172; **15**: 111; **25**: 319; **28**: 373
*King Lear* **31**: 77, 84
*The Taming of the Shrew* **9**: 334, 342, 362, 375, 407

**royalty**
*Antony and Cleopatra* **6**: 94

**Salic Law**
*Henry V* **5**: 219, 252, 260; **28**: 121

**as satire or parody**
*Love's Labour's Lost* **2**: 300, 302, 303, 307, 308, 315, 321, 324, 327; **23**: 237, 252
*The Merry Wives of Windsor* **5**: 338, 350, 360, 385; **38**: 278, 319; **47**: 354, 363,

**satire or parody of pastoral conventions**
*As You Like It* **5**: 46, 55, 60, 72, 77, 79, 84, 114, 118, 128, 130, 154

**satirical elements**
*The Phoenix and Turtle* **10**: 8, 16, 17, 27, 35, 40, 45, 48
*Timon of Athens* **27**: 155, 235
*Troilus and Cressida* **3**: 539, 543, 544, 555, 558, 574; **27**: 341

**Saturnalian elements**
*Twelfth Night* **1**: 554, 571, 603, 620, 642; **16**: 53

**schemes and intrigues**
*The Merry Wives of Windsor* **5**: 334, 336, 339, 341, 343, 349, 355, 379

**Scholasticism**
*The Phoenix and Turtle* **10**: 21, 24, 31

**School of Night, allusions to**
*Love's Labour's Lost* **2**: 321, 327, 328

**self-conscious or artificial nature of play**
*Cymbeline* **4**: 43, 52, 56, 68, 124, 134, 138; **36**: 99

**self-deception**
*Twelfth Night* **1**: 554, 561, 591, 625; **47**: 45

**self-indulgence**
*Twelfth Night* **1**: 563, 615, 635

**self-interest or expediency**
*Henry V* **5**: 189, 193, 205, 213, 217, 233, 260, 287, 302, 304; **30**: 273

**self-knowledge**
*As You Like It* **5**: 32, 82, 102, 116, 122, 133, 164
*Much Ado about Nothing* **8**: 69, 95, 100
*Timon of Athens* **1**: 456, 459, 462, 495, 503, 507, 515, 518, 526; **20**: 493; **27**: 166

**self-love**
*Sonnets* **10**: 372; **25**: 374

**Senecan or revenge tragedy elements**
*Timon of Athens* **27**: 235
*Titus Andronicus* **4**: 618, 627, 628, 636, 639, 644, 646, 664, 672, 680; **16**: 225; **27**: 275, 318; **43**: 170, 206, 227

**servitude**
See also **freedom and servitude**
*Comedy of Errors* **42**: 80

**setting**
*The Merry Wives of Windsor* **47**: 375
*Much Ado about Nothing* **18**: 173, 174, 183, 184, 185, 186, 187, 188, 189, 190, 191, 192, 193, 195, 197, 199, 201, 204, 206, 207, 208, 209, 210, 254
*Richard III* **14**: 516, 528
*The Two Gentlemen of Verona* **12**: 463, 465, 485

**sexual ambiguity and sexual deception**
*As You Like It* **46**: 134, 142
*Twelfth Night* **1**: 540, 562, 620, 621, 639, 645; **22**: 69; **34**: 311, 344; **37**: 59; **42**: 32
*Troilus and Cressida* **43**: 365

**sexual anxiety**
*Macbeth* **16**: 328; **20**: 283

**sexual politics**
*The Merchant of Venice* **22**: 3
*The Merry Wives of Windsor* **19**: 101; **38**: 307

**Sexuality in Shakespeare** (Volume 33: 1, 12, 18, 28, 39)
*As You Like It* **46**: 122, 127, 134, 142
*All's Well That Ends Well* **7**: 67, 86, 90, 93, 98, 126; **13**: 84; **19**: 113; **22**: 78; **28**: 38; **44**: 35
*Coriolanus* **9**: 112, 142, 174, 183, 189, 198; **30**: 79, 111, 125, 142
*Cymbeline* **4**: 170, 172; **25**: 319; **32**: 373; **47**: 245
*King Lear* **25**: 202; **31**: 133, 137, 142
*Love's Labour's Lost* **22**: 12
*Measure for Measure* **13**: 84; **16**: 102, 114; **23**: 321, 327, 335, 340, 352; **25**: 12; **33**: 85, 90, 112
*A Midsummer Night's Dream* **22**: 23, 93; **29**: 225, 243, 256, 269; **42**: 46; **45**: 107
*Othello* **22**: 339; **28**: 330, 344; **35**: 352, 360; **37**: 269; **44**: 57, 66
*Romeo and Juliet* **25**: 181; **33**: 225, 233, 241, 246, 274, 300
*Sonnets* **25**: 374; **48**: 325
*Troilus and Cressida* **22**: 58, 339; **25**: 56; **27**: 362; **43**: 365

**Shakespeare and Classical Civilization** (Volume 27: 1, 9, 15, 21, 30, 35, 39, 46, 56, 60, 67)
*Antony and Cleopatra*
  Egyptian versus Roman values **6**: 31, 33, 43, 53, 104, 111, 115, 125, 142, 155, 159, 178, 181, 211, 219; **17**: 48; **19**: 270; **27**: 82, 121, 126; **28**: 249; **47**: 96, 103, 113, 149
*The Rape of Lucrece*
  Roman history, relation to **10**: 84, 89, 93, 96, 98, 109, 116, 125, 135; **22**: 289; **25**: 305; **33**: 155, 190
*Timon of Athens* **27**: 223, 230, 325
*Titus Andronicus* **27**: 275, 282, 293, 299, 306
  Roman elements **43**: 206, 222
*Troilus and Cressida*
  Trojan versus Greek values **3**: 541, 561, 574, 584, 590, 596, 621, 638; **27**: 370

**Shakespeare's artistic growth, *Richard III*'s contribution to**
*Richard III* **8**: 165, 167, 182, 193, 197, 206, 210, 228, 239, 267; **25**: 164; **39**: 305, 326, 370

**Shakespeare's canon, place in**
*Titus Andronicus* **4**: 614, 616, 618, 619, 637, 639, 646, 659, 664, 668; **43**: 195
*Twelfth Night* **1**: 543, 548, 557, 569, 575, 580, 621, 635, 638

**Shakespeare's dramas, compared with**
*The Rape of Lucrece* **43**: 92

**Shakespeare's moral judgment**
*Antony and Cleopatra* **6**: 33, 37, 38, 41, 48, 51, 64, 76, 111, 125, 136, 140, 146, 163, 175, 189, 202, 211, 228; **13**: 368, 523; **25**: 257

**Shakespeare's political sympathies**
*Coriolanus* **9**: 8, 11, 15, 17, 19, 26, 39, 52, 53, 62, 80, 92, 142; **25**: 296; **30**: 74, 79, 89, 96, 105, 133
*Richard II* **6**: 277, 279, 287, 347, 359, 364, 391, 393, 402

*Richard III* **8:** 147, 163, 177, 193, 197, 201, 223, 228, 232, 243, 248, 267; **39:** 349; **42:** 130

**Shakespeare's Representation of Women (Volume 31:** 1, 3, 8, 12, 16, 21, 29, 34, 35, 41, 43, 48, 53, 60, 68)
- *Henry VI, Parts 1, 2, and 3* **3:** 103, 109, 126, 140, 157; **16:** 183; **39:** 196
- *King John* **9:** 222, 303; **16:** 161; **19:** 182; **41:** 215, 221
- *King Lear* **31:** 117, 123, 133
- *Love's Labour's Lost* **19:** 92; **22:** 12; **23:** 215; **25:** 1
- *The Merry Wives of Windsor* **5:** 335, 341, 343, 349, 369, 379, 390, 392, 402; **19:** 101; **38:** 307
- *Much Ado about Nothing* **31:** 222, 231, 241, 245
- *Othello* **19:** 253; **28:** 344
- *The Taming of the Shrew* **31:** 288, 300, 307, 315
- *The Winter's Tale* **22:** 324; **36:** 311; **42:** 301

**Shakespeare's romances, compared with**
- *Henry VIII* **41:** 171

**shame**
- *Coriolanus* **42:** 243

**sibling rivalry**
- *As You Like It* **34:** 109
- *Henry VI, Parts 1, 2, and 3* **22:** 193

**slander or hearsay, importance of**
- *Coriolanus* **48:** 230
- *Much Ado about Nothing* **8:** 58, 69, 82, 95, 104

**social action**
- *Sonnets* **48:** 352

**social and moral corruption**
- *King Lear* **2:** 116, 133, 174, 177, 241, 271; **22:** 227; **31:** 84, 92; **46:** 269

**social and political context**
- *All's Well That Ends Well* **13:** 66; **22:** 78; **38:** 99, 109, 150, 155

**social aspects**
- *Measure for Measure* **23:** 316, 375, 379, 395

**social milieu**
- *The Merry Wives of Windsor* **18:** 75, 84; **38:** 297, 300

**social order**
- *As You Like It* **37:** 1; **46:** 94
- *The Comedy of Errors* **34:** 238

**society**
- *Coriolanus* **9:** 15, 17, 18, 19, 26, 33, 43, 53, 62, 65, 73, 80, 92, 106, 110, 112, 121, 144, 153, 157, 164, 180; **22:** 248; **25:** 296; **30:** 58, 67, 79, 89, 96, 105, 111, 125
- *Troilus and Cressida* **43:** 298

**songs, role of**
- *Love's Labour's Lost* **2:** 303, 304, 316, 326, 335, 362, 367, 371, 375

**sonnet arrangement**
- *Sonnets* **10:** 174, 176, 182, 205, 226, 230, 236, 315, 353; **28:** 363; **40:** 238

**sonnet form**
- *Sonnets* **10:** 255, 325, 367; **37:** 347; **40:** 284, 303

**sonnets, compared with**
- *A Lover's Complaint* **48:** 336

**source of tragic catastrophe**
- *Romeo and Juliet* **5:** 418, 427, 431, 448, 458, 469, 479, 480, 485, 487, 493, 509, 522, 528, 530, 533, 542, 565, 571, 573; **33:** 210

**sources**
- *Antony and Cleopatra* **6:** 20, 39; **19:** 304; **27:** 96, 126; **28:** 249
- *As You Like It* **5:** 18, 32, 54, 59, 66, 84; **34:** 155; **46:** 117
- *The Comedy of Errors* **1:** 13, 14, 16, 19, 31, 32, 39; **16:** 3; **34:** 190, 215, 258
- *Cymbeline* **4:** 17, 18; **13:** 401; **28:** 373; **47:** 245, 265, 277
- *Hamlet* **1:** 76, 81, 113, 125, 128, 130, 151, 191, 202, 224, 259
- *Henry VI, Parts 1, 2, and 3* **3:** 18, 21, 29, 31, 35, 39, 46, 51; **13:** 131; **16:** 217; **39:** 196
- *Henry VIII* **2:** 16, 17; **24:** 71, 80
- *Julius Caesar* **7:** 149, 150, 156, 187, 200, 264, 272, 282, 284, 320; **30:** 285, 297, 326, 358
- *King John* **9:** 216, 222, 300; **32:** 93, 114; **41:** 234, 243, 251
- *King Lear* **2:** 94, 100, 143, 145, 170, 186; **13:** 352; **16:** 351; **28:** 301
- *Love's Labour's Lost* **16:** 17
- *Measure for Measure* **2:** 388, 393, 427, 429, 437, 475; **13:** 94
- *The Merry Wives of Windsor* **5:** 332, 350, 360, 366, 385; **32:** 31
- *A Midsummer Night's Dream* **29:** 216
- *Much Ado about Nothing* **8:** 9, 19, 53, 58, 104
- *Othello* **28:** 330
- *Pericles* **2:** 538, 568, 572, 575; **25:** 365; **36:** 198, 205
- *The Phoenix and Turtle* **10:** 7, 9, 18, 24, 45; **38:** 326, 334, 350, 367
- *The Rape of Lucrece* **10:** 63, 64, 65, 66, 68, 74, 77, 78, 89, 98, 109, 121, 125; **25:** 305; **33:** 155, 190; **43:** 77, 92, 148
- *Richard III*
  - chronicles **8:** 145, 165, 193, 197, 201, 206, 210, 213, 228, 232
  - Marlowe, Christopher **8:** 167, 168, 182, 201, 206, 218
  - morality plays **8:** 182, 190, 201, 213, 239
  - Seneca, other classical writers **8:** 165, 190, 201, 206, 228, 248
- *Romeo and Juliet* **5:** 416, 419, 423, 450; **32:** 222; **33:** 210; **45:** 40
- *Sonnets* **10:** 153, 154, 156, 158, 233, 251, 255, 293, 353; **16:** 472; **28:** 407; **42:** 375
- *The Taming of the Shrew*
  - folk tales **9:** 332, 390, 393
  - Old and New Comedy **9:** 419
  - Ovid **9:** 318, 370, 430
  - Plautus **9:** 334, 341, 342
  - shrew tradition **9:** 355; **19:** 3; **32:** 1, 56

*The Tempest* **45:** 226
*Timon of Athens* **16:** 351; **27:** 191
*Troilus and Cressida* **3:** 537, 539, 540, 541, 544, 549, 558, 566, 574, 587; **27:** 376, 381, 391, 400
*Twelfth Night* **1:** 539, 540, 603; **34:** 301, 323, 344; **46:** 291
*The Two Gentlemen of Verona* **6:** 436, 460, 462, 468, 476, 480, 490, 511, 547; **19:** 34; **40:** 320
*The Two Noble Kinsmen* **19:** 394; **41:** 289, 301, 363, 385
*Venus and Adonis* **10:** 410, 412, 420, 424, 429, 434, 439, 451, 454, 466, 473, 480, 486, 489; **16:** 452; **25:** 305; **28:** 355; **33:** 309, 321, 330, 339, 347, 352, 357, 370, 377; **42:** 347

**spectacle**
- *Love's Labour's Lost* **38:** 226
- *Macbeth* **42:** 258
- *Pericles* **42:** 352

**spectacle versus simple staging**
- *The Tempest* **15:** 206, 207, 208, 210, 217, 219, 222, 223, 224, 225, 227, 228, 305, 352; **28:** 415

**stage history**
- *As You Like It* **46:** 117
- *Antony and Cleopatra* **17:** 84, 94, 101
- *The Merry Wives of Windsor* **18:** 66, 67, 68, 70, 71

**staging issues**
*See also* **performance issues**
- *All's Well That Ends Well* **19:** 113; **26:** 15, 19, 48, 52, 64, 73, 85, 92, 93, 94, 95, 97, 114, 117, 128
- *Antony and Cleopatra* **17:** 6, 12, 84, 94, 101, 104, 110; **27:** 90; **47:** 142
- *As You Like It* **13:** 502; **23:** 7, 17, 19, 22, 58, 96, 97, 98, 99, 101, 110, 137; **28:** 82; **32:** 212
- *The Comedy of Errors* **26:** 182, 183, 186, 188, 190
- *Coriolanus* **17:** 172, 242, 248
- *Cymbeline* **15:** 6, 23, 75, 105, 111, 121, 122; **22:** 365
- *Hamlet* **13:** 494, 502; **21:** 11, 17, 31, 35, 41, 44, 50, 53, 78, 81, 89, 101, 112, 127, 139, 142, 145, 148, 151, 157, 160, 172, 182, 183, 202, 203, 208, 225, 232, 237, 242, 245, 249, 251, 259, 268, 270, 274, 283, 284, 301, 311, 334, 347, 355, 361, 371, 377, 379, 380, 381, 384, 386, 392, 407, 410, 416; **44:** 198
- *Henry IV, Parts 1 and 2* **32:** 212; **47:** 1
- *Henry V* **5:** 186, 189, 192, 193, 198, 205, 226, 230, 241, 281, 314; **13:** 194, 502; **14:** 293, 295, 297, 301, 310, 319, 328, 334, 336, 342; **19:** 217; **32:** 185
- *Henry VI, Parts 1, 2, and 3* **24:** 21, 22, 27, 31, 32, 36, 38, 41, 45, 48, 55; **32:** 212
- *Henry VIII* **24:** 67, 70, 71, 75, 77, 83, 84, 85, 87, 89, 91, 101, 106, 113, 120, 127, 129, 136, 140, 146, 150, 152, 155; **28:** 184
- *Julius Caesar* **48:** 240
- *King John* **16:** 161; **19:** 182; **24:** 171, 187, 203, 206, 211, 225, 228, 241, 245, 249
- *King Lear* **11:** 136, 137, 142, 145, 150, 151, 154, 158, 161, 165, 169; **32:** 212; **46:** 205, 218

*Love's Labour's Lost* **23:** 184, 187, 191, 196, 198, 200, 201, 202, 207, 212, 215, 216, 217, 229, 230, 232, 233, 237, 252
*Macbeth* **13:** 502; **20:** 12, 17, 32, 64, 65, 70, 73, 107, 113, 151, 175, 203, 206, 210, 213, 245, 279, 283, 312, 318, 324, 329, 343, 345, 350, 353, 363, 367, 374, 376, 379, 382, 387, 400, 406, 413; **22:** 365; **32:** 212
*Measure for Measure* **2:** 427, 429, 437, 441, 443, 456, 460, 482, 491, 519; **23:** 283, 284, 285, 286, 287, 291, 293, 294, 298, 299, 311, 315, 327, 338, 339, 340, 342, 344, 347, 363, 372, 375, 395, 400, 405, 406, 413; **32:** 16
*The Merchant of Venice* **12:** 111, 114, 115, 117, 119, 124, 129, 131
*The Merry Wives of Windsor* **18:** 74, 75, 84, 86, 90, 95
*A Midsummer Night's Dream* **3:** 364, 365, 371, 372, 377; **12:** 151, 152, 154, 158, 159, 280, 284, 291, 295; **16:** 34; **19:** 21; **29:** 183, 256; **48:** 23
*Much Ado about Nothing* **8:** 18, 33, 41, 75, 79, 82, 108; **16:** 45; **18:** 245, 247, 249, 252, 254, 257, 261, 264; **28:** 63
*Othello* **11:** 273, 334, 335, 339, 342, 350, 354, 359, 362
*Pericles* **16:** 399; **48:** 364
*Richard II* **13:** 494; **24:** 273, 274, 278, 279, 280, 283, 291, 295, 296, 301, 303, 304, 310, 315, 317, 320, 325, 333, 338, 346, 351, 352, 356, 364, 383, 386, 395, 402, 405, 411, 414, 419, 423, 428; **25:** 89
*Richard III* **14:** 515, 527, 528, 537; **16:** 137
*Romeo and Juliet* **11:** 499, 505, 507, 514, 517; **13:** 243; **25:** 181; **32:** 212
*The Tempest* **15:** 343, 346, 352, 361, 364, 366, 368, 371, 385; **28:** 391, 415; **29:** 339; **32:** 338, 343; **42:** 332; **45:** 200
*Timon of Athens* **20:** 445, 446, 481, 491, 492, 493
*Titus Andronicus* **17:** 449, 452, 456, 487; **25:** 245; **32:** 212, 249
*Troilus and Cressida* **16:** 70; **18:** 289, 332, 371, 395, 403, 406, 412, 419, 423, 442, 447, 451
*Twelfth Night* **26:** 219, 233, 257, 337, 342, 346, 357, 359, 360, 364, 366, 371, 374; **46:** 310, 369
*The Two Gentlemen of Verona* **12:** 457, 464; **42:** 18
*The Winter's Tale* **7:** 414, 425, 429, 446, 464, 480, 483, 497; **13:** 409; **15:** 518; **48:** 309

**Stoicism**
  *Hamlet* **48:** 195

**strategic analysis**
  *Antony and Cleopatra* **48:** 206

**structure**
  *All's Well That Ends Well* **7:** 21, 29, 32, 45, 51, 76, 81, 93, 98, 116; **22:** 78; **26:** 128; **38:** 72, 123, 142
  *As You Like It* **5:** 19, 24, 25, 35, 44, 45, 46, 86, 93, 116, 138, 158; **23:** 7, 8, 9, 10, 11; **34:** 72, 78, 131, 147, 155
  *Coriolanus* **9:** 8, 9, 11, 12, 13, 14, 16, 26, 33, 45, 53, 58, 72, 78, 80, 84, 92, 112, 139, 148; **25:** 263; **30:** 79, 96

  *Hamlet* **22:** 378; **28:** 280, 325; **35:** 82, 104, 215; **44:** 152
  *Henry V* **5:** 186, 189, 205, 213, 230, 241, 264, 289, 310, 314; **30:** 220, 227, 234, 244
  *Henry VI, Parts 1, 2, and 3* **3:** 31, 43, 46, 69, 83, 103, 109, 119, 136, 149, 154; **39:** 213
  *Henry VIII* **2:** 16, 25, 27, 28, 31, 36, 44, 46, 51, 56, 68, 75; **24:** 106, 112, 113, 120
  *Julius Caesar* **7:** 152, 155, 159, 160, 179, 200, 210, 238, 264, 284, 298, 316, 346; **13:** 252; **30:** 374
  *King John* **9:** 208, 212, 222, 224, 229, 240, 244, 245, 254, 260, 263, 275, 284, 290, 292, 300; **24:** 228, 241; **41:** 260, 269, 277
  *King Lear* **28:** 325; **32:** 308; **46:** 177
  *Love's Labour's Lost* **22:** 378; **23:** 191, 237, 252; **38:** 163, 172
  *Macbeth* **16:** 317; **20:** 12, 245
  *Measure for Measure* **2:** 390, 411, 449, 456, 466, 474, 482, 490, 491; **33:** 69
  *The Merchant of Venice* **4:** 201, 215, 230, 232, 243, 247, 254, 261, 263, 308, 321; **12:** 115; **28:** 63
  *The Merry Wives of Windsor* **5:** 332, 333, 334, 335, 343, 349, 355, 369, 374; **18:** 86; **22:** 378
  *A Midsummer Night's Dream* **3:** 364, 368, 381, 402, 406, 427, 450, 513; **13:** 19; **22:** 378; **29:** 175; **45:** 126, 175
  *Much Ado about Nothing* **8:** 9, 16, 17, 19, 28, 29, 33, 39, 48, 63, 69, 73, 75, 79, 82, 115; **31:** 178, 184, 198, 231
  *Othello* **22:** 378; **28:** 325
  *The Phoenix and Turtle* **10:** 27, 31, 37, 45, 50; **38:** 342, 345, 357
  *The Rape of Lucrece* **10:** 84, 89, 93, 98, 135; **22:** 294; **25:** 305; **43:** 102, 141
  *Richard II* **6:** 282, 304, 317, 343, 352, 359, 364, 39; **24:** 307, 322, 325, 356, 395
  *Richard III* **8:** 154, 161, 163, 167, 168, 170, 177, 184, 193, 197, 201, 206, 210, 218, 223, 228, 232, 243, 252, 262, 267; **16:** 150
  *Romeo and Juliet* **5:** 438, 448, 464, 469, 470, 477, 480, 496, 518, 524, 525, 528, 547, 559; **33:** 210, 246
  *Sonnets* **10:** 175, 176, 182, 205, 230, 260, 296, 302, 309, 315, 337, 349, 353; **40:** 238
  *The Taming of the Shrew* **9:** 318, 322, 325, 332, 334, 341, 362, 370, 390, 426; **22:** 48, 378; **31:** 269
  *The Tempest* **8:** 294, 295, 299, 320, 384, 439; **28:** 391, 415; **29:** 292, 297; **45:** 188
  *Timon of Athens* **27:** 157, 175, 235
  *Titus Andronicus* **4:** 618, 619, 624, 631, 635, 640, 644, 646, 647, 653, 656, 659, 662, 664, 668, 672; **27:** 246, 285
  *Troilus and Cressida* **3:** 536, 538, 549, 568, 569, 578, 583, 589, 611, 613; **27:** 341, 347, 354, 391
  *Twelfth Night* **1:** 539, 542, 543, 546, 551, 553, 563, 570, 571, 590, 600, 660; **26:** 374; **34:** 281, 287; **46:** 286
  *The Two Gentlemen of Verona* **6:** 445, 450, 460, 462, 504, 526
  *The Two Noble Kinsmen* **37:** 313
  *Venus and Adonis* **10:** 434, 442, 480, 486, 489; **33:** 357, 377

**style**
  *Henry VIII* **41:** 158

  *The Phoenix and Turtle* **10:** 8, 20, 24, 27, 31, 35, 45, 50; **38:** 334, 345, 357
  *The Rape of Lucrece* **10:** 64, 65, 66, 68, 69, 70, 71, 73, 74, 77, 78, 81, 84, 98, 116, 131, 135; **43:** 113, 158
  *Venus and Adonis* **10:** 411, 412, 414, 415, 416, 418, 419, 420, 423, 424, 428, 429, 439, 442, 480, 486, 489; **16:** 452

**subjectivity**
  *Hamlet* **45:** 28
  *Sonnets* **37:** 374

**substitution of identities**
  *Measure for Measure* **2:** 507, 511, 519; **13:** 112

**subversiveness**
  *Cymbeline* **22:** 302
  *The Tempest* **22:** 302
  *The Winter's Tale* **22:** 302

**supernatural grace versus evil or chaos**
  *Measure for Measure* **48:** 1

**suffering**
  *King Lear* **2:** 137, 160, 188, 201, 218, 222, 226, 231, 238, 241, 249, 265; **13:** 343; **22:** 271; **25:** 218
  *Pericles* **2:** 546, 573, 578, 579; **25:** 365; **36:** 279

**symbolism**
  *The Winter's Tale* **7:** 425, 429, 436, 452, 456, 469, 490, 493
  *The Tempest* **48:** 299

**textual arrangement**
  *Henry VI, Parts 1, 2, and 3* **24:** 3, 4, 6, 12, 17, 18, 19, 20, 21, 24, 27, 42, 45; **37:** 165
  *Richard II* **24:** 260, 261, 262, 263, 271, 273, 291, 296, 356, 390

**textual issues**
  *Henry IV, Parts 1 and 2* **22:** 114
  *King Lear* **22:** 271; **37:** 295
  *A Midsummer Night's Dream* **16:** 34; **29:** 216
  *The Taming of the Shrew* **22:** 48; **31:** 261, 276; **31:** 276
  *The Winter's Tale* **19:** 441, **45:** 333

**textual problems**
  *Henry V* **5:** 187, 189, 190; **13:** 201

**textual revisions**
  *Pericles* **15:** 129, 130, 132, 134, 135, 136, 138, 152, 155, 167, 181; **16:** 399; **25:** 365

**textual variants**
  *Hamlet* **13:** 282; **16:** 259; **21:** 11, 23, 72, 101, 127, 129, 139, 140, 142, 145, 202, 208, 259, 270, 284, 347, 361, 384; **22:** 258; **32:** 238

**theatrical viability**
  *Henry VI, Parts 1, 2, and 3* **24:** 31, 32, 34

**theatricality**
  Antony and Cleopatra **47**: 96, 103, 107, 113
  Macbeth **16**: 328
  Measure for Measure **23**: 285, 286, 294, 372, 406
  The Merry Wives of Windsor **47**: 325

**thematic disparity**
  Henry VIII **2**: 25, 31, 56, 68, 75; **41**: 146

**time**
  As You Like It **5**: 18, 82, 112, 141; **23**: 146, 150; **34**: 102; **46**: 88, 156, 164, 169
  Macbeth **3**: 234, 246, 283, 293; **20**: 245
  Richard II **22**: 137
  Sonnets **10**: 265, 302, 309, 322, 329, 337, 360, 379; **13**: 445; **40**: 292
  The Tempest **8**: 401, 439, 464; **25**: 357; **29**: 278, 292; **45**: 236
  Troilus and Cressida **3**: 561, 571, 583, 584, 613, 621, 626, 634
  Twelfth Night **37**: 78; **46**: **297**
  The Winter's Tale **7**: 397, 425, 436, 476, 490; **19**: 366; **36**: 301, 349; **45**: 297, 329, 366, 374

**time and change, motif of**
  Henry IV, Parts 1 and 2 **1**: 372, 393, 411; **39**: 89; **48**: 143
  As You Like It **46**: 156, 164, 169

**time scheme**
  Othello **4**: 370, 384, 390, 488; **22**: 207; **35**: 310; **47**: 51

**topical allusions or content**
  Hamlet **13**: 282
  Henry V **5**: 185, 186; **13**: 201
  Love's Labour's Lost **2**: 300, 303, 307, 315, 316, 317, 319, 321, 327, 328; **23**: 187, 191, 197, 203, 221, 233, 237, 252; **25**: 1
  Macbeth **13**: 361; **20**: 17, 350; **29**: 101

**traditional values**
  Richard III **39**: 335

**tragedies of major characters**
  Henry VIII **2**: 16, 39, 46, 48, 49, 51, 56, 58, 68, 81; **41**: 120

**tragic elements**
  The Comedy of Errors **1**: 16, 25, 27, 45, 50, 59; **34**: 229
  Cymbeline **25**: 319; **28**: 373; **36**: 129; **47**: 296
  Henry V **5**: 228, 233, 267, 269, 271
  King John **9**: 208, 209, 244
  A Midsummer Night's Dream **3**: 393, 400, 401, 410, 445, 474, 480, 491, 498, 511; **29**: 175; **45**: 169
  The Rape of Lucrece **10**: 78, 80, 81, 84, 98, 109; **43**: 85, 148
  The Tempest **8**: 324, 348, 359, 370, 380, 408, 414, 439, 458, 464
  Twelfth Night **1**: 557, 569, 572, 575, 580, 599, 621, 635, 638, 639, 645, 654, 656; **26**: 342

**treachery**
  Coriolanus **30**: 89
  King John **9**: 245

**treason and punishment**
  Macbeth **13**: 361; **16**: 328

**trickster, motif of**
  Cymbeline **22**: 302
  The Tempest **22**: 302; **29**: 297
  The Winter's Tale **22**: 302; **45**: 333

**triumph over death or fate**
  Romeo and Juliet **5**: 421, 423, 427, 505, 509, 520, 530, 536, 565, 566

**Trojan War**
  Troilus and Cressida
    as myth **43**: 293

**The Troublesome Reign (anonymous), compared with**
  King John **41**: 205, 221, 260, 269; **48**: 132

**Troy**
  Troilus and Cressida **43**: 287

**Troy passage**
  The Rape of Lucrece **43**: 77, 85

**Tudor doctrine**
  King John **9**: 254, 284, 297; **41**: 221

**Tudor myth**
  Henry VI, Parts 1, 2, and 3 **3**: 51, 59, 77, 92, 100, 109, 115, 119, 131; **39**: 222
  Richard III **8**: 163, 165, 177, 184, 193, 201, 218, 228, 232, 243, 248, 252, 267; **39**: 305, 308, 326, 387; **42**: 130

**Turkish elements**
  Henry IV, Parts 1 and 2 **19**: 170
  Henry V **19**: 170

**two fathers**
  Henry IV, Parts 1 and 2 **14**: 86, 101, 105, 108; **39**: 89, 100

**tyranny**
  King John **9**: 218

**unity**
  Antony and Cleopatra **6**: 20, 21, 22, 24, 25, 32, 33, 39, 43, 53, 60, 67, 111, 125, 146, 151, 165, 208, 211, 219; **13**: 374; **27**: 82, 90, 135
  Hamlet **1**: 75, 76, 87, 103, 113, 125, 128, 142, 148, 160, 184, 188, 198, 264; **16**: 259; **35**: 82, 215
  Henry VI, Parts 1, 2, and 3 **39**: 177, 222
  A Midsummer Night's Dream **3**: 364, 368, 381, 402, 406, 427, 450, 513; **13**: 19; **22**: 378; **29**: 175, 263

**unity of double plot**
  The Merchant of Venice **4**: 193, 194, 201, 232; **12**: 16, 67, 80, 115; **40**: 151

**unnatural ordering**
  Hamlet **22**: 378
  Love's Labour's Lost **22**: 378
  The Merry Wives of Windsor **22**: 378
  A Midsummer Night's Dream **22**: 378
  Othello **22**: 378

**as unsuccessful play**
  Measure for Measure **2**: 397, 441, 474, 482; **23**: 287

**usurpation**
  See also **rebellion**
  Richard II **6**: 263, 264, 272, 287, 289, 315, 323, 331, 343, 354, 364, 381, 388, 393, 397; **24**: 383
  The Tempest **8**: 304, 370, 408, 420; **25**: 357, 382; **29**: 278, 362, 377; **37**: 336

**utopia**
  The Tempest **45**: 280

**value systems**
  Troilus and Cressida **3**: 578, 583, 589, 602, 613, 617; **13**: 53; **27**: 370, 396, 400

**Venetian politics**
  Othello **32**: 294

**Venice, Elizabethan perceptions of**
  The Merchant of Venice **28**: 249; **32**: 294; **40**: 127

**Venus and Adonis**
  The Rape of Lucrece **43**: 148

**Vergil, influence of**
  Titus Andronicus **27**: 306; **28**: 249

**verisimilitude**
  As You Like It **5**: 18, 23, 28, 30, 32, 39, 125; **23**: 107

**Verona society**
  Romeo and Juliet **5**: 556, 566; **13**: 235; **33**: 255

**Violence in Shakespeare's Works (Volume 43: 1, 12, 24, 32, 39, 61)**
  Henry IV, Parts 1 and 2 **25**: 109
  Henry VI, Parts 1, 2, and 3 **24**: 25, 31; **37**: 157
  Julius Caesar **48**: 240
  Love's Labour's Lost **22**: 12
  Macbeth **20**: 273, 279, 283; **45**: 58
  Othello **22**: 12
  The Rape of Lucrece **43**: 148, 158
  Titus Andronicus **13**: 225; **25**: 245; **27**: 255; **28**: 249; **32**: 249, 265; **43**: 186, 203, 227, 239, 247, 255, 262
  Troilus and Cressida **43**: 329, 340, 351, 357, 365, 377

**virginity or chastity, importance of**
  Much Ado about Nothing **8**: 44, 75, 95, 111, 121, 125; **31**: 222

**Virgo vs. Virago**
*King Lear* **48**: 222

**visual arts, relation to**
*Sonnets* **28**: 407

**visual humor**
*Love's Labour's Lost* **23**: 207, 217

**war**
*Coriolanus* **25**: 263; **30**: 79, 96, 125, 149
*Henry V* **5**: 193, 195, 197, 198, 210, 213, 219, 230, 233, 246, 281, 293; **28**: 121, 146; **30**: 262; **32**: 126; **37**: 175, 187; **42**: 141

**Wars of the Roses**
*Richard III* **8**: 163, 165, 177, 184, 193, 201, 218, 228, 232, 243, 248, 252, 267; **39**: 308

**Watteau, influence on staging**
*Love's Labour's Lost* **23**: 184, 186

**wealth**
*The Merchant of Venice* **4**: 209, 261, 270, 273, 317; **12**: 80, 117; **22**: 69; **25**: 22; **28**: 249; **40**: 117, 197, 208; **45**: 17

**wealth and social class**
*Timon of Athens* **1**: 466, 487, 495; **25**: 198; **27**: 184, 196, 212

**wheel of fortune, motif of**
*Antony and Cleopatra* **6**: 25, 178; **19**: 304
*Henry VIII* **2**: 27, 65, 72, 81

**widowhood and remarriage, themes of**
*Hamlet* **32**: 238

**wisdom**
*King Lear* **37**: 213; **46**: 210

**wit**
*The Merry Wives of Windsor* **5**: 335, 336, 337, 339, 343, 351
*Much Ado about Nothing* **8**: 27, 29, 38, 69, 79, 91, 95; **31**: 178, 191

**witchcraft**
*See* Magic and the Supernatural

**women, role of**
*See* Shakespeare's Representation of Women

**wonder, dynamic of**
*The Comedy of Errors* **37**: 12

**wordplay**
*As You Like It* **46**: 105
*Romeo and Juliet* **32**: 256

**written versus oral communication**
*Love's Labour's Lost* **2**: 359, 365; **28**: 63

**youth**
*The Two Gentlemen of Verona* **6**: 439, 450, 464, 514, 568

**youth versus age**
*All's Well That Ends Well* **7**: 9, 45, 58, 62, 76, 81, 86, 93, 98, 104, 116, 126; **26**: 117; **38**: 109

# Cumulative Topic Index, by Play

The Cumulative Topic Index, by Play identifies the principal topics of discussion in the criticism of each play and non-dramatic poem. The topics are arranged alphabetically by play. Page references indicate the beginning page number of each essay containing substantial commentary on that topic. A parenthetical reference after a play indicates which volumes discuss the play extensively.

*All's Well That Ends Well* (Volumes 7, 26, 38)

appearance versus reality  7: 37, 76, 93; 26: 117
audience perspective  7: 81, 104, 109, 116, 121
bed-trick  7: 8, 26, 27, 29, 32, 41, 86, 93, 98, 113, 116, 126; 13: 84; 26: 117; 28: 38; 38: 65, 118
Bertram
    characterization  7: 15, 27, 29, 32, 39, 41, 43, 98, 113; 26: 48; 26: 117
    conduct  7: 9, 10, 12, 16, 19, 21, 51, 62, 104
    desire  22: 78
    transformation or redemption  7: 10, 19, 21, 26, 29, 32, 54, 62, 81, 90, 93, 98, 109, 113, 116, 126; 13: 84
comic elements  26: 97, 114; 48: 65
dark elements  7: 27, 37, 39, 43, 54, 109, 113, 116; 26: 85; 48: 65
*Decameron* (Boccaccio), compared with  7: 29, 43
desire  38: 99, 109, 118
displacement  22: 78
education  7: 62, 86, 90, 93, 98, 104, 116, 126
elder characters  7: 9, 37, 39, 43, 45, 54, 62, 104
conclusion  38: 123, 132, 142
gender issues  7: 9, 10, 67, 126; 13: 77, 84; 19: 113; 26: 128; 38: 89, 99, 118; 44: 35
genre  48: 65
Helena
    as agent of reconciliation, renewal, or grace  7: 67, 76, 81, 90, 93, 98, 109, 116
    as dualistic or enigmatic character  7: 15, 27, 29, 39, 54, 58, 62, 67, 76, 81, 98, 113, 126; 13: 66; 22: 78; 26: 117
    as "female achiever"  19: 113; 38: 89
    desire  38: 96; 44: 35
    pursuit of Bertram  7: 9, 12, 15, 16, 19, 21, 26, 27, 29, 32, 43, 54, 76, 116; 13: 77; 22: 78
    virginity  38: 65
virtue and nobility  7: 9, 10, 12, 16, 19, 21, 27, 32, 41, 51, 58, 67, 76, 86, 126; 13: 77
implausibility of plot, characters, or events  7: 8, 45
irony, paradox, and ambiguity  7: 27, 32, 58, 62, 67, 81, 86, 109, 116
King  38: 150
language and imagery  7: 12, 29, 45, 104, 109, 121; 38: 132; 48: 65
Lavatch  26: 64; 46: 33, 52, 68
love  7: 12, 15, 16, 51, 58, 67, 90, 93, 116; 38: 80
merit versus rank  7: 9, 10, 19, 37, 51, 76; 38: 155
"mingled yarn"  7: 62, 93, 109, 126; 38: 65
morality plays, influence of  7: 29, 41, 51, 98, 113; 13: 66
Parolles
    characterization  7: 8, 9, 43, 76, 81, 98, 109, 113, 116, 126; 22: 78; 26: 48, 73, 97; 26: 117; 46: 68
    exposure  7: 9, 27, 81, 98, 109, 113, 116, 121, 126
    Falstaff, compared with  7: 8, 9, 16
reconciliation  7: 90, 93, 98
religious, mythic, or spiritual content  7: 15, 45, 54, 67, 76, 98, 109, 116
romance or folktale elements  7: 32, 41, 43, 45, 54, 76, 104, 116, 121; 26: 117
sexuality  7: 67, 86, 90, 93, 98, 126; 13: 84; 19: 113; 22: 78; 28: 38; 44: 35
social and political context  13: 66; 22: 78; 38: 99, 109, 150, 155
staging issues  19: 113; 26: 15, 19, 48, 52, 64, 73, 85, 92, 93, 94, 95, 97, 114, 117, 128
structure  7: 21, 29, 32, 45, 51, 76, 81, 93, 98, 116; 22: 78; 26: 128; 38: 72, 123, 142
youth versus age  7: 9, 45, 58, 62, 76, 81, 86, 93, 98, 104, 116, 126; 26: 117; 38: 109

*Antony and Cleopatra* (Volumes 6, 17, 27, 47)

*All for Love* (John Dryden), compared with  6: 20, 21; 17: 12, 94, 101
ambiguity  6: 53, 111, 161, 163, 180, 189, 208, 211, 228; 13: 368
androgyny  13: 530
Antony
    characterization  6: 22, 23, 24, 31, 38, 41, 172, 181, 211; 16: 342; 19: 270; 22: 217; 27: 117; 47: 77, 124, 142
    Cleopatra, relationship with  6: 25, 27, 37, 39, 48, 52, 53, 62, 67, 71, 76, 85, 100, 125, 131, 133, 136, 142, 151, 161, 163, 165, 180, 192; 27: 82; 47: 107, 124, 165, 174
    death scene  25: 245; 47: 142
    dotage  6: 22, 23, 38, 41, 48, 52, 62, 107, 136, 146, 175; 17: 28
    nobility  6: 22, 24, 33, 48, 94, 103, 136, 142,

159, 172, 202; **25:** 245
political conduct **6:** 33, 38, 53, 107, 111, 146, 181
public versus private personae **6:** 165; **47:** 107
self-knowledge **6:** 120, 131, 175, 181, 192; **47:** 77
as superhuman figure **6:** 37, 51, 71, 92, 94, 178, 192; **27:** 110; **47:** 71
as tragic hero **6:** 38, 39, 52, 53, 60, 104, 120, 151, 155, 165, 178, 192, 202, 211; **22:** 217; **27:** 90
audience response **48:** 206
Cleopatra
Antony, relationship with **6:** 25, 27, 37, 39, 48, 52, 53, 62, 67, 71, 76, 85, 100, 125, 131, 133, 136, 142, 151, 161, 163, 165, 180, 192; **25:** 257; **27:** 82; **47:** 107, 124, 165, 174
characterization **47:** 77, 96, 113, 124
contradictory or inconsistent nature **6:** 23, 24, 27, 67, 76, 100, 104, 115, 136, 151, 159, 202; **17:** 94, 113; **27:** 135
costume **17:** 94
creativity **6:** 197; **47:** 96, 113
death, decay, and nature's destructiveness **6:** 23, 25, 27, 41, 43, 52, 60, 64, 76, 94, 100, 103, 120, 131, 133, 136, 140, 146, 161, 165, 180, 181, 192, 197, 208; **13:** 383; **17:** 48, 94; **25:** 245; **27:** 135; **47:** 71
personal attraction of **6:** 24, 38, 40, 43, 48, 53, 76, 104, 115, 155; **17:** 113
self-knowledge **47:** 77, 96
staging issues **17:** 94, 113
as subverter of social order **6:** 146, 165; **47:** 113
as superhuman figure **6:** 37, 51, 71, 92, 94, 178, 192; **27:** 110; **47:** 71, 174, 192
as tragic heroine **6:** 53, 120, 151, 192, 208; **27:** 144
as voluptuary or courtesan **6:** 21, 22, 25, 41, 43, 52, 53, 62, 64, 67, 76, 146, 161; **47:** 107, 174
comic elements **6:** 52, 85, 104, 125, 131, 151, 192, 202, 219; **47:** 77, 124, 149, 165
*contemptus mundi* **6:** 85, 133
dreams **45:** 28
dualisms **19:** 304; **27:** 82
Egyptian versus Roman values **6:** 31, 33, 43, 53, 104, 111, 115, 125, 142, 155, 159, 178, 181, 211, 219; **17:** 48; **19:** 270; **27:** 82, 121, 126; **28:** 249; **47:** 96, 103, 113, 149
Elizabethan culture, relation to **47:** 103
Enobarbus **6:** 22, 23, 27, 43, 94, 120, 142; **16:** 342; **17:** 36; **22:** 217; **27:** 135
gender issues **13:** 368; **25:** 257; **27:** 144; **47:** 174, 192
irony or paradox **6:** 53, 136, 146, 151, 159, 161, 189, 192, 211, 224
language and imagery **6:** 21, 25, 39, 64, 80, 85, 92, 94, 100, 104, 142, 146, 155, 159, 161, 165, 189, 192, 202, 211; **13:** 374, 383; **25:** 245, 257; **27:** 96, 105, 135
love and passion **6:** 51, 64, 71, 80, 85, 100, 115, 159, 165, 180; **25:** 257; **27:** 126; **47:** 71, 124, 174, 192
monument scene **13:** 374; **16:** 342; **17:** 104, 110; **22:** 217; **47:** 142, 165

moral relativism **22:** 217; **27:** 121
mythological allusions **16:** 342; **19:** 304; **27:** 110, 117; **47:** 71, 192
Octavius **6:** 22, 24, 31, 38, 43, 53, 62, 107, 125, 146, 178, 181, 219; **25:** 257
political and social disintegration **6:** 31, 43, 53, 60, 71, 80, 100, 107, 111, 146; **180, 197, 219; 22:** 217; **25:** 257; **27:** 121
reason versus imagination **6:** 107, 115, 142, 197, 228; **45:** 28
reconciliation **6:** 100, 103, 125, 131, 159, 181
religious, mythic, or spiritual content **6:** 53, 94, 111, 115, 178, 192, 224; **47:** 71
royalty **6:** 94
Seleucus episode (Act V, scene ii) **6:** 39, 41, 62, 133, 140, 151; **27:** 135
Shakespeare's major tragedies, compared with **6:** 25, 53, 60, 71, 120, 181, 189, 202; **22:** 217; **47:** 77
Shakespeare's moral judgment **6:** 33, 37, 38, 41, 48, 51, 64, 76, 111, 125, 136, 140, 146, 163, 175, 189, 202, 211, 228; **13:** 368, 523; **25:** 257
sources **6:** 20, 39; **19:** 304; **27:** 96, 126; **28:** 249
stage history **17:** 84, 94, 101
staging issues **17:** 6, 12, 84, 94, 101, 104, 110; **27:** 90; **47:** 142
strategic analysis **48:** 206
theatricality and role-playing **47:** 96, 103, 107, 113
unity **6:** 20, 21, 22, 24, 25, 32, 33, 39, 43, 53, 60, 67, 111, 125, 146, 151, 165, 208, 211, 219; **13:** 374; **27:** 82, 90, 135
wheel of fortune, motif of **6:** 25, 178; **19:** 304

*As You Like It* (Volumes 5, 23, 34, 46)
Appearance versus Reality **46:** 105
androgyny **23:** 98, 100, 122, 138, 143, 144; **34:** 172, 177; **46:** 134
anti-romantic elements **34:** 72
aristocracy **34:** 120
art versus nature **5:** 128, 130, 148; **34:** 147
Audrey **46:** 122
autobiographical elements **5:** 25, 35, 43, 50, 55, 61
bawdy elements **46:** 122
Celia **46:** 94
characterization **5:** 19, 24, 25, 32, 36, 39, 54, 82, 86, 116, 148; **34:** 72; **48:** 42
Christian elements **5:** 39, 98, 162
contradiction, paradox, and opposition **46:** 105
comic form **46:** 105
corruption in society **46:** 94
costume **46:** 117
courtship and marriage **34:** 109, 177; **48:** 32
death, decay, nature's destructiveness **46:** 169
deception, disguise, and duplicity **46:** 134
desire **37:** 43
domestic elements **46:** 142
dramatic shortcomings or failure **5:** 19, 42, 52, 61, 65
duration of time **5:** 44, 45
Elizabethan culture, relation to **5:** 21, 59, 66, 68, 70, 158; **16:** 53; **28:** 46; **34:** 120; **37:** 1; **46:** 142
Fathers and Daughters **46:** 94

feminism **23:** 107, 108
Forest of Arden
as "bitter" Arcadia **5:** 98, 118, 162; **23:** 97, 98, 99, 100, 122, 139
Duke Frederick's court, contrast with **5:** 46, 102, 103, 112, 130, 156; **16:** 53; **23:** 126, 128, 129, 131, 134; **34:** 78, 102, 131; **46:** 164
pastoral elements **5:** 18, 20, 24, 32, 35, 47, 50, 54, 55, 57, 60, 77, 128, 135, 156; **23:** 17, 20, 27, 46, 137; **34:** 78, 147; **46:** 88
as patriarchal society **5:** 168; **23:** 150; **34:** 177
as source of self-knowledge **5:** 98, 102, 103, 128, 130, 135, 148, 158, 162; **23:** 17; **34:** 102
as timeless, mythical world **5:** 112, 130, 141; **23:** 132; **34:** 78; **37:** 43; **46:** 88
theme of play **46:** 88
gender identity **46:** 127, 134,
genre **5:** 46, 55, 79
homoerotic elements **46:** 127, 142
homosexuality **46:** 127, 142
Hymen episode **5:** 61, 116, 130; **23:** 22, 48, 54, 109, 111, 112, 113, 115, 146, 147
irony **5:** 30, 32, 154
Jaques
love-theme, relation to **5:** 103; **23:** 7, 37, 118, 128
as malcontent **5:** 59, 70, 84
melancholy **5:** 20, 28, 32, 36, 39, 43, 50, 59, 63, 68, 77, 82, 86, 135; **23:** 20, 26, 103, 104, 107, 109; **34:** 85; **46:** 88, 94
pastoral convention, relation to **5:** 61, 63, 65, 79, 93, 98, 114, 118
Seven Ages of Man speech (Act II, scene vii) **5:** 28, 52, 156; **23:** 48, 103, 105, 126, 138, 152; **46:** 88, 156, 164, 169
Shakespeare, relation to **5:** 35, 50, 154
as superficial critic **5:** 28, 30, 43, 54, 55, 63, 65, 68, 75, 77, 82, 86, 88, 98, 138; **34:** 85
justice **46:** 94
juxtaposition of opposing perspectives **5:** 86, 93, 98, 141; **16:** 53; **23:** 119; **34:** 72, 78, 131
language and imagery **5:** 19, 21, 35, 52, 75, 82, 92, 138; **23:** 15, 21, 26; **28:** 9; **34:** 131; **37:** 43; **48:** 42
love **5:** 24, 44, 46, 57, 79, 88, 103, 116, 122, 138, 141, 162; **28:** 46, 82; **34:** 85
*Love in a Forest* (Charles Johnson adaptation) **23:** 7, 8, 9, 10
<male/female relationships
metadramatic elements **5:** 128, 130, 146; **34:** 130
mythological allusions **46:** 142
nature **46:** 94
Neoclassical rules **5:** 19, 20
Orlando
as ideal man **5:** 32, 36, 39, 162; **34:** 161; **46:** 94
as younger brother **5:** 66, 158; **46:** 94
pastoral characters (Silvius, Phebe, and Corin) **23:** 37, 97, 98, 99, 108, 110, 118, 122, 138; **34:** 147
pastoral convention, parodies of **5:** 54, 57, 72
pastoral convention, relation to **5:** 72, 77, 122; **34:** 161; **37:** 1

primogeniture **5:** 66, 158; **34:** 109, 120
psychoanalytic interpretation **5:** 146, 158; **23:** 141, 142; **34:** 109; **48:** 42
public versus private worlds **46:** 164
reconciliation of opposites **5:** 79, 88, 103, 116, 122, 138; **23:** 127, 143; **34:** 161, 172; **46:** 156
as romance **5:** 55, 79; **23:** 27, 28, 40, 43
Rosalind **46:** 94, 122,
    Beatrice, compared with **5:** 26, 36, 50, 75
    charm **5:** 55, 75; **23:** 17, 18, 20, 41, 89, 111
    disguise, role of **5:** 75, 107, 118, 122, 128, 130, 133, 138, 141, 146, 148, 164, 168; **13:** 502; **23:** 35, 42, 106, 119, 123, 146; **34:** 130; **46:** 134
    femininity **5:** 26, 36, 52, 75; **23:** 24, 29, 46, 54, 103, 108, 121, 146
    as Ganymede **46:** 127, 142
    love-theme, relation to **5:** 79, 88, 103, 116, 122, 138, 141; **23:** 114, 115; **34:** 85, 177
rustic characters **5:** 24, 60, 72, 84; **23:** 127; **34:** 78, 161
sexual ambiguity and sexual deception **46:** 134, 142
Sexuality in Shakespeare **46:** 122, 127, 134, 142
as satire or parody of pastoral conventions **5:** 46, 55, 60, 72, 77, 79, 84, 114, 118, 128, 130, 154
self-knowledge **5:** 32, 82, 102, 116, 122, 133, 164
sibling rivalry **34:** 109
social order **37:** 1; **46:** 94
sources **5:** 18, 32, 54, 59, 66, 84; **34:** 155; **46:** 117
stage history **46:** 117
staging issues **13:** 502; **23:** 7, 17, 19, 22, 58, 96, 97, 98, 99, 101, 110, 137; **28:** 82; **32:** 212
structure **5:** 19, 24, 25, 35, 44, 45, 46, 86, 93, 116, 138, 158; **23:** 7, 8, 9, 10, 11; **34:** 72, 78, 131, 147, 155
time **5:** 18, 82, 112, 141; **23:** 146, 150; **34:** 102; **46:** 88, 156, 164, 169
Touchstone
    callousness **5:** 88
    comic and farcical elements **46:** 117
    as philosopher-fool **5:** 24, 28, 30, 32, 36, 63, 75, 98; **23:** 152; **34:** 85; **46:** 1, 14, 18, 24, 33, 52, 60, 88, 105,
    relation to pastoral convention **5:** 54, 61, 63, 72, 75, 77, 79, 84, 86, 93, 98, 114, 118, 135, 138, 166; **34:** 72, 147, 161
    selflessness **5:** 30, 36, 39, 76
verisimilitude **5:** 18, 23, 28, 30, 32, 39, 125; **23:** 107
wordplay **46:** 105

## *The Comedy of Errors* (Volumes 1, 26, 34)

Adriana **16:** 3; **34:** 211, 220, 238
adultery **34:** 215
audience perception **1:** 37, 50, 56; **19:** 54; **34:** 258
autobiographical elements **1:** 16, 18
characterization **1:** 13, 21, 31, 34, 46, 49, 50, 55, 56; **19:** 54; **25:** 63; **34:** 194, 201, 208, 245
classical influence and sources **1:** 13, 14, 16, 31, 32, 43, 61

comic elements **1:** 43, 46, 55, 56, 59; **26:** 183, 186, 188, 190; **34:** 190, 245
composition date **1:** 18, 23, 34, 55
dramatic structure **1:** 19, 27, 40, 43, 46, 50; **26:** 186, 190; **34:** 190, 229, 233; **37:** 12
Elizabethan culture, relation to **26:** 138, 142; **34:** 201, 215, 233, 238, 258; **42:** 80
Dromio brothers **42:** 80
farcical elements **1:** 14, 16, 19, 23, 30, 34, 35, 46, 50, 59, 61; **19:** 54; **26:** 188, 190; **34:** 245
feminist criticism **42:** 93
food, meaning of **34:** 220
gender issues **34:** 215, 220
genre **34:** 251, 258
identity **34:** 201, 208, 211
illusion **1:** 13, 14, 27, 37, 40, 45, 59, 63; **26:** 188; **34:** 194, 211
language and imagery **1:** 16, 25, 39, 40, 43, 57, 59; **34:** 233
male/female relationships **16:** 3
marriage **34:** 251
mistaken identity **1:** 13, 14, 27, 37, 40, 45, 49, 55, 57, 61, 63; **19:** 34, 54; **25:** 63; **34:** 194
Plautus"s works, compared with **1:** 13, 14, 16, 53, 61; **16:** 3; **19:** 34
problem comedy **34:** 251
redemption **19:** 54; **26:** 188
romantic elements **1:** 13, 16, 19, 23, 25, 30, 31, 36, 39, 53
servitude **42:** 80
social order **34:** 238
sources **1:** 13, 14, 16, 19, 31, 32, 39; **16:** 3; **34:** 190, 215, 258
staging issues **26:** 182, 183, 186, 188, 190
supernatural, role of **1:** 27, 30
tragic elements **1:** 16, 25, 27, 45, 50, 59; **34:** 229
wonder, dynamic of **37:** 12

## *Coriolanus* (9, 17, 30)

aggression **9:** 112, 142, 174, 183, 189, 198; **30:** 79, 111, 125, 142; **44:** 11, 79
*Anthony and Cleopatra*, compared with **30:** 79, 96
appearance versus reality **30:** 142
Aufidius **9:** 9, 12, 17, 19, 53, 121, 148, 153, 157, 169, 180, 193; **19:** 287; **25:** 263, 296; **30:** 58, 67, 89, 96, 133
body politic, metaphor of **22:** 248; **30:** 67, 96, 105, 125
butterfly episode (Act I, scene iii) **9:** 19, 45, 62, 65, 73, 100, 125, 153, 157
capitulation scene (Act V, scene iii) **9:** 19, 26, 53, 65, 100, 117, 125, 130, 157, 164, 183
ceremonies, rites, and rituals, importance of **9:** 139, 148, 169
Christian elements **30:** 111
comic elements **9:** 8, 9, 14, 53, 80, 106
Cominius **25:** 245
Cominius"s tribute (Act II, scene ii) **9:** 80, 100, 117, 125, 144, 164, 198; **25:** 296
Coriolanus
    anger or passion **9:** 19, 26, 45, 80, 92, 157, 164, 177, 189; **30:** 79, 96
    as complementary figure to Aufidius **19:** 287
    death scene (Act V, scene vi) **9:** 12, 80, 100, 117, 125, 144, 164, 198; **25:** 245, 263

    as epic hero **9:** 130, 164, 177; **25:** 245
    immaturity **9:** 62, 80, 84, 110, 117, 142; **30:** 140
    inhuman attributes **9:** 65, 73, 139, 157, 164, 169, 189, 198; **25:** 263
    internal struggle **9:** 31, 43, 45, 53, 72, 117, 121, 130; **44:** 93
    introspection or self-knowledge, lack of **9:** 53, 80, 84, 112, 117, 130; **25:** 296; **30:** 133
    isolation or autonomy **9:** 53, 65, 142, 144, 153, 157, 164, 180, 183, 189, 198; **30:** 58, 89, 111
    manipulation by others **9:** 33, 45, 62, 80; **25:** 296
    modesty **9:** 8, 12, 19, 26, 53, 78, 92, 117, 121, 144, 183; **25:** 296; **30:** 79, 96, 129, 133, 149
    narcissism **30:** 111
    noble or aristocratic attributes **9:** 15, 18, 19, 26, 31, 33, 52, 53, 62, 65, 84, 92, 100, 121, 148, 157, 169; **25:** 263; **30:** 67, 74, 96
    pride or arrogance **9:** 8, 11, 12, 19, 26, 31, 33, 43, 45, 65, 78, 92, 121, 148, 153, 177; **30:** 58, 67, 74, 89, 96, 129
    reconciliation with society **9:** 33, 43, 45, 65, 139, 169; **25:** 296
    as socially destructive force **9:** 62, 65, 73, 78, 110, 142, 144, 153; **25:** 296
    soliloquy (Act IV, scene iv) **9:** 84, 112, 117, 130
    as tragic figure **9:** 8, 12, 13, 18, 25, 45, 52, 53, 72, 80, 92, 106, 112, 117, 130, 148, 164, 169, 177; **25:** 296; **30:** 67, 74, 79, 96, 111, 129; **37:** 283
    traitorous actions **9:** 9, 12, 19, 45, 84, 92, 148; **25:** 296; **30:** 133
    as unsympathetic character **9:** 12, 13, 62, 78, 80, 84, 112, 130, 157
domestic elements **42:** 223
England and Rome, parallels between **9:** 39, 43, 106, 148, 180, 193; **25:** 296; **30:** 67, 105
fable of the belly (Act I, scene i) **9:** 8, 65, 73, 80, 136, 153, 157, 164, 180, 183, 189; **25:** 296; **30:** 79, 105, 111
fame **30:** 58
fire and water **25:** 263
flattery or dissimulation **9:** 26, 45, 92, 100, 110, 121, 130, 144, 157, 183, 193; **25:** 296
friendship **30:** 125, 142
gender issues **30:** 79, 125, 142; **44:** 93
genre **9:** 42, 43, 53, 80, 106, 112, 117, 130, 164, 177; **30:** 67, 74, 79, 89, 111, 125
honor or integrity **9:** 43, 65, 73, 92, 106, 110, 121, 144, 153, 157, 164, 177, 183, 189; **30:** 89, 96, 133
identity **42:** 248
irony or satire **9:** 65, 73, 80, 92, 106, 153, 157, 164, 193; **30:** 67, 89, 133
Jacobean culture, relation to **22:** 248
language and imagery **9:** 8, 9, 13, 53, 64, 65, 73, 78, 84, 100, 112, 121, 136, 139, 142, 144, 153, 157, 174, 183, 193, 198; **22:** 248; **25:** 245, 263; **30:** 111, 125, 142; **37:** 283; **44:** 79
*Macbeth*, compared with **30:** 79
martial vs. civil law **48:** 230
Menenius **9:** 8, 9, 11, 14, 19, 26, 78, 80, 106, 148, 157; **25:** 263, 296; **30:** 67, 79, 89, 96, 111, 133

Midlands Revolt, influence of **22:** 248; **30:** 79
naming, significance of **30:** 58, 96, 111, 125
nature, philosophy of **30:** 74
nurturing or feeding **9:** 65, 73, 136, 183, 189; **30:** 111; **44:** 79
paradoxical elements **9:** 73, 92, 106, 121, 153, 157, 164, 169, 193
plebeians **9:** 8, 9, 11, 12, 15, 18, 19, 26, 33, 39, 53, 92, 125, 153, 183, 189; **25:** 296; **30:** 58, 79, 96, 111
Plutarch and historical sources **9:** 8, 9, 13, 14, 16, 26, 39, 92, 106, 130, 142, 164; **30:** 74, 79, 105
politics **9:** 15, 17, 18, 19, 26, 33, 43, 53, 62, 65, 73, 80, 92, 106, 110, 112, 121, 144, 153, 157, 164, 180; **22:** 248; **25:** 296; **30:** 58, 67, 79, 89, 96, 105, 111, 125; **37:** 283; **42:** 223; **48:** 230
psychoanalytic interpretations **44:** 93
public versus private worlds **37:** 283; **42:** 223
sexuality **9:** 112, 142, 174, 183, 189, 198; **30:** 79, 111, 125, 142
shame **42:** 248
Shakespeare"s political sympathies **9:** 8, 11, 15, 17, 19, 26, 39, 52, 53, 62, 80, 92, 142; **25:** 296; **30:** 74, 79, 89, 96, 105, 133
slander **48:** 230
society **9:** 15, 17, 18, 19, 26, 33, 43, 53, 62, 65, 73, 80, 92, 106, 110, 112, 121, 144, 153, 157, 164, 180; **22:** 248; **25:** 296; **30:** 58, 67, 79, 89, 96, 105, 111, 125
staging issues **17:** 172, 242, 248
structure **9:** 8, 9, 11, 12, 13, 14, 16, 26, 33, 45, 53, 58, 72, 78, 80, 84, 92, 112, 139, 148; **25:** 263; **30:** 79, 96
treachery **30:** 89
the tribunes (Brutus and Sicinius) **9:** 9, 11, 14, 19, 33, 169, 180
Virgilia **9:** 11, 19, 26, 33, 58, 100, 121, 125; **25:** 263; **30:** 79, 96, 133
Volumnia
   Coriolanus"s subservience to **9:** 16, 26, 33, 53, 62, 80, 92, 100, 117, 125, 142, 177, 183; **30:** 140, 149; **44:** 79
   influence on Coriolanus **9:** 45, 62, 65, 78, 92, 100, 110, 117, 121, 125, 130, 148, 157, 183, 189, 193; **25:** 263, 296; **30:** 79, 96, 125, 133, 140, 142, 149; **44:** 93
   as noble Roman matron **9:** 16, 19, 26, 31, 33
   personification of Rome **9:** 125, 183
war **25:** 263; **30:** 79, 96, 125, 149

## *Cymbeline* (Volumes 4, 15, 36, 47)

appearance versus reality **4:** 87, 93, 103, 162; **36:** 99; **47:** 228, 286
authorship controversy **4:** 17, 21, 35, 48, 56, 78
autobiographical elements **4:** 43, 46; **36:** 134
bawdy elements **36:** 155
Beaumont and Fletcher"s romances, compared with **4:** 46, 52, 138
Belarius **4:** 48, 89, 141
British nationalism **4:** 19, 78, 89, 93, 129, 141, 159, 167; **32:** 373; **36:** 129; **45:** 67; **47:** 219, 265

Cloten **4:** 20, 116, 127, 155; **22:** 302, 365; **25:** 245; **36:** 99, 125, 142, 155; **47:** 228
combat scenes **22:** 365
comic elements **4:** 35, 56, 113, 141; **15:** 111, 122; **47:** 296
dramatic structure **4:** 17, 18, 19, 20, 21, 22, 24, 38, 43, 48, 53, 64, 68, 89, 116, 129, 141; **22:** 302, 365; **25:** 319; **36:** 115, 125
dreams **4:** 162, 167; **44:** 28; **45:** 67, 75
dualisms **4:** 29, 64, 73
Elizabethan dramatic conventions **4:** 53, 124
family, theme of **44:** 28
Guiderius and Arviragus **4:** 21, 22, 89, 129, 141, 148; **25:** 319; **36:** 125, 158
historical elements **47:** 260
Iachimo **25:** 245, 319; **36:** 166
Imogen **4:** 21, 22, 24, 29, 37, 45, 46, 52, 56, 78, 89, 108; **15:** 23, 32, 105, 121; **19:** 411; **25:** 245, 319; **28:** 398; **32:** 373; **36:** 129, 142, 148; **47:** 25, 205, 228, 245, 274, 277
Imogen"s reawakening (Act IV, scene ii) **4:** 37, 56, 89, 103, 108, 116, 150; **15:** 23; **25:** 245; **47:** 252
irony **4:** 64, 77, 103
language and imagery **4:** 43, 48, 61, 64, 70, 73, 93, 108; **13:** 401; **25:** 245; **28:** 373, 398; **36:** 115, 158, 166, 186; **47:** 205, 286, 296
Lucretia, analogies to **36:** 148
misperception **19:** 411; **36:** 99, 115; **47:** 228, 237, 252, 277, 286, 296,
negative appraisals **4:** 20, 35, 43, 45, 48, 53, 56, 68; **15:** 32, 105, 121
patriarchy **32:** 373; **36:** 134; **47:** 237
Posthumus **4:** 24, 30, 53, 78, 116, 127, 141, 155, 159, 167; **15:** 89; **19:** 411; **25:** 245, 319; **36:** 142; **44:** 28; **45:** 67, 75; **47:** 25, 205, 228, 
psychological elements **36:** 134; **44:** 28; **45:** 67, 75
reconciliation **4:** 38, 64, 73, 93, 105, 113, 116, 129, 138, 141, 162, 170
religious, mythical, or spiritual content **4:** 22, 29, 78, 93, 105, 108, 115, 116, 127, 134, 138, 141, 159; **28:** 373; **36:** 142, 158, 186; **47:** 219, 260, 274
romantic elements **4:** 17, 20, 46, 68, 77, 141, 148, 172; **15:** 111; **25:** 319; **28:** 373
self-conscious or artificial nature of play **4:** 43, 52, 56, 68, 124, 134, 138; **36:** 99
sexuality **4:** 170, 172; **25:** 319; **32:** 373; **47:** 245
Shakespeare"s lyric poetry, compared with **13:** 401
sources **4:** 17, 18; **13:** 401; **28:** 373; **47:** 245, 265, 277
staging issues **15:** 6, 23, 75, 105, 111, 121, 122; **22:** 365
subversiveness **22:** 302
tragic elements **25:** 319; **28:** 373; **36:** 129; **47:** 296
trickster, motif of **22:** 302
vision scene (Act V, scene iv) **4:** 17, 21, 28, 29, 35, 38, 78, 105, 108, 134, 150, 167; **47:** 205
wager plot **4:** 18, 24, 29, 53, 78, 155; **22:** 365; **25:** 319; **47:** 205, 277

## *Hamlet* (1, 21, 35, 44)

ambiguity **1:** 92, 160, 198, 227, 230, 234, 247, 249; **21:** 72; **35:** 241

appearance versus reality **1:** 95, 116, 166, 169, 198; **35:** 82, 126, 132, 144, 238; **44:** 248; **45:** 28
aristocracy **42:** 217
audience response **28:** 325; **32:** 238; **35:** 167; **44:** 107
autobiographical elements **1:** 98, 115, 119; **13:** 487
Calvinist implications **48:** 195
classical Greek tragedies, compared with **1:** 74, 75, 130, 184, 212; **13:** 296; **22:** 339
Claudius **13:** 502; **16** 246; **21:** 259, 347, 361, 371; **28:** 232, 290; **35:** 104, 182; **44:** 119, 241
closet scene (Act III, scene iv) **16:** 259; **21:** 151, 334, 392; **35:** 204, 229; **44:** 119, 237
costume **21:** 81
death, decay, and nature"s destructiveness **1:** 144, 153, 188, 198, 221, 242; **13:** 502; **28:** 280, 311; **35:** 241; **42:** 284
dreams **45:** 28
dumbshow and play scene (Act III, scene ii) **1:** 76, 86, 134, 138, 154, 160, 207; **13:** 502; **21:** 392; **35:** 82; **44:** 241; **46:** 74
Elizabethan culture, relation to **1:** 76, 148, 151, 154, 160, 166, 169, 171, 176, 184, 202, 209, 254; **13:** 282, 494; **19:** 330; **21:** 407, 416; **22:** 258
Elizabethan and Jacobean politics, relation to **28:** 232; **28:** 290, 311; **35:** 140
fencing scene (Act V, scene ii) **21:** 392
Fortinbras **21:** 136, 347; **28:** 290
gender issues **35:** 144; **44:** 189, 195, 198,
genre **1:** 176, 212, 237
Gertrude **21:** 259, 347, 392; **28:** 311; **32:** 238; **35:** 182, 204, 229; **44:** 119, 160, 189, 195, 237, 248
Ghost **1:** 75, 76, 84, 85, 128, 134, 138, 154, 171, 218, 231, 254; **16:** 246; **21:** 17, 44, 112, 151, 334, 371, 377, 392; **25:** 288; **35:** 152, 157, 174, 237; **44:** 119
gravedigger scene (Act V, scene i) **21:** 392; **28:** 280; **46:** 74
grotesque elements **42:** 284
Hamlet
   delay **1:** 76, 83, 88, 90, 94, 98, 102, 103, 106, 114, 115, 116, 119, 120, 148, 151, 166, 171, 179, 188, 191, 194, 198, 221, 268; **13:** 296, 502; **21:** 81; **25:** 209, 288; **28:** 223; **35:** 82, 174, 212, 215, 237; **44:** 180, 209, 219, 229
   divided nature **16:** 246; **28:** 223; **32:** 288; **35:** 182, 215; **37:** 241
   elocution of the character"s speeches **21:** 96, 104, 112, 127, 132, 172, 177, 179, 194, 245, 254, 257
   as a fool **46:** 1, 29, 52, 74
   madness **1:** 76, 81, 83, 95, 102, 106, 128, 144, 154, 160, 234; **21:** 35, 50, 72, 81, 99, 112, 311, 339, 355, 361, 371, 377, 384; **35:** 117, 132, 134, 140, 144, 212; **44:** 107, 119, 152, 209, 219, 229
   melancholy **21:** 99, 112, 177, 194; **35:** 82, 95, 117; **44:** 209, 219
   as negative character **1:** 86, 92, 111, 171, 218; **21:** 386; **25:** 209; **35:** 167
   reaction to his father"s death **22:** 339; **35:** 104, 174; **44:** 133, 160, 180, 189
   reaction to Gertrude"s marriage **1:** 74, 120,

154, 179; **16**: 259; **21**: 371; **22**: 339; **35**: 104, 117; **44**: 133, 160, 189, 195
romantic aspects of the character **21**: 96; **44**: 198
as scourge or purifying figure **1**: 144, 209, 242; **25**: 288; **35**: 157
sentimentality versus intellectuality **1**: 75, 83, 88, 91, 93, 94, 96, 102, 103, 115, 116, 120, 166, 191; **13**: 296; **21**: 35, 41, 44, 72, 81, 89, 99, 129, 132, 136, 172, 213, 225, 339, 355, 361, 371, 377, 379, 381, 386; **25**: 209; **44**: 198
soliloquies **1**: 76, 82, 83, 148, 166, 169, 176, 191; **21**: 17, 31, 44, 53, 89, 112, 268, 311, 334, 347, 361, 384, 392; **25**: 209; **28**: 223; **44**: 107, 119, 229
theatrical interpretations **21**: 11, 31, 78, 101, 104, 107, 160, 177, 179, 182, 183, 192, 194, 197, 202, 203, 208, 213, 225, 232, 237, 249, 253, 254, 257, 259, 274, 311, 339, 347, 355, 361, 371, 377, 380
virility **21**: 213, 301, 355; **44**: 198
*Hamlet with Alterations* (David Garrick adaptation) **21**: 23, 334, 347
Horatio **44**: 189
idealism versus pragmatism **16** 246; **28**: 325
Laertes **21**: 347, 386; **28**: 290; **35**: 182
language and imagery **1**: 95, 144, 153, 154, 160, 188, 198, 221, 227, 249, 259, 270; **22**: 258, 378; **28**: 311; **35**: 144, 152, 238, 241; **42**: 217; **44**: 248
madness **19**: 330; **35**: 104, 126, 134, 140, 144; **44**: 107, 119, 152, 209, 219, 229
marriage **22**: 339
Marxist criticism **42**: 234
nunnery scene (Act III, scene i) **21**: 157, 381, 410
Ophelia **1**: 73, 76, 81, 82, 91, 96, 97, 154, 166, 169, 171, 218, 270; **13**: 268; **16**: 246; **19**: 330; **21**: 17, 41, 44, 72, 81, 101, 104, 107, 112, 136, 203, 259, 347, 381, 386, 392, 416; **28**: 232, 325; **35**: 104, 126, 140, 144, 182, 238; **44**: 189, 195, 248
Polonius **21**: 259, 334, 347, 386, 416; **35**: 182
prayer scene (Act III, scene iii) **1**: 76, 106, 160, 212, 231; **44**: 119
psychoanalytic interpretations **1**: 119, 148, 154, 179, 202; **21**: 197, 213, 361; **25**: 209; **28**: 223; **35**: 95, 104, 134, 237; **37**: 241; **44**: 133, 152, 160, 180, 209, 219
religious, mythic, or spiritual content **1**: 98, 102, 130, 184, 191, 209, 212, 231, 234, 254; **21**: 361; **22**: 258; **28**: 280; **32**: 238; **35**: 134
revenge **1**: 74, 194, 209, 224, 234, 254; **16**: 246; **22**: 258; **25**: 288; **28**: 280; **35**: 152, 157, 167, 174, 212; **44**: 180, 209, 219, 229
*Richard II*, compared with **1**: 264
ceremonies, rites, and rituals, importance of **13**: 268; **28**: 232
sources **1**: 76, 81, 113, 125, 128, 130, 151, 191, 202, 224, 259
staging issues **13**: 494, 502; **21**: 11, 17, 31, 35, 41, 44, 50, 53, 78, 81, 89, 101, 112, 127, 139, 142, 145, 148, 151, 157, 160, 172, 182, 183, 202, 203, 208, 225, 232, 237, 242, 245, 249, 251, 259, 268, 270, 274, 283, 284, 301, 311, 334, 347, 355, 361, 371, 377, 379, 380, 381, 384, 386, 392, 407, 410, 416; **44**: 198

Stoicism **48**: 195
structure **22**: 378; **28**: 280, 325; **35**: 82, 104, 215; **44**: 152
subjectivity **45**: 28
textual variants **13**: 282; **16**: 259; **21**: 11, 23, 72, 101, 127, 129, 139, 140, 142, 145, 202, 208, 259, 270, 284, 347, 361, 384; **22**: 258; **32**: 238
topical allusions or content **13**: 282
unity **1**: 75, 76, 87, 103, 113, 125, 128, 142, 148, 160, 184, 188, 198, 264; **16**: 259; **35**: 82, 215
unnatural ordering **22**: 378
widowhood and remarriage, themes of **32**: 238

### Henry IV, Parts 1 and 2 (Volumes 1, 14, 39)

carnival elements **28**: 203; **32**: 103
characterization **1**: 321, 328, 332, 333, 336, 344, 365, 383, 385, 389, 391, 397, 401; **19**: 195; **39**: 123, 137; **42**: 101, 164
comic elements **1**: 286, 290, 314, 327, 328, 336, 353; **19**: 195; **25**: 109; **39**: 72
contractual and economic relations **13**: 213
contrasting dramatic worlds **14**: 56, 60, 61, 84, 105; **48**: 95
critical history **42**: 187; **48**: 167
deception, disguise, and duplicity **1**: 397, 406, 425; **42**: 101; **47**: 1, 60; **48**: 95
Elizabethan culture, relation to **19**: 195; **48**: 117, 143, 151, 175
Elizabethan politics, relation to **22**: 395; **28**: 203; **47**: 60; **48**: 117, 143, 167, 175
Falstaff
 characterization **1**: 287, 298, 312, 333; **25**: 245; **28**: 203; **39**: 72, 134, 137, 143
 as comic figure **1**: 287, 311, 327, 344, 351, 354, 357, 410, 434; **39**: 89; **46**: 1, 48, 52
 as coward or rogue **1**: 285, 290, 296, 298, 306, 307, 313, 317, 323, 336, 337, 338, 342, 354, 366, 374, 391, 396, 401, 433; **14**: 7, 111, 125, 130, 133; **32**: 166
 dual personality **1**: 397, 401, 406, 434
 female attributes **13**: 183; **44**: 44
 Iago, compared with **1**: 341, 351
 Marxist interpretation **1**: 358, 361
 as parody of the historical plot **1**: 314, 354, 359; **39**: 143
 as positive character **1**: 286, 287, 290, 296, 298, 311, 312, 321, 325, 333, 344, 355, 357, 389, 401, 408, 434
 rejection by Hal **1**: 286, 287, 290, 312, 314, 317, 324, 333, 338, 344, 357, 366, 372, 374, 379, 380, 389, 414; **13**: 183; **25**: 109; **39**: 72, 89
 as satire of feudal society **1**: 314, 328, 361; **32**: 103
 as scapegoat **1**: 389, 414
 stage interpretations **14**: 4, 6, 7, 9, 15, 116, 130, 146; **47**: 1
 as subversive figure **16**: 183; **25**: 109
 as Vice figure **1**: 342, 361, 366, 374
flattery **22**: 395
gender issues **13**: 183; **25**: 151; **44**: 44; **48**: 175
Hal
 as the central character **1**: 286, 290, 314, 317, 326, 338, 354, 366, 374, 396; **39**: 72, 100

dual personality **1**: 397, 406; **25**: 109, 151
as Everyman **1**: 342, 366, 374
fall from humanity **1**: 379, 380, 383
general assessment **1**: 286, 287, 289, 290, 314, 317, 326, 327, 332, 357, 397; **25**: 245; **32**: 212; **39**: 134
as ideal ruler **1**: 289, 309, 317, 321, 326, 337, 342, 344, 374, 389, 391, 434; **25**: 109; **39**: 123; **47**: 60
as Machiavellian ruler **47**: 60
as negative character **1**: 312, 332, 333, 357; **32**: 212
*Richard II*, compared with **1**: 332, 337; **39**: 72
Henry **39**: 123, 137
historical content **1**: 310, 328, 365, 366, 370, 374, 380, 387, 421, 424, 427, 431; **16**: 172; **19**: 157; **25**: 151; **32**: 136; **39**: 143; **48**: 143, 167
historical epic, place in or relation to Shakespeare"s **1**: 309, 314, 328, 374, 379, 424, 427; **48**: 167
Hotspur **25**: 151; **28**: 101; **39**: 72, 134, 137; **42**: 101
kingship **1**: 314, 318, 337, 366, 370, 374, 379, 380, 383, 424; **16**: 172; **19**: 195; **28**: 101; **39**: 100, 116, 123, 130; **42**: 143; **48**: 143
language and imagery **13**: 213; **16**: 172; **25**: 245; **28**: 101; **39**: 116, 130; **42**: 155; **47**: 1
as medieval allegory or morality play **1**: 323, 324, 342, 361, 366, 373, 374; **32**: 166; **39**: 89; **47**: 60
Mortimer **25**: 151
Neoclassical rules **1**: 286, 287, 290, 293
Oldcastle, references to **22**: 114; **32**: 166; **48**: 117
politics **28**: 101; **39**: 130; **42**: 143; **48**: 143, 175
psychoanalytic interpretations **13**: 457; **28**: 101; **42**: 187; **44**: 44
rebellion **22**: 395; **28**: 101
relationship to other Shakespearean plays **1**: 286, 290, 309, 329, 365, 396; **28**: 101; **42**: 101, 155; **48**: 167
relationship of Parts 1 and 2 **32**: 136; **39**: 100
religious, mythic, or spiritual content **1**: 314, 374, 414, 421, 429, 431, 434; **32**: 103; **48**: 151
 as autonomous works **1**: 289, 337, 338, 347, 348, 373, 387, 393, 411, 418, 424
 comparison **1**: 290, 295, 329, 348, 358, 393, 411, 419, 429, 431, 441
 unity of both parts **1**: 286, 290, 309, 314, 317, 329, 365, 373, 374, 396, 402, 404, 419
staging issues **32**: 212; **47**: 1
textual issues **22**: 114
time and change, motif of **1**: 372, 393, 411; **39**: 89; **48**: 143
Turkish elements **19**: 170
two fathers **14**: 86, 101, 105, 108; **39**: 89, 100
violence **25**: 109

### Henry V (Volumes 5, 14, 30)

battle of Agincourt **5**: 197, 199, 213, 246, 257, 281, 287, 289, 293, 310, 318; **19**: 217; **30**: 181
Canterbury and churchmen **5**: 193, 203, 205,

213, 219, 225, 252, 260; **22:** 137; **30:** 215, 262
characterization **5:** 186, 189, 192, 193, 199, 219, 230, 233, 252, 276, 293; **30:** 227, 278
Chorus, role of **5:** 186, 192, 226, 228, 230, 252, 264, 269, 281, 293; **14:** 301, 319, 336; **19:** 133; **25:** 116, 131; **30:** 163, 202, 220
class distinctions, conflict, and relations **28:** 146
colonialism **22:** 103
comic elements **5:** 185, 188, 191, 192, 217, 230, 233, 241, 252, 260, 276; **19:** 217; **28:** 121; **30:** 193, 202,
economic relations **13:** 213
Elizabethan culture, relation to **5:** 210, 213, 217, 223, 257, 299, 310; **16:** 202; **19:** 133, 233; **28:** 121, 159; **30:** 215, 262; **37:** 187
English language and colonialism **22:** 103; **28:** 159
epic elements **5:** 192, 197, 246, 257, 314; **30:** 181, 220, 237, 252
<lvFalstaff **5:** 185, 186, 187, 189, 192, 195, 198, 210, 226, 257, 269, 271, 276, 293, 299; **28:** 146; **46:** 48
Fluellen **30:** 278; **37:** 105
French aristocrats and the Dauphin **5:** 188, 191, 199, 205, 213, 281; **22:** 137; **28:** 121
French language, Shakespeare"s use of **5:** 186, 188, 190; **25:** 131
gender issues **13:** 183; **28:** 121, 146, 159; **44:** 44
Henry
  brutality and cunning **5:** 193, 203, 209, 210, 213, 219, 233, 239, 252, 260, 271, 287, 293, 302, 304; **30:** 159,
  characterization in *1* and *2 Henry IV* contrasted **5:** 189, 190, 241, 304, 310; **19:** 133; **25:** 131; **32:** 157
  chivalry **37:** 187
  courage **5:** 191, 195, 210, 213, 228, 246, 257, 267
  disguise **30:** 169, 259
  education **5:** 246, 267, 271, 289; **14:** 297, 328, 342; **30:** 259
  emotion, lack of **5:** 209, 212, 233, 244, 264, 267, 287, 293, 310
  as heroic figure **5:** 192, 205, 209, 223, 244, 252, 257, 260, 269, 271, 299, 304; **28:** 121, 146; **30:** 237, 244, 252; **37:** 187
  humor **5:** 189, 191, 212, 217, 239, 240, 276
  intellectual and social limitations **5:** 189, 191, 203, 209, 210, 225, 226, 230, 293; **30:** 220
  interpersonal relations **5:** 209, 233, 267, 269, 276, 287, 293, 302, 318; **19:** 133; **28:** 146
  mercy **5:** 213, 267, 289, 293
  mixture of good and bad qualities **5:** 199, 205, 209, 210, 213, 244, 260, 304, 314; **30:** 262, 273
  piety **5:** 191, 199, 209, 217, 223, 239, 257, 260, 271, 289, 310, 318; **30:** 244; **32:** 126
  public versus private selves **22:** 137; **30:** 169, 207
  self-doubt **5:** 281, 310
  slaughter of prisoners **5:** 189, 205, 246, 293, 318; **28:** 146
  speech **5:** 212, 230, 233, 246, 264, 276, 287, 302; **28:** 146; **30:** 163, 227

historical content **5:** 185, 188, 190, 192, 193, 198, 246, 314; **13:** 201; **19:** 133; **25:** 131; **30:** 193, 202, 207, 215, 252
historical epic, place in or relation to Shakespeare"s **5:** 195, 198, 205, 212, 225, 241, 244, 287, 304, 310; **14:** 337, 342; **30:** 215
homoerotic elements **16:** 202
Hotspur **5:** 189, 199, 228, 271, 302
hypocrisy **5:** 203, 213, 219, 223, 233, 260, 271, 302
imperialism **22:** 103; **28:** 159
Irish affairs **22:** 103; **28:** 159
irony **5:** 192, 210, 213, 219, 223, 226, 233, 252, 260, 269, 281, 299, 304; **14:** 336; **30:** 159, 193,
Katherine **5:** 186, 188, 189, 190, 192, 260, 269, 299, 302; **13:** 183; **19:** 217; **30:** 278; **44:** 44
kingship **5:** 205, 223, 225, 233, 239, 244, 257, 264, 267, 271, 287, 289, 299, 302, 304, 314, 318; **16:** 202; **22:** 137; **30:** 169, 202, 259, 273
language and imagery **5:** 188, 230, 233, 241, 264, 276; **19:** 203; **25:** 131; **30:** 159, 181, 207, 234
Machiavellianism **5:** 203, 225, 233, 252, 287, 304; **25:** 131; **30:** 273
MacMorris **22:** 103; **28:** 159; **30:** 278
Marlowe"s works, compared with **19:** 233
metadramatic elements **13:** 194; **30:** 181,
Mistress Quickly **5:** 186, 187, 210, 276, 293; **30:** 278
morality **5:** 195, 203, 213, 223, 225, 239, 246, 260, 271, 293
obscenity **5:** 188, 190, 260
order **5:** 205, 257, 264, 310, 314; **30:** 193,
patriarchy **37:** 105; **44:** 44
nationalism and patriotism **5:** 198, 205, 209, 210, 213, 219, 223, 233, 246, 252, 257, 269, 299; **19:** 133, 217; **30:** 227, 262
Pistol **28:** 146
power **37:** 175
psychoanalytic interpretations **13:** 457; **44:** 44
religious, mythic, or religious content **25:** 116; **32:** 126
Salic Law **5:** 219, 252, 260; **28:** 121
self-interest or expediency **5:** 189, 193, 205, 213, 217, 233, 260, 287, 302, 304; **30:** 273
soldiers **5:** 203, 239, 267, 276, 281, 287, 293, 318; **28:** 146; **30:** 169,
staging issues **5:** 186, 189, 192, 193, 198, 205, 226, 230, 241, 281, 314; **13:** 194, 502; **14:** 293, 295, 297, 301, 310, 319, 328, 334, 336, 342; **19:** 217; **32:** 185
structure **5:** 186, 189, 205, 213, 230, 241, 264, 289, 310, 314; **30:** 220, 227, 234, 244
textual problems **5:** 187, 189, 190; **13:** 201
topical allusions or content **5:** 185, 186; **13:** 201
tragic elements **5:** 228, 233, 267, 269, 271
traitors (Scroop, Grey, and Cambridge) **16:** 202; **30:** 220, 278
Turkish elements **19:** 170
violence **43:** 24
war **5:** 193, 195, 197, 198, 210, 213, 219, 230, 233, 246, 281, 293; **28:** 121, 146; **30:** 262; **32:** 126; **37:** 175, 187; **42:** 143
Williams **13:** 502; **16:** 183; **28:** 146; **30:** 169, 259, 278

wooing scene (Act V, scene ii) **5:** 186, 188, 189, 191, 193, 195, 260, 276, 299, 302; **14:** 297; **28:** 121, 159; **30:** 163, 207

*Henry VI, Parts 1, 2, and 3* (Volumes 3, 24, 39)

  ambivalent or ironic elements **3:** 69, 151, 154; **39:** 160
  authorship controversy **3:** 16, 18, 19, 20, 21, 26, 27, 29, 31, 35, 39, 41, 55, 66; **24:** 51
  autobiographical elements **3:** 41, 55
  Bordeaux sequence **37:** 165
  Cade scenes **3:** 35, 67, 92, 97, 109; **16:** 183; **22:** 156; **25:** 102; **28:** 112; **37:** 97; **39:** 160, 196, 205
  carnival elements **22:** 156
  characterization **3:** 18, 20, 24, 25, 31, 57, 64, 73, 77, 109, 119, 151; **24:** 22, 28, 38, 42, 45, 47; **39:** 160
  class distinctions, conflict, and relations **37:** 97; **39:** 187
  dance **22:** 156
  decay of heroic ideals **3:** 119, 126
  disorder and civil dissension **3:** 59, 67, 76, 92, 103, 126; **13:** 131; **16:** 183; **24:** 11, 17, 28, 31, 47; **25:** 102; **28:** 112; **39:** 154, 177, 187, 196, 205
  Elizabethan literary and cultural influences **3:** 75, 97, 100, 119, 143; **22:** 156; **28:** 112; **37:** 97
  Folk rituals, elements and influence of **39:** 205
  Henry
    characterization **3:** 64, 77, 151; **39:** 160, 177; **47:** 32
    source of social disorder **3:** 25, 31, 41, 115; **39:** 154, 187
    as sympathetic figure **3:** 73, 143, 154; **24:** 32
  historical accuracy **3:** 18, 21, 35, 46, 51; **16:** 217; **24:** 16, 18, 25, 31, 45, 48
  historical epic, place in or relation to Shakespeare"s **3:** 24, 59; **24:** 51
  as humanistic play **3:** 83, 92, 109, 115, 119, 131, 136, 143
  Humphrey **13:** 131
  as inferior or flawed plays **3:** 20, 21, 25, 26, 35
  Joan of Arc **16:** 131; **32:** 212
  kingship **3:** 69, 73, 77, 109, 115, 136, 143; **24:** 32; **39:** 154, 177, 187; **47:** 32
  language and imagery **3:** 21, 50, 52, 55, 57, 66, 67, 71, 75, 76, 97, 105, 109, 119, 126, 131; **24:** 28; **37:** 157; **39:** 213, 222
  legitimacy **3:** 89, 157; **39:** 154,
  Machiavellianism **22:** 193
  Margaret
    characterization **3:** 18, 26, 35, 51, 103, 109, 140, 157; **24:** 48
    Suffolk, relationship with **3:** 18, 24, 26, 157; **39:** 213
  Marlowe"s works, compared with **19:** 233
  medieval literary influence **3:** 59, 67, 75, 100, 109, 136, 151; **13:** 131
  molehill scene (*3 Henry VI*, Act III, scene ii) **3:** 75, 97, 126, 149
  moral inheritance **3:** 89, 126
  multiple perspectives of characters **3:** 69, 154
  Neoclassical rules **3:** 17, 18

patriarchal claims **16:** 131 **25:** 102
nationalism and patriotism **24:** 25, 45, 47
play-within-the-play, convention of **3:** 75, 149
retribution **3:** 27, 42, 51, 59, 77, 83, 92, 100, 109, 115, 119, 131, 136, 151
Richard of Gloucester
    characterization **3:** 35, 48, 57, 64, 77, 143, 151; **22:** 193; **39:** 160, 177
    as revenger **22:** 193
    soliloquy (*3 Henry VI*, Act III, scene ii) **3:** 17, 48
sibling rivalry **22:** 193
sources **3:** 18, 21, 29, 31, 35, 39, 46, 51; **13:** 131; **16:** 217; **39:** 196
staging issues **24:** 21, 22, 27, 31, 32, 36, 38, 41, 45, 48, 55; **32:** 212
structure **3:** 31, 43, 46, 69, 83, 103, 109, 119, 136, 149, 154; **39:** 213
Talbot **39:** 160, 213, 222
textual arrangement **24:** 3, 4, 6, 12, 17, 18, 19, 20, 21, 24, 27, 42, 45; **37:** 165
theatrical viability **24:** 31, 32, 34
Tudor myth **3:** 51, 59, 77, 92, 100, 109, 115, 119, 131; **39:** 222
Unity **39:** 177, 222
violence **24:** 25, 31; **37:** 157
women, role of **3:** 103, 109, 126, 140, 157; **16:** 183; **39:** 196
York"s death **13:** 131

### *Henry VIII* (Volumes 2, 24, 41)

ambition or pride **2:** 15, 38, 67
authorship controversy **2:** 16, 18, 19, 22, 23, 27, 28, 31, 35, 36, 42, 43, 44, 46, 48, 51, 58, 64, 68; **41:** 129, 146, 158, 171,
Anne Boleyn **2:** 21, 24, 31; **41:** 180
Buckingham **22:** 182; **24:** 129, 140; **37:** 109
change **2:** 27, 65, 72, 81
characterization **2:** 17, 23, 25, 32, 35, 39; **24:** 106
composition date **2:** 19, 22, 35; **24:** 129
costumes **24:** 82, 87; **28:** 184
Cranmer"s prophecy **2:** 25, 31, 46, 56, 64, 68, 72; **24:** 146; **32:** 148; **41:** 120, 190
*Cymbeline*, compared with **2:** 67, 71
discrepancy between prophetic ending and preceding action **2:** 22, 25, 31, 46, 49, 56, 60, 65, 68, 75, 81; **32:** 148; **41:** 190
Elizabethan politics, relation to **22:** 395; **24:** 115, 129, 140; **32:** 148
Elizabethan dramatic conventions **24:** 155
English Reformation, influence of **2:** 25, 35, 39, 51, 67; **24:** 89
flattery **22:** 395
historical and romantic elements, combination of **41:** 129, 146, 180
historical epic, as epilogue to Shakespeare"s **2:** 22, 25, 27, 39, 51, 60, 65
historical relativity, theme of **41:** 146
King Henry
    as agent of divine retribution **2:** 49
    characterization **2:** 23, 39, 51, 58, 60, 65, 66, 75; **28:** 184; **37:** 109
    incomplete portrait **2:** 15, 16, 19, 35; **41:** 120
    as realistic figure **2:** 21, 22, 23, 25, 32

historical and romantic elements, combination of **2:** 46, 49, 51, 75, 76, 78; **24:** 71, 80, 146
historiography **37:** 109
inconsistencies **2:** 16, 27, 28, 31, 60
ironic aspects **41:** 129
Katherine
    characterization **2:** 18, 19, 23, 24, 38; **24:** 129; **37:** 109; **41:** 180
    Hermione, compared with **2:** 24, 51, 58, 76
    politeness strategies **22:** 182
    religious discourse **22:** 182
    as tragic figure **2:** 16, 18
kingship **2:** 49, 58, 60, 65, 75, 78; **24:** 113; **41:** 129, 171
language and imagery **41:** 180, 190
legitimacy **37:** 109
moral intent **2:** 15, 19, 25; **24:** 140
Norfolk **22:** 182
pageantry **2:** 14, 15, 18, 51, 58; **24:** 77, 83, 84, 85, 89, 91, 106, 113, 118, 120, 126, 127, 140, 146, 150; **41:** 120, 129, 190
patience **2:** 58, 76, 78
politics **2:** 39, 49, 51, 58, 60, 65, 67, 71, 72, 75, 78, 81; **24:** 74, 121, 124; **41:** 146
Porter **24:** 155
rebellion **22:** 395
rhetoric of politeness **22:** 182
Shakespeare"s romances, compared with **2:** 46, 51, 58, 66, 67, 71, 76; **41:** 171
sources **2:** 16, 17; **24:** 71, 80
staging issues **24:** 67, 70, 71, 75, 77, 83, 84, 85, 87, 89, 91, 101, 106, 113, 120, 127, 129, 136, 140, 146, 150, 152, 155; **28:** 184
Stephen Gardiner **24:** 129
structure **2:** 16, 25, 27, 28, 31, 36, 44, 46, 51, 56, 68, 75; **24:** 106, 112, 113, 120
style **41:** 158
thematic disparity **2:** 25, 31, 56, 68, 75; **41:** 146
tragedies of major characters **2:** 16, 39, 46, 48, 49, 51, 56, 58, 68, 81; **41:** 120
wheel of fortune, motif of **2:** 27, 65, 72, 81
Cardinal Wolsey **2:** 15, 18, 19, 23, 24, 38; **22:** 182; **24:** 80, 91, 112, 113, 129, 140; **37:** 109; **41:** 129

### *Julius Caesar* (Volumes 7, 17, 30)

anachronisms **7:** 331
Antony
    characterization **7:** 160, 179, 189, 221, 233, 284, 320, 333; **17:** 269, 271, 272, 284, 298, 306, 313, 315, 358, 398; **25:** 272; **30:** 316
    funeral oration **7:** 148, 154, 159, 204, 210, 221, 238, 259, 350; **25:** 280; **30:** 316, 333, 362
aristocratic values **16:** 231; **22:** 280; **30:** 379
the assassination **7:** 156, 161, 179, 191, 200, 221, 264, 272, 279, 284, 350; **25:** 272; **30:** 326
audience interpretation **48:** 240
audience response **7:** 179, 238, 253, 255, 272, 316, 320, 336, 350; **19:** 321; **48:** 240
Brutus
    arrogance **7:** 160, 169, 204, 207, 264, 277, 292, 350; **25:** 280; **30:** 351
    as chief protagonist or tragic hero **7:** 152, 159, 189, 191, 200, 204, 242, 250, 253, 264, 268, 279, 284, 298, 333; **17:** 272, 372, 387
    citizenship **25:** 272
    funeral oration **7:** 154, 155, 204, 210, 350
    motives **7:** 150, 156, 161, 179, 191, 200, 221, 227, 233, 245, 292, 303, 310, 320, 333, 350; **25:** 272; **30:** 321, 358
    nobility or idealism **7:** 150, 152, 156, 159, 161, 179, 189, 191, 200, 221, 242, 250, 253, 259, 264, 277, 303, 320; **17:** 269, 271, 273, 279, 280, 284, 306, 308, 321, 323, 324, 345, 358; **25:** 272, 280; **30:** 351, 362
    political ineptitude or lack of judgment **7:** 169, 188, 200, 205, 221, 245, 252, 264, 277, 282, 310, 316, 331, 333, 343; **17:** 323, 358, 375, 380
    self-knowledge or self-deception **7:** 191, 200, 221, 242, 259, 264, 268, 279, 310, 333, 336, 350; **25:** 272; **30:** 316
    soliloquy (Act II, scene i) **7:** 156, 160, 161, 191, 221, 245, 250, 253, 264, 268, 279, 282, 292, 303, 343, 350; **25:** 280; **30:** 333
Caesar
    ambiguous nature **7:** 191, 233, 242, 250, 272, 298, 316, 320
    arrogance **7:** 160, 207, 218, 253, 272, 279, 298; **25:** 280
    idolatry **22:** 137
    leadership qualities **7:** 161, 179, 189, 191, 200, 207, 233, 245, 253, 257, 264, 272, 279, 284, 298, 310, 333; **17:** 317, 358; **22:** 280; **30:** 316, 326
    as tragic hero **7:** 152, 200, 221, 279; **17:** 321, 377, 384
    weakness **7:** 161, 167, 169, 179, 187, 188, 191, 207, 218, 221, 233, 250, 253, 298; **17:** 358; **25:** 280
Caesarism **7:** 159, 160, 161, 167, 169, 174, 191, 205, 218, 253, 310; **30:** 316, 321
Calphurnia
    dream **45:** 10
Cassius **7:** 156, 159, 160, 161, 169, 179, 189, 221, 233, 303, 310, 320, 333, 343; **17:** 272, 282, 284, 344, 345, 358; **25:** 272, 280; **30:** 351; **37:** 203
construing the truth **7:** 320, 336, 343, 350; **37:** 229
Elizabethan culture, relation to **16:** 231; **30:** 342, 379
emulation or rivalry **16:** 231
gender issues **13:** 260
historical determinism versus free will **7:** 160, 298, 316, 333, 346, 356; **13:** 252
irony or ambiguity **7:** 167, 257, 259, 262, 268, 282, 316, 320, 333, 336, 346, 350
language and imagery **7:** 148, 155, 159, 188, 204, 207, 227, 242, 250, 277, 296, 303, 324, 346, 350; **13:** 260; **17:** 347, 348, 350, 356, 358; **19:** 321; **22:** 280; **25:** 280; **30:** 333, 342
liberty versus tyranny **7:** 158, 179, 189, 205, 221, 253; **25:** 272
love and friendship **7:** 233, 262, 268; **25:** 272
medieval physiology **13:** 260
moral choice **7:** 179, 264, 279, 343
Octavius **30:** 316
omens **22:** 137; **45:** 10
philosophical elements **7:** 310, 324; **37:** 203

the poets **7:** 179, 320, 350
politics **7:** 161, 169, 191, 205, 218, 221, 245, 262, 264, 279, 282, 310, 324, 333, 346; **17:** 317, 318, 321, 323, 334, 350, 351, 358, 378, 382, 394, 406; **22:** 137, 280; **25:** 272, 280; **30:** 285, 297, 316, 321, 342, 374, 379; **37:** 203
as "problem play" **7:** 272, 320
psychoanalytic interpretation **45:** 10
public versus private principles **7:** 161, 179, 252, 262, 268, 284, 298; **13:** 252
quarrel scene (Act IV, scene iii) **7:** 149, 150, 152, 153, 155, 160, 169, 188, 191, 204, 268, 296, 303, 310
retribution **7:** 160, 167, 200
revenge tragedy elements **7:** 316
ceremonies, rites, and rituals, importance of **7:** 150, 210, 255, 259, 268, 284, 316, 331, 339, 356; **13:** 260; **22:** 137; **30:** 374
role-playing **7:** 356; **37:** 229
Roman citizenry, portrayal of **7:** 169, 179, 210, 221, 245, 279, 282, 310, 320, 333; **17:** 271, 279, 288, 291, 292, 298, 323, 334, 351, 367, 374, 375, 378; **22:** 280; **30:** 285, 297, 316, 321, 374, 379; **37:** 229
Senecan elements **37:** 229
Shakespeare"s English history plays, compared with **7:** 161, 189, 218, 221, 252; **22:** 137; **30:** 369
Shakespeare"s major tragedies, compared with **7:** 161, 188, 227, 242, 264, 268
sources **7:** 149, 150, 156, 187, 200, 264, 272, 282, 284, 320; **30:** 285, 297, 326, 358
staging **48:** 240
structure **7:** 152, 155, 159, 160, 179, 200, 210, 238, 264, 284, 298, 316, 346; **13:** 252; **30:** 374
violence **48:** 240

**King John (Volumes 9, 24, 41)**

ambiguity **13:** 152; **41:** 243
anti-catholic rhetoric **22:** 120; **25:** 98
Arthur **9:** 215, 216, 218, 219, 229, 240, 267, 275; **22:** 120; **25:** 98; **41:** 251, 277
autobiographical elements **9:** 209, 218, 245, 248, 260, 292
characterization **9:** 222, 224, 229, 240, 250, 292; **41:** 205, 215
church versus state **9:** 209, 212, 222, 235, 240; **22:** 120
commodity or self-interest **9:** 224, 229, 245, 260, 275, 280, 297; **19:** 182; **25:** 98; **41:** 228
commodity versus honor **41:** 269
Constance **9:** 208, 210, 211, 215, 219, 220, 224, 229, 240, 251, 254; **16:** 161; **24:** 177, 184, 196
corruption in society **9:** 222, 234, 280, 297
Elizabethan politics, relation to **48:** 132
ethical or moral issues **9:** 212, 222, 224, 229, 235, 240, 263, 275, 280
excess **9:** 251
Faulconbridge, the Bastard **41:** 205, 228, 251, 260, 277

as chorus or commentator **9:** 212, 218, 229, 248, 251, 260, 271, 284, 297, 300; **22:** 120
as comic figure **9:** 219, 271, 297
development **9:** 216, 224, 229, 248, 263, 271, 275, 280, 297; **13:** 158, 163
as embodiment of England **9:** 222, 224, 240, 244, 248, 271
heroic qualities **9:** 208, 245, 248, 254, 263, 271, 275; **25:** 98
political conduct **9:** 224, 240, 250, 260, 280, 297; **13:** 147, 158; **22:** 120
Henry **41:** 277
historical content **9:** 216, 219, 220, 222, 235, 240, 254, 284, 290, 292, 297, 300, 303; **13:** 163; **32:** 93, 114; **41:** 234, 243
John **41:** 205, 260
death, decay, and nature"s destructiveness **9:** 212, 215, 216, 240
decline **9:** 224, 235, 240, 263, 275
Hubert, scene with (Act III, scene iii) **9:** 210, 212, 216, 218, 219, 280
moral insensibility **13:** 147, 163
negative qualities **9:** 209, 212, 218, 219, 229, 234, 235, 244, 245, 246, 250, 254, 275, 280, 297
positive qualities **9:** 209, 224, 235, 240, 244, 245, 263
kingship **9:** 235, 254, 263, 275, 297; **13:** 158; **19:** 182; **22:** 120
language and imagery **9:** 212, 215, 220, 246, 251, 254, 267, 280, 284, 292, 297, 300; **13:** 147, 158; **22:** 120; **37:** 132; **48:** 132
legitimacy or inheritance **9:** 224, 235, 254, 303; **13:** 147; **19:** 182; **37:** 132; **41:** 215
Neoclassical rules **9:** 208, 209, 210, 212
oppositions or dualisms **9:** 224, 240, 263, 275, 284, 290, 300
*Papal Tyranny in the Reign of King John* (Colley Cibber adaptation) **24:** 162, 163, 165
nationalism and patriotism **9:** 209, 218, 222, 224, 235, 240, 244, 275; **25:** 98; **37:** 132
politics **9:** 218, 224, 260, 280; **13:** 163; **22:** 120; **37:** 132; **41:** 221, 228
rebellion **9:** 218, 254, 263, 280, 297
Shakespeare"s other history plays, compared with **9:** 218, 254; **13:** 152, 158; **25:** 98
sources **9:** 216, 222, 300; **32:** 93, 114; **41:** 234, 243, 251
staging issues **16:** 161; **19:** 182; **24:** 171, 187, 203, 206, 211, 225, 228, 241, 245, 249
structure **9:** 208, 212, 222, 224, 229, 240, 244, 245, 254, 260, 263, 275, 284, 290, 292, 300; **24:** 228, 241; **41:** 260, 269, 277
tragic elements **9:** 208, 209, 244
treachery **9:** 245
*The Troublesome Reign* (anonymous), compared with **9:** 216, 244, 260, 292; **22:** 120; **32:** 93; **41:** 205, 221, 260, 269; **48:** 132
Tudor doctrine **9:** 254, 284, 297; **41:** 221
tyranny **9:** 218
women, role of **9:** 222, 303; **16:** 161; **19:** 182; **41:** 205, 221

**King Lear (Volumes 2, 11, 31, 46)**

Albany **32:** 308
allegorical elements **16:** 311

audience perception **19:** 295; **28:** 325
autobiographical elements **2:** 131, 136, 149, 165
characterization **2:** 108, 125, 145, 162, 191; **16:** 311; **28:** 223; **46:** 177, 210
Christian elements **2:** 137, 170, 179, 188, 191, 197, 207, 218, 222, 226, 229, 238, 249, 265, 286; **22:** 233, 271; **25:** 218; **46:** 276
as Christian play **48:** 222
*Clarissa* (Samuel Richardson), compared with **48:** 277
combat scenes **22:** 365
comic and tragic elements, combination of **2:** 108, 110, 112, 125, 156, 162, 245, 278, 284; **46:** 191
Cordelia
attack on Britain **25:** 202
characterization **2:** 110, 116, 125, 170; **16:** 311; **25:** 218; **28:** 223, 325; **31:** 117, 149, 155, 162; **46:** 225, 231, 242
as Christ figure **2:** 116, 170, 179, 188, 222, 286
rebelliousness **13:** 352; **25:** 202
self-knowledge **46:** 218
on stage **11:** 158
transcendent power **2:** 137, 207, 218, 265, 269, 273
cruelty of daughters **2:** 101, 102, 106; **31:** 84, 123, 137, 142
death, decay, and nature"s destructiveness **2:** 93, 94, 101, 104, 106, 109, 112, 116, 129, 131, 137, 143, 147, 149, 156, 160, 170, 179, 188, 197, 207, 218, 222, 226, 231, 238, 241, 245, 249, 253, 265, 269, 273; **16:** 301; **25:** 202, 218; **31:** 77, 117, 137, 142; **46:** 264
double-plot **2:** 94, 95, 100, 101, 104, 112, 116, 124, 131, 133, 156, 253, 257; **46:** 254
Dover Cliff scene **2:** 156, 229, 255, 269; **11:** 8, 151
Edgar **28:** 223; **32:** 212; **32:** 308; **37:** 295; **47:** 9
Edgar-Edmund duel **22:** 365
Edmund **25:** 218; **28:** 223
Edmund"s forged letter **16:** 372
Elizabethan culture, relation to **2:** 168, 174, 177, 183, 226, 241; **19:** 330; **22:** 227, 233, 365; **25:** 218; **46:** 276; **47:** 9
Fool **2:** 108, 112, 125, 156, 162, 245, 278, 284; **11:** 17, 158, 169; **22:** 227; **25:** 202; **28:** 223; **46:** 1, 14, 18, 24, 33, 52, 191, 205, 210, 218, 225
Gloucester **46:** 254
Goneril **31:** 151; **46:** 231, 242
grotesque or absurd elements **2:** 136, 156, 245; **13:** 343
implausibility or plot, characters, or events **2:** 100, 136, 145, 278; **13:** 343
Job, compared with **2:** 226, 241, 245; **25:** 218
Kent **25:** 202; **28:** 223; **32:** 212; **47:** 9
language and imagery **2:** 129, 137, 161, 191, 199, 237, 257, 271; **16:** 301; **19:** 344; **22:** 233; **46:** 177
Lear
curse on Goneril **11:** 5, 7, 12, 114, 116
love-test and division of kingdom **2:** 100, 106, 111, 124, 131, 137, 147, 149, 151, 168, 186, 208, 216, 281; **16:** 351; **25:** 202; **31:** 84, 92, 107, 117, 149, 155; **46:** 231, 242

madness **2:** 94, 95, 98, 99, 100, 101, 102, 103; 111, 116, 120, 124, 125, 149, 156, 191, 208, 216, 281; **46:** 264
   as scapegoat **2:** 241, 253
   self-knowledge **2:** 103, 151, 188, 191, 213, 218, 222, 241, 249, 262; **25:** 218; **37:** 213; **46:** 191, 205, 225, 254, 264,
legal issues **46:** 276
love **2:** 109, 112, 131, 160, 162, 170, 179, 188, 197, 218, 222, 238, 265; **25:** 202; **31:** 77, 149, 151, 155, 162
madness **19:** 330
Marxist criticism **42:** 234
medieval or morality drama, influence of **2:** 177, 188, 201; **25:** 218
misogyny **31:** 123
nihilistic or pessimistic vision **2:** 130, 143, 149, 156, 165, 231, 238, 245, 253; **22:** 271; **25:** 218; **28:** 325
pagan elements **25:** 218
patriarchal or monarchical order **13:** 353, 457; **16:** 351; **22:** 227, 233; **25:** 218; **31:** 84, 92, 107, 117, 123, 137, 142; **46:** 269
performance issues **2:** 106, 137, 154, 160; **11:** 10, 20, 27, 56, 57, 132, 136, 137, 145, 150, 154; **19:** 295, 344; **25:** 218
poetic justice, question of **2:** 92, 93, 94, 101, 129, 137, 231, 245
politics **46:** 269
providential order **2:** 112, 116, 137, 168, 170, 174, 177, 218, 226, 241, 253; **22:** 271
Regan **31:** 151; **46:** 231, 242
rhetorical style **16:** 301; **47:** 9
romantic elements **31:** 77, 84
sexuality **25:** 202; **31:** 133, 137, 142
social and moral corruption **2:** 116, 133, 174, 177, 241, 271; **22:** 227; **31:** 84, 92; **46:** 269
sources **2:** 94, 100, 143, 145, 170, 186; **13:** 352; **16:** 351; **28:** 301
staging issues **11:** 1-178; **32:** 212; **46:** 205, 218
structure **28:** 325; **32:** 308; **46:** 177
suffering **2:** 137, 160, 188, 201, 218, 222, 226, 231, 238, 241, 249, 265; **13:** 343; **22:** 271; **25:** 218
Tate's adaptation **2:** 92, 93, 94, 101, 102, 104, 106, 110, 112, 116, 137; **11:** 10, 136; **25:** 218; **31:** 162
textual issues **22:** 271; **37:** 295
*Timon of Athens,* relation to **16:** 351
Virgo vs. Virago **48:** 222
wisdom **37:** 213; **46:** 210

### *Love's Labour's Lost* (Volumes 2, 23, 38)

Armado **23:** 207
artificial nature **2:** 315, 317, 324, 330; **23:** 207, 233
authorship controversy **2:** 299, 300; **32:** 308
Berowne **2:** 308, 324, 327; **22:** 12; **23:** 184, 187; **38:** 194; **47:** 35
characterization **2:** 303, 310, 317, 322, 328, 342; **23:** 237, 250, 252; **38:** 232; **47:** 35
as comedy of affectation **2:** 302, 303, 304; **23:** 191, 224, 226, 228, 233
comic resolution **2:** 335, 340; **16:** 17; **19:** 92; **38:** 209
conclusion **38:** 172
dance and patterned action **2:** 308, 342; **23:** 191, 237
death, decay, and nature's destructiveness **2:** 305, 331, 344, 348
desire **38:** 185, 194, 200, 209
dramatic shortcomings or failure **2:** 299, 301, 303, 322
Elizabeth I **38:** 239
Elizabethan love poetry **38:** 232
feminist criticism **42:** 93
genre **38:** 163
gift exchange **25:** 1
grace and civility **2:** 351
Holofernes **23:** 207
illusion versus reality **2:** 303, 308, 331, 340, 344, 348, 356, 359, 367, 371, 375; **23:** 230, 231
knowledge **22:** 12; **47:** 35
language and imagery **2:** 301, 302, 303, 306, 307, 308, 315, 319, 320, 330, 335, 344, 345, 348, 356, 359, 362, 365, 371, 374, 375; **19:** 92; **22:** 12, 378; **23:** 184, 187, 196, 197, 202, 207, 211, 221, 227, 231, 233, 237, 252; **28:** 9, 63; **38:** 219, 226
love **2:** 312, 315, 340, 344; **22:** 12; **23:** 252; **38:** 194
male domination **22:** 12
male sexual anxiety **16:** 17
marriage **2:** 335, 340; **19:** 92; **38:** 209, 232
metadramatic elements **2:** 356, 359, 362
Neoclassical rules **2:** 299, 300
as satire or parody **2:** 300, 302, 303, 307, 308, 315, 321, 324, 327; **23:** 237, 252
physical versus intellectual world **2:** 331, 348, 367
public versus private speech **2:** 356, 362, 371
School of Night, allusions to **2:** 321, 327, 328
sexuality **22:** 12
songs, role of **2:** 303, 304, 316, 326, 335, 362, 367, 371, 375
sources **16:** 17
spectacle **38:** 226
staging issues **23:** 184, 187, 191, 196, 198, 200, 201, 202, 207, 212, 215, 216, 217, 229, 230, 232, 233, 237, 252
structure **22:** 378; **23:** 191, 237, 252; **38:** 163, 172
theme
   idealism versus realism **38:** 163
topical allusions or content **2:** 300, 303, 307, 315, 316, 317, 319, 321, 327, 328; **23:** 187, 191, 197, 203, 221, 233, 237, 252; **25:** 1
unnatural ordering **22:** 378
violence **22:** 12
visual humor **23:** 207, 217
Watteau, influence on staging **23:** 184, 186
women, role of **19:** 92; **22:** 12; **23:** 215; **25:** 1
written versus oral communication **2:** 359, 365; **28:** 63

### *Macbeth* (Volumes 3, 20, 29, 44)

antithetical or contradictory elements **3:** 185, 213, 271, 302; **25:** 235; **29:** 76, 127; **47:** 41
appearance versus reality **3:** 241, 248; **25:** 235
archetypal or mythic elements **16:** 317
audience response **20:** 17, 400, 406; **29:** 139, 146, 155, 165; **44:** 306
banquet scene (Act III, scene iv) **20:** 22, 32, 175
Banquo **3:** 183, 199, 208, 213, 278, 289; **20:** 279, 283, 406, 413; **25:** 235; **28:** 339
characterization **20:** 12, 318, 324, 329, 353, 363, 367, 374, 387; **28:** 339; **29:** 101, 109, 146, 155, 165; **44:** 289; **47:** 41
Christian elements **3:** 194, 239, 260, 269, 275, 286, 293, 297, 318; **20:** 203, 206, 210, 256, 262, 289, 291, 294; **44:** 341, 366; **47:** 41
combat scenes **22:** 365
dagger scene (Act III, scene i), staging of **20:** 406
evil **3:** 194, 208, 231, 234, 239, 241, 267, 289; **20:** 203, 206, 210, 374
free will versus fate **3:** 177, 183, 184, 190, 196, 198, 202, 207, 208, 213; **13:** 361; **44:** 351, 361, 366, 373
innocence **3:** 234, 241, 327
Jacobean culture, relation to **19:** 330; **22:** 365
Lady Macbeth
   ambition **3:** 185, 219; **20:** 279, 345
   characterization **20:** 56, 60, 65, 73, 140, 148, 151, 241, 279, 283, 338, 350, 406, 413; **29:** 109, 146
   childlessness **3:** 219, 223
   good and evil, combined traits of **3:** 173, 191, 213; **20:** 60, 107
   inconsistencies **3:** 202; **20:** 54, 137
   influence on Macbeth **3:** 171, 185, 191, 193, 199, 262, 289, 312, 318; **13:** 502; **20:** 345; **25:** 235; **29:** 133
   psychoanalytic interpretations **20:** 345; **44:** 289, 297, 324; **45:** 58
   as sympathetic figure **3:** 191, 193, 203
language and imagery **3:** 170, 193, 213, 231, 234, 241, 245, 250, 253, 256, 263, 271, 283, 300, 302, 306, 323, 327, 338, 340, 349; **13:** 476; **16:** 317; **20:** 241, 279, 283, 367, 379, 400; **25:** 235; **28:** 339; **29:** 76, 91; **42:** 263; **44:** 366; **45:** 58
laws of nature, violation of **3:** 234, 241, 280, 323; **29:** 120
letter to Lady Macbeth **16:** 372; **20:** 345; **25:** 235
Macbeth
   ambition **44:** 284, 324
   characterization **20:** 20, 42, 73, 107, 113, 130, 146, 151, 279, 283, 312, 338, 343, 379, 406, 413; **29:** 139, 152, 155, 165; **44:** 289
   courage **3:** 172, 177, 181, 182, 183, 186, 234, 312, 333; **20:** 107; **44:** 315
   disposition **3:** 173, 175, 177, 182, 186; **20:** 245, 376
   imagination **3:** 196, 208, 213, 250, 312, 345; **20:** 245, 376; **44:** 351
   as "inauthentic" king **3:** 245, 302, 321, 345
   inconsistencies **3:** 202
   as Machiavellian villain **3:** 280
   manliness **20:** 113; **29:** 127, 133; **44:** 315
   psychoanalytic interpretations **20:** 42, 73, 238, 376; **44:** 284, 289, 297, 324; **45:** 48, 58
   Richard III, compared with **3:** 177, 182, 186, 345; **20:** 86, 92; **22:** 365; **44:** 269

as Satan figure **3:** 229, 269, 275, 289, 318
self-awareness **3:** 312, 329, 338; **16:** 317; **44:** 361
as sympathetic figure **3:** 229, 306, 314, 338; **29:** 139, 152; **44:** 269, 306, 337
as tragic hero **44:** 269, 306, 315, 324, 337
Macduff **3:** 226, 231, 253, 262,; **25:** 235; **29:** 127, 133, 155
madness **19:** 330
major tragedies, relation to Shakespeare''s other **3:** 171, 173, 213; **44:** 269
Malcolm **25:** 235
manhood **3:** 262, 309, 333; **29:** 127, 133
Marxist criticism **42:** 234
medieval mystery plays, relation to **44:** 341
moral lesson **20:** 23
murder scene (Act II, scene ii) **20:** 175
Neoclassical rules **3:** 170, 171, 173, 175; **20:** 17
nightmarish quality **3:** 231, 309; **20:** 210, 242; **44:** 261
Porter scene (Act II, scene iii) **3:** 173, 175, 184, 190, 196, 203, 205, 225, 260, 271, 297, 300; **20:** 283; **44:** 261; **46:** 29, 78
primitivism **20:** 206, 213; **45:** 48
providential order **3:** 208, 289, 329, 336
psychoanalytic interpretations **3:** 219, 223, 226; **44:** 11, 284, 289, 297
regicide **16:** 317, 328; **45:** 48 248, 275, 312
religious and theological issues **44:** 324, 341, 351, 361, 366, 373
religious, mythic, or spiritual content **3:** 208, 269, 275, 318; **29:** 109
retribution **3:** 194, 208, 318; **48:** 214
sexual anxiety **16:** 328; **20:** 283
sleepwalking scene (Act V, scene i) **3:** 191, 203, 219; **20:** 175; **44:** 261
staging issues **13:** 502; **20:** 12, 17, 32, 64, 65, 70, 73, 107, 113, 151, 175, 203, 206, 210, 213, 245, 279, 283, 312, 318, 324, 329, 343, 345, 350, 353, 363, 367, 374, 376, 379, 382, 387, 400, 406, 413; **22:** 365; **32:** 212
structure **16:** 317; **20:** 12, 245
supernatural grace versus evil or chaos **3:** 241, 286, 323
theatricality **16:** 328
time **3:** 234, 246, 283, 293; **20:** 245
topical allusions or content **13:** 361; **20:** 17, 350; **29:** 101
treason and punishment **13:** 361; **16:** 328
violence **20:** 273, 279, 283; **45:** 58
witches and supernaturalism **3:** 171, 172, 173, 175, 177, 182, 183, 184, 185, 194, 196, 198, 202, 207, 208, 213, 219, 229, 239; **16:** 317; **19:** 245; **20:** 92, 175, 213, 279, 283, 374, 387, 406, 413; **25:** 235; **28:** 339; **29:** 91, 101, 109, 120; **44:** 351, 373,

### Measure for Measure (Volumes 2, 23, 33)

ambiguity **2:** 417, 420, 432, 446, 449, 452, 474, 479, 482, 486, 495, 505
Angelo
anxiety **16:** 114
authoritarian portrayal of **23:** 307
characterization **2:** 388, 390, 397, 402, 418, 427, 432, 434, 463, 484, 495, 503, 511; **13:** 84; **23:** 297; **32:** 81; **33:** 77
hypocrisy **2:** 396, 399, 402, 406, 414, 421; **23:** 345, 358, 362
repentance or pardon **2:** 388, 390, 397, 402, 434, 463, 511, 524
audience response **48:** 1
autobiographical elements **2:** 406, 410, 414, 431, 434, 437
Barnardine **13:** 112
bed-trick **13:** 84
characterization **2:** 388, 390, 391, 396, 406, 420, 421, 446, 466, 475, 484, 505, 516, 524; **23:** 299, 405; **33:** 77
Christian elements **2:** 391, 394, 399, 421, 437, 449, 466, 479, 491, 511, 522; **48:** 1
*Clarissa* (Samuel Richardson), compared with **48:** 277
comic form **2:** 456, 460, 479, 482, 491, 514, 516; **13:** 94, 104; **23:** 309, 326, 327
death, decay, and nature''s destructiveness **2:** 394, 452, 516; **25:** 12
displacement **22:** 78
Duke
as authoritarian figure **23:** 314, 317, 347; **33:** 85
characterization **2:** 388, 395, 402, 406, 411, 421, 429, 456, 466, 470, 498, 511; **13:** 84, 94, 104; **23:** 363, 416; **32:** 81; **42:** 1; **44:** 89
dramatic shortcomings or failure **2:** 420, 429, 441, 479, 495, 505, 514, 522
godlike portrayal of **23:** 320
noble portrayal of **23:** 301
speech on death (Act III, scene i) **2:** 390, 391, 395
Elbow **22:** 85; **25:** 12
Elbow, Mistress **33:** 90
Elizabethan betrothal and marriage customs **2:** 429, 437, 443, 503
Elizabethan culture, relation to **2:** 394, 418, 429, 432, 437, 460, 470, 482, 503
feminist interpretation **23:** 320
good and evil **2:** 432, 452, 524; **33:** 52, 61
homosexuality **42:** 1
immortality **16:** 102
inconsistency between first and second halves **2:** 474, 475, 505, 514, 524
Isabella **2:** 388, 390, 395, 396, 397, 401, 402, 406, 409, 410, 411, 418, 420, 421, 432, 437, 441, 466, 475, 491, 495, 524; **16:** 114; **23:** 278, 279, 280, 281, 282, 296, 344, 357, 363, 405; **28:** 92; **33:** 77, 85
judicial versus natural law **2:** 446, 507, 516, 519; **22:** 85; **33:** 58, 117
justice and mercy **2:** 391, 395, 399, 402, 406, 409, 411, 416, 421, 437, 443, 463, 466, 470, 491, 495, 522, 524; **22:** 85; **33:** 52, 61, 101
language and imagery **2:** 394, 421, 431, 466, 486, 505; **13:** 112; **28:** 9; **33:** 69
Lucio **13:** 104
marriage **2:** 443, 507, 516, 519, 524, 528; **25:** 12; **33:** 61, 90
as medieval allegory or morality play **2:** 409, 421, 443, 466, 475, 491, 505, 511, 522; **13:** 94
metadramatic elements **13:** 104
misgovernment **2:** 401, 432, 511; **22:** 85
misogyny **23:** 358;
moral seriousness, question of **2:** 387, 388, 396, 409, 417, 421, 452, 460, 495; **23:** 316, 321
Neoclassical rules **2:** 387, 388, 390, 394; **23:** 269
politics **23:** 379
power **13:** 112; **22:** 85; **23:** 327, 330, 339, 352; **33:** 85
as "problem play" **2:** 416, 429, 434, 474, 475, 503, 514, 519; **16:** 102; **23:** 313, 328, 351
providential order **48:** 1
psychoanalytic interpretations **23:** 331, 332, 333, 334, 335, 340, 355, 356, 359, 379, 395; **44:** 79
Puritanism **2:** 414, 418, 434
rebirth, regeneration, resurrection, or immortality **13:** 84; **16:** 102, 114; **23:** 321, 327, 335, 340, 352; **25:** 12
religious and theological issues **48:** 1
religious, mythic, or spiritual content **48:** 1
resolution **2:** 449, 475, 495, 514, 516; **16:** 102, 114
sexuality **13:** 84; **16:** 102, 114; **23:** 321, 327, 335, 340, 352; **25:** 12; **33:** 85, 90, 112
social aspects **23:** 316, 375, 379, 395
sources **2:** 388, 393, 427, 429, 437, 475; **13:** 94
staging issues **2:** 427, 429, 437, 441, 443, 456, 460, 482, 491, 519; **23:** 283, 284, 285, 286, 287, 291, 293, 294, 298, 299, 311, 315, 327, 338, 339, 340, 342, 344, 347, 363, 372, 375, 395, 400, 405, 406, 413; **32:** 16
structure **2:** 390, 411, 449, 456, 466, 474, 482, 490, 491; **33:** 69
substitution of identities **2:** 507, 511, 519; **13:** 112
supernatural grace vs. evil or chaos **48:** 1
theatricality **23:** 285, 286, 294, 372, 406
comic and tragic elements, combination of **16:** 102
as unsuccessful play **2:** 397, 441, 474, 482; **23:** 287

### The Merchant of Venice (Volumes 4, 12, 40)

Act V, relation to Acts I through IV **4:** 193, 194, 195, 196, 204, 232, 270, 273, 289, 300, 319, 321, 326, 336, 356
allegorical elements **4:** 224, 250, 261, 268, 270, 273, 282, 289, 324, 336, 344, 350
Antonio
excessive or destructive love **4:** 279, 284, 336, 344; **12:** 54; **37:** 86
love for Bassanio **40:** 156
melancholy **4:** 221, 238, 279, 284, 300, 321, 328; **22:** 69; **25:** 22
pitiless **4:** 254
as pivotal figure **12:** 25, 129
appearance versus reality **4:** 209, 261, 344; **12:** 65; **22:** 69
Bassanio **25:** 257; **37:** 86; **40:** 156
bonding **4:** 293, 317, 336; **13:** 37
casket scenes **4:** 226, 241, 308, 344; **12:** 23, 46, 47, 65, 117; **13:** 43; **22:** 3; **40:** 106
contrasting dramatic worlds **44:** 11
conflict between Christianity and Judaism **4:** 224, 250, 268, 289, 324, 344; **12:** 67, 70, 72,

76; **22:** 69; **25:** 257; **40:** 117, 127, 166, 181; **48:** 54, 77
desire **22:** 3; **40:** 142; **45:** 17
Economics and exchange **40:** 197, 208
Elizabethan culture, relation to **32:** 66; **40:** 117, 127, 142, 166, 181, 197, 208; **48:** 54, 77
genre **4:** 191, 200, 201, 209, 215, 221, 232, 238, 247; **12:** 48, 54, 62
homosexuality **22:** 3, 69; **37:** 86; **40:** 142, 156, 197
implausibility of plot, characters, or events **4:** 191, 192, 193; **12:** 52, 56, 76, 119
irony **4:** 254, 300, 321, 331, 350; **28:** 63
Jessica **4:** 196, 200, 228, 293, 342
justice and mercy **4:** 213, 214, 224, 250, 261, 273, 282, 289, 336; **12:** 80, 129; **40:** 127
language and imagery **4:** 241, 267, 293; **22:** 3; **25:** 257; **28:** 9, 63; **32:** 41; **40:** 106
Launcelot Gobbo **46:** 24, 60
love **4:** 221, 226, 270, 284, 312, 344; **22:** 3, 69; **25:** 257; **40:** 156
medieval homilies, influence of **4:** 224, 250, 289
Portia **4:** 194, 195, 196, 215, 254, 263, 336, 356; **12:** 104, 107, 114; **13:** 37; **22:** 3, 69; **25:** 22; **32:** 294; **37:** 86; **40:** 142, 156, 197, 208
psychoanalytic interpretation **45:** 17
resolution **4:** 263, 266, 300, 319, 321; **13:** 37
rings episode **22:** 3; **40:** 106, 151, 156
sacrificial love **13:** 43; **22:** 69; **40:** 142
sexual politics **22:** 3
Shylock
  alienation **4:** 279, 312; **40:** 175
  ambiguity **4:** 247, 254, 315, 319, 331; **12:** 31, 35, 36, 50, 51, 52, 56, 81, 124; **40:** 175
  forced conversion **4:** 209, 252, 268, 282, 289, 321
  Jewishness **4:** 193, 194, 195, 200, 201, 213, 214, 279; **22:** 69; **25:** 257; **40:** 142, 175, 181
  motives in making the bond **4:** 252, 263, 266, 268; **22:** 69; **25:** 22
  as Puritan **40:** 127, 166
  as scapegoat figure **4:** 254, 300; **40:** 166
  as traditional comic villain **4:** 230, 243, 261, 263, 315; **12:** 40, 62, 124; **40:** 175
  as tragic figure **12:** 6, 9, 10, 16, 21, 23, 25, 40, 44, 66, 67, 81, 97; **40:** 175
  staging issues **12:** 111, 114, 115, 117, 119, 124, 129, 131
  structure **4:** 201, 215, 230, 232, 243, 247, 254, 261, 263, 308, 321; **12:** 115; **28:** 63
  trial scene **13:** 43; **25:** 22; **40:** 106, 156
  unity of double plot **4:** 193, 194, 201, 232; **12:** 16, 67, 80, 115; **40:** 151
  Venetians **4:** 195, 200, 228, 254, 273, 300, 321, 331
  Venice, Elizabethan perceptions of **28:** 249; **32:** 294; **40:** 127
  wealth **4:** 209, 261, 270, 273, 317; **12:** 80, 117; **22:** 69; **25:** 22; **28:** 249; **40:** 117, 197, 208; **45:** 17

*The Merry Wives of Windsor* (Volumes 5, 18, 38, 47)

Anne Page-Fenton plot **5:** 334, 336, 343, 353, 376, 390, 395, 402; **22:** 93; **47:** 308

avarice **5:** 335, 353, 369, 376, 390, 395, 402
Caius, Doctor **47:** 354
caricature **5:** 343, 347, 348, 350, 385, 397
characterization **5:** 332, 334, 335, 337, 338, 351, 360, 363, 366, 374, 379, 392; **18:** 74, 75; **38:** 264, 273, 313, 319
class distinctions, conflict, and relations **5:** 338, 343, 346, 347, 366, 390, 395, 400, 402; **22:** 93; **28:** 69
comic and farcical elements **5:** 336, 338, 346, 350, 360, 369, 373; **18:** 74, 75, 84
*The Comical Gallant* (John Dennis adaptation) **18:** 5, 7, 8, 9, 10
deception, disguise, and duplicity **5:** 332, 334, 336, 354, 355, 379; **22:** 93; **47:** 308, 314, 321, 325, 344
desire **38:** 286, 297, 300
Elizabethan society **47:** 331
Elizabeth's influence **5:** 333, 334, 335, 336, 339, 346, 355, 366, 402; **18:** 5, 86; **38:** 278; **47:** 344
Evans, Sir Hugh **47:** 354
Falstaff
  characterization in *1* and *2 Henry IV*, compared with **5:** 333, 335, 336, 337, 339, 346, 347, 348, 350, 373, 400; **18:** 5, 7, 75, 86; **22:** 93
  diminishing powers **5:** 337, 339, 343, 347, 350, 351, 392; **28:** 373; **47:** 363
  as Herne the Hunter **38:** 256, 286; **47:** 358
  incapability of love **5:** 335, 336, 339, 346, 348; **22:** 93
  as Jack-a-Lent **47:** 363
  personification of comic principle or Vice figure **5:** 332, 338, 369, 400; **38:** 273
  recognition and repentance of follies **5:** 338, 341, 343, 348, 369, 374, 376, 397
  as scapegoat **47:** 358, 363, 375
  sensuality **5:** 339, 343, 353, 369, 392
  shrewdness **5:** 332, 336, 346, 355
  threat to community **5:** 343, 369, 379, 392, 395, 400; **38:** 297
  as unifying force **47:** 358
  vanity **5:** 332, 339
  victimization **5:** 336, 338, 341, 347, 348, 353, 355, 360, 369, 373, 374, 376, 392, 397, 400
  as villain **47:** 358
  as a woman **47:** 325
folk rituals, elements and influence of **5:** 353, 369, 376, 392, 397, 400; **38:** 256, 300
Ford, Francis **5:** 332, 334, 343, 355, 363, 374, 379, 390; **38:** 273; **47:** 321
Ford, Mistress Alice **47:** 321
insults **47:** 331
jealousy **5:** 334, 339, 343, 353, 355, 363; **22:** 93; **38:** 273, 307
Jonsonian humors comedy, influence of **38:** 319
knighthood **5:** 338, 343, 390, 397, 402; **47:** 354
language and imagery **5:** 335, 337, 343, 347, 351, 363, 374, 379; **19:** 101; **22:** 93, 378; **28:** 9, 69; **38:** 313, 319
male discontent **5:** 392, 402
marriage **5:** 343, 369, 376, 390, 392, 400; **22:** 93; **38:** 297
mediation **5:** 343, 392

morality **5:** 335, 339, 347, 349, 353, 397
Neoclassical rules **5:** 332, 334
Page, Anne **47:** 321
Page, Mistress Margaret **47:** 321
play and theatricality **47:** 325
play-within-the-play, convention of **5:** 354, 355, 369, 402
realism **38:** 313
reconciliation **5:** 343, 369, 374, 397, 402
revenge **5:** 349, 350, 392; **38:** 264, 307
as satire or parody **5:** 338, 350, 360, 385; **38:** 278, 319; **47:** 354, 363
schemes and intrigues **5:** 334, 336, 339, 341, 343, 349, 355, 379
setting **47:** 375
sexual politics **19:** 101; **38:** 307
social milieu **18:** 75, 84; **38:** 297, 300
sources **5:** 332, 350, 360, 366, 385; **32:** 31
stage history **18:** 66, 67, 68, 70, 71
staging issues **18:** 74, 75, 84, 86, 90, 95
structure **5:** 332, 333, 334, 335, 343, 349, 355, 369, 374; **18:** 86; **22:** 378
unnatural ordering **22:** 378
wit **5:** 335, 336, 337, 339, 343, 351
women, role of **5:** 335, 341, 343, 349, 369, 379, 390, 392, 402; **19:** 101; **38:** 307

*A Midsummer Night's Dream* (Volumes 3, 12, 29, 45)

adaptations **12:** 144, 146, 147, 153, 280, 282
ambiguity **3:** 401, 459, 486; **45:** 169
appearance, perception, and illusion **3:** 368, 411, 425, 427, 434, 447, 459, 466, 474, 477, 486, 497, 516; **19:** 21; **22:** 39; **28:** 15; **29:** 175, 190; **45:** 136
Athens and the forest, contrast between **3:** 381, 427, 459, 466, 497, 502; **29:** 175
autobiographical elements **3:** 365, 371, 379, 381, 389, 391, 396, 402, 432
Bottom
  awakening speech (Act IV, scene i) **3:** 406, 412, 450, 457, 486, 516; **16:** 34
  folly of **46:** 1, 14, 29, 60
  imagination **3:** 376, 393, 406, 432, 486; **29:** 175, 190; **45:** 147
  self-possession **3:** 365, 376, 395, 402, 406, 480; **45:** 158
  Titania, relationship with **3:** 377, 406, 441, 445, 450, 457, 491, 497; **16:** 34; **19:** 21; **22:** 93; **29:** 216; **45:** 160
  transformation **3:** 365, 377, 432; **13:** 27; **22:** 93; **29:** 216; **45:** 147, 160
brutal elements **3:** 445, 491, 497, 511; **12:** 259, 262, 298; **16:** 34; **19:** 21; **29:** 183, 225, 263, 269; **45:** 169
capriciousness of the young lovers **3:** 372, 395, 402, 411, 423, 437, 441, 450, 497, 498; **29:** 175, 269; **45:** 107
chastity **45:** 143
class distinctions, conflict, and relations **22:** 23; **25:** 36; **45:** 160
as dream-play **3:** 365, 370, 372, 377, 389, 391; **29:** 190; **45:** 117
dreams **45:** 96, 107, 117
duration of time **3:** 362, 370, 380, 386, 494; **45:** 175

erotic elements **3:** 445, 491, 497, 511; **12:** 259, 262; 298; **16:** 34; **19:** 21; **29:** 183, 225, 269
fairies **3:** 361, 362, 372, 377, 395, 400, 423, 450, 459, 486; **12:** 287, 291, 294, 295; **19:** 21; **29:** 183, 190; **45:** 147
feminist interpretation **48:** 23
Helena **29:** 269
Hermia **29:** 225, 269; **45:** 117
Hippolytus, myth of **29:** 216; **45:** 84
identity **29:** 269
imagination and art **3:** 365, 371, 381, 402, 412, 417, 421, 423, 441, 459, 468, 506, 516, 520; **22:** 39
language and imagery **3:** 397, 401, 410, 412, 415, 432, 453, 459, 468, 494; **22:** 23, 39, 93, 378; **28:** 9; **29:** 263; **45:** 96, 126, 136, 147; **45:** 143, 169, 175; **48:** 23, 32
male domination **3:** 483, 520; **13:** 19; **25:** 36; **29:** 216, 225, 243, 256, 269; **42:** 46; **45:** 84
marriage **3:** 402, 423, 450, 483, 520; **29:** 243, 256; **45:** 136, 143; **48:** 32
metadramatic elements **3:** 427, 468, 477, 516, 520; **29:** 190, 225, 243
*Metamorphoses* (Golding translation of Ovid) **16:** 25
Minotaur, myth of **3:** 497, 498; **29:** 216
music and dance **3:** 397, 400, 418, 513; **12:** 287, 289; **25:** 36
Oberon as controlling force **3:** 434, 459, 477, 502; **29:** 175
Ovid, influence of **3:** 362, 427, 497, 498; **22:** 23; **29:** 175, 190, 216
parent-child relations **13:** 19; **29:** 216, 225, 243
passionate or romantic love **3:** 372, 389, 395, 396, 402, 408, 411, 423, 441, 450, 480, 497, 498, 511; **29:** 175, 225, 263, 269; **45:** 126, 136
Pauline doctrine **3:** 457, 486, 506
Platonic elements **3:** 368, 437, 450, 497; **45:** 126
politics **29:** 243
power **42:** 46; **45:** 84
psychoanalytic interpretations **3:** 440, 483; **28:** 15; **29:** 225; **44:** 1; **45:** 107, 117
Puck **45:** 96, 158
Pyramus and Thisbe interlude **3:** 364, 368, 379, 381, 389, 391, 396, 408, 411, 412, 417, 425, 427, 433, 441, 447, 457, 468, 474, 511; **12:** 254; **13:** 27; **16:** 25; **22:** 23; **29:** 263; **45:** 107, 175
reason versus imagination **3:** 381, 389, 423, 441, 466, 506; **22:** 23; **29:** 190; **45:** 96
reconciliation **3:** 412, 418, 437, 459, 468, 491, 497, 502, 513; **13:** 27; **29:** 190
reversal **29:** 225
*Romeo and Juliet*, compared with **3:** 396, 480
rustic characters **3:** 376, 397, 432; **12:** 291, 293; **45:** 147, 160
sexuality **22:** 23, 93; **29:** 225, 243, 256, 269; **42:** 46; **45:** 107
sources **29:** 216
staging issues **3:** 364, 365, 371, 372, 377; **12:** 151, 152, 154, 158, 159, 280, 284, 291, 295; **16:** 34; **19:** 21; **29:** 183, 256; **48:** 23
structure **3:** 364, 368, 381, 402, 406, 427, 450, 513; **13:** 19; **22:** 378; **29:** 175; **45:** 126, 175
textual issues **16:** 34; **29:** 216
Theseus
    characterization **3:** 363
    Hippolyta, relationship with **3:** 381, 412, 421, 423, 450, 468, 520; **29:** 175, 216, 243, 256; **45:** 84
    as ideal **3:** 379, 391
    "lovers, lunatics, and poets" speech (Act V, scene i) **3:** 365, 371, 379, 381, 391, 402, 411, 412, 421, 423, 441, 498, 506; **29:** 175
    as representative of institutional life **3:** 381, 403
Titania **29:** 243
tragic elements **3:** 393, 400, 401, 410, 445, 474, 480, 491, 498, 511; **29:** 175; **45:** 169
unity **3:** 364, 368, 381, 402, 406, 427, 450, 513; **13:** 19; **22:** 378; **29:** 175, 263
unnatural ordering **22:** 378

## Much Ado about Nothing (Volumes 8, 18, 31)

appearance versus reality **8:** 17, 18, 48, 63, 69, 73, 75, 79, 88, 95, 115; **31:** 198, 209
battle of the sexes **8:** 14, 16, 19, 48, 91, 95, 111, 121, 125; **31:** 231, 245
Beatrice and Benedick
    Beatrice"s femininity **8:** 14, 16, 17, 24, 29, 38, 41, 91; **31:** 222, 245
    Beatrice"s request to "kill Claudio" (Act IV, scene i) **8:** 14, 17, 33, 41, 55, 63, 75, 79, 91, 108, 115; **18:** 119, 120, 136, 161, 245, 257
    Benedick"s challenge of Claudio (Act V, scene i) **8:** 48, 63, 79, 91; **31:** 231
    Claudio and Hero, compared with **8:** 19, 28, 29, 75, 82, 115; **31:** 171, 216
    marriage and the opposite sex, attitudes toward **8:** 9, 13, 14, 16, 19, 29, 36, 48, 63, 77, 91, 95, 115, 121; **16:** 45; **31:** 216
    mutual attraction **8:** 13, 14, 19, 24, 29, 33, 41, 75
    nobility **8:** 13, 19, 24, 29, 36, 39, 41, 47, 82, 91, 108
    popularity **8:** 13, 38, 41, 53, 79
    transformed by love **8:** 19, 29, 36, 48, 75, 91, 95, 115; **31:** 209, 216
    unconventionality **8:** 48, 91, 95, 108, 115, 121
    vulgarity **8:** 11, 12, 33, 38, 41, 47
    wit and charm **8:** 9, 12, 13, 14, 19, 24, 27, 28, 29, 33, 36, 38, 41, 47, 55, 69, 95, 108, 115; **31:** 241
Borachio and Conrade **8:** 24, 69, 82, 88, 111, 115
Christian elements **8:** 17, 19, 29, 55, 95, 104, 111, 115; **31:** 209
church scene (Act IV, scene i) **8:** 13, 14, 16, 19, 33, 44, 47, 48, 58, 63, 69, 75, 79, 82, 91, 95, 100, 104, 111, 115; **18:** 120, 130, 138, 145, 146, 148, 192; **31:** 191, 198, 245
Claudio
    boorish behavior **8:** 9, 24, 33, 36, 39, 44, 48, 63, 79, 82, 95, 100, 111, 115; **31:** 209
    credulity **8:** 9, 17, 19, 24, 29, 36, 41, 47, 58, 63, 75, 77, 82, 95, 100, 104, 111, 115, 121; **31:** 241; **47:** 25
    mercenary traits **8:** 24, 44, 58, 82, 91, 95
    noble qualities **8:** 17, 19, 29, 41, 44, 58, 75
    reconciliation with Hero **8:** 33, 36, 39, 44, 47, 82, 95, 100, 111, 115, 121
    repentance **8:** 33, 63, 82, 95, 100, 111, 115, 121; **31:** 245
    sexual insecurities **8:** 75, 100, 111, 115, 121
courtship and marriage **8:** 29, 44, 48, 95, 115, 121, 125; **31:** 191, 231
deception, disguise, and duplicity **8:** 29, 55, 63, 69, 79, 82, 88, 108, 115; **31:** 191, 198
Dogberry and the Watch **8:** 9, 12, 13, 17, 24, 28, 29, 33, 39, 48, 55, 69, 79, 82, 88, 95, 104, 108, 115; **18:** 138, 152, 205, 208, 210, 213, 231; **22:** 85; **31:** 171, 229; **46:** 60
Don John **8:** 9, 12, 16, 17, 19, 28, 29, 36, 39, 41, 47, 48, 55, 58, 63, 82, 104, 108, 111, 121
Don Pedro **8:** 17, 19, 48, 58, 63, 82, 111, 121
eavesdropping scenes (Act II, scene iii and Act III, scene i) **8:** 12, 13, 17, 19, 28, 29, 33, 36, 48, 55, 63, 73, 75, 82, 121; **18:** 120, 138, 208, 215, 245, 264; **31:** 171, 184
egotism or narcissism **8:** 19, 24, 28, 29, 55, 69, 95, 115
Elizabethan culture, relation to **8:** 23, 33, 44, 55, 58, 79, 88, 104, 111, 115
Friar **8:** 24, 29, 41, 55, 63, 79, 111
genre **8:** 9, 18, 19, 28, 29, 39, 41, 44, 53, 63, 69, 73, 79, 82, 95, 100, 104; **48:** 14
Hero **8:** 13, 14, 16, 19, 28, 29, 44, 48, 53, 55, 82, 95, 104, 111, 115, 121; **31:** 231, 245; **47:** 25
implausibility of plot, characters, or events **8:** 9, 12, 16, 19, 33, 36, 39, 44, 53, 100, 104
irony **8:** 14, 63, 79, 82; **28:** 63
justice and mercy **22:** 85
language and imagery **8:** 9, 38, 43, 46, 55, 69, 73, 88, 95, 100, 115, 125; **19:** 68; **25:** 77; **28:** 63; **31:** 178, 184, 222, 241, 245; **48:** 14
law versus passion for freedom **22:** 85
love **8:** 24, 55, 75, 95, 111, 115; **28:** 56
Messina **8:** 19, 29, 48, 69, 82, 91, 95, 108, 111, 121, 125; **31:** 191, 209, 229, 241, 245
misgovernment **22:** 85
music and dance **19:** 68; **31:** 222
"nothing," significance of **8:** 17, 18, 23, 55, 73, 95; **19:** 68
performance issues **18:** 173, 174, 183, 184, 185, 186, 187, 188, 189, 190, 191, 192, 193, 195, 197, 199, 201, 204, 206, 207, 208, 209, 210, 254
power **22:** 85; **25:** 77; **31:** 231, 245
repentance or forgiveness **8:** 24, 29, 111
resurrection, metamorphosis, or transformation **8:** 88, 104, 111, 115
romance or chivalric tradition, influence of **8:** 53, 125
self-knowledge **8:** 69, 95, 100
setting **18:** 173, 174, 183, 184, 185, 186, 187, 188, 189, 190, 191, 192, 193, 195, 197, 199, 201, 204, 206, 207, 208, 209, 210, 254
slander or hearsay, importance of **8:** 58, 69, 82, 95, 104
sources **8:** 9, 19, 53, 58, 104
staging issues **8:** 18, 33, 41, 75, 79, 82, 108; **16:** 45; **18:** 245, 247, 249, 252, 254, 257, 261, 264; **28:** 63
structure **8:** 9, 16, 17, 19, 28, 29, 33, 39, 48, 63, 69, 73, 75, 79, 82, 115; **31:** 178, 184, 198, 231
virginity or chastity, importance of **8:** 44, 75, 95, 111, 121, 125; **31:** 222

wit **8:** 27, 29, 38, 69, 79, 91, 95; **31:** 178, 191
works by Shakespeare or other authors, compared with **8:** 16, 19, 27, 28, 33, 38, 39, 41, 53, 69, 79, 91, 104, 108; **31:** 231

### *Othello* (Volumes 4, 11, 35)

autobiographical elements **4:** 440, 444
Brabantio **25:** 189
Cassio **25:** 189
*Clarissa* (Samuel Richardson), compared with **48:** 277
consummation of marriage **22:** 207
contrasts and oppositions **4:** 421, 455, 457, 462, 508; **25:** 189
Desdemona
  as Christ figure **4:** 506, 525, 573; **35:** 360
  culpability **4:** 408, 415, 422, 427; **13:** 313; **19:** 253, 276; **35:** 265, 352, 380
  innocence **35:** 360; **47:** 25
  as mother figure **22:** 339; **35:** 282
  passivity **4:** 402, 406, 421, 440, 457, 470, 582, 587; **25:** 189; **35:** 380
  spiritual nature of her love **4:** 462, 530, 559
  staging issues **11:** 350, 354, 359; **13:** 327; **32:** 201
dramatic structure **4:** 370, 390, 399, 427, 488, 506, 517, 569; **22:** 207; **28:** 243
Duke **25:** 189
Emilia **4:** 386, 391, 392, 415, 587; **35:** 352, 380
gender issues **32:** 294; **35:** 327
handkerchief, significance of **4:** 370, 384, 385, 396, 503, 530, 562; **35:** 265, 282, 380
*Hercules Furens* (Seneca) as source **16:** 283
Iago
  affinity with Othello **4:** 400, 427, 468, 470, 477, 500, 506; **25:** 189; **44:** 57
  as conventional dramatic villain **4:** 440, 527, 545, 582
  as homosexual **4:** 503
  Machiavellian elements **4:** 440, 455, 457, 517, 545; **35:** 336, 347
  motives **4:** 389, 390, 397, 399, 402, 409, 423, 424, 427, 434, 451, 462, 545, 564; **13:** 304; **25:** 189; **28:** 344; **32:** 201; **35:** 265, 276, 310, 336, 347; **42:** 278
  revenge scheme **4:** 392, 409, 424, 451
  as scapegoat **4:** 506
  as victim **4:** 402, 409, 434, 451, 457, 470
idealism versus realism **4:** 457, 508, 517; **13:** 313; **25:** 189
implausibility of plot, characters, or events **4:** 370, 380, 391, 442, 444; **47:** 51
jealousy **4:** 384, 488, 527; **35:** 253, 265, 282, 301, 310; **44:** 57, 66
justice **35:** 247
language and imagery **4:** 433, 442, 445, 462, 493, 508, 517, 552, 587, 596; **13:** 304; **16:** 272; **22:** 378; **25:** 189, 257; **28:** 243, 344; **42:** 278; **47:** 51
love **4:** 412, 493, 506, 512, 530, 545, 552, 569, 570, 575, 580, 591; **19:** 253; **22:** 207; **25:** 257; **28:** 243, 344; **32:** 201; **35:** 261, 317
love and reason **4:** 512, 530, 580; **19:** 253
madness **35:** 265, 276, 282
marriage **35:** 369

Marxist criticism **42:** 234
*Measure for Measure*, compared with **25:** 189
medieval dramatic conventions, influence of **4:** 440, 527, 545, 559, 582
military and sexual hierarchies **16:** 272
Othello
  affinity with Iago **4:** 400, 427, 468, 470, 477, 500, 506; **25:** 189; **35:** 276, 320, 327
  as conventional "blameless hero" **4:** 445, 486, 500
  credulity **4:** 384, 385, 388, 390, 396, 402, 434, 440, 455; **13:** 327; **32:** 302; **47:** 25, 51
  Desdemona, relationship with **22:** 339; **35:** 301, 317; **37:** 269
  divided nature **4:** 400, 412, 462, 470, 477, 493, 500, 582, 592; **16:** 293; **19:** 276; **25:** 189; **35:** 320
  egotism **4:** 427, 470, 477, 493, 522, 536, 541, 573, 597; **13:** 304; **35:** 247, 253
  self-destructive anger **16:** 283
  self-dramatizing or self-deluding **4:** 454, 457, 477, 592; **13:** 313; **16:** 293; **35:** 317
  self-knowledge **4:** 462, 470, 477, 483, 508, 522, 530, 564, 580, 591, 596; **13:** 304, 313; **16:** 283; **28:** 243; **35:** 253, 317
  spiritual state **4:** 483, 488, 517, 525, 527, 544, 559, 564, 573; **28:** 243; **35:** 253
perception **19:** 276; **25:** 189, 257
poetic justice, question of **4:** 370, 412, 415, 427
pride and rightful self-esteem **4:** 522, 536, 541; **35:** 352
psychoanalytic interpretations **4:** 468, 503; **35:** 265, 276, 282, 301, 317, 320, 347; **42:** 203; **44:** 57
racial issues **4:** 370, 380, 384, 385, 392, 399, 401, 402, 408, 427, 564; **13:** 327; **16:** 293; **25:** 189, 257; **28:** 249, 330; **35:** 369; **42:** 203
religious, mythic, or spiritual content **4:** 483, 517, 522, 525, 559, 573; **22:** 207; **28:** 330
revenge **35:** 261
*Romeo and Juliet*, compared with **32:** 302
sexuality **22:** 339; **28:** 330, 344; **35:** 352, 360; **37:** 269; **44:** 57, 66
sources **28:** 330
staging issues **11:** 273, 334, 335, 339, 342, 350, 354, 359, 362
structure **22:** 378; **28:** 325
time scheme **4:** 370, 384, 390, 488; **22:** 207; **35:** 310; **47:** 51
*'Tis Pity She's a Whore* (John Ford), compared with
unnatural ordering **22:** 378
Venetian politics **32:** 294
violence **22:** 12; **43:** 32
*The Winter's Tale*, compared with **35:** 310
women, role of **19:** 253; **28:** 344

### *Pericles* (Volumes 2, 15, 36)

archetypal structure **2:** 570, 580, 582, 584, 588; **25:** 365
art and nature **22:** 315; **36:** 233
audience perception **42:** 359; **48:** 364
authorship controversy **2:** 538, 540, 543, 544, 545, 546, 548, 550, 551, 553, 556, 558, 564, 565, 568, 576, 586; **15:** 132, 141, 148, 152; **16:** 391, 399; **25:** 365; **36:** 198, 244
autobiographical elements **2:** 551, 554, 555, 563, 581
brothel scenes (Act IV, scenes ii and vi) **2:** 548, 550, 551, 553, 554, 586, 590; **15:** 134, 145, 154, 166, 172, 177; **36:** 274
composition date **2:** 537, 544
Deconstructionist interpretation of **48:** 364
Diana, as symbol of nature **22:** 315; **36:** 233
doubling of roles **15:** 150, 152, 167, 173, 180
Gower chorus **2:** 548, 575; **15:** 134, 141, 143, 145, 149, 152, 177; **36:** 279; **42:** 359
incest, motif of **2:** 582, 588; **22:** 315; **36:** 257, 264
as inferior or flawed plays **2:** 537, 546, 553, 563, 564; **15:** 139, 143, 156, 167, 176; **36:** 198
innocence **36:** 226, 274
Jacobean culture, relation to **37:** 361
language and imagery **2:** 559, 560, 565, 583; **16:** 391; **19:** 387; **22:** 315; **36:** 198, 214, 233, 244, 251, 264
Marina **37:** 361
as miracle play **2:** 569, 581; **36:** 205
nature as book **22:** 315; **36:** 233
oaths, importance of **19:** 387
patience **2:** 572, 573, 578, 579; **36:** 251
Pericles
  characterization **36:** 251; **37:** 361
  patience **2:** 572, 573, 578, 579
  suit of Antiochus's daughter **2:** 547, 565, 578, 579
  Ulysses, compared with **2:** 551
politics **37:** 361
popularity **2:** 536, 538, 546; **37:** 361
recognition scene (Act V, scene i) **15:** 138, 139, 141, 145, 161, 162, 167, 172, 175
reconciliation **2:** 555, 564, 584, 586, 588; **36:** 205
religious, mythic, or spiritual content **2:** 559, 561, 565, 570, 580, 584, 588; **22:** 315; **25:** 365
riddle motif **22:** 315; **36:** 205, 214
Shakespeare's other romances, relation to **2:** 547, 549, 551, 559, 564, 570, 571, 584, 585; **15:** 139; **16:** 391, 399; **36:** 226, 257
spectacle **42:** 359
sources **2:** 538, 568, 572, 575; **25:** 365; **36:** 198, 205
staging issues **16:** 399; **48:** 364
suffering **2:** 546, 573, 578, 579; **25:** 365; **36:** 279
textual revisions **15:** 129, 130, 132, 134, 135, 136, 138, 152, 155, 167, 181; **16:** 399; **25:** 365

### *The Phoenix and Turtle* (Volumes 10, 38)

allegorical elements **10:** 7, 8, 9, 16, 17, 48; **38:** 334, 378
art and nature **10:** 7, 42
authenticity **10:** 7, 8, 16
autobiographical elements **10:** 14, 18, 42, 48
bird imagery **10:** 21, 27; **38:** 329, 350, 367
Christian elements **10:** 21, 24, 31; **38:** 326

complex or enigmatic nature **10**: 7, 14, 35, 42; **38**: 326, 357
consciously philosophical **10**: 7, 21, 24, 31, 48; **38**: 342, 378
constancy and faithfulness **10**: 18, 20, 21, 48; **38**: 329
Court of Love **10**: 9, 24, 50
Donne, John, compared with **10**: 20, 31, 35, 37, 40
satiric elements **10**: 8, 16, 17, 27, 35, 40, 45, 48
love **10**: 31, 37, 40, 50; **38**: 342, 345, 367
as metaphysical poem **10**: 7, 8, 9, 20, 31, 35, 37, 40, 45, 50
Neoplatonism **10**: 7, 9, 21, 24, 40, 45, 50; **38**: 345, 350, 367
as "pure" poetry **10**: 14, 31, 35; **38**: 329
Scholasticism **10**: 21, 24, 31
Shakespeare"s dramas, compared with **10**: 9, 14, 17, 18, 20, 27, 37, 40, 42, 48; **38**: 342
sources **10**: 7, 9, 18, 24, 45; **38**: 326, 334, 350, 367
structure **10**: 27, 31, 37, 45, 50; **38**: 342, 345, 357
style **10**: 8, 20, 24, 27, 31, 35, 45, 50; **38**: 334, 345, 357

### *The Rape of Lucrece* (Volumes 10, 33, 43)

allegorical elements **10**: 89, 93
Brutus **10**: 96, 106, 109, 116, 121, 125, 128, 135
Christian elements **10**: 77, 80, 89, 96, 98, 109
Collatine **10**: 98, 131; **43**: 102
Elizabethan culture, relation to **33**: 195; **43**: 77
irony or paradox **10**: 93, 98, 128
language and imagery **10**: 64, 65, 66, 71, 78, 80, 89, 93, 116, 109, 125, 131; **22**: 289, 294; **25**: 305; **32**: 321; **33**: 144, 155, 179, 200; **43**: 102, 113, 141
Lucrece
    chastity **33**: 131, 138; **43**: 92
    as example of Renaissance *virtù* **22**: 289; **43**: 148
    heroic **10**: 84, 93, 109, 121, 128
    patriarchal woman, model of **10**: 109, 131; **33**: 169, 200
    self-responsibility **10**: 89, 96, 98, 106, 125; **33**: 195; **43**: 85, 92, 158
    unrealistic **10**: 64, 65, 66, 121
    verbose **10**: 64, 81, 116; **25**: 305; **33**: 169
    as victim **22**: 294; **25**: 305; **32**: 321; **33**: 131, 195; **43**: 102, 158
male/female relationships **10**: 109, 121, 131; **22**: 289; **25**: 305; **43**: 113, 141
narrative strategies **22**: 294
Roman history, relation to **10**: 84, 89, 93, 96, 98, 109, 116, 125, 135; **22**: 289; **25**: 305; **33**: 155, 190
Shakespeare"s dramas, compared with **10**: 63, 64, 65, 66, 68, 71, 73, 74, 78, 80, 81, 84, 98, 116, 121, 125; **43**: 92
sources **10**: 63, 64, 65, 66, 68, 74, 77, 78, 89, 98, 109, 121, 125; **25**: 305; **33**: 155, 190; **43**: 77, 92, 148,

structure **10**: 84, 89, 93, 98, 135; **22**: 294; **25**: 305, **43**: 102, 141
style **10**: 64, 65, 66, 68, 69, 70, 71, 73, 74, 77, 78, 81, 84, 98, 116, 131, 135; **43**: 113, 158
Tarquin **10**: 80, 93, 98, 116, 125; **22**: 294; **25**: 305; **32**: 321; **33**: 190; **43**: 102
tragic elements **10**: 78, 80, 81, 84, 98, 109; **43**: 85, 148
the Troy passage **10**: 74, 89, 98, 116, 121, 128; **22**: 289; **32**: 321; **33**: 144, 179; **43**: 77, 85
*Venus and Adonis*, compared with **10**: 63, 66, 68, 69, 70, 73, 81; **22**: 294; **43**: 148
violence **43**: 148, 158

### *Richard II* (Volumes 6, 24, 39)

abdication scene (Act IV, scene i) **6**: 270, 307, 317, 327, 354, 359, 381, 393, 409; **13**: 172; **19**: 151; **24**: 274, 414
acting and dissimulation **6**: 264, 267, 307, 310, 315, 368, 393, 409; **24**: 339, 345, 346, 349, 352, 356
allegorical elements **6**: 264, 283, 323, 385
audience perception **24**: 414, 423; **39**: 295
Bolingbroke
    comic elements **28**: 134
    guilt **24**: 423; **39**: 279
    language and imagery **6**: 310, 315, 331, 347, 374, 381, 397; **32**: 189
    as Machiavellian figure **6**: 305, 307, 315, 331, 347, 388, 393, 397; **24**: 428
    as politician **6**: 255, 263, 264, 272, 277, 294, 364, 368, 391; **24**: 330, 333, 405, 414, 423, 428; **39**: 256
    Richard, compared with **6**: 307, 315, 347, 374, 391, 393, 409; **24**: 346, 349, 351, 352, 356, 395, 419, 423, 428
    his silence **24**: 423
    structure, compared with **39**: 235
    usurpation of crown, nature of **6**: 255, 272, 289, 307, 310, 347, 354, 359, 381, 385, 393; **13**: 172; **24**: 322, 356, 383, 419; **28**: 178
Bolingbroke and Richard as opposites **24**: 423
Bolingbroke-Mowbray dispute **22**: 137
carnival elements **19**: 151; **39**: 273
censorship **24**: 260, 261, 262, 263, 386; **42**: 120
ceremonies, rites, and rituals, importance of **6**: 270, 294, 315, 368, 381, 397, 409, 414; **24**: 274, 356, 411, 414, 419
comic elements **24**: 262, 263, 395; **39**: 243
contractual and economic relations **13**: 213
costumes **24**: 274, 278, 291, 304, 325, 356, 364, 423
deposition scene (Act III, scene iii) **24**: 298, 395, 423; **42**: 120
Elizabethan attitudes, influence of **6**: 287, 292, 294, 305, 321, 327, 364, 402, 414; **13**: 494; **24**: 325; **28**: 188; **39**: 273; **42**: 120
Essex Rebellion, relation to **6**: 249, 250; **24**: 356
family honor, structure, and inheritance **6**: 338, 368, 388, 397, 414; **39**: 263, 279
fate **6**: 289, 294, 304, 352, 354, 385
garden scene (Act III, scene iv) **6**: 264, 283, 323, 385; **24**: 307, 356, 414
Gaunt **6**: 255, 287, 374, 388, 402, 414; **24**:

274, 322, 325, 414, 423; **39**: 263, 279
gender issues **25**: 89; **39**: 295
historical sources, compared with **6**: 252, 279, 343; **28**: 134; **39**: 235
irony **6**: 270, 307, 364, 368, 391; **24**: 383; **28**: 188
King of Misrule **19**: 151; **39**: 273
kingship **6**: 263, 264, 272, 277, 289, 294, 327, 354, 364, 381, 388, 391, 402, 409, 414; **19**: 151, 209; **24**: 260, 289, 291, 322, 325, 333, 339, 345, 346, 349, 351, 352, 356, 395, 408, 419, 428; **28**: 134; **39**: 235, 243, 256, 273, 279, 289; **42**: 175
language and imagery **6**: 252, 282, 283, 294, 298, 315, 323, 331, 347, 368, 374, 381, 385, 397, 409; **13**: 213, 494; **24**: 269, 270, 298, 301, 304, 315, 325, 329, 333, 339, 356, 364, 395, 405, 408, 411, 414, 419; **28**: 134, 188; **39**: 243, 273, 289, 295; **42**: 175
Marlowe"s works, compared with **19**: 233; **24**: 307, 345; **42**: 175
medievalism and chivalry, presentation of **6**: 258, 277, 294, 327, 338, 388, 397, 414; **24**: 274, 278, 279, 280, 283; **39**: 256
mercantilism and feudalism **13**: 213
mirror scene (Act IV, scene i) **6**: 317, 327, 374, 381, 393, 409; **24**: 267, 356, 408, 414, 419, 423; **28**: 134, 178; **39**: 295
negative assessments **6**: 250, 252, 253, 255, 282, 307, 317, 343, 359
Northumberland **24**: 423
Richard
    artistic temperament **6**: 264, 267, 270, 272, 277, 292, 294, 298, 315, 331, 334, 347, 368, 374, 393, 409; **24**: 298, 301, 304, 315, 322, 390, 405, 408, 411, 414, 419; **39**: 289
    Bolingbroke, compared with **24**: 346, 349, 351, 352, 356, 419; **39**: 256
    characterization **6**: 250, 252, 253, 254, 255, 258, 262, 263, 267, 270, 272, 282, 283, 304, 343, 347, 364, 368; **24**: 262, 263, 267, 269, 270, 271, 272, 273, 274, 278, 280, 315, 322, 325, 330, 333, 390, 395, 402, 405, 423; **28**: 134; **39**: 279, 289
    dangerous aspects **24**: 405
    delusion **6**: 267, 298, 334, 368, 409; **24**: 329, 336, 405
    homosexuality **24**: 405
    kingship **6**: 253, 254, 263, 272, 327, 331, 334, 338, 364, 402, 414; **24**: 278, 295, 336, 337, 339, 356, 419; **28**: 134, 178; **39**: 256, 263
    loss of identity **6**: 267, 338, 368, 374, 381, 388, 391, 409; **24**: 298, 414, 428
    as martyr-king **6**: 289, 307, 321; **19**: 209; **24**: 289, 291; **28**: 134
    nobility **6**: 255, 258, 259, 262, 263, 391; **24**: 260, 263, 274, 280, 289, 291, 402, 408, 411
    political acumen **6**: 263, 264, 272, 292, 310, 327, 334, 364, 368, 374, 388, 391, 397, 402, 409; **24**: 405; **39**: 256
    private versus public persona **6**: 317, 327, 364, 368, 391, 409; **24**: 428
    role-playing **24**: 419, 423; **28**: 178
    seizure of Gaunt"s estate **6**: 250, 338, 388
    self-dramatization **6**: 264, 267, 307, 310, 315, 317, 331, 334, 368, 393, 409; **24**: 339; **28**: 178

self-hatred **13:** 172; **24:** 383; **39:** 289
self-knowledge **6:** 255, 267, 331, 334, 338, 352, 354, 368, 388, 391; **24:** 273, 289, 411, 414; **39:** 263, 289
spiritual redemption **6:** 255, 267, 331, 334, 338, 352, 354, 368, 388, 391; **24:** 273, 289, 411, 414
Shakespeare"s other histories, compared with **6:** 255, 264, 272, 294, 304, 310, 317, 343, 354, 359; **24:** 320, 325, 330, 331, 332, 333; **28:** 178
Shakespeare"s sympathies, question of **6:** 277, 279, 287, 347, 359, 364, 391, 393, 402
*Sicilian Usurper* (Nahum Tate adaptation) **24:** 260, 261, 262, 263, 386, 390
staging issues **13:** 494; **24:** 273, 274, 278, 279, 280, 283, 291, 295, 296, 301, 303, 304, 310, 315, 317, 320, 325, 333, 338, 346, 351, 352, 356, 364, 383, 386, 395, 402, 405, 411, 414, 419, 423, 428; **25:** 89
structure **6:** 282, 304, 317, 343, 352, 359, 364, 39; **24:** 307, 322, 325, 356, 395
textual arrangement **24:** 260, 261, 262, 263, 271, 273, 291, 296, 356, 390
time **22:** 137
usurpation **6:** 263, 264, 272, 287, 289, 315, 323, 331, 343, 354, 364, 381, 388, 393, 397; **24:** 383
York **6:** 287, 364, 368, 388, 402, 414; **24:** 263, 320, 322, 364, 395, 414; **39:** 243, 279

*Richard III* (Volumes 8, 14, 39)

ambivalence and ambiguity **44:** 11; **47:** 15
conscience **8:** 148, 152, 162, 165, 190, 197, 201, 206, 210, 228, 232, 239, 243, 252, 258; **39:** 341
Elizabethan politics, relation to **22:** 395; **25:** 141; **37:** 144; **39:** 345, 349; **42:** 132
family honor, structure and inheritance **8:** 177, 248, 252, 263, 267; **25:** 141; **39:** 335, 341, 349, 370
flattery **22:** 395
gender issues **25:** 141; **37:** 144; **39:** 345
genre **8:** 181, 182, 197, 206, 218, 228, 239, 243, 252, 258; **13:** 142; **39:** 383
ghost scene (Act V, scene iii) **8:** 152, 154, 159, 162, 163, 165, 170, 177, 193, 197, 210, 228, 239, 243, 252, 258, 267
*Henry VI,* relation to **8:** 159, 165, 177, 182, 193, 201, 210, 213, 218, 228, 243, 248, 252, 267; **25:** 164; **39:** 370
historical accuracy **8:** 144, 145, 153, 159, 163, 165, 168, 213, 223, 228, 232; **39:** 305, 308, 326, 383
historical principles **39:** 308, 326, 387
language and imagery **8:** 159, 161, 165, 167, 168, 170, 177, 182, 184, 186, 193, 197, 201, 206, 218, 223, 243, 248, 252, 258, 262, 267; **16:** 150; **25:** 141, 245; **39:** 360, 370, 383; **47:** 15
Margaret **8:** 153, 154, 159, 162, 163, 170, 193, 201, 206, 210, 218, 223, 228, 243, 248, 262; **39:** 345
Christopher Marlowe"s works, compared with **19:** 233
minor characters **8:** 154, 159, 162, 163, 168, 170, 177, 184, 186, 201, 206, 210, 218, 223, 228, 232, 239, 248, 262, 267
modernization **14:** 523
moral corruption of English society **8:** 154, 163, 165, 177, 193, 201, 218, 228, 232, 243, 248, 252, 267; **39:** 308
plot and incident **8:** 146, 152, 159; **25:** 164
popularity **8:** 144, 146, 154, 158, 159, 162, 181, 228; **39:** 383
rebellion **22:** 395
retribution **8:** 163, 170, 177, 182, 184, 193, 197, 201, 206, 210, 218, 223, 228, 243, 248, 267

Richard III
ambition **8:** 148, 154, 165, 168, 170, 177, 182, 213, 218, 228, 232, 239, 252, 258, 267; **39:** 308, 341, 360, 370, 383
attractive qualities **8:** 145, 148, 152, 154, 159, 161, 162, 165, 168, 170, 181, 182, 184, 185, 197, 201, 206, 213, 228, 243, 252, 258; **16:** 150; **39:** 370, 383
credibility, question of **8:** 145, 147, 154, 159, 165, 193; **13:** 142
death, decay, and nature"s destructiveness **8:** 145, 148, 154, 159, 165, 168, 170, 177, 182, 197, 210, 223, 228, 232, 243, 248, 252, 258, 267
deformity as symbol **8:** 146, 147, 148, 152, 154, 159, 161, 165, 170, 177, 184, 185, 193, 218, 248, 252, 267; **19:** 164
inversion of moral order **8:** 159, 168, 177, 182, 184, 185, 197, 201, 213, 218, 223, 232, 239, 243, 248, 252, 258, 262, 267; **39:** 360
as Machiavellian villain **8:** 165, 182, 190, 201, 218, 232, 239, 243, 248; **39:** 308, 326, 360, 387
as monster or symbol of diabolic **8:** 145, 147, 159, 162, 168, 170, 177, 182, 193, 197, 201, 228, 239, 248, 258; **13:** 142; **37:** 144; **39:** 326, 349
other literary villains, compared with **8:** 148, 161, 162, 165, 181, 182, 206, 213, 239, 267
role-playing, hypocrisy, and dissimulation **8:** 145, 148, 154, 159, 162, 165, 168, 170, 182, 190, 206, 213, 218, 228, 239, 243, 252, 258, 267; **25:** 141, 164, 245; **39:** 335, 341, 387
as scourge or instrument of God **8:** 163, 177, 193, 201, 218, 228, 248, 267; **39:** 308
as Vice figure **8:** 190, 201, 213, 228, 243, 248, 252; **16:** 150; **39:** 383, 387
Richmond **8:** 154, 158, 163, 168, 177, 182, 193, 210, 218, 223, 228, 243, 248, 252; **13:** 142; **25:** 141; **39:** 349
settings **14:** 516, 528
Shakespeare"s artistic growth, *Richard III*"s contribution to **8:** 165, 167, 182, 193, 197, 206, 210, 228, 239, 267; **25:** 164; **39:** 305, 326, 370
Shakespeare"s political sympathies **8:** 147, 163, 177, 193, 197, 201, 223, 228, 232, 243, 248, 267; **39:** 349; **42:** 132
sources
chronicles **8:** 145, 165, 193, 197, 201, 206, 210, 213, 228, 232
Marlowe, Christopher **8:** 167, 168, 182, 201, 206, 218
morality plays **8:** 182, 190, 201, 213, 239
Seneca, other classical writers **8:** 165, 190, 201, 206, 228, 248
staging issues **14:** 515, 527, 528, 537; **16:** 137
structure **8:** 154, 161, 163, 167, 168, 170, 177, 184, 193, 197, 201, 206, 210, 218, 223, 228, 232, 243, 252, 262, 267; **16:** 150
*The Tragical History of King Richard III* (Colley Cibber adaptation), compared with **8:** 159, 161, 243
traditional values **39:** 335
Tudor myth **8:** 163, 165, 177, 184, 193, 201, 218, 228, 232, 243, 248, 252, 267; **39:** 305, 308, 326, 387; **42:** 132
Wars of the Roses **8:** 163, 165, 177, 184, 193, 201, 218, 228, 232, 243, 248, 252, 267; **39:** 308
wooing scenes (Act I, scene ii and Act IV, scene iv) **8:** 145, 147, 152, 153, 154, 159, 161, 164, 170, 190, 197, 206, 213, 218, 223, 232, 239, 243, 252, 258, 267; **16:** 150; **19:** 164; **25:** 141, 164; **39:** 308, 326, 360, 387

*Romeo and Juliet* (Volumes 5, 11, 33)

accident or chance **5:** 418, 444, 448, 467, 470, 487, 573
adolescence **33:** 249, 255, 257
amour-passion or *Liebestod* myth **5:** 484, 489, 528, 530, 542, 550, 575; **32:** 256
androgyny **13:** 530
anxiety **13:** 235
balcony scene **32:** 276
*Caius Marius* (Thomas Otway adaptation) **11:** 377, 378, 488, 495
comic and tragic elements, combination of **46:** 78
contradiction, paradox, and opposition **5:** 421, 427, 431, 496, 509, 513, 516, 520, 525, 528, 538; **33:** 287; **44:** 11
costuming **11:** 505, 509
courtly love tradition, influence of **5:** 505, 542, 575; **33:** 233
detention of Friar John **5:** 448, 467, 470
divine will, role of **5:** 485, 493, 505, 533, 573
dramatic shortcomings or failure **5:** 416, 418, 420, 426, 436, 437, 448, 464, 467, 469, 480, 487, 524, 562
Elizabethan poetics, influence of **5:** 416, 520, 522, 528, 550, 559, 575
evil **5:** 485, 493, 505
as experimental play **5:** 464, 509, 528
fate **5:** 431, 444, 464, 469, 470, 479, 480, 485, 487, 493, 509, 530, 533, 562, 565, 571, 573; **33:** 249
feud **5:** 415, 419, 425, 447, 458, 464, 469, 479, 480, 493, 509, 522, 556, 565, 566, 571, 575; **25:** 181
Friar Lawrence
contribution to catastrophe **5:** 437, 444, 470; **33:** 300
philosophy of moderation **5:** 427, 431, 437, 438, 443, 444, 445, 458, 467, 479, 505, 538
as Shakespeare"s spokesman **5:** 427, 431, 437, 458, 467
ideal love **5:** 421, 427, 431, 436, 437, 450, 463, 469, 498, 505, 575; **25:** 257; **33:** 210, 225, 272
gender issues **32:** 256

lamentation scene (Act IV, scene v) **5**: 425, 492, 538
language and imagery **5**: 420, 426, 431, 436, 437, 456, 477, 479, 489, 492, 496, 509, 520, 522, 528, 538, 542, 550, 559; **25**: 181, 245, 257; **32**: 276; **33**: 210, 272, 274, 287; **42**: 271
love versus fate **5**: 421, 437, 438, 443, 445, 458; **33**: 249
medieval influence **5**: 480, 505, 509, 573
Mercutio
   bawdy **5**: 463, 525, 550, 575
   death, decay, and nature"s destructiveness **5**: 415, 418, 419, 547; **33**: 290
   as worldly counterpoint to Romeo **5**: 425, 464, 542; **33**: 290
comic and tragic elements, combination of **5**: 496, 524, 528, 547, 559
Neoclassical rules **5**: 416, 418, 426
Nurse **5**: 419, 425, 463, 464, 575; **33**: 294
*Othello*, compared with **32**: 302
Petrarchian poetics, influence of **5**: 416, 520, 522, 528, 550, 559, 575; **32**: 276
prose adaptations of Juliet"s character **19**: 261
psychoanalytic interpretation **5**: 513, 556
public versus private worlds **5**: 520, 550; **25**: 181; **33**: 274
reconciliation **5**: 415, 419, 427, 439, 447, 480, 487, 493, 505, 533, 536, 562
rhetoric **42**: 271
rival productions **11**: 381, 382, 384, 385, 386, 487
Romeo and Juliet
   death-wish **5**: 431, 489, 505, 528, 530, 538, 542, 550, 566, 571, 575; **32**: 212
   Romeo"s Dream **45**: 40
   immortality **5**: 536
   Juliet"s epithalamium speech (Act III, scene ii) **5**: 431, 477, 492
   Juliet"s innocence **5**: 421, 423, 450, 454; **33**: 257
   maturation **5**: 437, 454, 467, 493, 498, 509, 520, 565; **33**: 249, 257
   rebellion **25**: 257
   reckless passion **5**: 419, 427, 431, 438, 443, 444, 448, 467, 479, 485, 505, 533, 538, 542; **33**: 241
   Romeo"s dream (Act V, scene i) **5**: 513, 536, 556
   Rosaline, Romeo"s relationship with **5**: 419, 423, 425, 427, 438, 498, 542, 575
sexuality **25**: 181; **33**: 225, 233, 241, 246, 274, 300
source of tragic catastrophe **5**: 418, 427, 431, 448, 458, 469, 479, 480, 485, 487, 493, 509, 522, 528, 530, 533, 542, 565, 571, 573; **33**: 210
sources **5**: 416, 419, 423, 450; **32**: 222; **33**: 210; **45**: 40
staging issues **11**: 499, 505, 507, 514, 517; **13**: 243; **25**: 181; **32**: 212
structure **5**: 438, 448, 464, 469, 470, 477, 480, 496, 518, 524, 525, 528, 547, 559; **33**: 210, 246
tomb scene (Act V, scene iii) **5**: 416, 419, 423; **13**: 243; **25**: 181, 245
triumph over death or fate **5**: 421, 423, 427, 505, 509, 520, 530, 536, 565, 566
Verona society **5**: 556, 566; **13**: 235; **33**: 255
wordplay **32**: 256

**Sonnets (Volumes 10, 40)**

ambiguity **10**: 251, 256; **28**: 385; **40**: 221, 228, 268
authenticity **10**: 153, 154, 230, 243; **48**: 325
autobiographical elements **10**: 159, 160, 166, 167, 175, 176, 182, 196, 205, 213, 215, 226, 233, 238, 240, 251, 279, 283, 302, 309, 325, 337, 377; **13**: 487; **16**: 461; **28**: 363, 385; **42**: 303; **48**: 325
beauty **10**: 247
Christian elements **10**: 191, 256
composition date **10**: 153, 154, 161, 166, 196, 217, 226, 270, 277; **28**: 363, 385
Dark Lady **10**: 161, 167, 176, 216, 217, 218, 226, 240, 302, 342, 377, 394; **25**: 374; **37**: 374; **40**: 273; **48**: 346
deception, disguise, and duplicity **25**: 374; **40**: 221
dramatic elements **10**: 155, 182, 240, 251, 283, 367
editorial and textual issues **28**: 363; **40**: 273; **42**: 303
Elizabeth, audience of **48**: 325
the Friend **10**: 279, 302, 309, 379, 385, 391, 394
friendship **10**: 185, 279; **28**: 380
gender issues **37**: 374; **40**: 238, 247, 254, 264, 268, 273
homoerotic elements **10**: 155, 156, 159, 161, 175, 213, 391; **16**: 461; **28**: 363, 380; **37**: 347; **40**: 254, 264, 273
identities of persons **10**: 154, 155, 156, 161, 166, 167, 169, 173, 174, 175, 185, 190, 191, 196, 218, 226, 230, 233, 240; **40**: 238
Ireland, William Henry, forgeries of **48**: 325
irony or satire **10**: 256, 293, 334, 337, 346
Italian influences **28**: 407
language and imagery **10**: 247, 251, 255, 256, 290, 353, 372, 385; **13**: 445; **28**: 380, 385; **32**: 327, 352; **40**: 228, 247, 284, 292, 303,
love **10**: 173, 247, 287, 290, 293, 302, 309, 322, 325, 329, 394; **28**: 380; **37**: 347
love versus reason **10**: 329
*A Lover"s Complaint* (the Rival Poet) **10**: 243, 353
   gender issues **48**: 336
   pastoral tradition, compared with **48**: 336
   sonnets, compared with **48**: 336
magic **48**: 346
Mr. W. H. **10**: 153, 155, 161, 169, 174, 182, 190, 196, 217, 218, 377
Montaigne"s *Essais*, relation to **42**: 382
mutability, theme of **42**: 382
Neoplatonism **10**: 191, 205
occult **48**: 346
other sonnet writers, Shakespeare compared with **10**: 247, 260, 265, 283, 290, 293, 309, 353, 367; **28**: 380, 385, 407; **37**: 374; **40**: 247, 264, 303; **42**: 303
pedagogy **37**: 374
performative issues **48**: 352
poet-patron relationship **48**: 352
poetic style **10**: 153, 155, 156, 158, 159, 160, 161, 173, 175, 182, 214, 247, 251, 255, 260, 265, 283, 287, 296, 302, 315, 322, 325, 337, 346, 349, 360, 367, 385; **16**: 472; **40**: 221, 228
procreation **10**: 379, 385; **16**: 461

rhetoric of consolation **42**: 382
the Rival Poet **10**: 169, 233, 334, 337, 385; **48**: 352
self-love **10**: 372; **25**: 374
sexuality **25**: 374
as social action **48**: 352
sonnet arrangement **10**: 174, 176, 182, 205, 226, 230, 236, 315, 353; **28**: 363; **40**: 238
sonnet form **10**: 255, 325, 367; **37**: 347; **40**: 284, 303
sonnets (individual):
   3 **10**: 346
   12 **10**: 360
   15 **40**: 292
   18 **40**: 292
   20 **10**: 391; **13**: 530
   21 **32**: 352
   26 **10**: 161
   30 **10**: 296
   35 **10**: 251
   49 **10**: 296
   53 **10**: 349; **32**: 327, 352
   54 **32**: 352
   55 **13**: 445
   57 **10**: 296
   59 **16**: 472
   60 **10**: 296; **16**: 472
   64 **10**: 329, 360
   65 **10**: 296; **40**: 292
   66 **10**: 315
   68 **32**: 327
   71 **10**: 167
   73 **10**: 315, 353, 360
   76 **10**: 334
   79 **32**: 352
   82 **32**: 352
   86 **32**: 352
   87 **10**: 296; **40**: 303
   93 **13**: 487
   94 **10**: 256, 296; **32**: 327
   95 **32**: 327
   98 **32**: 352
   99 **32**: 352
   104 **10**: 360
   105 **32**: 327
   107 **10**: 270, 277
   116 **10**: 329, 379; **13**: 445
   117 **10**: 337
   119 **10**: 337
   121 **10**: 346
   123 **10**: 270
   124 **10**: 265, 270, 329
   126 **10**: 161
   129 **10**: 353, 394; **22**: 12
   130 **10**: 346
   138 **10**: 296
   144 **10**: 394
   145 **10**: 358; **40**: 254
   146 **10**: 353
sonnets (groups):
   1-17 **10**: 296, 315, 379, 385; **16**: 461; **40**: 228
   1-21 **40**: 268
   1-26 **10**: 176
   1-126 **10**: 161, 176, 185, 191, 196, 205, 213, 226, 236, 279, 309, 315, 372
   18-22 **10**: 315
   18-126 **10**: 379

23-40 **10**: 315
27-55 **10**: 176
33-9 **10**: 329
56-77 **10**: 176
76-86 **10**: 315
78-80 **10**: 334, 385
78-101 **10**: 176
82-6 **10**: 334
100-12 **10**: 337
102-26 **10**: 176
123-25 **10**: 385
127-52 **10**: 293, 385
127-54 **10**: 161, 176, 185, 190, 196, 213, 226, 236, 309, 315, 342, 394
151-52 **10**: 315
sources **10**: 153, 154, 156, 158, 233, 251, 255, 293, 353; **16**: 472; **28**: 407; **42**: 382
structure **10**: 175, 176, 182, 205, 230, 260, 296, 302, 309, 315, 337, 349, 353; **40**: 238
subjectivity **37**: 374
time **10**: 265, 302, 309, 322, 329, 337, 360, 379; **13**: 445; **40**: 292
visual arts, relation to **28**: 407

*The Taming of the Shrew* (Volumes 9, 12, 31)

appearance versus reality **9**: 343, 350, 353, 365, 369, 370, 381, 390. 430; **12**: 416; **31**: 326
Baptista **9**: 325, 344, 345, 375, 386, 393, 413
Bianca **9**: 325, 342, 344, 345, 360, 362, 370, 375
Bianca-Lucentio subplot **9**: 365, 370, 375, 390, 393, 401, 407, 413, 430; **16**: 13; **31**: 339
*Catherine and Petruchio* (David Garrick adaptation) **12**: 309, 310, 311, 416
class distinctions, conflict, and relations **31**: 300, 351
deception, disguise, and duplicity **12**: 416
Elizabethan culture, relation to **31**: 288, 295, 300, 315, 326, 345, 351
as farce **9**: 330, 337, 338, 341, 342, 365, 381, 386, 413, 426
folk elements **9**: 381, 393, 404, 426
gender issues **28**: 24 **31**: 261, 268, 276, 282, 288, 295, 300, 335, 351
genre **9**: 329, 334, 362, 375; **22**: 48; **31**: 261, 269, 276
induction **9**: 320, 322, 332, 337, 345, 350, 362, 365, 369, 370, 381, 390, 393, 407, 419, 424, 430; **12**: 416, 427, 430, 431, 441; **19**: 34, 122; **22**: 48; **31**: 269, 315, 351
irony or satire **9**: 340, 375, 398, 407, 413; **13**: 3; **19**: 122
Kate
 characterization **32**: 1
 final speech (Act V, scene ii) **9**: 318, 319, 329, 330, 338, 340, 341, 345, 347, 353, 355, 360, 365, 381, 386, 401, 404, 413, 426, 430; **19**: 3; **22**: 48
 love for Petruchio **9**: 338, 340, 353, 430; **12**: 435
 portrayals of **31**: 282
 shrewishness **9**: 322, 323, 325, 332, 344, 345, 360, 365, 370, 375, 386, 393, 398, 404, 413
 transformation **9**: 323, 341, 355, 370, 386, 393, 401, 404, 407, 419, 424, 426, 430; **16**: 13; **19**: 34; **22**: 48; **31**: 288, 295, 339, 351
*Kiss Me, Kate* (Cole Porter adaptation) **31**: 282
language and imagery **9**: 336, 338, 393, 401, 404, 407, 413; **22**: 378; **28**: 9; **31**: 261, 288, 300, 326, 335, 339; **32**: 56
Lucentio **9**: 325, 342, 362, 375, 393
marriage **9**: 322, 325, 329, 332, 329, 332, 334, 341, 342, 343, 344, 345, 347, 353, 360, 362, 375, 381, 390, 398, 401, 404, 413, 426, 430; **13**: 3; **19**: 3; **28**: 24; **31**: 288
metadramatic elements **9**: 350, 419, 424; **31**: 300, 315
metamorphosis or transformation **9**: 370, 430
pedagogy **19**: 122
performance history **31**: 282
performance issues **12**: 313, 314, 316, 317, 337, 338; **31**: 315
Petruchio
 admirable qualities **9**: 320, 332, 341, 344, 345, 370, 375, 386
 audacity or vigor **9**: 325, 337, 355, 375, 386, 404
 characterization **32**: 1
 coarseness or brutality **9**: 325, 329, 365, 390, 393, 398, 407; **19**: 122
 as lord of misrule **9**: 393
 love for Kate **9**: 338, 340, 343, 344, 386; **12**: 435
 portrayals of **31**: 282
 pragmatism **9**: 329, 334, 375, 398, 424; **13**: 3; **31**: 345, 351
 taming method **9**: 320, 323, 329, 340, 341, 343, 345, 355, 369, 370, 375, 390, 398, 407, 413, 419, 424; **19**: 3, 12, 21 **31**: 269, 295, 326, 335, 339
popularity **9**: 318, 338, 404
role-playing **9**: 322, 353, 355, 360, 369, 370, 398, 401, 407, 413, 419, 424; **13**: 3; **31**: 288, 295, 315
romantic elements **9**: 334, 342, 362, 375, 407
Shakespeare"s other plays, compared with **9**: 334, 342, 360, 393, 426, 430; **31**: 261
Sly **9**: 320, 322, 350, 370, 381, 390, 398, 430; **12**: 316, 335, 416, 427, 441; **16**: 13; **19**: 34, 122; **22**: 48; **37**: 31
sources
 Ariosto **9**: 320, 334, 341, 342, 370
 folk tales **9**: 332, 390, 393
 Gascoigne **9**: 370, 390
 Old and New Comedy **9**: 419
 Ovid **9**: 318, 370, 430
 Plautus **9**: 334, 341, 342
 shrew tradition **9**: 355; **19**: 3; **32**: 1, 56
structure **9**: 318, 322, 325, 332, 334, 341, 362, 370, 390, 426; **22**: 48, 378; **31**: 269
 play-within-a-play **12**: 416; **22**: 48
*The Taming of a Shrew* (anonymous), compared with **9**: 334, 350, 426; **12**: 312; **22**: 48; **31**: 261, 276, 339
textual issues **22**: 48; **31**: 261, 276; **31**: 276
violence **43**: 61

*The Tempest* (Volumes 8, 15, 29, 45)

allegorical elements **8**: 294, 295, 302, 307, 308, 312, 326, 328, 336, 345, 364; **42**: 327
Antonio and Sebastian **8**: 295, 299, 304, 328, 370, 396, 429, 454; **13**: 440; **29**: 278, 297, 343, 362, 368, 377
Ariel **8**: 289, 293, 294, 295, 297, 304, 307, 315, 320, 326, 328, 336, 340, 345, 356, 364, 420, 458; **22**: 302; **29**: 278, 297, 362, 368, 377
art versus nature **8**: 396, 404; **29**: 278, 297, 362
autobiographical elements **8**: 302, 308, 312, 324, 326, 345, 348, 353, 364, 380
Caliban **8**: 286, 287, 289, 292, 294, 295, 297, 302, 304, 307, 309, 315, 326, 328, 336, 353, 364, 370, 380, 390, 396, 401, 414, 420, 423, 429, 435, 454; **13**: 424, 440; **15**: 189, 312, 322, 374, 379; **22**: 302; **25**: 382; **28**: 249; **29**: 278, 292, 297, 343, 368, 377, 396; **32**: 367; **45**: 211, 219, 226, 259; **48**: 299
characterization **8**: 287, 289, 292, 294, 295, 308, 326, 334, 336; **28**: 415; **42**: 339; **45**: 219; **48**: 299
classical influence and sources **29**: 278, 343, 362, 368
colonialism **13**: 424, 440; **15**: 228, 268, 269, 270, 271, 272, 273; **19**: 421; **25**: 357, 382; **28**: 249; **29**: 343, 368; **32**: 338, 367, 400; **42**: 327; **45**: 200, 280
compassion, theme of **42**: 346
conspiracy or treason **16**: 426; **19**: 357; **25**: 382; **29**: 377
dreams **45**: 236, 247, 259
education or nurturing **8**: 353, 370, 384, 396; **29**: 292, 368, 377
exposition scene (Act I, scene ii) **8**: 287, 289, 293, 299, 334
Ferdinand **8**: 328, 336, 359, 454; **19**: 357; **22**: 302; **29**: 362, 339, 377
freedom and servitude **8**: 304, 307, 312, 429; **22**: 302; **29**: 278, 368, 377; **37**: 336
Gonzalo **22**: 302; **29**: 278, 343, 362, 368; **48**: 299
Gonzalo"s commonwealth **8**: 312, 336, 370, 390, 396, 404; **19**: 357; **29**: 368; **45**: 280
good versus evil **8**: 302, 311, 315, 370, 423, 439; **29**: 278; 297
historical content **8**: 364, 408, 420; **16**: 426; **25**: 382; **29**: 278, 339, 343, 368; **45**: 226
the island **8**: 308, 315, 447; **25**: 357, 382; **29**: 278, 343
language and imagery **8**: 324, 348, 384, 390, 404, 454; **19**: 421; **29**: 278; **29**: 297, 343, 368, 377
love **8**: 435, 439; **29**: 297, 339, 377, 396
magic or supernatural elements **8**: 287, 293, 304, 315, 340, 356, 396, 401, 404, 408, 435, 458; **28**: 391, 415; **29**: 297, 343, 377; **45**: 272; **48**: 299
the masque (Act IV, scene i) **8**: 404, 414, 423, 435, 439; **25**: 357; **28**: 391, 415; **29**: 278, 292, 339, 343, 368; **42**: 339; **45**: 188
Miranda **8**: 289, 301, 304, 328, 336, 370, 454; **19**: 357; **22**: 302; **28**: 249; **29**: 278, 297, 362, 368, 377, 396
Montaigne"s *Essais*, relation to **42**: 346
music **8**: 390, 404; **29**: 292; **37**: 321; **42**: 339
nature **8**: 315, 370, 390, 408, 414; **29**: 343, 362, 368, 377
Neoclassical rules **8**: 287, 292, 293, 334; **25**: 357; **29**: 292; **45**: 200
politics **8**: 304, 307, 315, 353, 359, 364, 401, 408; **16**: 426; **19**: 421; **29**: 339; **37**: 336; **42**: 327; **45**: 272, 280

Prospero
- characterization **8:** 312, 348, 370, 458; **16:** 442; **22:** 302; **45:** 188, 272
- as God or Providence **8:** 311, 328, 364, 380, 429, 435
- magic, nature of **8:** 301, 340, 356, 396, 414, 423, 458; **25:** 382; **28:** 391; **29:** 278, 292, 368, 377, 396; **32:** 338, 343
- psychoanalytic interpretation **45:** 259
- redemptive powers **8:** 302, 320, 353, 370, 390, 429, 439, 447; **29:** 297
- as ruler **8:** 304, 308, 309, 420, 423; **13:** 424; **22:** 302; **29:** 278, 362, 377, 396
- self-control **8:** 312, 414, 420; **22:** 302; **44:** 11
- self-knowledge **16:** 442; **22:** 302; **29:** 278, 292, 362, 377, 396
- as Shakespeare or creative artist **8:** 299, 302, 308, 312, 320, 324, 353, 364, 435, 447
- as tragic hero **8:** 359, 370, 464; **29:** 292

realism **8:** 340, 359, 464

reality and illusion **8:** 287, 315, 359, 401, 435, 439, 447, 454; **22:** 302; **45:** 236, 247

reconciliation **8:** 302, 312, 320, 334, 348, 359, 370, 384, 401, 404, 414, 429, 439, 447, 454; **16:** 442; **22:** 302; **29:** 297; **37:** 336; **45:** 236

religious, mythic, or spiritual content **8:** 328, 390, 423, 429, 435; **45:** 211, 247

romance or pastoral tradition, influence of **8:** 336, 348, 396, 404; **37:** 336

Shakespeare"s other plays, compared with **8:** 294, 302, 324, 326, 348, 353, 380, 401, 464; **13:** 424

spectacle versus simple staging **15:** 206, 207, 208, 210, 217, 219, 222, 223, 224, 225, 227, 228, 305, 352; **28:** 415

sources **45:** 226

staging issues **15:** 343, 346, 352, 361, 364, 366, 368, 371, 385; **28:** 391, 415; **29:** 339; **32:** 338, 343; **42:** 339; **45:** 200

Stephano and Trinculo, comic subplot of **8:** 292, 297, 299, 304, 309, 324, 328, 353, 370; **25:** 382; **29:** 377; **46:** 14, 33

structure **8:** 294, 295, 299, 320, 384, 439; **28:** 391, 415; **29:** 292, 297; **45:** 188

subversiveness **22:** 302

symbolism **48:** 299

*The Tempest; or, The Enchanted Island* (William Davenant/John Dryden adaptation) **15:** 189, 190, 192, 193

*The Tempest; or, The Enchanted Island* (Thomas Shadwell adaptation) **15:** 195, 196, 199

time **8:** 401, 439, 464; **25:** 357; **29:** 278, 292; **45:** 236

tragic elements **8:** 324, 348, 359, 370, 380, 408, 414, 439, 458, 464

trickster, motif of **22:** 302; **29:** 297

usurpation or rebellion **8:** 304, 370, 408, 420; **25:** 357, 382; **29:** 278, 362, 377; **37:** 336

utopia **45:** 280

## *Timon of Athens* (Volumes 1, 20, 27)

Alcibiades **25:** 198; **27:** 191
alienation **1:** 523; **27:** 161
Apemantus **1:** 453, 467, 483; **20:** 476, 493; **25:** 198; **27:** 166, 223, 235

appearance versus reality **1:** 495, 500, 515, 523
Athens **27:** 223, 230
authorship controversy **1:** 464, 466, 467, 469, 474, 477, 478, 480, 490, 499, 507, 518; **16:** 351; **20:** 433
autobiographical elements **1:** 462, 467, 470, 473, 474, 478, 480; **27:** 166, 175
Elizabethan culture, relation to **1:** 487, 489, 495, 500; **20:** 433; **27:** 203, 212, 230
as inferior or flawed plays **1:** 476, 481, 489, 499, 520; **20:** 433, 439, 491; **25:** 198; **27:** 157, 175
genre **1:** 454, 456, 459, 460, 462, 483, 492, 499, 503, 509, 511, 512, 515, 518, 525, 531; **27:** 203
*King Lear*, relation to **1:** 453, 459, 511; **16:** 351; **27:** 161; **37:** 222
language and imagery **1:** 488; **13:** 392; **25:** 198; **27:** 166, 184, 235
as medieval allegory or morality play **1:** 492, 511, 518; **27:** 155
mixture of genres **16:** 351; **25:** 198
nihilistic elements **1:** 481, 513, 529; **13:** 392; **20:** 481
pessimistic elements **1:** 462, 467, 470, 473, 478, 480; **20:** 433, 481; **27:** 155, 191
Poet and Painter **25:** 198
politics **27:** 223, 230
religious, mythic, or spiritual content **1:** 505, 512, 513, 523; **20:** 493
satirical elements **27:** 155, 235
self-knowledge **1:** 456, 459, 462, 495, 503, 507, 515, 518, 526; **20:** 493; **27:** 166
Senecan elements **27:** 235
Shakespeare"s other tragedies, compared with **27:** 166
sources **16:** 351; **27:** 191
staging issues **20:** 445, 446, 481, 491, 492, 493
structure **27:** 157, 175, 235
Timon
- comic traits **25:** 198
- as flawed hero **1:** 456, 459, 462, 472, 495, 503, 507, 515; **16:** 351; **20:** 429, 433, 476; **25:** 198; **27:** 157, 161
- misanthropy **13:** 392; **20:** 431, 464, 476, 481, 491, 492, 493; **27:** 161, 175, 184, 196; **37:** 222
- as noble figure **1:** 467, 473, 483, 499; **20:** 493; **27:** 212

wealth and social class **1:** 466, 487, 495; **25:** 198; **27:** 184, 196, 212

## *Titus Andronicus* (Volumes 4, 17, 27, 43)

Aaron **4:** 632, 637, 650, 651, 653, 668, 672, 675; **27:** 255; **28:** 249, 330; **43:** 176
amputations, significance of **48:** 264
authorship controversy **4:** 613, 614, 615, 616, 617, 619, 623, 624, 625, 626, 628, 631, 632, 635, 642
autobiographical elements **4:** 619, 624, 625, 664
banquet scene **25:** 245; **27:** 255; **32:** 212
ceremonies, rites, and rituals, importance of **27:** 261; **32:** 265; **48:** 264
characterization **4:** 613, 628, 632, 635, 640, 644, 647, 650, 675; **27:** 293; **43:** 170, 176

Christian elements **4:** 656, 680
civilization versus barbarism **4:** 653; **27:** 293; **28:** 249; **32:** 265
*Clarissa* (Samuel Richardson), compared with **48:** 277
Elizabethan culture, relation to **27:** 282
Euripides, influence of **27:** 285
language and imagery **4:** 617, 624, 635, 642, 644, 646, 659, 664, 668, 672, 675; **13:** 225; **16:** 225; **25:** 245; **27:** 246, 293, 313, 318, 325; **43:** 186, 222, 227, 239, 247, 262
language versus action **4:** 642, 644, 647, 664, 668; **13:** 225; **27:** 293, 313, 325; **43:** 186
Lavinia **27:** 266; **28:** 249; **32:** 212; **43:** 170, 239, 247, 255, 262
marriage as political tyranny **48:** 264
medieval literary influence **4:** 646, 650; **27:** 299
order versus disintegration **4:** 618, 647; **43:** 186, 195
Ovid, influence of **4:** 647, 659, 664, 668; **13:** 225; **27:** 246, 275, 285, 293, 299, 306; **28:** 249; **43:** 195, 203, 206
political content **43:** 262
politics **27:** 282; **48:** 264
rape **43:** 227, 255; **48:** 277
rightful succession **4:** 638
Roman elements **43:** 206, 222
Romans versus Goths **27:** 282
Senecan or revenge tragedy elements **4:** 618, 627, 628, 636, 639, 644, 646, 664, 672, 680; **16:** 225; **27:** 275, 318; **43:** 170, 206, 227
Shakespeare"s canon, place in **4:** 614, 616, 618, 619, 637, 639, 646, 659, 664, 668; **43:** 195
Shakespeare"s other tragedies, compared with **16:** 225; **27:** 275, 325
staging issues **17:** 449, 452, 456, 487; **25:** 245; **32:** 212, 249
structure **4:** 618, 619, 624, 631, 635, 640, 644, 646, 647, 653, 656, 659, 662, 664, 668, 672; **27:** 246, 285
Tamora **4:** 632, 662, 672, 675; **27:** 266; **43:** 170
Titus **4:** 632, 637, 640, 644, 647, 653, 656, 662; **25:** 245; **27:** 255
Vergil, influence of **27:** 306; **28:** 249
violence **13:** 225; **25:** 245; **27:** 255; **28:** 249; **32:** 249, 265; **43:** 1, 186, 203, 227, 239, 247, 255, 262,

## *Troilus and Cressida* (Volumes 3, 18, 27, 43)

ambiguity **3:** 544, 568, 583, 587, 589, 599, 611, 621; **27:** 400; **43:** 365
ambivalence **43:** 340
assignation scene (Act V, scene ii) **18:** 442, 451
autobiographical elements **3:** 548, 554, 557, 558, 574, 606, 630
body, role of **42:** 66
characterization **3:** 538, 539, 540, 541, 548, 566, 571, 604, 611, 621; **27:** 381, 391
Chaucer"s Criseyde, compared with **43:** 305
chivalry, decline of **16:** 84; **27:** 370, 374
communication, failure of **43:** 277
conclusion **3:** 538, 549, 558, 566, 574, 583, 594

comedy vs. tragedy **43**: 351
contradictions **43**: 377
costumes **18**: 289, 371, 406, 419
courtly love **22**: 58
Cressida
  as ambiguous figure **43**: 305
  inconsistency **3**: 538; **13**: 53; **16**: 70; **22**: 339; **27**: 362
  individual will versus social values **3**: 549, 561, 571, 590, 604, 617, 626; **13**: 53; **27**: 396
  infidelity **3**: 536, 537, 544, 554, 555; **18**: 277, 284, 286; **22**: 58, 339; **27**: 400; **43**: 298
  lack of punishment **3**: 536, 537
  as mother figure **22**: 339
  objectification of **43**: 329
  as sympathetic figure **3**: 557, 560, 604, 609; **18**: 284, 423; **22**: 58; **27**: 396, 400; **43**: 305
cynicism **43**: 298
desire **43**: 317, 329, 340
disillusioned or cynical tone **3**: 544, 548, 554, 557, 558, 571, 574, 630, 642; **18**: 284, 332, 403, 406, 423; **27**: 376
disorder **3**: 578, 589, 599, 604, 609; **18**: 332, 406, 412, 423; **27**: 366
double plot **3**: 569, 613
Elizabeth I
  waning power **43**: 365
Elizabethan culture, relation to **3**: 560, 574, 606; **25**: 56
food imagery **43**: 298
genre **3**: 541, 542, 549, 558, 566, 571, 574, 587, 594, 604, 630, 642; **27**: 366
Greece **43**: 287
inaction **3**: 587, 621; **27**: 347
language and imagery **3**: 561, 569, 596, 599, 606, 624, 630, 635; **22**: 58, 339; **27**: 332; 366; **42**: 66
love and honor **3**: 555, 604; **27**: 370, 374
love versus war **18**: 332, 371, 406, 423; **22**: 339; **27**: 376; **43**: 377
male/female relationships **16**: 70; **22**: 339; **27**: 362
marriage **22**: 339
master-slave relationship **22**: 58
medieval chivalry **3**: 539, 543, 544, 555, 606; **27**: 376
moral corruption **3**: 578, 589, 599, 604, 609; **18**: 332, 406, 412, 423; **27**: 366; **43**: 298
Neoclassical rules **3**: 537, 538; **18**: 276, 278, 281
nihilistic elements **27**: 354
patriarchy **22**: 58
politics **3**: 536, 560, 606; **16**: 84
as "problem play" **3**: 555, 566
  lack of resolution **43**: 277
psychoanalytical criticism **43**: 287
rape **43**: 357
satirical elements **3**: 539, 543, 544, 555, 558, 574; **27**: 341
sexuality **22**: 58, 339; **25**: 56; **27**: 362; **43**: 365
sources **3**: 537, 539, 540, 541, 544, 549, 558, 566, 574, 587; **27**: 376, 381, 391, 400
staging issues **16**: 70; **18**: 289, 332, 371, 395, 403, 406, 412, 419, 423, 442, 447, 451
structure **3**: 536, 538, 549, 568, 569, 578, 583, 589, 611, 613; **27**: 341, 347, 354, 391
Thersites **13**: 53; **25**: 56; **27**: 381
time **3**: 561, 571, 583, 584, 613, 621, 626, 634
Troilus
  contradictory behavior **3**: 596, 602, 635; **27**: 362
  Cressida, relationship with **3**: 594, 596, 606; **22**: 58
  integrity **3**: 617
  opposition to Ulysses **3**: 561, 584, 590
  as unsympathetic figure **18**: 423; **22**: 58, 339; **43**: 317
  as warrior **3**: 596; **22**: 339
*Troilus and Cressida, or Truth Found too late* (John Dryden adaptation) **18**: 276, 277, 278, 280, 281, 283
Trojan versus Greek values **3**: 541, 561, 574, 584, 590, 596, 621, 638; **27**: 370
Trojan War
  as myth **43**: 293
Troy **43**: 287
Ulysses"s speech on degree (Act I, scene iii) **3**: 549, 599, 609, 642; **27**: 396
value systems **3**: 578, 583, 589, 602, 613, 617; **13**: 53; **27**: 370, 396, 400
violence **43**: 329, 351, 357, 365, 377
  through satire **43**: 293

*Twelfth Night* (Volumes 1, 26, 34, 46)

ambiguity **1**: 554, 639; **34**: 287, 316
Antonio **22**: 69
appetite **1**: 563, 596, 609, 615
autobiographical elements **1**: 557, 561, 599; **34**: 338
bear-baiting **19**: 42
characterization **1**: 539, 540, 543, 545, 550, 554, 581, 594; **26**: 257, 337, 342, 346, 364, 366, 371, 374; **34**: 281, 293, 311, 338; **46**: 286, 324
Christian elements **46**: 338
comic elements **26**: 233, 257, 337, 342, 371
composition date **37**: 78
credibility **1**: 540, 542, 543, 554, 562, 581, 587
dark or tragic elements **46**: 310
Elizabethan culture, relation to **1**: 549, 553, 555, 563, 581, 587, 620; **16**: 53; **19**: 42, 78; **26**: 357; **28**: 1; **34**: 323, 330; **46**: 291
fancy **1**: 543, 546
Feste
  characterization **1**: 558, 655, 658; **26**: 233, 364; **46**: 1, 14, 18, 33, 52, 60, 303, 310
  role in play **1**: 546, 551, 553, 566, 570, 571, 579, 635, 658; **46**: 297, 303, 310
  song **1**: 543, 548, 561, 563, 566, 570, 572, 603, 620, 642; **46**: 297
festive or folklore elements **46**: 338
gender issues **19**: 78; **34**: 344; **37**: 59; **42**: 32; **46**: 347, 362, 369
homosexuality **22**: 69; **42**: 32; **46**: 362
language and imagery **1**: 570, 650, 664; **22**: 12; **28**: 9; **34**: 293; **37**: 59
love **1**: 543, 546, 573, 580, 587, 595, 600, 603, 610, 660; **19**: 78; **26**: 257, 364; **34**: 270, 293, 323; **46**: 291, 333, 347, 362
madness **1**: 554, 639, 656; **26**: 371
Malvolio
  characterization **1**: 540, 544, 545, 548, 550, 554, 558, 567, 575, 577, 615; **26**: 207, 233, 273; **46**: 286
  forged letter **16**: 372; **28**: 1
  punishment **1**: 539, 544, 548, 549, 554, 555, 558, 563, 577, 590, 632, 645; **46**: 291, 297, 338
  as Puritan **1**: 549, 551, 555, 558, 561, 563; **25**: 47
  role in play **1**: 545, 548, 549, 553, 555, 563, 567, 575, 577, 588, 610, 615, 632, 645; **26**: 337, 374; **46**: 347
music **1**: 543, 566, 596
Olivia **1**: 540, 543, 545; **46**: 286, 333, 369; **47**: 45
order **1**: 563, 596; **34**: 330; **46**: 291, 347
Orsino **46**: 286, 333; **47**: 45
philosophical elements **1**: 560, 563, 596; **34**: 301, 316; **46**: 297
Puritanism **1**: 549, 553, 555, 632; **16**: 53; **25**: 47; **46**: 338
psychoanalytic criticism **46**: 333
Saturnalian elements **1**: 554, 571, 603, 620, 642; **16**: 53
self-deception **1**: 554, 561, 591, 625; **47**: 45
self-indulgence **1**: 563, 615, 635
sexual ambiguity and sexual deception **1**: 540, 562, 620, 621, 639, 645; **22**: 69; **34**: 311, 344; **37**: 59; **42**: 32
Shakespeare"s canon, place in **1**: 543, 548, 557, 569, 575, 580, 621, 635, 638
Shakespeare"s other plays, relation to **34**: 270; **46**: 303
sources **1**: 539, 540, 603; **34**: 301, 323, 344; **46**: 291
staging issues **26**: 219, 233, 257, 337, 342, 346, 357, 359, 360, 364, 366, 371, 374; **46**: 310, 369
structure **1**: 539, 542, 543, 546, 551, 553, 563, 570, 571, 590, 600, 660; **26**: 374; **34**: 281, 287; **46**: 286
time **37**: 78; **46**: 297
tragic elements **1**: 557, 569, 572, 575, 580, 599, 621, 635, 638, 639, 645, 654, 656; **26**: 342
Viola **26**: 308; **46**: 286, 324, 347, 369

*The Two Gentlemen of Verona* (Volumes 6, 12, 40)

absurdities, inconsistencies, and shortcomings **6**: 435, 436, 437, 439, 464, 507, 541, 560
appearance versus reality **6**: 494, 502, 511, 519, 529, 532, 549, 560
audience versus character perceptions **6**: 499, 519, 524
authorship controversy **6**: 435, 436, 437, 438, 439, 449, 466, 476
characterization **6**: 438, 442, 445, 447, 449, 458, 462, 560; **12**: 458; **40**: 312, 327, 330, 365
Christian elements **6**: 438, 494, 514, 532, 555, 564
education **6**: 490, 494, 504, 526, 532, 555, 568
Elizabethan setting **12**: 463, 485

forest. **6:** 450, 456, 492, 514, 547, 555, 564, 568
genre **6:** 460, 468, 472, 516; **40:** 320
identity **6:** 494, 511, 529, 532, 547, 560, 564, 568; **19:** 34
ironic or parodic elements **6:** 447, 472, 478, 484, 502, 504, 509, 516, 529, 549; **13:** 12
Julia or Silvia **6:** 450, 453, 458, 476, 494, 499, 516, 519, 549, 564; **40:** 312, 327, 374
language and imagery **6:** 437, 438, 439, 445, 449, 490, 504, 519, 529, 541; **28:** 9; **40:** 343
Launce and Speed, comic function of **6:** 438, 439, 442, 456, 458, 460, 462, 472, 476, 478, 484, 502, 504, 507, 509, 516, 519, 549; **40:** 312, 320
love **6:** 442, 445, 456, 479, 488, 492, 494, 502, 509, 516, 519, 549; **13:** 12; **40:** 327, 335, 343, 354, 365
love versus friendship **6:** 439, 449, 450, 458, 460, 465, 468, 471, 476, 480; **40:** 354, 359, 365
marriage **48:** 32
mimetic rivalry **13:** 12; **40:** 335
morality **6:** 438, 492, 494, 514, 532, 555, 564
Proteus **6:** 439, 450, 458, 480, 490, 511; **40:** 312, 327, 330, 335, 359; **42:** 18
repentance and forgiveness **6:** 450, 514, 516, 555, 564
resolution **6:** 435, 436, 439, 445, 449, 453, 458, 460, 462, 465, 466, 468, 471, 476, 480, 486, 494, 509, 514, 516, 519, 529, 532, 541, 549; **19:** 34
romantic and courtly conventions **6:** 438, 460, 472, 478, 484, 486, 488, 502, 507, 509, 529, 541, 549, 560, 568; **12:** 460, 462; **40:** 354, 374
setting **12:** 463, 465, 485
sources **6:** 436, 460, 462, 468, 476, 480, 490, 511, 547; **19:** 34; **40:** 320
staging issues **12:** 457, 464; **42:** 18
structure **6:** 445, 450, 460, 462, 504, 526
youth **6:** 439, 450, 464, 514, 568

### *The Two Noble Kinsmen* (Volumes 9, 41)

amorality, question of **9:** 447, 460, 492
authorship controversy
  Shakespeare not a co-author **9:** 445, 447, 455, 461
  Shakespearean portions of the text **9:** 446, 447, 448, 455, 456, 457, 460, 462, 463, 471, 479, 486; **41:** 308, 317, 355
  Shakespeare"s part in the overall conception or design **9:** 444, 446, 448, 456, 457, 460, 480, 481, 486, 490; **37:** 313; **41:** 326
ceremonies, rites, and rituals, importance of **9:** 492, 498
characterization **9:** 457, 461, 471, 474; **41:** 340, 385
Emilia **9:** 460, 470, 471, 479, 481; **19:** 394; **41:** 372, 385; **42:** 368
free will versus fate **9:** 474, 481, 486, 492, 498
friendship **9:** 448, 463, 470, 474, 479, 481, 486, 490; **19:** 394; **41:** 355, 363, 372; **42:** 368
gender issues **42:** 368
innocence to experience **9:** 481, 502; **19:** 394
irony or satire **9:** 463, 481, 486; **41:** 301

the jailer"s daughter **9:** 457, 460, 479, 481, 486, 502; **41:** 340
language and imagery **9:** 445, 446, 447, 448, 456, 461, 462, 463, 469, 471, 498, 502; **41:** 289, 301, 308, 317, 326
love **9:** 479, 481, 490, 498; **41:** 289, 355, 301, 363, 372, 385
masque elements **9:** 490
Palamon and Arcite **9:** 474, 481, 490, 492, 502
sources **19:** 394; **41:** 289, 301, 363, 385
structure **37:** 313

### *Venus and Adonis* (Volumes 10, 33)

Adonis **10:** 411, 420, 424, 427, 429, 434, 439, 442, 451, 454, 459, 466, 473, 489; **25:** 305, 328; **28:** 355; **33:** 309, 321, 330, 347, 352, 357, 363, 370, 377
allegorical elements **10:** 427, 434, 439, 449, 454, 462, 480; **28:** 355; **33:** 309, 330
ambiguity **10:** 434, 454, 459, 462, 466, 473, 480, 486, 489; **33:** 352
beauty **10:** 420, 423, 427, 434, 454, 480; **33:** 330, 352
the boar **10:** 416, 451, 454, 466, 473; **33:** 339, 347, 370
the courser and the jennet **10:** 418, 439, 466; **33:** 309, 339, 347, 352
death, decay, and nature"s destructiveness **10:** 419, 427, 434, 451, 454, 462, 466, 473, 480, 489; **25:** 305; **33:** 309, 321, 347, 352, 363, 370
dramatic elements **10:** 459, 462, 486
eroticism or sensuality **10:** 410, 411, 418, 419, 427, 428, 429, 442, 448, 454, 459, 466, 473; **25:** 305, 328; **28:** 355; **33:** 321, 339, 347, 352, 363, 370
*Faerie Queene* (Edmund Spenser), compared with **33:** 339
*Hero and Leander* (Christopher Marlowe), compared with **10:** 419, 424, 429; **33:** 309, 357
comic elements **10:** 429, 434, 439, 442, 459, 462, 489; **33:** 352
hunt motif **10:** 434, 451, 466, 473; **33:** 357, 370
imagery **10:** 414, 415, 416, 420, 429, 434, 449, 459, 466, 473, 480; **25:** 328; **28:** 355; **33:** 321, 339, 352, 363, 370, 377; **42:** 348
love versus lust **10:** 418, 420, 427, 434, 439, 448, 449, 454, 462, 466, 473, 480, 489; **25:** 305; **28:** 355; **33:** 309, 330, 339, 347, 357, 363, 370
morality **10:** 411, 412, 414, 416, 418, 419, 420, 423, 427, 428, 439, 442, 448, 449, 454, 459, 466; **33:** 330
negative appraisals **10:** 410, 411, 415, 418, 419, 424, 429
Ovid, compared with **32:** 352; **42:** 348
pictorial elements **10:** 414, 415, 419, 420, 423, 480; **33:** 339
popularity **10:** 410, 412, 418, 427; **25:** 328
procreation **10:** 439, 449, 466; **33:** 321, 377
reason **10:** 427, 439, 449, 459, 462, 466; **28:** 355; **33:** 309, 330
rhetoric **33:** 377
Shakespeare"s plays, compared with **10:** 412, 414, 415, 434, 459, 462

Shakespeare"s sonnets, compared with **33:** 377
sources **10:** 410, 412, 420, 424, 429, 434, 439, 451, 454, 466, 473, 480, 486, 489; **16:** 452; **25:** 305; **28:** 355; **33:** 309, 321, 330, 339, 347, 352, 357, 370, 377; **42:** 348
structure **10:** 434, 442, 480, 486, 489; **33:** 357, 377
style **10:** 411, 412, 414, 415, 416, 418, 419, 420, 423, 424, 428, 429, 439, 442, 480, 486, 489; **16:** 452
Venus **10:** 427, 429, 434, 439, 442, 448, 449, 451, 454, 466, 473, 480, 486, 489; **16:** 452; **25:** 305, 328; **28:** 355; **33:** 309, 321, 330, 347, 352, 357, 363, 370, 377
Wat the hare **10:** 424, 451

### *The Winter's Tale* (Volumes 7, 15, 36, 45)

Antigonus
  characterization **7:** 394, 451, 464
  death scene (Act III, scene iii) **7:** 377, 414, 464, 483; **15:** 518, 532; **19:** 366
appearance versus reality **7:** 429, 446, 479
art versus nature **7:** 377, 381, 397, 419, 452; **36:** 289, 318; **45:** 329
audience perception, Shakespeare"s manipulation of **7:** 394, 429, 456, 483, 501; **13:** 417; **19:** 401, 431, 441; **25:** 339; **45:** 374
autobiographical elements **7:** 395, 397, 410, 419
Autolycus **7:** 375, 380, 382, 387, 389, 395, 396, 414; **15:** 524; **22:** 302; **37:** 31; **45:** 333; **46:** 14, 33
Christian elements **7:** 381, 387, 402, 410, 417, 419, 425, 429, 436, 452, 460, 501; **36:** 318
counsel **19:** 401
court society **16:** 410
dramatic structure **7:** 382, 390, 396, 399, 402, 407, 414, 429, 432, 473, 479, 493, 497, 501; **15:** 528; **25:** 339; **36:** 289, 295, 362, 380; **45:** 297, 344, 358, 366
ethnicity **37:** 306
folk drama, relation to **7:** 420, 451
forgiveness or redemption **7:** 381, 389, 395, 402, 407, 436, 456, 460, 483; **36:** 318
fusion of comic, tragic, and romantic elements **7:** 390, 394, 396, 399, 410, 412, 414, 429, 436, 479, 483, 490, 501; **13:** 417; **15:** 514, 524, 532; **25:** 339; **36:** 295, 380; **45:** 295, 329
grace **7:** 420, 425, 460, 493; **36:** 328
Hermione
  characterization **7:** 385, 395, 402, 412, 414, 506; **15:** 495, 532; **22:** 302, 324; **25:** 347; **32:** 388; **36:** 311; **47:** 25
  restoration (Act V, scene iii) **7:** 377, 379, 384, 385, 387, 389, 394, 396, 412, 425, 436, 451, 452, 456, 464, 483, 501; **15:** 411, 412, 413, 518, 528, 532
  supposed death **25:** 339; **47:** 25
as historical allegory **7:** 381; **15:** 528
homosexuality **48:** 309
hospitality **19:** 366
irony **7:** 419, 420
Jacobean culture, relation to **19:** 366, 401, 431; **25:** 347; **32:** 388; **37:** 306
language and imagery **7:** 382, 384, 417, 418, 420, 425, 460, 506; **13:** 409; **19:** 431; **22:** 324;

comedy vs. tragedy **43:** 351
contradictions **43:** 377
costumes **18:** 289, 371, 406, 419
courtly love **22:** 58
Cressida
    as ambiguous figure **43:** 305
    inconsistency **3:** 538; **13:** 53; **16:** 70; **22:** 339; **27:** 362
    individual will versus social values **3:** 549, 561, 571, 590, 604, 617, 626; **13:** 53; **27:** 396
    infidelity **3:** 536, 537, 544, 554, 555; **18:** 277, 284, 286; **22:** 58, 339; **27:** 400; **43:** 298
    lack of punishment **3:** 536, 537
    as mother figure **22:** 339
    objectification of **43:** 329
    as sympathetic figure **3:** 557, 560, 604, 609; **18:** 284, 423; **22:** 58; **27:** 396, 400; **43:** 305
cynicism **43:** 298
desire **43:** 317, 329, 340
disillusioned or cynical tone **3:** 544, 548, 554, 557, 558, 571, 574, 630, 642; **18:** 284, 332, 403, 406, 423; **27:** 376
disorder **3:** 578, 589, 599, 604, 609; **18:** 332, 406, 412, 423; **27:** 366
double plot **3:** 569, 613
Elizabeth I
    waning power **43:** 365
Elizabethan culture, relation to **3:** 560, 574, 606; **25:** 56
food imagery **43:** 298
genre **3:** 541, 542, 549, 558, 566, 571, 574, 587, 594, 604, 630, 642; **27:** 366
Greece **43:** 287
inaction **3:** 587, 621; **27:** 347
language and imagery **3:** 561, 569, 596, 599, 606, 624, 630, 635; **22:** 58, 339; **27:** 332; 366; **42:** 66
love and honor **3:** 555, 604; **27:** 370, 374
love versus war **18:** 332, 371, 406, 423; **22:** 339; **27:** 376; **43:** 377
male/female relationships **16:** 70; **22:** 339; **27:** 362
marriage **22:** 339
master-slave relationship **22:** 58
medieval chivalry **3:** 539, 543, 544, 555, 606; **27:** 376
moral corruption **3:** 578, 589, 599, 604, 609; **18:** 332, 406, 412, 423; **27:** 366; **43:** 298
Neoclassical rules **3:** 537, 538; **18:** 276, 278, 281
nihilistic elements **27:** 354
patriarchy **22:** 58
politics **3:** 536, 560, 606; **16:** 84
as "problem play" **3:** 555, 566
    lack of resolution **43:** 277
psychoanalytic criticism **43:** 287
rape **43:** 357
satirical elements **3:** 539, 543, 544, 555, 558, 574; **27:** 341
sexuality **22:** 58, 339; **25:** 56; **27:** 362; **43:** 365
sources **3:** 537, 539, 540, 541, 544, 549, 558, 566, 574, 587; **27:** 376, 381, 391, 400
staging issues **16:** 70; **18:** 289, 332, 371, 395, 403, 406, 412, 419, 423, 442, 447, 451
structure **3:** 536, 538, 549, 568, 569, 578, 583, 589, 611, 613; **27:** 341, 347, 354, 391
Thersites **13:** 53; **25:** 56; **27:** 381
time **3:** 561, 571, 583, 584, 613, 621, 626, 634
Troilus
    contradictory behavior **3:** 596, 602, 635; **27:** 362
    Cressida, relationship with **3:** 594, 596, 606; **22:** 58
    integrity **3:** 617
    opposition to Ulysses **3:** 561, 584, 590
    as unsympathetic figure **18:** 423; **22:** 58, 339; **43:** 317
    as warrior **3:** 596; **22:** 339
*Troilus and Cressida, or Truth Found too late* (John Dryden adaptation) **18:** 276, 277, 278, 280, 281, 283
Trojan versus Greek values **3:** 541, 561, 574, 584, 590, 596, 621, 638; **27:** 370
Trojan War
    as myth **43:** 293
Troy **43:** 287
Ulysses"s speech on degree (Act I, scene iii) **3:** 549, 599, 609, 642; **27:** 396
value systems **3:** 578, 583, 589, 602, 613, 617; **13:** 53; **27:** 370, 396, 400
violence **43:** 329, 351, 357, 365, 377
    through satire **43:** 293

*Twelfth Night* (Volumes 1, 26, 34, 46)

ambiguity **1:** 554, 639; **34:** 287, 316
Antonio **22:** 69
appetite **1:** 563, 596, 609, 615
autobiographical elements **1:** 557, 561, 599; **34:** 338
bear-baiting **19:** 42
characterization **1:** 539, 540, 543, 545, 550, 554, 581, 594; **26:** 257, 337, 342, 346, 364, 366, 371, 374; **34:** 281, 293, 311, 338; **46:** 286, 324
Christian elements **46:** 338
comic elements **26:** 233, 257, 337, 342, 371
composition date **37:** 78
credibility **1:** 540, 542, 543, 554, 562, 581, 587
dark or tragic elements **46:** 310
Elizabethan culture, relation to **1:** 549, 553, 555, 563, 581, 587, 620; **16:** 53; **19:** 42, 78; **26:** 357; **28:** 1; **34:** 323, 330; **46:** 291
fancy **1:** 543, 546
Feste
    characterization **1:** 558, 655, 658; **26:** 233, 364; **46:** 1, 14, 18, 33, 52, 60, 303, 310
    role in play **1:** 546, 551, 553, 566, 570, 571, 579, 635, 658; **46:** 297, 303, 310
    song **1:** 543, 548, 561, 563, 566, 570, 572, 603, 620, 642; **46:** 297
festive or folklore elements **46:** 338
gender issues **19:** 78; **34:** 344; **37:** 59; **42:** 32; **46:** 347, 362, 369
homosexuality **22:** 69; **42:** 32; **46:** 362
language and imagery **1:** 570, 650, 664; **22:** 12; **28:** 9; **34:** 293; **37:** 59
love **1:** 543, 546, 573, 580, 587, 595, 600, 603, 610, 660; **19:** 78; **26:** 257, 364; **34:** 270, 293, 323; **46:** 291, 333, 347, 362
madness **1:** 554, 639, 656; **26:** 371
Malvolio
    characterization **1:** 540, 544, 545, 548, 550, 554, 558, 567, 575, 577, 615; **26:** 207, 233, 273; **46:** 286
    forged letter **16:** 372; **28:** 1
    punishment **1:** 539, 544, 548, 549, 554, 555, 558, 563, 577, 590, 632, 645; **46:** 291, 297, 338
    as Puritan **1:** 549, 551, 555, 558, 561, 563; **25:** 47
    role in play **1:** 545, 548, 549, 553, 555, 563, 567, 575, 577, 588, 610, 615, 632, 645; **26:** 337, 374; **46:** 347
music **1:** 543, 566, 596
Olivia **1:** 540, 543, 545; **46:** 286, 333, 369; **47:** 45
order **1:** 563, 596; **34:** 330; **46:** 291, 347
Orsino **46:** 286, 333; **47:** 45
philosophical elements **1:** 560, 563, 596; **34:** 301, 316; **46:** 297
Puritanism **1:** 549, 553, 555, 632; **16:** 53; **25:** 47; **46:** 338
psychoanalytic criticism **46:** 333
Saturnalian elements **1:** 554, 571, 603, 620, 642; **16:** 53
self-deception **1:** 554, 561, 591, 625; **47:** 45
self-indulgence **1:** 563, 615, 635
sexual ambiguity and sexual deception **1:** 540, 562, 620, 621, 639, 645; **22:** 69; **34:** 311, 344; **37:** 59; **42:** 32
Shakespeare"s canon, place in **1:** 543, 548, 557, 569, 575, 580, 621, 635, 638
Shakespeare"s other plays, relation to **34:** 270; **46:** 303
sources **1:** 539, 540, 603; **34:** 301, 323, 344; **46:** 291
staging issues **26:** 219, 233, 257, 337, 342, 346, 357, 359, 360, 364, 366, 371, 374; **46:** 310, 369
structure **1:** 539, 542, 543, 546, 551, 553, 563, 570, 571, 590, 600, 660; **26:** 374; **34:** 281, 287; **46:** 286
time **37:** 78; **46:** 297
tragic elements **1:** 557, 569, 572, 575, 580, 599, 621, 635, 638, 639, 645, 654, 656; **26:** 342
Viola **26:** 308; **46:** 286, 324, 347, 369

*The Two Gentlemen of Verona* (Volumes 6, 12, 40)

absurdities, inconsistencies, and shortcomings **6:** 435, 436, 437, 439, 464, 507, 541, 560
appearance versus reality **6:** 494, 502, 511, 519, 529, 532, 549, 560
audience versus character perceptions **6:** 499, 519, 524
authorship controversy **6:** 435, 436, 437, 438, 439, 449, 466, 476
characterization **6:** 438, 442, 445, 447, 449, 458, 462, 560; **12:** 458; **40:** 312, 327, 330, 365
Christian elements **6:** 438, 494, 514, 532, 555, 564
education **6:** 490, 494, 504, 526, 532, 555, 568
Elizabethan setting **12:** 463, 485

forest. **6:** 450, 456, 492, 514, 547, 555, 564, 568
genre **6:** 460, 468, 472, 516; **40:** 320
identity **6:** 494, 511, 529, 532, 547, 560, 564, 568; **19:** 34
ironic or parodic elements **6:** 447, 472, 478, 484, 502, 504, 509, 516, 529, 549; **13:** 12
Julia or Silvia **6:** 450, 453, 458, 476, 494, 499, 516, 519, 549, 564; **40:** 312, 327, 374
language and imagery **6:** 437, 438, 439, 445, 449, 490, 504, 519, 529, 541; **28:** 9; **40:** 343
Launce and Speed, comic function of **6:** 438, 439, 442, 456, 458, 460, 462, 472, 476, 478, 484, 502, 504, 507, 509, 516, 519, 549; **40:** 312, 320
love **6:** 442, 445, 456, 479, 488, 492, 494, 502, 509, 516, 519, 549; **13:** 12; **40:** 327, 335, 343, 354, 365
love versus friendship **6:** 439, 449, 450, 458, 460, 465, 468, 471, 476, 480; **40:** 354, 359, 365
marriage **48:** 32
mimetic rivalry **13:** 12; **40:** 335
morality **6:** 438, 492, 494, 514, 532, 555, 564
Proteus **6:** 439, 450, 458, 480, 490, 511; **40:** 312, 327, 330, 335, 359; **42:** 18
repentance and forgiveness **6:** 450, 514, 516, 555, 564
resolution **6:** 435, 436, 439, 445, 449, 453, 458, 460, 462, 465, 466, 468, 471, 476, 480, 486, 494, 509, 514, 516, 519, 529, 532, 541, 549; **19:** 34
romantic and courtly conventions **6:** 438, 460, 472, 478, 484, 486, 488, 502, 507, 509, 529, 541, 549, 560, 568; **12:** 460, 462; **40:** 354, 374
setting **12:** 463, 465, 485
sources **6:** 436, 460, 462, 468, 476, 480, 490, 511, 547; **19:** 34; **40:** 320
staging issues **12:** 457, 464; **42:** 18
structure **6:** 445, 450, 460, 462, 504, 526
youth **6:** 439, 450, 464, 514, 568

*The Two Noble Kinsmen* (Volumes 9, 41)

amorality, question of **9:** 447, 460, 492
authorship controversy
Shakespeare not a co-author **9:** 445, 447, 455, 461
Shakespearean portions of the text **9:** 446, 447, 448, 455, 456, 457, 460, 462, 463, 471, 479, 486; **41:** 308, 317, 355
Shakespeare's part in the overall conception or design **9:** 444, 446, 448, 456, 457, 460, 480, 481, 486, 490; **37:** 313; **41:** 326
ceremonies, rites, and rituals, importance of **9:** 492, 498
characterization **9:** 457, 461, 471, 474; **41:** 340, 385
Emilia **9:** 460, 470, 471, 479, 481; **19:** 394; **41:** 372, 385; **42:** 368
free will versus fate **9:** 474, 481, 486, 492, 498
friendship **9:** 448, 463, 470, 474, 479, 481, 486, 490; **19:** 394; **41:** 355, 363, 372; **42:** 368
gender issues **42:** 368
innocence to experience **9:** 481, 502; **19:** 394
irony or satire **9:** 463, 481, 486; **41:** 301

the jailer's daughter **9:** 457, 460, 479, 481, 486, 502; **41:** 340
language and imagery **9:** 445, 446, 447, 448, 456, 461, 462, 463, 469, 471, 498, 502; **41:** 289, 301, 308, 317, 326
love **9:** 479, 481, 490, 498; **41:** 289, 355, 301, 363, 372, 385
masque elements **9:** 490
Palamon and Arcite **9:** 474, 481, 490, 492, 502
sources **19:** 394; **41:** 289, 301, 363, 385
structure **37:** 313

*Venus and Adonis* (Volumes 10, 33)

Adonis **10:** 411, 420, 424, 427, 429, 434, 439, 442, 451, 454, 459, 466, 473, 489; **25:** 305, 328; **28:** 355; **33:** 309, 321, 330, 347, 352, 357, 363, 370, 377
allegorical elements **10:** 427, 434, 439, 449, 454, 462, 480; **28:** 355; **33:** 309, 330
ambiguity **10:** 434, 454, 459, 462, 466, 473, 480, 486, 489; **33:** 352
beauty **10:** 420, 423, 427, 434, 454, 480; **33:** 330, 352
the boar **10:** 416, 451, 454, 466, 473; **33:** 339, 347, 370
the courser and the jennet **10:** 418, 439, 466; **33:** 309, 339, 347, 352
death, decay, and nature's destructiveness **10:** 419, 427, 434, 451, 454, 462, 466, 473, 480, 489; **25:** 305; **33:** 309, 321, 347, 352, 363, 370
dramatic elements **10:** 459, 462, 486
eroticism or sensuality **10:** 410, 411, 418, 419, 427, 428, 429, 442, 448, 454, 459, 466, 473; **25:** 305, 328; **28:** 355; **33:** 321, 339, 347, 352, 363, 370
*Faerie Queene* (Edmund Spenser), compared with **33:** 339
*Hero and Leander* (Christopher Marlowe), compared with **10:** 419, 424, 429; **33:** 309, 357
comic elements **10:** 429, 434, 439, 442, 459, 462, 489; **33:** 352
hunt motif **10:** 434, 451, 466, 473; **33:** 357, 370
imagery **10:** 414, 415, 416, 420, 429, 434, 449, 459, 466, 473, 480; **25:** 328; **28:** 355; **33:** 321, 339, 352, 363, 370, 377; **42:** 348
love versus lust **10:** 418, 420, 427, 434, 439, 448, 449, 454, 462, 466, 473, 480, 489; **25:** 305; **28:** 355; **33:** 309, 330, 339, 347, 357, 363, 370
morality **10:** 411, 412, 414, 416, 418, 419, 420, 423, 427, 428, 439, 442, 448, 449, 454, 459, 466; **33:** 330
negative appraisals **10:** 410, 411, 415, 418, 419, 424, 429
Ovid, compared with **32:** 352; **42:** 348
pictorial elements **10:** 414, 415, 419, 420, 423, 480; **33:** 339
popularity **10:** 410, 412, 418, 427; **25:** 328
procreation **10:** 439, 449, 466; **33:** 321, 377
reason **10:** 427, 439, 449, 459, 462, 466; **28:** 355; **33:** 309, 330
rhetoric **33:** 377
Shakespeare's plays, compared with **10:** 412, 414, 415, 434, 459, 462

Shakespeare's sonnets, compared with **33:** 377
sources **10:** 410, 412, 420, 424, 429, 434, 439, 451, 454, 466, 473, 480, 486, 489; **16:** 452; **25:** 305; **28:** 355; **33:** 309, 321, 330, 339, 347, 352, 357, 370, 377; **42:** 348
structure **10:** 434, 442, 480, 486, 489; **33:** 357, 377
style **10:** 411, 412, 414, 415, 416, 418, 419, 420, 423, 424, 428, 429, 439, 442, 480, 486, 489; **16:** 452
Venus **10:** 427, 429, 434, 439, 442, 448, 449, 451, 454, 466, 473, 480, 486, 489; **16:** 452; **25:** 305, 328; **28:** 355; **33:** 309, 321, 330, 347, 352, 357, 363, 370, 377
Wat the hare **10:** 424, 451

*The Winter's Tale* (Volumes 7, 15, 36, 45)

Antigonus
  characterization **7:** 394, 451, 464
  death scene (Act III, scene iii) **7:** 377, 414, 464, 483; **15:** 518, 532; **19:** 366
appearance versus reality **7:** 429, 446, 479
art versus nature **7:** 377, 381, 397, 419, 452; **36:** 289, 318; **45:** 329
audience perception, Shakespeare's manipulation of **7:** 394, 429, 456, 483, 501; **13:** 417; **19:** 401, 431, 441; **25:** 339; **45:** 374
autobiographical elements **7:** 395, 397, 410, 419
Autolycus **7:** 375, 380, 382, 387, 389, 395, 396, 414; **15:** 524; **22:** 302; **37:** 31; **45:** 333; **46:** 14, 33
Christian elements **7:** 381, 387, 402, 410, 417, 419, 425, 429, 436, 452, 460, 501; **36:** 318
counsel **19:** 401
court society **16:** 410
dramatic structure **7:** 382, 390, 396, 399, 402, 407, 414, 429, 432, 473, 479, 493, 497, 501; **15:** 528; **25:** 339; **36:** 289, 295, 362, 380; **45:** 297, 344, 358, 366
ethnicity **37:** 306
folk drama, relation to **7:** 420, 451
forgiveness or redemption **7:** 381, 389, 395, 402, 407, 436, 456, 460, 483; **36:** 318
fusion of comic, tragic, and romantic elements **7:** 390, 394, 396, 399, 410, 412, 414, 429, 436, 479, 483, 490, 501; **13:** 417; **15:** 514, 524, 532; **25:** 339; **36:** 295, 380; **45:** 295, 329
grace **7:** 420, 425, 460, 493; **36:** 328
Hermione
  characterization **7:** 385, 395, 402, 412, 414, 506; **15:** 495, 532; **22:** 302, 324; **25:** 347; **32:** 388; **36:** 311; **47:** 25
  restoration (Act V, scene iii) **7:** 377, 379, 384, 385, 387, 389, 394, 396, 412, 425, 436, 451, 452, 456, 464, 483, 501; **15:** 411, 412, 413, 518, 528, 532
  supposed death **25:** 339; **47:** 25
as historical allegory **7:** 381; **15:** 528
homosexuality **48:** 309
hospitality **19:** 366
irony **7:** 419, 420
Jacobean culture, relation to **19:** 366, 401, 431; **25:** 347; **32:** 388; **37:** 306
language and imagery **7:** 382, 384, 417, 418, 420, 425, 460, 506; **13:** 409; **19:** 431; **22:** 324;

25: 347; 36: 295; 42: 308; 45: 297, 333, 344
Leontes
  characterization 19: 431; 45: 366
  jealousy 7: 377, 379, 382, 383, 384, 387, 389, 394, 395, 402, 407, 412, 414, 425, 429, 432, 436, 464, 480, 483, 497; 15: 514, 518, 532; 22: 324; 25: 339; 36: 334, 344, 349; 44: 66; 45: 295, 297, 344, 358; 47: 25
  Othello, compared with 7: 383, 390, 412; 15: 514; 36: 334; 44: 66; 47: 25
  repentance 7: 381, 389, 394, 396, 402, 414, 497; 36: 318, 362; 44: 66
love 7: 417, 425, 469, 490
Mamillius 7: 394, 396, 451; 22: 324
metadramatic elements 16: 410
myth of Demeter and Persephone, relation to 7: 397, 436
nationalism and patriotism 32: 388
nature 7: 397, 418, 419, 420, 425, 432, 436, 451, 452, 473, 479; 19: 366; 45: 329
Neoclassical rules 7: 376, 377, 379, 380, 383, 410; 15: 397
Ovid"s *Metamorphoses*, relation to 42: 308
*Pandosto*, compared with 7: 376, 377, 390, 412, 446; 13: 409; 25: 347; 36: 344, 374
Paulina 7: 385, 412, 506; 15: 528; 22: 324; 25: 339; 36: 311
Perdita
  characterization 7: 395, 412, 414, 419, 429, 432, 452, 506; 22: 324; 25: 339; 36: 328
  reunion with Leontes (Act V, scene ii) 7: 377, 379, 381, 390, 432, 464, 480
plot 7: 376, 377, 379, 382, 387, 390, 396, 452; 13: 417; 15: 518; 45: 374
rebirth, regeneration, resurrection, or immortality 7: 397, 414, 417, 419, 429, 436, 451, 452, 456, 480, 490, 497, 506; 25: 339 452, 480, 490, 497, 506; 45: 366
sheep-shearing scene (Act IV, scene iv) 7: 379, 387, 395, 396, 407, 410, 412, 419, 420, 429, 432, 436, 451, 479, 490; 16: 410; 19: 366; 25: 339; 36: 362, 374; 45: 374
staging issues 7: 414, 425, 429, 446, 464, 480, 483, 497; 13: 409; 15: 518; 48: 309
statue scene (Act V, scene iii) 7: 377, 379, 384, 385, 387, 389, 394, 396, 412, 425, 436, 451, 456, 464, 483, 501; 15: 411, 412, 518, 528, 532; 25: 339, 347; 36: 301
subversiveness 22: 302
symbolism 7: 425, 429, 436, 452, 456, 469, 490, 493
textual issues 19: 441; 45: 333
Time-Chorus 7: 377, 380, 412, 464, 476, 501; 15: 518
time 7: 397, 425, 436, 476, 490; 19: 366; 36: 301, 349; 45: 297, 329, 366, 374
trickster, motif of 22: 302; 45: 333
Union debate, relation to 25: 347
violence 43: 39
witchcraft 22: 324
women, role of 22: 324; 36: 311; 42: 308

ISBN 0-7876-3143-4